MARKETING CHANNELS

BARRY BERMAN

JOHN WILEY & SONS, INC.

NEW YORK • CHICHESTER • BRISBANE • TORONTO • SINGAPORE

To Linda, Glenna, and Lisa
With all of my love.

Acquisitions Editor   Petra Sellers
Assistant Editor   Ellen Ford
Marketing Manager   Leslie Hines
Production Manager   Linda Muriello
Production Editor   Edward Winkleman
Designer   Harry Nolan
Cover Illustration   Marjory Dressler
Manufacturing Coordinator   Dorothy Sinclair
Photo Editor   Mary Ann Price
Illustration Coordinator   Rosa Bryant
Illustrator   Boris Starosta

This book was set in Cheltenham by General Graphic Services and printed and bound by Donnelley/Crawfordsville. The cover was printed by New England Book.

Recognizing the importance of preserving what has been written, it is a policy of John Wiley & Sons, Inc. to have books of enduring value published in the United States printed on acid-free paper, and we exert our best efforts to that end.

The paper in this book was manufactured by a mill whose forest management programs include sustained yield harvesting of its timberlands. Sustained yield harvesting principles ensure that the number of trees cut each year does not exceed the amount of new growth.

Copyright © 1996 by John Wiley & Sons, Inc.

All rights reserved. Published simultaneously in Canada.

Reproduction or translation of any part of
this work beyond that permitted by Sections
107 and 108 of the 1976 United States Copyright
Act without the permission of the copyright
owner is unlawful. Requests for permission
or further information should be addressed to
the Permissions Department, John Wiley & Sons, Inc.

Library of Congress Cataloging-in-Publication Data
Berman, Barry.
    Marketing channels / Barry Berman.
      p.   cm.
    Includes indexes.
    ISBN 0-471-57748-0 (cloth   :   alk. paper)
     1. Marketing channels.   2. Marketing—Management.   I. Title.
HF5415.129.B47   1996
658.8′4—dc20
                                                                                           95-36680
                                                                                           CIP

Printed in the United States of America

10 9 8 7 6 5 4 3 2

About the Author

Barry Berman earned his Ph.D. in Business (with majors in Marketing and Behavioral Sciences) from the City University of New York. During his doctoral program studies, he was a National Defense Education Act Fellow.

Dr. Berman is the Walter H. "Bud" Miller Distinguished Professor of Business and Professor of Marketing and International Business at the Zarb School of Business at Hofstra University. He is co-director of the university's Business Research Institute and Retail Management Institute. Dr. Berman was co-director of the American Marketing Association's Special Interest Group in Retailing and Retail Management. In 1995, he was co-director of the American Marketing Association's Faculty Consortium on "Ethics and Social Responsibility in Marketing."

Dr. Berman has served as consultant to such orgainzations as Fortunoff's, Singer Company, Associated Dry Goods, Price/Costco, the State Education Department of New York, and professional and trade groups. He is the author or editor of numerous books and articles and is active in various professional associations. With Joel R. Evans, he is co-author of *Marketing,* Sixth Edition; *Retail Management: A Strategic Approach,* Sixth Edition; *Principles of Marketing,* Third Edition; and *Readings in Marketing Management: A Strategic Perspective.*

Dr. Berman regularly teaches undergraduate and graduate courses to a wide range of students. In 1984, he was selected as Teacher of the Year by the Hofstra M.B.A. Association.

PREFACE

As in the case of many other authors, I began my plans to write a channels text after teaching a channels course and being unhappy with the available texts. In addition, no available text had the types of ancillary materials that I needed as a faculty member. Out of this dissatisfaction *Marketing Channels* was born.

Several characteristics differentiate *Marketing Channels* from other texts:

- A full complement of pedagogical aids. Each chapter has chapter objectives, two boxed "Channels in Action" extracts, a listing of key terms, a chapter summary keyed to chapter objectives, and questions for discussion.
- Two inserts for four-color art.
- Many tables, figures, and flowcharts.
- A strategic emphasis, with a focus on decision making in a changing environment.
- Inclusion of the latest developments in channels management, specifically:

  - Chapter 1: Marketing Channels: An Introduction—switching costs in channels and channel management as a competitive advantage.
  - Chapter 2: The Channel Environment—building scenarios and developing a contingency plan, micromarketing, and value orientation.
  - Chapter 3: Retail Channel Members—conglomerate merchants, leveraged buyouts and channel competition, and the strategic profit model.
  - Chapter 4: Wholesale Channel Members—power retailers, modular corporations, and integrated distributors.
  - Chapter 5: Relationship Marketing and Customer Service—relationship marketing, customer service, and total quality management.
  - Chapter 6: Physical Distribution Strategy in Channels—logistics, deregulation of intrastate trucking, third-party transportation service providers, just-in-time inventory management, Efficient Consumer Response, and ABC inventory analysis.
  - Chapter 7: Market Research and Information Systems in Channels—all commodity volume, percent category volume, single-source data, electronic data interchange, bar coding, and database marketing.
  - Chapter 8: Product Management Strategy in Channels—the product life cycle and channel management, the role of resellers in the diffusion process, pay to stay fees, failure fees, private-label strategies, product recall, product recycling, and packaging and channels.

- Chapter 9: Pricing Strategy in Channels—direct product profitability, high-low pricing, everyday low pricing, gray market goods, and legal aspects of pricing.
- Chapter 10: Promotion Strategy in Channels—developing and implementing a push-oriented promotional strategy, street money, pay-for-performance allowances, push money, developing and implementing a pull-oriented promotional strategy, cooperative advertising, rebates, trade shows, and legal aspects of channel promotional strategy.
- Chapter 11: Channel Design and Selection—relationship between channel length and market, product, consumer, and intermediary factors; hybrid channel arrangements; and reseller checklists.
- Chapter 12: Administrative Structures in Marketing Channels—programmed merchandising agreements, conversion franchising, area development franchising, methods of coordination in franchising, and legal aspects of vertical marketing systems.
- Chapter 13: Channel Power: Conflict and Cooperation—coercive power, noncoercive power, methods of manufacturer dominance, methods of wholesaler dominance, methods of buyer dominance, and channel satisfaction.
- Chapter 14: Channels for Services and International Marketing—locational flexibility in production and consumption of services, physical distribution concerns in the delivery of services, piggybacking, foreign franchising, international physical distribution decision making, export automation software, and legal aspects of international channels.
- Chapter 15: Evaluation of Channels—channel performance measures, activity-based costing, channel audits, channel partnerships, and Efficient Consumer Response.

- Use of the American Marketing Association's *Dictionary of Marketing Terms,* Second Edition (Lincoln, Nebr.: NTC Business Books, 1995) for many definitions.
- Use of the latest data available from such sources as *American Demographics, Fortune, Harvard Business Review, Industrial Distribution, Industrial Marketing Management, Journal of Marketing, Progressive Grocer,* and *Wall Street Journal.*
- Incorporation of data from the most current *Census of Retail Trade* and *Census of Wholesale Trade.*
- A total of 34 cases (30 end-of-chapter cases and four integrative cases).
- Four appendixes:
  - Appendix A   The Information Superhighway and Channel Management
  - Appendix B   Ethics in Channel Management
  - Appendix C   Careers in Channel Management
  - Appendix D   Glossary

- A full package including an Instructor's Manual, a computer package, and a four-hour selection of videos.

Please feel free to communicate with me regarding *Marketing Channels* at the Zarb School of Business, 134 Hofstra University, Hempstead, NY 11550-1090. I welcome your comments and promise to respond as soon as possible.

ABOUT THE CASES IN MARKETING CHANNELS

Each chapter has two end-of-chapter cases. There are also four integrative cases in the text, one for each of the first four part sections. All cases, with the exception of the integrative case for Part Four, are based on real companies and situations. Real, current data are used for all the cases. Faculty may wish to assign "How to Solve a Case Study" (at the end of Chapter 1), prior to the first case discussion.

Although the questions for all cases were designed especially for the chapter in which the cases are placed, many cases can be used in conjunction with other chapters. A matrix in the Instructor's Manual indicates suggested chapters for each case.

I have used cases dealing with a variety of situations, channel levels, and different-sized channels to show students the applicability of channel management principles to a variety of situations.

ABOUT THE BOXED MATERIALS IN MARKETING CHANNELS

As indicated in the Preface, there are two boxed "Channels in Action" extracts in each chapter of the text. Each box has been carefully chosen to be stimulating to students, to integrate with material in the chapter, and to demonstrate the applicability of channels management principles to different types of channel members (based on level, size, and strategy). Faculty may use the boxes for class discussion or as caselets.

ABOUT THE VIDEOS THAT ACCOMPANY *MARKETING CHANNELS*

Four hours of videos (from a variety of firms) are provided to adopters. The video package includes two teaching videos appropriate as a class lecture: "Channels of Distribution" (Video 1) and "Wholesaling" (Video 5).

Each of the 18 videos are summarized in the *Instructor's Manual.* A grid in the *Instructor's Manual* also matches each video to the appropriate text chapter. The following videos are available: 1) "Channels of Distribution"; 2) "Crisis Management"; 3) "Macy's: Introduction to BPS"; 4) "Lands' End"; 5) "Wholesaling"; 6) "Relationship Marketing"; 7) "CSX Corporation: Winning in the World Marketplace"; 8) "Roadway Package Service: Multiship"; 9) "Block Pallets: The Distribution Solution"; 10) "Texas Mill Supply-Louisiana Mill Supply Story"; 11) "Information Resources Inc.: The Power of Information"; 12) Reynolds Metals: A Shining Example" (recycling); 13) "Fordstar: The Newest American Road"; 14) "The Independent Electrical Distributors: Discover the Advantage"; 15) "Sunkist Growers: A Heritage of Quality"; 16) "Roadway Express: Making a World of Difference"; 17) "Coop Switzerland"; and 18) "ECR."

ABOUT THE COMPUTER SUPPLEMENT THAT ACCOMPANIES *MARKETING CHANNELS*

An IBM-PC compatible computer diskette is available free to adopters. This supplement contains a variety of computer exercises pertinent to a marketing channels course. Among the types of exercises are spreadsheets, simulations, and questionnaire analysis. All exercises are user-friendly with self-prompting features.

All exercises are keyed to the text through use of a computer-disk symbol. The titles include 1) Channel Costs; 2) Management Horizons' Impact Model; 3) Strategic Profit Model; 4) Physical Distribution (Total Cost) Concept; 5) Economics of Inventory Turnover; 6) All Commodity Volume; 7) Chain-Markup Pricing; 8) Aspinwall's Characteristics of Goods and Parallel Systems Theory; 9) Independent Representative Checklist; 10) Costs of Different Channel Arrangements; 11) Measurement of Supplier Power; and 12) Distribution Cost Analysis.

ACKNOWLEDGMENTS

The writing of a book is a team effort. The Marketing Channels team was intelligent, hardworking, persistent, and, above all, a pleasure to work with. During this entire project, I have always felt that I was working with friends who also were respected colleagues.

Many people assisted in this project. My colleagues at the Zarb School have always provided a supportive environment for me. I must especially mention my best friend, Joel R. Evans, with whom I have worked since 1976. While this was a solo flight, I could always count on him for his assistance. Other colleagues that have been helpful include Benny Barak, Herman Berliner, Dorothy Cohen, Andrew Forman, Joel Greene, Ulric Haynes, Jr., William James, Keun Lee, William McDonald, Rusty Moore, James Neelankavil, Ehsan Nikbakht, Ralph Polimeni, Elaine Sherman, and Yong Zhang. I also very much enjoyed working with Victor V. Cordell, Monterey Institute of International Studies, on the Part Four integrative case.

I also wish to thank my reviewers for their hard work and thought-provoking comments. It has always been clear to me that the review process for this book was a "labor of love" for them. These reviewers made a significant impact on *Marketing Channels:* Stephen C. Cosmas, California State Polytechnic University at Pomona; Ed Chung, York University, Canada; Sid C. Dudley, Eastern Illinois University; Donald A. Fuller, University of Central Florida; Sharon Gregg, Middle Tennessee State University; Ann T. Kuzma, Mankato State University; Arnold Maltz, New Mexico State University; Brian J. McNeeley, University of Wisconsin, Parkside; Joseph C. Miller, Indiana University; Thomas G. Ponzurick, West Virginia University; and Rodney Stump, Morgan State University

Special thanks are due to the Wiley team who worked on this edition. This includes Rosa Bryant, Ellen Ford, Leslie Hines, Linda Muriello, Harry Nolan, Betty C. Pessagno, Mary Ann Price, Petra Sellers, and Edward A. Winkleman. I also wish to thank Tim Kent, my initial editor, and William F. Oldsey, who was instrumental in signing this project. Several graduate students assisted me on this project; they include Gregg Lombardo, Eileen Murphy, and Susan Parker. Special thanks is also due to Chip Galloway for his work on the computer supplement. As usual, Diane Schoenberg, my editorial assistant, was a pleasure to work with. Proudly, I thank my daughter Lisa for her work on the *Instructor's Manual.* Lastly, my wife, Linda, helped me out throughout this project from the encouragement to write this book through the preparation of the indexes.

Barry Berman
Hofstra University

BRIEF CONTENTS

Part One: An Overview of Marketing Channels 1

1. Marketing Channels: An Introduction 3
2. The Channel Environment 47

Part Two: Major Channel Members 105

3. Retail Channel Members 107
4. Wholesale Channel Members 145

Part Three: Channel Management and the Marketing Mix 199

5. Relationship Marketing and Customer Service 201
6. Physical Distribution Strategy in Channels 241
7. Market Research and Information Systems in Channels 287
8. Product Management Strategy in Channels 333
9. Pricing Strategy in Channels 381
10. Promotion Strategy in Channels 421

Part Four: Channel Planning, Coordination, and Organization 473

11. Channel Design and Selection 475
12. Administrative Structures in Marketing Channels 519
13. Channel Power: Conflict and Cooperation 555
14. Channels for Services and International Marketing 589

Part Five: Channel Assessment and Control 635

15. Evaluation of Channels 637

Appendix A: The Information Superhighway and Channel Management A1
Appendix B: Ethics in Channel Management B1
Appendix C: Careers in Channel Management C1
Appendix D: Glossary D1
Name Index N1
Subject Index S1

Contents

PART ONE: AN OVERVIEW OF MARKETING CHANNELS   1

1   **Marketing Channels: An Introduction**   3
Chapter Objectives   3
Marketing Channel Defined   5
Functions Performed by Intermediaries   10
Alternative Channel Structures   14
Special Characteristics of Channel Relationships   17
Importance of Channel Management to the Firm   21
Importance of Channel Management in the Economy   29
Organization of the Text   33
Summary   34
Key Terms   37
Questions for Discussion   37
Case 1: Wal-Mart's Decision to Eliminate Purchasing Goods Through Wholesalers   41
Case 2: ComputerLand's Decision to Change Its Distribution Strategy   42
How to Solve a Case Study   44

2   **The Channel Environment**   47
Chapter Objectives   47
Overview of the Channel Environment   49
The Final Consumer: Demographic Characteristics   52
The Final Consumer: Consumer Life-Styles   58
Channel Competition   66
The Economy   72
The Legal Environment   75
Technological Environment   80
Summary   84
Key Terms   86
Questions for Discussion   87
Case 1: Avon Cosmetics' Initial Difficulties with Its Dual Distribution Strategy   91
Case 2: Prodigy: Evaluating a Computer-Ordering System   92
Part One Integrative Case: The Coca-Cola Company   94

PART TWO: MAJOR CHANNEL MEMBERS   105

3   **Retail Channel Members**   107
Chapter Objectives   107

Retail Structure   107
The Special Characteristics of Retailing   112
Retail Trends   116
A Typology of Retail Institutions   121
Retail Buying Organizations   133
Summary   137
Key Terms   138
Questions for Discussion   139
Case 1: The Gap: Examining the Strategy of a Successful Retailer   142
Case 2: Home Depot: A Power Retailer Dominates Home Improvement Sales in the Do-It-Yourself and Contractor Segments   143

4 Wholesale Channel Members   145
Chapter Objectives   145
Wholesale Structure   147
The Special Characteristics of Wholesaling   156
A Typology of Wholesalers   159
Manufacturer/Supplier—Wholesaler Contracts   169
Summary   177
Key Terms   179
Questions for Discussion   180
Case 1: Anheuser-Busch: Territorial Restrictions in Beer Distribution   183
Case 2: Wakefern: A Retailer-Owned Wholesale Cooperative   184
Part Two Integrative Case: Dell Computer Corporation   186

PART THREE: CHANNEL MANAGEMENT AND THE MARKETING MIX   199

5 Relationship Marketing and Customer Service   201
Chapter Objectives   201
An Introduction to Relationship Marketing   203
Evaluating the Use of a Relationship Marketing Strategy   212
Developing a Customer Service Strategy   214
Implementing a Customer Service Strategy   221
Customer Service Standards in Physical Distribution   227
Evaluating Suppliers on the Basis of Multiple Customer Service Standards   229
Summary   230
Key Terms   232
Questions for Discussion   233
Case 1: Relationship Marketing at Kodak   237
Case 2: Public Service Electric and Gas Company: Total Quality Management   238

6 Physical Distribution Strategy in Channels   241
Chapter Objectives   241
Introduction to Physical Distribution   243
Transportation Decision Making   250

Warehouse Decision Making   257
Inventory Management Principles   261
Inventory Decision Making   265
Summary   275
Key Terms   277
Questions for Discussion   278
Case 1: OTR Express: The Physical Distribution Strategy of a Motor Carrier   282
Case 2: Coleman Company: Implementing a Just-in-Time Inventory System   284

7 Market Research and Information Systems in Channels   287
Chapter Objectives   287
Introduction to Marketing Research in Channels Management   289
The Marketing Research Process In Channels Management   291
An Introduction to Channel Member Marketing Information Systems   308
Special Topics in Channel Information Systems   310
Summary   322
Key Terms   324
Questions for Discussion   325
Case 1: InfoScan: Single-Source Data   329
Case 2: Kmart's Use of Channel Information Systems   330

8 Product Management Strategy in Channels   333
Chapter Objectives   333
Overview of Product Management Strategy in Channels   335
New Product Planning Process and Channel Management   335
Channel Management Implications of the Product Life Cycle Concept   339
Reverse Channels   356
Packaging and Channels   365
Legal Aspects of Channel Management Relating to Product Strategy   367
Summary   370
Key Terms   372
Questions for Discussion   372
Case 1: Goodyear Tire & Rubber Company: Reevaluating Channels   377
Case 2: OPW Fueling: The Anatomy of a Product Recall   378

9 Pricing Strategy in Channels   381
Chapter Objectives   381
Introduction to Pricing Strategy in Channels   383
Price Versus Nonprice Competition   383
Pricing Objectives   385
Developing an Overall Pricing Strategy: Cost-, Demand-, and Competition-Oriented Approaches to the Setting of Price   386

Cost-Oriented Pricing   386
Demand-Oriented Pricing   391
Competition-Oriented Pricing   393
Developing an Integrated Approach to Pricing   394
Determining Pricing Policies   395
Discounts and Terms   404
Adapting the Price Strategy   407
Legal Aspects of Pricing   408
Summary   412
Key Terms   414
Questions for Discussion   414
Case 1: Dealing with Diverters   417
Case 2: Everyday Low Pricing at Procter & Gamble   418

10 Promotion Strategy in Channels   421
Chapter Objectives   421
Special Factors to Consider in the Development and Implementation of a Channel Promotional Strategy   423
Developing and Implementing a Push-Oriented Promotional Strategy   426
Developing and Implementing a Pull-Oriented Promotional Strategy   438
Legal Aspects of Channel Promotional Strategy   452
Summary   453
Key Terms   455
Questions for Discussion   455
Case 1: Dealer Training at Caterpillar   459
Case 2: Selling at Saturn Dealers   460
Part Three Integrative Case: Baxter International Inc.   462

PART FOUR: CHANNEL PLANNING, COORDINATION, AND ORGANIZATION   473

11 Channel Design and Selection   475
Chapter Objectives   475
Introduction to Channel Design and Selection   477
Determining Channel Objectives   478
Assessing Channel Length, Width, and Types of Intermediary Requirements   480
Evaluating Market Product Manufacturer Intermediary Factors That Affect Channel Length   486
Allocating Channel Tasks among Channel Members   493
Selection of Specific Channel Resellers   496
Revising Channel Arrangements   507
Summary   510
Key Terms   511
Questions for Discussion   512
Case 1: Snap-On Incorporated: Evaluating Channel Design   515
Case 2: Alberto-Culver: Channel Strategy for Sally Beauty Supply   516

12 Administrative Structures in Marketing Channels 519
Chapter Objectives 519
Conventional Channel Arrangements Versus Vertical Marketing Systems 521
Corporate Marketing Systems 523
Administered Marketing Systems 525
Contractual Marketing Systems 529
Legal Aspects of Vertical Marketing Systems 541
Summary 545
Key Terms 547
Questions for Discussion 548
Case 1: Sherwin-Williams: Use of Conventional and Corporate Channels 552
Case 2: AlphaGraphics: From Conflict to Cooperation 553

13 Channel Power: Conflict and Cooperation 555
Chapter Objectives 555
Overview of Channel Power: Conflict and Cooperation 557
Channel Power 557
Methods of Channel Dominance 562
Nature of Channel Conflicts 568
Channel Cooperation 573
Conflict Management and Resolution 576
Channel Satisfaction 578
Summary 579
Key Terms 581
Questions for Discussion 581
Case 1: Compaq and Intel: Channel Conflict 585
Case 2: Channel Cooperation Between Suppliers and Customers 586

14 Channels for Services and International Marketing 589
Chapter Objectives 589
Introduction to Channels for Services and International Marketing 591
Channels for Services 591
Channels for International Marketing 600
Channel Length and Width in International Markets 608
International Physical Distribution 611
Examples of International Channels and Physical Distribution 612
Legal Aspects of International Channels 615
Summary 616
Key Terms 618
Questions for Discussion 619
Case 1: Travel Agents Battle Airlines over Commission Cuts 623
Case 2: Toys "R" Us in Japan 624
Part Four Integrative Case: Thermashield Distributors, Poland 626

PART FIVE: CHANNEL ASSESSMENT AND CONTROL 635

15 Evaluation of Channels 637
Chapter Objectives 637
Introduction to Channel Assessment and Control 639
Overall Measures of Channel Performance Used by Dealers and Suppliers 639
Financial Performance Measures 643
Distribution Cost Analysis 647
The Channel Audit 651
Improving Overall Channel Productivity Through Channel Partnerships and Efficient Consumer Response 653
Summary 657
Key Terms 659
Questions for Discussion 659
Case 1: The Use of ABC Analysis 661
Case 2: Simpson Timber Company: The Use of a Channel Audit 662

APPENDIXES

A: The Information Superhighway and Channel Management A1
Introduction A1
    Interactive Television Shopping A2
    Internet A2
    World Wide Web A3
    CD-ROM Disks A4

B: Ethics in Channel Management B1
Introduction B1
    Examples of High Ethical Standards by Channel Resellers B1
    Examples of Unethical Standards by Channel Resellers B1
        Honda Sales Executives B2
        Prudential Sales Agents B2
        A J. C. Penney Buyer B3
How to Reduce Unethical Behavior B3

C: Careers in Channel Management C1
Introduction C1
    Channel Careers with Manufacturers C2
    Channel Careers in Wholesaling C3
    Channel Careers in Retailing C3
    Channel Careers in Logistics C3
Sources of Additional Information C4

D: Glossary D1

Name Index N1

Subject Index S1

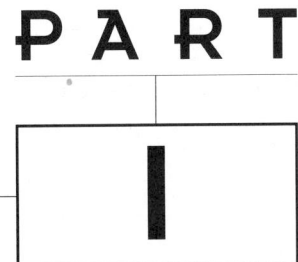

AN OVERVIEW OF MARKETING CHANNELS

In Part One, we begin our study of marketing channels and discuss important channel concepts that form the foundation for the text.

CHAPTER 1
Marketing Channels: An Introduction In this chapter, we define the term *marketing channels,* explore channel functions, and study alternative channel structures. We evaluate the special characteristics of channel relationships and illustrate the importance of channel management to the firm and the economy. Although there are various approaches to the study of channel management, this text uses a strategic approach.

CHAPTER 2
The Channel Environment Here we depict the complex environment within which marketing channels operate. Channel implications of the current environment and of environmental trends are explained.

CHAPTER 1

MARKETING CHANNELS: AN INTRODUCTION

CHAPTER OBJECTIVES

1. To define marketing channel.
2. To describe the functions performed by channel members.
3. To study alternative channel structures.
4. To evaluate the special characteristics of channel relationships.
5. To illustrate the importance of channel management to the firm and the economy.
6. To analyze the orientation and format of the text.

Although many of General Motors' (GM) car subsidiaries are facing difficulties as a result of poor consumer acceptance, GM appears to have a winner with Saturn. GM research indicates that 70 percent of Saturn buyers would not have purchased a GM car if they had not purchased a Saturn. Fully half of Saturn buyers would have purchased Japanese brands (such as the Honda Civic and the Toyota Corolla). Therefore, most of Saturn's sales are new business to GM, not sales taken from other GM cars. At a time when most new car dealers were losing money, 90 percent of Saturn dealers were profitable. Demand for the Saturn is so high that close to 95 percent of Saturn buyers paid full sticker price for their new car. Each Saturn dealer currently sells over 1000 new cars per year, versus 650 for every Honda dealer and 340 for Nissan.

Among the reasons for the success of the Saturn are its dealer organization, dealer relations, customer service, and inventory management system. Although many of these channel management concepts are new to GM, they are similar to those used by Acura, Infiniti, and Lexus (imports costing as much as four times the price of an average Saturn).

GM created a new dealership organization to market its line of Saturn cars. This organization allowed GM to reward its best dealers (as measured by customer satisfaction and financial soundness). To entice its best GM dealers to open Saturn showrooms, each Saturn dealer received the right to an exclusive geographic market area. Unlike the typical auto franchise agreement which restricts a dealer to one showroom, this contract allows Saturn dealers to add more showrooms in their market area with GM's approval. In addition, Saturn dealers are rewarded with large territories.

GM has also worked hard to maintain good dealer relations. To reduce the impact of slow production on new Saturn dealers, GM delayed the opening of 25 additional dealerships by three to five months. GM also agreed to refund fees of $50,000 to $100,000 to those dealerships that were already opened. And while many dealers buy cars at 12 percent off list price, Saturn dealers receive 17 percent discounts.

GM and its Saturn dealers are committed to customer service. For example, GM subsidized its Saturn dealers so that early Saturn customers could be reimbursed for car rental costs (owing to longer than anticipated delays in producing early models). When close to 2000 Saturn cars were recalled due to a faulty coolant, Saturn offered to replace the cars rather than just changing the antifreeze. If a comparable car was not available at the dealership, Saturn again offered to reimburse customers for their rental car costs. In some cases, Saturn consumers were even offered in-stock cars with pricier options (such as a sun roof) as an even exchange for their recalled car. Each dealer is also equipped with a sophisticated computerized information system for two-way data and one-way video information sharing. This facilitates the ordering of parts and the identification of problem repair areas. In 1993 Saturn scored third in a J. D. Powers customer satisfaction study, just behind Lexus and Infiniti.

GM even changed its traditional inventory management system. Unlike its traditional system that relies on the accumulation of large inventories at the factory and at nearby warehouses, Saturn cars are produced using a just-in-time (JIT) inventory system. In a JIT system, suppliers of Saturn's components deliver these parts directly to Saturn's assembly line. Shipments are also closely coordinated with production requirements so that inventory accumulations average to be a one-day supply of parts on hand. JIT enables Saturn to minimize inventory holding costs; it helps it increase product quality. According to Saturn's vice president of manufacturing, "When you bank parts, little problems tend to get ignored. This way [JIT], we have little choice but to fix them."[1]

In this chapter, we define the term *marketing channels,* describe channel functions, and discuss the importance of channel management to the firm and to the economy. We will see how an effective channel management strategy can be used to secure a long-term competitive advantage to channel members, as in the case of Saturn.

MARKETING CHANNELS DEFINED

Marketing channels can be defined as an organized network (system) of agencies and institutions which, in combination, performs all the activities required to link producers with users to accomplish the marketing task.[2] The important components of this definition—an organized network (system), agencies and institutions, channel activities, the linkage of producers and users, and the marketing task—are explained in the next section where marketing channels are also compared and contrasted with retailing, wholesaling, and physical distribution.

COMPONENTS OF MARKETING CHANNELS

The definition of marketing channels can best be explained by analyzing its components: an organized network (system), agencies and institutions, channel functions, the linkage of producers and users, and the marketing task.

An organized network in a channel refers to the need for channel participants to work together in an integrated and coordinated manner. For example, channel members need to share common objectives concerning customer service and product image. The simplest means of developing an organized network is through common ownership of channel participants. For example, Sherwin-Williams distributes its paint through 2046 company-owned stores as well as independently owned paint channels.[3] Developing an integrated strategy is more difficult when channel members are independently owned. An organized network can be created and maintained among independently owned channel members through the use of long-term contracts (such as franchise agreements between Coca-Cola and its independently owned wholesaler bottlers), and through the development of common goals among channel members (as in the case of O. M. Scott & Sons, a manufacturer of lawn fertilizers, which provides promotional materials and extensive dealer training to its garden supply dealers).

The second part of the definition of marketing channels relates to the agencies and institutions that are channel participants. Channel participants include consumers, **intermediaries** (manufacturers, wholesalers, and retailers) and marketing research firms, warehouses, transportation firms, insurance companies, financial institutions, advertising agencies, and consultants (called **facilitators**). Although intermediaries generally take title to and possession of goods, directly contact prospective customers, and offer credit to their customers, facilitators do not perform these activities. Facilitators also typically perform more specialized functions than intermediaries.

The third component of the definition refers to channel member activities. Activities undertaken by channel members include physical possession, ownership, promotion, negotiation, financing, risking, ordering, and payment. These activities are further explained in Table 1-1. Although these activities are common to almost all channel relationships, it is important to note that some wholesalers (drop shippers) do not take physical possession and that others (agents and brokers) do not assume product ownership. Figure 1-1 describes the channel flows for these activities.[4] Note that the physical possession and ownership flows in this diagram move downward, whereas the other flows are more complex. For example, negotiation flows and capital flows are two-way. In capital flows, channel members both grant credit and pay back short-term loans. There are multiple possible directions to each flow. For example, in the case of the risking flow, risk can go back to the manufacturer, wholesaler, and

TABLE 1-1 MARKETING CHANNEL ACTIVITIES

Activity	Explanation
Physical possession	All channel members (except drop shippers) take physical possession of inventory. Possession requires warehousing facilities.
Ownership	All channel members (except agents and brokers) assume ownership of inventory.
Promotion	Channel members are responsible for customer contact. Contact can be mass (such as advertising, publicity, and sales promotion) or individual (such as personal selling).
Negotiation	Channel members negotiate price, selling terms, delivery dates, and functions performed with their suppliers and their customers.
Financing	Credit terms enable buyers to finance their purchases.
Risking	Risks include product obsolescence, perils such as fire and flooding, seasonality, economic downturns, increased competition, reduced demand, poor acceptance of a manufacturer's products, and product recalls.
Ordering	Channel members order merchandise periodically from their suppliers. Some orders are based on direct customer requests; others are based on the channel member's desire to build up inventory to meet anticipated demand, or to reduce costs owing to anticipated price increases.
Payment	Although channel members generally offer credit to other members, payment is based on when a purchasing channel member purchases goods and services, not when these goods and services are sold.

FIGURE 1-1 Marketing channel flows.

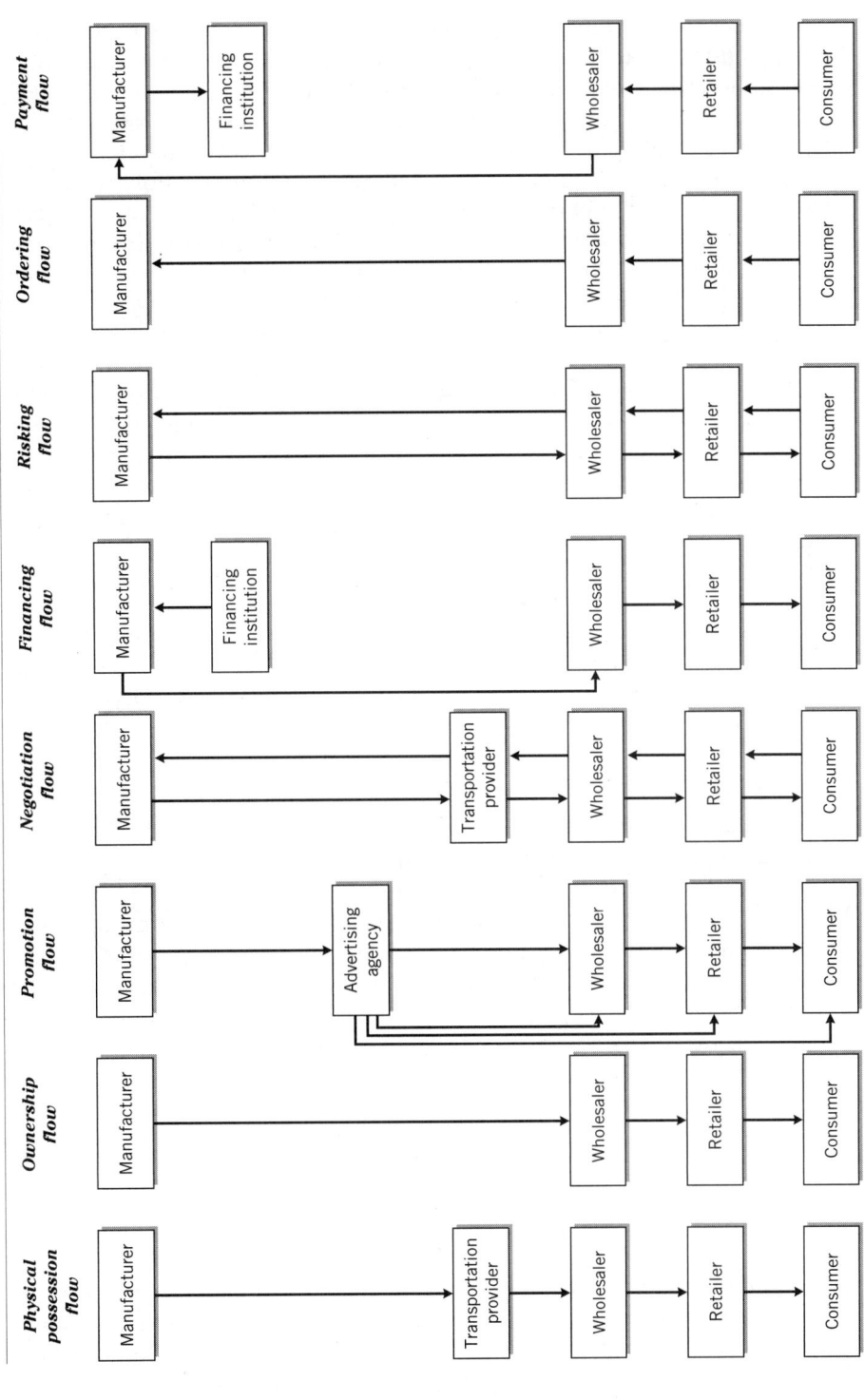

Source: Adapted from Roland S. Vaile, E. T. Grether, and Reavis Cox, *Marketing in the American Economy* (New York: Ronald Press, 1952), p. 133.

retailer even after the product is sold in the case of a product recall or after the merchandise is sold with return privileges. Final consumers can also receive promotion from retailers as well as manufacturers.

The fourth part of the definition refers to the linkage of producers and users. Producers are linked with users through one of several channel arrangements. In a conventional channel arrangement, manufacturers, wholesalers, and retailers are independently owned and may have conflicting goals. For example, although a food manufacturer may seek additional space for a new line of frozen yogurt, a supermarket chain may feel that the new line will not add new sales to the store but merely take sales from existing lines. In contrast, in franchising, a fast-food franchise has a much closer relationship with its franchisees and a higher degree of control over its channel members. Alternative channel structures are discussed later in this chapter. There are also differences in the extent to which channel relationships are routinized. For example, in contract pricing, manufacturers and customers agree on a constant price for a fixed time period, such as two years. Therefore, there is only one negotiation during this time interval. In contrast, in transactional marketing, prices are separately negotiated for each individual transaction. Similarly, some channel members share information on a routine basis through the exchange of scanned sales data, whereas others share information on a sporadic basis.

The last part of the definition refers to the accomplishment of the marketing task. All channel activities should lead to an exchange of goods and services among channel members as well as to satisfaction by both buyers and sellers.

THE RELATIONSHIP AMONG RETAILING, WHOLESALING, PHYSICAL DISTRIBUTION, AND MARKETING CHANNELS

Although retailing, wholesaling, and physical distribution are each part of marketing channels, there are important differences among these marketing activities. An explanation of these concepts and their interrelationship with marketing channels follows.

Retailing consists of those business activities involved in the sale of goods and services to consumers for personal, family, or household use.[5] It is the final stage in the distribution process. In comparison to channel management, which covers the linkage among manufacturers, wholesalers, retailers, and consumers, in retailing, the last linkage is with final consumers (see Figure 1-2a). Consumers tend to think of retailing as being store-related, but it also covers nonstore purchases such as vending machines, direct selling, catalog sales, and mail-order sales.

Wholesaling involves the buying or handling of merchandise and its subsequent resale to organizational users, retailers, and/or other wholesalers, but not the sale of significant volume to final consumers.[6] Whereas retailing is strictly concerned with the sale of goods and services to the final consumer, wholesaling is involved with the sale of goods and services for resale by channel members or use by organizational consumers. The sale of goods and ser-

FIGURE 1-2 Differences between retailing and wholesaling.

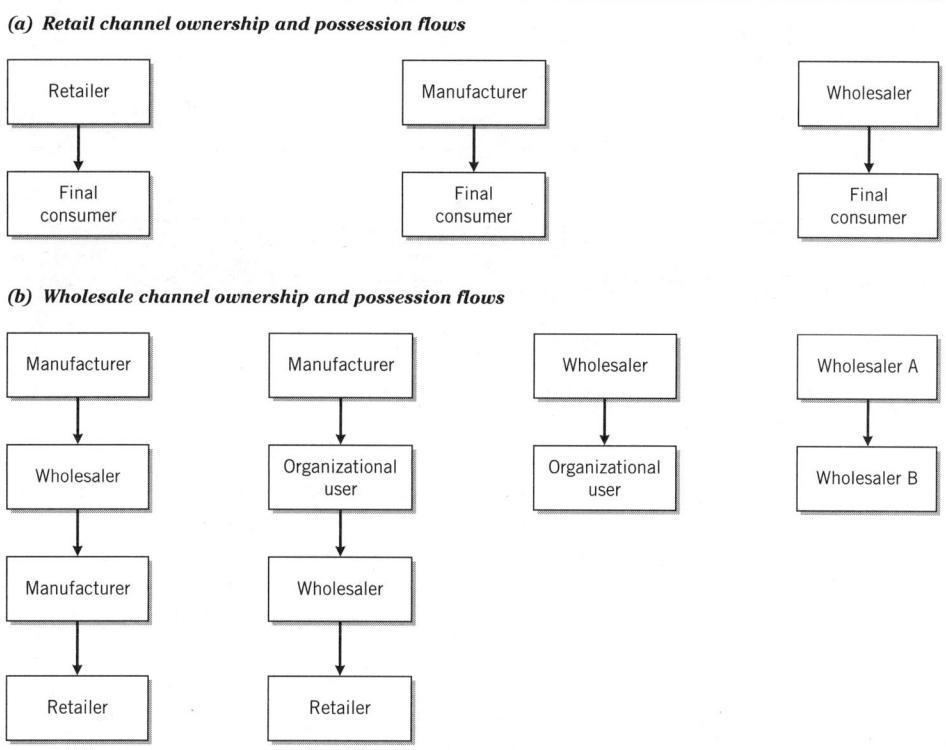

vices to a dentist for use in his or her office is wholesaling, as is the sale of goods to a retailer for resale to final consumers. Wholesaling includes the linkage of manufacturers and wholesalers, manufacturers and organizational users, wholesalers and organizational users, wholesalers and other wholesalers, manufacturers and retailers, and wholesalers and retailers (see Figure 1-2b).

The study of channel management from the perspective of wholesaling and retailing looks at channel management from an institutional perspective. All channel flows are either retailing or wholesaling. If the destination of the flow is a final consumer, then it is retailing; if the destination is any other channel participant, it is considered to be wholesaling.

In contrast to retailing and wholesaling, which look at channel management from an institutional perspective, physical distribution views channel management from an activity perspective. **Physical distribution** describes a concept or an approach to managing the finished goods inventory of the firm. It includes the transportation, warehousing, inventory, and order processing functions of the firm.[7] Physical distribution activities can be conducted by any channel member. However, not all channel activities are physical distribution. For example, promotion, negotiation, financing, risking, and payment are not considered aspects of physical distribution. Channel activities related to physical possession and ownership generally have high physical distribution components.

FUNCTIONS PERFORMED BY INTERMEDIARIES

Wholesalers and retailers have been the subject of much scorn. A common misunderstanding is that these intermediaries do not perform any useful function,

CHANNELS IN ACTION

Factors: Important Channel Facilitators

Factors, firms that provide financing primarily to small businesses (such as clothing manufacturers and suppliers of goods to government agencies), are an important channel member. The small business clients of factors typically would not qualify for financing from traditional lenders such as banks. In 1993 factors financed at least $62 billion in receivables according to the publisher of *Edwards Directory of American Factors*. Although a few large firms (such as Barclay's Commercial Corporation, CIT Group, and Heller Financial Inc.) dominate the market, many other factors are small firms that have been in business less than 10 years.

Factors provide financing to manufacturers on the basis of their retailer customer's credit rating. Factors purchase a manufacturer's receivables at a discount (typically 1 percent) and make their profits from the difference of the price paid to the manufacturer and the amount received from the retailer customer. Factors typically guarantee a manufacturer's accounts receivable; they have no recourse against the manufacturer if the retailer cannot pay its bills. Therefore, factors are extremely sensitive to any development that can affect a retailer's ability to pay. In contrast, banks and other traditional lenders lend against a firm's receivables, with the burden of collection on the small business.

Since retailers pay a manufacturer's bill directly to the factor, factors are generally the first to learn of a retailer's financial difficulties. Competing factors typically trade information about the payment record of major retailers. Some observers feel that retailers may seek to pay factors faster than manufacturers, owing to their informal, but effective, communication network.

Recent bankruptcies of such retailers as Federated Department Stores, R. H. Macy, B. Altman, Ames Department Stores, Hill's, and Carter Hawley Hale, have made factors especially sensitive to any change in a retailer's financial situation. For example, a major factor told suppliers in 1991 that it would only guarantee up to $25,000 of orders to Saks Fifth Avenue. The factor was upset that privately held Saks refused to provide it with copies of recent financial statements. Factors were also extremely cautious about guaranteeing payment for merchandise purchased by R. H. Macy in the several-month period preceding Macy's bankruptcy.

Sources: Udayan Gupta, "Factoring and Venture Firms' Roles in Financing Grow," *Wall Street Journal* (April 18, 1994), p. B2; and Laura Zinn, "Sniffing Trouble on Seventh Avenue," *Business Week* (August 26, 1991), p. 52.

and their presence in a transaction unnecessarily raises the cost of goods. This criticism of intermediaries suggests that, by bypassing them in a transaction, consumers (either final or organizational) will be able to reduce costs without having suffered any loss of services. This section responds to this criticism by describing the common functions of intermediaries and by discussing the channel principle that channel functions can be shifted, but not eliminated.

CHANNEL FUNCTIONS

Five channel member functions can be identified: the sorting process (including breaking bulk and contractual efficiency), mass distribution, customer contact, credit, and market research. The activities listed in Table 1-1 support these channel functions. For example, promotion, negotiation, ordering, and payment all support the customer contact function.

Through the **sorting process**, wholesalers and retailers resolve the conflicting orientations of manufacturers (their suppliers) and their organizational and final consumers. Although many manufacturers produce a narrow variety or shallow assortments of goods, both final and organizational consumers desire the benefits of one-stop shopping. The sorting process resolves these orientations through accumulation, allocation, sorting, and assorting functions. In accumulation, wholesalers and retailers collect shipments from multiple manufacturers. Through allocation, these goods and services are distributed to various consumer markets. In sorting, wholesalers and retailers divide their inventory into grades, sizes, capacities, and colors. In assorting, intermediaries purchase and store a broad range of merchandise from multiple manufacturers.[8] Through these four functions, manufacturers are able to specialize while offering consumers the benefit of one-stop shopping.

Breaking bulk and contractual efficiency are two important aspects of the sorting process. **Breaking bulk** refers to the wholesaler or retailer function of purchasing goods in case lots and reselling them to their customers in smaller quantities. In fact, the word "retailing" comes from the old French term *retailler,* which means "to cut up."

Another important aspect of the sorting process is **contactual efficiency**.[9] Through the use of intermediaries, a manufacturer reaches thousands of final consumers through the sale of its product via a wholesaler or retailer. See Figure 1-3 for a model that contrasts the number of required consumer contacts with and without intermediaries. Contactual efficiency enables both manufacturers, wholesalers, and retailers and their customers to reduce time and financial expenditures. For example, the cost of a business-to-business field sales call now exceeds $250; it is also costly to maintain retail stores that specialize in the goods and services of a single manufacturer.[10] Both organizational and final consumers would rather purchase from a few intermediaries with a wide and deep product mix than from a large number of manufacturers each having a narrow and shallow product mix.

Contactual efficiency enables mass distribution. By reducing the costs of an average sale (through the selling of related merchandise produced by multiple manufacturers), manufacturers are able to sell their goods and services in market areas

FIGURE 1-3 A model of contactual efficiency.

(a) Number of required consumer contacts without wholesalers or retailers

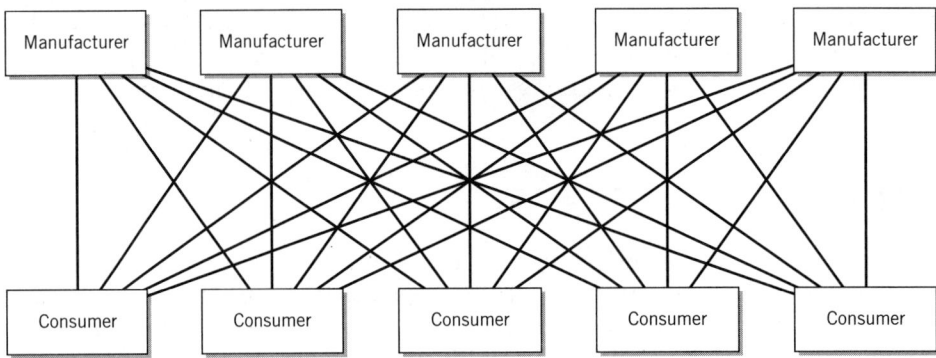

Number of required contacts without wholesalers or retailers
= number of manufacturers (M) x number of consumers (C)
= 5 x 5
= 25 contacts

(b) Number of required consumer contacts with one intermediary (wholesaler or retailer)

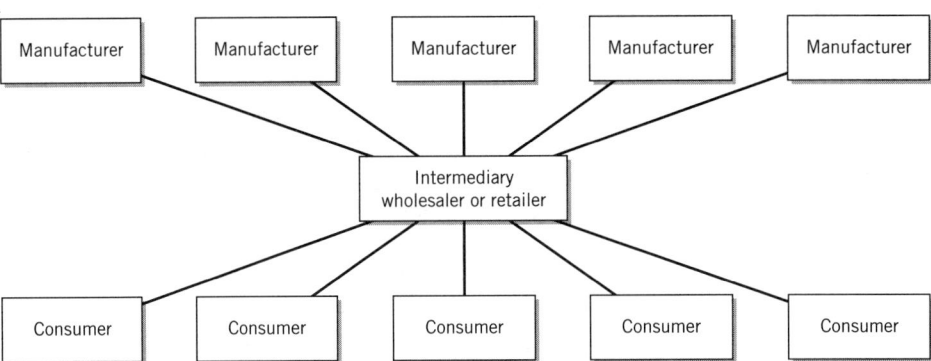

Number of required contacts with one wholesaler or retailer
= number of manufacturers (M) + number of consumers (C)
= 5 + 5
= 10 contacts

(c) Net saving due to one wholesaler or retailer

= (M x C) - (M + C)
= 25 - 10
= 15 contacts

that would have been otherwise unprofitable. Since intermediaries sell the products of multiple manufacturers (assorting), final and organizational consumers will prefer to purchase from intermediaries with large selections. Mass distribution is enabled through shared selling, warehousing, transportation, and billing costs. Mass distribution may even lower production costs through economies of scale.

Consumer contact refers to the task of meeting and communicating with consumers. Consumer contact generally occurs before the sale (as in searching for prospects), during the sale (the sales presentation), and after the sale (following up with consumers). In retailing, customer contact often occurs in a store environment; in wholesaling, customer contact typically occurs when a salesperson visits the organizational consumer.

Although wholesalers and retailers typically purchase goods and services on the basis of terms, they still provide an important credit function for their suppliers. Payment for the purchased goods is almost always based on the purchase date, and not the date when the goods and services are ultimately sold to the wholesaler's or retailer's customers. This credit function allows manufacturers that sell goods through wholesalers and retailers, and wholesalers that sell goods through other channel members, to plan their cash flows accurately.

In market research, channel members generate, collect, and disseminate important information to manufacturers. Wholesalers and retailers are a vital source of information to manufacturers for several reasons. First, they are close to the market in that they see their customers on a continuing basis. Second, many channel members sell the products of competing manufacturers, which helps them be a better judge of consumer reactions. Third, point-of-sales systems enable wholesalers and retailers to share timely data with manufacturers.

CHANNEL FUNCTIONS CAN BE SHIFTED BUT NOT ELIMINATED

An important principle in channels is that channel functions can be shifted, but not eliminated. This concept suggests that the elimination of an intermediary does not necessarily mean that the channel function will no longer be performed. In contrast, the elimination of a wholesaler or retailer reallocates channel functions among channel members. A distribution function may be performed by a manufacturer, shared with other firms, contracted out, or shifted backward or forward in the marketing channel.[11] For example, a computer manufacturer that decides to bypass retailers and to sell goods directly to customers must now seek to maintain proper assortments, sell in small quantities, accept credit cards, employ a sales force, maintain attractive retail facilities, and conduct market research on its own. These functions were formerly performed by its retailer channel members. Similarly, a manufacturer that ships goods to its own sales branches has shipping costs that are comparable to transporting these same goods to an independent wholesaler or retailer.

If the manufacturer insisted on cash purchases or used a self-service operation, performance of these functions would be shifted to final consumers. According to one industry analyst in commenting on the shifting of functions among channel members in the computer industry, "Somebody has to provide support; either the manufacturer, or the dealer, or the customer must do it himself. If ComputerLand (now Vanstar) can do it cheaper, then that's a potential edge."[12]

According to the **Bucklin's system of service outputs** concept, consumers prefer to deal with marketing channels that provide them with higher levels of service outputs. Professor Bucklin identified four service outputs that a channel member can provide: spatial convenience or market decentralization, lot size, product variety or assortment breadth, and waiting or delivery time. Spatial convenience reduces transportation time and costs by providing convenient access to goods. Shopping centers and central business district locations provide spatial convenience. Lot size reduces minimum purchasing requirements for consumers, while enabling mass production for manufacturers. There is high overlap between Bucklin's service outputs and the sorting process. For example, spatial convenience is provided through the sorting process and through contactual efficiency. The assorting/breaking bulk process also provides lot size. Lastly, sorting provides product variety and assortment breadth. Waiting time, the time differential between ordering and receiving goods, is reduced through the channel member's maintenance of inventories of desired merchandise as well as through product delivery. According to Bucklin's theory, the more service outputs required by consumers, the less likely intermediaries will be bypassed.[13]

ALTERNATIVE CHANNEL STRUCTURES

The assignment of channel functions among channel members is based on the concept of channel specialization. In **channel specialization**, channel members perform those tasks in which they have a comparative advantage.

In a **short channel (direct distribution)**, manufacturers sell their goods and services directly to final or organizational consumers. No channel specialization is used, for one channel member performs all functions. For example, Sherwin-Williams sells some of its paint (such as its Sherwin-Williams brand) through company-owned outlets. In this way, Sherwin-Williams can control the quality of its in-store merchandising efforts, establish the assortment and variety in its stores, ensure that its stores will be open appropriate hours (for both its contractor and do-it-yourself customers), and legally determine the final selling prices for its merchandise. In a **long channel (indirect distribution)**, independent channel members (manufacturers, wholesalers, and retailers) take on specified responsibilities. Long channels are generally associated with high channel specialization. The sale of convenience goods through independent manufacturers, wholesalers, and retailers illustrates a long channel. Although long channels reduce the financial requirements of each member, they require coordination of channel activities and functions (see Figure 1-4a).

Channels can also be described in terms of channel width. **Channel width** refers to the degree of competition at any channel level as well as the intensity of distribution in a market area. For example, in **intensive distribution**, all channel members that meet minimum credit requirements can purchase a manufacturer's goods and services. Although competition among channel members is high, the market coverage of a product or service is also generally high. In **exclusive distribution**, only one channel member at any level can sell a manufacturer's goods and services in a given geographic area. Competition in a market

FIGURE 1-4 Alternative channel arrangements.

(a) Short and long channels of distribution

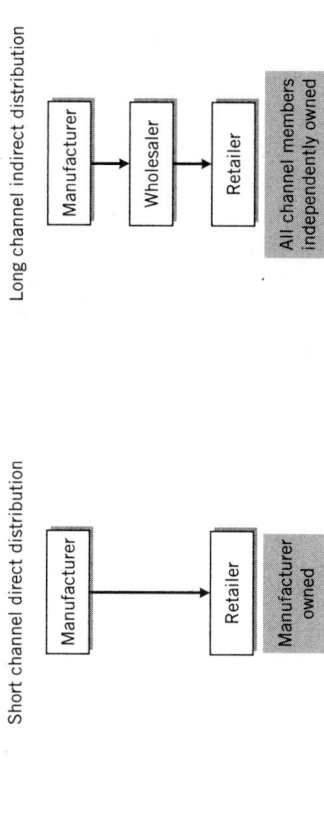

(b) Exclusive, selective, and intensive distribution

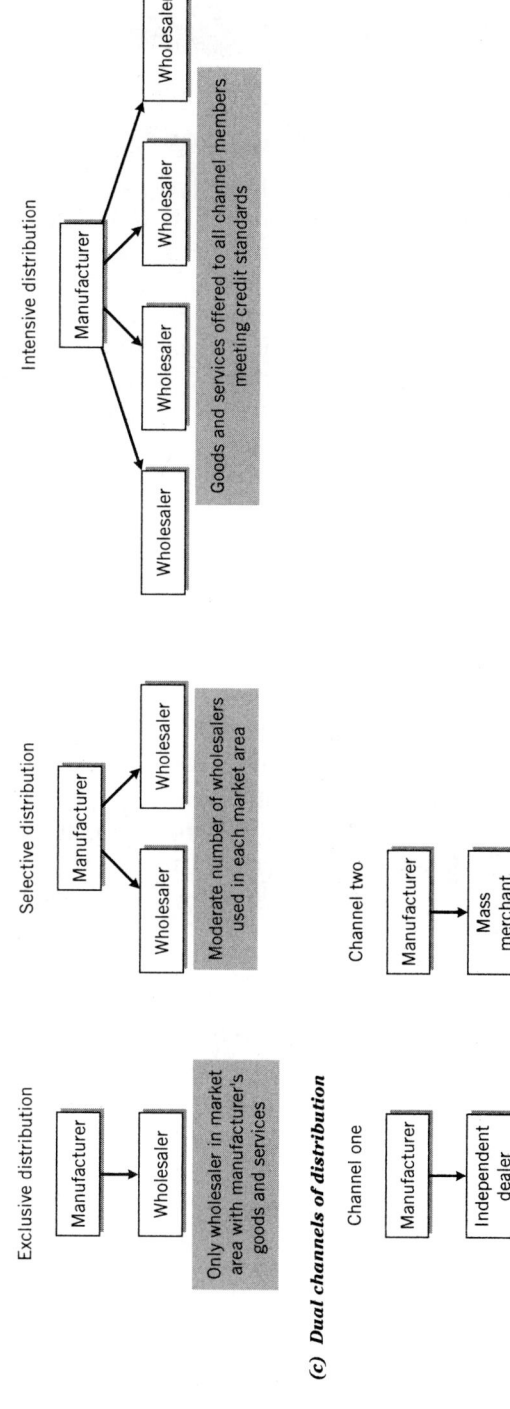

(c) Dual channels of distribution

CHANNELS IN ACTION

The Role of a Distributor in the Success of Birkenstock in the United States

When Margot Fraser, a dress designer on vacation in Germany, purchased a pair of Birkenstock's sandals in the late 1960s, she was an immediate convert. The anatomically molded sandals were in sharp contrast to the uncomfortable shoes that she typically wore.

Unfortunately, Fraser's initial enthusiasm was unmatched by both Birkenstock and U.S. retailers. It took Fraser three years of almost constant badgering for Birkenstock to appoint her as the sole U.S. distributor. In the intervening period, Fraser simply purchased Birkenstock sandals directly from the factory, typically 6 to 12 pairs at a time.

The initial response from U.S. retailers was also poor. Many traditional shoe retailers in the United States viewed the sandals as ugly and clunky. Most refused to carry them. Undeterred, Fraser decided to sell the shoes through health food stores. Many of her early customers were health food store owners and small stores near college campuses. The store owners raved so much about the shoes to their counterculture customers that the sandals became associated with hippies and "flower children." To many of its initial customers, Birkenstocks were the only alternative to bare feet.

Fraser was an active force in working with its supplier to extend the target market of Birkenstock to a much broader customer base:

- Fraser worked with Birkenstock to expand its line from one unisex style to 125 varieties of Birkenstocks (including separate lines for men, women, and kids). Birkenstocks are now even available in a patent leather version for dress and in a synthetic fabric model (for nonleather wearers). She also made frequent trips to Germany to ensure that new styles and colors would appeal to American tastes.
- A semiannual catalog was developed by Fraser to reposition Birkenstock's image from "flower children" to "trendy" customers. A typical scene features male and female models at a cafe wearing Birkenstocks.
- Fraser expanded distribution to include conventional shoe stores, department stores, and mail-order merchants such as L.L. Bean and the Sharper Image. The Sharper Image's catalog features the new Birkenstock Professional model that is designed to be worn with business attire.

Fraser's wholesale operation, Birkenstock Footprint Sandals, Inc., had wholesale sales of $50 million (about 1 million pairs of Birkenstock sandals) in fiscal 1992 (up from $8.6 million in 1986). The firm plans to sell over $100 million in Birkenstocks in 1995.

Source: Leslie Brokaw, "Feet Don't Fail Me Now," *Inc.* (May 1994), pp. 70–74 ff.

Beachwood Place, Cleveland, Ohio, is a modern multi-level enclosed regional shopping center. Part of the mall's common fountain area is used to display fashions. (Chapter 3) Photo courtesy of the Rouse Company.

Beachwood Place, Cleveland, Ohio

The unobtrusive columns in this photo are part of Sensormatic's Pro-Max® system which is used to prevent pilferage through electronic article surveillance (EAS). (Chapter 3) Photo courtesy of Sensormatic Electronics Corporation.

Marriott Distribution Services has seven distribution centers to service its own operations as well as those of its wholesale customers in the limited menu and casual dining segment. (Chapter 4) Photo © Jeff Zaruba.

A manufacturer should be evaluated by its wholesaler customers on the basis of multiple customer service standards as well as the quality of marketing support. (Chapter 5) Courtesy of Warren Tool Group.

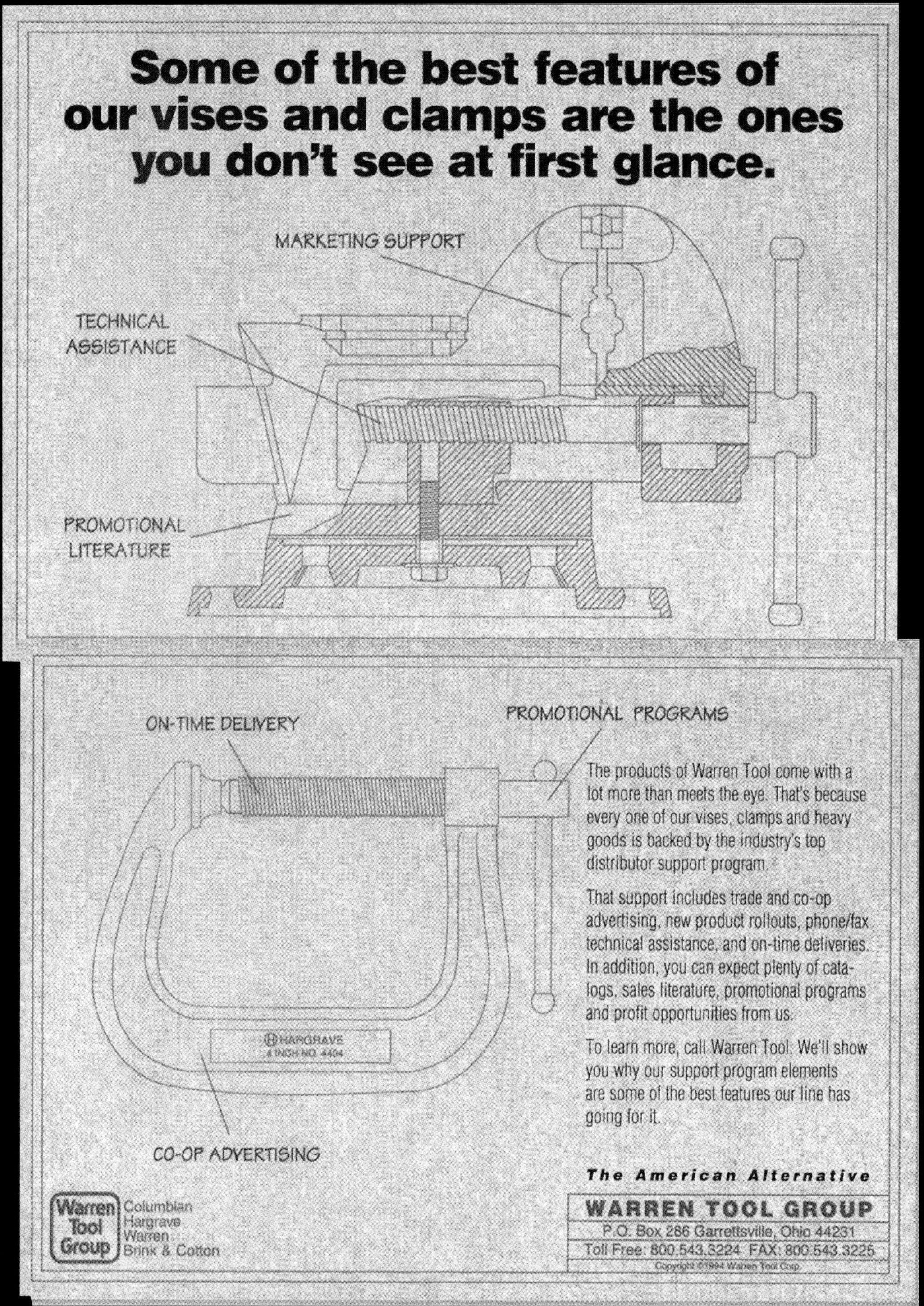

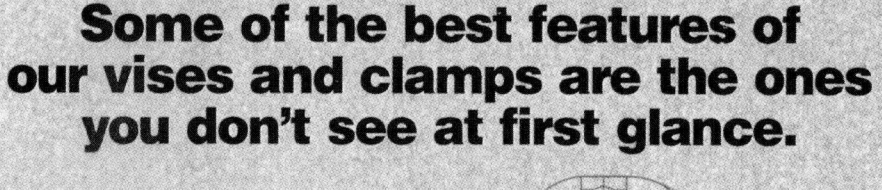
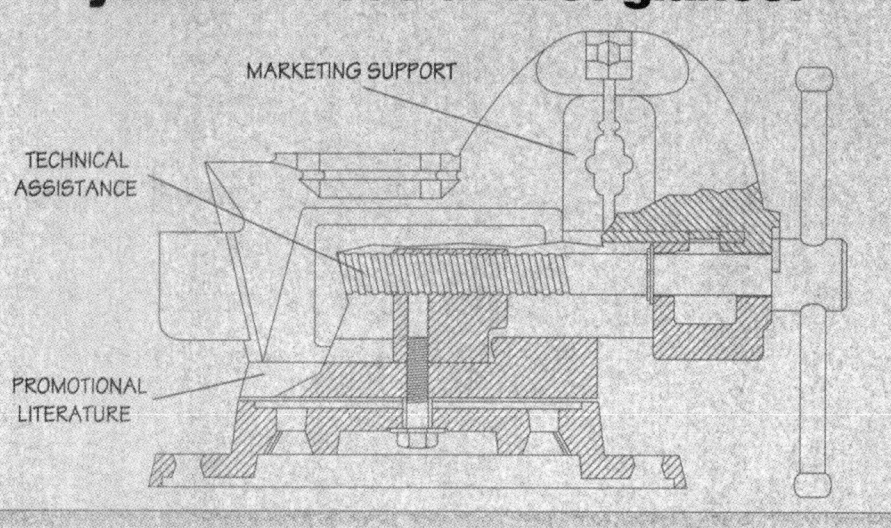

Air Products has used relationship marketing (partnering) for over 50 years. The Florida cogeneration facility shown here has been designed, built, and operated by Air Products and Chemicals. (Chapter 5) Photo courtesy of Air Products and Chemicals.

A Krautkramer Ultrasonic Weld Flaw Detector scans weld joints on a high pressure natural gas pipeline. The detector's software produces a printed record of weld flaws. (Chapter 6) Photo courtesy of Emerson Electric.

area is low, but the degree of market coverage is generally lower than in intensive distribution. **Selective distribution** seeks to balance the amount of channel member competition and degree of market coverage (see Figure 1-4b).

In addition to channel length and width, channels can also be described by their diversity. In **dual channels of distribution**, for example, the same good or service is sold through different channel arrangements. For example, Goodyear Tire & Rubber sells tires to mass merchandisers such as Sears and to independent tire dealers. These channel arrangements are illustrated in Figure 1-4c. Although dual channels of distribution may be costly to set up and maintain, they allow a manufacturer, wholesaler, or retailer to satisfy multiple market segments.

SPECIAL CHARACTERISTICS OF CHANNEL RELATIONSHIPS

In this section, we review the special characteristics of channel relationships: the divided loyalty of retailers and wholesalers in their relationships with suppliers and customers, the concepts of selling to and selling through intermediaries, the long-term relationships among channel members, and the high switching costs in channels. Other special characteristics that pertain only to retail or wholesale channels are covered in Chapters 3 and 4, respectively.

DIVIDED LOYALTY OF RETAILERS AND WHOLESALERS IN THEIR RELATIONSHIPS WITH SUPPLIERS AND CUSTOMERS

A study of the relationships of retailers and wholesalers with their suppliers and customers needs to reflect the multiple roles of each channel member. Wholesalers and retailers have two roles: (1) as salespersons for suppliers, and (2) as sources of supply for certain groups of customers. As a salesperson, wholesalers and retailers seek to build demand among their customers for particular brands. As a source of supply for customers, wholesalers and retailers assemble a group of products that can solve the needs of their customers. The ideal product selection for their customers may not include products produced by a given manufacturer.[14]

The importance of wholesalers as marketers and as sources of supply can be seen from a recent study by *Industrial Distribution* that was based on hundreds of interviews with 200 distributors. The study showed that in half of all transactions, an industrial distributor is asked to recommend a brand; in the other half, the customer asks for a specific brand. When asked to recommend a brand, 83 percent of all distributors do so, and nearly all customers buy the brand recommended. When distributors were asked whether they served as the purchasing arm for their customers, 59 percent agreed that is a highly accurate statement and 26 percent stated that it is somewhat accurate.[15]

Manufacturers and suppliers selling through wholesalers or retailers must also develop capabilities in their roles as sources of product and revenues for their wholesalers and retailers, and as the locus of brand preference with end-users. In their first role, suppliers are the marketing partner of the wholesaler and retailer through active support of their product lines. In the brand preference role, suppliers seek to develop brand loyalty for their products by end-users.

These roles generate a mutual interest in selling the goods of the manufacturers as well as divided loyalties. For example, wholesalers may not know whether they should give their loyalty to either their manufacturer/supplier or their customers. For example, although a wholesaler may be aware that a manufacturer's product is priced too high relative to competition, the wholesaler may need to sell the product to meet a sales quota or a manufacturer's sales incentive program. The wholesaler, however, does not want to lose the buyer's trust or lose the account.

Figure 1-5 describes the various capabilities and roles of wholesalers and their manufacturer/suppliers through a seesaw analogy. According to the figure, how the seesaw tips depends on such factors as the profit margin available to each party, the ability of the supplier to maintain brand preference with end-

FIGURE 1-5 Multiple roles of wholesalers and their manufacturer/suppliers.

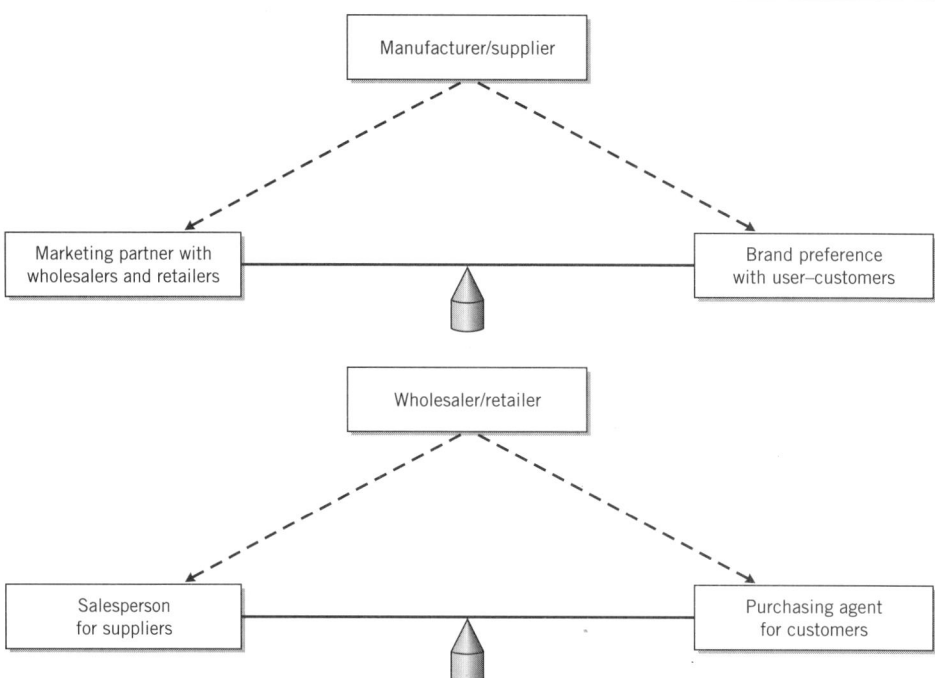

The direction of the seesaw depends on the relative channel power of the manufacturer/supplier and the wholesaler/retailer. Sources of channel power include profit margins, a supplier's brand pull, and other available sourcing options for wholesalers and retailers.

Source: Frank V. Cespedes, *Channel Management* (Boston: Harvard Business School, case 590-045, 1989), p. 13. Copyright ©1989 by the President and Fellows of Harvard College. Reprinted by permission.

users, and the other sourcing options of wholesalers and retailers. These variables all relate to **channel power**, the ability of one channel member to control the marketing strategy of another member at a different level of distribution in the same channel. For example, a high profit margin available to a wholesaler and high brand loyalty each contribute to a manufacturer's channel power. In contrast, the ability of a wholesaler to get a comparable product from another source provides the wholesaler with channel power.

SELLING TO (PUSH) AND SELLING THROUGH (PULL) INTERMEDIARIES

The roles of manufacturers and suppliers as the marketing partner of wholesalers and retailers and in developing brand preference with users/customers, as well as the role of wholesalers and retailers as selling agents for suppliers, implies the need for manufacturer and supplier marketing support.

Promotional support directed to wholesalers and retailers to get them to stock, display, and promote a manufacturer's products is referred to as **selling to the wholesaler/retailer**, or **push**. Examples of push are manufacturer training for wholesale and retail salespersons, sales contests directed at wholesale and retail sales persons, and incentives for wholesalers and retailers to load up on inventory (through quantity discounts and seasonal discounts). Push is often used by manufacturers and suppliers to gain adequate market coverage in competitive markets.

In contrast, **selling through the wholesaler/retailer**, or **pull**, emphasizes the importance of the final customer and the need for the producer to stimulate the final customer. Sometimes, the producer uses pull to get distribution that it could not otherwise obtain. Figure 1-6 illustrates push and pull. In practice, producers need to use both push and pull. Unless demand is generated at the final user stage through pull, inventories assembled at wholesalers and retailers through push will accumulate and prevent future sales from being made. Similarly, push-related promotional effort helps provide for adequate market coverage for products with little initial demand, such as a new product. Lastly, many intermediaries will not stock an item that is not effectively supported with advertising directed at consumers.

LONG-TERM RELATIONSHIPS AMONG CHANNEL MEMBERS

Many of the relationships among channel members are long term. For example, contracts between fast-food franchisors and franchisees are typically for 20 years. Contracts between manufacturers/suppliers and wholesalers are also typically long term. Even when the initial and subsequent contracts are for shorter terms (as the five-year contract between an auto manufacturer and a car dealer), a 30-year relationship between a car dealer and an auto manufacturer is not uncommon. In other cases, long-term relationships among channel members have existed for years without formal contracts.

FIGURE 1-6 Selling to (push) versus selling through (pull) the wholesaler/retailer.

Selling to the wholesaler and retailer (push)

In selling to the wholesaler and retailer (push), a producer's promotional support is directed at wholesalers and retailers to persuade them to stock, display, and promote the manufacturer–supplier's goods. The producer ultimately relies on the wholesaler and retailer to generate demand at the final customer level.

Selling through the wholesaler and retailer (pull)

In selling through the wholesaler and retailer (pull), a producer's promotional support is directed at the final consumer. The producer ultimately relies on demand from the final customer to generate demand at the retailer, wholesaler, and ultimately the manufacturer level.

Long-term relationships allow relationship marketing among channel participants to be developed and fostered. **Relationship marketing (partnering)** is based on building and maintaining long-term relationships between buyers and sellers that are based on trust and commitment. In relationship marketing, there is mutual recognition and understanding that the success of both the manufacturer/supplier and the wholesaler/retailer depends in part on the other firm. Through coordinated effort, these channel members can satisfy the requirements of the marketplace.[16] To build and maintain an effective long-term relationship, a manufacturer must understand its reseller's needs, develop reseller training and incentive programs, and actively manage these partnerships.[17]

Important components of effective partnerships include the monitoring of wholesalers and retailers through market research and through distributor councils, obtaining wholesaler and retailer input for the firm's overall marketing plan, and ensuring that two-way communication exists (through face-to-face contacts, newsletters, and the sponsoring of retreats for executives of both distributors and manufacturers).[18]

HIGH SWITCHING COSTS IN CHANNELS

The long-term relationship between manufacturer/supplier and its wholesalers and retailers is often due to high investment and costs for each. Technical and sales training costs, testing equipment, and electronic data interchange hardware and software all involve large investments in time and money.

Another type of cost involves **switching costs**, the costs facing a manufacturer, wholesaler, or retailer when they change channel arrangements. Switching costs for wholesalers and retailers include the cost of hiring or retraining sales and technical personnel, the lost profits due to some accounts staying with the old manufacturer, loss in productive sales time, the cost of establishing new physical distribution systems, and the psychic costs of severing a relationship.[19] Other costs include liquidating inventories, converting record-keeping to new product code numbers, and training sales personnel in particular features and applications of the new product line.[20]

A manufacturer's switching costs include such takedown costs as contractual restrictions on termination, the magnitude of a wholesaler's or retailer's reactions, and the reaction of the wholesaler and retailer network.[21]

High switching costs create a barrier to entry and suggest that wholesalers and retailers will have long-term relationships with their manufacturer/suppliers.[22] In a study of the effects of switching costs on termination of manufacturers' representatives in 243 firms, the researchers found that there is considerable inertia in the manufacturer/manufacturers' representative relationship. A manufacturer's perception of the level of switching costs has a significant negative impact on the firm's likelihood of converting to a direct sales force. High switching costs can block dissatisfied manufacturers from terminating their relationships with their manufacturers' representatives.[23]

IMPORTANCE OF CHANNEL MANAGEMENT TO THE FIRM

Channel management can be defined as the process of planning, managing, and controlling channel activities. This section explores the eight channel management strategies that can lead to a competitive advantage, the advantages of a channel-based strategy, and the relationship of channel management to the other elements of a firm's overall marketing strategy.

CHANNEL MANAGEMENT AS A COMPETITIVE ADVANTAGE

A channel member can use channel management as a means of developing and sustaining a long-term competitive advantage. Eight distinct channel management strategies that can lead to a competitive advantage can be identified: using exclusive distribution, using dual channels of distribution, using nontraditional channels, creating and maintaining a network of superior channel members, using technology, providing superb customer service, being a low-cost channel member, and having access to a specialized consumer market.[24] Unlike other strategies that may be easy for a competitor to copy, these strategies are long term in effectiveness. This section describes each strategy (see Table 1-2).

USING EXCLUSIVE DISTRIBUTION

Exclusive distribution enables full-service intermediaries to give their customers a high level of service without the fear of price competition from limited-service competitors. Exclusive distribution allows manufacturers to de-

TABLE 1-2 CHANNEL MANAGEMENT AS A COMPETITIVE ADVANTAGE

Competitive Advantage	Description of Advantage	Sources of Advantage
Using exclusive distribution	Enables full-service intermediaries to offer a high level of customer service without fear of price competition; allows manufacturers to develop close associations with wholesalers and retailers; fosters high mutual dependence among channel members.	Exclusive distribution agreement between channel members.
Using dual channels of distribution	Allows a manufacturer, wholesaler, or retailer to have access to a broader market with the same offering. Dual channels increase a firm's market coverage.	Access to different channels increases shopper convenience, and provides access to new target markets.
Using nontraditional channels	Expands product availability at convenient locations.	Identification of nontraditional channel members, being aware of special needs of these channel members, and satisfaction of special needs.
Having access to a broad network of channel members	Enables a channel member to use national advertising, to develop and maintain a regional or national brand image, and to provide a satisfactory level of market coverage.	Developing and maintaining strong channel members on a regional and national basis.
Using technology	Improves communication among channel members, lowers costs, and improves inventory management.	Computer software and hardware, communication linkages between channel members, and warehouse automation.
Providing superb customer service	Improves brand and dealer loyalty, reduces the impact of price competition, and increases customer satisfaction.	Fast delivery, maintenance of customer service records, high-quality order fulfillment, and stocking a wide assortment and variety of goods.
Being a low-cost distributor	Appeals to a price-conscious market segment, allows channel members to pass cost savings to customers and to earn a satisfactory profit while matching prices of competitors.	Automation, low-cost rental facilities, reducing services to customers, and charging additional fees for additional services.
Having access to a specialized market	Allows a channel member to better appeal to specialized needs of its target market, and to reach a target market more efficiently than competitors.	Targeted distribution directed at specialized target market.

velop a close association with their intermediaries. In exclusive distribution, the success of a manufacturer in a geographic area is dependent on the success of its intermediaries. Similarly, a retailer cannot succeed without an adequate level of manufacturer support. Exclusive distribution also enables an intermediary to develop its territory without the fear that a manufacturer will appoint additional wholesalers or retailers to take advantage of the high sales generated by its hard work.

Through use of exclusive distribution, Nautica (a manufacturer of men's and children's sportswear) was able to expand from a small firm in 1983 to a firm with sales of approximately $65 million in 1990. Only one or two department stores sell its product mix in each market, except New York. Exclusive distribution enables Nautica to work closely with its retailer customers on new merchandising ideas and to track sales by product category. Lower competition in their markets also enables department store customers to sell a high proportion of Nautica's line at its suggested list price. About 65 percent of Nautica's men's sportswear sales are made without markdowns; this compares favorably with 55 percent for all men's sportswear brands. With high sales per square foot and low markdowns, many department stores have begun to open Nautica boutiques within their stores. This has enabled Nautica to further expand its line of goods.[25]

Using Dual Channels of Distribution

Though costly to establish and maintain, dual channels allow a manufacturer, wholesaler, or retailer to satisfy multiple markets (such as price versus service-oriented consumers, and final versus organizational consumers) with the same or a similar product offering.

Although Goodyear Tire & Rubber sells its tires to both new car manufacturers and tire stores, it also maintains different channels for its retailers. For example, its Goodyear tire line is distributed among Goodyear's 6000 small dealers as well as through mass merchants.[26] This strategy allows Goodyear to increase its market coverage by selling in two markets, and to satisfy both the price and service-oriented market segments.

Using Nontraditional Channels

In nontraditional channels, manufacturers, wholesalers, and retailers are able to sell goods and services that are generally not associated with their facility. Two examples of the use of nontraditional channels are Timex and L'eggs. Timex sells its watches through such retail channels as supermarkets, convenience stores (such as 7-Eleven), airport newsstands, and Benetton stores. L'eggs intensively distributes its pantyhose through drug stores, convenience stores, and supermarkets. These channels were traditionally ignored by other competing manufacturers of watches and pantyhose. In 1993 Sara Lee Corporation's L'eggs brand was the best-selling pantyhose brand in the United States with a 42 percent share of the market in mass markets, according to data from Information Resources Inc.[27]

Nontraditional channels allow consumers to purchase goods and services at convenient locations. For example, Timex knows that consumers shop more frequently in its nontraditional channels for watches than in jewelry stores. L'eggs also understands that females shop more in food-based outlets than in clothing-based outlets. Timex and L'eggs also understand the self-service nature of these markets. To increase the acceptance of their products by self-service retailers and to better enable consumers to use self-service, both Timex and L'eggs developed special display racks for retailers to display their uniquely shaped containers.[28]

CREATING AND MAINTAINING A BROAD NETWORK OF CHANNEL MEMBERS

The creation and maintenance of a broad network of channel members allow a manufacturer to utilize regional and national advertising (providing the distribution network matches the coverage of the advertising), to develop and maintain a regional or national brand image, and to provide a satisfactory level of market coverage.

Although most first-tier Japanese car manufacturers (Honda, Toyota, and Nissan) have an extensive distribution network throughout the United States, second-tier Japanese car manufacturers (such as Mazda, Mitsubishi, Subaru, and Isuzu) have a less consistent dealer network in terms of market coverage. Without a sufficient number of high-quality dealers in a market area, these manufacturers cannot hope to obtain their market potential on either a local, regional, or national basis.

For years, Mitsubishi has had a poor level of brand awareness among U.S. car-buying consumers. It entered the U.S. market late (in 1982), had a small number of dealers that were clustered on the East and West Coasts, and had its image blurred by supplying cars under the Dodge and Plymouth as well as Mitsubishi brands. Mitsubishi is now changing its marketing strategy by developing a full line of cars (including a sportscar—the 3000GT—and a luxury sedan—the Diamante) as well as by strengthening its dealership network. It has expanded its number of dealers from 204 (at the end of 1987) to 550 (as of the middle of 1993). Unlike other Japanese competitors, Mitsubishi has decided that it will not create a separate dealer network for its Diamante luxury car. This decision increased existing dealer loyalty to the firm and made it easier for Mitsubishi to attract new dealers. Mitsubishi has purchased Value Rent-A-Car, a Florida-based car rental agency. The rental car operation should increase the visibility and trial rate of Mitsubishi cars. Lastly, to increase dealer loyalty, it spent $30 million on advertising to introduce its 1994 Galant model, more than it ever spent on a new model launch. It gives its dealers additional training and even tests their product knowledge with written examinations.[29]

USING TECHNOLOGY

Channel members can utilize technology to develop and maintain a competitive advantage. Computers can be used to schedule appointments, to maintain an up-to-date list of inventory, to isolate fast and slow-selling goods, and to target promotions at selected customers. Warehouse automation can reduce errors in order fulfillment, speed delivery, and decrease labor costs.

An example of an innovative use of technology as a competitive channel advantage is Baxter International's ValueLink automated purchasing system. ValueLink enables large customers, such as major hospitals, to order goods directly from Baxter using a telephone-linked terminal. Goods ordered through this system are delivered by Baxter directly to the ordering department (such as an operating room or a nursing floor) in the exact quantity requested. Thus, hospitals using Baxter's system benefit from a stockless inventory system. Stockless systems reduce both ordering and inventory carrying costs. These costs can equal the direct costs of the product.

ValueLink also provides important benefits to Baxter. Baxter is the leading distributor to hospitals with an estimated 28 percent market share. Its ValueLink service is acknowledged by Baxter to be a contributing cause of high market share. ValueLink also allows Baxter to impose extra charges for this service and to become a hospital's sole source of medical supplies. Although Baxter's price is higher than competitors that use traditional ordering and delivery methods, the hospital's total costs are typically lower with Baxter, owing to cost savings from inventory management.[30]

Providing Superb Customer Service

Channel members can develop and maintain a long-term competitive advantage by providing superb customer service. Examples of superb customer service include making fast delivery, maintaining customer service records, fulfilling over 95 percent of customer orders from stock-on-hand, stocking a wide assortment and variety of goods, and repairing equipment on-site.

Invacare Corporation, a manufacturer and distributor of home health-care products, has succeeded by offering its dealers superior service. Although its competitors offered low prices on comparable goods to home health-care retailers, these retailers had to buy goods in large quantities. Furthermore, retailers often had to wait as long as three weeks for deliveries. As a result, retailers needed a sizable inventory to properly service customer needs. In contrast, Invacare's channel strategy is based on daily deliveries, through a chain of 32 warehouses. Although Invacare's prices include freight charges, most competitors charge separately for freight costs. Invacare has also expanded its product mix from wheelchairs to the manufacture of hospital beds and rehabilitation equipment and to the distribution of items such as mattresses and batteries for motorized wheelchairs. Invacare's retailer customers can now purchase goods at Invacare that at one time required going to 30 different manufacturers.[31]

Being a Low-Cost Channel of Distribution

The development of a distribution strategy based on low cost enables a channel member to appeal to a price-conscious market segment, to pass on cost savings to its consumers, and to earn a satisfactory profit while matching the prices of competitors.

A channel member can reduce its costs through automation (of ordering, warehousing, and bookkeeping operations); through use of low-cost rental facilities (for showrooms, warehouses, and retail facilities); and minimizing the services offered to its customers (through self-service merchandising; through catalog sales; or through extra charges for delivery, installation, and on-premises repairs).

An example of the use of a low-cost approach to competitive advantage is Gateway, a mail-order computer retailer. Gateway's annual sales increased from about $1 million in 1986 to $275 million in 1990 and to $2.6 billion in 1994. The company went public in 1992, raising $143 million from its initial public offering. According to experts, Gateway's computers are not state-of-the-art, nor is its level of customer support extraordinary. What differentiates Gateway from other firms is its low-cost distribution system; this system enables Gateway to undercut most competitors' prices by at least 10 percent. Gateway has no showroom, assembles and distributes computers in South Dakota (which offers low-cost labor and rent), sells all of its computers on a prepaid basis (to reduce credit costs and inventory risks), and offers little technical support to its customers. As a result, Gateway's operating costs are only 5.4 percent of its revenues, as compared with 13 percent for Compaq. Although this strategy would not be successful for all target markets, Gateway's target customers are sophisticated computer users who require little technical assistance and who are driven to the firm on the basis of price—not service.[32]

HAVING ACCESS TO A SPECIALIZED MARKET

The last competitive advantage is having access to a specialized market. Access to this market allows a firm to better appeal to the specialized needs of its target market and to reach its market more efficiently than competitors. Without access to the specialized market, a marketer would have to promote its goods and services to the mass market. This would involve considerable waste.

In 1993 Merck, the nation's largest pharmaceutical company, purchased Medco Containment Services, one of the country's largest managers of prescription drug plans in a $6 billion transaction. In 1992 Medco processed 64.5 million prescriptions through retail pharmacies and dispensed 31 million prescriptions from its own mail-order pharmacies. Medco's customers include large medical plan sponsors such as companies, unions, and health maintenance organizations. These organizations insure 33 million patients. While Merck reaches the country's 653,000 physicians through its 5500 sales representatives, it acknowledges that this is an inefficient process. It also did not have access to the large and growing market of medical plan sponsors. Medco also has a database showing which doctors are in particular need of its drugs. It also keeps elaborate records of each patient's drug needs.[33]

ADVANTAGES OF A CHANNEL-BASED STRATEGY

These competitive advantages are applicable to manufacturers, wholesalers, and retailers; to sellers of both goods and services; to users of both short and long marketing channels; to channel members that utilize both single and dual distribution channels; to domestic and international firms; and to channel members that base their overall strategy on price versus service philosophies.

Although the competitive advantages were discussed separately, a firm can combine these strategies. For example, a firm can use technology to lower costs (through better management of its inventory) or to provide better customer service (through maintaining a repair record for customer equipment), and a firm can use nontraditional channels as part of a dual channel of distribution strategy (by selling goods through both traditional and nontraditional channels).

A common feature of the effective use of a distribution-related competitive advantage is that a firm's channel strategy is integrated with its overall marketing strategy. For example, L'eggs developed innovative packaging for self-service merchandising, used an egg-shaped container to increase brand recognition, and provided displays for supermarkets. Goodyear developed and maintained separate channels to increase its overall market share. Mitsubishi introduced innovative products and a full product line to attract customers as well as dealers. And Gateway used its low-cost distribution network to lower its prices to a cost-conscious market segment.

A key strength of channel management as a competitive advantage is its long-term nature. For example, many contracts with franchises are based on 20-year renewable contracts. An effective retailer network can take years to develop, and it is extremely difficult for a product to meet its potential without an adequate presence in the market. Many wholesalers will not represent manufacturers with competing brands and products. A manufacturer may not be able to get access to the most effective wholesaler because of this restriction.

In addition to being long term, channel relationships are among the most difficult for a competitor to duplicate.[34] Although a competitor may seek to copy a successful pricing strategy by meeting a firm's low price, by developing a similar line of products, or by imitating a firm's promotional theme, channel relationships are much more difficult to imitate. For example, the best dealers may also be already committed to competing brands. A manufacturer, wholesaler, or retailer may also find that the best retail locations have already been taken by a major competitor.

The next section explores the relationship of channel management to the other elements of marketing strategy.

THE RELATIONSHIP OF CHANNEL MANAGEMENT TO THE OTHER ELEMENTS OF A FIRM'S OVERALL MARKETING STRATEGY

Channel management can be undertaken by marketing personnel that handle channel decisions as part of their overall responsibilities or by specialized channel managers. In the most common form of channel management organization, product managers, pricing executives, advertising executives, sales managers, credit managers, franchise relations personnel, customer service personnel, market researchers, and vice presidents of marketing undertake channel management tasks as part of their overall responsibilities. For example, a manufacturer's sales manager may be responsible for motivating, training, and evaluating the firm's wholesalers.[35]

This form of organization has a number of advantages, namely: channel management is undertaken by functional specialists, no additional marketing personnel are required, and responsibility is clearly focused with the functional executive. Its disadvantages include: the lack of coordination among marketing executives relating to channels, no executive has a specialized channels perspective, and channel-related activities may be given inadequate attention.

An alternative form of organization is the use of a specialized channels manager position. In this organization, the channel manager is responsible for planning, coordinating, and controlling channel-related activities.[36] Table 1-3 outlines the intrafirm relationships of the channels manager. The advantages of the use of a specialized channel manager are the use of a channels specialist, better coordination among marketing executives, and the development of stan-

TABLE 1-3   INTRAFIRM RELATIONSHIPS OF THE CHANNELS MANAGER

Position	Channels Manager Relationship
Vice president of marketing	Reports to the vice president of marketing and coordinates activities with other marketing personnel
Sales manager	Ensures proper allocation of selling time to various channels
	Maintains channel support such as distributor training and selling aids
	Promotes effective communication and education of channel members in the areas of cooperative advertising, sales promotion campaigns, and trade discounts
Advertising manager	Coordinates trade promotion in terms of media budgets, advertising allowances, and consistency of themes
Product manager	Coordinates channel-related activities among various products
	Ensures that products flow through the most efficient and effective channels
Physical distribution manager	Coordinates the firm's physical distribution efforts with those of other channel members
	Strives to eliminate duplication of efforts to reduce costs
Marketing research director	Requests and assists in designing studies of channel attitudes, conflict, and consumer preferences for alternatives
Controller	Obtains financial data necessary to evaluate and control the channel and to ensure budgets sufficiently large to support channel development and maintenance
Legal counsel	Communicates with the legal department to ensure legality of territorial restrictions, exclusive dealing, pricing, dual distribution, and vertical integration

Source: Donald W. Jackson, Jr. and Bruce J. Walker, "The Channels Manager: Marketing's Newest Aide?" *California Management Review,* Vol. 23 (Winter 1980), p. 52.

dardized channel policies. The disadvantages of the channels manager position include the increased costs of a channels manager and his or her staff, coordination problems among the channels manager and other functional marketing personnel, and the difficulty in finding a person with the necessary background.[37]

The most recent study of channel organization, reported in 1985, examined large manufacturing companies with annual sales of $50 million or more.[38] Fourteen percent of the marketing executive respondents reported that their firm has a channels manager within the firm's marketing organization. This is a significant increase over the less than 2 percent of firms reporting a channels manager position in a study conducted in 1976.[39] Channel management activities were most commonly undertaken by a variety of marketing executives including marketing managers, the vice president of marketing, sales managers, and product managers.[40]

It is possible that franchisors and wholesalers have a greater proportion of channel managers than manufacturers. For example, franchisors require channel management personnel to evaluate franchisees, determine whether territories need to be redefined (on the basis of sales and population patterns), to help franchisees manage their businesses, and to determine criteria for franchise renewal. Wholesalers may also require larger proportions of channel management personnel. The low proportion of channel managers should not be taken to mean that a low percentage of marketing personnel are employed in channel-related activities. Data on employment in channels are discussed in the next section.

Regardless of the form of organization of channel activities, it is important for a firm to make sure that channel management considerations are reflected in its short-term and long-term marketing strategy. A firm also needs to coordinate its channel strategy with the other elements of its overall marketing strategy. Table 1-4 contains a listing of channels-related decisions that need to be analyzed by marketing personnel involved in product planning, pricing management, and promotion management.

IMPORTANCE OF CHANNEL MANAGEMENT IN THE ECONOMY

A problem in evaluating the importance of channel management in the U.S. economy is the scarcity of channel-related data on channel management activities by manufacturers. For example, although data on channel costs and/or channel-related employment are reported for retailers and wholesalers by the government, trade associations, and market research firms, little or no corresponding data are reported for manufacturers.

Obtaining channel costs and employment data for retailers and wholesalers is relatively easy, since all activities performed by retailers and wholesalers are related to channel management. Although a manufacturer's physical distribution and dealer support activities (dealer training, dealer incentives, and troubleshooting) can be easily classified as channel management, other activities

TABLE 1-4 CHANNEL-RELATED DECISIONS THAT NEED TO BE ANALYZED BY MARKETING PERSONNEL

Product planning	Can potential new products be sold through the same channels as existing products?
	Do we use channel members as input for new product ideas?
	How will existing channel members respond to a new private-label strategy?
	How can we get channel member cooperation in handling a product recall?
	Will channel members give our new products adequate shelf space?
	What products and services should we require franchises to purchase from us to help ensure a consistent image across outlets?
	How can we implement a strategy of providing specialized products to small geographical markets?
	Under what conditions should we refuse to sell our products to a retailer?
Pricing management	Are profit margins adequate for wholesalers and retailers to adequately service the product?
	How will dealers respond to a manufacturer's reduction in list price to increase retail sales of a slow-selling product?
	What price differentials should we maintain between small and large retailer customers?
	How should we handle distributors that purchase our products through unauthorized distribution channels and then resell them at a discount to traditional customers?
	What quantity discount schedule enables us to maximize our market share?
	How can we control retailers that discount our products' prices and then "ruin the market" for full-service retailers?
	What price differentials should we maintain between direct store delivery to retailers and delivery to the retailer's distribution center?
	What seasonal discount structure can be used to encourage intermediaries to purchase goods off-season?
Promotion management	How much of our advertising budget should go to trade-related promotions (push)?
	How much of our advertising budget should go to final consumer-related promotions (pull)?
	What is the best mix of advertising, publicity, selling, and sales promotion for an intermediary?
	What is the best mix of advertising, publicity, selling, and sales promotion for final consumers?
	How can we get intermediaries to effectively use our cooperative advertising allowances?
	What cooperative advertising allowance should we provide to an intermediary?
	What types of sales contests and other incentives will best motivate a wholesaler's and retailer's salespersons?
	How should we determine wholesaler quotas?

are more difficult to categorize properly. For example, point-of-purchase materials provided to wholesalers and retailers by manufacturers and cooperative advertising allowances are clearly channel management activities. However, image-related advertising is generally not considered as channel management. It is difficult to obtain accurate data on these costs.

ESTIMATING CHANNEL COSTS

Channel costs include customer communication, paperwork flows, physical distribution, financial risk assumption, and reseller net margins and commissions (see Table 1-5). Channel costs vary greatly among channel members. For example, on the average, about 38 to 40 cents of every sales dollar spent in department and specialty stores go to retailers as channel costs and profit.[41] The corresponding number for independent supermarkets is 22 cents on the sales dollar.[42] Channel costs should not be confused with channel profits. The average profits as a percentage of sales for specialty stores is a little over 2 percent of sales, and supermarkets typically have net profit margins of between 1 and 2 percent. One study of channel costs for three leading industrial goods manufacturers found that channel costs were 39.4 and 43.3 percent of sales for two major electrical equipment suppliers, and 32.2 percent of sales for a leading industrial supplies manufacturer for 1985.[43]

Although no data exist on overall wholesale channel costs, annual data are compiled by Robert Morris Associates for wholesalers by product line. In data

TABLE 1-5 ELEMENTS OF CHANNEL COSTS

Customer communications
  Personal selling
  Travel
  Sales meetings
  Telemarketing
  Computer interfaces with customers
  Trade shows and demonstrations
  Advertising
    Media: print, television, radio
    Direct mail
Paperwork flows
  Billing and collections
Physical distribution
  Order receipt and processing
  Shipping
  Physical handling and storage
Financial risk assumption
  Sales credit
  Inventory financing
Reseller net margins and commissions

Source: Adapted from E. Raymond Corey, *A Note on Industrial Distribution Costs* (Boston: Harvard Business School, 1989), pp. 1–2.

reflecting wholesalers with annual sales of $25 million or more (for the time period October 1, 1993 to April 1, 1993 through March 31, 1994), the median wholesaler had channel costs and profits of 20.4 percent of sales. The range was 8 percent for meat and meat products wholesalers to 34.5 percent for toys, hobby goods, and supplies. The median wholesaler had a profit margin of 1.8 percent of sales. The range was −1.2 percent for piece goods (woven fabrics) wholesalers to 8.4 percent for footwear wholesalers.[44]

The most recent published study of manufacturer channel costs was conducted by the National Council of Physical Distribution Management in 1976. The study estimated that physical distribution costs accounted for 13.6 percent of each sales dollar for all manufacturers.[45] This study did not estimate channel management expenses other than physical distribution.

Although no study is available that quantifies channel management costs as a percentage of a retail sales dollar, a rough estimate of channel management expenses can be estimated by making several reasonable assumptions. These assumptions are that a product is sold by a manufacturer through both a wholesaler and a retailer, that the retailer's gross profit margin is 35 percent, that a wholesaler's gross profit margin is 20 percent, and that a manufacturer's channel costs are 15 percent of its wholesale selling prices. Using these assumptions, we see that channel costs (including profits to the wholesaler and retailer) would equal 55.8 percent of sales (see Table 1-6). Total channel costs would be even greater if additional channel members were involved, if gross profit margins of these intermediaries were higher, and if a manufacturer's channel costs were higher.

Although the numbers used are hypothetical, the gross profit numbers and the number of channel members used in this example are realistic. The important aspect of these numbers is that channel costs are higher than the manufacturer's costs for producing the product.

TABLE 1-6 AN ESTIMATE OF CHANNEL COSTS

Assuming:
- Retailer gross profit of 35 percent
- Wholesaler gross profit of 20 percent
- Manufacturer channel costs of 15 percent of sales

Selling price =	$1.00
Retailer costs and profit =	
35 percent of retail selling price =	.35
Wholesale cost to retailer =	.65
Wholesale costs and profit =	
20 percent of wholesale selling price =	.13
Cost to wholesaler =	.52
Total manufacturer channel costs =	
15 percent of wholesale selling price =	.078

Total channel costs = 35 cents + 13 cents + 7.8 cents = 55.8 cents

Note: Wholesalers base their profit margin on the selling price to retailers (not retail selling price). A manufacturer's channel costs are also based on its wholesale selling price, not retail selling price.

EMPLOYMENT

As is the case for channel costs, data on employment in channels are also available for retailers and wholesalers, but not for manufacturers. According to the U.S. Bureau of Labor Statistics, about 19.5 million people are employed by traditional retailers in the United States. This does not include several million persons employed by various service firms, seasonal employees, proprietors, and unreported employees in a family business or partnership. And about 4.8 million people are employed in wholesaling. This represents about one-fifth of all civilian employees 16 years of age and over.[46]

SALES

According to the U.S. Department of Commerce, annual retail store sales (including some mail-order sales by store retailers) are close to $2 trillion. In addition, $175 billion in yearly sales are derived from telephone and mail-order sales by nonstore retailers, vending machines, and direct selling. These data do not include personal consumption expenditures on services (such as financial, medical, and educational).

Wholesale sales are well over $2 trillion. Wholesaler sales are higher than retailing because some products move through several levels of wholesalers. An item can be sold through two or more wholesale levels; in contrast, an item can only be sold through one retailer. Wholesale sales also include purchases made by organizational consumers as well as wholesale sales made by manufacturers to organizational consumers.

Not counting direct sales to final consumers by manufacturers through nonstore channels, over $4 trillion in sales transactions moves through wholesale and retail channels of distribution. Some of these sales may be double-counted. For example, the same good may be sold through a long channel such as manufacturers to wholesalers, wholesalers to retailer (both wholesaling activities), and then retailer to consumer (a retailing activity).

ORGANIZATION OF THE TEXT

There are four different approaches to the study of channel management: an institutional approach, a functional approach, a behavioral approach, and a strategic approach.

An institutional approach focuses on the characteristics of channel members, their size, compensation, trends, organization, and responsibilities. Such a study would look at such institutions as wholesalers, retailers, transportation firms, financial institutions, advertising agencies, and market research firms. A functional approach describes such channel functions as sales management, advertising, market research, and credit that are undertaken by channel members. A behavioral approach stresses the relations among channel members;

this approach studies such factors as power, conflict, and cooperation among channel members, and the effect of channel member satisfaction on performance. A **strategic approach** focuses on the development, implementation, and control of a long-term competitive advantage through efficient and effective channel management.

All four approaches are used in the text, but the main focus of the text is on the strategic approach. A strategic approach differs from the other approaches in that it

- Defines the scope of a firm's business in terms of both goods and services and markets.
- Has a decision-making orientation.
- Bases a firm's strategy on its overall strengths and weaknesses.
- Focuses on opportunities and threats in the environment.
- Anticipates change and sets strategy on a proactive (rather than a reactive) basis.
- Has a long-term orientation.

This text is divided into five parts. The balance of Part One discusses the channel environment. Among the parts of the environment covered are consumers, channel competition, the economy, the legal environment, and the technological environment. Part Two analyzes the major channel members: wholesalers and retailers. These chapters cover the structure, special characteristics, channel members, and channel management issues in retailing and wholesaling. Part Three describes channel management from the perspective of the marketing mix. The marketing mix for channels includes market research and information systems, product management, physical distribution, pricing strategy, and promotion strategy of channel members. Part Four analyzes channel planning, coordination, and organization. This part covers such important topics as channel structure and design, administrative structures in marketing channels, channel conflict and cooperation, and channels for services and international marketing. Part Five discusses channel assessment and control. Appropriate productivity measures and the channel member audit are covered in this section.

SUMMARY

1 *To define marketing channels.* A marketing channel is an organized network (system) of agencies and institutions which, in combination, perform all the activities required to link producers with users to accomplish the marketing task.

2 *To describe the functions performed by channel members.* Five channel members can be identified: the sorting process (including breaking bulk and contactual efficiency), mass distribution, customer contact, credit, and market research. Through the sorting process, wholesalers and retailers resolve the conflicting orientations of manufacturers (their suppliers) and their organizational and final consumers. Breaking bulk refers to the wholesaler or retailer function of purchasing goods in case lots and reselling them to their customers in smaller quantities. Consumer contact refers to the task of meeting and communicating with consumers. Channel members enable mass distribution to occur through shared selling, warehousing, transportation, and billing costs. Mass distribution may even lower production costs owing to economies of scale. The credit function allows manufacturers that sell goods through wholesalers and retailers, and wholesalers that sell goods through other channel members, to accurately plan their cash flows. In market research, channel members generate, collect, and disseminate important information to manufacturers.

3 *To study alternative channel structures.* The assigning of channel functions among channel members is based on the concept of channel specialization. In channel specialization, channel members perform those tasks in which they have a comparative advantage. In a short channel (direct distribution), manufacturers sell their goods and services directly to final or organizational consumers. No channel specialization is used, for one channel member performs all functions. In a long channel (indirect distribution), independent channel members (manufacturers, wholesalers, and retailers) take on specified responsibilities. Channels can also be described in terms of channel width. In intensive distribution, all channel members that meet minimum credit requirements can purchase a manufacturer's goods and services. In exclusive distribution, only one channel member in any level can sell a manufacturer's goods and services in a given geographic area. Selective distribution seeks to balance the amount of channel member competition and degree of market coverage. In addition to channel length and width, channels can also be described by their diversity. In dual channels of distribution, for example, goods and services are sold through different channel arrangements.

4 *To evaluate the special characteristics of channel relationships.* The special characteristics of channel relationships include the divided loyalty of retailers and wholesalers in their relationships with suppliers and customers, the concept of selling to (push) versus selling through (pull) intermediaries, the long-term relationships among channel members, and the high switching costs in channels.

5 *To illustrate the importance of channel management to the firm and the economy.* A channel member can use channel management as a means of developing and sustaining a long-term competitive advantage. Eight distinct channel management strategies that can lead to a competitive advantage have been identified: using exclusive distribution, using a dual channel of distribution, using nontraditional channels, creating and maintaining a network of superior channel members, using technology, providing superb customer service, being a low-cost channel member, and having access to a specialized consumer market.

Channel costs vary greatly among retailers and wholesalers. For example, on the average, about 38 to 40 cents of every sales dollar spent in department and specialty stores go to retailers as channel costs and profit. The corresponding number for independent supermarkets is 22 cents on the sales dollar. While no data exist on overall wholesale channel costs, annual data are compiled by Robert Morris Associates for wholesalers by product line. In data reflecting wholesalers with annual sales of $25 million or more, the median wholesaler had channel costs and profits of 17.7 percent of sales. The most recent published study of manufacturer channel costs estimated that physical distribution costs accounted for 13.6 percent of each sales dollar for all manufacturers. This study did not estimate channel management expenses other than physical distribution. Although no study is available that quantifies channel management costs as a percentage of a retail sales dollar, a rough estimate of channel management expenses can be made by making several reasonable assumptions. Based on these assumptions, channel costs (including profits to the wholesaler and retailer) would equal 55.8 percent of sales. Total channel costs would be even greater if additional channel members were involved and if gross profit margins of these intermediaries were higher.

Data on employment in channels are also available on retailing and wholesaling, but not manufacturing. According to the U.S. Bureau of Labor Statistics, about 20 million people are employed by traditional retailers in the United States. And about 6 million people are employed in wholesaling. This represents about one-fifth of all civilian employees 16 years of age and over.

According to the U.S. Department of Commerce, annual retail store sales (including some mail-order sales by store retailers) are close to $2 trillion. Wholesale sales are well over $2 trillion.

6 *To analyze the orientation and format of the text.* There are four different approaches to the study of channel management: an institutional approach, a functional approach, a behavioral approach, and a strategic approach. Although all four approaches are used in the text, the major focus is on a strategic approach. A strategic approach focuses on the development, implementation, and control of a channel management strategy.

KEY TERMS

marketing channels
intermediaries
facilitators
retailing
wholesaling
physical distribution
sorting process
breaking bulk
contactual efficiency
consumer contact
Bucklin's system of service outputs

channel specialization
short channel (direct distribution)
long channel (indirect distribution)
channel width
intensive distribution
exclusive distribution
selective distribution
dual channels of distribution

channel power
selling to the wholesaler/retailer (push)
selling through the wholesaler/retailer (pull)
relationship marketing (partnering)
switching costs
channel management
strategic approach

QUESTIONS FOR DISCUSSION

1. Define marketing channels. Be sure to differentiate among retailing, wholesaling, physical distribution, and marketing channels in your explanation.

2. Describe and explain each channel management activity.

3. a. Describe the sorting process stages of accumulation, allocation, sorting, and assorting using the example of a department store buyer purchasing high fidelity components from 15 different manufacturers.

   b. What are the benefits from the perspective of the manufacturer? the retailer? the final consumer?

4. A wholesaler buys its supplies from 30 different manufacturers; the wholesaler has over 10,000 retailer customers. Describe the concept of contactual efficiency as it applies to the firm. Compute the number of consumer contacts with and without the wholesaler.

5. Explain the following statement from the perspective of a manufacturer considering converting its distribution strategy from a long to a short channel: "Channel functions can be shifted, but not eliminated."

6. According to the concept of channel specialization, "Channel members perform those tasks in which they have a comparative advantage." Describe the comparative advantages of retailers in comparison to manufacturers.

7. Differentiate between the following channel structures:
   a. Short and long channels.
   b. Intensive, exclusive, and selective distribution.
   c. Single and dual channels of distribution.

8. Explain the importance of both push and pull to a manufacturer/supplier in generating and maintaining good channel relations.

9. Describe how a firm can use channel management as a means of developing and sustaining a long-term competitive advantage.

10. "Many of the means of using channel management as a competitive advantage involve opposite concepts: exclusive and intensive distribution, high service and low costs, broad market access and access to a market niche." Explain this concept.

11. a. Describe the concept of a channels manager.
    b. What are the advantages of a channels manager form of organization in comparison to a functional form of marketing organization?
    c. What are the disadvantages of a channels manager form of organization in comparison to a functional form of marketing organization?

12. Estimate total channel costs on the basis of retailer gross profits of 40 percent, wholesaler gross profits of 15 percent, and manufacturer channel costs of 20 percent.

13. Differentiate between the following approaches to the study of channel management:
    a. An institutional approach.
    b. A functional approach.
    c. A behavioral approach.
    d. A strategic approach.

14. What are the advantages of studying channels management from a strategic approach?

END NOTES

1. Robert R. Rehder, "Is Saturn Competitive?" *Business Horizons,* Vol. 37 (March–April 1994), pp. 7–15; Jaclyn Fierman, "The Death and Rebirth of the Salesman," *Fortune* (July 25, 1994), pp. 80–82 ff.; Doron P. Levin, "Bringing a Slow-Moving Auto Giant Up to Speed," *New York Times* (September 5, 1993), p. F5; David Woodruff, "Saturn: May We Help Kick the Tires," *Business Week* (August 3, 1992), pp. 49–50; and David Woodruff et al., "Saturn Moves into High Gear," *Business Week* (August 17, 1992), pp. 86–91.

2. Peter D. Bennett, ed., *Dictionary of Marketing Terms* (Chicago: American Marketing Association, 1988), p. 29.

3. *Sherwin Williams Company 1994 Annual Report,* p. 4.

4. The material on marketing channel flows is based on Roland S. Vaile, E. T. Grether, and Reavis Cox, *Marketing in the American Economy* (New York: Ronald Press, 1952), pp. 113–129.

5. Barry Berman and Joel R. Evans, *Retail Management: A Strategic Approach,* 6th ed. (Englewood Cliffs, N.J.: Prentice Hall, 1995), p. 4.

6. Joel R. Evans and Barry Berman, *Marketing,* 6th ed. (Englewood Cliffs, N.J.: Prentice Hall, 1994), p. 516. This definition has been adapted from the U.S. Bureau of the Census.

7. Peter D. Bennett, ed., *Dictionary of Marketing Terms,* Second Edition (Chicago: American Marketing Association, 1995), pp. 206–207.

8. Wroe Alderson, *Marketing Behavior and Executive Action* (Homewood, Ill.: Richard D. Irwin, 1957), Ch. 7.

9. Wroe Alderson, "Factors Governing the Development of Marketing Channels," in *Marketing Channels for Manufacturers,* Richard M. Clewett, ed. (Homewood, Ill.: Richard D. Irwin, 1954), pp. 5–22.

10. The costs of a business-to-business field sales call are estimated annually in the "Survey of Selling Costs," *Sales & Marketing Management.*

11. See Ronald D. Michman, "Managing Structural Changes in Marketing Channels," *Journal of Business and Industrial Marketing,* Vol. 5 (Summer 1990), pp. 5–13.

12. John Markoff, "Computerland's Survival Strategy," *New York Times* (November 13, 1991), p. D4.

13. See Louis P. Bucklin, *Competition and Evolution in the Distributive Trades* (Englewood Cliffs, N.J.: 1972), pp. 18–31.

14. Frank V. Cespedes, *Channel Management* (Boston: Harvard Business School, 1989), pp. 6–7.

15. Jack Keough, "Distributors: The New Purchasing Arm for Their Customers," *Industrial Distribution* (May 1994), pp. 40–41.

16. James C. Anderson and James A. Narus, "A Model of Distributor Firm and Manufacturer Firm Working Partnerships," *Journal of Marketing,* Vol. 54 (January 1990), p. 42.

17. See James Narus and James C. Anderson, "Turn Your Industrial Distributors into Partners," *Harvard Business Review,* Vol. 64 (March–April 1986), pp. 66–71.

18. Ibid.

19. Michael E. Porter, *Competitive Strategy: Techniques for Analyzing Industries and Competitors* (New York: Free Press, 1980), p. 114.

20. E. Raymond Corey, *Industrial Marketing Systems* (Boston: HBS Case Services, 1982), p. 15.

21. Allen M. Weiss and Erin Anderson, *The Effects of Switching Costs on the Termination of Distribution Channel Relationships* (Cambridge, Mass.: Marketing Science Institute, April 1991), p. 10.

22. For a discussion of role performance of current channel members, an alternative channel member, and switching costs, see Robert Ping and F. Robert Dwyer, "Relationship Termination in Marketing Channels," in *1988 American Marketing Educators' Proceedings,* Gary Frazier, Charles Ingene, and David Aaker et al., eds. (Chicago: American Marketing Association, 1988), pp. 245–249.

23. Weiss and Anderson, *The Effects of Switching Costs on the Termination of Distribution Channel Relationships.*

24. The first four reasons are drawn from Allan J. Magrath, "Differentiating Yourself Via Distribution," *Sales & Marketing Management* (March 1991), pp. 50, 56–57.

25. Katherine Weisman, "Kismet on Seventh Avenue," *Forbes* (November 25, 1991), pp. 152–153.

26. *The Goodyear Tire & Rubber Company 1993 Annual Report,* p. 8.

27. Teri Agins, "Women Show What They Think of Pantyhose: Less and Less," *Wall Street Journal* (March 10, 1994), pp. B1, B6.

28. Anthony Ramirez, "L'eggs Makes Big Switch from Plastic to Cardboard," *New York Times* (July 10, 1991), pp. D1, D7.

29. Doron P. Levin, "Mitsubishi's Big Campaign in U.S.," *New York Times* (April 30, 1991), pp. D1, D4; Karen Lowry Miller, Larry Armstrong, and James B. Treece, "Mitsubishi Pulls Out the Stops," *Business Week* (May 6, 1991), pp. 64, 66; and Krystal Miller, "Mitsubishi Restyles Galant to Anchor Line," *Wall Street Journal* (June 23, 1993), p. B1.

30. *Baxter International Annual Report 1993;* Marcia Berss, "2 + 2 = 3," *Forbes* (February 28, 1994), pp. 82–83; and Susan Caminiti, "Finding New Ways to Sell More," *Fortune* (July 27, 1992), p. 100.

31. Harlan S. Byrne, "The Right Rx," *Barron's* (July 18, 1994), p. 19; Elizabeth Ehrlich, "The Quality Management Checkpoint," *International Business* (May 1993), pp. 56–62; and Christopher Palmeri, "Wheel-to-Wheel Combat," *Forbes* (February 15, 1993), pp. 62–65.

32. Peter Burrows, "The Computer Is in the Mail," *Business Week* (January 23, 1995), pp. 76–77; John Dvorak, "The Udder Truth Is No Bull," *Marketing Computers* (February 1994), p. 20; and Bronwyn Fryer, "Marketers to Watch," *Marketing Computers* (January 1994), pp. 28–30.

33. Brian O'Reilly, "Why Merck Marries the Enemy," *Fortune* (September 20, 1993), pp. 60–64; and Milt Freudenheim, "Merck Is Buying Drug Discounter, Seeing a Future of Price Restraint," *New York Times* (July 29, 1993), pp. A1 ff.

34. Donald W. Jackson, Jr. and Bruce J. Walker, "The Channels Manager: Marketing's Newest Aide?" *California Management Review,* Vol. 23 (Winter 1980), p. 54.

35. See Bert Rosenbloom and Rolph Anderson, "Channel Management and Sales Management: Some Key Interfaces," *Journal of the Academy of Marketing Science,* Vol. 13 (Summer 1985), pp. 97–106.

36. Bruce J. Walker, Janet E. Keith, and Donald W. Jackson, Jr., "The Channels Manager: Now, Soon or Never?" *Journal of the Academy of Marketing Science,* Vol. 13 (Summer 1985), p. 84.

37. Adapted from Jackson and Walker, "The Channels Manager: Marketing's Newest Aide?" pp. 57–58.

38. Walker, Keith, and Jackson, "The Channels Manager: Now, Soon or Never?" pp. 82–96.

39. James R. Moore and Donald W. Eckrich, "Marketing Channels from a Manufacturer's Perspective: Are They Really Managed?" in Kenneth L. Bernhardt, ed., *Marketing 1776–1976 and Beyond* (Chicago: American Marketing Association, 1976), pp. 248–252.

40. Donald W. Jackson, Janet E. Keith, and Bruce J. Walker, "Who Is Responsible for Managing Marketing Channels in Manufacturing Firms?" in *1985 American Marketing Association Educators' Proceedings,"* Robert F. Lusch, Gary T. Ford, and Gary L. Frazier et al., eds. (Chicago: American Marketing Association, 1985), pp. 215–221.

41. David P. Schulz, "NRF's New FOR: Profits Dip," *Stores* (December 1990), pp. 27–28.

42. "62nd Annual Report of the Grocery Industry," *Progressive Grocer* (April 1995), p. 26.

43. E. Raymond Corey, *A Note on Industrial Distribution Costs,* (Boston: Harvard Business School, 1989), p. 5.

44. *Robert Morris Associates: Annual Statement Studies* (Philadelphia: 1994), pp. 372–487.

45. B. J. LaLonde and P. H. Zinszer, *Customer Service: Meaning and Measurement* (National Council of Physical Distribution Management, 1976).

46. *Statistical Abstract of the United States,* 1993 (Washington, D.C.: U.S. Bureau of the Census), p. 409.

CASE 1

WAL-MART'S DECISION TO ELIMINATE PURCHASING GOODS THROUGH WHOLESALERS

In a November 1990 letter, David D. Glass, chairman of the board of Wal-Mart, told the firm's suppliers that it would no longer purchase goods through any wholesaler (such as brokers and independent representatives). According to the letter, Wal-Mart would insist on dealing directly with suppliers. Wal-Mart is the nation's largest retailer, with $67.3 billion in retail sales in 1994. The practice of a large firm insisting on dealing directly with suppliers is called power buying.

Wal-Mart claims that power buying will allow it to improve communications with manufacturers concerning its current sales and inventory requirements. Wal-Mart's new computer system enables it to place orders directly to the manufacturer. It also enables Wal-Mart's vendors to analyze sales to the retailer, determine inventory levels at Wal-Mart stores and warehouses, and verify their invoices. This will enable Wal-Mart to maintain lower inventories, reduce the number of stockouts, and increase reorders on fast-selling merchandise more quickly. Wal-Mart vehemently denies that it is engaging in power buying to reduce its merchandise costs. According to industry analysts, many other large retailers, such as Sears, Roebuck & Co., have also insisted that they deal direct with manufacturers.

Competitors are concerned that Wal-Mart's decision to eliminate brokers will give Wal-Mart an important price advantage. Although suppliers give brokers commissions that generally range from 5 to 15 percent of sales, commissions to Wal-Mart are generally in the 2 to 3 percent-of-sales range, owing to the firm's size. Competitors feel that power buying will enable suppliers to pass on the commissions to Wal-Mart in the form of lower prices. Federal antitrust laws forbid a manufacturer from offering discounts to customers in place of commissions or brokerage fees.

This decision can have disastrous effects on independent reps and on manufacturers with low sales to Wal-Mart. Many contracts between independent representatives and manufacturers can generally be canceled on 30 days' notice. For some major brokers, sales to Wal-Mart account for more than half of their total sales. These brokers will have a very difficult time replacing that business.

Some manufacturers argue that using brokers and reps is more economical than hiring their own direct sales force. Brokers enable manufacturers of noncompeting and complementary products to share the expenses involved in sales calls and in servicing accounts. The use of direct selling will be especially troublesome for small manufacturers or for manufacturers with narrow product lines. Among the firms troubled by this announcement is a snack-foods manufacturer that uses a broker sales force exclusively. According to the firm's chief executive, "Our entire sales force is a broker sales force." The firm relies on its brokers to sell promotions as well as new products to Wal-Mart. In addition, these brokers visit stores and resolve problems.

Other manufacturers that are concerned about Wal-Mart's new strategy take orders directly from Wal-Mart but use independent reps to handle the day-to-day needs of each account. Still other firms take orders directly from Wal-Mart but allow store managers to make special orders through a representative.

The legality of Wal-Mart's decision has been questioned. In a similar incident, Fingerhut Companies, a catalog retailer, agreed to settle a suit which charged that the firm interfered with agreements between contracts between manufacturers and reps when Fingerhut asked the firms to sell direct. Although the terms of the settlement are not public, Fingerhut agreed to pay the affected reps any monetary damages and to notify manufacturer reps that they were welcome back. Because the Fingerhut case was settled out of court, the issues raised by both sides were never adjudicated.

QUESTIONS

1. What are the advantages of Wal-Mart's decision to eliminate purchasing goods through wholesalers (beyond those mentioned in the case)?

2. What are the disadvantages of Wal-Mart's decision to eliminate purchasing goods through wholesalers?

3. Evaluate Wal-Mart's decision to eliminate purchases from wholesalers from the perspectives of contactual efficiency and the notion that "channel functions can be shifted but not eliminated."

4. How can brokers and independent representatives respond to Wal-Mart's objections?

Sources: Karen Blumenthal, "Wal-Mart Set to Eliminate Reps, Brokers," *Wall Street Journal* (December 2, 1991), pp. A1, A8; Richard Halverson, "Vendor Reps Rap Wal-Mart Effort to Deal Direct," *Discount Store News* (January 6, 1992), pp. 1, 72; Michael Sansolo, "Wal-Mart: Going for Brokers," *Progressive Grocer* (April 1993), p. 5; Michael Selz, "Independent Sales Reps are Squeezed by the Recession," *Wall Street Journal* (January 27, 1991), p. B2; and Eben Shapiro, "Wal-Mart Is Making Supermarkets Edgy," *New York Times* (December 30, 1991), pp. D1, D4.

CASE 2

COMPUTERLAND'S DECISION TO CHANGE ITS DISTRIBUTION STRATEGY

In the past several years, few industries have seen distribution channels change more than the computer industry. Major factors that can explain shifts in distribution channels are the increased popularity of personal computers and the increased sophistication of computer users (particularly among purchasers of second computers). Among the important distribution changes have been the increased popularity of mail-order firms (such as Dell Computer and Gateway 2000), the growth of discount computer superstores that feature a wide assortment of competing brands in one showroom), and the sale of simpler machines at appliance and department stores (such as Sears, Roebuck).

The changes in distribution have forced many traditional computer distributors to reexamine their channel strategy. One such firm is ComputerLand, a firm with retail sales of about $3 billion in 1990 at its 637 franchised and company-owned stores. ComputerLand Corporation is the nation's largest franchiser of personal computer stores. In 1990 ComputerLand had net profits of about $6 million (largely from its royalty payments of $424 million from its franchised dealers). According to William Tauscher, ComputerLand's chief executive, in 1990 its typical store, with a high-rent location and attentive staff, was similar to specialty retailing. In its place will be an operation that more closely resembles a wholesaling operation. Tauscher argues that "We don't have a price advantage or an equipment advantage. What we do have is a cost advantage." Tauscher feels that under its new distribution system, his firm can deliver an order for 10 percent of the sales price. In its old system, total distribution costs made up 20 percent of revenues.

Under the new wholesale approach, ComputerLand has bought out franchised operations in about 20 major cities and converted them to company-owned sales offices. The new offices will deal in large-volume sales to medium and large corporate accounts, instead of walk-in customers. To attract its larger customers, ComputerLand provides its corporate customers with improved service and support. One example of this support is a direct electronic link that allows these customers to shop by computer. ComputerLand's

12 largest customers have a computer-based linkup that enables them to receive price quotes and to place orders from their phones. ComputerLand plans to add three to four major customers to this network per month. No traditional mail-order computer firm has such a linkup.

In smaller cities, the firm will continue to use the traditional franchisees that will market computers using a traditional store approach. Tauscher argues that many customers in small cities are too small to warrant the expense of an external sales force. The firm is also experimenting with a superstore format in Atlanta, called ComputerLand Express. If the superstore is successful, ComputerLand is prepared to implement this format on a nationwide basis.

To meet cost competition, ComputerLand has increased its sales of machines from such low-priced, but respected firms as AST Research and NEC. While it continues to sell IBM computers, Tauscher hopes that the firm will be able to win back lost market share through lowering its selling price and through developing high-performance software. If IBM falters, ComputerLand has plans to assemble its own brand of clone.

ComputerLand handles its physical distribution from three warehouses. In its Indianapolis warehouse, just 68 people handle close to $1 billion in annual orders. The warehouse configures each personal computer to the customer's specifications. (These relate to hard drive size and brand, the number and types of floppy drives, and the type of graphics board.) ComputerLand then arranges for a contract trucking firm to ship computers directly to the customer. Orders are typically received by the customer within two days of being shipped out. In fact, ComputerLand's inventory system is so efficient that its inventory at branches is confined to demonstration machines.

QUESTIONS

1. Describe and evaluate ComputerLand's competitive advantages in channel management.
2. Analyze the advantages and disadvantages of ComputerLand's dual channel of distribution strategy.
3. Discuss the channel functions performed by ComputerLand.
4. Discuss Tauscher's comment that ComputerLand is shifting from a specialty retailing-based strategy to wholesaling.

Sources: John Markoff, "ComputerLand's Survival Strategy," *New York Times* (November 13, 1991), pp. D1, D4; and Kathleen K. Wiegner, "Retailing Without Shelves," *Forbes* (November 11, 1991), p. 340.

HOW TO SOLVE A CASE STUDY

Two cases accompany each chapter; there are also four integrative cases in this text—one case per part in Parts One through Four. Each case is based on a real company, with actual data, and on an important situation (problem area or opportunity) affecting the firm. This appendix is designed to help you better solve these cases.

A case study describes a business situation that requires you to analyze data, determine the problem/opportunity, list appropriate solutions, evaluate each solution, and determine an optimal response. The case method of instruction has been extensively used by major business schools and by firms in their training programs. In developing your solution, you should be able to integrate much of the material from the applicable chapter(s).

The following are hints to help improve your analysis of a case.

- Reread each case several times before attempting to solve it. Often, facts and material that are not apparent during your first reading will become clearer in subsequent readings.
- Make sure that you have isolated the major, secondary, and peripheral issues in the case and that your solution addresses these areas.
- Pay particular attention to the data within the case. For example, if the case presents sales over a five-year time period, calculate the annual percent sales increase and the average sales increase over the five-year period. You should address changes in growth rates, a firm's growth rate as it compares to competitors, and so on.
- Compute ratios that are meaningful to the case. These can include sales per square foot, average sales, the percentage of sales calls that result in sales, the average cost per call, the number of retail outlets per 100,000 population, gross profit as a percentage of sales, and net profit as a percentage of sales. Compare these ratios with other data that appear in this text. In comparing these ratios, make sure that the comparisons are made in a meaningful manner.
- After each reading, you should jot down some tentative conclusions on the basis of comments made by each person in the case, the data presented in the case, and the ratios you have computed.
- Draft your tentative analysis and suggested courses of action. Be sure to include the ramifications of each action. For example,
    - Does the firm have the funds to undertake each action? If not, is it likely that it can finance the intended course of action?
    - Is each course of action ethical?
    - Is each course of action legal?
    - Is each channel strategy consistent with the firm's overall marketing strategy?

- What are the short-run and long-run competitive advantages and disadvantages of each course of action?
- What likely course of action would a competitor take to each strategy?
- What is the impact (short and long term) of each strategy on sales, profits, and channel member relations?

Reread the case several times before you plan to hand it in. Make sure that your paper focuses on the questions asked, is analytical, and is not merely a summary of the case.

As with any assignment, your grade on the case will reflect the clarity of your thoughts, the techniques used to analyze a situation, and the solution chosen. Be sure that the appearance of your paper reflects the care you took in its writing. For example, spelling errors, mistakes in grammar, graphs and charts that are sloppily drawn, and careless mathematical errors all detract from a paper's value. These factors will affect your grade.

CHAPTER 2

THE CHANNEL ENVIRONMENT

CHAPTER OBJECTIVES

1. To describe how channel members can plan in an uncertain environment through building scenarios, developing a contingency plan, and using market research.

2. To study final consumer demographic characteristics: population, age distribution, income distribution, number of households, marital status, and working women and their impact on channel members.

3. To analyze final consumer life-style characteristics: poverty of time, the greening of America, value orientation, blurring of gender roles, component life-styles, and VALS 2 and other typologies and their impact on channel members.

4. To view channel competition: horizontal competition, intertype competition, vertical competition, and vertical marketing system competition and their impact on channel members.

5. To analyze the effect of economic conditions on channel members.

6. To examine federal legislation and its effect on channel members and legal issues in channel management.

7. To determine the technological environment and its impact on channel members.

Tupperware, a division of Premark International, is the world's leading manufacturer of high-quality plastic, food-storage, and serving containers. Tupperware uses a direct selling approach throughout the world; salespeople sell Tupperware products to consumers at their homes, in factories, and at office buildings. While Tupperware has a two-thirds market share of the U.S. market, high brand recognition, and a reputation for high-quality products, its U.S. market has had a declining trend in both sales and profits. This contrasts with its success in foreign markets. More than 80 percent of sales comes from outside the United States. Tupperware is particularly successful in the Pacific Rim (including Japan) and Central Europe. It also plans a major expansion into China, the Indian subcontinent, and Eastern Europe; these areas are conducive to Tupperware's direct selling methods.

A major demographic factor that impedes Tupperware's sales in the United States is the high proportion of working women, which hurts Tupperware several ways. First, it makes it more difficult to attract and keep salespeople since many females prefer working in an office environment. Second, the high percentage of working women makes it less likely that a Tupperware salesperson will find consumers home during the day. Third, the high proportion of working women gives them access to competing brands. These brands are distributed through department, houseware, home improvement centers, and variety stores—channels not used by Tupperware. Many of these brands are also less expensive than Tupperware.

Tupperware is working on restoring its U.S. operations to profitability. In 1993 the Tupperware division earned $12.5 million, as compared with a loss of $22 million in 1992. Sales also increased by 11 percent from 1992 to 1993. Tupperware's channel strategy consists of strengthening the size of the field sales organization, increasing the supervision of its dealers, and building a more effective delivery system.

The size of Tupperware's active sales force is a driving factor to its sales. The active number of salespeople is important since not all Tupperware dealers work each week. From 1986 to 1990, the size of Tupperware's active U.S. dealer sales force decreased from 31,400 to 27,800 salespersons. In contrast to the U.S. numbers, during the same time period, Tupperware's international active dealer sales force increased from 80,400 to 96,300.

Tupperware is strengthening dealer supervision by increasing the number of its regional vice presidents. While there are now 40 distributors per vice president, Tupperware plans to decrease this ratio to 20 to 1. The increased number of vice presidents will increase activities relating to dealer recruiting, training, and dealer support.

Lastly, Tupperware has completed tests on Tupperware Express (TE), a direct-to-the-customer delivery system. TE allows dealers to spend a higher percentage of their time selling; according to one estimate, dealer delivery accounts for 40 percent of a dealer's time. TE is expected to be applied on a national basis within two years. In addition to allowing dealers to spend more time selling, TE should be able to increase Tupperware's market penetration in three other ways. First, it enables distributors to be placed in market areas that would otherwise be too small to be profitable. Second, TE reduces the need for costly warehouse space in central cities. And third, it enables improved marketing research. Since products are shipped directly to final consumers by Tupperware, Tupperware can determine areas of geographic strength and weakness, and determine whether product purchases vary by geographic area.[1]

In this chapter, we will study the role of the channel environment on distribution. The chapter also explains how a firm can react to its channel environment through use of contingency planning. In addition to such factors as consumer demographics (including working women) and life-styles that can affect a channel member, in this chapter, we will see the impact of channel competition, the economy, the legal environment, and the technological environment on channel management.

OVERVIEW OF THE CHANNEL ENVIRONMENT

The channel environment facing manufacturers, wholesalers, and retailers consists of consumer demographics, consumer life-styles, channel competition, the economy, legal issues, and technology. This environment is often ever-changing and difficult to forecast. For example, although it may be difficult to determine whether a change in life-styles is short-lived or the beginning of a significant trend, it is important that marketing analysts, economists, and demographers provide realistic assumptions for each significant area of the channel environment to channel members.

This section describes how channel members can deal with the uncertain environment. Among the topics to be covered are building scenarios, developing a contingency plan, and conducting market research to monitor the channel environment.

BUILDING SCENARIOS AND DEVELOPING A CONTINGENCY PLAN

A difficulty in market planning is the need to accurately forecast demographic variables, consumer life-styles, competitive reactions, economic factors, the legal environment, and technological developments. Some of the environmental variables can be forecast with greater accuracy than others. For example, it is generally more difficult to forecast an area's population growth than the total U.S. population growth. And population growth can typically be forecast with greater accuracy than interest rates. Lastly, short-run forecasts are often more accurate than long-term forecasts.

One way of dealing with the uncertainty in environmental forecasting is through the development of scenarios. A **scenario** is a description of a possible or probable future event or level of an activity that is likely to occur in the future. By developing scenarios, a channel member increases his or her awareness of key opportunities, critical risks, and decision alternatives. Without a scenario, these managers may not have considered these opportunities, risks, and alternative strategies.

Although a channel member can develop scenarios with regard to a wide variety of activities, scenario building should be limited to those events that are very likely to occur and/or that would have a major impact (either opportunity or threat) on the company. Three types of scenarios that should be studied by channel managers are a continuation of a current trend (such as population growth), a scenario in which all conditions are favorable (such as high regional population growth, an economic recovery, and an absence of aggressive competition), and a disaster scenario (such as a manufacturer threatening to cut off the channel member as a distributor through use of direct distribution). Scenarios are an important element in the development of a contingency plan.

A **contingency plan** specifies a series of events that are designed to take full advantage of a business opportunity or to reduce the impact of an event that would generally be disastrous to a firm. Three important steps in developing and implementing a contingency plan are identifying the critical event, specifying the trigger point, and determining the appropriate response. The **contingent event** is a key opportunity or threat facing the channel member. The **trigger point** signifies that the contingent event has reached a critical level that requires some action. The trigger point should be at such a level that the channel member is reasonably sure that the contingent event is about to occur or has occurred. A trigger point can be a predetermined percentage increase or decrease in a relevant indicator such as employment rates, foreign exchange rates, or bad debts. It can also be confirmation that an important competitor has entered your market area (through requesting a zoning variance, signing a lease, or advertising for employees), or that a letter has been received from a supplier detailing a major disruption in supplies owing to a labor strike. An advantage of specifying the contingent event and the trigger point in advance is that a firm can plan its strategy in a proactive manner.

In a product recall contingency plan, the critical event is an accidental injury or death attributable to product usage; the trigger point is the first product-related injury that is confirmed by a reliable source; and the response involves notifying distributors, the Consumer Product Safety Commission, recalling the goods, and arranging for collection and repair of the affected goods. See Table 2-1 for a listing of critical events, trigger points, and appropriate responses for different contingency plans for a manufacturer, a wholesaler, and a retailer.

THE NEED FOR MARKET RESEARCH TO MONITOR THE CHANNEL ENVIRONMENT

A marketing information system (including marketing research) is required to scan the channel member's environment for both threats and opportunities. Many marketing experts feel that the earlier a firm is able to determine an environmental factor that is significant to its success, the larger the number of plausible strategies and tactics it can implement, and the greater its chance of taking advantage of an opportunity or minimizing the impact of a threat.

Channel members need to determine the environmental data to be scanned, how frequently the data should be collected, and how the data are to be analyzed. The topic of channel market research and information systems is covered in detail in Chapter 7.

TABLE 2-1 EXAMPLES OF CHANNEL MEMBER CONTINGENCY PLANS

Channel Member/ Contingent Event	Trigger Point	Response
MANUFACTURER Product recall	Report from hospital indicates that product contributed to patient illness.	Confirm cause of illness with independent investigation. Seek to determine which product and production lot, if any, need to be recalled. Notify retailers and wholesalers to immediately withhold affected product from further distribution. Notify the Consumer Product Safety Commission; designate a spokesperson to contact media. Develop toll-free telephone number for customer contact. Arrange with dealers to repair/replace affected products.
WHOLESALER Increase in population	Population increases at 5 percent per year in regional area.	Seek out additional retail customers within high-growth market area. Search for new distribution channels that serve additional customers. Evaluate ability of existing warehouses to serve additional channel members with appropriate level of service.
RETAILER Increased competition due to aggressive competitor entering market area	New competitor announces plans to enter your market; applies for zoning change, building permit, or signs lease; advertises for employees.	Evaluate firm's strengths and weaknesses with respect to competitor. Develop programs to reinforce store loyalty. Increase salesperson training. Improve customer service.

In the next section of this chapter, we describe and analyze the overall environment of channel members. The environments include consumer demographic trends, life-style trends, channel competition, the economy, the legal environment, and the technological environment. The implications of these trends on channel members are also discussed.

THE FINAL CONSUMER: DEMOGRAPHIC CHARACTERISTICS

Consumer demographics involve such population characteristics as population, age distribution, income, number of households, marital status, and number of working women. Data on consumer demographics are available from a variety of sources. Government demographic data are available from the *Census of Population.* Commercial sources of demographic data include *Sales & Marketing Management's Survey of Buying Power, Editor & Publisher Market Guide, American Demographics, Rand McNally Commercial Atlas & Market Guide,* and *Standard Rate & Data Service.*

The major advantage of *Census of Population* data is its availability in small aggregated units. Census data are available on blocks, census tracts, cities, counties, regions, and the total United States. Block and census tract data are particularly important for channel members that serve small geographic regions and for those with territories that do not neatly correspond to cities or counties. Channel members that need to determine the demographic characteristics of a part of a city or county can add demographic data from individual blocks and census tracts. For example, a beer distributor may have a territory the size of half a county. Although county data are available from a large number of sources, the distributor cannot assume that the demographic characteristics of the county as a whole match those of its territory. By adding the data from census blocks and tracts that comprise its territory, the distributor can learn about the demographic characteristics of his or her customers.

The major disadvantage of *Census of Population* data is that it is available only every 10 years. And while the *1990 Census of Population* is the latest available, the full complement of 1990 data was not available until sometime in 1992. Thus, in 1992 some census data were as little as two years old; other elements of data were as much as 12 years old. Where population mobility is high and the characteristics of new entrants differ from existing consumers, 12-year-old data may be of little value.

Commercial demographic data sources such as *Sales & Marketing Management's Survey of Buying Power, Editor & Publisher Market Guide, Rand McNally Commercial Atlas & Market Guide,* and *Standard Rate & Data Service* are available on an annual basis. In addition, a number of commercial research firms provide annual demographic data in computer disk format. Each of these sources provides important demographic information such as the number of households, median income, total retail sales, climate, major employers, and five-year population projections. The most important disadvantage of these data sources is that they report data on a city and county basis only. These sources do not further break out geographic data into census tracts and blocks as in the *Census of Population.* These data sources are further discussed in Chapter 5 in the section on secondary data sources.

Next, we look at national U.S. trends regarding such important demographic characteristics as population growth, age distribution, income distribution, number of households, marital status, and working women and their impact on channel management (see Figure 2-1).

FIGURE 2-1 Final consumer demographic characteristics.

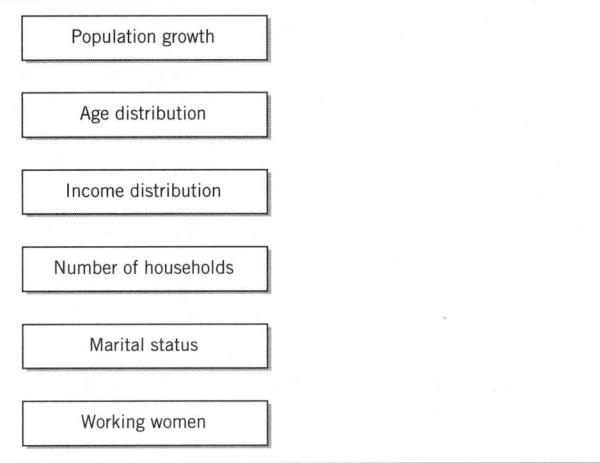

POPULATION GROWTH

The most significant fact about population is the low overall population growth rate forecast between now and the year 2000. Despite higher birth rates, higher forecast immigration into the United States, and increased longevity, the overall U.S. population is growing less than 1 percent per year.

Not all ethnic groups, however, are growing at the same rate. For example, Asian Americans are the fastest growing ethnic group. According to one source, the average annual growth rate for Asian Americans in the 1990s will be 5 percent. This is in contrast to a 3 percent annual growth rate for Hispanics, 1.3 percent for African Americans, and 0.6 percent for non-Hispanic whites.[2] Channel members need to be aware that the Asian-American market may be difficult to target. The 7 million Asian Americans are comprised of Chinese, Filipino, Japanese, Indian, Korean, Vietnamese, and others. Each of these groups has a different culture and even a different language.

Another fast-growing population group is the Hispanic. Between 1990 and 2010, the Hispanic population will grow to account for over 12.9 percent of the total U.S. population (versus 12.5 percent for African Americans).[3] About 22 million Americans now have an Hispanic background, over 8 percent of the total population. These Hispanics have a disposable income of $144 billion. Spanish consumers spend an estimated $175 billion yearly.[4] As with Asian Americans, the Hispanic market is made up of a variety of nationalities and cultures. For example, both the language and culture of a Puerto Rican, an Argentinian, and a Mexican are different. Marketers also have to understand the different levels of assimilation of the Hispanic segment; this is reflected by Acculturation Influence Groups (AIG). In the AIG I market, the Spanish culture dominates; members of this group speak little or no English. In the AIG II group, consumers are bilingual. Although they are fluent in English, they prefer to speak Spanish at home. In the AIG III group, the American culture dominates.[5]

A third large and growing market is the African-American market. African-American consumers spend about $250 to $270 billion a year.[6] This market represents the largest ethnic group in the United States. In 1990 African Americans earned about $263 billion.[7]

Channel members focusing on these ethnic markets need to be aware of significant differences in terms of median household income across these markets. The median household income among white, Hispanic, and black households in 1990 was $30,000, $22,000, and $18,000, respectively.[8]

Population growth is also projected not to be equal by geographic area within the United States. For the period 1990 to 2000, the greatest growth will take place in the Mountain, Pacific, South Atlantic, and Southwest regions. Relative declines will occur in the Central Northeast, Central Southeast, Middle Atlantic, and Northern Midwest regions.

In general, the population growth means that channel members increasingly must meet growth objectives through either **market penetration** (increasing market share within existing markets) or **market development** (expanding into new market areas both within and outside the United States). Market penetration strategies consist of making better appeals to ethnic markets and micromarketing.

Among the firms that are seeking to improve their appeal to ethnic markets are Quaker, Procter & Gamble, Kmart, and Toys "R" Us. Quaker employs a black-owned promotions company, Segmented Marketing Services Inc. (SMSI), to make sure that its products and promotional materials are well-displayed in neighborhoods with large proportions of black consumers. SMSI also distributes product samples for Quaker and Procter & Gamble through a network of 7000 black churches.[9] Both Kmart and Toys "R" Us seek to better appeal to ethnic markets through special promotional campaigns. Each firm has hired advertising agencies that specialize in marketing to Hispanic Americans and African Americans. Other major retailers (such as Sears, Roebuck and Dayton Hudson) and manufacturers (such as Procter & Gamble, Maybelline, and RJR Nabisco) have also used agencies that specialize in minority marketing.

Another market penetration-based strategy is micromarketing. **Micromarketing** involves satisfying the needs and wants of a special consumer segment by specifically adapting the marketing strategy to appeal to that segment's special needs.[10] Micromarketing is a special type of differentiated (multiple segmentation) target marketing strategy. Unlike traditional differentiated marketing, each of the markets in micromarketing may be very small. Frito-Lay is an example of a marketer that successfully uses micromarketing. The firm changes potato chip flavors to match regional taste preferences. In the Northeast, for example, consumers prefer a darker, greasier chip; southeastern consumers, in contrast, prefer a lighter tasting, heavier textured chip. Frito-Lay distributes the desired flavor on a regional basis only. This enables the firm to maximize its market share on a regional basis without having to incur costs of national distribution and poor demand outside of the desired target area. To successfully implement micromarketing, a channel member needs access to sales, cost, competitive, and profit data on a local basis. The firm also needs to be able to develop and implement decentralized marketing plans. For example, Frito-Lay needs to use regional warehouses and distribution systems.

Market development consists of entering new market areas. Examples of firms using market development strategies include Toys "R" Us (entering Japan and Germany as well as new territories within the United States), Wal-Mart (seeking new locations in the North and West, Canada, and South America), and Smith's Food and Drug Centers (expanding into new market areas in California).

Other areas of significant population growth include the 35-and-older population, the number of households, and the increase in downscale and affluent households. These will now be discussed.

AGE DISTRIBUTION

Both the 18- to 24-year-old and the 25- to 34-year-old age groups will shrink during this decade. The fastest growing segments will be the 35- to 44-year-old, 45- to 54-year-old, and older age groups. Much of the growth in the 35- to 54-year-old age segments will be due to baby boomers (those born between 1946 and 1964) reaching middle age. According to one forecast, by the year 2030, 21 percent of the population will be over 65. The increased importance of the elderly is due to longer life expectancy, lower birth rates, and the aging of the baby boomer population.

The Georgia State University Center for Mature Consumer Studies estimates that the 55-plus age group already controls 75 percent of the nation's total financial assets and more than half of discretionary income.[11] Some market analysts predict that by the year 2000, baby boomers will represent over half of U.S. households earning $50,000 and up.[12]

Some analysts regard "comfort, security, and convenience as the key concerns of older people."[13] Channel members should assess their ability to cater to the special needs of older people. Manufacturers, wholesalers, and retailers need to provide desired goods and services for the elderly. These include leisure activities (such as grandparent/grandchild vacations, medical services, financial services, and winter homes). Retailers must also consider the elderly in terms of making access to shopping areas easier (through wide aisles for wheelchairs and motorized carts, and elimination of steps), using large print for in-store signs, hiring older salespersons, training younger employees to become more sensitive, promoting telephone and mail-order sales, providing home delivery, using early-bird specials (to appeal to senior citizens with low prices in off-peak hours), and even utilizing on-premises services (such as a bank located in a senior citizen housing complex).

As with population growth, there are significant differences in age distribution by race and ethnic makeup. And while the median age is increasing for all racial and ethnic groups, Hispanics and African Americans will remain younger than non-Hispanic whites. The Census Bureau predicts that the median age for non-Hispanic whites in 2010 will be 41.4, versus 31.4 for African Americans and 29.3 for Hispanics.[14]

INCOME DISTRIBUTION

Despite overall favorable income trends, there has been a widening gap between the poorest and the wealthiest people in the United States—which will continue in the 1990s. Income can be measured on the basis of **money income** (actual dollar income) and **real income** (income that reflects the cost of living). Since the cost of living changes periodically, real income is always expressed in terms of a base year. At present, the base year for real income is the 1982–1984 price index; the price index for this time period is expressed as 100. If money income rises faster than the price index, real income is increasing; if it rises more slowly than the price index, real income is decreasing.

Although overall median real family income should rise during much of the period from 1990 to 2000, the growth rate will not approach that of the 1960s and early 1970s. Much of the increase will be due to the greater number of two-income households. A report by the Conference Board entitled *The Great Income Reshuffle* estimates that three of four families with an income of $50,000 have working wives.[15]

Two significant distribution implications can be drawn from income distribution trends. First, many lower- and middle-income consumers are finding it difficult to keep pace with the cost of living. *American Demographics* defines **downscale households** as those having a household income of less than $25,000 in 1989. Since the median income of all households in that year was $28,900, 43 percent of households could be classified as downscale. One-quarter of all households had an annual income of less than $15,000 in 1989.[16]

Eighteen percent of downscale householders are single women heads of families; this is double the percentage in midscale families (having incomes between $25,000 and $49,999) and about four times more than in upscale households (with household incomes of $50,000 or more).[17]

Appropriate distribution responses to the large number of downscale households include offering more basic models of products, providing flexible financing arrangements, marketing do-it-yourself products, stressing value through the sale of private and generic brands, reducing costs through second-use locations (locations where fixtures and storefronts were provided by a prior tenant), opportunistic buying (buying specials and closeouts), and using unbundled pricing (to allow those wishing to deliver and install purchases themselves to pay lower prices). The use of rental centers for household appliances for those unable to get credit from additional stores is another example of an appeal to downscale households.

Second, affluent consumers represent a lucrative market, and that segment is becoming larger all the time. This means considerable possibilities for luxury products, luxury car dealers, fashion retailers, personal services retailers, fine restaurants, and other upscale goods and services providers.

NUMBER OF HOUSEHOLDS

A **household** consists of a person or group of persons occupying a dwelling unit; these persons may be related or unrelated. In contrast, a **family** consists of two or more related persons who live together.

The number of U.S. households is expected to rise from 94 million in 1990 to 106 million by 2000. At the same time, the average size of the U.S. household will decline from 2.6 in 1990 to 2.5 in 2000. The decrease in the size of households is due to the larger number of older people who live apart from their grown children, the high divorce rate (about 60 percent of marriages end in divorce), and the later age of first marriages.

An important segment of households is single-person households. The 1990 census shows that about 23 million Americans live by themselves, a 91 percent increase for women, and a 156 percent increase for men since 1970.[18] According to research conducted by J. Walter Thompson, middle-aged singles are the fastest growing group of singles. The firm estimates that singles have a combined earning power of $660 billion.

It is difficult to generalize about the singles market other than to say that singles as a group tend to spend more on travel, convenience foods, and restaurants than married adults.[19] Marketers can appeal to the singles market through the distribution of single-serving sizes, salad bars in supermarkets, and "meet your neighbor nights" at housing complexes with large proportions of singles. Hyatt hotels even provide roommates at its ski resorts for singles; if it can't find a roommate, a single still pays half price. According to the most recent survey of first-time home buyers by the National Association of Realtors (NAR), one-third of first-time home buyers were single adults in 1989 versus one-quarter in 1987. According to the chief economist for NAR, "The homeownership rate is lowest among singles, and they are likely to make the greatest gains in the 1990s."[20]

MARITAL STATUS

In 1970 married couples represented 71 percent of all households; in 1991 they represented 56 percent of all households[21] (see Table 2-2). Although three-fifths of U.S. adults aged 18 and older are married, several major changes in the traditional family structure have occurred. One-third of all children born in the last 10 years will probably live in a stepfamily before they are 18 years old, and 9 percent of all households are single-parent households (versus 6 percent in 1970). In 1970, 38 percent of all households were childless; in 1990 the percent-

TABLE 2-2 COMPARISON OF NINE HOUSEHOLD TYPES, 1970 AND 1990

	Percentage of All Households	
Household Type	1970	1990
Dual-earner married couples with children	20	19
Other married couples with children	21	8
Childless married couples with householders under age 45 (Young couples)	6	7
Childless married couples with householders aged 45 to 64 (Empty nesters)	15	13
Childless married couples with householders aged 65 or older (Mature couples)	9	9
Single parents	6	9
Young singles under age 45	3	9
Older singles aged 45 and older	14	16
Other multiple-member (Shared households)	6	10
Total households	100	100

Source: Bureau of the Census, Current Population Surveys, 1970 and 1990.

age of childless households increased to 45. The greatest difference in the percentage of childless households occurred within the young singles (under the age of 45) group. This group increased from 3 percent of all households in 1970 to 9 percent of all households in 1990.

As with other demographic characteristics, consumer markets are heavily fragmented with regard to marital status. Single parents require in-store child care services (for both customers and employees), convenience foods, and direct marketing. Dual-earner married couples with children require similar goods and services. However, these products are less meaningful to childless single parents and to childless married couples. In contrast, leisure products and services, such as vacations, restaurants, and hobby-related products, are more important for this group.

WORKING WOMEN

A major change in parenting relates to the decrease in the traditional breadwinner-homemaker model. About 57 percent of all U.S. women aged 16 and older are employed; the percentage of female participation in the workforce increased from 38 percent in 1961 to 43 percent in 1971, and to 52 percent in 1981.[22] By the year 2000, over 60 percent of women are forecast to be working outside the home. In addition, the profile of working women has changed. In the past, many working women were divorced, separated, or widowed; now 56 percent of working women have children.

These numbers do not explain the sequencing arrangement that has been adopted by many working women with children. In sequencing, working mothers step off career ladders to focus on child-rearing and household obligations when children are born. They then return to full-time jobs when children reach school age. In a variation of the sequencing theme, other working mothers temporarily switch to jobs requiring a lower time commitment so that they have more time to spend with their families.[23] Opportunities exist for all sorts of convenience-oriented goods and services, ranging from convenience foods to direct marketing to longer store hours. And in-store child care services (for both consumers and employees) are becoming much more important to working mothers. The decline in traditional homemakers has had a major effect on direct sellers. Instead of appealing to homemakers through selling at an in-home market, direct sellers such as Avon and Tupperware have shifted to selling goods through office and factory settings.

THE FINAL CONSUMER: CONSUMER LIFE-STYLES

This section explores consumer life-style trends and their impact on channel members. **Consumer life-styles** represent the manner in which people conduct their lives, including their activities, interests, and opinions.[24] Although demographic data are easily observed and measurable, it is substantially more difficult to measure life-style trends reliably. And while many demographic data are available from the *Census of Population* and the Bureau of Labor Statistics, life-style data are generally available from commercial market research and polling organizations. Among the best known sources of data are the *Yankelovich Monitor* (published by Yankelovich, Clancy, and Shulman), VALS 2 (conducted by SRI International), and PRIZM (Potential Rating Index by Zip Market). Although consumer demographics and life-styles are covered separately in this chapter, in practice, both demographic and life-style characteristics are used in combination to explain and forecast consumer behavior.

This section explores the following facets of life-styles: poverty of time, the greening of America, value orientation, blurring of gender roles, component life-styles, and VALS 2, an important means of classifying life-styles (see Figure 2-2).

POVERTY OF TIME

Poverty of time relates to the perceived shortage of leisure time among consumers despite the shorter time spent at work. Poverty of time may be due to greater travel time to and from work, increased time spent on hobbies, and greater time obligations of working wives, who have responsibilities both at home and at work.[25] Americans' expectations for leisure time have also increased.

Based on responses to a national survey conducted for Hilton Hotels, four of ten Americans report cutting back on sleep to gain time for daily activities.[26] The Hilton survey reports that there is a 42 percent gap between respondents' estimates of the free time they have (19 hours per week on average) and the ideal amount of free time desired (27 hours per week). The gap rises to 47 percent among full-time workers. Single working mothers have the highest time crunch of any demographic group. Divorced and separated women also feel more of a time crunch than married women.[27]

FIGURE 2-2 Final consumer life-style characteristics.

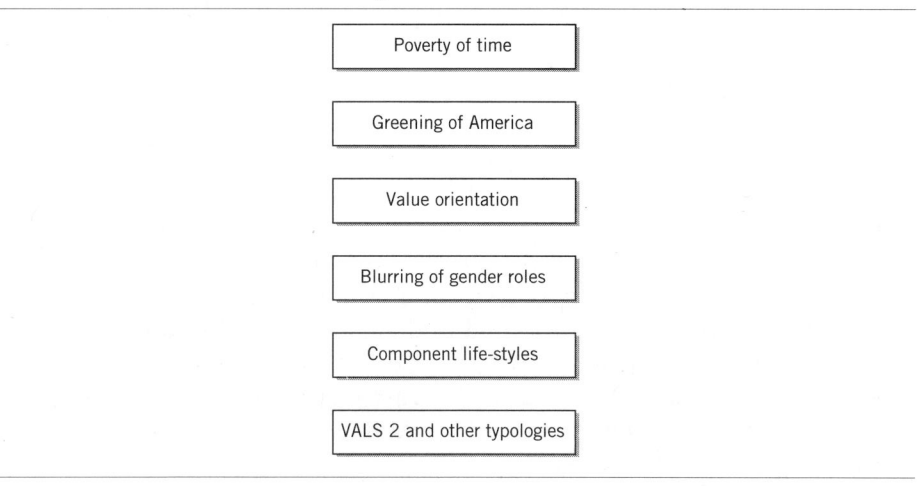

Market analysts expect direct marketers to do well based on the poverty-of-time life-style. There is no waiting on line, no parking, no going to stores to find they are out-of-stock; consumers can order 24 hours a day, and returns are as close and convenient as your mailbox. Mail-order sales, for example, are increasing at a rate of 12 percent, according to mail catalog consultant Maxwell Sroge.[28] Channel members should also evaluate goods and services that are time saving. These include home delivery and installation, in-home repair (for items such as computers), assembly of products that are normally shipped unassembled (such as inexpensive furniture), and acceptance of telephone orders by supermarkets.

Kroger is appealing to poverty-of-time life-styles by seeking to increase checkout speed. Kroger places express checkouts in every major department (such as floral, bakery, and ready-made meals). This eliminates the need for customers to wait on long central checkout lines. Other retailers have conducted research on customer perceptions of waiting in line and have analyzed methods for making the waiting times more tolerable.[29]

THE GREENING OF AMERICA

The **greening of America** reflects the increased concern of Americans for the ecological soundness of products. Ecological considerations generally relate to the entire **ecological life cycle of a product**. This includes natural resource depletion in a product's manufacture, the effect of product use on the environment (air and noise pollution, and desecration of the landscape), natural resource depletion associated with a product's use (such as gasoline mileage), and the ease of product recycling.

A nationwide poll of over 1000 consumers by the *Wall Street Journal*/NBC News shows that 8 of 10 Americans view themselves as "environmentalists." Most of these consumers recognize the need for substantial and profound changes in their life-styles. Environmental concerns have become a significant factor in buying decisions, but are still one factor out of others such as price and convenience. Some analysts argue that these numbers may be inflated by the desire of many respondents to appear responsible.

Among the findings in this *Wall Street Journal* poll are that[30]

- Fifty-three percent of respondents say that it will take fundamental changes in life-style, rather than scientific advances, to bring about dramatic changes in the environment.
- Almost 70 percent of respondents say the best way to deal with the nation's trash crisis is to use less packaging and to do more recycling.
- More than 80 percent state that protecting the environment is generally more important than keeping prices down.
- Three-fourths of those surveyed say a product's or manufacturer's environmental reputation is important to them in deciding what to buy.
- Fifty-four percent say they have purchased a more expensive product than a less expensive one because of environmental concerns. And 53 percent say they have avoided buying something because of environmental fears about the product.

Albertson's, a regional supermarket chain, responded to the growing environmental awareness by initiating a major program in 1990. Its program includes recyclable bins for plastic bags and aluminum cans, refunds for reusing bags, and the sale of reusable canvas shopping bags and recyclable egg cartons. In addition, the firm introduced environmentally safe paper products under the HOPE (Helping Our Planet's Ecology) label.[31] McDonald's is composting food scraps on a pilot basis, testing refillable coffee cups, and thinking about using biodegradable cutlery. Wal-Mart uses special shelf markers to highlight new versions of products on their packaging that is environmentally friendly. The markers state that "Wal-Mart Recommends . . ." and identify the improvement.

All channel members need to cooperate to meet the ecological expectations of consumers. Manufacturers can employ **life-cycle costing** to study the environmental impact of the production and use of a product. With this technique, likely future costs are projected to every feature of a product's life span, from product development to manufacture, use, and eventual disposal. Two or more products or packaging alternatives are then compared.[32]

A number of state-based laws are being proposed that would force manufacturers to be accountable for a package after it is sold. Among the objectionable practices that are being examined by legislators are redundant packaging (such as boxes within boxes for perfume), single-serving packages (these produce far more waste per ounce of food than larger sized servings), and compact disk packaging. (This packaging is 10 times the volume of the disk itself.)[33] Sears, Roebuck is working with suppliers to reduce packaging by 25 percent by the end of 1994. Sears estimates that this program will effect a 1.5-ton reduction of packaging materials a year, as well as save $5 million a year. Currently, Sears is displaying its Craftsman brand hand tools such as hammers, pliers, and screwdrivers on racks without any packaging. When this program is expanded to 500 stores, the firm estimates that it will save 78 tons of plastic a year.[34]

VALUE ORIENTATION

Value orientation is the increased concern among consumers for "the right combination of product quality, fair price, and good service."[35] "It means giving more: an improved product, with added features and enhanced service—all at a better price."[36] A value orientation changes the role of marketing from being a means of image enhancement to being an efficient delivery system.[37]

Value marketing will be most successfully practiced by lean and efficient channel members. For example, Wal-Mart's efficiency in comparison to Kmart partially accounts for its success in competing against Kmart. Wal-Mart is able to make a satisfactory profit at a retail price that Kmart could not match. Wal-Mart's motto is "The low price on the brands you trust." Kmart's selling, general, and administrative expenses accounted for 22 cents of every sales dollar in fiscal year 1994; these expenses were 15 percent of sales revenue at Wal-Mart in the same time period.[38] The Gap also does well as a result of value orientation. Although its prices are not rock-bottom, the quality is good, and the fashion fits an age when "it's almost immoral to be ostentatious."[39]

Value orientation also fuels the growth of factory outlets, off-price chains, and off-price malls. **Factory outlets** are owned and operated by a manufacturer to dispose of excess inventory in an out-of-the-way location (so as not to alienate the manufacturers' traditional customers). Some 468 manufacturers were operating outlet stores in mid-1990.[40] Where once only midpriced manufacturers such as Van Heusen or Hanes operated factory outlets, now status-oriented manufacturers such as Ralph Lauren, Donna Karan, Liz Claiborne, Calvin Klein, and Jones New York have begun to develop outlets.

In comparison to a factory outlet, **off-price chains** are owned and operated by retailers. These retailers specialize in opportunistic buying of canceled orders, slightly irregular, and end-of-season merchandise that is sold in a no-frills retail setting.

In the past, both factory outlets and off-price chains were located in out-of-the-way locations. The factory outlet stores sought to control distribution of their merchandise so as not to alienate the factory's traditional customers, which included department and specialty stores. This meant that many factory outlets were located in areas where the manufacturer did not have traditional distribution. In many cases, factory outlets were 30 miles from a major department store customer. Off-price chains were also located in isolated locations so as not to alienate the manufacturers' traditional retailer customers. In addition, these locations enabled the retail operators to pay low rents.

Increasingly, both factory outlets and off-price chains have begun to locate in **outlet malls**, a grouping of factory outlets and off-price chains that are planned as a unit with common property management. These malls attract consumers from considerable distance, allow retailers to share customer traffic, and enable retailers to use mall-based cooperative advertising programs with other merchants. Many of the newer malls use more costly fixturing, are built new (not an abandoned mill), and are opening up closer to major cities. Some even have arrangements with tour buses to bring consumers from long distances for a day of shopping.[41] In 1981 there were 26 outlet malls in the United States; in 1993 there were 340 factory outlet malls with $10 billion in sales.[42]

Value-based marketing also helps shift the importance of retail channels. For example, membership-based wholesale clubs (such as Price/Costco and Sam's) increased sales six times in the 1984–1990 period. **Buying clubs (membership clubs)** service both wholesale and final consumers, charge retail shoppers an annual membership fee, locate in low rental locations, and typically resemble a warehouse. Unlike other retailers, these clubs engage in opportunistic buying, and they typically limit their selection of popular brands to those that offer them special discounts. Manufacturers are responding to buying clubs by redesigning products, packaging, promotional strategies, and delivery to meet special needs. Heinz, for example, is combining condiments such as ketchup and relish into a single package. It is also shipping 64-ounce ketchup bottles on customized display pallets that are easy for wholesale clubs to store and handle.[43]

BLURRING OF GENDER ROLES

Blurring of gender roles refers to the broadening of typical household duties between male and female heads of households. The primary notion of the blurring of gender roles is that the typical role structure of male breadwinner and female homemaker is no longer universally applicable. For example, husbands often do household chores that are traditionally thought of as women's work, and a wife may frequently assume tasks generally regarded as male-oriented.

In a survey conducted by the Conference Board using a representative national sample of 5000 homes, over 25 percent of husbands almost always or often shop for food or wash the dishes. The most significant factor affecting a man's housekeeping participation rate in these tasks is his age. Young men are much more prone to perform all household chores such as shopping for food, cooking, dishwashing, doing the family laundry, and cleaning the house.[44]

Men who are full-time homemakers are still rare, but men are taking on more of the everyday responsibilities of running a household. A Maritz poll found that one-third of men do all or most of the food shopping. The average household spends a total of $172 a week on household shopping, according to this poll. About a third of men spend all or most of the weekly total, compared with two-thirds of women.[45] Men shop almost as frequently as women but have different habits. For example, research by Simmons Market Research Bureau found that men are less likely than women to refer to shelf offers or brochures, but are more likely to read shopping-cart ads and to see overhead aisle markers.[46]

In line with the blurring of gender, a study by the Families and Work Institute, a not-for-profit policy research center, found that in households where only the husband works, the wife does 94 percent of the cooking and 93 percent of the child care. Where both parents work, the wife's share drops to 80 percent of the cooking and 70 percent of the child care.[47]

Channel members need to consider blurring of gender in designing channels. For example, a large proportion of females buy tires for the family car. They want to be comfortable waiting for their tires to be installed, want appropriate reading material, and do not care to be treated in a condescending manner by tire installers. Similarly, an increased number of supermarket shoppers are men. Men need to be comfortable purchasing cuts of meat or shopping for ripe vegetables.

COMPONENT LIFE-STYLES

According to the concept of **component life-styles**, consumer attitudes and behavior vary by purchase situation; thus, typecasting or stereotyping people may not be particularly valid. In the future, more and more U.S. consumers will adopt component life-styles because they are less constrained by social customs and standards than in the past or because they treat purchases differently, depending on the product or the occasion of use: "A consumer may own a BMW but fill it with self-service gasoline. Buy take-out fast food for lunch but good wine for dinner. Own sophisticated photographic equipment and low-priced home stereo equipment. Shop for socks at Kmart and suits or dresses at Brooks

Brothers."[48] While component life-styles are most noticeable among affluent consumers, they are applicable to consumers of any age or income level.

The component life-style concept suggests that consumers may lack consistency and predictability regarding their purchase behavior. Component life-styles also make it difficult for firms to define their customer base accurately. As suggested by the previous quote, upper-income consumers might shop at discount stores for items viewed as unimportant, while lower income consumers might shop at upscale stores for items viewed as very important.

Component life-styles also create opportunities for channel members in scrambled merchandising (carrying goods and services that are not usually associated with its merchandise lines). The concept of scrambled merchandising and its implications for channel members are covered later in this chapter under intertype competition.

VALS 2 AND OTHER TYPOLOGIES

In order to appeal to life-style segments, market researchers have sought to divide consumers into classification systems on the basis of attributes of psychographic research. **Psychographic research** classifies consumers into life-styles by investigating how they live, what interests them, and what they like. An important means of classifying consumers in terms of a broad range of demographic and life-style factors is SRI International's **VALS (Values and Life-Styles) program**, which divides Americans into eight life-style categories.

VALS 1 was introduced in 1978 and was the first life-style psychographic system to incorporate social values in its framework. VALS 1 divided consumers into two basic categories: inner-directed consumers and outer-directed consumers. It then subdivided consumers into two additional segments: belongers and achievers.

VALS 2 was introduced in 1989 to replace the VALS 1 typology, which did not reflect how well consumer motivations actually matched their ability to purchase the goods and services they desired. VALS 1 life-style segments had also become too fragmented to predict behavior. VALS 2 seeks to explain why and how consumers make purchase decisions, and divides them into groups on the basis of self-orientation and resources. Self-orientation comprises the attitudes and activities that help people reinforce, keep, or modify their social self-image. The self-orientation categories are principle-, status-, and action-oriented consumers. Principle-oriented consumers are guided in their choices by beliefs and principles; status-oriented consumers are heavily influenced by the actions, approval, and opinions of others; and action-oriented consumers are guided by their desire for social or physical activity, variety, and risk taking. The resources available to consumers include their education, income, self-confidence, health, eagerness to buy, intelligence, and energy level. Resources increase from youth to middle age and decline with old age.

VALS 2 has eight basic segments: actualizers, fulfilleds, believers, achievers, strivers, experiencers, makers, and strugglers. Although the actualizer group is small (with 8 percent of the population), the size of the other segments ranges from 10 percent to 17 percent of the population.[49] The VALS 2 segments are summarized in Table 2-3.

TABLE 2-3 CHARACTERISTICS OF THE VALS 2 LIFE-STYLE SEGMENTS

Actualizers	Status-oriented, highest resources. Successful, sophisticated. Can indulge in any or all self-orientations. Interested in developing and expressing themselves in a variety of ways: sometimes by principle and sometimes by a desire to change. Have cultivated a taste for the finer things in life. Receptive to new products, technologies, distribution. Skeptical of advertising. Frequent readers of a wide variety of publications. Represent 8 percent of the population.
Fulfilleds	Principle-oriented, abundant resources. Mature, satisfied, comfortable, and reflective. Value order, knowledge, and responsibility. Most are professionals and well educated. Above-average consumers of products for the home. As consumers, they are concerned with functionality, value, and durability. Fulfilleds have little interest in image or prestige. They read widely and often. Represent 12 percent of the population.
Believers	Principle-oriented, lower resources. Conservative and conventional with concrete beliefs and strong attachments to traditional institutions. Follow routines organized around their homes, families, and social or religious organizations; believers are slow to change habits. Want American products and established brands. Look for bargains. Read retirement, home and garden, and general-interest magazines. Represent 17 percent of the population.
Achievers	Status-oriented, second highest resources. Committed to their jobs and families, and get satisfaction from them. Like to feel in control of their lives and value structure, predictability, and stability. Favor premium products that demonstrate their success to their peers. Prime target for a variety of products. Average television watchers. Read business, news, and self-help publications. Represent 10 percent of the population.
Strivers	Status-oriented, lower resources. Values similar to achievers but fewer resources. Image conscious. Limited discretionary income but carry credit balances. Seek to be stylish. Prefer television to reading. Spend on clothing and personal-care products. Represent 14 percent of the population.
Experiencers	Action-oriented, abundant resources. Young, enthusiastic, and rebellious. Seek variety and excitement, and desire the offbeat and risky. Spend much of their income on clothing, fast food, music, movies, videos, and socializing. Follow fashion and fads. This is the youngest segment, with a median age of 25. Listen to rock music. Represent 11 percent of the population.
Makers	Action-oriented, lower resources. Live in a traditional context of family, practical work, and physical recreation. Unimpressed by material possessions other than those with a practical purpose. Shop for comfort, durability, and value. Like to fix their own cars and conduct do-it-yourself projects. Read auto, home improvement, fishing, and outdoor magazines. Represent 12 percent of the population.
Strugglers	Status-oriented, lowest resources (too few to be included in any self-orientation). Chronically poor, ill educated, older, and low in skills. Concerned about health, safety, and security. Within their limited means, they are brand loyal and cautious consumers. They use coupons and watch for sales. They trust advertising. Read tabloids and women's magazines. Represent 16 percent of the population.

Source: SRI International.

Although life-style segments and their respective sizes may vary over time, VALS 2 is an important conceptual example of how consumers may be categorized. Channel members can better plan and implement their strategies by studying the life-style characteristics of their customers and determining the segments to which they are appealing. For instance, a strategy aimed at fulfilleds should be different from one aimed at strivers because the fulfilled are less status conscious owing to their self-satisfaction. In addition, adjacent VALS 2 segments can be combined for purposes of targeting customers.

In some cases, channel members found that VALS is not applicable to their customers. For example, the Coca-Cola Research Council developed a typology of supermarket shoppers on the basis of their eating, cooking, and shopping needs and attitudes. Six distinct life-style groups were identified: avid shoppers, hurried shoppers, unfettered shoppers, kitchen strangers, kitchen birds, and constrained shoppers.[50] As with any other typology, this system forms an excellent basis for segmenting consumer markets. For example, avid shoppers are price conscious and look for weekly specials and store-based coupons. Hurried shoppers dislike cooking, lack the time to prepare meals, and seek out quality take-out food. And kitchen strangers rarely cook dinner and eat out breakfast as well as lunch. While the size of the avid shopper and hurried markets are predicted to be relatively stable, the size of the kitchen stranger market is forecast to grow from 17.1 million households in 1985 to 22.6 million households by the year 2000. Supermarkets and food-based manufacturers and wholesalers need to be concerned about the loss of revenues owing to the growth of the kitchen stranger life-style segment. They should attempt to appeal to this segment with restaurant-quality take-out food (that only needs to be heated), fine wines, and in-home and in-office catering.

CHANNEL COMPETITION

This section describes the nature of channel competition among channel members both at the same stage and at different stages of distribution. Channel competition takes one of four forms: horizontal, intertype, vertical, and vertical marketing system (see Figure 2-3). The arrows go up and down to reflect a firm's competitive action and the competitor's reaction. In the vertical marketing system competition model, there are no arrows between the manufacturer, wholesaler, and retailer within a box since these channel members function in an integrated manner. This will be explained in the vertical marketing system section on channel competition.

Horizontal competition consists of competition among channel members of the same type, such as among Dillard's and Bloomingdale's, two department store chains. **Intertype competition** relates to competition among different types of channel members at the same level within a channel. For example, a full-service wholesaler may compete with a limited-service wholesaler. There is generally greater diversity between the characteristics of each channel member and their overall marketing strategy in intertype versus horizontal competition.

FIGURE 2-3 Examples of horizontal, intertype, vertical, and vertical marketing system competition.

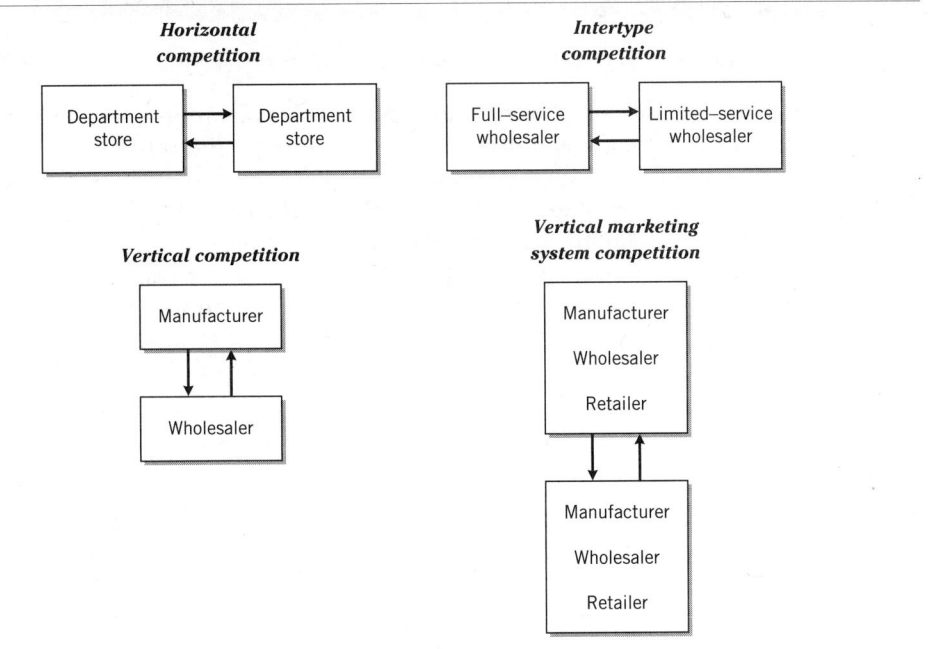

Vertical competition describes competition among different channel members at different levels within the channel, such as a manufacturer competing with a retailer. In **vertical marketing system competition**, horizontally coordinated and vertically aligned establishments that are professionally managed and centrally coordinated compete against each other. For example, Sherwin-Williams performs manufacturing, wholesaling, and retailing functions. It can compete with another vertical marketing system or through independently owned manufacturers, wholesalers, and retailers.

HORIZONTAL COMPETITION

Horizontal competition represents competition among similar channel members at the same level in the channel of distribution. Horizontal competition can be a department store versus a department store, a full-service wholesaler versus another full-service wholesaler, or a manufacturer versus a manufacturer.

Although it is difficult to generalize, the strategy of competing firms in horizontal competition is more similar than that of competing with channel members in intertype competition. To a manufacturer, horizontal competition also results in a more consistent image, more comparable customer service, and possibly less price competition among resellers (owing to the similar cost structures of each channel member).

CHANNELS IN ACTION

A Life-Style Typology of Fashion Shoppers

Management Horizons, a consulting firm, developed a six-classification shopper typology especially for clients that sell clothes, home furnishings, and other fashion-based goods. These clients found that general typologies such as VALS 2 were not useful in describing their customers. The Management Horizons typology is based on a national survey of 5000 primary shoppers of households.

The six-shopper types are Progressive Patrons, Power Purchasers, Social Strivers, Fashion Foregoers, Dutifuls, and Yester Years. The most important shoppers in terms of total fashion-based purchases are Progressive Patrons, Power Purchasers, and Social Strivers.

- Progressive Patrons: This group will pay high prices for top-quality clothing. Comprised mainly of young couples or midlife families with higher incomes.
- Power Purchasers: Power Purchasers are fashion risk takers who are self-indulgent. This group has the highest income.
- Social Strivers: Social Strivers purchase a lot of clothes and desire the latest styles. This group is comprised primarily of young women with low income.
- Fashion Foregoers: This group consists primarily of men who couldn't care less about their appearance.
- Dutifuls: Dutifuls are careful shoppers who like guarantees and low prices. They are middle-aged to mature shoppers, the poorest income group.
- Yester Years: This group purchases few clothes and responds mainly to low prices. Yester Years shoppers are comprised of both older women and young parents.

Management Horizons found that the typology was useful in predicting retailer choice. For example, Power Purchasers are two times more likely than the average woman to purchase dresses at Macy's; and Progressive Patrons are three times more likely than the average shopper to shop for dresses at The Limited. And Fashion Foregoers are the best customers for men's dress shirts at Sears, JC Penney, and Mervyn's. Shopper type has also been associated with selling emphasis. Social Strivers, for example, respond well to friendly salespeople; in contrast, Progressive Patrons prefer interactive computer systems.

Source: Rebecca Piirto, "Clothes with Attitude," *American Demographics* (October 1990), pp. 10 ff.

INTERTYPE COMPETITION

Intertype competition consists of competition among different types of channels at the same level in the channel of distribution. In some cases, intertype competition involves new channel formats that are competing against traditional formats or competition between price and service-oriented channel members. Manufacturers often sell their goods and services through different channel members to maximize sales. For example, while Coach, a division of Sara Lee that specializes in leather accessories (such as belts, pocketbooks, and wallets) originally sold its leather goods in catalogs and department stores, it now also sells through boutiques devoted exclusively to Coach products as well as in factory outlets. According to an executive at Sara Lee, "We aim to sell in every channel where people would want to buy."[51] Since Sara Lee acquired Coach in 1985, the leather goods company has increased its sales from $20 million to $150 million.

Another type of intertype competition is multiple channels of distribution. With **multiple channels of distribution**, a manufacturer sells different product lines to different channel members. Multiple channels of distribution enables a manufacturer to reach multiple target markets. For example, Sara Lee sells L'eggs to drug store and mass-merchandise shoppers, Hanes Silk Reflections and Sheer Elegance to department stores, and Donna Karan designer hose (as much as $35 per pair) to specialty boutiques. Multiple channels has the advantage of enabling a manufacturer to reach multiple market segments and to minimize direct competition among channel members. The disadvantages of multiple channels of distribution are the high distribution costs, the high necessary investment, possible inconsistent service, and possible price competition.

An extreme case of intertype competition involves scrambled merchandising. In **scrambled merchandising**, a channel member adds goods and services that are not usually associated with its merchandise lines. Examples of scrambled merchandising are Timex's sale of watches in a variety of retail formats, the sale of hosiery by L'eggs in supermarkets, and the sale of health and beauty aids in grocery stores. Scrambled merchandising is practiced extensively in the grocery industry in both health and beauty aids and in general merchandise. For example, in 1990 grocery stores had a 42.3 percent market share of health and beauty aids.[52] The market share of total health and beauty aids sales for drug stores and mass merchandisers was 38.3 percent and 19.4 percent, respectively.

Although scrambled merchandising is often associated with retailing, wholesalers can add unrelated lines as well. There are a number of reasons for scrambled merchandising by an intermediary: the appeal to one-stop shopping convenience, the desire to sell goods and services with higher profit margins, and the need for goods that build overall retail traffic (for retailers) or that generate sales leads (for retailers and wholesalers).

The implications of scrambled merchandising are very important for all channel members. For manufacturers, scrambled merchandising means that they now need to distribute their products in additional forms of distribution outlets. This means higher distribution costs, reliance on dual channels of distribution, and greater competition among disparate channel members. For example, Campbell Soups and Kraft General Foods are dedicating special teams to stock their goods in discount outlets, convenience stores, and even candy and tobacco concessions. Herbert Baum, former president of Campbell Soup North America, said "We've got to respond to the fact that 50 percent of food isn't being purchased in conventional grocery stores."[53] A problem associated with scrambled merchandising for manufacturers is that different wholesalers and retailers may require different gross profit margins to stock and sell their products. Thus, scrambled merchandising may also generate increased price competition.

For wholesalers and retailers, scrambled merchandising means increased opportunity for sales and higher profit margins. However, these intermediaries face certain problems with scrambled merchandising. First, scrambled merchandising has a major ripple effect. If a firm successfully scrambles merchandise, it ultimately reduces sales of a product by another channel member at the same level of distribution. The firm whose merchandise line was scrambled now must seek to scramble lines to restore its lost sales. Thus, scrambled merchandising, if successful, can create a self-perpetuating cycle. Second, too much scrambling can result in a channel member losing its identity or having an inconsistent image. Finally, there are limits to a firm's ability to engage in scrambled merchandising. Beyond a given point, a firm may not be able to properly determine a customer's needs, or to demonstrate or service merchandise.

VERTICAL COMPETITION

Vertical competition relates to competition between channel members at different levels in the channel of distribution. For example, a wholesaler of appliances may be competing with a manufacturer that sells direct to large builders. Increasingly, channel members are competing with suppliers or customers as a result of vertical integration.

Vertical integration can be forward or backward. In **forward vertical integration**, manufacturers acquire or build up retail channels, or wholesalers acquire or develop retail channels. In **backward vertical integration**, retailers purchase or develop wholesale operations, wholesalers acquire or build manufacturing operations, or retailers purchase or develop manufacturing operations.

An example of forward vertical integration is the development of retail store chains by such manufacturers as Ralph Lauren, Liz Claiborne, and Nike. Nike, for instance, operates Nike Town, a manufacturer-owned and operated retail chain that sells Nike products exclusively. Nike Town's initial stores in Portland, Oregon; West Hollywood, California; Boston, Massachusetts; and Freeport, Maine, have been so successful that waiting time at some branches can run 15 to 20 minutes during weekends.

Food-based wholesalers such as SuperValu, Fleming, Wakefern, Nash Finch, and Scriver also operate a significant number of supermarket chains. For example, not only is SuperValu the major supplier to over 4350 retail food stores, but it also owns and operates 246 stores.[54] In some cases, the wholesalers operate these stores as a means of obtaining a prime location, to take over a marginally performing retailer, to preserve a customer when it is up for sale, to maintain and build warehouse volume, to open large retail facilities that traditional retailers could not afford owing to large investment requirements, and/or to test innovations. Ownership can be either on a long-term or transitional basis.

Channel members using vertical integration need to be concerned with other channel member reactions and potential conflict of interest situations. For example, will a wholesaler keep the most profitable locations for itself and sell the less profitable ones? Are profits generated from wholesale sales used to purchase retail units that compete for retail customers? For example, SuperValu's senior vice president of marketing states: "We are cognizant of who our retailers are and where, and we consult with them. We avoid conflict by doing our research and our homework very carefully. We feel we have dealt with our retailers very fairly." To avoid potential conflicts with its retail customers, SuperValu typically sells stores purchased through the acquisition of another wholesaler to its independent retailer customers.[55]

An example of backward vertical integration is Kroger, a major supermarket chain that produces ice cream, baked goods, and dairy products in company-owned and operated plants. As with channel members using forward vertical integration, there is a high potential for channel conflict in backward vertical integration.

VERTICAL MARKETING SYSTEM COMPETITION

Vertical marketing systems can be defined as a channel system that consists of horizontally coordinated and vertically aligned establishments that are professionally managed and centrally coordinated to achieve optimum operating economies and maximum market impact.[56] Table 2-4 describes the major differences between conventional channels and vertical marketing systems. Three

TABLE 2-4 DIFFERENCES BETWEEN CONVENTIONAL CHANNELS AND VERTICAL MARKETING SYSTEMS

Characteristic	Conventional Channel Arrangement	Vertical Marketing System
Nature of contacts	Negotiation on an individual basis	Advanced joint planning for an extended time period
Information considered	Supplier sales presentation data	Retailer's merchandising data
Supplier participants	Supplier's territorial salesperson	Salesperson and major regional or headquarters executive
Retailer participants	Buyer	Various executives, perhaps top management
Retailer's goals	Sales gain and percentage markup	Programmed total profitability
Supplier's goals	Big order on each call	Continuing profitable relationship
Nature of performance evaluation	Event-centered; primarily related to sales volume and other short-term performance criteria	Specific performance criteria written into the program

Source: Ronald L. Ernst, "Distribution Channel Détente Benefits Suppliers, Retailers, and Consumers," *Marketing News* (March 7, 1980), p. 19.

types of vertical marketing systems are administered, contractual, and corporate channel systems. Vertical marketing systems involve coordinated channel functions and activities among channel members at different levels (administered systems), linkages between channel members by contracts (contractual systems), and ownership-based relationships (corporate channel systems).

The major advantages of vertical marketing systems for manufacturers are better inventory planning owing to sharing of sales data from wholesalers and retailers, trust developed from a long-term relationship, better control over product merchandising at the retail level, and improved coordination of efforts throughout the channel. Among the benefits of vertical marketing systems for wholesalers and retailers are improved marketing, financial, and troubleshooting assistance from manufacturers and suppliers; association with a product that has a strong brand image; dealing with manufacturers and suppliers that take a long-term perspective with a wholesaler and retailer; and limited horizontal and intertype competition through use of exclusive or selective distribution.

A major disadvantage of vertical marketing systems for most wholesalers and retailers is **constrained decision making**. Through constrained decision making, decision making related to store hours, involvement in a cooperative advertising program, merchandise depth and width, and vendor selection may be severely limited by contract, or manufacturer and supplier channel power. This topic is fully discussed in Chapter 12: Administrative Structures in Marketing Channels.

THE ECONOMY

This section explores the measurement of the economic climate using leading indicators. Two important measures of economic health, the unemployment rate and consumer confidence, are discussed in depth. The second section describes the relative value of the dollar, an important economic variable for channel members that are involved with importing and/or exporting.

MEASURING ECONOMIC TRENDS

Economic trends are judged by 11 leading indicators: workweek, unemployment claims, orders for consumer goods, slower deliveries, plant and equipment orders, building permits, durables order backlog, materials prices, stock prices, money supply, and consumer confidence. These indicators and commentary concerning economic predictions are typically listed and discussed in both the *Wall Street Journal* and *Business Week* on a national basis, and in local business periodicals for local and regional predictions. The Commerce Department also has an index of **coincident indicators**, which is designed to track the current economic climate.

Perhaps one of the most visible measures of economic health is the unemployment rate. In November 1994, for instance, the unemployment rate was 5.6

percent of the civilian workforce. The **unemployment rate** is the percentage of the civilian workforce that is looking for work that is unemployed. This index is somewhat confusing in that it excludes people who are not looking for work. Thus, the unemployment rate can actually increase when the economy improves, since more people seek work in an improving economy. For example, the civilian labor force as of November 1994 was 131.9 million persons; of this group, 7.3 million were unemployed (but looking for work). This translates into a 5.6 percent unemployment rate (7.3 million/131.9 million). If the economy declined and 1 million unemployed civilians who had given up finding a job resumed their search, the unemployment rate would decrease to 4.8 percent (6.3 million/131.9 million).

Consumer spending accounts for two-thirds of all economic activity and is a major ingredient in the country's economic health. Economists believe that consumer spending is related not only to actual income but also to consumer perceptions of the economy. **Consumer confidence surveys** of consumer attitudes about current and business conditions are conducted by the Conference Board and the University of Michigan. The University of Michigan survey is included in the Commerce Department's Index of Leading Indicators. Many newspapers conduct research into regional consumer confidence using the same questions as those in the nationally based surveys.

A major problem in using consumer confidence studies is that the Conference Board survey and the University of Michigan survey do not always coincide. For example, in November 1994 the Conference Board measure of consumer confidence was at 101.3, while the University of Michigan measure was at 91.6. At that time the Conference Board measure increased to its highest level in four years, whereas the Michigan measure was less than the level of January 1994. The questions asked and the survey methodologies of each survey differ[57] (see Table 2-5). One research study suggests that the Conference Board measure should be used as a means of forecasting economic activity and that the University of Michigan measure is the preferable measure for predicting purchases of consumer durables.[58]

The economy has a major impact on both final consumer purchases and purchases by manufacturers and wholesalers. Poor economic conditions or poor consumer confidence causes many final consumers to defer major purchases. This affects manufacturers and wholesalers since the demand for many organizational goods and services is a derived demand. In **derived demand**, the market for organizational goods sold through manufacturers and wholesalers is affected by the ultimate demand at the final consumer level. For example, a slowdown in air travel ultimately affects the demand for replacement aircraft. This affects manufacturers as well as wholesalers of aircraft components. Although the economy has a greater impact on certain products and services than others, in many cases an economic downturn results in a lower demand for both consumer and organizational goods; fear of excess inventories by manufacturers, wholesalers, and retailers; and the use of temporary price reductions to seek to move this inventory.

A novel way to stimulate growth during a poor economic climate (with a high unemployment rate) and low consumer confidence was Volkswagen's recent "Payment Protection Plus" promotion. In this promotion, workers who lost their jobs would not have to make car-loan and car-insurance payments for up to 12 months (up to $500 per month for car insurance and lease or loan payments) in

TABLE 2-5 COMPARING THE CONFERENCE BOARD AND THE UNIVERSITY OF MICHIGAN MEASURES OF CONSUMER CONFIDENCE

The Conference Board Consumer Confidence Measure

- How would you rate the general present conditions in your area (good, normal, or bad)?
- Six months from now, do you think they will be better, the same, or worse?
- What would you say about available jobs in your area right now (plentiful, not so many, or hard to get)?
- Six months from now, do you think there will be more jobs, the same, or fewer jobs?
- What would you guess your total family income to be six months from now (higher, the same, or lower)?

Methodology

Monthly sample of 5000 households, conducted on a nationwide basis for the Conference Board by National Family Opinion Inc. The consumer confidence index has an index of 100. The Conference Board releases its consumer confidence data once a month. This measure of consumer confidence tends to be more volatile than the University of Michigan survey.
Source: The Conference Board.

The University of Michigan Consumer Confidence Measure

- Would you say that you are better off or worse off than you were a year ago?
- Now looking ahead, do you think that a year from now you will be better off financially or worse off or just about the same as now?
- Now turning to business conditions in the country as a whole, do you think that during the next 12 months we'll have good times financially or bad times or what?
- Looking ahead, which would you say is more likely—that in the country as a whole we'll have continuous good times during the next five years or so, or that we will have periods of widespread unemployment or depression or what?
- Generally speaking, do you think now is a good or a bad time for people to buy major household items?

Methodology

Questions 500 households by telephone twice per month. Although the University of Michigan consumer confidence data are released to subscribers immediately, it is released to the general public after a one-month lag.
Source: University of Michigan.

the event they got laid off. The promotion was designed to reduce consumer fears about buying a car in the midst of a recession. The new car buyer was not required to reimburse Volkswagen in the event that he or she was laid off.[59]

RELATIVE VALUE OF THE DOLLAR

A country's **foreign exchange rate** is how much of another country's currency its currency can trade for. The sensitivity of the cost of foreign goods to the exchange rate can be seen in examining the trading range of the dollar and

Mexican peso between December 1994 and February 1995. During this time period, the value of the peso was drastically reduced as a result both of the Mexican government's devaluation of the peso and investor uncertainty.

In the beginning of December 1994, a U.S. dollar could be traded for 3.46 Mexican pesos. The exchange rate can be noted as 1 U.S. dollar = 3.46 Mexican pesos or 1 peso = 0.2890 U.S. dollar. If a Mexican-produced industrial part cost 5000 pesos, its cost in dollars was equal to $1445.00.

Cost in dollars of Mexican goods

$$= \text{The exchange rate in pesos per dollar} \times \text{Cost in Mexican pesos}$$
$$= \$0.2890 \times 5000 \text{ Mexican pesos}$$
$$= \$1445.00$$

As of the beginning of February, the relative value of the dollar was much stronger, and one U.S. dollar equaled 5.75 pesos. Then when 1 peso equaled $0.1739, the cost of the industrial product was $869.50. The industrial product's price, in effect, would be reduced by the equivalent of $575.50 if there were no increase in the cost of the part:

$$= \$0.1739 \times 5000 \text{ Mexican pesos}$$
$$= \$869.50$$

The relative value of a peso dropped so much during this time period that the Clinton administration had to develop a rescue program to shore up the value of the peso. In contrast, a decline in the value of the dollar relative to the peso would increase the cost of Mexican goods.

Fluctuations in exchange rates give rise to risks and opportunities in foreign trade. As the value of the dollar improves, imports are less costly, but exports are more expensive. On the other hand, as the value of the dollar decreases, imports are more costly, but exports become less expensive.

Channel members need to continually adjust U.S. prices to match currency fluctuations. This is particularly the case when currency fluctuations have wide and sudden swings in value. A special case involving exchange rates centers on gray market goods. **Gray market goods** are generally foreign goods purchased abroad that were not intended for the U.S. domestic market. In many instances, these goods compete for market share with goods purchased by authorized importers. A strong foreign exchange rate for the U.S. dollar contributes to the presence of gray market goods. Gray market goods are covered in Chapter 9: Pricing Strategy in Channels.

THE LEGAL ENVIRONMENT

The legal environment comprises federal, state, and local legislation. Table 2-6 lists major federal legislation affecting channel members in chronological order. The legislation relating to channels can be classified according to purpose: antitrust, discriminatory pricing, and unfair trade practices; consumer protection

TABLE 2-6 MAJOR FEDERAL LEGISLATION AFFECTING CHANNELS

Sherman Act (1890)—Prevents organizations from monopolizing markets and from engaging in activities that restrain trade in interstate and foreign commerce. Outlawed monopolies and conspiracies that restrain trade. Enforced by the Antitrust Division of the U.S. Department of Justice.

Clayton Act (1914)—Clarifies and strengthens the provisions of the Sherman Act by prohibiting such anticompetitive practices as price discrimination, requirements contracts, reciprocity, and tying and exclusive agreements.

Federal Trade Commission Act (1914)—Restricts firms from using unfair methods of competition, such as monopolies, and from restraining trade.

Cellar-Kefauver Act (1950)—Amends the Clayton Act. Regulates acquisition of assets and/or stock of another company. Regulates vertical and horizontal integration.

Robinson-Patman Act (1936)—Amends the Clayton Act's provisions concerning pricing policies. Regulates price differentials and price-related discounts, advertising allowances, quantity discounts, and brokerage fees paid to customers.

Wheeler-Lea Amendment (1938)—Revises the Federal Trade Commission Act to include unfair or deceptive practices.

Consumer Products Safety Act (1972)—Created the Consumer Product Safety Commission (CPSC), the federal agency with major responsibility for product safety.

Consumer Goods Pricing Act (1975)—Repealed the Miller-Tydings Act, which permitted retail price maintenance.

Deregulation of Airline, Trucking, and Railroads (1978, 1980):
  Airline Deregulation Act (1978)—Eliminated route restrictions and price controls.
  Motor Carrier Act (1980)—Eliminated many restrictions on interstate trucking.
  Staggers Rail Act (1980)—Eliminated the obligation for railroads to provide service along unprofitable routes.

legislation; and industry deregulation legislation. All three types of legislation are represented in this table. The Sherman Act is the earliest federal legislation relating to antitrust; the Clayton Act clarified the Sherman Act by prohibiting specific anticompetitive practices; the Federal Trade Commission Act restricts firms from unfair methods of competition; the Cellar-Kefauver Act regulates vertical and horizontal integration; the Robinson-Patman Act specifically addresses unfair pricing practices; the Wheeler-Lea Amendment strengthened the Federal Trade Commission Act; the Consumer Products Safety Act created the Consumer Product Safety Commission, the major federal agency empowered to create and enforce standards with regard to product safety; the Consumer Goods Pricing Act made retail price maintenance illegal; and the Airline Deregulation Act, Motor Carrier Act, and Staggers Rail Act resulted in deregulation of airlines, interstate trucking, and railroads, respectively.

The legal environment affects product-, pricing-, and advertising-related distribution strategies. Table 2-7 covers legal issues in channel management. Product-related legal issues in channel management include exclusive dealing,

Table 2-7 Legal Issues in Channel Management

PRODUCT-RELATED ISSUES

Exclusive dealing	—Is the requirement by a seller that its customers sell only its products, or at least no products in direct competition with its products. —Exclusive dealing gives a ready-available market to the seller. However, exclusive dealing limits buyer choice in vendor selection.
Tying agreements	—Require that a buyer must purchase one good to secure another. —Generally, an undesirable good must be purchased by a wholesaler or retailer for it to receive a desired one. This is common in franchising where the franchise is the tied product. Tying agreements have the effect of limiting competition by forcing wholesalers and retailers to purchase a large selection of a manufacturer's product mix.
Full-line forcing	—When a wholesaler or retailer is forced to order, inventory, and display each type of product produced by a manufacturer that is applicable to its trade area. —Full-line forcing is a type of tying contract.
Resale restrictions	—Involve a manufacturer restricting authorized distributors from selling its products to unauthorized distributors. A territorial restriction either prevents or discourages an intermediary from selling outside a particular area, while a customer restriction prohibits an intermediary from selling to specific customers or classes of customers. A common territorial restriction is granting an exclusive distribution or franchise. —Territorial and customer restrictions reduce intrabrand competition—competition among wholesalers or retailers of the same brand.
Reciprocity	—The practice of buying goods and services from your major customers; in turn, these customers then purchase goods and services from your firm. —Reciprocity severely limits the competition among noncustomers.
Refusal to deal	—Involves a manufacturer or wholesaler refusing to sell goods to selected intermediaries. For example, a manufacturer can refuse to sell goods to a retailer that does not meet the manufacturer's sales quota. —A seller can select its own distributors or dealers according to its own criteria and judgment. One of the main legal issues involved in refusal to deal is whether the refusal can be characterized as a conspiracy between firms that excludes other firms from being able to buy from that channel member.
Vertical or horizontal integration	—Relates to the legality of a firm acquiring channel members at different stages of the channel of distribution (vertical integration) or at the same stage of the channel (horizontal integration). —Courts are biased toward internal expansion by growth versus external expansion by merger or acquisition.

TABLE 2-7 LEGAL ISSUES IN CHANNEL MANAGEMENT (*CONTINUED*)

PRICING-RELATED ISSUES

Price discrimination	—Refers to price differences charged to competing channel members at the same level in a channel of distribution. In general, prices charged to competing channel members must be the same unless there are cost differences in selling and manufacturing goods to each channel member, a channel member meets another seller's lower price, or when conditions change (such as technological obsolescence). In addition, promotional allowances or services cannot be given unless they are offered to all competing customers on proportionately equal terms. —Price discrimination legislation severely restricts the ability of channel members to charge different prices to competing channel members unless the channel members are able to cost-justify these differences.
Resale price maintenance	—Relates to the right of manufacturers to set final retail selling prices for goods and services performed by retailers. Generally in resale price maintenance cases, manufacturers seek to force dealers to sell products at specified prices, attempt to terminate dealers because of their failure to adhere to suggested prices, and ask dealers to report discounting dealers to them. —Generally, manufacturers and wholesalers do not have the right to impose resale price maintenance on their customers.
Gray market distribution	—Refers to goods that are distributed through unauthorized channels of distribution. While gray market distribution generally refers to foreign goods purchased abroad that were not intended for the U.S. domestic market, it also includes goods that were transshipped from authorized dealers to unauthorized dealers. Manufacturers may refer to gray market goods as diversionary importing; gray market operators typically refer to them as parallel importing. —Imported gray market goods typically compete for market share with goods that are imported through authorized channels. Gray market goods infuriate authorized importers and retailers who pay higher prices and are forced to contribute to cooperative advertising programs. In some cases, gray market goods may not meet U.S. safety standards.
Taxation of mail-order sales	—In a May 1992 ruling, the Supreme Court ruled that states would have to get the permission of Congress to tax mail-order sales concluded in other states. —In the short run, large mail-order firms could continue to have price advantages for consumers who live in the 35 states with sales taxes. Consumers in high sales-tax states would continue to save as much as 8 percent through purchasing by mail or phone. National mail-order firms would also be freed from having to remit sales taxes, a cumbersome process due to different sales tax rates and sales tax regulations on a national basis.
Unit pricing	—Channel members are required to post not only the total price of an item, but also the price per standard unit of measure. This allows consumers to compare prices when package sizes vary among brands or when different size packages of the same brand make price comparisons difficult.

TABLE 2-7 LEGAL ISSUES IN CHANNEL MANAGEMENT (*CONTINUED*)

ADVERTISING-RELATED ISSUES

Former price comparisons	—If a former price is advertised, it must be a true one. The former price is not necessarily fictitious merely because no sales were made at that price. However, the price must be one at which the product was openly and actively offered for sale for a reasonably substantial period of time, and in the normal course of business. —Reductions from former price claims need to be substantiated.
Bait advertising	—Involves the promotion of a product at an unusually low price. When a consumer seeks to purchase the advertised good, it is either unavailable or is disparaged by sales personnel. —A channel member must have reasonable quantities of promoted items in stock. Bait advertising cannot be used by channel members to increase customer inquiries or store traffic.
Credit advertising	—All interest rates expressed in advertisements must be expressed in terms of an annual percentage rate. Credit terms advertised must be available at the stated terms.

tying agreements, full-line forcing, resale restrictions, reciprocity, refusal to deal, and vertical or horizontal integration. Exclusive dealing is the requirement that customers cannot sell products in competition with their suppliers' products. Tying agreements specify that a buyer must purchase one good to be able to purchase another. In full-line forcing, a buyer is required to purchase all of a supplier's goods or services that are applicable to the buyer's market area. Resale restrictions restrain a distributor from selling a manufacturer's products to unauthorized distributors. Reciprocity is the practice of a supplier's buying goods and services from its major customers. In refusing to deal, a manufacturer or wholesaler refuses to sell goods to selected intermediaries. In vertical or horizontal integration, a channel member seeks to expand by purchasing channel members at different stages of distribution (vertical integration) or by purchasing channel members at the same stage of the channel (horizontal integration).

Pricing-related issues include price discrimination, resale price maintenance, gray market distribution, taxation of mail-order sales, and unit pricing. Price discrimination legislation concerns the legality of charging different prices to competing channel members at the same channel stage. Resale price maintenance legislation refers to the right of a manufacturer to set final retail selling prices. Gray market distribution refers to goods that are sold through unauthorized distribution channels. Taxation of mail-order sales refers to the right of states to tax mail-order sales conducted with mail-order retailers located in other states. Unit pricing legislation requires channel members to post total prices and price per standard unit of measure.

Advertising-related issues relate to former price comparisons, bait advertising, and credit advertising. Former price comparisons relate to claims of price reductions. In bait advertising, a product is promoted by a channel member, even though the firm has no intention of selling the product. Credit advertising legislation requires annual credit costs to be listed in all advertising statements concerning interest rates.

This material is covered in greater detail in future chapters. Product-related legal issues are covered in Chapter 8, pricing-related legal issues in Chapter 9, and promotion-related legal issues in Chapter 10.

TECHNOLOGICAL ENVIRONMENT

Important technological developments in channels relate to recording sales and monitoring inventory, computer-based sales support and technical problem-solving systems, and video-ordering systems. Most of these technological developments involve computerization, either on a manufacturer, wholesaler, retailer, or consumer level.

RECORDING SALES AND MONITORING INVENTORY

Three major technological developments relating to sales and inventory data are scanning, point-of-sale inventory systems, and electronic data interchange. **Bar code scanners** can be used to keep track of sales and inventory on hand at manufacturers, wholesalers, and retailers by reading and recording Universal Product Codes. According to the Fifth Annual Barcode/EDI/Quick Response survey prepared by Deloitte & Touche for the National Retail Federation, 92 percent of retailers (mass merchants, nonapparel specialty retailers, department stores, and apparel specialty retailers) stated that they were committed to scanning. Retailers were also making greater use of scanning for inventory taking and warehouse functions.[60]

Scanning enables channel members to have real-time data on sales. For example, data on sales are read by scanners at local Kmart stores and are instantaneously fed into Kmart's centralized computer-based inventory system located at Kmart's headquarters (in Troy, Michigan). This centralized system enables goods to be reordered instantaneously on the basis of current sales trends. Data on current sales performance enable Kmart to reduce its inventory investment by concentrating on fast-selling merchandise, and to improve profits by concentrating on appropriate selections for local needs and by reducing stockouts. Manufacturers and distributors can also use scanning to verify inventory quantities, to pick outgoing inventory, and to verify outgoing inventory against orders.

While scanning systems keep track of sales by product classification and item, point-of-sales terminals are able to perform more complex functions directly on the sales floor. New **point-of-sale terminals** can perform such functions as price lookup (allowing chains to vary prices by region and by store); determine sales by item, product line, merchandise category, and salesperson;

CHANNELS IN ACTION

Pizza Hut Gains Access to Institutional Markets

Although many firms take a reactive approach to the legal environment and change their strategies to adapt to changes in the law, Pizza Hut has taken a proactive approach. Through a proactive approach, Pizza Hut was able to change the legal environment to its advantage.

The school and other institutional market for pizza is a huge one. Over $500 million in pizza is sold through school cafeterias. The college market is estimated to be worth an additional $1 billion in annual sales. This does not include the market for pizza sold through other private and nonprofit institutions such as hospitals and prisons.

Pizza Hut lobbied successfully to break the frozen pizza industry's virtual monopoly on meat pizza sales to these institutions. Under the old law, only frozen pizza met the 85-year-old inspection requirement for all meat products distributed to restaurants and institutions for resale. To meet the old requirements, fresh pizza makers would have to spend millions of dollars to upgrade their kitchens. They would also have to pay for federal inspectors to approve their operations. According to a lobbyist for Pizza Hut, "The real issue isn't health and safety. They just don't want any competition."

The National Frozen Pizza Institute argued unsuccessfully that the exemption would undermine public health safeguards. It also contended that Pizza Hut intended to convert its operation from "sit down restaurants to a pizza distribution company."

To take advantage of the changes in the law, Pizza Hut plans to rapidly expand its distribution into the institutional market. According to a Pizza Hut spokesperson, "We'd like to have every one of our (4000) delivery-capable units nationwide serving at least one school." Pizza Hut intends to prepare the pizza at local restaurant locations and then to deliver the pizza to the schools.

Since fresh meat pizza has become exempt, many channel analysts feel that manufacturers of such products as burritos, eggrolls, and tacos will apply for exemption as well.

Source: Bruce Ingersoll, "Pizza Hut Gains Fast-Food Entree to Institutions," *Wall Street Journal* (November 29, 1991), pp. B1, B6; and Malcolm Gladwell, "The Pepperoni Pizza Pickle," *Washington Post* (May 27, 1992), p. A17.

---

evaluate returns and exchanges; take markdowns associated with special one-day sales; and track customers by zip code to evaluate a store's location. Sears' new cash register terminals accept payment for merchandise, issue temporary Sears charge cards, print gift certificates, and even process charge card payments. The expanded functions allow Sears to eliminate the use of separate customer service departments.[61]

Electronic data interchange (EDI), the systematic sharing of sales and inventory data between channel members, is generally used in conjunction with scanning and point-of-sales systems. According to the *Fifth Annual Barcode/EDI/Quick Response Survey* prepared by Deloitte & Touche for the National Retail Federation, more than 39 percent of retailers were using electronic data interchange in 1992 with selected vendors.[62] Whereas in traditional order systems data are mailed to suppliers and then rekeyed by them, in electronic data interchange, data are sent via a telecommunications link. There is no need to print, mail, or reenter data. The advantages of electronic data interchange are speed of information transmission, ability of a vendor to determine sales trends in a timely manner, reduced reorder times, lower inventory levels, and fewer errors.[63] Electronic data interchange allows **quick response inventory management**. In quick response inventory management, retailers and wholesalers receive multiple small orders from their suppliers to match sales patterns. Through quick response inventory systems, channel members can minimize inventory investment and focus on producing those items with high sales performance. Such a system minimizes ordering costs incurred in the routinizing of information flow.

Wal-Mart was the first major retailer to insist that all ordering be done computer to computer. It has also entered into agreements with suppliers (such as a jeans manufacturer) wherein the vendor (not the retailer) is responsible for inventory for a specific number of racks. The vendor gets space in Wal-Mart's warehouse, but Wal-Mart does not "buy" the merchandise until it is moved into the store. To enable this relationship to work, Wal-Mart tells its supplier how fast and at what price it is selling jeans. Sharing information with suppliers has been viewed by some as "giving foxes membership at the henshouse country club." In contrast to this position, Wal-Mart uses electronic data interchange to create increased opportunities for sharing information.[64]

COMPUTER-BASED SALES SUPPORT AND TECHNICAL PROBLEM-SOLVING SYSTEMS

Many manufacturer sales reps and wholesalers use **computer-based sales support systems**. In a sales support system, salespeople (field or telemarketing) are linked via terminals or modems to the firm's central computer. This linkage provides important customer information to the salesperson, such as allowing the salesperson to verify whether an item is currently in stock or to check on the delivery status of an order.

Technical problem-solving systems give customers access to technical data such as which products meet customer needs.[65] For example, DEC, a computer manufacturer, has an electronic store that gives customers access to every product and service that DEC sells. Nearly 100,000 DEC users can dial into the electronic store via a PC or terminal to view product descriptions, specifications, and prices; see a five-minute software demonstration; and get updates on new products.[66] To induce DEC's sales personnel to get their customers to use the electronic store, DEC gives the rep credit for all orders placed through the store.[67]

VIDEO-ORDERING SYSTEMS

Consumers can order goods and services by computer, telephone, or an in-store computer terminal through **video-ordering systems**. Prodigy, a computer ordering system jointly owned by IBM and Sears, offers more than 800 on-line features to 2 million subscribers. The videotext service delivers news, ads, and mail-order shopping all through a PC. Other computer-based ordering systems are CompuServe (owned by H&R Block), GEnie (owned by General Electric), and America Online. Supporters of on-line services argue that by the end of the decade, Prodigy will have more than 10 million members. Despite the high enrollment, Prodigy has yet to return any profit despite a $1 billion investment over a nine-year period.[68] U.S. West, Nordstrom, and JC Penney are also collaborating to create a service that will enable shoppers to browse through the retailers' offerings and to purchase merchandise through their remote-control equipped television set.

At least one retail scholar argues that computer-based ordering systems more closely resemble wholesaling than retailing. According to the expert, the distinguishing characteristic of retailing is inspection by the consumer within a store environment. In wholesaling, the wholesaler has a warehouse, sales are made by specifying an order number, and delivery is made with the item in the box. "If the sale is made from a warehouse, by the number, and shipped in the box, it is conceptually (functionally) a wholesale transaction even though the sale is made to the final consumer."[69] According to this notion, consumers have taken on many functions formerly performed by retailers, and retailers more closely resemble wholesaler suppliers.

Telephone-ordering systems include Home Shopping Network, which operates the home shopping network, the largest retailer in this category, QVC, and Cable 1, a new cable shopping channel developed by Time Warner and Spiegel. (Both Home Shopping Network and QVC can handle live operator and voice response computer modes.) Computers also provide marketing managers with on-line access to product sales, inventory levels, and sales per minute. Their network's programming is run 24 hours a day, 7 days a week. Catalog 1 features merchandise from Eddie Bauer (a Spiegel subsidiary), Williams-Sonoma, the Sharper Image, the Nature Company, Crate and Barrel, and the Bombay Company. While Home Shopping Network and QVC charge participants between 40 and 50 percent of their sales, these firms handle all warehousing, sorting, packaging, and shipping responsibilities. In contrast, catalog participants pay between 20 and 30 percent of sales, but handle their own order processing.[70]

In-store computer terminals can be illustrated with Price Club/Costco's Quest automated touch screen catalog which are placed in many of the firm's stores. Each kiosk contains more than 8000 products, in 30 product categories (including collectibles, computers, jewelry, watches, power tools, sporting goods, gourmet foods, and electronics). None of the goods in the catalog is found in the stores. The customer also has the convenience of the computer printing out the order form, shipment to one's own home or to recipient (in the case of a gift), and low prices. The consumer gets low prices because products are shipped directly from the manufacturer or importer.

Some experts argue that video-ordering systems can become the 1990s version of mail order. In the early 1990s, consumers were already doing 7 percent of their retail buying by mail. Video ordering enables a retailer to receive orders from around the country and to appeal to poverty-of-time life-styles. Others argue that it will be years before some shopping services (such as interactive home shopping) will reach a mass audience since they are now only in the test marketing stage. Some cable operators may also resist carrying the new programming owing to their current success with the Home Shopping Network and QVC.[71] See Appendix B: The Information Superhighway and Channel Management for additional coverage on important topics such as interactive television, the Internet, the World Wide Web, and CD-ROM–based shopping.

The technological environment is rapidly evolving. Important developments that affect all channel members are the increased sophistication of consumers and managers, the increased ownership of personal computers and modems by final consumers, the lower hardware and software costs, and an increased desire among many suppliers and customers to share both sales and inventory data.

SUMMARY

1 *To describe how channel members can plan in an uncertain environment through building scenarios, developing a contingency plan, and using market research.* One way of dealing with uncertainty in forecasting the environment is through the development of scenarios. Three types of scenarios that should be studied by channel managers are a continuation of a current trend, a scenario in which all conditions are favorable, and a disaster scenario. Scenarios are an important element in the development of a contingency plan. Three important steps in developing and implementing a contingency plan are identifying the critical event, specifying the trigger point, and determining the appropriate response. Marketing research and marketing information are required to survey the firm's environment for both threats and opportunities. Many marketing experts feel that the earlier that a firm can detect an issue that is significant to its success, the greater will its range of strategies and tactics be, and the greater its chance of resolving the issue in its favor.

2 *To study final consumer demographic characteristics: population growth, age distribution, income distribution, number of households, marital status, and working women and their impact on channel members.* Among the effects of demographic trends on channel members are the need for market penetration and market development strategies, the increased importance of micromarketing, the increase in importance of the 35-plus age group, the need to appeal to both downscale and upscale markets, the increase in importance of single-person households, the increase in single-parent households, and the importance of the working woman market.

3. *To analyze final consumer life-style characteristics: poverty of time, the greening of America, value orientation, blurring of gender roles, component life-styles, and VALS 2 and other typologies and their impact on channel members.* The poverty of time trend should positively impact mail-order sales, home delivery, assembly of products, and acceptance of phone orders. The greening of America signifies the importance of recyclable bins, refunds for reusing bags in supermarkets, life-cycle costing by manufacturers, and use of less packaging by manufacturers and retailers. Value orientation should increase sales at factory outlets, off-price chains, outlet malls, and membership-based wholesale clubs. The blurring of gender roles forces marketers to rethink the traditional stereotypical roles of males and females in buying. Component life-styles suggest that consumers may lack consistency and predictability regarding their purchase behavior. VALS 2 and other typologies can be used by channel members to segment their markets and to decide their appeal to various segments.

4. *To view channel competition: horizontal competition, intertype competition, vertical competition, and vertical marketing system competition and its impact on channel members.* Horizontal competition consists of competition among channel members of the same type. Intertype competition relates to competition among different types of channel members at the same level within a channel. There is generally greater diversity between the characteristics of each channel member and their overall marketing strategy in intertype versus horizontal competition. Dual channels of distribution and scrambled merchandising are two common strategies used with intertype competition. Vertical competition describes competition among different channel members at different levels within the channel, such as a manufacturer competing with a retailer. Manufacturers and wholesalers using vertical competition need to be concerned with retailer reactions and potential conflict-of-interest situations. In vertical marketing system competition, horizontally coordinated and vertically aligned establishments that are professionally managed and centrally coordinated compete against each other. Coordination is due to power, contracts among channel members, and ownership.

5. *To analyze the effect of economic conditions on channel members.* Economic trends are judged by 11 leading indicators. Two important leading indicators are the unemployment rate and consumer confidence surveys. Although these factors have an immediate effect on consumer spending, there is a derived demand relationship between consumer and organizational goods.

6. *To examine federal legislation and its effect on channel members and legal issues in channel management.* Major federal legislation that affects channel decision making includes the Sherman Act, the Clayton Act, the Federal Trade Commission Act, the Cellar-Kefauver Act, the Robinson-Patman Act, the Wheeler-Lea Amendment, the Consumer Products Safety Act, the Consumer Goods Pricing Act, and various acts that deregulated the airline, motor carrier, and rail industries. These acts affect channel member decisions in the areas of product, pricing, and advertising.

7. *To determine the technological environment and its impact on channel members.* Important technological developments in channels relate to recording sales and monitoring inventory, computer-based sales support and technical problem-solving systems, and video-ordering systems. Most of these technological developments involve computerization, either on a manufacturer, wholesaler, retailer, or consumer level. Through such systems, channel members can receive better information on inventory turnover, better communicate with vendors and with salespeople and customers, and simplify ordering by retail customers.

KEY TERMS

scenario
contingency plan
contingent event
trigger point
consumer demographics
market penetration
market development
micromarketing
money income
real income
downscale households
household
family
consumer life-styles
poverty of time
greening of America
ecological life cycle of a product
life-cycle costing
value orientation
factory outlets
off-price chains
outlet malls
buying clubs (membership clubs)
blurring of gender roles
component life-styles
psychographic research
VALS (Values and Life-Styles) program
horizontal competition
intertype competition
vertical competition
vertical marketing system competition
multiple channels of distribution
scrambled merchandising
forward vertical integration
backward vertical integration
constrained decision making
coincident indicators
unemployment rate
consumer confidence surveys
derived demand
foreign exchange rate
gray market goods
bar code scanners
point-of-sale terminals
electronic data interchange (EDI)
quick response inventory management
computer-based sales support systems
technical problem-solving systems
video-ordering systems

QUESTIONS FOR DISCUSSION

1. Determine recommended trigger points and responses for the following scenarios:
   a. A decrease in population of school-aged children to a regional school supply wholesaler.
   b. Increased ecological awareness among new car buyers to a car dealer.
   c. Increased value orientation among consumers to a manufacturer of washing machines.
2. a. What are the advantages of using *Census of Population* data (versus commercial demographic data sources) in determining the demographic environment by a consumer electronics wholesaler? The wholesaler's territory corresponds to half the area of a major county.
   b. What are the disadvantages of using *Census of Population* data (versus commercial demographic data sources) in determining the demographic environment by a consumer electronics wholesaler?
3. Differentiate between the use of micromarketing and differentiated marketing by a Frito-Lay distributor.
4. Develop a marketing strategy for a major appliance retailer (selling refrigerators, VCRs, and room air conditioners) to appeal to downscale households.
5. What marketing opportunities and threats can be traced to the increase in working women? Differentiate among opportunities and threats for manufacturers and for department store retailers.
6. Explain the interrelationship between the increase in working women (as a demographic trend) and the poverty of time (as a consumer life-style trend).
7. What is the impact of component life-styles on a manufacturer of upscale shoes?
8. Discuss how a manufacturer can use VALS 2 to better segment markets.
9. Differentiate among horizontal, intertype, vertical, and vertical marketing system competition.
10. "An extreme case of dual distribution involves scrambled merchandising." Comment on this statement.
11. Show how changes in the foreign exchange rate can generate opportunities for marketers of gray market goods.
12. Differentiate among exclusive dealing, tying arrangements, and full-line forcing.
13. Describe the interrelationship between electronic data interchange and quick response inventory management.
14. "Computer-based ordering systems more closely resemble wholesaling than retailing." Comment on this statement.

END NOTES

1. Tim R. Davis, "The Distribution Revolution," *Planning Review* (March/April 1994), pp. 46–49; Laurie M. Grossman, "Families Have Changed But Tupperware Keeps Holding Its Parties," *Wall Street Journal* (July 21, 1992), pp. A1, A4; Gene G. Marcial, "Get Ready for a Tupperware Party," *Business Week* (May 9, 1994), p. 80; and *Premark International, Inc. 1993 Annual Report,* pp. 6–8.

2. Thomas G. Exter, "The Declining Majority," *American Demographics* (January 1993), p. 59; and Betsy Wiesendanger, "Asian-Americans: The Three Biggest Myths," *Sales & Marketing Management* (September 1993), pp. 86–88 ff.

3. See Thomas G. Exter, "The Largest Minority," *Progressive Grocer* (February 1993), p. 59.

4. Stuart Elliott, "2 Big Retailers Reach Out to Minorities," *New York Times* (December 31, 1991), p. D16.

5. Teresa Andreoli, "Experts Probe Major Influences in Marketing to Minorities," *Discount Store News* (June 20, 1994), p. 12.

6. Laurie M. Grossman, "After Demographic Shift, Atlanta Mall Restyles Itself as Black Shopping Center," *Wall Street Journal* (February 26, 1992), pp. B1, B7; and Elliott, "2 Big Retailers Reach Out to Minorities," p. D16.

7. Maria Mallory and Stephanie Anderson Forest, "Waking Up to a Major Market," *Business Week* (March 23, 1992), pp. 72–73.

8. Christopher Palmeri and Joshua Levine, "No Habla Español," *Forbes* (December 23, 1991), pp. 140, 142.

9. Mallory and Forest, "Waking Up to a Major Market," pp. 72–73.

10. See Spencer L. Hapoienu, "The Rise of Micromarketing," *Journal of Business Strategy,* Vol. 11 (November–December 1990), p. 39; and "Micromarketing Flourishes in Sporting Goods," *Discount Store News* (August 15, 1994), p. 84.

11. Rick Christie, "Marketers Err by Treating Elderly as Uniform Group," *Wall Street Journal* (October 31, 1988), p. B1.

12. Penny Gill, "Who's Counting," *Stores* (May 1988), p. 34.

13. Marianne Wilson, "Sixty Something," *Chain Store Age Executive* (July 1991), pp. 31–33.

14. Martha Farnsworth Riche, "We're All Minorities Now," *American Demographics* (October 1991), p. 29.

15. See Bill Kelley, "The New Consumer Revealed," *Sales & Marketing Management* (May 1993), p. 51.

16. See Jan Larson, "Reaching Downscale Markets," *American Demographics* (November 1991), pp. 38–40 ff.

17. Ibid., p. 40.

18. Laura Zinn, Heather Keets, and James B. Treece, "Home Alone—With $660 Billion," *Business Week* (July 29, 1991), p. 76.

19. Ibid.

20. Blayne Cutler, "Housing: Single and Settled," *American Demographics* (May 1991), p. 10.

21. See Gordon Green and Edward Welniak, "The Nine Household Markets," *American Demographics* (October 1991), pp. 36–40.

22. Diane Crispell, "People Patterns: Proportion of Women in Work Force Drops," *Wall Street Journal* (March 16, 1992), p. B1.

23. Jerrold K. Footlick, "What Happened to the Family?" *Newsweek* (Winter/Spring 1990), p. 16.

24. Peter D. Bennett, ed., *Dictionary of Marketing Terms* (Chicago: American Marketing Association, 1988), p. 106.

25. See Blayne Cutler, "Where Does the Free Time Go?" *American Demographics* (November 1990), pp. 36–38.

26. John P. Robinson, "Your Money or Your Time," *American Demographics* (November 1991), p. 26.

27. Ibid., pp. 22-26.

28. Laura Zinn, "Shopper Sightings Reported," *Business Week* (January 13, 1992), p. 81.

29. Karen L. Katz, Blaire M. Larson, and Richard C. Larson, "Prescription for the Waiting-in-Line Blues: Entertain, Enlighten, and Engage," *Sloan Management Review,* Vol. 39 (Winter 1991), pp. 44–53.

30. Rose Gutfeld, "Eight of 10 Americans Are Environmentalists, At Least They Say," *Wall Street Journal* (August 9, 1991), pp. A1, A10.

31. *Albertson's, Inc. 1990 Annual Report,* p. 8.

32. See Art Klenier, "What Does It Mean to Be Green?" *Harvard Business Review,* Vol. 69 (July–August 1991), pp. 38–42 ff.

33. John Holusha, "Learning to Wrap Products in Less—or Nothing at All," *New York Times* (January 19, 1992), p. F8.

34. Ibid.

35. Christopher Power, Walecia Konrad, Alice Z. Cuneo, and James B. Treece, "Value Marketing: Quality, Service, and Fair Pricing Are the Keys to Selling in the '90s," *Business Week* (November 11, 1991), p. 132.

36. Ibid., p. 134.

37. See Rahul Jacob, "Meet the New Consumer: Beyond Quality and Value," *Fortune* (Autumn/Winter 1993), pp. 6–11; and Bill Kelley, "The New Consumer Revealed," *Sales & Marketing Management* (May 1993), pp. 46–51 ff.

38. *Kmart 1994 Annual Report and 10K for the Year Ending January 31, 1994* and *Wal-Mart 1994 Annual Report and 10K for the Year Ending January 31, 1994.*

39. Zinn, "Shopper Sightings Reported," p. 81.

40. Claudia H. Deutsch, "Unlikely Malls, Unlikely Tenants, Unheard-of-Places," *New York Times* (February 23, 1992), p. R11.

41. See "A Retailing Hub Grows in Virginia's Countryside," *New York Times* (December 23, 1991), p. D4, and Laura Zinn, "Shopper Sightings Reported," *Business Week* (January 13, 1992), p. 81.

42. Deutsch, "Unlikely Malls, Unlikely Tenants, Unheard-of-Places," p. R11; and Kerry J. Smith, "Getting into the Outlets," *Promo* (December 1993), pp. 69–71.

43. Patricia Sellers, "Winning over the New Consumer," *Fortune* (July 29, 1991), p. 124.

44. Fabian Linden, "How We Live: Women's Work Is Almost Never Done—By Men," *Across the Board* (October 1990), pp. 10–11.

45. Diane Crispell, "The Brave New World of Men," *American Demographics* (January 1992), pp. 40–41.

46. Ibid., p. 40.

47. Douglas Martin, "For Many Fathers, Roles Are Shifting," *New York Times* (June 20, 1993), p. L20.

48. "31 Major Trends Shaping the Future of American Business," Roper's *The Public Pulse,* Vol. 2, No. 1 (1988), p. 1.

49. See Judith Waldrop, "Markets with Attitude," *American Demographics* (July 1994), pp. 22-33; and Martha Farnsworth Riche, "Psychographics for the 1990s," *American Demographics* (July 1989), pp. 25–26 ff.

50. *Supermarket Merchandising for the 1990s: A Framework for Competing* (Atlanta: Coca-Cola Retailing Research Council, 1989).

51. Stephanie Strom, "A Women's Chain Beckons to Men," *New York Times* (July 24, 1991), pp. D1 ff.

52. "Supers Yield a Bit in HBA Share," *Progressive Grocer* (January 1992), pp. 57–58.

53. Sellers, "Winning over the New Consumer," p. 124.

54. *SuperValu 1993 Annual Report,* p. 1.

55. "Retailing: A Wholesale Dilemma," *Progressive Grocer* (November 1990), p. 36.

56. Peter D. Bennett, ed., *Dictionary of Marketing Terms,* Second Edition (Chicago: American Marketing Association, 1995), p. 300.

57. See Louis Uchitelle, "Confidence Index Has a Surge," *New York Times* (November 30, 1994), pp. D1 ff.

58. William L. Huth, David R. Eppright, and Paul M. Taube, "The Indexes of Consumer Sentiment and Confidence: Leading or Misleading Guides to Future Buyer Behavior," *Journal of Business Research,* Vol. 29 (March 1994), pp. 199–206.

59. Jacqueline Miller, "Buyers of VWs Receive Cushion Against Layoffs," *Wall Street Journal* (January 29, 1992), pp. B1, B5; and Adam Bryant, "Buyers of New Volkswagens Get Hedge Against Job Loss," *New York Times* (January 29, 1992), p. D2.

60. "Quick Resonse Grows," *Chain Store Age Executive* (May 1993), p. 160.

61. See Suzanne Biello, "Sears Cutting 7,000 Jobs," *Newsday* (January 8, 1992), pp. 35–36; and Francine Schwader, "Sears Roebuck to Streamline Catalog Business," *Wall Street Journal* (January 8, 1992), pp. B1, B5.

62. "Quick Response Grows," p. 160.

63. Brian Dearing, "The Strategic Benefits of EDI," *Journal of Business Strategy,* Vol. 11 (January–February 1990), pp. 4–6.

64. Bill Saporito, "Is Wal-Mart Unstoppable?" *Fortune* (May 6, 1991), p. 58.

65. See James A. Narus and Tom Guimaraes, "Computer Usage in Distributor Marketing," *Industrial Marketing Management,* Vol. 16 (February 1987), pp. 43–57.

66. See Thayer C. Taylor, "DEC Gets Its House in Order," *Sales & Marketing Management* (July 1990), pp. 63–64.

67. See William C. Moncrief III, Charles W. Lamb, Jr., and Jane M. Mackay, "Laptop Computers in Industrial Sales," *Industrial Marketing Management,* Vol. 20 (November 1991), pp. 279–285.

68. See Glenn Rifkin, "At Age 9, Prodigy On-Line Reboots," *New York Times* (November 8, 1993), pp. D1, D2.

69. See Wilke D. English, "The Impact of Electronic Technology upon the Marketing Channel," *Journal of the Academy of Marketing Science,* Vol. 13 (Summer 1985), pp. 57–71.

70. Stephanie Strom, "Mail Order Shifts Its Pitch to Cable," *New York Times* (March 21, 1994), pp. D1, D7.

71. See "Interactive Home-Shopping Channel Slated by US West, Nordstrom, Penney," *Wall Street Journal* (May 19, 1994), p. B9.

CASE 1

AVON COSMETICS' INITIAL DIFFICULTIES WITH ITS DUAL DISTRIBUTION STRATEGY

Avon has been beset with a variety of problems with its traditional direct sales distribution system in the United States. Its sales representative turnover rate has been very high, and many of its traditional customers, homemakers, are now working. The increase in the percentage of females in the workforce poses a double-edged problem for Avon. This has the joint effect of reducing the number of qualified reps as well as the number of the company's prospects.

In addition to its direct selling (where Avon's average sale is $20 or less), Avon has begun to distribute its products through a combination of direct mail and telemarketing called Avon Select. To build up this new form of distribution, Avon reps are asked to supply the firm with the names of current Avon users and other potential customers. Each prospect is then mailed a catalog. Avon plans to share catalog mailing expenses with its direct sales representatives. The Avon sales representatives then follow up the catalog with a telephone call. The direct mail customer can also mail her order directly to the firm or place the order with her sales representative. In addition, Avon has instituted a toll-free telephone number, and will take orders for cosmetics via facsimile machine. To increase awareness of the new form of distribution, Avon has invested in a $34 million national advertising campaign, the largest in the firm's 108-year history.

When it was initially announced, Avon's chief executive officer predicted that Avon Select would become a $300 million to $500 million business within a three- to five-year period. The executive assumed that this program would attract new customers who either did not know an Avon lady, were in an area served by a poorly motivated Avon lady, or chose not to buy from an Avon lady. Some of the optimism was based on an initial test of Avon Select wherein 12 percent of western Connecticut customers responded to Avon's direct mail campaign, well above the average 3 percent response rate. In 1993 Avon Select generated about $45 million in sales, about 3.2 percent of Avon's total U.S. revenues. Avon's marketing executives acknowledge that this performance was disappointing. Other market analysts also contend that some of these sales would have come from Avon's traditional customers via direct selling.

There are several explanations as to what went wrong with Avon Select. According to the president of the Direct Selling Association, a professional association, "the key is not to undercut the field sales force." Although Mary Kay Corporation is testing a direct mail catalog, its catalog carries different merchandise than its sales force. Mary Kay, unlike Avon, also forwards a commission to the local sales representative based on total direct mail sales in her territory. At the same time as it introduced Avon Direct, Avon restructured its sales commission structure; this required Avon sales representatives to sell more products to earn the same commission. It also reduced the value of vacations and other prizes it awarded to its top performers. In addition, although Avon had given its sales representatives points that were redeemable for a wide variety of gifts, this policy was discontinued. Points were now redeemable for savings bonds. These changes resulted in severe morale problems among Avon's 400,000-person traditional sales force in the United States.

Another explanation for the failure of Avon Select was the firm's inability to establish a brand image that did not require a sales representative. According to a marketing consultant, the sales representative developed confidence in the brand. "When you take away that selling relationship, you're left with a brand that's relatively naked." Some analysts are especially concerned that Avon has recently announced a major reduction in its advertising budget.

QUESTIONS

1. Develop a scenario including critical event, trigger point, and response for Avon's new form of distribution.
2. How can catalog sales enable Avon to better utilize micromarketing? Explain your answer.
3. a. What is the impact of working women on Avon's traditional means of distribution?
   b. What is the impact of working women on Avon's new catalog form of distribution?
4. Describe Avon's channel competition.

Sources: Claudia H. Deutsch, "Relighting the Fires at Avon," *New York Times* (April 3, 1994), p. F6; Suein L. Hwang, "Updating Avon Means Respecting History Without Repeating It," *Wall Street Journal* (April 4, 1994), pp. A1, A9; Mark Poirer, "Yet Another Avon Select Makeover," *Catalog Age* (May 1994), pp. 1 ff.; and Jeffrey A. Trachtenberg, "Catalogs Help Avon Get a Foot in the Door," *Wall Street Journal* (February 28, 1992), pp. B1, B10.

CASE 2

PRODIGY: EVALUATING A COMPUTER-ORDERING SYSTEM

Prodigy is an electronic buying and information service owned by Sears and IBM. It enables consumers with personal computers to receive news and advertising, and to conduct mail-order shopping. Sears and IBM invested an estimated $650 million to develop Prodigy. As of 1993 Prodigy claims that it has 2 million members (people who can access the system). Prodigy's market share is 41 percent versus 33 percent for CompuServe, a unit of H&R Block. Yet as of 1993, Prodigy has lost as much as $1 billion for Sears and IBM. Supporters of on-line services argue that by the end of the decade, Prodigy will have more than 10 million members and that on-line services will become the 1990s version of direct mail. In 1994 Prodigy had 30 to 40 retailer clients (including Sears, JC Penney, Lands' End, Spiegel, Hammacher Schlemmer, L'eggs, PC Flowers, and the Sunglass Shop). This compares to more than 125 vendors at CompuServe and seven vendors on America Online. Some retailers such as Sears, JC Penney, Lands' End, Hammacher Schlemmer, and L'eggs subscribe as merchants to both Prodigy and CompuServe.

A special feature of Prodigy is its Gift Reminder Service. This service tracks the dates of up to 50 events (such as birthdays and anniversaries) and then sends an E-mail message to the subscriber to remind him or her of the event. Gift Sender contains 400 gifts in a wide variety of categories (such as meats, stuffed animals, and novelties). It also has a section of gifts below $25.

An example of a successful firm that sells its goods and services through Prodigy is PC Flowers. Although PC Flowers is the second largest generator of business (out of 25,000 North American members) in the FTD flower-delivery network, virtually all of its sales are through Prodigy or an audiotex retail service. Through Prodigy, PC Flowers can be reached by either searching through a menu of shopping choices or by noticing one of its ads, which are interspersed with general information. PC Flowers' menu contains two dozen digitized pictures of bouquets, along with a written description and price. Orders can be placed by credit card; the PC Flowers computer then checks the buyer's credit. A search based on zip codes determines the FTD member closest to where the flowers are to be delivered. In 1990 PC Flowers generated 25,000 wire transfers; as originator of a wire transfer, PC Flowers collects a fee of 20 percent of the order. In contrast, in 1993 it generated 110,000. The nice part of PC Flowers' Prodigy business is that the firm also does not need an inventory, doesn't have payables, has no collectibles, and involves no major overhead.

It more recently began to sell its flowers through an audiotex floral retail service. PC Flowers runs a color page ad with 18 floral arrangements in selected telephone directories. Each display has a digital code that enables a caller without a computer to order a floral arrangement. Ten percent of audiotex revenues are shared with the directory's publisher, in place of advertising fees. Each publisher has a separate 800 number so that PC Flowers can easily track sales and payments.

Based on its success with flowers, PC Flowers is now considering delivery of merchandise other than flowers, such as fruit, cookies, and baskets for new mothers.

Still, PC Flowers is not without difficulties. As a member of FTD, PC Flowers had to develop software to translate orders from Prodigy's format into FTD's. Prodigy also had to revise its software to allow PC Flowers to collect orders every two to three hours instead of on a daily basis. PC Flowers also had to purchase and operate a florist shop to become a FTD member, despite the fact that the vast majority of its sales are through Prodigy. Lastly, the graphics available on Prodigy and on consumers' home computers do not do justice to the floral arrangements available through FTD.

QUESTIONS

1. What life-style trends have positive ramifications for PC Flowers?
2. a. Discuss the nature of channel competition for PC Flowers.
   b. What are its advantages and disadvantages with respect to traditional florists?
3. a. What impact would the economy have on PC Flowers?
   b. How can PC Flowers minimize the effect of a recession?
4. What technological developments impact on PC Flowers?

Sources: Paul B. Brown, "On-Screen Sales," *Inc.* (January 1991), pp. 108-109; Paul B. Carroll, "Computer-Ordering Method Helps Newcomer Blossom," *Wall Street Journal* (January 22, 1991), p. B2; Scott Donaton, "In Fast-Changing World, A Sense of Urgency at Prodigy," *Advertising Age* (April 5, 1993), pp. S1–S2; Stuart Elliott, "Prodigy Makes Pitch to Marketers," *New York Times* (February 13, 1992), p. D10; Mark Fitzgerald, "Newspapers Are Buying into On-Line Services But Will They Sell?" *Editor and Publisher* (February 19, 1994), pp. 22–23 ff., Gregg Keizer, "Electronic Shopping," *Ziff-Davis Personal Computing* (Fall 1994), pp. 46–48; and Steven Ramos, "Kick the Tires on the Screen," *Forbes* (January 21, 1991), pp. 100–101.

PART ONE CASE

THE COCA-COLA COMPANY

OVERVIEW OF THE SODA INDUSTRY

Coca-Cola Company, the world's largest soft-drink company, is a truly global firm. Coca-Cola makes its syrup and concentrates at 44 plants worldwide; its soft-drink products are sold in over 160 countries throughout the world.

Sales growth in the soft-drink industry as a whole varies by sector. In general, sales growth is much faster in foreign than in domestic markets. And in domestic markets, the fastest sales growth rates are in the diet drink, private label (store brand), and the premium-priced soft-drink sectors (largely comprised of New Age fruit-flavored drinks). Cola flavors from all manufacturers account for nearly 60 percent of all domestic soft-drink sales (see Table 1). Many analysts feel that domestic cola sales have peaked.

The soft-drink business is marked by a high degree of product proliferation. In 1991, 1805 new beverages were introduced in the United States. The largest number of new beverage products were fruit and fruit-flavored drinks (480), teas (293), and bottled waters (181). Many new soft-drink products have been introduced by small firms, such as Snapple Natural Beverage. Snapple now sells over 25 million cases a year.

Market analysts refer to natural sodas, flavored sparkling waters, and sparkling fruit juices as New Age drinks. In general, the New Age drinks are less sweet and lighter in both taste and appearance than colas. Much of the popularity of New Age drinks is due to consumer perceptions that they are healthier than traditional soft drinks and to the reluctance of some consumers to drink tap water. Many market analysts believe that the sales of New Age beverages especially affect the consumption of diet beverages. The New Age category was

TABLE 1 MARKET SHARE OF THE 1993 SUPERMARKET SOFT-DRINK MARKET (IN PERCENT)

Beverage Type	Market Share
Cola (caffeinated and caffeine-free)	59.8
Citrus (includes orange and lemon-lime)	20.2
Dr Pepper	7.4
Root beer	2.2
Ginger ale	1.7
Other	8.7
TOTAL	100.0

Source: Author's calculations based on the sales of six companies: Coca-Cola, PepsiCo, Dr Pepper/7-Up, Royal Crown Companies, Cadbury Schweppes, and National Beverage. These firms accounted for 93.3 percent of cases sold in 1993. Data from *Standard & Poor's Industry Surveys: Food, Beverages & Tobacco* (August 18, 1994), p. F25.

estimated to be growing at 25 percent per year in 1993. In comparison, the overall domestic soft-drink market is growing at about 2 to 3 percent per year. More importantly, the market share for colas fell from 63 percent in 1988 to 60 percent in 1993.

Retailers like New Age products because of their relatively high profit margins. For instance, when Kroger Company opened a new supermarket, it devoted one side of a 48-foot aisle to bottled waters and New Age drinks (some 150 different varieties). New Age beverages are also increasingly sold through convenience stores and gas stations.

COCA-COLA'S DOMESTIC DISTRIBUTION STRATEGY

Coca-Cola's sales and market strategy (both domestic and foreign) have often been compared with PepsiCo's. Coca-Cola's domestic market share was 40.9 percent in 1990 versus Pepsi-Cola's 33.2 percent, according to *Beverage Digest*.

Both Coca-Cola and PepsiCo use multiple forms of distribution for their products. One way of distinguishing between types of distribution is to discuss fountain versus can/bottle sales. The fountain and can/bottle distribution differs significantly. In fountain sales, soft drinks are purchased either for on-premises or take-out consumption. Fountain sales are typically through the fast-food and restaurant business. In comparison to the can/bottle business, where a single outlet may sell multiple competing brands, only one brand of soft drink is sold through fountain sales per establishment. Fountain sales generally limit customer selection to not only one brand, but also to four selections of that one brand. Typically, the selection includes a traditional cola, a diet cola, and two other products of the same manufacturer.

COCA-COLA'S FOUNTAIN SALES

The competition for fountain distribution is especially high in the fast-food franchise business. A large franchisor such as McDonald's controls purchasing for thousands of franchisee- and franchisor-owned units. In total, fast-food restaurants accounted for about two-thirds of U.S. restaurant traffic in 1990 (see Table 2). Fast-food franchises are generally slow to switch between Coca-Cola Company and PepsiCo. In 1990, for instance, Burger King shifted from PepsiCo to Coca-Cola.

PepsiCo's ownership of Taco Bell, Pizza Hut, and KFC gives PepsiCo a large captive market in fountain sales. As of the beginning of 1994, there were about 16,500 Taco Bell, Pizza Hut, and KFC units in the United States. Combined, they represent more eating units than McDonald's. Although these units give PepsiCo an advantage in the fountain sales sector over Coca-Cola through captive distribution, many competing fast-food franchise competitors see PepsiCo's ownership of restaurants as a disadvantage. To many fast-food franchisors and franchisees, the purchase of a Pepsi product is seen as providing "support for a major competitor."

To appeal to niche fountain markets (such as small offices, stores, and factories), Coca-Cola developed BreakMate, a vending machine that can dispense

TABLE 2 U.S. RESTAURANT TRAFFIC BY RESTAURANT TYPE, 1990 (IN PERCENT TRAFFIC)

Type of Restaurant	Percent Traffic
Quick service	
Fast-food restaurants such as McDonald's, Wendy's, and Pizza Hut	67
Midscale	
Family restaurants and cafeterias such as Shoney's, Denny's, and Morrison's	25
Casual dining	
Dinner houses such as T.G.I. Friday, Ground Round, and Olive Garden	7
Fine dining	
High-ticket, white-tablecloth restaurants	1
TOTAL	100

Source: NPD Crest, Laurie M. Grossman, "Pizza Hut Cooks Up an Italian Theme," *Wall Street Journal* (August 15, 1991), p. B1.

eight different soft-drink products using one-liter syrup dispensers (which can make between 20 and 30 drinks per liter of syrup). Coca-Cola planned to lease its BreakMate vending machine at little cost to the using company if the company used a minimum of 20 drinks a day. The BreakMate machine is about the size of a countertop microwave unit and is self-contained. The program was designed to replace a traditional vending machine in the roughly 1 million U.S. offices with 45 or fewer employees. Unfortunately, the program did not come close to meeting Coca-Cola's original estimates of sales and profitability. Coca-Cola is now attempting to market BreakMate to hospitals and doctors' offices.

COCA-COLA'S BOTTLE AND CAN SALES

The bottle and can segment is also marked by high competition in all distribution channels. Competition is especially high in supermarkets. Part of Coca-Cola's long-term strategy in the supermarket field is to bring out brand extensions of its popular products in an attempt to dominate supermarket shelf space. Within three years of introducing diet Coke, Coca-Cola brought out caffeine-free Coke, caffeine-free diet Coke, cherry Coke, new Coke, and diet cherry Coke. These brand extensions made it increasingly difficult for smaller brands to get shelf space for their current and new products. To encourage supermarket and other large retailers to stock new products, Coca-Cola typically provides cash fees for functions performed and grants these retailers special promotional discounts.

Both Coca-Cola and PepsiCo are aware of the need to increase domestic distribution as a means of increasing sales. Both have begun to sell their products in such important channels as buying clubs, warehouse stores, mass merchandisers, and convenience stores.

A major segment of the bottle and can market is vending machines. About 15 percent of domestic soft drinks are sold through vending machines. In the

United States, there are 1.9 million vending machines; these machines dispense 570 million cases of soft drinks annually (90 percent in cans). Almost 1 million of these vending machines dispense Coca-Cola's products. Increased outdoor sports and leisure activity as well as new technology has forced both Coca-Cola and PepsiCo to commit major resources to vending machines.

Coca-Cola is studying the use of a vending machine that will ask a consumer if he or she wants another product if his or her first choice is out-of-stock. This type of vending machine will provide data to bottlers on the second, third, and fourth choices of consumers by initial product choice. Coca-Cola has also designed a vending machine that will dispense cold soft drinks as well as magazines and candy in conjunction with Mead Merchandising. This unit is especially designed for placement in the front of supermarkets by the cash registers. Not to be outdone by Coca-Cola, Pepsi is experimenting with the use of debit cards instead of cash in vending machines.

Lastly, a number of niche markets for canned and bottled soda include colleges and universities, hotels, food service operations, airlines, and mobile lunch coaches. In an innovative strategy, PepsiCo received exclusive rights to stock its products in all soda vending machines and to supply all soda fountains at Penn State's 21 campuses by outbidding rival Coca-Cola. It also received the exclusive right to advertise in Penn State University's Beaver Stadium. Through a 10-year contract with the university, Pepsi effectively limited Coca-Cola's presence on its campus. The contract will provide Penn State with an estimated $14 million over its 10-year term. Rutgers signed a similar contract in 1994 with Coca-Cola, giving the firm exclusive rights to sell soft drinks at its three New Jersey campuses.

Coca-Cola states that it is available at 80 percent of the college campuses in the United States and that it outsells Pepsi 2-to-1 among college students. The college market is especially important; some research studies suggest that teenagers drink about 75 gallons of soft drinks a year, versus 48 gallons for the average consumer.

In a similar manner, PepsiCo outbid Coca-Cola as the exclusive soft drink of the Ohio State Fair. PepsiCo's winning bid for a five-year exclusive contract was $2.6 million.

COCA-COLA'S DOMESTIC WHOLESALE DISTRIBUTION SYSTEM

Coca-Cola uses a franchise system of distribution. Local bottlers purchase syrup or concentrate from Coca-Cola, mix the concentrate with sweetener and carbonated water, and fill bottles and cans with the liquid. The bottlers then sell the filled bottles and cans to independent distributors that typically operate on 15-year contracts.

Increasingly, Coca-Cola has begun to consolidate its independently owned bottlers. Consolidation is used as a strategy to replace weaker bottlers with stronger ones. It also gives the larger bottlers economies of scale in manufacturing, marketing, and distribution. At the same time, consolidation gives Coca-Cola more control over marketing. Coca-Cola has purchased many of the family-owned bottlers that were up for sale during the early 1980s. When Coca-Cola resold these firms to larger bottlers, it generally kept at least a 20 percent equity interest in each bottler.

Coca-Cola's largest domestic bottler is Coca-Cola Enterprises (CCE), a publicly owned corporation. CCE is also the nation's largest domestic bottler. In 1986 Coca-Cola consolidated the U.S. bottling operations it owned into Coca-Cola Enterprises (CCE). Fifty-one percent of CCE was sold to the public in a stock offering; the balance is owned by Coca-Cola. CCE closed down several outdated plants and built up its distribution system. By decentralizing its organization structure and increasing the responsibility into its 10 regions, CCE was able to save more than $100 million in manufacturing and raw materials expenses in its first two years of operation. Subsequently, CCE merged with Johnson Coca-Cola Bottling Group of Chattanooga, then the second largest bottler of Coca-Cola. CCE and Johnson Coca-Cola together produce 55 percent of all Coca-Cola sold in the United States.

Coca-Cola Company also owns 30 percent of Coca-Cola Consolidated, which is currently the second largest domestic Coke bottler (after its acquisition of Sunbelt Coke). Coca-Cola now owns a financial interest in bottlers that account for 70 percent of its volume. Although PepsiCo has also purchased several of its large bottlers, it has kept full ownership. PepsiCo owns the bottling and distribution operations for half of its system (up from 21 percent in 1981).

Coca-Cola's relationship with its bottlers can result in conflicts when competition keeps soda prices low. Although low soda prices increase sales and profits to Coca-Cola, its bottlers lose profits because Cola-Cola keeps syrup prices constant.

Bottlers sell the bottles or canned products to independent Coca-Cola distributors that service specific routes in a given territory. These distributors deliver Coca-Cola products directly to the retail outlets under individual contracts with the local bottling company. Many contracts are for 15 years; this gives the distributors ample time to build up their territories. A 15-year contract also enables independent distributors to sell their route. The value of a route is dependent on the time remaining on the lease, the number of cases sold in a territory, the concentration of accounts, the value of the equipment, and profits. In some regions, routes have been sold for $300,000 to $800,000.

The distributors are responsible for delivering, purchasing, or leasing delivery trucks, vending machines, and refrigerators (for retailers such as pizzerias); stocking supermarket shelves; building displays; making credit collections; and picking up empties. Distributors pick up soda directly from the bottlers. Although they are paid on terms from the retailers they sell to, the distributors are responsible for paying the bottler on a daily basis. The independent distributors earn a gross profit of about $1.25 a case.

In some areas, the relationship between Coca-Cola's bottlers and their independent distributors is strained. In the New York metropolitan region, Coca-Cola Bottling Company of New York (which has used independent distributors since 1965) has refused to renew its contract with 340 independent distributors after the contracts expire in 1995. Coca-Cola has argued that it must vertically integrate its distributor system owing to the demand for tractor-trailer deliveries and electronic data interchange by larger retailers. Coca-Cola feels that smaller independent distributors could not offer these services. In March 1995 the Coca-Cola Bottling Company of New York reached a settlement with the distributors by which the distributors will be replaced by Coca-Cola employees, and Coca-

Cola will offer the distributors $140 million, purchase their trucks and equipment for an additional $10 million to $15 million, and give each distributor a job.

COCA-COLA'S DOMESTIC PHYSICAL DISTRIBUTION SYSTEM

Transportation costs (depreciation of equipment, drivers' salaries, fuel, insurance, and maintenance) represent a large cost to Coca-Cola's bottlers and to its independent distributors. These wholesalers are constantly reevaluating any means to lower costs while keeping customer service at high levels.

At CCE, the routing problem is a very complicated one. Through 200 different distribution centers, CCE sells over 2 million cases a day of up to 150 different products to 560,000 outlets, along 6500 routes. CCE has planned a $50 million investment (over a three-year period) to develop a state-of-the-art computer-based routing management system. As part of this system, each of CCE's 1800 salespeople will be equipped with a hand-held computer terminal. At the end of the day, each salesperson will transmit all orders to the bottler. The next day's routing is planned on the basis of the previous day's orders. CCE tested a prototype of the new routing system in Los Angeles; this region has been acknowledged to be one of the best run of Coca-Cola's 200 distribution centers. After the prototype system was implemented, the total distance traveled by route trucks declined by 8 percent, total hours spent on deliveries dropped by 13 percent, and the number of required vehicles and delivery employees was reduced by 14 percent.

Coca-Cola/Dr Pepper of Albuquerque, an independent distributor, began leasing trailers from Ryder to handle its peak loads (owing to seasonality and special promotions). Later on, the distributor contracted with Ryder to supply it with replacement trucks on an as-needed basis (to replace trucks that were being repaired). More recently, Coca-Cola/Dr Pepper of Albuquerque has begun to use Ryder's full-service leasing arrangements. In a full-service lease, Ryder provides the distributor with specially designed trucks with the distributor's signage, periodically washes and paints the vehicles, performs preventative maintenance and repairs, and provides replacement vehicles when needed.

Other Coca-Cola distributors have contracted with Ryder and other leasing firms for either contract maintenance (wherein the firm provides preventative maintenance, road service, tires, and mechanics), full-service leasing (as described with Coca-Cola of Albuquerque), or dedicated contract carriage (wherein the leasor provides all physical distribution functions from the shipping dock to in-store delivery, including providing truck drivers and all equipment).

Sunbelt Coca-Cola Bottling Company of Charleston, South Carolina, uses nighttime and daytime operations to eliminate warehouses and to maximize vehicle utilization. Beverage containers are loaded in the evening at its main production facility in Morgantown, West Virginia. During the night, 21 dedicated contract carriers take loaded double trailers to six distribution points. These double trailers return with empty double trailers from the previous day's deliveries. This backhauling operation makes the equipment productive on the transportation run from the distribution point to the main production facility. The next morning, Coca-Cola route drivers operating Ryder full-service leased tractors leave their empty trailers at their distribution point and pick up full single trailers to run that day's delivery route. According to Ryder's national account manager, "the product is only handled when it is loaded at the bottling plant, and when it reaches the consumer. In addition to eliminating at least six satellite warehouses and their attendant costs, reduced handling means reduced breakage." Coca-Cola's products are delivered to grocery stores on pallets. This reduces handling costs for the retailer.

Johnston Coca-Cola Bottling Company's Eagan, Minnesota, facility is state-of-the-art. The plant runs two 10-hour shifts a day and has an annual capacity of 45 million cases. The bottling facility is fully automated and is designed to load 300 route and bulk trucks every 10 hours. This equals 30 trucks per hour or a truck every two minutes. Trailers are loaded using a "double-bottoming" philosophy. The tractor pulls two fully loaded trailers to remote sales centers. These satellite locations are actually no more than parking lots where the tandems are split into single trailers for preassigned routes by the local drivers. In line with its automated production facility, its Eagan warehouse facility is fully automated. Aisles are 300 feet deep; pallets are stored 13 units high. All product handling is also fully automated.

COCA-COLA'S FOREIGN DISTRIBUTION STRATEGY

Foreign operations have very high growth potential. Although the U.S. market consumes on average 303 8-ounce servings of company soft drinks per person per year, the average per-capita non-U.S. yearly consumption of company soft drinks is only 40 servings. Many market analysts believe that foreign market consumption will quickly rise as a result of such factors as the rising standard of living in foreign markets, the opening of foreign trade, and the ability of mass communications to reach more consumers. During 1988–1991, the international soft-drink industry grew at more than twice the U.S. volume. Coca-Cola is forecasting 8 to 10 percent growth rates for international sales. In contrast, the annual growth in domestic sales is forecast in the 1 to 2 percent range.

In 1993 foreign operations generated 67 percent of Coca-Cola's sales and 71 percent of its profits. Japan alone accounted for about one-fifth of Coca-Cola's profits. In comparison to PepsiCo, Coca-Cola's market share in foreign markets is high. Although Pepsi Cola is available in at least 150 countries, its foreign beverage sales are only one-quarter those of Coca-Cola. In Western Europe, Coca-Cola outsells Pepsi 6-to-1. Coca-Cola also has the leading market share in Japan.

Part of the reason for Coca-Cola's success in foreign markets (relative to PepsiCo) is its early entry into foreign markets. Coca-Cola entered many foreign markets in the 1940s seeking distribution to markets with large concentrations of American soldiers. In comparison, Pepsi Cola entered many foreign markets in the 1950s. Coca-Cola was also the first soft-drink manufacturer to enter China.

Coca-Cola has also been quick to adapt its distribution strategy to foreign opportunities. Its western German bottlers handed out samples to eastern Germans when the Berlin Wall fell in November 1989. Since 1989, Coca-Cola has invested $450 million in the eastern part of Germany, including starting a sales and distribution system from ground zero. In little time, even the giant Sports Hall in eastern Berlin had a giant Coke sign near its skating rink, a dozen Coca-Cola vending machines, and three cafeterias that serve Coca-Cola beverages. Coca-Cola also quickly set up 8000 vending machines in prime eastern German locations. Excluding west Berlin, it is estimated that Coca-Cola sold over 100 million cases of its soda in 1994, up from zero in 1990.

Coca-Cola's leading market share in Japan is largely due to its 750,000 vending machines. (There are approximately 2 million total vending machines in Japan.) Whereas vending machines can be routinely vandalized in the United States, vandalism is unheard of in Japan. Vending machine channels are so important in Japan that a well-placed vending machine can sell as many as 10,000 cans of soft drink per year, as much as a medium-size convenience store. As a consequence, the demand for excellent vending machine locations is very high. Coca-Cola's bottlers have even begun to develop contracts with office building developers to build vending machines into office walls, in a manner similar to built-in furniture.

Initially, Coca-Cola's Japanese bottlers would sell or lease the vending machines to store owners. Now, the vending machines are provided by the bottlers, and retailers receive as much as $8000 per machine as "key money." The ownership of vending machines by Coca-Cola's Japanese bottlers allows Coca-Cola to control the mix of products sold, keep out competitive products, and control the level of customer services. To retain its market share, Coca-Cola's Japanese bottlers have invested in 120,000 to 130,000 new vending machines per year at a cost of about $4000 per machine.

In the past, Pepsi held the greatest advantage in Eastern Europe and the old Soviet Union. In the former Soviet Union in 1991, Pepsi sold about 45 million cases, about double Coke's output, according to *Beverage Digest*. Future prospects in these markets are uncertain. As with domestic markets, PepsiCo's ownership of Taco Bell, Pizza Hut, and KFC gives it an advantage in fountain sales owing to the captive market for its products. As of the beginning of 1992, there were 5051 Taco Bell, Pizza Hut, and KFC units in foreign markets. PepsiCo is also seeking to strengthen foreign distribution through the purchase of Britain's leading snack companies: Smiths Crisps and Walker Crisps. These help provide distribution strength on the Continent. According to Pepsi-Cola's head of international operations, "We'll do joint purchasing and marketing programs for snacks and soft drinks in European hypermarkets. Eventually we're looking for ways to put them together in the same vending machine."

COCA-COLA'S FOREIGN WHOLESALE DISTRIBUTION SYSTEM

Coca-Cola's foreign wholesale distribution in several ways mirrors its domestic strategy. First, the main source of earnings for Coca-Cola overseas is the shipment of concentrates. Second, Coca-Cola has many joint ventures overseas with its bottlers. As in domestic markets, Coca-Cola typically has a minority ownership in these bottlers to provide them with additional financial and managerial strength. Third, Coca-Cola has promoted the international expansion of anchor bottlers. These are especially strong bottlers who operate outside their home territories.

An example of its aggressiveness internationally has been Coca-Cola's return to India after a 16-year absence. Coca-Cola formed a strategic alliance with Parle Exports, an Indian bottler, which provided Coca-Cola with immediate access to Parle's distribution facilities and its 60-plant bottling network. Coca-Cola invested over $60 million in India, renovating two bottling plants and purchasing a new fleet of six-ton delivery trucks. The new trucks provide direct-to-store delivery for larger stores. Traditional tricycle carts, fitted for pallet loading, are used to service smaller stores in less accessible areas.

KEY DIFFERENCES BETWEEN DOMESTIC AND FOREIGN MARKETS FOR SOFT DRINKS

There are some important differences between the domestic and international market for soft drinks that affect Coca-Cola's distribution strategy:

- In international markets, most soft drinks are sold in single-serving bottles. Market analysts forecast that the growth of supermarkets in foreign markets will increase the demand for larger size bottles.
- Coca-Cola has only three products that are sold around the world: Coca-Cola, Sprite, and Fanta. Coca-Cola adapts other products to customer tastes. For example, the firm bottles a cream-type soda in the Latin American market.
- Coca-Cola changes package designs on a country or regional basis. There are also major differences in Coca-Cola's promotional strategy on a country or regional basis. Some countries do not allow any advertising.
- The United States is generally more diet conscious than the average foreign market.
- In the United States, vending machines account for about 12 to 15 percent of soft-drink sales. While vending machines are still rare in many foreign countries, a major exception is Japan. In Japan, an estimated 50 percent of soft drink retail sales are made through vending machines.

QUESTIONS

1. Describe the relationship between retailing, wholesaling, physical distribution, and marketing channels for Coca-Cola. Refer to the firm's domestic strategy.
2. Outline the channel functions of the Coca-Cola Company, its bottlers, and its independent distributors.
3. Describe the concept that "channel functions can be shifted, but not eliminated." Refer to examples pertinent to the soft-drink market.
4. Contrast the environment facing Coca-Cola in domestic versus foreign markets.
5. Explain the concept of forward vertical competition as it pertains to Coca-Cola's independent New York metropolitan area distributors.

6. Evaluate Coca-Cola's overall domestic channel strategy.
7. Evaluate Coca-Cola's overall foreign channel strategy.

Sources: The Coca-Cola Company 1993 Annual Report; "Efficient Transportation Is a 24-Hour Operation," *The Ryder Resource* (Spring 1991), p. 5; John R. Emshwiller and Michael J. McCarthy, "Coke's Soda Fountain for Offices Fizzles, Dashing High Hopes," *Wall Street Journal* (June 14, 1993), pp. A1, A8; Carl Hoover, Alta Campbell, and Patrick J. Spain, eds., *Hoover's Handbook of American Business 1994* (Austin: Reference Press: 1994), pp. 360–361; "Distributors Sue Coca-Cola over Routes," *Newsday* (February 7, 1995), p. A42; Stuart Elliott, "Coca-Cola's 'Alternative' Beverages," *New York Times* (March 2, 1994), pp. D1, D18; Scott Hume, "Fast-Food Giants Fume as State Fair Gets Pepsi Backing," *Advertising Age* (July 13, 1992), pp. 3 ff.; Sharen Kindel, "The Route Case," *Financial World* (August 20, 1991), p. 70; Walecia Konrad and Igor Reichlin, "The Real Thing Is Thundering Eastward," *Business Week* (April 13, 1992), pp. 96–97; Michael J. McCarthy, "Soft-Drink Firms Search for Answers as Volumes Drop," *Wall Street Journal* (July 27, 1992), p. B3; "Right Here, Right Now," *Beverage World* (February 1992), pp. 54–56, 58; Maria Mallory, "The Cola Wars Go to College," *Business Week* (September 19, 1994), p. 42; *PepsiCo, Inc. 1991 Annual Report*, pp. 9–11; Paul Schreiber, "A Forced Departure and a Fresh Start," *Newsday* (March 6, 1995), p. C3; Paul Schreiber, "Dealers Fear Coke Deals Them Out" *Newsday* (June 29, 1992), pp. 21, 29; Eben Shapiro, "A Dowdy Soft Drink in Search of a New Age Remake," *New York Times* (May 3, 1992), p. F10; Eric Sfilogoj, "Super Convenience," *Beverage World* (March 1992), pp. 58 ff.; and Jeffrey A. Tannenbaum, "FTC Assures Lawmakers It's Enforcing Franchise Rules," *Wall Street Journal* (January 5, 1993), p. B2.

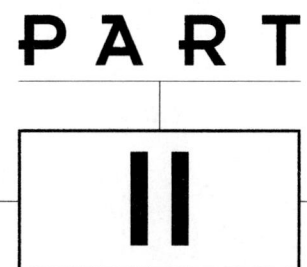

MAJOR CHANNEL MEMBERS

In Part Two, we study the characteristics of two important channel members: retailers and wholesalers. Important concepts in retailing and wholesaling are defined and explained from a strategic perspective.

CHAPTER 3
Retail Channel Members In this chapter, we examine the economic structure of retailing, explore the special characteristics of retailing, and study a typology of retail institutions.

CHAPTER 4
Wholesale Channel Members Here, we study the economic structure of wholesaling, describe the special characteristics of wholesalers, and examine a typology of wholesale institutions. The key provisions of supplier-wholesaler contracts are studied.

CHAPTER 3

RETAIL CHANNEL MEMBERS

CHAPTER OBJECTIVES

1. To examine the structure of retailing, including total retail sales and retail sales growth.

2. To describe the special characteristics of retailing: immediacy, the importance of location, low average sale, high proportion of impulse purchases, and high seasonality.

3. To determine important trends affecting retailing: the growth of conglomerate merchants, increased market saturation, leveraged buyouts, and performance differences among discounters.

4. To study a classification system of retailers according to ownership, retail strategy, and nonstore retailing.

5. To analyze alternative buying organizations.

According to some analysts, the department store is as extinct as the dinosaur. These analysts cite the large number of bankruptcies in the industry and the increased competition from specialty stores (on service and selection) and from off-price chains and warehouse stores (on price). Major bankruptcies of department stores include: B. Altman, Macy's, Carter Hawley Hale, Garfinckel's and Federated/Allied (this chain emerged from bankruptcy as of February 1992). According to a marketing professor, "Department stores are islands surrounded by vicious competitors. On the right, the attackers are specialty retailers like The Gap and J. Crew. On the left are the so-called category killers such as Toys "R" Us and Circuit City. At the bottom are discounters like Wal-Mart. Everybody's taking a piece." Another skeptical view on the future of department stores argues that "They're the beached whales of the retail industry. Too sick to live and too big to die."

A more balanced view suggests that many of the current problems of department stores are due to high debt incurred as a result of leveraged buyouts (the taking on of debt to finance the purchase of stock in a buyout plan). These leveraged buyouts were conducted by the outside firm's or the store's existing management to finance the purchase of the department store. For example, Macy's bankruptcy can be largely attributed to the high debt generated as a consequence of Macy's going private and then acquiring Bullock's and I. Magnin.

Three particularly successful department stores are Bloomingdale's, Burdine's, and Parisian. Bloomingdale's is increasingly using a store-within-a-store program, which resembles high-fashion boutiques within the department store. Bloomingdale's and Giorgio Armani have opened A/X: Armani Exchange within Bloomingdale's stores. The boutique will feature moderately priced Armani apparel (generally priced below $100) such as jeans, skirts, sweaters, and jackets. To make the boutique even more distinctive, each A/X: Armani Exchange will feature a separate street entrance. Burdine's, a Florida-based department store chain, now houses its furniture department in a separate store facility, and uses the freed space to increase the size of profitable and high-turnover merchandise such as women's shoes. Parisian, an Alabama-based chain, marks down merchandise only once during the selling season, guarantees that the price will not be further reduced, and has few cumbersome anti-shoplifting devices. This strategy attempts to assure shoppers that it does not pay to wait for a sale and makes it easier for shoppers to try on garments. According to the firm's chief executive officer, "You won't see anything chained down. We feel that makes it awful hard to try on."

Analysts who argue that the department store is a viable retail institution state that major department stores have a valuable consumer franchise. This franchise consists of access to designer goods (such as fragrances and cosmetics), a credit system with a large customer base, and the convenience of a one-stop shopping environment for an entire family's needs.[1]

In this chapter, we study the economic environment of retailing and the special characteristics of retailing, and analyze the retail strategies of a large number of different retail institutions, including department stores. The impact of leveraged buyouts on retailers and other channel members is also described.

RETAIL STRUCTURE

As noted in Chapter 1, **retailing** consists of those business activities involved in the sale of goods and services to consumers for personal, family, or household use.[2] Several key elements in this definition need to be explained further. These relate to the types of institutions that can be considered as retailers and nonstore sales.

Retail activities can be performed by a variety of marketing channel members other than retailers. For example, a manufacturer or wholesaler selling goods directly to final consumers would be considered to be performing retail functions. On the other hand, the sale of goods and services by one retailer to another would be considered a wholesaling activity. Some institutions such as buying clubs can be classified as both a wholesale and a retail operation based on their sales to both final customers and retail establishments.

Although many people associate retailing with store locations, retailing can involve such nonstore retailers as vending machines, direct selling, and direct marketing. These are further described in the classification of retail institutions portion of this chapter.

TOTAL RETAIL SALES

Total retail store sales were $2.2 trillion in 1994, up from $1.4 trillion in 1985; retail sales grew at a compound yearly rate of 5.7 percent from 1985 to 1994 (see Table 3-1). The highest annual sales growth rate by retail category was 8.5 percent for family and other apparel stores; the lowest growth rate was for variety stores (with an average rate of decline of 1.0 percent over this time period). Note that growth rates in this table reflect a given merchandise category, not for retail institutional type (except variety and department stores).

The numbers in Table 3-1 include the effects of inflation. **Real sales growth** equals dollar sales growth in percent minus the inflation rate for the corresponding period. Although annual total retail store sales grew at an annual compound rate of 5.7 percent from 1985 to 1994, the annual average compound rate of inflation during this period was 3.7 percent. Thus, real compound annual sales growth was only 2.0 percent during the 1985–1994 time period.

We can also gain some perspective into retailing by examining the characteristics of leading retailers. In the past, *Fortune* listed data on the 50 largest retailers in the United States separately. As of its May 1995 issue, *Fortune* began to combine data on industrial and service companies in one report. Along with information on retail sales, *Fortune* lists data on number of employees, assets, and stockholders' equity. Table 3-2 lists information on the 25 largest retailers in the United States for 1994; these data are derived from the *Fortune 500* listing. Although Wal-Mart overtook Sears' position as the largest retailer in the United States as of the 1995 *Fortune* listing, in actuality, Wal-Mart has had larger retail sales than Sears since 1990. The *Fortune* data include Sears' sales from its financial divisions.

TABLE 3-1 RETAIL STORE SALES BY KIND OF BUSINESS, 1985-1994 (MILLIONS OF DOLLARS)[a]

Type of Retailing	1985	1986	1987	1988	1989	1990	1991	1992	1993	1994	Average Yearly Percentage Increase
All retail stores	1,375,027	1,449,636	1,541,229	1,656,202	1,758,971	1,844,611	1,855,937	1,951,589	2,074,499	2,236,966	5.7
Durable goods stores, total	498,125	540,688	575,863	629,154	657,154	668,835	649,974	703,604	777,539	880,426	6.8
Automotive group	303,199	326,138	342,896	372,570	386,011	387,605	372,647	406,935	456,890	526,319	6.8
Furniture and appliance group	68,287	75,714	78,072	85,390	91,301	91,545	91,676	96,947	105,728	119,626	6.9
Lumber, building materials, and hardware group	61,237	67,244	72,338	78,690	80,094	82,865	80,344	88,087	95,657	106,950	6.4
Nondurable goods stores, total	876,902	911,948	965,436	1,027,048	1,101,817	1,175,776	1,205,963	1,247,985	1,296,690	1,356,540	5.0
General merchandise group	158,636	169,397	181,970	192,521	206,306	215,514	226,730	246,420	264,617	282,541	6.5
Department stores	126,412	134,486	144,017	151,523	160,524	165,808	172,922	186,423	200,494	218,069	6.1
Variety stores	8,459	7,447	7,134	7,458	7,936	8,306	8,341	9,516	9,044	7,891	−1.0
Apparel group	70,195	75,626	79,322	85,307	92,341	95,819	97,441	104,212	107,184	109,603	5.5
Men's and boys' wear group	8,458	8,646	9,017	9,826	10,507	10,450	10,435	10,196	10,291	12,157	4.0
Women's apparel, accessory stores	26,149	28,600	29,208	30,567	32,231	32,812	32,865	35,750	36,820	34,867	3.9
Family and other apparel stores	17,827	19,336	21,472	23,902	26,375	28,398	30,521	33,222	34,892	37,054	8.5
Shoe stores	13,054	13,947	14,594	15,444	17,290	18,043	17,504	18,122	18,206	18,345	4.1
Gasoline service stations	113,341	102,093	104,769	110,341	122,882	138,504	137,295	136,950	138,299	142,193	2.8
Eating and drinking places	127,949	139,415	153,461	167,993	177,829	190,149	194,424	200,164	213,663	228,351	6.5
Food group	285,062	297,019	309,461	325,493	347,045	368,333	374,523	377,099	385,386	397,800	3.9
Drug and proprietary stores	46,994	50,546	54,142	57,842	63,343	70,558	75,540	77,788	79,645	81,536	6.4
Liquor stores	19,532	19,929	19,826	19,638	20,099	21,722	22,454	21,698	21,567	21,823	1.8

[a]Includes some mail-order sales for the retail categories shown in the table.
Sources: Bureau of the Census, U.S. Department of Commerce; and Standard & Poor's Industry Surveys: Retailing (June 15, 1995), p. R76.

TABLE 3-2 THE 25 LARGEST RETAILING COMPANIES, 1994

1994 Rank	Company	Sales (thousands)	Net Income (thousands)	Employees
1	Wal-Mart	$ 83,412,400	$ 2,681,000	600,000
2	Sears, Roebuck[a,b]	54,559,000	1,454,000	360,000
3	Kmart	34,313,000	296,000	335,000
4	Kroger[c]	22,959,100	242,200	200,000
5	Dayton Hudson	21,311,000	434,000	194,000
6	JC Penney	21,082,000	1,057,000	202,000
7	American Stores	18,355,100	345,200	118,000
8	Price/Costco	16,480,600	−112,400	47,000
9	Safeway Stores	15,626,600	239,700	109,969
10	Home Depot	12,476,700	604,500	70,000
11	May Department Stores	12,223,000	782,000	119,000
12	Albertson's	11,894,600	400,400	76,000
13	Melville	11,285,600	307,500	117,414
14	Winn-Dixie Stores	11,082,200	216,100	112,000
15	Great Atlantic & Pacific Tea (A&P)	10,384,100	4,000	94,000
16	Walgreen	9,235,000	281,900	61,900
17	Toys "R" Us	8,745,600	531,800	58,000
18	Publix Super Markets	8,742,500	238,600	90,000
19	McDonald's	8,320,800	1,224,400	183,000
20	Federated Dept. Stores	8,315,900	187,600	111,700
21	Woolworth	8,293,000	47,000	119,000
22	The Limited	7,320,800	448,300	105,600
23	Supermarkets General	7,226,500	−41,800	30,000
24	Lowe's	6,110,500	223,600	37,555
25	Dillard Department Stores	5,728,600	251,800	37,832
	TOTAL 25 LARGEST RETAILERS	$435,494,200	$12,344,400	3,588,970

[a]Includes merchandising, insurance, and banking income.
[b]Reflects extraordinary gain of greater than 10 percent.
[c]Reflects extraordinary loss of greater than 10 percent.
Source: "The Fortune 500 Largest U.S. Corporations," *Fortune* (May 15, 1995), pp. F1–F9, F51–F53, F61. Reprinted from the FORTUNE Directory by permission; © 1995 Time Inc. All rights reserved.

GROWTH OF RETAIL SALES

Growth of retail sales can be measured in several ways. We previously looked at sales growth as measured by real growth (after taking inflation into account) versus dollar sales growth.

Many analysts evaluate the maturity of retail institutions (such as variety stores, department stores, and supermarkets) and firms by looking at growth in terms of same-store sales. **Same-store sales** examines sales in stores open at least one year. Same-store sales growth removes the effect of increases in sales due to new locations; it is an especially important measure to use for retailers with large expansion programs. For example, whereas Kmart's sales increased 10.0 percent to $34.16 billion from 1992 to 1993, same-store sales increased only 3.6 percent. Included within the same-store sales figure were newly renovated Kmart stores (which experienced a 7 percent increase) and expanded Kmart stores (which had a 14 percent increase in sales) over this time period.[3] A retailer or retail institutional format with low same-store sales growth can be viewed as mature.

THE SPECIAL CHARACTERISTICS OF RETAILING

In addition to the special characteristics of all channel members that were noted in Chapter 1, retailing is characterized by immediacy, the importance of location, a low average sale, a high proportion of impulse purchases, and high seasonality. Each of these characteristics imposes special requirements on a retailer's strategy. These are examined next.

IMMEDIACY

Immediacy relates to the short-run focus of most retail advertising and retail promotions. Generally, there is a lag of no more than several days between a retailer's seeing a customer response to an advertisement, a special price offer, or a special promotion. In many cases, consumers limit their shopping trip to one or a limited number of retailers. Thus, a retailer being out-of-stock or a poor sales presentation may reduce sales drastically.

Unlike much of advertising by manufacturers that may be informational or image oriented, most of retail advertising is sales oriented. Retail advertising seeks to generate immediate sales or store traffic. It is relatively easy to determine the effectiveness of retail advertising. Advertising for specific goods and services can be correlated with sales of the advertised product, with coupon redemptions, or with total store traffic.

Because many goods have short selling seasons, sales and inventory levels of important goods need to be monitored on a daily basis. Monitoring of sales and inventory status is particularly important for high-fashion goods and for imported goods that require several weeks for receipt after they are ordered. An important criterion in vendor appraisal for retailers with this type of goods is both order lead time (the time difference between when an order is originated with a vendor and the time the good is received by the retailer) and the reliability of lead time.

IMPORTANCE OF LOCATION

Location is a very important part of a retailer's strategy. In comparison to wholesaling, in retailing, shoppers customarily visit the retailer at its store location. Location is not equally important for all retailers. Notable exceptions are direct marketing (where shoppers respond to mail order, telemarketing, or television-based advertisements) and direct selling (where the salesperson visits the prospect at his or her home, office, or factory location). Although vending machines are another form of nonstore retailing, location is of prime consideration for vending machine operators. Off-price chains and warehouse clubs are also often able to attract shoppers to otherwise poor locations because of their low-price strategy.

For the most part, however, location is a critical aspect of a retailer's strategy. Unlike other strategic elements, it is a long-term strategy component. Many leases are long term (10 years and longer); in addition, many leases have renewal options. In other cases, retailers seek to own their store facilities to achieve tax advantages through depreciation allowances, capital appreciation possibilities, and the freedom from concern over a property owner not renewing a lease.

Retail locations are evaluated by such criteria as trading area characteristics, affinities, pedestrian traffic counts, vehicular traffic counts, visibility, and lease terms.

Trading area characteristics refer to the demographic and life-style characteristics of the geographic area from which a retailer draws its shoppers. A retailer's strategy needs to reflect the trading area's characteristics. Since retail leases are typically long term, a retailer needs to monitor the trading characteristics and to reassess its strategy as the characteristics of consumers change.

The term **affinities** refers to the composition of neighboring stores. Stores have affinities for one another to the extent that shoppers visit neighboring retail stores. Affinities are particularly important with shopping goods where consumers seek to compare price levels and offerings among competing retailers. An example of affinities is a shopping center location where a high degree of store interchange exists among selected retailers in the center and the center's anchor tenants (supermarket, variety store, or department store). In contrast, an isolated location offers no affinities for a retailer. An isolated location can be effectively used when the retailer is able to attract and retain its own customer traffic and when low rent is an important part of a retailer's overall strategy.

Pedestrian traffic counts are the number of people passing by a given location. Some retailers only include in their pedestrian traffic counts people who are likely shoppers, such as those carrying shopping bags. This type of traffic count discounts people who are going to and from work. Other retailers only include those people who match their target market, such as a career-oriented men's clothing store counting only males over 25. Pedestrian traffic counts vary by time of day, day of week, and even by side of street. Therefore, when conducting a pedestrian traffic count, a retailer needs to study the variation in traffic by these parameters. For example, a downtown central business district may have high pedestrian traffic counts during weekdays, but very poor pedestrian traffic on weekends when offices are generally closed.

Vehicular traffic counts measure the number of vehicles passing by a given location. A vehicular traffic count should reflect the number of vehicles on the right side of a highway relative to the retail location. The count should discount cars going in the opposite direction, especially when a divided highway must be crossed. The vehicular traffic count also should discount traffic going above a given speed.

Transportation refers to public transportation facilities that serve the retail location. Factors such as the nearness to location, transportation cost, relative safety, and frequency need to be evaluated.

Visibility refers to the ability of a retail location to be seen from the road. Visibility is especially important for locations that are recessed from major highways; these locations can be seen only as the site is being passed. Visibility is also an important consideration for retailers based in shopping centers that are open at early or late hours.

Lease terms refer to the duration of a lease, renewal options, and rental amounts. Lease terms for retail locations are especially complex owing to the long-term duration of most leases. A retailer wants a long-term lease to protect his or her investment and to facilitate the sale of his or her business. In contrast, the property owner is concerned about inflation limiting the value rental receipts as well as cost increases (for costs such as insurance, utilities, and property taxes). To enable retailers to have long-term leases, property owners often insist that rents be based on a percentage of sales, that rental amounts be graduated, and that retail tenants pay increases in such expenses as insurance, utilities, and property taxes.

LOW AVERAGE SALE

Although the average sale varies depending on the type of retailer, and there is variation within a retail type, in general, the average sale in retailing is low. For example, the average sale for an independent supermarket was $14.81 in 1994 and $19.19 for chains.[4] The average sale for department stores in 1993 was $36.80 and in specialty stores, $53.50.[5] Even with the low average sales for both department and specialty stores, 49.3 percent of department store sales and 44.6 percent of specialty store sales were made on credit (through both in-house and outside cards).[6]

Low average sales mean that retailers must work hard at processing transactions efficiently. For example, the average independent supermarket had 8583 transactions per week, and the average chain supermarket had 13,865 transactions per week.[7] To process transactions effectively, 70 percent of independent supermarkets and 95 percent of supermarket chains used scanning.[8]

The low average sale makes impulse sales very important for all retailers. This area is covered next.

HIGH PROPORTION OF IMPULSE SALES

Impulse sales are generally defined as nonplanned purchases. A major study by the Point-of-Purchase Advertising Institute (POPAI) found that 53 percent of supermarket purchases were unplanned. POPAI research also found that 66 percent of all supermarket purchases were due to in-store marketing efforts. POPAI studied three categories of planned purchases: specifically planned, generally planned, and substitute purchases. **Specifically planned purchases** are identified by the shopper at the preshopping phase; specific items that are listed are actually purchased; 34 percent of total purchases are specifically planned. **Generally planned purchases** are identified by the product category, but not by brand, prior to the shopping experience; 10 percent of total purchases are generally planned. **Substitute purchases** are brands or products that are switched from the ones that were originally planned; 4 percent of purchases are substitute.

Based on these data, the **in-store decision rate** (generally planned purchases + substitute purchases + unplanned purchases) equals 66 percent. The in-store decision rate relates to the percentage of purchase decisions that are made owing to the store environment. The study also found that displays increase the level of impulse shopping. For all product categories, the percentage of impulse purchases increases to 64 percent versus 53 percent (when a display may or may not be present). With a display, specifically planned purchases decrease from 34 percent to 24 percent for the items displayed. The in-store decision rate increases to 76 percent for displayed items from 66 percent for all items.[9]

Figure 3-1 represents Management Horizons' Impact Model. According to the model, store traffic is a function of three factors: market coverage (the size of the markets served), penetration level (market share within markets served), and average shopping frequency (how often the average shopper shops at a particular retail store). Market coverage times penetration level times average shopper frequency equals store traffic. Closure rate is the number of shoppers that actually buy merchandise. Store traffic times closure rate equals the number of transactions. And the number of transactions times the average transaction equals total gross sales.[10]

According to this model, retailers have an opportunity to generate impulse sales within their existing stores by increasing store traffic, the closure rate, and the average transaction size. A retailer can increase store traffic through special sales and promotions, demonstrations, and longer hours. Closure rate depends on salespeople, whether a store had the desired goods in stock, merchandise presentation, merchandise quality, the number and quality of point-of-purchase displays, and whether consumers view pricing as fair.

FIGURE 3-1 Management Horizons' Impact Model.

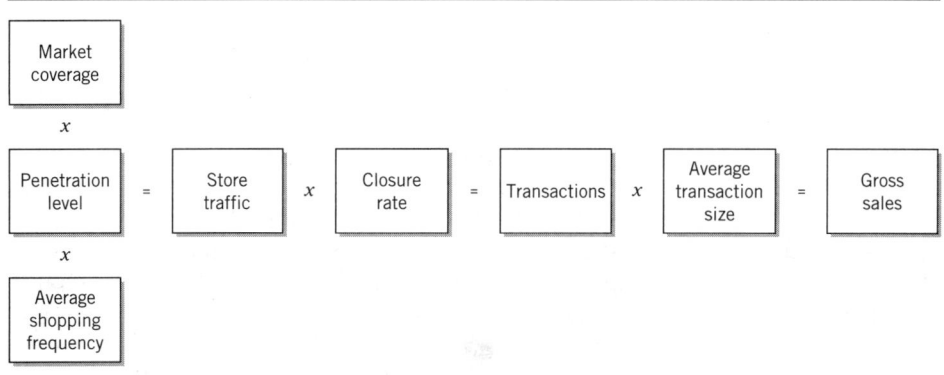

Source: Management Horizons Retailing 2000 Report.

According to the Point-of-Purchase Advertising Institute, the use of in-store promotions and advertising has been increasing by 10 to 15 percent annually between 1985 and 1990 versus an increase of 4 to 6 percent for traditional advertising.[11]

HIGH SEASONALITY

Overall retail sales are highly seasonal. For example, the fourth quarter of the year accounted for 32.7 percent of conventional department store sales (including leased departments) in 1993.[12] The fourth quarter includes November, December, and January sales. Most department stores end their fiscal year as of January 31. The height of the season for most department stores and fashion-based specialty stores is from Thanksgiving to Christmas. In contrast, the other quarters have relatively low sales: first quarter (20.7 percent), second quarter (22.2 percent), and third quarter (24.4 percent).[13]

High seasonality makes planning especially difficult. It makes overall performance for the year difficult to predict until late in the year. Furthermore, fourth-quarter sales are highly susceptible to weather as well as to economic conditions. High seasonality also makes employee utilization difficult to plan and may pose a strain on a retailer's facilities. Many retailers need to hire and train part-time employees for short time periods. Although a retailer's parking area may be perfectly adequate nine months out of the year, it could easily be strained during key weekends between Thanksgiving and Christmas.

RETAIL TRENDS

This section examines several important trends in retailing: the growth of conglomerate merchants, increased market saturation, leveraged buyouts, and performance differences among retailers.

CONGLOMERATE MERCHANTS

Although many retailers are part of chain units, retailers are increasingly part of conglomerate merchant organizations. A **conglomerate merchant (conglomerchant)** operates disparate retailers. Examples of conglomerchants include Dayton Hudson, Woolworth, and Melville. Dayton Hudson now has three divisions: department stores (Dayton's, Hudson's, and Marshall Field's), discount department stores (Mervyn's), and discount stores (Target).[14] Woolworth operates such disparate retail operations as Woolworth variety stores, Kinney shoe stores, Afterthoughts Accessories, and Champs Sports. Melville operates more than 7200 stores including Thom McAn shoes, CVS (a drug store chain), Marshalls (an off-price chain), Kay-Bee (a hobby and toy chain), and This End Up (a furniture chain) as well as other retail units.[15]

The advantages of the conglomerate merchant form of organization are less reliance on one type of retail operation (diversification), ability to better control growth through the mix of retail formats, operation of economies through the operation of different retail formats in the same shopping center, better bargaining power with major shopping center owners and managers, ability to shift retail operations in a leased location as an area's demographics and life-styles change, ability to shift resources among divisions based on opportunities and risks, and the appeal to multiple target markets. And while Melville started as a shoe retailer with Thom McAn, CVS and Marshalls accounted for 63 percent of Melville's net sales in 1994.[16]

The disadvantages of a conglomerate merchant form of organization are difficulty in centralizing buying, selling, and store operations functions, as well as in managing disparate units; an unclear image for the firm; the need for a complex retail organization; and the lack of quantity discounts in buying. Recently two conglomerate merchants changed their organizational format. The Limited, which had multiple store groupings in a conglomerate merchant format, split into two broad units: women's apparel (made up of Limited Stores, Express, Lerner's, and Lane Bryant) and lingerie/personal care (made up of Victoria's Secret, Cacique, Bath & Body Works, and Penhaligon's).[17] Kmart began to sell off its specialty stores (Border Books & Music, Waldenbooks, OfficeMax, and the Sports Authority) in 1993.[18] In 1995 its specialty stores accounted for less than 10 percent of its total sales.[19]

INCREASED MARKET SATURATION

Many retail markets are now overstored. In evaluating retail growth opportunities, retail analysts need to consider the population size, disposable income within the area, and the number of retail facilities located within the area.

An **understored trading area** has too few retail facilities selling a specific good or service to satisfy the needs of the area's population. In contrast, an **overstored trading area** has too many retailers selling a specific good or service to satisfy the needs of its population. A **saturated trading area** has the proper amount of retail facilities to satisfy the needs of its population.[20]

A retailer can determine the degree of market saturation by calculating saturation ratios. These **saturation ratios** include the number of persons per establishment, average sales per retail store, sales per capita or household, and sales per square foot of selling space. For example, if two adjacent areas are equal in terms of demographics and life-styles, yet one area has twice the sales per capita as another, the area with twice the retail sales can be viewed as overstored relative to the other area. In general, a retailer is expected to generate high profits in understored areas, satisfactory profits in saturated areas, and below-average profits in oversaturated markets.

The conventional thought is that most U.S. markets are overstored. "There are too many malls, too many strip shopping centers, and too many stores," says the chairman of Dayton Hudson Corporation. According to a major retail consulting firm, in 1992 the United States had 18.4 square feet of retail space per person, about twice as much as in 1974 and 40 percent more than in 1980.[21]

Market saturation issues may intensify as major retailers such as Wal-Mart, Toys "R" Us, and Home Depot seek out new market areas for growth. In the past, for example, Arkansas-based Wal-Mart stuck to rural areas of the South and Midwest. By the year 2000, it will be fully established in California and the Northeast. These areas are current market strongholds of rivals Kmart and Target (a division of Dayton Hudson). In 1990 Wal-Mart operated in only 35 percent of Kmart's markets. By 1995 the common trading areas will be 75 percent. While in 1991 all three discount stores (which control 70 percent of the discount department store business) had 15 percent overlap in their territories, the overlap was estimated to be about 40 percent as of 1995. According to one analyst, "anytime a lot of square footage is added, it takes a little bit away from everyone."[22]

Overstoring has several important implications for retailers. First, rents will be reduced as a result of increased store space and reduced demand. Second, retail competition will intensify and perhaps force weaker retailers into bankruptcy. Third, retailers may seek to increase sales opportunities through scrambled merchandising.

LEVERAGED BUYOUTS

In a **leveraged buyout (LBO)**, a retailer is acquired by an outside firm (as in the case of Federated Department Stores) or by the firm's existing management (as in the case of R. H. Macy and Southland Corporation, the parent company of 7-Eleven). The purchase of stock in the acquired firm is financed by high-risk, high-interest bonds, commonly referred to as junk bonds.[23] LBOs are in sharp contrast to The Gap Inc. and The Limited, two very successful chains with almost no debt.

Many retail bankruptcies—Federated Department Stores and R. H. Macy, in department stores, and Southland (7-Eleven), in convenience stores—can be attributed, in large part, to the high-interest payments in the leveraged buyouts. For example, in the case of Macy's, not only did the firm have high debt, but also interest costs on bonds was in excess of 14.5 percent on two bond issues and 16.5 percent on the third.[24] Although some LBO-based retailers have been successful (such as Safeway), other firms have become vulnerable to high debt, owing to the reluctance of suppliers to ship merchandise, and to the inability to take advantage of growth opportunities. The recessionary economy of the early 1990s has made many LBOs especially weak.

A large proportion of the LBOs of the 1980s involved retailers. Many acquiring firms felt retailers had **hidden assets**, assets that were not reflected in the firm's balance sheet at near their market values. Hidden assets for retailers were property that was owned by the retailer for years and heavily depreciated, or long-term leases at below-market rentals. In many cases, the acquiring firms felt that they could sell these assets and then reduce debt. Unfortunately, many acquiring firms had little knowledge of retailing or did not have financial resources to ride out the recession of the early 1990s.

The next section reinforces coverage of leveraged buyouts by defining the concept of financial leverage on profits and by providing financial leverage data for a number of major retailers.

HIGH- AND LOW-PERFORMANCE RETAILERS

Many retailers have not performed well in terms of such measures as net profit margin (net profit as a percentage of sales) and return on stockholders' equity. Others can be classified as high-performance retailers based on these and other measures.

Among the high-performance retailers are Dillard Department Stores, Home Depot, The Limited, Toys "R" Us, Wal-Mart, The Gap, and Nordstrom. These chains are characterized as having exciting merchandising programs, using new technology in an innovative manner, effectively using marketing research and marketing information, having a clear market position, and having a high recent annual growth rate in sales.[25] For example, the average annual growth rate for these retailers over a recent five-year period was: Dillard Department Stores (15 percent), Home Depot (36.2 percent), The Limited (12.9 percent), Toys "R" Us (14.5 percent), Wal-Mart (27.4 percent), The Gap (22.1 percent), and Nordstrom (9.0 percent).[26]

Although retailers can be analyzed by several performance measures, an important means of assessing retailer performance is the strategic profit model. The **strategic profit model** assesses retailer performance on the basis of asset turnover (net sales/total assets), net profit margin (net profit/net sales), and financial leverage (total assets/net worth).

Multiplying each of these measures by each other results in return on investment (net profit/net worth). The strategic profit model computes net return on investment (net profit/net worth) on the basis of multiplying asset turnover, net profit margin, and financial leverage (see Figure 3-2). Table 3-3 shows the variation in net profits/net worth among these retailers. It also provides some indication of the differences in performance among these retailers.

Asset turnover represents the sales made from the equivalent of one dollar of assets. A retailer can increase asset turnover by having a fresh inventory, dealing with vendors that offer favorable credit terms, using second-use locations (in which other retailers have invested fixtures and renovations), using inexpensive store fixtures, and increasing store traffic and impulse sales through special promotions. Table 3-3 shows asset turnover for a sample of major retailers. No data are included on Sears, Roebuck due to the firm's owning insurance companies and credit operations. Among general-merchandise retailers studied in this table, the highest asset turnover ratio was Wal-Mart (2.54); the lowest was Dillard (1.25). Among food-based retailers, Winn-Dixie had the highest asset turnover ratio (5.16); Stop & Shop's asset turnover was 2.16 (the lowest).

FIGURE 3-2 Strategic profit model.

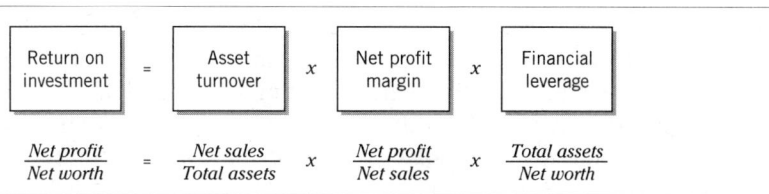

TABLE 3-3 APPLICATION OF STRATEGIC PROFIT MODEL TO RETAILERS, 1994 DATA

Retailer	Asset Turnover	×	Net Profit Margin	×	Financial Leverage	=	Net Profit / Net Worth
General-Merchandise Retailers							
Wal-Mart	2.54		3.21		2.58		21.04
JC Penney	1.30		5.01		2.89		18.82
Home Depot	2.16		4.84		1.68		17.56
Service Merchandise	2.10		1.39		5.73		16.73
Toys "R" Us	1.33		6.08		1.92		15.53
The Limited	1.60		6.12		1.66		16.25
Lowe's	1.97		3.66		2.19		15.79
Nordstrom	1.62		5.21		1.78		15.02
Dillard Department Stores	1.25		4.40		1.97		10.84
Food-Based Retailers							
Stop & Shop	2.16		1.92		7.13		29.57
Albertson's	3.28		3.37		2.15		23.77
Winn-Dixie	5.16		1.95		2.03		20.43
Publix	3.80		2.73		1.56		16.18
Giant Food	2.63		2.67		1.90		13.34
Bruno's	3.06		1.32		2.20		8.89
Vons	2.25		0.53		4.02		4.79

Source: Author's calculation of data from "The Fortune 500 Largest U.S. Corporations," *Fortune* (May 15, 1995), pp. F1–F13.

Net profit margin represents a retailer's net profit as a percentage of its sales. A retailer can increase its profit margin by making special buys from vendors, by increasing the percentage of high markup goods that are sold, through scrambled merchandising, by reducing operating costs (such as using low-rent locations), by automation and mechanization, and by use of self-service merchandising. Table 3-3 depicts net profit margins for a number of major retailers. Among general-merchandise retailers, the highest net profit margin was attained by The Limited (6.12), and the lowest, by Service Merchandise (1.39). For food-based retailers, Albertson's had the highest net profit margin (3.37); the lowest was Vons (with 0.53).

Financial leverage is the percentage of net worth that is represented by assets. A firm with a high financial leverage ratio has a high degree of debt. A financial leverage ratio of 1 means that the retailer has no debt (assets equal net worth). Although a retailer can increase its return on net worth by increasing debt, this debt must be repaid. Too high financial leverage can result in bankruptcy in the worse case or in a short-run philosophy due to the need to make large interest payments on a periodic basis. High financial leverage can also have a negative effect on a firm's net profit margins as high financial leverage involves high-interest costs. On the other hand, too low financial leverage may mean that a firm is overcautious or too conservative. Having too low financial leverage may limit a firm's ability to renovate and expand existing stores, and to expand into current and new markets. Service Merchandise's high net profit/net worth is due to its high financial leverage. Stop & Shop also has high financial leverage.

LBOs (with high debt and interest costs), increased market saturation, the recessions of the early 1990s, as well as changes in consumer demographics and life-styles, combined to make the retail environment a precarious one for many retailers. During the late 1980s and early 1990s, a large number of major retailers went bankrupt: Federated Department Stores (it emerged from bankruptcy in February 1992), Macy's, Circle K, and Ames Department Stores. According to one analyst, 23 percent of department store sales in the United States in 1991 were made by firms that were in bankruptcy.[27] Dun & Bradstreet estimates that 12,575 retailers failed in 1994, a 19.7 percent decrease over 1993. The failure rate per 10,000 listed retailers for 1994 was 66; this compares favorably with 78 per 10,000 retailers in 1993.[28]

In 1989 David Glass, chief executive officer of Wal-Mart, shook up the retail industry with his prediction that 50 percent of all retailers would not be around in the year 2000. In 1991 Glass was quoted as saying: "I may have underestimated."[29]

It is uncertain as to what will happen to firms as they emerge from bankruptcy. For example, Federated Department Stores wiped out $5 billion in debt as it emerged from bankruptcy.[30] The elimination of this debt will enable it to be a more effective competitor.

A TYPOLOGY OF RETAIL INSTITUTIONS

This section classifies retailers according to ownership, retail strategy (for food-based and general-merchandise retailers), and nonstore retailing. The purpose is to show not only the diversity of retail institutions, but also how the institution type affects the retailer's buying arrangements.

Where possible, current data on size of the retailer type by both number of firms and overall sales are provided. The reader should be careful in summarizing these data since the retail categories overlap. For example, a retailer can be both an independent and a specialty retailer. Combining sales in these overlapping classifications would overstate retail sales for the affected units.

BY OWNERSHIP

There are three major different types of ownership arrangements in retailing: independent, chain, and franchises. An **independent retailer** owns and operates only one retail outlet. As can be seen from Table 3-4 (which shows the latest data available at the time of publication), independent retailers make up 95 percent of all retail firms, 80 percent of retail establishments, but less than half of retail sales and retail payrolls. Since 1972, the relative importance of chains has grown (at the expense of independents) in terms of number of firms, number of establishments, dollar sales, and dollar payrolls.

TABLE 3-4 INDEPENDENT VERSUS CHAIN RETAILING[a]

	Number of Firms	Number of Firms as Percentage of Total[b]		Establishments as Percentage of Total[b]		Sales as Percentage of Total[b]		Payrolls as Percentage of Total[b]	
	1992	1992	1987	1992	1987	1992	1987	1992	1987
Total U.S. retailers	1,066,358	100.00	100.00	100.00	100.0	100.0	100.0	100.9	100.0
Total independent retailers	1,013,520	95.04	94.80	66.4	80.0	41.8	47.1	42.7	46.4
Total chain retailers	52,838	4.95	5.20	33.6	20.0	58.2	52.9	57.3	53.6
2 to 4 units	40,837	3.83	4.13	6.6	4.5	7.9	8.2	8.8	9.3
5 to 9 units	7,032	0.66	0.63	2.9	1.8	4.0	3.8	4.2	4.1
10 to 24 units	3,144	0.29	0.28	3.0	1.8	4.4	4.3	4.3	4.3
25 to 99 units	1,285	0.12	0.11	3.8	2.3	7.7	6.7	7.4	6.4
100 or more units	540	0.05	0.04	17.3	9.6	34.2	29.9	32.5	29.5

[a]This table does not include independent retailers that are run entirely by the owners and/or their families.
[b]Rounding errors appear in some of the percentages.

Sources: *1992 and 1987 Censuses of Retail Trade Subject Series: Establishment and Firm Size* (Washington, D.C.: U.S. Bureau of the Census); and author's estimates and calculations.

Independent retailers have the following advantages over chain organizations: flexibility in developing strategies (independents do not need to develop and maintain a uniform image with their other branch units or to meet stringent franchisor requirements), speed in changing strategy (there are no board of directors or committee meetings), and ability to provide expert personal service (based on the abilities and personality of the owner-manager). The disadvantages of independent retail organizations include lack of specialists, difficulty in raising capital, lack of quantity discounts and bargaining power with vendors, and inefficiency of certain advertising media owing to waste circulation. (The medium's geographic coverage is greater than the trading area of the retailer.) An additional disadvantage of independents is management succession. **Management succession** refers to the ability of a retail operation to successfully continue to operate in the event of the sudden disability or death of a retail owner or partner.

Chain retailers consist of two or more similar retail establishments that are owned and operated by one firm. While in 1992 less than 5 percent of all retail firms were chains, chain retailers accounted for 34 percent of retail establishments and 57 percent of both retail sales and retail payrolls. The relative importance of chains varies by type of retailer. For example, according to the *1992 Census of Retail Trade,* chains accounted for over 99 percent of sales in department stores and 88 percent of variety store sales, but only 50 percent of sales in furniture stores and 30 percent of liquor store sales.

As was discussed in the section on independents, for almost every category of chain retailer (2 to 4 units, 5 to 9 units, 10 to 24 units, 25 to 99 units, and 100 or more units), the importance of chain retailers as measured by establishments, sales, and payroll increased between 1987 and 1992 (see Table 3-4).

The advantages of chain retailers over independents include the use of specialists, high bargaining power with vendors, ability to use regional and perhaps national media efficiently, less dependence on any one executive, ability to buy directly from manufacturers, and economies of scale due to the operation of multiple stores. The disadvantages include difficulty in meeting local and regional needs owing to extreme centralization of buying and selling staffs, high required investment for multiple units, and difficulty in implementing common policies across diverse retail units.

With regard to the third major retail ownership form, franchising, there are two types of retail franchises: product/trademark franchising and business format franchising. In **product/trademark franchising**, franchised dealers acquire the identity of their suppliers by agreeing to sell the suppliers' products and/or operate under the suppliers' names. In product/trademark franchising, retailers have considerable freedom in establishing store hours, in choosing locations, and in setting their retail strategies. Product/trademark franchising represents about 70 percent of all retail franchising. In contrast, **business format franchising** is characterized by tight control and coordination between franchisors and retail franchisees. Franchisors require business format franchisees to participate in cooperative advertising programs, to use prototype stores, and to adhere to policies and procedures so that individually owned store units closely resemble chains.[31]

The advantages of franchising to the franchisor include ability to develop regional and/or national distribution capabilities with low capital requirements; ability to secure profits from franchisees through initial franchise fees, royalties, and sale of goods and services; perhaps more highly motivated franchisees than traditional retail managers owing to investment risk; ability of franchisors to control franchisees through cancellation provisions in franchise contracts; and payment to the franchisor for goods and services based on when these goods and services are ordered by the franchisee, not sold to retail customers.

The disadvantages of franchising to the franchisor are as follows: franchisors have less control over franchisees than through expansion by ownership; a poorly run franchise may adversely affect the franchise's overall image; the franchisor is an independent businessperson and not an employee; and the franchisor may have to buy back marginally successful franchises to restore the image of the franchise.

The advantages of franchising to the franchisee are the ability to use a proven retail format, troubleshooting assistance from the franchisor, access to regional and national media, development and maintenance of a chainlike image, a protected territory (if provided for in the contract), and legal rights (such as federal laws that require the franchisor to disclose profitability, franchisee success rates, and so on). In the past, many franchisors believed that franchisees enjoyed higher rates of success than independents. A recent study using Census Bureau data concluded that, despite higher initial sales and greater investments, franchises had lower chances of survival than independents. Three-year-old franchises also had lower average pretax earnings than independents.[32]

The disadvantages of franchising to the franchisee include limited decision making with respect to store hours, merchandise purchases, and store operations; higher prices paid for goods and services from the franchisor than traditional market prices; high channel power to the franchisor relative to the franchisee; and payment to the franchisor on the basis of sales, not profits.

The characteristics of franchising are discussed further in Chapter 12.

BY STRATEGY

Retailers can be categorized according to strategy by two dimensions: merchandise width, depth, and consistency; and price-service emphasis. **Merchandise width** consists of different product lines stocked and sold; this is referred to as variety. **Merchandise depth** consists of the selection within any product line; this is described as a retailer's assortment. Depth can consist of different price lines, different vendors, different styles, different colors, and different sizes. **Merchandise consistency** refers to the differences among product lines covered. For example, a toy-based retailer that uses a scrambled merchandising strategy has a less consistent merchandise mix than one that does not (see Figure 3-3).

One can also classify retailers by price versus service emphasis. **Low-end strategy retailers** generally seek to appeal to a price-conscious market segment through a low-cost retail format. In contrast, **high-end strategy retailers** seek to

FIGURE 3-3 Merchandise depth and width of food-oriented retailers.

appeal to a consumer segment that is more concerned with high service levels than with a low price. Table 3-5 describes the major differences between these two strategies. Although these strategies are presented as dichotomy, obviously there are middle-ground positions between low-end and high-end retail strategies.

TABLE 3-5 DIFFERENCES BETWEEN LOW-END AND HIGH-END RETAIL STRATEGIES

	Low-End Retail Strategy	**High-End Retail Strategy**
Target market served	Price-conscious market.	Market segment more concerned with high-service levels than low price.
Location choice	Isolated retail locations, and strip mall locations which enable retailer to have low rental costs.	High-rent locations in regional shopping centers and in downtown central business districts.
Services mix	Self-service. Centralized cashier. Shopping carts provided by retailer. Returns, exchanges, layaway services provided. Credit cards and checks accepted. If delivery, installation, and alterations are provided; they involve additional costs to consumer.	High level of salesperson assistance. Separate cashier in each department. Provides all services of low-end retailers. In addition, provides delivery, installation, and alterations at no additional cost.
Price levels	Low-price emphasis. Will meet or beat competitors' prices. May use everyday low pricing.	Price is compatible with services provided. Sales often limited to off-season specials.
Product mix	Features private labels or products that are intensively distributed. May purchase on an opportunistic basis (such as manufacturer overruns, special purchases, off-season merchandise, or canceled orders).	Features products that are selectively or exclusively distributed.

(Continued)

TABLE 3-5 DIFFERENCES BETWEEN LOW-END AND HIGH-END RETAIL STRATEGIES (*CONTINUED*)

	Low-End Retail Strategy	High-End Retail Strategy
Promotion mix	Promotes low prices in its advertising. May advertise it will beat prices of competitors. Promotes goods on basis of current prices charged by competitors in market area. Low levels of sales force training. Few or no special events and demonstrations.	Promotes special services. Attempts to differentiate retailer on basis of special services or on exclusive merchandise. Prices not featured in advertising. High levels of sales force training. Many special events and demonstrations.
Store atmosphere	Inexpensive, standardized fixtures. Linoleum or tile floors. Standardized storefront. Use of inexpensive paneling.	Costly, custom fixtures. Carpeted and parquet floors. Custom storefront. Use of wood and marble in interior area.

FOOD-ORIENTED RETAILERS

Six different food-oriented retailers can be distinguished by their merchandise width and depth as well as by their strategy mix: convenience stores, conventional supermarkets, superstores, combination stores, warehouse stores, and buying clubs. Table 3-6 classifies food-oriented retailers based on merchandise depth and width.

Convenience stores offer a limited line of convenience goods and services such as cigarettes, milk, candy, beer, and video rentals. As of 1994, 58,000 convenience stores accounted for 6.9 percent of total grocery store sales. (This sales analysis does not include gasoline sales by convenience stores.)[33] Convenience stores fulfill a fill-in demand function for consumers. These stores are often busiest when a local conventional supermarket is closed or when consumers do not wish to make a special trip to the conventional supermarket for one or two items. In many cases, convenience stores are operated in conjunction with gasoline stations. The growth of convenience stores occurred at the same time that many gasoline stations shifted to self-service gas-only outlets. This freed up the area previously devoted to repair facilities. In addition, a large percentage of gasoline buyers sought out sandwiches, tobacco, automotive products, dairy products, and video rentals.[34]

Supermarkets are defined as large departmentalized retail establishments offering a relatively broad and complete stock of dry groceries, fresh meat, per-

TABLE 3-6 LOW-END AND HIGH-END RETAIL STRATEGIES OF FOOD-ORIENTED RETAILERS

Low-End Retail Strategies	High-End Retail Strategies
Warehouse store	Convenience store
	Conventional supermarket
	Combination store
	Superstore

CHANNELS IN ACTION

Is McDonald's Really McRisky?

McDonald's, once looked upon with envy by competitors, is now facing major problems of its own.

- In 1990 total burger consumption as a percentage of all restaurant orders dropped to 17 percent versus 19 percent in 1982.
- Total fast-food sales, which grew at an average rate of 8.7 percent during the 1980s, will probably only grow at the same rate as inflation during the 1990s.
- McDonald's share of the fast-food market decreased from a peak of 18.8 percent in 1986 to 16.3 percent in 1991.
- A new value menu that resulted in price reductions of about 20 percent on a large variety of items increased sales by only 4 to 5 percent. Profits are down 10 to 15 percent at many franchises.
- In 1972 there were over 2500 Americans per fast-food outlet. That number dropped to 2000 in 1982 and to less than 1500 in 1993.

An obvious solution for the current problems faced by McDonald's is to concentrate more of its efforts on its foreign operations. However, nearly one-quarter of McDonald's revenues come from franchise fees that are based on a percentage of domestic revenues.

To increase domestic sales, McDonald's has given considerable freedom to its franchisees. In some cases, these franchisees have experimented with new foods such as fruit cups, lasagna, oven-roasted chickens, and even corn on the cob. Others have changed their unit's decor. A Chicago location has rock-and-roll memorabilia, while a Wall Street location boasts a baby grand piano and a ticker tape. In 1993 McDonald's also opened 130 satellite sites including more than 80 outlets inside Wal-Mart stores. Other nontraditional sites include a McDonald's inside the MGM Grand Hotel in Las Vegas and in a Mobil gasoline station. While proponents of this new flexibility cite its ability to meet local needs, some critics feel that localized strategies may blur McDonald's current chainlike image.

Source: Barnaby J. Feder, "McDonald's Finds There's Still Plenty of Room to Grow," *New York Times* (January 9, 1994), p. F5.

---

ishable produce, and dairy products, supplemented by a variety of convenience, nonfood merchandise and operated primarily on a self-service basis.[35] According to the Food Marketing Institute and *Progressive Grocer,* to be characterized as a supermarket a food-based retailer requires annual sales of at least $2 million. Four types of retail establishments can be classified as supermarkets: conventional supermarkets, superstores, combination stores, and warehouse stores. The major differences among these supermarkets are in both store size and major product emphasis.

Conventional supermarkets average 15,000 to 30,000 square feet in size and specialize in food-related merchandise. (Less than 5 percent of sales comes from general-merchandise sales.) In 1994 conventional supermarkets accounted for 63.2 percent of supermarkets' stores and 45.8 percent of total supermarket sales. Average annual sales for a conventional supermarket is $7,360,000.[36]

Superstores average 30,000 to 65,000 square feet in size and offer a large selection of general merchandise. Between 20 and 25 percent of sales comes from general merchandise. In comparison to conventional supermarkets, superstores generally have a larger trading area, offer one-stop shopping convenience, and are more likely to engage in scrambled merchandising. They have a less consistent merchandise mix than a conventional supermarket.

Combination stores combine in a single-store format a supermarket and a pharmacy or a supermarket and a general-merchandise retailer. These stores average 30,000 square feet in size. Unlike superstores, typically 25 percent of the space in a combination store is devoted to nonfoods. Combination stores have a synergy between the combined units. The general-merchandise or pharmacy retail operation benefits from the frequency of the supermarket shopper. The supermarket operation benefits from higher profit margins of general merchandise, pharmacy, and health and beauty aids; an increased trading area; and a higher average sale.

Warehouse stores vary in size. They can be classified as limited assortment, warehouse, super warehouse, and hypermarket/supercenter depending on their size.[37] All warehouse stores offer low prices in a no-frills setting. Warehouse stores reduce costs of operation by utilizing low-cost locations (such as in an industrial park), low fixture costs (such as used store fixtures or cut case displays), and opportunistic buying (concentrating on special buys from vendors). Because of opportunistic buying, warehouse stores may not stock the same brand on a consumer's next shopping trip. In total, warehouse stores accounted for 15 percent of supermarket sales in 1994.[38]

Buying clubs (membership clubs) charge shoppers an annual membership fee (typically $25 to $35), locate in low-rental locations, and typically resemble a warehouse. These clubs sell products to both retail and wholesale customers. Like warehouse stores, these clubs engage in opportunistic buying and typically limit their selection of popular brands in which they can secure special discounts. Unlike warehouse stores, buying clubs limit their sales to small businesses that buy wholesale quantities and to retail customers that are members of unions. According to one consultant, the typical consumer member spends $75 per visit, while the average wholesale customer spends $1000 per shopping trip. In buying clubs, food and related products account for half of sales. The other half consists of general-merchandise items such as appliances, electronics, domestics, and clothing.[39] Sales of the more than 600 U.S. buying clubs were estimated to be $39 billion in 1994. Membership fees comprise approximately two-thirds of the profits of buying clubs.[40]

Some marketers are redesigning products, packaging, promotional strategies, and delivery to meet the special needs of buying clubs. Heinz, for example, is combining condiments such as ketchup and relish into a single package. It is also shipping 64-ounce ketchup bottles on customized display pallets that are easy for buying clubs to store and handle. Traditional supermarkets have begun to fight back with "warehouse" sections and club-size packaging.[41]

FIGURE 3-4 Merchandise depth, width, and consistency of general-merchandise retailers.

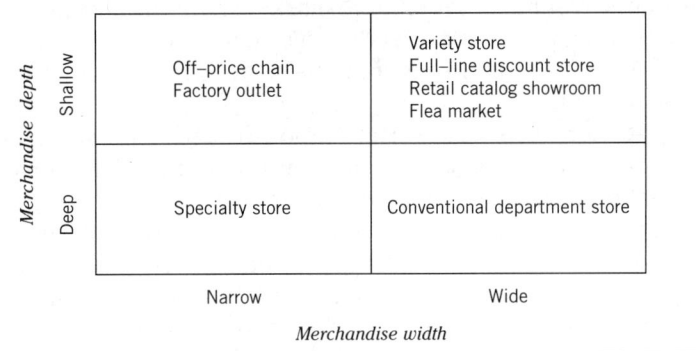

GENERAL-MERCHANDISE RETAILERS

General-merchandise retailers can be categorized as specialty stores, variety stores, department stores, full-line discount stores, retail catalog showrooms, off-price chains, factory outlets, and flea markets. Figure 3-4 shows the merchandise depth and width of these retailers. Table 3-7 classifies these retailers by merchandise depth and width.

Specialty stores stock and sell one line or limited lines of related merchandise. In 1993 the top 100 specialty stores had sales of over $104 billion; these chains operated more than 67,000 retail stores.[42] Data on sales by specialty stores are difficult to obtain because of the various lines of merchandise that can be sold. The advantages of specialty stores over other general-merchandise retail formats include greater depth of selection, high salesperson knowledge, higher levels of sales assistance, and ability to provide technical assistance. The disadvantages of specialty stores are lack of diversification and domination by key vendors. In addition, full-service specialty stores often have competition from price-oriented discount stores. This is especially true because of the free-rider phenomenon. In the **free-rider phenomenon**, consumers seek information from specialty stores, get the brand name and model number of the preferred product, and then seek to purchase the product at a retailer that offers a discount.

TABLE 3-7 LOW-END AND HIGH-END RETAIL STRATEGIES OF GENERAL-MERCHANDISE RETAILERS

Low-End Retail Strategies	High-End Retail Strategies
Variety store	Specialty store
Full-line discount store	Conventional department store
Retail catalog showroom	
Off-price chain	
Factory outlet	
Flea market	

A specific type of specialty store is a **category killer**, an especially large specialty store that dominates other retailers in a merchandise category. Category killers have large trading areas, a large market share in their product category, and high bargaining power with vendors. For example, the average Toys "R" Us store stocks 18,000 items throughout the year versus Wal-Mart's 3500 items around Christmas.[43]

A **variety store** sells a wide variety of low-priced general merchandise in a self-service, cash-and-carry format. In comparison to full-line discount stores, variety stores typically have no store-related credit card. In comparison to conventional department stores, variety stores are not decentralized by department for either buying or selling responsibilities. Variety stores are an important seller of notions, housewares, and health and beauty aids. The variety stores category is the only one in Table 3-1 to have recorded a decrease in sales growth over the most recent 10-year period. Variety stores have been particularly hard hit by scrambled merchandising from other retail formats. Firms such as Woolworth Corporation have decreased the number of its variety stores. In late 1993 it began to close half of its remaining variety stores. This reorganization further moved Woolworth to become a specialty retailing conglomerate.[44]

According to the U.S. Bureau of the Census, **department stores** must meet three criteria: (1) they must employ at least 50 people; (2) apparel and soft goods must account for 20 percent or more of total sales; and (3) the merchandise assortment must include each of these three groups of items: furniture, home furnishings, appliances, radios, and television sets; a general line of family apparel; and household linens and dry goods. If a store's annual sales are below $10 million, no more than 80 percent of a store's sales can be from any one merchandise line. If a store's sales are $10 million or more, there is no limitation on the percentage of sales from any one merchandise category, as long as combined sales of the two smallest lines are at least $1 million. Few stores are classified as department stores as a result of the $10 million or more exclusion; most of the stores that are classified as a result of this exception would otherwise be apparel-based specialty stores. Department stores comprise the largest category in sales for general merchandise, apparel, and furniture (GAF) sales.[45]

Two types of stores meet the Bureau of Census definition for a department store: the conventional department store and the full-line discount department store. In comparison to the full-line discount store, the **conventional department store** has decentralized customer service and customer assistance, sells soft and hard goods, and has greater customer service, higher merchandise depth, greater emphasis on fashion merchandise, more attractive overall store atmosphere and fixturing, and a higher proportion of sales at higher price points. Conventional department stores appeal to fashion-conscious shoppers and to the one-stop shopping needs of the entire family. In many cases, conventional department stores have copied the success of specialty stores by arranging departments in boutiques. In a conventional department store, shoppers seeking to purchase a coordinated clothing line by a single manufacturer, such as Ralph Lauren, are able to fulfill their shopping needs by visiting one department, without having to shop the entire department store.

Conventional department stores have been particularly hard hit by bankruptcies including B. Altman, Carter Hawley Hale, Federated Department

Stores, and R. H. Macy. As noted earlier, leveraged buyouts (LBOs) with high debt structure and high-interest payments contributed to these bankruptcies in several of these instances. Some retail analysts argue that conventional department stores have been particularly hard hit by specialty stores and category killers that have outmerchandised them and by full-line discount stores and off-price chains that have outpriced them. Off-price chains have had a major effect on department stores because they have the same customer demographics as the department store shopper.[46]

Unlike the conventional department store, the **full-line discount store** uses central checkouts (often shopping carts are provided), emphasizes hard goods, has lower fixturing costs, stocks soft goods that are sold on the basis of function rather than fashion, and does not typically accept mail orders or deliver merchandise. Full-line discount stores are important sellers of such product categories as ladies' wear, housewares, children's wear, hardware, and consumer electronics.[47] The full-line discount store industry also has had a number of bankruptcies and reorganizations, including such firms as Zayre, Ames, Lechmere, and Heck's.

Retail catalog showrooms sell items via a catalog (the catalog is generally delivered to the shopper's home) in a warehouse-type setting. Typically, shoppers pre-select merchandise from a catalog in their homes and then order merchandise by catalog number in the store. In many cases, goods are not demonstrated or even visible to the consumer. A high proportion of a typical retail catalog showroom's sales are in jewelry. Other key product categories are electronics, housewares, gifts, and watches.

The concept of the catalog showroom epitomizes the low-cost approach to retailing. Most retail catalog showrooms utilize low-rent locations, have a relatively low pilferage expense (because most merchandise is not accessible to consumers until it is paid for), have a low fixturing cost (a large portion of the retail store is actually a warehouse), and a low labor element (because many items are presold).

A major problem associated with retail catalog showrooms is that the catalog must be prepared nine months to one year prior to distribution. Catalog prices are then valid for one year. If costs rise between the preparation and the expiration date of the catalog, the retail catalog showroom can either raise prices and anger consumers, or keep prices at the published levels and reduce its profitability. This problem is increased by the large amount of jewelry sales and the changing value of gold.

Off-price chains specialize in the opportunistic buying of canceled orders, slightly irregular, and end-of-season merchandise that is sold in a no-frills retail setting. Off-price chains generally specialize in such items as apparel, shoes, linens, fabrics, cosmetics, and/or housewares. Opportunistic buying means that offerings to consumers change week-to-week and even day-to-day on the basis of the chain's ability to purchase selected goods at below wholesale cost (often less than half the customary wholesale price). Although opportunistic buying may result in poor distribution of merchandise (on the basis of size, style, and brand), it generates excitement to the shopping experience for value-oriented shoppers.

Retail prices in off-price chains may be 30 to 40 percent less than traditional prices, but these chains are highly profitable. Off-price chains are efficient in distribution owing to low-rent locations, self-service operations, no alterations, and very high inventory turnover.

Years ago, off-price chains typically removed a manufacturer's label to protect the image of the manufacturer and its relationship with its traditional specialty and department store customers. Now the manufacturer's label is customarily kept on the garment intact. The label signifies value to a consumer. However, to retain their long-term relationship with vendors, most off-price chains do not advertise the brand name of merchandise in their ads.

Factory outlets are owned and operated by a manufacturer to dispose of excess inventory in an out-of-the-way location (so as not to alienate the manufacturer's traditional customers). Many manufacturers utilize factory outlets rather than off-price chains so as to have greater control over the distribution of goods. Factory outlets reduce the fear that off-price chains can transship goods to more traditional retailers that are located near manufacturers' coveted traditional specialty and department store customers. Factory outlets also enable manufacturers to obtain profits (and pay costs) associated with running a retail outlet. Sales in factory outlets were about $9.9 billion in 1993, about 2 percent of total retail sales. In total, there were 10,500 factory outlets in the United States in 1993, triple the number six years earlier.[48]

Flea markets are typically open several days a week. These retailers often are located in an unconventional retail location such as a race track parking lot or a former discount store location. In some cases, the same retailers occupy the same locations throughout the year; in other cases, retail locations are rented on a daily basis. Consumers can be charged either a parking fee or an admission fee. Generally, sales taxes are absorbed by the retailer; the prices quoted by the retailer typically include sales tax.

Flea market operators include a broad spectrum of retailers, including consumers seeking to sell or trade surplus items, part-time retailers that sell and trade antiques and used furniture, traditional retailers that sell surplus stock or special buys to a price-conscious segment, and wholesalers seeking to establish a retail outlet. Low overhead costs, low investment, and the part-time nature of selling activities make flea markets particularly attractive.

Nonstore-Based Retailers

Retail strategies can also be classified by nonstore activities. Three nonstore-based strategies are vending machines, direct selling, and direct marketing.

Vending machines involve the sale of goods and services through coin- and card-operated machinery. Many marketers have tried to expand the line of goods and services that can be sold through this distribution medium. Still, 97 percent of merchandise sold through vending machines consists of hot and cold beverages, food items, and cigarettes.[49] While vending machines are viewed as automatic, operating costs are high because of the need to constantly refill and service the machines. These machines are also prone to vandalism and theft. New technology enables machines to accept credit cards and to trace malfunctions. In 1993 total vending machine sales in the United States were $26 billion.[50]

Direct selling involves sales made on the basis of house-to-house canvassing or telemarketing. Direct selling can be based on cold canvassing (without leads that have been qualified) or the party plan method of selling. As compared with traditional store-based retailing, direct selling offers these advantages: increased customer convenience, ability to demonstrate in one's home, and the customer not being exposed to competing brands. The disadvantages include very high sales turnover, little control over the external sales force, the large number of working wives who are unavailable during business hours, and high selling costs. According to the Direct Selling Association, direct retail sales were $15 billion in 1993.[51]

Direct marketing is a form of retailing in which a customer is first exposed to a good or service through a nonpersonal medium (such as direct mail, conventional or cable television, radio, magazines, or newspapers) and then orders by mail or telephone (usually through a toll-free telephone number)—sometimes by computer.[52] Direct marketing includes video-ordering systems (see Chapter 2). Annual U.S. sales to final consumers are over $140 billion (including charitable contributions), and almost 90 million people make one or more direct-marketing purchases during a typical year.[53] The advantages of direct marketing are low rent with no offsetting customer inconvenience, capability to sell and service customers 24 hours a day, and ability to effectively service sparsely populated rural areas. Traditional retailers can use direct marketing as an addition to their regular store sales. As compared to store-based retailing, in direct marketing does not enable consumers to examine an item, profits are sensitive to postal rates and paper costs, obtaining and updating mailing lists are difficult and time-consuming processes, and large clutter exists from multiple mailings received by consumers.

RETAIL BUYING ORGANIZATIONS

The buying organization of retailers can be described on the basis of formality; centralization; a buying versus merchandising orientation; an inside-, outside-, and cooperative-buying organization; and regularity (see Table 3-8).

Formality refers to whether buying is a separate function within the organization with a specialized staff. In an informal organization, the person with responsibility and authority for buying also is involved with other activities such as store operations, budgeting, and financial management. Independents are generally organized informally with little or no specialization; large chain organizations generally have a formal buying department. Although formal buying organizations may be more costly, a formal organization treats buying as a separate activity, acknowledges that the skills necessary for buying and other retailer functions may be different, and ensures that adequate attention is given to buying activities.

Buying responsibilities can be centralized or decentralized. In a **pure centralized buying organization**, one buyer purchases all goods for all retail store units. Centralization reduces costs, provides opportunities for quantity discounts, allows common advertising across all store units, and provides for a

Table 3-8 Alternative Retail Buying Organizations

Formality	Formal buying organizations specify that buying is a specialized function with a specialized staff. In an informal buying organization, the person responsible for the buying function is also responsible for disparate activities such as store operations and budgeting.
Centralization	In a pure centralized buying organization, one buyer purchases all goods for all retail store units. In most retail chains, buying is typically organized either on a geographic or product basis. This ensures that special target market needs are fulfilled and that buyers have appropriate technical skills.
Buying versus merchandising	In a buying philosophy, authority and responsibility for buying is held by a buying specialist (single person or group). In a merchandising orientation, responsibility for both buying and selling is held by a single person or group.
Inside, outside, and cooperative buying	In an inside buying organization, buying specialists are employees of the retailer. In an outside buying organization, a retailer employs a private firm to perform the buying function. In cooperative buying, noncompeting retailers share buying responsibility and costs.
Regularity	In some cases, retailers routinely submit orders and reorders for merchandise. In other cases, they seek to purchase opportunistically.

uniform store image. The disadvantages of a pure centralized buying organization relate to the ability to meet regional preferences and the ability of one buyer to purchase goods involving different degrees of style and different levels of technical expertise.

In most retail chains, the buying function is typically organized on a decentralized basis either by geography or product. In a **geographic-based buying organization**, responsibilities are divided on the basis of state or region. Geographic organizations help assure that the special needs of geographic target markets are satisfied. **Product-based buying organizations** utilize product-based specialists. Product-based buying organizations recognize that special expertise is needed for distinct products and product lines.

Retail chains also utilize different forms of centralization/decentralization with respect to buying and selling activities. Responsibility for buying and selling may be wholly placed in a central buying office, or each branch unit may be given some autonomy for buying and selling. In general, the centralization of buying and selling involves cost economies (owing to the ability to use regional and national advertising, and to shift merchandise among retail units) and helps establish and maintain a consistent retail image across all retail units. A disadvantage of centralization is the inability to meet special local preferences. A chain can gain the benefits of both centralization and decentralization by having centralized buying but allowing some discretion to branches to meet local and regional preferences.

A type of centralization/decentralization decision relates to whether a firm uses a buying or a merchandising philosophy. In a **buying philosophy**, authority and responsibility for buying is held by buying specialists. A buying philosophy is common in large department stores where buyers are placed in the main store and sales managers are placed in the smaller branch stores. The buying philosophy is also common with variety stores and specialty stores. The advantages of a buying organization are that it provides for staff specialists; it recognizes that different skills are essential for success in buying and selling; and it recognizes that buyers spend a great deal of time in the field and may not be able to effectively manage and control a sales force. Major disadvantages of a buying organization are the need for buying and selling activities to be coordinated, and the expenses incurred in maintaining both functional areas.

In contrast, in a **merchandising orientation**, retailers combine responsibility and authority for buying and selling in a single person or group. A merchandising orientation assures proper coordination between buying and selling activities. A merchandising orientation also clearly assigns responsibility for failure and success. In a buying organization, for example, a buyer can argue that the right goods were purchased, but sales effort was poor. In contrast, the sales manager could argue that despite excellent sales efforts, the goods could not be sold since they were inappropriate for the local target market.

Large retail organizations generally employ an inside buying organization. In an **inside buying organization**, buying specialists are employees of the retailer. They may be located at a retail location or in a resident buying office. **Resident buying offices** are used when a retailer seeks to have an office in an important buying center for a major product. Many apparel-based retailers, for example, have resident buying offices in New York City, a major market for apparel. In an **outside buying organization**, a retailer employs a private firm to perform the buying function. The outside buying organization conducts market research, evaluates trends, contacts appropriate vendors, and orders and reorders merchandise. In some cases, the outside buying organization even arranges with a manufacturer to supply private-label goods. Outside buying organizations are typically paid either by a retailer (on the basis of the retailer's overall sales volume) or by commissions paid by vendors. In a **cooperative buying organization**, retailers share buying responsibility and costs. The retailers can be independents that are noncompeting (owing to lack of geographic proximity), or can be members of franchise wholesaling organizations (such as IGA and Walgreens) or retailer-owned wholesale cooperatives (such as Ace Hardware). Cooperative buying organizations allow small retailers and franchises to increase their bargaining power in dealing with vendors. It also enables independent retailers to use a more sophisticated analysis of vendors' products. A potential criticism of cooperative buying organizations is excessive merchandise uniformity among retailer members.

Buying organizations also differ in terms of their regularity. In many cases, retailers deal with the same vendors, having orders routinely filled. Conventional supermarkets utilize routine buying arrangements with most of their vendors. Franchisees are often constrained by their franchise contract to limit their purchases with approved vendors or with the franchisor. In other cases such as with warehouse stores, buying clubs, and off-price chains, buyers purchase opportunistically. In **opportunistic buying**, buyers seek to buy goods at 20 to 50

CHANNELS IN ACTION

Price/Costco Inc.: A Buying Club's Buying and Operating Philosophy

Price/Costco is the second largest buying club in the United States, after Wal-Mart's Sam's Wholesale Club. The firm was formed from the merger of Price Company and Costco Wholesale in 1993. The company operates more than 200 stores that serve its more than 9 million members.

Like other buying clubs, Price/Costco limits what it sells to what it can sell at competitive prices. According to the firm's president, "When we see a branded television for $329, we try to get it to sell for $249. We always try to buy smarter. But if we can't get that set for $249, we get an equivalent set to sell at that price." And when supermarkets in Oregon began selling sugar below cost, Price/Costco stopped selling sugar in the affected market area.

While traditional discounters may stock 40,000 to 50,000 different items, Price/Costco (and its buying club competitors) generally stock only 3500 items. Unlike a typical supermarket that may stock multiple brands of tuna fish in three different sizes and in multiple varieties (chunk, albacore, oil-packed, and water-packed), Price/Costco may limit its sales of tuna to one size, one brand, and one variety. The smaller inventory allows it to have greater bargaining power with its vendors and better inventory management. Price/Costco stocks a broad variety of goods ranging from perishables, groceries, major appliances, jewelry, and electronics.

According to one market analyst, buying clubs have low operating costs because of four factors: limited advertising expenses, low labor costs, below-average pilferage and bad check losses, and a cash-and-carry philosophy. Price/Costco's markup is generally 8.5 percent versus 25 to 28 percent for discounters and 45 to 50 percent for department stores and full-service specialty shops. Since 1986, the firm's operating costs have decreased from 10.1 percent of sales to 8.2 percent of sales. Markups are so low that an important contribution to Price/Costco's profitability is the annual membership fee to businesses and final consumers.

Source: Isadore Barmash, "A Flourishing Industry's Shining Star," *New York Times* (December 22, 1991), p. F7; James M. Regan, "Warehouse Clubs Move from Revolution to Evolution," *Marketing News* (August 3, 1992), p. 8; and "Warehouse Clubs Face Mid-Life Crisis: Industry Shakeout Leaves Two Giants," *Chain Store Age Executive* (August 1994), pp. 26A–28A.

percent below wholesale prices. In contrast to buying arrangements with typical chains, opportunistic buyers seek out special opportunities and may purchase lots of uneven size and color distributions (of 100 men's shirts purchased, 35 are size 15 with a sleeve length of 34 inches). This offering would be unsuitable to a typical department store (see Table 3-9).

It is important to consider that, while they represent retailers, buying organizations (whether corporate or cooperative) are performing a wholesale function for the retailers they represent.

TABLE 3-9 DIFFERENCES BETWEEN REGULAR BUYING AND OPPORTUNISTIC BUYING

Regular Buying	Opportunistic Buying
Multiple levels of decision making are required to approve a special order.	Buyers are empowered to make decisions quickly.
Buyers are concerned about controlling buying activities at the item level.	Buyers are concerned about controlling buying at a broad classification level.
Purchase commitments are made early in the selling season. Late season orders are largely limited to reorders.	A large amount of purchasing flexibility is left for later on in the selling season.
Purchasing is generally confined to first-quality goods.	An active search is made for irregulars, end-of-season merchandise, canceled orders, excess stock due to packaging changes, and bankruptcy stocks.
The concern is that special buys may limit sales of full-price merchandise.	The concern is about the salability of special buys. The impact on sales of traditional merchandise is less important.
The concern is about the impact of special buys on overall retail image, especially when buys consist of merchandise with uneven size and color distributions.	Special buys create store traffic and reinforce store image as a smart place to shop.

SUMMARY

1 *To examine the structure of retailing, including total retail sales and retail sales growth.* Total retail sales were $2.1 trillion in 1993, up from $1.3 billion in 1984. These numbers do not reflect inflation; the real sales growth in this time period was 2.3 percent. Many analysts evaluate the maturity of retail institutions by examining same-store sales growth.

2 *To describe the special characteristics of retailing: immediacy, the importance of location, a low average sale, a high proportion of impulse purchases, and high seasonality.* Immediacy relates to the short-run focus of retailing. Unlike much of advertising by manufacturers that is informational or image-oriented, most retail advertising is sales-oriented. In comparison to wholesaling, in retailing shoppers customarily visit the retailer at its store location. Location is also a long-term aspect of a retailer's overall strategy. The average sale in retailing is low, yet a large proportion of department and specialty store sales are on credit. Impulse sales are generally defined as nonplanned purchases. A major study by the Point-of-Purchase Advertising Institute found that 53 percent of supermarket purchases were unplanned and that 66 percent of purchases were due to in-store marketing efforts. Overall, retail sales are highly seasonal; the fourth quarter of the year accounts for about one-third of total department store yearly sales.

3. *To determine important trends affecting retailing: the growth of conglomerchants, increased market saturation, leveraged buyouts, and performance differences among discounters.* A conglomerate merchant operates disparate retailers. Dayton Hudson, Woolworth, and Melville are examples of conglomerchants. Many retail markets are now overstored. In 1992 the United States had 18.4 square feet of retail space per person, about twice as much as in 1974 and 40 percent more than in 1980. In a leveraged buyout, a retailer is acquired by an outside firm or the firm's existing management. The purchase of the stock is financed by high-risk, high-interest bonds. Many retail bankruptcies can be attributed to the high-interest payments in the leveraged buyout. High-performance and low-performance retailers can be differentiated through the strategic profit model. This model assesses a retailer's performance on the basis of asset turnover, net profit margin, and financial leverage.

4. *To study a classification system of retailers according to ownership, retail strategy, and nonstore retailing.* There are three different ownership arrangements in retailing: independent, chain, and franchise. Retailers can also be categorized on the basis of merchandise width, depth, and consistency and by low-end strategy retailers and high-end strategy retailers. Six different food-oriented retailers can be distinguished: convenience stores, conventional supermarkets, combination stores, superstores, warehouse stores, and buying clubs. General-merchandise retailers can be categorized as specialty stores, variety stores, department stores, full-line discount stores, retail catalog showrooms, off-price chains, factory outlets, and flea markets. Three nonstore retailer strategies are vending machines, direct selling, and direct marketing.

5. *To analyze alternative buying organizations.* Buying organizations can be described on the basis of formality; centralization; a buying versus a merchandising orientation; an inside, outside, and cooperative buying organization; and regularity.

KEY TERMS

retailing
real sales growth
same-store sales
trading area characteristics
affinities
pedestrian traffic counts
vehicular traffic counts
transportation
visibility
lease terms
impulse sales
specifically planned purchases
generally planned purchases
substitute purchases
in-store decision rate

conglomerate merchant (conglomerchant)
understored trading area
overstored trading area
saturated trading area
saturation ratios
leveraged buyout (LBO)
hidden assets
strategic profit model
asset turnover
net profit margin
financial leverage
independent retailer
management succession
chain retailers
product/trademark franchising
business format franchising
merchandise width
merchandise depth
merchandise consistency
low-end strategy retailers
high-end strategy retailers
convenience stores
supermarkets
conventional supermarkets
superstores
combination stores
warehouse stores
buying clubs (membership clubs)
specialty stores
free-rider phenomenon
category killer
variety store
department stores
conventional department store
full-line discount store
retail catalog showrooms
off-price chains
factory outlets
flea markets
vending machines
direct selling
direct marketing
formality
pure centralized buying organization
geographic-based buying organization
product-based buying organizations
buying philosophy
merchandising orientation
inside buying organization
resident buying offices
outside buying organization
cooperative buying organization
opportunistic buying

QUESTIONS FOR DISCUSSION

1. Evaluate the argument that the department store is as "extinct as the dinosaur."
2. a. Distinguish among sales growth, real sales growth, and same-store sales growth.
   b. How can each of these measures be used to assess the maturity of a retail institution type?
3. How can a retail furniture chain increase its average sale? Refer to Management Horizons' impact model in your answer.
4. What problems and opportunities arise due to high seasonality in retailing?
5. Describe the implications of retail market saturation to retailers.
6. a. Why have many leveraged buyouts involved retailers?
   b. What is the impact of a leveraged buyout on a retailer's overall retail strategy?
7. a. Describe each element in the strategic profit model.
   b. How can a retailer increase its asset turnover? net profit margin? financial leverage?
8. What are the competitive advantages of a retail chain versus an independent retailer? Explain your answer.

9. What are the competitive advantages of a franchise system of organization versus chain ownership from the perspective of the franchisor? Explain your answer.
10. Differentiate among a convenience store, a conventional supermarket, a superstore, and a buying club.
11. Differentiate among a conventional department store, a full-line discount store, and a retail catalog showroom.
12. a. Differentiate among direct selling and direct marketing.
    b. What environmental factors will affect direct selling? direct marketing?
13. Develop an appropriate buying organization for a department store chain.
14. Differentiate between an appropriate buying organization in an off-price chain versus a buying club.

END NOTES

1. Amy Feldman, "But It Wasn't Broken," *Forbes* (March 14, 1994), pp. 66–67; and Annetta Miller, Dody Tsiantar, Peter Annin, et al., "Remaking a Dinosaur," *Newsweek* (February 10, 1992), pp. 42–43.

2. Barry Berman and Joel R. Evans, *Retail Management: A Strategic Approach,* 6th ed. (Englewood Cliffs, N.J.: Prentice Hall, 1995), p. 4.

3. *Kmart Corporation Annual Report Fiscal 1993,* p. 3; and *Kmart Corporation Corporate Profile 1993.*

4. "62nd Annual Report of the Grocery Industry," *Progressive Grocer* (April 1995), p. 26.

5. "Retailing: Basic Analysis," *Standard & Poor's Industry Surveys* (June 15, 1995), p. R82

6. Ibid.

7. "62nd Annual Report of the Grocery Industry," p. 26.

8. Ibid.

9. See *POPAI Consumer Buying Habits Study* and Jonathan Rabinovitz, "Influencing Shoppers During the Moment of Decision," *New York Times* (August 18, 1991), p. F4.

10. See Christopher J. Carey, "Boost Sales by Converting Browsers into Buyers," *Discount Store News* (September 23, 1991), pp. 16 ff.

11. Rabinovitz, "Influencing Shoppers During the Moment of Decision," p. F4.

12. Author's computations from *Current Business Reports, Monthly Retail Trade: Sales and Inventories* (Washington, D.C.: Bureau of the Census, February 1994), p. 4.

13. Ibid.

14. *Dayton Hudson Annual Report 1993.*

15. *Melville Annual Report 1993.*

16. *Melville Annual Report 1994.*

17. Laura Bird, "Limited Directors Approve Plan to Split Most Operations into Two Companies," *Wall Street Journal* (May 16,1995), p. B10.

18. *Kmart Annual Report 1994.*

19. Kmart investor relations.

20. Berman and Evans, *Retail Management: A Strategic Approach,* 6th ed., p. 289.

21. Eben Shapiro, "Retailing: Sick Merchants, Capitalist 'Cure,'" *New York Times* (January 6, 1992), p. F2; and Laura Zinn, "Fewer Rings on the Cash Registers," *Business Week* (January 14, 1991), p. 85.

22. Bill Saporito, "Is Wal-Mart Unstoppable?" *Fortune* (May 6, 1991), p. 51.

23. See Steve Weinstein, "The Legacy of Leverage," *Progressive Grocer* (June 1993), pp. 70–72 ff.

24. Stephanie Strom, "Suppliers Set to Ship to Macy," *New York Times* (January 29, 1992), pp. D1, D6.

25. Susan Caminiti, "The New Champs of Retailing," *Fortune* (September 24, 1990), pp. 85–86 ff.; and Susan Caminiti, "Toys "R" Us: After You Win the Fun Begins," *Fortune* (May 2, 1994), p. 76.

26. Zina Moukheiber, "Retailing," *Forbes* (January 2, 1995), pp. 190–193.

27. Patricia Sellers, "Winning over the New Consumer," *Fortune* (July 29, 1991), p. 113.

28. *Business Failure Record* (Wilton, CT: The Dun & Bradstreet Corporation, 1994), p. 8.

29. Saporito, "Is Wal-Mart Unstoppable?" p. 50.

30. See Laura Zinn, "As If Macy's Didn't Have Enough to Worry About," *Business Week* (January 13, 1992), p. 34; and Laura Zinn with Michele Galen, "Short Chapter, Happy Ending," *Business Week* (February 10, 1992), pp. 126–127.

31. See *Franchising in the Economy: 1991–1993* (Washington, D.C.: International Franchise Association, 1994).

32. Jeffrey A. Tannenbaum, "Franchise Failure Rate Is High, Study Says," *Wall Street Journal* (December 17, 1993), p. B2.

33. "62nd Annual Report of the Grocery Industry," p. 9.

34. Teresa D. Williams, "Gasoline Fuels Growth of the Convenience Store Industry," *Chain Store Age Executive* (August 1991), pp. 37A–38A.

35. Peter D. Bennett, ed., *Dictionary of Marketing Terms,* Second Edition (Chicago: American Marketing Association, 1995), p. 279.

36. "62nd Annual Report of the Grocery Industry," p. 9.

37. See Steve Weinstein, "The Hypermarket Jury Is Still Out," *Progressive Grocer* (January 1990), pp. 68–70 ff.

38. "62nd Annual Report of the Grocery Industry," p. 9.

39. Steve Weinstein, "The Power of the Club," *Progressive Grocer* (February 1991), pp. 26–28 ff.

40. Wendy Zellner, "Warehouse Clubs Butt Heads—And Reach for the Ice Pack," *Business Week* (April 19, 1993), p. 34; Alice Bredin, "The Fight Begins," *Stores* (September 1993), p. 23; and "Discount Dynamos Pull in Over $290B," *Discount Store News* (July 3, 1995), p.w 1.

41. Steve Weinstein, "Living with Clubs," *Progressive Grocer* (March 1993), pp. 45–46; and Sellers, "Winning over the New Consumer," p. 124.

42. Computed by the author from David P. Schulz, "The Top 100 Specialty Stores," *Stores* (August 1994), pp. 18–20 ff.

43. Seth Lubove, "Toys "R" Us: The Growing Gets Tough," *Forbes* (April 13, 1992), p. 69.

44. Andrea Adelson, "Woolworth to Shutter 970 Stores," *New York Times* (October 14, 1993), pp. D1, D6.

45. "Retailing: Basic Analysis," p. R76.

46. See Richard A. Rauch, "Retailing's Dinosaurs: Department Stores and Supermarkets," *Business Horizons,* Vol. 34 (September/October 1991), pp. 21–25.

47. "Full-Line Discount Store Productivity," *Discount Store News* (August 5, 1991), p. 37.

48. Christina Duff, "Brighter Lights, Fewer Bargains: Outlets Go Upscale," *Wall Street Journal* (April 11, 1994), p. B1.

49. *Vending Times Census of the Industry 1992.*

50. Sana Siwolop, "Vending-Machine Technology Pushes Electronics Frontier," *New York Times* (July 17, 1994), p. F7.

51. *Direct Selling Association Fact Sheet* (Washington, D.C.: Direct Selling Association).

52. Berman and Evans, *Retail Management: A Strategic Approach,* 6th ed., p. 160.

53. Estimated by the author from N. R. Kleinfeld, "Even for J. Crew, the Mail-Order Boom Days Are Over," *New York Times* (September 2, 1990), Section 3, p. 5; and Edward R. Silverman, "Catalog Companies Struggle to Keep Shoppers at Home," *Newsday* (December 23, 1990), p. 61.

CASE 1

THE GAP: EXAMINING THE STRATEGY OF A SUCCESSFUL RETAILER

The Gap has been called "the most popular and profitable specialty chain in American retailing today." In 1994 sales of The Gap and its GapKids, GapShoes, BabyGap, Old Navy Clothing, and Banana Republic stores increased 11.3 percent over 1993 levels. Profits in 1993 were a healthy 7.8 percent of sales. And over the 1989 to 1994 period, the chain maintained an average sales growth rate of 22 percent per year while maintaining a 35.7 percent return on equity. In 1991 The Gap became the second best-selling clothing brand in the United States after displacing Liz Claiborne Inc. Levi Strauss is the best-selling brand.

On a simplistic level, the long-term strategy of The Gap can be described as "Good style, good quality, good value." But there is much more to the Gap's success.

- The Gap enjoys high sales among a diverse population consisting of all age groups from tots to baby boomers, including the important young adult segment.
- All of The Gap's merchandise is private label. This means less price competition and greater coordination with suppliers than the typical clothing specialty retailer. The Gap designs its clothes, chooses the materials, and closely watches quality control.
- Currently, there are 767 Gap stores in 700 of the country's largest 1500 malls. In 1994 it was set to open an additional 55 stores. There are many opportunities for additional stores in major shopping centers and shopping districts.
- The Gap has also barely tapped opportunities abroad. As of 1993, The Gap only had 39 stores overseas, with nearly all of them in England. It plans a major expansion into Japan.
- The Gap closely monitors its stores to ensure uniformity of presentation. Gap management tells store managers exactly where merchandise is placed in stores; this is called *rationalized retailing*. Rationalized retailing makes a customer immediately comfortable in a new Gap location, since he or she knows where merchandise is. To The Gap, rationalized retailing simplifies fixturing and enables goods to be placed in locations that increase a store's total sales due to impulse purchases.

Several market analysts once forecast a 20 percent annual growth rate in sales for The Gap through 1997, but other analysts are not as optimistic. Particularly distressing to some analysts is The Gap's 1992 profit decline; this was the first drop in profits since 1984. The price of Gap Inc.'s stock also slid more than 50 percent between early 1992 and September 1993. Among the concerns of market analysts and stockholders are oversaturating markets; increased competition from such retailers as department stores, The Limited, and Dayton Hudson's new Everyday Hero chain; and The Gap's inability to adapt (when tastes change from denim and khaki to other fibers).

Gap management acknowledged its disappointing results in 1992 as being due to a decline in the importance of basic clothing and increased competition. The Gap plans to refine its long-term strategy to include:

- The addition of more fashionable and higher priced clothing. Although these goods carry higher profit margins, they also involve greater risk. Gap's president conceded, "We're going to make mistakes, but we have a reasonably good record in figuring these things out." Many Gap locations now sell shoes and workout gear. And jewelry and small leather accessories are now sold at Banana Republic.

- The Gap has reached out to the low-end clothing customer through its warehouse concept called Old Navy Clothing Company. The new chain is designed to target customers who traditionally shop at JC Penney, Target, Sears, Mervyn's, and Marshalls. The Gap has tested the warehouse concept at 48 of its least profitable stores in an attempt to turn them around in 1993. In 1995 it plans to open between 40 and 45 Old Navy stores. About 80 percent of Old Navy's merchandise sells for $22 or less. The firm recognizes that this strategy can backfire if it attracts The Gap's traditional customers. Some analysts think that Old Navy can generate as much as $3 billion in sales by the end of the decade and could grow at 20 percent per year.

- Lastly, The Gap is increasingly opening up in more downtown and urban neighborhood locations. Leasing space in shopping strips built around either a Wal-Mart or a Sports Authority store is less costly. Rent is typically 5 percent less than in a regional mall. In addition, property owners often pay for site improvements.

QUESTIONS

1. How do the special characteristics of retailing affect The Gap?
2. Apply Figure 3-1, "Management Horizons' Impact Model," to The Gap.
3. a. How can a traditional department store effectively compete against The Gap?
   b. What are The Gap's competitive advantages as compared to a traditional department store?
4. What is the most appropriate buying organization for The Gap? Explain your choice.

Source: Christina Duff, "Gap's New Line Goes Beyond the Basics," *Wall Street Journal* (August 12, 1993), p. B1; *Gap Inc. 1993 Annual Report;* Russell Mitchell, "The Gap," *Business Week* (March 9, 1992), pp. 58–64; Zina Moukheiber, "Retailing," *Forbes* (January 2, 1995), pp. 190–191; and Stephanie Strom, "How Gap Inc. Spells Revenge," *New York Times* (April 24, 1994), pp. F1, F6.

CASE 2

HOME DEPOT: A POWER RETAILER DOMINATES HOME IMPROVEMENT SALES IN THE DO-IT-YOURSELF AND CONTRACTOR SEGMENTS

Home Depot is recognized by retail experts as the premier power retailer in the home improvement sector. Before Home Depot, the home improvement retail market was dominated by small, fragmented lumber yards and plumbing wholesalers that catered to contractors and knowledgeable do-it-yourselfers. Home Depot reformatted the market as the leading national home improvement retailer. Even though Home Depot operated in only 23 states with 264 stores in 1993, its estimated total U.S. market share has been estimated by market analysts at 7 percent. The firm's national presence will expand significantly when its expansion plans in the Midwest are completed.

Some of the important elements in the firm's retail strategy relate to choice of product lines, staff selection, staff training, inventory management, and everyday low pricing.

Home Depot carries only items for which it can be the dominant supplier. For example, it discontinued selling unfinished furniture despite its having a profitable $80 million in sales when it realized that it could not displace IKEA as a leading furniture retailer. And while half of its customers are female, the chain does not sell such items as pantyhose.

According to the firm's chief executive, "We could be the biggest pantyhose seller in America, but we don't want to weaken the link in shoppers' minds between Home Depot and do-it-yourself projects."

In contrast with many competitors that have hired traditional salespeople with little or no technical knowledge, Home Depot seeks out carpenters and electricians as salespeople. These salespeople not only can answer technical questions posed by customers (such as how to install a replacement electric switch), but also conduct workshops on a regular basis (such as demonstrations on how to install kitchen cabinets). Home Depot keeps turnover among its sales staff low by promoting from within. High growth in terms of store openings and same-store sales growth gives these salespeople a fast career path.

Home Depot invests heavily in training its sales staff. Whereas competitors hire salespeople who are asked to immediately go on the floor, Home Depot requires that its salespeople learn every item in the aisle of their store—and in the two adjacent aisles. Salespeople are also given updates on products from vendors. Salespeople receive specialized training in salesmanship. Staff visit factories to be given updated information on new products, and they learn about products through the retailer's own closed-circuit television. While many of Home Depot's competitors hire salespeople with little technical knowledge, Home Depot seeks out retired or out-of-work contractors who can offer consumers practical advice on home repairs or product choice.

Each Home Depot store stocks over 30,000 different types of building materials, home improvement supplies, and lawn and garden products. No other competitor stocks such variety and depth of merchandise. The majority of stores also feature the installation of home improvement products. Large inventories coupled with high customer service make Home Depot a destination store. Many consumers bypass several conventional home improvement retailers to shop at Home Depot. To ensure high customer service, the firm is especially watchful of its inventory levels. According to one top manager, the worst three words that can be heard by a customer are that "It's on order." Despite high inventory stocks on fast-selling goods, Home Depot's inventory turnover is six times per year; this is the highest in the industry.

Home Depot uses an everyday low pricing strategy. In everyday low pricing, goods are priced at the same price throughout the year. (There are some exceptions because of special buys and sales to clear out seasonal merchandise.) Proponents of everyday low pricing suggest that this strategy reduces a retailer's advertising expense, reduces wide fluctuations in sales (between a sales price and regular price offer), increases trust in the retailer, and results in a more value-oriented retail image. For example, this strategy enabled Home Depot to reduce its advertising expense from 3.2 percent of sales in 1985 to 0.5 percent of sales in 1993.

QUESTIONS

1. Evaluate Home Depot's overall retail strategy.
2. How can a department store effectively compete against Home Depot? Explain your answer.
3. What buying organization is most appropriate for Home Depot? Explain your answer.
4. Evaluate Home Depot as a potential retailer for a brand of nationally advertised replacement windows; for a line of portable phones with no national image.

Sources: Isadore Barmash, "The 'How' in Home Improvement," *New York Times* (June 14, 1992), p. F5; Claudia H. Deutsch, "With Much Hand-Holding, Retailers Are Turning Hobbyists into Builders," *New York Times* (June 2, 1991), p. F5; Gary Hoover, Alta Campbell, and Patrick J. Spain, eds., *Hoover's Handbook of American Business 1995* (Austin, Tex.: Reference Press, 1994), pp. 610–611; *The Home Depot 1993 Annual Report;* and Lee Montgomery, "Home Depot: Role Model for DIY Competition," *Discount Store News* (August 17, 1992), pp. 3 ff.

CHAPTER 4

WHOLESALE CHANNEL MEMBERS

CHAPTER OBJECTIVES

1. To analyze the structure of wholesaling, including wholesale sales volume, wholesale trends, and important statistics relating to wholesaling.

2. To determine the special characteristics of wholesaling: multiple layers of wholesalers, representation of multiple manufacturers, and geographic concentration of wholesale sales and establishments.

3. To study a classification system of wholesalers according to manufacturer wholesaling, merchant wholesalers, and agents and brokers.

4. To describe the components of manufacturer/supplier—wholesaler contracts.

Premier Industrial Corporation is a broad line distributor of electronic and electrical components. The firm is a major supplier of maintenance products for industrial, commercial, and institutional applications, as well as a manufacturer of high-performance fire-fighting accessories.

Premier Industrial is viewed by many market analysts as one of the most aggressive and successful industrial distributors in the United States. Premier mails its 1500+ page catalog to some 1 million customers; the catalog lists the 120,000 products the firm has in stock. The catalog includes detailed product information, technical drawings, and reference tools to facilitate ordering the correct product. In addition to the catalog, Premier uses 1000 telemarketing salespeople to follow up on catalog sales.

Premier prides itself on fast service. It is able to ship most of the items in its catalog within 24 hours; the company can even accommodate emergency shipments with faster speed. Premier Industrial has recorded many incidents that verify its ability to quickly handle an emergency order. Recently, Disney World, a regular Premier customer, called Premier with an emergency request for a replacement part necessary to reopen a closed ride. The wholesaler supplied the part to Disney World within hours. According to Premier's chief executive officer, "That kind of service is a customer's right and we're fanatics about it."

In an industry where price discounting is relatively common, Premier does not discount prices. Instead, it concentrates on providing value-added services to its customers. For example, customers purchasing its premium diesel oil can receive a computer analysis of their used oil. The analysis is helpful in determining an engine's condition. For example, excessive levels of copper in the oil means that the engine bearings are worn; too much chrome in the used oil means that the engine's piston rings need replacement. This analysis is extremely important to Premier's customers in that it determines what maintenance is necessary; it also avoids costly engine breakdowns.

Fast order-response times and excellent customer service are practiced by many of Premier's competitors. What sets Premier apart from these competitors is that Premier's average order size is only $130. Many competitors would not fill an order this small. In fact, Premier sales personnel often get referrals from other distributors who cannot profitably handle small accounts. Premier Industrial also stocks some low-turnover items that many competitors would not handle. For example, the firm stocks 50-cent clips that attach chrome to older cars. It also stocks innovative items such as a new special pen used by automobile mechanics to reconnect damaged rear-window defroster wiring.

A one-stop shopping environment, high levels of customer service, value-added services, the acceptance of small orders, and the stocking of unique items all combine to give Premier high levels of customer loyalty. They also contribute to high profitability and sales growth. In fiscal year 1994, Premier had net income as a percentage of sales of 12.7 percent (on sales of $739 million); its return on equity was also an impressive 23 percent.[1]

In this chapter, we learn about the structure of wholesaling and the special characteristics of wholesaling. We study a classification system for wholesalers, including full-service merchant wholesalers such as Premier Industrial Corporation. The chapter also covers the components of manufacturer/supplier—wholesaler contracts.

WHOLESALE STRUCTURE

This section describes the structure of wholesaling. Included here are the definition of wholesaling, wholesale sales volume, and important statistics relating to wholesaling.

As stated in Chapter 1, **wholesaling** involves the buying or handling of merchandise and its subsequent resale to organizational users, retailers, and/or other wholesalers but not the sale of significant volume to final consumers.[2]

Wholesaling, by definition, includes all sales to organizational users. Thus, the sale of an automobile transmission component to Ford Motor Company and the sale of cleaning supplies to a supermarket are both considered part of wholesaling. Wholesaling does not have to directly involve a manufacturer. The sale of caviar by a fish specialty wholesaler to a supermarket is also part of wholesaling. In some cases, wholesalers resell goods to other wholesalers, such as the sale of caviar by a fish specialty wholesaler to a general-merchandise wholesaler.

Lastly, some institutions straddle the line between wholesaling and retailing such as a buying club that sells significant volume to both small businesses and to final consumers, a home improvement chain that sells goods to both contractors and do-it-yourselfers, and an office supply chain that sells stationery, computers, and computer supplies to small businesses, students, and the general public.

TOTAL WHOLESALE SALES

The U.S. wholesaling industry had $3.2 trillion in sales in 1992 (see Table 4-1). Wholesale sales are higher than retail sales since they include purchases made by organizational users. They are also higher owing to double-counting. Unlike in retailing, where goods are sold through only one retailer before reaching the final consumer, in wholesaling, many goods are sold through multiple levels of wholesalers.

Thirty-two percent of wholesale sales volume for 1992 (the latest year for which data are available) was accounted for by manufacturers' sales branches and offices, manufacturers that perform the wholesale function (see Table 4-2). Sixty-eight percent of the sales volume of products in 1992 were distributed through independent wholesalers. The largest category of independent wholesaler is the merchant wholesaler. Merchant wholesalers take title to goods and are compensated on the basis of discounts received for services rendered, for purchasing in large quantities, for participating in promotions, and so on. Merchant wholesalers accounted for 57.2 percent of wholesale sales volume in 1992.

Unlike merchant wholesalers, agents, brokers, and commission merchants do not take title to goods. These wholesalers are primarily responsible for matching buyers and sellers and are typically paid on the basis of commissions from manufacturers. Agents, brokers, and commission merchants accounted for 10.8 percent of 1992 wholesale sales volume.

TABLE 4-1 WHOLESALE TRADE ESTABLISHMENTS, SALES, AND PAYROLL, 1992

Type of Wholesaler	Establishments	Sales ($000)	Annual Payroll ($000)
Manufacturers' sales branches and offices	35,953	1,039,729,165	36,724,453
Merchant wholesalers	414,836	1,858,627,115	127,987,185
Agents, brokers, and commission merchants	44,668	351,517,671	8,560,848
Total wholesale trade	495,457	3,249,873,951	173,272,486

Source: 1992 Census of Wholesale Trade: Geographic Area Series (Washington, D.C.: Bureau of the Census, January 1995), US 9.

WHOLESALE TRENDS

The three-year period 1990–1993 was not a good one for the nation's wholesalers. During these years, wholesalers were subject to increased actions by large mass-market discounters (such as Wal-Mart) that have attempted to bypass wholesalers by buying direct from manufacturers, and increased pressure to maintain health-care costs (for hospital distributors). In addition, traditional wholesalers have been subject to competition from new distribution channels. According to the National Association of Wholesaler-Distributors (NAW), gross profits as a percentage of sales was 21.1 percent in 1993.[3] Table 4-3 shows profit and operating expense data for a sample of wholesalers.

A 1993 survey of more than 700 manufacturing and distribution executives conducted by the NAW, as summarized in a report entitled *Facing the Forces of Change 2000,* concluded that distributors need to add new products and services to customers, internationalize their operations to a greater extent, and improve productivity.[4] The next section reviews the major trends facing whole-

TABLE 4-2 WHOLESALE TRADE ESTABLISHMENTS, SALES, AND PAYROLL, 1992 (IN PERCENT)

Type of Wholesaler	Establishments	Sales ($000)	Annual Payroll ($000)
Manufacturers' sales branches and offices	7.3	32.0	21.2
Merchant wholesalers	83.7	57.2	73.9
Agents, brokers, and commission merchants	9.0	10.8	4.9
Total wholesale trade	100.0	100.0	100.0

Source: 1992 Census of Wholesale Trade: Geographic Area Series (Washington, D.C.: Bureau of the Census, January 1995), US 9.

TABLE 4-3 SELECTED PERFORMANCE DATA FOR U.S. WHOLESALERS BY PRODUCT CATEGORY[a] (DATA COVER THE PERIOD OCTOBER 1, 1993, THROUGH MARCH 31, 1994, FOR WHOLESALERS WITH ANNUAL SALES OF $25 MILLION OR OVER)

Product Category of Wholesaler	Gross Profit (As Percent of Sales)[b]	Operating Expenses (As Percent of Sales)	All Other Expenses (As Percent of Sales)	Profit Before Taxes (As Percent of Sales)
Books, periodicals, and newspapers	25.7	23.5	0.1	2.1
Building materials	18.1	16.8	0.4	0.9
Chemicals and allied products	19.9	16.7	0.7	2.5
Computers, peripheral equipment, and software	22.4	19.7	0.5	2.1
Drugs, drug proprietaries, and druggists' supplies	18.2	14.5	0.5	3.2
Electrical supplies and apparatus	20.5	18.9	0.8	0.8
Electrical appliances, television, and radio sets	16.2	14.9	0.3	1.0
Farm supplies	14.0	12.8	0.2	1.0
Fish and seafood	10.6	9.1	0.6	1.0
Floor coverings	21.2	19.4	0.5	1.3
Footwear	34.4	25.1	0.9	8.4
General groceries	16.1	14.4	0.3	1.4
General merchandise	25.2	22.7	0.9	1.6
Hardware and paints	27.4	22.7	0.4	4.2
Jewelry	22.5	17.7	1.0	3.8
Industrial machinery and equipment	24.6	20.5	0.4	3.7
Motor vehicle supplies and new parts	29.3	24.2	0.7	4.5
Tires and tubes	20.0	17.9	0.2	2.0
Wine, liquor, and beer	21.0	18.1	0.4	2.6

[a]In interpreting these data, Robert Morris Associates cautions that the Studies be regarded only as a general guideline and not as an absolute industry norm. This is due to limited samples within categories, the categorization of firms by their primary Standard Industrial Classification (SIC) number only, and different methods of operations by firms within the same industry. For these reasons, RMA recommends that the figures be used only as general guidelines in addition to other methods of financial analysis.
[b]Total costs of wholesaling, which include expenses and profit. There may be some small discrepancies in the numbers due to rounding.
Source: Adapted from '94 Annual Statement Studies (Philadelphia: Robert Morris Associates, 1994). © 1994, Robert Morris Associates; reprinted by permission.

salers. These include increased competition from power retailers, broadening of merchandise lines, manufacturer downsizing, the growth of the modular corporation, international expansion, increased computerization, and the increased importance of large distributors due to mergers and acquisitions.

INCREASED COMPETITION FROM POWER RETAILERS

Wholesalers are now being subject to increased competition from **power retailers**, retailers that have a high market share in their merchandise category, high store loyalty, and high bargaining power relative to their suppliers. Examples of power retailers include Wal-Mart, Sam's, Price/Costco, CompUSA, and Staples. Many of these retailers have begun to bypass traditional wholesalers and to purchase directly from manufacturers. The wholesaler loses direct sales from the power retailer and indirect sales from consumers who now buy from the power retailer versus traditional resellers (that were supplied from the wholesaler)[5] (see Figure 4-1).

BROADENING OF MERCHANDISE LINES

Wholesalers have broadened their merchandise lines to take advantage of growth opportunities and of scrambled merchandising by their retailer customers and to offer a wider variety of merchandise. This strategy better enables a wholesaler's customers to successfully compete against new competitors, to have the convenience of ordering goods for one supplier, and increases their opportunities for additional sales owing to related-item selling. For example, Stationers Distributing Company added furniture and computers to its product lines. This change enables its traditional office supply customers to compete more effectively against such discounters as Office Depot, OfficeMax, and Staples. These goods are provided to its office supply retailer customers on an overnight delivery basis. Bearings Inc. has also added products and services such as motors, belts, and drives to the firm's traditional line of industrial bearings. It also has begun to do energy audits of motors.[6]

In an extension of broadening merchandise lines, some large industrial distributors have become integrated supply wholesalers. An **integrated supply contract** is a long-term contract that names the wholesaler as sole supplier for the firm's needs in a given product area (such as maintenance, repair, and operating supplies) and geographic area. The integrated supply wholesaler generally sets up third-party supply arrangements with other distributors to carry the products and brands needed by its customers.[7] As with scrambled merchandising by retailers, wholesalers need to be concerned about their ability to adequately service these products.

MANUFACTURER DOWNSIZING

For many distributors, manufacturer downsizing has created opportunities for additional business. As a consequence of downsizing, many manufacturers have cut out smaller customers and begun to concentrate on larger accounts.

FIGURE 4-1 The effect of power retailers on wholesalers.

A distribution channel without a power retailer

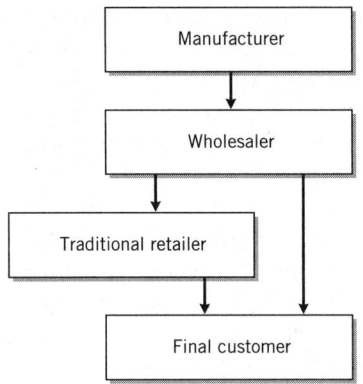

A distribution channel with a power retailer

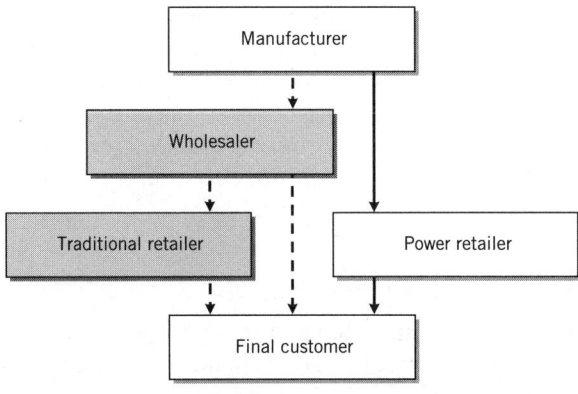

Source: Robert F. Lusch and Deborah Zizzo, *Competing for Customers* (Washington, D.C.: Distribution Research and Education Foundation, 1995), p. 14. Reprinted by permission.

Many are also walking away from lower margin accounts.[8] Many of these accounts can be profitably handled by wholesalers that service the accounts of multiple manufacturers.

There are opportunities for wholesalers at both ends of the price-service spectrum. Price-based wholesalers can service small accounts through catalog sales and telemarketing. In contrast, service-based wholesalers can offer smaller accounts high levels of customer service but at higher prices.

GROWTH OF THE MODULAR CORPORATION

A trend related to manufacturer downsizing is the growth of the modular corporation. In a **modular corporation,** a manufacturer outsources production activities to independent, but closely coordinated, organizations. The modular corporation enables firms to perform as wholesalers through outsourcing marketing functions to others. According to Professor Webster,

> *Across the board—for all factors of production including parts and subassemblies, services such as transportation and maintenance, and professional marketing services such as marketing research, some selling functions, and most distribution functions—the bias has shifted from "make" to "buy," from ownership to partnership, from fixed cost to variable cost, but in the context of stable, long-term relationships.*[9]

Two examples of modular corporations are Reebok and Dell.[10] Through the use of modular corporation formats, these traditional manufacturers function as wholesalers. Although Reebok designs and markets high-tech footwear, it does not own a single plant. Instead, all production is contracted out to independent suppliers located in Taiwan, South Korea, and other parts of Asia. Through outsourcing production, Reebok is technically a wholesaler. Outsourcing enables Reebok to conserve capital and to focus on its marketing competencies while leaving production to others.

Dell now sells 650 computer programs, a full range of modems, and much more. But it does not produce or even stock the items. Dell orders goods from Merisel, a large distributor, which then delivers the goods directly to the buyer. Dell's buyers now have the advantage of being able to order a wide variety of goods from a single source. And the ordering and delivery process is so well integrated between Dell and Merisel that most customers do not even know multiple parties are involved.

INTERNATIONAL EXPANSION

Like other marketers, wholesalers have increased their international expansion plans. By the year 2000, the National Association of Wholesaler-Distributors (NAW) predicts that U.S.-based wholesalers will generate 18 percent of their revenues in foreign markets; this compares to about 9 percent in 1993.[11] Part of the increased push on foreign markets can be attributed to the North American Free Trade Agreement (prior to NAFTA, Mexico restricted joint ventures involving foreign firms), partly because of the realization that sales opportunities are greater abroad than in the United States and partly because of customer needs. For example, VWR, a $500 million a year distributor of laboratory equipment, began selling to Canada as a result of pressure from Du Pont Corporation, a major customer. Du Pont wanted to deal with fewer suppliers and sought a supplier who would be able to meet its customer service and quality expectations. VWR is now the third largest wholesaler of lab equipment in Canada.[12] Other examples of foreign expansion are McKesson's Canadian pharmaceutical operations, Fleming's supermarket operations in Mexico, and Wetterau's extensive foreign operations.

INCREASED COMPUTERIZATION

Wholesalers have also increased their use of computerization to improve customer service and to lower costs. Inventory management, sales force reporting, and credit management activities are particularly conducive to computerization. Some of these functions, such as inventory management, can be tied in directly to suppliers and customers.[13]

New tools such as electronic data interchange (EDI), which enables paperless communication between wholesalers, their suppliers, and customers; bar coding of inventory; and computerized order entry are being used by an increasingly large number of wholesalers to increase customer service as well as to reduce costs. For example, Bergen Brunswig Company, a major pharmaceutical distributor, recently opened four fully automated distribution centers that can take electronically transmitted purchase orders. The center can fulfill these orders automatically in its computerized warehouse.[14]

Unfortunately, the use of computerization appears to be related to a wholesaler's size. The NAW study found that 60 percent of large wholesalers (with annual sales of $5 million or more), but only 15 percent of small wholesalers (with annual sales of under $1 million), use EDI. Similarly, 8 percent of the large wholesalers use bar coding, but only 3 percent of small wholesalers do.[15]

Increased Importance of Large Distributors Due to Mergers and Acquisitions

Mergers and acquisitions among wholesalers have increased the ability of wholesalers to serve their manufacturer/suppliers on one hand and their customers on the other. They also can provide economies of scale to the larger firm.[16] The NAW study predicts a 15 percent reduction in wholesalers between 1993 and 2000 owing to the net effect of mergers and acquisitions, business failures, and business startups. The NAW study forecasts that large distributors will have a 52 percent market share in the year 2000 (up from 43 percent in 1993). Economies of scale was cited as the major reason for mergers and acquisitions among larger wholesalers, according to the partner in charge of Arthur Andersen's Worldwide Distribution Practice. Among small and medium-sized businesses, the primary reason was to build business by gaining market share.[17]

Recent mergers and acquisitions among wholesalers include SuperValu's acquisition of Wetterau; United Stationers Inc.'s purchase of Stationers Distributing Co.; Fleming Companies Inc.'s acquisition of Serivner (the third largest food distributor in the United States); Owens & Minor Inc.'s acquisition of Stuart Medical Inc. (a major medical distributor); Bergen Brunswig Corporation's purchase of Durr-Fillauer Medical; and General Medical Corporation's acquisition of F. D. Titus Inc. (another medical wholesaler). The mergers and acquisitions will increase the relative strength and market share of large distributors. Merger activity among wholesalers is also being driven by manufacturers such as Du Pont and Union Carbide that prefer to deal with few large suppliers rather than many smaller ones. In some cases, these manufacturers have sole-sourcing agreements with selected wholesalers.

A potential problem associated with the increase in merger activity among both wholesalers and manufacturer/suppliers is the increased potential for a wholesaler to represent a competing line of products. In many cases, manufacturer/supplier contracts with their wholesalers prohibit wholesalers from representing directly competing products from other manufacturers.

Large wholesalers that are able to undertake functions such as inventory management and market research more efficiently than some manufacturers through economies of scale, mechanization, and computerization are called **integrated distributors**.[18] For example, W. W. Grainger, a wholesaler of electric motors and accessories, has 160 branches in more than 30 states. Its annual sales exceeded $2.3 billion in 1994, and it employs over 1100 salespeople. Other integrated distributors are WESCO, G. E. Supply, and Graybar Electric. These firms have high power in the channel of distribution. They can determine which manufacturer's products they will stock, they can exercise control over product quality, and in many cases they have better resources than the manufacturers they represent.[19]

It is also probable that large wholesalers will increasingly go into retailing to increase sales opportunities, to give themselves a captive market, and to foreclose markets to competitors. For example, major food wholesalers such as SuperValu and Fleming operate approximately 258 and 315 corporate stores, respectively.[20] This may generate increased conflict between wholesalers and retailers.

To more effectively compete with large distributors, smaller wholesalers will need to compete by specializing in narrow product lines, by selling to smaller accounts not serviced by larger distributors or manufacturers, and by increasing the services offered to their manufacturer/suppliers and to their wholesale customers. Many wholesalers will also have increased opportunities in serving low-margin accounts that are no longer being serviced by manufacturers owing to their downsized sales forces or increased pressures to lower costs.[21]

IMPORTANT STATISTICS RELATING TO WHOLESALERS

As of the end of 1992 (the most recent data available), operating expenses were 11 percent of sales for all wholesalers. This percentage varied from 4.6 percent for agents, brokers, and commission merchants to 14.3 percent for merchant wholesalers (see Table 4-4).

TABLE 4-4 WHOLESALE TRADE SALES 1992, SELECTED RATIOS BY TYPE OF WHOLESALER

Type of Wholesaler	Sales per Establish.	Sales per Employee	Employees per Establish.	Oper. Exp. (Percent of Sales)
Manufacturers' sales branches and offices	$28,919,121	$1,109,508	26	7.4
Merchant wholesalers	$ 4,480,390	$ 405,105	11	14.3
Agents, brokers, and commission merchants	$ 7,869,564	$1,320,110	6	4.6
Total wholesale trade	$ 6,559,346	$ 561,155	12	11.0

Source: 1992 Census of Wholesale Trade: Geographic Area Series (Washington, D.C.: Bureau of the Census, January 1995), US 22.

WHOLESALE STRUCTURE

TABLE 4-5 WHOLESALE TRADE ESTABLISHMENTS, 1992, BY THE 4, 8, 20, AND 50 LARGEST WHOLESALERS BY TYPE OF WHOLESALER

Type of Wholesaler	4 Largest Firms	8 Largest Firms	20 Largest Firms	50 Largest Firms	Total All Firms
Manufacturers' sales branches and offices	466	1,035	2,822	5,436	35,953
Merchant wholesalers	268	424	1,516	3,700	414,836
Agents, brokers, and commission merchants	74	94	162	261	44,668
Total wholesale trade	508	1,089	2,695	5,935	495,457

Source: 1992 Census of Wholesale Trade: Subject Area Series Establishment and Firm Size (Washington, D.C.: Bureau of the Census, March 1995), 1–194.

Many distributors are still small firms, despite the increase in mergers and acquisitions. For example, as of 1992, the average wholesaler had 12 employees. The average number of employees per establishment ranged from 6 for agents, brokers, and commission merchants to 26 for manufacturers' sales branches and offices (see Table 4-4). Overall, the largest 50 wholesale firms accounted for 12 percent of all wholesale establishments (see Table 4-5) and 20.4 percent of all wholesale sales (see Table 4-6) in 1992 (the latest data available).

The greatest degree of wholesale concentration occurs among manufacturers' sales branches and offices where the top 50 firms account for 15.1 percent of establishments and 49.9 percent of wholesale sales as of 1992. In 1992 the lowest degree of concentration is among agents, brokers, and commission merchants where the largest 50 firms account for 5.8 percent of all wholesale establishments and 17.7 percent of sales.

TABLE 4-6 WHOLESALE TRADE SALES, 1992, BY THE 4, 8, 20, AND 50 LARGEST WHOLESALERS BY TYPE OF WHOLESALER ($000)

Type of Wholesaler	4 Largest Firms	8 Largest Firms	20 Largest Firms	50 Largest Firms	Total All Firms
Manufacturers' sales branches and offices	174,184,106	233,912,696	358,906,773	518,946,337	1,039,729,165
Merchant wholesalers	67,320,267	112,854,272	195,644,749	304,476,226	1,858,627,115
Agents, brokers, and commission merchants	22,146,013	29,892,029	44,689,417	62,384,730	351,517,671
Total wholesale trade	178,156,053	250,971,453	407,169,824	663,999,663	3,249,873,951

Source: 1992 Census of Wholesale Trade: Subject Area Series Establishment and Firm Size (Washington, D.C.: Bureau of the Census, March 1995), 1–194.

THE SPECIAL CHARACTERISTICS OF WHOLESALING

In addition to the special characteristics of all channel members noted in Chapter 1, wholesaling is characterized by multiple layers of wholesaling, wholesaler representation of multiple manufacturer/suppliers, and a high geographic concentration of wholesalers. These are now examined.

MULTIPLE LAYERS OF WHOLESALING

There is generally only one level of retail institution in a channel, but there can be more than one level of wholesale institution. For example, a specialty goods wholesaler may sell goods to a full-line wholesaler. Manufacturers' agents often also sell to other distributors. Lastly, foreign goods often involve multiple wholesalers. See Figure 4-2 for illustrations of multiple layers of wholesalers.

Profit margins assigned to wholesalers need to reflect services performed for other wholesalers in contrast to those performed for retailers and industrial users. Multiple layers of wholesalers also create long channels.

WHOLESALER REPRESENTATION OF MULTIPLE MANUFACTURER

Many wholesalers represent multiple manufacturers. Thus, wholesalers can profitably call on small accounts, serve geographic areas with low sales poten-

FIGURE 4-2 Multiple layers of wholesalers.

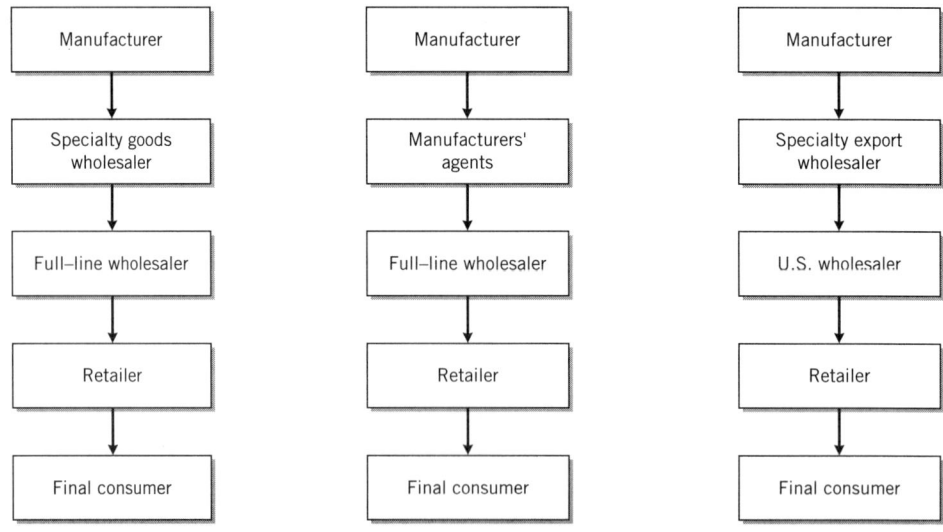

TABLE 4-7 QUESTIONS WHOLESALERS AND MANUFACTURERS SHOULD CONSIDER RELATING TO CONFLICTS DUE TO CARRYING COMPETING BRANDS

1. Will single representation of multiple manufacturers compromise the market or financial objectives of either or both brands?
2. Should a wholesaler be given a trial period to show its ability to effectively merchandise and sell each brand?
3. Can a wholesaler effectively handle promotions on each brand when the promotions overlap in time?
4. Will dual representation hinder the flow of information between each manufacturer and the wholesaler?
5. Can the wholesaler handle all communication in a confidential manner?
6. Does dual representation produce benefits for either or both manufacturers?

Source: Adapted from *Guides for Developing Food Broker-Principal Agreements* (Washington, D.C.: National Food Brokers Association, 1990), p. 5.

tial, and become a one-stop shopping resource for other retailer and end-user customers. A potential difficulty associated with representation of multiple manufacturers is conflict among manufacturers when goods from different manufacturers compete for the same target market. Table 4-7 contains a checklist for manufacturers and wholesalers to consider regarding wholesaler representation of multiple manufacturers.

The National Food Brokers Association and Grocery Manufacturers of America, Inc. differentiates among three levels of conflict: potential, allowable, and real. In a **potential conflict**, conflict occurs when a manufacturer expects to be entering a new product category or to expand the selling area of a product. In an **allowable conflict**, conflicts can be effectively managed without loss of sales or communication for either the company or the broker. With a **real conflict**, the conflict affects sales objectives and communication for one or more of a manufacturer's brands.[22]

According to a policy paper of the National Food Brokers Association and Grocery Manufacturers of America, a potential conflict should not be declared until a product is actually in production and offered for sale in the wholesaler's territory. For allowable conflict, the joint council recommends that clear objectives be established for the wholesaler, that the wholesaler be evaluated against goals, that the manufacturer and wholesaler communicate as to their attitudes toward conflict, and that different account executives be responsible for each brand. When real conflict exists, the council recommends that the wholesaler's contract be terminated and that an orderly transition to a newly appointed wholesaler be planned and implemented.[23]

The code of ethics of the Manufacturers' Agents National Association specifies that the sales agency should "refrain from representing lines, products and goods which compete with those lines, products and goods already contracted for representation" (see Table 4-8).

TABLE 4-8 CODE OF ETHICS OF THE MANUFACTURERS' AGENTS NATIONAL ASSOCIATION

1. To be accorded the Manufacturer by the Sales Agency:

- Comply with established policies of the Manufacturer;
- Conscientiously cover the territory assigned;
- Avoid misrepresentation in any form or manner;
- Restrict lines or accounts with Principals to those which can well be handled;
- Refrain from representing lines, products and goods which compete with those lines, products and goods already contracted for representation; and
- Give the Manufacturer the same loyal service as the Sales Agency, operating its own business, expects from its own employees.

2. To be accorded the Sales Agency by the Manufacturer:

- Enter into a fair and clearly worded written agreement with the Manufacturers' Sales Agency;
- Make the agreement terminable by either party during its first year on suitable cause and advance written notice, but subsequently only for failure of either party to comply with its terms, or by mutual consent;
- Refrain from any modification whatever of the terms of such agreement, except by mutual written consent after full and friendly discussion of the reasons of such desired modification;
- Refrain from absorbing, refusing or cutting the Manufacturers' Sales Agency's established commissions, territory or accounts, except by mutual consent; and
- Agree to practical and dignified means for friendly negotiation of all controversial points that may arise, between Sales Agency and Principal.

3. To be accorded one Manufacturers' Sales Agency by another:

- Exchange trade information, in the mutual interest;
- Avoid any suggestion or agreement to divide commissions with those representing other than the Sales Agency's own Principals;
- Refrain from soliciting from manufacturers the known lines or accounts of other established Manufacturers' Sales Agencies by unfair methods;
- Act in good faith and deal fairly so as not to deprive the other of the fruits of their performance; and
- Cooperate to enhance the professional relationship of the Manufacturers' Sales Agency and its Principal by supporting the National Association established for that purpose, subscribing to its aims and objectives, and in every practical way working to advance the marketing interests of all Manufacturers' Sales Agencies and their Principals.

Source: Reprinted by permission from *Agency Sales Magazine,* Copyright 1995, Manufacturers' Agents National Association, 23016 Mill Creek Road, P.O. Box 3467, Laguna Hills, CA 92654-3467, (714) 859-4040; fax (714) 855-2973. All rights reserved. Reproduction without permission is strictly prohibited.

GEOGRAPHIC CONCENTRATION OF WHOLESALE SALES AND ESTABLISHMENTS

Table 4-9 lists the 10 states with the highest concentrations of wholesale sales as of 1992. In total, the 10 largest states in terms of wholesale sales volume (California, New York, Texas, Illinois, New Jersey, Florida, Ohio, Pennsylvania, Michigan, and Georgia) accounted for 62 percent of total U.S. wholesale sales. These states comprised 56 percent of total U.S. wholesale establishments. Average sales per wholesale establishment were also 11 percent higher in the top-selling 10 wholesale states than for the nation as a whole.

Although many of these establishments are concentrated in the East, one researcher reports a gradual movement of wholesalers from the East to the Midwest and Far West. Part of this movement can be attributed to better transportation facilities, lower operating costs, and the need to better serve the growing far-western markets.[24]

A TYPOLOGY OF WHOLESALERS

There are three broad categories of wholesalers: manufacturer wholesaling, merchant wholesaling, and agents and brokers. The primary difference among the wholesaler categories relates to ownership of the wholesaler, whether the wholesaler takes title to goods, and the method of compensation (see Table 4-10).

In **manufacturer wholesaling**, the manufacturer performs all wholesale functions and owns and controls goods until they are sold. The gross profitability of

TABLE 4-9 THE 10 STATES WITH LARGEST WHOLESALE SALES, 1992

State	Wholesale Sales ($000)	Number of Establishments	Average Sales per Establishment ($000)
California	432,945,928	58,437	7,409
New York	287,738,537	40,934	7,029
Texas	281,273,414	36,611	7,683
Illinois	219,361,442	24,637	8,904
New Jersey	176,021,592	18,444	9,544
Florida	132,562,218	30,137	4,399
Ohio	127,343,908	19,305	6,596
Pennsylvania	126,369,922	20,230	6,247
Michigan	125,670,957	15,517	8,099
Georgia	113,803,382	14,608	7,790
Top 10 states	2,023,091,443	278,860	7,255
Total 50 states	3,249,873,951	495,457	6,559

Source: 1992 Census of Wholesale Trade: Geographic Area Series (Washington, D.C.: Bureau of the Census, January 1995), US 32.

Table 4-10 Key Differences among Manufacturer Wholesaling, Merchant Wholesaling, and Agents and Brokers

	Manufacturer Wholesaling	Merchant Wholesaling	Agents and Brokers
Ownership of goods	Manufacturer	Wholesaler	Manufacturer
Method of compensation	Difference between selling price and transfer price	Difference between selling price and cost of goods sold (reflects functional and other discounts).	Commission rate paid by seller
Control over wholesaling	Maximum	Control varies.	Control varies.
Timing of payment from wholesaler	Based on terms provided to accounts of manufacturer wholesaler.	Based on terms provided to merchant wholesaler. Manufacturer can be paid before merchant wholesaler sells goods.	Based on when goods are sold by agents and brokers.
Capital requirements for wholesaling activities	Manufacturer must finance warehousing, delivery system, inventory, sales force salaries, wholesaling administration costs, and final consumer advertising expenses.	Manufacturer is able to reduce capital expenditures by sharing costs of warehousing, delivery, inventory, personal selling, and advertising with merchant wholesaler.	Manufacturer must finance warehousing, delivery system, inventory expenses, and final consumer advertising expenses. Agents and brokers finance personal selling expenses.
Ideal application	Manufacturer has high capital; manufacturer seeks to tightly control distribution; product is highly technical; customers are large and geographically concentrated; manufacturer has wide and/or deep product mix.	Manufacturer has limited capital; control over wholesaler is not a major issue; wholesalers can be trained in technical aspects of product; customers are small and scattered; manufacturer has narrow and/or shallow product mix.	Manufacturer has limited capital; control over wholesaler is not a major issue; wholesalers can be trained in technical aspects of product; customers are small and scattered; manufacturer has narrow and/or shallow product mix.

manufacturer wholesaling (profits before operating expenses to the wholesaler) is determined by the difference in the wholesale cost charged to the wholesaler and the selling price. The wholesale cost is the **transfer price**, the price charged for goods and services sold through a company-owned channel. Since the manufacturer is also a wholesaler, a higher transfer price yields a higher profit to manufacturing and a lower profit to wholesale operations.

In **merchant wholesaling**, independent wholesalers purchase and take title to products and undertake all wholesale functions. Merchant wholesalers are compensated on the basis of the difference of the cost of goods sold less their sales revenues. Merchant wholesalers generally receive discounts from list price from the manufacturer on the basis of trade discounts for their channel level, functional discounts for undertaking specific activities, quantity discounts for purchasing in quantities, promotional discounts for promotional activities, and cash discounts for early payment of invoices.

Unlike merchant wholesaling, **agents and brokers** do not take title to goods or services. They are compensated on the basis of sales commissions that are typically paid for by sellers. See Figure 4-3 for a typology of wholesale institutions. Table 4-11 details the major functions of wholesale institutions.

FIGURE 4-3 A typology of wholesale institutions.

```
Manufacturer Wholesaling
    Manufacturers' sales office
    Manufacturers' branch office
```

```
Merchant Wholesaling
    Full-service merchant wholesalers
        General merchandise wholesalers
        Specialty merchandise wholesalers
        Rack jobbers
        Franchise wholesalers
        Cooperative wholesalers
            Producer-owned cooperatives
            Retailer-owned cooperatives
    Limited-service merchant wholesalers
        Cash-and-carry wholesalers
        Drop shippers
        Truck/wagon wholesalers
        Mail-order wholesalers
```

```
Agents and Brokers
    Agents
        Manufacturers' agents
        Selling agents
        Commission agents
    Brokers
        Food brokers
        Export brokers
```

TABLE 4-11 MAJOR FUNCTIONS OF WHOLESALE INSTITUTIONS

Institution	Financing	Storage & Delivery	Title	Promotion	Personal Sales Force	Research & Planning	Negotiation	Transportation
Manufacturer Wholesaling								
Manufacturers' sales office	Yes	No	Yes	Yes	Yes	Yes	Yes	Yes
Manufacturers' branch office	Yes	Yes	Yes	Yes	Yes	Yes	Yes	Yes
Merchant Wholesalers								
Full-service merchant wholesalers	Yes	Yes	Yes	Yes	Yes	Yes	Yes	Yes
General-merchandise wholesalers	Yes	Yes	Yes	Yes	Yes	Yes	Yes	Yes
Specialty-merchandise wholesalers	Yes	Yes	Yes	Yes	Yes	Yes	Yes	Yes
Rack jobbers	Yes	Yes	Yes	No[a]	Yes	Yes	Yes	Yes
Franchise wholesalers	Yes	Yes	Yes	Yes	Yes	Yes	Yes	Yes
Cooperative wholesalers								
Producer-owned cooperatives	Yes	Yes	Yes	Yes	Yes	Yes	Yes	Yes
Retailer-owned cooperatives	Yes	Yes	Yes	Yes	Yes	Yes	Yes	Yes
Limited-service merchant wholesalers								
Cash-and-carry wholesalers	No	Stores[b]	Yes	No	No	No	Yes	No
Drop shippers	Yes	Delivers[c]	Yes	Yes	Yes	Some	Yes	Yes
Truck/wagon wholesalers	Yes	Some	Yes	Yes	Yes	No	Yes	Yes
Mail-order wholesalers	Some	Yes	Yes	No	No	Some	Yes	Yes
Agents and Brokers								
Agents								
Manufacturers' agents	No	Some	No	Yes	Yes	Some	Yes	Some
Selling agents	Some	Yes	No	Yes	Yes	Yes	Yes	Some
Commission (factor) merchants	Some	Yes	No	Yes	Yes	Yes	Yes	Some
Brokers								
Food brokers	No	No	No	Yes	Yes	Yes	Yes	Some
Export brokers	No	No	No	Yes	Yes	Yes	Yes	Some

[a]Provides merchandising assistance.
[b]Stores but does not deliver.
[c]Delivers but does not store.

MANUFACTURER WHOLESALING

Manufacturer wholesaling can be accomplished through either manufacturers' sales offices or manufacturers' branch offices. In a **manufacturers' sales office**, a manufacturer conducts wholesale activities in an office that does not contain inventory. Generally, the sales office is located either near the firm's factory or near large concentrations of customers. In contrast, in a **manufacturers' branch office**, the manufacturers have facilities for storing inventory.

Manufacturer wholesaling accounts for 32 percent of wholesale sales and only 7.3 percent of wholesale establishments (see Table 4-2). Sales per establishment are the highest for any wholesaler type. Manufacturers' sales branches and offices have sales per establishment of $28,919,121, over three times that of agents, brokers, and commission merchants (see Table 4-4). Manufacturer wholesaling has operating expenses equal to 7.4 percent of sales (see Table 4-4). Manufacturer wholesaling is more concentrated than other forms of wholesaling. The four largest firms control 16.8 percent of sales, and the 20 largest firms control 34.5 percent of total sales through this wholesale form (see Table 4-6).

Manufacturers' sales offices and branch offices are considered **captive distributors** in that they are owned and operated by their manufacturers. For example, Mead, a forest products, paper, and paperboard manufacturer, sells its products through both independent wholesalers and Mead Merchants, a manufacturer wholesaler.

Manufacturers' sales offices and branch offices often are used when the manufacturer has high capital, when it seeks to tightly control distribution elements such as customer service and wholesale prices, when the product is highly technical, when customers are large and geographically concentrated, when the manufacturer has a wide and/or deep product mix, or when the manufacturer does not want to be represented by a firm that carries competing lines. Manufacturer wholesaling is also especially suitable when major retailers seek electronic data interchange (which requires direct computer hookups between retailer and manufacturer to record sales), or when ideal wholesalers are not available.

In some cases, manufacturer wholesaling evolves when independent wholesalers are forced out by retailers that wish to deal directly with manufacturers, or when manufacturers terminate contracts with independent wholesalers.

The disadvantages of using manufacturer wholesaling versus independent wholesalers are that high turnover of manufacturer personnel makes establishing long-term relationships with accounts difficult, independent wholesalers have greater incentive to build up territories than manufacturers, independent wholesalers can more profitably service smaller accounts, and independent wholesalers are more prone to service an entire account's needs.

MERCHANT WHOLESALING

As defined previously, in merchant wholesaling independent wholesalers purchase and take title to products. Merchant wholesalers are the largest category of wholesalers, accounting for 57.2 percent of wholesale sales and 83.7 percent of wholesale establishments (see Table 4-2). However, of the three categories of wholesalers, sales per establishment and sales per employee are lowest for merchant wholesalers. Sales per establishment are less than $4.5 million (less than 16 percent of the average for manufacturers' sales branches and offices), and sales per employee are approximately $400,000 (about 37 percent of the average manufacturers' sales branches and offices) (see Table 4-4).

Merchant wholesaling is ideally used when a manufacturer has limited capital, control over the wholesaler is not a major issue, wholesalers can be trained in technical aspects of the product, customers are small and geographically scattered, and the manufacturer has a narrow and/or shallow product mix.

Generally, merchant wholesalers are further classified into full-service and limited-service merchant wholesalers on the basis of functions performed.

FULL-SERVICE MERCHANT WHOLESALERS

Full-service merchant wholesalers generally conduct a wide variety of wholesale functions that include provision of credit to customers, storage and delivery of goods, merchandising and promotional assistance, and market research. In contrast, **limited-service merchant wholesalers** do not perform all the services that full-service wholesalers perform. They may not provide one or more of the following functions: credit, storage and delivery of goods, merchandising and promotional assistance, and marketing research.

An example of a full-service merchant wholesaler is Baxter International Inc., a manufacturer and distributor of a diversified line of products used primarily in the health-care field. Through the firm's ValueLink automated purchasing system, large customers such as major hospitals can order goods directly from Baxter using a telephone-linked terminal. The ValueLink system also provides the hospital with computerized price information and order confirmation. ValueLink enables the hospital to reduce ordering costs. It also permits major hospitals to reduce inventory carrying costs by delivering health-care products to individual hospital departments on a just-in-time basis. The ValueLink program virtually eliminates the need for a hospital to warehouse products. As of 1993, 53 hospitals were on Baxter's ValueLink program. In 1994 annual sales through the ValueLink program were expected to exceed $400 million.[25]

Five types of full-service merchant wholesalers are general merchandise, specialty merchandise, rack jobbers, franchise wholesalers, and cooperative wholesalers.

General-merchandise (full-line) merchant wholesalers generally carry almost all of the items required by their customers. A general-merchandise industrial distributor such as a mill supply house may stock such items as paint, small hand tools, nuts and bolts, abrasives, and maintenance supplies. In addition to offering one-stop shopping convenience for their customers, general-merchandise wholesalers make it easier for their customers to receive quantity discounts. Full-line wholesalers may be defined in product terms such as chemical wholesaler or steel warehouses, or may be classified by a customer category such as a hospital supply house or office supply dealer.

CHANNELS IN ACTION

Customer Service: Direct Distribution Versus Industrial Distributors

A study of British firms that buy industrial products (such as hand tools, fasteners, raw materials, lubricants, and routine office supplies) compared the ability of direct versus distributor channels to provide customer service. Respondents were asked to indicate on a five-point scale the influence of each of 21 factors in their selection of suppliers. The scale ranged from 1 (no influence) to 5 (very strong influence). Fifteen of the 21 factors were mentioned by over 90 percent of the sample; the least cited criterion was cited by 69 percent of the sample. The top 10 criteria in order of influence were price competitiveness, keeps promises, helpful in emergencies, product quality, fair and trustworthy, previous performance, product availability, delivery service, technical know-how, and response to complaints.

Neither direct nor distributor channels adequately met industrial customer needs. Of the 14 highest ranking buyer influences, distributors underperformed on 13 influences and direct sellers underperformed on 12 influences.

Performance on buyer influences differed significantly among distributors and direct sellers. Distributors performed significantly better than direct sellers on the following attributes: keeps promises, helpful in emergencies, product availability, delivery service, and relations with buyer. On the other hand, direct sellers outperformed distributors on these dimensions: price competitiveness, product quality, technical know-how, and adapt to specifications. There were no significant differences in the other variables studied. Four of the competitive advantages of distributors can be attributed to their narrow geographic coverage and their ability to build customer relations and react rapidly when required. In contrast, direct sellers outperformed distributors on such product-related attributes as technical know-how, product customization, and quality.

Forty-five percent of the buyers preferred purchasing from direct sellers, and 7 percent preferred distributors. Forty-eight percent of respondents cited no preference in dealing with either direct sellers or distributors.

Source: David Shipley, Colin Egan, and Scott Edgett, "Meeting Source Selection Criteria," *Industrial Marketing Management,* Vol. 20 (November 1991), pp. 297–303.

Specialty-merchandise (limited-line) merchant wholesalers generally specialize in a narrow range of products and have an extensive assortment within that range (such as paint or small hand tools). These wholesalers often sell products and have specialized expertise that is not offered by general-merchandise wholesalers. In industrial products, specialty-merchandise merchant wholesalers can be very highly specialized and cover a broad geographic area.

Rack jobbers provide and maintain general merchandise that is sold on a consignment basis to self-service-based mass merchants. In addition to retaining title to goods until they are sold by retailers, rack jobbers maintain inventory records, pricemark goods, provide racks, and fill in merchandise on racks as needed. Rack jobbers typically handle nonfood merchandise (such as housewares, books, tools, cosmetics, health-and-beauty aids, and stationery) that is sold in supermarkets, combination stores, hardware, variety, and drug stores. Rack jobbers are a major factor behind the sales of nonfoods in grocery stores and behind scrambled merchandising.

In **franchise wholesaling**, independently owned retailers affiliate with an existing wholesaler and use a common retail strategy. Common elements of retail strategy generally include a common store name, cooperative advertising, access to private-label merchandise, and use of prototype store construction and layouts. IGA is a franchise wholesaler. Its shares are owned completely by its 19 member wholesalers. These 19 wholesalers account for nearly half of the wholesale food business in the United States.[26] In the grocery-related business, there were 99 voluntary chains in 1991 versus 161 in 1985.[27]

Cooperative wholesalers can be differentiated from other full-service merchant wholesalers through their ownership: they are owned by either their producer or retail members. Producer-owned cooperatives are common in farming. **Producer-owned cooperatives** purchase supplies; perform such wholesale tasks as storage, transportation, grading products, and arranging to sell output; and promote products through a common brand name. Ocean Spray, Land O'Lakes, Blue Diamond, Sun-Maid, and Welch's are examples of producer-owned cooperatives.

In contrast to producer-owned cooperatives, **retailer-owned cooperatives** are owned and operated by their retailer members. Profits from the retailer-owned cooperatives are divided among their retailer members at the end of the year. Retailer-owned cooperatives "level the playing field" by giving independent retailers many of the advantages of chains. These cooperatives often help retailer members develop strategies relating to location, merchandising, computerization, cost control, and marketing support. Producer-owned cooperatives are an important factor in the hardware, supermarket, and drug store market.

Common problems associated with retailer-owned cooperatives include high reliance on retailer board members, competition from producer-owned cooperatives for members, conflicts over whether patronage dividends should be withdrawn or reinvested, and the level of retailer service provided. (Some members feel that some retailer-owned cooperatives are more concerned with warehouse profits than with member services.)[28]

Two major retailer-owned cooperatives are Ace Hardware and Wakefern, the wholesaler arm of the ShopRite supermarket cooperative. Ace Hardware has over 5000 members and runs 25 promotions per year that include circulars, free-standing inserts, and radio and television ads. Ace Hardware aids retailer members in securing lower costs on merchandise due to quantity discounts. Dealers pay Ace's cost of merchandise plus 10 percent on most items.[29] In the grocery-related business, there were 53 retailer-owned cooperatives in 1991 versus 70 in 1985.[30]

Limited-Service Merchant Wholesalers

Limited-service merchant wholesalers include cash-and-carry wholesalers, drop shippers, truck/wagon wholesalers, and mail-order wholesalers. In contrast to full-service merchant wholesalers, these wholesalers generally operate with lower profit margins due to reduced wholesale functions. Limited-service merchant wholesalers may not offer credit, warehouse goods, or have a personal sales force. Some limited-service merchant wholesalers closely resemble full-service merchant wholesalers. For example, a truck/wagon wholesaler performs all the functions of a rack jobber except it does not offer trade credit.

As the name implies, **cash-and-carry wholesalers** do not offer credit or delivery and are self-service operations. Cash-and-carry wholesalers are typically used by small retailers for fill-in merchandise, or by contractors and auto repair shops for goods that are needed immediately. Wholesale customers of a cash-and-carry wholesaler must drive to the wholesaler, load their truck, and pay cash. These customers receive no promotional or market research assistance from the wholesaler. Cash-and-carry wholesalers are similar to buying clubs used by wholesalers but require no membership and do not typically sell to final customers. An example of a cash-and-carry wholesaler is Smart & Final, a 112-unit company that serves independent food service operators, restaurants, and caterers.[31]

Drop shippers (desk jobbers) perform all the traditional wholesale tasks of full-service wholesalers except that they do not handle or store goods. The drop shipper is the only merchant wholesaler that does not have warehouse facilities. As a result, the manufacturer/supplier needs to ship goods directly to the customer, based on an order received from the drop shipper. Drop shippers are not considered agents since they take title to goods. Drop shippers are commonly used in the sale of goods with high weight in relation to value such as coal, oil, lumber, aluminum ore, and building materials. These goods are typically sold in carload shipments.

Truck/wagon wholesalers typically have a regular route and deliver goods at the same time they are sold. Truck/wagon wholesalers are viewed as a limited-service wholesaler because they do not extend trade credit. These wholesalers commonly deal with perishables such as tobacco, bakery products, and snack foods and semi-perishables such as beer and candy. Truck/wagon wholesalers commonly service grocery stores, hospitals, hotels, restaurants, and cafeterias.

Mail-order wholesalers utilize catalogs to promote and to communicate with potential buyers. Mail-order wholesalers can effectively deal with small accounts, profitably cover rural areas or territories where customers are geographically scattered, and handle small order sizes. Mail-order wholesalers are common in jewelry and in sporting goods.

AGENTS AND BROKERS

Agents and brokers can be differentiated from other wholesalers in that they do not take title to goods and they are paid on a commission basis (with the commission being paid by the seller). The basic function of agents and brokers is to bring together a buyer and seller to complete a transaction. Agents and brokers concentrate on customer contact and negotiation functions. Although the responsibilities of agents and brokers are the same, **agents** are likely to be employed on a permanent basis whereas **brokers** are typically employed on a temporary basis (for a particular project or deal). Brokers may represent different principals at different times and may not have a long-term relationship with any principal.

In 1992, the latest year for which data are available, agents and brokers accounted for 10.8 percent of wholesale sales. It is the smallest category for wholesale trade (see Table 4-2). Sales by agents and brokers are also less concentrated than sales by other wholesalers. The four largest agent and broker firms accounted for only 6.3 percent of total sales by agents and brokers (see Table 4-6).

Agents

Three categories of agents are manufacturers' agents, selling agents, and commission (factor) merchants.

Manufacturers' agents are employed by several manufacturers with non-competing and complementary product lines. A manufacturers' agent is typically given an exclusive territory from each manufacturer it represents and carries limited lines within that territory. A manufacturer can employ several manufacturers' agents, as long as each agent has a unique territory and product mix. Several types of companies should consider the use of manufacturers' agents: a firm too small to be able to afford the number of required salespeople, a midsized firm that gives only superficial coverage to selected geographic areas, a larger firm with fragmented markets, and a larger firm with relatively large-sized markets that are ignored by its present sales force.[32] The major professional association of manufacturers' agents is the Manufacturers' Agents National Association (MANA) which has over 8000 members.[33] Table 4-12 contains a profile of a typical manufacturers' agent for selected years 1987 through 1994.

Selling agents assume responsibility for the entire marketing operation of a single manufacturer. Unlike manufacturers' agents, selling agents can negotiate price and other conditions of sales without need to contact the seller on each transaction. And while a manufacturer can use several manufacturers' agents, it can only employ a single selling agent. Selling agents are common in textiles and electronics.

Commission (factor) merchants receive goods on consignment from producers, accumulate them from local markets, and arrange for their sales in a central market location. Unlike manufacturers' agents and brokers, commission merchants take possession of products. Generally, commission merchants are used to sell specific goods on a short-term basis, and they can only sell goods at the market price or above a minimum price. Commission merchants are commonly used in agriculture.

Brokers

Brokers are important channels for crude oil, agricultural commodities, and industrial machinery. Two categories of brokers are food brokers and export brokers.

Food brokers specialize in the sale of foods and related items to food service retailers. Food brokers generally represent several manufacturers or producers

TABLE 4-12 PROFILE OF A TYPICAL MANUFACTURERS' AGENT, 1987, 1990, 1992, 1994

	1987	1990	1992	1994
Average number of offices	1.50	1.68	1.62	1.69
Average number of states covered	5.17	4.88	5.56	5.87
Average number of manufacturers represented	10.10	10.40	10.14	10.41
Average gross profits (from previous year)	$ 280,100	$ 378,982	$ 442,830	$ 465,411
Average gross sales (from previous year)	$4,402,986	$5,879,244	$6,512,355	$6,944,793
Average agency net (after taxes—from previous year)	$ 55,922	$ 55,841	$ 68,233	$ 62,877
Average number of salespeople	3.46	3.60	3.68	3.90
Major markets sold to[a]				
Original equipment manufacturers	56%	57%	54%	55%
Wholesale/distributor	n/a	50%	43%	44%
Capital equipment in primary market	22%	25%	24%	20%
Retail/mass merchandisers	14%	12%	11%	12%
Capital equipment manufacturing	27%	25%	25%	26%
Government/municipalities	15%	12%	16%	17%
Contractors/architects	n/a	n/a	20%	20%

[a]Totals equal more than 100 percent owing to multiple response nature of question.

Source: Reprinted from *Agency Sales Magazine,* Copyright 1994, Manufacturers' Agents National Association, 23016 Mill Creek Road, P.O. Box 3467, Laguna Hills, CA 92654-3467, (714) 859-4040; fax (714) 855-2973. All rights reserved. Reproduction without permission is strictly prohibited.

of food, equipment, and related products. Food brokers typically cover such outlets as grocery stores, restaurants, hotels, motels, airlines, and delicatessens.[34] As of 1990, there were about 1600 food brokerage firms; these firms employ about 40,000 people. Although the fee varies by product category and by services rendered, the average charged by food brokers in 1990 was 3.1 percent of sales.[35]

Export brokers specialize in international trade. They are particularly knowledgeable of foreign market conditions and of the rules relating to the sale and distribution of goods in specific foreign countries, and they have contacts in specific foreign countries.

MANUFACTURER/SUPPLIER—WHOLESALER CONTRACTS

Figure 4-4 contains a sample contract between a manufacturer/supplier and a food broker. This contract was prepared by the National Food Brokers Association. Other sample contracts are available from the Electronics

FIGURE 4-4 Sample contract between a manufacturer/supplier and a food broker.

This Agreement is made this _____ day of _____, 19__, by and between _____ of _____, (insert either: "a corporation duly organized under the laws of the State of _____"; other form of enterprise or "an individual"), herein called the PRINCIPAL, and _____ of , (designate as above whether corporation, other form of business enterprise, or an individual), herein called the BROKER.

WITNESSETH:

WHEREAS, PRINCIPAL is a manufacturer (or processor or other appropriate designation) and seller, among other things, of certain merchandise or products, as listed in Attachment No. 1 to this Agreement and desires to secure the services of a broker in the territory hereinafter described, to negotiate the sales of said merchandise or products in PRINCIPAL's name and for his account, and

WHEREAS, BROKER is desirous in securing the exclusive right to negotiate sales of said PRINCIPAL's products of merchandise in said territory.

NOW THEREFORE, in consideration of the premises and covenants and undertakings herein contained.

IT IS MUTUALLY AGREED AS FOLLOWS:

(1) TERRITORY. PRINCIPAL hereby appoints BROKER, and BROKER hereby agrees to act for PRINCIPAL, as its (or his/her, as the case may be) sole and exclusive Representative for negotiations of sales of the merchandise or products hereinabove enumerated, subject to the terms, provisions and conditions hereof, within the territory as described in Attachment No. 2 to this Agreement.

(2) SALES NEGOTIATIONS. All sales negotiations by BROKER for the account of PRINCIPAL shall be conducted in accordance with such process, terms and conditions as specified by PRINCIPAL.

(3) AGENCY. It is further understood that BROKER shall act as Agent of PRINCIPAL, that neither BROKER nor its employees shall be considered employees of PRINCIPAL, and neither party shall in any event be held liable or accountable for any obligations incurred by either party other than as specified herein, it being specifically understood that the respective businesses of each of the parties shall be operated separate and apart from each other.

(4) CONFLICTS. In the event of product conflicts, both parties shall make every reasonable effort to reach an agreement on a method for BROKER to represent the products involved. The general policy on conflicts is described in Attachment No. 3.

(5) APPLICABLE LAW. The laws of the State of _____ shall govern the application and interpretation of this Agreement.

(6) ENTIRE AGREEMENT. It is understood that this Agreement cancels and supersedes any and all prior agreements, oral and written, made between the parties hereto, and can only be modified by an agreement in writing, signed by all applicable parties.

(7) ARBITRATION. Any controversy or claim arising out of or relating to this Agreement shall be settled by arbitration in accordance with the rules of the American Arbitration Association and judgment may be entered in any court having jurisdiction thereof.

THE PRINCIPAL AGREES AS FOLLOWS:

(8) EXCLUSIVE REPRESENTATION. BROKER shall be the sole and exclusive Representative of PRINCIPAL for negotiating sales of the merchandise and products herein specified in the described territory and PRINCIPAL will either (a) make no sales of said merchandise and products in such territory other than those negotiated by BROKER, or (b) in case of sales made by PRINCIPAL in such territory other than those negotiated by BROKER, or on sales otherwise for shipment of PRINCIPAL's merchandise or products into said territory for resale, PRINCIPAL will pay BROKER a commission or brokerage on the merchandise and products so sold at the rate specified in the following paragraph. Further, PRINCIPAL agrees not to enter into any contract with any other Sales Representative in the territory specified herein during the life of this Agreement.

(9) COMMISSIONS. To pay Broker, without deduction or offset, a commission, or brokerage of ___ percent on each and every sale, as provided herein, the said percentage rate of commission, or brokerage, to be computed on the price of the merchandise or products sold before discounts and allowances are figured, said brokerage payment to be made promptly within ___ days after the end of each month. A delinquency charge of ___ percent per month (but not in excess of the lawful maximum) may be added on any amount ___ days in arrears. Such other special services shall be compensated as agreed from time to time.

(10) ELIGIBLE BUYERS. To permit BROKER, consistent with the terms of this Agreement, to negotiate sales to any and all prospective Buyers of PRINCIPAL's said products throughout the entire territory mentioned as specified.

(11) SHIPMENTS. To ship the merchandise or products sold as BROKER may specify. PRINCIPAL shall be given reasonable notice with respect to the required shipments. PRINCIPAL accepts full responsibility for granting credit to BUYERS.

(12) SALES AND PROMOTIONAL POLICIES. To keep BROKER fully informed on all sales and promotional policies and programs affecting the specified territory.

(13) INDEMNIFICATION. If any claim or action be made or filed against BROKER, claiming loss or injury of any nature whatsoever, as a result of defect in any merchandise, purchase or use of any product manufactured, produced, or distributed by PRINCIPAL, to defend, hold harmless and indemnify BROKER from any and all loss or damage, costs, and expenses, including legal fees, incurred by it.

THE BROKER AGREES AS FOLLOWS:

(14) PRINCIPAL'S INSTRUCTIONS. To carry-out PRINCIPAL's instructions with respect to the sales of the merchandise and products specified herein.

(15) COMPETITIVE PRODUCTS. To keep PRINCIPAL informed with respect to the representation of a competitive product by BROKER.

(16) REPORTING PURCHASE ORDERS AND NEGOTIATIONS. To promptly report all negotiations and purchase orders of specified merchandise and products for confirmation or approval by PRINCIPAL, and in negotiating sales to prospective Buyers within the specified territory, to report negotiations to PRINCIPAL.

(17) ASSIST IN COLLECTIONS. To assist PRINCIPAL in effecting prompt and full payment by BUYERS for all deliveries of merchandise and products sold. The final determination as to credit and credit terms shall be made only by PRINCIPAL.

(18) CONTACT PROSPECTIVE BUYERS. To contact prospective Buyers in the assigned territory in furtherance of sales of specified merchandise and products of PRINCIPAL.

DURATION OF AGREEMENT

(19) TERM/TERMINATION. This agreement shall continue in full force and effect from year to year; provided that either party may terminate this Agreement by giving ____ months written notice of such intention to the other party.

- (a) Double brokerage will be paid to BROKER as severance pay during the termination period as defined in Paragraph 19.
- OR (b) In the event PRINCIPAL elects to terminate this Agreement, it is understood that BROKER will be paid on the date of termination as severance payment to be the average monthly brokerage based on the previous two years' earnings, for as many months as there were years of representation, not to exceed ____ years.
- OR (c) Brokerage payments will continue for ____ months after the notice of termination, such payments to be based on the previous years' average monthly brokerage.

IN WITNESS THEREOF, the parties hereto have signed this Agreement, thereunto duly authorized on the day and year above written.

Attest: (seal)   PRINCIPAL:
By _____   By _____

(Title)   (Title)

Attest: (seal)   BROKER:
By _____   By _____

(Title)   (Title)

IMPORTANT NOTE: This contract is prepared as a general reference and guide only. Professional legal advise should be secured prior to signing any agreement.

Source: Guides for Developing Food Broker-Principal Agreements (Reston, Va.: National Food Brokers Association, 1990), pp. 7–9. Reprinted by permission. This document is scheduled to be revised and updated by December 1995.

Representatives Association (Chicago, Illinois) and from the Manufacturers' Agents National Association (Laguna Hills, California).

Important aspects of all contracts between manufacturer/suppliers and wholesalers relate to the services-responsibility mix of each party, wholesaler compensation, territorial rights and the right of a manufacturer/supplier to add distributors, resale restrictions, and the length of the contract and conditions of termination.

THE SERVICES-RESPONSIBILITY MIX OF EACH PARTY

A contract should attempt to clearly outline the services-responsibilities mix of each party. A manufacturer's services-responsibilities mix typically includes training (technical, marketing, and account management) for the wholesaler's staff, financing of inventory, a **hold-harmless agreement** (stating that the manufacturer will reimburse the distributor for product liability cases), provision of promotional material for use by the wholesaler's salespeople, a cooperative advertising program, and a provision for the speedy replacement of defective products.[36]

A wholesaler's responsibilities commonly include order solicitation among new and existing accounts, customer contact, inventory levels to be stocked, sales quotas to be achieved, physical distribution requirements (including minimum inventory requirements and customer service-level requirements), technical advice and customer service, and market information.[37] It is important to be as specific as possible in outlining both the frequency of required account coverage and the types of accounts to be contacted.

Some contracts require that wholesalers carry the manufacturer's entire line and not directly competing products. Full-line selling provides market coverage for all of a manufacturer's products. A contract provision that stipulates that the wholesaler not carry competing products ensures a manufacturer that the distributor will give the manufacturer's products proper attention. Manufacturers that prohibit a wholesaler from taking on a second line argue that the additional line reduces the amount of time a wholesaler spends on its products, decreases the interdependence between a wholesaler and the manufacturer, lessens the confidentiality between a manufacturer and its wholesalers, and allows wholesalers to use a manufacturer's sales and technical training for a competitive product.

Other manufacturer/suppliers allow wholesalers to take on a second line of merchandise in addition to the primary manufacturer's line. Advocates of this position argue that a second line enables the wholesaler to support additional sales calls, gives the salesperson more than one reason to call on an account, and provides the wholesaler with greater security against decline in sales from one product or loss of a manufacturer/supplier.[38] In some cases, manufacturers have accepted wholesalers with conflicting lines owing to their outstanding overall performance. According to the chairman of a food brokerage firm, "Manufacturers have decided they would rather live with a first-rate broker with some conflicts than a third-rate broker with no conflicts."[39]

> ## CHANNELS IN ACTION
>
> ### Use of Food Brokers by Clorox
>
> The Clorox Company sells a wide variety of products that are distributed through grocery stores and other retail outlets. These products include cleaning products (such as Clorox bleach, Pine-Sol cleaner, Soft Scrub cleanser, and Tilex instant mildew remover), grill products (such as Kingsford and Match Light charcoal briquets), salad dressings and specialty foods (such as Hidden Valley Ranch salad dressings and K.C. Masterpiece barbecue sauce), insecticides (such as Combat), and professional products (such as Formula 409, Liquid-Plumr, and Hidden Valley Ranch salad dressings that are marketed in institutional sizes).
>
> Clorox has more than 100,000 direct and indirect customers worldwide. Its retailer customers include supermarket chains, convenience stores, and warehouse clubs. While many competitors use a direct sales force for sales to these retailers, Clorox distributes to retailer customers through a network of 174 food brokerage firms. According to Clorox's management, "Brokers offer the great advantages of being local to their markets and having a reservoir of knowledge that comes from years of calling on the same customers—getting to know and understand their accounts all the way from the local store level to their accounts' senior management."
>
> According to the chief executive officer and president of a firm that has been a Clorox food broker since 1916, "We're seen as partners in the quest for increasing profitability. Clorox has made our jobs easier because the integrity of the Company and its products has helped us gain the trade's confidence."
>
> Food brokers have been instrumental in improving customer service. For example, through the cooperation of its food brokers, Clorox is now able to deliver its goods directly to retail customers during special promotions. This eliminates warehousing costs for retailers. Clorox's on-time delivery rates have also increased from the low 80 percent range to better than 96 percent. Order fill rates, the number of cases shipped versus the number of cases ordered, has also increased from 95 percent to 98 percent. One way of increasing on-time delivery rates has been food brokers' providing Clorox with as much advance notice of a major order as possible.
>
> Clorox has recently consolidated its food broker network. Now a single broker organization represents all of Clorox's retail brands rather than just one line of products. This new organization format has improved communication as well as reduced Clorox's distribution costs by $4 million per year.
>
> Source: *The Clorox Company Annual Report for the Year Ended June 30, 1991* and *The Clorox Company 1994 Annual Report.*

In adopting a position with regard to second lines, it is important to determine whether a wholesaler can sell and merchandise conflicting brands and the impact of the second line on competitive information. To reduce the possible conflict, different account executives within a wholesaler's organization should be responsible for each manufacturer's brand.[40]

WHOLESALER COMPENSATION

Merchant wholesalers are compensated on the basis of discounts from list price, whereas brokers and agents are compensated by commissions from the seller. Discounts to merchant wholesalers include trade discounts, functional discounts, quantity discounts, cash discounts, and payments for other services. A **trade discount** represents a discount from a product's list price given to all resellers on the basis of the level of trade. For example, a merchant wholesaler may receive a 40 percent discount, while a retailer may receive a 25 percent discount. A **functional discount** is received by a reseller for assuming a function that would otherwise be performed by a seller (such as storage, customer service, customer contact, and selling). Without a functional discount, a wholesaler would only earn profits through breaking bulk, purchasing in larger quantities, and selling in smaller quantities. **Quantity discounts** are earned by wholesalers for buying specified quantities of merchandise. **Terms** involve credit provided by a manufacturer/supplier for wholesalers and retailers. **Cash discounts** are given to wholesalers for early payment. In addition to these discounts, wholesalers also receive compensation for conducting work associated with test marketing, trade shows, and demonstrations; setting up displays for new products; handling unsalable merchandise; and assisting with product recall programs.[41] Most discount schedules are difficult to change once established.

Wholesalers typically require price protection. In **price protection**, wholesalers are reimbursed by manufacturers when a manufacturer reduces the list price of its goods. Without price protection, wholesalers would suffer a decline in inventory value and would stock as little inventory as possible.

If a wholesaler is a broker or an agent, the contract must specify a timetable for payment of commissions (upon booking of an order, product shipment, or payment by the customer), the commission rate for different goods and services, and whether the commission rate changes at different levels of sales activity. In some cases, agents and brokers are paid incentive commissions for new products and for exceeding sales quotas.

TERRITORIAL RIGHTS AND THE RIGHT OF A MANUFACTURER/SUPPLIER TO ADD WHOLESALERS

Clauses relating to territorial rights outline a wholesaler's territory in terms of getting credit for sales. Wholesalers often seek to get credit for all sales in their territory whether or not they initiate the sales. Such an agreement protects the wholesaler when accounts seek out information from the wholesaler and then seek to buy directly from manufacturers to secure lower prices.

The contract also needs to specify how orders for the wholesaler's territory will be handled if they arise outside the territory. For example, an order for goods to be delivered within the wholesaler's territory may have originated from a customer's main office located in another state. Through **profit passover arrangements**, payment is given to a wholesaler that sells goods and services to accounts that are located outside of that wholesaler's territory by the wholesaler having those territorial rights.

In some cases, a manufacturer using dual channels of distribution plans to sell and service some accounts through manufacturer wholesaling and other accounts through independent wholesalers. Accounts serviced through manufacturer wholesaling are generally large accounts or accounts that have had long relationships with manufacturers and seek to continue these relationships. These accounts are called **direct accounts**. Usually, wholesalers are not given credit for sales from direct accounts and have no responsibilities in servicing them. If a wholesaler has any obligation to service direct accounts, it should be appropriately paid for these services. For example, the contract may call for lower commission rates for these sales, as well as a lower level of responsibility. To minimize confusion and potential conflict, the names of each direct account, wholesaler responsibilities for direct accounts, and wholesaler compensation for direct account sales should be covered in the contract.

Some contracts divide direct accounts by size of order or by product type. **Size-of-order boundaries** specify that the role of independent wholesalers is to serve smaller accounts; larger accounts are then served by direct distribution. Size-of-order boundaries as a means of account allocation may generate channel conflict between a manufacturer and a wholesaler and may be difficult to enforce. For example, in the size-of-order boundaries system, a customer gets shifted to a direct account as it grows, even if the wholesaler was responsible for developing the account. A larger order that would be considered a direct account could be split into several smaller orders.[42] For these reasons, many wholesalers and manufacturers recommend that direct accounts be specifically named in the contract.

Territorial rights can also create conflict when a manufacturer attempts to reduce a wholesaler's territory to ensure better coverage of an expanded market. In these instances, the manufacturer appoints additional wholesalers in the original territory, reduces the size of the original wholesaler's territory, or seeks to restrict each wholesaler to a specific product line or customer category. A common argument from the original wholesaler is that it was responsible for market expansion and that it should therefore benefit from larger market size. For example, Procter & Gamble (P&G) had difficulties with its bottler wholesalers regarding distribution of its Crush product. Its bottlers made more money by distributing Crush through vending machine, food service, and convenience store channels, and so were ignoring supermarkets. To enforce bottler sales through supermarkets, P&G began to remove the territorial rights of its franchised bottlers. P&G assumed that this would increase sales to supermarkets. In fact, many bottlers merely switched sales from Crush to other competitors such as A&W and Canada Dry. P&G ultimately sold its soda business to Cadbury Schweppes.[43]

RESALE RESTRICTIONS

Resale restrictions involve a manufacturer restricting authorized distributors from selling its products to unauthorized distributors or authorized distributors outside his or her territory. A **territorial resale restriction** prevents or discourages a wholesaler from selling outside a particular area. A **customer resale restriction** prohibits a wholesaler from selling to specific customers or classes of customers. Territorial and customer restrictions reduce intrabrand competition. Violations of territorial and customer resale restrictions are referred to as transshipping. The classic cases involving resale restrictions are 1967 *U.S. v. Arnold Schwinn* and 1977 *Continental T.V. v. GTE*. Both of these Supreme Court decisions have been heavily quoted.

A key difference in these cases is the application of the per se rule versus the rule of reason. A **per se rule** action by its nature is illegal. For example, actions such as a conspiracy among resellers not to sell to a discounting wholesaler would be illegal by their nature. These practices have no positive competitive characteristics. Under the per se rule, the complaining party only needs to show that the illegal practice occurred. In contrast, under the **rule of reason**, the court must first ascertain the reasonableness of the restraint and its effect on the overall competitive environment and then determine whether an act is illegal. Under the rule of reason doctrine, courts look at facts peculiar to the case, the reasons why the actions were implemented, and their competitive significance.

On the wholesale level, Schwinn limited distributor sales to exclusive territories. Schwinn also restricted the customers to whom wholesalers and retailers could sell. The Supreme Court argued in the *Schwinn* case that once Schwinn parted with title, risk, and possession of its bicycles, it could not control to whom its distributors could resell Schwinn bicycles. In the *Schwinn* case, territorial restrictions were judged as a per se violation of Section 1 of the Sherman Act. Schwinn could legally control the resale of its products through either selling on a consignment basis (title remained with Schwinn until the goods were sold) or through ownership of its wholesale and retail operations. Schwinn could also legally designate areas of prime responsibility for its distributors and state the location of the place of business in its franchise agreements.[44]

In the *Continental T.V. v. GTE* case, the Supreme Court ruled that distributor territorial restrictions should be evaluated on the basis of the "rule of reason"; that each instance should be judged on a case-by-case basis. The Court recognized that while territorial restrictions might reduce intrabrand competition, desirable interbrand competition might be fostered owing to the manufacturer's ability to "achieve certain efficiencies in the distribution of its products." Furthermore, the Court held that the location clause "was one of the least restrictive methods the manufacturer might have employed to strengthen its market position."[45] The Court sided with Sylvania, which argued that its territorial allocation policy allowed it to better compete with rival manufacturers. At the time of the case, RCA had a 60 to 70 percent market share, Zenith and Magnavox were also major competitors, and Sylvania's market share was between 1 and 2 percent.[46] The *Continental* case eliminated the per se interpretation of territorial restrictions and began the rule of reason interpretation.

In a much more recent case, the District Court for the District of New Jersey (in *Michael Haleblan, N.J. Inc. v. Roppe Rubber Corp. et al.*) found a central issue relating to resale restrictions was whether a manufacturer had a uniform policy that is developed and communicated in advance (and not a specific response to a given situation) against sales by authorized distributors to unauthorized distributors by transshipment. These policies should be based on legitimate marketing concerns such as the need to carry the full line of products, to make adequate presentations and promotions of the product, and to resolve warranty claims and customer complaints.[47]

LENGTH OF CONTRACT AND CONDITIONS OF TERMINATION

Wholesalers generally desire a long-term contract in order to protect their investment in developing a new territory for a manufacturer. Many wholesalers fear that a manufacturer may use the wholesaler to develop a territory and then change to direct distribution when the territory can be profitably covered by manufacturer wholesaling.

Since wholesaler termination is likely to result in legal action, it is important that reasons for termination be identified and communicated to wholesalers. There is also a need to have a uniform policy instead of merely an ad hoc response to a given situation.[48] Several states, such as Maryland, have passed laws that protect distributors against sudden termination.[49]

A common condition of termination is transshipping. As in the case of retailers, a manufacturer/supplier cannot terminate a distributor as a means of controlling the distributor's wholesaler prices.[50] Other legitimate reasons for terminating a distributor are not meeting reasonable sales performance, poor credit, failure to develop and maintain adequate sales and service facilities, improper or inadequate market representation, and inability of a manufacturer to provide adequate products for all wholesalers owing to product shortages.[51]

The termination clause also needs to specify the amount of notice to be given to a wholesaler prior to termination and to detail how a wholesaler's inventory will be sold. If at the time of termination, orders are in process or about to be placed, the contract needs to indicate who gets credit for the sale.

SUMMARY

[1] *To analyze the structure of wholesaling, including wholesale sales volume, wholesale trends, and important statistics relating to wholesaling.* The U.S. wholesaling industry was a $3.2 trillion industry in 1992. Wholesale sales are higher than retail sales since they include purchases made by organizational users. They are also higher due to double-counting since many goods are sold through multiple levels of wholesalers. Thirty-two percent of wholesale sales volume for 1992 (the latest year for which data are available) was accounted for by manufacturers' sales branches and offices. Merchant wholesalers accounted for 57.2 percent of wholesale sales volume in 1992. Agents, brokers, and commission merchants accounted for 10.8 percent of 1992 wholesale sales volume.

Seven major trends affecting wholesalers have been identified: increased competition from power retailers, the broadening of merchandise lines, increased opportunities due to manufacturer downsizing, the growth of the modular corporation, international expansion, increased computerization, and the increased importance of large distributors due to mergers and acquisitions.

Many distributors are still small firms, despite the increase in mergers and acquisitions. For example, as of 1992, the average wholesaler had 12 employees.

2 *To determine the special characteristics of wholesaling: multiple layers of wholesalers, representation of multiple manufacturers, and geographic concentration of wholesale sales and establishments.* Although there is generally only one level of retail institution in a channel, there can be more than one level of wholesale institution. For example, a specialty goods wholesaler may sell goods to a full-line wholesaler. Multiple layers of wholesalers also create long channels.

Many wholesalers represent multiple manufacturers. This allows wholesalers to profitably call on small accounts, to serve geographic areas with low sales potential, and to become a one-stop shopping resource for other retailer and end-user customers. A potential difficulty with representation of multiple manufacturers is conflict among manufacturers when goods from different manufacturers compete for the same target market.

In total, the 10 largest states in terms of wholesale sales volume accounted for 62 percent of total U.S. wholesale sales. These states comprised 56 percent of total U.S. wholesale establishments.

3 *To study a classification system of wholesalers according to manufacturer wholesaling, merchant wholesalers, and agents and brokers.* There are three broad categories of wholesalers: manufacturer wholesaling, merchant wholesaling, and agents and brokers. The primary difference among wholesaler categories relates to ownership of the wholesaler, whether the wholesaler takes title to goods, and the method of compensation.

In manufacturer wholesaling, the manufacturer performs all wholesale functions and owns and controls goods until they are sold. The profitability of manufacturer wholesaling is determined by the difference in the firm's transfer price and the selling price. In merchant wholesaling, independent wholesalers purchase and take title to products and undertake all wholesale functions. Merchant wholesalers are compensated on the basis of the difference of the cost of goods sold less their sales revenues. Merchant wholesalers generally receive discounts from list price from the manufacturer on the basis of trade, functional, quantity, promotional, and cash discounts. Unlike merchant wholesalers, agents and brokers do not take title to goods or services. They are compensated on the basis of sales commissions that are typically paid for by sellers.

Manufacturer wholesaling can be accomplished through either manufacturers' sales offices or manufacturers' branch offices. Merchant wholesalers are generally further classified into full-service and limited-service merchant wholesalers on the basis of functions performed. Five types of full-service merchant wholesalers are general merchandise, specialty merchandise, rack jobbers, franchise wholesalers, and cooperative wholesalers. Limited-service merchant wholesalers include cash-and-carry wholesalers, drop shippers, truck/wagon wholesalers, and mail-order wholesalers. Three categories of agents are manufacturers' agents, selling agents, and commission (factor) merchants. Two categories of brokers are food brokers and export brokers.

To describe the components of manufacturer/supplier—wholesaler contracts. Important aspects of all contracts between manufacturer/suppliers and wholesalers relate to the services-responsibility mix of each party, wholesaler compensation, territorial rights and the right of a manufacturer/supplier to add distributors, resale restrictions, and the length of the contract and conditions of termination.

KEY TERMS

wholesaling
power retailers
integrated supply contract
modular corporation
integrated distributors
potential conflict
allowable conflict
real conflict
manufacturer wholesaling
transfer price
merchant wholesaling
agents and brokers
manufacturers' sales office
manufacturers' branch office

captive distributors
full-service merchant wholesalers
limited-service merchant wholesalers
general-merchandise (full-line) merchant wholesalers
specialty-merchandise (limited-line) merchant wholesalers
rack jobbers
franchise wholesaling
producer-owned cooperatives
retailer-owned cooperatives

cash-and-carry wholesalers
drop shippers (desk jobbers)
truck/wagon wholesalers
mail-order wholesalers
agents
brokers
manufacturers' agents
selling agents
commission (factor) merchants
food brokers
export brokers
hold-harmless agreement
trade discount
functional discount

quantity discounts
terms
cash discounts
price protection
profit pass-over arrangements

direct accounts
size-of-order boundaries
resale restrictions
territorial resale restriction

customer resale restriction
per se rule
rule of reason

QUESTIONS FOR DISCUSSION

1. How can a traditional industrial distributor successfully compete against Premier Industrial Corporation?
2. a. What are the advantages and disadvantages to a manufacturer/supplier's selling through an integrated distributor?
   b. Explain the implications of large wholesalers going into retailing.
3. Differentiate among potential conflict, allowable conflict, and real conflict as they relate to wholesaler representation of multiple manufacturers.
4. Under what circumstances would you recommend that a manufacturer/supplier utilize manufacturer wholesaling? merchant wholesaling? agents and brokers?
5. What are the disadvantages of using manufacturer wholesaling?
6. Discuss Baxter International's ASAP system from the perspective of its competitive advantage to the wholesaler.
7. Differentiate among rack jobbers, franchise wholesalers, and producer-owned cooperatives.
8. Why is a rack jobber considered to be a full-service merchant wholesaler, while a truck/wagon wholesaler is characterized as a limited-service merchant wholesaler?
9. Differentiate among a manufacturers' agent, a selling agent, and a commission (factor) merchant.
10. Develop a services-responsibility mix for a food broker that has taken on a new line of specialty light bulbs (such as decorator-type vanity bulbs and heating lamps for bathrooms) for sale through grocery stores.
11. Explain how the wholesaler compensation contract would differ depending if the wholesaler were a manufacturer wholesaler, a merchant wholesaler, or an agent or broker.
12. What are the critical issues that relate to the territorial rights of a wholesaler?
13. Differentiate between territorial and customer resale restrictions.
14. Develop five conditions of termination for a contract between a manufacturer/supplier and a merchant wholesaler. Explain your choice.

END NOTES

1. Ret Autry, "Premier Industrial," *Fortune* (April 8, 1991), p. 82; and *Premier Industrial Corporation 1994 Annual Report.*

2. Joel R. Evans and Barry Berman, *Marketing,* 6th ed. (Englewood Cliffs, N.J.: Prentice Hall, 1994), p. 516. This definition has been adapted from the U.S. Bureau of the Census.

3. Richard A. Melcher, "Cut Out the Middleman? Never," *Business Week* (January 10, 1994), p. 96.

4. *Facing the Forces of Change 2000: The New Realities in Wholesale Distribution* (Washington, D.C.: Distribution Research and Education Foundation, 1993).

5. See Robert F. Lusch and Deborah Zizzo, *Competing for Customers* (Washington, D.C.: Distribution Research and Education Foundation, 1995).

6. Melcher, "Cut Out the Middleman? Never," p. 96.

7. James P. Morgan, "A Decade of Shrinking Numbers, Larger Entities?" *Purchasing* (May 20, 1993), p. 67.

8. See Paul Herbig and Bradley S. O'Hara, "Industrial Distributors in the Twenty-First Century," *Industrial Marketing Management,* Vol. 24 (July 1994), p. 201.

9. Frederick E. Webster, "The Changing Role of Marketing in the Corporation," *Journal of Marketing,* Vol. 56 (October 1992), p. 9.

10. Shawn Tully, "The Modular Corporation," *Fortune* (February 8, 1993), pp. 106–108 ff.

11. Joseph A. Weber, "Wholesaling: On a Fast Boat to Anywhere," *Business Week* (January 11, 1993), p. 94.

12. Ibid.

13. See *U.S. Industrial Outlook 1993* (Washington, D.C.: U.S. Department of Commerce, International Trade Administration, 1993), pp. 38-1–38-4.

14. Ned C. Hill and Michael J. Swenson, "The Impact of Electronic Data Interchange on the Sales Function," *Journal of Personal Selling and Sales Management,* Vol. 14 (Summer 1994), pp. 79–87.

15. Morgan, "A Decade of Shrinking Numbers, Larger Entities?" p. 61.

16. See Christine Forbes, "Acquisitions Drive Industry Change," *Industrial Distribution* (March 1993), pp. 22–24.

17. Forbes, "Acquisitions Drive Industry Change," pp. 22–24.

18. See Ronald D. Michman, "Managing Structural Changes in Marketing Channels," *Journal of Business and Industrial Marketing,* Vol. 5 (Summer/Fall 1990), pp. 8–9.

19. Jim Morgan, "How Will Goliaths Change Distribution?" *Industrial Distribution* (June 1994), pp. 39–40 ff.

20. Kathryn Jones, "A Move Along the Food Chain," *New York Times* (July 2, 1994), pp. 33 ff.; and Matthew Schifrin, "Middleman's Dilemma," *Forbes* (May 23, 1994), pp. 67 ff.

21. See Herbig and O'Hara, "Industrial Distributors in the Twenty-First Century," pp. 199–203.

22. *Handling Product Conflicts: A Joint Subcommittee White Paper* (Washington, D.C.: National Food Brokers Association and Grocery Manufacturers of America, Inc., n.d.).

23. Ibid.

24. Michman, "Managing Structural Changes in Marketing Channels," pp. 9–10.

25. *Baxter International 1993 Annual Report,* p. 25.

26. See Bruce Fox, "Preaching the Way to a New IGA," *Chain Store Age Executive* (April 1990), pp. 26–29.

27. Steve Weinstein, "Climate for Co-Ops: Partly Cloudly," *Progressive Grocer* (November 1991), p. 43.

28. Ibid.

29. See Mike McDermott, "The Revenge of the Little Guy," *Adweek's Marketing Week* (September 17, 1990), pp. 21 ff.

30. Weinstein, "Climate for Co-Ops: Partly Cloudly," p. 43.

31. See Marjorie Wold, "Just Call It Smart for Short," *Progressive Grocer* (September 1991), p. 44.

32. Harold J. Novick, "When to Use Independent Reps," *Business Marketing* (December 1987), p. 65.

33. Melissa Campanelli, "Manufacturers' Reps: Agents of Change," *Sales & Marketing Management* (February 1995), p. 72.

34. *Foodservice Brokers: Moving the Industry* (Washington, D.C., n.d.).

35. Steve Weinstein, "Banking on Brokers," *Progressive Grocer* (November 1990), p. 73.

36. For a discussion of product liability concerns of wholesalers, see Jere W. Morehead, "Products Liability: Exposure for Everyone in the Chain of Marketing?" *Journal of the Academy of Marketing Science,* Vol. 19 (Winter 1991), pp. 69–70.

37. See Frederick E. Webster, Jr., *Industrial Marketing Strategy* (New York: John Wiley & Sons, 1991), pp. 236–240.

38. Nicholas Nickolaus, "Marketing New Products with Industrial Distributors," *Industrial Marketing Management,* Vol. 19 (November 1990), p. 292.

39. Weinstein, "Banking on Brokers," p. 73.

40. *Handling Product Conflicts: A Joint Subcommittee White Paper.*

41. *Guides for Developing Food Broker-Principal Agreements* (Washington, D.C.: National Food Brokers Association, 1990), p. 2.

42. Kenneth G. Hardy, "Manufacturers: Use Distributors Profitably," *Business Quarterly* (Spring 1990), pp. 27–30.

43. Allan Magrath, "The Hidden Clout of Marketing Middlemen," *Journal of Business Strategy,* Vol. 11 (March/April 1990), pp. 38–41.

44. Louis W. Stern and Thomas L. Eovaldi, *Legal Aspects of Marketing Strategy* (Englewood Cliffs, N.J.: Prentice-Hall, 1984), p. 330.

45. Ray O. Werner, "Marketing and the United States Supreme Court, 1975–1981," *Journal of Marketing,* Vol. 46 (Summer 1982), p. 74.

46. Stern and Eovaldi, *Legal Aspects of Marketing Strategy,* p. 321.

47. Brad Reid, "*Michael Halebian, N.J. Inc. v. Roppe Rubber Corp. et al.,*" *Journal of Marketing,* Vol. 55 (January 1991), pp. 85–86.

48. Ibid.

49. John R. Johnson, "Distributor Termination: You Can Fight Back," *Industrial Distribution* (February 1994), pp. 20–22.

50. See Brad Reid, "*Richard J. Kowalski et al. v. Chicago Tribune Co.,*" *Journal of Marketing,* Vol. 53 (April 1989), pp. 103–104.

51. E. Raymond Corey, *Industrial Marketing Systems* (Boston: HBS Case Services, 1982), p. 27.

CASE 1

ANHEUSER-BUSCH: TERRITORIAL RESTRICTIONS IN BEER DISTRIBUTION

Anheuser-Busch Inc., the marketer of such beers as Budweiser, Busch, and Michelob, is seeking to better control distribution of its beers in New York City. The firm has raised the wholesale prices of its popular brands throughout the state and will issue a rebate of $1.00 to $1.15 to those retailers who buy all their beer from the company's four New York City franchised wholesalers. These wholesalers are expected to retain the old pricing on Anheuser-Busch products. The 15 cent difference between the cost increase is an incentive for grocery stores and other retailers to buy all their beer from the franchised wholesaler.

According to the Empire State Beer Distributors Association, which has 325 independent wholesaler members, this strategy is an attempt to eliminate transshipping of Anheuser-Busch beers. These independent wholesalers supply small restaurants, delicatessens, and bodegas with beer that has been purchased from authorized Anheuser-Busch wholesalers that are located upstate. These upstate wholesalers have lower wholesale prices than those of authorized New York City-based wholesalers. Under the proposed plan, independent distributors would not be entitled to any rebate. Many of these distributors have a large market presence in inner-city neighborhoods.

The impact of the price increase and rebate plan is to change the price advantage back to the New York City authorized wholesaler and away from the independent distributor.

According to the publisher of a trade publication, "Anheuser Busch is trying very hard . . . to keep its product within the territory it assigned to its distributor so that it can monitor its product quality." According to this argument, the use of franchised wholesalers assures greater control in shipping and greater product freshness. Many New York City-based beer wholesalers were also angry that they had to handle recycling of Anheuser-Busch beer containers that they did not sell.

An independent distributor argued that the price difference could force him to abandon Anheuser-Busch products. The brand is so important to most independents that cutting this brand could drive them out of business. Another independent distributor argued that the price difference of $1.15 on a $10.55 wholesale price of a case of Budweiser beer is significant. The bars, restaurants, groceries, and bodegas that the independent serves will quickly switch to the franchise distributors.

What is particularly disturbing to many of the independent distributors is that they have distributed Anheuser-Busch products in inner-city areas that were avoided by Anheuser-Busch's franchised wholesalers. Only after the independents built up distribution for Anheuser-Busch products to the point where it was profitable for Anheuser-Busch's franchised wholesalers did Anheuser-Busch change its pricing strategy.

New York City-based authorized Anheuser-Busch wholesalers argue that their contracts with Anheuser-Busch give them territorial protection and that competition from distributors with lower cost structures is unfair, and contrary to their agreements with Anheuser-Busch. The new pricing strategy protects their investment in their territories.

The New York State Attorney General's office filed an antitrust suit against Anheuser-Busch and its four New York City-based distributors. The suit charged that distribution contracts that restrict wholesalers to sell beer in designated territories artificially increases the price of beer. The Consumer Affairs commissioner of New York City is concerned that once Anheuser-Busch drives out the independent distributors, it will gradually raise the prices of its beers between $1 and $2 a case. A federal judge ruled that the state did not prove its allegations that Anheuser-Busch improperly assigned exclusive territories to its wholesalers to drive up the price of beer. A spokesperson for the attorney general of New York argued that the state had evidence that the lawsuit had caused Anheuser-Busch to allow some beer to be shipped outside normal distribution channels. This strategy had the impact of increasing competition and lowering beer prices.

QUESTIONS

1. Evaluate Anheuser-Busch's planned strategy.
2. Assess the argument of independent wholesalers that only after they built up distribution did Anheuser-Busch seek to bypass them.
3. What other strategies can Anheuser-Busch utilize to better control its distribution? Explain your answer.
4. What options (other than the lawsuit described in the case) should independent wholesalers pursue?

Sources: Allen R. Myerson, "Are Champagne Prices in Store for Beer?" *New York Times* (January 31, 1992), pp. B1, B3; Alan J. Wax, "This Bud's for Just a Few Chosen as Distributors," *Newsday* (January 31, 1992), p. 45; and Alan J. Wax, "Judge Dumps State's Beer Case," *Newsday* (January 23, 1993), p. 16.

CASE 2

WAKEFERN: A RETAILER-OWNED WHOLESALE COOPERATIVE

Wakefern is a major retailer-owned wholesale cooperative. Its members operate grocery stores under the ShopRite name. Wakefern began with a handful of independents in 1947 and by 1993 grew to 181 supermarkets, 100 pharmacies, and 49 liquor stores in five states (New Jersey, New York, Pennsylvania, Connecticut, and Delaware). In that year, its wholesale sales to its members exceeded $3.7 billion. Wakefern's members range in size from independents to corporate chains; larger members have annual sales volumes as high as $700 million.

What sets Wakefern apart from traditional general-merchandise, full-service wholesalers is the retailer ownership of the wholesaler. Wakefern is organized through a committee and corporate staff member structure. There are about 20 to 30 members who are really active at Wakefern. Committees are involved with such activities as sales and merchandising, advertising, and site development. In addition to committees, Wakefern has product manager staff members responsible for buying, merchandising, and pricing. The Wakefern staff members work actively together with committees. While the merchandising committee approves new items and programs, the staff members are responsible for implementing the plan. Staff product managers also have to bring programs to the relevant committee for approval.

Wakefern's facilities include grocery warehouses, a perishables depot, and a general-merchandise warehouse with a combined capacity of 2.5 million square feet of space. Its distribution system enables Wakefern to serve stores within 200 miles of its warehouses. Wakefern is especially concerned about using its warehouse space capacity. According to one observer, "Forget about the stores. The warehouse has to grow to develop more patronage dividends." To help ensure that the warehouses are used to their capacity, Wakefern members must purchase at least 85 percent of their needs from Wakefern on items stocked in the Wakefern warehouse. If a Wakefern member sells its stores to a company not approved by Wakefern, the seller must pay a portion of certain warehouse facility costs. The purchaser must also agree to be a Wakefern member, if it qualifies.

The purchaser also cannot own or operate non-ShopRite supermarkets in 12 northeastern states. (These include five states where ShopRite does not operate stores.)

As with other grocery wholesalers, there is some controversy about Wakefern's developing corporate-owned stores. Wakefern originally got into corporate stores in the 1980s when a Wakefern member had problems with one location. In 1987 Wakefern purchased the Connecticut and Massachusetts stores of one member. These stores were originally purchased as a defensive measure. Currently, Wakefern will open corporate stores only when Wakefern sees a need to expand stores, but where no member is able to open a new store. The same criteria are used to evaluate a proposed location regardless of ownership. For example, to operate under the ShopRite format, a grocery store must have a minimum size of 40,000 to 45,000 square feet. Their prototype store is 55,000 square feet, including a pharmacy.

Wakefern has been viewed as being on the forefront of computerization, but it is not complacent. A new computer system will handle check cashing, pharmacy, labor scheduling, and labor attendance on a store-by-store basis. The new system may also handle credit cards. Wakefern has been doing computer-assisted ordering for years, and it is moving to computer-generated ordering for products that are directly delivered to each store (direct store delivery—DSD items). Wakefern plans to better control pricing and inventory management for DSD items.

Wakefern is very aggressive in buying. Unlike other wholesalers, it seeks to takes advantage of quantity discounts to sell at reduced prices to final consumers, not to generate additional profits through forward buying. Its members also love to run half-price sales. ShopRite has agreed to hold the price on specific items for 60 days. These items are highlighted in bag stuffers and ads.

Wakefern uses its private-label programs effectively. The co-op has about 3000 private-label items, and about 28 percent of its total sales are in these items. Wakefern has three private brands: the standard quality ShopRite brand; Elizabeth York, a premium quality private label; and Farm Flavor, a lower grade.

QUESTIONS

1. Discuss the differences between Wakefern and a traditional general-merchandise full-service wholesaler.
2. What are the advantages of Wakefern's retailer ownership organization? the disadvantages?
3. Evaluate Wakefern's strategy of developing corporate stores.
4. Assess Wakefern's warehouse policies.

Sources: Glenn Snyder, "Wakefern/ShopRite Thinks Big," *Progressive Grocer* (January 1992), pp. 61–62; Steve Weinstein, "Wakefern: A Co-Op That Works," *Progressive Grocer* (October 1991), pp. 27–32; *Wakefern Food Corporation: Press Release* (July 1994); and Steve Weinstein, "Wakefern Operations: Overcoming Obstacles," *Progressive Grocer* (November 1991), pp. 28–42.

PART TWO CASE

DELL COMPUTER CORPORATION

INTRODUCTION

Even though Michael Dell started off at the University of Texas at Austin in 1983 as a premed major, his real long-term ambition was to market personal computers. Some observers have commented that Dell saw college more as a potential market for his computer products than as a place of higher learning. As a college freshman at the University of Texas at Austin, he sold PCs out of his dormitory room. He assembled and sold hard drive kits (made up of a hard drive, software, and cables) that were used to upgrade early-model IBM PCs. During his first semester at school, Michael purchased the excess inventories of authorized IBM dealers and sold them through advertisements in local newspapers and national computer magazines. The IBM dealers were anxious to sell these parts to Dell at cost since their contract with IBM required them to maintain relatively high sales quotas. These sales quotas commonly exceeded demand.

Since Dell had no overhead, he could easily undercut traditional retail computer stores. His products were sold at 10 to 15 percent below traditional retail prices.

As of his second semester, Dell was grossing big money: $30,000 in the month of January and $80,000 in April 1984. And he was only 19! Despite his business success, both of Dell's parents were upset. During a surprise visit to his dorm room, his parents quickly realized that he did not buy any books for his spring courses and that he concentrated all of his energies on his computer business. Michael made a deal with his parents; if he finished all of his spring classes, he could continue with his business in the summer. If the business didn't work out, he would agree to return to school in the fall.

As of the summer, Dell started PC's Limited, with 1000 square feet of office space in Austin. As with his old dormitory operation, Michael Dell advertised in newspapers and computer trade magazines. By that September, he was selling $180,000 worth of computers a month. Dell quickly realized that while sales were strong, his firm's profit margins were very low. He then decided to design his own personal computers, to sell them directly to consumers using advertising and telemarketing, and to support his personal computer machine sales with outstanding customer service. Dell was one of the first to make inexpensive IBM clones. He was soon selling personal computers for as little as $795, about 40 percent less than what IBM charged. By cutting his marketing and distribution costs by selling direct to consumers, Dell has been able to undersell traditional manufacturers (including Compaq) and retailers (such as Computerland and JWP Businessland) and produce a satisfactory profit.

In 1986 Dell hired E. Lee Walker, a venture capitalist who started as a consultant and later became president and chief operating officer. Lee Walker helped

Dell raise capital by taking Dell Computer Corporation public (with the sale of 3.5 million shares of stock for $30 million) in 1987. Dell still owned 80 percent of the stock. His share of the company was worth $120 million. Dell now had the capital to go beyond direct marketing to individuals to sell to corporations. He subsequently sold off all but a 35 percent share in the company. His 35 percent stake in the firm is now worth $300 million.

Just nine years after his first sales out of his dormitory room, Dell Computer topped $2 billion in sales. Over the 1985 to 1990 time period, Dell's sales increased at a compound rate of 75 percent per year. During this time period, the firm's net profits increased at a compound rate of more than 100 percent per year. Although net profit for 1993 rose to $101.6 million, the company suffered a loss of $36.9 million in 1994; this was its first full-year loss as a public company. The loss was due in large part to inventory writedowns, and to costs associated with delayed and canceled notebook products and with the consolidation and restructuring of international operations (see Table 1).

DIRECT-MARKETING PERSONAL COMPUTER SALES

Mail-order computers accounted for 22 percent of the $29 billion a year market for personal computers and peripherals. According to Maxwell Sroge, a catalog consultant, computer suppliers are the fastest growing sector of the mail-order business. As a group, mass merchants and direct-marketing sales of personal computers grew more than 20 percent in 1991, whereas overall sales of personal computers experienced no growth. Another market research firm, WorkGroup Technologies, estimates that mail-order companies will account for 29 percent of all personal computer sales in 1995 versus their 22 percent market share as of 1991.

The success of the mail-order segment has come at the expense of traditional manufacturers and their traditional dealer-oriented channels. One market analyst estimates that mail-order retailers accounted for between 15 and 20 per-

TABLE 1   DELL COMPUTER CORPORATION, SELECTED FINANCIAL DATA, 1986–1994

Year	Sales ($ mil)	Net Income ($ mil)	Employees
1986	34	1	—
1987	70	2	—
1988	159	9	—
1989	258	14	1,175
1990	389	5	1,500
1991	546	27	2,050
1992	890	51	2,970
1993	2,014	102	4,650
1994	2,873	(36)	5,980

Source: Dell Computer Corporation 1994 Annual Report.

cent of the total $45 billion personal computer sales as of the beginning of 1995. Four out of five of the world's largest personal computer manufacturers have incorporated direct marketing into their marketing strategies.

Mail-order operations such as Dell Computer do not have the expense of running stores and are not confined to six-day-a-week and 10-hour-a-day operations. The best mail-order computer vendors have used the strategies of such excellent mail-order operations as L.L. Bean and Lands' End. Customers are treated with respect, salespersons are knowledgeable, the firms' return policies are generous, and customer service is superb. To reduce concerns among consumers that are leery of buying a computer over the phone, most major computer direct marketers offer free trial periods (of between 30 and 60 days) with money-back guarantees, one- to two-year warranties, toll-free phone lines, and in-home or in-office repair services. Dell's customers, for example, can place orders or have technical questions answered by knowledgeable technicians seven days a week and 15 hours a day on weekdays. Dell even maintains a toll-free fax service that provides detailed specifications of Dell Systems for potential buyers.

DELL'S CHANNEL STRATEGY

Dell's overall marketing strategy can be separated into two components: its channels strategy, and its marketing strategy other than channels. The channels strategy includes direct marketing, dual channels of distribution, inventory management, and customer service. Its marketing strategy other than channels consists of target market selection, product strategy, pricing strategy, advertising strategy, and international sales.

Although these areas are covered separately, they are interconnected. For example, direct marketing provides Dell with better access to consumer preferences for new products, a database of past customers for promotions, and the ability to undercut competitors that use traditional dealer channels.

DIRECT MARKETING

There are three broad channel arrangements among personal computer manufacturers: conventional channels, direct marketing, and mass market channels. (See Table 2 for a listing and description of these channel arrangements.)

TABLE 2 ALTERNATIVE CHANNEL ARRANGEMENTS FOR PERSONAL COMPUTERS

CONVENTIONAL CHANNELS	
Manufacturer's sales force	Sells one brand of personal computers. Manufacturer's sales representatives visit important accounts and use telemarketing for smaller accounts and for reorders.
Authorized dealers	Salespeople and technicians are manufacturer trained. Dealers participate in cooperative advertising with manufacturer. May maintain repair facilities at the dealer's premises. Used by manufacturers such as IBM, Apple, and Hewlett-Packard.

(Continued)

TABLE 2 (CONTINUED)

Franchises	Dealers join franchises to take advantage of buying power, cooperative advertising, and technical assistance of franchisor. Examples of franchises are Intelligent Electronics and Computerland.
Computer superstores	Stores with over 25,000 square feet of space that specialize in computers. Sell leading brands such as Apple, Compaq, and Hewlett-Packard. Computer City SuperCenter is a computer superstore and a subsidiary of Tandy.
Computer specialty stores	Often independently owned. May cooperatively purchase parts with other independents to reduce costs through greater bargaining power. Generally offer on-dealer premises service. Many repair machines purchased through other dealers. Often assemble computers through purchasing components from multiple manufacturers.
Value-added resellers	Sell computer systems bundled with software for use by professionals, manufacturers, wholesalers, and retailers. May add hardware to standard systems to accommodate special needs of users.
DIRECT MARKETING Direct-marketing channel	Mail-order manufacturers that typically offer on-site repair service through firms such as TRW and GE, and toll-free technical assistance. Examples include Dell, Zeos, and Gateway 2000.
MASS MARKETING Office supply stores	Sell two to three brands. Products are often configured with popular software. Consumer cannot vary computer options in store. Level of customer service varies from dealer to dealer. Technical assistance and repair service provided by manufacturer. Examples include Staples and OfficeMax.
Consumer electronics stores	Sell multiple brands. Products are often configured with popular software. Consumer may be able to vary computer options in store. Technical assistance and repair service provided by manufacturer; some technical assistance provided by retailer. May have large mail-order sales. Salespeople may have high technical knowledge. Examples include J & R Music World and 47th Street Camera.
Buying clubs	Sell two to three brands. Products are often configured with popular software. Consumer cannot vary computer options in store. Technical assistance and repair service provided by manufacturer. Examples include Price/Costco and Sam's.
Department stores	Sell two to three brands. Products are often configured with popular software. Consumer cannot vary computer options in store. Technical assistance and repair service provided by manufacturer. An example is Sears, Roebuck.

Source: Loosely adapted from "Computer Stores: Getting What You Pay For," *New York Times: The 1992 Review of Computers,* p. 24; and Steve Kichen, "Pick a Channel," *Forbes* (March 2, 1992), pp. 108, 110.

Table 3 compares Dell's 1993 sales by distribution channel to the personal computer industry as a whole. In the conventional channel arrangement, a manufacturer of personal computers uses its own sales force to sell and service major accounts; a dealer network (comprised of authorized dealers, franchises, computer superstores, and computer specialty stores) to cover small firms, the home office, and the final consumer segments; and value-added resellers (VARs) to sell computer systems that are bundled with software and training to specialized users such as attorneys, dentists, and insurance brokers. Firms such as IBM, Unisys, and Digital Equipment Corporation use this channel. In a direct-marketing channel arrangement, the manufacturer sells direct to consumers (including large and small accounts). Dell, Austin Computer Systems, CompuAdd, Gateway 2000, and Swan Technologies are among the firms that use direct marketing. In a mass market channel, computer manufacturers sell their products through retailers such as Sears, Wal-Mart, and Price/Costco. Packard Bell and KLH are among the manufacturers using this channel arrangement.

Conventional channels recognize the need for different channel arrangements for the various types of customers. For instance, home hobbyists buying a computer for the first time are given instruction by dealers, whereas professionals requiring special software can utilize value-added resellers. A potential problem with conventional channels is that declining prices in the computer field often pit the manufacturer against its dealer. For example, Compaq attempted to protect its 41 percent gross margin by cutting its discounts to computer stores. In the past its highest volume stores received wholesale discounts of about 40 percent; these retailers now get only 30 percent off the retail suggested list price. As a result, some dealers have chosen not to push Compaq computers. Dell also views this channel strategy as a high-cost channel arrangement.

Direct channels enable a computer manufacturer to control the level of customer service, control final retail selling price, utilize low-cost locations for computer assembly and repair, and sell and provide customer assistance 18 hours a day between 5 and 7 days per week. Dell has always used a direct-marketing strategy. It claims that its direct-marketing strategy gives it several important advantages over manufacturers that utilize conventional channels. Specifically, direct marketing enables Dell to:

- Lower costs by conducting channel functions more efficiently than retailers. This enables Dell to undercut the prices of firms using traditional channel structures while still making a satisfactory profit. Dell estimates

TABLE 3   DELL COMPUTER VERSUS PC INDUSTRY DISTRIBUTION CHANNELS, 1993 (PERCENT OF TOTAL SALES)

	Dell Computer	PC Industry
Direct sales	75	36
Dealers	0	31
Retail dealers	10	16
Other resellers	15	17
Total	100	100

Source: Peter Burrows, "Dell Computer: Beyond Rock Bottom," *Business Week* (March 14, 1994), p. 82.

that it has a 15 percent cost advantage over such competitors as Compaq.
- Track every contact with a customer from initial inquiry to calls for technical support. Dell receives more than 35,000 sales and service calls on a worldwide basis per day.
- Use its database for specialized promotions and market research. In 1994 Dell began to target customers through five broad end-user categories based on their personal computer usage patterns. For example, a Techno-wizard is a power user that wants to own the fastest and highest performance system on the market. In contrast, a Techno-critical user is responsible for maintaining one or more local area networks. Each has different needs.
- Control the quality of customer service. At Dell, all customer inquiries calls are handled by computer-literate salespeople who are trained by Dell. If the customer calls back, he'll speak with the same salesperson again.
- Reduce its inventory levels. Dell has the equivalent of 35 days worth of sales in its inventory. In comparison, Compaq Computer has 110 days.

Mass market-based computer manufacturers aim their sales at first-time computer buyers who like to buy personal computers at office supply stores, consumer electronics stores, buying clubs, and department stores. Firms such as Packard Bell were among the first to use the mass-market channel. Packard Bell has sold its computers through such channels as Wal-Mart, consumer electronics outlets, department stores, and buying clubs. Its products received prime shelf space in these retail outlets and high levels of advertising support. In the first quarter of 1994, Packard Bell shipped more PCs in the United States than either IBM or Apple, despite a six-day shutdown of its manufacturing facilities due to an earthquake. Packard Bell is growing fast due to its distribution channels, as well as its knack for anticipating consumer needs. Packard Bell had these channels to themselves. Other competitors eschewed the home market because of the high return rate (about 20 percent versus single-digit returns in the industrial market). Packard Bell was also the first major vendor to ship personal computers with multimedia capabilities and among the first to ship personal computers with the Pentium microprocessor chip.

DUAL CHANNELS OF DISTRIBUTION

In 1988 Dell added a sales force to deal with large corporate customers and signed up value-added resellers who customize Dell computers with their own software and sell them to specialized markets such as dentists. Its corporate customers enable Dell to sell a large number of computers in a single order and to deal with experienced buyers that require little hand-holding. These corporate customers accounted for 50 percent of Dell's 1994 sales. All of Dell's mail-order customers do not save sales tax, as Dell charges sales tax on all of these sales.

Dell also sells to value-added retailers recognizing that some customers are willing to pay a premium for additional support and better software–hardware integration. As of 1994, 11 percent of its sales were to these value-added resellers.

Dell had broadened its market coverage through the sale of Dell computers to some buying clubs (such as Sam's Wholesale Club) as of 1990, but the firm pulled out of this distribution channel in the summer of 1994. At one point, Dell sold its products in more than 2000 consumer retail outlets in 10 countries in addition to its mail-order operations. Sales through consumer outlets accounted for less than 2 percent as of Dell's announced pullout. Retail store sales never exceeded 10 percent of Dell's overall sales. According to Dell's chairman, its retail store sales were not profitable. According to Michael Dell, "There are 180 million telephones in the United States, and anyone can reach us."

INVENTORY MANAGEMENT

Dell has developed a sophisticated inventory management system. The system enables Dell to have the lowest inventory level in the industry (just a four-week supply as of the beginning of 1995), yet ship orders for personal computers within five days of its receipt.

Unlike other vendors that keep large inventories in stock, Dell assembles most computers only after they have been ordered. It can customize an order and ship it within five days. Specifications are sent via computer network to a nearby plant. This allows Dell's customers to order a computer with a hard disk, graphics board, and memory to meet their unique needs. For customers in a hurry or for those who desire popular models with standard configurations, Dell will ship computers within a day of receiving an order.

Dell understands that inventory management is a very sensitive issue in the personal computer business. First, consumers typically want a computer as soon as possible. Even a wait of only several days seems like a long time to many consumers. Second, from a consumer choice perspective, a computer purchase is more similar to the purchase of a car than to that of an appliance. There are at least three different types of microprocessors, five different sizes of hard disks, and four different levels of memory. This makes for 60 different computer configurations. Third, with chip prices constantly fluctuating and with overall computer prices generally decreasing over time, there are dangers in keeping too high a level of inventory. For example, in 1988 Dell loaded up on DRAM chips, anticipating high machine sales levels and higher chip prices. Not only did these sales not materialize, but also chip prices dropped 70 percent. Dell tried to sell off its $104 million in chip inventory through machine sales instead of taking a charge against earnings. However, owing to a decline in prices for machines, Dell was unable to recoup its chip costs. As a result, in fiscal 1990, Dell's profits dropped to $5.1 million, down from $14.4 million in fiscal 1989.

Unlike other competitors, Dell relies on an assemble-to-order production philosophy. While this concept may reduce its ability to fill an order quickly, it reduces inventory accumulations, ensures that the correct configurations are built, and reduces costs. Some users, however, are critical of Dell's inventory policy. According to an account representative of the leasing and financing arm of AIG Insurance, "The machines are good, but Dell's idea of just-in-time is not the same as ours." While the account representative purchases up to 100 machines a day, Dell meets the promised delivery schedule of six days only about half of the time.

Dell sells software, modems, CD-ROMS, and other computer peripherals through an arrangement with Merisel, a large distributor. Merisel typically delivers the ordered goods directly to the buyer, saving Dell the need to stock and ship the goods itself. Many customers like to deal with one supplier and to order the computer, peripherals, and software from one supplier with a single phone call.

CUSTOMER SERVICE

Michael Dell understands that personal computers have become a commodity for many customers. He also understands that many buyers are reluctant to spend $3000 or so on a product that cannot be examined until after it has been paid for. As a result, the firm has a long-term commitment to high levels of customer service. According to Dell's director of marketing, "Customer service is not a department, it's a philosophy." Dell's customer service strategy not only established the company as a bona fide alternative to the local computer store, but it also made the mail order a viable channel for buying computers. "Dell raised people's perceptions of what mail order is all about," states a market researcher.

Dell Computer Corporation holds onto customers through what Michael Dell calls "direct relationship marketing." As he states, "We take direct responsibility for the complete satisfaction of each and every customer."

Other elements of Dell's customer service strategy are as follows:

- Dell was the first personal computer maker to offer guaranteed next-day on-site service (1987) and the first to provide replacement machines by overnight delivery (1989).

- Dell Computer was the first-place winner in J. D. Power & Associates' first personal computer customer satisfaction survey. The rating is based on a survey of customers in office-based businesses with fewer than 500 employees.

- Results of a *PC Magazine* "Service and Reliability" study (of 8592 reader responses to a mail survey of randomly selected subscribers) shows a higher than average rating for Dell on the basis of its four service and reliability criteria: satisfaction with the repair experience, satisfaction with technical support, reliability, and future likelihood of buying another Dell computer.

- Dell claims that 70 percent of its sales are to existing customers. This loyalty attests to overall customer satisfaction.

- Every Friday morning at 7:30, Dell managers have a Customer Advocate meeting. At the weekly meeting, managers review customer complaints, with the goal of turning solutions to specific problems into policy changes.

- Dell claims that its toll-free technical hotline solves 91 percent of all technical problems through its staff of 150 technicians. If a problem cannot be solved by telephone, Dell dispatches BancTec Service Corporation (BSC) employees to the customer's home or office within four hours in 17 major cities. If a technical problem occurs with a Dell laptop, Dell will even transfer all data from the unit sent in for repair to a replacement unit. The replacement unit will be shipped out by Dell the next business day.

In contrast to Dell's positive experiences with customer service during a time period of rapid sales growth, growth has created difficulties for some of Dell's direct-marketing competitors. According to a Compaq executive, high sales growth is "almost an albatross. The more success you have, the higher the level of customer expectations." For example, competitor Gateway 2000, which has nearly 500,000 machines in circulation, receives 9000 calls on its toll-free customer service phone number on a typical Monday morning. Gateway has experienced difficulty in training technical personnel in an area where the largest employers are meat-packing houses.

DELL'S MARKETING STRATEGY (OTHER THAN CHANNELS)

Dell's marketing strategy other than channels is made up of target market selection, product strategy, pricing strategy, advertising strategy, and international strategy.

TARGET MARKET SELECTION

Major corporations, government units, medical, and educational institutions now account for about half of Dell's total sales. Dell claims that 80 percent of the Fortune 100 are Dell customers. Dell has dedicated sales and management teams that are headed by account representatives to work with major accounts. It even works with large customers on disposing of and reselling their older systems. Sales to medium-sized companies, smaller businesses, and individuals increased 31 percent (to $1.03 billion) between 1993 and 1994.

Dell also aims its sales at the experienced business user and knowledgeable final consumer. According to Michael Dell, "We're not interested in home PCs. We can grow at a rapid rate by focusing on our core business."

PRODUCT STRATEGY

Unlike other competitors that buy generic components from well-known suppliers on a competitive bid or low-cost basis, Dell is active in research and development. Dell has been one of the industry's pioneers in the development of upgradable computers. With an upgradable computer, a home user can change a computer's microprocessor chip in about 15 minutes with a screwdriver and a simple installation procedure. Upgradables offer many advantages to computer users: there is no need to transfer data from the old to the new computer, a computer owner does not have to go through the hassle of selling an old computer, and business users report that it is easier to sell firms on the purchase of upgradable models.

Upgradable models also offer advantages to Dell. They are typically easier to repair than models not designed for upgrading. Upgradable models also use standardized components for multiple models. Standardized components lower Dell's inventory costs and give Dell greater buying power with suppliers.

Dell's direct-marketing channel strategy allows the company to ask customers what they want directly. According to Dell's senior vice president of the product group, "We get 5000 sales calls a day. We take all that information into account in computer design. We won't do something where there isn't a market." Dell also has access to its 750,000 personal computer owners through a database. The database enables Dell to better focus on important product improvements.

Dell is aware that product life cycles in the personal computer industry are very short. On average, Dell has introduced a new product every three weeks. Its oldest product is 11 months old.

PRICING STRATEGY

Dell's pricing strategy is especially attractive when compared to IBM and Compaq. According to the editor of a newsletter, IBM and Compaq machines retail for 30 percent more than comparable machines sold by leading direct marketers. Although both IBM and Compaq feel that they do not have to match low-end competitors on a dollar-for-dollar basis, Compaq was forced to cut prices by as much as 34 percent in 1991. Price cuts are costly to Compaq, since the company refunds to dealers the difference between the old and new wholesale prices on their inventory.

Despite deep cuts owing to competition from direct marketers and a slowdown in overall demand for personal computers, IBM and Compaq cannot match the prices of direct marketers. The high-cost structures at these firms prevent them from being profitable even at gross profit margins of 40 to 50 percent. In contrast, Dell reported a 5.0 percent net profit as a percentage of sales in 1993, with a 22.3 percent gross margin.

Dell Computer's overall pricing strategy is to offset declining gross margins by reducing operating expenses as a percentage of sales. This keeps net income as a percentage of sales constant and enables the firm to chase market share through price reductions. "It's the same thing Wal-Mart has done for years," states Michael Dell. Dell is also aware that a low-overhead upstart can take business away from it just as his firm took away business from IBM and Compaq. As a result, Dell is adding value to its computers by bundling software programs from Lotus and Microsoft. It has also reduced its prices. At one point, Dell's prices were 60 percent above Gateway; they are now within 10 to 15 percent above Gateway and, in some cases, even below Gateway. Dell figures that as long as its prices are in the ballpark, the firm's reputation for quality and service will enable it to gain market share. According to Michael Dell, "Price attracts customers, but service retains them."

ADVERTISING STRATEGY

Dell's overall marketing expenses in 1990 were $87.8 million (about 16.1 percent of sales) in 1990. This figure includes an estimated $16.9 million in advertising expenditures. Dell spends less on advertising than smaller competitors (such as Northgate Computer Systems) and proportionately less than other direct-marketing companies.

Dell's director of advertising states that each advertisement has a specific code and telephone number. The firm tracks the effectiveness of each periodical by recording the advertising code when a purchase is made as the result of an advertisement. This allows Dell to determine the relative pulling power of different advertising strategies, of different media, and the effective duration of each advertisement.

Dell is also noted for quickly implementing its advertising strategy. When Dell was awarded first place in the J. D. Power quality poll, its print and televised media campaign was ready within six weeks, not the four months considered typical for such a campaign. Dell's campaign was effective in generating a high degree of brand awareness and in positioning Dell as a major computer manufacturer, according to Dell's director of advertising. The campaign was also successful in reaching prospects who do not normally read computer magazines.

Dell also has used comparative advertising, focusing on the large price differences between comparable Dell and Compaq equipment. Compaq has filed legal suit seeking to ban Dell from poking fun at Compaq's high prices. According to Michael Dell, "We've been running ads comparing ourselves to Compaq since 1987. It wasn't until Dell became a threat to their business that they sued." According to Compaq's chief executive Joseph R. Canion, "We're just trying to keep them from misleading the public."

INTERNATIONAL STRATEGY

Dell began selling in Europe in 1987. It realized that European sales would be difficult since Europeans had never in the past purchased big-ticket items through mail-order sales. "In every country they told us mail order would not work," recalls Andrew R. Harris, senior vice president for international operations for Dell. Dell received 30 percent of its total sales in Europe as of the beginning of 1995.

To get European customers to try its personal computers, Dell developed an educational program. The campaign that ran throughout Britain and the continent was in seven languages. The ads stressed Dell's reputation for quality, service, and price. Most ads included the tagline: "It's Best to Be Direct." Dell's current goal in Europe is to develop and maintain a single price throughout the continent as well as a five-day delivery policy.

Originally, Dell maintained separate distribution facilities in each major country in Europe. It has now consolidated its distribution network in Europe in one location (Ireland) and pulled out of such marginal markets as Finland. Its assembly plant in Limerick, Ireland, will be important in fulfilling its customer service standards. Ninety-five percent of Dell's European sales have come from business customers. Dell still needs to penetrate the home office and hobbyist markets.

Dell is aggressively selling its products in Central and South America and the Caribbean as well. It is building a new factory in Malaysia. Dell has a contract with Xerox Corporation to distribute its computers in these markets.

In 1993 Dell announced that it would begin to implement its direct-marketing strategy in Japan. Although Dell would welcome orders from the general public, it plans to target business customers. As in the United States, Dell would provide free technical service by telephone and on-site service (through a

Japanese company). Dell's computer would be priced at the equivalent of $1200; this compares favorably to NEC's least expensive product, which has a list price of $1745. Some market analysts question whether Dell's strategy will be successful since many Japanese customers are accustomed to personalized service. Japanese customers also do not typically order expensive products through the mail or by telephone.

LONG-TERM OUTLOOK

Dell's past performance has been outstanding. Few companies can boast reaching $1 billion in sales in their first nine years of operation, or have a 75 percent compounded sales growth per year over a five-year period. Although its sales revenue for the year ended January 30, 1994 grew 42 percent from the prior year to $2.8 billion, during this time period, it suffered its first net loss as a public corporation.

Dell has a well-integrated marketing strategy with several strengths: control of distribution due to direct marketing, access to multiple target markets through dual channels of distribution, a superior inventory management system, and excellent customer service. In addition, the firm has a lower cost structure than major traditional channel competitors, a solid financial position, a positive brand image, and opportunities for growth in both domestic and international markets. These advantages cannot easily be copied by its competitors.

Of concern to Dell is increased price competition among all competitors, the increased feeling among consumers that personal computers are a commodity, lower gross profit margins throughout the industry, and limited domestic growth owing to market saturation.

QUESTIONS

1. a. Describe the marketing channel activities that must be undertaken by Dell due to its direct-marketing strategy.
   b. Which of these activities would ordinarily be conducted by retailers if Dell used a traditional channel arrangement? Explain your answer.
2. Outline the pros and cons of Dell's dual channels of distribution strategy.
3. Which of Dell's competitive advantages can be attributed to its channel strategy?
4. How can Dell Computer use data on the demographic environment of final consumers to improve its channel strategy?
5. Describe the nature of horizontal, intertype, vertical, and vertical marketing system competition for Dell Computer. Refer to Tables 2 and 3.
6. Develop specific criteria that Dell can use to evaluate a potential new value-added retailer as a channel member for its computers.
7. Evaluate the pros and cons of Dell's overall channel strategy.

Sources: Michael Allen, "Low-Cost PC Makers Have Come on Strong But Difficulties Loom," *Wall Street Journal* (May 11, 1992), pp. A1, A2; Peter Burrows, "Dell Computer: Beyond Rock Bottom," *Business Week* (March 14, 1994), pp. 80 ff; Peter Burrows, "The Computer Is in the Mail (Really)," *Business Week* (January 23, 1995), pp. 76–77; "Computer Stores: Getting What You Pay For," *New York Times: The 1992 Review of Computers,* p. 24; Jim Carlton, "Packard Bell Prospers Despite PC

Industry Shake-Up," *Wall Street Journal* (June 11, 1994), p. B4; *Dell Computer Corporation 1994 Annual Report;* Joseph Desposito, "Dell Computer Corporation," *PC Magazine* (May 26, 1992), pp. 120 ff.; Alan Deutschman, "America's Fastest Risers," *Fortune* (October 7, 1991), pp. 46–48 ff.; Stephanie Anderson Forest, "PC Slump? What PC Slump?" *Business Week* (July 1, 1991), pp. 66–67; Stephanie Anderson Forest, Catherine Arnst, Kathy Rebello, and Peter Burrows, "The Education of Michael Dell," *Business Week* (March 22, 1993), pp. 83–88; "Dell to Sell Computers Directly to Japan," *New York Times* (January 22, 1993), p. D4; Mark Ivey, "Does Compaq's Formula Still Compute?" *Business Week* (May 13, 1991), pp. 100 ff.; Steve Kichen, "Pick a Channel," *Forbes* (March 2, 1992), pp. 108 ff.; Hal Lancaster and Michael Allen, "Dell Computer Battles Its Rivals with a Lean Machine," *Wall Street Journal* (March 30, 1992), p. B4; Peter H. Lewis, "Michael Dell Says He's More Than Ready for a Good Fight," *New York Times* (July 5, 1992), p. F12; Steve Lohr, "How Did Dell Computer Stumble?" *New York Times* (May 28, 1993), pp. D1–D2; Toni Mack, "Michael Dell's New Religion," *Forbes* (June 6, 1994), pp. 45–45; Gary McWilliams, "Mail-Order Madness," *Business Week* (October 26, 1991), p. 128; Patrick Oster and Igor Reichlin, "Dell: Mail Order Was Supposed to Fail," *Business Week* (January 20, 1992), p. 89; Claire Poole, "The Kid Who Turned Computers into Commodities," *Forbes* (October 21, 1991), pp. 318–319 ff.; Donna Tapellini, "The Advertising Shots Heard 'Round the World," *Electronic Business* (October 7, 1991), pp. 160 ff.; and Shawn Tully, "The Modular Corporation," *Fortune* (February 8, 1993), pp. 106–108 ff.

PART III

CHANNEL MANAGEMENT AND THE MARKETING MIX

In Part Three, we study channel management and the marketing mix: relationship marketing and customer service, physical distribution, market research and information systems, product management, pricing strategy, and promotion strategy.

CHAPTER 5
Relationship Marketing and Customer Service   Here, we describe the concept of relationship marketing and its implications for channel strategy. We then discuss the pros and cons of the use of relationship marketing and its most appropriate use. The development and implementation of a customer service strategy are discussed in depth. Lastly, we explain how a firm can develop customer service standards in physical distribution and how suppliers can be evaluated on the basis of multiple customer service standards.

CHAPTER 6
Physical Distribution Strategy in Channels   In this chapter, we examine important topics in physical distribution and their impact on channel management. Topics covered include an introduction to physical distribution, transportation decision making, warehousing, inventory management principles, and inventory management decision making.

CHAPTER 7
Market Research and Information Systems in Channels   In this chapter, we examine introductory topics in marketing research and the marketing research process in channels management. Introductory concepts in channel member marketing information systems and special topics in channel information systems are also analyzed.

CHAPTER 8
Product Management Strategy in Channels Here, we discuss the channel management implications of the product life cycle concept, including the new product planning process. Reverse channels of distribution—product recall and product recycling—are described. The channel management implications of packaging are analyzed, and the legal aspects of product management that relate to channels are studied.

CHAPTER 9
Pricing Strategy in Channels Here, we study the development, implementation, and control of a channel pricing strategy. Pricing is covered from a cost-, demand-, and competition-based perspective. Alternative pricing policies, discount structures, and adaptive pricing strategies are analyzed. The legal aspects of pricing in channels are also discussed.

CHAPTER 10
Promotion Strategy in Channels In this chapter, we study the role of advertising, publicity, personal selling, and sales promotion in channels. The channel promotional budgeting process is discussed and analyzed. Push and pull promotional strategies are covered. Alternative means of evaluating the effectiveness of channel promotional strategies are studied. Legal implications of a firm's channel promotional strategy are described.

CHAPTER 5

RELATIONSHIP MARKETING AND CUSTOMER SERVICE

CHAPTER OBJECTIVES

1. To introduce the concept of relationship marketing, the different forms of relationship marketing, and the implications of using a relationship marketing strategy.

2. To evaluate the use of a relationship marketing strategy.

3. To describe key issues in the development of a customer service strategy.

4. To discuss the implementation of a customer service strategy.

5. To study the development of customer service standards in physical distribution.

Allen-Edmonds is a high-quality shoe manufacturer. Its men's and ladies' shoes, which average $230 a pair, are sold in shoe departments in over 3000 retail stores in 33 countries around the world. Many of its shoes are sold in upscale retail department stores (such as Nordstrom's) and in fine men's clothing shops. Allen-Edmonds also sells its shoes in its own retail stores that are located in the United States and overseas. Allen-Edmonds's current yearly sales revenues are about $44 million.

Allen-Edmonds is firmly committed to building long-term relationships with its retailer channel members. Its interactions with its retailers are based on trust and shared responsibilities; it also conducts many important wholesaling, warehousing, and promotion activities for its retailer customers. This viewpoint is termed *relationship marketing.* Some of Allen-Edmonds's activities are as follows:

- Allen-Edmonds distributes its shoes to its retailer customers through manufacturer wholesaling. It does not use independent wholesalers since it desires to have total control over the quality of its customer service.

- Even though Allen-Edmonds has 12 retail stores and four leased departments in the United States, it is careful not to jeopardize its established relationships with its retailer customers. For example, while the firm advertises the availability of its catalog in The *Wall Street Journal, Business Week,* and *Gentlemen's Quarterly,* the catalog contains the name of the closest retailer where they can make the purchase. Although it could offer to ship the goods directly from the manufacturer, Allen-Edmonds does not want to lessen its trust among its resellers.

- Allen-Edmonds currently has a mailing list of 107,000 final customers by zip code. It uses this list in developing special promotions geared to specific retailers. For example, if a Philadelphia retailer is interested in a special promotion, Allen-Edmonds will send a mailing to customers located in its trading area (based on the zip code of the customer in Allen-Edmonds's mailing list). In addition to direct mailings, Allen-Edmonds encourages its retailer customers to use cooperative advertisements (in which the costs of the ads are shared between Allen-Edmonds and the retailer). This promotion generates store traffic for the retailer.

- Allen-Edmonds also sends hundreds of thousands of catalogs each year to its retailer customers for distribution to their final consumers. The catalogs help customers choose an Allen-Edmonds style or color that a store does not stock, and increase store traffic for its retailers.

- If a particular size or color is not available at any of its retailers, Allen-Edmonds will ship it directly to the customer on the store's behalf. This policy enables the customer to get his or her shoes without going back to the retailer. It also enables the retailer to obtain its full profit margin even though it did not purchase, stock, or ship the shoe.

- Allen-Edmonds sets up special "trunk shows" for its retailer customers to feature its new styles. It often sends a special representative to work with the retailer's sales personnel at these shows. Although the cost of the representative is paid by Allen-Edmonds, this activity increases store traffic for the retailer.

- Allen-Edmonds keeps communications open with its retailer customers through its quarterly newsletter. The newsletter features information on the stores that sell its shoe products, retailers' success stories with Allen-Edmonds products, and short stories on public figures that are loyal Allen-Edmonds customers.[1]

In this chapter, we study relationship marketing and customer service as applied to marketing channels. We will see the importance of trust and commitment in dealing with other channel members. We also examine how firms can develop and implement a customer service strategy.

AN INTRODUCTION TO RELATIONSHIP MARKETING

A firm's relationships with its suppliers and clients can be described from the perspective of two contrasting models: transactional marketing and relationship marketing. Transactional marketing represents the traditional view of marketing. In **transactional marketing**, a customer uses multiple sources of supply, tends to switch frequently among suppliers, and buys largely on the basis of price. The focus of marketing under transactional marketing is on exchanges in single transactions. Transactional marketing is also adversarial in nature. Both suppliers and buyers seek to maximize their short-term profitability (often at their exchange partner's expense). Sellers seek to make as much money from their customers, and buyers attempt to secure the best price relative to product quality and customer services. There is also little trust or commitment between buyers and sellers. Finally, the major marketing emphasis in transactional marketing is on attracting new customers (rather than keeping existing customers).

According to one academic researcher, transactional marketing rests on three fundamental assumptions:[2]

1. The buyer relies on a large number of suppliers who can be played off against each other to gain price concessions and to ensure continuity of supply.
2. The buyer allocates an amount to suppliers to keep them in line.
3. The buyer assumes an arms-length posture and uses only short-term contracts.

Critics of the transactional view of marketing state that marketing has overemphasized individual transactions at the cost of spending too little time on analyzing the relationship between the firm and its customers, suppliers, and other key markets. These critics also argue that transactional marketing has given too little attention to holding onto existing customers through superior customer service and to developing and maintaining buyer loyalty. Lastly, they state that transactional marketing has overemphasized the role of price relative to customer service.

In contrast to transactional marketing, **relationship marketing (partnering)** is based on building and maintaining long-term relationships between buyers and sellers that are based on trust and commitment. Relationship marketing proponents argue that the elements that comprise relationships in marketing are similar to those in personal relationships: shared values, trust, mutual respect, mutual benefit, frequent communications, honest feedback, cooperation, flexibility, understanding, and relationship commitment.[3]

Instead of being adversaries, in relationship marketing, buyers and sellers view each other as partners or collaborators in improving quality and managing costs. As partners, they involve each other in product development, inventory management, and sales processes through the sharing of information and technology. Thus, the emphasis in relationship marketing is on keeping existing customers and on forming and maintaining strong long-term ties that can be social (e.g., friendship), economic (e.g., joint investment), and technical (e.g., joint development of products).[4] Although relationship marketing concepts have been recognized in business-to-business marketing for some time now, they have more recently been expanded to final consumer marketing.

Evidence of the use of relationship marketing can be communications linkages between buyers and sellers (automated, such as electronic data interchange or nonautomated), a salesperson that is seen as a valuable consultant (instead of an order taker or order getter), an established means of conflict resolution (such as a distributor advisory council), the addition of value-added services (such as a supplier providing new research and development services for a buyer), coordination of responsibilities among channel members (such as a just-in-time inventory management system), and a focus on long-term relationships (such as a distributor's supplier helping the distributor plan and implement a sales call to an important client).

Proponents of the relationship marketing model argue that a firm cannot sustain long-term growth without a strong base of loyal customers. This need for customer loyalty causes relationship marketing to be more concerned with providing high levels of customer service and customer satisfaction to existing customers. Thus, relationship marketing focuses on the need to "market to customers *after* they have become customers."[5] Unlike transactional marketing which seeks to maximize the profit of a single transaction, relationship marketing is concerned with maximizing the long-term value of an association with a given customer.

Figure 5-1 distinguishes between transactional and relationship marketing on the basis of a two-by-two matrix. In transactional marketing, relationships between sellers and buyers are characterized on the basis of conflict and ad hoc-based relationships, whereas relationship marketing is characterized by cooperative and ongoing relationships. For example, channel members in transactional marketing think of relationships in terms of a single short-term

FIGURE 5-1 Forms of customer-marketer interaction.

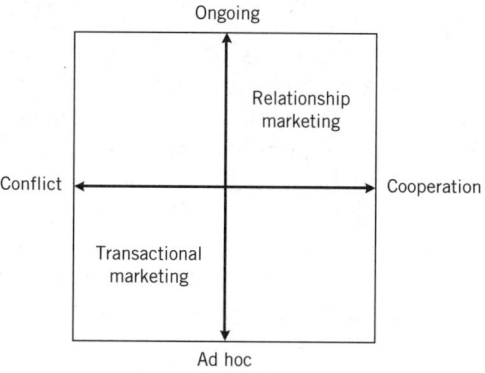

Source: Joseph P. Cannon and Jagdish N. Sheth, "Developing a Curriculum to Enhance Teaching of Relationship Marketing," *Journal of Marketing Education* (Summer 1994), p. 5. Reprinted by permission. The *JME* is published by the Business Research Division, University of Colorado at Boulder.

transaction, whereas relationship marketing views transactions from a multiple transactions and long-term perspective. Since exchanges are long term in relationship marketing, they often are preplanned. In addition, greater cooperation, mutual trust, and commitment between trading partners are seen in relationship marketing than in transactional marketing.

Table 5-1 outlines the major differences between transactional and relationship marketing on the basis of 15 interrelated attributes. In reviewing these dif-

TABLE 5-1 DIFFERENCES BETWEEN TRANSACTIONAL MARKETING AND RELATIONSHIP MARKETING

Attribute	Transactional Marketing	Relationship Marketing
Analysis perspective	Single transaction	Multiple transactions
Time perspective	Short term	Long term
Measurement of customer satisfaction	Ad hoc measurement	Ongoing
Transaction cost perspective	Single transaction	Multiple transactions
Marketing focus	One-time sale	Buyer loyalty
Number of suppliers	Many	Few
Nature of exchange relationship	Ad hoc exchange	Preplanned exchange
Customer understanding	Independent buyer and seller	Interdependent buyer and seller
Switching costs	Low	High
Nature of goals	Individual	Shared
Benefit to customer	Higher service/price mix than competitor	Long-term problem solving
Marketing emphasis	Get new customers	Keep present customers
Trust	Low	High
Commitment	Low	High
Level of communication	Low	High

ferences, it is important that a series of single-event transactions not be confused with relationship marketing.[6] Like relationship marketing, transactional exchanges can also be long term, such as when an industrial buyer awards the contract to Company A for five years on the basis of its low bid each year. However, unless Company A is the lowest bidder in the sixth year, it will have no edge over newcomers in a transactional exchange. If a relationship model depicted this situation, the current supplier would be told, "We would like to continue to do business with you, but you are not the lowest bidder. If you cut your price by 3 percent, we will place the order with you."[7]

Similarly, a customer can still use multiple sources of supply in relationship marketing. However, these exchanges would be less price driven and would involve a smaller group of suppliers than exchanges in transactional marketing.

LEVELS OF RELATIONSHIP MARKETING

Relationship marketing can be described as a hierarchy consisting of three different levels. Each level has different characteristics.[8] See Table 5-2 for a summary of the three levels of relationship marketing and their features.

Level one relationships are based on financial benefits to the customer such as a lower price owing to high cumulative purchases, or membership in a frequent flier or hotel club (that provides free or upgraded flights or rooms). In a level one relationship, there is no special social relationship with the service provider. The service is not especially differentiated for the client. The bond to the customer is basically a lower price or an upgraded service.

Level two relationships add social relationships and a medium level of service customization to a price-based relationship. An example of a level two relationship is a long-term social relationship as well as a special billing or a direct store delivery arrangement between a service provider and client. A level two arrangement is more difficult for a new competitor to copy than a level one relationship.

An example of the importance of the social relationship component to a customer can be seen by describing the experience of United Parcel Service (UPS). UPS always assumed that on-time delivery was the most important concern of its customers, but research revealed that its clients wanted more interaction with drivers and were less concerned with on-time delivery. "We've discovered

TABLE 5-2 THE THREE LEVELS OF RELATIONSHIP MARKETING

Level	Primary Bond	Marketing Orientation	Degree of Service Customization	Potential for Sustained Competitive Differentiation
One	Financial	Customer	Low	Low
Two	Social	Client	Medium	Medium
Three	Structural	Client	Medium to high	High

Source: Adapted from Leonard L. Berry and A. Parasuraman, *Marketing Services: Competing Through Quality* (New York: Free Press, 1991), p. 137.

that the highest-rated element we have is our drivers," says UPS's service-quality manager. As a result, the company is encouraging its 62,000 delivery drivers to get out and visit customers along with its salespeople. It also allows drivers to spend an additional 30 minutes a day at their discretion to strengthen ties with customers. This strategy helps cement their level two relationships.[9]

Level three relationships are characterized by high levels of service customization (such as use of proprietary software, sharing of sales data, joint technical support assistance, supplier assistance in parts design, and shared inventory management responsibilities), as well as a structural change in the customer relationship. In contrast to level one and level two relationships, a firm generally conducts level three relationships with a very small number of its total customers. Level three relationships also represent the greatest degree of competitive advantage and are most difficult for a competitor to copy.

Federal Express and Martin Supply are examples of two different ways a level three relationship can be established and maintained. Federal Express Corporation has compiled a list of more than 20,000 major customers. Through

CHANNELS IN ACTION

The Use of Relationship Marketing by MCI

The MCI Communications Company's "Friends & Family" long-distance program has signed up 10 million people in its first 22 months of service. After joining this program, members can save 20 percent on long-distance calls (over MCI's regular rates), providing both the caller and the called party are members.

This program gives MCI several benefits. First, the initial member helps recruit new MCI subscribers. Thus, one member becomes a salesperson to his or her friends and family. MCI subscribers can also give a list of friends and family directly to MCI for solicitation by them. A second advantage is that AT&T cannot directly copy this program. AT&T does not have centralized records of individual phone calls since it bills its customers directly through local phone companies.

AT&T began a new campaign directly designed to target "Friends & Family" customers. The campaign featured actors who portrayed MCI customers who had alienated their mothers and girlfriends. The Friends & Family advocates in the ad conclude that "It's not worth it." AT&T has also conducted research that revealed that "a substantial number" of long-distance customers felt that MCI was invading their privacy by getting their phone numbers from friends and family.

A marketing consultant also questions the use of "Friends & Family" from the perspective of relationship marketing. "What it (Friends & Family) conveys to MCI customers is they are valued only so far as they are successful salespeople. When relationship marketing is done correctly, you slowly move people up a loyalty ladder from trial buyer, to client, to advocate." According to the consultant, in this program "the advocacy stage is self-initiated, not manipulated by the marketer."

Source: Aimee L. Stern, "Courting Consumer Loyalty with the Feel-Good Bond," *New York Times* (January 17, 1993), p. F10.

its Powership program, Federal Express provides these major customers with personal computers that are linked to Federal Express's headquarters. By using Powership, a Federal Express customer can track a package and then inform its customers of the package's expected delivery date. To further its customer service quality and to increase its customer loyalty, Federal Express also polls 1000 of its Powership customers on a monthly basis to determine ways to improve its relationship with its clients.[10]

Unlike Federal Express which bases its service customization strategy on its proprietary technology, Martin Supply, an industrial distributor, bases its customization on fulfilling important channel functions. Many of these functions would ordinarily be fulfilled by Martin's key customers. For example, not only is Martin Supply listed on a key customer's organization chart, but also Martin's employees work full time at the customer's plant, attend the customer's production scheduling meetings, participate in the client's quality team, and even chair some of its customers' standing plant committees. According to a Martin Supply spokesperson, "We work as full-time partners with them. When they have a problem, we feel it is our problem. When they win, so do we."[11]

IMPLICATIONS OF RELATIONSHIP MARKETING

A major implication of relationship marketing is that there are a limited number of relationship marketing exchanges that any supplier or buyer can maintain. This means that an active partnership with one client may necessarily limit the number of potential relationship exchanges with other clients. The limited number of relationships causes both sellers and buyers to evaluate a relationship from the perspective of opportunity costs. In **opportunity costs**, existing relationships may preclude a firm from undertaking additional relationship marketing programs with new partners. The high opportunity costs associated with relationship marketing should force both buyers and sellers to be very careful in selecting their relationship partners. The questions in Table 5-3 represent the range of concerns a buyer should have when selecting a partner. Many of these questions cannot be answered by the buyer alone.

Relationship marketing is also characterized by a long-term commitment. A contract purchase, for example, at Raytheon (a major defense contractor and appliance manufacturer) is generally for two years. Other contracts are often for longer time periods. The two-year duration at Raytheon is needed because of the difficulty in understanding Raytheon's inventory requirements and the time required to set up appropriate inventory systems.[12] Long-term commitments require buyers and suppliers to structure each partner's responsibilities carefully. The structure also has to be sufficiently flexible so that the relationship can evolve as the nature of the product or competition shifts. For example, the division of responsibilities among the parties may change as a new competitor emerges or as a patent for an important process expires.

Lastly, in relationship marketing, buyers and sellers seek out collaborative relationships, which means that both parties have to work toward common goals.[13] The goals may be related to long-term problem solving (such as suppliers working with a buyer on product development). In contrast, in transactional

TABLE 5-3 QUESTIONS TO ASK SUPPLIERS UNDER RELATIONSHIP MARKETING

1. How has the supplier signaled commitment?
2. How early into the design stage is the supplier willing or able to participate?
3. Does the supplier understand the level of commitment to help achieve long-term gains?
4. As we grow and become more expert, is the supplier able to grow with us?
5. Does the supplier have adequate technical support?
6. Does the supplier represent a team solution to purchasing, manufacturing, or quality problems?
7. Is the supplier's senior management committed to the processes inherent in strategic partnerships?
8. How much planning is the supplier willing to share with us?
9. How well does the supplier know our business?
10. What does the supplier demand from us?

Source: Robert E. Spekman, "Strategic Supplier Selection: Understanding Long-Term Buyer Relationships," *Business Horizons,* Vol. 31 (July–August 1988), pp. 80–81.

marketing, the goals may be related to obtaining higher services per dollar cost than from a competing firm.

Table 5-4 shows why relationship marketing has become more popular. One major reason is the need for long-term relationships, trust, and the sharing of information between buyers and sellers to secure the advantages of electronic data interchange (EDI) and just-in-time (JIT) inventory management. Other reasons relate to the increased use of a long-term perspective, the concern with efficiency, the increased concern of retailers and wholesalers to avoid out-of-stock situations, and increased recognition of the role of channel member partners in providing high levels of customer service.

TABLE 5-4 REASONS FOR POPULARITY OF RELATIONSHIP MARKETING

- Recognition that unnecessary capacity and inventories bloat production and working capital costs and adds to labor, storage, and obsolescence costs. Popularity of just-in-time inventory requires data interchange.
- Recognition of the usefulness of new information and communication technologies (UPC, scanning, EDI, and so on).
- Increased trust among channel members.
- Concern of wholesalers and retailers to reduce out-of-stock levels.
- Channel members that were concerned with total system costs.
- Relationships between buyers and sellers more efficient in the long run than transactional exchanges.
- Willingness of firms to take a long-term view.
- Willingness of marketers to customize products and services for individual services.
- Concern for high levels of customer service to win over and keep customers.

Source: Adapted from Walter Salmon, "Origins of Partnering Relationships," in Sandy D. Jap, ed., *Evolving Relationships of Retailers and Manufacturers* (Cambridge, Mass.: Marketing Science Institute, 1992), p. 3.

Distribution Decision Making

Relationship marketing features much more open sharing of information between buyer and seller. For example, there is a sharing of information pertaining to inventory levels and sales by product between buyer and seller. This sharing of information is not common in transactional marketing. The sharing of information between intermediaries and suppliers through electronic data interchange and other means is covered in detail in Chapter 7.

A second important aspect of relationship marketing relating to distribution concerns the high levels of commitment between buyers and sellers. Both distributors and manufacturers look for different signs of channel partner commitment. For example, a study by Anderson and Weitz of 378 manufacturer-supplier relationships found that a distributor's confidence that the manufacturer's commitment to them increases if[14]

- The manufacturer grants them an exclusive territory.
- The distributor sees the manufacturer making investments (pledges) in their relationship (e.g., training and assigning dedicated personnel).
- The manufacturer really is committed to them (distributors appear to sense the manufacturer's state of mind).

But it decreases if the relationship has been plagued by a history of conflict.

Distributors are also more committed to manufacturers when there is a strong two-way communication and the manufacturer is reputed to treat other distributors fairly. Surprisingly, manufacturers seem to feel less committed when they grant distributors territorial exclusivity. This may reflect the power dynamics of certain distributor relationships.

A manufacturer can build trust through a number of services that are offered to distributors. These can include electronic data interchange, lead-generation programs, joint sales calls, equipment on loan, and the development of special software.[15] Manufacturers are also more committed to relationships with distributors in which they have made investments and with whom there is strong two-way communication.[16]

In turn, confidence that the distributor is committed to the manufacturer increases if[17]

- The distributor grants product class exclusivity (refrains from promoting competing brands).
- The distributor is perceived to invest in the relationship.
- The distributor is committed (manufacturers sense the distributor's sentiments).

But it decreases if the relationship has a serious history of conflict.

Product Decision Making

Product strategies also differ substantially in transactional and relationship marketing. In relationship marketing, the nature of product decision making changes drastically, depending on the degree of customer commitment.

For example, product strategies in relationship marketing depend on whether a supplier currently is a supplier (an in-supplier) or not (an out-supplier). An in-supplier should attempt to increase switching costs by using specially designed products; proprietary ordering, status checking, and billing systems; and emphasizing systems selling (to increase an account's purchases of related items). These strategies will make it more difficult for new suppliers to gain access to the account. In contrast, an out-supplier should produce parts that are compatible with a customer's system, easy to install, and easy to learn how to operate.[18] These strategies will facilitate trial and usage by a new client.

Pricing Decision Making

Instead of negotiating each exchange separately, relationship marketing is often characterized by the use of long-term supply contracts. These contracts are negotiated on a one-time basis instead of on a transaction basis. For example, in a long-term supply contract, the long-term price may be related to the market price for raw material, or it may be tied to a cost-plus agreement. It is also important for firms to set different pricing levels to distinguish between transactional and relationship marketing. The pricing levels should reflect the additional services associated with relationship marketing.

A true relationship marketing relationship may also have less emphasis on price. For example, Raytheon uses the following criteria (in order of importance) to evaluate the bids of alternative suppliers in relationship marketing contracts: service, price, brands carried, computerized systems, and location.[19]

Promotional Decision Making

Personal selling is more important than advertising and other forms of mass communication in relationship marketing. In contrast with advertising, personal selling has an important social bond. Personal selling can also be used as a mechanism of building trust and as a means of problem solving. In fact, once a contract is signed, a salesperson in relationship marketing may spend more time servicing than selling.

The personal selling process also differs significantly between relationship marketing and transactional marketing. In relationship marketing, the salesperson functions more as a consultant and a problem solver; in transactional marketing, the salesperson is seen as a revenue generator or persuader. Salespersons also have fewer accounts and conduct less prospecting in relationship marketing than in transactional marketing.

In order to fulfill their increased responsibilities, sales territories in relationship marketing may have to be reduced in order for salespeople to provide the higher expected levels of customer service. Some salespeople in relationship marketing may even confine their activities to one customer and to a single factory. Some relationship-oriented salespeople may even have an office in their key customer's plant. It is also important for suppliers to minimize the turnover for both the sales and support staff; this encourages the development of long-term social bonds with clients. One study found that it takes nearly five years for a securities broker to rebuild relationships with customers as a result of a salesperson's turnover. Thus, a securities firm can lose $2.5 million in commissions for each successful securities broker that leaves his or her firm.[20] The concern for minimizing employee turnover also calls into question the practice of rotating sales personnel among accounts and territories.

Lastly, sales personnel in relationship marketing should be evaluated on the quality of customer service and on retaining accounts.[21] This may require a firm to rethink its salesperson compensation system. For example, State Farm Insurance agents receive as high a commission for renewing a policy (10 percent on auto and 15 percent on homeowner's) as for opening a new account.[22]

EVALUATING THE USE OF A RELATIONSHIP MARKETING STRATEGY

This section describes the development and implementation of an appropriate exchange strategy. We begin by discussing the advantages and disadvantages of a relationship marketing strategy. We then discuss when transational and relationship marketing are best used.

ADVANTAGES AND DISADVANTAGES OF RELATIONSHIP MARKETING

One study of business-to-business marketers found that suppliers considered the following four factors as primary advantages of long-term relationships: price/production stability, enhanced marketing efficiency, optimal capacity planning, and customer orientation.[23] Price/production stability derives from the supplier's ability to offer better prices owing to the reliability of reorders and the resulting efficiencies in production. Enhanced marketing efficiency means that a supplier has lower marketing costs owing primarily to its base of established customers. Optimal capacity planning relates to planning advantages stemming from an ability to forecast sales more accurately. And customer orientation assumes that long-term relationships give suppliers better insight into customer needs and preferences than transactional marketing relationships.

Two disadvantages of relationship marketing relate to the need for trust and the increased dependence of each partner on one another. Relationship marketing can easily fall apart from lack of trust. An example of lack of trust occurs when a supplier (who has shared technical information with a customer) discovers a buyer's employee showing the information to another company, asking his or her firm to "Make the product for less."[24] Although this behavior might be an accepted part of transactional marketing, it would be viewed as inappropriate in relationship marketing.

Relationship marketing is also characterized by high interdependence among channel partners. For suppliers, a very high percentage of sales can be derived from a few buyers. Thus, the loss of a major account could substantially reduce a firm's short-term sales and profits. Similarly, buyers may be overdependent on a single supplier and may have difficulties getting alternative sources of supply because of a labor disruption or a raw material shortage at its key supplier.[25]

Both buyers and sellers have to make a careful study of the advantages and disadvantages. It is important to realize that transactional marketing may be preferable in certain situations and relationship marketing in others.

WHEN TRANSACTIONAL MARKETING AND RELATIONSHIP MARKETING ARE BEST USED

A common error is to assume that suppliers are limited in choosing between two extreme positions: the use of transactional marketing with all its customers or relationship marketing with all its customers. In practice, firms can utilize relationship marketing with larger customers and transactional marketing with smaller customers. Alternatively, a client that requires high levels of customer service can be given a level two relationship marketing experience, while a customer concerned solely with a low price may be given a transactional marketing exchange relationship.[26] Customers can also change their desired exchange relationship over time. For example, they can shift from transactional marketing to relationship marketing on the basis of increased trust and the development of social bonds.

The decision to use a given form of exchange relationship should be based on an analysis of customer and supplier attributes, as well as on an examination of the products sold. For example, relationship marketing is best used when a customer looks at the total cost of a product (including value of the information exchange), when there is mutual interest in cooperating and in sharing the benefits, and when a firm is concerned with being a leader in technological innovation.[27] In contrast, transactional marketing may be more effective for a small customer, for a customer concerned solely with delivered price, and for situations where little trust and interest in sharing benefits exist.

One researcher differentiates between two levels of supplier-customer commitment: lost-for-good customers and always-a-share customers. **Lost-for-good customers** favor long-term commitments to one vendor, do not change vendors often, and switch vendors only with considerable reluctance. These customers have high switching costs, are less able to mix and match parts from different suppliers, have large investments in procedures and lasting assets, and have long time horizons. In contrast, **always-a-share customers** share their patronage over multiple vendors. These customers do not view their commitment to a single supplier from a long-term perspective. Lost-for-good customers represent relationship marketing, whereas always-a-share customers are best served through transactional marketing.[28]

A firm should also consider the nature of the product when deciding on the appropriate form of exchange relationship. A high-technology product may be more appropriate for relationship marketing owing to the need for technical support, whereas a commodity may be more effective for transactional marketing or a level one relationship marketing experience. According to Barbara Bund Jackson, lost-for-good customers include computer, aircraft engine, and communications equipment manufacturers; always-a-share customers include purchasers of commodity chemicals, carbon steel, computer services, and shipping services.[29]

DEVELOPING A CUSTOMER SERVICE STRATEGY

Customer service is related to the first part of this chapter inasmuch as it is an important means of differentiating a firm's products and services in both transactional and relationship marketing. It is also a major factor in the development of customer loyalty in relationship marketing.

DEFINITION OF CUSTOMER SERVICE

Customer service can be defined as a customer-oriented corporate philosophy that integrates and manages all the elements of the customer interface to meet or exceed expectations of customer service quality.[30]

In defining customer service, we need to focus on three dimensions: customers, customer interface, and predetermined cost-service mix. Customers can be any channel member: manufacturers, wholesalers, retailers, or final consumers. We can also differentiate between downstream customer relationships (with ultimate customers) and upstream relationships (with suppliers and with a supplier's suppliers). The customer interface relates to activities that can be performed either before, during, or after the sale. See Table 5-5 for a listing of customer services at various stages in the buying process. Included within the definition of customer service are personal selling, inventory availability, delivery, instructions, installation, repair, and after-sale followup.

Although marketers like to think of services in terms of tangibles such as minimization of billing errors, store hours, credit options, and whether delivery is offered, customers typically measure customer services in terms of expectations and experiences. A consumer-based definition of customer service is based on the difference between expectations and experiences as judged by consumers; this difference is referred to as a **customer service gap**.

Overall, a consumer's judgment of the customer service gap is based on the difference between that consumer's expectations and experiences. Figure 5-2 identifies four possible scenarios: two where experiences and expectations coincide, and two where experiences do not match expectations. Where experiences and expectations coincide, consumer expectations are confirmed. In the two where experiences do not match expectations, a consumer encounters either a pleasant surprise (where experiences are significantly above expectations) or an unpleasant surprise (where experiences are significantly below expectations).

TABLE 5-5   COMPONENTS OF CUSTOMER SERVICE, BY STAGE IN THE PURCHASE TRANSACTION

Pretransaction
  Internal Operations
    Systematic lead times
    Formal production schedules
    Order-driven production schedules
    Physical inventory control
    Order forecast accuracy
Transaction
  Physical Appearance
    Employee appearance to customers
    Facilities appearance to customers
  Order Status
    Providing order status information
    Ability to expedite shipments
  Order Accuracy
    Billing accuracy
    Shipping accuracy
    Telephone etiquette
Post-Transaction
  Startup
    Product installation
    Product training
  Problem Handling
    Preventing stockouts
    Variability of delivery
    Product tracing for recalls

Source: Michael H. Morris and Duane L. Davis, "Measuring and Managing Customer Service in Industrial Firms," *Industrial Marketing Management,* Vol. 21 (November 1992), p. 348. Reprinted by permission. Copyright 1992 by Elsevier Science Inc.

FIGURE 5-2   A customer service evaluation model.

	Poor experience	Excellent experience
Poor expectation	No gap Confirmation of poor expectation	Large gap Pleasant surprise
Excellent expectation	Large gap Unpleasant surprise	No gap Confirmation of excellent expectation

Source: Barry Berman, "Developing and Implementing an Effective Customer Service Strategy," in *The Dartnell Marketing Manager's Handbook,* 3rd ed., Sidney J. Levy, George R. Frerichs, and Howard L. Gordon, eds. (Chicago: Dartnell Corporation, 1994), p. 804.

Consumer perceptions of expectations and experiences apply to both process- and outcome-related activities. **Process-related activities** accompany a service (such as a store's cleanliness, the friendliness of its personnel, and waiting lines at cash resisters). Customers judge process-related activities as the service is being delivered. In contrast, **outcome-related activities** pertain to the reliability of the service (how accurately a repair was made and whether a repair was done correctly the first time). Consumers, in evaluating their expectations and experiences, consider both process-related and outcome-related activities. For example, while a rental car may be dependable (an outcome measure), poor performance in terms of waiting lines, faulty instructions, and a dirty rental facility may result in a less than satisfactory or poor overall customer service judgment. Opinion Research Corporation surveyed 400 executives of the nation's largest companies. The vast majority reported that how much an airline "cares about its customer" (a process measure) was as important to them as were prompt baggage delivery and efficient check-in (an outcome measure).[31]

In evaluating his or her experiences, each customer has a **zone of tolerance**; this zone separates desirable from adequate service levels.[32] The zone of tolerance varies from customer to customer and from situation to situation for the same customer. For example, more experienced customers may have higher service expectations and may be more prone to complain if they are not satisfied. A customer may also be more tolerant of an airline delay when the weather is poor than when weather conditions are favorable.

THE ECONOMICS OF CUSTOMER SERVICE

Three approaches can be used to calculate the economics of customer service. The first approach calculates the loss in profits owing to a defecting customer; the second determines the impact of small changes in customer retention on sales and profits; and the third approach develops a model in which the impact of changes in customer service is determined on sales (holding constant other factors that can affect sales).

Mathematically, the loss in profits caused by a defecting customer equals the present value of that customer's lifetime sales potential times the average profit margin on that customer's incremental sales. A similar approach calculates the cost of replacing a lost customer in terms of advertising, sales promotion, and personal selling expense.

Professor Barbara Bund Jackson extends the lifetime value of a customer approach by treating each customer as an uncertain investment, where the length of the customer's purchase commitments, the timing of purchases, and the purchase quantities are unknown. According to this approach, the purpose of customer service is to extend the probability of purchase, the length of purchase, and the frequency of purchase to maximize the value of this investment.[33] Note that calculations relative to the length and frequency of a customer's purchase relate to the customer's loyalty.

A second approach to the economics of customer service determines the sensitivity of sales and profits to small changes in customer retention. For example, studies by Arthur D. Little, a major consulting firm, suggest that the quality of a company's service can cause it to gain or lose as much as 10 percent of its sales revenues.[34] Other researchers have concluded that reducing the customer defection rate by 5 percent can boost profits by 25 percent to 95 percent.[35] Another study found that a 5 percent increase in customer loyalty can produce profit increases from 25 to 85 percent.[36] All of these studies assume that the incremental profits from additional sales (due to high loyalty and excellent customer service) are high.

The third approach develops a mathematical model in which changes in customer satisfaction scores are correlated with changes in sales. This approach holds the impact of other variables (such as price changes or economic factors) constant. Using this approach, a senior IBM executive determined that every percentage-point change in customer satisfaction scores translates into a gain or loss of $500 million in sales over a five-year period.[37]

All of these approaches must examine a customer's lifelong sales potential. Thus, the loss of an industrial customer should be measured in terms of the customer's lifetime sales, not the loss of a single transaction. Similarly, the new customer needs to have a lifelong sales pattern similar to that of the customer that defected. The lifelong sales concept significantly increases the importance of excellent customer service. Although much of the evidence concerning the economics of the customer is anecdotal, these data clearly suggest that continuous improvement in service quality should be seen as an investment, not as a cost.

CUSTOMER SERVICE MODELS

Two important models that depict service quality are Porter's value chain and SERVQUAL, a model of service-quality dimensions developed by Professors Zeithaml, Parasuraman, and Berry. According to Michael Porter, buyers seek out suppliers that offer them the greatest added value. SERVQUAL defines service quality on the basis of five dimensions: reliability, responsiveness, assurance, empathy, and tangibles.

Porter's Value Chain

Professor Porter developed the value chain as a means of creating added value for buyers. The **value chain** consists of the collection of activities that are performed to design, produce, market, deliver, and support its products.[38] The chain classifies value-creating activities into primary and support activities. Primary activities include the physical creation of the product, the product's sale, transfer to the buyer, and after-sales assistance; support activities support the primary activities.

The value chain concept should force a firm to examine all of the linkages between a manufacturer and its wholesale customers and retailer and its final consumer buyer to determine how a channel member can provide a unique competitive advantage. The competitive advantage for a manufacturer can be faster delivery, shipping merchandise directly to a wholesaler's accounts, and so on. An example of a value chain benefit is 3M's ability to speed up delivery for Boise Cascade by affixing locations that mapped out slot locations in Boise Cascade's

TABLE 5-6 SOURCES OF CUSTOMER SERVICE COMPETITIVE ADVANTAGE BASED ON VALUE CHAIN ANALYSIS

Competitive Advantage Element	Source of Competitive Advantage
High reliability	Increase reliability through selling only products that have excellent serviceability and excellent records for mechanical performance, and that exceed a marketer's laboratory standards.
	Test all major purchases before they leave the warehouse for shipment to a customer.
Ease of use	Study buyers' level of expertise in use.
	Design effective manuals and instructions for use (beyond instructions provided by manufacturer).
	Offer workshops for recent buyers.
Product adequacy determination	Produce printed checklists for buyers to use in estimating product needs.
	Train salespeople in identifying consumer needs, in gaining product knowledge, and in matching needs with specific product types.
	Offer on-site product evaluation assistance.
Ease of repair	Sell only those products with excellent manufacturer-supported repair facilities or those for which manufacturers offer on-site repair to consumers.
	Own and operate repair facilities.

Source: Barry Berman, "Developing and Implementing an Effective Customer Service Strategy," in *The Dartnell Marketing Manager's Handbook,* 3rd ed., Sidney J. Levy, George R. Frerichs, and Howard L. Gordon, eds. (Chicago: Dartnell Corporation, 1994), p. 808.

warehouse. This resulted in lower costs to Boise Cascade, since it reduced inventory handling costs as well as inventory storage costs.[39] The competitive advantage in terms of wholesale service can be service manuals and procedures, spare parts, technical service, inspection by the vendor, and high quality control.

Table 5-6 describes how use of value chain analysis can help a retailer better service its final customers. This analysis focuses on four customer benefits: reliability, ease of use, product adequacy determination, and ease of repair. Note that this value chain analysis has implications for the retailer's choice of suppliers, as well as for the range of services that are offered.

A reseller can increase reliability to a buyer by lowering the risk of product failure. For example, although the furniture industry has a poor record in terms of defects, too few retailers seek to develop a competitive advantage by inspecting furniture before it leaves the retailer's warehouse. Such a strategy would lower the inconvenience of waiting at home for a repair, increase the consumer's quality perceptions of both the product and the service, and also allow retailers to conduct such repairs centrally (which saves travel time).

Increasing ease of use is a second competitive advantage. Retailers need to recognize that a personal computer is among the most technically complex products that a typical consumer purchases in his or her lifetime. Some consumers even get overwhelmed just on seeing the web of wires in the computer box. In the past, Packard Bell had return rates of nearly 20 percent; many of these returns were based on consumers' inability to set up its computers properly. To combat this problem, Packard Bell has developed a giant illustrated setup guide to show users where cables are to be located. In addition, the company has created a shell called Navigator that better enables its unsophisticated buyers to use the Windows interface.[40]

Determining product adequacy is a third source of a competitive advantage. A home improvement center can produce guidelines in estimating air conditioning capacity needs (based on size of area, exposure, degree of insulation, etc.) and clearly post them in the store. This ensures self-service customers that their air conditioner is the most suitable size. These "fact-tags," which can be used in selling other complex items, reduce the level of required sales assistance and can be used to expand the range of goods sold by a self-service retailer.

CHANNELS IN ACTION

Varian Associates Inc.: Putting the Value Chain to Work

Varian Associates Inc. is a scientific equipment maker that makes vacuum systems for computer clean rooms. In the late 1980s, Varian adopted the total quality management concept. It put 1000 managers through a four-day course on quality, reinvented the way it conducted its business, and even adopted a quality mascot. Even though its radiation equipment service department ranked Number 1 in the industry for prompt customer visits, sales grew by only 3 percent between 1989 and 1990. Worse, profits dropped from a $32 million profit in 1989 to a $4.1 million loss in 1990. Obsessed with meeting production schedules, Varian lost sight of its customers. For example, during this time period, Varian's staff did not return phone calls.

Varian recently changed its procedures to please customers and to increase service quality. For example, it now focuses on less costly ways of increasing the value chain for its customers. So when customers complained about the long time it took to set up its radiology equipment at hospitals, Varian identified several hundred solutions (ranging from the way it shipped products to how they were installed). The company then chose to redesign key parts to make them fit together better. These changes in product design saved 95 hours of setup time, worth as much as $50,000 per order. Varian also decided to ship its cables in plastic bags as opposed to using the popcorn-shaped material that it used in the past. This strategy alone saved 30 minutes of cleanup time per installation.

As opposed to its past strategies, Varian's customer service strategies are now carefully evaluated on the basis of their economic feasibility. For example, the changes in product design for its radiology equipment saved Varian $1.8 million per year, in addition to saving setup and cleanup time for its customers.

Source: David Greising, "Quality: How to Make It Pay," *Business Week* (August 8, 1994), pp. 54–59.

A fourth source of competitive advantage is ease of repair. A retailer can increase ease of repair by purchasing products only from vendors that offer comprehensive repair services, including on-site customer service. Many of these competitive advantages are also applicable to industrial products.

Marketers need to communicate these competitive advantages to increase inquiries, to generate marketer loyalty, and to reduce price competition.

SERVQUAL DIMENSIONS

An important contribution to the service-quality literature was the development of a scale for measuring customers' perceptions of service quality. The SERVQUAL customer service measure includes five independent dimensions: reliability, responsiveness, assurance, empathy, and tangibles. Although there have been some criticisms of this measure, it has won broad acceptance.[41] Each of these dimensions is defined and illustrated in Table 5-7.

TABLE 5-7 SERVICE-QUALITY COMPONENTS OF SERVQUAL

Service Element	Definition of Service Element	Examples of Service Element
Reliability	Ability to perform the promised service dependably and accurately	Will an employee call me back when promised? Are my billing statements correct? Are repairs performed properly the first time?
Responsiveness	Willingness to help customers and provide prompt service	When there is a problem, will the marketer resolve it quickly? Will the salesperson answer my specific questions? Will I be given a specific time for home delivery?
Assurance	Knowledge and courtesy of employees and their ability to convey trust and confidence	Are employees able to answer questions? Are employees polite? Does the marketer have a good reputation? Can I be confident that repairs/installations/alterations were performed properly?
Empathy	Caring, individualized attention the firm provides its customers	How easy is it for me to talk with senior executives, when a problem cannot be resolved in the regular manner? Do employees avoid technical language? Am I recognized as a regular customer?
Tangibles	Appearance of physical facilities, equipment, personnel, and communication materials	Are the marketer's facilities attractive? Are employees appropriately dressed? Are statements easy to understand?

Source: Adapted from Valarie A. Zeithaml, A. Parasuraman, and Leonard L. Berry, *Delivering Quality Service: Balancing Customer Perceptions and Expectations* (New York: Free Press, 1990), pp. 21–22, 25.

Professors Zeithaml, Parasuraman, and Berry found that respondents considered all five dimensions critical. At the same time, these researchers found that the reliability dimension was the most critical in consumers' assessments of service quality. These service dimensions were ranked in a five-company study (when the total responses were combined) in the following order: reliability, responsiveness, assurance, empathy, and tangibles.[42]

These attributes are defined as follows:

Reliability—Customers want companies to perform the desired service dependably, accurately, and consistently. They want companies to keep the promises they make.

Responsiveness—Prompt service is desired.

Assurance—Company employees should be knowledgeable and courteous.

Empathy—Customers want individualized attention, and they want to be heard.

Tangibles—Physical facilities should be attractive and clean; employees should be well groomed.

The researchers also found that the reliability dimension is primarily a service outcome measure, whereas tangibles, responsiveness, assurance, and empathy are more concerned with a process outcome measure.

IMPLEMENTING A CUSTOMER SERVICE STRATEGY

This part is divided into two sections: total quality management and customer service, and common principles of excellent customer service. The first section reviews the literature on total quality management to determine its characteristics and usage. The second develops common principles of customer service by examining the practices of firms with excellent customer service reputations.

TOTAL QUALITY MANAGEMENT AND CUSTOMER SERVICE

Total quality management was developed on the basis of the teachings of management consultants W. Edwards Deming and Joseph Juran.[43] **Total quality management (TQM)** can be defined as the ongoing process of improving product and service quality through constant feedback, examination of quality leaders' strategies, use of teams, and total employee involvement (see Figure 5-3).

Specifically, TQM utilizes constant user feedback on its performance, and the feedback becomes the basis of a continual improvement program. Feedback may be in the form of standardized questionnaires that are given to customers at fixed intervals, as well as periodic monitoring of delivery times, stockouts, and waiting times.

TQM studies the practices of competitors and noncompetitors to reduce shortages, delays, and defects. Through **benchmarking**, a firm continually com-

FIGURE 5-3 Components of total quality management.

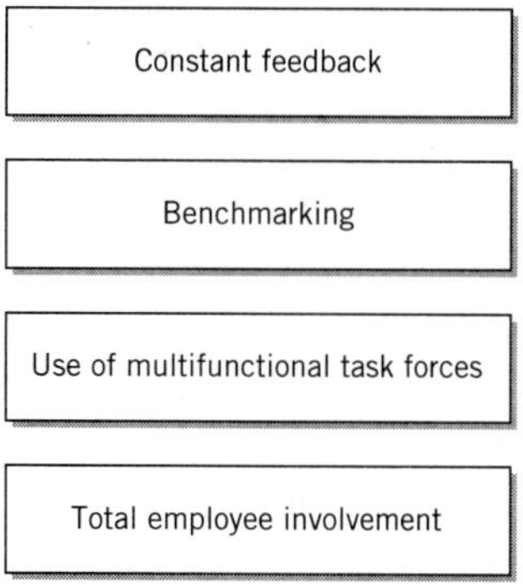

```
┌─────────────────────────────┐
│      Constant feedback      │
└─────────────────────────────┘

┌─────────────────────────────┐
│        Benchmarking         │
└─────────────────────────────┘

┌─────────────────────────────┐
│ Use of multifunctional task forces │
└─────────────────────────────┘

┌─────────────────────────────┐
│  Total employee involvement │
└─────────────────────────────┘
```

pares and measures its performance against that of business leaders anywhere in the world. This information is used to improve the company's performance.[44] See Table 5-8 for a listing of good, bad, and questionable benchmarking practices.

When something goes wrong, TQM users employ multifunctional task forces or teams to resolve the problem. TQM also uses employee teams to reexamine a firm's procedures.

TQM also entails a firm's total employee involvement. Through TQM, every person in the organization is part of the customer service team, from the accounts payable clerk to the elevator operator. For example, Infiniti insists that every dealer employee attend its training program. According to one of the firm's instructors, "The receptionist probably talks to more customers than any other person in the showroom."[45]

TABLE 5-8 GOOD, BAD, AND QUESTIONABLE BENCHMARKING PRACTICES

Good Benchmarking Practices
- Using secondary research to locate public documents about a target company
- Conducting market research and customer satisfaction surveys
- Gathering information at trade shows
- Soliciting other companies to share information about their processes

Bad Benchmarking Practices
- Bribing individuals to act as informants
- Requiring suppliers to participate in a benchmarking study as a condition of obtaining or keeping your business

Questionable Benchmarking Practices
- Recruiting employees from competing companies for the purpose of obtaining information
- Asking questions at a professional meeting without disclosing your company and name

Source: International Benchmarking Clearinghouse, Houston, Texas. Adapted from Betsy Wiesendanger, "Benchmarking for Beginners," *Sales & Marketing Management* (November 1992), p. 61.

TQM has been used successfully by firms such as Xerox, Motorola, Federal Express, and Harley-Davidson.[46] TQM principles have also been effective in improving customer service at Hillenbrand Industries' American Tourister division and at the McNeil unit of Johnson & Johnson.

Hillenbrand Industries' American Tourister division used TQM principles in forming a cross-functional team to solve major problems with excessive inventories. The firm had an excess of vacuum-formed plastic shells that were used to make its cases for its pullman luggage. By studying the process, Hillenbrand's team was able to reduce the accumulated shell inventory from 10 days to no days through conversion to a true just-in-time inventory management system. The team also studied American Tourister's factory outlet stores. As a result of its analysis, inventory receipts are now electronically processed, merchandise is rearranged to enable easier stocking and customer selection, and procedures for ordering goods have been revised.[47]

The McNeil unit of Johnson & Johnson began a TQM initiative to reduce the time and expense it takes the firm to develop customized retail displays for chain drug stores and supermarkets. Displays that once took three to four months to develop are now put together in 30 days.[48]

Despite the number of firms that have successfully used TQM, there is concern over how well firms practice TQM. One study, for example, found that most users of total quality management received a D or F grade on their efforts to increase market share, decrease costs, and improve customer satisfaction.[49] In another study, a major management consulting firm found that the total quality management process was having "a significant impact" on their ability to outdistance themselves from competitors in only 36 percent of the firms studied.[50]

Finally, a major study of 584 companies in the United States, Canada, Germany, and Japan found a number of problems in the auto, computer, banking, and health care industries. Among the study's findings with its U.S.-based sample are that:

- Computer firms involve only 12 percent of their employees in idea suggestion programs. Auto manufacturers, which involve more participation than any other kind of firm studied, involve only 28 percent of their workers.
- Customer complaints are of "major or primary" importance in identifying new products and services among only 19 percent of banks and 26 percent of hospitals.
- Quality performance measures, such as defect rates and customer satisfaction levels, are part of senior management incentive programs in less than one in five of the companies studied.

The results appear to be even poorer when we compare them to practices at competing foreign firms. For example, idea suggestion boxes are used by 34 percent of responding Canadian banks and 78 percent of Japanese auto manufacturers. And 73 percent of Japanese and 60 percent of German computer maker respondents, respectively, use consumer complaints to identify new products versus 26 percent of U.S. respondents.[51]

TABLE 5-9 COMMON PRINCIPLES OF CUSTOMER SERVICE

Customer Service Leaders
- Have a written customer service policy.
- Monitor their customer service levels on a regular basis.
- Get their employees close to the customer.
- Study customer service as defined by the customer.
- Empower their employees to resolve consumer complaints.
- Facilitate customer access to the company.
- Resolve complaints on the side of the customer.
- Think in terms of the lifetime income or profit stream of the customer.
- Utilize technology in improving customer services.
- Make customer service personnel part of a career path, not a dead-end job.
- Are concerned with customer retention, as well as obtaining new customers.

Source: This listing is adapted from Barry Berman, "Developing and Implementing an Effective Customer Service Strategy," in *The Dartnell Marketing Manager's Handbook,* 3rd ed., Sidney J. Levy, George R. Frerichs, and Howard L. Gordon, eds. (Chicago: Dartnell Corporation, 1994), pp. 814–817.

COMMON PRINCIPLES OF CUSTOMER SERVICE

This section describes the common principles of excellent customer service that are listed in Table 5-9. These principles were obtained by evaluating the customer service practices of those firms with excellent customer service records. In evaluating these principles, it is important to look beyond the firm or industry to see broad principles that can be universally applied.

HAVE A WRITTEN CUSTOMER SERVICE POLICY

Based on research conducted among a sample of industrial firms in six different industries (silicate, concrete, oil, gas, rubber, and agriculture), firms with a written customer policy were far more likely to use customer service as a competitive weapon than those with no written policy. Only 3 percent of respondents with a written policy did not view customer service as a strategic tool.[52]

A firm with a written customer service policy is United Services Automobile Association (USAA), the nation's fifth largest insurer of privately owned automobiles and homes. According to the firm's CEO, "the mission and corporate culture of this company are, in one word, service. As a company objective, service comes ahead of either profits or growth. . . . But I submit that it's because service comes first at USAA that profits and growth have been so healthy."[53]

MONITOR CUSTOMER SERVICE LEVELS

Standardized, ongoing measurement of customer service levels leads to a benchmark against which managers can be evaluated and rewarded. This process also enables a firm to track complaints and to search for a cause. For example, MBNA tracks its average balance per card, as well as 15 measures of customer satisfaction, on a daily basis. MBNA's average balance is $2500 against the industry average of $1600. And MBNA's retention rate of profitable customers—cardholders who resolve their charges—is 98 percent.[54]

Federal Express's service-quality indicators are weighted as to their importance. For example, a delivery that is late by a few hours is weighted as a 1, while a missed pickup or a damaged shipment has a weight of 10. These weights give Federal Express personnel something to shoot for, and they also explain customer priorities in terms of customer needs and preferences.[55]

GET EMPLOYEES CLOSE TO THE CUSTOMER

Excellent customer service providers commonly do not rely on the sales force as the sole contact with consumers. For example, Weyerhaeuser requires its employees to work for a customer for a week so that its employees can see things from their customers' point of view. It also gives its employees greater awareness of problems, such as a company bar code on newsprint sticking to a printing press, even though a customer has never complained.[56]

Similarly, Procter & Gamble requires some executives to man the customer service phones periodically. Hewlett-Packard also assigns executives to key clients to maintain executive-level contact.[57]

STUDY CUSTOMER SERVICE AS DEFINED BY THE CUSTOMER

Customer service should be defined in terms of the customer's measure of satisfaction, not the supplier's. One way to ensure that customer service is acceptable is through a customer service guarantee.

Hampton Inns, for example, will not charge for a room if it fails to meet the customer's, *not the motel's,* standard for cleanliness, comfort, or safety. Refunds totaled a mere $1.1 million in 1993. Promus, the owner of Hampton Inns, calculated that as a result of the program, it received $10 in revenue for every dollar paid to a dissatisfied guest.[58] The extra profits were due to the willingness of dissatisfied guests to come back, even though their prior experience was poor. The service guarantee also gave Promus access to its main customer gripes.

Similarly, Delta Dental, the largest group dental insurer in Massachusetts, has a "Guarantee of Service Excellence" that includes seven promises (everything from no-hassle customer relations to fast processing of claims). It pays restitution to its customers if it does not meet promises. Since the program was instituted in April 1990, Delta has paid $100,015 for service failures involving 1086 incidents.[59]

EMPOWER EMPLOYEES

High-quality service providers empower employees to correct a customer complaint. Employee empowerment enables complaints to be resolved quickly, improves employee morale, and provides greater recognition to employees. For example, the Ritz-Carlton Hotel Company allows employees to spend up to $2000 to redress a guest grievance. The firm's employees are also free to leave their routine job responsibilities to make a guest happy. As a result, more than 90 percent of Ritz-Carlton's guests return; the rate is even higher for customers that hold meetings there.[60]

Xerox authorizes its frontline service employees to replace up to $250,000 worth of equipment if customers are not getting results.[61]

FACILITATE CUSTOMER ACCESS TO THE COMPANY

Making it easy to complain provides companies with immediate feedback on problem areas and even potential opportunities. A 1992 study found that callers who had their complaint solved quickly told five people, on average, about the helpful service. Those who were not satisfied told 9 to 10 people.[62] To facilitate comments from consumers, University Brands, a children's shoe manufacturer, even puts its toll-free phone number on the bottom of all its shoes.

RESOLVE COMPLAINTS FAVORABLY FOR THE CUSTOMER

The owner of a Seattle-based restaurant chain, Satisfaction Guaranteed Eateries, adopted a "replace plus one" philosophy. To compensate for the customer's hassle—if an item is late, doesn't taste right, and so on—not only is the item free (with no need for explanation), but also the patron is offered a drink or dessert. If consumers wait more than 20 minutes beyond their reservation time, the whole meal might be free. Any employee from the busboy up has the right to placate a dissatisfied guest.[63]

THINK IN TERMS OF THE LIFETIME INCOME OR PROFIT STREAM

The average Home Depot buyer only spends $38 per visit but visits a store 30 times per year, year after year; therefore, the average buyer spends $25,000 over his or her lifetime. Thus, losing a customer is significant for Home Depot. Clearly, the problem of customer satisfaction is more important when it is perceived from the perspective of the loss of $25,000 in lifetime sales rather than the loss of a single sale.[64]

UTILIZE TECHNOLOGY

Federal Express can track a package's location, determine when it was picked up, what plane it is on, what truck will pick it up, and when it will be delivered, based on bar coding of all packages and the use of scanners. This technology gives the firm a major advantage in the fiercely competitive market for specialized package delivery. Similarly, laptop computers and modems allow a field sales force to log in orders quickly, determine inventory availability, and generate customized letters to follow up on recent sales.

USAA retains 98 percent of its auto insurance customers each year versus about 85 percent of the industry as a whole, even though many of its military customers move each year. USAA's use of a computerized database centrally located in San Antonio allows clients to use the same agent regardless of where they live.[65]

Make Customer Service Personnel Part of a Career Path

Firms need to position customer service as an important function within their organization, to describe its impact on sales and profits to all employees, and to attract and maintain top-caliber people in customer service positions. Customer service cannot flourish in an environment that seeks to minimize costs or where customer service is viewed as expendable. For example, Bethlehem Steel sent a positive signal that customer service was important to its employees, customers, and competitors when its chief metallurgist at a major plant was assigned to the customer service department.

Be Concerned with Customer Retention, as Well as Obtaining New Customers

MBNA America, the credit card operation of MNC Financial, holds onto 95 percent of its customers every year, compared with 88 percent for its competitors. A new cardmember costs $100 to acquire, but a five-year customer brings in an average of $100 in profits annually, and a ten-year customer produces $300. The firm has 68 phone service agents who call every customer who wants to close an account. Agents have broad powers to win customers back, including waiving annual fees. Agents typically rescue one-half of the accounts.[66]

CUSTOMER SERVICE STANDARDS IN PHYSICAL DISTRIBUTION

This section examines customer service from the perspective of getting the right goods to the right customers at the right time at the right cost. It relates to the transportation, warehousing, inventory, and order processing functions of the firm.[67] Whereas the previous section dealt with customer service standards as perceived by the customers, this section focuses on objective standards that can be assessed by a service provider.

It is important that both types of standards be used at the same time. Many of the physical distribution standards may appear to be objective, but they do not reflect consumer perceptions. These perceptions may be drastically different from those predicted by these objective standards. For example, at one company, the in-house measurement system found that 98 percent of all orders went out on time. However, another survey found that only 50 percent of the firm's customers reported satisfaction with deliveries. The company reconciled the two conflicting figures when it discovered that the customer survey reflected the date when the customer received the order, whereas the company's data reflected the shipping date.[68]

According to a study by the Council of Logistics Management, customer service standards in physical distribution have the following characteristics:[69]

- Ease of inquiry, order placement, and order transmission.
- Timely, reliable order delivery and communications.
- Accurate, complete, undamaged orders and error-free paperwork.
- Accurate, timely generation and transmission of information to support the planning, management, and execution of the above activities.

In 1992, two researchers studied a sample of senior marketing managers of industrial products with 50 or more employees that were located in Florida. Table 5-10 shows the percentage of firms that collect and set performance data for specific service activities. These standards can be combined into three major customer service dimensions: availability, timeliness, and quality.

Availability relates to the in-stock rate and percentage of orders, units, and lines filled. For example, a **customer service level** corresponds to the percentage of orders for a particular good that are in-stock. A 98 percent customer service level means that a customer wanting a particular model could get it 98 times out of 100 requests.

The **timeliness** dimension relates to such factors as consistent delivery, order cycle time reliability, and minimum order cycle time. Consolidated Rail Corporation asked its customers what they expected from its transportation service. Customers expected a fast response to inquiries and pricing, prompt pickup, consistent delivery, timely communication en route, and timely billing and handling of claims.

The **quality** dimension includes such measures as minimum damage in transit, order-filling accuracy, billing accuracy, and shipping accuracy.[70]

A service provider can operationalize service standards through the use of various ratios and measures. Among the more important measures are reliabil-

TABLE 5-10 MEASUREMENT PRACTICES IN THE CUSTOMER SERVICE AREA FOR FLORIDA-BASED INDUSTRIAL MANUFACTURING FIRMS

Service Activity	Collect Data	Set Performance Standards
Customer complaints	55.6%	31.1%
Inventory levels	52.2	43.3
Order status information	48.9	34.4
Order cycle time	46.1	31.5
Product tracing for recalls	46.0	19.5
Variability of delivery	43.8	21.3
Preventing stockouts	43.0	33.7
Customer satisfaction	34.4	42.2
Shipping accuracy	33.7	47.2
Order forecast accuracy	33.3	30.0
Billing accuracy	27.8	35.6
Customer notification of problems	23.3	34.4
Employee courtesy	22.2	45.6

Source: Michael H. Morris and Duane L. Davis, "Measuring and Managing Customer Service in Industrial Firms," *Industrial Marketing Management,* Vol. 21 (November 1992), p. 349. Reprinted by permission. Copyright 1992 by Elsevier Science Inc.

ity, service failures, the fraction of demand filled from stock, and the minimum sum of the cost of inventory and backorders.[71]

The **reliability measure** is the fraction of order or replenishment cycles with no stockouts. It is expressed mathematically as

$$\text{Reliability} = 1 - \frac{\text{Number of stockouts}}{\text{Number of replenishments}}$$

If, in 200 orders, there are 4 stockouts, reliability = [1 − (4/200)] = 0.98. This means that, on average, 98 percent of items are filled from stock on hand. It is important to examine differences in reliability with fast- versus slow-moving inventory.

Service failures are the expected stockouts per unit of time. This measure examines stockouts per week, month, or year.

$$\text{Service failures} = \frac{\text{Number of stockouts}}{\text{Unit of time}}$$

A service failure of 12 per day means that there are 12 stockouts per day.

The **fraction of demand filled from stock** examines the percentage of orders that can be filled from existing inventory:

$$\frac{\text{Fraction of demand}}{\text{filled from stock}} = \frac{\text{Number of orders that can be completely filled}}{\text{Total number of orders}}$$

This measure does not differentiate among orders where one item is out-of-stock or among orders where all items are out-of-stock. It also does not reflect customers who did not place an order because a product was not available. In this manner, a 95 percent fill rate can actually be a 75 percent rate when these customers are reflected in the data.[72]

The **minimum sum of the cost of inventory and backorders** standard seeks to minimize the total of the costs of stockouts and of carrying inventory to prevent stockouts. Stockouts are costly because of additional order processing and handling costs, as well as loss of customer goodwill. This standard seeks to balance the costs of stockouts with the costs of having large inventory levels.

EVALUATING SUPPLIERS ON THE BASIS OF MULTIPLE CUSTOMER SERVICE STANDARDS

The diagram in Figure 5-4 shows the hierarchy of quality measures collected at the General Business Systems Division of AT&T. This figure breaks down product quality into business processes, customer needs, and internal metrics. As the diagram shows, business processes are comprised of products, sales, installation, repair, and billing. In this example, 30 percent of the variation in overall quality is explained by product, 30 percent by sales, 10 percent by installation, 15 percent by repair, and 15 percent by billing. Service accounts for 70 percent of the total variation. Obviously, these percentages can change to reflect different weights at different companies, for different products, and at different times.[73]

FIGURE 5-4 The linkage between quality measures.

Overall Quality			
	Product (30%)	Reliability (40%)	% Repair calls
		Easy to Use (20%)	% Calls for help
		Features/Functions (40%)	Function performance test
	Sales (30%)	Knowledge (30%)	Supervisor observations
		Response (25%)	% Proposals made on time
		Follow-up (10%)	% Followups made
	Installation (10%)	Delivery Interval (30%)	Average order interval
		Does Not Break (25%)	% Repair reports
		Installed When Promised (10%)	% Installed on due date
	Repair (15%)	No Repeat Troubles (30%)	% Repeat reports
		Fixed Fast (25%)	Average speed of repair
		Kept Informed (10%)	% Customers informed
	Billing (15%)	Accuracy, No Surprises (45%)	% Billing inquiries
		Resolve on First Call (35%)	% Resolved first call
		Easy to Understand (10%)	% Billing inquiries

Note: The weights used are for illustrative purposes only.
Source: Raymond E. Kordupleski, Roland T. Rust, and Anthony J. Zahorik, "Why Improving Quality Doesn't Improve Quality," *California Management Review,* Vol. 35 (Spring 1993), p. 89. Copyright 1993 by The Regents of the University of California. By permission of The Regents.

Kodak's Office Imaging Unit uses a similar system to assess suppliers. Each month, Kodak sends suppliers a quality rating report that uses a 100-point rating standard. Suppliers can earn up to 60 points on quality and up to 40 points for on-time delivery. In the quality category, a minimum of 80 percent acceptance is required to earn any points. Forty points are awarded when the supplier achieves the 80 percent mark. An additional point is added for each percentage point over 80. Kodak rates delivery performance on the percentage of lots delivered within an agreed time period. Forty points are awarded for 100 percent on-time delivery. Suppliers who fail to achieve at least an 80 percent delivery rate receive no points.[74]

SUMMARY

1 *To introduce the concept of relationship marketing, the different forms of relationship marketing, and the implications of using a relationship marketing strategy.* Relationship marketing is based on building and maintaining long-term relationships between buyers and sellers that are based on trust and commitment. Instead of being adversaries, in relationship marketing, buyers and sellers view each other as partners or collaborators in improving quality and in managing costs.

Relationship marketing can be described as a hierarchy consisting of three different levels. Level one relationships are based on financial benefits to the customer. Level two relationships are comprised of social relationships and a medium level of service customization to a price-based relationship. Level three relationships are characterized by high levels of service customization, as well as a structural change in the nature of the relationship.

Relationship marketing affects the overall marketing process. A limited number of relationship exchanges can be maintained, the relationship is based on commitment, and both parties work toward common goals. Relationship marketing also has an impact on distribution, product, pricing, and decision making.

2 *To evaluate the use of a relationship marketing strategy.* There are four major advantages to the use of relationship marketing: price/production stability, enhanced marketing efficiency, optimal capacity planning, and customer orientation. Two disadvantages of relationship marketing are the need for trust and the increased interdependence of each channel partner.

The decision to use either transactional marketing or relationship marketing should be based on an analysis of customer and supplier attributes as well as on an analysis of the products sold. For example, relationship marketing is best used when a customer is looking at the total cost of a product (including the value of information exchange), when there is a mutual interest in cooperating and in sharing the benefits, and when a firm is concerned with being a leader in technological innovation. High technological products may also be more appropriate for relationship marketing. In contrast, transactional marketing may be more effective for a small customer, a customer solely concerned with delivered price, and where there is little interest and trust in sharing the benefits. Commodity type products are more appropriate for transactional marketing.

3 *To describe key issues in the development of a customer service strategy.* Customer service can be defined as a customer-oriented corporate philosophy that integrates and manages all the elements of the customer interface to meet or exceed customer service quality expectations. A customer-based definition of customer service quality is based on the difference between expectations and experiences as judged by consumers. This difference is referred to as the customer service gap.

There are three approaches to calculating the economics of customer service: calculate the loss in profits owing to a defecting customer; determine the impact of small changes in customer retention on sales and profits; and develop a model in which the impact of changes in customer service is determined on sales (holding all other factors constant).

Two important models that depict service quality are Porter's value chain and SERVQUAL, a model of customer service dimensions. Porter's model provides a way for channel members to focus on value-creating activities. SERVQUAL breaks down customer service into five independent dimensions: reliability, responsiveness, assurance, empathy, and tangibles.

4 *To discuss the implementation of a customer service strategy.* Total quality management is based on four principles: constant feedback from users, benchmarking, use of multifunctional task forces, and total employee involvement.

A number of practices exemplify superior customer service: having a written customer policy, regular monitoring, encouraging employees to be close to the customer, studying customer service as defined by the customer, empowering employees, making it easy for customers to complain and for the firm to respond, resolving complaints on the side of the customer, viewing customers from a lifetime income stream, utilizing technology, making customer service a career path, and being concerned with customer retention, as well as obtaining new customers.

5 *To study the development of customer service standards in physical distribution.* Customer service standards relate to availability, timeliness, and quality. Specific measures of customer service quality are reliability, service failures, fraction of demand filled from stock, and the minimum sum of the cost of inventory and backorders.

KEY TERMS

transactional marketing
relationship marketing (partnering)
level one relationships
level two relationships
level three relationships
opportunity costs
lost-for-good customers
always-a-share customers
customer service
customer service gap
process-related activities

outcome-related activities
zone of tolerance
value chain
reliability
responsiveness
assurance
empathy
tangibles
total quality management (TQM)
benchmarking
availability

customer service level
timeliness
quality
reliability measure
service failures
fraction of demand filled from stock
minimum sum of the cost of inventory and backorders

QUESTIONS FOR DISCUSSION

1. Differentiate between transactional and relationship marketing.
2. Identify the fundamental assumptions of relationship marketing.
3. Provide an example of a level one, level two, and level three relationship for a manufacturer of personal computers.
4. Discuss the view of personal selling in transactional marketing versus the view of selling in relationship marketing.
5. Examine the view of distribution in transactional marketing versus the view of distribution in relationship marketing.
6. Differentiate between process- and outcome-related activities using the example of an airline trip.
7. Discuss the ramifications of the lifelong sales concept in determining an appropriate level of customer service.
8. Show how Baxter International uses the value chain concept. Refer to the Part 3 integrative case.
9. Relate the SERVQUAL components to process- and outcome-related activities.
10. Explain the basic components of total quality management.
11. Describe the role of benchmarking in total quality management.
12. List and describe five common principles of customer service.
13. Compute an availability, timeliness, and quality measure used in developing customer service standards in physical distribution. List your assumptions.
14. Discuss a pitfall of using the fraction of demand filled from stock measure.

END NOTES

1. Mollie Neal, "If the Shoe Fits . . . Market It," *Direct Marketing* (January 1992), pp. 19–22.

2. Robert E. Spekman, "Strategic Supplier Selection: Understanding Long-Term Buyer Relationships," *Business Horizons,* Vol. 31 (July–August 1988), p. 76.

3. Leonard L. Berry, "Educational Perspectives of Relationship Marketing," Presentation at the AMA Faculty Consortium on Relationship Marketing (June 9, 1994); and Shelby D. Hunt, "Seven Questions for Relationship Marketing," Presentation at the AMA Faculty Consortium on Relationship Marketing (June 9, 1994).

4. Jagdish N. Sheth and Atul Parvatiyar, "The Evolution of Relationship Marketing," Sixth Conference on Historical Thought in Marketing (May 22–25, 1993), Atlanta, Georgia; and James C. Anderson and James A. Narus, "Partnering as a Focused Strategy," *California Management Review,* Vol. 34 (Spring 1991), p. 96.

5. Leonard L. Berry, "Educational Perspectives of Relationship Marketing," Presentation at the AMA Faculty Consortium on Relationship Marketing (June 9, 1994).

6. Jeffrey P. Geibel, "Dealer Development," *Sales & Marketing Management* (May 1993), p. 56.

7. Ravindranath Madhavan, Reshma H. Shah, and Rajiv Grover, "Relationship Marketing: An Organizational Process Perspective," in Jagdish N. Sheth and Atul Parvatiyar, eds., *Relationship Marketing: Theory, Methods, and Applications* (Atlanta, Ga.: Center for Relationship Marketing, 1993).

8. Leonard L. Berry and A. Parasuraman, *Marketing Services: Competing Through Quality* (New York: Free Press, 1991).

9. David Greising, "Quality: How to Make It Pay," *Business Week* (August 8, 1994), p. 59.

10. See Aimee L. Stern, "Courting Consumer Loyalty with the Feel-Good Bond," *New York Times* (January 17, 1993), p. F10.

11. Jack Keough, "Distributors: The New Purchasing Arm for Their Customers," *Industrial Distribution* (May 1994), p. 41.

12. Ibid., p. 42.

13. See Joel R. Evans and Richard L. Laskin, "The Relationship Marketing Process: A Conceptualization and Application," *Industrial Marketing Management,* Vol. 23 (December 1994), p. 441.

14. Erin Anderson and Barton Weitz, *The Use of Pledges to Sustain Commitment in Distribution Channels* (Boston: Marketing Science Institute, 1991).

15. See Allan McGrath and Kenneth G. Hardy, "Manufacturer Services for Distributors," *Industrial Marketing Management,* Vol. 21 (May 1992), p. 121.

16. Anderson and Weitz, *The Use of Pledges to Sustain Commitment in Distribution Channels*.

17. Ibid.

18. Barbara Bund Jackson, *Winning and Keeping Industrial Customers: The Dynamics of Customer Relationships* (Lexington, Mass.: D. C. Heath, 1985), pp. 102–116.

19. Keough, "Distributors: The New Purchasing Arms for Their Customers," p. 42.

20. James L. Heskett, Thomas O. Jones, Gary W. Loveman, W. Earl Sasser, Jr., and Leonard A. Schlesinger, "Putting the Service Profit Chain to Work," *Harvard Business Review,* Vol. 72 (March–April 1994), pp. 164–174.

21. See Jean Perrien, Pierre Filiatrault, and Line Ricard, "The Implementation of Relationship Marketing in Commercial Banking," *Industrial Marketing Management,* Vol. 22 (May 1993), pp. 141–148.

22. Patricia Sellers, "Keeping the Buyers You Already Have," *Fortune* (Autumn/Winter 1993), p. 58.

23. Sang-Lin Han, David T. Wilson, and Shirish P. Dant, "Buyer-Supplier Relationships Today," *Industrial Marketing Management,* Vol. 22 (November 1993), p. 335.

24. See Martin Everett, "Why Partners Sometimes Part," *Sales & Marketing Management* (April 1993), pp. 69–74.

25. See Han, Wilson, and Dant, "Buyer-Supplier Relationships Today," pp. 335–337.

26. See Anderson and Narus, "Partnering as a Focused Market Strategy," pp. 95–113.

27. Ibid., pp. 100–103.

28. Jackson, *Winning and Keeping Industrial Customers*.

29. Ibid.

30. Adapted from Peter D. Bennett, ed., *Dictionary of Marketing Terms,* Second Edition (Chicago: American Marketing Association, 1995), p. 73.

31. Patricia Sellers, "What Customers Really Want," *Fortune* (June 4, 1990), p. 58.

32. A. Parasuraman, Leonard L. Berry, and Valarie Zeithaml, "Understanding Customer Expectations of Service," *Sloan Management Review,* Vol. 39 (Spring 1991), p. 42.

33. Jackson, *Winning and Keeping Industrial Customers,* p. 5.

34. See Harvey N. Shycon, "Improved Customer Service: Measuring the Payoff," *Journal of Business Strategy,* Vol. 13 (January–February 1992), p. 13.

35. Rahul Jacob, "Why Some Customers Are More Equal Than Others," *Fortune* (September 24, 1994), p. 216.

36. Frederick F. Reicheld and W. Earl Sasser, "Zero Defections: Quality Comes to Services," *Harvard Business Review,* Vol. 68 (September–October 1990), pp. 105–111.

37. Jaclyn Fierman, "The Death and Rebirth of the Salesman," *Fortune* (July 25, 1994), p. 82.

38. Michael E. Porter, *Competitive Advantage: Creating and Sustaining Superior Performance* (New York: Free Press, 1985), p. 36.

39. Jacob, "Why Some Customers Are More Equal Than Others," p. 216.

40. Bill Howard, "What Goes into a Great Home PC?" *PC Magazine* (December 20, 1994), pp. 156–157.

41. For an assessment of the SERVQUAL measure, see Tom J. Brown, Gilbert A. Churchill, Jr., and J. Paul Peter, "Research Note: Improving the Measurement of Service Quality," *Journal of Retailing,* Vol. 69 (Spring 1993), pp. 127–139; James A. Carman, "Consumer Perceptions of Service Quality," *Journal of Retailing,* Vol. 66 (Spring 1990), pp. 33–55; J. Joseph Cronin, Jr. and Steven A. Taylor, "Measuring Service Quality: A Reexamination and Extension," *Journal of Marketing,* Vol. 56 (July 1992), pp. 55–68; and A. Parasuraman, Leonard L. Berry, and Valarie A. Zeithaml, "Refinement and Reassessment of the SERVQUAL Scale," *Journal of Retailing,* Vol. 67 (Winter 1991), pp. 420–450.

42. See Parasuraman, Berry, and Zeithaml, "Refinement and Reassessment of the SERVQUAL Scale," p. 431.

43. See J. M. Juran, *Juran on Quality by Design: The New Steps for Planning Quality into Goods and Services* (New York: Free Press, 1992), pp. 300–333.

44. See Betsy Wiesendanger, "Benchmarking for Beginners," *Sales & Marketing Management* (November 1992), pp. 59–64.

45. Larry Armstrong, "The Customer as 'Honored Guest'," *Business Week* (Quality 1991), p. 104.

46. See Jay Mathews and Peter Katel, "The Cost of Quality," *Newsweek* (September 7, 1992), pp. 48–49.

47. *Hillenbrand Industries Annual Report 1991,* p. 10.

48. Rahul Jacob, " 'TQM' More Than a Dying Fad," *Fortune* (October 18, 1993), p. 68.

49. Mathews and Katel, "The Cost of Quality," pp. 48–49.

50. Ibid.

51. Ibid.

52. Myroslaw J. Kyj, "Customer Service as a Competitive Tool," *Industrial Marketing Management,* Vol. 16 (August 1987), p. 228.

53. Thomas Teal, "Service Comes First: An Interview with USAA's Robert F. McDermott," *Harvard Business Review,* Vol. 69 (September–October 1991), p. 118.

54. Jacob, "Why Some Customers Are More Equal Than Others," p. 218.

55. Frank Rose, "Now Quality Means Service Too," *Fortune* (April 22, 1991), p. 106.

56. Jacob, "Why Some Customers Are More Equal Than Others," p. 222.

57. Earl Naumann and Patrick Shannon, "What Is Customer-Driven Marketing?" *Business Horizons,* Vol. 35 (November–December 1992), p. 47.

58. Greising, "Quality: How to Make It Pay," pp. 56–57.

59. Cyndee Miller, "Dental Insurer Offers Absolute Guarantee on Its Service," *Marketing News* (March 14, 1994), pp. 8, 18.

60. Jacob, "Why Some Customers Are More Equal Than Others," p. 224.

61. Heskett, Jones, Loveman, Sasser, and Schlesinger, "Putting the Service Profit Chain to Work," pp. 164–174.

62. Carl Quintanilla and Richard Gibson, " 'Do Call Us': More Companies Install 1-800 Phone Lines," *Wall Street Journal* (April 20, 1994), p. B1.

63. Timothy W. Firnstahl, "My Employees Are My Service Guarantee," *Harvard Business Review,* Vol. 67 (July–August 1989), pp. 28–30 ff.

64. Patricia Sellers, "Companies That Serve You Best," *Fortune* (May 31, 1993), p. 75.

65. Sellers, "Keeping the Buyers You Already Have," p. 57.

66. Sellers, "What Customers Really Want," p. 61.

67. Peter D. Bennett, ed., *Dictionary of Marketing Terms* (Chicago: American Marketing Association, 1988), p. 144.

68. Benson P. Shapiro, V. Kasturi Rangan, and John J. Sviokla, "Staple Yourself to an Order," *Harvard Business Review*, Vol. 70 (July–August 1992), pp. 120–121.

69. David P. Schulz, "Flow Management: Study Measures Quality, Productivity in Order Cycle," *Stores* (June 1992), p. 41.

70. See John T. Mentzer, Roger Gomes, and Robert E. Krapfel, Jr., "Physical Distribution Service: A Fundamental Marketing Concept?" *Journal of the Academy of Marketing Science,* Vol. 17 (Winter 1989), p. 59.

71. This section is adapted from John F. Magee, William C. Copacino, and Donald B. Rosenfield, *Modern Logistics Management: Integrating Marketing, Manufacturing, and Physical Distribution* (New York: John Wiley and Sons, 1985), pp. 82–86.

72. Neil S. Novich, "Leading-Edge Distribution Strategies," *Journal of Business Strategy,* Vol. 11 (November–December 1990), p. 50.

73. Raymond E. Kordupleski, Roland T. Rust, and Anthony J. Zahorik, "Why Improving Quality Doesn't Improve Quality," *California Management Review,* Vol. 36 (Spring 1993), pp. 82–95.

74. Joseph P. Aleo, Jr., "Redefining the Manufacturer-Supplier Relationship," *Journal of Business Strategy,* Vol. 13 (September 1, 1992), p. 11.

CASE 1

RELATIONSHIP MARKETING AT KODAK

Kodak's Office Imaging Unit is fully committed to relationship marketing. Good supplier relations and supplier input are especially critical to the imaging unit since half of Kodak's components used in the manufacture of imaging products are supplied by outside vendors. Kodak also plans to reduce its number of vendors for two reasons. First, Kodak feels that a smaller number of suppliers is easier to manage. Second, Kodak wants to concentrate its purchases among those vendors with the best product quality and on-time performance records.

Relationship marketing effectively characterizes Kodak's involvement with its suppliers in its initial supplier selection process, in Kodak's relationships after selection of a supplier, and after a supplier is certified. In its Early Supplier Improvement Program (ESIP), Kodak asks suppliers to sign a nondisclosure and a supplier agreement early in the new product development process. The nondisclosure part of the agreement ensures that suppliers and Kodak can share important confidential information. The supplier agreement also outlines the specific responsibilities for Kodak and its suppliers.

The supplier's involvement in the ESIP program can be characterized as a level three relationship. This relationship is distinguished by joint decision making, trust, and information sharing. The following describes Kodak's product development process with its key suppliers:

- Working together, Kodak engineers and selected suppliers jointly produce drawings and other information to better define the product. The supplier then submits engineering samples to be evaluated and tested to make sure that they meet product standards. Any problems with test results on the samples are jointly resolved by the Kodak-supplier team.

- After the supplier's product meets quality tests and budget needs, the supplier must demonstrate that it can meet the delivery requirements. At this stage, the Kodak-supplier team identifies whatever quality, delivery, and communication requirements are necessary.

- When all objectives have been resolved (such as cost, delivery, and functional requirements), Kodak and the supplier jointly outline the product's final specifications and agree as to whether the product can be consistently produced for the agreed price.

- A quality plan is then jointly drafted by Kodak and the supplier. After the supplier creates a process flowchart that summarizes the entire production process, a Kodak team reviews the submitted material and determines whether it meets certification requirements. Kodak then gives the supplier Class A certification and permission to manufacture. Class A certification recognizes that selected products from a given supplier consistently meet functional and quality requirements.

Kodak continues to utilize relationship marketing concepts after a supplier is certified. For example, Kodak provides its vendors with a questionnaire that evaluates the suppliers' adherence to quality specifications that have been jointly agreed to by Kodak and the supplier. Kodak's supply team (made up of supplier quality assurance, product engineering, procurement, material quality assurance, and parts planning) also jointly agrees on short- and long-term improvement goals.

Kodak's Imaging Division has identified several advantages of relationship marketing. These include shortened lead times in new product development, improved communication with suppliers, lower defect rates, and higher delivery standards.

QUESTIONS

1. Show how Kodak's relationship with its suppliers would differ if it used transactional marketing.
2. Describe how Kodak could use a level two relationship marketing program.
3. What potential problems are associated with the use of relationship marketing by Kodak?
4. Comment on Kodak's use of multiple standards in evaluating customer service. (Note: See page 230.)

Source: Joseph P. Aleo, Jr., "Redefining the Manufacturer-Supplier Relationship," *Journal of Business Strategy,* Vol. 13 (September 1, 1992), pp. 10–14.

CASE 2

PUBLIC SERVICE ELECTRIC AND GAS COMPANY: TOTAL QUALITY MANAGEMENT

Public Service Electric and Gas Company (PSE&G) is a regulated utility providing electric and gas service to more than 2 million customers and more than 5.5 million residents of New Jersey. PSE&G is the state's largest utility and one of America's largest combined electric and gas companies. PSE&G is a subsidiary of Public Service Enterprise Group Incorporated (Enterprise).

Beginning in 1987, when PSE&G developed its current "core values" statement, the firm began to intensively study customer satisfaction and customer expectations. In particular, the firm is concerned with how its energy product is being used, what the customer's perception of satisfactory service is, what types of services its customers prefer, and how its customers want the service supplied.

PSE&G compares its operating methods with those of the best firms in the industry and other leading businesses throughout the United States (even though they are not direct competitors of PSE&G). The firm benchmarks its services on the basis of customer perceptions, not by some internal performance index. Data on customer satisfaction are obtained using such measures as overall satisfaction with the firm's gas and/or electric service, how consumers judge that service, how much they are impacted by the cost of energy, and what their future business prospects are.

Market research on customer satisfaction is part of an ongoing process that involves questionnaires, visits to its largest industrial and commercial accounts, customer panels with a cross section of customers, and surveys to consumers who have experienced service problems.

During 1993, PSE&G initiated a Customer Satisfaction Management system; this process relies on continually surveying its customer population on the key factors that shape their perception of the company. As surveys are completed, their results are compared with results from previous years; trends are then studied. Its marketing representatives visited more than 10,000 important industrial and commercial accounts in a two-year time period. Customer panels with a cross section of customers focus on such issues as billing literature, environmental concerns, safety, and the needs of special groups such as the elderly or the disabled. Lastly, customers who have experienced service problems are asked, "How fast and efficiently did PSE&G respond after your service was interrupted?"

On the basis of the data collected, PSE&G implemented a number of important changes in its strategies and tactics.

- It enlarged print size on bills to senior citizens wherever possible.
- It instituted plain-language customer bills.
- It scheduled meter readings on weekends to accommodate working couples.
- It provided translators to communicate with consumers in languages other than English.
- It provided carefully calculated estimates of restoration time during a power outage.
- It expanded its use of protective devices to reduce lightning damage.

As a result of these strategies and tactics, PSE&G has been able to decrease executive and regulatory customer complaints from 13,000 in 1986 to slightly over 4000 in 1991. More than 90 percent of PSE&G customers now rate the firm as good or excellent in supplying electric and gas service, with especially high marks for reliability and prompt response to calls for service. PSE&G also has the best regional record in providing reliable service at a low cost to its customers. For example, it has the lowest average number of interruptions per customer. This is lower than six of its seven regional competitors. Its cost in dollars per customer to maintain service is less than $60; only one of seven regional competitors has a lower cost.

QUESTIONS

1. Develop a questionnaire for PSE&G that uses the concepts of reliability, responsiveness, assurance, empathy, and tangibles to measure the quality of PSE&G's customer service.
2. Explain how PSE&G can improve its customer service using total quality management.
3. Can PSE&G use the common principles of customer service even though its product is intangible? Explain your answer.
4. Develop three customer service standards in physical distribution for PSE&G. Explain each standard.

Source: Public Service Enterprise Group Incorporated Annual Report for 1991; and *Public Service Enterprise Group Incorporated Annual Report for 1993.*

CHAPTER 6

PHYSICAL DISTRIBUTION STRATEGY IN CHANNELS

CHAPTER OBJECTIVES

1. To discuss basic concepts in physical distribution.
2. To study transportation decision making.
3. To describe warehouse decision making.
4. To introduce basic concepts in inventory management.
5. To study inventory decision making.

During the spring of 1985, Levi Strauss began to pre-ticket its products with UPC codes. It was one of the first apparel producers to use this code. Levi Strauss was also the first manufacturer to use the Uniform Code Council's new shipping label on all of its cartons. This label produces electronic packing slips, which enable Levi Strauss's retailers to scan carton labels and find out which style, size, and color is contained within any carton.

In September 1986, Levi Strauss launched its LeviLink technology. The heart of LeviLink is an electronic data interchange system that links Levi Strauss and its major retailers. Levi Strauss's retailer customers can electronically order and plan their inventories through LeviLink. In addition, LeviLink enables retailers to computerize the process of ordering, stocking, and receiving goods, and to analyze their sales data.

Levi Strauss and Designs Inc., a 111-store chain, have developed a model stock management system that specifies an ideal inventory level for each item, style, and color. Designs Inc. transmits sales data to Levi Strauss by item; Levi matches each store's stock level against the model level and then replenishes each store's core items. Model stock requirements are developed on a store-by-store basis. According to Designs Inc.'s treasurer and chief financial officer, "Just by taking human things out of the ordering process, we've cut the lead time for orders down to a week to ten days." Prior to this system, the average turnaround time for an order was as much as four weeks. The chain's inventory level has also been reduced by 10 to 15 percent since the model stock plan was implemented. The model stock plan also allows Designs to support its $243.5 million in annual sales with a buying staff consisting of the firm's president and six staffers. Lastly, Levi now ships its products directly to Designs' stores, so that the retailers do not need warehouse or distribution facilities.

LeviLink has been further expanded to Levi's suppliers so that they can fine tune the amounts and kinds of fabrics needed to meet customer demand. LeviLink practically eliminated the need for large fabric warehouses that were located near Levi's apparel plants. As a result of electronic data interchange, Levi's shipping cycle was reduced from three weeks to six days for some accounts. Levi's goal "is to order electronically the manufacture of a pair of jeans when the customer buys one in the store."

LeviLink has also enabled many of Levi Strauss's retailers to eliminate their warehouses. A senior vice president for KG Retail Stores, a Denver-based chain of 126 stores west of the Mississippi, finds that an important benefit of LeviLink is that goods can be shipped directly to each store, where personnel simply open the carton and immediately place the jeans on a shelf. This bypasses a retailer's central distribution facility. KG Retail Stores no longer has to maintain a warehouse. A new addition to the LeviLink program is electronic funds transfer (EFT); Levi Strauss is using EFT with Sears and with KG Retail Stores.

Levi Strauss's physical distribution activity is not confined to LeviLink. In 1994, the company began to implement a program for customized-fit jeans which cost $10 more at retail than a ready-made pair. After a customer's dimensions are transmitted electronically to Levi's factory, a robotic tailor cuts a bolt of denim to the customer's measurements. Levi Strauss can either ship these jeans directly to the store where they were measured or to the customer's home or office via Federal Express (for an additional $5 fee). Levi Strauss plans to offer this service at more than 30 original Levi's stores throughout the United States. To successfully implement the customized-fit jeans program, Levi Strauss uses bar codes on its custom-cut pieces to identify each customer. After cutting, these jeans are sent through regular mass production lines, where they are sewn. The bar code is then used to identify where the jeans are to be delivered.

In this chapter, we review physical distribution strategy, including transportation, warehouse, and inventory management decision making. We will see how superior physical distribution profit can become a major competitive advantage to producers and resellers.[1]

INTRODUCTION TO PHYSICAL DISTRIBUTION

Physical distribution describes a concept or approach to managing the finished goods inventory of a firm. A good physical distribution system seeks to get the right goods, to the right customers, at the right time, and at the right cost. Physical distribution activities relate to transportation, facility structures (such as warehouse and distribution center management), inventory management, materials handling, and communication and information. These activities are outlined in Table 6-1. We discuss each of these areas in this chapter.

A firm's physical distribution costs are affected by its product, pricing, and promotional strategies. For example, a wholesaler's decision to stock a manufacturer's complete product line increases the retailer's inventory investment and may lower its inventory turnover. A retailer's use of everyday low pricing (instead of providing price reductions various times throughout a year) can improve inventory planning by flattening variations in sales caused by special price reductions. And sales promotions such as rebates, coupons, and sales contests can be used to clear a manufacturer's and its resellers' inventory of discontinued products.

Like other areas of channels marketing, there are ample opportunities to develop and maintain long-term relationships through physical distribution. Increasingly, channel members have developed **logistics alliances** in which members maintain long-term alliances, coordinate tasks, and share investment requirements to lower costs and improve customer service. The service provider, in these alliances, usually agrees to a penalty when performance is poorer than specified. On the other hand, these agreements reward excellent performance.[2]

Physical distribution has been recognized as an important component of a firm's overall marketing strategy owing to its high costs, its contribution to customer service, and its ability to provide a firm with a long-term competitive advantage.

According to some market analysts, physical distribution often constitutes a firm's largest controllable cost element.[3] According to a senior official of the

TABLE 6-1 PHYSICAL DISTRIBUTION ACTIVITIES

TRANSPORTATION
  Inbound traffic
  Outbound traffic
  International traffic
  Carrier selection
  Mode selection
  Public versus private carriage

FACILITY STRUCTURE
  Warehouse management
  Warehouse planning
  Distribution center management
  Distribution center planning
  Plant site selection

INVENTORY MANAGEMENT
  Purchasing
  Raw material inventory
  Work-in-process inventory
  Finished goods inventory
  Parts/service support
  Returned goods handling

MATERIALS HANDLING
  Salvage/scrap disposal
  Materials handling
  Packaging

COMMUNICATION AND INFORMATION
  Order processing
  Demand forecasting
  Production scheduling

Source: Kenneth C. Williamson, Daniel M. Spitzer, Jr., and David J. Bloomberg, "Modern Logistics Systems," *Journal of Business Logistics,* Vol. 11 (Number 2, 1990), p. 72.

Council of Logistics Management, a professional association, managing the supply chain can account for 10 to 15 percent of a company's total costs.[4] For many products, distribution costs (including selling costs) can be as much as 30 to 40 percent of a product's costs. Another estimate places distribution costs at 10.5 percent of Gross Domestic Product.[5]

It is important to evaluate a firm's physical distribution system on the basis of customer service, as well as costs. One argument is that the output of the physical distribution system can be measured in terms of customer service standards. Many of these standards were covered in Chapter 5. In many cases, the overall quality of a firm's customer service can be improved at the same time as expenses are reduced. Examples of companies with effective physical distribution strategies are Wal-Mart, Circuit City, and Helene Curtis.

According to Wal-Mart's president, David Glass, "Our distribution facilities are one of the keys to our success. . . . if we do anything better than other folks, that's it."[6] Wal-Mart's distribution costs have been estimated to be about 1.5

percent of sales, or anywhere from one-third to one-half less than its competitors. Wal-Mart's savings are due to a number of innovations. Wal-Mart commonly requires manufacturers to ship goods already tagged and ready for the selling floor. Wal-Mart also uses electronic data interchange with its important vendors to provide them with up-to-date sales information. This enables vendors to replenish goods from their suppliers as they are sold. Wal-Mart stores reserve only about 10 percent of their square footage for inventory versus 25 percent for the average store.[7]

Circuit City, an electronics retailer, has a computerized inventory and distribution system that reduces its inventory investment and provides higher levels of customer service. Through its computerized inventory and distribution system, Circuit City is able to track the shipment of nearly every box to all of its 229 store locations. As a result, its inventory arrives just when needed. This system avoids the loss of sales attributable to stockouts, reduces warehousing and inventory carrying costs, and provides a higher level of customer service. The firm's new inventory control system also reduces employee theft to half of the industry average. As a result of its low-cost distribution system, Circuit City has been estimated to add at least one percentage point to its overall profitability.[8]

Chronically slow, or error-prone, physical distribution systems create ill will and contribute to the loss of customers. In contrast, a system that performs well frees up sales personnel time to devote to prospecting for new customers and for selling, versus explaining mishaps, to current customers. For example, according to an executive at Helene Curtis, "Ten years ago salesmen would have to spend the first five minutes of their presentation apologizing for what happened with the last shipment. Just giving them five more minutes to sell is a big competitive weapon."[9] In addition to reducing customer defections, Helene Curtis's new physical distribution system enables it to reduce the prices on some of its items by as much as 5 percent through savings in distribution and inventory costs.[10]

SYMPTOMS OF A POOR PHYSICAL DISTRIBUTION SYSTEM

Table 6-2 lists several important symptoms of a poor physical distribution system. These symptoms relate to transportation, facility structure, inventory management, materials handling, and communication and information activities. Each symptom indicates the existence of a larger problem. Note that some of the problems such as low order size can be solved through minimum order quantities or quantity discounts, areas not normally considered as part of physical distribution. Other problem areas such as stockouts or high defect rates on delivery can be solved through proper inventory management or improvements in packaging or transportation.

A common physical distribution problem is uneven utilization of motor carriers between delivery to a firm's customers and return trips to the firm's distribution center or factory. Some firms attempt to balance low utilization by providing customers with allowances when they pick up freight at a reseller's warehouse. Other firms, such as PepsiCo, have used creative solutions to this problem. In balancing its freight utilization, Pepsi-Cola was able to reduce its to-

TABLE 6-2 SELECTED SYMPTOMS OF A POOR PHYSICAL DISTRIBUTION SYSTEM

Symptom	Implication
TRANSPORTATION	
Unprofitable transactions due to low order size, little opportunity for peripheral hauls, and little opportunity for backhauling	Need for reevaluation of minimum order quantities and quantity discount schedules. Use of freight forwarders and transportation service companies should be explored.
FACILITY STRUCTURE	
Uneven warehouse utilization throughout the year	Poor warehouse utilization on an annual basis. Can also smooth out demand through special pricing incentives or deferred payment plans in slow demand periods. Also need to use public warehouses in peak periods.
INVENTORY MANAGEMENT	
Frequent stockouts	Lost sales and profits; poor customer loyalty. Inventory levels are too low for selected goods.
High proportion of emergency shipments to customers	Physical distribution costs too high. While customers are given good customer service, the firm has high shipping costs. Inventory management needs to be improved.
Inventory turnover too slow	Too high an investment in inventory. Inventory holding costs (interest, warehousing, insurance, and so on) are too high. Inventory may also not be fresh or current.
MATERIALS HANDLING	
A high proportion of goods received by customers in defective condition	Low customer retention; high customer complaints. Evaluate alternative packaging materials and transportation forms.
COMMUNICATION AND INFORMATION	
Inability to determine order status information for customers	Firm unable to track merchandise availability or shipment status.
Inconsistent customer service levels	Accuracy in customer billing, on-time delivery, and/or response time on order information is inconsistent. Customer service is not dependable.

tal distribution expenses by $56 million, about 20 percent of total distribution expenses, between 1987 and 1991. In addition to shipping its soda products, Pepsi-Cola's trucks now ship cartons of Frito-Lay's products (a PepsiCo division) and even outside firms' products (such as Purina Dog Chow or Rubbermaid wastebaskets). According to the president of Pepsi Cola North America, "We even tried hauling chickens for a while, but that got too messy."[11]

LOGISTICS

Logistics, an important extension of physical distribution, can be defined as a single logic that guides the usage of financial and human resources committed to physical distribution, manufacturing support, and purchasing operations.[12] Logistics focuses on all activities from raw material choice to final delivery of a product, including the required information flows. Logistics also examines the interrelationships among components of a physical distribution system. It views all physical distribution elements such as transportation, storage, order processing, distribution, packaging, and customer service as interdependent.

For example, a firm can increase the quality of its overall customer service through a combination of events: a higher proportion of popularly ordered goods in inventory, better communication between a seller and its buyers, use of a faster transportation form, use of local warehouses, and improved order processing. Logistics recognizes that the physical distribution channels are often complex. For instance, a product can travel from a supplier to a manufacturer's warehouse, a wholesaler's warehouse, a retailer's distribution center, the retailer's stores, and ultimately to a final customer's home. As the product travels through the supply chains, decisions need to be made about transportation, inventory management, order processing, and so on. Unfortunately, without a total logistics perspective, many of these decisions are made independently. For example, a person responsible for package design may use a package design that minimizes his or her firm's costs, but the box may not stack properly in a retailer's point-of-sale display, may increase shipping costs, or may reduce the amount of inventory that can be stocked per square foot of display space.

Logistics management principles are being increasingly used by channel members to reduce costs, improve customer service, and maintain lean inventories. For example, before it implemented logistics management, Laura Ashley shipped all of its blouses made in Hong Kong to the firm's distribution center in Wales, which then filled all of its orders. This policy required that blouses ordered in Tokyo be sent back to the Orient. Because of this roundabout supply chain, while Laura Ashley had fully loaded warehouses, some of its stores were commonly out-of-stock on popular items. After studying its total supply chain, Laura Ashley now uses Federal Express to ship its blouses from the manufacturer to its stores around the world; blouses are no longer stored at the firm's distribution center. This new strategy reduced Laura Ashley's total distribution costs and increased the speed of its inventory replenishment process.[13]

Procter & Gamble (P&G) has streamlined its logistics system so that its customers can now order almost all of its products with just one phone call. All items ordered can now be listed on one invoice with one set of payment terms. In addition, the entire order is now shipped on one truck. This change in P&G's policy required a very high level of coordination among P&G's order processing, billing, warehouse, and transportation personnel. The revised system represents a major competitive advantage for P&G because it has simplified the receiving, ordering, warehousing, and accounts payable operations of its reseller customers.[14]

TABLE 6-3 A LIST OF QUESTIONS NEEDED TO BE RESOLVED IN TAILORING A LOGISTICS STRATEGY

1. Is the product a high-margin or low-margin item when all carrying and handling costs are reflected?
2. Do we sell many or few of these products during a year? Does the sale of this product prompt the sale of others?
3. Does the product need to arrive with others in a kit, or is it simple?
4. Must the people delivering the product perform a service along with the delivery?
5. Does the customer need rapid response, routine response, or a response during an extended time period?
6. Does the customer typically buy the product in small or large quantities?
7. What are the special handling and storage characteristics of the product? Does it need to be stored in a bucket, pallet, box, or refrigerated container? How much needs to be on hand?
8. Is the product substitutable by another product?

Source: Adapted from Joseph B. Fuller, "Tailored Logistics: The Next Advantage," *Harvard Business Review,* Vol. 71 (May–June 1993), pp. 93, 96.

A good logistics management strategy should reflect the specialized needs of different types of products and customers at a reasonable cost. These needs are satisfied through a **tailored logistics package**. A principal component of the tailored logistics package concept is the need to offer different logistics strategies based on a product's characteristics or a customer's needs. For example, although some products typically require emergency shipments (regardless of the extra cost), other products can be shipped through low-cost, but slower, transportation forms. A technically complex product may also have to be delivered by a specially trained employee, while another product can be delivered by a delivery service. Table 6-3 presents a checklist of items that need to be evaluated in developing a tailored logistics strategy.[15]

A firm cannot typically maximize the quality of its overall logistics system at the lowest cost level. For example, lowest cost levels may be associated with frequent stockouts, the need for emergency shipments, a high proportion of goods that are received by customers in defective condition, or a supplier's inability to provide order status information to its customers.

THE PHYSICAL DISTRIBUTION (TOTAL COST) CONCEPT

The **physical distribution (total cost) concept** examines the total costs of providing a given level of customer service. The concept recognizes important cost tradeoffs among warehousing, inventory, transportation, and ordering alternatives. For example, with a just-in-time inventory management system, higher per-unit product costs may be offset through cost savings on inspection and reinspection, warehousing, inventory, scrap, and rework operations. High transportation costs for air freight (versus motor carriers) can also be offset by reducing the need for regional warehouses and by maintaining lower inventory levels in a central warehouse. The physical distribution concept recognizes that a firm should examine the interrelationship among costs (including lost sales and profits resulting from stockouts).

Compaq, for example, used to make its computer retailers pay for freight. As a result, its loading docks were so crowded that logjams were common. At one point, Compaq had 156 different firms hauling its goods. To increase the efficiency at its loading dock areas, Compaq now pays the freight costs; as a result, only six freight carriers are used. Compaq's current ability to load 40 percent more merchandise per day more than offsets its added freight costs.[16]

Some physical distribution costs must be estimated or imputed. An example of estimated costs are lost business caused by stockouts. For example, a study of National Association of Purchasing Management buyers (employed in a variety of industries, including defense, medical equipment, electronics, electrical equipment, food processing, and telecommunications) found that 13 percent of industries that experienced a stockout stopped purchasing the particular brand. Some of these customers may be lost forever.[17] Forty-five percent of these buyers also estimated losses from stockouts to include a production slowdown, and 32 percent reported a production stoppage as a result of stockouts. Eighty-seven percent of the buyers reported that administrative costs increased from stockouts. These findings are applicable where the buyer could find alternatives to the product that was out-of-stock.

Imputed costs include loss in interest owing to significant investment in large inventory levels and decline in a stock's value owing to deterioration or obsolescence. These costs may not be reflected on a firm's profit-and-loss statement unless the inventory is financed or the value of a good is reduced at the time of sale. It is important that the imputed costs reflect the level of risk incurred. For example, the imputed inventory interest costs should be high enough to reflect technological obsolescence or inventory held in a good that widely fluctuates in value.

A firm should seek to minimize physical distribution costs only at customer service levels that meet or exceed customer expectations of their target market. Otherwise, lower costs will be offset by customer dissatisfaction, an erosion of brand or dealer loyalty, and long-term customer defections. Optimal total cost rarely occurs at the lowest possible physical distribution costs since this cost level would not generally satisfy the firm's target market.

An example of a company that uses the physical distribution concept is National Semiconductor. Over a two-year period, the firm has cut its standard delivery time 47 percent, reduced distribution costs 2.5 percent, increased sales 34 percent, and closed 6 of its 10 warehouses. Formerly, National Semiconductor had stockpiles of chips at its assembly plants, at its customer's warehouses, and at all points in between: consolidators, forwarders, customs clearers, and distributors. To reach the customers, the chips traveled 20,000 different routes (in planes flown by 12 different airlines) and then were shipped to National Semiconductor's 10 warehouses. Now, Federal Express handles all of the company's storage, sorting, and shipping activities out of a single 125,000-square-foot distribution center in Singapore where the chips are sorted and air-freighted to its customers.[18]

TRANSPORTATION DECISION MAKING

Producers and resellers need to continually review the efficiency and effectiveness of their transportation system. According to two consultants, those companies maximizing transportational efficiency can frequently lower freight costs by 10 to 30 percent by making a thorough review of their operations. Cost savings are commonly achieved by reducing the number of carriers, negotiating more favorable rates, and eliminating overbuying of domestic and international freight services.[19]

Table 6-4 lists relative operating characteristics for railroads, motor carriers, waterways, pipelines, and airways. Each transportation mode excels in different areas. Railroads have the highest rating for range of products carried; motor carriers for number of locations served; waterways for the lowest cost per ton-mile; pipelines for delivery time dependability, frequency of shipments, and losses and damages; and airways for door-to-door delivery time. Similarly, each transportation mode has unique disadvantages. For example, railroads have the poorest rating for losses and damages, whereas airways have the highest cost per ton-mile.

RAILROADS

Railroads are the major transportation mode for shipping heavy, bulky commodity items that have low value relative to their bulk or weight (such as coal, grains, and other commodities). Railroads are used primarily for long-distance hauls. Although they represent a relatively low-cost transportation mode, they are not generally that economical for small packages or short distances. A significant disadvantage of railroads in comparison to motor carriers is that they generally offer less frequent and less flexible service.

Overall, the use of railroads has declined since World War II, when nearly 70 percent of the nation's freight was shipped by rail, to about 38 percent today.[20] However, there has been some evidence of the regrowth of railroads in response to the development of customized services, increased productivity through double-stacking and mergers, and the railroads' increased ability to track shipments.

Some railroads have also increasingly developed **customized services** involving the use of specially configured trains. Burlington Northern, for example, runs a special train from Boise Cascade's mills in International Falls, Minnesota, to St. Paul, which carries paper that is then relayed to other Burlington Northern points. To get the business, Burlington Northern acquired new flatcars and set up new computer linkages with Boise Cascade. To woo the automobile sector, railroads have also built specially equipped closed-door freight cars. These cars reduce costly damage in transit to the new automobiles (such as dents, scratches, and even bullet holes).[21]

Railroads have launched an aggressive campaign to increase productivity in order to better compete with motor carriers and other transportation forms.

TABLE 6-4 RELATIVE OPERATING CHARACTERISTICS OF FIVE TRANSPORTATION FORMS

	Ranking by Transportation Form[a]				
Operating Characteristics	Railroads	Motor Carriers	Waterways	Pipelines	Air Freight
Cost per ton-mile	3	4	1	2	5
Door-to-door delivery time	3	2	4	5	1
Number of locations served	2	1	4	5	3
Delivery time dependability[b]	3	2	4	1	5
Range of products carried	1	2	3	5	4
Frequency of shipments	4	2	5	1	3
Losses and damages	5	4	2	1	3

[a]1 = highest ranking, 5 = lowest ranking.
[b]Delivery time dependability relates to the relative variation from anticipated delivery time.
Sources: Adapted from Donald J. Bowersox, David J. Closs, and Omar K. Helferich, *Logistical Management,* 3rd ed. (New York: Macmillan, 1986), p. 166; and Ronald H. Ballou, *Business Logistics Management: Planning and Control,* 2nd ed. (Englewood Cliffs, N.J.: Prentice-Hall, 1985), p. 194.

For example, through use of double-stacking of truck containers on low-slung railcars, railroads can move freight long distances, saving as much as 30 percent, as compared with over-the-road trucking.[22] An additional factor contributing to the increased efficiency is the increased merger activity among railroads. Burlington Northern Inc. and the Santa Fe Pacific Corporation may merge into a new carrier called the Burlington Northern and Santa Fe Railway Company. The merger will create the nation's largest railroad, with combined revenues of more than $7.1 billion and with 31,000 miles of track in the Midwest, Southeast, and West.[23] This merger must be approved by the Interstate Commerce Commission. Other mergers that have been proposed (but not yet approved) are Illinois Central and Kansas City Southern, Norfolk Southern and Conrail, and Union Pacific and Southern Pacific. Mergers can increase productivity through elimination of overlapping routes, economies of scale, and lower capital costs.

Lastly, railroads have increasingly sought to woo new customers by offering on-time delivery good enough to mesh with just-in-time manufacturing processes. Many railroads now use computer links with other carriers that enable merchandise to be tracked as shipments are passed from one carrier to another.

MOTOR CARRIERS

Trucks now transport about 25 percent of the nation's freight, compared with a little more than 5 percent at the end of World War II.[24] In many cases, motor carriers compete directly with railroads. Unlike rail, which concentrates on heavy, bulky shipments over long distances, motor carriers concentrate on lower weight shipments over shorter runs. As compared with railroads, motor carriers offer greater ability to provide door-to-door service and greater flexibility in scheduling shipments over a dispersed geographic area. The increased flexibility of motor carriers is increased by the wide range of vehicles (which range in size from vans to double trailers), and the availability of specialized motor carriers equipment. (Some motor carriers can carry refrigerated products and liquid gasses.) A shipper can also own its trucks, lease them, or hire a third-party provider (such as Ryder) to perform all trucking services, including payment for drivers, mechanics, and maintenance.

Motor carriers have three major disadvantages: limitations on weight of shipments (based on highway and bridge load limits), higher costs on longer hauls (as compared with both rail and water transportation alternatives), and longer travel times on long routes. For instance, trains can make the Los Angeles to Chicago run in about 50 hours. To travel this distance in 50 hours, a motor carrier would need to operate around the clock using two drivers per cab. It is generally difficult to hire and retain truckers on such long routes.

The American Trucking Association divides the industry into two major segments: full truckload and less-than-full truckload. **Less-than-truckload (LTL) shipments** include freight shipments that are under 10,000 pounds. In contrast, **truckload (TL) shipments** comprise a full truckload. Freight costs per pound are significantly lower for truckload shipments than less-than-truckload shipments. The logistics of sending a fully loaded truck container from a single company to a single destination are quite different from those of routing less-than-full truckloads to several destinations. Yellow Freight, Consolidated Freightways, Roadway Express, Overnite Transportation, and ABF Freight System are the five largest firms in the less-than-full segment.[25] In the less concentrated full-truckload segment, the five leading companies are United Parcel Service, Schneider National Carriers Inc., J. B. Hunt, Ryder Dedicated Logistics, and Werner Enterprises.[26]

The major change in motor carriers has been the deregulation of interstate trucking as a result of the **Motor Carrier Act of 1980**. This act lowered barriers to entry in the motor carrier industry and encouraged competitive pricing. Thousands of new trucking firms were formed in the decade after deregulation. In 1980, 18,045 companies were regulated by the Interstate Commerce Commission; in 1993, this figure had grown to 54,629 companies.[27] However, in 1980, the top four overall trucking firms (United Parcel Service, Consolidated Freightways, Roadway Express, and Yellow Freight Systems) had 29 percent of the total revenue of the 100 largest trucking firms; in 1993, the top four firms (United Parcel Service, Yellow Freight Systems, Roadway Express, and Consolidated Freightways) had 46 percent of the total business of the top 100 trucking firms.[28] And of the top 50 trucking companies operating in 1978, all but 9 had closed or merged as of 1992.[29]

Intrastate trucking was deregulated by federal mandate as of January 1, 1995. Until this date, 41 states continued to regulate in-state trucking. Interstate regulations were designed to protect local truckers that served unpopular rural routes. Now, intrastate shippers can obtain the same benefits of deregulation as interstate shippers. Some market analysts estimate potential savings of $6 to $8 billion in lower freight costs owing to deregulation.[30]

Three important innovations in motor carriers have been the use of cages, curtainside trailers, and computer modeling in the routing and scheduling of motor carriers. Caged parts holders are increasingly used by automakers to deliver parts to dealers. These cages enable automakers to make unattended nighttime delivery to the dealerships, reduce packaging requirements, and facilitate the loading and unloading of shipments. Evening deliveries reduce delivery time and costs. For example, a driver can make from 15 to 20 stops on a typical nighttime route, reducing the amount of equipment, fuel, and time required to service each dealership.[31]

Another recent motor carrier design innovation is the use of **curtainside trailers**, trailers with flexible "walls" on the sides of a truck that are made of a tough fabric material. The fabric moves over a series of rollers on the top of the trailer; the fabric used is so durable that it will not be pierced even if a truck trailer turns on its side. Curtainside trailers allow goods to be reached from all sides, including the top. This innovation facilitates the loading and unloading of merchandise. Seventy percent of Federal Express's truck fleet uses curtainside trailers. Curtainside trailers are also used by Toyota for just-in-time deliveries to its Georgetown, Kentucky, plant.[32]

Computer models are increasingly being used in routing and scheduling motor carriers. Ryder has a number of route models, with each one to fit a set of business needs. In one such system, called "meets and relays," remotely based tractors perform local deliveries and then rendezvous with linehaul tractors to trade their empty trailers for loaded ones. Such a system does not require a warehouse; it also eliminates the costs and damages associated with repeatedly handling a product.[33] Ryder's computer model system evaluates a number of factors such as deliveries to be made, when customers are open, times of delivery appointments, amount of product to be delivered, availability of vehicles, and available time for each driver.

WATERWAYS

Waterways are used primarily for transporting low-value, high-bulk freight. Although transportation costs on waterways are low, waterways are slow, may be closed in winter, and are limited to shipments along the water. Waterways compete with railroads for basic bulk commodities such as iron ore, grains, cement, coal, and petroleum products. These products may be shipped by barge on inland waterway, or on bulk dry cargo carriers, oil tankers, and liquid gas ships. Like railroads and motor carriers, waterway shipments are often used in conjunction with containers that speed up handling and provide protection from weather and theft.

The waterway market is generally divided into inland waterways (such as the Great Lakes, Atlantic Coast rivers, Pacific Coastal rivers, the Mississippi River and its tributaries, and the St. Lawrence Seaway), domestic coastwise, and international.

PIPELINES

Pipelines are characterized by continuous movement, with no inventory accumulation. In contrast with other transportation modes, pipelines typically involve one-direction product flows and are designed to carry one type of product. Pipelines are used primarily for petroleum, natural gas, chemicals, and liquid fertilizer, as well as products that can be suspended in liquid (such as particles in hydraulic suspension).

The major advantages of pipelines are dependability, low maintenance and low operating costs, and continuous operation capability. (Pipelines can operate 24 hours per day, seven days per week.) The disadvantages are the limited range of goods that can be shipped by pipeline, the very high fixed investment, and the slow speed (3 to 4 miles per hour is common).

AIR FREIGHT

Air freight is the smallest, but fastest growing, mode of transportation. It is used primarily for high-value, perishable, and emergency shipments over long distances. Air freight is typically used when the cost of the shipment is small relative to the cost of the product's unavailability or to the decline in the useful life of a product (such as for a perishable good).

Air freight services are performed by specialized express companies or by scheduled passenger lines. In comparison to scheduled passenger lines with a low proportion of evening flights, express companies are able to pick up goods in the early evening hours and deliver goods by the next day in most major markets in the United States. This gives a marketer greater opportunity to service customers. Air freight has been deregulated since the late 1970s. (Specialized air freight carriers are covered in more detail in the following section.)

The primary advantage of air freight is speed of service from a package's origin to its destination. Other advantages are cost savings achieved through reduced inventories (both in transit and at a warehouse), through delivery speed, and through reduced need for regional warehouses. Air freight can also expand the geographic market for a product or a marketer.

A major disadvantage of air freight is its high cost. Despite delivery speed, most shipments of less than 400 to 500 miles are still carried faster by motor carrier. In addition, with scheduled airlines, air freight must generally be coordinated with other shipment forms to arrange for parcel pickup and delivery.

THIRD-PARTY PROVIDERS OF TRANSPORTATION SERVICES

Third-party transportation service providers include an array of facilitators that operate between carriers and shippers. These providers deliver such services as brokerage, freight forwarding, freight consolidation, warehousing, auditing of goods received against purchase orders, information processing, and fleet operations.[34] For example, Sears uses a third-party logistics services firm to manage the shipment of imported goods.[35] Third-party services are now available from subsidiaries of most major logistics providers. Among the major third-party providers are government parcel post, private parcel companies, express companies, and freight forwarders.

Government parcel post operates both surface and air parcel services. Government parcel post charges for services on the basis of weight and distance as established for eight postal zones. For the most part, parcels must be delivered to the post office, but a large user may be able to obtain post office service at its site.

Private parcel companies include United Parcel Service (UPS), a firm owned by its managers. UPS is by far the largest transportation company in the United States, with annual sales of $17.8 billion in 1993. UPS now controls more than three-quarters of the ground-parcel market in the United States and is a growing force in the air-express market (where it is about half the size of Federal Express). Though a minor player overseas, UPS is growing abroad at 10 percent per year.[36]

Express companies include firms such as Federal Express, Airborne Express, United Parcel Service (air-express service), and the U.S. Postal Service. Federal Express created the express company industry. Prior to Federal Express, air freight was handled largely by scheduled air passenger lines that did not travel at night. Express companies have seen some drastic changes in their business. First, although the growth in the overnight-delivery segment has slowed down, the market for two-day deliveries (known in the trade as deferred services) has increased drastically. Some market analysts believe that some express companies such as Federal Express will increase their presence in the light-trucking business owing to the popularity of two-day deliveries and the lower costs associated with motor carriers. Demand in the express business has also shifted from documents to goods as more companies have shifted to express carriers for just-in-time inventory systems and as the popularity of facsimile machines has soared.[37]

The express market is now highly competitive. To gain market share, Federal Express has made contracts with large firms and organizations such as the federal government and General Electric which have drastically reduced user costs. For instance, Federal Express's overnight rates to the federal government are as low as $3.75 per package (versus $13 for traditional 10:30 A.M. next-day delivery).[38]

Freight forwarders are service providers that consolidate small shipments from several companies. These third-party transportation providers pick up merchandise at the shipper's location and then deliver the shipped goods directly to a buyer. Freight forwarders earn part of their profits based on the difference between carload versus less-than-carload shipping rates. In some industries, member firms develop nonprofit shipper associations to perform freight forwarding functions. International channels almost always involve freight forwarders because of customs and other specilized transportation issues.

COORDINATING TRANSPORTATION MODES

In **intermodal transportation**, different transportation modes are used for the same shipment; in some cases, the transportation also involves multiple vendors. Intermodal transportation is generally used in conjunction with contain-

CHANNELS IN ACTION

Overnight Replacement Parts for Tractors

The speed of replacement parts delivery is particularly important for costly goods such as tractors. Rapid and reliable delivery of tractor parts represent a major competitive advantage for a particular brand. This is especially important for custom cutters, harvesters who travel in groups that follow crops from south to north. Custom cutters need to get picked crops to market as quickly as possible owing to the high perishability of crops.

All major tractor manufacturers have now developed warehousing and delivery systems that can deliver spare parts within a day of a tractor's breakdown, sometimes even within hours. After being called for a part by a farmer (many farmers have cellular telephones or C.B. radios in their tractor cabs), a tractor dealer searches his or her inventory and delivers the part(s) immediately, if in stock. If the part(s) must be ordered, the dealer then dials the tractor manufacturer's computer system. This system uses a satellite communication network to search for the part in the manufacturer's worldwide parts depots. The computer searches the closest depot first and then goes to the next closest until the part is located. Deere & Company and Case Corporation (formerly a division of Tenneco) each have nearly a dozen parts depots throughout North America.

A computer then generates a written order for the part. Parts are picked and packed by robots, and delivered to the farmer by Federal Express or United Parcel Service. High competition among these firms has increased customer service levels in remote areas. The costs of overnight shipping are high, but according to a marketing vice president in Case's tractor group: "When you consider the cost of the downtime associated with a $100,000 machine, it becomes pretty cost effective to deliver that part."

Source: Eric N. Berg, "An Uncertain Reprieve for Tractor Makers," *New York Times* (December 30, 1990), p. F4.

---

ers, rail flatcars, and trailers. Among the types of intermodal transportation are fishyback (waterways and motor carrier), piggyback (rail and motor carrier), COFC (container on flatcar), rail-water, airtruck, and trainship. A major difference between piggyback and COFC is that trailers cannot be double-stacked. Many transportation experts argue that the use of intermodal transportation should grow rapidly as a result of the deregulation of transportation. For example, as a result of deregulation, some railroads have purchased motor carriers.

The objective of multiple transportation modes is to use the most efficient transportation mode over each portion of a trip. For example, piggyback service (the use of rail and motor carrier) combines the advantages of railroads or waterways (low-cost operations) with motor carriers (flexibility in pickup and delivery locations). The use of containers also lowers pilferage, permits power loading and unloading, and reduces handling and storage costs at terminals. Other advocates of intermodal transportation are environmentalists who cite the reduced oil consumption, pollution, and highway traffic resulting from lower use of motor carrier versus railroad and waterway. According to a market analyst, 15 years ago, intermodal transport was a stepchild even within the railroad industry. "Now it is being embraced by virtually everyone in surface transportation" as a way to reduce freight costs.[39]

An example of the use of intermodal transportation is an agreement between J. B. Hunt Transportation Services Inc. and Santa Fe. Whereas, in the past, J. B. Hunt Transportation Services Inc. moved its trailers by truck from Chicago to the West Coast, it now lifts the trailers onto Santa Fe rail flatcars that are dedicated to containers and trailer transportation. According to Hunt's president and chief executive, "We're combining competitive strengths." In 1992, between 14 and 15 percent of Hunt's loads moved by rail; the firm forecasts that this amount may increase to 50 percent as of 1997.[40] The alliance enables Hunt to charge lower rates and to better compete with firms that rely solely on trucking. So far, Hunt has been concentrating on very long trips, but the firm will soon begin to use piggyback on trips of 700 to 1000 miles.

The use of multiple transportation modes and multiple vendors should be **seamless**, or invisible, to the customer. This requirement indicates the need for a consistent, reliable exchange of traffic and information among transportation modes. A true seamless operation involves negotiation with a single transportation firm, the ability to call one transportation provider to determine a shipment's delivery status, and the use of one firm for billing.

WAREHOUSE DECISION MAKING

A **warehouse** is a physical facility used primarily to store goods held in anticipation of sale or transfer within the marketing channel.[41] Inventories kept at warehouses serve as buffers to minimize stockouts resulting from difficulty in forecasting demand.

There are two broad types of warehouses: private and public. **Private warehouses** are owned or leased by a supplier or reseller. **Public warehouses** are for-hire facilities that are available to any business requiring storage or handling of goods. The public warehouse usually operates on a monthly contract and charges users based on a storage fee in addition to a handling fee (for receiving products and moving products out of storage).

PRIVATE WAREHOUSES

Private warehouses are especially important when a product requires special handling or storage such as perishable products. A private warehouse also signals a company's commitment to a product and a geographic region. A manufacturer or reseller should consider using private warehouses when there is little seasonal variation and when demand is stable on a year-to-year basis in the geographic area close to the warehouse.

In comparison with public warehouses, private warehouses provide a marketer with more control over hours of operation and special handling needs. Private warehouses can also be used as a firm's regional sales office. Finally, private warehouses enable the development of better communication linkages between suppliers and customers. A major disadvantage associated with a private warehouse is the significant investment required; this investment can tie up much of a firm's capital.

One type of private warehouse is a distribution center. A **distribution center** is a privately owned major warehouse facility used to serve a regional market by consolidating large shipments from multiple vendors. Goods are typically shipped by vendors to a distribution center; these goods are then shipped to a channel member's factory, intermediaries, or retail stores. Newer distribution centers are often 250,000 to 1 million square feet in size, versus 52,300 square feet for the average-sized U.S. warehouse.[42] As compared with older private warehouses, newer distribution centers typically have superflat floors (which vary less than one-eighth of an inch overall) and high ceilings (which are 30 feet to 50 feet high). Superflat floors prevent forklift trucks from weaving as they fetch goods, whereas high ceilings allow goods to be stacked higher in one spot. Smaller private warehouses typically have 24-foot ceilings.

The advantages of central distribution to a wholesaler or retailer are less inventory required owing to use of a centralized location; greater ability to earn quantity discounts attributable to large-volume purchases; ability to take advantage of special buying opportunities; greater opportunity for automation and mechanization owing to large-scale operations; and lower transportation costs accruing from the use of a hub-and-spoke distribution network.[43]

Cadillac, for example, is testing the use of a distribution center in Florida as an alternative to stocking cars at individual dealers. In this program, about 1400 Cadillacs will be stored at a single distribution center in Orlando to await delivery to that state's 42 dealerships within 24 hours of receiving an order. The costs of running the distribution center will be jointly funded by the Florida dealers and General Motors. The distribution center will enable dealers to reduce the number of cars in stock. (For example, one dealer will reduce its inventory from 60 cars to 25 cars.) Cadillac also believes that the distribution center will enable dealers to better locate hot-selling cars. In the current system, dealers must call other dealers to locate cars that are in short supply or to pinpoint cars with special factory-installed options. Cadillac acknowledges losing business when popular models are out-of-stock.[44]

For resellers, alternatives to use of a private warehouse are direct store delivery of merchandise, cross docking, and the storefront system. In **direct store delivery**, goods are delivered by the vendor directly to the retailer's store location instead of to the store's private warehouse. The advantages of direct store delivery to retailers are a reduced need for warehouse space and facilities, lower freight costs, reduced investment in warehousing and trucking facilities, and decreased time between an order and delivery to the store (for products are delivered directly to the store instead of the retailer's distribution center). The disadvantages of direct store delivery to retailers are higher product prices, less flexibility (it is more difficult to shift inventory among stores), need to check orders against shipments on a store-by-store (versus centralized) basis, less opportunity for automation and mechanization, need for higher inventory levels (additional inventory needs to be kept on at each store instead of at a centralized private warehouse), and greater difficulty in determining whether a retailer is getting all applicable deals and allowances.[45]

There is no simple correct answer to determine whether direct store delivery or the use of a private warehouse is more effective. According to a vice president of a major consulting firm, factors such as density of store clusters, types of products, and whether services (such as pre-ticketing of merchandise) are performed by the suppliers or retailer affect which system is optimal.[46]

Some market analysts view cross docking as a cousin to direct store delivery since it also bypasses warehouses. In **cross docking**, the supplier ships its goods directly to the receiving dock, where these goods are divided up for each retailer's or wholesaler's branch location. Goods are then immediately dispatched in trucks at the receiving dock, never having spent a minute in storage. In cross docking, the supplier does not deliver goods directly to any final destination. Cross docking requires that a reseller's loading dock have a sufficiently large staging area.

In a more sophisticated form of cross docking, the supplier is responsible for preparing store-specific multi-stockkeeping pallets and making sure that these goods arrive on the reseller's receiving dock in time for delivery on a specific outgoing truck. This form of cross docking requires that both distributors and retailers use EDI to facilitate advance shipping notices, that cases be coded, and that inbound shipments be scheduled to match outbound shipments. In this form of cross docking, a reseller needs to carefully forecast its daily needs using complex software that reflects past sales patterns, current sales levels, seasonality, and so on.[47]

For resellers, cross docking saves costs on the high fixed costs and investment associated with a private warehouse. Cross docking also increases inventory turnover owing to the absence of goods at a private warehouse. A 1994 study found that 60 percent of chain supermarkets use cross docking for some health and beauty care items, and 43 percent for general merchandise. In contrast, 43 percent of wholesalers were using cross docking for some health and beauty care items, and 42 percent for general merchandise.[48]

An additional alternative to direct store delivery is the storefront system. This system maintains some of the characteristics of the private warehouse and direct store delivery systems. In a **storefront system**, a reseller maintains, in addition to a centralized distribution network, storefront locations where orders are taken, customer contacts are initiated, spare parts are maintained, and some inventory is kept. The storefront system enables customers to visit a branch office and to speak with a salesperson while still centralizing some portion of warehousing operations. Delivery of some products would be from a private warehouse or a distribution center.[49]

PUBLIC WAREHOUSES

Public warehouses are particularly useful for satisfying customers in a new geographic market, when seasonal peak demand requirements cannot be met through a firm's private warehouse, when demand is unstable on a year-to-year basis, or when a firm seeks to use selected products for collateral for a loan. With a **bonded warehouse**, tax payments (on products such as cigarettes and liquor) can be postponed until products are sold. A special type of bonded warehouse, a **customs bonded warehouse**, defers duties on imported merchandise until these goods are sold. In a **field warehouse**, products are kept in a special area, and product movement is monitored by the public warehouse manager. These products can be used as collateral for loans.

The use of a public warehouse also reduces a company's investment in its physical distribution facilities. For example, Sun Microsystems has outsourced its distribution center to Federal Express, giving FedEx's Business Logistics Services group responsibility for moving Sun machines from the factory floor to the customer. "Every time we invest in a material handling resource, we don't have that money to invest in an engineer," says a Sun executive. Sun also wanted distribution to be a variable cost rather than a fixed cost in its manufacturing process.[50]

HUB-AND-SPOKE DISTRIBUTION SYSTEMS

Decision making relative to the optimal number of warehouses needs to consider the required levels of customer service (as measured by delivery service frequency and reliability), as well as the costs of developing, stocking, and operating multiple warehouse locations. These decisions generally involve a tradeoff, with fewer warehouses being associated with lower costs but longer delivery frequencies. In making decisions as to the number of warehouses, one needs to consider the geographic distance that could be served by a warehouse using alternative transportation modes. For example, with motor carriers, a single warehouse can serve a market area of 200 miles within one travel day, 450 to 500 miles within two days, and 700 to 750 miles within three days (depending on weather and road conditions). With air freight, a single warehouse can serve the entire United States and some major foreign cities within one day.

A popular configuration for warehouses is a **hub-and-spoke distribution system**. In this system, small shipments are consolidated in a regional warehouse and then shipped to customers. In many cases, this system reduces transportation costs since large trailers can be used for shipments to a firm's distribution center, while smaller trailers can be used for delivery to a customer. The opposite of a hub-and-spoke system is direct shipment to customers from a centralized warehouse.

Firms use the hub-and-spoke distribution system to determine the number of warehouses and their configuration. It is also used in assessing a firm's ability to adequately fill orders in a new geographic area. For example, in its early days, Wal-Mart could not get any large distributors to call on its firm at its remote Bentonville, Arkansas, location. So Wal-Mart planned a growth strategy on the basis of concentric circles growing from Bentonville. As the circles grew, Wal-Mart supplied them with its own distribution centers and truck fleet.[51] In 1994, Wal-Mart operated 32 food, general merchandise, and apparel distribution centers. Its McLane convenience store subsidiary operated 16 distribution centers, and its Western Merchandisers subsidiary operated five distribution centers that supply music and video materials to 850 Wal-Mart stores.[52]

In addition to warehouses, hub-and-spoke distribution systems are common in the airline and air-express business. In these examples, large hubs bring in traffic from smaller destinations served by smaller airports (spokes). Originally, the hub system used by airlines was a great success. The hub-and-spoke system enabled major airlines to envelop large geographic regions, to capture traffic for long-distance flights by pulling in passengers from smaller cities, to increase passenger options over a traditional linear route structure, and to integrate remote cities into a national and international route network. For example, United Airlines' domestic route system is distinguished by its four hubs (Chicago, Denver, San Francisco, and Washington, D.C.), which are strategically positioned across the United States for efficient east/west and north/south coverage.[53]

Critics of the hub-and-spoke system argue that the system worked well in the 1980s in response to the demand for an increased number of flights. When demand slackened, however, the cost of maintaining the hub became prohibitive. The most vulnerable hubs are those in smaller cities that do not generate a lot of traffic. Also in peril are those hubs that are operated by airlines in Chapter 11 bankruptcy proceedings.[54]

INVENTORY MANAGEMENT PRINCIPLES

The inventory management section of this chapter is divided into two sections. In this section, we study some fundamental concepts relating to inventory. We discuss the types of inventory, three ways to compute inventory turnover, and the advantages and disadvantages of fast versus slow inventory turnover.

The second part of inventory management focuses on inventory decision making. In this section, we discuss just-in-time and quick response inventory planning, reorder point calculations, economic order quantities, and the application of ABC analysis to inventory management.

TYPES OF INVENTORY

Four types of inventory are process stock, lot size (cycle stock), safety stock, and seasonal and smoothing stocks.[55] **Process stocks** are inventory in transit. This inventory is needed because of the time required to get inventory from one channel member to another. A firm can reduce its process stocks by locating warehouses closer to customers, by using regional versus centralized warehouses, and by selecting transportation modes with faster delivery times.

Lot size stocks (cycle stocks) are carried whenever a firm manufactures, ships, or purchases an item in larger lots than is needed for its immediate needs. Firms purchase lot size inventories owing to economies of transportation (to receive TL versus LTL shipping rates), quantity discounts, the higher level of bargaining power associated with a larger order, or the need to spread ordering costs over more units. Obviously, decisions as to the size of lot stocks involve a tradeoff of economies possible with larger quantity discounts or lower freight costs versus the additional holding costs associated with larger lot sizes.

Firms use **safety stocks** to meet unanticipated variations in consumer demand or unplanned delays in order cycle time from vendors. The function of safety stocks is to avoid a stockout. A firm can reduce safety stocks by using (1) perpetual inventory systems that continually monitor inventory levels, (2) delivery forms with reliable delivery times, and (3) vendors with high quality control.

Lastly, **smoothing and seasonal stocks** are needed to reflect differences between production and demand. For instance, a perishable product may be grown in the summer months but sold throughout the year. Christmas cards may be produced over a period of several months but sold over a one-month period. One tradeoff with smoothing and seasonal stocks involves the use of overtime production to minimize smoothing and seasonal stocks. But this increases production costs owing to higher labor and excess capacity of machinery in nonpeak sales periods.

The specific functions of each type of inventory are shown in Table 6-5. None of these inventory types reflects inventory used in production or inventory needed for sales. The four types of inventory suggest that inventory holdings need to be considerably larger than necessary because of factors relating to inventory in transit (process stock), bargaining power (lot stock), uncertainty in delivery or demand (safety stock), and seasonality (seasonal and smoothing stocks). An example of the need for high inventory levels comes from a study in which the head of manufacturing at a major plant of Corning Inc. found that just 6 percent of inventory at the plant was "live" or in use at any given moment.[56] We will soon see how just-in-time and quick response inventory systems seek to minimize each of these types of inventory.

COMPUTING INVENTORY TURNOVER

Inventory turnover is the relationship between a firm's sales and the inventory required by the firm to support that sales level. Inventory turnover can be computed in units or in dollars (both retail and cost). Although inventory turnover is generally computed on an annual basis, computing turnover on a monthly basis is preferred when sales tend to peak in a few key months. For example, many retailers compute inventory turnover on a monthly basis:

$$\text{Inventory turnover (in units)} = \frac{\text{Number of units sold during a year}}{\text{Average inventory on hand during year (in units)}}$$

$$\text{Inventory turnover (in \$ retail)} = \frac{\text{Net annual sales in dollars}}{\text{Average inventory on hand during year (at retail)}}$$

$$\text{Inventory turnover (in \$ cost)} = \frac{\text{Cost of goods sold during the year}}{\text{Average inventory at hand at cost}}$$

Table 6-5 Functions of Each Type of Inventory

Inventory Type	Inventory Function
Process stock	1. To provide storage of raw materials 2. To reflect large distances between production and distribution
Lot size (cycle stock)	1. To defer increasing plant capacity 2. To handle variations in production 3. To store overruns 4. To take advantage of a favorable raw material price 5. To speculate against price and cost changes
Safety stock	1. To provide acceptable customer service due to uncertainty in sales patterns 2. To provide acceptable customer service due to uncertainty in order cycles 3. To protect against strikes or work stoppages 4. To protect against acts of nature such as frost
Seasonal and smoothing stocks	1. To reflect seasonal differences in demand 2. To smooth production throughout the year despite heavy seasonal demand

Source: Inventory functions from James I. Morgan, "Questions for Solving the Inventory Problem," *Harvard Business Review,* Vol. 41 (July–August 1963), p. 95.

There are some key differences in each of the three measures of turnover. For example, the unit-based turnover measure may skew results if low-cost units have higher turnover than higher-cost units. Distributors or retailers that keep their inventory values at retail levels generally would use the second measure, whereas firms that keep inventory valuations at cost levels would use the third measure. Note that all of these measures use average inventory levels in their denominator. The time periods used to take a physical inventory must be representative. Some retailers have large sales prior to taking a physical inventory, and many retailers take inventory during a poor selling season. These actions may artificially inflate a firm's inventory turnover rates.

Although these are the most commonly used measures of inventory turnover, days' supply or stock-to-sales ratios represent inventory (in dollars or units) divided by a firm's average sales rate (in dollars or units). Automobile dealers commonly measure turnover in terms of days' supply using a unit-based measure. Many dealers commonly accept the notion that a 60-day supply of a new car is optimal. A less than 60-day supply is viewed as too low an inventory, while a greater than 60-day supply suggests oversupply of a particular model.

ADVANTAGES AND DISADVANTAGES OF FAST VERSUS SLOW INVENTORY TURNOVER

A fast inventory turnover means that a firm uses its inventory investment efficiently. A fast inventory turnover is also associated with fresh and current merchandise, the need for fewer markdowns (owing to technological shifts, style changes, or perishability), and lower costs of maintaining inventory (owing to lower need for insurance, capital, lower warehousing costs, and lower pilferage).

A firm that generally has high inventory turnover is The Gap. One industry analyst estimates that The Gap replaces its inventory 7.5 times a year; this compares to 3.5 times a year for specialty apparel retailers as a whole. High replenishment rates also mean that The Gap's merchandise is fresh and that it has less need for markdowns to clear stale merchandise.[57]

Table 6-6 outlines the economics of a fast turnover rate. This example assumes that the firm has annual sales of $300 million, an average markup at retail of 50 percent, and inventory carrying costs equal to 10 percent of the value of its inventory. Using these figures, a firm increasing its inventory turnover from three to five times would save $2 million a year. These figures do not include lost profits resulting from stockouts, or the loss in quantity discounts resulting from frequent ordering in small quantities.

There are some major disadvantages to too fast an inventory turnover. Too fast a turnover may mean that a firm cannot take advantage of noncumulative quantity discount opportunities, that a firm may have lost sales because of frequent stockouts, that a firm's customers cannot purchase their total requirements from a single source, and that a firm's customer service response time is poor. For example, GE Appliances found that low inventories on some parts—it gets 475 parts from 75 suppliers—prevented it from responding to customer demands quickly. So it recently increased its inventory of parts with long delivery times by 24 percent. The change helped GE Appliances respond to customer orders in 3.6 weeks, down from 18 weeks in 1990.[58]

The advantages of a slow inventory turnover are the ability to obtain quantity discounts, high in-stock levels, and a client's ability to obtain total requirements from a single source. The disadvantages are high capital costs, poor utilization of capital investment, and a high proportion of stock on hand that may be unsalable or old.

TABLE 6-6 ECONOMICS OF FAST TURNOVER RATES

Turnover Rate	Inventory Cost ($)	Carrying Cost ($)	Annual Reduction in Carrying Costs ($)
2.0	75 mil	7.5 mil	—
2.5	60 mil	6.0 mil	1.5 mil
3.0	50 mil	5.0 mil	2.5 mil
3.5	43 mil	4.3 mil	3.2 mil
4.0	37.5 mil	3.8 mil	3.7 mil
5.0	30 mil	3.0 mil	4.5 mil
6.0	25 mil	2.5 mil	5.0 mil

Assume annual sales = $300,000,000.
Average gross profit = 50 percent of retail.
Assume carrying cost = 10 percent of inventory cost.

Source: "Inventory Management: New Rules, New Game Plan," *Chain Store Age Executive* (March 1991), p. 13B.

INVENTORY DECISION MAKING

Among the strategies used to better manage inventories are the use of just-in-time and quick response inventory systems, Efficient Consumer Response, reorder point determination, economic order quantity determination, and ABC inventory analysis. This section explores several important characteristics of inventory management. A concern of inventory decision making is to examine the major tradeoffs. For example, in determining the optimal inventory level at hand, one must balance high inventory holding costs with high opportunities at sales. Although large inventories can be costly to maintain, they minimize the possibility of a stockout. Another important inventory management decision seeks to determine the optimal order quantity. While large purchase quantities lower ordering costs, they increase holding costs.

JUST-IN-TIME AND QUICK RESPONSE INVENTORY SYSTEMS

Just-in-time (JIT) inventory management systems seek to minimize inventory investment through frequent deliveries and low average order sizes from a small group of suppliers. Just-in-time inventory management systems are called **quick response inventory systems** by retailers. Proponents of JIT inventory management systems argue that excessive inventories are wasteful. In addition, inventory is viewed as a means of masking problems in purchasing (such as poor vendor delivery performance or poor supplier quality) or in manufacturing (such as the need for large lot sizes to cover high fixed setup costs).[59] JIT started in 1977 when TRI-CON, a supplier of motorcycle seats, delivered its products on a just-in-time basis to Kawasaki.[60] Though originally associated with Japanese manufacturing systems and the automobile industry, JIT is being used by such firms as the American Tourister division of Hillenbrand Industries, Boeing, DuPont, Ford, General Electric, General Motors, Harley Davidson, Hewlett-Packard, IBM, Lever Brothers, Procter & Gamble, Wal-Mart, and Xerox.[61]

The basics of a just-in-time and quick response system are the tracking of inventory and sales on an item level, the use of high technology, the packing of goods on a customer level, and the availability of goods ready to use or sell directly out of the shipping container:

- Both inventory and sales are tracked on an item level. Automatic replenishment systems constantly monitor inventory levels relative to demand to support smaller inventory levels. A survey of general managers of strategic business units or divisions of 200 consumable goods manufacturing companies and of merchandising managers at 80 retailing companies found that leaders in implementing JIT and quick response inventory systems were far ahead of other companies in the industry in sharing sales, stockout, and inventory data.[62]
- UPC bar coding, point-of-sale scanning, shipper container marking, and electronic data interchange (discussed in Chapter 5) are needed to sup-

port communication of sales data and documents among retailers, vendors, and textile mills and suppliers.

- Goods are packed on a store basis. Retailers do not need to break down large shipments in their distribution center, repackage the merchandise, and then allocate it to their various stores. Similarly, manufacturers receive goods at the factory floor instead of at a warehouse. This reduces labor costs and required warehouse space.

- Goods are ready to use or sell when taken out of the shipping container. For example, Federated Department Stores is asking some apparel suppliers to upgrade the hangers used for shipping so that Federated will no longer have to change hangers.[63]

See Table 6-7 for a listing of other important characteristics of JIT. Four other important elements in a JIT system that need further clarification are a pull ori-

TABLE 6-7 CHARACTERISTICS OF JIT PURCHASING

Suppliers
- Few suppliers
- Nearby suppliers
- Repeat business with same suppliers
- Active use of analysis to enable desirable suppliers to become/stay competitive
- Clusters of remote suppliers
- Competitive bidding limited mostly to new part numbers
- Buyer plant resists vertical integration and subsequent wipeout of supplier business
- Suppliers encouraged to extend JIT buying to *their* suppliers

Quantities
- Steady output rate (a desirable prerequisite)
- Frequent deliveries in small lot quantities
- Long-term contract agreements
- Minimal release paperwork
- Delivery quantities variable from release to release but fixed for whole contract term
- Little or no permissible overage or underage of receipts
- Suppliers encouraged to package in exact quantities
- Suppliers encouraged to reduce their production lot sizes (or store unreleased material)

Quality
- Minimal product specifications imposed on supplier
- Help suppliers to meet quality requirements
- Close relationships between buyers' and suppliers' quality assurance people
- Suppliers encouraged to use process control charts instead of lot sampling inspection

Shipping
- Scheduling of inbound freight
- Gain control by use of company-owned or contract shipping, contract warehousing, and trailers for freight consolidation/storage where possible—instead of using common carriers

Source: Richard J. Schonberger and James P. Gilbert, "Just-in-Time Purchasing: A Challenge for U.S. Industry," *California Management Review*, Vol. 26 (Fall 1983), p. 58.

entation, inventory flow, relationship marketing, and suppliers located near important customers.

First, many observers argue that, while traditional inventory systems are push-oriented, JIT is pull-oriented. The basic difference between pull and push is that a **pull system** initiates production as a reaction to present demand, whereas in a **push system**, production is initiated in anticipation of present demand.[64] In a pull system, materials are not produced until they are requested from the preceding work center. In contrast, in the traditional push system, parts are made as scheduled and sent to the next work center where they are scheduled for use.[65] A traditional push system requires higher safety stocks owing to poor estimates of demand and anticipated machine breakdowns. A hallmark of a pull inventory system is the use of Japanese-style kanban cards. In the **kanban system**, cards or other objects are used to initiate the production or delivery of inventory. Conventional blanket orders or electronic data interchange also can be used to pull inventory. These systems are used in place of traditional purchase order systems to minimize the paperwork associated with monitoring inventory levels and printing purchase orders on small order quantities.

Second, the flow nature of JIT relates to the coordination between a buyer's requirements and the seller's production and delivery schedules. According to two experts, "This emphasis on flow rather than production process can be accomplished by conceding that factors such as large lot sizes, high setup times, high vendor and production scrap rates, and high machine downtime have no place in a just-in-time material flow."[66]

Third, JIT inventory management systems are characterized by such relationship marketing characteristics as long-term contracts between suppliers and customers, few suppliers servicing a manufacturer, the sharing of inventory and sales information between vendors and customers, trust and cooperation between vendors and customers, and buyer control of transportation. For example, companies such as Deere and Caterpillar organize joint workshops with their suppliers and increasingly work with contracts of between 24 and 36 months.[67]

Fourth, suppliers need to relocate closer to major buyers. The need for closeness is related to the absence of safety stocks at the buyer's location. Closeness of suppliers helps reduce the variability in shipping times. Japanese JIT manufacturers such as Toyota surround themselves with nearby suppliers who ship directly to the assembly line every few minutes from dedicated mini-factories or transit warehouses.[68] The closeness of suppliers to buyers enables buyers to view a supplier's warehouse as an extension of the buyer's factory. Shipping times in a JIT system are typically every 24, 48, or 72 hours.

Other important characteristics of JIT include the importance of on-time deliveries, perfect quality of goods-in-process and finished goods, efficient materials handling, and floor layouts to arrange for delivery from suppliers directly to the factory (versus warehouse delivery in a traditional inventory system).

Saturn and Compaq are two examples of firms with fine-tuned JIT systems. Saturn's JIT system is so well coordinated with suppliers that in four years, it had to halt production just once—for only 18 minutes—because the right part was not delivered on time. Saturn maintains almost no inventory of components. Instead, a central computer directs trucks to deliver pre-inspected and pre-sorted parts at precise times to the factory's 56 receiving docks, 21 hours a day, 6 days a week. Most of Saturn's 339 suppliers are not near the plant—they average 550 miles away from Spring Hill, Tennessee.[69]

Prior to its use of JIT, Compaq used to store between five and seven days' worth of sheet-metal casings in its own warehouse. Now these casings are stored in suppliers' warehouses. This enabled Compaq to clear out its own warehouse and to add an additional manufacturing line without acquiring additional square footage. Phelps Tool & Die Company opened a 60,000-square-foot assembly plant in Houston. Phelps can now deliver casings to Compaq in 15 minutes.[70]

Among the benefits of just-in-time and quick response are reduced inventory investment and carrying costs, higher sales (less stockouts), fewer markdowns,

CHANNELS IN ACTION

Procter & Gamble: Relationship Marketing and Inventory Management

Procter & Gamble (P&G) has often been cited as the leading advocate of partnerships with major food retailers. The purpose of such partnerships has been to reduce inventory management costs for both parties, to smooth out production schedules, and to quickly determine service and quality problems. For example, P&G has assigned teams to such major retailers as Kmart to automate and harmonize their order and recordkeeping systems with P&G's. Both Kmart's and P&G's logistics managers share information and coordinate delivery schedules. Their marketing and finance managers also share timely sales data and long-range plans.

According to P&G's senior vice president in charge of sales, "When we started looking at this, we saw a potential savings of $1 billion annually in the United States for P&G and just as much, if not more, for our customers. But the elephants have to dance together to get there."

The combination of improved information exchange and logistical adjustments has led to a wide variety of improvement in service to firms such as Wal-Mart. Wal-Mart's inventories of Tide detergent have been cut from 30 to 2 days. In another instance, Shaw's Supermarkets worked with P&G to standardize the language and structure of electronic order processing forms. While at first, P&G was only able to electronically process 10 percent of Shaw's computerized orders, now the figure is over 90 percent. P&G has also automated replenishment of supplies for 12 retailers. In one case, the automation reduced the inventory of P&G products by 80 percent.

According to P&G's top logistics executive, the firm is now saving about $500 million annually due to its new inventory management systems.

Source: Barnaby J. Feder, "Moving the Pampers Faster Cuts Everyone's Costs," *New York Times* (July 14, 1991), p. F5.

less need for warehouses, better reaction to sales trends, higher quality control, improved responsiveness to changes in demand, faster detection of defects, and less need for paperwork. Retailers that are leaders in quick response have improved their in-stock positions in basic/seasonal merchandise from 70 percent to 80 percent to more than 90 percent. They have also increased the sales of fashion merchandise by as much as 28 percent by reducing order delivery times. Automatic replenishment systems and electronic data interchange have reduced the time required to create, communicate, and track purchase orders by as much as 80 percent. Finally, inventory turnover in basic/seasonal merchandise has increased by 25 percent to 35 percent and by 40 to 45 percent in fashion merchandise.[71]

A study of the impact of JIT on industrial marketers examined firms in the steel, home entertainment equipment, agricultural machinery, computer, home appliance, and automotive industries. The study found that:[72]

- About one-half of the responding companies felt that the purchase prices of goods bought through JIT were slightly lower.
- Sixty percent of the buyers reported significantly higher supplier quality.
- Three-quarters of the respondents stated that handling costs were unchanged with the implementation of JIT.
- Most respondents did not feel that JIT increased company profits.
- The average firm reported that average backorders declined by 20 to 30 percent, order cycle times were cut by over 40 percent, damaged products were reduced by 40 percent, and supplier delivery frequency increased by over 200 percent.

In a landmark study, Andersen Consulting, commissioned by the Voluntary Interindustry Communications Standards (VICS) Committee, estimated that the benefits of quick response in 1989 to the retail industry were $9.6 billion in savings, roughly 4.9 percent of retail industry sales.[73]

Many experts argue that JIT works best when a buyer's production schedules are predictable and smooth; when larger, steady orders are given to a smaller number of suppliers; when purchase agreements are long term; and when suppliers are responsive to the need for improved containers and labeling.

A number of potential difficulties are associated with JIT. First, critics of JIT argue that it is not appropriate with highly seasonal goods whose sales are difficult to predict, such as toys.[74] Second, JIT is often associated with high freight costs owing to fewer opportunities to consolidate shipments and with the need for substantial air freight usage, especially in the early stages of a JIT conversion.[75] Third, quality control and delivery scheduling need to be nearly perfect to avoid stockouts and the costs associated with factory closings. Fourth, although the intent of JIT is to minimize inventories throughout the manufacturer-reseller channel, suppliers with low capacity may still be forced to stock large inventories to protect against sudden surges in demand.[76] Some critics argue that much of JIT's success is due to the shifting of inventory responsibility between customers and suppliers. This can cause confrontations between customers and their suppliers, particularly when JIT is imposed on a supplier by a large customer.

EFFICIENT CONSUMER RESPONSE

Efficient Consumer Response (ECR) is a term used in the food distribution industry to describe efforts to maximize the effectiveness of the entire supply chain. ECR gives special emphasis to the linkages among all of a firm's trading partners. For example, manufacturers need to push quick response-related technologies back into their plants and material procurement systems. The primary efforts of ECR have been centered around inventory replenishment and promotional practices. These two areas account for 70 percent of the savings expected through ECR. ECR projects center on activity-based costing, category management, direct store delivered items, electronic data interchange, cross docking, and continuous replenishment.

ECR proponents argue that firms can achieve efficiencies through joint category planning between manufacturers and distributors, computer-assisted ordering, space management, just-in-time delivery, continuous replenishment, joint promotion planning, contract pricing, cross docking, and automated coupon administration. The operating cost reductions for the entire channel—manufacturers, suppliers, retailers, wholesalers, and brokers—have been estimated at $24 billion in one study and $30 billion in another for total dry grocery goods alone.[77]

The Efficient Consumer Response Performance Measures Operating Committee (PMOC) examined the role of trading partners for the three product distribution channels (direct store delivery, the self-distributing retailer, and the wholesaler-supplied system) and found that multiple trading partners often perform the same activity. The committee has attempted to eliminate redundancy by eliminating activities that add no value, by adding activities that improve communication, and by striving to eliminate poorly performing products. For example, the Grocery Manufacturers of America (GMA) estimates that dry grocery products spend an average of 84 days in supply chain inventories and make an average of 2.5 warehouse stops. It is estimated that a flow-through process can reduce inventories in supply channels by as much as 65 percent, or about $16 billion annually.[78]

According to a study by Meyers Research Center, only 24 percent of the grocery industry was pursuing an ECR strategy in 1993. However, 45 percent were actively working towards ECR.[79] There are some major stumbling blocks to industrywide implementation of ECR: (1) Some wholesalers and retailers see more benefits accruing to manufacturers and wholesalers than to themselves; and (2) others fear that ECR may reduce price allowances to those retailers that do not use everyday low pricing. In particular, they see ECR as a threat to current profits derived from forward buying and from reduced cooperative advertising allowances.[80]

REORDER POINT DETERMINATION

The **reorder point** formula sets the inventory level at which a firm must place an order or risk a stockout. The traditional reorder point formula has three variables: order cycle time, usage rate, and safety stock.

Order cycle time is the time span between when an order is placed and when the goods are ready for sale or use in a production process. Order cycle time needs to incorporate time to verify shipments against an order, product inspection, and other necessary tasks before the product is ready for use or sale (such as merchandise ticketing, placing goods on hangers, and pressing garments for a retailer or getting the products to the factory floor for a manufacturer). A firm can lower the order cycle time by making faster shipments (such as use of air freight), placing orders with suppliers who can deliver quickly, locating plants closer to key customers, and using EDI, JIT, and floor-ready merchandise. For example, Wal-Mart demands that goods be in its stores three days after an order is placed.[81] In **floor-ready merchandise**, goods come from a vendor pre-ticketed with store label and bar codes, pre-priced, and pre-hung. These tactics enable a retailer to take merchandise out of a carton and place it directly on the selling floor. For example, Mercantile Stores Company expects to have 90 to 95 percent of its merchandise floor ready by the spring of 1996.[82]

According to a study conducted by A. T. Kearney Inc. for the Council of Logistics Management, order cycle time in the general merchandise industry decreased from 7.9 days in 1985 to 5.8 days in 1990. Executives who participated in the study hoped to reduce order cycle time to 3.8 days as of 1995.[83]

Usage rate represents the rate at which a good is sold or the rate at which a good is used in a production process for a manufacturer. Safety stock (cushion) is additional inventory required in the event that demand is higher than expected or order cycle time is longer than expected (such as delivery delays or the product being temporarily out-of-stock at the supplier). Safety stock is the difference between the reorder point level and the expected demand during the order cycle time period. The safety stock quantity is based on the degree of variation in demand or usage rates, and service reliability. For example, if a manufacturer seeks to fulfill 90 percent of demand from stock on hand, the manufacturer needs higher safety stock than if the manufacturer seeks an 80 percent reliability policy.

The traditional formula for computing reorder points assumes that a firm has a perpetual inventory system that monitors up-to-date inventory levels on important products:

$$\text{Reorder point} = (\text{Order cycle time} \times \text{Usage rate}) + \text{Safety stock}$$

The following problem illustrates the reorder point calculation. A retailer that generally receives belts from a local supplier can expect to receive his or her order within five days of placing it. This retailer anticipates a usage rate of 10 belts per day. Without any safety stock, the retailer must reorder the belts when his or her inventory reaches 50 units. If either the order cycle time is greater than five days or the usage rate is greater than 10 units a day, the retailer faces a stockout. A safety stock of 10 units gives the retailer an additional cushion against an additional day of order cycle time, or an additional 2 units per day for his or her usage rate. With the addition of the 10-unit safety stock, the reorder point equals 60 units.

This traditional formula can be modified to reflect conditions in which a firm monitors inventory only periodically (versus on a perpetual basis). The formula for reorder point (assuming periodic review form inventory) is

Reorder point
$$= (\text{Order cycle time}) \times \left[(\text{Usage rate}) + \frac{(\text{Review period})}{2}\right] + \text{Safety stock}$$

In this formula, the **review period** is the frequency with which inventory counts are made. Using the numbers in the above example for order cycle time, usage rate, and safety stock, with a 10-day review period, we find that the reorder point is 85 units:

$$\text{Reorder point} = 5 \times [10 + (10/2)] + 10 = 85 \text{ units}$$

This formula provides additional inventory to compensate for the review period being five days greater than the order cycle time. If the review period were daily, the reorder point would be 65 units. These formulas all assume that the inventory level could fall below the reorder point calculated value on one-half of the review times.

Another method of incorporating uncertainty into usage rate estimation is accurate response. **Accurate response** is a new approach to forecasting for products with unpredictable demand patterns. This approach makes the supply chain fast and flexible, so that managers can postpone decisions about their most unpredictable items until they have some market signals (such as early-season sales results) that will help correctly match supply with demand. For example, goods with the most predictable demand should be made the longest in advance of demand in order to reserve greater manufacturing capacity for producing unpredictable items closer to the selling season.[84]

The Timberland Company, maker of shoes and sportswear, employs a sophisticated production planning system that is linked to its sales tracking system used to update demand forecasts. Those systems, along with efforts to reduce order cycle times in obtaining leather from tanners, have enabled the company to significantly reduce lost sales owing to stockouts, as well as mark down costs.

ECONOMIC ORDER QUANTITY DETERMINATION

The quantity to be ordered at a given time is referred to as **economic order quantity (EOQ)**. This order quantity has the lowest sum of inventory holding and order processing costs per unit. EOQ involves tradeoffs of inventory holding costs versus order processing costs. **Inventory holding costs** are associated with keeping inventory in stock. These costs are interest costs on inventory, insurance costs, markdowns due to obsolescence, pilferage, taxes on inventory, and warehousing costs. Inventory holding costs tend to increase exponentially as a firm seeks never to have a stockout. **Order processing costs** are the costs of implementing and verifying a transaction (such as an effort to prepare and validate a purchase order, merchandise inspection, and verification of products received versus order). As order size increases, inventory holding costs per unit increase while order placement costs per unit decrease. In contrast, as order size decreases, inventory holding costs per unit decrease while order placement costs per unit increases.

The formula for computing EOQ is:

$$EOQ = \sqrt{\frac{2DS}{IC}}$$

where

EOQ = economic order quantity in units
D = annual demand in units
S = order placement costs in dollars
I = holding costs on an annual basis (as a percentage of unit costs)
C = unit cost per item in dollars

See Table 6-8 for a computation of economic order quantity.

The estimated cost of carrying $1 of inventory varies, but carrying costs of $1 of inventory typically cost manufacturers 20 cents to 25 cents.[85] One study found that for the typical retailer, the cost of carrying inventory averages 17 percent of its net value.[86] Costs would be higher for retailers stocking goods with high technological obsolescence (such as computers) or with high seasonality or fashion components.

Order processing costs can be reduced through relationship marketing, which reduces negotiating time, and EDI, which simplifies the process of implementing a purchase order.

The EOQ formula is somewhat simplistic in that it assumes that there are no safety stock requirements, no quantity discounts, no discounts through using TL versus LTL rates, no costs to being out of stock, and no seasonality. For example, in a peak sales period, the traditional formula would use the same order quantity but would require a more rapid reorder period to reflect increased demand. The effect of these factors on EOQ can be studied by comparing total holding and ordering costs associated at the standard EOQ quantity versus the total costs of other quantities under any of these special conditions.

ABC INVENTORY ANALYSIS

ABC inventory analysis seeks to reduce total inventory needs by assigning different customer service-level requirements to goods based on such factors as sales and profits. The primary concern of ABC analysis is to divide goods into two or more groupings so that the best-selling items have the highest safety stocks. ABC analysis resembles the 80/20 rule, which states that 80 percent of sales comes from 20 percent of products. For example, 80 percent of dollar sales come from only 20 percent of items. These are called A items; B items represent 15 percent of dollar sales and 30 percent of items; and C items constitute 5 percent in dollar sales but 50 percent of all inventory items (see Table 6-9).

ABC analysis assigns different levels of priorities to A, B, and C items. For example, A items have the highest safety stocks, and B items have lower safety stocks. A firm may even develop inventory policies for C goods based on suggesting specific substitutes. A firm could use EDI to generate timely data for A

TABLE 6-8 COMPUTATION OF ECONOMIC ORDER QUANTITY

Table Example

Order Quantity	(a) Average Inventory on Hand[a]	(b) Annual Inventory Holding Costs[b]	(c) Annual Order Processing Costs[c]	(d) = (b)+(c) Total Annual Inventory Costs
50	25	50	3200	3250
100	50	100	1600	1700
200	100	200	800	1000
300	150	300	533.33	833.33
400	200	400	400	800 ← EOQ
500	250	500	320	820
600	300	600	266.67	866.67
700	350	700	228.57	928.57

Mathematical computation:

$$EOQ = \sqrt{\frac{2DS}{IC}}$$

$$= \sqrt{\frac{2(4000)(40)}{.20(10)}}$$

$$= \sqrt{160{,}000}$$

$$= 400$$

where

EOQ = economic order quantity in units
D = annual demand in units
S = order placement costs in dollars
I = holding costs on an annual basis (as a percentage of unit costs)
C = unit cost per item in dollars

[a]Average inventory on hand = 1/2 of order quantity. Assumes inventory at time of order receipt = zero (no safety stock).
[b]Annual inventory holding costs = Annual holding costs as a percentage of unit costs × Unit costs × Average inventory on hand. Annual holding costs are $2 per unit in this example.
[c]Annual order processing costs = Number of orders × Order placement costs. Number of orders = (Annual demand/Order quantity). Order placement costs are $40 per order in this example.

goods, whereas the inventory of C level goods is taken on a monthly basis. Another way to plan A, B, and C goods is to require a 98 percent service level for A goods, a 95 percent service level for B goods, and an 80 percent service level for C goods.

TABLE 6-9 ABC ANALYSIS

Product Grouping	Percent of Company's Total Sales	Percent of Company's Total Products	Customer Service Level
A	80	20	98
B	15	30	95
C	5	50	80

SUMMARY

1 *To discuss basic concepts in physical distribution.* Physical distribution describes a concept or approach to managing the finished goods inventory of the firm. Physical distribution activities relate to transportation, facility structures, inventory management, materials handling, and communication and information. Symptoms of a poor physical distribution system include unprofitable transactions, uneven warehouse utilization, frequent stockouts, slow inventory turnover, a high proportion of goods received by customers in defective condition, inability to determine order status information for customers, and inconsistent customer service levels. An important extension of physical distribution is logistics. Logistics focuses on the interrelationships among components of a physical distribution system. The physical distribution (total cost) concept examines the total costs of providing a given level of customer service. This concept recognizes that there are tradeoffs among warehousing, inventory, transportation, and ordering alternatives.

2 *To study transportation decision making.* Railroads are the major transportation mode for shipping heavy, bulky commodity items that have low value relative to their bulk or weight. Railroads have been aggressive in attracting customers through customized services, increased productivity (due to double-stacking and mergers), and the increased ability of railroads to track shipments. Motor carriers concentrate on lower weight shipments over shorter runs. The motor carrier industry is divided into two major segments: less-than-truckload and truckload shipments. Three important innovations in motor carriers have been the use of cages, curtainside trailers, and computer modeling in the routing and scheduling of motor carriers. Waterways are used primarily for transporting low-value, high-bulk freight. Like railroads and motor carriers, waterway shipments are often used in conjunction with containers that speed up handling and provide protection from weather and theft. Pipelines are characterized by continuous movement with no inventory accumulation. In contrast with other transportation modes, pipelines involve one-direction product flows and are designed to carry one type of product. Air freight is used primarily for high-value, perishable, and emergency shipments over long distances. Air freight can be specialized air freight carriers or freight carried by scheduled passenger lines.

Third-party providers of transportation services include an array of facilitators that operate between carriers and shippers. These providers deliver such services as brokerage, freight forwarding, freight consolidation, warehousing, auditing of goods received against purchase orders, information processing, and fleet operations.

In intermodal transportation, different transportation modes are used for the same shipment; in some cases, the transportation also involves multiple vendors. Intermodal transportation is generally used in conjunction with containers, rail flatcars, and trailers.

3 *To describe warehouse decision making.* There are two broad types of warehouses: private and public. Private warehouses are especially important when a product requires special handling or storage. Private warehouses provide a marketer with control over hours of operation and special handling needs. One type of private warehouse is a distribution center.

Alternatives to the use of a distribution center are direct store delivery of merchandise, cross docking, and the storefront system. A public warehouse is a for-hire facility that is available to any business requiring storage or handling of goods. Public warehouses are particularly useful for satisfying customers in a new geographic market, when seasonal demand requirements cannot be met through a firm's private warehouse, when demand is unstable on a year-to-year basis, or when a firm seeks to use selected products as collateral for a loan.

In a hub-and-spoke-distribution system, small shipments are consolidated in a regional warehouse and then shipped to customers. In many cases, this system reduces transportation costs since large trailers can be used for shipments to a firm's distribution center, while smaller trailers can be used for delivery to a customer. In addition to warehouses, hub-and-spoke distribution systems are popular in the airline and air-express business.

4 *To introduce basic concepts in inventory management.* There are four types of inventory: process stock, lot size (cycle stock), safety stock, and smoothing stocks. None of these types of inventory is used in production or inventory needed for sales. Inventory holdings need to be considerably larger than necessary due to the need for inventory in transit (process stock), bargaining power (lot stock), uncertainty in delivery and demand (safety stock), and seasonality (seasonal and smoothing stocks).

Inventory turnover is the relationship between a firm's sales and the inventory required by the firm to support that sales level. Inventory turnover can be computed in units and in dollars (both retail and cost). A fast inventory turnover is associated with fresh merchandise, the need for fewer markdowns, and lower costs of maintaining inventory. Too high an inventory turnover may mean that a firm cannot take full advantage of noncumulative quantity discounts, that a firm may have lost sales because of frequent stockouts, that a firm's customers cannot purchase all of their requirements from a single source, or that its customer service is poor.

To study inventory decision making. Inventories can be better managed through the use of just-in-time and quick response inventory systems, Efficient Consumer Response, reorder point determination, economic order quantity formulas, and ABC inventory analysis. Just-in-time inventory (JIT) management systems seek to minimize investment through frequent deliveries and low average sizes from a small group of suppliers. JIT inventory management systems are called a quick response inventory system by retailers. Efficient Consumer Response is a term used in the food distribution industry to describe efforts to maximize the effectiveness of the entire supply chain. The reorder point formula sets the inventory level at which a firm must place an order or risk a stockout. An economic order quantity has the lowest sum of inventory holding and order processing costs per unit. ABC inventory analysis seeks to reduce total inventory needs by assigning different customer service-level requirements to goods based on such factors as sales and profits.

KEY TERMS

physical distribution
logistics alliances
logistics
tailored logistics package
physical distribution (total cost) concept
customized services
less-than-truckload (LTL) shipments
truckload (TL) shipments
Motor Carrier Act of 1980
curtainside trailers
third-party transportation service providers
freight forwarders
intermodal transportation
seamless
warehouse
private warehouses
public warehouses
distribution center
direct store delivery
cross docking
storefront system
bonded warehouse
customs bonded warehouse
field warehouse
hub-and-spoke distribution system
process stocks
lot size stocks (cycle stocks)
safety stocks
smoothing and seasonal stocks
inventory turnover
just-in-time (JIT) inventory management systems
quick response inventory systems
pull system
push system
kanban system
Efficient Consumer Response (ECR)
reorder point
order cycle time
floor-ready merchandise
usage rate
review period
accurate response
economic order quantity (EOQ)
inventory holding costs
order processing costs
ABC inventory analysis

QUESTIONS FOR DISCUSSION

1. Differentiate between physical distribution and logistics.
2. What are the advantages and disadvantages of the use of a tailored logistics package?
3. Describe the tradeoffs in the physical distribution (total cost) concept between the use of air freight and motor carrier.
4. "A firm should seek to minimize physical distribution costs only at customer service levels that meet or exceed customer expectations of their target market." Explain this statement.
5. Describe the pros and cons of the use of motor carriers versus railroads as a transportation mode.
6. Describe the difficulties in developing and implementing a seamless transportation system in intermodal transportation.
7. Under what circumstances would you recommend that a firm utilize a public warehouse? a private warehouse?
8. Discuss the relative merits of the following forms of warehousing arrangement: distribution center, direct store delivery, and cross docking.
9. Under what situations would you recommend that a firm organize its warehouse locations to conform to a hub-and-spoke distribution system?
10. Differentiate among process stocks, lot size (cycle stocks), safety stock, and seasonal and smoothing stocks.
11. "A fast inventory turnover is preferable to a slow turnover." Explain this statement.
12. Examine the role of process stocks, lot size (cycle stocks), safety stock, and seasonal and smoothing stocks in a just-in-time inventory system.
13. Explain the role of the review period in the computation of a reorder point.
14. How can the economic order quantity formula reflect safety stock requirements, quantity discounts, and seasonality?

END NOTES

1. "Chain's One and Only Vendor Makes Quick Response Easy," *Chain Store Age Executive* (March 1991), pp. 18B–19B; *Designs Inc. Form 10K for the Fiscal Year Ended January 10, 1993*, pp. 10–11; Penny Gill and Glenn Rifkin, "Digital Blue Jeans Pour Data and Legs into Customized Fit," *New York Times* (November 8, 1994), pp. D1 ff.; and Richard S. Teitelbaum, "Designs Inc.," *Fortune* (February 8, 1993), p. 127.

2. See Donald J. Bowersox, "The Strategic Benefits of Logistics Alliances," *Harvard Business Review*, Vol. 68 (July–August 1990), pp. 36–38 ff.

3. Rita Koselka, "Distribution Revolution," *Forbes* (May 25, 1992), p. 58.

4. Stephanie Strom, "Logistics Steps onto Retail Battlefield," *New York Times* (November 3, 1993), p. D2.

5. Ronald Henkoff, "Delivering the Goods," *Fortune* (November 28, 1994), p. 64.

6. Arthur Markowitz, "State-of-the-Art Distribution a Must to Survive," *Discount Store News* (August 3, 1992), p. 12.

7. Koselka, "Distribution Revolution," p. 58.

8. Dean Foust, "Circuit City's Wires Are Sizzling," *Business Week* (April 27, 1992), p. 76.

9. Koselka, "Distribution Revolution," p. 58.

10. Ibid., p. 60.

11. Patricia Sellers, "Pepsi Keeps on Going after No. 1," *Fortune* (March 11, 1991), p. 70.

12. Adapted from Peter D. Bennett, ed., *Dictionary of Marketing Terms,* Second Edition (Chicago: American Marketing Association, 1995), p. 156.

13. Stephanie Strom, "Logistics Steps onto Retail Battlefield," *New York Times* (November 3, 1993), p. D1.

14. Zachary Schiller, "Ed Artzt's Elbow Grease Has P&G Shining," *Business Week* (October 10, 1994), p. 86.

15. See Joseph B. Fuller, "Tailored Logistics: The Next Advantage," *Harvard Business Review,* Vol. 71 (May–June 1993), pp. 87–98.

16. Stephanie Losee, "How Compaq Keeps the Magic Going," *Fortune* (February 21, 1994), p. 92.

17. Paul A. Dion, Loretta M. Hasey, Patrick C. Dorin, and Jean Lundin, "Consequences of Inventory Stockouts," *Industrial Marketing Management,* Vol. 20 (February 1991), pp. 23–27.

18. Henkoff, "Delivering the Goods," pp. 66, 74.

19. Phil Ramsdale and Steve Harvey, "Make Freight Cost Control Part of Planning," *Journal of Business Strategy,* Vol. 11 (March–April 1990), p. 42.

20. Agis Salpukas, "When Trucks and Trains Unite," *New York Times* (June 21, 1992), p. F5.

21. Joseph Weber, "Big Rail Is Finally Rounding the Bend," *Business Week* (November 11, 1991), p. 129.

22. Daniel Machalaba, "Shippers Prepare to Jump on Rail-Truck Combinations," *Wall Street Journal* (December 29, 1992), p. B4.

23. Adam Bryant, "$2.7 Billion Merger for Big Railroads," *New York Times* (July 1, 1994), pp. D1 ff.; Adam Bryant, "Bid Ended in Battle for Santa Fe," *New York Times* (February 1, 1995), pp. D1, D5; and Daniel Machalaba and Greg Steinmetz, "Santa Fe Leaves the Door Open to Rival Offer," *Wall Street Journal* (November 23, 1994), p. C19.

24. Salpukas, "When Trucks and Trains Unite," p. F5.

25. *American Trucking Associations. 1993 Top 200 Motor Carriers* (Alexandria, Virg.: American Trucking Associations, 1993), pp. 1,2.

26. Ibid.

27. *American Trucking Trends 1993–1994 Edition* (Alexandria, Virg.: American Trucking Associations, 1993), p. 10.

28. Author's calculations from *American Trucking Associations 1993 Top 200 Motor Carriers,* pp. 1–10.

29. Adam Bryant, "A Victim of the Deregulated Road," *New York Times* (June 15, 1993), p. 1.

30. Jonathan Marshall, "Cheap Truckin'," *National Review* (November 7, 1994), p. 54; and David P. Schulz, "Retailers See Gains from Trucking Deregulation," *Stores* (April 1995), pp. 53–54.

31. *The Ryder Resource* (Spring 1991), pp. 3, 5.

32. Agis Salpukas, "Use of Fabric Sides Are Opening Up Trucking," *New York Times* (November 4, 1992), p. D13.

33. *The Ryder Resource,* p. 7.

34. Yosef Sheffi, "Third Party Logistics: Present and Future Prospects," *Journal of Business Logistics,* Vol. 11 (Number 2, 1990), p. 27.

35. "Third-Party Handles Sears Overseas Freight," *Chain Store Age Executive* (November 1991), p. 130.

36. Robert Frank, "As UPS Tries to Deliver More to Its Customers, Labor Problems Grow," *Wall Street Journal* (May 23, 1994), pp. A1 ff.

37. Robert Frank, "Federal Express Grapples with Changes in U.S. Market," *Wall Street Journal* (July 5, 1994), p. B6.

38. Daniel Pearl, "Airborne Express Rushes to Keep Pace with Its Rivals," *Wall Street Journal* (July 13, 1992), p. B3.

39. Machalaba, "Shippers Prepare to Jump on Rail-Truck Combinations," p. B4.

40. Salpukas, "When Trucks and Trains Unite," p. F5.

41. Bennett, ed., *Dictionary of Marketing Terms,* p. 303.

42. Susan Scherreik, "New Warehouses: Big, Bright, Efficient," *New York Times* (May 30, 1993), p. R9.

43. See Donald R. Rosenfeld, "Storefront Distribution for Industrial Products," *Harvard Business Review,* Vol. 67 (July–August 1989), pp. 44–45 ff.

44. Gabriella Stern, "Cadillac Will Test Distribution Method to Cut Delivery Time and Dealer Stock," *Wall Street Journal* (August 16, 1994), p. A4; and Gabriella Stern, "GM Expands Its Experiment to Improve Cadillac's Distribution, Cut Inefficiency," *Wall Street Journal* (February 8, 1995), p. C29.

45. See Michael Garry, "More Joy of Dex," *Progressive Grocer* (January 1992), pp. 65–66.

46. David P. Schulz, "Flow Management: Study Measures Quality, Productivity in Order Cycle," *Stores* (June 1992), p. 41.

47. Michael Garry, "Cross Docking: The Road to ECR," *Progressive Grocer* (August 1993), p. 111.

48. Glenn Snyder, "ECR: A Survival Tool," *Progressive Grocer* (September 1994), p. 104.

49. See Rosenfeld, "Storefront Distribution for Industrial Products," pp. 44–45 ff.

50. Koselka, "Distribution Revolution," p. 58.

51. John Huey, "America's Most Successful Merchant," *Fortune* (September 21, 1991), p. 50.

52. Richard Halverson, "Logistical Supremacy Secures Merchandise—But Will It Translate Abroad?" *Discount Store News* (December 5, 1994), p. 108.

53. See Wilton Woods, "Goodbye Hub and Spoke," *Fortune* (December 13, 1993), pp. 160–161.

54. See James S. Hirsch, "Big Airlines Scale Back Hub-Airport System to Curb Rising Costs," *Wall Street Journal* (January 12, 1993), pp. A1, A8.

55. This section is adapted from John F. Magee, William C. Copacino, and Donald B. Rosenfield, *Modern Logistics Management: Integrating Marketing, Manufacturing, and Physical Distribution* (New York: John Wiley and Sons, 1985), pp. 86–95.

56. Thomas F. O'Boyle, "Firms' Newfound Skill in Managing Inventory May Soften Downtown," *Wall Street Journal* (November 11, 1990), p. A6.

57. Maria Shao and Laura Zinn, "Everybody's Falling into the Gap," *Business Week* (September 23, 1991), p. 36.

58. Amal Kumar Nal, "Some Manufacturers Drop Efforts to Adopt Japanese Techniques," *Wall Street Journal* (May 7, 1993), p. A6.

59. Larry C. Giunipero and Charles O'Neal, "Obstacles to JIT Procurement," *Industrial Marketing Management,* Vol. 17 (February 1988), p. 36.

60. Richard J. Schonberger and James P. Gilbert, "Just-in-Time Purchasing: A Challenge for U.S. Industry," *California Management Review,* Vol. 26 (Fall 1983), p. 56.

61. *Hillenbrand Industries Annual Report 1991;* Gary L. Frazier, Robert E. Spekman, and Charles O'Neal, "Just-in-Time Exchange Relationships," *Journal of Marketing,* Vol. 52 (October 1988), p. 53; Paul H. Zipkin, "Does Manufacturing Need a JIT Revolution?" *Harvard Business Review,* Vol. 69 (January–February 1991), p. 40; and Robert O. Knorr and John L. Neuman, "Quick Response

Technology: The Key to Outstanding Growth," *Journal of Business Strategy,* Vol. 13 (September 1, 1992), pp. 61–64.

62. Knorr and Neuman, "Quick Response Technology: The Key to Outstanding Growth," pp. 61–64.

63. Christina Duff, "Nation's Retailers Ask Vendors to Help Share Expenses," *Wall Street Journal* (August 8, 1993), p. B4.

64. See Uday Karmarkar, "Getting Control of Just-in-Time," *Harvard Business Review,* Vol. 67 (September–October 1989), p. 123.

65. Giunipero and O'Neal, "Obstacles to JIT Procurement," p. 36.

66. Roger Gomes and John T. Mentzer, "The Influence of Just-in-Time Systems on Distribution Channel Performance in the Presence of Environmental Uncertainty," *Transportation Journal,* Vol. 30 (Summer 1991), p. 36.

67. Paul Matthyssens and Christophe Van den Bulte, "Getting Closer and Nicer: Partnerships in the Supply Chain," *Long Range Planning,* Vol. 27 (February 1994), p. 74.

68. Malcolm Wheatley, "Management Method: Partners in Purchasing," *Management Today* (October 1991), p. 86.

69. Henkoff, "Delivering the Goods," p. 76.

70. Scott McCartney, "Compaq Borrows Wal-Mart's Idea to Boost Production," *Wall Street Journal* (June 17, 1994), p. B4.

71. "Measuring the Impact: Quick Response and the Bottom Line," *Chain Store Age Executive* (March 1991), p. 8B.

72. Paul A. Dion, Peter M. Banting, and Loretta M. Hasey, "The Impact of JIT on Industrial Marketers," *Industrial Marketing Management,* Vol. 19 (February 1990), pp. 41–46.

73. "Why Aren't More Retailers Implementing Quick Response—Or Are They?" *Chain Store Age Executive* (March 1991), p. 14B.

74. See Joseph Pereira, "Toy Industry Finds It's Harder and Harder to Pick the Winner," *Wall Street Journal* (December 21, 1993), pp. A1 ff.

75. Ramsdale and Harvey, "Make Freight Cost Control Part of Planning," p. 43.

76. Zipkin, "Does Manufacturing Need a JIT Revolution?" pp. 41, 44.

77. Ryan Mathews, "A New Look at ECR," *Progressive Grocer* (June 1994), pp. 29–32.

78. Homer Dunn, "Cross Docking Concepts Promise Huge Gains in Efficiency," *Progressive Grocer Executive Report: Part II* (January 1994), p. n–10.

79. Tim Triplett, "More U.S. Grocers Turning to ECR to Cut Waste," *Marketing News* (September 12, 1994), p. 5.

80. See Steve Weinstein, "Small Firms Need Help," *Progressive Grocer* (February 1994), pp. 40–46.

81. Leslie Baylor, "Wal-Mart Exec Notes Need for Efficiency," *Advertising Age* (March 8, 1993), p. 32.

82. Susan Reda, "Floor-Ready Merchandise," *Stores* (April 1994), pp. 41–44.

83. David P. Schulz, "Flow Management: Study Measures Quality, Productivity in Order Cycle," *Stores* (June 1992), p. 41.

84. See Marshall L. Fisher, Janice H. Hammond, Walter R. Obermeyer, and Ananth Raman, "Making Supply Meet Demand in an Uncertain World," *Harvard Business Review,* Vol. 72 (May–June 1994), pp. 83–93.

85. O'Boyle, "Firms' Newfound Skill in Managing Inventory May Soften Downtown," p. A6.

86. "Inventory Management: New Rules, New Game Plan," *Chain Store Age Executive* (March 1991), p. 12B.

CASE 1

OTR EXPRESS: THE PHYSICAL DISTRIBUTION STRATEGY OF A MOTOR CARRIER

The motor carrier business is a tough one. According to one source, as many as 10 percent of the trucking companies in the United States go bankrupt each year. OTR Express (OTR) is a small trucking firm based in Olathe, Kansas. The firm started with one truck in the early 1980s; it now has 230 trucks, estimated sales of over $22 million, and a net profit margin of 3.2 percent. OTR's high sales and profitability are not due to old equipment, poor maintenance, or underpaid employees. In fact, OTR has some of the most modern equipment in the industry. In addition, the motor carrier pays its drivers (who average 14 years' experience) 20 percent above the industry norm.

The company's founder, Bill Ward, attributes his success to his lack of knowledge of the trucking business and his computer expertise. Bill, a former real estate investor, entered the trucking business with no preconceptions of how the business should operate. Some of OTR's current strategies are the opposite of its competitors. OTR's business utilizes Bill's extensive computer expertise. According to a staff writer of a trucking management trade publication, "We're not aware of any other single company that does business this way, because no one else has gone into the business the way it has."

The conventional wisdom in the trucking business is based largely on the core-carrier concept. With the core-carrier concept, a trucking company develops close ties with comparatively few customers. These core customers receive higher-than-average service rates in return for offering the motor carrier steady volume and higher than average rates. There are, however, several potential disadvantages to the core-carrier concept. First, a motor carrier operator needs additional equipment to fulfill a core customer's emergency or peak-season shipping requirements. Second, there are fewer opportunities to backhaul freight because of the need to accommodate a shipper's last-minute requests. Finally, the core-customer concept makes the trucker very dependent on a few key customers. Bill decided to pursue the spot or "intermittent" market; this market is comprised of small shippers that move freight on a less-than-regular basis. With this strategy, OTR has 600 customers; its largest customer accounts for less than 4 percent of its total revenues.

OTR makes extensive use of computers to help it move its trucks. Its computers position OTR's motor carrier fleet, determine the amount of fuel each truck consumes, and also compare the cost of purchasing a spare tire in different locations. OTR's computer system even manages OTR's routes and destinations. Its software considers what percentage of OTR's fleet is already in a specific area and what percentage should arrive in the area within the next two days. OTR's strategy is to position its trucks on the basis of computer-generated data that detail the most profitable opportunities for freight. For example, most truckers look only to the initial, and not the subsequent, moves of a truck. However, the profitability of moving freight from Kansas City to Los Angeles is also based on finding a good load of freight in Los Angeles.

OTR's computer system scans all of the firm's Los Angeles customers according to revenue potential. It then ranks at the top of its list the Los Angeles-based customer that in the past month shipped the most freight the greatest distance via OTR. Other customers would then be ranked in descending order based on their potential. In the near future, OTR will evaluate all of its customers based on revenues generated during the past 15 days. When an OTR truck is heading into a geographic region to drop off a load, OTR's dispatchers begin to call those customers at the top of its priority list. If the first list does not find a customer with a profitable run, the dispatcher then moves to an adjacent area. Finally, the dispatcher will resort to using

Table 1 Selected Financial and Operating Data OTR Express Inc.

	OTR Express	Trucking Industry Average
Net profit margin	3%	2–5%
Trucker's annual compensation	Up to $50,000	Up to $30,000
Trailer/tractor ratio[a]	1.2:1	2.5:1
Employees/tractor ratio	1:6	1:3
Proportion of total miles traveled by empty trucks	6.05%	10%
Average haul	1451 miles	700 miles
Accidents per million miles driven	Less than 1	3

[a] A ratio of 1:1 is optimal.
Source: Edward O. Welles, "Riding the High-Tech Highway," *Inc.* (March 1993), pp. 72–74 ff.

freight brokers to fill up a tractor. Since freight brokers charge a commission, they are used only if OTR cannot find a profitable load on its own.

Table 1 provides some financial and operating data on OTR. The motor carrier business is capital intensive; a tractor and trailer costs about $85,000. OTR's efficiency is due to several factors. First, it operates at close to the optimal ratio of trailers per tractor since it does not need extra trailers for emergency or peak seasonal use by core customers. Second, OTR's proportion of total miles traveled by empty trucks means that it has a 4-cents-per-mile edge over competitors (since the average freight rate is $1 per mile). And third, OTR's longer than average hauls gives it higher-than-average profits since longer hauls require less loadings, less unloadings, and less paperwork.

OTR's personnel strategy is also unusual. Its 230 drivers average 43 years of age and 14 years' experience. OTR will not hire any driver who has had an accident within the past two years. Each driver is viewed as a profit center. Drivers can increase their compensation based on purchasing fuel in low-tax states, washing trucks themselves, staying off high-toll roads, and being accident-free. Smart drivers can also plan to purchase fuel at one of five unmanned company-owned depots, where they can purchase fuel at wholesale prices (which can be as much as 15 cents cheaper per gallon than retail prices). Drivers can also benefit by getting repairs done at wholesale cost at designated service centers and by having work covered by warranty performed at authorized dealers. The expense of accidents is also charged to each driver. Currently, the bonus paid to each driver averages about $900 per quarter across the entire fleet.

QUESTIONS

1. Interpret Table 1.
2. Would you use OTR Express as a motor carrier on the basis of the information contained in this case? Explain your answer.
3. What additional computer-based opportunities are present for OTR?
4. How can OTR develop and maintain additional competitive advantages? Refer to the examples in this chapter.

Source: Edward O. Welles, "Riding the High-Tech Highway," *Inc.* (March 1993), pp. 72–74 ff.

CASE 2

COLEMAN COMPANY: IMPLEMENTING A JUST-IN-TIME INVENTORY SYSTEM

Coleman Company is a well-known manufacturer of camping stoves and lanterns. Its products (such as lanterns, portable stoves, jugs, and ice coolers) have a long-time reputation as being reasonably priced and well-built camping products. The Coleman Company has a rich history. The firm was founded in 1900 by W. C. Coleman, a former schoolteacher. In 1940 Sheldon Coleman, son of W. C. Coleman, took over as chief executive officer. During World War II, the company's pocket stove was voted by servicemen as one of the two most useful pieces of noncombat equipment. (The other product was the Jeep.) Sheldon's son, Sheldon, Jr., took over as chief executive officer in 1988. Coleman was purchased in 1989 by MacAndrews & Forbes, a holding company that also owns Revlon. Although Coleman controls about 90 percent of the market for coolers and jugs, it faces strong competition from firms such as Rubbermaid and Igloo in the ice cooler and jug markets.

At the time of its purchase by MacAndrews & Forbes, the new owners hired a consulting firm, Thomas Group, to analyze the firm's inventory management strategy. The consulting firm recommended that Coleman adopt a just-in-time inventory management system because of the firm's high inventory holding costs. So much of Coleman's inventory was work-in-process that Coleman had to build ceiling racks just to store parts for its stoves, lanterns, and coolers. The ceiling racks spanned the entire length of the factory. The previous owners used these inventories as a cushion for breakdowns in equipment. Since it often took days to repair broken equipment, Coleman used these inventories. This inventory also served as safety stock in the event that suppliers furnished defective parts. To Thomas Group, however, this inventory hid manufacturing problems. The consultants viewed the inventory as "a sea: As you lower the level of the sea, you can see dangerous rocks, or manufacturing problems, that had been covered up for years."

Coleman was able to reduce the time period from obtaining an order to shipping it. Although the shipping order cycle time used to be eight days, Coleman can now ship an order within two days of its receipt. And while Coleman used to require two months of inventory to provide its customers with adequate supplies of its products, it now requires only a week's worth of sales in inventory. At least a day of this interval was reduced by electronic data interchange involving key customers such as Wal-Mart and Kmart. Coleman's total reduction in order cycle time and in inventory requirements did not occur at once. Its order cycle time, for example, dropped from eight days to four days, from four days to two, and so on. At each stage, problems were studied and corrected. For example, the company realized that it could improve response time to factory problems by relocating its tool and tie shop to the factory; it had formerly been 12 miles away.

Coleman's reductions in order cycle time and inventory are especially noteworthy in that the firm now offers 140 models of ice coolers in 12 color combinations. In comparison, in 1990, it sold 20 different models in just three color combinations. During the same time period, Coleman has also reduced its inventory costs by $10 million. All of its huge overhead storage bins are now empty. While Coleman is a privately owned firm and does not release data on profitability, one source estimates that its operating profit in a recent year was $32 million on sales of $435 million.

QUESTIONS

1. Describe the advantages of Coleman's just-in-time inventory system.
2. Describe the disadvantages of Coleman's just-in-time inventory system.
3. What is the impact of Coleman's use of JIT on its suppliers?
4. What other methods could Coleman use to increase its inventory turnover? Explain your answer.

Source: Brian Dumaine, "Earning More by Moving Faster," *Fortune* (October 7, 1991), pp. 89–90 ff.

CHAPTER 7

MARKET RESEARCH AND INFORMATION SYSTEMS IN CHANNELS

CHAPTER OBJECTIVES

1. To study introductory topics in channel management, including the definition of market research, and the differences between market research in channels management and market research in other areas of marketing.

2. To describe the market research process in channels management.

3. To illustrate introductory topics in marketing information systems, including the differences between market research and marketing information systems, the types of channel information systems, and the structure of a channel information system.

4. To discuss special topics in channel information systems: the use of scanning-based data, electronic data interchange, database marketing, and channel information system reports.

Frito-Lay Inc., the snack-food division of PepsiCo, produces more than 100 different snack-food products. Its products are distributed to over 400,000 retail stores. As part of its overall marketing information system, Frito-Lay Inc. provides hand-held computers to each of its 10,000 route sales representatives. Frito-Lay then combines information from the field representatives with scanner data purchased from Information Resources Inc. (IRI), a market research provider, to study its performance in each market area.

According to Frito-Lay's vice president of management information services, "We pick up every sale of every bag made to every customer every day." This information is then relayed to Frito-Lay's manufacturing and distribution centers on a daily basis. The data are summarized and analyzed by territory at Frito-Lay's headquarters; the completed analysis is sent back to Frito-Lay's regional and divisional levels within 24 hours of receipt.

Frito-Lay's marketing information system enables it to keep track of prices, special promotions, stale and returned products, shelf space allocations, share of displays, market share, and actual retail prices. Important data are also tracked for major competitors in each market. Frito-Lay uses this information to monitor, evaluate, and implement changes in its marketing strategy and tactics.

For example, based on analyzing the inventory on hand in stores, Frito-Lay can reduce its current production quantities. This enables the company to reduce the number of its customer returns due to stale merchandise. This information system also allows Frito-Lay to evaluate the impact of a competitor's special promotion on such factors as Frito-Lay's shelf space allocation and on Frito-Lay's short- and long-term sales.

The information system helps the firm uncover and evaluate micromarketing opportunities. Recently, the marketing information system enabled Frito-Lay's president to attribute the cause of a recent downturn in sales performance in a local market to a chain of stores that sold a new white-corn chip. As a result of this timely data, Frito-Lay was able to quickly develop and commercialize a white-corn version of its Tostitos corn chip. Other managers have used the information system to determine what package sizes sell best in each market and how specific market areas respond to promotions.

Frito-Lay spent about $2500 to equip each of its route salespeople with the hand-held computer (called "bricks" because of their size) and a printer for their delivery van. The software for the central system and for the system that returns the information to manufacturing and distribution centers took 18 months to develop. Frito-Lay estimates that the system "paid for itself well within a year." The firm calculated that its marketing information system saved it more than $40 million in its first year as a result of reduced paperwork, lower losses due to stale products, and consolidation of routes. Since salespeople have less paperwork, they are also able to devote more time to selling and to managing their territories.

Frito-Lay is now studying computer systems that would hook up directly into a customer's computer. Such a system would handle accounts payable and receivables, and allow a store manager to determine which Frito-Lay products are the most profitable in his or her stores.[1]

In this chapter, we explore the topics of market research and marketing information systems from a channels perspective. We define market research and examine the differences between marketing research in channels management and marketing research in other areas of marketing. We also describe the marketing research process in channels management. Introductory topics in marketing information systems are discussed. In addition, we look at special topics in channel information systems, such as scanning-based data and the types of channel information system reports that Frito-Lay uses so effectively.

INTRODUCTION TO MARKETING RESEARCH IN CHANNELS MANAGEMENT

In this section, we define marketing research and study the major differences between marketing research in channels and in other areas of marketing. This material is an important foundation for the other topics covered in this chapter.

DEFINITION OF MARKETING RESEARCH

Marketing research consists of the systematic gathering, recording, and analyzing of relevant data to reduce uncertainty in marketing decision making. This definition can be further clarified by examining each of its major components. The term *systematic* refers to being objective and to using the scientific method to identify and reduce potential sources of bias in the study. For example, a channel researcher can reduce potential bias by studying the characteristics of both wholesaler respondents and nonrespondents in a study of channel members' satisfaction. Nonrespondents may have different characteristics than respondents and may also have different levels of channel member satisfaction. Systematic research seeks to uncover the actual relationships; it does not "start with a conclusion and seek to prove it." Common alternatives to the use of a systematic research process are the use of a convenient sample that may not be representative, relying on intuition to determine the nature of a problem, or foregoing research and then copying the strategy of a competitor.

The "gathering, recording, and analyzing of relevant data" part of the marketing research definition refers to using data that currently exist but that were gathered for some other purpose (secondary data) or generating data specifically for the problem/opportunity at hand (primary data). It is important that the researcher focus the data gathering, recording, and analyzing process on relevant data. For example, a channel member needs to distinguish between adding total sales on a yearly basis (due to a special price promotion) and the shifting of sales throughout the year (due to customers' stocking up on the product at the special sales prices). The relevant data for this analysis are annual, not seasonal, sales. Similarly, the relevant data for evaluating a retailer's productivity for a retailer with a high amount of store openings are sales per square foot

TABLE 7-1   KEY COMPONENTS IN THE DEFINITION OF MARKETING RESEARCH

Definition Component	Description/Implication
Systematic	Description: Objectivity of investigator, use of scientific method, efforts to identify and reduce potential sources of bias in a market research study.
	Implication: Concern over investigator objectivity, need to reduce potential biases that can affect outcome: evaluate characteristics of respondents and nonrespondents to a survey; pretest all questionnaires on small sample (to avoid loaded questions, ambiguity, and alterative responses not anticipated by researchers); carefully select, train, and supervise interviewers; analyze sampling methodology.
Gathering, recording, and analyzing	Description: Information search and analysis for data from a variety of sources (secondary and primary).
	Implication: Information may require participation and cooperation of other channel members. The investigator should first seek out secondary sources (data already gathered for other purposes) prior to gathering, recording, and analyzing primary data specifically collected for this study.
Relevant data	Description: The investigator must define the problem carefully so that only relevant data are gathered, recorded, and analyzed.
	Implication: Not all data are relevant. Need to properly define problem to clarify and better focus data gathering, recording, and analysis. Without proper problem definition, the incorrect data may be gathered, recorded, and analyzed, and the incorrect conclusion may be drawn.
To reduce uncertainty in marketing decision making	Description: The ultimate goal of marketing research is to reduce the risk in decision making by "buying information" through market research.
	Implication: A channel member needs to develop tradeoffs between the cost of additional information and its value in reducing uncertainty.

for stores open at least one year, not total sales, or sales growth. Focusing on the wrong data may result in a channel's member misinterpreting its strategies.

The ultimate goal of research is to reduce uncertainty in marketing decision making. Uncertainty exists owing to lack of understanding of the dynamics of the marketing environment and to the uncontrollable nature of the channel environment. Table 7-1 describes the components of market research in channels management.

DIFFERENCES BETWEEN MARKETING RESEARCH IN CHANNELS MANAGEMENT AND MARKET RESEARCH IN OTHER AREAS OF MARKETING

The marketing research process in channels differs from the research process in other areas of marketing. In channels research, information is often interorganizational, a cooperative relationship often exists, data gathering is based on long-term commitments, and much data gathering is based on a census (studying all members of a population).

Researchers have differentiated among three different types of information on the basis of the direction of its source: downstream information, upstream information, and internal information. **Downstream information** describes an information flow between a firm and its customers (intermediaries and final consumers). In **upstream information**, the flow of information is between the firm and its manufacturers/suppliers. The information flow in **internal information** is within the firm itself.[2] In both downstream and upstream information, the flow of information is interorganizational. Channel research typically involves interorganizational (both downstream and upstream) and internal information.

A second major difference between channel and traditional market research is that much channel research is based on a cooperative relationship and trust among channel members. Channel members often view data sharing as a strategy in which each member gains a strategic advantage. For example, data provided by retailers on sales of a manufacturer's/supplier's products help the retailer get faster replenishment of its inventory, and aid the manufacturer in better planning its production levels.

Third, the market research data collection process among channel members often represents a significant long-term commitment by each channel member.[3] For example, the establishment of a computer linkage between channel members for data sharing (such as electronic data interchange) represents a significant investment by each channel member in computer software, computer hardware, communications interfaces, and training. The topic of electronic data interchange is covered later in this chapter.

Lastly, although much of traditional market research is based on sampling, in many cases, channels research can be conducted based on a **census**, whereby the entire population is questioned or observed. For example, a manufacturer selling to 30 wholesalers in a region can gather data from all of the wholesalers rather than a sample. Upstream research and downstream research that does not involve final consumers is especially likely to involve a census. In this respect, marketing research in channels management resembles market research in business-to-business marketing.

THE MARKETING RESEARCH PROCESS IN CHANNELS MANAGEMENT

The marketing research process in channels management consists of six interrelated steps: problem definition (defining the problem to be researched), examination of secondary data, generation of primary data, analysis of data, recommendations for action, and implementation of findings (see Figure 7-1). Note that the box around the generation of primary data has broken lines. The broken lines signify that primary data generation is not always necessary in marketing research. An examination and analysis of secondary data may be suffi-

FIGURE 7-1 The marketing research process in channels.

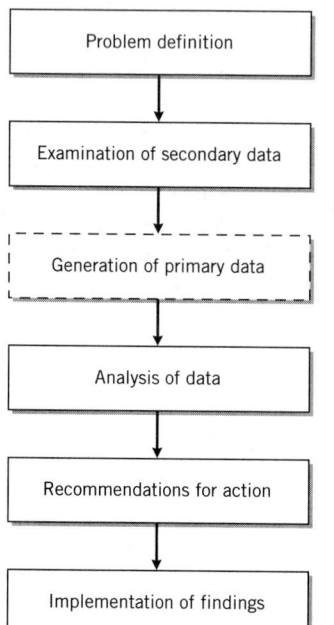

cient to resolve a problem or explain an opportunity if the secondary data are available, relevant, accurate, and timely. This topic is explored further in the analysis of secondary data section of this chapter.

PROBLEM DEFINITION

Problem definition seeks to develop a clear statement of the topic to be studied. In the problem definition stage, the researcher seeks to better understand the research problem through exploratory research. In **exploratory research**, the investigator uses unstructured or semistructured research techniques (such as discussions with consultants, analysis of published data of a similar problem in a different industry, or study of a focus group) to develop a more precise statement of the research problem. Exploratory research is the first phase of the problem definition stage of the marketing research process.

After the dynamics of the market research problem are better understood, more structured conclusive research techniques can be used. **Conclusive research** leads to the development of a methodology to understand the problem at hand. It is more structured than exploratory research. Conclusive research techniques include secondary data analysis, surveys, observation, experimentation, and simulation.

It is important to consider that the quality of conclusive research is based on the exploratory research that preceded it. If exploratory research is done poorly, then the data collection and analysis in conclusive research may focus on the wrong problem/opportunity and may not shed light on the marketing problem.

TABLE 7-2 EXAMPLES OF EXPLORATORY AND CONCLUSIVE RESEARCH IN CHANNELS MANAGEMENT

Vague Research Topic	Exploratory Research	Precise Research Topic	Conclusive Research
Study the willingness of major wholesalers to conduct promotional activity.	Discussions with representative sample of wholesalers to determine acceptability of various promotional programs offered by manufacturer.	What percent of major wholesalers will use a cooperative advertising program with a specific reimbursement program?	Survey all major wholesalers. Determine planned usage of cooperative advertising through personal interviews.
Determine the channel coverage of major competitors.	Discussions with wholesalers and retailers to determine most effective regional competitors within specific product lines and their channels of distribution.	Determine coverage as a percent of all commodity volume (ACV) in grocery stores for three major competitors in each of its three major product lines.	Determine channel coverage as a percent of ACV using IRI InfoScan scanner data.
Evaluate the channel performance of major retailers.	Discussions with consultant to determine major elements of channel performance.	Measure channel performance on the basis of 10 specific criteria.	Determine channel performance on the basis of secondary data (such as annual reports and IRI InfoScan scanner data) and on the basis of primary data (such as surveys and observation).

Table 7-2 presents examples of exploratory and conclusive research in channel management and identifies three vague research topics: to study the willingness of wholesalers to conduct promotional activity; to determine the channel coverage of major competitors; and to evaluate the channel performance of major retailers. This table shows how these vague research problems can be clarified through exploratory and then conclusive research. Note how each successive step more closely defines the nature of the research topic and better structures the data gathering, analysis, and interpretation process.

EXAMINATION OF SECONDARY DATA

Secondary data consist of "statistics not gathered for the immediate study at hand but for some other purpose."[4] Secondary data may be internal (gathered by the company) or external (gathered by a commercial research firm, a governmental entity, a periodical, or other source).

In comparison to generating data specifically for the purpose of the study at hand (primary data), secondary data have the following advantages:

- Secondary data often include data that would normally not be available to a firm (such as governmental data or data conducted by a major trade association).
- Secondary data are generally low cost, for the channel member has no data costs in gathering or interpreting data. Even when secondary data costs may involve a sizable fee (as with data collected and sold by commercial research houses), the data costs are still much less than what it would cost a single channel member to gather, record, and analyze comparable data exclusively for its own use. Commercial research houses have economies of scale; they may sell the same data to multiple channel members.
- Unlike primary data, secondary data are often quickly available.
- Secondary data are especially suitable for background information for use in problem definition.

In comparison to primary data, the disadvantages of secondary data are as follows.

- Secondary data may not be timely. For example, although the *Census of Wholesale Trade* is a very important source of information on sales by manufacturer wholesalers, merchant wholesalers, and agents and brokers, this source is only available every five years (for years ending in 2 and 7, as in 1987 and 1992). There is also generally a two-year lag between the collection and publication of data. Thus, as of 1995, the most current *Census of Wholesale Trade* data are from 1992.
- The secondary source may use a classification system that is not directly usable to the channel member investigating a problem. For example, the data collected by the secondary source may report sales of housewares by all discounters (without separating out sales by buying clubs), may evaluate the shopping behaviors of retired persons (without giving separate data among different ages of retired persons), or may study inventory management effectiveness of wholesalers on the basis of low, medium, and high inventory turnover levels without providing data on the basis of wholesaler size and geographic region.
- The secondary source may not directly relate to the problem/opportunity at hand. A manufacturer seeking to study channel member satisfaction of wholesalers wishes to obtain data relating to wholesaler attitudes toward manufacturers. Instead, the manufacturer is only able to secure studies of wholesalers that have voluntarily terminated their relationships with manufacturers, of wholesaler-manufacturer litigation, and of the use of wholesaler advisory boards by manufacturers.
- The accuracy of data collection and analysis needs to be assessed. The user of secondary sources must assess the methodology used by the investigator. The user of secondary sources should be suspicious of data where the research design for data collection is not available or when the sponsor of the secondary data research has a financial stake in its findings (such as research used in litigation).

Sources of Internal Secondary Data in Channels Management

Internal secondary data consist of market research data that have already been gathered by the firm. These data were originally generated for another purpose. Sources of internal secondary channel data include invoices, accounting data, inventory records, shipping records, customer correspondence, and company-based research reports (conducted for other purposes or done in a prior time period). Internal secondary data sources, the information supplied, and the channel application of each source are detailed in Table 7-3.

TABLE 7-3 SOURCES OF INTERNAL SECONDARY DATA IN CHANNELS

Source	Information	Channel Application
Invoices	Average order size to each account	Quantity discount schedules, evaluation of minimum order size quantities
	Sales price as a percentage of list price by type of account	Profitability analysis, substantiate legality of pricing structure
	Yearly sales to each distribution channel	Sales analysis
	Sales price as a percentage of list price to each distribution channel	Profitability analysis, substantiate legality of pricing structure
	Seasonality by distribution channel	Production and inventory planning
	Time differential from order to delivery	Customer service analysis
	Percentage of incomplete deliveries due to out-of-stock inventory	Inventory management
	Products that have been out-of-stock during past week	Inventory management, vendor analysis
	Fast-selling products	Inventory management
Accounting data		
Budgets	Planned costs per distribution channel	Channel planning and evaluation
	Planned total distribution costs	Channel planning and evaluation
Distribution cost data	Actual versus planned costs per distribution channel	Channel planning and evaluation

TABLE 7-3 (CONTINUED)

Source	Information	Channel Application
	Warehousing cost data	Physical distribution management
	Transportation cost data	Physical distribution management
Profit-and-loss statements	Profit by distribution channel	Profit planning
Balance sheets	Investment in distribution channels	Channel planning and evaluation
Inventory records	Out-of-stock reports by product	Inventory management
	Slow-moving stock reports	Inventory management
	Fast-moving stock reports	Inventory management
	Backorder reports	Inventory management, vendor analysis
Shipping records	Planned versus actual delivery times	Customer service and physical distribution management
	Costs by shipping source	Physical distribution management
	Number of emergency shipments	Inventory and distribution management
	Backhaul loads (such as shipments from a wholesaler to a manufacturer)	Physical distribution management
Customer correspondence	Customer inquiries	Technical service assessment, inventory management
	Customer complaints	Customer service management
	Customer letters commending customer service	Customer service management, employee reward programs
Company-based research reports conducted for other purposes or done in a prior time period	Depends on subject of report	Depends on time of report, methodology, and applicability in current environment

Invoices have a broader range of applications than any other internal secondary data source. By analyzing the data in invoices, a channel member can determine the average order size by account, sales price as a percentage of list price by type of account, yearly sales through each distribution channel, sales price as a percentage of list price to each distribution channel, seasonality by distribution channel, the time span from a customer's placing an order to delivery, percentage of incomplete deliveries because of out-of-stock inventory, products that have been out-of-stock, and fast-selling products. This information is useful for developing and evaluating quantity discount schedules, determining minimum order size quantities, making profitability analyses, substantiating the legality of the channel member's pricing structure, production planning, inventory planning, preparing customer service analyses, and developing vendor analysis.

Accounting data include budgets, distribution cost data, profit-and-loss statements, and balance sheet data. Accounting data include planned costs per distribution data, planned overall distribution costs, actual versus planned distribution costs per distribution channel, warehousing cost data, transportation cost data, profit by distribution channel, and investment in distribution channels. Accounting data can be used for channel planning and evaluation, physical distribution management, and profit planning.

Inventory records include out-of-stock reports, slow-moving stock reports, fast-moving stock reports, and backorder reports. These reports can be used for inventory management and vendor analysis functions. Shipping records include planned versus actual delivery times, costs by shipping source, number of emergency shipments, and backhaul load reports. These shipping records can be used to analyze customer service, physical distribution management, and inventory management. Customer correspondence includes customer inquiries, customer complaints, and customer letters commending customer service. These reports can be used for technical service assessment, inventory management, customer service management, and the development of employee reward programs.

Company-based research reports conducted for other purposes or done in a prior time period are also an important source of internal secondary data. As with external secondary data, the channel member needs to assess the relevancy of these data to the current problem/opportunity in terms of timeliness, classification system used, methodology, and purpose of the prior study.

Sources of External Secondary Data in Channel Management

External secondary data include data generated by sources other than the channel member directly involved in conducting a market research study. External secondary data should be studied if internal secondary data are too old, not directly applicable (such as the need to study competitors), or if the results of several types of internal secondary data are conflicting. External secondary data sources include other channel members, government entities, periodicals, trade associations, and commercial research firms.[5]

TABLE 7-4 SOURCES OF EXTERNAL SECONDARY DATA IN CHANNELS: INFORMATION PROVIDED BY MANUFACTURERS/SUPPLIERS

Source	Information	Channel Application
Backorder reports	Out-of-stock inventory, inventory lead times	Inventory management
Facility inspection reports	Cleanliness, quality of sales presentation, accuracy of inventory records	Evaluation of operations
Survey data on customer satisfaction provided by manufacturer/supplier	Customer satisfaction	Evaluation of customer service
Product recall notices	Notification to customers of product recall due to safety defects	Evaluate effectiveness of product recall notification among consumers
Cooperative advertising utilization reports	Advertising budgeting	Advertising management

The type of information provided by manufacturers/suppliers depends on the nature of the relationship. A high degree of information flow between manufacturers/suppliers and their customers generally occurs in franchising and in exclusive distribution arrangements. In some cases, this information is electronically transferred between channel members. Table 7-4 lists some of the sources of information provided by manufacturers/suppliers. These include backorder reports, facility inspection reports, customer satisfaction reports, product recall notices, and cooperative advertising utilization reports. These reports are useful in inventory management, evaluation of operations, customer service management, product recall programs, and advertising management. Similarly, retailers and wholesalers provide downstream information to manufacturers/suppliers on such important areas as sales, inventory levels, and consumer response to special promotions.

External secondary data are collected by governmental units, publications, trade associations, and commercial research firms. Governmental units (federal, state, and local) are important sources of channel data. Especially important are the *Census of Population, Census of Wholesale Trade,* and *Census of Retail Trade.* Government data are comprehensive, contain information that could not be obtained through nongovernment sources, typically is either free or available for a low fee, and is not copyrighted. A disadvantage of much government data is its lack of currency. The *Census of Population,* for example, is taken every 10 years, and the *Census of Wholesale Trade,* the *Census of Service Industries,* and the *Census of Retail Trade,* as noted earlier, are conducted every 5 years (with years ending in 2 and 7, as in 1992 and 1997). In many cases, the full report is not available until two to three years after the cover date.

Many publications and trade associations publish annual reports of interest to channel members. A listing and description of these reports as well as reports provided by governmental units are presented in Table 7-5. A channels researcher should be familiar with the standard reference sources described in Table 7-5, the channels-related periodicals in Table 7-6, and the general reference periodicals, which often contain articles on important channels topics in Table 7-7. Many of the periodicals in Tables 7-6 and 7-7 are referenced in the *Business Periodicals Index, Predicasts F&S Index,* and *Reader's Guide to Periodical Literature.* The *New York Times Index* and the *Wall Street Index* also reference important articles on channels topics. All of these indexes are typically bound on an annual basis and updated on a monthly or quarterly basis. In addition to these printed reference guides, a number of computerized databases are available on-line.

TABLE 7-5 SELECTED EXTERNAL SECONDARY SOURCES OF CHANNEL-RELATED DATA PROVIDED BY BOTH GOVERNMENT AND NONGOVERNMENT UNITS

Source	Description
Annual Report of the Grocery Industry published by *Progressive Grocer*	Annual. Includes important data on grocery sales by types of store, industry outlook surveys, competition, buyer/seller relations, operations, costs and prices, consumers, and market saturation by geographic area.
Annual Survey of Promotional Practices published by Donnelly Marketing Services	Annual. Covers types of promotions used and redemption rates for coupons.
Business Failure Record by Dun & Bradstreet	Annual. Contains data on retail and wholesale failures by line of business, age of failed business, and causes of business failure.
Discount Industry Annual Report by *Discount Store News*	Annual. Includes important sales and financial data on discount retailing.
Editor and Publisher Market Guide	Annual. Includes important demographic, retail shopping center, and newspaper data for major cities in the United States and Canada.
Franchising in the Economy published by the International Franchise Association Educational Foundation	Biannual. Provides data on franchising sales and outlets, and investment and startup costs by goods and services category.
Industry Norms and Key Business Ratios by Dun & Bradstreet	Annual. Provides selected financial ratios by line of business for manufacturers, wholesalers, and retailers.
Journal of Marketing	Quarterly. Contained "Legal Developments in Marketing" section through 1993 outlining important legal cases involving channels. Currently has "Marketing Literature Review" section that abstracts articles relating to channels management and other areas of marketing.
Journal of the Academy of Marketing Science	Quarterly. Contains a "Marketing and the Law" section that outlines important legal developments.

Table 7-5 (Continued)

Million Dollar Directory, Dun and Bradstreet	Annual. Lists businesses that meet at least one of these criteria: 250 or more employees, $25 million in annual sales, and a tangible net worth in excess of $500,000. Lists addresses, sales volume, SIC codes, company officers, and year started.
National Retail Federation's Financial and Operating Results (FOR)	Annual. Provides financial data for department and specialty stores. Data include markdowns, stock shortages, stock turnover, pretax earnings, and net operating expenses.
National Retail Federation's Merchandising and Operating Results (MOR)	Annual. Provides selected performance data for department stores organized by product category. Data include net sales as percentage of total store, expenses as percentage of department sales, gross margin per dollar of inventory investment, and stock turnover.
1992 *Census of Retail Trade.*	Every five years ending with 2 and 7. Contains statistics for about 100 different kinds of retail establishments, by geographic area and by subject. Data classified by state, SMSA, county, and city.
1992 *Census of Service Industries*	Every five years ending with 2 and 7. Contains number of establishments, receipts, and payroll by geographic area and kind of business. Data are classified by state, SMSA, county, and city.
1992 *Census of Wholesale Trade*	Every five years ending with 2 and 7. Contains number of establishments, sales, payroll, employment, operating expenses, and legal form of organization for all forms of wholesaling establishments. Data classified by manufacturers' sales branches and sales offices, merchant wholesalers, and agents and brokers.
1990 *Census of Population*	Every 10 years. Provides comprehensive breakdown of U.S. population by geographic area, age, sex, marital status, education, race, employment, and income.
Restaurant Franchising in the Economy by *Restaurant Business*	Annual. Provides data on restaurant franchising such as company-owned and franchised units, and foreign units.
Robert Morris Associates Annual Statement Studies	Annual. Includes selected balance sheet, income statement data, and financial ratios for manufacturers, wholesalers, and retailers by SIC classification.
Standard & Poor's Industry Surveys—Retailing: Basic Analysis	Annual with periodic updates. Provides summary of major developments affecting retailing. Includes important retailing statistics for industry as well as specific companies.
Survey of Buying Power by *Sales & Marketing Management*	Annual. Includes data on population, households, income, and retail sales for six retail categories. Five-year projections of data are also provided.
Survey of Industrial and Commercial Buying by *Sales & Marketing Management*	Annual. Provides data on number of plants and total shipments by SIC classification.

Table 7-5 (Continued)

Survey of Selling Costs by *Sales & Marketing Management*	Annual. Provides selling costs for major markets in the United States and Canada. Also contains data on sales compensation and transportation costs.
Vending Times Census of the Vending Industry	Annual. Provides data on the vending machine such as total sales, sales by merchandise line, sales by location, and sales by firm size.

Table 7-6 Sources of External Secondary Data in Channels: Selected Periodicals with Channels Management Emphasis

PROFESSIONAL SOURCES
- *Agency Sales Magazine,* monthly
- *Chain Drug Review,* biweekly
- *Chain Store Age Executive,* monthly
- *Chilton's Distribution,* monthly
- *Current Business Reports: Annual Retail Trade,* annual
- *Direct Marketing,* monthly
- *Discount Merchandiser,* monthly
- *Discount Stores News,* biweekly
- *Distribution,* monthly
- *Drug Store News,* biweekly
- *Editor and Publisher Market Guide,* annual
- *Handling & Shipping Management,* monthly
- *Industrial Distribution,* monthly
- *Marketing News,* 26 times a year
- *Progressive Grocer,* monthly
- *Rand McNally Commercial Atlas & Marketing Guide,* annual
- *Retail Control,* monthly
- *Sales & Marketing Management* "Survey of Buying Power I and II," "Survey of Industrial and Commercial Buying," and "Survey of Selling Costs" issues
- *Stores,* monthly
- *Supermarket Business,* monthly
- *Supermarket News,* weekly
- *Traffic Management,* monthly
- *Transportation and Distribution,* monthly
- *Women's Wear Daily,* five times per week

ACADEMIC SOURCES
- *International Journal of Physical Distribution & Materials Management,* eight times a year
- *Journal of Business Logistics,* semiannual
- *Journal of Direct Marketing,* quarterly
- *Journal of Marketing Channels,* quarterly
- *Journal of Public Policy & Marketing,* semiannual
- *Journal of Purchasing and Materials Management,* quarterly
- *Journal of Retailing,* quarterly
- *Logistics and Transportation Review, The,* quarterly
- *Transportation Journal,* quarterly

TABLE 7-7 SOURCES OF EXTERNAL SECONDARY DATA IN CHANNELS: SELECTED PERIODICALS

GENERAL SOURCES
  Advertising Age, weekly
  American Demographics, monthly
  Barron's, weekly
  Business Horizons, bimonthly
  Business Marketing, monthly
  Business Week, weekly
  California Management Review, quarterly
  Columbia Journal of World Business, quarterly
  European Journal of Marketing, eight times per year
  European Management Journal, quarterly
  Forbes, biweekly
  Fortune, semimonthly
  Harvard Business Review, bimonthly
  Inc., monthly
  Industrial Marketing Management, quarterly
  Industrial Marketing Review, quarterly
  Journal of Academy of Marketing Science, quarterly
  Journal of Advertising, quarterly
  Journal of Advertising Research, bimonthly
  Journal of Business, quarterly
  Journal of Business and Industrial Marketing, quarterly
  Journal of Business Logistics, semiannual
  Journal of Business Strategy, bimonthly
  Journal of Consumer Marketing, quarterly
  Journal of Consumer Research, quarterly
  Journal of Global Marketing, quarterly
  Journal of Macromarketing, semiannual
  Journal of Marketing, quarterly
  Journal of Marketing Research, quarterly
  Journal of Personal Selling and Sales Management, quarterly
  Journal of Product Innovation Management, quarterly
  Journal of Services Marketing, quarterly
  Management Science, monthly
  Psychology and Marketing, quarterly
  Sales & Marketing Management, monthly (except bimonthly in February, April, July, and October)
  Sloan Management Review, quarterly
  Strategic Management Journal, ten times per year
  Wall Street Journal, five times per week

Nongovernment external secondary data are also collected by commercial research firms that sell data to channel members. Some of these data are based on irregular research reports on a given topic; in other cases, commercial research firms provide data on a continuous basis. This is useful in ascertaining trends or determining relationships between variables. An important type of continuous secondary data collected by commercial research firms is single-source data. **Single-source data** use household panels and seek to explain purchases (which are recorded either in stores or at the respondent's home using scanners) through correlating purchases to television viewing (which is monitored), past purchases, in-store promotions, couponing effort by manufacturers, and life-style and demographic data.[6]

Single-source data are collected and analyzed by firms such as A. C. Nielsen (a unit of Dun & Bradstreet) and Information Resources Inc. (IRI). For example, the current IRI household data collection methodology requires only that the panelist show an ID card at a checkout, thereby allowing the supermarket scanner to record his or her purchase. Coupons redeemed by the panelist are subsequently added to his or her purchase data by IRI field personnel. The level and nature of in-store display and newspaper promotional activity are also monitored and recorded by IRI personnel. Lastly, a household's television viewing behavior is also recorded.

The services offered by competing single-source data firms differ in terms of where the scanning data are collected (in-store or in-home), the retail institutions covered (some cover convenience stores, mass merchants, and drug stores, in addition to grocery stores), and sample size and composition.[7] For example, although IRI relies on in-store purchase information among households with appropriate identification cards, Nielsen uses scanner data compiled in-home through a panel of 40,000 households.[8]

An important use of single-source data to channel members is the analysis of the importance of distribution intensity on sales. IRI's InfoScan service includes these data. Table 7-8 shows sales and distribution intensity for two similar products: product "Y" and product "X." While product "X" sells more volume (70 million pounds versus 50 million for your product), it has 95 percent **all commodity volume (ACV)**. A 95 percent ACV means that the product is distributed in grocery stores that account for 95 percent of total grocery store sales in that

TABLE 7-8 COMPARISON OF SALES OF COMPETING PRODUCTS DUE TO DISTRIBUTION INTENSITY

	Your Product "Y"	Competitor "X"
Total sales (in pounds)	50 million	70 million
Percent ACV distribution[a]	46	95
Pounds per distribution point[b]	1087	737
Total sales with 100 percent distribution[c] (in million pounds)	108.7	73.7

[a] An analysis of competitor's distribution is that it is distributed in stores that account for 95 percent of total store sales in that market, versus your product's 46 percent ACV.

[b] Pounds per 1 percent ACV distribution = $\dfrac{\text{Total sales (in pounds)}}{\text{Percent ACV distribution}}$

[c] Total sales with 100 percent distribution = (Pounds per distribution point) × 100

A major assumption of this analysis is that the product will continue to sell at its old sales rate (pounds per distribution point) as the intensity of its distribution (percent ACV distribution) increases.

Source: InfoScan (Chicago: Information Resources Inc., 1990), p. 10.

market. In contrast, product "Y" has 46 percent ACV. An analysis of these data shows that product "Y" has a higher sales rate (1087 pounds per 1 percent distribution versus 737 pounds per distribution point for product "X"). Given 100 percent ACV distribution, product "Y" should sell 108.7 million pounds versus 73.7 million pounds for product "X" with 100 percent distribution. This analysis shows the impact of increasing distribution on a product's overall sales. A major assumption of this analysis is that the product will continue to sell at its old sales rate (pounds per distribution point) as the intensity of its distribution (percent ACV distribution) increases. A better measure would be to weigh the stores by the percentage of the relevant product category they sell. This is called **percent category volume (PCV)**. If there were only one brand in a product category, it would have 100 percent PCV, by definition. Therefore, ACV would be a more meaningful measure. However, in established product categories, the PCV measure is generally more meaningful. PCV is normally not provided by commercial audit firms.[9]

The advantages of single-source data collection are as follows:

- There is no bias owing to exaggerated self-reported purchasing (as with diary-based data collection) or to the respondent's poor memory.
- Scanner data report actual sales. Prior to scanning, commercial research firms reported sales based on warehouse withdrawals. Sales to a retailer may not correspond to retail sales, for a retailer can build up its inventory in anticipation of higher wholesaler prices or deplete its inventory in anticipation of a special promotional offer from a manufacturer/supplier.
- Single-source data enable a channels researcher to examine the association of promotions and short- and long-term sales, shelf space and sales, advertising and sales, and so on.

The disadvantages of single-source data include the following.

- Current panels are not nationally representative. Single-source data panels are in markets where television exposure is being electronically measured.
- Television watching is based on household, not individual data.[10]
- Single-source data collection is generally restricted to food and drug store products.
- Customers that do not identify themselves at the point-of-sale would not have these transactions counted.
- Single-source data collection and analysis involve a high investment for the channel member. Single-source data collection can cost as little as $10,000 or so for a one-time measurement of a single brand in a single region, and up to $10 million a year for an array of studies covering several product categories.
- A number of privacy issues exist. For example, do single-source data collection firms have the right to sell information on individual households to marketers? For example, should a commercial research firm have the right to sell household consumption data on ketchup to manufacturers?

Based on these data, Heinz can mail 50-cent coupons to brand-loyal Del Monte Ketchup users to induce them to try its brand, but not mail coupons to loyal Heinz ketchup users.[11]

Because of the speed of the secondary data collection process as well as its low cost, a firm should first try to clarify a problem or opportunity or to resolve the research question through a secondary data search. If data are unavailable, are conflicting, or are not adequate (owing to timeliness, bias in methodology, or poor classification methods), a channels researcher needs to collect primary data.

GENERATION OF PRIMARY DATA

Primary data consist of information collected specifically for the purpose of the investigation at hand.[12] Sources of primary data include surveys (personal interview, mail questionnaire, telephone interview), observation, experimentation, and simulation.

In comparison to secondary data collection, primary data collection offers these advantages:

- It is current.
- It fits with the problem at hand.
- A channels researcher can maintain secrecy in data collection and analysis.
- The researcher can control the methodology to meet his or her unique needs (sample methodology, secrecy, timeliness).

In comparison to secondary data collection, primary data collection offers these disadvantages:

- High cost.
- A long lag time between statement of the problem and collection and analysis of data.
- A significant amount of expertise needed to properly conduct primary research.
- Difficulty in collecting data.

THE RESEARCH DESIGN

A **research design** consists of the framework or plan that guides the collection and analysis of data.[13] Data collection includes sampling and primary data collection sources. In **sampling**, selected respondents or observations are used to generate conclusions about a larger group. Often in channels research, a census is used whereby the entire population is questioned or observed. A census is likely to be used when a channel member seeks to question key customers or important wholesalers. The advantages of a census are that no sampling error is present and clients feel they have participated in decision making.

Sampling is typically used when a large number of manufacturers/suppliers or customers exist. The costs of questioning or observing every member of this group would be prohibitive. In developing a sampling plan, the channels researcher needs to specify both the sampling methodology and sample size. The two general approaches to sampling are probability and nonprobability.

In a **probability-based sample**, every unit (final customer, retailer, wholesaler, or manufacturer/supplier) has an equal chance of being chosen as a member of the sample. The rules relating to measuring precision or sampling error relate only to probability-based samples. Despite the value of a probability-based sample, many channels researchers use nonprobability samples. In a **nonprobability sample**, the researcher chooses sampling units. Nonprobability samples are often called either judgment or convenience samples. These samples are generally easier to implement and less costly to research than probability samples. The level of uncertainty about value being measured, **precision (sampling error)**, is related to the square of the sample size. As a rule of thumb, if channels researchers want to double the precision of an estimate, they have to increase the sample size by four times.

There are four basic sources of primary data: survey, observation, experimentation, and simulation. In a **survey**, data are gathered from a respondent through communication. Surveys can be used to measure attitudes, opinions, awareness/knowledge, behavior, demographic/socioeconomic characteristics, intentions, and motivations. Communication between the researcher and the respondent can be in the form of a personal interview, mail questionnaire, or telephone interview. Generally, a personal interview is most appropriate when product samples or advertising copy need to be observed, when the respondent has to be probed for additional information, and when the investigator does not want the respondent to see the entire questionnaire at once. A mail questionnaire is most appropriate when the information desired of the respondent is confidential (or when the respondent will be more honest if he or she cannot be identified), when the questionnaire is very long, or when a firm's research funds are restricted. The telephone interview is most appropriate when personal interviewing is too costly (or does not warrant the additional expense), the data need to be gathered as quickly as possible, and the researcher does not want the respondent to see the entire questionnaire form at one time.

Observation is a form of data collection in which the behavior of respondents is observed and recorded. Unlike surveys, observation does not rely on the willingness or ability of respondents to report behavior. However, unlike surveys, observation cannot be used to measure the attitudes, motivations, and plans of respondents. There are four types of observation: natural, controlled, mechanical, or human. In **natural observation**, a person is observed in a regular setting such as the shopping environment of a grocery store. In **controlled observation**, the setting of the data collection area is part of an experiment. Observation can also be **mechanical** when a machine measures behavior (such as a scanner or Nielsen television rating measurement), or **human** when a trained interviewer/observer records a subject's behavior (as in the case of a manufacturer evaluating a wholesaler's display-making capability).

Experimentation is a controlled setting whereby one or more variables are manipulated. Experiments can be either laboratory or field. In a **laboratory experiment**, a highly controlled, but unnatural, environment is used. In a **field experiment**, the environment is more realistic but control is reduced. Often, researchers use a combination of the two approaches. For example, real shoppers in a field experiment can be exposed to an **experimental treatment** (the controllable variable being studied), the effect of an increased number of shelf facings (the number of rows of a product on a supermarket shelf), to determine its effect on sales. Experiments are the only primary data source that can show a cause-effect relationship.

In **simulation**, mathematical descriptions are developed to explain a given situation. An example of simulation is a mathematical model that predicts the impact on wholesale sales if the manufacturer increases its advertising to channel members by 10 percent. Simulation enables a channel researcher to manipulate a model to predict what would happen in a real-life situation. Through simulation, a researcher can determine the costs of increasing sales through a variety of strategies (increasing shelf facings, lowering prices, increasing personal selling effort, and so on).

ANALYSIS OF DATA

Information generated through surveys, observation, experimentation, and simulation needs to be coded, tabulated, and then interpreted. In **coding**, each completed data form is numbered and response categories are labeled. For example, a "no" response to a given question can be coded as a 0, while a "yes" response to that question can be coded as a 1. Coding is more difficult for open-ended questions. For example, a researcher will have to decide whether the terms *dependable, reliable,* and *trustworthy* should be assigned the same or separate response categories or coding numbers. In **tabulation**, summary data (averages, totals, and percents) are calculated for each response category. The total number of responses to each question is determined. In **data analysis**, responses are evaluated in the form of cross-classification tables (where the impact of changing the level of one variable on another variable can be studied), correlations, and other statistical measures and techniques.

RECOMMENDATIONS FOR ACTION

In the recommendations-for-action stage of the marketing research process, recommendations are made to management on the basis of the data that have been collected and analyzed.

The recommendations-for-action stage lists possible short- and long-term strategies for the firm to undertake based on the data within the report, examines the advantages and disadvantages associated with each strategy, and then recommends one of the strategies. The reasons for the recommended strategy are explained. For example, a research study for a limited-service wholesaler reveals that the firm's customer service image is poor. However, a number of its customers utilize the wholesaler because of its low prices and convenient location. A number of alternatives are possible: retain the present strategy; improve customer service, keep prices constant (to increase overall sales); and improve customer service but raise prices (to keep gross profit constant). The pros and cons of each strategy need to be studied. For example, the firm needs to investigate what percentage of its current customers would pay a higher price for better service, the overall costs of improving customer service, the effect of improved customer service on customer loyalty, and whether the changed strategy would result in a blurred image among its customers. On the basis of exploring each of these options, the report recommends improving customer service while keeping the price constant. However, customer service improvements that are recommended are low-cost ones: increasing the number of telephone lines to reduce waiting time, installing a toll-free order number, and training employees to be more responsive.

IMPLEMENTATION OF FINDINGS

The last stage of the marketing research process reflects the use of the research findings in a manner most suitable for the firm. The implementation process deals with timetables, budgets, and intermediate objectives, and with delegation of responsibility. For example, the wholesaler implemented the research findings in an efficient, low-cost manner.

AN INTRODUCTION TO CHANNEL MEMBER MARKETING INFORMATION SYSTEMS

In this section, we explore some fundamental concepts in marketing information systems: the differences between marketing research and marketing systems, the types of marketing information systems, and the structure of a channel information system.

DIFFERENCES BETWEEN MARKETING RESEARCH AND MARKETING INFORMATION SYSTEMS

Marketing research was defined earlier as the systematic gathering, recording, and analyzing of relevant data to reduce uncertainty in marketing decision making. In contrast, a **third-generation information system (marketing decision support system)** can be defined as "an interactive, computer-based information system designed to assist with semistructured and unstructured management decisions."[14]

Marketing information systems have the following components:[15]

- They support but do not replace management decision making.
- They are directed at semistructured decisions of middle and upper management.

- They are interactive.
- They have data and models organized and dedicated to a specific decision or group of closely related decisions.
- They are user-friendly.

Major differences exist between marketing research and marketing information systems. Marketing research is often reactive, responding to a problem or an opportunity. In contrast, a marketing information system is proactive; the system anticipates a problem or opportunity early enough to minimize its threat or to take full opportunity of a change. Whereas marketing research is typically project-oriented, marketing information systems are continuous. In marketing research, data are collected and stored, often with no meaningful structure. In a marketing information system, data are stored in a manner to assist in better understanding behavior. For example, a marketing information system will plot trends, highlight differences from predicted performance, and examine relationships among data.

TYPES OF CHANNEL INFORMATION SYSTEMS

We can differentiate among three different levels of channel information systems. **First-generation information systems** consist of computerized information from a single source, such as A. C. Nielsen. The data in these systems are not combined with other related data to explain behavior. **Second-generation information systems** are characterized by the development of integrated marketing databases that combine data from commercial research firms with internal secondary data (such as sales, advertising, coupon redemption, and distribution effectiveness). A firm can evaluate the impact of increasing distribution, lowering prices, and increasing advertising expenditures in a second-generation marketing system. Third-generation channel information systems extend the second-generation systems to use scanners to continuously record sales data.[16] Third-generation systems are also called marketing decision support systems (MDSS). A third-generation marketing information system combines the ease of desktop computing with the power of centralized data processing. It enables users to tap a variety of internal databases as well as external ones.[17]

STRUCTURE OF A CHANNEL INFORMATION SYSTEM

The physical structure of a channel information system consists of a database, display, model, and analysis.[18]

The **database** consists of internal and external secondary data (such as shipments, coupon redemptions, distribution intensity, and so on). Some of the data are included on a continuous basis such as sales; other elements of the database are included in an irregular manner (such as distribution intensity). Managers need to be aware of potential problems with database integrity and accuracy.[19] (The use of scanning and electronic data interchange is covered in the next section of this chapter.)

The **display** consists of traditional reports, exception reports, and graphics, in paper or on screen formats. Traditional reports list performance on all attributes, including those in which the firm has met its planned performance levels. In contrast, in exception reports, outstanding or significantly below planned performance levels are highlighted. Exception reports result in shorter reports that flag problem areas as well as opportunities. Displays can also be in the form of graphics, such as bar charts, graphs, and histograms. (Channel reports are covered in greater depth in the next section.)

The **model** portion of the channel information system consists of interrelationships among data that can be used for prediction. A spreadsheet with an "if, then" analysis is an example of a model. Models can be simple (such as cross-classification tables showing sales levels at two price points) or complex (such as the development of a mathematical relationship between sales and price through multiple regression analysis).

Analysis consists of manipulating data in order to better understand a marketing-related issue. For example, a firm can determine the relative merits of conducting alternative strategies in terms of sales, profits, and return on investment.

SPECIAL TOPICS IN CHANNEL INFORMATION SYSTEMS

Four broad special topics in channel management are the use of scanning-based data, electronic data interchange, database marketing, and channel information system reports.

USE OF SCANNING-BASED DATA

The most common bar code symbol, and the generally accepted bar code for the retail industry, is the **Universal Product Code (UPC)**, a 12-digit number used for merchandise identification down to the lowest level (color and size for apparel). All UPC bar codes include digits that identify vendor and items as well as leading and trailing control digits. According to UPC guidelines, vendors are required to assign different UPC codes to all variations of the same basic product. Thus, products that are similar but differ by color, size, or label should receive a different UPC designation. The data bank for UPC identification numbers for manufacturer/suppliers, wholesalers, and retailers is the Uniform Code Council. Uniform Code Council membership fees are based on the firm's gross dollar sales in addition to a one-time fee. Uniform Code Council members receive one set of Uniform Communication Standards (UCS), admission to the UCS User Group, and the support services of UCS staff.

Among the earliest users of UPC scanning was Levi Strauss, which preticketed its apparel products with UPC codes in the spring of 1985. Levi was also the first manufacturer to use the Universal Product Code on shipping labels placed on all cartons.[20] A recent study of the use of the UPC among retailers conducted by Deloitte & Touche found that 83 percent of the responding retailers stated that they were either currently using UPC scanning or planned to establish UPC programs with vendors. Virtually all large and medium-size retailers are scanning or planning to do so. Mass merchants are also more likely to be committed to scanning than other types of retailers.[21]

Although many people associate the UPC with its use in a retail setting, bar coding is not confined to grocery store shelves or checkout counters. Manufacturers use bar codes to track work-in-progress, shipping, receiving, and distribution.[22] Bar coding is also used by all channel members for warehouse functions and for inbound and outbound shipping containers. For example, through bar codes, a firm can determine the appropriate conveyor lane for each package in a warehouse, sort merchandise by truck, build a manifest for each truck, and sort parcels by drop point number.[23] Bar codes are even used by airlines to keep track of luggage.

The Universal Product Code is used in conjunction with **electronic scanning**; either hand-held or stationary laser-based devices that read and transmit UPC data as items are passed over or by the scanner. Scanners, which read the various symbols, contain a source of intense light or light-emitting diode aimed at the bar code. The dark bars absorb the light, and the spaces reflect it back onto the scanner. The scanner then transforms the patterns of light and dark into electrical impulses that are measured by a decoder and translated into a binary code for transmission into a computer. Scanners read the bar codes and enter the information directly into a computer. The code identifies an item. Scanning a bar code can cause inventory to be debited or credited, or other actions.[24]

Not all product codes are bar codes. For example, UPS's product code, called Maxicode, is only slightly larger than a postage stamp and resembles an array of black hexagons. UPS says that Maxicode can hold 100 characters of data in a square inch, much more than a typical UPC bar code. In addition, a sensor can read the Maxicode on packages moving as fast as 500 feet a minute.[25] UPS will initially use Maxicode to carry destination and tracking information.

In the Fifth Annual Barcode/EDI/Quick Response Survey of retailers (respondents included executives from department stores, mass merchants, and specialty stores) conducted by Deloitte & Touche, 92 percent of the respondents indicated that they had installed scanning or planned to scan at the point of sale as of 1992. This represents an increase in usage of more than 20 percent over the previous year. The study also found high overall commitment to use scanning to look up retail selling prices. Ninety percent of retailer respondents noted commitment use of price lookup (PLU), which was up from 69 percent in 1991. For the first time, smaller retailers have the same degree of commitment to PLU as larger retailers.[26] Approximately 91 percent of chain and 75 percent of independent supermarkets are scanning. Scanning rates are very high among mass merchandisers, and chain drug stores with these retailers ring up about 70 percent of their all commodity volume (ACV) on scanners. All but one of the major buying club chains use scanners.[27]

Scanning benefits are as follows:[28]

- The scanning of bar codes is faster and more accurate than manual systems that require keyboard entry. There is no need to reenter data.

- Scanning improves inventory management. A firm can track its merchandise down to the stockkeeping unit (SKU) level throughout the entire distribution pipeline. Scanning reduces stockouts and the number of slow-selling items kept in inventory.
- Scanning improves price accuracy by eliminating manual price entry at the point of sale. Through scanning, prices can be continuously updated. The automatic price lookup capability of most scanning systems also simplifies verification of the prices on returned goods.
- Scanning improves the productivity of channel members. There are shorter checkout lines thanks to the speed of price lookup. Retailers also do not have to re-mark merchandise for promotions. Reducing or eliminating manual receiving and checking procedures also improves distribution center productivity for manufacturers, wholesalers, and retailers.
- Scanner data from individual stores can be integrated with single-source data provided by commercial research firms.
- Scanning data reflect actual sales. Prior to scanning, much of the data on sales was based on warehouse withdrawal data.

Among the typical problems associated with scanning are the following.

- A sales clerk can punch in one black pair of socks three times instead of the one black, one blue, and one brown pair of socks that were actually purchased. This action incorrectly increases the sales of black socks and decreases the sales of blue and brown socks.
- Some items, such as large bags of dog food, are not scanned by sales clerks.
- Some vendors incorrectly use the same UPC code for different items.
- Currently, scanners correctly record product bar codes between 80 and 85 percent of the time on the first pass. Industrywide goals are to reach a 97 percent correct reading on the first pass.[29] Poor reading of scanners has been attributed to poor quality printing, improper bar code location, or inaccurate UPC codes. Industry estimates place the added labor costs due to multiple scans as high as $145 million annually.[30]

Because of some problems with UPC bar codes supplied by some vendors, Wal-Mart has instituted a fines policy of 10 percent of the order for the first offense, and the larger of $50,000 or 10 percent of the purchase order for the second offense. The third offense is the larger of $100,000 or 10 percent.[31]

ELECTRONIC DATA INTERCHANGE

Electronic data interchange (EDI) enables electronic transmission and exchange of standard format documents (such as product transfer and resale, purchase orders, order status, invoices, remittance advice, bills of lading, and advance shipping notices) among companies or a network of companies for the purpose of facilitating the flow of information through a channel. EDI cannot be used for unstructured documents such as business letters.[32]

EDI usage involves four steps.[33] In the first step, an electronic scanner compiles sales data on all items that final consumers purchase at a retailer. In step two, the retailer analyzes the sales data, generates an order, and uploads the data file to the supplier. In the third step, the supplier ships the retailer's order. In some cases, the supplier analyzes the data and ships the most appropriate replenishment order without an actual purchase order from the retailer. Lastly, the supplier uploads shipping, billing, and account information to the retailer.

According to the Fifth Annual Barcode/EDI/Quick Response Survey, 39 percent of respondents stated that they were using EDI with their vendors in 1992, compared with 20 percent in 1991 and 15 percent in 1990. Specialty retailers lagged behind other retailers in the use of EDI. Most retailers that have implemented EDI have used it for purchase orders.[34]

Electronic data interchange has been used at Kmart since 1989. The system electronically links Kmart's stores to half of its suppliers. EDI allows Kmart to replenish supplies of commodities such as motor oil in 2 or 3 days instead of the customary 21 days. It also reduces stockouts while minimizing inventory levels. Kmart plans to expand electronic data interchange internationally to further reduce lead times on international shipments; these lead times are now 120 days (for imported toys, sporting goods, hardware, and stationery products). Kmart hopes to reduce this lead time to 90 days with electronic data interchange.[35]

Levi Strauss uses an electronic data interchange system with its retailers called "LeviLink," which enables customers to order and plan their inventories electronically. LeviLink has been further expanded to Levi's suppliers so that they can fine tune the amounts and kinds of fabrics needed to meet customer demand. LeviLink practically eliminated the need for large fabric warehouses that were located near Levi's apparel plants. It also enabled many Levi retailers to eliminate their warehouses. As a result of electronic data interchange, Levi's shipping cycle was reduced from three weeks to six days for some accounts. Levi's goal "is to order electronically the manufacture of a pair of jeans when the customer buys one in the store."[36]

EDI systems can be industrywide or proprietary. In 1976, a joint industry committee was formed from the Cooperative Food Distributors of America, the Food Marketing Institute, the Grocery Manufacturers of America, the National Association of Retail Grocers of the United States, the National American Wholesale Growers Association, and the National Food Brokers Association to develop a method of electronic data communication that could be standardized throughout the industries represented by the member organizations. The VICS EDI committee is now administered by the Universal Code Council, the same trade organization that administers UPC.

Industry standards have now been developed for EDI. The American Standards Institute developed a committee in 1979 known as ANSC X.12 to develop uniform standards for interindustry electronic interchange of business transactions. This committee developed standards for purchase orders, invoices, and payment. The current standard is referred to as VICS ANSI X.12. Sixty-nine percent of retailer respondents to the Fifth Annual Barcode/EDI/Quick Response survey are either currently using or plan to use the VICS ANSI X.12 standard as their EDI communications protocol.[37] There are other common standards for the motor, ocean, and rail industries.

In an industrywide system, all firms in the same industry use the same message formats and communication protocols. **Message formats** are the structured data that represent forms, such as purchase orders and invoices. The data areas covered include purchase orders and related adjustments, invoices and related adjustments, order acknowledgments, shipping advice, receiving advice, credit/debit memos, price change and promotional announcements, and administrative messages.[38] **Communications protocols** describe in technical terms how computers interface. Communications protocols are dictated by specific hardware or software. A standard communications protocol enables one communications language to be used with all trading partners.[39] In a proprietary system, message formats or communications protocols are unique to two trading partners.

EDI systems can also be direct or third-party networks. In **direct communication**, each trading partner communicates directly with each other. Direct communications are typically used by larger firms that have a high volume of transactions with a limited number of trading partners.

In a **third-party network**, a service bureau establishes an electronic mailbox in which companies can send and retrieve electronic documents. These networks maintain an electronic mailbox that sorts and deposits messages throughout the day. Third-party networks also provide an interconnect facility that allows electronic mail from different service bureaus (when one trading partner uses another service bureau than that of the other trading partner).[40] Third-party networks offer flexibility in the number of companies that can communicate; they are often used by firms that sell to firms in industries with different message formats and communication protocols, by small manufacturers/suppliers, or by channel members that lack computer expertise. The advantages of third-party networks include simplicity for the trading partners, ability to communicate with a larger number of firms, lower investment requirement, and reduced need for technical staff.

According to Dayton Hudson's vice president of merchandising, GE Information Services, its third-party organization, "takes our proprietary computer language and translates it to the VICS ANSI X.12 standards. GE then acts as a mailbox, storing the information until the vendor is ready to pick it up." Dayton Hudson has 5000 vendors and would have to adjust its sending modes for each. Dayton Hudson pays GE to send its orders; the vendors pay for receiving them.[41] According to the Fifth Annual Barcode/EDI/Quick Response survey, among respondents committed to EDI third-party networks, mailbox service was by far the preferred implementation approach.[42]

The advantages of EDI can be classified as direct, indirect, or strategic.[43] **Direct benefits** stem from the fact that the data are sent electronically from one application to another and do not rely on either business's making other changes in business practices. These benefits include lower transaction costs through reduced paperwork and fewer errors owing to the elimination of the need to print, mail, and rekey data. Direct computer-to-computer or terminal-to-terminal linkages eliminate the need for rekeying orders. This results in reductions in clerical and administrative costs associated with key entry, correction, and tracking of huge volumes of business documents. EDI enables sales reps to spend more time learning about clients rather than filling in order forms. The result is a faster cycle of sales, invoice, and payment.[44] A study by Deloitte & Touche found that by implementing EDI, supermarket retailers can reduce the cost of processing a typical transaction by $23, wholesalers can save $11.30 per transaction, and brokers between $4.62 and $8.06.[45] SuperValu Corporation eliminated $600,000 a year in clerical expense by automating the match between purchase orders (sent electronically to suppliers), invoices (received electronically from suppliers), and receiving information (entered by its receiving dock personnel).[46]

Indirect benefits come from leveraging EDI to enable the technology to change the way one does business. EDI (together with bar code scanning, UPC,

CHANNELS IN ACTION

The Use of EDI by Wal-Mart and Its Major Suppliers

The major reason behind the success of Wal-Mart is its close contact with suppliers. Closeness with suppliers has been a relatively new concept for Wal-Mart. As late as the mid-1980s, Wal-Mart's relationships with its manufacturers/suppliers was in many cases strained. The firm then realized that these turbulent relationships could impede Wal-Mart's growth.

Wal-Mart's sophisticated computers analyze sales data regularly and alert suppliers with data on both fast- and slow-selling merchandise. As part of Wal-Mart's new cooperative style, it shares data with most of its major suppliers down to even color and size distributions. With this system, the right goods are rushed to Wal-Mart's. As a result, Wal-Mart's stores are able to devote only 10 percent of their square footage for inventory versus 25 percent for the average store.

Market analysts feel that Wal-Mart has an advantage in relaying sales information. Between 1990 and 1991, Wal-Mart has hooked most of its suppliers to an electronic data interchange computer network that collects information on sales, shipping, and order information on a daily basis. Manufacturers can view this information at will. According to Wal-Mart's senior vice president for information services, "Customers tell us what they like or don't like every day, with every purchase they make. But our merchants had to guess before at what our demand would be. Now they can know tomorrow what we sold today." For example, when Wal-Mart's Bentonville, Arkansas, store sells a pair of women's size 10 jeans, Wal-Mart's supplier is now able to replace them automatically.

The president of J. P. Stevens, a manufacturer of towels and linens, says that Wal-Mart's electronic data interchange system gives his company instantaneous access to sales data on Stevens's products. According to the president, "Every part of our relationship with Wal-Mart will evolve around this. Technology has always been important to Wal-Mart. Now, we can test styles fast, see the sales results and plan accordingly."

Source: Thomas C. Hayes, "Behind Wal-Mart's Surge, A Web of Suppliers," *New York Times* (July 1, 1991), pp. D1, D2; and Rita Koselka, "Distribution Revolution," *Forbes* (May 25, 1992), p. 60.

and shipping container marking) enables a firm to develop a quick response (just-in-time capability) and to reduce inventory levels. The indirect benefits of EDI are reduced inventory requirements, a faster order cycle, lower warehousing costs, faster transmission of data, better product and order status information, and shorter lead times for order processing. For example, better coordination with its suppliers through EDI enabled Navistar to reduce its use of premium freight charges by 90 percent.[47]

Strategic benefits come from sharing information among channel members, from open communication, and from greater trust. The strategic benefits of EDI include better relationships with suppliers, the use of EDI as an element in high switching costs, and greater coordination among trading partners. The use of EDI may result in an increased share of the target firm's business.[48] For example, retailers such as May Department Stores and Wal-Mart are concentrating on purchases to suppliers with whom they can link inventories electronically. A study of independent property and casualty insurance agents found that agents did more business with insurance carriers with whom they had an EDI linkage. The share of business with these carriers increased after EDI linkage.[49]

The disadvantages of electronic data interchange involve use of batch processing, need to still use paper documents, lack of security when third-party processing is used, need for coordination between vendor and retailer, and high investment for hardware and software. Let us explain these disadvantages. First, electronic data interchange messages generally are transmitted in batch form and remain in the receiver's mailbox until the receiver is ready to pick up messages. They are not instantaneously recorded. Second, although EDI enables firms to eliminate paperwork, in many cases paperwork still accompanies the transaction, "just to be sure." In addition, not all vendors have EDI, so a retailer or wholesaler still needs a traditional paper-based system in addition to EDI. Third, there is a lack of security when third-party networks are used to transmit data. Fourth, there is a high need for extensive coordination and planning between vendor and retailer. Thus, EDI is most useful in long-term channel relationships. Fifth, EDI involves high one-time costs. EDI requires hardware, application and translation software, and communication vehicles as well as an organization to manage and control the entire process.

DATABASE MARKETING

Database marketing is the creation and maintenance of a bank of information about individual customers (e.g., taken from orders, inquiries, and external lists), with the objective of analyzing consumer buying patterns and targeting promotions aimed at specific types of customers.[50] As this definition suggests, database marketing can be used as a means of communicating with individual customers as well as a marketing research tool.

Database marketing can be differentiated from other forms of marketing in that sales and purchase pattern data are kept at the individual customer level. Among the benefits of database marketing over traditional marketing are addressability, measurability, flexibility, and accountability.[51]

- Addressability—the ability to identify each customer and to reach each customer on a one-by-one basis.

- Measurability—knowledge of what, how, where, and when a consumer purchased at a point in time. The purchase history of a customer can also be determined.
- Flexibility—the opportunity to appeal to different customers using a separate marketing mix.
- Accountability—the development of profit data for specific marketing programs. Database marketing can also determine the types of customers who participated in any program.

Database marketing has been used by a large variety of firms at different levels of resellers. For example, General Motors has a proprietary database of more than 6 million households that are enrolled in a credit card program that provides rebates toward new car purchases. General Motors provides data on these households to local GM dealers.[52] Blockbuster Entertainment Corporation uses its customer database of 40 million names to determine children's titles and product features for its rental video game business.[53] Philip Morris is generating a database of cigarette smokers, recording such information as the type of cigarette used, how long they smoked their regular brand, and their degree of cigarette consumption. Some analysts have suggested that Philip Morris is preparing the database in the event that over-the-counter sales of cigarettes are prohibited through traditional retailer channels. The database would enable Philip Morris to reach customers and to sell cigarettes through direct mail.[54]

As a channel information system, database marketing is commonly used to describe behavior. A firm can track all of its interactions with a customer—for example, whether or not a consumer responded to a special promotion, purchased a specific item, returned a warranty card, and required a special service call. Researchers can also link information generated from surveys or from other sources with the database.[55] To be successful, a database should capture material from field sales reports, customer comments, sales invoices (including purchase quantities, payment form, use of special incentives), owner registration cards, and other sources. A firm can also add external data to its internal customer files. Examples of external database providers include R. L. Polk, Donnelley Marketing, TRW, Infobase Marketing, and Claritas.

A number of operational issues need to be resolved in properly maintaining a database. Databases must be continually maintained to be current. For example, merge/purge software has to be used to determine whether J. Jones and John Jones are the same person. Different reporting sources may report inconsistent information about the same customer. Some small firms delegate these responsibilities to service bureaus. There are also important issues relating to customer privacy.

The next section describes the different forms of channel information systems reports that can be generated from scanning, electronic data interchange, and database marketing. This is the display portion of the channel information system.

CHANNEL INFORMATION SYSTEM REPORTS

Different types of channel members want different system reports. For example, manufacturers want market share data in different cities and supermarket chains under different conditions of advertising and pricing. This allows manufacturers to determine the short- and long-term sales and profit impact of alternative advertising and pricing levels. Wholesalers want to study market shares of their brands within selected territories. Retailers want to analyze their private-label strategy, and sales and profits per linear foot of shelf space allocated to alternative products and brands.

Despite the differences, each of these channel members needs to be able to examine data on a disaggregated (small-unit) basis. Thus, although a manufacturer is most interested in its overall market share, it still needs to be able to track sales to major chains and smaller geographic areas in order to ascertain weaknesses or opportunities. A wholesaler also needs to track sales by salesperson and by product.

Large volumes of data can be assembled by all channel members. The amount of data can especially increase for channel members that use scanning for tracking sales, inventory, and shipping. Although supermarkets, for example, can track purchases at the individual consumer level, such data tracking can generate one megabyte of data per day for a single supermarket.[56] Often because of large amounts of data, channel members use exception reports. **Exception reports** flag outstanding or significantly below planned performance and list these performance levels. Reports of performance within an acceptable range of performance are not listed. This results in shorter reports that highlight problems and opportunities, but do not list performance levels for all products, stores, customers, and wholesalers. For example, an inventory exception report would list items that need a buyer's immediate attention, such as fast-selling items, slow-selling items, and out-of-stock situations. The report would not list the inventory status of items selling within planned levels or items with acceptable levels of stock. Exception reports offer the following advantages: they highlight problem or opportunity areas, they result in shorter reports, and a marketer does not have to read several columns (such as current inventory levels, anticipated sales rate, and planned reorder time interval) to determine situations requiring action. A disadvantage of exception reports is that they do not show all performance levels. The channels manager would need to examine additional reports to see the performance levels for all products, stores, customers, and wholesalers.

Reports can include graphics options along with data. Increasingly, managers incorporate data from reports into spreadsheet format in order to see the impact of changes in sales and costs on profit and on return on investment.

In the next sections, we examine a sample of channel information system reports—sales reports, markdown reports, lists of prospective and current customers, inventory management system, reports, and computer-aided ordering reports. Inventory management systems and computer-aided ordering reports have been covered in depth in Chapter 6.

SALES REPORTS

Sales reports contain important data relating to actual sales, planned sales, and sales for the corresponding time period one year ago. Table 7-3 (Sources of Internal Secondary Data in Channels) outlines selected sales report information that can be derived from invoices: average order size, yearly sales to each channel of distribution, seasonality by distribution channel, and fast-selling products. Other sales reports cover total sales, sales by geographic region, by sales representative, by product, by product line, and by major account. This information is useful in ascertaining sales trends as well as turning points in performance (such as the loss of a major account or the increased importance of a distribution channel).

Although much sales information at the retail level regarding sales comes from scanning, at industrial firms much of the data input comes from laptop computers supplied to salespeople. In a study of industrial firms, 57 percent of the responding firms used laptop or portable computers for sales call reporting, and 17 percent of the firms used these computers for order entry.[57] Much of the information needed for sales reports can be generated from sales call reports and order entry.

Pall Corporation and James River Corporation use sales reporting systems. Pall Corporation, an industrial specialty filter manufacturer, tracks and develops sales trends from customer invoices (which do not reveal price information) that are sent to it on a monthly basis from each Pall wholesaler. Sales trends are tracked by distributor, salesperson, customer, market, and product. On the basis of these trends, Pall develops and updates a Sales Action Plan for each distributor.[58]

James River Corporation, a manufacturer of paper products (such as toilet tissue, napkins, and disposable cups) shares proprietary marketing information on sales with its customers. It knows, for example, how often its final customers buy paper goods and which items are generally purchased together. It also understands differences in consumption patterns by type of store and by a store's location. On the basis of its research, it told Lucky Stores, a major West Coast supermarket chain, to reshelve all of its paper products. As a result, Lucky's market share in this important category increased.[59]

Markdown Reports

Manufacturers, wholesalers, and retailers need periodically to examine inventory and designate products that should be reduced in price owing to slow sales, lack of a full assortment in a product category, the product's being superceded by a new model, or lateness in a selling season. These products are candidates for markdowns, that is, reductions from traditional selling prices. Merry-Go-Round, a retailer of reasonably priced teenage clothing, uses its computerized merchandise tracking system to track its best-selling as well as slow-selling merchandise. If the system shows that a particular color or style is selling poorly, Merry-Go-Round slashes the price to get it out of the stores fast. According to the firm's chief executive officer, "This is not French wine we're selling. The clothes don't get better with age just by hanging there."[60]

Lists of Prospective and Current Customers

Channel information systems can be used to generate lists of current and prospective customers. These lists can include current customers, past customers, and potential customers (on the basis of their SIC code, zip code, or inquiry). A customer database can be developed internally from customer files, order records, service reports, merchandise return records, sales force records, inquiries, and warranty cards.[61] They also can be rented or purchased from mailing list firms, professional associations, and magazines.

A customer list is particularly useful when the consumer or business name is matched with important data relating to past purchase dates, purchase quantities, and product categories. In this manner, specific promotions can be targeted to customers with special needs. Two examples of firms with highly targeted customer lists are GTE's Sylvania Lighting Division and Williams-Sonoma.

GTE's Sylvania Lighting Division recently introduced its Prestige Partnership Program, which is designed to help its 2200 distributors target the most promising accounts in each of their territories. To help its distributors (primarily small and medium-sized independent electrical supply wholesalers) better sell its lighting products, Sylvania developed an integrated database that can be used to identify prospects in each distributor's territory. The database contains the name of the business, address, phone number, name of the person responsible for ordering lighting materials, the annual lighting potential of the business, and the number of fixtures the business has.[62]

Williams-Sonoma, a cooking supplies catalog and store-based retailer, uses its marketing information system to keep track of its 4.5 million customers. It tracks up to 150 different pieces of information per customer. Williams-Sonoma can determine what each customer purchased from each of its five catalogs (an estimated 60 percent of customers have bought from more than one), what time of the year the customer tends to buy, how often he or she makes a purchase, the category of merchandise purchased, and so on. Through a complex system, Williams-Sonoma's two full-time statisticians are able to project with a plus or minus 5 percent accuracy, on average, each catalog's sales. This database also helps the company determine the most promising locations for new stores.[63]

INVENTORY MANAGEMENT SYSTEM REPORTS

Inventory represents one of the largest investments for wholesalers and retailers and a large investment for manufacturers. Furthermore, stockouts are especially costly in terms of the potential loss of business resulting from poor customer service. A good inventory management system needs to determine stock-on-hand by product, the amount of stock at various points in the distribution pipeline, and order status information desired by customers.

Federated Department Stores maintains an excellent inventory management system. Its Sabre Group (not connected with American Airlines' computer reservation system) enables buyers and managers at any of its divisions to compare that unit's performance with that of any other Federated division. Sabre tracks inventory from the time a purchase order is placed until the good is sold. Information supplied by Sabre enables Federated's buyers to mark down slow-selling inventory, to avoid bad decisions made by colleagues, and to transship merchandise from one division to another. Federated's buyers can also order merchandise directly through Sabre's electronic data interchange capabilities.[64] Other retailers can purchase the right to use Sabre.

> # CHANNELS IN ACTION
>
> ## Computer-Aided Ordering
>
> Computer-aided ordering (CAO) began in the supermarket field in 1978 when Shaw's Supermarkets pioneered this concept. According to some estimates, Shaw's is saving at least 0.5 percent of sales through use of this technique. With CAO, Shaw's was able to increase its annual inventory turnover from 30 to 44 times. Within the supermarket field, few firms are using CAO. A study of leading supermarket chains and wholesalers conducted by Deloitte & Touche in 1992 found that 20 percent of the retailer/wholesaler respondents were using CAO (up from 14 percent in 1990).
>
> Benefits of CAO include better inventory management, less need for physical inventories, lower ordering costs, fewer stockouts, fewer markdowns, and fresher merchandise. A Deloitte & Touche study found that 55 percent of its supermarkets and wholesaler respondents identified fewer stockouts as an expected benefit of CAO, 54 percent cited store labor savings, and 54 percent named fewer overstocks as an expected benefit.
>
> Despite potential benefits, people familiar with CAO feel that users need to be aware of the need for extensive information and for clean scanning data. CAO requires that a firm continually update information relating to sales, purchases, and inventory on hand. For example, for CAO to work well, a firm needs to provide information concerning breakage, shrinkage, and returns to vendors. Unreliable scanner data are viewed by 25 percent of the respondents as hindering further development of CAO. For example, register operators need to be trained not to run the multiple key for one scanned item when multiple flavors (selling for the same price) are purchased. For example, by incorrectly using the multiple key for one flavor of Jello gelatin dessert (raspberry) when seven different flavors were purchased, the raspberry flavor would be overordered while the other flavors would be underordered. Scanning data would also have to be adjusted to reflect new products and special promotional packaging (such as "buy one, get one free" deals) from manufacturers.
>
> CAO varies significantly in complexity. Some retailers are using simplistic systems such as "sell a case/ship a case" or to "simply replace what has been sold plus what is expected to be sold" before the actual delivery of the product. Some retailers do not believe that slow-moving or frequently promoted items do not belong in a CAO system.
>
> *Source:* Michael Garry, "Inventory Control: Moving Ahead," *Progressive Grocer* (January 1993), pp. 63 ff.

COMPUTER-AIDED ORDERING REPORTS

A marketer can use its inventory management system as the basis of computer-aided ordering. In **computer-aided ordering (CAO)**, the computer report determines the minimum in-stock inventory level for each product based on current sales patterns and vendor delivery times. The program prints purchase orders for items whose inventory level is below the minimum. Computer-aided ordering is ideal for products with predictable sales patterns, such as nonseasonal products, and for products with little fashion.[65] Computer-aided ordering enables firms to minimize inventory investment while reducing the chance of a stockout.

SUMMARY

1 *To study introductory topics in channel management, including the definition of market research, and the differences between market research in channels management and market research in other areas of marketing.* Market research consists of the systematic gathering, recording, and analyzing of relevant data to reduce uncertainty in marketing decision making.

The marketing research process in channels differs from the research process in other areas of marketing. In channels research, information is often interorganizational, a cooperative relationship often exists, data gathering is based on long-term commitments, and much data gathering is based on a census.

2 *To describe the market research process in channels management.* The market research process in channels management consists of six interrelated steps: defining the problem to be researched, examining secondary data, generating primary data, analyzing data, making recommendations, and implementing findings. Problem definition seeks to develop a clear statement of the topic to be studied. Secondary data consist of statistics that are gathered not for the immediate study at hand but for some other purpose. Secondary data can be internal or external. Primary data consist of information collected specifically for the purpose of the investigation at hand. Sources of primary data include surveys, observation, experimentation, and simulation. Data analysis consists of coding, tabulation, and data analysis. In the making recommendations for action stage, recommendations are made to management on the basis of the data that have been collected and analyzed. The last stage of the marketing research process, implementation of findings, reflects the use of the research findings in a manner most suitable for the firm.

3 *To illustrate introductory topics in marketing information systems, including the differences between market research and marketing information systems, the types of channel information systems, and the structure of a channel information system.* A marketing information system is an interactive, computer-based information system designed to assist with semistructured and unstructured management decisions.

There are major differences between marketing research and a marketing information system. Marketing research is often reactive; in contrast, a marketing information system is proactive. While marketing research is typically project-oriented, marketing information systems are continuous. In marketing research, data are collected and stored, often with no meaningful structure. In a marketing information system, data are stored in a manner to assist in better understanding behavior.

First-generation information systems consist of computerized information from a single source. The data in these systems are not combined with other related data to explain behavior. Second-generation information systems are characterized by the development of integrated marketing databases that combine data from commercial research firms with internal secondary data (such as sales, advertising, coupon redemption, and distribution effectiveness). Third-generation information systems extend the second-generation systems to use scanners to continuously record sales data.

The physical structure of a marketing information system consists of a database, display, model, and analysis. The database consists of internal and external secondary data (such as shipments, coupon redemptions, and distribution intensity). The display consists of traditional reports, graphics, in-paper, or in-screen formats. The model portion of the marketing information system consists of interrelationships among data that can be used for prediction. Analysis consists of manipulating data in order to better understand a marketing-related issue.

4 *To discuss special topics in channel information systems: the use of scanning-based data, electronic data interchange, database marketing, and channel information system reports.* The most common bar code symbol, and the generally accepted bar code for the retail industry, is the Universal Product Code (UPC), a 12-digit number used for merchandise identification down to the lowest level (color and size for apparel). Products that are similar but differ by either color, size, or label should receive a different UPC designation. The Universal Product Code is used in conjunction with electronic scanning, either hand-held or stationary laser-based devices that read and transmit UPC data as an item is passed over or by the scanner. Scanning a bar code can cause inventory to be debited or credited, or other actions.

Electronic data interchange (EDI) enables electronic transmission and exchange of standard format documents (such as product transfer and resale, purchase orders, order status, invoices, remittance advice, bills of lading, and advance shipping notices) among companies or a network of companies for the purpose of facilitating the flow of information through a channel. EDI cannot be used for unstructured documents such as business letters. EDI systems can be industry-wide or proprietary. EDI systems can also be direct or third-party networks. Advantages of the use of EDI can be classified as being direct, indirect, or strategic. The disadvantages of electronic data interchange involve use of batch processing, need to still use paper documents, lack of security when third-party processing is used, need for coordination between vendor and retailer, and high investment for hardware and software.

Database marketing is the creation and maintenance of a bank of information about individual customers (e.g., taken from orders, inquiries, and external lists), with the objective of analyzing consumer buying patterns and targeting promotions aimed at specific types of customers. Database marketing can be used as a means of communicating with individual customers as well as a marketing research tool. Among the benefits of database marketing over traditional marketing are addressability, measurability, flexibility, and accountability. A number of operational issues need to be resolved in properly maintaining a database. Databases must be continually maintained to be current. Different reporting sources may report inconsistent information about the same customer. There are also important issues relating to customer privacy.

Channel information system reports are often exception reports. These reports flag outstanding or significantly below planned performance and list these performance levels. Channel information system reports include sales reports, markdown reports, mailing lists, inventory management systems, and computer-aided ordering reports.

KEY TERMS

marketing research
downstream information
upstream information
internal information
census
problem definition
exploratory research
conclusive research
secondary data
internal secondary data
external secondary data
single-source data
all commodity volume (ACV)
percent category volume (PCV)
primary data
research design
sampling
probability-based sample
nonprobability sample
precision (sampling error)
survey
observation
natural observation
controlled observation
mechanical observation
human observation
experimentation
laboratory experiment
field experiment
experimental treatment
simulation
coding
tabulation
data analysis
third-generation information system (marketing decision support system)
first-generation information systems

second-generation information systems
database
display
model
analysis
Universal Product Code (UPC)
electronic scanning
electronic data interchange (EDI)
message formats
communications protocols
direct communication
third-party network
direct benefits
indirect benefits
strategic benefits
database marketing
exception reports
computer-aided ordering (CAO)

QUESTIONS FOR DISCUSSION

1. a. Describe the concept of relevant data in marketing research.
   b. How does the concept of relevant data relate to the problem definition stage of the marketing research process?
2. Differentiate between marketing research in channels management and market research in other areas of marketing.
3. Apply the market research process to a bicycle manufacturer that seeks to sell specialty bicycles (such as $500 French-made racing bicycles) via mail order. Focus separately on each stage of the process.
4. "Invoices have a broader range of applications than any other internal secondary data source." Explain this statement.
5. Describe the advantages and disadvantages of single-source data collection.
6. a. Discuss the advantages of primary data in comparison to secondary data.
   b. Describe the disadvantages of primary data in comparison to secondary data.
7. Under what circumstances should a channel member collect primary data through
   a. Observation?
   b. Experimentation?
   c. Simulation?
8. Contrast marketing research with marketing information systems.
9. Differentiate among first-, second-, and third-generation information systems.
10. Why do so many channel members rely on scanning-based data?
11. Describe the advantages and disadvantages of the use of electronic data interchange.
12. Distinguish among direct benefits, indirect benefits, and strategic benefits to the use of electronic data interchange.
13. a. Contrast exception reports with traditional reports.
    b. Develop an exception report for a sales reporting system.
14. Discuss the benefits and risks to computer-aided ordering reports.

END NOTES

1. Dan Fost, "Frito Lay's Adds High Tech Crunch," *American Demographics* (March 1991), pp. 18–20; and Peter H. Lewis, "Looking Beyond Innovation, an Award for Results," *New York Times* (June 23, 1991), p. F8.

2. Rashi Glaser, "Marketing in an Information-Intensive Environment: Strategic Implications of Knowledge as an Asset," *Journal of Marketing*, Vol. 55 (October 1991), p. 4.

3. See Gerrit K. Janssens and Ludo Cuyvers, "EDI—A Strategic Weapon in International Trade," *Long Range Planning*, Vol. 24 (April 1991), p. 46.

4. Peter D. Bennett, ed., *Dictionary of Marketing Terms*, Second Edition (Chicago: American Marketing Association, 1995), p. 257.

5. An excellent annotated bibliography of external secondary sources is Lorna M. Daniells, *Business Information Sources* (Berkeley and Los Angeles: University of California Press, 1993).

6. See Scott Hume, "Scanner Research Snared in Discounting Web," *Advertising Age* (June 11, 1990), p. S10.

7. See Bill Carter, ". . . And Arbitron Tries to Track Buying Habits," *New York Times* (November 4, 1991), p. 8; Jack Honomichl, "Top 50 Research Firms Profiled," *Marketing News* (May 27, 1991), p. H2; Howard Schlossberg, "IRI Expands Tracking to Drugstores, Mass Merchandisers," *Marketing News* (May 27, 1991), pp. 1, 10; and Howard Schlossberg, "IRI, Nielsen Slug It Out in 'Scanning Wars'," *Marketing News* (September 9, 1991), pp. 1, 47.

8. George Shababb, "To Understand Consumers: Start at Home," *Progressive Grocer Executive Report: Part II* (January 1994), pp. n–4—n–5.

9. James M. Olver and Paul W. Farris, "Push and Pull: A One-Two Punch for Packaged Goods," *Sloan Management Review*, Vol. 37 (Fall 1989), p. 54.

10. See Henry Assael and David F. Poltrack, "Using Single Source Data to Select TV Programs Based on Purchasing Behavior," *Journal of Advertising Research*, Vol. 31 (August–September 1991), p. 10.

11. See Michael W. Miller, "Citicorp Creates Controversy with Plan to Sell Data on Credit-Card Purchases," *Wall Street Journal* (August 21, 1991), pp. B1, B7.

12. Bennett, *Dictionary of Marketing Terms*, p. 216.

13. Peter D. Bennett, ed., *Dictionary of Marketing Terms* (Chicago: American Marketing Association, 1988), p. 172.

14. Alan J. Greco and Jack T. Hogue, "Developing Marketing Decision Support Systems," *Journal of Business and Industrial Marketing*, Vol. 5 (Summer/Fall 1990), p. 28.

15. Ibid., p. 28.

16. See Thayer C. Taylor, "Strategic Information Systems for Marketing," *Sales & Marketing Management* (July 1990), p. 90.

17. Tom Eisenhart, "After 10 Years of Marketing Decision Support Systems: Where's the Payoff?" *Business Marketing* (June 1990), p. 46.

18. See Greco and Hogue, "Developing Marketing Decision Support Systems," pp. 28–30; and John D.C. Little and Peter Guadagni, "Making Scanner Data Work for Marketing Management," in *1988 American Marketing Educators' Proceedings*, Gary Frazier, Charles Ingene, and David Aaker et al., eds. (Chicago: American Marketing Association, 1988), p. 327.

19. See William M. Bulkeley, "Databases Are Plagued by Reign of Error," *New York Times* (May 26, 1992), p. B6.

20. Penny Gill, "QR Keeps Jeans Moving," *Stores* (February 1991), pp. 23–24.

21. "Quick Response Grows," *Chain Store Age* (May 1993), p. 158.

22. See "Quick Response Technologies," *Chain Store Age Executive* (March 1991), p. 6B.

23. See "East Meets West in Minnesota," *Chain Store Age Executive* (June 1990), p. 76.

24. Susan Avery, "Bar Codes Take Off from Factory Floor," *Purchasing* (November 7, 1991), p. 52.

25. Clifford J. Levy, "A Product Code Leaves the Straight and Narrow," *New York Times* (November 16, 1993), p. D4.

26. "Quick Response Grows," p. 160.

27. "Two Decades On, Scanners Are Still Under-Used," *Progressive Grocer* (July 1994), p. S5.

28. "Quick Response Technologies," *Chain Store Age Executive* (March 1991), p. 6B; and "Barcoding Continues Gains: Scanning Greatest among Mass Merchants," *Chain Store Age Executive* (May 1991), p. 159.

29. Howard Schlossberg, "Scanning Improvements Introduced: IRI, Nielsen Services Designed to Increase First-Pass Efficiency," *Marketing News* (February 17, 1992), p. 1; and *Information Resources Inc. 1991 Annual Report,* p. 42.

30. *Information Resources Inc. 1991 Annual Report,* p. 42.

31. Richard Halverson, "Wal-Mart Cracks Down on UPC Errors," *Discount Store News* (July 8, 1991), pp. 1, 42.

32. See Brian Dearing, "The Strategic Benefits of EDI," *Journal of Business Strategy* (January–February 1990), p. 4.

33. Bill Stack, "Small Firms Can Reap Huge Gains with Electronic Data Interchange," *Marketing News* (April 1, 1991), p. 14.

34. "Quick Response Grows," p. 160.

35. Francine Schwadel and Damon Darlin, "Retailers Hope for 2nd Half Recovery But Plan for Less-Than-Robust Sales," *New York Times* (May 8, 1992), p. A2.

36. Brenton R. Schlender, "How Levi Strauss Did an LBO Right," *Fortune* (May 7, 1990), p. 106.

37. *Fifth Annual Bar Code/EDI/Quick Response Survey Results* (New York: National Retail Federation, 1992), p. 10.

38. *Uniform Communication Standard (UCS) and the Food Broker* (Washington, D.C.: National Food Brokers Association, n.d.), p. 2.

39. Tamala L. Barrier and Michael Morris, "Industrial Marketing Implications of Electronic Data Exchange," in *1987 American Marketing Association Educators' Proceedings,* Susan P. Douglas, Michael P. Solomon, and Vijah Maharajan et al., eds. (Chicago: American Marketing Association, 1987), p. 35.

40. "EDI and Quick Response: Easy Money," *Chain Store Age Executive* (March 1991), p. 20B.

41. "Quick Response: The Right Thing," *Chain Store Age Executive* (March 1990), p. 50.

42. *Fifth Annual Bar Code/EDI/Quick Response Survey Results,* p. 10.

43. Dearing, "The Strategic Benefits of EDI," p. 4.

44. Janssens and Cuyvers, "EDI—A Strategic Weapon in International Trade," p. 51.

45. Denise Zimmerman, "Study Tracks Savings from EDI, Two Pilots," *Supermarket News* (January 16, 1995), p. 33.

46. Dearing, "The Strategic Benefits of EDI," p. 5.

47. Ibid.

48. Ramon O'Callaghan, Patrick J. Kaufmann, and Benn R. Konsynski, "Adoption Correlates and Share Effects of Electronic Data Interchange Systems in Marketing Channels," *Journal of Marketing,* Vol. 56 (April 1992), p. 46.

49. Ibid., pp. 51–52.

50. Robert Shaw and Merlin Stone, *Database Marketing: Strategy and Implementation* (New York: John Wiley and Sons, 1990), p. 4.

51. Terry G. Vavra, "The Database Marketing Imperative," *Marketing Management,* Vol. 2, No. 1 (1993), p. 48.

52. Gary Levin, "'Keeping in Touch' Easy with Database," *Advertising Age* (March 28, 1994), p. S–8.

53. Jeffrey D. Zbar, "Blockbuster's Database to Fuel Future Expansion," *Advertising Age* (July 18, 1994), p. 26.

54. Vavra, "The Database Marketing Imperative," p. 48.

55. See Phyllis Ezop, "Database Marketing Research," *Marketing Research,* Vol. 6 (Fall 1994), pp. 35–41.

56. "It's Not As Easy As It Looks," *Chain Store Age Executive* (August 1991), p. 52.

57. William C. Moncrief III, Charles W. Lamb, Jr., and Jane M. Mackay, "Laptop Computers in Industrial Sales," *Industrial Marketing Management,* Vol. 20 (November 1991), p. 283.

58. Nicholas Nickolaus, "Marketing New Products with Industrial Distributors," *Industrial Marketing Management,* Vol. 19 (November 1990), p. 290.

59. Jaclyn Fierman, "The Death and Rebirth of the Salesman," *Fortune* (July 25, 1994), p. 88.

60. Susan Caminiti, "If It's Hot, They've Got It," *Fortune* (June 3, 1991), p. 103.

61. See Shaw and Stone, *Database Marketing: Strategy and Implementation,* p. 90.

62. Cyndee Miller, "Sylvania Targets Brightest Prospects with 'Prestige Partnership' Marketing," *Marketing News* (March 4, 1991), p. 12.

63. Fleming Meeks, "Preserving the Magic," *Forbes* (February 18, 1991), pp. 60–61.

64. Stephanie Strom, "Computerized Record-Keeping for Retailers," *New York Times* (May 20, 1992), p. D6.

65. For difficulties with implementing automatic reordering systems, see Warren Thayer, "Computer-Aided Ordering is Ready . . . Should You Care?" *Progressive Grocer* (March 1991), pp. 81–84.

CASE 1

INFOSCAN: SINGLE-SOURCE DATA

InfoScan is a national scanning service that is owned by Information Resources Inc. (IRI). InfoScan is the leading source of single-source data; it also has the largest base of panelists in the single-source data collection and analysis industry. InfoScan is currently sold to about 740 U.S. clients.

InfoScan evaluates the sales of 2.5 million UPC-coded products sold in a nationwide sample of 2700 supermarkets, 500 drug stores, and 250 mass merchandisers through tracking consumer purchases of some 60,000 nationally projectable households. As of 1991, InfoScan also began to include drug store and mass merchandisers. InfoScan enables a manufacturer, wholesaler, or retailer to monitor sales of a product, a brand, a store merchandise category, a chain, a market, a region, or the total U.S. market. InfoScan estimates that it gathers 100 million new records each week.

InfoScan collects and integrates four types of data: retail store sales, consumer purchases, retail and consumer promotion, and television viewing. These data are recorded and distributed on a weekly basis.

Data are collected on retail store sales based on scanners located in thousands of retail grocery stores, convenience stores, drug stores, and mass merchandisers. Each panelist is provided with an identification card that is presented to the store's cashier (so that data can be collected at checkout). Their purchases are automatically recorded and identified by individual household. This passive data collection results in a higher participation rate (with a 40 percent cooperation rate) than in-home wand and paper diaries (with a 10 percent cooperation rate). Since electronic scanners track sales, reporting errors and self-reporting biases are also eliminated.

IRI's field staff monitors all UPCs in each InfoScan store and market on a weekly basis. Important retail and consumer promotion data (such as the average number of units per display, space allocated to specific sections, and number of shelf facings) are monitored. Users can then match in-store merchandising conditions (price reductions, features, and displays) and couponing activity to their retail and consumer data. Each household is also monitored for television viewing; meters automatically record a television set's status every five seconds. Television advertising effectiveness can then be linked to purchases of a given brand.

Table 1 outlines data available from Information Resources Inc. These data are available as hard copy, on magnetic tape, and on PC diskette.

As of 1991, InfoScan added a national sample of drug store chains (including a sample of stores from each of the top 10 drug store chains, such as Walgreen's, Osco, Eckerd, Rite Aid, and Thrifty) as well as stores from the leading deep discounters and wholesalers such as F&M, Drug Emporium, Hooks-Super X, and Bergen Brunswig. Mass merchandisers added to the sample include Wal-Mart, Kmart, and Target. The addition of drug store and mass merchandiser coverage opens up added marketing information for health and beauty aid marketers such as Bristol-Myers, Clairol Inc., and Johnson & Johnson/Merck.

An important element of InfoScan's service is its Distribution Opportunity Report. This report shows for paired items (yours and competitors) the current ACV distribution for each paired item as well as the dollar sales rate for each brand. On a market and chain level, competitive products (defined by the manufacturer as being competitive) with high distribution but a low sales rate are paired with the manufacturer's like products, which have lower distribution but a higher sales rate. On the basis of chain and market data, the system then calculates the annual sales impact, for both the retailer and manufacturer, of delisting the competitive product and authorizing the manufacturer's product.

TABLE 1 DATA AVAILABLE FROM INFOSCAN

Variable	Specific Measures
Volume	• Volume/Share • Base Volume/Share (everyday movement achieved outside the influence of trade promotion) • Incremental Volume/Share from Promotion Activity (additional sales due to promotional activity)
Price	• Average Price (average price good is sold at in each market area) • Merchandised Price (deal price) • Regular Everyday Shelf Price (nonsale price) • Percent Price Reduction
Distribution	• Percent All Commodity Volume (ACV) Selling • Sales Rate per Million ACV • Base/Incremental Sales per Million ACV (outside the influence of trade promotion)
In-store merchandising	• Percent ACV with Price Reduction Only • Incremental Volume Due to Price-Reduction Activity • Features by Size: A,B,C (existence of large advertisements and/or displays for each product) • Displays by Location • Features and Displays
Couponing	• Circulation • Average Value

Source: InfoScan (Chicago: Information Resources Inc., 1990), p. 4.

QUESTIONS

1. Describe the advantages of single-source data collection over traditional forms.
2. Describe the disadvantages of single-source data collection.
3. Discuss how a retailer could use the Distribution Intensity Report. Refer to Table 7-8.
4. Describe how a manufacturer could use single-source data to convince a retailer to stock its products.

Source: Richard Gibson, "Amid Share Slump, Market Researcher Plays 'Patch-Up'," *Wall Street Journal* (April 25, 1994), p. B4; and *InfoScan* (Chicago: Information Resources Inc., 1990), p. 4.

CASE 2

KMART'S USE OF CHANNEL INFORMATION SYSTEMS

According to Kmart's chairman and president, "... after store modernization, technology is probably the second most important building block to improve profitability and market share." As of 1991, Kmart completed installation of point-of-sales scanning and satellite communication systems in all its stores. This enables Kmart to begin to develop a chainwide automatic reordering program and to phase in just-in-time inventory management.

Over 75 percent of Kmart's merchandise is now ordered through EDI purchase orders and invoices and is received in just-in-time deliveries. EDI has been instrumental in Kmart's being able to get much of its merchandise within two days of ordering.

Kmart is also finishing implementing its Kmart Information Network II (KIN II) information system project. This system

- Monitors sales and develops reports to spot important emerging trends. Through this system, merchandisers can fine tune purchases and plan markdowns. KIN II has been used to predict how "hot" a fad (such as Teenage Mutant Ninja Turtles towels) will be.
- Monitors and reorders merchandise by evaluating inventory levels. The new system assigns products to stores based on actual sales of the same or similar items, with consideration to such variables as time period and price level. For example, the system is able to retrieve data on the sales of comparable units on a store-by-store basis for purchase planning. Retail buyers are able to use their data to adjust inventory requirements on a store-by-store basis. The system is then able to process the orders.
- Tracks store traffic.
- Evaluates personnel.
- Prints in-store display signs, black and white shelf labels, UPC merchandise tags, and store signs (up to 8½ by 11 inches).
- Receives batch orders from stores and transmits the orders to Kmart's distribution centers.
- Records charge transactions.
- Verifies shelf prices.
- Handles inquiries about the availability of goods.
- Assists in inventory ordering.

Kmart relies heavily on scanning data to make better use of its shelf space, to efficiently process its immense database, and to accurately buy seasonal merchandise. It is also studying the use of scanning data to customize shelf sets for individual stores. According to Dave Carlson, Kmart's senior vice president of corporate information systems, "We do use individual store scan data to determine, for example, what amount of product goes into a store to support an ad or for a seasonal sales period. So when we decide how many 3-foot-high Santa Clauses at $49 go into a particular store at Christmas time, it will be based on information collected at that store."

One of Kmart's biggest information challenges is seasonal planning. According to Dave Carlson, "Mass merchants do a lot of business in support of particular seasons. Medium-priced Christmas ornaments carry good margins and aren't in stores long; if you make a good buying decision, the return on investment can be quite extraordinary. If you do a bad job, you carry over a substantial inventory and face markdowns. This is one of the richest areas for use of scan data and all of us are working on it."

In a test of its ability to effectively plan inventory levels, Kmart management compared the inventory levels recommended by both the new system and the old manual method for the peak Christmas selling season in two departments. While the old system recommended well over $50 million in inventory, the new system recommended only one-third as much. Using the new system recommendation, Kmart experienced no significant shortages of merchandise.

QUESTIONS

1. Describe the advantages of using scanner data for Kmart.
2. Discuss the disadvantages of using scanner data for Kmart.
3. What types of marketing information system reports can Kmart generate through scanning?
4. Explain the advantages to Kmart of using KIN II for computer-aided ordering.

Sources: Jeffrey Arlen, "Cyber Trust: Will It Work?" *Discount Store News* (June 20, 1994), pp. A11–A13; Bruce Fox, "Kmart Tackles Distribution with 'Clas'," *Chain Store Age Executive* (January 1991), pp. 60–61 ff.; "Retail Technology Charges Up Kmart," *Discount Store News* (February 17, 1992), pp. 121–122; and Warren Thayer, "The View for Kmart: Grocers Are Still Catching Up," *Progressive Grocer* (August 1990), pp. 147–148.

CHAPTER 8

PRODUCT MANAGEMENT STRATEGY IN CHANNELS

CHAPTER OBJECTIVES

1. To discuss the channel management implications of the new product planning process.

2. To discuss the channel management implications of the product life cycle concept.

3. To describe reverse channels: product recall and product recycling.

4. To analyze the channel management implications of packaging.

5. To study the legal aspects of product management relating to channels: exclusive dealing, tying arrangements, full-line forcing, reciprocity, refusal to deal, private-label strategy, and slotting allowances.

In a 1992 landmark case, the Supreme Court ruled that Kodak must stand trial in an important antitrust case. Eighteen independent service companies sued Kodak, alleging that Kodak illegally refused to sell them replacement parts for Kodak's photocopy and microfiche machines. The service firms alleged that Kodak attempted to monopolize the market for services by tying the sales of service for its machines to the sale of parts. Tying agreements are illegal according to the Sherman Antitrust Act if a seller possesses high economic power in the market for one of the goods (such as replacement parts) to force the buyer to purchase another product (service). This decision is in marked contrast to other recent Supreme Court cases that have given manufacturers greater control in the distribution and repair of their products.

While Kodak controls nearly the entire market for its replacement parts (these are not interchangeable with parts from other companies' machines) and between 80 to 95 percent of the service market for its machines, its market share in the high-volume copier and microfiche market is only 20 percent. As in all antitrust lawsuits, the affected parties are seeking triple damages.

Prior to 1985, Kodak sold replacement parts for its equipment without significant restrictions to independent service firms and large customers with their own service personnel. In 1985, Kodak shifted its policy and refused to sell replacement parts to customers unless they promised not to have their equipment serviced by independent firms. Kodak also stopped selling parts to the independent service firms. To get around Kodak's refusal to sell parts to them, independent service organizations, posed as customers, bought cloned parts from foreign firms or purchased parts from Kodak copier dealers. Some Kodak copier dealers have sold these parts, even though they are required to sign agreements promising not to resell the parts.

Kodak argued that it needs to prevent independents from "freeriding" on its investments. It also stated that its low market share prevents it from exercising market power. Kodak alleges that if it overcharged for repairs, its consumers would stop buying Kodak equipment. It also suggested that it wants its customers to receive a higher level of service than the independent service providers could achieve.

The outcome of this case will affect the ability of independent service organizations in all fields (such as computer, auto repair, and consumer electronics) to compete for replacement parts and service business with the product's manufacturer. The Supreme Court ruling also generates a warning for manufacturers that seek to control the market for repair services and replacement parts. For example, the Auto Service Industry Association is concerned about the "recent push [by big manufacturers] to restrict sales" of car parts. This action affects the 5000 manufacturers of replacement parts, 26,000 wholesale distributors, and thousands of repair garages and supply stores. One estimate of the size of the aftermarket in service and replacement parts for all products is $100 billion a year. The case also threatens manufacturers' ability to expect sales revenues and profits from equipment servicing. About 30 percent of the photocopier's $18 billion annual revenues comes from service contracts. Some analysts estimate that large computer manufacturers have gross profit margins of 40 percent to 50 percent on servicing.[1]

In this chapter, we explore the impact of product management strategy on channels. In addition to legal questions such as tying agreements, the chapter examines channel management implications of the product life cycle concept, reverse channels (such as product recall and product recycling), and channel management implications of packaging.

OVERVIEW OF PRODUCT MANAGEMENT STRATEGY IN CHANNELS

This chapter describes channel implications of a firm's product management strategy. Among the topics covered are the new product planning process, the product life cycle, reverse channels (product recall and product recycling), packaging, and legal aspects.

Although these topics are treated separately, they are interrelated. For example, a channel member can increase the proportion of recycled goods through effective new product planning. Much of the waste of raw materials can also be reduced by proper packaging decisions. These interrelationships are discussed in this chapter.

The channel implications of a firm's product management strategy are covered in a sequential manner beginning with the new product planning process, then going to the product life cycle concept, and finally ending with product recall and product recycling. The fourth area covered is channel management implications of packaging. Lastly, the legal aspects of product management relating to channels packaging are analyzed.

NEW PRODUCT PLANNING PROCESS AND CHANNEL MANAGEMENT

The **new product planning process** describes the series of steps undertaken by a manufacturer in introducing a new product. These steps typically include idea generation, product screening, concept testing, business analysis, product development, test marketing, and commercialization.

Channel members are important participants in the new product planning process:

- Manufacturers can secure new product ideas from other channel members. Wholesalers and retailers can be used to evaluate a new product concept. They can also forecast a new product's potential sales.

- In evaluating new product alternatives, manufacturers need to consider the channel overlap of the firm's new products with its existing products.
- A manufacturer needs channel member cooperation in test marketing. Test marketing is used to measure a new product's sales potential as well as a channel member's willingness to stock and display the new product.

USE CHANNEL MEMBERS TO GENERATE NEW PRODUCT IDEAS AND TO EVALUATE NEW PRODUCT CONCEPTS

Often channel members (such as suppliers, wholesalers, retailers, and key personnel such as retail buyers or a wholesaler's salespersons) are used by manufacturers to generate new product ideas and to evaluate potential product candidates. These channel members are used to generate and evaluate new product ideas because

- They are closer to the market than manufacturers. They are exposed to customer objections, comments, and concerns on a first-hand and continuous basis. They are also in an ideal position to comment on competitor offerings.
- Channel member support may be essential for the success of a new product. Channel members function as purchasing agents for their customers. Without their stocking a new product, the product would be inaccessible to consumers. Channel members can also encourage or discourage potential buyers from purchasing new products on the basis of their comments.
- Many channel members are likely to give an honest response, not what a manufacturer would want to hear. For example, in franchising and in exclusive distribution arrangements, the success of the manufacturer and that of its wholesalers and retailers are intertwined. A successful new product would benefit all channel members. A new product failure, on the other hand, would have a detrimental impact on the wholesalers and retailers as well as the manufacturer.
- Suppliers of parts may have greater expertise in designing a new product than their customers. Since suppliers can sell parts to multiple manufacturers, they can transfer knowledge among their customers. In addition, the use of suppliers to develop new products reduces its customers' engineering costs.

Many of McDonald's new products such as the Big Mac and the Egg McMuffin came from its franchisees. Black & Decker developed a new reciprocating saw on the basis of the recommendation of a Black & Decker power tool distributor. Weldon Tool Company, a manufacturer of cutting tools, entered the glazing and auto body market with a tool requested by a distributor.[2] Whirlpool uses Eaton Corporation, a supplier, to design the burner system for its gas ranges. And

Intermodal transportation is generally used in conjunction with containers, rail flat cars, and trailers. (Chapter 6) Courtesy CSX Corporation.

Containers and trailers are being loaded at Santa Fe's intermodal facilities. (Chapter 6) Photo by ATSF Railway Company.

Nicor's Tropical Shipping division consolidates small shipments at this warehouse for delivery to the 22 ports it serves. (Chapter 6) Photographer: Mark Joseph, Chicago.

This bar code has a total of ten digits. The first five of these numbers refer to the manufacturer's code; the last five numbers specify a unique product designation. (Chapter 7) Courtesy of Symbol Technologies, Inc.

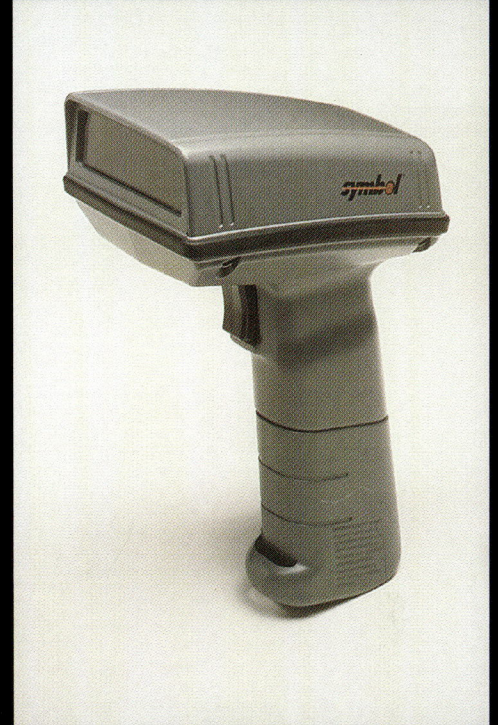

This hand-held bar code scanner uses a laser beam to read the bar code. The scanner reads the black bars of the bar code as zeros; the white spaces are read as ones. (Chapter 7) Courtesy of Symbol Technologies, Inc.

James River produces its own premium quality recycled fiber using a new K-1 paperboard machine. This machine has an annual capacity to produce 200,000 tons of 100 percent recycled coated paperboard. (Chapter 8) Courtesy James River Corporation.

Sales demonstrators for S-B Power Tool Company are shown explaining the features and benefits of their power tools to final consumers and contractors at hardware stores and home centers. Sales demonstrators provide a valuable service for both retailers and their consumers. (Chapter 10) Photo courtesy of Emerson Electric.

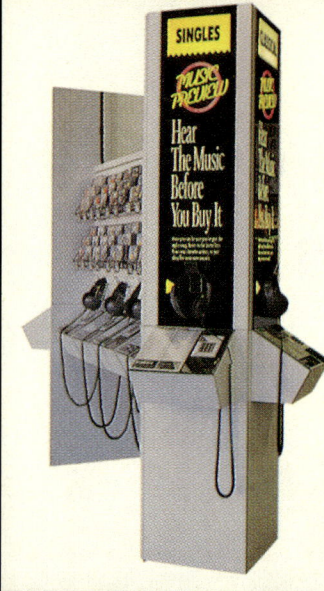

At Coconuts, a Music Preview station enables customers to preview hundreds of songs. (Chapter 13) Courtesy Trans World Entertainment Corporation.

Chrysler uses its suppliers to design everything from car seats to drive shafts.[3] Channel members may also suggest new markets for existing products.

STUDY THE FIT OF EXISTING CHANNELS FOR NEW PRODUCTS

A manufacturer must study the fit of existing channels for new products. There are two dimensions of channel fit: functional fit and channel overlap. **Functional fit** deals with assessing the ability of existing channels to store, sell, repair, and service a new product. For example, a new product may require special warehousing, continuing maintenance, and special installation. This is especially important when the new product is technologically different from existing products (see Table 8-1).

Channel overlap refers to the extent to which two or more products share distribution channels (see Figure 8-1). A high channel overlap of a new product with existing products is a significant advantage for a new product:

- The incremental costs of adding a new product with high channel overlap with existing products is small.
- High channel overlap means that the manufacturer or wholesaler already has a relationship with its customers. Positive relationships from past transactions can carry over to the new product.
- With high channel overlap, a wholesaler or retailer may be eligible for additional discounts owing to purchasing larger quantities or through cooperative advertising allowances.

TABLE 8-1 A FUNCTIONAL FIT CHECKLIST

Can existing resellers store a proposed new product in terms of
- Size of warehouse?
- Perishability of good?
- Concern for protection of good from theft?

Can existing resellers properly sell goods in terms of
- Overall sales ability?
- Overall technical knowledge?
- Market knowledge?
- Awareness of competitive offerings?
- Knowledge of our company's competitive advantages?

Can existing resellers properly repair products in terms of
- Ability to stock replacement parts?
- Training of technicians?
- Availability of diagnostic equipment?

Can existing resellers properly service accounts in terms of
- Experience with specialized target market?
- Knowledge of special needs of individual customers?
- Closeness of existing warehouse facilities to customers?

FIGURE 8-1 Illustration of channel overlap.

NO CHANNEL OVERLAP

Distribution channels for existing products	Ideal Distribution channels for proposed product
Conventional supermarket Superstore Combination store	Buying club Cash-and-carry wholesaler

HIGH CHANNEL OVERLAP

Distribution channels for existing products	Ideal Distribution channels for proposed product
Conventional supermarket Superstore Combination store	Conventional supermarket Superstore Combination store

- Many wholesalers and retailers prefer to deal with one supplier. Fewer sources enable wholesalers and retailers to reduce order costs, and to have single-source accountability in the event of compatibility problems.
- High channel overlap saves a manufacturer the expense of seeking out and evaluating alternative wholesalers and retailers.

The advantages of high channel overlap can exist even when the product's use differs from that of the firm's existing products or when the product's technology differs. For example, Kodak has high channel overlap between its battery and film sales owing to common retail institutions that sell both products. Baxter International sells products to hospitals ranging from needle-free syringes for drawing fluids to a new disposable bedpan liner (made from recycled telephone books). Although Baxter International produces about 70 percent of the products it sells, it is also Johnson & Johnson's largest customer of hospital supplies. Among the major benefits of high channel overlap among Baxter's products is the desire of hospital purchasing agents to deal with as few salespeople as possible.[4]

Manufacturers need to be aware that a new product may have low channel overlap with a firm's previous products despite a common use. For example, market analysts are concerned about possible distribution outlets for a new light bulb, designated as the E-lamp (for electronic lamp). The bulb will sell at $12 to $15 each and last up to 14 years. According to the president of Intersource Technologies, the lamp's inventor, the E-Lamp was "not a disposable good, but a durable good, like an appliance."[5] The high price of the bulb and its long life span may make the product unacceptable to those retailers who currently sell bulbs for home use. On the other hand, analysts expect brisk sales in wholesalers that sell maintenance supplies and equipment to factories, hotels, and office buildings, for these businesses would save lamp replacement costs as well as energy costs.[6]

SECURE CHANNEL COOPERATION IN TEST MARKETING

In **test marketing**, a manufacturer places a new or modified product for sale in one or more cities to observe sales performance under a given marketing plan. The objectives of test marketing relate to acceptance of the new or revised product by both final and intermediate consumers. Appropriate objectives among final consumers are to determine initial sales, repeat sales, the impact of sales of the new product on the firm's existing products, and competitive positioning. Appropriate objectives of test marketing among intermediate consumers relate to their willingness to initially stock a product, to continue to stock the product beyond an initial period, to set up and maintain displays, and to provide the product with a given number of **shelf facings** (columns of the same product displayed on a shelf). On the basis of test marketing, a firm can determine its distribution intensity in terms of its percentage of all commodity volume (ACV) in a given merchandise category in the test market.

Manufacturers also need the cooperation of intermediaries in determining the response of competitors to the test market in terms of coupon offers, price reductions, and increased promotions. Channel cooperation is also needed to determine buyer attributes, the products considered by buyers as direct substitutes for new products, and buyer objections to the new product.

CHANNEL MANAGEMENT IMPLICATIONS OF THE PRODUCT LIFE CYCLE CONCEPT

The **product life cycle** describes the stages in the history of a product: introduction, growth, maturity, and decline. The product life cycle concept was first popularized by Theodore Levitt in a classic article in 1965.[7] The product life cycle concept has been used to explain a product's marketing objectives, competition, industry profits, appropriate target market, and marketing strategy as it moves from the introduction through the decline stages. Figure 8-2 illustrates a traditional product life cycle curve.

The product life concept is a useful framework for channel members:

- A manufacturer must realize that different channel strategies are required at each stage of the product life cycle. For example, many new products have difficulty getting access to appropriate distribution channels in the introduction stage. In contrast, there is a need to limit sales to channel members in the decline stage. The amount of distributor training also varies depending on the life cycle stage.

- Wholesaler and retailer strategies also differ by product life cycle stage. For example, the need for customer training and assistance, the type of customer, and the extent of price competition are based on the product life cycle stage.

FIGURE 8-2 The traditional product life cycle curve.

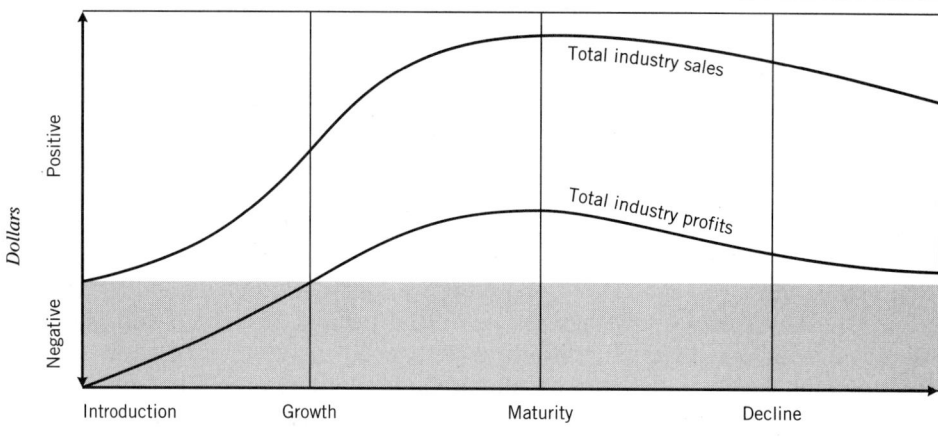

Characteristics of each stage

	Introduction	Growth	Maturity	Decline
Sales growth	Low	High	Sales peak	Negative growth in sales
Company profits	Negative profits	Positive	Profits plateau	Profits decline from prior levels
Industry profits	Negative profits	Positive	Begin to decline	Profits decline from prior levels
Competition	Little or no competition	Competition begins to emerge	Highest degree of competition	Competition declines as weak firms drop out from market

- Wholesalers and retailers control the diffusion of new products in their roles as gatekeepers (by controlling the availability of new products) and change agents (by influencing the purchasing decisions of intermediate and final customers).
- Wholesalers and retailers face a derived demand situation. Distributor sales growth is dependent on the sales growth of the products they sell. An effective channel member needs to evaluate its product mix by the percentage of products in each product life cycle stage.

The role of channel members in each product life cycle stage is summarized in Table 8-2.

Although the product life cycle concept has received some criticism, it is a good means of describing appropriate channel strategies under different envi-

TABLE 8-2 APPROPRIATE CHANNEL STRATEGIES IN EACH PRODUCT LIFE CYCLE STAGE

Product Life Cycle Stage	Appropriate Channel Strategy
New product planning process	• Use channel members to generate new product ideas and to evaluate new product concepts. • Study the fit of existing channels for new products. • Secure channel cooperation in test marketing.
Introduction	• Evaluate the role of wholesalers and retailers in the diffusion of new products. • Obtain channel cooperation in stocking new products. • Determine channel member criteria in selecting new products. • Study the differences in success among channel members in the marketing of new products.
Growth	• Reevaluate market coverage. • Reevaluate the appropriateness of channels.
Maturity	• Reevaluate market coverage. • Increase dealer enthusiasm and shelf space allocation. • Evaluate a private-label strategy. • Appeal to new market segments.
Decline	• Reduce the number of channel members. • Discontinue product and distribution outlets. • Develop new products and a new distribution strategy.

ronments. In response to criticisms of the product life cycle, channel members need to realize that a channel member can manage a product to prolong the growth and maturity stages, and to fight off the decline stage. A channel manager also needs to be aware that the decline stage is not inevitable. The product life cycle can be managed through an effective channel and overall marketing strategy. (The product life cycle concept is evaluated in the last part of this section.)

INTRODUCTION STAGE

The **introduction stage** of the product life cycle corresponds to a product's commercialization and its intended sale to its full target market. This stage is characterized by increasing industry sales and little or no industrywide competition for the new product. During the introduction stage, a manufacturer generally loses money owing to low initial sales, high marketing costs, and high production costs (there are no economies of scale). Often there is difficulty in getting adequate distribution for the new product. In many instances, much promotional effort needs to be directed at initial distributors to encourage them to stock the product in sufficient quantities.

A manufacturer's overall channel strategy in the introduction stage is to build a sufficient distribution network to satisfy early demand and to provide high levels of intermediate and final customer assistance. Depending on the product, this may also involve customer training and high levels of technical service.

This section describes the following activities of channel members in the introduction stage:

- The role of wholesalers and retailers in the diffusion of new products.
- Channel criteria in stocking new products.
- The need for channel cooperation in stocking new products.
- Differences in success in marketing new products among distributors.

EVALUATE THE ROLE OF WHOLESALERS AND RETAILERS IN THE DIFFUSION OF NEW PRODUCTS

An important concept in understanding the product life cycle concept is the diffusion process. The **diffusion process** explains the manner in which different members of a population purchase a new product. This process covers the entire product life cycle from product introduction to product decline.

Wholesalers and retailers influence consumer diffusion of new products in their dual roles as gatekeeper and change agent. Channel members function as **gatekeepers** by controlling the availability of new products and the physical flow of goods to the consumer. As a gatekeeper, these channel members pre-select products that will ultimately be available to consumers. As a gatekeeper, wholesalers and retailers may limit the size of the potential consumer market based on the availability of a given good in various geographic and end-use markets.

In their role as **change agents**, wholesalers and retailers attempt to influence the purchase decisions of intermediate and final consumers. As a change agent, wholesalers and retailers interpret the needs and desires of their organizational and final customers. Innovative wholesalers and retailers can also serve as opinion leaders for more conservative intermediaries.[8]

Research on the new product diffusion process based on a study of consumer electronics retailers found that there are two types of retailers: scouts (innovators) and troops (followers). The classification is based on the extent to which one retailer influences others. **Scouts** are the first retailers to adopt a new product. They are likely to try a new product or commit themselves to a new product through a small order. On the other hand, **troops** purchase a product only when scouts experience satisfactory sales levels. If scouts turn up negative signs such as poor sales, troops back off in making purchase commitments. As a consequence, distribution may fall to a very low level. Figure 8-3 shows typical diffusion patterns for retailers for a successful and an unsuccessful innovation. Note the sharp dropoff in sales for the unsuccessful innovation shortly after being adopted by troops. In contrast, the successful innovation has high sales volume during the same time period.

FIGURE 8-3 Typical retailer diffusion patterns.

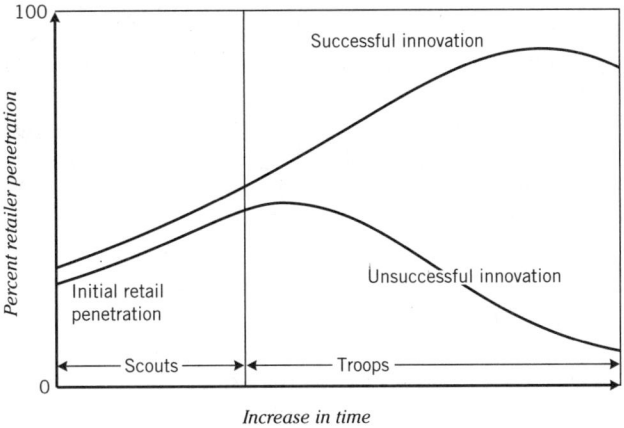

Source: J. Morgan Jones and Charlotte H. Mason, *The Role of Distribution in the Diffusion of New Durable Consumer Products* (Cambridge, Mass.: Marketing Science Institute, 1990), p. 9. Reprinted by permission.

According to this scout-troop concept, the speed of the product life cycle is dependent on the early success of the products by scouts. Early success by scouts will lead to quick growth due to copying by troops. Similarly, early failure signifies that the product's future is limited. Scouts and troops each tend to evaluate products on the basis of different criteria.

DETERMINE CHANNEL MEMBER CRITERIA IN SELECTING NEW PRODUCTS

A study of new product-adoption decisions among consumer electronic retailers found that scouts use different criteria in selecting new products than troops. Scouts are more likely to evaluate a new product's potential to generate store traffic, a manufacturer's reputation, the fit with a customer's needs, and desire to have a complete product assortment and to have the "latest." Scouts also want the benefits of relatively higher margins, are more likely to subjectively assess expected long-term potential, want the product to be available from a current vendor or supplier, and desire good trade promotions.[9] Criteria important to troops are decreasing prices, past consumer demand, sufficient volume in the product class, wish to keep pace with the competition, and increased availability of related or complementary items.[10]

The amount of reseller support in terms of advertising directed at final consumers and end-users is especially critical with new products. In many cases, manufacturers have to provide special demonstrations and informative advertising, and to accompany resellers' salespeople on sales trips. For industrial products, special technical service programs may also be required.

A summary of research on new product acceptance by supermarkets for nondurable consumer packaged goods identified these criteria in the selection of new products: whether a product would compete with an existing private-label brand, the volume in the product's category, the manufacturer's reputation, the newness of the product, the amount of supplier advertising, and credit terms.[11]

Another study of buyer criteria for a large northwestern supermarket chain focused on four categories of variables: financial (gross margin, profit, and opportunity cost), competition (firm and brand), marketing strategy (product uniqueness, vendor effort, marketing support, terms of trade, and price), and other (category growth and synergy).[12] The researchers found that product uniqueness (based on ratings of product performance, quality, and package design), expected category growth, and the number of competing firms have a positive effect on new product acceptance. Billback terms of trade had a negative impact on new product acceptance. The study also found a higher acceptance rate for new products introduced by large manufacturers.[13]

In addition to the research cited, wholesalers and retailers need to be assured that new products are properly tested in terms of effectiveness, efficiency, and safety, and that the new products are available on the promised delivery date. Wholesalers and retailers do not want to alienate their customers either with a nonperforming or poorly performing product, with a new product that is quickly recalled because of a safety defect, or with a product that is unavailable on the promised delivered date. A common error is for a manufacturer to introduce a new product before it was fully tested in an attempt to increase dealer and customer enthusiasm or to reduce the time lag between its own and a competitor's new product introduction.[14]

OBTAIN CHANNEL COOPERATION IN STOCKING NEW PRODUCTS

A study of food industry buyers found that resellers have a much more favorable attitude for **pioneer brands** (the first entrants into a new market) as opposed to **follower brands** (products that the reseller perceives to be very similar to a previously introduced item). Resellers feel that pioneer brands are more likely to meet an unmet need, contribute to incremental sales, generate excitement, and achieve high sales volume.[15]

It is often difficult to obtain channel member cooperation in stocking new products (especially follower brands) because of the large number of new products that become available in a given year and because of the high channel member costs in adding a new product.

A large number of new products compete for warehouse and display space, as well as for the attention of wholesaler and retailer salespeople. For instance, almost 14,000 new products were introduced to be sold through supermarkets in 1990; this was double the number of new product introductions of 1984 and five times the level of 1980 new product introductions.[16] New product introductions have increased at a much faster rate than the average size of supermarkets. The typical grocery store now carries 30,000 different items, more than twice the number of 10 years ago.

The increase in new products creates many problems for supermarkets. First, there is a shortage of shelf space for all new products. Second, many of the new products do not represent increased sales for the retailers but merely compete with a retailer's existing sales. Third, the increase of product alternatives generates confusion for shoppers who may be overwhelmed with product choice. Fourth, retailers need to ensure that the new products do not crowd out the shelf space that they have reserved for their private labels (store brands).

Retailers incur high costs when they add a new product. For example, each new product involves inventory control and handling costs, specialized retail shelf space requirements, and production of shelf signs and price tags. Retailers also face product discontinuance costs if the new product fails.[17]

A manufacturer wants to get as much shelf space as possible (it keeps competitors out), but at the same time needs to be careful in that it can push retailers too far. For example, at one point, Fisher-Price began developing large numbers of new products, causing its number of stockkeeping units (SKUs) to balloon. However, many of its new products were nothing more than variations on a theme that did not bring in incremental business to a retailer. (They were viewed as substitute items by consumers.) As a result, many retailers eventually canceled orders, leaving Fisher-Price with large inventories.[18]

The difficulty in securing shelf space (in the face of such competitors as Procter & Gamble's Folger brand; Philip Morris's Maxwell House, Sanka, and Yuban brands; and Nestlé's Hills Bros., Taster's Choice, and Nescafé brands) was a contributing factor in Chock Full o' Nuts Corporation's decision to seek out the institutional market for coffee: restaurants and businesses. In 1986, 85 percent of Chock Full o' Nuts' sales came from supermarkets; in 1992, less than half of its revenues come from this channel.[19]

With industrial products, getting channel cooperation in stocking new technical products is especially difficult. The manufacturer needs to overcome distributors' inertia. Distributors may be comfortable with established products, know how to sell them, and understand their applications. Distributors often want to be able to handle technical questions on their own. As a result, a manufacturer needs to show commitment to the new product. The manufacturer also needs to explain the selling of the new product, provide technical service, and show quantifiable benefits of the new product to end-users.[20]

To obtain shelf space, manufacturers often pay supermarket owners for the use of its shelf space, as well as discounts and other special deals. With a **slotting allowance**, retailers (generally large supermarket chains) require that manufacturers pay for the use of in-store shelf space for new products. The distinguishing feature of slotting allowances versus other allowances (such as promotional allowances, placement allowances, and cooperative advertising) is that a slotting allowance is usually a fixed fee for each stockkeeping unit (SKU) that a retailer places in inventory. It is paid only at the time that the product is first placed in inventory.[21]

Slotting allowances do not guarantee that retailers will keep a product on their shelf. A retailer can pull a product from its shelf if it does not meet sales expectations. Slotting allowances need to be differentiated from pay to stay fees or failure fees. A **pay to stay fee** keeps a product on a shelf for a specified period. A **failure fee** would be paid to the trade after the product's launch, if the new product failed to sell at a predetermined rate.

To manufacturers, slotting allowances represent the power of large grocery chains relative to product manufacturers. A slotting allowance also represents a barrier to new product introduction. To retailers, slotting allowances represent an additional source of revenue as well as a shifting of the risk of new product failure (in terms of the value of the shelf space occupied by the new product) from the retailer to the manufacturer. It also represents a means of ensuring that a manufacturer has high commitment to a new product.

STUDY THE DIFFERENCES IN SUCCESS AMONG CHANNEL MEMBERS IN MARKETING NEW PRODUCTS

In addition to studying criteria used by wholesalers and retailers in choosing new products, a manufacturer needs to study those factors that explain differences in the success of wholesalers in marketing new products. A manufacturer should consider choosing distributors on the basis of the identified criteria.

A study of the heating, ventilating, and air conditioning (HVAC) industry distributors in two southern U.S. states identified characteristics of both high-performing and low-performing distributors. High-volume distributors of heat pumps were more likely to

- Coordinate more sales and installations with electrical and building contractors.
- Desire better distributor education.
- Expect more input from the heat pump association, utility company, and manufacturer to support their higher levels of marketing activity.
- Sell the product on the basis of financing through a utility versus cash payment.
- Sell heat pumps to individuals with functioning equipment.
- Sell equipment on the basis of increased comfort, cleanliness, and quietness of operation.
- Desire support from the manufacturer and utility company regarding advertising, employee training, and getting qualified leads.
- Support customer education programs for the product.
- Participate in marketing support programs offered by other channel members (such as financing programs for buyers).
- Communicate with manufacturers, electrical contractors, and other channel members.[22]

GROWTH STAGE

The **growth stage** of the product life cycle corresponds to rapid sales growth attributable to increased product acceptance among consumers and the emergence of competition. In this stage, distribution needs to be expanded rapidly to accommodate the increased demand levels. Innovators comprise the major target market in the introduction stage; in the growth stage, the market has expanded to include part of the mass market. In the growth stage, firms are most

CHANNELS IN ACTION

Slotting Allowances and Failure Fees

For years, grocery product manufacturers provided wholesalers and retailers with an introductory deal at the time of a new product launch. Typically, the introductory deal was in the form of a temporary off-invoice case allowance on the retailer's initial order or free goods (such as a free case for each 10 cases purchased). In the early 1980s, slotting allowances emerged as an added administrative charge ($25 to $50 per item per store). The slotting allowance was initially designed to cover a retailer's adding a new product to its inventory system as well as a charge for warehouse space and store display space. Over time, slotting allowances increased, especially in the Northeast and in the refrigerated and frozen product categories where shelf space was at a premium. For example, soft-drink makers pay as much as $25,000 per package type (for example, a six pack or a 1.5 liter bottle requires a separate payment) to guarantee shelf space for up to one year. Then they must pay maintenance fees to continue. In other instances, supermarkets require two or three cases of free product per flavor to receive first-time access to shelf space.

Campbell Soup Company agreed to pay failure fees as an alternative to slotting allowances. The failure fee would be paid to the trade after the product's launch, if the new product failed to sell at a predetermined rate. Campbell agreed to buy back any unsold product in full case lots and to compensate channel members for lost profits due to the space being tied up. This proposal was rejected by the major grocery chains. J. M. Jones Company, Urbana, Illinois, a division of SuperValu, charged the first publicly acknowledged failure fee. The wholesaler charged $2000 per SKU for new items that do not achieve agreed-upon sales goals within a 90 day-period. In many cases, these failure fees were in addition to slotting allowances.

Sources: Richard H. Buskirk, Edward T. Popper, and Bruce D. Buskirk, "Retail Power, Slotting Allowances, Market Entry Barriers, and Entrepreneurs," *1991 American Marketing Association's Educators' Proceedings,* Mary C. Gilly, F. Robert Dwyer, and Thomas W. Leigh et al., eds. (Chicago: American Marketing Association, 1991), pp. 512–513; Marj Charlier, "Beer Makers Frothing over Plan to Charge for Retail Shelf Space," *Wall Street Journal* (April 22, 1994), pp. B1, B5; Kenneth Kelly, "The Antitrust Analysis of Grocery Slotting Allowances: The Procompetitive Case," *Journal of Public Policy & Marketing,* Vol. 10 (Spring 1991), pp. 187–198; John A. Quelch and Aimee L. Stern, "Sorrell Ridge: Slotting Allowances" (Boston: Harvard Business School, 1991), pp. 7–8; and Steve Weinstein, "New Deal: Out of the Case and into the Street," *Progressive Grocer* (February 1990), pp. 42–43.

likely to begin to expand the product line beyond the one or two models that were available during the introduction stage, and both company and industry profits begin to emerge.

A critical channel decision during growth is for a firm to reevaluate its market coverage to ensure that a firm can capitalize on the growth opportunities in the market. This decision may also involve a channel member's considering scrambled merchandising opportunities.

REEVALUATE MARKET COVERAGE

Market coverage is typically low in the introduction stage of the product life cycle. The relatively low levels of market demand cannot support a large number of wholesalers and retailers. Manufacturers often limit the number of wholesalers and retailers in a product's introduction because of the need for high levels of training, technical service for industrial products, and the low profitability of products. As the market for a product expands, however, a manufacturer needs to expand the product's distribution. The new level of distribution needs to be adequate to take advantage of market growth opportunities.

For goods distributed in grocery stores, convenience stores, mass merchants, and drug stores, data on market coverage are available as part of the single-source data provided by such firms as Information Resources Inc. and A. C. Nielsen. As discussed in Chapter 3, these firms compute market coverage on the basis of a product's percentage of all commodity volume (ACV). A product with a 40 percent ACV measure in grocery stores is stocked in grocery stores that comprise 40 percent of total grocery store sales in that market.

To increase market coverage, some manufacturers may shift from selective to intensive distribution or from exclusive to selective distribution during the growth stage. The shift to broader distribution may increase competition at the retail level both within and between retailers. Retailers may take on competing brands as other retailers directly compete with them on the same brands.

Pharmacy manufacturers also have to reevaluate market coverage when a drug goes from prescription to over-the-counter status. For example, firms that have distributed their products exclusively through pharmacies have to examine the appropriateness of such outlets as grocery stores, full-line discount stores, hypermarkets, and convenience stores. In addition to new packaging with appropriate warning labels, manufacturers need to promote the product directly to consumers.[23]

In some cases, channel members begin to use scrambled merchandising in the growth stage of the product life cycle. With the increase in scrambled merchandising, manufacturers and wholesalers need to consider the degree of sales support available through self-service retailers. These channel members may have to help these new retailers with appropriate point-of-sale promotional materials, product fact-tags (which outline the product's appropriate uses and specifications), and toll-free customer assistance phone lines that can be used to explain product features to potential customers.

REEVALUATE APPROPRIATENESS OF CHANNELS

Manufacturers need to reevaluate channels particularly when a product's price has been reduced significantly since introduction (generating increased demand among new market segments). For example, while $2000 to $4000 photocopy machines were customarily sold through photocopy specialty firms that delivered, installed, and repaired machines in small offices and in home offices, a photocopy retailer cannot economically distribute $500 to $1000 photocopiers in the same manner. To increase sales to these segments, photocopier manufacturers have increasingly relied on channels such as electronics stores, retail catalog showrooms, camera shops, and appliance stores.

Manufacturers also have to reevaluate the appropriateness of channels when the consumer's product knowledge increases. Higher product knowledge may signal opportunities in terms of self-service merchandising, limited-service wholesalers, and mail-order sales. Compaq is a good example of a firm that reevaluated the appropriateness of its channels.

> *Consider Compaq, the classic 80's company. Its strategy was to build powerful PC's and to sell those machines exclusively through a rigidly controlled dealer channel, producing powerful profits. That worked well in the 80's when corporate computer buyers were still a bit naive about PC technology, wary of clones and willing to pay premium prices for brand names. Compaq became one of the fastest-growing companies in American history.*[24]

Now Compaq sells its personal computers through superstores, electronics stores, catalogs, and telemarketing. The new channels resulted in rapid increases in Compaq's sales. The firm's goal is to become the world's largest personal computer maker by 1996.

MATURITY STAGE

The **maturity stage** of the product life cycle corresponds to a product's reaching its sales peak (both for the company and the industry) and the highest level of product competition. At this stage, both industry and company profits begin to decline. Although few laggard buyers exist who have not purchased the product, most sales in the maturity stage are based on population and household growth and replacement demand. The maturity stage of the product life cycle is particularly important since more products are in this product life cycle stage than any other.

Low overall sales growth in maturity may be due to high levels of product ownership within a market segment or to a lack of new products. An example of a mature industry is home electronics. The Electronic Industries Association (EIA) forecast a 2 percent increase in industry sales in 1992; some retailers even regard that amount as optimistic. Sales in core categories (such as videocassette recorders, camcorders, and portable stereos) have slowed, and there are no new gangbuster products (such as digital recorders or high definition televisions). For example, sales of VCRs and camcorders in 1988 were $5 billion; in 1992, EIA estimated sales to be a little more than $4.5 billion. At the same time, the average price of a VCR dropped from $265 to $225 and that of a camcorder from $1000 to $690.[25] Lower prices mean that retailers need to make more unit sales to stay even with the previous year's profitability.

In maturity, the channel emphasis is to reevaluate market coverage, increase dealer enthusiasm and shelf space allocation, consider a private-label strategy, and appeal to new market segments. These strategies seek to lengthen the maturity stage of the product life cycle.

Reevaluate Market Coverage

As in any stage of the product life cycle, the relative importance of different channel members may change as a product enters maturity. In maturity, channels that were important in introduction and growth may become less important and new retail institutions may emerge. For example, the maturity of the electronics market contributed to the bankruptcy of two major retail chains—47th Street Photo and Newmark & Lewis—but other types of retailers have increased in importance. One is the **superstore**, which uses massive amounts of floor space, a deeper selection of products (such as personal computers and home appliances), product demonstration areas, and low prices.

One manufacturer that avoided maturity by changing channels is Hewlett-Packard. The firm cleverly exploited growth in mail-order outlets and at supermarket-style computer stores to avoid the sales slump of competitors that relied on traditional channels for printers and computers.[26]

Increase Dealer Enthusiasm and Shelf Space Allocation

Manufacturers and wholesalers can increase dealer enthusiasm in maturity through vehicles such as sales contests, cooperative advertising, push money (incentives for distributor salespeople to sell selected models), and ability to keep dealer profit margins at satisfactory levels. Monitoring dealer enthusiasm is particularly important at the maturity stage. With stable sales and high-price competition, wholesaler and retailer profitability can be eroded by lower sales levels and lower profit margins. Many dealers may be vulnerable to a better deal from a competing manufacturer.

In attempting to increase shelf space with different product varieties (such as size, flavor, and colors), manufacturers need to understand a retailer's reluctance to stock additional products that are viewed as substitutes, and not as complementary offerings. Product-line extensions may be subject to slotting allowances much as any new product is.

A manufacturer is particularly vulnerable when sales of its products decline at greater than industrywide levels. For example, after Schwinn experienced a decline in its market share (because of quality problems with its foreign-produced bicycles and lack of investment in product design), many of its dealers deserted it for other brands. In order to win the dealers back, Schwinn needs to increase its advertising budget, improve dealer relations, and develop important new product features.[27]

Evaluate a Private-Label Strategy

A **private label (dealer brand)** is a brand-name designation developed by a wholesaler or retailer. Examples of private brands include White Rose, Shop Rite, Kenmore, and Craftsman. In contrast to a private label, a **national brand (manufacturer's brand)** is a brand designation developed by a manufacturer. The term *national brand* is a misnomer since it does not indicate anything about a brand's scope of distribution or consumer brand awareness. A private label, such as Kenmore, can have broader distribution and a higher degree of brand recognition than a national brand of a small regional manufacturer.

The use of private labels began in the early 1900s. The first private label is commonly attributed to A&P, which created the brand Quaker Maid for its own packaged breads, canned goods, teas, and coffees. While market shares for private labels differ by merchandise category and by distribution outlet, private brands had a market share of 19.7 percent in food stores, drug stores, and mass merchandisers. Total dollar volume for private labels was estimated as $30 billion in 1993 by Information Resources Inc.[28] A Gallup Poll conducted for the Private Label Manufacturers Association found consumer acceptance of private labels at an all-time high, with nearly 90 percent of those surveyed buying them.[29] Although private labels traditionally have sold for lower prices than national brands, some supermarkets have begun to develop premium private-label brands that directly compete with more costly national branded products.[30] See Table 8-3 for a listing of the top private labels in terms of dollar volume.

The duration of relationships between manufacturers and retailers in private branding varies. Some supermarkets, for example, may frequently switch suppliers on the basis of a competitive bidding process, but in other instances, relationships can be long term. Whirlpool, for example, has been Sears, Roebuck's principal supplier of home laundry appliances for over 70 years and of room air conditioning equipment for over 25 years. Whirlpool is also Sears's principal supplier of residential trash compactors and a major supplier to Sears of dishwashers and home refrigeration equipment. Whirlpool sells products to Sears under the Kenmore, Capri, and Whirlpool brand names.[31]

There are three ways to develop and implement a private-label program. In the first, a wholesaler or retailer seeks out a reliable contractor, manufacturer, or packer that also produces its own national brand. This manufacturer produces private labels to ensure a steady stream of work for its employees, to uti-

TABLE 8-3 THE TOP 10 PRIVATE-LABEL BRAND CATEGORIES, BY DOLLAR SALES FOR 1993[a] (IN $ MILLION)

Product Category	1993 Dollar Volume
Dog food	283
Vitamins	177
Carbonated beverages	163
Diapers	138
Internal analgesics	135
Juice	67
Snack foods	62
Hosiery	61
Cat food	56
Cold & sinus tablets/cough drops	53

[a]For the 52 weeks ending January 2, 1994.

Source: Dawn Wilensky, "Store Brands Take Paramount Importance as Retailers Scale Back National Brands," *Discount Store News* (May 16, 1994), p. 24. Data from Information Resources Inc. and Private Label Manufacturers Association.

lize excess plant capacity, to promote cash flow from a major retailer, and to appeal to a different market segment. For example, in 1993 R. J. Reynolds Tobacco developed two private-label tobacco products for an association of 148 distributors.[32] In the second manner, a wholesaler or retailer contracts with a firm that specializes as a private-label manufacturer that can go into production on the retailer's or wholesaler's terms. In the third manner, a wholesaler or retailer can work with a private-label broker that provides private labels to them under their own brand designation. Private-label brokers are paid by vendors.[33]

Use of private labels has some major advantages for the wholesaler or retailer.

- Private labels convert brand loyalty from a manufacturer to a wholesaler or retailer. At the retail level, brand loyalty becomes store loyalty.
- Private labels reduce price competition at the wholesaler or retailer level, since the brand is unavailable elsewhere.
- For durables, such as appliances, the wholesaler or retailer gets the replacement parts business.
- With private labels, a high degree of channel power is given to the wholesaler or retailer. The wholesaler or retailer can change a vendor without loss in sales to end-users or final customers. In most cases, final customers will not even be aware of the change in vendors.
- Private labels often have higher profit margins than national brands.[34]

The disadvantages of a wholesaler's or retailer's use of private label are as follows.

- Private labels involve greater risk than national brands. Wholesalers and retailers must commit to large production quantities well in advance of a selling season. In general, wholesalers and retailers cannot cancel orders for private-label merchandise.
- Private labels involve high-inventory investment for wholesalers and retailers. These channel members may have to stock both national brands and private labels. They have to pay for goods earlier or have to agree to minimum purchase quantities.
- Too great a reliance on a poor-selling private label can attract the wrong target market and lead to poor overall sales performance.
- Private labels receive less manufacturer support than do national brands. For example, typically no manufacturer sales assistance and no cooperative advertising programs are available with private labels.

Use of private labels has a number of advantages for the manufacturer.

- Private labels are an excellent distribution outlet for excess capacity.
- Private-label merchandise may not directly compete for the same target market as the manufacturer's national brand.
- A large order from a large retailer may allow a smaller manufacturer to receive more favorable bank financing.
- A private-label strategy may involve high coordination with retailers. Private labels can be an important element in a manufacturer's overall partnership with its retailers.

The disadvantages of a manufacturer's use of private labels are as follows.

- A manufacturer may find that its private-label strategy takes sales away from its national brand. The private label may compete for the same target market as the manufacturer's national brand and may sell for less at the retailer level.
- Wholesalers and retailers may have too much power in the channel. A strong retailer that is a major customer of a small manufacturer may bargain hard, and secure favorable terms. The retailer may also terminate the vendor as its private-label manufacturer with little advance notice.
- Too great a reliance on one customer or a few customers for a large proportion of sales puts a manufacturer into jeopardy. The severing of an important private-label relationship can drive a small manufacturer into bankruptcy.
- A private label builds up the retailer's image and power in the channel at the price of the manufacturer's.
- Retailers can stock both national brands and private labels. In some cases, retailers engage in **selling against the brand**. In this practice, retailers charge artificially high prices for the national brand to encourage consumers to purchase their private label.

APPEAL TO NEW MARKET SEGMENTS

In maturity, channel members need to appeal to those market segments that did not originally buy because of high price, difficulty in operating the product, and so on. This appeal may involve dual branding (as with national brands and private labels) and dual channels of distribution. In some cases, manufacturers begin to sell to channel members that they avoided in the past owing to image, reputation, or servicing capabilities.

IBM has begun to sell its own low-price "clone" computer in Europe through a subsidiary, Individual Computer Products International Ltd. (ICPI). ICPI's Ambra-brand computer is made with mostly Asian parts. ICPI units will be sold in many of the outlets that currently sell IBM products; ICPI will also sell its computers directly to consumers via a toll-free telephone line. According to ICPI's general manager, the Ambra product line will be sold "in any part of the world where it makes sense."[35] Models are designed to compete for a market segment that IBM ignored in Europe, the clone buyer. The clone buyer is more likely to treat brands of computers as interchangeable, to be more price conscious than an IBM buyer, and to require less assistance in setting up a system.

OshKosh B'Gosh Inc., a children's clothing manufacturer, originally sold its clothing almost exclusively through department and specialty stores. Now the firm has begun to sell its products through Sears and J. C. Penney. According to OshKosh's senior vice president for marketing, for years "Chain stores had a negative connotation."[36] OshKosh reacted positively to Sears and J. C. Penney on the basis of several factors. First, J. C. Penney is now the nation's top seller of children's clothing. Second, many department stores were either in or just emerging from bankruptcy, and OshKosh was concerned about the financial stability of its traditional retailer customers. Third, the success of GapKids threatened OshKosh's sales and profits.

In appealing to new market segments, channel members need to seek out new customers without alienating their current customers. Manufacturers have to be particularly cautious about adding channel members if existing wholesalers and retailers feel threatened or want to drop the manufacturer's line. A second important consideration is the need to differentiate products sold through multiple channels. This is especially important when similar products are sold at significantly different prices. Often, product differentiation is in the form of either different levels of service or different products based on channel members.

In the case of IBM's selling clones, IBM will not give the new organizational unit any support from its marketing and service organizations. Third-party organizations will provide these functions. ICPI will also not mention its association with IBM. For its part, OshKosh is seeking to maintain the loyalty of its department store final and organizational customers by offering department stores exclusive items such as a new novelty denim line. According to OshKosh's senior vice president for marketing, "It's important that OshKosh stays on the shelves at Saks, Bloomingdale's, and Marshall Field's."[37]

DECLINE STAGE

The **decline stage** of the product life cycle corresponds to a drop in industry sales and profits. This stage may be due to technological factors as well as to changes in customer tastes. In decline, a manufacturer has several channel options: to reduce the number of outlets through which a product is sold, to discontinue the product and its distribution, or to revive sales through the development of new products and new distribution channels.

REDUCE THE NUMBER OF CHANNEL MEMBERS

In reducing the number of channel members, the manufacturer strives to increase the chance that those channels that continue to stock the product will still be profitable. The point of this strategy is to reduce the number of channels to ensure that each remaining channel member will have an acceptable profit despite declining sales and profit margins. This strategy seeks to maintain the loyalty of major channel members.

DISCONTINUE THE PRODUCT AND DISTRIBUTION CHANNEL

This strategy implicitly assumes that a product cannot be revived and that the manufacturer cannot continue as a viable competitor. The manufacturer needs to inform channel members that it is no longer producing or marketing the product in a timely manner. It must also decide how replacement parts and product servicing will be conducted. Product servicing is especially important for durables, for products with warranties still in effect, and for products that were formerly serviced by distributors.

In instances where the firm has large quantities of existing products in inventory, the manufacturer needs to seek alternative distribution channels for discontinued and abandoned products. Potential buyers include closeout buyers, export channels, barter arrangements, and off-price chains (for clothing). The popularity of these channels is based on the fact that these sales will not "spoil the market for regular-priced goods" in current markets.

Develop New Products and a New Distribution Channels Strategy

This strategy seeks to revive sagging sales and profits through the development of new distribution channels. Firms pursuing this strategy need to notify channel members that an item is about to be superceded. In this way, wholesalers and retailers will not load up on goods that are about to be discontinued. Stockpiles of old inventory will limit sales of the newly introduced goods.

In some cases, manufacturers provide dollar adjustments to compensate wholesalers and retailers for the decline in inventory values associated with the discontinued goods.

EVALUATION OF THE PRODUCT LIFE CYCLE CONCEPT

Although the product life cycle concept is popular among marketing scholars and practitioners, channel members need to evaluate it in light of its potential shortcomings.[38]

- There are different cycles for product categories (personal computers), product forms (486s), and brands (IBM personal computers). A brand may be in maturity while a product category is within growth, or vice versa.

- A firm can influence the product life cycle stage and its duration through appropriate strategies. The product life cycle is not inevitable. Firms must give products appropriate support in each stage. Through a **self-fulfilling prophecy**, a firm falsely predicts that its product is in the maturity or decline stage and consequently reduces the level of marketing support. This false prediction shortens the life of a product.

- Product life cycles vary in shape and do not necessarily look like a bell-shaped curve. In a fad life cycle, sales growth is low, and the time from introduction to decline is very short. On the other hand, in a classic product life cycle, maturity is prolonged, and the time span from introduction to maturity is long. In a cycle-recycle pattern, sales increase after the decline stage, and the product goes through another full product life cycle. The recycle portion, however, does not reach the sales level of the product in the earlier cycle stage.

REVERSE CHANNELS

Reverse channels signify the movement of products from buyer back to manufacturer. These channels occur in the case of returned goods (returned for repair or for consumer credit), product recall, and product recycling.[39]

Although all three cases involving reverse channels differ, they do share some common characteristics.

- In forward channels, the direction of the flow of goods and services is from manufacturer to wholesaler to retailer to final customer. In reverse channels, the flow is from final consumer to manufacturer. This change in direction provides opportunities for **backhauling**, using vendors' transportation facilities that are often not used to capacity after goods are shipped from manufacturers to wholesalers or from wholesalers to retailers.

- In forward channels, a major function in distribution is breaking bulk. Wholesalers and retailers buy in large quantities and sell goods to their consumers in smaller quantities. In reverse channels, wholesalers and retailers accumulate small quantities from their customers. These quantities are sorted and then shipped to the appropriate vendors.

- In forward channel arrangements, wholesalers and retailers separate merchandise into grades, colors, and sizes for the benefit of their customers. In reverse channels, channel members combine separate goods into appropriate categories for the benefit of their vendors.

- In forward channels, manufacturers often deal with few wholesalers and retailers. In reverse channels, manufacturers deal with large numbers of final consumers.

- In forward channels, manufacturers and wholesalers often deal with authorized distributors. In reverse channels, suppliers may not be past customers. For example, recalled products may have been resold by original buyers. Recycled products may also be collected by school children and charities.

Two important reverse channels are product recall and product recycling.

PRODUCT RECALL

Product recall involves products that require repair or replacement. These products may be in the manufacturer's finished goods inventory, in the inventory of wholesalers or retailers, or may have been sold to organizational final consumers. Product recall can be voluntary, as in a manufacturer's repainting car finishes that are subject to premature weathering; or mandatory, to comply with the requirement of a government agency.

Almost a dozen agencies have some jurisdiction over product recalls, with different agencies controlling different products. Automobiles and tires fall under the jurisdiction of the National Highway Traffic Safety Administration, whereas food, drug, and cosmetic products are controlled by the Food and

Drug Administration. The Consumer Product Safety Commission regulates the safety of all consumer products other than cars, boats, airplanes, guns, drugs, airplanes, and food. The Commission was created in 1972 by Congress following a study by a panel of safety experts that identified many household hazards. Each of these agencies has the power to order a mandatory product recall. In 1993, the Consumer Product Safety Commission handled 176 product recalls, almost all of them voluntary.[40]

Recall programs can involve millions of units. In 1991, DeLonghi S.p.A. agreed to repair 3.6 million portable electric heaters that could pose a fire risk.[41] In 1993, Honda recalled 1.8 million vehicles with a defective fuel filler pipe that was prone to corrode under certain circumstances.[42] While Intel's recall of its Pentium chip in 1994 did not involve a safety problem, the chip made errors in complex mathematical calculations. Intel produced 5.3 million flawed chips.[43]

Recall programs are particularly costly to a manufacturer, sometimes totaling tens of millions of dollars. Recall generally involves advertising and mail costs to wholesalers, retailers, and intermediate and final consumers; physical distribution costs of recovering the old product and returning the new product to consumers; disposal of the affected product; replacement or repair costs; and loss in profits from lost sales. One estimate of Perrier's cost in a worldwide product recall (following the discovery of traces of benzene in its bottled water) of 160 million bottles in 1990 was $30 million after taxes.[44] This cost estimate did not include loss in future sales caused by the product's tainted image. Honda's recall has been estimated to have cost between $15 and $20 million. The cost of Intel's Pentium replacement program has been estimated between $200 and $260 million.[45]

It is often costly to identify current owners, especially when products have been resold. A successful product recall program needs to identify the affected products (by serial number or model number and date of manufacture) as well as the channel member that purchased the affected lot. In this way, promotion concerning the product recall can be targeted at a specific region as well as specific stores within that region. Recall programs are also particularly difficult when a good is recalled a long time after its initial sale. For instance, in January 1992, General Motors announced the recall of about 1.5 million cars to replace defective V6 engines that were subject to sudden stalling. The problem was not determined until July 1990, nearly five years after the first engines were built.

The effectiveness of recalls is measured by the **completion rate**. The percentage of products that are either returned or destroyed is quite low. For example, of the 176 recalls initiated by the Consumer Product Safety Commission in 1993, only about 11 percent of the recalled products were returned by retailers and consumers.[46] The completion rate varies by product, with some major appliances approaching 80 percent. Sears, Roebuck has found that the completion rate for a toaster recall involving a safety defect can be as high as 40 percent.[47] The low overall completion rate is in part due to the difficulty in tracking down customers. One study found, for instance, that fewer than 10 percent of customers fill out product warranty cards.[48] Another reason for the low completion rate may be the low proportion of firms that set performance standards with regard to product tracing for recalls. A study of Florida-based industrial manufacturers found that while 46 percent collect data on product tracing for recalls, only 19.5 percent set performance standards in this important area.[49]

The difficulty in implementing a product recall program is illustrated in Table 8-4. This table divides the difficulty into three groupings: not as difficult as other groupings, difficult, and very difficult. There are also differences in difficulty within each section. The most difficult recall programs to implement are at the bottom of each section. For example, it is easier to locate affected goods as work-in-process inventory (that is not fabricated) than to locate affected products that are stored at a retailer's warehouse. All of the cases categorized as "not as difficult as other groupings" are either in the possession of the manufacturer or its traditional wholesalers or retailers (except for goods sold by and delivered by the manufacturer). For example, since most of Dell's sales of its computers are made directly to its customers, it can more easily track down its computers than a manufacturer that sells computers through a variety of indirect channels. Products classified as difficult have been sold to consumers, transshipped by their original buyers, or have been sold to final consumers who have registered ownership. The most difficult product recall cases are those involving a manufacturer who cannot directly contact current owners. In these instances, ownership is not registered, the products were subsequently resold by their original owners, or the products were exported.

The costs of correcting a problem increase geometrically as a product travels down the channel and gets closer to the consumer. According to a business school professor at Harvard, "The difference [in cost] between finding a problem at the supplier versus finding one when it's in the customer's hands is a factor of 100,000."[50] A firm can reduce the costs of a recall through a combination of measures designed to reduce the probability of recalling a good, the costs of contacting customers, the time period between a product's being confirmed to

TABLE 8-4 DIFFICULTY IN LOCATING AFFECTED PRODUCTS IN PRODUCT RECALL

Not As Difficult As Other Groupings in Table
Work-in-process inventory at manufacturer
Finished goods inventory at manufacturer
Finished goods in transit to wholesalers
Finished goods in transit to retailers
Products stored in wholesaler warehouses
Products stored in retailer warehouses
Products sold using direct distribution and delivered by manufacturer

Difficult
Products transshipped to other wholesalers and retailers by their original purchasers
Products sold to customers within past year that have registered ownership with manufacturer
Products sold to customers five years ago or longer that have registered ownership

Most Difficult
Products sold to customers within past year that have not registered ownership
Products sold used to other consumers as used
Products exported to foreign countries

be defective and the recall notification, and lost business after a recall notification (see Table 8-5).

The completion rate can be increased by encouraging consumers to complete warranty cards (some firms offer inducements such as the chance of winning a new product), by offering a payment for each recalled product brought in (or a credit toward the purchase of a new product), by mailing prepaid shipping cartons to consumers, and by extending hours to implement the recall in

TABLE 8-5 REDUCING THE COSTS OF PRODUCT RECALLS

Reduce costs of contacting customers:

Include a safety registration self-addressed postcard with each new product. Ask buyers to register ownership with this form. Use this form only for customer ownership identification information, not for market research purposes.

Develop and maintain records of components that have been installed in specific serial numbers or in lots produced on specific dates.

Record serial numbers of goods that have been sold to specific channel members.

Ask vendors to record customers purchasing goods by serial number.

Encourage customers to send the manufacturer notification of the new owner of product.

Record new owners of product during service call. Also record new owner of product by serial number, if owner requests replacement parts.

Reduce time period between a product's being suspected of having to be recalled and the recall notification:

Immediately react to instances where product safety is at question. Send investigators to determine cause of problem. If accident is product-related, order recall as soon as possible.

Develop a product recall program in advance of its need. The program should include choice of a company spokesperson, an advertising/publicity plan, notification forms, a policy as to reimbursement for handling and shipping, and the development of toll-free telephone numbers.

Reduce lost business after a recall notification:

Acknowledge problem as being a real and significant one. Do not hide behind uncertainty. Be open and honest in dealing with media. Do not attempt to cover up the problem.

Reissue product in new package, model number, or style to differentiate it from recalled product. This reduces confusion among both final consumers and distributors as to the recalled and new product.

Offer customers options in handling the recall to reduce consumer inconvenience. For example, Chrysler is testing three approaches to a recall on its Dodge Ram pickup (to fix a seat-latch problem) to determine which strategy consumers prefer. Options include: dropping off the vehicle for repairs, offering customers a free car wash and a loaner vehicle, or having a dealer employee pick up and return the truck at the customer's home or place of business.

cases where the product has to be brought in for modification (such as a car). Some products need more aggressive strategies. For example, one study showed that the completion rate for car recalls is higher for owners of American cars (versus European and Japanese vehicles), for owners of newer vehicles, and for owners of vehicles with serious safety concerns. The authors suggest increasing the completion rate via multiple recall notices and the use of periodic safety inspections.[51]

Table 8-6 contains a product recall checklist that can be used to determine a firm's preparation for a product recall. A particularly well-designed and implemented product recall was Lexus's recall of its LS 400 model. The same day the recall was announced, dealers contacted their customers about the recall. In most recalls, customers have to seek dealers out, after they have read about the recall in newspapers or after receiving a written recall notification. After the dealers modified the cars, they washed them and filled up the gas tank. If the owners lived more than 100 miles away from the dealership, they were given the option to have a technician repair the car at the person's home. In one case, a technician even flew from Los Angeles to Anchorage to service a car that had originally been purchased in Portland.[52]

PRODUCT RECYCLING

Like product recalls, product recycling is an example of reverse channels. **Product recycling** deals with the recovery of natural resources from the return of used products and its packaging. Recycling affects manufacturers in terms of

TABLE 8-6   A PRODUCT RECALL CHECKLIST

1. What programs are in place to reduce the likelihood of a recall requirement, such as total quality programs and product safety audits?
2. Are product recalls explicitly considered throughout the new product development process and in the design and development of logistics systems and company databases?
3. Does field monitoring include reviews of the safe performance of older products, perhaps no longer made by the company, and their safe disposal?
4. How quickly and from whom would senior management learn of a recall requirement?
5. Does the company have a comprehensive recall plan or manual identifying recall scenarios and appropriate responses? Is the plan reviewed regularly?
6. Who is the senior executive responsible for product recalls?
7. How quickly could a recall be implemented? (Is this response time confirmed by mock recalls?)
8. Do the company's products, packages, and shipping containers carry easy-to-read identifiers that designate the product's date and place of manufacture?
9. Where possible, do customer and end-user records show sales by product identifiers?
10. How would a recall be funded?

Source: N. Craig Smith and John A. Quelch, *Ethics in Marketing* (Homewood, Ill.: Richard D. Irwin, Inc., 1993), p. 367. Reprinted by permission.

design of products (with a high proportion of recycled goods and with ease of recycling), wholesalers and retailers in terms of legal requirements (such as state-mandated recycling programs for soda beverages), and final consumers (in terms of the costs of recycling programs).

It is important to differentiate the place in distribution at which recycling activity takes place. The paper industry, for example, differentiates among post-consumer waste, comparable waste, and pre-consumer waste. **Post-consumer waste** is paper that has serviced its intended use, been collected from consumers, and been diverted from landfills for reprocessing into recycled pulp. **Comparable waste** is made up of press overruns or unsold magazines that have never reached the final buying public. **Pre-consumer waste** consists of paper generated in the papermaking process such as scraps and paper shavings.[53] The category with the largest potential is post-consumer waste: it also presents the most difficult challenge.

According to the director of commodities of the Institute of Scrap Recycling Industries, recycling operations divert approximately 100 million tons of metal, paper, plastic, glass, and textiles from the nation's waste stream. In 1991, mills in the United States consumed 40 million tons of scrap steel. This scrap steel provided 41 percent of the 96 million tons of steel demanded by the milling industry.[54]

The recycling business has two segments: the scrap industry that has been reusing industrial waste, and the "post-consumer" business that aims to convert the stream of municipal waste flowing from homes and commercial businesses into something useful.[55] The recycling process differs by product. For example, the largest percentage of plastics packaging recycling occurs in states with deposit laws. In contrast, corrugated cardboard is recycled through a vast collection network that feeds cartons to some 1700 paper-packing plants. The baled fibers are then sent to domestic and foreign paperboard mills for re-pulping.[56]

Ways to Promote Recycling

State and local government efforts to promote recycling consist of financial incentives, disincentives, educational programs, and laws. In some cases, a combination of incentives, disincentives, educational programs, and laws drive down the value of recycled materials because of an increase in supply. For example, old newsprint prices dropped from $60 a ton in the Northeast at the end of 1987 to below zero at the beginning of 1992.[57] The supply side of America's recycling revolution has been growing at an explosive rate, but the demand side is still barely under way. Many manufacturers simply are not equipped to absorb the huge volumes of recycled products that are now available.

Financial incentives include the return of deposits on aluminum cans and bottles. A dozen states offer low-interest loans, grants, or tax credits to companies that make products from recycled materials. About 35 states have recently adopted purchasing programs designed to lift the demand for paper products, construction materials, and soil additives with recycled content.[58] States such as Illinois and New York offer low-interest loans and grants to help businesses buy recycling machines or develop recycled products. Other states offer tax credits for inventing machines that help recycle. About 30 states are willing to pay 5 to 10 percent more to buy recycled goods, and 16 states specify that a certain percentage of their purchases involve recycled goods. In addition, about 10 states have rules that will force a minimum recycled content in paper, plastic containers, and other goods in the next few years.[59]

The National Solid Wastes Management Association estimates that the number of curbside collection programs grew to 3500 in 1992 from 600 in 1989. About 40 percent of these curbside programs are mandatory, and most of them are in the Northeast, California, and Minnesota.[60] Between 1989 and 1991, a dozen states passed laws requiring local newspapers to use a minimum content of recycled newsprint. Since either 1991 or 1992, most laws have required 10 percent to 25 percent recycled paper content. These percentages have been phased in to increase to 50 percent by the year 2000.[61] State and federal recycled-content laws requiring that a set percentage of all packages be made from recycled material would benefit aluminum. The aluminum industry now recycles 64 percent of all cans, up from 15 percent in 1972.[62]

Financial disincentives consist of having people pay for garbage disposal services. **Tipping fees**, the price of dumping municipal waste in landfills, rose 30 percent in 1988 to a national average of $27 a ton.[63]

Educational services seek to make the public aware of the importance of recycling.[64] Materials such as corrugated paper and fat renderings have been recycled for years. Spartan Stores, a Grand Rapids, Michigan, grocery wholesaler, has backhauled corrugated paper from stores they supply. According to Spartan's corporate and government relations manager: "It may be expensive initially, since the average compactor costs $17,000. But you have to look at the long run. Trash disposal costs generally are $95 a load, and you have a one-year ROI on the purchase of a compactor."[65] A pilot program in Minneapolis of 28,000 households found that despite an aggressive public education program, the number of people who actually sorted their garbage ranged from a paltry 22 percent to a modest 62 percent.[66]

Germany has taken the lead in passing legislation on recycling of packaging materials. Its regulations require business and industry to recycle all packaging (including bottles, cans, cardboard, paper, and plastic materials). German law requires that 80 percent of packaging materials be recycled as of the middle of 1995. France and Austria have adopted similar laws. The laws also require that manufacturers prove a component cannot be reused before it can be discarded. These laws also apply to products made in the United States and other countries for sale in Germany.[67]

STRATEGIES TO REDUCE WASTE AND INCREASE PRODUCT RECYCLING

Channel members can reduce waste and increase product recycling by designing products for ease of disposal, and by using innovative packaging, a closed-loop production cycle, and raw materials with a high recycling rate.

DESIGN PRODUCTS FOR EASE OF DISPOSAL. Several industries have begun to design products that are easy to disassemble. Minnesota Mining and Manufacturing, for example, has a plastic desk organizer designed for recycling. Each of its three parts is labeled with the recycling symbol (three arrows in a circle) and a number indicating the type of plastic resin. BMW's Z1 limited production model has plastic body panels that were designed to come off easily with the removal of a few fasteners. In designing for recycling, the resulting product must be easy to take apart, with each piece made from a distinct, easily recycled material.[68] BMW can now recycle 80 percent of a car, by weight; its aim is 95 percent. In contrast, traditional cars must be stripped of glass and lead-acid batteries, and gas tanks. These can leak or explode during traditional recycling operations.[69] Most automotive glass also ends up in landfills because it contains plastic that prevents it from shattering. As a result, the glass-plastic materials are almost impossible to recycle.[70]

USE INNOVATIVE PACKAGING. Clorox Company's new gallon bleach bottle is made with 20 percent recycled plastic. With distribution in 10 percent of the United States, this new bottle will prevent the equivalent of 4.6 million gallon-size plastic bottles from entering landfills. On a national basis, that would be 46 million bottles.[71] Clorox is currently planning to expand recycled plastic packaging for additional products such as its Pine-Sol cleaner, Soft Scrub and Soft Scrub with bleach, mild abrasive cleaners, and its Formula 409 all-purpose cleaner. In Europe, many of Procter & Gamble's (P&G) basic household items, such as cleaners and detergents, are available in refills that come in disposable pouches. Instead of pouches, P&G uses cartons and bottles in the United States, which contain less plastic for its refills. Refills now account for 40 percent of the sales of P&G's Downy fabric softener; these refills typically sell for 15 percent less than the full-size bottle. Ultra Tide also is available in a refill; the refill has 40 percent less plastic per ounce than the regular bottles.[72] Since refills use less storage and shelf space, they are popular with wholesalers and retailers.

USE OF A CLOSED-LOOP RECYCLING OPERATION. In a **closed-loop cycle**, production, distribution, collection, and recycling are controlled by one company. This system enables manufacturers to encourage users to recycle, ensures manufacturers of a continuous supply of recycled materials, and reduces distribution costs. Closed-loop recycling operations are particularly important in the recycling of hazardous products, for distribution of these products is tightly controlled. In a closed-loop system, Stone Container Corporation, working with Recycling International, uses waste-paper supplies for mill, produces paper, and picks up used papers. These recycled materials are used to produce new papers. Stone Container Corporation's 142 converting plants worldwide recover and recycle all paper waste generated in the manufacturing process. Many of its facilities have launched additional in-house programs for recycling newspapers, office paper, and rollstock cores.[73]

USE PRODUCTS WITH HIGH RECYCLING RATES. Recycling rates vary by material. In packaging materials, the highest recycling rate is for aluminum; about 64 percent of aluminum is recycled. In contrast, the recycling rate for steel is only 25 percent.[74] The advantage of recycling aluminum is that it reduces energy costs by 95 percent and capital costs by 90 percent (see Table 8-7). The value of aluminum and steel to industry further guarantees that they

TABLE 8-7 RECYCLABILITY OF DIFFERENT PACKAGING MATERIALS

	Aluminum	Steel	Plastic	Glass	Paper-Board
Recycling rate	64%	25%	1–30%	20–30%	0–50%
Recycled content	50–55%	Under 10%	Almost none	20–80%	30–100%
Price per ton of scrap	$600	$60	$160–$220	$50	$30
Advantages	Closed loop; high value	Closed-loop potential; easy sorting by magnetic collection	High value	High recycled content; closed loop	High recycling rate for some products
Disadvantages	Foil has low recycling rate and recycled content	Also contains aluminum and tin; low value	Recycling reduces quality	Difficulty mixing colors; low value	Low value; reduced quality

Source: Dana Milbank, "Aluminum's Envious Rivals Turn Green, Rush to Show They, Too, Are Recyclable," *Wall Street Journal* (September 18, 1991), p. B1. Reprinted by permission of *Wall Street Journal*, copyright 1991 Dow Jones & Company, Inc. All Rights Reserved Worldwide.

will be economically feasible components of recycling programs. In 1993, 33 companies joined the "Buy Recycled Alliance" to foster the purchase (for internal use) and sale to the general public of recycled content products and materials. In less than one year, the steering committee members have accounted for $3 billion of recycled-content products and materials.[75]

PACKAGING AND CHANNELS

Packaging has a major impact on channel members. An effective product-packaging program should protect a product; lower distribution, shipping, and disposal costs; reduce shelf space usage; and encourage self-service merchandising.

Packaging should protect the product's contents from spoilage, breakage, and deterioration. The product needs to be protected in shipping to the wholesaler and retailer, in storage at the wholesaler or retailer, and in shipping to the final user. International Paper Company uses sensors that are attached to a package during shipment. The sensors record information about vibrations, shocks, and atmospheric conditions. They can record sudden shock, determine whether a package fell to the floor from where it was stacked, and measure the distance of the drop. In response to the sensor, International Paper was able to modify some of its package designs. For example, the firm was able to reduce cigarette containers used to ship cigarettes from a thickness of 12 one-thousandths to 10 one-thousandths of an inch. Lighter packaging reduces distribution costs and also lowers dumping fees for wholesalers and retailers.[76]

Retailers and wholesalers are increasingly using direct product profitability to determine the distribution, shipping, and disposal costs for different packaging materials and designs. For example, the shape of a bottle affects such factors as the number of units shipped in each case, the number of cases shipped on each pallet, and the number of pallet loads that can be stored in the warehouse. The shape also affects the number of units that can be displayed on store shelves and the labor associated with handling cases, pallet loads, and individual units. For example, a manufacturer of hair-care products recently test marketed a new formulation in a teardrop-shaped bottle. While the new shape was chosen mainly as a means of enhancing the shampoo's shelf presence, retailers discovered that a more square or barrel-shaped container would save distributors of the shampoo 29 cents a case. This information prompted the manufacturer to make subtle but profitable alterations to the bottle.[77]

Packaging impacts shelf space usage. L'eggs is by far the largest seller of panty hose, in large part because of its distribution strategy. Although its past distinctive egg shape generated a lot of brand awareness, it also resulted in substantial dead space (and increased transportation costs and shelf space requirements for retailers). The new package design now allows a retailer to place 992 L'eggs packages into the typical supermarket display, 264 more than could be placed with the old package design. The new package also uses almost 40 percent less packaging material than the old one; it is also made of cardboard that can easily be recycled.[78]

CHANNELS IN ACTION

Herman Miller Uses Recycling

Herman Miller Inc., a manufacturer of office furniture, uses recycled materials, recycles its own products, and nips toxic spills in the bud. By reducing packaging and building an $11 million waste-to-energy heating-and-cooling plant, it has cut the trash it hauls to landfills by 90 percent since 1982. It plans to send nothing to landfills by 1995. According to the vice president of the Michigan Audubon Society, "Herman Miller has been doing a superb job." Even the firm's scrap fabric is shredded and made into insulation for car-roof linings and dashboards—saving Miller $50,000 in dumping fees. The firm has adopted a "cradle-to grave" design. Miller favors the use of materials such as scrap aluminum that take little energy to fabricate, generate few pollutants, and come apart easily for recycling. For its part in recycling, the firm won the 1993 Waste Reduction Program Award administered by California's Integrated Management Board. It also received the Wildlife Federation Corporate Conservation Council's 1993 Environmental Achievement Award.

The company has also reduced its costs by cutting down on unnecessary packaging materials. For example, it has saved $250,000 a year in materials and shipping costs by eliminating 70 percent of the styrofoam and cardboard packaging for the cloth-covered panels of its Ethospace office partitions. One of its suppliers for office chairs helped design returnable bins to enable the firm to reuse cardboard and plastic shipping wrap. This saves Herman Miller an additional $300,000 a year.

Herman Miller will invest in capital equipment to reduce pollution. It has recently invested $800,000 for two incinerators that burn 98 percent of the toxic solvents that escape from booths in which wood is stained and varnished. The furnaces exceed the standards of the Clean Air Act. Miller even maintains a spill-response team.

Miller does not "toot its own horn." Its senior vice president of sales sees "green marketing as a ploy that will eventually wear thin with customers." The firm is convinced that it has a long way to go. For example, it now recycles only 15 percent of its corrugated cardboard while the rest is burned at its energy plant; this is not considered optimal. The firm is considering how to modify its energy plant so that it can safely burn 1820 tons of sawdust per year. After it modifies the plant, all cardboard can then be recycled.

Source: Joseph A. Azzarello, "Long-Time Environmental Leadership Pays Off in Many Ways at Herman Miller," *Total Quality Environmental Management* (Winter 1992/1993), pp. 187–191; David Woodruff, "Herman Miller: How Green Is My Factory," *Business Week* (September 16, 1991), p. 54; *Herman Miller, Inc. and Subsidiaries 1994 Annual Report;* and Faye Rice, "Who Scores Best on the Environment," *Fortune* (July 26, 1993), pp. 114–122.

Packaging enables retailers to use self-service merchandising through a visible brand name, describing directions, fitting neatly on a rack or display area, and inhibiting pilferage. For example, some items such as computer modems may need larger sized packages so as to include a photograph of the modem and describe its features.

LEGAL ASPECTS OF CHANNEL MANAGEMENT RELATING TO PRODUCT STRATEGY

Among the topics covered in this section are exclusive dealing, tying arrangements, full-line forcing, reciprocity, refusal to deal, private label strategy, and slotting allowances.

EXCLUSIVE DEALING

Exclusive dealing is the seller's requirement that its customers sell only its products, or at least no products in direct competition with its products.[79] Exclusive dealing provides a ready-available market to the seller. Exclusive dealing also develops a close relationship between channel members at different levels. For example, the success of a manufacturer in a market area and the success of its wholesalers and retailers in that area are interconnected. It also limits competition and lowers investment costs for a wholesaler or retailer.

On the negative side, exclusive dealing limits a buyer's choice and increases a channel member's risk owing to the importance of a relationship with one vendor.

Exclusive dealing is evaluated by the courts under the rule of reason. Exclusive dealing can be considered illegal if a manufacturer has a large market share in the served market. The power of a dealer in a given market reduces competition.

TYING ARRANGEMENT

A **tying arrangement** is an agreement whereby a seller conditions the sale of one product or service (the tying product) on the buyer's purchase of a second product or service (the tied product). A tying arrangement that poses an unacceptable risk of stifling competition in the sale of a tied product or service constitutes a violation of antitrust laws.[80]

Under the rule of reason, five elements must be present to prove an illegal tying agreement:[81]

1. The existence of a tying and a tied product.
2. Actual coercion by the seller forcing the buyer to purchase the tied product.
3. Evidence that the seller had sufficient market power to force the purchase of the tied product.
4. Anticompetitive effects in the tied market.
5. A "not insubstantial" amount of interstate commerce in the tied product.

In general, tying agreements are illegal if the seller possesses sufficient clout in the market for one product to force consumers to buy another product.

Tying agreements may not work if retailers have enough clout to stand up to a manufacturer. When Zenith Data Services developed a new distribution policy that required its laptop dealers to sell its unpopular office models as well, more than 1000 dealers including large chains such as ComputerLand Corporation simply dropped all of the firm's computer lines. To lure these large chains back, Zenith Data Systems increased the incentives for dealers.[82]

FULL-LINE FORCING

Full-line forcing exists when a wholesaler or retailer is forced to order, stock, and display each type of product produced by a manufacturer that is applicable to its trade area. Full-line forcing is a type of tying contract.

In a recent case, a farm equipment manufacturer's forcing full lines on its dealers was not ruled to be a per se illegal tying agreement, but instead was judged to be a nonprice vertical restraint subject to the rule of reason analysis. The retailer was contractually obligated by the manufacturer to "order, keep on hand, and display a representative sample of each type of the manufacturer's product applicable to retailer's trade area." The retailer refused to stock a new model of the manufacturer, claiming that the manufacturer was guilty of an illegal tying contract. The court concluded that the manufacturer's actions were legal and that full-line forcing had the economic impact of increasing interbrand competition (competition among wholesalers or retailers of the same brand) by making another tractor available for sale to the public. Central to the court's judgment was the fact that the manufacturer did not prohibit the dealer from carrying competing brands.[83]

RECIPROCITY

Reciprocity involves the practice of buying goods and services from major customers; in turn, these customers then purchase goods and services from the firm. Although reciprocity reduces selling costs for each party, it severely limits the competition among noncustomers. Reciprocity is similar to a tying arrangement where the tied good is a buyer's. Reciprocity is generally illegal when it involves pressure or when a reciprocity program occurs as a result of a merger.[84] There are comparatively few cases involving reciprocity.

REFUSAL TO DEAL

Refusal to deal involves a manufacturer or wholesaler refusing to sell goods to selected intermediaries. The classic legal case involving refusal to deal is *U.S. v. Colgate*. In 1919, the Supreme Court formally recognized the right of a manufacturer to select his own dealers or distributors based on his own criteria and judgment. The *Colgate* case held that refusal to deal must be exercised unilaterally. This case reinforced the right of a manufacturer to refuse to deal with channel members that did not meet its stated criteria. The *Colgate* case allows a seller to select its own distributors or dealers according to its own criteria and judgment. The criteria can deal with poor credit, failure to meet sales quotas, or poor service.

One of the main legal issues involved in refusal to deal is whether the refusal can be characterized as a conspiracy between firms that excludes other firms from being able to buy from that channel member. This often occurs when a manufacturer refuses to sell its products to a retailer that discounts the manufacturer's products. In a recent case, the District Court for the Southern District of New York ruled that two swimwear manufacturers legally were allowed to refuse to sell their primary merchandise lines to Toys "R" Us, despite complaints by Macy's. Although the manufacturers communicated to Macy's, there was no evidence of an agreement between Macy's and the manufacturers not to sell to Toys "R" Us.[85]

PRIVATE LABEL

A central issue in pricing private-label goods versus pricing national brands produced by the same manufacturer is whether the private-label products are subject to the Robinson-Patman Act's "like grade and quality" notion. This act prohibits the granting of discriminatory prices for products of like grade and quality.

In a 1966 landmark case, the Supreme Court ruled that Borden had engaged in price discrimination by selling the same canned evaporated milk at two prices, a higher price for cans sold under Borden's national brand, and a lower price for cans sold under private labels.[86] The Supreme Court ruled that product differences need to be based on real differences, not on basis of perception. As a result of this case, price differences between private labels and national brands are now subject to the traditional Robinson-Patman Act guidelines if the two products are identical, except for brand-name designation.

Manufacturers that produce both national brands and private labels in order to avoid Robinson-Patman Act influence could develop different specifications for the private-label product. The specifications should be based on meaningful performance measures (such as material content, recipe, motor horsepower), and not on factors such as packaging.

SLOTTING ALLOWANCES

Slotting allowances are also subject to the Robinson-Patman Act. A manufacturer needs to offer equivalent allowances to all trade accounts in any market area. Although the Federal Trade Commission originally viewed a slotting allowance as a potential antitrust violation, it currently is concerned with only "the discriminatory purchase of shelf space." Thus, under the FTC's revised program, slotting allowances must be shown to be discriminatory before they can be challenged as anticompetitive.[87]

SUMMARY

1 *To discuss the channel management implications of the new product planning process.* The new product planning process describes the series of steps undertaken by a manufacturer in the introduction of a new product. Channel members are important in the new product planning process. Manufacturers can secure new product ideas from channel members. They can also forecast sales of a new product. In evaluating product alternatives, manufacturers need to consider the channel overlap of new products with the firm's existing products. Manufacturers also need to secure the cooperation of channel members in test marketing.

2 *To discuss the channel management implications of the product life cycle concept.* The product life cycle describes the stages in the history of a product: introduction, growth, maturity, and decline. While most texts limit the discussion of the product life cycle to the last four stages, this chapter also examines the role of channel members in the new product planning process.

The introduction stage of the product life cycle corresponds to a product's commercialization and its intended sales to the full target market. A manufacturer's overall channel strategy in the introduction stage is to build a sufficient distribution network to satisfy demand and to provide high levels of intermediate and final customer assistance. Depending on the product, this may involve customer training and technical support. Important channel considerations in the introductory stage are the role of wholesalers and retailers in the diffusion of new products, channel criteria in stocking new products, need for channel cooperation in stocking new products, and differences in the success in marketing new products among distributors.

The growth stage of the product life cycle corresponds to a period of rapid sales growth due to increased product acceptance among consumers and the emergence of competition. In this stage, distribution needs to be rapidly expanded to accommodate increased demand. While innovators comprise the major market target in the introduction stage, in the growth stage, the market has expanded to include part of the mass market. Critical channel decisions in this stage are to reevaluate market coverage and the appropriateness of channels to ensure that a firm can capitalize on the growth opportunities in the market.

The maturity stage of the product life cycle corresponds to a product's reaching its sales peak (both for the company and the industry) and the highest level of competition. In maturity, the channel emphasis is to reevaluate market coverage, increase dealer enthusiasm and shelf space allocation, consider a private-label strategy, and appeal to new market segments. These strategies seek to lengthen the maturity stage of the product life cycle.

The decline stage of the product life cycle corresponds to a drop in industry sales and profits. The decline stage may be due to technological factors (such as technological advances) as well as changes in customer tastes. In decline, a manufacturer has several channel options: reduce the number of channel members that a product is sold through, discontinue the product and its distribution, or attempt to revise sales through development of a new product and new distribution channels.

3 *To describe reverse channels: product recall and product recycling.* Reverse channels signify the movement of products from the buyer back to the manufacturer. Reverse channels occur in the case of returned goods, in product recall, and in product recycling.

Common characteristics of reverse channels are: the direction of the flow of goods and services is from final consumer to manufacturer, wholesalers and retailers accumulate small quantities from their customers, channel members combine separate goods into appropriate categories for the benefit of their vendors, and suppliers may not be past customers.

Product recalls involve products that require repair or replacement. Product recalls can be voluntary or mandatory. Different government agencies have jurisdiction over product recalls, depending on the type of product. Product recalls are costly. A firm can reduce the costs of a recall through a combination of measures designed to reduce the probability of recalling a good, the time period between determining that a product is defective and its actual recall, and lost business after a recall notification.

Product recycling deals with the recovery of natural resources from the return of a used product or its packaging. Product recycling can be promoted through financial incentives, financial disincentives, educational programs, and laws. Channel members can reduce waste and increase product recycling by designing products for ease of disposal, using a closed-loop production cycle, and using product components with a high recycling rate.

4 *To analyze the channel management implications of packaging.* Packaging has a major impact on channel members. An effective package should protect a product; lower distribution, shipping, and disposal costs; reduce shelf space usage; and encourage self-service merchandising.

5 *To study the legal aspects of product management relating to channels: exclusive dealing, tying arrangements, full-line forcing, reciprocity, refusal to deal, private-label strategy, and slotting allowances.* Exclusive dealing is the requirement by a seller that its customers sell only its products, or at least no products in direct competition with its products. A tying arrangement is an agreement whereby a seller conditions the sale of one product upon the buyer's purchase of a second product. Full-line forcing exists when a wholesaler or retailer is forced to order, stock, and display each type of product produced by a manufacturer that is applicable to its trade area. Reciprocity is the practice of buying goods and services from major customers; in turn, these customers then purchase goods and services from the firm. Refusal to deal involves a manufacturer or wholesaler refusing to sell goods to selected intermediaries. Both private-label goods and slotting allowances are subject to the Robinson-Patman Act.

KEY TERMS

new product planning process
functional fit
channel overlap
test marketing
shelf facings
product life cycle
introduction stage
diffusion process
gatekeepers
change agents
scouts
troops
pioneer brands
follower brands

slotting allowance
pay to stay fee
failure fee
growth stage
maturity stage
superstore
private label (dealer brand)
national brand (manufacturer's brand)
selling against the brand
decline stage
self-fulfilling prophecy
reverse channels
backhauling

product recall
completion rate
product recycling
post-consumer waste
comparable waste
pre-consumer waste
tipping fees
closed-loop cycle
exclusive dealing
tying arrangement
full-line forcing
reciprocity
refusal to deal

QUESTIONS FOR DISCUSSION

1. Why are channel members important resource people in the new product planning stage?
2. Explain the concept of channel overlap as a competitive advantage in channels management.
3. Differentiate between the use of test marketing to determine final customer and distributor acceptance of a new product.

4. Why is the product life cycle concept a useful framework for channel members? Explain your answer from the perspective of a retailer.

5. Explain the gatekeeper and change agent roles of wholesalers and retailers.

6. Differentiate among a slotting allowance, a pay to stay fee, and a failure fee.

7. Comment on Compaq's channel strategy in the 1980s and the 1990s. Relate the strategy to the product life cycle concept.

8. What are the pros and cons of a private-label strategy to a manufacturer that also manufactures a major national brand?

9. Differentiate between reverse and forward channels.

10. Develop a product recall strategy for a pharmaceutical manufacturer with a tainted product.

11. Develop a strategy for a soda manufacturer to increase product recycling in a state with a mandatory deposit law. Five-cent deposits are charged for the container and redeemed in local stores.

12. Explain the role of packaging to channel members.

13. Differentiate between the per se rule and the rule of reason.

14. Differentiate among tying agreements, full-line forcing, and reciprocity.

END NOTES

1. Paul M. Barrett, "Supreme Court Clears Trial of Kodak in Antitrust Case," *Wall Street Journal* (June 9, 1992), p. A3; Brent Bowers and Jeffrey A. Tannenbaum, "Small Businesses Laud High Court Ruling on Kodak," *Wall Street Journal* (June 10, 1992), p. B2; Linda Greenhouse, "Kodak Dealt a Setback in Antitrust Case Ruling," *New York Times* (June 6, 1992), p. D2; Joan E. Rigdon, "Small Repair Firms Fight Manufacturers," *Wall Street Journal* (June 22, 1992), p. B2; and Tim Smart, Gary McWilliams, and Alice Z. Cuneo, "Kodak Takes a Shot in the Mug," *Business Week* (June 22, 1992), p. 40.

2. See Christopher S. Eklund, "How Black & Decker Got Back in the Black," *Business Week* (July 12, 1987), pp. 86–90; and John R. Johnson, "Promoting Profits Through Partnerships," *Industrial Distribution* (March 1994), p. 23.

3. See Neal Templin and Jeff Cole, "Manufacturers Use Suppliers to Help Them Develop New Products," *Wall Street Journal* (December 19, 1994), pp. A1, A8.

4. See Milt Freudenheim, "Removing the Warehouse from Cost-Conscious Hospitals," *New York Times* (March 3, 1991), p. F5; and Christopher Palmeri, "Unwelcome Attention," *Forbes* (October 14, 1991), pp. 45–46.

5. "Radio-Wave Light Bulb May Last Up to 14 Years," *New York Times* (June 1, 1992), p. D4.

6. Joan E. Rigdon and Meredith K. Wadman, "Long-Life Lightbulb May Lose Brilliance in a Crowded Market," *Wall Street Journal* (June 2, 1992), p. B4.

7. Theodore Levitt, "Exploit the Product Life Cycle," *Harvard Business Review*, Vol. 43 (November–December 1965), pp. 81–94.

8. J. Morgan Jones and Charlotte H. Mason, *The Role of Distribution in the Diffusion of New Durable Consumer Products* (Cambridge, Mass.: Marketing Science Institute, 1990), pp. 6, 12. Also see Elizabeth C. Hirschman and Ronald W. Stampfl, "Roles of Retailing in the Diffusion of Popular Culture: Microperspectives," *Journal of Retailing*, Vol. 56 (Spring 1980), pp. 16–36.

9. Jones and Mason, *The Role of Distribution in the Diffusion of New Durable Consumer Products*, p. 8.

10. Ibid., pp. 8–9.

11. Ibid., p. 5.

12. Vithala R. Rao and Edward W. McLaughlin, "Modeling the Decision to Add New Products by Channel Intermediaries," *Journal of Marketing,* Vol. 53 (January 1989), p. 83.

13. Ibid., pp. 84–87.

14. See Nicholas Nickolaus, "Marketing New Products with Industrial Distributors," *Industrial Marketing Management,* Vol. 19 (November 1990), pp. 295–296.

15. Frank H. Alpeer, Michael A. Kamins, and John L. Graham, "An Examination of Reseller Buyer Attitudes Toward Order of Brand Entry," *Journal of Marketing,* Vol. 55 (July 1992), pp. 25–37.

16. *Nash Finch 1990 Annual Report,* p. 4; and Patricia Sellers, "Winning over the New Consumer," *Fortune* (July 29, 1991), p. 113.

17. See Rao and McLaughlin, "Modeling the Decision to Add New Products by Channel Intermediaries," p. 81.

18. See Bill Saporito, "How Quaker Oats Got Rolled," *Fortune* (October 8, 1990), pp. 129 ff.

19. Jason Zweig, "Chock Full o' Potential," *Forbes* (June 22, 1992), pp. 52, 54.

20. See Nickolaus, "Marketing New Products with Industrial Distributors," pp. 296–298.

21. See Marj Charlier, "Beer Makers Frothing over Plan to Charge for Shelf Space," *Wall Street Journal* (April 22, 1994), pp. B1, B5; and Kenneth Kelly, "The Antitrust Analysis of Grocery Slotting Allowances: The Procompetitive Case," *Journal of Public Policy & Marketing,* Vol. 10 (Spring 1991), p. 189.

22. Elizabeth J. Wilson and Arch G. Woodside, "Marketing New Products with Distributors," *Industrial Marketing Management,* Vol. 15 (February 1992), pp. 15–21.

23. See Steven W. Kopp and Mary Jane Sheffet, "A Proposal for Change in the Distribution of OTC Drugs: A Third Category of Drugs," *1991 American Marketing Association Educators' Proceedings,* Mary C. Gilly, F. Robert Dwyer, and Thomas W. Leigh et al., eds. (Chicago: American Marketing Association, 1991), pp. 343–349.

24. Peter H. Lewis, "As Price Wars Heat Up, the Victors Seem to Be Customers," *New York Times* (June 28, 1992), p. F8.

25. Patrick M. Reilly, "Electronics Retailers Revamp Stores and Inventories as Sales Begin to Cool," *Wall Street Journal* (April 20, 1992), p. B8.

26. Stephen Kreider Yoder, "Hewlett-Packard Is Too Busy to Notice Industry Slump," *Wall Street Journal* (May 11, 1992), p. B5.

27. Timothy L. O'Brien, "Beleaguered Schwinn Seeks Partner to Regain Its Luster," *Wall Street Journal* (May 20, 1992), p. B2; and Andrew Tanzer, "Bury Thy Teacher," *Forbes* (December 21, 1992), pp. 90–94 ff.

28. Dawn Wilensky, "Store Brands Take Paramount Importance as Retailers Scale Back National Brands," *Discount Store News* (May 16, 1994), p. 24.

29. Wendy Zellner, "The Sam's Generation," *Business Week* (November 25, 1991), pp. 36, 38.

30. Suein L. Hwang, "Healthy Eating, Premium Private Labels Take a Bite Out of Nabisco's Cookie Sales," *Wall Street Journal* (July 13, 1992), pp. B1, B4.

31. *Whirlpool Corporation Annual Report on Form 10K for the Year Ended December 31, 1990,* p. 5.

32. See Betsy Wiesendanger, "Bigger Sales, Same Budget," *Sales & Marketing Management* (July 1993), pp. 46–48.

33. See Steve Weinstein, "Managing Store Brands," *Progressive Grocer* (May 1994), pp. 115–120.

34. See Sharon Reier, "Branding the Company," *Financial World* (November 26, 1991), pp. 32–33.

35. Laurence Hooper, "IBM Opens a European Unit to Sell Low-Priced PC Clones Made in Asia," *Wall Street Journal* (June 5, 1992), p. B8.

36. Julia Flynn Siler and Stephanie Anderson Forest, "Oshkosh B'Gosh May Be Risking Its Upscale Image," *Business Week* (July 15, 1991), p. 140.

37. Ibid.

38. See Mary Lambkin and George Day, "Evolutionary Processes in Competitive Markets: Beyond the Product Life Cycle," *Journal of Marketing*, Vol. 53 (July 1989), pp. 4–20; and Susan L. Holak and Y. Edwin Tang, "Advertising's Effect on the Product Evolutionary Process," *Journal of Marketing*, Vol. 53 (July 1990), pp. 16–29.

39. For a classic article on reverse channels, see James H. Barnes, Jr., "Recycling: A Problem in Reverse Logistics," *Journal of Macromarketing* (Fall 1982), pp. 31–37.

40. "Product Recalls: Less Than Meets the Eye," *Consumer Reports* (November 1994), p. 732.

41. Barry Meier, "Product Safety Commission Is Criticized as Too Slow to Act," *New York Times* (September 21, 1991), p. 46.

42. Neal Templin, Oscar Suris, and Gregory N. Racz, "Honda Doubles Size of Recall to Biggest Ever," *Wall Street Journal* (June 16, 1993), p. B1.

43. Jim Carlton and Stephen Kreider Yoder, "Humble Pie: Intel to Replace Its Pentium Chips," *Wall Street Journal* (December 21, 1994), p. B6.

44. Stewart Toy and Lisa Driscoll, "Can Perrier Purify Its Reputation?" *Business Week* (February 26, 1990), p. 45.

45. Carlton and Yoder, "Humble Pie: Intel to Replace Its Pentium Chips," p. B6.

46. "Product Recalls: Less Than Meets the Eye," p. 732.

47. Carlton and Yoder, "Humble Pie: Intel to Replace Its Pentium Chips," pp. B1, B6.

48. "Product Recalls: Less Than Meets the Eye," p. 732.

49. Michael H. Morris and Duane L. Davis, "Measuring and Managing Customer Service in Industrial Firms," *Industrial Marketing Management*, Vol. 21 (1992), p. 349.

50. Roberta Furger and Daniel Tynan, "For Better or Worse," *PC World* (November 1994), p. 160.

51. George E. Hoffer, Stephen W. Pruitt, and Robert J. Reilly, "When Recalls Matter: Factors Affecting Owner Response to Automotive Recalls," *Journal of Consumer Affairs*, Vol. 28 (Summer 1994), pp. 96–106.

52. See J. Davis Illingworth, "Relationship Marketing: Pursuing the Perfect Person-to-Person Relationship," *Journal of Service Marketing*, Vol. 5 (Fall 1991), pp. 49–52.

53. See Tim Triplett, "Economics Meets Ecology As Recycled Paper Matures," *Marketing News* (February 28, 1994), p. 2.

54. John T. McQuiston, "Comes a Hunk of Junk, Goes a Chunk of Steel," *New York Times* (June 6, 1992), p. L29.

55. See Peter Nulty, "Recycling Becomes a Big Business," *Fortune* (August 13, 1990), pp. 81–82 ff.

56. See Jerry Powell, "Realities of Recycling," *Progressive Grocer Special Report* (June 1990), pp. 37–40.

57. See Marcia Berss, "No One Wants to Shoot Snow White," *Forbes* (October 14, 1991), p. 40.

58. Frank Edward Allen, "As Recycling Surges, Market for Materials Is Slow to Develop," *Wall Street Journal* (January 17, 1992), p. A6.

59. Laurie M. Grossman, "Florida to Buy Back Its Recycled Waste," *Wall Street Journal* (June 19, 1992), p. B1.

60. Allen, "As Recycling Surges, Market for Materials Is Slow to Develop," p. 1.

61. Berss, "No One Wants to Shoot Snow White," p. 40.

62. Dana Milbank, "Aluminum's Envious Rivals Turn Green, Rush to Show They, Too, Are Recyclable," *Wall Street Journal* (September 18, 1991), pp. B1, B7.

63. See Nulty, "Recycling Becomes a Big Business," pp. 81–82 ff.

64. Joshua L. Wiener and Ajay Sukdial, "Recycling of Solid Waste: Directions for the Future," *1990 American Marketing Association Educators' Proceedings,* A. Parasuraman, William Bearden, and Rohit Deshpande, eds. (Chicago: American Marketing Association, 1990), p. 389.

65. Steve Weinstein, "Trashing the Trash," *Progressive Grocer* (August 1991), p. 86.

66. George C. Lodge and Jeffrey F. Rayport, "Knee-Deep and Rising: America's Recycling Crisis," *Harvard Business Review,* Vol. 69 (September–October 1991), p. 130.

67. Ferdinand Protzman, "Germany's Push to Expand the Scope of Recycling," *New York Times* (July 4, 1993), p. F8.

68. Gene Bylinsky, "Manufacturing for Reuse," *Fortune* (February 6, 1995), pp. 104–105.

69. See John Holusha, "Car Recycling: An Afterlife for Automobiles," *New York Times* (June 16, 1991), p. F10.

70. See Krystal Miller, "Economics and Environmental Concerns Underlie Push for Fully Recyclable Cars," *Wall Street Journal* (April 30, 1991), p. B1.

71. *The Clorox Company Annual Report for the Year Ended June 30, 1991,* p. 15.

72. Valarie Reitman, "'Green' Products Sales Seem to Be Wilting," *Wall Street Journal* (May 18, 1992), p. B1.

73. *Stone Container Corporation 1990 Annual Report,* p. 13.

74. Milbank, "Aluminum's Envious Rivals Turn Green, Rush to Show They, Too, Are Recyclable," p. B1.

75. David Biddle, "Recycling for Profit: The New Green Business Frontier," *Harvard Business Review,* Vol. 71 (November–December 1993), p. 148.

76. Jonathan P. Hicks, "Sensors That Tell Just How Good the Packaging Is," *New York Times* (September 15, 1991), p. F7.

77. Greg Erickson, "High-Profit Packages," *Packaging* (June 1988), p. 8.

78. Anthony Ramirez, "L'eggs Makes Big Switch: From Plastic to Cardboard," *New York Times* (July 10, 1991), pp. D1, D7.

79. Louis W. Stern and Thomas L. Eovaldi, *Legal Aspects of Marketing Strategy* (Englewood Cliffs, N.J.: Prentice-Hall, 1984), p. 302.

80. Dorothy Cohen, "Faulkner Advertising Associates, Inc. v. Nissan Motor Corp. in U.S.A.," *Journal of Marketing,* Vol. 55 (April 1991), p. 60.

81. Nick L. Nicholas, "Dean O. Webb, Regency Consultants, Inc., and Primo's Partners, Ltd., v. Primo's Inc., Ferris Anthony and Carmelo Tringali," *Journal of Marketing,* Vol. 54 (July 1990), p. 95.

82. Gary McWilliams, "Zenith Data, Act II: Enter New Chief, Swinging," *Business Week* (May 27, 1991), pp. 102–103.

83. Brad Reid, "Smith Machine Co., Inc. v. Hesston Corp." *Journal of Marketing,* Vol. 54 (April 1990), pp. 96–97.

84. See Stern and Eovaldi, *Legal Aspects of Marketing Strategy,* pp. 319–321.

85. Brad Reid, "Toys 'R' Us v. R.H. Macy & Co., Inc." *Journal of Marketing,* Vol. 54 (October 1990), p. 106.

86. *FTC v. Borden Co.,* 383 U.S. 636 (1966).

87. Ken Rankin, "FTC May Relax Opposition to 'Slotting Fees'," *Discount Store News* (September 17, 1990), p. 8. For a comprehensive analysis of the legality of slotting allowances, see Joseph P. Cannon and Paul N. Bloom, "Are Slotting Allowances Legal under the Antitrust Laws?" *Journal of Public Policy & Marketing,* Vol. 10 (Spring 1991), pp. 167–186.

CASE 1

GOODYEAR TIRE & RUBBER COMPANY: REEVALUATING CHANNELS

Goodyear Tire & Rubber, under the leadership of Stanley C. Gault, the former chairman of Rubbermaid, wants to recapture the lost market share of its flagship Goodyear brand. The brand's share of the replacement tire business fell from approximately 15 percent in 1987 to about 12 percent in 1992.

Part of Goodyear Tire & Rubber's problems have been its poor response to changes in channel purchasing behavior by final consumers. Goodyear management realized that it needed broader distribution of its tires since people were no longer willing to seek out a specialty tire dealer when their tires needed replacement (see Table 1). Consumers increasingly purchase tires at discount tire shops, mass merchandisers, and warehouse clubs (these outlets sell multiple brands), but until recently, the Goodyear brand was sold almost exclusively through 1000 company-owned stores and 2500 independent dealers (who sell the Goodyear brand exclusively). In 1992, Goodyear began selling its Goodyear brand of tires through Sears, Wal-Mart, and several tire chains such as Discount Tire Company of Arizona. On March 3, 1992, Goodyear Tire & Rubber announced that it would begin to sell seven of its Goodyear-brand tire product lines to Sears, Roebuck & Company. Sears sells 9.5 million tires a year, more than any other retailer.

The sale of tires to these channel members resulted in poor relations between Goodyear and many of its independent dealers. These independent dealers still sell over 50 percent of Goodyear's replacement tires. According to the president of a 10-store tire chain, "You feel like after 35 years of marriage your wife is stepping out on you." Hundreds of Goodyear Tire & Rubber's 2500 independent dealers have begun to stock additional tire brands as a reaction to Goodyear's sales to Sears. Many dealers have started stocking private-label tires (some of which are made by Goodyear's Kelly-Springfield unit). These brands offer dealers higher profit margins and less price competition. Other dealers picked up competitive brands such as Michelin and Bridgestone. Several California dealers have even sued Goodyear, arguing that it unfairly cut the dealers' profit margins by selling tires through mass merchandisers. Although a top Goodyear executive argued that Goodyear dealers have reported record sales increases

TABLE 1 SHARE OF U.S. REPLACEMENT TIRE MARKET BY CHANNEL, 1982 AND 1992

Channel Outlet	1982	1992[a]
Traditional multibrand	44	44
Discount multibrand	7	15
Mass merchandisers	20	14
Company-owned	10	9
Service stations	11	8
Warehouse clubs	—	6
Other	8	4
Total	100	100

[a]Estimate.

Source: Zachary Schiller, "Goodyear Is Gunning Its Marketing Engine," *Business Week* (March 16, 1992), p. 42.

over this time period, several dealers reported lower profit margins due to competition from mass merchandisers.

On January 24, 1995, Goodyear announced that it plans to offer its independent tire retailers and company-owned stores an exclusive line of tires. Many of the tires will be comparable or identical to Goodyear's existing products, but they will be sold under different model designations. Some tires will be offered in different sizes and tread depths, while others will be available only through dealers. These strategies were designed to reduce price competition between Goodyear's distribution channels. Although other tire manufacturers have offered exclusive products to different channel members, this is the first time that Goodyear has used this strategy. As part of this strategy, Goodyear will develop a new discount structure that will make it more profitable for dealers to purchase more Goodyear tires. Goodyear hopes that the discount structure will stop dealers from selling an additional brand. Goodyear will also help dealers open additional branches in underserved markets.

Goodyear's distribution differs from competitors in terms of private-label emphasis. Cooper Tire & Rubber distributes half of its production as private label (through oil companies, large independent distributors, and mass marketers). The other half is sold through independent dealers. Cooper also does not compete against its dealers through company-owned stores.

QUESTIONS

1. Apply the product life cycle concept to Goodyear's past and new distribution strategy.
2. Compare Goodyear's distribution with Cooper Tire & Rubber.
3. Evaluate Table 1.
4. Evaluate the strengths and weaknesses of Goodyear's overall distribution strategy.

Sources: Seth Lubove, "The Last Bastion," *Forbes* (February 14, 1994), pp. 56 ff.; "Kmart Rolling Out Exclusive Michelin Tire Line," *Discount Store News* (July 6, 1992), p. 43; Myron Magnet, "Goodyear Tire & Rubber: The Marvels of High Margins," *Fortune* (May 2, 1994), pp. 73–74; Dana Milbank, "Independent Goodyear Dealers Rebel," *Wall Street Journal* (July 18, 1992), p. B2; Raju Narisetti, "Goodyear Plans to Offer Dealers Exclusive Lines," *Wall Street Journal* (January 23, 1995), p. A4; Peter Nulty, "The Bounce Is Back at Goodyear," *Fortune* (September 7, 1992), pp. 70–72; Zachary Schiller, "Goodyear Is Gunning Its Marketing Engine," *Business Week* (March 16, 1992), p. 42; and Alex Taylor III, "Cooper Tire & Rubber: Now Hear This, Jack Welch," *Fortune* (April 6, 1992), pp. 94–95.

CASE 2

OPW FUELING: THE ANATOMY OF A PRODUCT RECALL

OPW Fueling Components manufactures a wide range of petroleum-handling equipment such as automatic service station nozzles and aircraft fueling equipment. One of its products is a tight-fill adaptor that is used in below-ground storage tanks. The groove on the end of the tight-fill adaptor is used to make a leak-tight connection for the delivery and storage of fuel.

In 1985, OPW replaced its metal adaptor with Duratuff, an OPW registered trademark for Dupont Zytel, a fiberglass-reinforced nylon resin. Duratuff was used instead of metal because of its ability to resist rusting; rust is a common problem with below-ground installations. Between 1985 and 1989, more than 50,000 Duratuff connections were sold. In early 1989, several incidents involving fires were reported to OPW. OPW engineers speculated that the flames were due to static electricity generated by the movement of product delivery and the increase in the sale of gasoline blended with methanol (which began in 1985).

OPW management made the difficult decision to recall all of its 50,000 Duratuff tight-fill adaptors (as well as the several thousand in the hands of distributors or in the inventory of end-use consumers). The most difficult aspect of the recall procedure was determining the locations where the adaptors were installed.

To help locate the recalled units installations, OPW

- Contacted OPW's 450 active fueling components distributors with a telegram that was sent on the same day the firm decided to recall the adaptor.
- Mailed press releases to over 40 publications announcing the product recall. The recall notice contained a photograph of the adaptor.
- Advertised the product recall in nine important trade publications such as *Convenience Store News, Journal of Petroleum Marketing,* and *Modern Bulk Transport.*
- Sent letters announcing the recall to different types of customers. Letters were sent to former distributors, original equipment manufacturer (OEM) customers that use the adaptor as part of the systems they assemble or manufacture, distributors that have purchased the product since its introduction, end-users that could be identified, and members of trade associations who were likely to be end-users. Distributors were asked to contact their customers and inform them of the recall.
- Designated other publics (such as state fire marshalls, members of the Petroleum Equipment Institute, and chief marketing officers of major petroleum marketers) to receive specifically targeted letters.

In all communication, OPW agreed to replace the adaptor with a similar product made from conductive Duratuff or from a metal material, or to provide a full refund or credit plus the cost of freight. All correspondence also contained the firm's toll-free telephone number and encourages users to contact the firm regarding the adaptor, the installation, or the product recall program.

The firm replaced conductive adaptors with a line of nonconductive adaptors. Current sales of the conductive adaptors are "robust." Part of the credit for the success of the recall was the advance planning, the close relationship between OPW's law firm, advertising/public relations firm, and strategic planners, and the nonadversarial relationship among the parties involved.

QUESTIONS

1. How can OPW evaluate the success of its product recall program?
2. Compare OPW's recall procedure to Table 8-4 in the text. This table lists three different degrees of difficulty in locating affected products in a product recall program.
3. Evaluate OPW's recall program from the perspective of Table 8-6 in the text.
4. How would the product recall program differ if it involved a product ultimately sold to final consumers, such as the filler adaptor in the gas tank of a car? Explain your answer.

Source: Ron Jackson, "Preparation's the Backbone in the 'Anatomy of a Recall'," *Marketing News* (August 6, 1990), p. 10.

CHAPTER 9

PRICING STRATEGY IN CHANNELS

CHAPTER OBJECTIVES

1. To compare and contrast the use of price and nonprice competition.

2. To differentiate among sales-based, profit-based, and status quo-based pricing objectives.

3. To study the three general approaches to the development of an overall pricing strategy: cost-oriented, demand-oriented, and competition-oriented and their integration.

4. To evaluate alternative pricing policies: high-low pricing, everyday low pricing, gray market goods, price guarantees, and selling against the brand.

5. To analyze the use of different discounts and terms.

6. To describe how a reseller can adapt its pricing strategy.

7. To determine the legal aspects of pricing decision making.

In October 1993, an Arkansas judge ruled that Wal-Mart Stores Inc., the nation's largest retailer, was guilty of trying to drive a handful of small-town pharmacies out of business by selling some merchandise below cost. In addition to Arkansas, 22 other states have similar below-cost pricing statutes.

In their lawsuit, three Arkansas pharmacy owners accused Wal-Mart of predatory pricing. In predatory pricing, a large retailer typically sells goods below cost in an effort to drive selected competitors into bankruptcy. Often, the prices set by the larger retailer are lower in areas where it seeks to destroy competition than in areas with no competition. The three pharmacy owners contended that Wal-Mart offered below-cost prices on everything from toothpaste to mouthwash to over-the-counter medicines at its Conway store. One pharmacy owner even acknowledged that he shopped for certain merchandise to stock his store at Wal-Mart's Conway store, since the store's retail prices were less than his wholesale cost. While Wal-Mart acknowledged that it sold some products for less than its cost, it insisted that its actions did not destroy competition in the Conway area.

An Arkansas judge awarded the Arkansas pharmacists treble damages totaling $289,407. The judge also ordered Wal-Mart to stop selling drugs and health and beauty products below cost at its Conway store. The judge based his ruling on Wal-Mart's stated policy to "meet or beat the competition without regard to cost," as well as in-store comparisons of prices at its competitors. In his awarding judgment, the judge stated that Wal-Mart broke a state law barring the sale of items at a loss "for the purpose of injuring competitors and destroying competition." Although this is the first time the Arkansas sales-below-cost law was invoked, it was not the first time that Wal-Mart lost a predatory pricing case. After Wal-Mart lost a similar case in Oklahoma in 1986, it agreed to raise prices in the state.

Critics of the judgment argued that it did not accurately reflect the current and historical market conditions in Conway. For example, since Wal-Mart opened its Conway store, the combined gross profit margins at the three pharmacies increased from 24.9 percent in 1986 to 29.2 percent in 1990. In addition, while there were 12 pharmacies in Conway in 1987, in 1993, there were 14 pharmacies. All of the original 12 pharmacies remained. Lastly, the number of pharmacists in Faulker County (where Conway is located) increased from 38 in 1987 to 58 in 1992.

In an appeal, the Arkansas Supreme Court in a 4-to-3 decision overturned the lower court decision. The court's majority stated that "The loss-leader strategy employed by Conway Wal-Mart is readily justifiable as a tool to foster competition and to gain a competitive edge as opposed to simply being viewed as a stratagem to eliminate rivals altogether." In its decision, the Arkansas Supreme Court ruled that the practice of selling some items below cost is "markedly different from a sustained effort to destroy competition." The court also noted that the three pharmacies that sued Wal-Mart are still profitable and are "far from destroyed." In addition, the court found that Wal-Mart's policies had little negative effect on other competitors. A Wal-Mart vice president referred to the Supreme Court's decision as "a clear victory for consumers and the competitive free enterprise system."

According to several legal experts, the Arkansas Supreme Court's decision is more in line with federal guidelines than the initial lawsuit. Federal laws require that the court examine the impact of predatory pricing on overall competition, not the effect on an individual competitor. Federal courts are also more prone to look at a retailer's overall pricing strategy, not the prices of just 10 or so items.[1]

In this chapter, we examine how prices are set and maintained by channel members. We also focus on legal issues relating to pricing, such as state sales-below-cost laws.

INTRODUCTION TO PRICING STRATEGY IN CHANNELS

Although pricing strategy is typically covered in retail management, business-to-business marketing courses, and marketing management courses, the coverage in a channels course is somewhat different. First, wholesalers and retailers generally set prices using markup forms of pricing. Therefore, this chapter gives special attention to markup and other cost-oriented pricing techniques. Second, channels management must consider the interrelationship among manufacturers, wholesalers, retailers, and final consumers in the price-setting process. While each intermediary needs to earn an adequate profit (to compensate them for their channel functions and risk), the ultimate price to the consumer must also be competitive to the consumer as well as profitable to the manufacturer. Third, special topics related to channels management such as high-low pricing, everyday low pricing, the gray market, and discounts are extensively covered.

This chapter describes the development and implementation of a channel pricing strategy. Figure 9-1 lays out the structure of the chapter. Although the process is sequential (beginning with the evaluation of price versus nonprice competition and ending with revising the strategy), the adaptation process can cause a channel member to reexamine any stage. For example, a price may have to be changed to reflect poor profitability, the opening of a major competitor, or a shortage of a major raw material ingredient.

PRICE VERSUS NONPRICE COMPETITION

The first step in developing an overall pricing strategy is to evaluate the relative use of pricing in the overall marketing mix. For example, in **price competition**, manufacturers, wholesalers, and retailers seek to increase or decrease demand

FIGURE 9-1 Developing and implementing a channels pricing strategy.

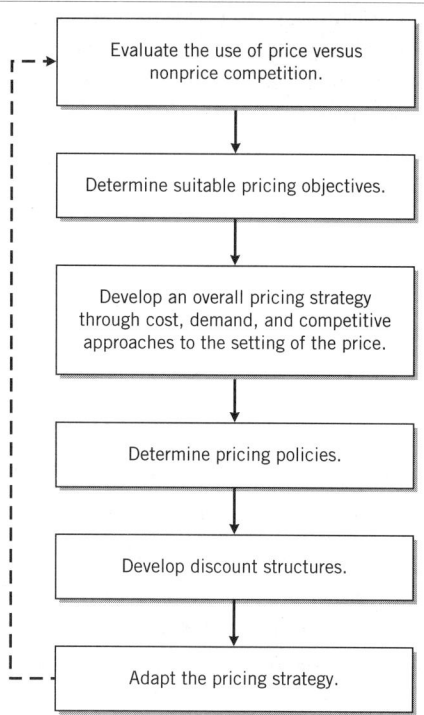

on the basis of changes in price. In contrast, in **nonprice competition**, sellers seek to change demand on the basis of distinctive benefits, and special pre-sale, during the sale, and post-sale services. Nonprice competition enables a manufacturer, wholesaler, or retailer to minimize the impact of price on demand.

Price competition may be a preferred strategy when a channel member has a long-term cost advantage over competition, when a product sold is a commodity that cannot be easily differentiated, and when consumers are very price conscious. On the other hand, nonprice competition is preferable if a channel member has distinctive products and services, or if a reseller seeks to appeal to a market segment that is not price sensitive.

While this chapter studies the development and implementation of a pricing strategy, it is important to discuss the difficulties using an overall marketing strategy that places too high a reliance on price. First, a pure price competition strategy suggests that a good is a commodity and cannot be differentiated through service. This requires a firm to sell goods at the market price. In contrast, a nonprice competition strategy suggests that even a commodity can be differentiated through service. Number 6 fuel oil, for example, is a pure commodity, but a fuel oil dealer can command a premium price on the basis of offering free warranties on a homeowner's heating system, and the professionalism of its service personnel. Second, a price strategy can more easily be copied by a competitor than a strategy based on nonprice competition. Any competitor can match a low price, whereas not every competitor can match a brand's image, a retailer's reputation for fair dealing, or a wholesaler's well-trained sales force. Third, price competition can erode profitability, tarnish a brand's image, and reduce the level of service an intermediary can provide.

One area where price competition can be welcomed is when a channel member is a low-cost provider. For example, an upstart airline that has low labor costs because of its nonunion status, flies used planes that are purchased at low cost, and uses small airports where landing fees are low, may be able to earn a profit at fares that are below the cost of those traditional airlines with higher cost structures. Retailers can be low-cost providers on the basis of low-rent, self-service formats, the use of second-use locations (where fixturing costs are low), and so on.

PRICING OBJECTIVES

There are three types of pricing objectives for all resellers: sales-, profit-, and status quo-based. With **sales-based pricing objectives**, resellers seek to increase sales. Sales can be measured in terms of dollars, units, or market share. Sales objectives can also be set for specific product lines, markets, or geographic areas. For example, a medical supplies wholesaler may wish to increase sales to the hospital market within downtown Memphis. Many resellers and market analysts also measure retailer success in terms of sales per square feet, or the sales increase on the basis of same-store sales (the percentage increase in sales for stores that have been open at least one year). This measure minimizes the effect of new stores on sales growth. Market share measures are generally used by large manufacturers, wholesalers, or retailers.

With **profit-based pricing objectives**, firms set pricing objectives in terms of profits, early recovery of cash, or return-on-investment measures. Some firms seek to maximize profitability, others seek satisfactory levels of profit, and still others seek to produce steady returns on a year-in-year-out basis. These steady returns are often desired by investors. An early recovery of cash objective is commonly used by resellers seeking to finance high growth, or by those with a high-interest expense (caused by a recent acquisition or a leveraged buyout).

One special form of return on investment pricing objectives used by many distributors and retailers is **gross margin return on investment (GMROI)**, or average gross profit per dollar of inventory investment. Mathematically, gross margin return on investment equals:

Gross margin return on investment

$$= \frac{\text{Gross profit}}{\text{Net sales}} \times \frac{\text{Net sales}}{\text{Average inventory at cost}}$$

GMROI has two components: gross profit as a percentage of sales and inventory turnover. GMROI recognizes that the largest investment for many wholesalers and retailers is its inventory. GMROI shows the importance of both gross profit and inventory turnover. For example, a low price that yields a very high inventory turnover (such as 20 percent gross profit and a five-times-a-year turnover) would produce a higher GMROI than a much higher price (such as a 60 percent gross profit and a one-time-a-year turnover).

With **status quo-based pricing objectives**, resellers seek to minimize the impact of a new competitor, anticipated government action, or change in market condition. Status quo-based pricing objectives attempt to keep sales at the level that existed prior to this event. We should not infer that status quo objectives are easy to accomplish. For example, a small hardware retailer that is confronted by the opening of a new Wal-Mart may have to totally revise its overall pricing strategy.

In practice, pricing objectives may be combinations of sales-, profit-, and status quo-based pricing objectives. For example, a wholesaler may seek to keep sales at last year's level in a tough economic climate (a combined sales- and status quo-based pricing objective), subject to achieving a 30 percent GMROI (a profit-based pricing objective).

DEVELOPING AN OVERALL PRICING STRATEGY: COST-, DEMAND-, AND COMPETITION-ORIENTED APPROACHES TO THE SETTING OF PRICE

There are three approaches to the development of an overall pricing strategy: the cost-oriented approach, the demand-oriented approach, and the competition-oriented approach. In their purest form, each approach focuses on only one element (cost, demand, or competition) in price setting. For example, cost-oriented techniques focus on adding a fair profit margin to cover a reseller's expenses and fair profit. This approach does not reflect demand or competitive conditions. Similarly, a price set on the basis of demand-oriented pricing would not reflect cost or competitive factors.

Cost-oriented approaches generally set the lowest price acceptable to the reseller; any lower price would not return a fair profit to the reseller. In contrast, demand-oriented approaches reflect the prices that a market segment is willing to pay. And competitive-oriented approaches focus on the amount of discretion any one firm has in the setting of price. Since each of these approaches looks at different factors, the resulting price level suggested by each approach can vary drastically. The integration of these three approaches is covered directly after this section.

COST-ORIENTED PRICING

In **cost-oriented pricing**, a reseller examines its total costs and adds a suitable profit to determine its price. Cost-oriented pricing is simple, since it does not require any understanding of demand or competition. It is also the most widely used overall approach to pricing by wholesalers and retailers. This section covers the following cost-oriented techniques: markup, the computation of the required initial markup percentage, and direct product profitability.

MARKUP PRICING

In **markup pricing**, channel members add operating expenses and profit requirements as a percentage of sales to determine their price. Markup pricing is widely used by wholesalers and retailers. Mathematically, the **markup percentage** is calculated as

$$\text{Markup percentage (at retail)} = \frac{\text{Selling price} - \text{Merchandise cost}}{\text{Retail selling price}}$$

$$\text{Markup percentage (at cost)} = \frac{\text{Selling price} - \text{Merchandise cost}}{\text{Merchandise cost}}$$

Although markup percentages can be computed on the basis of either merchandise costs or selling price, wholesalers and retailers have historically computed markup percentages on the basis of selling price. There are a number of reasons why selling price is used rather than merchandise cost. First, most expenses are computed as a percentage of selling price. Trade, functional, and quantity discounts are also computed on the basis of selling price. Therefore, the computation of markups based on selling price facilitates profit planning. For example, if a markup is 45 percent and operating expenses total 38 percent of sales, then net profit before tax would equal 7 percent of sales. This computation could not be easily made if markups were computed on the basis of merchandise cost. Second, selling price data can be obtained from scanners, sales receipts, and invoices; merchandise cost is not as easily obtained. And many retailers also keep inventories on the basis of retail inventory values, not wholesale cost. Third, markups are smaller if they are computed on the basis of selling price than at cost. For example, a 50 percent markup at selling price is equal to a 100 percent markup at cost.

Although most texts argue that markups are a pure cost-based pricing technique, markups can also reflect demand. Let's examine a typical markup problem to uncover its demand and competitive implications.

Problem: *A retailer requires a 30 percent markup at retail for its electronics products. The retailer can purchase a discontinued Walkman-type personal stereo for $40 wholesale. What should the retailer charge for the personal stereo?*

$$\text{Markup percentage (at retail)} = \frac{\text{Selling price} - \text{Merchandise cost}}{\text{Retail selling price}}$$

$$.30 = \frac{SP - 40}{SP}$$

$$.30\, SP = SP - 40$$

$$.70 SP = 40$$

$$SP = \$57.14$$

This problem incorporates demand considerations since the retailer needs to determine whether it can sell the good at $57.14 or more. The retailer also needs to ascertain the impact of the sale of this model at $57.14 on the sale of its other personal stereos (a competitive implication).

Another common way in which markups reflect differences in cost or demand is through a variable markup policy. In a **variable markup policy**, different markup requirements are set for specific goods to reflect differences in costs, demand, and competition. For example, a retailer could accept a lower markup on the basis of a wholesaler providing direct store delivery of certain goods (versus delivery of goods to the retailer's warehouse). This strategy is explained further in the direct product profitability section of this chapter. A wholesaler or retailer could also set a higher markup to reflect unusually high demand for a new product or to take advantage of its being an exclusive distributor in a given territory. The use of variable markups is covered in the direct product profitability section of this chapter.

COMPUTATION OF PLANNED INITIAL MARKUP PERCENTAGES BY RESELLERS

There are two broad types of markups: the **initial markup**, which uses planned levels for expenses, profit, reductions, and sales, and the **maintained markup**, which measures actual profit as a percentage of sales. The **initial markup percentage** is used in profit planning. It determines the overall markup percentage that is required for a reseller based on planned operating expenses, profits, and reductions (stock shortages, employee discounts, and planned markdowns).

Required initial markup percentage

$$= \frac{\text{Planned operating expenses} + \text{Planned profit} + \text{Planned reductions}}{\text{Planned net sales} + \text{Planned reductions}}$$

In the above formula, the required initial markup percentage is based on planned levels for operating expenses, profit levels, reductions, and sales. Thus, if a retailer has planned operating expenses of $450,000, a planned profit of $50,000, planned sales of $3.5 million, and planned reductions (such as markdowns and special discounts) of $35,000, it requires an initial markup percentage of 15.1 percent.

$$\begin{aligned}
\text{Required initial markup percentage} &= \frac{\$450{,}000 + \$50{,}000 + \$35{,}000}{\$3{,}500{,}000 + \$35{,}000} \\
&= \frac{\$535{,}000}{\$3{,}535{,}000} \\
&= 15.1\%
\end{aligned}$$

In contrast to the initial markup percentage, the **maintained markup percentage** uses actual operating expenses, profits, and sales data. The computation of maintained markup percentage is:

$$\text{Maintained markup} = \frac{\text{Actual operating expenses} + \text{Actual profit}}{\text{Actual net sales}}$$

While reductions are not specifically stated in this formula, they reduce profits in the numerator and net sales in the denominator. In the initial markup example, if profits and operating expenses were as planned, but sales were $3 million (instead of the planned $3.5 million), the maintained markup would be 16.6 percent.

$$= \frac{\$450{,}000 + \$50{,}000}{\$3{,}000{,}000}$$

$$= \frac{\$500{,}000}{\$3{,}000{,}000}$$

$$= 16.6\%$$

This is greater than the initial markup percentage. Higher than planned sales, and higher operating expenses would result in the initial markup being greater than the maintained markup. Resellers need to compare their initial and maintained markup percentages to explain why actual profit performance has been either better or worse than anticipated. These data should be used by resellers in modifying future profit goals, as well as in correcting problem areas.

DIRECT PRODUCT PROFITABILITY

Resellers that have diverse product lines (each with different cost structures) should consider using a variable markup policy. An important technique in planning and implementing a variable policy is direct product profitability. **Direct product profitability** seeks to assign warehouse, store transportation, labor, occupancy, inventory, and other store costs to categories of products to more accurately assess their profitability. Direct product profitability also adjusts gross margins to reflect special deals, allowances, and other revenues such as slotting fees.

Direct product profitability seeks to overcome the notion that costs and revenues associated with each product category are equal. Although two products could have markups that are equal, one could be much more profitable than the other owing to lower costs. For example, a comprehensive study of profitability by department for a major supermarket chain found that while a service deli generates a $1 gross profit per sale, it has only 29 cents per sale in direct product profits owing to high labor costs. In contrast, the frozen food department has less labor costs but higher equipment costs. Therefore, while its gross profit per unit sold is 59 cents, its average direct product profitability is 43 cents.[2] See Figure 9-2 for the components of direct product profitability.

Direct product profitability can also be used to plan a wholesaler's or retailer's overall product strategy. In Figure 9-3, heavy-duty liquid detergents are plotted on a two-by-two matrix. The columns in this figure categorize detergents on the basis of inventory turnover; the rows divide the detergents into one of two categories on the basis of direct product profitability. High-profit and high-inventory turnover make a category a **winner**, whereas low-profit and low-inventory turnover make a product a **dog**. High profit and low turnover characterizes a **sleeper**, while **traffic builders** have low profits but high turnover. In planning merchandise assortments, a retailer needs to assess traffic builders

FIGURE 9-2 Components of direct product profitability.

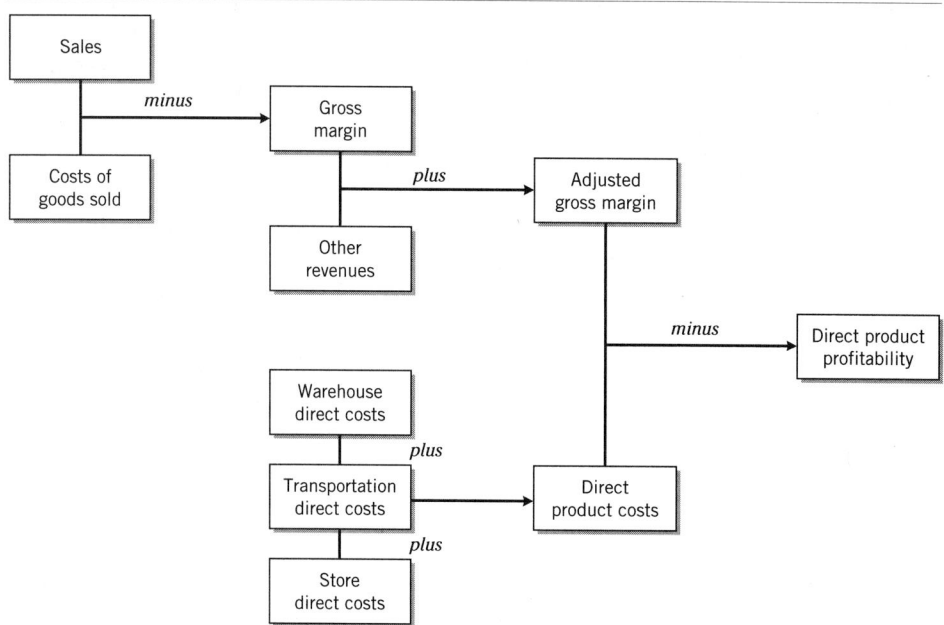

Other revenues include deals, allowances, and other direct revenues such as slotting fees.

Source: Norm Borin and Paul Farris, "An Empirical Comparison of Direct Product Profit and Existing Measures of SKU Productivity," *Journal of Retailing,* Vol. 66 (Fall 1990), p. 301. Reprinted by permission.

from their impact on the overall store. Thus, a retailer may retain a traffic builder based on its contribution to a store's overall sales levels. A retailer may also seek to turn a sleeper into a winner through better displays, better store positioning, and increased use of store sampling.

SOURCES OF GROSS MARGIN DATA ON WHOLESALERS AND RETAILERS

Gross margin data on wholesalers and retailers are available from a number of sources: Robert Morris Associates, *Dun & Bradstreet Annual Statement Studies, Progressive Grocer Annual Report of the Grocery Industry,* the National Retail Federation, and specialized trade associations. All of these organizations report data for specific categories of retailers or wholesalers. These categories can be based on chain versus independents, type of goods sold, and size of reseller. These data are an important source in determining markup percentages used by competing resellers or by channel members that are suppliers or customers.

Resellers should be aware of several difficulties in using these data sources. First, these data sources use relatively small samples. The sample sizes get even smaller when one examines a reseller category based on a particular size.

FIGURE 9-3 Application of direct product profitability to planning product strategy.

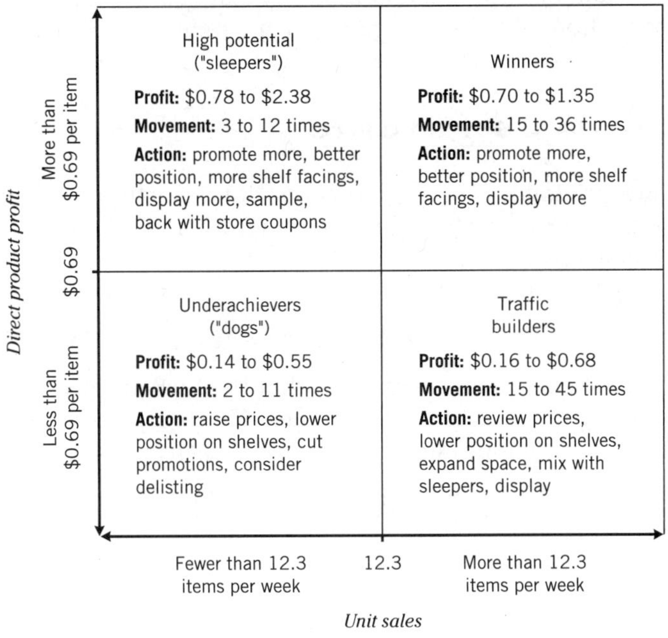

	Fewer than 12.3 items per week	More than 12.3 items per week
More than $0.69 per item	**High potential ("sleepers")** Profit: $0.78 to $2.38 Movement: 3 to 12 times Action: promote more, better position, more shelf facings, display more, sample, back with store coupons	**Winners** Profit: $0.70 to $1.35 Movement: 15 to 36 times Action: promote more, better position, more shelf facings, display more
Less than $0.69 per item	**Underachievers ("dogs")** Profit: $0.14 to $0.55 Movement: 2 to 11 times Action: raise prices, lower position on shelves, cut promotions, consider delisting	**Traffic builders** Profit: $0.16 to $0.68 Movement: 15 to 45 times Action: review prices, lower position on shelves, expand space, mix with sleepers, display

Vertical axis: Direct product profit (break at $0.69). Horizontal axis: Unit sales (break at 12.3).

Note: The break points for profitability and inventory turnover used in this example are the average performance for heavy-duty liquid detergents. The averages will be different for other product categories.
Source: "Profitability: Where It's Really At," *Progressive Grocer* (December 1992), p. 27. Reprinted by permission.

Second, different firms can respond to the sample on a year-to-year basis; newer firms could have a different profit margin performance that differs from the sample in a preceding year. Third, the data can also be misleading in that the resellers listed can be in different geographic areas from a firm's competitors. They also can have different marketing strategies. For example, while Robert Morris Associates lists the markups for a wholesaler, it describes the wholesaler on the basis of the goods sold, not whether the wholesaler is a full-service or limited-service wholesaler.

DEMAND-ORIENTED PRICING

Two important demand-oriented pricing techniques are demand-minus and chain-markup pricing. Each technique starts with the maximum price a customer (either intermediate or final) will pay for a product and then works backward to compute maximum costs for the manufacturer and each intermediary. Of the two demand-oriented techniques, demand-minus pricing is appropriate to direct distribution and chain-markup pricing to indirect distribution.

DEMAND-MINUS PRICING

Demand-minus pricing is useful in direct distribution where a manufacturer determines the appropriate final selling price and then works backward to compute its allowable costs.

The demand-minus pricing formula is:

Maximum product cost = Final selling price × [(100 − Markup percent)/100]

For example, if a manufacturer estimates that the final selling price for a product is $200 and the manufacturer determines that its markup requirements are 55 percent, the maximum product costs become $90:

$$\text{Maximum product cost} = \$200 \times (.45)$$
$$= \$90$$

CHAIN-MARKUP PRICING

Chain-markup pricing extends the concepts in demand-minus pricing to reflect the use of wholesalers and retailers as channel intermediaries. **Chain-markup pricing** works backward from the final selling price to the final customer in order to determine the acceptable price levels for each reseller. It incorporates a fair markup for merchant wholesalers, as well as retailers.

In a channel consisting of a manufacturer, a wholesaler, and a retailer, the chain markup computation formula is:

1. Maximum selling price to retailer = Final selling price × [(100 − Retailer's markup)/100]
2. Maximum selling price to wholesaler = Selling price to retailer × [(100 − Wholesaler's markup)/100]
3. Maximum product cost to manufacturer = Selling price to wholesaler × [(100 − Manufacturer's markup)/100]

For example, if the final selling price for a product is $200, and the retailer requires a 40 percent markup, a wholesaler requires a 30 percent markup, and a manufacturer a 35 percent markup, then:

1. Maximum selling price to retailer = $200 × [(100 − 40)/100]
 = $120
2. Maximum selling price to wholesaler = $120 × [(100 − 30)/100]
 = $84

3. Maximum product cost to manufacturer = $84 \times [(100 - 35)/100]$
= $54.60

Chain-markup pricing anticipates pricing opportunities and problems at each channel level. In this example, the maximum selling price to a wholesaler is $84. If a manufacturer attempts to sell the good to the wholesaler for more than $84, the merchant wholesaler cannot obtain its 20 percent markup requirement. If a wholesaler cannot receive its fair markup, it may refuse to sell the good or it may reduce the level of its services. Similarly, the maximum selling price to the retailer is $120.

Chain-markup pricing can also be used to determine the impact of different channel arrangements on a product's price. For example, chain markup allows a manufacturer to determine the impact of adding or deleting a channel member on its channel costs. It also enables a manufacturer to evaluate the impact of providing a higher or lower markup on the manufacturer's gross profit or on the ultimate cost to the final consumer. Lastly, chain-markup pricing forces a manufacturer to review its cost structure as a consequence of not being able to meet each channel member's maximum selling price levels. For example, a manufacturer can attempt to produce the good for less (by substituting materials, simplifying production processes, or using standardized parts), or even undertake certain distribution functions itself. Although a manufacturer could attempt to get a wholesaler or retailer to accept a lower markup, this strategy is generally a difficult one. Many wholesalers and retailers have strong feelings about the fairness of specific markups and may refuse to sell a product with too low a markup.

COMPETITION-ORIENTED PRICING

Unlike cost- or demand-oriented pricing, competition-oriented pricing first sets price on the basis of evaluating the offerings of competitors. A firm can choose to sell at, above, or below the competition on the basis of evaluating differences in offerings, as well as the economic environment affecting its products. Obviously, for a good considered a commodity, all resellers have little choice but to sell the good at the market price. A reseller can charge above the market to the extent that its goods are unique and its customer service levels are differentiated from other competitors. Finally, poor levels of customer service, incomplete selections, and the ability to reduce costs as the result of very high sales volumes may be accompanied by below-market price levels.

A common competition-oriented pricing technique in business-to-business marketing is competitive bidding. In **competitive bidding**, a seller submits a written offer to produce a given product or service based on specifications determined by the buyer. The specifications outline product quality criteria, architectural specifications, and delivery dates. In some markets like large municipal projects, competitive bidding is generally required by municipal law. Many firms also often require competitive bids for projects above a given dollar size.

TABLE 9-1 COMPETITIVE BIDDING MODEL

Bid Amount	Cost of Fulfilling Contract	Profit at Each Bid Level	Probability of Winning Contract	Long-Term Profit at Bid
$ 80,000	$87,000	−$ 7,000	.90	−$6,300
$ 90,000	$87,000	$ 3,000	.70	$2,100
$100,000	$87,000	$13,000	.60	$7,800
$120,000	$87,000	$23,000	.30	$6,900

All competitive bidding models rely on the **expected value concept**. This concept states that the long-term profitability at each bid level equals the profit at that bid level times the probability of that bid being accepted. An important component of the expected value concept is that while higher bid prices have higher profits, higher bid prices have lower probabilities of winning a contract than lower bid levels.

Table 9-1 illustrates competitive bidding and the expected value concept. Based on this example, the optimal bid is $100,000. This assumes a cost of $87,000 and a long-term profit of $7,800 (.60 × $13,000). Of the components in the competitive bidding model, the most difficult element to estimate is the probability of winning the contract (the probability of your bid being the lowest). One way of estimating the probability of winning the contract is to determine the chances of winning a bid using your firm's historical data at various bid amounts divided by the cost of fulfilling the contract. As your firm's bid gets larger relative to its costs, the probability of winning a bid is reduced. Conversely, the probability of winning a contract increases as the bid amount becomes small relative to a firm's costs.

Although this overall approach provides a structured means of assessing bid levels, it has several shortcomings. First, different firms may be present in each bid situation. Second, other factors may affect a competitor's bid price besides the probability of winning and the profit level at each bid. For example, a competitor may bid very low in an off-season to keep its full-time employees employed. A firm can also bid very high on the basis of being especially busy and being reticent to accept additional work. Third, competitors may have different cost structures than your firm. For example, a small firm may be able to secure a profit at a price level that would be unprofitable for a larger firm.

DEVELOPING AN INTEGRATED APPROACH TO PRICING

Although the cost-, demand-, and competitive-oriented approaches look at pricing decisions differently, all three are interrelated in practice. Since cost-oriented approaches examine pricing from the perspective of a firm's costs, they generally focus on the minimum acceptable price to a reseller. In contrast, demand-oriented approaches typically center on the market value of a good or service as perceived by a customer or market segment. This orientation assures a reseller that the calculated price is appropriate for the intended market. Finally, competitive-oriented approaches compare a firm's pricing decision with that of competition. It helps a firm determine whether it must price at the market, below the market, or above the market after considering the firm's differential advantage and its economic environment.

In reality, the setting of a price level must reflect all three considerations. For example, while a wholesaler may initially set a ballpark price based on the product's cost, its overhead, and a fair markup, the wholesaler's final price determination needs to reflect both demand and competition. A product in high demand without a direct competitor can command a higher than anticipated markup, whereas a product with lower than anticipated demand and a lot of competition may require a downward pricing adjustment.

Any reseller must determine the answers to such questions as "what is the lowest price I can charge for a product and still earn a profit?" (a cost orientation), "what is the maximum price that I can obtain from a channel member for this product?" (a demand orientation), and "can my firm charge 10 percent more than competitor X?" (a competitive orientation). These questions reflect cost, demand, and competition orientations.

DETERMINING PRICING POLICIES

Price policies enable a reseller to maintain buyer loyalty, increase sales, lower promotional expense, and maintain cost advantages over competitors. Among the pricing policies covered in this section are high-low pricing, everyday low pricing, gray market goods, price guarantees, and selling against the brand.

HIGH-LOW PRICING

In **high-low pricing**, a reseller charges higher prices on an everyday basis but runs frequent promotions in which these goods are offered at lower prices on a temporary basis. A high-low price is also characterized by heavy forward buying by wholesalers and retailers, and reductions offered to final consumers. In **forward buying**, retailers and wholesalers purchase large quantities at special discount prices that are offered to them by manufacturers. The channel intermediary typically orders a product at the end of the manufacturer's special price promotion-planning to charge consumers the full price after the promotion is over.

Four major advantages are associated with the use of high-low pricing. First, during periods of high inflation, the forward buying associated with high-low pricing increases an intermediary's profits by building large inventories at low prices. One major study, "Wholesale Food Distribution Today and Tomorrow," prepared by Andersen Consulting, found that 34 percent of wholesaler profits (based on the six wholesalers studied) came from the use of forward buying and similar buying practices.[3] Second, manufacturers use forward buying as a

CHANNELS IN ACTION

Price Setting By British Distributors

Two researchers studied the pricing practices used by engineering and paper distributors in Britain. A mail questionnaire was sent to 351 paper and 261 engineering distributors; usable responses were received from 33 percent of the paper companies and 31 percent of the engineering firms.

While the questionnaire dealt with a number of pricing practices, we will examine the findings relating to pricing methods used by the industrial distributors. Six overall pricing methods were listed by the researchers: contribution over direct costs, reference to competitor prices, full cost plus markup, price as high as customers will pay, suppliers stipulate process, and follow the market leader. These techniques reflect cost-, demand-, and competitive-oriented approaches to price setting.

Both paper and engineering distributors were more likely to use contribution over direct costs, reference to competitor process, and full cost plus markup than the other techniques listed. The competitive nature of both types of distributors can be seen in that at least 50 percent of each group set prices by referring to rivals' prices. Large proportions of both samples also used multiple methods to set price. With the exception of no engineering firm using follow the leader pricing, each of the six pricing methods was used by at least 9 percent of the respondents from both industries. This indicates that the distributors were flexible in their choice of technique. It also means that distributors sought to use the most applicable technique to a given situation. The low usage of follow the market leader by paper distributors (9 percent) and by no engineering firm may reflect the fragmented nature of these markets.

The paper distributors were more likely to use full cost plus markup and price as high as customers will pay methods than the engineering distributors. Each pricing method was also more widely used by the paper than the engineering distributors.

Source: David Shipley and Elizabeth Bourdon, "Distributor Pricing in Very Competitive Markets," *Industrial Marketing Management,* Vol. 19 (August 1990), pp. 215–224.

means of reaching short-term sales targets. The use of forward buying by manufacturers as a means of loading up resellers to increase short-term sales is referred to as **trade loading**. Sales of impulse goods especially thrive on the special promotions associated with high-low pricing. For example, according to data from Information Resources Inc., there was a 138 percent increase in sales of soft drinks that were put on display.[4] Third, high-low pricing generates high levels of store traffic and high excitement among customers. Fourth, some manufacturers also use forward buying hoping to increase longer term sales by building large inventory levels at their resellers.[5]

Critics of high-low buying cite its high costs, the lack of intended savings being passed onto customers, and poor price credibility as disadvantages of high-low pricing. The high costs of high-low pricing can be divided into three groups: carrying costs of excess inventory; high production and distribution costs; and high costs of advertising, continually repricing goods, and setting up displays. A 1991 study by the Grocery Manufacturers Association of America found that there is $60 to $80 billion worth of excess inventory in the total food distribution system. Forward buying has contributed to this practice.[6] There are also high costs for production and distribution caused by the high peaks and valleys of production. For instance, high-production utilization for a manufacturer is often followed by a major downswing as wholesalers, retailers, and final consumers use up their inventories. Lastly, high costs are associated with the use of frequent promotions, the cost of setting up and disassembling displays, and costs associated with continually repricing merchandise.

Since resellers do not pass onto final consumers all of their special pricing incentives, they do not accomplish the desired sales increase sought by manufacturers.[7] Severe price swings reduce a store's credibility.

There are three different ways to avoid the problems associated with forward buying in a high-low pricing policy. One is to use coupons given to final consumers instead of price reductions to resellers. (This method is discussed in Chapter 10). A second strategy is to verify that a manufacturer's price reduction is actually passed onto final consumers through a manufacturer's auditing of scanning tapes.[8] A third is to use everyday low pricing.

EVERYDAY LOW PRICING

In its purest form, everyday low pricing (EDLP) is set by manufacturers and enables retailers to sell their products at a single price throughout the year. There are no temporary price reductions in a pure EDLP system. In EDLP, long-term contracts are negotiated between a supplier and a customer based on a weighted average price that reflects the proportion of merchandise bought on deal and the proportion bought at regular price. For example, after Procter & Gamble eliminated trade promotions for its Dawn dishwashing liquid, it set the brand's price to a standard average of $1.32, rather than at 99 cents one week and $1.49 another.

A pure EDLP manufacturer or retailer would not have price reductions, but in reality, EDLP manufacturers and retailers still must use temporary price reductions and coupons to obtain shelf space and to stimulate consumer interest for new products or for products with lagging sales.

Although EDLP is the opposite of high-low pricing, there is not as much of a dichotomy as it may appear if the difference between high and low prices is small. A major research study of 3000 supermarkets found that EDLP is not typically practiced in its pure format. The research concluded that most of the EDLP stores sold as much merchandise on deal as high-low operators. Twenty-six percent of store volume was sold with some form of merchandising support in EDLP stores, versus 24 percent of volume in high-low stores. However, price reductions are less deep in EDLP stores than in high-low stores.[9]

In return for receiving a favorable EDLP price, retailers generally agree to support the manufacturer's product with a given number of events and to guarantee to sell the goods ordered at the reduced price. Many manufacturers ask for the right to evaluate a retailer's scanner tapes to verify that the retailer has actually sold the goods at the reduced price level.[10]

EDLP started in grocery products (particularly with Procter & Gamble) and buying clubs, and it has expanded into department stores and car dealerships.[11] According to a recent study of pricing practices by supermarkets in the top 50 markets in the United States, 26 percent of supermarket retailers are using some form of EDLP. However, the use of EDLP is more prevalent in the South and less popular in the Northeast.[12] In department stores, EDLP means that retailers will not initially set prices so high as to assume intermediate markdowns. Instead, retailers set initial prices and intend to stick to them (except for markdowns at the end of the season). In car dealerships, the use of EDLP is associated with dealers that post firm prices on selected models and do not allow negotiation.

For manufacturers, wholesalers, and retailers, EDLP helps restore price credibility that has been tarnished by frequent sales. The advantages of EDLP for manufacturers stem more from lower production and distribution costs than from high-low pricing (due to a greater opportunity to practice just-in-time inventory management and better plant utilization), reduction in forward buying, reduced allowances, less opportunity for wholesalers and retailers to sell diverse goods to other resellers, and lower administrative costs associated with deals. EDLP saves retailers the costs of changing prices on products, shelves, and in computer systems; lowers advertising expense; enables a retailer to change displays less frequently; and lowers inventory and warehouse handling expenses associated with forward buying. EDLP also enables them to be more competitive on a day in–day out basis with membership clubs.

The disadvantages associated with EDLP relate to the difficulty in generating and maintaining customer excitement through price-related promotions, and the difficulty in stimulating short-term and long-term sales. According to some market analysts, EDLP works best with products that have high market share and high brand and store loyalty.

Manufacturers, wholesalers, and retailers need to examine the impact of switching from a high-low pricing strategy to EDLP on both sales and profits. Some market analysts are particularly concerned about how EDLP would work in a situation where a manufacturer wanted to build up market share. Retailers in particular need to be concerned as to how they plan to build and maintain store traffic and how to replace excitement, given there are fewer price-oriented promotions.

GRAY MARKET GOODS

The two types of gray market goods are domestic and imports. With **domestic gray market goods**, manufacturer-authorized channel members sell trademarked goods to unauthorized channel members who then resell these goods domestically. In contrast to domestic gray market goods, **foreign gray market goods** are foreign goods that bear a valid U.S. trademark and are imported into the United States without the approval of the U.S. trademark owner. These goods are purchased abroad and were not intended for sale in the U.S. domestic market. In many cases, both domestic and foreign gray market goods compete directly with goods purchased by authorized importers. The distribution channels for both types of gray market goods are referred to as **parallel channels of distribution** since at least one vendor in the channel of distribution is not an authorized distributor of the manufacturer.

The practice of selling gray market goods is commonly called diverting. Through **diverting**, a retailer or wholesaler can also ship excess inventory it has ordered to regions that have not received a special deal from a manufacturer or wholesaler. The new retailer can sell the good at the regular retail price or at a discounted price.

Diverting can be contrasted with forward buying. In diverting, wholesalers or retailers plan to sell excess inventory sold to others or to shift merchandise

CHANNELS IN ACTION

Does EDLP Increase a Supermarket's Profitability?

Three academic researchers studied the impact of EDLP on supermarket profitability. All 86 units of Dominick's, a Chicago-based regional supermarket chain, were randomly assigned to three pricing conditions: EDLP, high-low, or control. In EDLP stores, the prices of each brand in a product category were decreased by a constant factor (ranging from 6 percent in bath tissue to 24 percent in soft drinks). On average, EDLP prices were decreased by 10 percent across all 19 categories. In high-low stores, prices of each brand in a category were increased an average of 10 percent across all product categories. While EDLP prices varied from store to store, the price of a complete market basket of goods across all 19 product categories remained unchanged during the experiment. The test ran for a minimum of 16 weeks. Promotional activity occurred as in the normal course of business.

The experiment's results showed that the 10 percent higher high-low prices led to a 15 percent increase in profitability. On the other hand, 10 percent lower EDLP prices led to an 18 percent decrease in profits. Profit results were significant in all 19 categories. Consumer demand was inelastic: 10 percent changes in EDLP levels resulted in 3 percent changes in unit sales.

The authors found that EDLP's lower prices did not increase volume to compensate for the lower profit margins in comparison to high-low pricing. In some product categories (analgesics, canned soup, and hot cereal), the differences in profitability between high-low pricing and EDLP were especially large.

A second study involving all 86 stores produced similar results. A 9 percent change in EDLP produced a 3 percent increase in unit sales in the EDLP stores compared with a 2 percent decrease in unit sales in high-low stores. Since consumer demand was inelastic, profits decreased by 18 percent in EDLP pricing and increased 17 percent with high-low pricing.

Source: Stephen J. Hoch, Xavier Drèze, and Mary E. Purk, "EDLP, Hi-Lo, and Margin Arithmetic," *Journal of Marketing*, Vol. 58 (October 1994), pp. 16–27.

from store to store within the same chain (for a national retailer).[13] In contrast, in forward buying, wholesalers or retailers purchase additional inventory for sale to their traditional customers.

Like authorized resellers, unauthorized resellers can purchase goods from authorized resellers or manufacturers in a foreign county. In many instances, foreign wholesalers or manufacturers are unaware that goods will be shipped to the United States. Figure 9-4 shows channel flows with authorized and gray markets.

Examples of foreign gray market goods that have directly competed against authorized imports are Seiko watches, Olympus cameras, Mercedes-Benz automobiles, Mallory batteries, and Caterpillar tractors. Although it is difficult to determine the overall size of the foreign gray market, one trade group estimates it to be as high as $15 billion annually. Some analysts also estimate that as much as 25 percent of the fragrances sold in the United States are foreign gray market products.[14] Traditional vendors and foreign manufacturers formed a trade group called COPIAT (Coalition to Preserve the Integrity of American Trademarks) in 1983 to fight foreign gray marketing practices. COPIAT now has more than 40 company members, including Ford, Givenchy, Benetton, Chanel, Macy's, and Procter & Gamble.

Some retail chains openly practice diverting as a means of increasing their profits. These chains have computers that enable executives to compare prices for the same merchandise in different regions. According to a Kroger spokesperson, "If we weren't into diverting, we'd be at a cost disadvantage."[15] Diverting is especially common in the food and health and beauty aids industries.

Some resellers have sold both traditional and gray market goods, but have effectively differentiated between both types of products through different service levels, warranty coverages, and so on. This is a multiple segmentation strategy, with different service offerings for the traditional product and the gray

FIGURE 9-4 Authorized markets and gray markets.

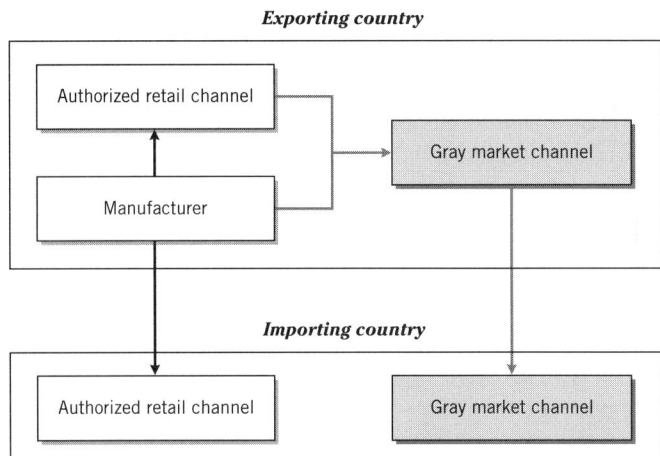

Source: Louis P. Bucklin, *The Gray Market Threat to International Marketing Strategies* (Cambridge, Mass.: Marketing Science Institute, 1990), p. 5. Reprinted by permission.

market segment. For example, traditional import channel cameras would include a guarantee covered on a worldwide basis through manufacturer-authorized repair service centers. Gray market cameras, on the other hand, would be covered through the dealers' special arrangements with individual local repair shops. Dealers selling both types of products allow the consumer to determine which combination of product, service, and price is most appropriate.

Three conditions are necessary for gray markets (either domestic or foreign) to develop. First, the price differentials across markets must be great enough to provide the motivation for gray marketing. In domestic markets, price differentials may be caused by differences in demand, the need for a manufacturer to gain access to a new market, and especially difficult competitive conditions in one market relative to other market areas. In foreign markets, price differentials can arise owing to exchange rate fluctuations, differences in demand, differences in consumer wealth, or differences in price elasticity across markets. Second, the product(s) must be well known in multiple markets. This condition allows a product to be easily sold across two or more market areas without extensive sales support or advertising. And third, tariffs and transportation costs must be low enough so that unauthorized resellers can move the product from one market to another.[16]

Other conditions that facilitate gray markets are relative shortages of desirable foreign-made products and the ease of use of a product in multiple markets. (Film would be easy to use, while a product with specific safety features would have to be modified.)[17]

THE RISKS OF THE GRAY MARKET

While gray market sales can increase a reseller's short-run sales, the gray market can severely affect the overall quality of a product's distribution system. Among the channel-related difficulties of gray market sales are the erosion of a firm's overall pricing strategy, problems in obtaining dealer support, reduction of a brand's image, and lack of control over resellers by manufacturers or wholesalers.

First, the low prices offered by gray marketers may cause consumers to view the authorized reseller's price as being much too high. Many of these customers are unconcerned with differences in the responsibilities between authorized and unauthorized distributors. For example, authorized distributors have to participate in cooperative advertising, have minimum purchase requirements, need to maintain costly repair facilities, and must handle product recall responsibilities; gray marketers do not conduct these activities.

Second, the gray market generates difficulties in obtaining support by authorized dealers. Authorized dealers are particularly resentful of the differences in pricing structures if a significant degree of free-riding occurs. In the **free-rider phenomenon**, customers ask full-service, authorized dealers for product information and then purchase goods at discounters or gray market dealers for less money. Gray market dealers also benefit from the advertising, display, servicing, and inventory maintenance of authorized dealers.[18]

Third, the reduction in brand image may be due to frequent sales at a low price, the existence of instructions in a foreign language, the absence of replacement parts in this country, or poor product quality. In some cases, such as with European-built Caterpillar tractors, foreign products may not meet U.S. safety standards. Gray market goods may also be poor in quality. Givenchy, for example, argued that unauthorized distributors sold perfumes that had spoiled as a result of being too long on foreign docks in the hot sun. According to the president of Givenchy, "It's very damaging to the image of quality we have spent millions to build."[19] Lastly, a brand's image may be tarnished when an authorized dealer refuses to repair a good purchased from a gray marketer.

Fourth, gray market sales are made through unauthorized channel members that have never been evaluated by their suppliers. Some of these gray market resellers engage in unscrupulous behavior (such as selling factory remanufactured goods as new), repair goods with parts manufactured by independent firms, and improperly adapt products to meet U.S. safety standards. Since these dealers are unauthorized, the manufacturer has no control over their selection or continuance.

Channel Strategies Designed to Limit Gray Market Goods

Many reseller strategies to limit the presence of gray market goods (see Table 9-2) are applicable to both domestic and foreign gray market products.[20]

An important manufacturer and wholesaler strategy is to identify firms that have resold goods to unauthorized resellers. A manufacturer or wholesaler can track down transshippers by a product's serial numbers, warranty card information, and factory rebate data to determine where the item was purchased versus who the item was sold to. Some manufacturers and wholesalers take a more aggressive position and employ "shoppers" to purchase products from unauthorized resellers. Manufacturers and wholesalers should also make resellers aware that they will carefully monitor all reselling activity and will take away authorized distributor or dealer status from authorized representatives that transship goods. These strategies should enable a manufacturer or retailer to stop transshipping early.

A second strategy is for a manufacturer or wholesaler to carefully evaluate its overall quantity discount schedule and price strategy by market area in order to reduce the incentive for transshipping. Large price differences between two purchase quantities and between two adjacent market areas also create an incentive to transship goods. Some manufacturers have limited the size of the gray market by offering special financing plans, leasing options, rebate offers,

Table 9-2 Channel Strategies To Reduce the Impact of Gray Market Goods

- Identify firms that have resold goods to unauthorized resellers.
- Evaluate quantity discount schedule and price strategy by market area to reduce the incentive for transshipping.
- Differentiate products sold to different markets.
- Make customers aware of the dangers of purchasing these products.
- Develop and maintain a marketing information system that monitors above-average purchases by specific wholesalers and retailers.

and guarantee programs that are not applicable to gray market products. For example, Concord watch dealers offered rebates as large as $1000 to combat unauthorized sales. In its advertising, Concord admitted that exchange rate differences created a major price differential between the United States and other markets throughout the world.

A third strategy is for manufacturers to differentiate products sold to different markets by appealing to local tastes, using a specific language, or meeting the safety standards of only one country. This makes it more difficult for trans-shipping to occur across foreign markets.

A fourth strategy is to make customers aware of the risk in purchasing gray market products. Kodak cautions film buyers that its gray market film can be spoiled because of high temperature and humidity conditions in transit. IBM also reinforces the risk in purchasing its gray market computers by withholding warranty coverage. This was a difficult decision for IBM since this policy can reduce the brand's quality image.

Fifth, a manufacturer should develop a marketing information system that monitors above-average purchases by specific wholesalers and retailers, sales of specific goods to wholesaler and retailer by serial number, and warranty card information that identifies place of purchase to more closely identify leakages in distribution channels.

PRICE GUARANTEES AND SELLING AGAINST THE BRAND

This section covers two important channel-related pricing strategies: price guarantees and selling against the brand. Price guarantees are a form of channel cooperation, whereas selling against the brand is a form of channel conflict.

Price guarantees protect merchant wholesalers and retailers from a decline in a product's list price. Price guarantees protect wholesalers and retailers by compensating them for the difference between past and current wholesale costs multiplied by a wholesaler's or retailer's stock on hand. Unless they were compensated in this manner, wholesalers and retailers would have to reduce their initial markup or would not be able to price the affected goods on a competitive basis. Price guarantees can be seen as a form of insurance offered to wholesalers and retailers by manufacturers as consideration for their having ample quantities of stock on hand. Conversely, if a manufacturer's list price goes up, its wholesalers and retailers benefit through higher markups (if the resellers plan to increase selling prices for goods purchased at lower prices) or through faster sales (if the reseller plans to sell stock on hand on the basis of its earlier product costs). Price guarantees are a form of channel cooperation. Another way of protecting resellers from a drop in list prices is for a manufacturer to keep the list price the same by offering a rebate program or coupon offer. These are discussed in Chapter 10.

In **selling against the brand**, wholesalers and retailers set an artificially high price on a national brand relative to a dealer brand to make its private label brand more easily saleable. This strategy is used to increase sales of private labels, to increase dealer or store loyalty, and to give consumers the perception that a store's private labels are very competitively priced. In a pure selling against the brand strategy, the reseller has no or little intention of even selling the national brand. To emphasize selling against the brand, some resellers will feature national brands and private label of the same product side by side in one ad, noting the price differences between both brands. Selling against the brand is an example of channel conflict.

DISCOUNTS AND TERMS

Historically, prices are quoted to resellers in terms of a single list price. The use of a single list price enables a manufacturer's catalog to be shown to all channel members, even though each member is eligible to buy a product at a different price. Price differences to each reseller are reflected through different types, and levels of discounts are applicable to resellers. These discounts are based on a reseller's channel functions, purchase quantities, promotional allowances, and so on. This section explains the nature of these discounts. Promotional allowances, rebates, street money (temporary deals and discounts often tied to promotions), and pay-for-performance incentives (payment to wholesalers and retailers for the performance of specific activities or for meeting specific objectives) are covered in Chapter 10. While these are often in the form of price discounts, they are tied to promotional performance.

TRADE AND FUNCTIONAL DISCOUNTS

Trade and functional discounts are often confused in textbooks. Properly defined, a **trade discount** is a discount given to buyers on the basis of the level of trade at which they operate.[21] For instance, the discount structure for a wholesaler and a retailer would differ because each operates at a different channel level. A mixed-level distributor that sells directly to final consumers, as well as to retailers, should then get different discounts depending on level of trade. It is easy to differentiate on sales to each segment, in those states where a state sales tax is collected on sales to final consumers.

All resellers need to receive adequate discounts. For example, a reseller may stop purchasing from a supplier whose trade discount level is considered inappropriate. Conversely, a reseller may push the goods of a supplier that offers its resellers a trade discount viewed as generous. One market analyst attributes part of Compaq's success in personal computers to the generous trade discount it gives its authorized retailers. This larger-than-average discount could be passed onto customers or kept by each retailer to increase profit margins. As a result of this trade discount, computer resellers gave Compaq shelf space and pushed Compaq computers.[22]

A **functional discount** is a discount offered by a seller to a reseller for assuming and performing a function that otherwise would be performed by the seller.[23] Any intermediary can use functional discounts to shift channel functions to downstream channel members.

QUANTITY DISCOUNTS

Most quantity discounts are based on the size of an individual order. A **noncumulative discount** is limited to one order. A special form of a noncumulative quantity discount is a **buying allowance** (an off-invoice allowance), which is a short-term offer of a special discount keyed to a minimum purchase requirement. Noncumulative quantity discounts should reflect a supplier's invoicing, transportation, insurance, and delivery cost savings due to filling fewer orders. Other savings derive from longer production runs, volume purchasing opportunities, the shifting of inventory holding costs from a supplier to a customer, and earlier payment by the channel member.

In contrast to a noncumulative discount, a **cumulative discount** is offered on the basis of combined purchases over a given time period. The advantage of the cumulative discount is that it encourages repeat sales. For example, General Electric has used cumulative discounts to encourage home builders to purchase all of their appliances from GE. One type of cumulative quantity discount is a **buyback allowance**, which is a reduction in price for new purchases that is based on the quantity purchased on a prior deal. Buyback allowances seek to increase sales in two consecutive buying periods.

A reseller must make three types of decisions in developing a cumulative or noncumulative quantity discount schedule:[24]

1. Whether the discount will apply to all units purchased or only the units incremental to a certain break point.
2. The number of break points that will be used.
3. The depth of the discount.

Providing discounts solely on purchases up to a given break point especially encourages resellers to increase purchases above that level. As mentioned previously, manufacturers and wholesalers need to be concerned that too high a break point, too many break points, or too deep a discount can encourage forward buying or the development of a gray market.

SEASONAL DISCOUNTS

Seasonal discounts provide an incentive for wholesalers and retailers to purchase goods early in the selling season by granting an additional reduction in price. Seasonal discounts provide several important benefits to the manufacturer. First, they enable a manufacturer to smooth out its production over a longer time period. Second, by increasing inventories at the wholesaler and retailer levels, seasonal discounts provide its resellers with the motivation to push the product. Third, by starting the sales process early, seasonal discounts enable all resellers to better forecast demand. And, fourth, early buying through seasonal discounts may extend the length of the selling season for a seasonal product.

TERMS

Terms relate to when payment is due from wholesalers and retailers. Generally, terms are standard to all firms that have a satisfactory credit record. Sometimes, increased terms are used to augment sales of goods off-season. For example, a wholesaler or retailer buying room air conditioners in February may be given terms such as net 30, as of May 1.

Some large channel members, such as Kmart and Compaq, have begun to demand increased payment terms from their vendors. Kmart is drawing out payments to its toy vendors by refusing to pay for toys until they go to its stores, no matter how long they sit in Kmart's own distribution centers. Similarly, Compaq doesn't pay for its parts or the cost of warehousing them until it actually takes delivery.[25]

INTEGRATING A FIRM'S OVERALL DISCOUNT STRUCTURE

All of the discounts a reseller obtains are taken sequentially. Thus, a trade discount of 40 percent, a functional discount of 10 percent, a quantity discount of 5 percent, and a cash discount of 2 percent is typically quoted as "less 40, 10, 5, and 2." This should not be viewed as a discount of 57 percent. The cumulative effect of these four discounts is equal to 49.7 percent (see Table 9-3). Discounts are never taken off freight or shipping charges.

Several advantages are associated with the discount system. First, all prices can be quoted in a single list price format, so that consumers can view a manufacturer's and wholesaler's catalog without being aware of the intermediary's

TABLE 9-3 THE CUMULATIVE EFFECT OF SEQUENTIAL DISCOUNTS

List price	$100.00
Less:	
Trade discount of 40 percent (.40 × $100) =	40.00
Balance	60.00
Functional discount of 10 percent (.10 × $60) =	6.00
Balance	54.00
Quantity discount of 5 percent (.05 × $54) =	2.70
Balance	51.30
Cash discount of 2 percent (.02 × $51.30) =	1.03
Balance	$ 50.27
Plus:	
Freight costs	6.00
Balance due	$ 56.27

cost. Second, the sequential nature of the discount may be viewed as a form of psychological pricing. For example, a discount of 40, 10, 5, and 2 percent may seem like a larger discount than its 49.7 percent off list price. Third, the discount system is useful in negotiation. The higher up a discount is achieved, the greater its impact. For example, a manufacturer may offer a retailer a discount structure of 40, 10, and 2 (for function, trade, and cash discounts), while the retailer may request 50 and 2. Fourth, this structure unbundles the components of pricing. Thus, the actual price paid reflects payment for specific activities.

At the same time, use of the traditional discount structure has several limitations. First, this structure bases all discounts on invoice prices as opposed to **pocket prices**, the price actually paid by a reseller. In the example shown in Table 9-4, the invoice price is $5.78, while the pocket price is $4.47 (a 22.7 percent difference between invoice and pocket price). A major difficulty in planning discounts on the basis of pocket prices is that traditional accounting systems do not collect data on payment terms, cooperative advertising allowances, and freight reimbursement.

A second difficulty with all these discounts is the high possibility it poses for accounting and billing errors among manufacturers, wholesalers, and retailers. Third, wholesalers and retailers also often ask for discounts that they have not earned. It is not uncommon for a retailer to remit a balance that reflects earning an early payment discount, even though it has paid the invoice after the discount period.

ADAPTING THE PRICE STRATEGY

The last stage in the pricing process is to adapt the price strategy to reflect special cost, demand, or competitive conditions. **Adaptive pricing** recognizes that initial prices may have to be changed to reflect differences between the planned pricing environment and actual conditions. Unusually high costs, less then an-

TABLE 9-4   THE POCKET PRICE WATERFALL

Dealer list price		$6.00
Order-size discount	$ .10	
Competitive discount	.12	
Total discounts		.22
Invoice price		5.78
Payment terms discount	$ .30	
Annual volume bonus	.37	
Off-invoice promotions	.35	
Co-op advertising allowance	.20	
Freight	.09	
Total discounts		1.31
Pocket price		$4.47

Source: Michael V. Marn and Robert L. Rossiello, "Managing Price, Gaining Profit," *Harvard Business Review*, Vol. 63 (September–October 1992), pp. 84–94.

ticipated demand, or a new model introduced by a competitor reflect conditions that require the use of adaptive pricing. Rebates, coupons, and additional discounts in the form of free goods (such as merchandise allowances) are examples of stimulating demand covered in Chapter 10.

Additional discounts are markdowns from a firm's initial price due to end of season sales, the need to move incomplete assortments of merchandise, discounts in anticipation of new models, and so on. Sometimes, additional discounts are partially funded by the manufacturer (such as special rebates to auto dealers to reduce end-of-model-year inventories). In other cases, additional discounts are funded exclusively by the wholesaler or retailer. In contrast to additional discounts, **additional markups** are upward adjustments to price levels attributable to unexpected high demand, increased list prices for new shipments, a weak dollar relative to foreign currency for imported merchandise, and so on.

LEGAL ASPECTS OF PRICING

This section covers important legal aspects of pricing: resale price maintenance, state sales below-cost laws, gray market goods, price discrimination, and discounts and terms.

RESALE PRICE MAINTENANCE

Resale price maintenance (also known as **fair trade**) is an agreement between a supplier and a retailer stating that the retailer will not sell a particular good below a minimum price level. Resale price maintenance was initially introduced as a means of preventing price cutting by large retail chains. It was also used by suppliers as a means of reducing price competition. These suppliers argued that continued price reductions would cheapen a product's or brand's image or ultimately reduce the quality of a retailer's customer service due to increased price competition. Critics of resale price maintenance argued that this practice resulted in increasing prices to a level where even inefficient retailers would be profitable. They also maintained that not all suppliers were equally effective in enforcing fair trade.

In 1977, the Consumer Goods Pricing Act was passed. This statute repealed federal legislation that permitted state resale price maintenance laws to apply to interstate commerce. All resale price maintenance contracts were then considered to be a violation of federal antitrust laws. Attempts by the Reagan and Bush administrations to revive resale price maintenance have not been successful.[26]

Two important cases involving resale price maintenance are *Monsanto v. Spray-Rite Service Corp.* and *Business Electronics Corp. v. Sharp Electronics Corp.* In the *Monsanto* case, the Supreme Court increased the evidence requirements in cases involving resale price maintenance. Although Spray-Rite, a Monsanto distributor, argued that its contract with Monsanto was canceled because competing distributors had complained to Monsanto, the Supreme Court ruled that such an agreement cannot be inferred solely on the basis of complaints. In the *Sharp* case, the Supreme Court maintained that an agreement between a full-price merchant and a manufacturer wherein the manufacturer terminates sales to a discounter is not a price-fixing agreement. To be considered illegal, such an agreement must state that the manufacturer and full-service merchant also agree to maintain a specific price or price level.[27]

Two important recent resale price maintenance cases involved Kreepy Krauly (a manufacturer of a swimming pool cleaning device) and Reebok. The 1991 action against Kreepy Krauly was the first federal case involving resale price maintenance in almost a decade.[28] In the second case, under the terms of its consent agreement, Reebok agreed to pay $9.5 million as damages. Under Reebok's Centennial Plan, "retailers were not allowed to price shoes below a suggested price level for the upper-end premier shoe and not allowed to discount a shoe more than 10 percent on less expensive lines," according to an assistant attorney general. Retailers that did not agree to these guidelines had the implied threat of being cut off from future business with Reebok.[29]

A number of recommendations can be made to suppliers that wish to legally maintain their suggested resale prices. For both new and established resellers, a manufacturer can establish a retail pricing policy and refuse to sell to retailers that do not follow this policy. It is also important that a manufacturer stop dealing with an offending reseller without threatening it or without responding to complaints of other resellers.[30] For new intermediaries, suppliers should consider vertical integration, establish performance criteria that are difficult for discounters to meet, and announce resale price maintenance policy when initial distribution arrangements are made. A manufacturer has the right to establish a pricing policy and to refuse to deal with resellers that do not follow this policy.[31]

STATE SALES BELOW-COST LAWS

Twenty-three states have **sales below-cost laws**.[32] Although the statutes differ in each state (as well as the method of computing the cost and the relative degree of enforcement), in general, these statutes forbid the sale of goods below cost when the intent is to destroy competition or injure a competitor. **Loss leaders** are goods sold below cost (defined as either purchase costs, replacement costs, or merchandise cost plus a fixed percentage to cover overhead), depending on state jurisdiction.

Sales below-cost laws exist to protect smaller retailers from discriminatory price cutting by larger retailers. They are based on the concern that larger retailers could willfully offer sales below cost in order to destroy their smaller competitors. After competition was destroyed, these large retailers could then raise their prices.

The most important recent state below-cost law case involved Wal-Mart. As discussed in the opening vignette of this chapter, the Arkansas Supreme Court overturned a lower Arkansas Court decision that ruled against Wal-Mart. The ruling of the Arkansas Supreme Court was based on its view of loss leaders as an acceptable form of building store traffic when the overall effect on competition is small.

GRAY MARKET GOODS

The United States Supreme Court ruled in May 1988, in a landmark case (*Kmart Corporation v. Cartier, Inc.*), that American trademark owners cannot prevent unauthorized importation of products bearing their own names or marks. The court ruled that the Tariff Act of 1930 allows imports to be blocked only when the foreign manufacturer and trademark owner are not subject to common control. For instance, only when a foreign company gives exclusive distribution rights to an unaffiliated U.S. company, and then competes with it in the United States, can Customs bar the foreign company's goods entry into the United States.[33] According to one source, about 90 percent of the foreign gray market was not affected by the ruling.[34] This ruling was a major setback for those American firms that control the supply of foreign gray market goods.

In a new legal approach to gray marketing, firms have begun to use copyright law, instead of trademark law, to stop foreign gray market goods. In an important recent case, Parfums Givenchy U.S.A. won a copyright infringement case against Drug Emporium Inc., a retailer that sold Givenchy's Amariage brand gray market perfumes. One provision of the copyright law prohibits the importation of copyrighted material without the permission of the copyright owner. Based on a similar case, Parfums Givenchy obtained a copyright on the Amariage box before it introduced the product in department stores; this was the first time the company sought a copyright for a box.[35] Givenchy contended that Drug Emporium had violated its copyright rights by importing and selling without permission its Amariage perfume, or at least the box in which the fragrance is packaged. The retailer sold Givenchy's Amariage perfume reduced by as much as 35 percent off list price. The Federal Appeals Court stopped Drug Emporium from selling Amariage perfume obtained from unauthorized channels.

According to some legal experts, the copyright defense can be used for every product that is manufactured overseas, providing the box is found to have artistic merit. As a result of its victory, Givenchy has filed copyright infringement cases against other unauthorized discounters including Wal-Mart, Sears, and Kmart. Swarovski America Ltd., a subsidiary of the Austrian crystal company, has also begun to sue Price/Costco on the basis of copyright law.[36] (A discussion of the Schwinn and Sylvania cases involving resale restrictions can be found in Chapter 4.)

PRICE DISCRIMINATION

The Robinson-Patman Act (an amendment to the Clayton Act) covers price discrimination. **Price discrimination** is the practice of charging different buyers different prices for goods of "like grade and quality." The intent of the Robinson-Patman Act is to curb the strong bargaining power of major retail chains. The government was concerned that price concessions offered to secure chain business would put smaller retailers at a major cost disadvantage. Detractors state that the Act protects competitors from competition and that it encourages price uniformity.

The Robinson-Patman Act prohibits manufacturers and wholesalers from charging different prices to different channel member purchasers for products of "like grade and quality" if such prices injure competition. There are several exceptions where price discrimination is legal under the Robinson-Patman Act: cost justification, meeting competition, and marketability. The **cost justification defense** allows sellers to pass onto their customers cost savings due to the manufacture, sale, or delivery to a buyer. The burden of proof is on the seller to maintain comprehensive cost accounting records. The **meeting competition defense** allows a seller to offer a lower price to a buyer to meet (but not beat) a competitor's lower bid.[37] The last defense, **marketability**, enables a seller to lower its price to reflect a product's seasonality, perishability, or obsolescence.

The Robinson-Patman Act also restricts buyers' actions. Buyers are liable for damages if they knowingly induce a seller to offer a price that is considered illegal. Experts argue that buyers should not bargain too hard, attempt to get too low a price, or lie about a competitor's lower price offer to unwittingly get the seller to "meet" the competitor's price. Comparatively few Robinson-Patman Act cases have been against wholesalers or retailers.

The Federal Trade Commission revised its guidelines to assist businesses in complying with these provisions in 1990. These allowances must be granted in connection with the customer's resale of the product. The guidelines also recognize two ways of measuring proportional equality: one based on customer cost and the other based on seller cost.[38]

DISCOUNTS AND TERMS

In addition to a product's price, quantity discounts, functional discounts, and terms all fall under the jurisdiction of the Robinson-Patman Act. These discounts have to be offered on a proportionately equal basis to all competing buyers. Like differences in a product's price, a seller needs to explain differences in discounts and terms on the basis of the cost justification, meeting competition, and marketability defenses. For example, a seller may justify a large-quantity discount on the basis of cost savings in delivery and/or manufacture. Generally, noncumulative quantity discounts are easier to prove than cumulative quantity discounts.

Functional discounts provided to distributors also fall under the Robinson-Patman Act. Functional discounts were meant to provide compensation for purchasers' actual completion of marketing functions. Although different levels in a distribution channel can legally be charged different prices, discounts given to higher level distributors may be illegal if they are substantial, are unrelated to the costs associated with the distributor's functions, and directly or indirectly result in an injury to competition or a competitor at the wholesale or retail level.[39]

To be legal, functional discounts need to be based on a channel member's responsibilities. For example, if a wholesaler member sells to both retailers and final consumers, the wholesaler can be eligible for different discounts as long as the manufacturer asks the channel member to verify sales. This requires that the channel member have a comprehensive recordkeeping system. This recordkeeping is facilitated when sales to end-users are subject to a state sales tax.

There are two contradictory court standards in interpreting functional discounts. One standard, called the Doubleday rule, argues that as long as the discount matches a channel member's cost of completing the function, the discount is legal. The standard is based on the buyer's costs. A second standard, referred to as the Mueller standard, argues that a channel member could receive a competitive advantage owing to its performing the marketing function paid for by the discount.[40]

Functional discounts are also subject to the **availability rule**. This rule states that functional discounts must be available to all customers, even if some customers choose not to receive them. Two important standards must be met for availability: all buyers must be notified of the discounts, and the conditions for qualifying for a discount must be achievable by all of a seller's customers.[41]

SUMMARY

1. *To compare and contrast the use of price and nonprice competition.* In price competition, manufacturers, wholesalers, and retailers seek to increase or decrease demand on the basis of changes in price. In contrast, in nonprice competition, sellers seek to change demand on the basis of distinctive benefits, and special pre-sale, during the sale, and post-sale services. Price competition may be a preferred strategy when a channel member has a long-term cost advantage over competition, when a product sold is a commodity that cannot be easily differentiated, and when consumers are very price conscious. Nonprice competition is preferable if a channel member has distinctive products and services, or if a reseller seeks to appeal to a market segment that is not price sensitive.

2. *To differentiate among sales-based, profit-based, and status quo-based pricing objectives.* With price-based pricing objectives, resellers seek to increase sales. Sales can be measured in terms of dollars, units, or market share. With profit-based pricing objectives, firms set pricing objectives in terms of profits, early recovery of cash, or return on investment measures. With status quo pricing objectives, resellers seek to minimize the impact of a new competitor, anticipated government action, or change in market condition. In practice, pricing objectives may be combinations of sales-, profit-, and status quo-based pricing objectives.

3. *To study the three general approaches to the development of an overall pricing strategy: cost-oriented, demand-oriented, and competition-oriented and their integration.* In cost-oriented pricing, a reseller examines its total costs and adds a suitable profit to determine its price. Markup pricing and direct product profitability are forms of cost-

oriented pricing. Demand-oriented pricing starts with the maximum price a customer will pay for a product and then works backward to compute maximum costs for the manufacturer and each intermediary. Demand-minus pricing and chain-markup pricing are forms of demand-oriented pricing. Competition-oriented pricing first sets price on the basis of evaluating the offerings of competitors. A common competition-oriented pricing technique is competitive bidding. In practice, these three approaches are integrated.

4 *To evaluate alternative pricing policies: high-low pricing, everyday low pricing, gray market goods, price guarantees, and selling against the brand.* In high-low pricing, a reseller charges higher prices on an everyday basis, but runs frequent promotions where these goods are offered at lower prices on a temporary basis. In its purest form, everyday low pricing is a practice set by manufacturers that enables retailers to sell their products at a single price throughout the year. However, in reality, EDLP manufacturers and retailers still must use temporary price reductions and coupons to obtain shelf space and to stimulate consumer interest for new products or for products with lagging sales. There are two types of gray market goods: domestic and foreign. While gray market goods can increase a manufacturer's short-run sales, the gray market can severely affect the overall quality of a manufacturer's distribution system. Price guarantees protect merchant wholesalers and retailers from a decline in a product's list price. They are a form of channel cooperation. Selling against the brand is used by wholesalers and retailers to increase sales of private labels at the expense of national brands.

5 *To analyze the use of different discounts and terms.* A trade discount is a discount given to buyers on the basis of the level of trade at which they operate. A functional discount is a discount offered by a seller to a reseller for assuming and performing a function that otherwise would be performed by the seller. Quantity discounts are based on the size of an individual order; they may be noncumulative or cumulative. Seasonal discounts provide an incentive for wholesalers and retailers to purchase goods early in the selling season by granting an additional reduction in price. Terms relate to when payment is due from wholesalers and retailers. All of the discounts a reseller obtains are taken sequentially.

6 *To describe how a reseller can adapt its pricing strategy.* A seller can adapt its selling strategy through the use of adaptive pricing. Forms of adaptive pricing are additional discounts and additional markups.

7 *To determine the legal aspects of pricing decision making.* Pricing strategies that are regulated include resale price maintenance, state sales below-cost laws, gray market goods, price discrimination, and discounts and terms.

KEY TERMS

price competition
nonprice competition
sales-based pricing objectives
profit-based pricing objectives
gross margin return on investment (GMROI)
status quo-based pricing objectives
cost-oriented pricing
markup pricing
markup percentage
variable markup policy
initial markup
maintained markup
initial markup percentage
maintained markup percentage
direct product profitability
winner
dog
sleeper
traffic builders
demand-minus pricing
chain-markup pricing
competitive bidding
expected value concept
high-low pricing
forward buying
trade loading
domestic gray market goods
foreign gray market goods
parallel channels of distribution
diverting
free-rider phenomenon
price guarantees
selling against the brand
trade discount
functional discount
noncumulative discount
buying allowance
cumulative discount
buyback allowance
seasonal discounts
terms
pocket prices
adaptive pricing
additional discounts
additional markups
resale price maintenance (fair trade)
sales below-cost laws
loss leaders
price discrimination
cost justification defense
meeting competition defense
marketability
availability rule

QUESTIONS FOR DISCUSSION

1. In what situation should a wholesaler use price competition? Nonprice competition?

2. How does gross margin return on investment differ from the standard return on investment measure used by most firms?

3. Explain how a reseller could use sales-, profit-, and status quo-based pricing objectives at the same time.

4. Differentiate between an initial markup and a maintained markup.

5. a. Describe how direct product profitability can be computed.
   b. Why is direct product profitabilty an important measure for a reseller?

6. a. Explain how chain-markup pricing is used.
   b. How does chain-markup pricing differ from demand-minus pricing?

7. a. Explain each of the elements involved in computing the optimal competitive bid price.
   b. Which is the most difficult to compute? Why?

8. What are the pros and cons of the use of high-low versus everyday low pricing?
9. Compare and contrast diverting with forward buying.
10. Describe the three conditions necessary for gray markets to develop.
11. "Price guarantees are a form of channel cooperation. Selling against the brand is a form of channel conflict." Explain this statement.
12. Explain the difference between an invoice price and a pocket price.
13. How can a manufacturer limit the quantity of gray market goods through legal action?
14. a. Explain the role of the Robinson-Patman Act in pricing decisions.
    b. Describe the cost justification, meeting competition, and marketability defenses.

END NOTES

1. Blant Hurt, "The Irrational Antitrust Case Against Wal-Mart," *Wall Street Journal* (October 20, 1993), p. A15; "Court Backs Wal-Mart on Pricing," *New York Times* (January 10, 1995), p. D4; Martin Everett, "Drugstore Cowboys Shoot It Out," *Sales & Marketing Management* (August 1994), p. 15; Kathryn Jones, "Wal-Mart on Trial on 'Predatory Pricing' Charges," *New York Times* (August 24, 1993), p. D1; Kathryn Jones, "Wal-Mart's Pricing on Drugstore Items Is Held to Be Illegal," *New York Times* (October 13, 1993), pp. A1 ff.; Louise Lee, "Arkansas Court Rules Wal-Mart Didn't Use Illegal Pricing Practices," *Wall Street Journal* (January 10, 1995), p. B10; and Theodore Spencer, "'Predator' Wal-Mart Loses Case to Its Prey," *Newsday* (October 13, 1993), pp. 87–88.

2. "Profitability: Where It's Really At," *Progressive Grocer* (December 1992), pp. 27, 30.

3. Michael Sansolo and Steve Weinstein, "Wholesalers: A Blueprint for Change," *Progressive Grocer* (April 1993), p. 5.

4. "What's in Store for EDLP?" *Sales & Marketing Management* (August 1993), p. 58.

5. See Patricia Sellers, "The Dumbest Marketing Ploy," *Fortune* (October 5, 1992), pp. 88–94.

6. Eben Shapiro, "P&G Takes on the Supermarkets with Uniform Pricing," *New York Times* (April 26, 1992), p. F5.

7. See Robert D. Buzzell, John A. Quelch, and Walter J. Salmon, "The Costly Bargain of Trade Promotion," *Harvard Business Review,* Vol. 61 (March–April 1990), pp. 141–149.

8. See "A Question of Will?" *Progressive Grocer* (July 1994), pp. S10–S11.

9. Stephen J. Hoch, Xavier Drèze, and Mary E. Purk, "EDLP, Hi-Lo, and Margin Arithmetic," *Journal of Marketing,* Vol. 58 (October 1994), p. 17.

10. See Buzzell, Quelch, and Salmon, "The Costly Bargain of Trade Promotion," p. 147.

11. See Gregory A. Patterson, "More Stores Switch from Sales to 'Everyday Low Prices'," *Wall Street Journal* (November 12, 1992), p. B1; and Stephanie Strom, "Retailers' Latest Tactic: If It Says $15, It Means $15," *New York Times* (September 29, 1992), pp. D1 ff.

12. Ken Patch, "Why the Issue of EDLP Won't Go Away," *Supermarket Business* (October 1992), pp. 19–22.

13. For a comprehensive analysis of diverting, see Matthew Schifrin, "Arbitraging Dog Food," *Forbes* (May 10, 1993), pp. 78–81.

14. Sallie Hofmeister, "Unable to Protect Product Trademarks, Manufacturers Copyright the Boxes," *New York Times* (November 11, 1994), p. B16.

15. Schifrin, "Arbitraging Dog Food," p. 80.

16. Dale F. Duhan and Mary Jane Sheffet, "Gray Markets and the Legal Status of Parallel Importation," *Journal of Marketing,* Vol. 52 (July 1988), p. 76.

17. See S. Tamer Cavusgil and Ed Sikora, "How Multinationals Can Counter Gray Market Imports," *Columbia Journal of World Business,* Vol. 23 (Winter 1988), pp. 75–85.

18. See Larry Lowe and Kevin F. McCrohan, "Minimize the Impact of the Gray Market," *Journal of Business Strategy,* Vol. 9 (November/December 1989), pp. 47–50.

19. Hofmeister, "Unable to Protect Product Trademarks, Manufacturers Copyright the Boxes," p. B16.

20. Much of this material is adapted from Frank V. Cespedes, E. Raymond Corey, and V. Kasturi Rangan, "Gray Markets: Causes and Cures," *Harvard Business Review,* Vol. 59 (July–August 1988), pp. 75–82; S. Tamer Cavusgil and Ed Sikora, *How Multinational Can Cope with Gray Market Imports* (Cambridge, Mass.: Marketing Science Institute, 1987), pp. 8–21; and Robert E. Weigand, "Parallel Import Channels—Options for Preserving Territorial Integrity," *Columbia Journal of World Business,* Vol. 26 (Spring 1991), pp. 53–60.

21. Mark T. Spriggs and John R. Nevin, "The Legal Status of Trade and Functional Price Discounts," *Journal of Public Policy & Marketing,* Vol. 13 (Spring 1994), p. 64.

22. Michael Gianturco, "Lessons from the Clone War," *Forbes* (February 28, 1994), p. 110.

23. Spriggs and Nevin, "The Legal Status of Trade and Functional Price Discounts," p. 65.

24. George S. Day and Adrian B. Ryans, "Using Price Discounts for a Competitive Advantage," *Industrial Marketing Management,* Vol. 17 (February 1988), p. 6.

25. Scott McCartney, "Compaq Borrows Wal-Mart's Idea to Boost Production," *Wall Street Journal* (June 17, 1994), p. B4.

26. "The Repeal of Fair Trade," *Chain Store Age Executive* (June 1994), p. 76.

27. See Dorothy Cohen, *Legal Issues in Marketing Decision Making* (Cincinnati, Ohio: South-Western College Publishing, 1995), pp. 225–226.

28. Paul M. Barrett, "FTC's Hard Line on Price Fixing May Foster Discounts," *Wall Street Journal* (January 11, 1991), pp. B1 ff.

29. Viveca Novak and Joseph Pereira, "Reebok and FTC to Settle Price Fixing Charges," *Wall Street Journal* (May 1, 1995), pp. B1, B10.

30. Cohen, *Legal Issues in Marketing Decision Making,* p. 228; and Mary Lou Steptoe, "Unfair Trade Practices," *Consumer Reports* (March 1995), p. 132.

31. Mary Jane Sheffet and Debra L. Scammon, "Resale Price Maintenance: Is It Safe to Suggest Retail Prices?" *Journal of Marketing,* Vol. 49 (Fall 1985), p. 89.

32. "The Irrational Antitrust Case Against Wal-Mart," p. A15.

33. Dorothy Cohen, "Trademark Strategy Revisited," *Journal of Marketing,* Vol. 55 (July 1991), p. 55.

34. Paula Dwyer and Amy Dunkin, "A Red-Letter Day for Gray Marketers," *Business Week* (June 13, 1988), p. 30.

35. Stephanie Strom, "Enlisting the Copyright Law in Battling the 'Gray Market'," *New York Times* (July 21, 1992), pp. D1 ff.

36. Hofmeister, "Unable to Protect Product Trademark, Manufacturers Copyright the Boxes," p. B16.

37. See C. Burk Tower, "Reserve Supply Corp. v. Owens-Corning Fiberglas Corp. and CertainTeed Corp.," *Journal of Marketing* (July 1993), pp. 117–118, for an analysis of a case that involved the meeting of the competition defense.

38. See C. Burk Tower, "Federal Trade Commission's Guides for Advertising Allowances and Other Merchandising Payments and Services," *Journal of Marketing* (July 1991), p. 64.

39. See C. Burk Tower, "Texaco v. Hasbrouck," *Journal of Marketing,* Vol. 55 (January 1991), p. 84.

40. Spriggs and Nevin, "The Legal Status of Trade and Functional Price Discounts," pp. 67–69.

41. Ibid., pp. 70–71.

CASE 1

DEALING WITH DIVERTERS

According to some observers, diverting is a disease that is spreading throughout the grocery industry. Diverters are now aided by personal computers and elaborate databases that enable them to determine the price for any product (such as a given brand, size, and flavor of a dog food) in every city in the United States. Such an information base is invaluable in determining whether it is worthwhile to move sufficient quantities from a low-cost area to a high-cost area. While profits are generally as little as a few cents per can, diverters are capable of moving hundreds of thousands of cases on a daily basis. One estimate is that diverting in the grocery industry alone accounts for $25 billion in yearly volume.

As an illustration of the profitability of diverting, RJR Nabisco recently offered case quantities of whole cashews to supermarkets and wholesalers in the mid-Atlantic region for $50.76 per case, including shipping. In comparison, one diverter was offering the same goods at $36.38 per case, with shipping included (a savings of 28 percent). While the diverter would not disclose the source of its goods, it more than likely was a wholesaler that was either overstocked or engaged in forward buying. Contributing to the low cost was Nabisco's reducing the price of its cashews in some areas to gain regional market share.

Although manufacturers will not deal directly with diverters, diverters generally have no problem securing desired goods from other retailers. For example, let's take the case of H. J. Heinz, which offers a special discount of $5 a case to supermarkets in Milwaukee that purchase at least 3000 cases (three truckloads). A small grocery chain may purchase that quantity to get the quantity discount, but will immediately sell the remaining 2000 cases to a diverter. The large quantity purchased enables a small supermarket to obtain ketchup at the same price as its larger competitors. In addition, the supermarket is able to secure a profit by selling excess goods above its cost to the diverter. The diverter benefits by obtaining ketchup at a lower price than it could otherwise obtain. According to one source, in such a transaction the small supermarket chain could easily earn $2200 profit on its investment. In addition, the diverter could earn $4000 profit on a $41,000 investment. And large diverters could conduct hundreds of such transactions each week.

In some cases, employees of the manufacturer know that goods sold eventually are resold to a diverter, but they agree to the sale to make their sales quota or to win a sales contest. Some diverters may even maintain diverting desks in the buying office of traditional wholesalers or supermarket chains.

To catch diverters, some firms such as Tropicana place control numbers on juice cases and spot check distribution. This enables them to determine that juice originally sold to a retailer in one city is now available for sale in another city. Another way to stop diverting is simply to sell the same goods at the same prices in different markets. A third way is to reduce the size of its quantity discounts to discourage accounts from overordering.

There are differences of opinion as to the ethics of diverting. Some wholesalers and retailers see diverting as an honest way of enhancing their profitability. These resellers note that many manufacturers "look the other way" at diverting. Some pride themselves by only buying (but not selling) diverted goods, or by the relative small size of their diverting activity. In contrast to these positions, the National Food Brokers Trade Relations Committee issued a "White Paper" on diverting that takes an opposite position. Among the recommendations to manufacturers are to clearly state the firm's policy on diverting, to refuse shipments to known diverters, and to develop a system to monitor customer volumes.

QUESTIONS

1. Explain how databases can make diverting easier to implement.
2. How can a manufacturer eliminate forward buying as a source of gray market goods?
3. Describe the economics of diverting using the RJR and Heinz examples cited in this case. Take both a buyer's and a seller's perspective.
4. a. Evaluate the ethics of diverting from a manufacturer's perspective. From a retailer's perspective.
   b. Reconcile these two viewpoints.

Sources: Diverting: Recommendations for Brokers and Manufacturers Regarding Diverting (Washington, D.C.: National Food Brokers Association, n.d.), pp. 1–3; Matthew Schifrin, "Arbitraging Dog Food," *Forbes* (May 10, 1993), pp. 78 ff.; Michael Sansolo and Steve Weinstein, "Hale-Halsell: Changing with the Times," *Progressive Grocer* (June 1992), pp. 98–100.

CASE 2

EVERYDAY LOW PRICING AT PROCTER & GAMBLE

Procter & Gamble (P&G) announced in late 1991 that it would convert some of its products to an everyday low pricing (EDLP) strategy. Its EDLP program first started with household products, was later extended to beauty and personal care, and ultimately expanded to P&G's mass cosmetics line (such as Cover Girl, Noxell, and Clarion). For example, under P&G's EDLP strategy, P&G will offer Dawn (a liquid dishwashing soap) for $1.32. In the old high-low system, Dawn could wholesale from 99 cents to $1.89 (with an average price of $1.37). As of 1994, P&G has reduced its list prices by 12 percent to 24 percent on nearly all of its U.S. brands. Most of the reduction was accomplished by cutting the level of P&G's trade promotions.

According to Edwin L. Artzt, chairman and chief executive of Procter & Gamble, "Swings in price create variability and massive inefficiency in the manufacturing and distribution system. To meet heavy demand, manufacturers must build raw material inventory and design peaks and valleys in production schedules, which entail excessive warehousing costs, excessive shipping rates, and new handling costs. In some cases, our factory would have to run around the clock for four weeks and then operate at less than capacity for several months, until supermarkets depleted their inventories." P&G estimated that it can save as much as $175 million a year through EDLP owing to flatter volume forecasts, more efficient plant utilization, and better raw material supply ordering.

As of 1994, about 70 percent of Procter & Gamble's products were priced using EDLP. As a result of EDLP, P&G has reduced the number of price changes from 55 a day to one, and the number of pricing brackets from 17 to three. There are several reasons behind the shift of P&G to EDLP from high-low pricing. First, membership warehouse clubs (such as Price/Costco) and discount stores (such as Wal-Mart) want to consistently sell a product at a single price throughout the year. EDLP enables these retailers to reduce their advertising costs and to consistently maintain a low-price image. Second, P&G had large administrative costs in maintaining its high-low pricing strategy. P&G was making 55 daily price changes on some 80 brands, necessitating rework on every third order. Retailers also began to dispute more of their bills; according to one source, 80 percent of these disputes were resolved in the customer's favor. Third, some analysts argue that EDLP is an especially viable strategy for P&G given its high market share and high brand loyalty. P&G has either the number 1 or 2 product in terms of market share in 32 of its 44 product categories. EDLP is better suited to P&G because of its low need to use special discounts to build market share. Fourth, EDLP eliminates opportunities for forward buying and for gray market goods.

Initially, P&G's major competitors (such as Colgate-Palmolive, General Mills, Unilever, and Nestlé) stated that they would continue using high-low pricing. For example, a Colgate-Palmolive spokesperson said that it would continue to offer large discounts to wholesalers and "will deal with (customers) as they wish to be dealt with." Now, a majority of competitors are using a menu approach in which customers can choose among a continuous but much lower deal or an allowance level. General Mills, for example, cut prices on eight brands (which represented about 40 percent of its cereal volume) and reduced spending on couponing and price promotions (such as half-price deals and buy one, get one free promotions).

P&G has had some fallout among some of its major accounts concerning its EDLP strategy. Some resellers such as Rite-Aid, A&P, Safeway, and SuperValu have reduced the number of P&G sizes or eliminated marginal P&G brands (such as Prell and Gleem). Others have even considered moving P&G's products from prime eye-level positions to knee or ankle level. Some executives at these firms attributed much of their dissatisfaction to the loss of forward buying opportunities. An estimated 70 percent of wholesalers' profits and 40 percent of supermarkets' profits come from forward buying. Other executives felt that P&G poorly communicated its new strategy.

QUESTIONS

1. Can a supermarket still use a high-low pricing strategy despite the fact that it purchases all of its goods at EDLP? Explain your answer.
2. Comment on the statement that EDLP is "much better suited to firms with a large market share."
3. Describe the specific cost savings to P&G made possible by using EDLP versus high-low pricing.
4. Describe the specific cost savings to a major supermarket attributable to using EDLP versus high-low pricing.

Sources: Joseph B. Fuller, James O'Connor, and Richard Rawlinson, "Tailored Logistics: The Next Advantage," *Harvard Business Review,* Vol. 64 (May–June 1993), pp. 87–98; Valarie Reitman, "Eliminated Discounts on P&G Goods Annoy Many of Them Who Sell Them," *Wall Street Journal* (August 11, 1992), pp. A1 ff.; Bill Saporito, "Behind the Tumult at P&G," *Fortune* (March 7, 1994), pp. 74–82; Matthew Schifrin, "Arbitraging Dog Food," *Forbes* (May 10, 1993), pp. 78–91; Zachary Schiller, "Ed Artzt's Elbow Grease Has P&G Shining," *Business Week* (October 10, 1994), pp. 84–86; Eben Shapiro, "P&G Takes on the Supermarkets with Uniform Pricing," *New York Times* (April 26, 1992), p. F5; "What's in Store For EDLP?" *Sales & Marketing Management* (August 1993), pp. 56–57; Steve Weinstein, "To Buy or Not to Buy?" *Progressive Grocer* (June 1994), pp. 19–20 ff.; Michael Sansolo and Steve Weinstein, "Will Procter's Gamble Work?" *Progressive Grocer* (July 1992), pp. 36–40.

CHAPTER 10

PROMOTION STRATEGY IN CHANNELS

CHAPTER OBJECTIVES

1. To study the special factors in developing and implementing a channel promotional strategy.

2. To examine the development and implementation of a push-oriented promotional strategy, including media usage, and how push promotions can be improved.

3. To describe the development and implementation of a pull-oriented promotional strategy, including media usage and how pull promotions can be improved.

4. To discuss the legal aspects of a channel promotional strategy.

Walter R. Hammond is a regional cutting tool distributor based in Minneapolis, Minnesota. Most of its accounts are located in Minnesota and surrounding states.

Hammond's promotional strategy is based on the integrated use of multiple promotional tools, including outside salespeople, inside salespeople, direct mail, and manufacturer-sponsored videos. Each promotional form has a unique role at Hammond. For example, its direct mail campaign is used to support the sales staff. Direct mail is also used to attract smaller accounts; many of these could not be profitably reached using Hammond's regular outside sales force. Hammond also works with its manufacturer-suppliers in developing, coordinating, and implementing its promotional plan. Many of these suppliers contribute promotional materials and funds to Hammond. While suppliers provide sales training support to its sales force, others contribute to the cost of Hammond's direct mail promotions.

Hammond works closely with manufacturers on sales training. Sales training is especially important to Hammond since its customers have increasingly shifted from high-speed steel to the use of carbide tooling. Hammond needs to inform both its sales force and customers about the opportunities and pitfalls in making this transition through continuous sales training sessions. Hammond uses its salespeople who are most knowledgeable in carbide tooling to train those salespeople with less experience. Hammond also uses product videos supplied by manufacturers for both sales and customer training.

Hammond began to use direct mail in 1985 when it started to sell to smaller maintenance accounts that were not covered by the firm's outside sales force. It has always assured its sales force that direct mail will be used to complement, not replace, the efforts of its traditional sales force. For example, Hammond views direct mail as an important source of new customers; many of these customers will ultimately be served by the firm's sales force as their average purchases increase. Each direct mail piece contains up to 10 product sheets.

Direct mail has been particularly effective at Hammond for four major reasons. First, since each sheet contains special prices on advertised items, these direct mail pieces are typically studied very carefully by its customers. Second, mailings are tailored to different types of industries, with specialized products appropriate to that end-user category. Third, even though the mailings contain a lot of copy, the product sheets are carefully designed to be both readable and attractive. And fourth, Hammond encourages its suppliers to contribute to the cost of preparing, printing, and mailing the product sheets. This lowers Hammond's costs and helps establish supplier commitment to Hammond's promotional program. While Hammond's hand-tool suppliers were quick to contribute to its direct mail costs, cutting-tool manufacturers were initially reluctant to compensate Hammond. These manufacturers quickly joined the program after they became aware of its success.

In addition to direct mail, Hammond extensively uses its 5 outside and 10 inside salespeople. Its inside sales group handles between 400 and 500 sales calls per day. Both its inside and outside salespeople get listings of sales prospects from multiple sources. These include asking for referrals from current customers, visiting new industrial manufacturers, and obtaining sales leads from directories of manufacturers located in Minnesota and surrounding states.

According to the firm's vice president of marketing and sales, "it's a laborious job, but it pays off." According to one of Hammond's major suppliers, "Hammond Co. knows how to handle promotions and how to follow up on the leads they produce."[1]

This chapter studies the promotional strategies by manufacturers, wholesalers, and retailers using a variety of promotional tools. The chapter is organized from the perspective of push (promotional efforts aimed at resellers) and pull (promotional efforts aimed at consumers). We will soon see the importance of coordinating the use of promotional materials from a variety of sources and the need for push and pull to work together to achieve a reseller's promotional objectives.

SPECIAL FACTORS TO CONSIDER IN THE DEVELOPMENT AND IMPLEMENTATION OF A CHANNEL PROMOTIONAL STRATEGY

Any promotional strategy that utilizes channel members should consider four basic factors: (1) Downstream channel members need to be motivated to support promotional programs that have been developed by an upstream channel member; (2) promotions geared to intermediaries and promotions oriented to final consumers need to be integrated; (3) upstream channel members need to recognize that promotions aimed at final consumers also have an indirect effect on wholesalers and retailers; and (4) the promotional functions of channel members at different levels need to be ascertained.

In developing a promotional program, a manufacturer or wholesaler needs to motivate its downstream resellers to support the promotional program. Implementing any channel promotional strategy is especially difficult when downstream channel intermediaries are independently owned. For example, a manufacturer or supplier needs to understand that an independent wholesaler or a retailer is not directly accountable to the manufacturer's sales or advertising manager. In addition, the sales or advertising manager must compete for attention with programs developed at competing manufacturers. It is especially difficult to secure reseller motivation for goods that have wide distribution channels or for goods whose supplier accounts for a low percentage of the reseller's total sales. The difficulty in motivating resellers explains why such a high proportion of cooperative advertising funds and manufacturer-sponsored sales incentives for its intermediary's salespeople go unused.

A second difficulty relates to the need to coordinate promotions geared for intermediaries with those targeted at final consumers or end-users. A manufacturer cannot develop an integrated promotional campaign when its promotions to intermediaries reinforce its excellent customer service, while its resellers' promotions are totally price-based. To add to the difficulty in integrating promotions, in many organizations the sales organization develops materials for use by channel members, while advertising agencies are used to develop materials for use by final consumers. This process disintegrates the communication form.[2]

A manufacturer-supplier can facilitate the integration of messages by increasing the participation of intermediaries in promotional planning, providing channel resellers with ample notice of impending promotions, and using the same organization unit for all resellers and final consumer promotions. Figure 10-1 shows how different channel members can be jointly involved in promotional planning for lead generation, cooperative advertising, and demonstrations. The figure differentiates among three levels of involvement: planning, implementing, and monitoring success.

The development of any channel promotional strategy must recognize the indirect impact of any promotion. For example, the impact of advertising on

FIGURE 10-1 Involvement of channel members in promotional planning.

	Lead Generation	Cooperative Advertising	Demonstrations
Manufacturer			
Marketing manager		P	
General sales manager			
Regional sales manager	P, M		
Salespeople	I		
In-house agency			
Advertising Agency			
Manufacturer's advertising agency		P, M	
Wholesaler's advertising agency		P, I, M	
Retailer's advertising agency		P, I, M	
Public Relations Firm			
Manufacturer's public relations firm			P, M
Wholesaler's public relations firm			
Retailer's public relations firm			
Wholesaler			
Wholesaler's general sales manager	P, M		
Wholesaler's salespeople	I		
Wholesaler's advertising personnel			
Wholesaler's public relations staff			
Retailer			
Retailer's centralized advertising personnel		I, M	
Retailer's decentralized advertising personnel			
Retailer's centralized public relations staff			P, M
Retailer's decentralized public relations staff			I
Retailer's salespeople			I

Legend for level of involvement:
  P = Plan
  I = Implement
  M = Monitor success

Source: Loosely adapted from Benson P. Shapiro, "Improve Distribution with Your Promotional Mix," *Harvard Business Review,* Vol. 55 (March–April 1977), p. 120.

FIGURE 10-2 Indirect communication effects of advertising.

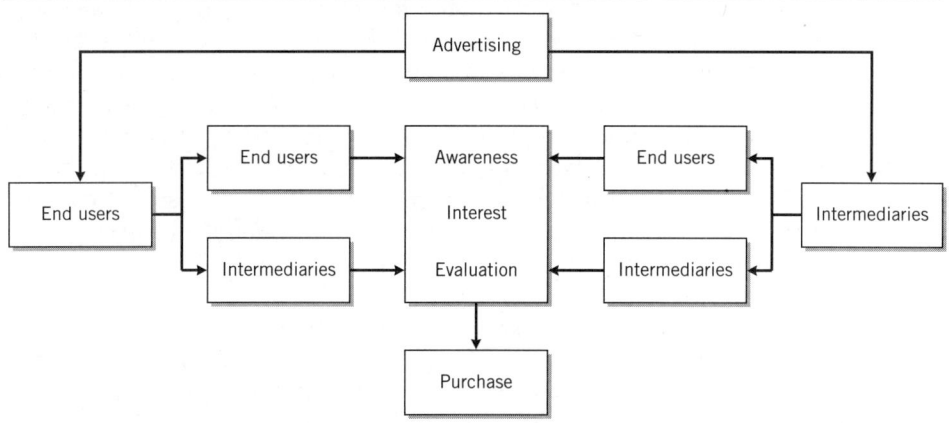

Source: C. Whan Park, Martin S. Roth, and Philip F. Jacques, "Evaluating the Effects of Advertising and Sales Promotion Campaigns," *Industrial Marketing Management,* Vol. 17 (June 1988), p. 131. Reprinted by permission. Copyright 1988 by Elsevier Science Inc.

end-users may have a positive effect on distributors. Similarly, advertising or trade literature primarily aimed at distributors may be read by consumers. These are referred to as an **indirect promotional effect**[3] (see Figure 10-2). The indirect promotional effects have two important ramifications. First, the potential audience of any promotional media may be broader than anticipated. Second, the indirect promotional effect underscores the importance of a common promotional theme across all channel members. The common theme presents a unified image and enables promotions aimed primarily at different channel levels to reinforce each other.

Lastly, different promotional responsibilities need to be allocated among channel members at different levels. For example, manufacturers are typically best suited to stimulate **primary demand**, demand for the entire product category, while intermediaries can be particularly effective in stimulating **selective demand**, demand for a manufacturer's brand. Specific promotional functions such as stimulating a reseller's sales force, developing store displays, creating advertising copy, and so on have to be allocated among channel members. In many cases, the proper allocation of promotional responsibilities depends on a channel member's size and skills. For example, a large distributor may be better able to create advertising copy than a small manufacturer.

The next section differentiates between push versus pull promotional strategies.

PUSH VERSUS PULL PROMOTIONAL STRATEGIES

As discussed in Chapter 1, promotional support to channel members can be characterized as either push or pull. All forms of promotional activity directed toward intermediaries to encourage them to stock, display, and promote a manufacturer's products is referred to as **selling to the wholesaler/retailer (push)**. Examples of push are manufacturer training for wholesale and retail salespersons, and sales contests directed at a reseller's salespersons. Manufacturers and suppliers often use push to gain and maintain promotional support among its resellers. In contrast, **selling through the wholesaler/retailer (pull)** emphasizes the importance of stimulating final customer demand by a manufacturer. Examples of pull are rebate offers to final consumers, advertising by a manufacturer that is directed at the final consumer, and free samples to final consumers that are provided by a manufacturer. Often, a manufacturer/supplier uses pull to encourage resellers to stock a product and to increase sales throughout all intermediary channels.

Often, the distinction between push versus pull is blurry; this can be seen by carefully examining cooperative advertising. **Cooperative advertising** is local advertising placed by a retailer or wholesaler that is partially or fully reimbursed by a manufacturer. Cooperative advertising can be classified as pull based on its role in increasing a consumer's awareness, preference, and purchase for a manufacturer's products. In contrast, the role of cooperative advertising in encouraging a retailer or wholesaler to stock a product in anticipation of increased sales is clearly push. While the direct effect of the cooperative advertising can be viewed as pull, the indirect effect is push.

Any planned promotional mix needs to have elements of both push and pull. For example, a manufacturer needs to attract final consumers to purchase its products while motivating intermediaries to stock and push its products. The most successful pull-oriented promotion could also result in inventories of goods that accumulate at wholesalers and retailers. Similarly, the most successful pull-oriented promotion will be unsuccessful unless resellers stock sufficient quantities of a product. Rust-Oleum's promotional program for its floor-coating business combines pull and push. It includes training videos for end-users (pull), direct mail assistance for distributors (push), incentives for its distributor's salespersons (push), and free samples for end-users (pull).[4]

According to the 16th Annual Survey of Promotional Practices, media advertising accounted for 25.2 percent of advertisers' total promotional expenditures, trade promotion for 46.9 percent, and consumer promotion for 27.9 percent of expenditures.[5] Although media advertising can be both push and pull, much of trade promotion is push, and most of consumer promotion is pull.

The next section of this chapter describes the design and implementation of push-oriented promotional strategies.

DEVELOPING AND IMPLEMENTING A PUSH-ORIENTED PROMOTIONAL STRATEGY

All promotional strategies, whether they are push or pull, involve decision making related to the development of promotional objectives, choice of media, budgeting, the special needs of downstream channel members, and evaluation of promotional effectiveness. This section concentrates on the major factors relating to push promotional strategies. The indirect effect of these objectives is to increase overall demand at the final consumer or end-user levels.

Promotional objectives in a push promotional strategy relate to downstream intermediaries. Like any promotional objective, these objectives can be information-, preference-, or demand-based. Making intermediate sellers aware of a new product is an example of an information-based promotional objective. Preference-based promotional objectives seek to increase a reseller's awareness of a manufacturer's or supplier's competitive advantage. An example of a preference-based promotional objective is increasing awareness of a manufacturer's new warranty policy among resellers. Lastly, promotional objectives may be demand-oriented. These objectives attempt to stimulate purchases by intermediaries. Upstream channel members ultimately aim to increase sales throughout all levels of the channel by first increasing sales to intermediaries.

Table 10-1 provides a list of media to implement push promotional strategies organized by media. The listing is organized in the same order as the promo-

TABLE 10-1 PUSH PROMOTIONAL STRATEGIES FOR DOWNSTREAM RESELLERS ORGANIZED BY MEDIA

Advertising
  Cooperative advertising (both push and pull)
  Preparation of direct mail pieces for wholesalers and retailers (both push and pull)
  Catalog materials prepared for wholesalers and retailers
  Product literature
  Dealer listing promotion

Personal Selling
  Sales contests for distributor and dealer employees
  Sales aids
  Product/sales training seminars
  Sales training programs for distributors

Sales Promotion
  Distributor recognition programs
  Street money
  Pay-for-performance allowances
  Push money
  Gifts to channel members
  Free merchandise given to distributors and dealers
  Sales literature for channel members
  Newsletters to distributors and retailers

Publicity
  Press releases on new products
  Press releases on new technical support capability
  Press release on distributor's winning sales contest
  Press release on new rebate program
  Press release for distributor recognition award

Sources: Many of the items are drawn from Allan J. Magrath and Kenneth G. Hardy, "Manufacturer Services for Distributors," *Industrial Marketing Management,* Vol. 21 (May 1992), pp. 120, 121; and Benson P. Shapiro, "Improve Distribution with Your Promotional Mix," *Harvard Business Review,* Vol. 55 (March–April 1977), pp. 122–123.

tional forms in this section: advertising, personal selling, sales promotion, and publicity. These strategies are reviewed in detail later in the chapter.

Table 10-2 describes the relative use of these media by industrial distributors for information about new and existing products. Distributors stated that the most frequently used source of information about both new and existing product lines was manufacturer's representatives. Advertising in trade publications and catalogs were the second and third most used media, respectively, for both types of products. Although trade shows and direct mail were tied for fourth greatest usage for new product lines, respectively, these sources were ranked fourth and fifth in usage, respectively, for existing products. Newsletters were the least used media for both new and existing product lines.

Budgeting for push promotional strategies is particularly difficult since the costs to an upstream channel member are dependent on the degree of a reseller's usage. For example, a manufacturer needs to estimate its reseller's use of cooperative advertising, sales incentives, sales training programs, sales literature, and joint sales calls. An upstream channel member's being below budget on push promotional expenditures may signify that its resellers have not bought into the program. Similarly, being over budget on push promotional media can signify wide acceptance for the promotional program.

Budgeting decisions should ultimately be related to profitability, not to a minimum promotional allowance. Professors Levy, Webster, and Kerin have devised an overall four-stage process to identify effective push promotional strategies. This process consists of (1) identifying the salient marketing activities affecting reseller support for a product class; (2) determining the level or amount of each activity that would differentially affect reseller support; (3) estimating the sales levels and costs associated with each of these different levels of marketing activities; and (4) calculating the profit impact of alternative marketing activities.[6]

Profit planning may be easier with those programs that are demand-based (such as cooperative advertising or sales incentives for distributors' or retailers' salespersons), since these costs are directly related to a reseller's sales. For example, a manufacturer may provide an advertising allowance of 2 1/2 percent of sales, or a $25 payment to a retailer's salesperson, as an incentive for selling a top-of-the-line appliance. However, profit planning is more difficult if a pro-

TABLE 10-2 SOURCES INDUSTRIAL DISTRIBUTORS USE MOST FOR INFORMATION ABOUT NEW AND EXISTING LINES (PERCENT)

Sources	New Lines	Existing Lines
Manufacturer's representatives	59	67
Advertising in trade publications	45	30
Catalogs	25	34
Trade shows	16	10
Direct mail	16	15
Newsletters	4	6

Source: Jack Keough, "Distributors: The New Purchasing Arm for Their Customers," *Industrial Distribution* (May 1994), p. 41. Reprinted by permission.

gram is information- or preference-based, such as a dealer listing programs and sales literature.

Promotional planning must reflect the special needs of individual channel intermediaries. Some manufacturers have developed a flexible approach to push-oriented promotions based on a reseller's size. This approach to promotional planning assumes that larger resellers have greater access to functional specialists (such as a specialized advertising and market research staff) and a greater degree of computerization than smaller distributors. This overall approach to promotional planning assumes that cooperative advertising, training, lead generation, and incentive programs are more appropriate for larger distributors that have larger staffs, more professional managers, and better financing than their smaller counterparts.[7]

One study examined how the importance of specific promotions was affected by an industrial distributor's size. Use of price discounts was the variable of greatest importance to both medium and large distributors, while the amount of advance notice was most important to small distributors. Medium-sized distributors, for example, considered contests and sweepstakes of greater importance than larger industrial distributors. Variables unimportant to small distributors (but not to large distributors) were contests and sweepstakes, use of sales quotas, use of cooperative advertising, and use of missionary salespeople.[8]

Upstream channel members should design overall push promotions by determining the mix of their resellers and their individual needs. One approach to this problem is to design promotions in two modules: a **universal core support module**, which contains promotional programs that are applicable to all resellers, and **optional support modules**, which are promotional elements offered only to specific groups of resellers based on their individual needs. Although universal core supports are offered across the board to all resellers, resellers must select among the optional support modules. A reseller can become eligible for specific optional support modules on the basis of its sales history, quality of customer service, stocking of specific products, and so on. Universal core supports can include national contests, literature, and catalogs; whereas optional supports can be training courses, technical backup assistance, local lead programs, and joint calls to target markets.[9]

According to the 16th Annual Survey of Promotional Practices, the leading trade promotion practice is that of account-specific trade promotions. These promotions are used by 98 percent of the respondents surveyed.[10] Account-specific trade promotions were ranked high in importance by over half of the respondents.

Finally, the effectiveness of a push promotional program must be evaluated. The effectiveness of any promotional program should be related to the specific information-, preference-, or demand-based objectives. For example, the quality of a promotional program based on an information-based objective can be assessed based on the number of requests for technical service from sales representatives that completed a comprehensive sales training program. A promotional program based on a preference-based objective can be related to higher importance rankings assigned to an energy conservation feature. Demand-based objectives can be measured in terms of sales both to and through resellers. In addition to these measures, the effectiveness of a promotional program should be evaluated based on downstream channel member participation (the amount of cooperative advertising dollars used and the number of distributors that participated in a special sales training program).

The next section explores the use of advertising, personal selling, sales promotions, and publicity as media in a push promotional strategy.

ADVERTISING

Much advertising to resellers occurs in trade periodicals; other advertising media include a firm's own newsletters, a company-based magazine, and direct mail. As compared with mass media oriented to final consumers, trade media involve less waste because of their highly targeted audience. For example, *Industrial Distribution* has large circulation among maintenance, repair, and operating supplies distributors; *Progressive Grocer* has a large readership among independent and chain supermarket operators and managers; and *Computer Reseller News* is widely read by computer wholesalers and retailers.

Like advertising aimed at final consumers, trade advertising can be timed to coincide with peak seasonal periods. However, as compared with final consumer advertising, much trade advertising occurs prior to a final consumer's peak selling period to reflect lead times in ordering, receiving, and making goods ready for sale. Trade advertising by a manufacturer is also planned to coincide with major industry trade shows or with the use of cooperative advertising (implemented by resellers) aimed at final consumers.

A specific form of push advertising is a **dealer listing promotion** in which a manufacturer's advertisement includes the names of distributors and resellers that stock its products. Dealer listing promotions refer potential customers directly to stocking resellers.

PERSONAL SELLING

A discussion of a manufacturer's sales representative's duties needs to focus on the representative's multiple roles as teacher, reviewer, working partner, ambassador, ombudsman, and motivator for its resellers.[11] Each role is described in Table 10-3. These roles also have to be considered in selecting, training, motivating, and evaluating a manufacturer's sales representative.

The importance of the **teacher role** reflects the need to train a reseller's sales and support staff in sales techniques and a product's technical attributes. In his or her **reviewer role**, a manufacturer's salesperson needs to assess a reseller's overall performance. As a **working partner**, a manufacturer's salesperson should offer assistance at trade shows and work jointly with a reseller's own sales force on important sales. Through the **ambassador role**, the salesperson explains the manufacturer's policies and their benefit to the distributor. As an **ombudsman**, a manufacturer's sales representative at times must take the reseller's side. And lastly, through the **motivator role**, a manufacturer's sales rep attempts to get a distributor to achieve the manufacturer's objectives.

The relative use of each role changes with the degree of a reseller's sophistication and through shifts in a product's life cycle. For example, while a large in-

TABLE 10-3 ROLES OF A MANUFACTURER'S OR SUPPLIER'S SALES REPRESENTATIVES IN DEALING WITH RESELLERS

Salesperson Role	Tasks	Key Skills
Teacher	of selling skills of product applications knowledge of market knowledge of display techniques	Excellent presenter; listener; counselor; coach
Reviewer	of sales by product mix of sales versus forecast sales of competitive activity in reseller's area of inventory stocking versus targets of reseller's participation in promotions	Analyzer; prober; trader of information; forecaster
Working Partner	on joint sales calls at reseller and end-user accounts on sales blitzes at targeted industries on trade show activity at shared booths on lead program followup on demonstrations and reseller programs	Hands-on demonstrator; leader by showing sales professionalism
Ambassador	about terms of sale, credit, warranties, leasing about promotions, contests, new product launches about cooperative promotions about ordering policies, assortments about pricing schedules, margins	Motivational; selling-in of programs
Ombudsman	for complaints about product performance for credit, accounts receivable problems for reseller dissatisfaction about deliveries, backorders for problems on order mixups, policies on assortments, minimum order sizes, nonstandard products	Negotiator; conciliator; empathic; confidant to distributor
Motivator	to achieve sales goals to partake in manufacturer's sales contests to adequately stock required inventory levels to aggressively sell manufacturer's products and services	Excellent inspirator; developer of goals; leader

Source of teacher, reviewer, working partner, ambassador, and ombudsman: Allan J. Magrath and Kenneth G. Hardy, "Factory Salesmen's Roles with Industrial Distributors," *Industrial Marketing Management*, Vol. 16 (August 1987), p. 165. Reprinted by permission. Copyright 1987 by Elsevier Science Inc.

tegrated distributor may have a sophisticated sales training staff (that can rival the staff of some small manufacturers), smaller distributors generally rely heavily on manufacturers for their sales training. A product in the introduction stage of the product life cycle also requires different degrees of technical service than a more mature product.

A manufacturer needs to periodically review its sales organization. Most manufacturer sales forces are either centralized, product-, or market-based.

Centralized sales organizations are appropriate for a small firm with a homogeneous product mix. Product-based sales organizations are most appropriate for technically sophisticated products. Market-based sales organizations are appropriate when product needs are based on industry, usage, or geographic factors. For example, since Hallmark, a greeting card and gift manufacturer, reorganized its sales force by market, it improved its ability to tailor its selection of cards and gift items to specific retailer customers. James River, a manufacturer of paper products that are sold to supermarkets, has also reorganized its sales force. In the past, three or four James River salespeople would call on a single retail customer. For example, one sales rep would sell plates, another cups, and a third toilet paper. As a result, its customers' purchasing agents had to see all three salespeople. In addition, its supermarket customers had to purchase three separate truckloads (one for each product category) to receive the lowest price. Now, a unified James River team sells all products to each major retailer. Major supermarket customers can now secure the best price by purchasing only one truckload (with a mix of paper products). The team-selling concept also makes it easier for James River and its supermarket customers to plan a unified promotion featuring all three product categories.[12]

Manufacturers must understand that their sales force needs to motivate their resellers to use specific sales promotions, as well as to stock additional inventory. In an innovative pilot program, about 100 Hallmark employees have taken a 15 percent cut in pay and have agreed to have a portion of their income based on performance. These sales representatives are eligible to receive a bonus of up to 15 percent of their income, based on retail, *not* wholesale, sales of Hallmark products.[13]

SALES TRAINING PROGRAMS

Sales training programs offered to resellers generally cover sales techniques and technical product information. Sales training programs are commonly categorized by degree of formality. Informal reseller sales training programs are based on conversations, demonstrations, and joint sales calls with the manufacturer and the distributor. Often, informal training occurs in conjunction with some other type of activity. In contrast, formal reseller training programs are based on lectures, video instruction, and role-playing sessions. Formal training programs are often conducted by a manufacturer's professional dealer or distributor development staffs.

Reseller training can also be categorized by stages, with a **stage one program** consisting of basic product training (such as a product demonstration), a **stage two program** being a joint sales call (where the dealer assists the manufacturer's representative in demonstrating a new product), and a **stage three program** (where the dealers swap roles with a manufacturer's sales staff).[14]

A 1993 survey of more than 700 manufacturing and distribution executives conducted by the National Association of Wholesale Distributors found that 40 percent of manufacturers offered training for distributors in 1994 and that 50 percent plan to offer such training by the year 2000.[15]

SALES INCENTIVES

Sales incentives include bonuses, contests, plaques, membership in an annual club of high-performing resellers, paid vacations, and other monetary and nonmonetary awards. Generally, sales incentives are based on the cumulative performance of a reseller's sales staff. Awards can be based on sales revenue, performance against quota, increases over a prior year's sales, and customer service (based on customer evaluation). In large manufacturers, sales incentive programs are often administered by a staff specialist (who also monitors performance). In small- to medium-sized manufacturers, a sales incentive program can be administered by a vice president of marketing, a sales manager, or even an outside firm.

It is especially difficult to develop a sales incentive program for resellers that represent multiple manufacturers for at least two reasons. First, these resellers may be subject to sales incentives from multiple suppliers at the same time; thus, they are subject to conflicting goals. Second, each wholesaler or retailer may have a different goal than its supplier. For example, although the manufacturer may seek to increase its market share, the wholesaler or retailer may desire to sell off excess inventory, to reduce stock in a good about to be discontinued, or to sell those goods with the highest profit margins.

In budgeting for incentives, manufacturers need to retain sufficient funds to effectively communicate and promote the incentive program. One market analyst argues that the value of awards should be 70 to 75 percent of the overall budget, 20 percent should be allocated to communication and promotions (to keep up interest among participants during promotion), and 5 to 15 percent should be for administrative costs (for either internal staffers or an outside service).[16]

There are several advantages of the use of sales incentives. Aside from a monetary award, the sales incentive provides recognition to an excellent sales force. Sales incentives are also flexible. Incentives can be based on slow moving goods, on improvement in sales, on achieving high levels of customer service, and so on. The incentive award can also be structured based on season, number of awards, and award distribution (many small awards versus few but large awards).

Often, manufacturers do not sufficiently plan their sales incentive programs or underestimate the difficulty in implementing them. Among the difficulties in administering a distributor sales incentive program are poor program publicity, too many programs occurring simultaneously, programs that do not meet a distributor's goals, programs that are too complicated, programs that last too long, and programs that fail to reward the proper persons.[17]

TABLE 10-4 A PUSH-ORIENTED PERSONAL SELLING AUDIT

- Does my channel member's sales force have proper training in product information, customer needs assessment, and characteristics of competition?
- Am I providing the same training for the reseller's sales force that is provided for the manufacturer's own sales force?
- Does my organization's sales force have a clear understanding of my reseller's buying priorities and decision-making process?
- Am I giving my reseller's sales force the proper training and tools needed to differentiate my products?
- Do I continuously offer some form of sales training to my channel member's sales force?

Source: Some of the material is from Marty Jones and Steve Kratz, "The Channel Empowerment Solution," *Sales & Marketing Management* (March 1993), p. 46.

Data on sales incentives are not broken down further, but the total amount of sales incentives exceeds $6 billion for manufacturers' and resellers' sales forces. Sales support personnel receive an additional $6 billion in incentive programs per year.[18] One study of sales incentive plans reported that 12 percent of sales incentives were aimed at wholesalers' sales representatives and an additional 12 percent at independent representatives.[19]

Table 10-4 contains a push-oriented personal selling audit that assesses the quality of a firm's personal selling efforts aimed at distributors.

SALES PROMOTION

Sales promotion includes all promotional effort that is not classified as personal selling, advertising, and publicity—often with the objective of stimulating demand. In contrast to other promotional forms, sales promotions generally are much more demand-based than either information- or preference-based. Generally, sales promotions are used to generate short-term sales increases for a product or service; most sales promotions have a limited time span.

In a major study of trade-oriented sales promotions, Professor Kenneth Hardy analyzed 113 trade promotions among 27 Canadian package goods firms that sold food and pharmaceutical products through food and/or drug retail channels.[20] The researcher found that, on average, unsuccessful promotions spent one-half to three-quarters as much as successful promotions. The study also found that achieving trade support was the critical variable related to success for each trade promotion objective: short-term volume, long-term market share, building trade inventories, and consumer trial. Overall, the major reasons for achieving trade objectives were high incentives, good trade support, good sales force support, and absence of competitive activity. The reasons for unsuccessful promotions were built trade inventories from previous deals, insufficient incentives, competitive promotions, and lack of trade support.

A variety of push sales promotions are aimed at stimulating reseller effort. The use of street money and pay-for-performance allowances, push money, and distributor recognition programs are discussed in the following section.

Street Money and Pay-for-Performance Allowances

A popular sales promotion is **street money**, a temporary deal or discount used on a short-term basis to increase shelf space, promote sales, introduce a new product, or increase market share in a region where sales are low. Street money is also called flexible funds or discretionary marketing funds. For example, in an R. J. Reynolds street money allowance, distributors were given $1 per carton, with the freedom to use these funds in a variety of ways. The distributor could give its retailer customers 50 cents off per carton, or give its own salespeople 10 cents for each carton sold to designated retailers. Street money recognizes differences among markets by providing flexibility to its distributors.[21]

A variation of street money is a **pay-for-performance allowance**, in which a manufacturer provides its intermediaries with a financial incentive to reimburse them for selling its goods at a reduced retail sales price, for increasing display activity, and for generating increased sales. Unlike street money, a pay-for-performance allowance requires a reseller to verify completion of each activity to be reimbursed. For example, a retailer would have to submit scanner data to verify performance on a pay-for-performance allowance based on reduced selling prices.[22]

An example of a pay-for-performance allowance is Philip Morris's estimated $150 million program which offered wholesalers cash rewards for meeting sales quotas and for compiling and forwarding up-to-date sales data. While Philip Morris's brands have about a 40 percent share, these promotional funds are based on wholesalers' commitment to increase the volume of Philip Morris's brands up to 49 percent of their business. Participants were also required to file weekly sales figures with Philip Morris. According to a wholesaler, "This is the first time Philip Morris has paid us for sales instead of space or buy-ins. They are making us part of the sales force because you have to meet specific sales objectives to get anything. That makes you work harder for Philip Morris."[23]

As mentioned in Chapter 9, a major difficulty with the use of street money and pay-for-performance allowances is that they encourage forward buying and diverting. Part of the rationale of everyday low pricing is to eliminate or severely reduce the use of temporary deals. Duracell is among the firms that have reduced their use of these short-term promotions. At one point, the promotions, which took place 32 weeks of the year, accounted for 90 percent of Duracell's total yearly sales. Duracell has now shifted to new displays and to helping retailers plan events to draw shoppers.[24]

Dial has also altered its strategy of using street money and pay-for-performance allowances. Dial has now begun to empower its field sales force to work with individual accounts in developing flexible deal structures that are best suited for each account instead of using the same program for all accounts.[25]

Push Money

Push money (PMs, promotional money, spiffs) is an incentive paid by a manufacturer directly to a retailer's salesperson to stimulate the sale of a particular brand or specific product. Push money is typically used to stimulate a retail salesperson to promote brand or product switching at the point of sale. Push money is often used for brands with a low degree of consumer recognition (such as a brand with a low advertising budget, or a new brand), for products that require extra sales effort (such as a product that utilizes a new technology which is difficult to explain), or for purposes of increasing sales of products that have not met a manufacturer's sales expectations.

Push money can be seen from the perspective of either channel conflict or cooperation. It is a form of channel conflict since a reseller's sales representa-

CHANNELS IN ACTION

Loctite's and Rust-Oleum's Use of Reseller Promotions

Almost every distributor can recount promotions in which they purchased large inventories only to find that the product was not bought by consumers. More and more manufacturers are now seeking the advice of distributors in planning promotions. Often, advice is sought out during distributor advisory councils or during brainstorming sessions.

An example of a particularly effective manufacturer promotion developed in conjunction with a distributor was Loctite's Survival Kit. This promotion was developed at a distributor advisory council with input from distributors. Since both Loctite's chairman of the board and president participate in the advisory council, they are also able to see that good ideas are properly planned and quickly implemented. Loctite's Survival Kit campaign featured six different products, a Swiss army knife, and a $1 per kit sales incentive paid to the distributor's salespeople. The kit was priced at 25 percent less than what it would cost the end-user to purchase the products individually. An important component of the plan was Loctite's guarantee that distributors would earn a 30 percent profit margin. The success of the plan was based on satisfying both intermediate and final consumers. The distributor's sales force received a popular incentive, the distributor was guaranteed a favorable profit level, and the end-user received a highly regarded premium.

The result? Loctite distributors reported that they earned more from this promotion than from any other Loctite program. One distributor sold 60 kits at a single plant. Another distributor sold 1200 kits in the first five days of the promotion.

Rust-Oleum, a paint specialty manufacturer, recently changed its entire marketing plan based on input from its distributor advisory board. According to Rust-Oleum's vice president of industrial marketing, "We used to have a load 'em and leave 'em approach. Now, we've developed a 'have it your way' system, a menu of different marketing options to choose from that can be implemented at the branch level." Rust-Oleum's new plan enables its distributors to choose the promotional program best suited for their territory among a variety of customized marketing promotions. And since promotion plans vary each quarter, they ensure distributors that they are fresh, as well as reflect seasonal factors. Among Rust-Oleum's programs are training videos, free end-user samples, and distributor salesperson incentives.

Source: John R. Johnson, "Promoting Profits Through Partnerships," *Industrial Distribution* (March 1994), pp. 22–24.

tive is now being motivated by the manufacturer or wholesaler rather than the retailer. For instance, a manufacturer's push money campaign may result in lower sales of the retailer's own private label brand. On the other hand, push money can be seen as a form of channel cooperation due to a manufacturer's providing a sales incentive at no cost to the retailer. The channel cooperation perspective is correct when retailers have little concern over which brand or model consumers purchase.

Push money is legal if the manufacturer notifies each retailer and obtains its permission to use this sales incentive.[26]

Distributor Recognition Programs

Distributor recognition awards are designed to motivate resellers by communicating a distributor's accomplishments at an annual meeting, an awards banquet, or a convention banquet. Generally, distributor recognition awards are accompanied by major publicity. The award is often in the form of a plaque, certificate, or membership in a special group. Often, distributor recognition awards are based on a distributor's performance in a specific time period. For example, a supplier can have an overall "Distributor of the Year" award or have individual awards within specific industry sectors, such as the "Automotive Distributor of the Year."

Unlike sales contests for the distributor's sales force, a distributor's recognition award recognizes the total accomplishments of all its employees. These awards are generally based on a variety of factors such as meeting a quota, superior customer service (as judged by customers), and even nominations. When nominations are required, an appropriate panel should be convened to prepare packets, evaluate recommendations, and recommend award winners.[27]

PUBLICITY

Publicity is nonpaid communication about a company or its products in the mass media. Publicity is a favored medium owing to the absence of media costs, as well as its high believability. A reseller can seek to use publicity as a push medium by developing press releases geared to its resellers, a distributor winning a "Distributor of the Year" award, and its quantity discount schedule.

Push publicity is often targeted at trade magazines that can be organized on the basis of industry, geographic area, or technology. To be effective, the manufacturer needs to understand the slant of the magazine, as well as its targeted audience. For example, sending a press release that a local distributor won an award may be perfectly appropriate for a business weekly newspaper with a local circulation. On the other hand, the manufacturer may have to send a product sample, independent test reports, and photographs to get publicity in a major trade magazine.

A major disadvantage of the use of publicity is that the marketer has no control over the media where the message will run, what the message will say, and when the story will run. For example, a magazine may not pick up the material in the press release, may place the coverage in the human interest section rather than the business section, may rewrite the material in a manner that is not complimentary, or may run the story three weeks too late. Due to the lack of control, upstream channel members should use publicity to supplement other media, not as the firm's entire promotional program.

Publicity can be evaluated on the basis of the traditional measures used to evaluate push advertising (such as increased shelf space, a higher proportion of distributors that use cooperative advertising programs, and increased distributor participation in a sales contest). A special measure used to evaluate publicity is the value of comparable space (for print media) and time (for broadcast media) if the firm had to pay for the media usage. In preparing this analysis, a marketer should be aware that the only element of publicity where there are no costs is for media placement. There can be considerable costs in the form of retainer fees for a public relations firm, photography costs, and significant time spent to woo reporters.

IMPROVING PUSH PROMOTIONS

Push-oriented promotions can be improved through a series of interrelated activities.[28] These can be categorized as timing-, administrative-, theme-, and product-related measures.

Timing-related measures include the importance of intermediaries receiving notice of the promotions in advance of the campaign, the need for a manufacturer's representative to contact the distributor throughout a promotional campaign, planning promotions on an annual (not piecemeal) basis, and running trade promotions at the same time as consumer promotions. Administrative-related measures include reducing paperwork and recordkeeping requirements which can be done by shifting some of the work to manufacturers or independent firms, or by providing specialized software for resellers to track data. Theme-related measures include having a sufficient variety of promotions for a channel member to choose from and providing flexibility to meet the diverse needs of both small and large resellers. Product-related measures include promoting larger sizes to accelerate in-home product usage of a product. The use of larger sizes also inhibits the effectiveness of competitive promotions since a final consumer may be fully stocked with a given product.

DEVELOPING AND IMPLEMENTING A PULL-ORIENTED PROMOTIONAL STRATEGY

According to one market analyst, "many manufacturers tend to view resellers as the final destination for their products. They reinforce the attitude by totaling revenues and paying commissions when the products are shipped to the reseller rather than when they are sold to the end-user. The manufacturer assumes that once the pallets are resting in the reseller's storage facility, the primary responsibility to move product into the hands of the customer lies with the reseller."[29]

· The argument that a sale is not complete until the product is ultimately sold to the consumer is a compelling one.[30] This argument has several ramifications for the manufacturer or supplier. One is that a manufacturer should reward its sales force on the basis of sales at the final consumer level, not sales to intermediaries. For instance, at Ocean Spray, a major producer of cranberry juice drinks, the promotional goal is measured on the basis of retail sales, not wholesale sales.[31] Rewarding salespeople on the basis of retail sales (as measured by scanner data) reinforces the role of a manufacturer's sales force work in setting up displays, training a distributor's or retailer's sales force, and assisting final consumers in the selection of alternative products. Objectives based on retail sales also reduce the current reward associated with forward buying and diverting.

Table 10-5 contains a listing of pull-related promotional strategies for distributors and retailers. Note that each of these strategies seeks to directly increase sales at the final consumer or end-user level.

TABLE 10-5 MANUFACTURERS' PULL PROMOTIONAL STRATEGIES FOR DISTRIBUTORS AND RETAILERS

Advertising
   Product advertising aimed at final consumers
   Cooperative advertising (both push and pull)
   Brand advertising

Personal Selling
   Joint sales calls (both push and pull)
   Personal selling aimed at end-users

Sales promotion
   Coupons for final consumers
   Rebate programs
   Trade shows
   Premiums
   Frequent users clubs
   Free samples
   Contests
   Sweepstakes
   Point-of-purchase displays (both push and pull)
   In-store materials

Publicity
   Press release on new products
   Press release on new rebate program

Sources: Many of these items are from Allan J. Magrath and Kenneth G. Hardy, "Manufacturer Services for Distributors," *Industrial Marketing Management,* Vol. 21 (May 1992), pp. 120, 121; and Benson P. Shapiro, "Improve Distribution with Your Promotional Mix," *Harvard Business Review,* Vol. 55 (March–April 1977), p. 122.

ADVERTISING

Part of the function of a manufacturer's advertising is to develop leads for its resellers. The listing of leads generated by this advertising can then be forwarded to distributors. In some cases, a manufacturer will ship goods for a distributor and give the distributor credit for all sales in its territory.

As is true of push advertising, not all pull-related advertising is demand-based; rather, much pull advertising is image- or information-based. For example, Brother International plans to spend $4 million to support its new low-cost laser printer via a television, radio, print, and outdoor advertising campaign. Its low-cost laser printer, which retails at $400, features a straight paper pass that minimizes paper jams. Although most consumers have associated Brother with typewriters or with facsimile machines, the objective of this campaign is to increase Brother's image to encompass laser printers.[32]

Sometimes, there is conflict between the goals of the manufacturer in its pull-related advertising and its customers. For example, Intel has spent $80 million on television advertising to persuade customers that they need personal computers based on its Pentium microprocessor chip. In contrast, Compaq has spent $100 million on advertising that communicates that it's not the chip, but the brand of personal computer, that is important.[33] While Intel hopes its advertising will get more customers to specify the Pentium chip, Compaq reports that 87 percent of its sales are of the older 486 variety.

Several important trends relate to pull advertising: increased use is being made of direct mail; more and more manufacturers are now developing specialized advertising programs for specific retailers; and dealers and distributors are becoming increasingly involved in planning pull advertising.

Direct mail is being increasingly used as an advertising medium. Advances in computer technology have lowered the cost of maintaining a database (consisting of the names and addresses of customers). And the increased use of notebook computers by salespersons has better enabled them to target specific accounts with special promotions. For example, a salesperson can now easily customize sales letters based on the past buying behavior of customers.

Manufacturers are increasingly using **account-specific advertising**, that is, specialized advertising programs that are planned for a specific retailer. Account-specific advertising can be used to better blend a manufacturer's advertisement with a retailer's image. For example, Warner-Lambert developed custom-tailored advertising for 100 major retailers. Its $1 million plus promotional budget, which ran in 60 markets, prominently features retailer logos along with product information on such products as its Arm & Hammer Dental Care products. Account-specific advertising has been used by Johnson & Johnson, Reckitt & Coleman, and Procter & Gamble.[34]

Increasingly, dealers have been actively involved in the development, implementation, and review of pull advertising programs through distributor or dealer councils. For example, four Oldsmobile dealers sitting on the advertising review committee provoked a review of General Motors' $140-million-a-year advertising account at Leo Burnett USA. Similarly, Pontiac and Mercedes Benz are among the car makers that now give their dealers more input into its advertising program.[35]

Much of pull-related advertising activity is cooperative advertising.

Cooperative Advertising

Cooperative advertising is local advertising placed by a distributor or retailer that is partially or fully reimbursed by a manufacturer. Cooperative advertising funds are generally used in local advertising campaigns. A common agreement in cooperative advertising is for the distributor or retailer to receive one-half or more of the cost of advertising of a manufacturer's products (sometimes even the total cost) up to a set limit (such as 5 percent of purchases). The amount of the cost sharing is usually based on the quantity of merchandise a distributor or retailer purchases within a specific period. (The time period is determined by the size, scope, and length of the cooperative advertising agreement.) Cooperative advertising allowances are given only to a distributor's or retailer's advertising programs that meet specific guidelines established by the manufacturer. Distributors and retailers are generally required to submit proof of placement of ads (generally tearsheets) to the manufacturer, its advertising agency, or a third party prior to payment.

Conditions for cooperative advertising outline the duration of the cooperative advertising fund, the manufacturer's maximum contribution, policies regarding approvals, the types of media that qualify, how dealers are reimbursed (credit towards future purchases or outright payment), and reasons for rejection of claims.[36] For example, some manufacturers have special requirements in terms of the use of competing products in the same ad, or the mention of price.[37] Conditions for cooperative advertising help assure that retail advertising builds on a manufacturer's national advertising efforts.

The Newspaper Advertising Bureau (NAB) estimates that about $15 billion worth of cooperative advertising funds are made available each year. Of that amount, about $5 billion will not be used.[38] Of the cooperative advertising funds used, NAB estimates that 64 percent will be used in newspapers, while the balance will be used in radio, television, outdoor, and increasingly, direct mail.[39] Although cooperative advertising is generally associated with distributors and retailers, one estimate is that up to 10 percent of all cooperative advertising is for business-to-business marketing.[40]

A 1993 survey of more than 700 manufacturing and distribution executives conducted by the National Association of Wholesaler-Distributors found that 20 percent of manufacturers offered cooperative advertising programs in 1994 and that 30 percent planned to offer such programs by the year 2000.[41]

Whereas retail cooperative advertising is generally oriented to reimburse distributors or retailers for the cost of advertising space, business-to-business cooperative advertising has been broadened to reimburse wholesalers for the costs of organizing seminars for prospects, sales staff training, trade shows, telemarketing, direct mail, and even for the salary of a salesperson dedicated to the manufacturer's line.[42]

In computing a manufacturer's or supplier's total advertising expenditures, resellers must be careful to add their share of cooperative advertising costs for budgeting purposes.

Cooperative advertising offers two major advantages for a manufacturer. First, a manufacturer pays a higher rate for advertising in either broadcast or print media; its rate is called a **national rate**. In contrast, the rate quoted to a distributor or retailer for space or time is referred to as a **local rate**. The difference between a national or local rate is based on whether a manufacturer or a reseller is billed for an advertisement; there is no difference in market coverage. In addition to the savings to a manufacturer based on the use of a local rate, a manufacturer pays for only a portion of the total costs of an ad (often one-half of the cost of the ad) in cooperative advertising.

Second, cooperative advertising has both pull and push promotional elements. A reseller's use of cooperative advertising increases the likelihood that it will stock an item, give it preferred display space, and train its sales personnel. In addition, cooperative advertising is designed to increase sales at the final consumer or end-user levels.

Resellers benefit from the promotional materials associated with cooperative advertising. For example, many manufacturers supply advertising copy and layout for their cooperative advertising. The quality of the artwork and copy is com-

CHANNELS IN ACTION

Push and Pull Reseller Promotions

Gemaire Distributors is a wholesaler that represents Rheem Air Conditioning and Heating Products. Gemaire used a sales incentive program for its local dealers which offered them a $100 U.S. Savings Bond for every ton of cooling capacity of Rheem air conditioners purchased. This sales program was supplemented with a cooperative advertising program to stimulate final consumer demand. Working with the *Palm Beach Post's* cooperative advertising department, the Newspaper Co-op Network (NCN), and the Florida Newspaper Co-op Association, Gemaire was able to invest more than $250,000 in cooperative advertising in 22 newspapers. The combined program was so successful that many dealers ran out of stock before the program ended.

This program was successful because dealers were involved in planning the program from its inception. Local dealers participated in the newspaper selection process. They were also given the chance to assign their advertising dollars to this promotion. To ensure a consistent presentation to consumers, Gemaire and the *Palm Beach Post* prepared camera-ready ads in a variety of sizes and formats. While dealers were able to use other media, most opted for the prepared newspaper format. A one order/one bill arrangement simplified recordkeeping. One phone call was all that was needed to place advertisements in multiple markets. And finally, administrative costs were reduced through the involvement of NCN.

Without the involvement of the NCN, Gemaire Distributors would have had to hire a staff of media buyers, customize the listings of its dealers, obtain cooperative rates, coordinate the placement of ads, and provide documentation (to prove that the advertisements actually ran in the newspapers). The NCN was also able to earn additional discounts from the media.

Source: Julie S. Newhall, "The Care and Feeding of a Cash Cow," *Sales & Marketing Marketing* (May 1992), pp. 40–46.

monly better than a small or medium-sized retailer could possibly implement on its own. They also benefit from sharing promotional costs with the manufacturer.

Cooperative advertising presents some disadvantages only to manufacturers, and others only to resellers. Other disadvantages apply to all of these channel members.

To the manufacturer, a retailer's use of cooperative advertising may also not be in line with a manufacturer's overall plans. For example, although much of the manufacturer's promotional budget may be used to increase its brand image, retailers may devote cooperative advertising monies to price promotions. Large retailers may also use cooperative advertising to generate store traffic, with little regard for impact on any brand's sales or image.

Distributors and retailers also have to fit cooperative advertising into their overall media plan, despite the conditions for cooperative advertising. For example, some advertisers insist that the cooperative advertising states a minimum price level in order to qualify for media reimbursement costs. In addition, some advertising formats prepared by a manufacturer may not reflect the retailer's image. For example, a manufacturer's advertising format may devote too much copy on a product's features (such as a Lexan interior) and too little copy on why a consumer should buy the dishwasher at a given retailer (lower price, same-day delivery, low-cost installation, or free carting away of the old appliance). Restrictions on cooperative advertising usage have also been found to be related to negative perceptions by retailers, such as being pressured to purchase more of a manufacturer's product.[43]

To all of these channel members, cooperative advertising imposes heavy administration duties (such as preparing copies of advertisements, verifying that cooperative advertisements actually ran, determining whether any conditions have been met, and so on). One indication of the difficulty of administering cooperative advertising reimbursements is that one review of 10 retail chains (selected at random by the Advertising Checking Bureau) found that even the most efficient chain could have increased its cooperative advertising reimbursement dollars by 22 percent. Another chain could have tripled its cooperative advertising allowances.[44] Both manufacturers and resellers are also liable for meeting the terms of the Robinson-Patman Act for cooperative advertising allowances. This topic is covered in the discussion of the legal aspects of channel promotional strategy area under price discrimination and promotional allowances.

Cooperative advertising programs can be improved through the use of a number of programs.[45] First, a cooperative advertising program should be based on objectives that are significant for a reseller. If not, reseller participation will be low. The conditions for cooperative advertising should not overly impede retailer participation. Conditions should be included to the extent that a reseller's ads reinforce a manufacturer's current advertising campaign.

Second, all of the communication materials should be provided to the retailer. These include samples of ads of various sizes that support the manufacturer's advertising campaign. Many manufacturers also prepare different advertising samples for each season. Still others supply pre-formatted ads for insertion into Yellow Pages, or prepare direct mail pieces for retailers. All of these materials should allow the retailer to insert its name, address, phone number, and other information in each advertisement.

Third, a manufacturer should review the appropriateness of its current marketing organization in terms of designing, implementing, and reviewing a cooperative program. Alternative organization formats to consider include an advertising agency with a high level of experience in cooperative advertising, an internal cooperative advertising coordinator, a newspaper industry organization, such as the Newspaper Advertising Bureau (NAB), and the Newspaper Co-op Network, and **third-party documentation agencies**. These agencies are outside firms that are paid to document print cooperative claims. Some third-party firms even advise retailers on how much cooperative advertising is initially available and what conditions it must meet; collect tearsheets as documentation; file the claims for cooperative funds; and then inform the retailers as to how much funding remains.[46]

PERSONAL SELLING

There are two types of personal selling programs in pull promotion. In the first type, the manufacturer's sales force participates in joint sales calls with a distributor's sales personnel. In the second format, the manufacturer's sales force sells directly to end-users.

A manufacturer's involvement with its distributor's sales force through joint sales calls serves several functions. This program indirectly provides sales assistance to the distributor, bolsters the manufacturer's image of the buyer, and increases the chance that the manufacturer's products (versus a competitor's) will be used if the distributor gets the sale. A special problem that needs to be resolved in joint sales calls is the identification of each party's responsibilities before, during, and after the sale.

Manufacturers and distributors are becoming more aware of the high costs of selling directly to end-users through an external sales force. The high median cost per call by an external sales force (over $200) necessitates examining alternatives to personal selling, especially for selling to smaller accounts. Few national firms now have field sales reps who call on customers with fewer than 20 employees. Often, an external sales force is used to sell to a firm's largest accounts, while an internal sales force, telemarketing, and catalog selling are used to handle smaller accounts and accounts with less potential.

One major change is to think of internal salespeople as order getters as well as order takers. In many instances, a manufacturer needs to better train and motivate its inside sales force to cross-sell related items (such as a service contract with a laser printer), recommend better alternatives (trading up), and sell a substitute item (when the desired item is unavailable). When the role of an inside salesperson is changed, a manufacturer may have to rethink its overall compensation system. Some firms reimburse inside salesmen on a commission basis in order to reflect the increased sales activity; others use team commissions (to compensate for the effort that inside salespeople expend on outside salespersons' accounts).[47]

Many manufacturers use telemarketing to reach small accounts, as well as accounts in rural areas. The use of telemarketers has been drastically restricted by the Telephone Consumer Protection Act of 1991. This law bars commercial ventures from using autodialers to deliver pre-recorded messages. However, **predictive dialers**, which ring many phones simultaneously to immediately transfer an answered call to a live operator, are allowed.[48]

Finally, catalog selling is also used to reach small accounts. A manufacturer can use catalogs in conjunction with databases to customize catalog sheets for individual customers based on their ordering history. Different catalogs can also be developed for different markets.

SALES PROMOTION

Professor Hardy also studied consumer promotions by 27 major Canadian package goods companies. Pull sales promotions had five objectives: short-term volume, long-term market share, building trade inventories, consumer trial, and consumer loading (building inventory in the consumer's home). Different factors were responsible for the success of sales promotions based on objectives. For example, in building short-term volume, it was important to have both consumer and trade promotions during the same time period. For long-term market share, sales force support was the major factor. For building trade inventories by consumer promotions, the major factors were avoiding competitive promotions, gaining trade sales force support, and offering a high level of incentives. For the consumer trial objective, the key variables were trade sales force support, a long promotion period, and a high level of incentives. Lastly, to obtain the consumer loading objective, the two key variables were trade sales force support and a high promotional cost. Promotional cost refers to high expenditures for increased advertising, point-of-purchase materials, and special shipping bins.[49]

Donnelley Marketing Inc., on an annual basis, outlines the promotional practices of large consumer products manufacturers. Table 10-6 presents data on

TABLE 10-6 TYPES OF PULL SALES PROMOTIONS USED, 1989–1993 (PERCENT OF RESPONDENTS USING EACH TYPE OF SALES PROMOTION)

Type of Sales Promotion	1989	1990	1991	1992	1993
Couponing consumer direct	93	95	100	100	100
Cents-off promotions	64	88	87	77	90
Couponing in retailers' ads	63	57	66	65	88
Sampling new products	66	75	64	73	84
Couponing—in store (electronic, handouts)	NA	54	49	75	82
Money back offers/cash refunds	74	72	77	88	80
Premium offers	73	62	70	69	78
Sampling established products	57	62	43	66	78
Sweepstakes	70	68	64	61	63
Contests	41	31	40	47	51
Pre-priced products	44	35	45	41	51

Source: 16th Annual Survey of Promotional Practices (Oakbrook Terrace, Ill.: Donnelley Marketing Inc., 1994), pp. 31, 35. Reprinted by permission.

the usage of selected sales promotions directed at final consumers from Donnelley's most recent study. The next section details the use of coupons, rebates, trade shows, and miscellaneous promotions.

Coupons

Coupons are certificates prepared for manufacturers that entitle consumers to price reductions for a limited time period. Generally, manufacturers distribute coupons in newspapers, in product packages (with the same or different products), in-store, by direct mail, by electronic form, or through magazines. Coupons found in newspaper freestanding inserts or on the package itself are the two most popular forms of coupon placement.[50] While the number of coupons distributed for 1993 was flat at 323 billion (the first time in 20 years that the number of coupons distributed had not increased), redemption declined to 7.2 billion coupons (a 2.2 per cent redemption rate). Part of the decline was due to the reduced expiration period, which currently averages 3.8 months. This is about half the average expiration period in 1988.[51]

While final consumers redeem the coupons with retailers, retailers typically submit coupons to a clearinghouse for redemption. Manufacturers or clearinghouses also typically pay retailers a small fee to compensate them for the paperwork associated with coupons. Some manufacturers directly reimburse retailers rather than use a clearinghouse. To ensure the same coupons are not reused, many manufacturers shred the coupons.

In a study using scanner data, coupon effectiveness was evaluated on the basis of incremental sales produced by the coupon and coupon efficiency (incremental sales per redemption). Databases for three different product categories (each consisting of the evaluations of 50 to 90 coupons by Information Resources, Inc.) have been studied cross-sectionally. Researchers sought to determine how market share, face value, and other coupon characteristics affect coupon effectiveness. The study found that:[52]

- Brand share has a negative effect on coupon effectiveness.
- Coupon face value and time since the last event had a positive effect on coupon effectiveness.
- The following coupon characteristics have negative effects on coupon effectiveness:
  - Unit requirements or restrictions.
  - Presence of an overlay (sweepstakes, contest) in conjunction with a coupon offer.
  - Coupon clutter (presence of other coupon events dropped in the same week).
  - Longer fuse length (number of days between the coupon drop and the expiration date.

New technological developments associated with scanning are point-of-sales equipment that prints coupons for competitive products, coupon-dispensing equipment located on a supermarket's shelves, and equipment to scan coupons to facilitate redemption. Some manufacturers are using equipment that automatically prints coupons for a competitive product at a supermarket's point-of-sale terminal. Thus, the purchaser of one brand of mouthwash can receive a coupon for a competing brand at the cash register. Other manufacturers have also begun to use coupon-dispensing equipment on supermarket shelves. Some 3500 supermarkets have also begun to reduce their coupon-processing costs through scanning coupons as of the beginning of 1993. To facilitate payment in as little as five days, some supermarkets have begun to electronically transmit coupons for redemption to manufacturers.[53]

Many positive elements are associated with the use of coupons. First, coupons are a flexible promotional medium. A manufacturer can issue coupons in an off-season in an effort to stimulate a trial for a new product and to indirectly increase shelf space allocations by generating demand. A manufacturer can also issue a coupon for a related item purchase. For example, a coupon in a shampoo package can provide for a half-price offer for a hair spray. This attempts to transfer brand preference from one manufacturer's product to another.

Two major difficulties associated with coupons are the high potential for coupon fraud by retailers and the high costs of printing, distributing, handling, and redeeming coupons. Some unscrupulous retailers cut coupons from newspapers and magazines and mail them to a manufacturer or clearinghouse as if a final consumer had redeemed the coupon at its store. **Chargebacks** are coupons a retailer submitted for payment but were denied. Coupons are denied if they are submitted after the expiration date or if the manufacturer or clearinghouse suspects fraud. It is important for manufacturers to be on the lookout for misredeemed coupons. Warning signs of misredemption are mint-condition coupons, coupons submitted with consecutive serial numbers, coupons that have all been cut with a paper cutter, coupons that have wrinkles that have been simulated to appear worn, and too high a redemption rate.[54]

According to General Mills, a 50 cent coupon costs the firm about 75 cents (after considering the cost to print, distribute, handle, and redeem.)[55]

REBATES

Rebates provide special money-back incentives directly to final consumers and end-users. Unlike reductions in a product's list price that reduce the inventory valuation of all resellers, rebates keep inventory values constant. In addition, unlike special discounts and allowances, rebates do not encourage forward buying by wholesalers and retailers. Manufacturers can ensure that rebates are passed onto the final consumer with rebates. Lastly, rebates present less potential for retailer fraud than coupons.

Rebates have been used with a wide variety of goods from inexpensive products to automobiles. Rebates can be several dollars off a product to over $1000 off the price of a car. In the fourth quarter of 1993, the average rebate offer for a U.S.-produced vehicle was $700, down from $900 in the previous quarter and about $1200 in the fourth quarter of 1992.[56] Instead of rebates, more automakers are offering a fixed set of auto options (such as air conditioning, power windows, and cassette players) at a nonnegotiable price.

From a positive point of view, rebates offer the attractiveness of reductions in list price, special discounts, and coupons without the difficulties associated with reductions in reseller inventory values, forward buying, and retailer fraud. They are also a flexible medium. The goods eligible for a rebate, the amount of a rebate, and the expiration date of a rebate can all be modified. A manufacturer can also use rebates to counter gray market price differentials (by providing rebates only to goods imported and sold through authorized channel members), and to increase brand loyalty (by providing rebates to past purchasers).

Like coupons, a major difficulty with rebates is the administrative paperwork. While final consumers must clip the rebate coupon, the manufacturer must verify that rebate conditions have been met (in terms of item, purchase quantity, and time period). As in any sales promotional tool, rebates can also lose their impact if they are used too frequently. Consumers may expect to receive a rebate and refuse to purchase goods without it.

Trade Shows

Trade shows are a periodic exhibition in a single location of a group of manufacturers and distributors where products and services are displayed to potential buyers. Trade shows can be a push or a pull promotional form. They are a pull promotion if developed by manufacturers to gain interest among end-users for a manufacturer's products. They can be a push promotion if designed for distributor attendance.

Trade shows accounted for between 22 and 25 percent of the typical U.S. business market promotional budget, second only to personal selling and ahead of print advertising and direct mail. In total, U.S. businesses spent $9 billion annually on exhibitors' travel and labor costs and $12 billion on actual exhibit costs in 1993.[57] Data from Simmons Market Research show that more than 70 percent of trade show buyers have the authority to purchase and that the average buyer makes purchases ranging from $31,000 to $78,000 on the floor.[58]

Trade shows can be classified by the types of visitors, as well as the types of exhibitors (see Figure 10-3). A **focused trade show** appeals to visitors and exhibitors from one industry. For example, the National Shoe Fair of America show attracts visitors from all levels of shoe distribution channels (distributors, retailers, and agents). In direct contrast, a **diversified trade show** appeals to visitors and exhibitors from a wide grouping of industries. A **multi-industry exhibitor trade show** appeals to the complete needs of potential customers in a given industry with exhibitors that have a wide range of products. In contrast, a **multi-industry visitor trade show** is designed to attract visitors' exhibitors from many industries with a focused selection of products and services.

Firms hold trade shows to seek new products, to discuss products with technical people, to compare alternative solutions to needs, and to collect new information. Trade shows provide the opportunity to meet many suppliers in a short time, the ability to gain hands-on experience with products and systems on display, and the potential for immediate followup.[59] Trade shows are also an ideal place to learn about offerings of competitors and new forms of competition.

There is a need to give salespeople special training to sell at trade shows. For example, a salesperson may see more people at a trade show in an hour than the salesperson would normally call on in a week. They need to separate out

FIGURE 10-3 A classification system for trade shows.

	Visitors	
Exhibitors	**Vertical**	**Horizontal**
Vertical	Focused shows. For example, a trade show where only producers and customers of the car replacement market meet.	Multi-industry visitors. For example, a trade show where packaging processes, materials, and machinery are shown to users in many industries.
Horizontal	Multi-industry exhibitors. For example, a trade show for producers of hospital supplies and pharmaceuticals to present their products to the health-care industry.	Diversified trade shows. For example, where producers from the electronics, subcontracting, and energy industries meet customers from the home building, industrial, and general contracting industries.

Source: Aviv Shaham, "Selecting and Evaluating Trade Shows," *Industrial Marketing Management,* Vol. 21 (November 1992), p. 336. Reprinted by permission. Copyright 1992 by Elsevier Science Inc.

buyers from lookers. Salespeople at a trade show also need to know trade show etiquette (how to handle multiple prospects at the same time), how to qualify leads (after the show ends), how to handle competitors who want to exchange information, how to handle distributors that are requesting information about handling the line, and so on.[60]

Miscellaneous Sales Promotions

Miscellaneous promotions include premiums, frequent user clubs, free samples, contests and sweepstakes, point-of-purchase displays, and in-store materials.

A **premium** is an item of value, other than the product itself, given as an additional incentive to influence the purchase of a product.[61] With **self-liquidating premiums**, the cost of the premium is equal to or less than the price charged. In other cases, the cost of a premium is entirely borne by the manufacturer. Many firms use **fulfillment houses**, independent firms that ship premiums directly to consumers. This reduces the manufacturer's expense in maintaining a part-time staff, setting aside warehouse space, and purchasing shipping equipment for seasonal promotions.

Many channel members use **frequent user clubs** to increase loyalty by providing free products or upgrades to loyal customers. They range in sophistication from airline mileage clubs to restaurants that provide one meal free with every ten purchased. For example, A&P's frequent shopper club gives members access to special discounts each week. It also provides A&P with important and timely information on its markets. For instance, A&P can offer regular shoppers of a brand a low discount, and can provide a high discount to attempt to get a consumer to switch brands.[62]

Free samples, contests and sweepstakes, point-of-purchase displays, and in-store materials are other forms of sales promotion. Free samples can be mailed, delivered door to door, or attached or inserted in another package. Contests and sweepstakes can also be used. While **contests** require skill, **sweepstakes** are based solely on chance.

Point-of-purchase displays are fixtures for stocking merchandise to increase a product's visibility and sales. Displays are sometimes provided by manufacturers specifically to stock their goods. Point-of-purchase displays are designed to increase impulse purchasing activity, as well as to efficiently store merchandise. Among the types of displays are refrigerated cases to hold perishables, specialized displays (such as heavy duty shelving to hold heavy goods such as paint), pegboard-based racks (with standardized hooks to contain carded merchandise), and so on. Some retailers, such as membership clubs, use standard pallets that are used in warehouses instead of conventional displays. Though austere looking, these pallets reinforce the retailer's low-cost image and reduce materials-handling costs.

One major study found that the impact of displays is often highest when combined with price cuts and advertising. A study of light bulb sales in a regional supermarket found that a sales gain was 9.6 percent with a temporary price reduction alone, 137.1 percent when the price reduction was accompanied with an ad, and 147.2 percent when the price reduction was joined with a display. However, when price, advertising, and display were all combined, the sales increase was 430.1 percent.[63]

In-store materials include sales and product information materials that are provided to manufacturers and distributors for final customer use. These materials include product specification sheets, brochures, fact tags (such as technical data on a high fidelity receiver's specifications), and video materials. These materials provide important information, particularly for technical products sold in a self-service shopping environment. For example, to increase shopper information, Compaq put cardboard strips around its monitors. The so-called monitor hood, which was printed on glossy paper stock, contained information on the computer's features. On the basis of the $240,000 sales promotion cost for the hood, sales for those models increased by 11 percent. The idea for the monitor hood was from a marketing expert that Compaq hired from Smith Corona (a typewriter manufacturer with considerable experience selling through store-based channels).[64]

PUBLICITY

Unlike push publicity that is often aimed at trade magazines, pull publicity is aimed at mass media. In general, the competition for space or time in mass media is much greater than with trade publications or local weekly business publications. Manufacturers may need to obtain the assistance of a professional public relations firm with its pull publicity or to consider hiring a separate public relations staff. A manufacturer may have to consider using a professional spokesperson and investing in more elaborate press releases (with samples), a planned factory tour, glossy photographs (capable of being reproduced in print media), and a video to receive the appropriate space and time.

A manufacturer can seek publicity on the basis of a variety of events: a new patent, record profits reported by the firm, a new president, receipt of a major contract, or the opening of a new factory.

The manufacturer can find that its distributors and retailers have appropriate media contacts and can assist in gaining favorable publicity. This may especially be the case with larger distributors and retailers.

IMPROVING PULL PROMOTIONS

Table 10-7 contains the evaluation of selected supplier pull-related strategies as rated by supermarket chain managers, independents, chain executives, and wholesalers. Although chains had higher ratings for some services than independents, in general, ratings for each service were a little above fair; none of these services was rated as good or excellent. The data in this table suggest that there is considerable room for improvement in push promotions, at least from the perception of supermarket managers, executives, and wholesalers.

There are several suggestions as to how to improve push promotions. First, pull promotions and push promotions need to be integrated to provide a common image and to reinforce each other. Conditions for cooperative advertising can be used to better align pull and push promotions, and the provision of standardized advertisements for resellers can be used to better coordinate push and pull.

Second, manufacturers and suppliers need to reexamine their traditional promotional organization structure in light of the media used. For example, different structures (such as an internal cooperative advertising coordinator, or a newspaper industry organization) may be more appropriate than the firm's current organization.

TABLE 10-7 QUALITY OF SUPPLIER PULL SERVICES AS RATED BY SUPERMARKET CHAIN MANAGERS, INDEPENDENTS, CHAIN EXECUTIVES, AND WHOLESALERS[a]

Service	Chain Managers	Independents	Chain Executives	Wholesalers
Amount of merchandising and display materials	37.3	28.9	44.3	31.9
Quality of manufacturers' store materials	48.8	45.9	46.7	45.9
Usage of manufacturers' materials	48.6	47.8	40.3	32.1
Amount of salesmen's services at store level	38.2	34.5	42.4	27.1

[a]The quality ratings have been converted to a score with 0 equaling poor performance, 33 fair performance, 67 good performance, and 100 excellent performance.

Source: "62nd Annual Report of the Grocery Industry," *Progressive Grocer* (April 1995), p. 20. Reprinted by permission.

Third, the media used have to be properly coordinated. In **integrated marketing**, computer databases are used to plan and implement all of the aspects of promotional strategies. For example, when Hewlett-Packard wanted to upgrade its business customers to new equipment, it developed an integrated marketing program by segmenting its customer listing, identifying individuals to be targeted at each company, and making sure that each category of buyer was offered an appropriate incentive.[65]

Fourth, a manufacturer needs to evaluate the differences between alternative promotional media that, on the surface, seem to accomplish the same objective. For example, coupons, rebates, special discounts and allowances, and reductions in list price are all flexible media that can effectively increase sales in the short run. However, each of these media is most appropriate under different situations.

Fifth, continuous sales force training is needed when new media or a new promotional program is implemented. For instance, a salesperson new to a trade show experience may not know how to handle multiple prospects at the same time, or what information can be exchanged with a competitor's salesperson.

LEGAL ASPECTS OF CHANNEL PROMOTIONAL STRATEGY

This section reviews the legal aspects of channel promotional strategy and covers promotional allowances and reimbursement for marketing expenses.

PROMOTIONAL ALLOWANCES

As stated in Chapter 9, promotional allowances also fall under the jurisdiction of the Robinson-Patman Act. These discounts have to be offered on a proportionately equal basis to all competing buyers. Like differences in price, a seller could explain differences in terms or discounts due to the exceptions. For example, a seller may justify a large promotional discount on the basis of cost savings in delivery and/or manufacture.

Slotting fees may also be subject to the Robinson-Patman Act if it can be shown that these fees are a form of promotional allowance that is available only to certain forms of retailers. If the Robinson-Patman Act is held applicable, then vendors, according to the act, have to offer these fees to "all retailers on a proportionate, nondiscriminatory and functionally equivalent basis."

REIMBURSEMENT FOR PROMOTIONAL EXPENSES

Many manufacturers and suppliers reimburse resellers for promotional expenses such as on brochures, mailings, and advertising. The firm's reimbursement should be based on actual incurred costs.

In a major case, Intelligent Electronics, a major computer wholesaler, allegedly charged its suppliers $32.4 million for marketing-related expenses, when, in fact, its actual costs were only $13.1 million. The $19.3 million profit was equal to approximately one-half of the firm's annual income for 1991. Intelligent Electronics is now subject to shareholder suits that claim that the firm misrepresented its profitability, as well as wrongful discharge suits from some of its former key employees. Several suppliers clearly did not get documentation for expenses such as tear sheets of advertising, or actual bills from printers prior to reimbursing Intelligent Electronics.

Although some competitors of Intelligent Electronics have acknowledged that they commonly charge as much as 10 to 15 percent above cost for marketing services, they stated that additional funds were for marketing administrative overhead and not profit.[66]

SUMMARY

1 *To study the special factors in developing and implementing a channel promotional strategy.* Any promotional strategy that utilizes channel members needs to consider four basic factors. First, downstream channel members need to be motivated to support promotional programs that have been developed by an upstream channel member. Second, promotions geared to intermediaries and promotions oriented to final consumers need to be integrated. Third, upstream channel members need to recognize that promotions aimed at final consumers also have an indirect effect on wholesalers and retailers. Fourth, the promotional functions of channel members at different levels need to be ascertained.

2 *To examine the development and implementation of a push-oriented promotional strategy, including media usage and how push promotions can be improved.* Promotional objectives in a push promotional strategy relate to downstream intermediaries. These objectives can be information-, preference-, or demand-based. Budgeting for push promotional strategies is particularly difficult since the costs to an upstream channel member depend on the degree of a reseller's media usage. Being underbudget is not necessarily good since this may signify that resellers have not bought into a manufacturer's promotional program. Upstream channel members should design overall push promotions by determining the mix of their resellers and their individual needs. Lastly, the effectiveness of a push promotional program needs to be evaluated.

Advertising, personal selling, sales promotions, and publicity are all appropriate media in a push promotional strategy. Much advertising to resellers occurs in trade publications; other media include a firm's own newsletters, a company magazine, and direct mail. Like advertising aimed at final consumers, trade advertising can be timed to coincide with peak seasonal periods. An evaluation of a manufacturer's personal selling function needs to consider the multiple roles of its sales representatives: teacher, reviewer, working partner, ambassador, ombudsman, and motivator. A manufacturer also needs to periodically review its sales organization. These organizations are generally either centralized, product-, or market-based. Sales training programs and sales incentives are also important aspects of sales force management. Sales promotions are used to generate short-term sales increases for a product or service; most sales promotions have a limited time span. A variety of push sales promotions are aimed at stimulating reseller effort. These include street money, pay-for-performance allowances, push money, distributor recognition programs, and sales aids. Publicity is a favored medium owing to the absence of media costs, as well as its high believability. A reseller can use publicity as a push medium by developing press releases geared to its resellers. Push promotions can be improved through a series of timing-, administrative-, theme-, and product-related measures.

3. *To describe the development and implementation of a pull-oriented promotional strategy, including media usage and how pull promotions can be improved.* There are several important trends relating to pull advertising: the increased use of direct mail, the use of specialized advertising programs for specific retailers, and the increased involvement of dealers and distributors in planning pull advertising. Much of pull-related advertising is cooperative advertising. There are two types of personal selling programs in pull promotion. In the first type, the manufacturer's sales force participates in joint sales calls with a distributor's sales personnel. In the second format, the manufacturer's sales force sells directly to end-users. The high median cost per sales call is forcing many manufacturers to make greater use of their internal sales force, telemarketing, and catalog selling. Specific sales promotions aimed at final consumers and end-users include coupons, rebates, trade shows, and other promotions (such as premiums, frequent user clubs, point-of-purchase displays, and in-store materials). Pull publicity is aimed at the mass media. A manufacturer can seek publicity on the basis of a variety of events: a new patent, record profits, a new president, receipt of a new contract, and the opening of a new factory. Manufacturers should seek to improve their pull promotions through better integrating pull and push promotions, reviewing their traditional promotional organization structures, coordinating media through integrated marketing, evaluating alternative media, and making continuous use of sales training.

4. *To discuss the legal aspects of a channel promotional strategy.* Promotional allowances fall under the Robinson-Patman Act. These allowances have to be offered on a proportionately equal basis to all competing buyers. The reimbursement received for promotional expenses should be on the basis of actual incurred costs.

KEY TERMS

indirect promotional effect
primary demand
selective demand
selling to the wholesaler/retailer (push)
selling through the wholesaler/retailer (pull)
cooperative advertising
universal core support module
optional support modules
dealer listing promotion
teacher role
reviewer role
working partner
ambassador role
ombudsman
motivator role
stage one program
stage two program
stage three program
sales incentives
sales promotion
street money
pay-for-performance allowance
push money (PMs, promotional money, spiffs)
distributor recognition awards
publicity
account-specific advertising
conditions for cooperative advertising
national rate
local rate
third-party documentation agencies
predictive dialers
coupons
chargebacks
rebates
trade shows
focused trade show
diversified trade show
multi-industry exhibitor trade show
multi-industry visitor trade show
premium
self-liquidating premiums
fulfillment houses
frequent user clubs
contests
sweepstakes
point-of-purchase displays
in-store materials
integrated marketing

QUESTIONS FOR DISCUSSION

1. Describe the special factors that need to be considered in planning a promotional strategy when downstream channel intermediaries are independently owned.

2. "Cooperative advertising has both push and pull promotional elements." Explain this statement.

3. Why is budgeting for a push promotional strategy particularly difficult? Explain your answer.

4. Why is the usage of promotions often related to a distributor's size?

5. Differentiate among the multiple roles of a manufacturer's salespersons.

6. a. As a manufacturer, would you rather offer a distributor street money or a pay-for-performance allowance? Explain your answer.

   b. As a distributor, would you rather be offered street money or a pay-for-performance allowance? Explain your answer.

7. Describe how the effectiveness of publicity can be evaluated.

8. Discuss five measures to improve push promotions.

9. Identify three major trends relating to pull advertising.

10. a. Design a cooperative program for a local nursery. Take the perspective of O. M. Scott, a major manufacturer of fertilizers and garden chemicals.

    b. Design a cooperative program for Home Depot, the nation's largest home improvement chain. Take the perspective of O. M. Scott, a major manufacturer of fertilizers and garden chemicals.

11. a. Under what circumstances would you as vice president-marketing for a manufacturer of a line of inexpensive laser printers prefer a coupon to a rebate?

    b. Under what circumstances would you as vice president-marketing for a manufacturer of a line of inexpensive laser printers prefer a rebate to a coupon?

12. What types of specialized training would salespeople require prior to "working the booth" at their first trade show? Explain.

13. Are frequent user clubs a form of relationship marketing? Explain your answer.

14. Explain the basic elements in an integrated marketing program.

END NOTES

1. John R. Johnson, "Direct Mail Drives Cutting Tool Sales," *Industrial Distribution* (November 1993), pp. 43–44.

2. Don E. Schulz, "How Communications Dis-Integrate," *Marketing News* (June 20, 1994), p. 12.

3. See C. Whan Park, Martin S. Roth, and Philip F. Jacques, "Evaluating the Effects of Advertising and Sales Promotion Campaigns," *Industrial Marketing Management,* Vol. 17 (June 1988), pp. 129–140.

4. See "Distributors Have It Their Way," *Industrial Distribution* (March 1994), p. 23.

5. *16th Annual Survey of Promotional Practices* (Oakbrook Terrace, Ill.: Donnelley Marketing Inc., 1994), p. 13.

6. Michael Levy, John Webster, and Roger A. Kerin, "Formulating Push Marketing Strategies: A Method and Application," *Journal of Marketing,* Vol. 47 (Winter 1983), pp. 25–34.

7. See Allan J. Magrath and Kenneth G. Hardy, "Gearing Manufacturer Support Programs to Distributors," *Industrial Marketing Management,* Vol. 18 (November 1989), pp. 239–244.

8. Donald R. Glover, "Distributor Attitudes Toward Manufacturer-Sponsored Promotions," *Industrial Marketing Management,* Vol. 20 (August 1991), pp. 245, 246.

9. See Magrath and Hardy, "Gearing Manufacturer Support Programs to Distributors," pp. 239–244.

10. 16th Annual Survey of Promotional Practices, p. 57.

11. This section is adapted from Allan J. Magrath and Kenneth G. Hardy, "Factory Salesmen's Roles with Industrial Distributors," *Industrial Marketing Management,* Vol. 16 (August 1987), pp. 163–168.

12. Jaclyn Fierman, "The Death and Rebirth of the Salesman," *Fortune* (July 25, 1994), p. 88.

13. Ibid., p. 91.

14. See Jeffrey P. Geibel, "Dealer Development," *Sales & Marketing Management* (May 1993), pp. 54–57.

15. "The Future of the Distributor-Manufacturer Relationship," *Industrial Distribution* (February 1994), p. 22.

16. Melissa Campanelli, "How to Reward All Your Sales Forces," *Sales & Marketing Management* (April 1993), p. 67.

17. Cynthia R. Milsap, "Conquering the Distributor Incentive Blues," *Business Marketing* (November 1985), pp. 122–125.

18. Campanelli, "How to Reward All Your Sales Forces," p. 63.

19. Bob Donath, "Readers' Report: How We Use Incentives," *Sales & Marketing Management* (June 1993), p. 34.

20. Kenneth G. Hardy, "Key Success Factors for Manufacturers' Sales Promotions in Package Goods," *Journal of Marketing,* Vol. 50 (July 1986), pp. 13–23.

21. Betsy Wiesendanger, "Bigger Sales, Same Budget," *Sales & Marketing Management* (July 1993), pp. 46–48.

22. See "A Question of Will," *Progressive Grocer* (July 1994), p. S11.

23. Fara Warner, "Philip Morris Wholesaler Program Aimed to Net Greater Share," *Brandweek* (March 28, 1994), pp. 1 ff.

24. See Patricia Sellers, "The Dumbest Marketing Ploy," *Fortune* (October 2, 1992), p. 94.

25. Steve Weinstein, "New Brand Strategies," *Progressive Grocer* (October 1993), p. 74.

26. Dorothy Cohen, *Legal Issues in Marketing Decision Making* (Cincinnati, Ohio: South-Western College Publishing, 1995), p. 192.

27. Leonard J. Kistner, C. Anthony di Benedetto, and Sriraman Bhoovaraghavan, "An Integrated Approach to the Development of Channel Strategy," *Industrial Marketing Management,* Vol. 23 (October 1994), pp. 320–321.

28. Much of the material in this section comes from Glover, "Distributor Attitudes Toward Manufacturer-Sponsored Promotions," pp. 245–247; John A. Quelch, "It's Time to Make Trade Promotion More Productive," *Harvard Business Review,* Vol. 61 (May–June 1983), pp. 130–136; and Benson P. Shapiro, "Improve Distribution with Your Promotional Mix," *Harvard Business Review,* Vol. 55 (March–April 1977), p. 120.

29. Marty Jones and Steve Kratz, "The Channel Empowerment Solution," *Sales & Marketing Management* (March 1993), p. 46.

30. Shapiro, "Improve Distribution with Your Promotional Mix," p. 120.

31. See "What Is the Formula for Making Promotions Work for Manufacturer and Retailer?" *Conference on Sales Promotions from the Consumer, Manufacturer, and Retailer Perspectives,* George Low, ed. (Cambridge, Mass.: February 1992), p. 10.

32. Gerry Khermouch, "Brother Sets $4 Million Laser Blast," *Brandweek* (August 8, 1994), p. 10.

33. Peter Burrows and Robert D. Hof, "Watch Out for Flying Chips," *Business Week* (September 26, 1994), p. 64.

34. Betsy Spethmann, "Warner-Lambert, Stores Team," *Brandweek* (October 11, 1993), p. 6.

35. Mary Connelly, "Auto Dealers Flex Their Muscles," *Advertising Age* (March 22, 1993), p. S–6.

36. G. A. Marken, "Firms Can Maintain Control over Creative Co-Op Programs," *Marketing News* (September 28, 1992), p. 7.

37. William Panczak, "Co-Op Advertising: Cutting Through the Confusion," *Discount Store News* (October 21, 1991), p. 10.

38. Julie S. Newhall, "The Care and Feeding of a Cash Cow," *Sales & Marketing Management* (May 1992), p. 40.

39. Ibid.

40. Miles David, "Business to Business Is Co-Op Bright Spot," *Sales & Marketing Management* (May 1992), p. 44.

41. "The Future of the Distributor-Manufacturer Relationship," p. 22.

42. David, "Business to Business Is Co-Op Bright Spot," p. 44.

43. See Sydney Roslow, Henry A. Laskey, and J. A. F. Nicholls, "The Enigma of Cooperative Advertising," *Journal of Business and Industrial Marketing,* Vol. 8 (Number 2, 1993), pp. 70–79.

44. Panczak, "Co-Op Advertising: Cutting Through the Confusion," p. 10.

45. See Mark Vogel and Walter J. Fiorentini, "Redefining Co-Op," *Sales & Marketing Management* (May 1993), p. 64.

46. See Robert D. Wilcox, "Getting Your Money's Worth," *Sales & Marketing Management* (May 1991), pp. 64–68.

47. See Louise King, "The Changing Role of Inside Sales," *Industrial Distribution* (April 1994), pp. 38–40.

48. See Mary Lu Carnevale, "Telemarketers Fight Banning of Autodialers," *Wall Street Journal* (January 20, 1993), pp. B1, B2.

49. Hardy, "Key Successful Factors for Manufacturers' Sales Promotions," pp. 19–20.

50. 16th Annual Survey of Promotional Practices, p. 37.

51. Tim Triplett, "Report of Coupon's Death Has Been Greatly Exaggerated," *Marketing News* (October 10, 1994), p. 1.

52. John Little, "A Look at Coupon Effectiveness," *Conference on Sales Promotions from the Consumer, Manufacturer, and Retailer Perspectives,* George Low, ed. (Cambridge, Mass.: February 1992), p. 16.

53. Steve Weinstein, "Coupons: Can the Problems Be Solved?" *Progressive Grocer* (February 1993), p. 66.

54. For a case study of coupon fraud, see Larry Krasnick, "Confessions of the Coupon King," *Across the Board* (December 1990), pp. 48–49.

55. Triplett, "Report of Coupon's Death Has Been Greatly Exaggerated," p. 1.

56. Brian S. Moska, "Consumer Age Begets Value Pricing," *Industry Week* (February 21, 1994), p. 38.

57. Paul Herbig, Brad O'Hara, and Fred Palumbo, "Measuring Trade Show Effectiveness: An Effective Exercise?" *Industrial Marketing Management,* Vol. 23 (April 1994), p. 166.

58. Joseph Conlin, "Beyond the Booth," *Sales & Marketing Management* (November 1994), p. 109.

59. Aviv Shaham, "Selecting and Evaluating Trade Shows," *Industrial Marketing Management,* Vol. 21 (November 1992), p. 336.

60. See Jerome D. Williams, Srinath Gopalakrishna, and Jonathan M. Cox, "Trade Show Guidelines for Smaller Firms," *Industrial Marketing Management,* Vol. 22 (November 1993), pp. 265–275.

61. Peter D. Bennett, ed., *Dictionary of Marketing Terms,* Second Edition (Chicago: American Marketing Association, 1995), p. 213.

62. See Jim Bessen, "Riding the Marketing Information Wave," *Harvard Business Review,* Vol. 70 (September 1992), pp. 150–160.

63. Glenn Synder, "Shedding Light on Bulb Sales," *Progressive Grocer* (June 1993), p. 117.

64. See Stephanie Losee, "How Compaq Keeps the Magic Going," *Fortune* (February 21, 1994), p. 91.

65. See Martin Everett, "Integrated Marketing: It's No Fluke," *Sales & Marketing Management* (April 1994), pp. 67–73.

66. Raju Narisetti, "Intelligent Electronics Made Much of Its Profit at Suppliers' Expense," *Wall Street Journal* (December 6, 1994), pp. A1 ff.

CASE 1

DEALER TRAINING AT CATERPILLAR

When confronted with competition from Komatsu, a major Japanese heavy equipment manufacturer, Caterpillar realized that one of its major competitive advantages was its dealer network and the marketing support programs it provided for its dealers. These programs include inventory financing plans, merchandising assistance, and advertising programs. Caterpillar has now begun to focus increased attention on strengthening its existing dealer network through training. Caterpillar is well aware that its dealer represents the final linkage in its distribution channel. It also understands that its customers rely on its dealer for pre-sale product information, as well as post-sales service.

Caterpillar's training program, known as the Sales Team Development System (STDS), is 12 months long. Caterpillar's objective is to provide professional assistance to dealers through the use of a consulting team. The consulting team works directly with the dealer's sales manager and salespeople to improve the dealer's effectiveness. In addition to the STDS program, Caterpillar has a self-study training program called Management-Minded Supervision (MMS) that is implemented by its dealers on a worldwide basis. Unlike STDS, MMS allows trainees to progress at their own rate. The principal objective of MMS is to make employees think like managers.

In developing the STDS training program, Caterpillar considered the following questions:

What are the objectives of the training program?
Who should receive the training?
What topics should be covered?
Where should the training take place?
Who should conduct the training? and
What training methods should be used?

What are the objectives of the training program? Caterpillar had three general objectives for STDS: to increase dealers' sales performance, to teach dealers to be more competitive in a global economy, and to train dealers in overcoming client objections, creating a team selling network, and improving time management skills.

Who should receive the training? In selecting dealers to receive training, Caterpillar gave preference to dealers that were fully committed to the training program, were financially stable, had a stable organization structure, were located in a stable and economically promising country, and had high-growth opportunities.

What topics should be covered? Caterpillar's STDS training program covers product knowledge, selling techniques, and forecasting and customer orientation. The product knowledge module covers such topics as servicing products and engine diagnosis. Selling techniques focus on negotiating skills, selling skills, and salesmanship. The forecasting and customer orientation portion of the training helps dealers better plan inventory management. Customer orientation focuses on developing profiles of customers and identifying sales opportunities.

Where should the training take place? Caterpillar uses a combination of field training and centralized training. U.S.-based dealers receive two to four days of training at Caterpillar's training facilities in Peoria, Illinois. Sixty percent of the training time is in class, and 40 percent is hands-on training in a laboratory environment. Overseas dealers receive training at either the dealer's location or at regional headquarters.

Who should conduct the training? Caterpillar uses three different types of trainers: staff specialists, line trainers, and outside specialists. Staff specialists prepare training materials and conduct the classes; they are employees at the centralized dealer training facility. Line trainers are Caterpillar line employees that have sales backgrounds. Outside specialists are hired to conduct training on a fee basis.

What training methods should be used? Caterpillar is using teleconferencing for some types of training. It has set up a satellite system for worldwide training.

Dealers that participated in the program increased their net sales on average by 102 percent during the pilot period. The STDS training program resulted in the following benefits as determined by attendees:

- All participating dealers felt they significantly improved their organizational skills.
- 80 percent stated that they significantly improved their planning skills, product/technical knowledge, and general marketing/sales skills.
- 50 percent felt they significantly improved their application knowledge, financial knowledge, and followup skills.

QUESTIONS

1. How does Caterpillar's approach to dealer sales training differ from its setting up and implementing a sales training program for its own employees?
2. a. What other training methods could be used in STDS?
   b. What are the appropriate uses of each of these methods?
3. Differentiate between the objectives of MMS and STDS.
4. How can Caterpillar evaluate the results of STDS?

Source: S. Tamer Cavusgil, "The Importance of Distributor Training at Caterpillar," *Industrial Marketing Management,* Vol. 19 (February 1990), pp. 1–9.

CASE 2

SELLING AT SATURN DEALERS

Buying a car is not fun to many buyers, especially when confronted with "hard-sell" practices at many dealerships. The automotive industry is widely associated with the use of a series of unethical selling practices. In one such practice, called the "slam dunk," a salesperson earns a huge commission in selling a car (at above the customary price) to an unsuspecting buyer. In another practice, a salesperson holds the customer's car keys and refuses to return them until the customer puts down a deposit on a new car.

In addition to unethical practices, some dealer salespeople have had problems selling cars to women, a large segment of the car-buying public. Contributing to unethical sales practices and poor skills is the high turnover and nonexistent sales training. The average annual turnover for a car dealer's sales force is 50 percent; no wonder many salespeople are not concerned with repeat business or recommendations. And until recently, car manufacturers have only invested in sales training for sales managers, not salespersons.

There are two simple means of doing away with some of these unpleasant experiences: one is for dealers to sell cars at one price, and the other is to provide increased sales training for salespeople at dealerships. The one-price policy is called the "no-dicker sticker." In such a program, car prices are prominently displayed on each car in the lot, and the car dealer pledges not to accept a lower offer.

The other approach is to institute dealer training programs. In 1992, Chrysler began a $25 million program to train 100,000 employees at its 5000 dealers. Much of the training has been earmarked in dealing with traditional import shoppers that have come into Chrysler showrooms to see the Dodge Intrepid, Eagle Vision, and Chrysler Concorde. After the program is implemented, Chrysler sends mystery shoppers into the dealers to see how well its dealers' salespeople implement the training. Ford has also begun to develop and impose new performance standards for its dealers. Among the new standards will be how many times the phone can ring unanswered.

The object at many sales training programs is to avoid the combative atmosphere present at many dealerships. According to one dealer, "you have to let people walk out the door and not harass them. That way they may come back or refer a friend to you."

Among the most advanced in selling are Saturn dealers, according to market analysts. Saturn dealers historically sell more cars per dealer than any other car brand. Saturn dealers also avoid problems with unethical pricing practices by selling cars at list price and by giving full book value for trade-ins. The suggested list price gives Saturn dealers a $1200 gross profit per car. Options are also sold as a group, making consumer choice easier. To reinforce the professional image of the Saturn sales staff, they are called "associates" or "customer assistance representatives." Saturn also uses the following ritual to reinforce customer satisfaction. When a car is picked up, a team consisting of representatives from service, sales, parts, and reception let out a cheer and then hand you the keys.

One convert to "Saturnization," Jack Pohanka, trains all of his employees (including mechanics and receptionists) in a three-day off-site sales training program. As a result of the training, Pohanka's dealerships had a 25 percent increase in sales for the first five months of 1994, twice the national average for comparable vehicles. All cars taken in for body work at a Pohanka dealership will get their car back not only properly repaired, but also vacuumed, washed, and even waxed.

Saturn's program differs significantly from traditional programs at many other General Motors dealers, where prices are negotiated, high-pressure tactics are used, and good guy-bad guy (the sales rep is the good guy, the sales manager is the bad guy) routines are still common.

Car dealers still have a long way to go in increasing the professionalism of their sales forces. A J. D. Power & Associates study found that only 35 percent of consumers felt well treated by their dealers in 1993, and only 26 percent of car buyers rated their car dealer's integrity as either very good or excellent.

QUESTIONS

1. Develop a job description for a district sales manager for Saturn. Use the multiple roles discussed in Table 10-3.
2. Identify training objectives for a dealer's sales force where only 20 percent of consumers stated that they were "well treated."
3. How can car dealers be trained to better sell cars to women?
4. Take the role of a prospective car buyer (mystery shopper) at a local Saturn and another car dealer. Critique your experiences at each dealership.

Sources: Jack Falvey, "The Selling of Saturn," *Sales & Marketing Management* (October 1994), pp. 26 ff.; Jaclyn Fierman, "The Death and Rebirth of the Salesman," *Fortune* (July 25, 1994), pp. 80–82 ff.; and David Woodruff, "What's This—Car Dealers with Souls," *Business Week* (April 6, 1992), pp. 66–67.

PART THREE CASE

BAXTER INTERNATIONAL INC.

INTRODUCTION

Baxter International Inc. is the world's largest manufacturer and distributor of hospital and institutional medical supplies and medical specialty products. The company sells more than 200,000 products that are used primarily by hospitals, clinical and medical research laboratories, blood and dialysis centers, rehabilitation centers, nursing homes, doctors' offices, and at home (under the supervision of a physician). The products Baxter manufactures and/or distributes include surgical gloves, surgical gowns, surgical instruments, urological products, blood bags, blood therapy products, biopsy needles, intravenous solutions, and dialysis equipment. Baxter estimates that it can provide 70 percent of the supplies needed by a typical hospital.

In 1994, Baxter's sales totaled $9.3 billion; products manufactured by Baxter represent 68 percent of its total sales. The balance of sales represents Baxter's distribution business. As a pure distributor, some market analysts estimate that Baxter's net profit margin was about 1 percent of sales (see Table 1).

Baxter's overall strategy can be depicted from the viewpoints of growth through acquisition, centralized management operations, and the use of relationship marketing with its hospital customers. These areas will now be described.

An important part of Baxter's overall strategy has been growth through acquisition. In 1984, Baxter acquired American Hospital Supply (AHS); AHS was a

TABLE 1   BAXTER INTERNATIONAL INC. SELECTED FINANCIAL DATA, 1984–1994

Year	Sales ($ mil)	Net Income ($ mil)	Employees
1984	1,800	29	—
1985	2,355	137	60,000
1986	5,543	219	60,000
1987	6,223	323	60,000
1988	6,861	388	61,500
1989	7,399	446	61,000
1990	8,100	40	60,600
1991	8,921	591	60,400
1992	8,471	606	61,300
1993	8,879	(268)	60,400
1994	9,324	596	53,500

Source: Baxter International 1994 Annual Report.

Baxter distributor from 1932 to 1962. While AHS had larger sales than Baxter, it concentrated more on lower margin products. Baxter, in comparison, manufactured most of its products. Baxter paid almost $4 billion in cash and stock for AHS, a company that was almost twice Baxter's size at the time of the acquisition.

On November 30, 1992, Baxter spunoff its Caremark International division to Baxter's shareholders. This division had sales of $1.2 billion in 1991. Caremark concentrated on "alternate site" segments, such as home infusion therapy, and mail-order drugs. Part of the reason for the spinoff was that many of Baxter's traditional hospital customers viewed Caremark as a supplier to its direct competitors. This did not reflect well on Baxter's intent to have long-term relationships with customers based on trust and commitment. Despite this concern, Baxter still retained Caremark's alternate site renal division (which provides dialysis treatment for kidney patients outside traditional hospital-based dialysis centers). Baxter reportedly has a 75 percent worldwide market share in ambulatory dialysis. And many market analysts agree that this division has plenty of room to grow in countries such as France, Germany, and Japan, where the overwhelming majority of kidney patients still go to hospital-based dialysis centers for treatment.

Baxter's management structure is highly centralized. Baxter purchases all of its products at one central location. (At one point in time, it had 16 purchasing locations.) Similarly, Baxter fills orders for both Baxter-produced and non-Baxter-produced goods from a single location. Credit collection locations are also centralized at one location (from 12 locations). Centralization offers Baxter the advantage of economies of scale. It also provides a single integrated distribution organization to serve all health-care providers. Baxter has had four major restructurings since 1984. These restructurings resulted in the loss of 16,500 jobs. As a result of these restructurings, Baxter hopes to achieve savings of almost $400 million by late 1996.

The last important part of Baxter's overall strategy is its use of relationship marketing with its important hospital accounts. Relationship marketing at Baxter is characterized by the use of just-in-time inventory systems, an EDI interface with customers, long-term contracts, the use of Baxter as a hospital's major supplier, the shifting of responsibilities between Baxter and its hospital customers, the importance of customer service, and Baxter's use of relationship marketing with its own vendors.

USE OF RELATIONSHIP MARKETING

Several aspects of Baxter's use of relationship marketing are also covered in separate sections of this case as they relate to customer service, inventory management, market research and information systems, product strategy, pricing strategy, and promotion strategy.

JUST-IN-TIME INVENTORY MANAGEMENT

Baxter uses just-in-time inventory management with its key customers through its ValueLink and other programs. As hospitals phase in ValueLink, they will reduce their stock-on-hand to two to three days of supplies. For example, St. Luke's

Episcopal Hospital (a 950-bed hospital) in Houston, Texas, closed its warehouse and sold its inventory to Baxter. The use of just-in-time inventory management will be further described in the inventory management section of this case.

ELECTRONIC DATA INTERCHANGE

Baxter is one of the four initial sponsors that established a common data communications standard for both hospitals and suppliers. Other sponsors are Eastman Kodak (imaging products), Boise Cascade Corporation (office supplies), and Bergen Brunswig (a pharmaceutical distributor). The new standard enables vendors and their clients to process orders, deliver price and product information, and make and receive payments electronically. The standard aims to facilitate the use of just-in-time inventory management, to increase the flow of information between suppliers and customers, and to reduce order processing costs. According to a market analyst, a large 500-bed hospital spends $30 to $40 in overhead every time it places an order. Electronic data interchange could reduce costs to hospitals to about $12 an order and to just 32 cents for suppliers.

LONG-TERM CONTRACTS WITH KEY CUSTOMERS

Baxter has found that 80 percent of its incremental sales are from large customers with which it already has a relationship. Baxter seeks to extend the range of products it sells and services through five-year contracts with its key customers. These long-term contracts enable Baxter to develop and implement special programs that are geared to each hospital and to make significant investments in special computer and delivery systems.

USE OF BAXTER AS A MAJOR SUPPLIER

Many major hospitals rely on Baxter as their sole or prime supply source. Part of Baxter's advantage over other suppliers is its ability to supply over 120,000 items on a one-stop shopping basis. Baxter sees itself as a one-stop shopping service for its hospital customers.

SHIFTING OF RESPONSIBILITIES BETWEEN BAXTER AND ITS MAJOR CUSTOMERS

In Baxter's ValueLink inventory management program, Baxter does not limit itself to delivering materials to a hospital's loading dock, but will distribute these products to the point of use (such as a nursing station in a specific floor of a hospital). Through Baxter's ValueLink program, Baxter delivers orders in exact quantities as needed on a daily basis. Baxter has even taken over the task of cleaning and sterilizing equipment at some hospitals. This frees hospital staff to care for patients. For example, Baxter has become a full-time partner with St. Luke's Hospital through managing, ordering, and delivering Baxter's products, as well as the products of 400 other firms.

IMPORTANCE OF CUSTOMER SERVICE

Although some firms may view customer service to be a post-sale activity or to be concerned only with delivery time and accuracy, Baxter takes a broad-based view of customer service. Baxter also has a senior vice president responsible for customer service. According to this vice president, "We look at the products that we produce as only one of the capacities that we share with customers. We look at the whole cycle from the time that anything is ordered, to the time that the order is processed, the goods are delivered, the product is used and the cash is paid."

Baxter has conducted substantial market research to determine customer service needs. Part of this research was to interview 100 key customers. In total, researchers spent six to seven months with purchasing agents and materials managers at these firms. The research study concluded that any delivery system had to be both reliable and accurate. Baxter also found that its customers would willingly trade off longer delivery dates for improved reliability on less important products.

Baxter also analyzed how it measures customer service so as to develop priorities and evaluate its managers and employees. For example, Baxter found that line fill rates (core/noncore), the number of rush orders, and the number of split purchase orders from accounts were key quality measurements.

USE OF RELATIONSHIP MARKETING WITH BAXTER'S OWN VENDORS

Baxter has also applied relationship marketing to its own vendors. In the past, Baxter did not want vendors in its plants for fear that they would disclose the company's operations to its competitors. Now, qualified vendors are asked to participate in Baxter's research and development projects.

As a result of its use of relationship marketing with its own suppliers, Baxter has been able to use just-in-time inventory management principles in some of its production lines. For example, Baxter's North Carolina plant (which produces more than 1 million units of intravenous solution a day) does not have more than an hour of corrugated box on hand due to just-in-time deliveries from its key suppliers. Under just-in-time, the number of corrugated suppliers to this plant has declined from over 30 to just 3 suppliers.

AN OVERVIEW OF BAXTER'S DOMESTIC AND INTERNATIONAL CHANNEL MANAGEMENT STRATEGY

This section describes Baxter's channel management organization in the United States and in foreign markets.

DOMESTIC CHANNEL STRATEGY

Baxter conducts its domestic selling effort through subsidiaries and divisions. Baxter's domestic distribution business covers four major market segments: medical/surgical, laboratory, alternate-site health care, and the industrial marketplace. According to Baxter's group vice president, U.S. Distribution, "No other distributor is poised in those four markets. By leveraging our operational costs and distribution technology, we now are not only the largest distributor in health care but [also] the low-cost distributor as well." Baxter's distribution centers, which may serve more than one division, are stocked with adequate inventories to facilitate prompt customer service.

Baxter is in the process of shifting its channel management systems to reflect the growth in importance of the alternate-site market as an important market. For instance, although hospitals still accounted for 63 percent of Baxter's revenues in 1993, hospitals have rapidly lost ground to new types of clinics and to in-home care. Baxter is aware that the average inpatient hospital stay has declined 7 percent since the mid-1980s and that outpatient visits to surgery centers, clinics, and other alternative treatment centers have risen by 66 percent during the same time period.

As of 1990, Baxter only sold its own manufactured products to the alternate-site market. By 1993, 70 percent of the goods sold to this market were made by Baxter. Baxter executives argue that this shows Baxter's commitment to becoming a broad-based distributor of products to this market. Baxter is also paying increased attention to the physician group practice market segment.

Despite its claims of being in touch with alternate-site markets, some market analysts question whether Baxter's distribution system is appropriate for this market segment. These analysts argue that Baxter is too tied to the hospital market. For example, according to the corporate program director of a Chicago-based hospital that has developed alternate treatment sites, "Baxter doesn't have ambulatory and alternate-site programs."

INTERNATIONAL CHANNEL STRATEGY

In 1994, 28 percent of Baxter International's revenues came from outside the United States. By the end of the decade, the company plans to double sales in Europe and in Japan, and to almost triple sales in Latin America. In the Pacific Rim, where the firm has had a small presence in 1993, Baxter International anticipates that revenues will grow to $600 million a year. In total, Baxter feels that revenues outside the United States will account for more than one-third of its revenue by the year 2000.

Baxter manufactures health-care products in 21 countries. International sales and distribution are made in about 100 countries either on a direct basis or through the use of independent local distributors. International sales are concentrated in five countries including Canada. International subsidiaries employ their own field sales forces in Argentina, Australia, Austria, Belgium, Brazil, Brunei, Canada, China, Colombia, Denmark, Ecuador, Finland, France, Germany, Hong Kong, India, Indonesia, Italy, Japan, Malaysia, Mexico, the Netherlands, New Zealand, Norway, Pakistan, the Philippines, Singapore, Spain, Sweden, Switzerland, Taiwan, Thailand, and the United Kingdom.

On March 25, 1993, Baxter agreed to enter a guilty plea acknowledging that it violated the United States anti-boycott laws by sending a letter that contained information concerning the company's business relationships with Israel to Arab boycott authorities. Baxter's actions stemmed from its attempts to increase its business with Arab customers. Baxter paid a $500,000 fine. The company and two of its subsidiaries also signed consent agreements of the Commerce Department Office of Anti-Boycott Compliance. In response to concerns by some of Baxter's customers and through a management initiative, Baxter established the formation of a corporate responsibilities office to oversee business ethics.

CHANNEL MANAGEMENT AND THE MARKETING MIX

This section covers customer service, physical distribution and inventory management, market research and information systems, and product management, pricing, and promotion strategies.

CUSTOMER SERVICE STRATEGY

In 1985, Baxter management initiated a corporate commitment to improve quality in Canada. This process was called the Quality Leadership Process (QLP). Similar initiatives were undertaken in other geographic areas. The foundations of QLP are:

1. Quality means meeting requirements.
2. The organization for achieving quality is total employee involvement.
3. The method is prevention.
4. The standard is defect-free products and services.
5. The attitude is ongoing improvement.

The primary objective of the QLP, according to Baxter Canada's Production, Planning and Inventory Control Manager, was the "management of premium service to the customer." A second and important goal was to reduce Baxter's inventory without reducing customer service reliability and accuracy. Over 500 QLP programs have since been implemented throughout Baxter worldwide (in over 20 countries) with customers and suppliers. Successful programs have achieved fill rates of between 97 and 99 percent. In addition, customers received faster delivery time, easier access to information on order status, consolidated shipments, and lower expense. Baxter also has begun to pay its sales representatives, in part, based on customer service surveys.

PHYSICAL DISTRIBUTION AND INVENTORY MANAGEMENT STRATEGY

Baxter is often cited as the classic textbook example of how to implement a physical distribution and inventory management strategy. Baxter has four levels of inventory management relationships: (1) Baxter's development of a core and noncore product list, (2) Baxter's Enhanced Distribution Services program, (3) Baxter's ASAP system; and (4) Baxter's assuming stockroom management functions for its clients through its ValueLink program.

Baxter's lowest level of inventory management is the development of a list of core and noncore products for each country and then stocking these products in each regional warehouse. Baxter's second-level program is Baxter's Quality Enhanced Distribution Services (QED) program which was introduced in 1991. Based on each customer's requirements, Baxter develops a delivery system to facilitate the efficient processing of products and related documents. For example, Baxter strategically positions products on pallets, applies labels that are matched to the hospital's receiving papers, and includes the hospital's own inventory codes on the boxes. In hospitals where QED has been implemented, Baxter has reduced the amount of labor associated with the receipt and storage of supplies by an average of 90 percent. Baxter benefits by a more predictable distribution schedule that has fewer but larger deliveries. As of the beginning of 1995, 732 customers participated in the Enhanced Distribution Services program (as compared with 536 at the beginning of 1993 and 117 at the beginning of 1992).

Through Baxter's third-level program, called ASAP, customers can order supplies directly from Baxter through use of a telephone-linked terminal. The ASAP system provides customers with computerized price information and order confirmation. This facilitates the ordering process by eliminating much of the paperwork, reduces a hospital's ordering costs, and provides Baxter with a market advantage over vendors who do not have a comparable system.

In its fourth-level program, called ValueLink, Baxter reduces its clients' expenses by assuming stock room management for its clients. Under ValueLink, Baxter takes over a hospital's entire purchasing and warehousing system. Baxter personnel are now responsible for all ordering, supply, and inventory responsibilities. In many instances, Baxter employees work on-site at the hospital 24 hours a day, to stock shelves as needed. Baxter supplies these customers on a just-in-time basis from a nearby Baxter distribution center. ValueLink enables hospitals to reduce their costs. According to Baxter's chairman, "There's at least a dollar of hospital overhead for every dollar of supply costs, so we can get better-margin products in there and the hospital still comes out ahead." Other analysts place overhead costs as high as $3 per dollar of supply costs for inventory ordering, holding, and handling costs.

As of the beginning of 1995, 108 hospitals participated in Baxter's ValueLink program. Baxter estimates that these hospitals saved over $22 million through one-time inventory reduction initiatives, and an additional $16 million in annual operating expenses (involved in managing supplies—from continuously determining replenishment needs to receiving and moving large quantities of inventory from multiple vendors). Baxter plans to sign a minimum of 23 new accounts and to open four additional distribution centers to have sales of $400 million through this program in 1994.

Since hospitals with large supply volumes and the operational capabilities to perform stockless distribution realize the largest savings from the ValueLink services, this program has been targeted primarily at large hospitals in major metropolitan areas. With some hospitals banding together on a regional basis, Baxter is now seeking many of these joint programs as potential ValueLink customers.

Some detractors argue that Baxter's maintenance of a hospital's inventory places it in conflict with its customers. While Baxter seeks to maximize its sales, a customer would seek to minimize its inventory. For example, Baxter could meet its objective by writing larger orders than the hospital needed.

MARKET RESEARCH AND INFORMATION SYSTEMS STRATEGY

Although EDI has been used successfully by suppliers, wholesalers, and retailers, it has just begun to be used in the hospital industry. Two large hospital associations, Voluntary Hospitals of America (in Dallas) and Premier Health Alliance (in Chicago) are developing an EDI system for their members. Baxter and other large vendors have systems (such as Baxter's ASAP system) that allow hospitals to place orders electronically. However, a hospital has to use a different system (and perhaps even a different computer terminal) for each individual vendor. In addition, many EDI systems only work with mainframe computers, which are costly to purchase and maintain.

A new EDI standard, partially developed by Baxter, will run on desktop computers. While the new standard will initially be used to automate purchasing functions, later versions should include electronic invoices, a catalog that will enable hospitals to compare prices of competing goods on-line, and electronic payment capabilities.

Baxter International also has used market research to determine the causes of customer dissatisfaction and to recommend corrective action. For example, MicroScan, a Baxter division that produces costly medical instruments, began to survey its customers and those of its key competitors on an annual basis. These customers were asked questions such as "How long did your equipment perform before it required a service call?" and "How quickly did the technical people come to fix it?" The purpose of its research was to determine the causes of customer dissatisfaction and to reduce customer defection to competitors.

PRODUCT STRATEGY

Baxter produces about 70 percent of the products that it sells to hospitals, but it distributes products of other firms, too, such as Johnson & Johnson. In 1993, 66 additional suppliers began distributing their products through Baxter. This accounted for about 15 percent of Baxter's new sales in 1993. In contrast, Johnson & Johnson, a major competitor in the hospital market, does not distribute supplies that have been manufactured by other firms.

Baxter's program provides large hospitals and multi-hospitals with a single point of contact for all of the firm's products, services, and special value-added programs. For instance, Baxter's ACCESS program enables hospitals to order products and services from leading companies in related industries that go beyond Baxter's offerings. Baxter maintains alliances with Waste Management of America, Inc. for the handling and disposal of medical waste; with Comdisco, Inc. for high-technology asset management and contingency services; and with Kraft General Foods to distribute and market a broad array of hospital food service products.

Baxter is also working with its important accounts to create standardized "product modules" that are delivered to the point of therapy. It anticipates providing cost savings from standardizing some supplies and packaging related products together (so that a hospital staff does not have to pull individual items from inventory every time a surgical procedure is performed). An example of this strategy is Baxter's agreement with Duke University Medical Center. A key component of this agreement is the creation of ten teams of physicians, nurses, other medical specialists, and Baxter representatives to establish standards for which products should routinely be supplied for use in different types of surgery. While physicians will still have some choice as to what equipment is available, the range of choice will be narrowed. Doctors will also be encouraged to adjust their supply and equipment usage habits to match those of colleagues with the best surgical and recovery track records.

PRICING STRATEGY

Distributors such as Baxter International profit from stockless services because they are able to impose additional charges (the service fee for ValueLink is between 3 and 6 percent of sales) and to raise prices more readily as they become the hospital's sole source of medical supplies. Baxter argues that even if its price for comparable products may be higher than a competitor's, the hospital's total costs are reduced owing to its additional services. According to Baxter's chairman, "We generally take about 30 percent of whatever is saved. The hospital is picking up 70 percent."

Two ways to reduce costs are to force Baxter and other competitors to bid against each other on each proposal and to enforce cost containment contracts. To guard against higher prices, some hospitals, such as St. Paul-Ramsey Medical Center (in St. Paul, Minnesota), require Baxter and two additional suppliers to bid against each other. All three suppliers provide just-in-time deliveries to the loading dock; the hospital then handles internal distribution. The hospital believes that this pricing strategy keeps prices low as the result of constant competition.

Cost-containment contracts involve basing ultimate prices on cost savings. For instance, Baxter's five-year contract with Duke University Medical Center specifies that Baxter will pay part of Duke's expenses if surgical supply costs are higher than projected. The contract also allows Baxter to be paid a bonus based on the amount saved if Duke spends less than budgeted. Baxter has also signed agreements stating that it be paid on the basis of cost savings. Unlike the Duke contract, these contracts did not require Baxter to compensate the hospital if Baxter did not meet cost targets.

PROMOTION STRATEGY

The total promotional strategy used by Baxter includes frequent contact by sales representatives, automated hospital communications via versions of the ASAP automated purchasing system, circulation of catalogs and merchandising bulletins, direct mail campaigns, trade publications, and advertising. However, as with most industrial products, the personal sales force is a particularly important promotional vehicle for Baxter. Unfortunately, Baxter has experienced a number of difficulties with its sales force. These problems relate to perceived favoritism to Baxter-produced products and to high sales force turnover.

Because 68 percent of Baxter's hospital business is in goods that Baxter produces in its own factories (such as intravenous solutions and surgical products), some hospital customers believe that Baxter's sales representatives push Baxter-made products over those produced by competitors. This feeling was reinforced when Baxter paid its sales representatives higher commissions on goods it had produced. As a result of this policy, many competing manufacturers have sought other distributors that do not have competing products. Some hospital customers also prefer to do business with other distributors to receive the non-Baxter products that they favored. According to the chairman of a large hospital group purchasing organization, "They [Baxter] wouldn't distribute C. R. Bard's products, but we were not willing to drop Bard [as a supplier]."

Baxter recently changed its strategy and now pays its sales reps the same commission for selling Baxter-made surgical gloves or a similar product made by Johnson & Johnson. As a result of this strategy, it is selling more non-Baxter goods; however, Baxter has had to cut its profit margins to make its goods more competitive. Even after this change in strategy, however, some market analysts believe that Baxter is working harder at pushing its own products. According to one analyst, "I still hear from hospitals that they are suspicious Baxter tries to get its own products onto the [delivery] skids. Hospitals simply don't want to deal with this."

Baxter's U.S. hospital business did not meet its profit goal in 1993 partially as a result of high sales representative turnover. Many sales reps attributed the staff turnover to Baxter's lower commission payment package. Baxter claims that this reduction was planned to bring Baxter in line with commissions at key competitors.

Baxter also recently introduced changes in its sales organization both domestically and abroad. As of February 1994, Baxter began to sell its products and services through a consolidated sales staff (derived from 20 divisions) rather than through salespeople who represented individual product lines and divisions. A regional account manager, called the new "single point of contact sales and marketing approach" by industry analysts, will be the single point of contact for all facilities in the region. The regional account manager will be responsible for sales and distribution of all Baxter products.

Baxter has also changed the organization of its sales force in Europe to reflect the European Union. It now organizes its European Union sales force on the basis of business lines instead of geography. For example, there is now one Baxter manager responsible for renal therapy products, and another for intravenous products in all the countries that belong to the European Union. This enables Baxter's sales force to allocate its activities by location and to more easily switch its market emphasis to reflect growth prospects.

LONG-TERM OUTLOOK

Overall, Baxter has several positive attributes. Clearly, its technological superiority over competition (in terms of the development of EDI and sophisticated inventory management systems) is difficult for competitors to match. Its five-year contracts with important hospital chains also make it difficult for new competitors to enter these markets. In addition, its large inventory of products gives it the advantage of using one distributor for a large proportion of a hospital's total orders. Lastly, the savings in costs to hospitals are particularly important to hospitals owing to the high scrutiny given to health-care costs.

Still, Baxter needs to resolve some key problem areas. The firm has had an uneven record of profitability in recent years. Most notable was its net loss in 1993 that amounted to 3 percent of sales. Baxter also needs to gain market penetration in the growth sectors of medical care without alienating its traditional hospital customers. Lastly, Baxter needs to resolve the concerns of its hospital and manufacturer clients over its fairness in representing competitive products. These elements of channel strategy need to be resolved promptly.

Baxter also has some large competitors. While Baxter attempted to acquire Stuart Medical (the country's third largest hospital supplies distributor with annual sales of almost $1 billion), Baxter's deal fell through. Stuart was eventually sold to Owens & Minor, the country's second largest hospital distributor. The combined Owens & Minor and Stuart operations will be equal in size to Baxter's overall distribution business.

QUESTIONS

1. Describe the pros and cons of Baxter's relationship marketing strategy.
2. Should Baxter have four different levels of inventory management strategies? Explain your answer.
3. Describe the benefits and risks of EDI to Baxter and its hospital clients.
4. How can Baxter resolve the difficulties associated with representing directly competing manufacturers?
5. Develop an overall pricing strategy for Baxter.
6. Evaluate Baxter's overall sales force strategy.
7. Can Baxter effectively sell to both the ambulatory care and hospital segments? Explain your answer.

Sources: Baxter International 1994 Annual Report; Baxter International 1994 Form 10-K; Marcia Berss, "2 + 2 = 5," *Forbes* (February 28, 1994), pp. 82–83; Thomas M. Burton, "Baxter Seeks Hit Products and Swings the Job Ax Again," *Wall Street Journal* (March 31, 1994), p. B4; Thomas M. Burton, "Baxter's Chairman Says Illegal Actions over Arab Boycott Were Unintentional," *Wall Street Journal* (May 3, 1993), p. A4; Susan Caminiti, "Finding New Ways to Sell More," *Fortune* (July 27, 1992), pp. 100–102 ff.; Barnaby J. Feder, "Hospital Supplier in Novel Deal," *New York Times* (July 14, 1994), pp. D1, D6; Deborah G. Fliehman, "How an Innovative Distribution Portfolio Can Strengthen Customer Relationships," *SAM Advanced Management Journal* (Winter 1990), pp. 26–29; Rahul Jacob, "Why Some Customers Are More Equal Than Others," *Fortune* (September 19, 1994), pp. 215–216 ff.; "New Baxter Could Emerge Following Restructuring," *Health Industry Today* (December 1993), pp. 1 ff.; Richard Ringer, "Big Baxter Customer Cuts Order," *New York Times* (May 26, 1993), p. D3; Patricia Sellers, "Keeping the Buyers You Already Have," *Fortune* (Autumn/Winter 1993), pp. 56–58; Susan Scherreik, "New Warehouses: Big, Bright, Efficient," *New York Times* (May 30, 1993), pp. R1 ff.; Lisa Scott, "Baxter, Duke to Share Risk," *Modern Healthcare* (July 18, 1994), p. 16; Lisa Scott, "Big Two's Control of Market to Change Supply Industry," *Modern Healthcare* (February 28, 1994), pp. 45–46; and Ron Winslow, "Four Hospital Suppliers Will Launch Common Electronic Ordering System," *Wall Street Journal* (April 12, 1994), p. B7.

PART IV

CHANNEL PLANNING, COORDINATION, AND ORGANIZATION

In Part Four, we study channel planning, coordination, and organization: channel design and selection, administrative structures in marketing channels, channel conflict and cooperation, and channels for services and international marketing.

CHAPTER 11
Channel Design and Selection Here, we discuss channel structure and design as part of a six-part process. First, we determine channel objectives. Second, we describe the assessment of channel length, width, and types of intermediary requirements. Third, the evaluation of market, product, manufacturer, and intermediary factors that affect channel length are summarized. Fourth, channel tasks are allocated among channel members. Fifth, we select specific channel resellers. And sixth, we examine the process of revising channel arrangements.

CHAPTER 12
Administrative Structures in Marketing Channels In this chapter, we examine important topics relating to administrative structures. Topics covered include contrasting conventional channel arrangements with vertical marketing systems, describing the characteristics of corporate and administrative marketing systems, and discussing the forms of corporate marketing systems. Lastly, we analyze the legal aspects of vertical marketing systems.

CHAPTER 13
Channel Power: Conflict and Cooperation In this chapter, we examine such topics as channel power, methods of channel dominance, the nature of channel conflicts, channel cooperation, conflict management and resolution, and channel satisfaction. The impact of channel dominance, channel conflict, and channel satisfaction on performance is also discussed.

CHAPTER 14

Channels for Services and International Marketing Here, we discuss the development of a channel strategy for services and international marketing. For services, we discuss the types and special characteristics of services as applied to channel management, channel activities of service-based intermediaries, types of service channels, and physical distribution concerns in the delivery of services. For international channels, channel length and width decision making, international physical distribution, and legal aspects are covered.

CHAPTER 11

CHANNEL DESIGN AND SELECTION

CHAPTER OBJECTIVES

1. To determine channel objectives.

2. To assess channel length, width, and types of intermediary requirements.

3. To evaluate market, product, manufacturer, and intermediary factors that affect channel length.

4. To discuss the allocation of channel tasks among channel members.

5. To study the selection process for specific channel resellers.

6. To describe the process of revising channel arrangements.

In 1993, women spent more than $2.4 billion a year on pantyhose in mass-market outlets, department stores, and specialty shops, according to the National Association of Hosiery Manufacturers. The average woman purchases about 17 pairs of pantyhose per year. In 1993, Sara Lee Corporation's L'eggs brand was the best-selling pantyhose brand in the United States, with a 42 percent share of the market in mass markets. The next best-selling brand, Kayser-Roth, had a 21.8 percent market share.

Sara Lee Corporation's channel strategy with its L'eggs and Underall brands can be best referred to as "selling to customers where they shop." Sara Lee sells more than $1 billion a year of hosiery through its L'eggs and Hanes divisions. In the early 1970s, L'eggs became the first major brand of pantyhose that was sold through grocery and drug stores. Prior to that, virtually all pantyhose was sold through discount department stores, traditional department stores, and specialty apparel stores. To increase acceptance of their products by self-service retailers and to better enable consumers to use self-service, L'eggs developed special display racks for retailers to display L'eggs' uniquely shaped containers.

Sara Lee used a similar channel strategy with its Underalls pantyhose brand. Sara Lee followed the movement of women who purchased more and more hosiery in discount stores. Originally, Underalls were only sold in department stores and other upscale outlets. In 1978, Sara Lee first introduced Underalls into Kmart and other discounters. It phased out Underalls completely from department stores in 1985; in 1988, the firm transferred Underalls to its L'eggs division. Under this division, Underalls were then distributed to groceries, drug stores, and mass merchandisers.

Since L'eggs and Underalls are sold to the same outlets, Sara Lee has carefully distinguished each brand. Each brand has a unique package, separate displays are used when a store carries each brand, and different price strategies are used. The L'eggs brand designation is also not used on either the Underalls package or in its advertising. According to a company spokesperson, "We made the move because the growth potential is better in mass distribution outlets, and the transition wasn't that hard because L'eggs was already there."

To appeal to more fashion-conscious and less price-conscious consumers, Sara Lee markets its Hanes Silk Reflections and Sheer Elegance product lines (which are sold in department stores), and its Donna Karan designer hose (which are sold in specialty boutiques) for as much as $35 per pair. These products are marketed through Sara Lee's Hanes division. In contrast to L'eggs and Underalls, these lines have extensive selections. For example, Silk Reflections is available in 447 different styles, colors, and nylon and spandex combinations.

Sara Lee's channel strategy with its L'eggs and Underall brands is based on maximizing consumer convenience via self-service merchandising. Its Hanes' division strategy enables more fashion-oriented consumers to benefit from the assistance of sales personnel and from larger selections. Sara Lee's use of multiple channels is an excellent choice for the firm; this strategy enables Sara Lee to maximize its market coverage and to appeal to multiple market segments. Sara Lee's sale of different brands and products to each channel also reduces competition among channel members.[1]

In this chapter, we study channel design and selection decision making. We examine such decisions as determining channel objectives; assessing channel width and depth requirements; studying market, product, company, and intermediary factors; allocating channel tasks among channel members; selecting specific channel members; and revising channel arrangements.

INTRODUCTION TO CHANNEL DESIGN AND SELECTION

Channel design decision making involves the choice of an optimal channel arrangement. Included in this process are questions relating to channel width and depth, the types of intermediaries to be used, and the specific responsibilities of each channel member. It is important to realize that, even though a channel member's contract may be long term, a firm needs to constantly reevaluate its channel member design and selection process.

This text views the channel design and selection process as a series of sequential activities (see Figure 11-1). These activities are determining channel objectives; assessing channel width and depth requirements; studying market,

FIGURE 11-1 The channel design and reseller selection process.

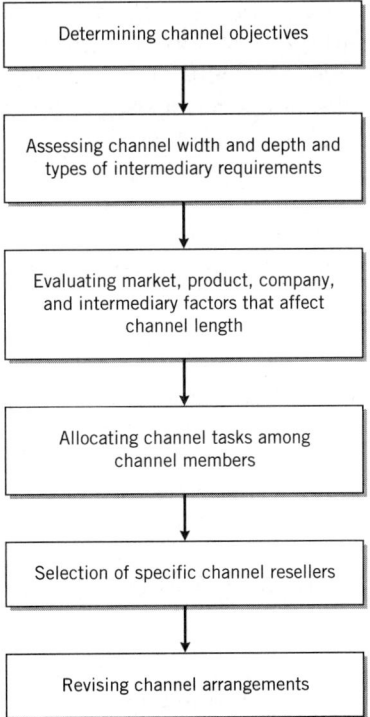

product, company, and intermediary factors; allocating channel tasks among channel members; determining the optimal channel arrangement; and revising channel arrangements.

A channel intermediary needs to reexamine its current channel design under several conditions. Channel designs need to be reevaluated prior to a merger or a major acquisition since both firms can have different channel structures or channels structures that overlap. For example, Kraft and General Foods recently merged their distribution channels into a single food business called Kraft Foods. According to the chairman and chief executive of Kraft Foods North America, "in any territory you'd have two people visiting supermarkets, fighting for spaces in the supermarket and vying for time with the store manager." Under the new channel structure, five different groups were combined into a single direct sales force of 3500 sales representatives. The new channel structure enables employees to cover more territories.[2]

A firm must also evaluate its channel structure whenever it undertakes a major change in its marketing strategy (such as the development of a new product or a focus on a new target market). Although a firm's current channel structure may be perfectly appropriate for its current strategy, it may be inappropriate for its planned strategy. For example, when Xerox recently began to sell an inexpensive copier aimed at the small office/home office market, it had to revise its channel strategy which successfully sold larger copiers through sales representatives visiting larger offices. Xerox continues to use its sales representatives to sell its larger copiers, but it now sells smaller machines through office supply chains, home electronics retailers, and buying clubs.

A firm also needs to reexamine its channel strategy based on new geographic markets that are serviced. For instance, a firm with a domestic market strategy generally cannot successfully export goods to foreign markets without the assistance of a foreign export specialist. One export management company, Dreyfus & Associates, handles practically all export functions for eight tool manufacturers. The company finds foreign buyers, pays the manufacturers for the goods, ships the product, extends credit to distributors, and collects payment.[3]

Lastly, a firm needs to reevaluate its current strategy as a result of the loss of a major client, an increase in gray market activity, changes in the importance of new channels, and changes in buyer behavior. For example, Black & Decker gained an important market advantage for its do-it-yourself power tool and accessory business through its ability in quickly responding to the growth of home improvement centers. Other competitors were slower to see this growth and continued to stress sales through neighborhood hardware stores and lumber yards.[4]

We will now explore the channel design and reseller selection process beginning with the first phase of this process, determining channel objectives.

DETERMINING CHANNEL OBJECTIVES

Typical objectives for a channel member can be to successfully integrate the channel coverage of two firms (in a merger or acquisition), to secure widespread distribution in a particular channel (such as supermarkets), to reduce sales by unauthorized dealers (where a sizable gray market exists), or to increase distribution for a product to new markets while keeping investment requirements to a minimum level.

Specific channel objectives can be determined by identifying a customer's distribution needs based on an examination of the **service output** requirements of its target customers. To the extent that producers and end-users are unable to perform these service outputs or cannot perform these outputs efficiently, intermediaries are needed.[5] Service output requirements may be grouped into five categories: lot size, market decentralization, waiting time, product variety,

CHANNELS IN ACTION

Hallmark: The World's Largest Card Company at a Transition

Hallmark is the world's largest card company with 1993 sales of $3.4 billion and net profits of at least $200 million. (Since Hallmark is privately held, its sales and profit figures are estimates.) In 1993, its largest competitor, American Greetings, had $1.7 billion in sales and net profits of $112 million. Since 1990, Hallmark's market share has dropped from 45 percent to 42 percent; in addition, its profits have been either stagnant or declining. Many analysts argue that much of the blame for Hallmark's sales and profit slippage can be attributed to its distribution strategy.

Of the more than 10,000 card shops that sell the Hallmark brand greeting card products, 9800 are independents and 216 are company owned. While Hallmark sells its Hallmark brand of cards to Walgreen and Osco drug chains, it has repeatedly refused to sell this brand to Wal-Mart. Hallmark has sold a lower priced line of cards to discounters under the Ambassador brand since 1959. The Ambassador brand now accounts for 19 percent of Hallmark's total sales; most analysts argue that it has taken sales away from Hallmark.

Hallmark is currently reassessing its distribution strategy as a result of the growth in importance of discounters, supermarkets, drug store chains, and other retail outlets. In 1975, Americans purchased half of their greeting cards at specialty shops; today, less than 30 percent are purchased at these stores. According to a market analyst, "Traditional Hallmark became a victim of one-stop shopping."

According to some market analysts, Hallmark is now at a crossroads and needs to commit itself more strongly to mass merchandisers to maintain its current sales and profitability. Changing its strategy also has considerable risk. Hallmark does not want to give up its strength among card shops. Hallmark feels strongly committed to these retailers and realizes that it will be vulnerable to the mass merchandisers. Since Hallmark's major competitors, American Greetings Corporation and Gibson Greetings, Inc., do not have distribution through independent card shops, they have been able to more easily make the transition into such mass merchandisers as discount stores and supermarkets.

Source: William M. Stern, "Loyal to a Fault," *Forbes* (March 14, 1994), pp. 58–59.

and service backup.[6] **Lot size** describes the consumer's desire to purchase a product in small quantities. **Market decentralization** concerns the importance of convenient locations. Although some customers may travel a long distance for a product, others want accessible retailers. **Waiting time** reports on delivery speed. **Product variety** measures the need to see competing brands and products. And **service backup** assesses the importance of having a product repaired in-home or in-office. Other service outputs can include technical service, or routinization of the buying process (as in just-in-time inventory management systems).

Channel objectives can relate to improvement in any of the service outputs. A firm can also segment a market based on differences in needs of different customer groups. For example, a reseller may seek to increase sales to price-conscious consumers through additional sales to buying clubs. The firm can continue to sell to variety- and convenience-conscious consumers through traditional supermarkets.

ASSESSING CHANNEL LENGTH, WIDTH, AND TYPES OF INTERMEDIARY REQUIREMENTS

A channel's service output specifications directly affect the channel's length and depth. Small lot size requirements, for example, may dictate that a manufacturer sell its products through resellers that are willing to break up case lots. This may determine that the manufacturer consider the use of a long channel arrangement. The consumer's need for high product variety may also dictate that long channels be used; long channels may be especially appropriate for those manufacturers that produce a single product. On the other hand, the need for high market decentralization may require that a wide channel arrangement be implemented.

Three major elements of channel design are channel length, channel width, and the different types of intermediaries used at each channel level. **Channel length requirements** specify the number of channel levels that are required to fulfill a supplier's objectives. In contrast, **channel width requirements** specify the number of intermediaries that are needed at each level in the channel. A related question to channel width is the degree of competition at each channel level; this determines whether different types of intermediaries will be used at different levels within the channel.

In total, a supplier has a large number of potential channel choices. For example, if a channel arrangement has three levels (not counting the manufacturer and the final consumer), with three intermediaries at each level, and two different types of intermediaries, there are 18 different alternatives to consider ($3 \times 3 \times 2 = 18$). Increasing the number of levels to four would increase the number of channel alternatives to 24 ($4 \times 3 \times 2 = 24$).

CHANNEL LENGTH

The alternatives for channel length range from direct distribution (with two levels: a manufacturer and a final consumer) to five levels (a product sold through a manufacturer to an exporter to a wholesaler to a retailer and then to a final consumer). In a **short channel (direct distribution)**, a manufacturer sells goods and services directly to final and organizational consumers without the use of independent resellers. The presence of a short channel generally indicates some degree of vertical integration, or the presence of a large-scale intermediary such as a large multinational enterprise that has engaged in forward integration.[7]

One of the major tradeoffs associated with channel length is the relationship between channel control and resource utilization. This relationship is depicted in Figure 11-2. Although long channels require limited financial resources, they provide a supplier with a low degree of control over the distribution process. In contrast, short channels provide more control but require greater utilization of a firm's resources.

Through short channels, a manufacturer can control final retail selling prices, store atmosphere, the range of competitive products offered to consumers, and the overall quality of customer service. However, short channels require that a manufacturer have high capital levels to finance inventories, build retail and warehouse facilities, assume wholesale and retail customer contact functions, and so on. Short channels also assume that manufacturers can conduct these activities as efficiently as wholesalers, retailers, and channel facilitators. The use of short channels is common in a number of situations. Large manufacturers, for example, often use them with large overall sales. Short channels are often associated with products in the early stages of a product life cycle, because of the need for highly trained employees to explain a product's features and to handle complex installations. In general, short channels are highly efficient when there are a few large customers as with industrial products.

FIGURE 11-2   Control versus financial resources in channel design.

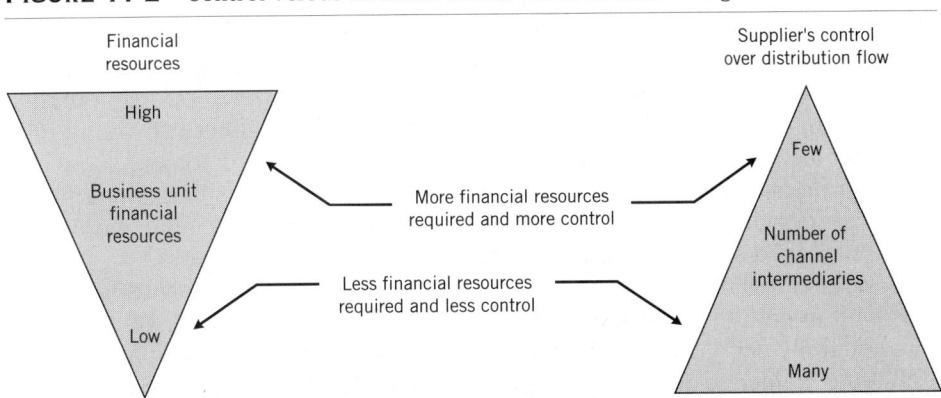

Source: Frank V. Cespedes, *Channel Management* (Boston: Harvard Business School, case 590-045, 1989), p. 8. Copyright © 1989 by the President and Fellows of Harvard College. Reprinted by permission.

Short channels enable a manufacturer to have maximum channel control. Short channels recognize that it is easier to control your own employees than the employees of an independent distributor, retailer, and even franchisees. In addition, some consumers prefer dealing directly with a manufacturer, especially when EDI is implemented, or when a product is complex and must be tailored to the individual customer's needs.

The two major disadvantages commonly associated with short channels are their requirement that a manufacturer have sufficient capital to conduct all channel activities and that a manufacturer have sufficient knowledge and the additional human resources to conduct these activities efficiently.

In a **long channel (indirect distribution)**, each independent channel member (manufacturers, wholesalers, and retailers) takes on specified channel responsibilities. A long channel indicates that a relatively large number of independent firms are involved in the channel arrangement. Long channels are generally associated with high channel specialization and with wide geographic coverage.

Long channels give the user the ability to distribute to a large number of customers, reduce financial requirements for manufacturers, allocate channel member responsibilities among channel members, and enable consumers to purchase a large proportion of their needs from one source.

Long channels enable a marketer to efficiently handle large numbers of widely dispersed customers. For example, a long channel might consist of a producer, manufacturer's sales branch, industrial distributor, and end-user. A manufacturer could have 36 sales branches, each dealing with 20 industrial distributors, for a total of 720 distribution points. If each distribution point had 100 customers, the channel could then cover 72,000 customers. A single manufacturer could not handle this number of customers through sales branches alone.[8]

A long channel reduces the financial and human resource requirements of each reseller, for other channel members would now undertake warehousing, shipping, credit, and field-selling activities. Some channel members could undertake these channel activities more efficiently than a producer. Long channels also enable each channel member to perform specific responsibilities based on their competitive strength. A wholesaler, for example, may be able to contact potential clients at a lower cost than a manufacturer, based on the wholesaler's representation of multiple manufacturers on a single sales call. Long channels are also desirable when consumers want to purchase a large proportion of their needs from one source. This one-stop shopping appeal reduces the number of contacts a customer needs to make with sellers, enables customers to receive goods from multiple vendors in one shipment, increases the bargaining power of customers, and reduces a customer's administrative costs. (One wholesaler could be paid a single check for purchases from multiple vendors.)

Long channels have several disadvantages. First, the more intermediaries involved in getting a supplier's product to market, the less control a supplier can generally exercise over the product's flow and transportation. A supplier's ability to influence prices to its final customers also decreases as channel length increases. Second, a long channel also increases the chance of transshipment and provides differing service levels at different channel levels. Third, long channels also require that channel activities and functions be properly coordinated among the independent channel members. Channel members that are independent have to be motivated to service smaller accounts, participate in cooperative advertising programs, and instruct their sales forces on new products, technologies, and markets.

CHANNEL WIDTH

Channel width refers to the degree of competition at any channel level, as well as the intensity of competition in a market area. Three factors that determine channel width are the required level of channel investments, buyer behavior of target consumers, and the volume of business in a market area.[9] Channel investments relate to the need for inventory to support a sales level and the need for specialized equipment and personnel. When channel investment is high relative to a market's sales potential, a supplier's representation in the market area should be low enough to attract and retain resellers. Buyer behavior relates to the degree of search activity by consumers. Consumers often conduct search activity to determine the characteristics of competing products, general technical information, and current prices and service-level offerings by competing vendors. For example, if purchasing convenience is of prime concern to buyers, more intensive channels are required. Finally, brands with higher market shares can support wider channels than brands with low market shares.

An important characteristic related to market width for final consumer-based products is the marketer's market coverage. Without high enough market coverage, a manufacturer may be unable to meet its sales goals. For products that are distributed through grocery stores, market coverage is generally measured by a product's percentage of **all commodity volume (ACV)**. For example, a product with 60 percent ACV in grocery stores is distributed in grocery stores that account for 60 percent of total grocery store sales in that market. ACV is only a rough measure of market coverage. For example, a 60 percent ACV measure does not mean that a product is distributed in stores that account for 60 percent of the sales of the affected product, or in 60 percent of the grocery stores in that region. ACV percentages in the grocery industry are available from market research firms such as Information Resources Inc. and A. C. Nielsen. A better measure would be to weight the stores by the percentage of the relevant product category that they sell. This is called **percent category volume (PCV)**. Both the ACV and PCV measures have been discussed in Chapter 7.

Market coverage should be analyzed by market segment. While a product's overall market coverage is satisfactory, it could be poor when market coverage is analyzed for a specific target market. For example, although Texas Instruments has good coverage for its line of notebook computers in small independent computer outlets and retail computer superstores, its coverage is poor among those independent distributors that serve medium to large-size businesses (a group that constitutes a major market for its notebook computers). Texas Instruments is currently trying to get additional coverage in this important market segment by adding distributors that are important resellers of personal computers to large corporations.[10]

There are three degrees of channel width: exclusive distribution, intensive distribution, and selective distribution.

Exclusive Distribution

In **exclusive distribution**, only one channel member at any level can sell a manufacturer's goods and services in a given geographic area. Exclusive distribution is characterized by low competition, as well as a low degree of market coverage. Exclusive distribution is generally used when a manufacturer wants a close relationship with its channel partners. The success of the manufacturer and its resellers is more closely intertwined in exclusive distribution than in any other form of distribution. Exclusive distribution is common with specialty goods.

Exclusive distribution shelters dealers, enabling them to service customers without fear of competition from other resellers. Exclusive distribution also enables resellers to build their businesses by increasing the number of sales representatives and branches without the fear of a supplier adding additional resellers. In addition, manufacturers use exclusive distribution with the expectation that this form of channel width will induce strong selling support by the reseller.

The disadvantages of exclusive distribution relate to reseller power due to low competition and lower convenience for customers. Exclusive distribution may enable a dealer to assume that it can take advantage of customers because of its monopoly position via a protected territory. Exclusive distribution also entails greater travel requirements for consumers than any other form of distribution.

Intensive Distribution

In **intensive distribution**, all channel members that meet a manufacturer's minimum credit arrangements can purchase its goods and services. Intensive distribution involves high competition among channel members, and high market coverage of a product or service. Intensive distribution is common with convenience goods.

Intensive distribution promotes increased sales through greater consumer convenience. The fundamental assumption of intensive distribution is that share of distribution (such as share of distribution outlets) equals market share.[11] The more intensive a product's distribution, the higher its sales potential.

On the negative side, with intensive distribution there may be a real limit as to the number of dealers that any manufacturer can service. A manufacturer needs to assess its dealer training, distribution support systems, and dealer communications networks to determine whether these are strained with intensive distribution. The sales efforts of competing dealers may also overlap within a given territory. Intensive distribution can increase competition among these resellers to such a degree that reseller loyalty to the manufacturer will be reduced, price competition increased, and the reseller's willingness to properly service an account diminished.

Selective Distribution

Selective distribution seeks to balance the amount of channel member competition and the degree of market coverage. This is the middle ground in channel width. Selective distribution has a higher level of reseller support than intensive distribution and offers better shopper convenience than exclusive distribution. Generally, shopping goods use selective distribution.

A common issue related to selective distribution is the degree to which dealer territories should overlap. The amount of overlap in selective distribution determines how closely selective distribution approximates exclusive or intensive distribution within a given territory. While high overlap increases customer choice and convenience, it may create some conflict among retailers. Low overlap increases reseller loyalty but reduces customer convenience.[12]

TYPES OF INTERMEDIARIES AT EACH LEVEL IN A CHANNEL

In evaluating channel width, marketers need to think of market coverage for specific segments of consumers. This approach recognizes that different market segments will patronize different dealer systems.

Three different types of competitive environments are horizontal competition, intertype competition, and vertical competition. A fourth type, vertical marketing systems, is covered in Chapter 12.

Horizontal Competition

Horizontal competition consists of competition among channel members of the same type. It is greatest with intensive distribution and least with exclusive distribution. Although it is difficult to generalize, the overall marketing strategy of competing dealers is more similar with horizontal competition than in intertype competition. To a manufacturer, horizontal competition also results in a more consistent image, more comparable customer service, and possibly less price competition among resellers (owing to the similar cost structures of each channel member).

Intertype Competition

Intertype competition relates to competition among different types of channel members at the same level within a channel, for example, a full-service retailer and a discounter. Intertype competition results when a manufacturer sells its goods and services through different channel members to maximize its total sales. Intertype competition can also involve the sale of a good or service through a new channel format. Two forms of intertype competition are multiple channels of distribution and dual channels of distribution.

With **multiple channels of distribution**, a manufacturer sells different product lines to different channel members. One product line can involve a private-label product, whereas another can use a national brand. For example, General Electric uses multiple marketing channels to sell large home appliances through retail outlets directly to new-home builders and through remodelers. Multiple channels of distribution enable a manufacturer to reach multiple target markets while minimizing direct competition among channel members. For example, the use of different models that are sold through each channel lowers price competition at all levels in a channel. The disadvantages of intertype competition are high distribution costs, the need for high investments, possible inconsistent service, and possible price competition.

A manufacturer seeks to minimize potential channel conflicts with multiple channels through specific product-based demarcations that limit sales with a given channel.[13] For example, at Ingersoll-Rand's air compressor division, large compressors are available for direct sales only, and manufacturers' representatives sell the low-end line to retail customers. Similarly, Sherwin-Williams sells its Sherwin-Williams paint brand exclusively through its own retail stores, but sells the Dutch Boy brand of paint to unaffiliated home centers, mass merchandisers, independent dealers, and distributors.

With **dual channels of distribution**, the same good or service is sold through different channel arrangements. Dual channels of distribution may be costly to set up and maintain, but they allow a manufacturer, wholesaler, or retailer to satisfy multiple market segments. A common form of dual channels of distribution is to use a direct channel for major accounts, but to sell through intermediaries for smaller accounts. Manufacturers can also use different channel arrangements for different territories. A mature territory can be handled by a manufacturer's sales representatives, whereas a new territory may be handled by food brokers. Dual channels of distribution have similar advantages and disadvantages to multiple channels of distribution, although with dual channels, there is a greater possibility of channel conflict owing to the sameness of product being sold through each channel.

Vertical Competition

Vertical competition describes competition among different channel members at different levels within the channel. Some vertical competition is due to vertical integration. In **forward vertical integration**, manufacturers acquire or build up retail channels, or wholesalers acquire or develop retail channels. In **backward vertical integration**, retailers purchase or develop wholesale operations, wholesalers acquire or build manufacturing operations, or retailers purchase or develop manufacturing operations. For example, Sherwin-Williams distributes its paint through 2046 company-owned stores, as well as indendently owned paint channels.[14]

Vertical integration suggests that channel efficiency can be improved through joint ownership of channel members or that channel member control is important.[15] Channel members using vertical integration need to be concerned with other channel member reactions and potential conflict of interest situations.

EVALUATING MARKET/PRODUCT/ MANUFACTURER/INTERMEDIARY FACTORS THAT AFFECT CHANNEL LENGTH

This section studies market, product, manufacturer, and intermediary factors that affect a channel's length. We will first explore several theories relating to channel length (by Aspinwall, Miracle, and Bucklin). We will then analyze individual market, product, manufacturer, and intermediary factors that affect length. Finally, we will summarize these factors and discuss their validity.

The classic theory that has been used to prescribe channel length is **Aspinwall's characteristics of goods and parallel systems theory**.[16] In this major work, Professor Aspinwall argues that a firm's channel structure should reflect a product positioning on the basis of its replacement rate, gross margin, adjustment, time of consumption, and searching time. These factors are defined as follows:

Replacement rate—the rate at which a product is purchased by users.

Gross margin—the total channel costs measured by the difference between production costs and the final selling price for a good.

Adjustment—services applied to a product to meet customers' needs or product customization requirements.

Time of consumption—the time period during which the product is used. In general, goods with a low time of consumption are likely to have a high replacement rate. However, some products such as aspirin have a short time of consumption but a long replacement rate.

Searching time—the amount of effort expended by customers to shop for a particular good. Searching time is measured by the travel time and distance consumers will travel to shop for a given product.

Many of Aspinall's factors have both market and product characteristics. A product's replacement rate, for instance, may be based on its usage rate as well as its perishability. Adjustment also reflects a product's characteristics as well as market factors. Aspinwall classified all products based on the degree to which they possess these factors. For example, **red goods** have a high replacement rate, low gross margin, low need for adjustment, low consumption time, and low searching time. According to Aspinwall, red goods should have long channels. **Orange goods** have medium characteristics for each of the five factors. Orange goods should have medium-length channels. Lastly, **yellow goods** are low in replacement rate but high in the other four factors. According to Aspinwall, yellow goods should have short channels (see Table 11-1).

Professor Miracle included several factors in addition to the factors studied by Aspinwall: consumer buying behavior elements (such as the significance of purchase and purchasing effort) and some technological characteristics (such as rate of technological change, technical complexity, and need for service).[17]

Neither Aspinwall's theory nor the research conducted by Miracle explains why a short or long channel should be selected on the basis of factors studied.

TABLE 11-1 ASPINWALL'S CHARACTERISTICS OF GOODS AND PARALLEL SYSTEMS THEORY

Characteristics of Goods	Red Goods	Orange Goods	Yellow Goods
Replacement rate	High	Medium	Low
Gross margin	Low	Medium	High
Adjustment	Low	Medium	High
Time of consumption	Low	Medium	High
Searching time	Low	Medium	High
Ideal channel length	Long	Medium	Short

Professor Bucklin argues that the explanation should be based on the costs of performing the four service output levels: market decentralization (fragmentation), lot size, assortment, and waiting time.[18] According to Professor Bucklin, a supplier should choose the channel system that minimizes the distribution costs associated with the delivery of these service outputs.

A large body of research has been published detailing the relationship between channel length and market, product, consumer, and intermediary factors (see Table 11-2).

TABLE 11-2 RELATIONSHIP BETWEEN CHANNEL LENGTH AND MARKET, PRODUCT, CONSUMER, AND INTERMEDIARY FACTORS

	Direct Distribution If—	Long Channel If—
Market Factors		
Size of customer base	Small	Large
Geographic dispersion	Low	High
Customer density	High	Low
Sales gestation period	Long	Short
Level of customer	High	Low
Average order size	Large	Small
Product Factors		
Bulk	High	Low
Perishability	High	Low
Unit value	High	Low
Product standardization	Low	High
Technical nature	High	Low
Gross margin	Low	High
Manufacturer Factors		
Size	Large	Small
Financial capability	High	Low
Desire for control	High	Low
Managerial expertise	High	Low
Customer knowledge	High	Low
Intermediary Factors		
Availability	Low	High
Cost	High	Low
Quality	Low	High

Sources: Many of these factors are from Leo V. Aspinwall, "The Characteristics of Goods Theory," in *Managerial Marketing: Perspectives and Viewpoints,* William Lazer and Eugene I. Kelley, eds., (Homewood, Ill.: 1962), pp. 633–643; Louis P. Bucklin, *A Theory of Distribution Channel Structure* (Berkeley, Calif.: IBER Special Publications, 1966); James D. Hlavacek and Tommy J. McCuistion, "Industrial Distributors—When, Who, and How?" *Harvard Business Review,* Vol. 61 (March–April 1983), p. 97; Donald W. Jackson, Robert F. Krampf, and Leonard J. Konopa, "Factors That Influence the Length of Industrial Channels," *Industrial Marketing Management,* Vol. 11 (October 1982), pp. 263–268; Gary L. Lilien, "ADVISOR 2: Modeling the Marketing Mix Decision for Industrial Products," *Management Science,* Vol. 25 (February 1979), pp. 191–204; and Gordon E. Miracle, "Product Characteristics and Marketing Strategy," *Journal of Marketing,* Vol. 29 (January 1965), pp. 18–24.

MARKET FACTORS

Channel length is affected by the size of the customer base, geographic dispersion, customer density, sales gestation period, level of customer, and average order size.

A large potential customer base favors the use of intermediaries. For example, if there are 3000 potential end customers for an industrial product, and a manufacturer could only effectively deal with 50 accounts, then a maximum of 50 intermediaries would have to be developed for the first level of the channel. This would leave each first-level intermediary with 60 final consumers. If there were 2500 potential consumers, a firm would need four levels of intermediaries to adequately staff all consumers, providing the number of consumer contacts at each level were limited to 50 (1 manufacturer × 50 manufacturer's representatives × 50 final consumers = 2500 potential consumers).

A broad sales territory (such as the United States as a whole) may favor a long channel, whereas a limited territory (such as a suburban part of a major city) may be efficiently covered by a short channel. Broad territories demand high resources from any channel reseller because these accounts have to be serviced from multiple warehouses, sales offices, and so on.

High customer density of buyers (which may occur in a major metropolitan area) favors the use of direct distribution owing to the lower cost of contacting and servicing each buyer. On the other hand, a manufacturer may have to use a long channel in a less densely populated area.

The **sales gestation period** reflects the average length of time from the first contact to a product's purchase. Long gestation periods (as in the purchase of complex industrial equipment) are more apt to use direct distribution. Direct distribution is also more appropriate for products with long gestation periods when a broker or wholesaler has a short-term contract or a contract that will soon expire.

The lower in the organization the person responsible for purchasing an item is, the more likely the item will be sold through a distributor. High-level executive decisions are more likely to be conducted with direct distribution.

Lastly, if the average order size is large, the transaction will probably be handled through direct distribution. Smaller average transactions are more likely to involve longer channels.

PRODUCT FACTORS

The product factors that affect channel length are bulk, perishability, unit value, product standardization, technical nature, and gross margin.

Goods of large bulk relative to value are more prone to use short channels. Short channels minimize physical distribution costs, when these costs are high relative to a good's value. On the other hand, long channels can be used when a product's bulk is low relative to its value.

Highly perishable goods should be sold through shorter channels to minimize travel time and distance; a large proportion of a product's shelf life should not be used up in transit. Goods that have longer lives, however, can be distributed through longer channels.

CHANNELS IN ACTION

Millstone Coffee: Evaluation of Distribution Channels

Millstone Coffee was already distributed in 125 supermarkets when Philip Johnson acquired the Seattle-based coffee bean wholesaler. Like other fresh roasted coffees, Millstone Coffee is sold in clear bins, where its whole beans can be purchased in any quantity desired by consumers. Millstone supplies each supermarket with the displays and coffee grinders; the company's route delivery drivers regularly refill the store's stock. The bin strategy is important to Millstone, for it limits entry by competitive firms due to space constraints at most supermarkets. Supermarket managers also like bulk coffees, since much of the labor in restocking and reordering is done by a firm's delivery drivers, not supermarket personnel.

In 1986, Philip Johnson reviewed Millstone's direct distribution strategy in light of the firm's high sales growth and relatively low capital. Johnson estimated that it cost the firm about $75,000 for a single truck and driver. Among the options explored were using food brokers, developing a network of coffee roasters, and franchising routes. According to Johnson, "After three solid months of debate, we agreed that it was in our best interests to keep distributing the coffee ourselves. If we went through distributors, our coffee could get lost among the 10,000 products in their warehouses. We weren't going to buy the best beans and roast them to perfection only to have them languish on the shelves and be ruined."

Direct distribution also enables Millstone to more easily develop and implement an inventory control system. This is especially important for coffee, which has a limited shelf life and limited product substitution for many customers. Customers desiring an expresso blend, for example, may not purchase a French Roast blend. Millstone's computer system enables its drivers to transmit inventory data on a bin-by-bin basis directly to Millstone's headquarters. These data are used to initiate roasting and shipping schedules.

Realizing that direct distribution could reduce Millstone's growth rate, Johnson chooses his markets carefully and provides incentives to his route drivers. He prefers market areas in the Midwest where coffee consumption is high and metropolitan areas with more than two or three major grocery chains. Sales from only one chain are generally not profitable since Millstone's route drivers sell only bulk coffee. Millstone also offers its drivers a performance-based incentive. Millstone Coffee is now sold in 42 states; its 1994 sales were $72 million.

Source: Teri Lammers Prior, "Channel Surfers," *Inc.* (February 1995), p. 66.

Items with high unit value are generally more prone to be sold direct. It is easier to justify high sales costs for these items. In contrast, products selling for several dollars can be sold by distributors. Low-value products produced by noncompeting manufacturers can be combined into a single sale.

Standardized products are generally sold through longer channels than tailored products. It may be difficult for custom designed products to be sold through distributors owing to the need for distributor training.

Technically complex factors are generally more prone to be distributed directly. With regard to these products, the advice of the manufacturer is needed on product selection, product use, and so on.

MANUFACTURER FACTORS

The manufacturer factors that affect channel length are size, financial capability, desire for control, managerial expertise, and customer knowledge.

Generally, larger firms have greater choice in channel arrangement, and greater choice is, in part, related to higher financial capability and managerial expertise. Thus, larger firms are more likely to use direct distribution, and smaller forms are more prone to use long channels.

Firms with limited financial capability need longer channels. Long channels enable these firms to receive payment based on when sales are made to downstream channel members (versus sales to the final consumer or end-user) and to minimize investment in inventory, warehouse, and retail facilities.

Firms need managerial expertise to carry out wholesale and retail functions. Firms with high managerial expertise in these areas can use direct distribution, whereas, as already noted, firms with low expertise need long channels.

The higher the degree of customer knowledge possessed by a manufacturer, the greater the chance the firm will use direct distribution. Manufacturers with low customer knowledge would benefit from the expertise of downstream resellers (long channels).

INTERMEDIARY FACTORS

The three intermediary factors that affect channel length are availability, cost, and service quality.

Availability relates to whether effective resellers can be found in the relevant market areas. Resellers may be unavailable because of prior obligations. (Most wholesaler contracts do not allow a wholesaler to represent competitive manufacturers.) In some instances, because of the low availability of qualified resellers, direct distribution may be the only feasible alternative.

Intermediary costs may be so high (in terms of commission rates in the case of agents and brokers and discounts required in the case of merchant wholesalers and retailers) that direct distribution is a more feasible alternative than a long channel. In evaluating intermediary costs, a supplier needs to be careful to include all costs for direct distribution and intermediaries, as well as to compare costs at different sales levels.

Manufacturers need to determine the ability of intermediaries to meet minimum customer service criteria. If a distributor's customer service is poor, then direct distribution may be the only alternative.

SUMMARY OF FACTORS AFFECTING CHANNEL LENGTH

Several concerns need to be addressed in using the factors in the prior sections in determining the ideal channel length. These difficulties stem from the lack of independence in these variables, the need to consider multiple factors, and the oversimplification of many of these relationships.

The factors studied are not wholly independent. For example, a relationship probably exists between level of customer and average order size. Higher level executives are more likely to make larger orders. A manufacturer's size, financial capability, managerial expertise, and customer knowledge may be interrelated. In an important literature review, a model of eight channel functions and their impact on channel choice was developed. The authors summarized the work of Aspinwall, Miracle, Bucklin, and others, and found that the channel functions that are most closely related to channel length are product information, product customization, product quality assurance, lot size, assortment, availability, after-sales service, and logistics.[19]

1. Product information—Product information requirements are high for products that are new or technically complex and those that have a rapidly changing technological component. Customers prefer a direct channel when information requirements are high.
2. Product customization—Customers prefer a direct channel when a product must be sized, graded, or adjusted to fit a customer's requirements.
3. Product quality assurance—Customers prefer a direct channel to ensure high product quality when a product is important to the customer.
4. Lot size—If a product has a high unit value, if it is used extensively, represents a major financial decision, or is likely to lead to a concerted purchasing effort, then customers seek a direct channel.
5. Assortment—Customers seek indirect channels when they have assortment needs, need complementary products, or seek one-stop shopping.
6. Availability—Customers seek indirect channels when they have intense product availability needs. Product availability needs are related to a buyer's difficulty in predicting a product's usage rates or in determining safety stock requirements.
7. After-sales service—Customers usually seek indirect channels to support high need for such after-sales services as installation, repair, maintenance, and warranty services.
8. Logistics—When logistics requirements (such as transporting, storing, and supplying products to the end-user) are complex, customers seek direct channels.

Another difficulty in studying these factors is the notion that channel strategy is the result of the relationship of multiple factors, not a single factor (with all other variables held constant). Figure 11-3 classifies business units based on their available financial resources and their relative need for direct control over distribution functions in order to determine the impact of both of these variables on channel design. The upper right quadrant depicts institutions with high financial resources and a high need for control. In this situation, a direct sales channel is appropriate. Conversely, in the lower left cell, the business unit's financial resources are limited and the need for control is low. Here, a longer distribution channel is most plausible. This channel alternative enables the supplier to delegate tasks and to conserve its financial resources. In the up-

FIGURE 11-3 The impact of financial resources and need for control on channel design.

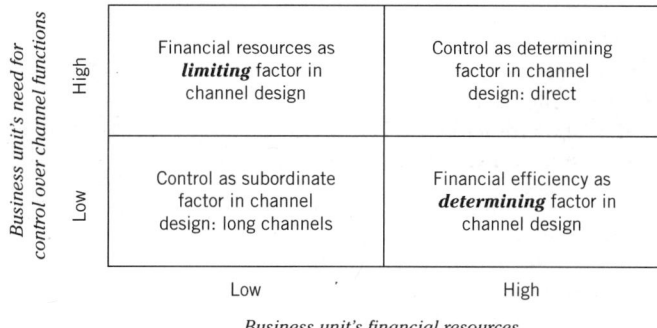

Source: Frank V. Cespedes, *Channel Management* (Boston: Harvard Business School, case 590-045, 1989), p. 9. Copyright © 1989 by the President and Fellows of Harvard College. Reprinted by permission.

per left cell, financial resources are low, but the need for control is high. In this case, the supplier tends to perform as many important channel functions as possible within the limits of its financial resources. Here, distribution costs are a constraint rather than a determinant of the supplier's channel management policies. In this instance, a producer would perform more functions if its financial condition improved. Conversely, in the bottom right-hand corner, financial resources are high, but the need for control is low. In this sector, low-cost distribution is the determining factor in channel design decisions.

These relationships oversimplify the channel length determination process. A manufacturer with low financial capability can use direct marketing to minimize capital investment. Postage expense, mailing list preparation costs, and brochure preparation expenses may involve a smaller investment than developing displays, paying slotting fees, and training and motivating a distributor's sales force in some cases. In 1988, Lifetime Automotive Products did not have the financial resources to sell its Tripledge windshield wipers through traditional retail channels. Instead, the firm used a direct marketing strategy that reached consumers through credit card inserts, catalogs, and print advertising. According to the firm's chief executive officer, "We get immediate cash flow from every ad we run. The same growth rate at retail would have taken $10 million in equity capital." If it decided to use traditional channels, Lifetime would have had to use national advertising before auto stores would accept the product. In addition, these retailers would have demanded payment terms of 120 days."[20]

ALLOCATING CHANNEL TASKS AMONG CHANNEL MEMBERS

The allocation of channel tasks among channel members can be broken down into two subactivities: listing reseller responsibilities and allocating tasks to the manufacturer and its resellers.

TABLE 11-3 CHANNEL MEMBER TASKS

Selling
    New account solicitation
    Solicitation of current accounts
    Promotion to final consumers
    Maintaining retail showrooms
    Negotiating prices and terms of sale

Channels Support
    Market research
    Sharing knowledge of local market conditions
    Providing information to customers
    Negotiation with final consumers
    Recruiting resellers
    Training reseller sales force

Physical Distribution
    Inventory storage
    Order processing
    Product transportation
    Conducting credit checks on final consumers
    Billing customers
    Handling collections

Product Modification and After-Sale Service
    Providing technical service
    Customizing a product to meet a user's needs
    Product maintenance and repair
    Handling returned products
    Handling product recalls

Risk Assumption
    Inventory financing
    Providing credit to final consumers
    Ownership of inventories
    Product liability
    Warehouse investments

Source: The broad headings are from E. Raymond Corey, *Industrial Distribution Systems* (Boston: Harvard Business School, 1989), p. 7.

LISTING CHANNEL MEMBER RESPONSIBILITIES

Table 11-3 lists channel member tasks in distribution. These tasks are organized by activity: selling, channels support, physical distribution, product modification and after-sale service, and risk assumption. These channel responsibilities must be allocated among the channel participants.

ALLOCATING RESPONSIBILITIES AMONG THE CHANNEL PARTICIPANTS

Each of the tasks identified in Table 11-3 must be allocated among the channel participants. Many of these tasks can be retained by a manufacturer, shifted to resellers, to final consumers/end-users, to a facilitator (such as a consultant, advertising agency, or transportation company), or even shared among channel members. For example, a manufacturer can provide product transportation directly to the end-user, require a wholesaler to pick up goods at the manufacturer's warehouse, require final consumers to arrange for pickup and delivery, arrange for shipment by a common carrier, or ship goods to a wholesaler but require wholesalers to ship goods to retailers.

According to Professor Corey, from the producer's perspective, the primary criteria in allocating responsibilities among channel members are:[21]

- Reducing distribution costs.
- Maximizing market share, sales revenues, and profits.
- Optimizing the return on distribution-specific investment risks.
- Meeting customer needs for product technical information, product availability, product customization, and after-sale service so as to gain a competitive edge.
- Maintaining sources of market information.

For example, according to the criterion of reducing distribution costs, a wholesaler or retailer (rather than the manufacturer) should place advertising in media because the wholesaler or retailer receives a local versus a national rate. However, the manufacturer may develop promotional copy on the basis of its sources of market information and higher expertise.

Several other considerations must be taken into account in allocating responsibilities among channel participants: namely, the willingness of channel members to undertake certain responsibilities, the quality of the services performed by different channel members, the level of customer contact desired by the manufacturer, the importance of specific customers, and the applicability of hybrid channel arrangements.

Not all channel members are willing to undertake specific tasks. For example, a wholesaler may be unwilling to provide technical service or to handle product recalls for a manufacturer. A manufacturer may not be able to allocate credit responsibilities to final consumers unless they are willing to forgo customary credit arrangements. The extent to which a manufacturer can induce a downstream intermediary to perform certain responsibilities is related to the attractiveness of the manufacturer's products and the manufacturer's power in the channel. (This topic is covered in Chapter 13.)

Similarly, not all channel members have the same ability to perform a responsibility well. For example, a study by Shipley, Egan, and Edgett suggests that senior buyers of engineering companies rate direct versus distributor channels differently. Distributors performed significantly better than direct sellers on keeping promises, helpfulness in emergencies, availability of products, quality of delivery service, and relationship with buyer variables. On the other hand, direct sellers significantly outperformed distributors on price competitiveness, product quality, technical knowledge, and adapt to specifications variables.[22]

With regard to the level of customer contact desired, three different degrees of customer contact for resellers are selling intermediary, stocking intermediary, and stocking/selling intermediary.[23] A selling intermediary initiates consumer contact; a stocking intermediary maintains stock but provides little technical support; and a stocking and service intermediary has the highest degree

TABLE 11-4 INTERMEDIARY ALTERNATIVES ON THE BASIS OF CHANNEL CONTACT, COST, AND CONTROL

Channel Member Type Required Based on Level of Contact	Possible Intermediaries	
	Low Cost and Control	High Cost and Control
Selling intermediary	Manufacturer's representative	Company sales force
Stocking intermediary	General industrial distributor	Manufacturer's branch or warehouse location
Stocking/servicing intermediary	Specialty industrial distributor	Manufacturer's sales branch

Source: Thomas L. Powers, "Industrial Distribution Options: Trade-Offs to Consider," *Industrial Marketing Management,* Vol. 18 (1989), p. 160. Reprinted by permission. Copyright 1989 by Elsevier Science Inc.

of customer contact. If the primary task assigned to the distributor is to arrange sales, then an agent or broker seems logical. If the handling of returned products and product recalls is required, then a stocking/selling intermediary is needed. See Table 11-4 for an analysis of intermediary alternatives based on channel contact, cost, and control.

A firm can also use different channel arrangements based on a customer's size. A direct sales force can be employed to handle all demand-generation tasks for large customers; midsize accounts can be sold through direct catalogs and telephone sales; and small accounts and nonusers can be serviced through indirect channels. A difficulty with this arrangement is that some sales representatives may improperly classify accounts to continue serving them as they grow.

Finally, a manufacturer can reach different segments through the same channel network (comprised of both direct and indirect channels), but perform different functions (for the entire product line) depending on the customer segment. This is referred to as a **hybrid channel arrangement**.[24] For example, at Becton Dickinson's Vacutainer Systems Division (BDVS), BDVS's direct salespeople actively negotiate contracts with large multihospital buying groups but have its distributors supply and deliver the products. With smaller hospitals, distributors initiated selling efforts and the BDVS's direct sales force performed technical assistance functions.[25]

SELECTION OF SPECIFIC CHANNEL RESELLERS

This section is divided into three main parts: determining the availability of channel resellers, evaluating resellers on a preliminary basis, and conducting a comprehensive analysis of resellers.

DETERMINING THE AVAILABILITY OF CHANNEL RESELLERS

A manufacturer can determine the availability of channel resellers by contacting professional associations for leads. Although many professional associations maintain directories of their members, they will not evaluate or recommend specific resellers. Table 11-5 provides a listing of major trade associations

TABLE 11-5   TRADE ASSOCIATIONS OF WHOLESALERS

Agricultural and Industrial Manufacturers Representatives Association
5818 Reeds Road
Mission, KS 66202
913 262-4511

Association of Industry Manufacturers Representatives
5818 Reeds Road
Mission, KS 66202
913 262-0163

Electronic Representatives Directory
Harris Publishing Co.
2057-2 Aurora Road
Twinsburg, OH 44087
216 425-9143

Electronics Representatives Association
20 East Huron Street
Chicago, IL 60611
312 649-1333

Incentive Manufacturers Representative Association
710 Ogden Avenue, Suite 113
Naperville, IL 60540
312 369-2425

Manufacturers' Agents National Association
23016 Mill Creek Road
P.O. Box 3467
Laguna Hills, CA 92654
714 859-4040

Manufacturers Representatives of America
P.O. Box 150229
Arlington, TX 76015
817 465-5511

National Association of General Merchandise Representatives
111 East Wacker Drive, Suite 600
Chicago, IL 60601
312 644-6610

National Electrical Manufacturers' Representatives Association
Suite 330
222 Westchester Avenue
White Plains, NY 10604
914 428-1307

TABLE 11-5 (*CONTINUED*)

National Food Brokers Association
1010 Massachusetts Avenue, NW
Washington, DC 20001
202 789-2844

Office Products Representatives Association
600 South Federal Street, Suite 400
Chicago, IL 60606
312 922-6222

Society of Manufacturers Representatives
29200 Vassar, Suite 520
Livonia, MI 48152
313 473-2002

---

of wholesalers organized by product category. Trade shows and advertisements in trade magazines can also provide the names of potential wholesalers and retailers. A list of potential channel resellers can also be developed based on recommendations from noncompeting manufacturers, valued customers, and suppliers.

Even though a channel intermediary is on a list, it does not mean that it is available. Some may have commitments to competing manufacturers; others may not have the resources to handle another product line. Some retailers, for example, do not want to take on a competing line since it would involve loss of quantity discounts on current lines, or the product may be viewed as not adding incremental sales.

The next section describes a four-stage process to evaluate channel resellers. This process consists of a preliminary screening, an interview, a checklist, and a comprehensive analysis.

EVALUATING RESELLERS THROUGH PRELIMINARY SCREENING, INTERVIEWS, AND CHECKLISTS

The selection of resellers should take place in sequential stages, with low-cost screening techniques being used to quickly eliminate resellers that do not meet minimum expectations, an interview to resolve questions and obtain additional information, a channel checklist, and higher cost techniques to further evaluate the most promising wholesalers and retailers. By dividing reseller evaluation into a four-part process, a manufacturer can limit its exhaustive investigation to the most promising resellers. As can be seen in Figure 11-4, the reseller evaluation process can terminate at any stage.

An example of a manufacturer that uses the retailer selection process is Lexus, Toyota's luxury car line. Lexus has been very selective in its choice of dealers. It favors dealers with a proven track record in customer satisfaction, broad management experience, high capitalization, and the willingness to build

FIGURE 11-4 The channel member selection process.

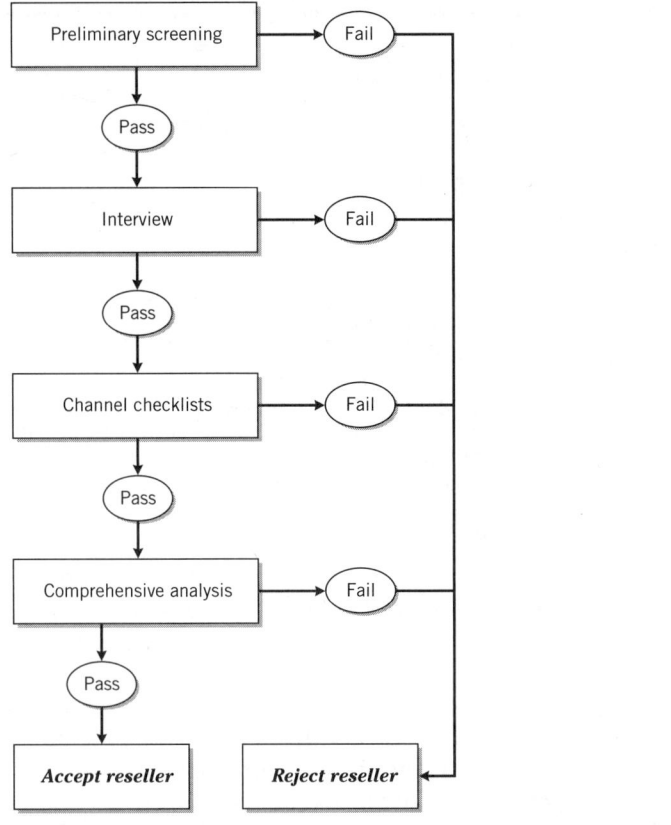

new facilities or to renovate existing facilities to meet Toyota's exacting standards. Potential dealers also have to demonstrate that they are committed to building long-lasting relationships with their final customers. Before Lexus was introduced to the market, over 1500 candidates for dealerships contacted Toyota. Of this group, 650 submitted complete proposals for review by Toyota; those that were currently non-Toyota dealers made presentations to Toyota executives in California. Initially, less than 100 of this group were approved. By the end of Lexus's first year, about 120 dealerships were operational.[26]

PRELIMINARY SCREENING

An example of a firm that uses preliminary screening for its wholesalers is Electric Liquid Fillers Inc. (ELF), a $140 million manufacturer of packaging systems. ELF uses a Representation Application Form, designed to be faxed by a prospective wholesaler, that enables ELF to quickly determine vital information about each potential representative. The form includes data on a representative's mechanical aptitude, size, current products that it distributes, size of technical staff, and credit rating.[27]

TABLE 11-6 KEY AREAS FOR A MANUFACTURER TO COVER WITH A PROSPECTIVE WHOLESALER DURING AN INTERVIEW

1. Wholesaler size
2. Growth patterns of wholesaler
3. Territory
4. Product line
5. Facilities and equipment
6. Company policies
7. Customers
8. Principals
9. Marketing and sales promotion abilities
10. Special services abilities

Source: Adapted from "Important Points to Cover with a Prospective Agent," *Pre-Screening Prospective Principals and Agents: Some Guidelines* (Laguna Hills, Calif.: Manufacturers' Agents National Association, 1990), p. 3.

THE INTERVIEW

The second stage of the selection process is to interview resellers that meet the minimum criteria to further explore their suitability. The preliminary screening application can serve as part of the basis of this interview. For example, a manufacturer may want to obtain additional information about the representative's current products, the markets it serves, and its technical staff based on the reseller's response on the screening form. Tables 11-6 and 11-7 list some key areas that should be covered during a preliminary interview between a prospective wholesaler and a manufacturer.

The following are some of the questions that a reseller needs to answer during an interview:

TABLE 11-7 KEY AREAS FOR A WHOLESALER TO COVER WITH A PROSPECTIVE SUPPLIER DURING AN INTERVIEW

1. Product information
2. Pricing information
3. Market information
4. Customer information
5. Competitive information
6. Sales information
7. Production situation
8. Advertising and sales promotion information
9. Sales leads
10. Wholesaler/supplier relationship
11. Written agreement

Source: Adapted from "Important Points to Cover with a Prospective Agent," *Pre-Screening Prospective Principals and Agents: Some Guidelines* (Laguna Hills, Calif.: Manufacturers' Agents National Association, 1990), p. 2.

- Will the wholesaler send its salespeople to attend seminars offered by manufacturer/suppliers?
- Does the wholesaler train its sales force on a periodic basis?
- What are the educational and professional qualifications of the wholesaler's sales force and sales managers?
- Does the wholesaler have a technical support group?
- Does the wholesaler have product testing and repair facilities?
- Does the wholesaler have resources to warehouse goods?
- Has the wholesaler successfully handled complementary accounts with high service levels?
- What other major retailer and end-user accounts does the wholesaler serve?
- What is the turnover of the wholesaler's sales staff?
- Are the wholesaler's current facilities adequate to handle an additional line?

CHANNEL CHECKLISTS

After the interview, the manufacturer needs to evaluate a prospective reseller on the basis of a channel checklist. The **channel checklist** contains specific criteria and weights for reseller evaluation. On the basis of a reseller's score on individual questions and the weight of each question, a final summary score can be determined for each intermediary. In comparison to less formal methods, the checklist ensures that all wholesalers are evaluated on the same criteria. Checklists also enable a manufacturer to determine whether a revised rating on several questions would significantly affect the wholesaler's overall rating. Table 11-8 represents a channel checklist for a merchant wholesaler, and Table 11-9 presents a checklist for an independent representative. The weights in Table 11-9 are merely suggestive; they can be changed to reflect the unique concerns or competitive environment of each manufacturer.

A manufacturer should use a checklist to determine whether a specific reseller meets the minimum rating for a more comprehensive analysis. For example, a manufacturer needs to determine minimum cutoff scores that constitute essential performance and desirable performance levels. For example, in the checklist in Table 11-9, the minimum essential performance score would be 50 points, whereas the minimum desirable performance score would be 60 points. Potential resellers with a score below 50 points should not be considered further. On the other hand, a potential wholesaler with a score of 80 or above should be quickly contacted and wooed.[28]

A COMPREHENSIVE ANALYSIS OF RESELLERS

In comparison to the preliminary analysis of resellers, the comprehensive analysis is designed to focus on several important decision criteria in a more systematic manner. Two areas that need to be examined in greater detail are an intermediary's costs under different sales levels and the ability of an intermediary to influence sales.

TABLE 11-8 MERCHANT WHOLESALER CHECKLIST

Attribute	Attribute Rating
1. Provides manufacturer with adequate market information	_____
2. Quality of staff in terms of technical service	_____
3. Willingness to help retailers effectively merchandise manufacturer's products	_____
4. Willingness to purchase total product line of manufacturer	_____
5. Ability to provide adequate territory coverage	_____
6. Market share in assigned geographic area	_____
7. Financial ability to maintain adequate inventory levels for good customer service	_____
8. Ethical reputation of wholesaler in market area	_____
9. Willingness to maintain manufacturer's price policies	_____
10. Technical ability to recommend and service products	_____
11. Importance of our line versus competitor's line to wholesaler	_____
12. Adequacy of warehouse	_____
13. Ability to invest resources for market growth	_____
14. Overall financial capability of wholesaler	_____

Scoring:

Rate a prospective channel member on a 7-point scale with 7 being a perfect score, 4 an average score, and 1 an unsatisfactory performance.

TABLE 11-9 INDEPENDENT REPRESENTATIVE CHECKLIST

Does the independent representative

1. Have an internal customer service or telemarketing staff to work, as a team, with its field salespeople? **(up to 15 points)**
2. Clearly understand the time needed to properly develop account relationships? **(up to 10 points)**
3. Initiate lead followup internally (rather than using field sales) to gain more information about needs rather than focusing on immediately offering a quote or making a sale? **(up to 15 points)**
4. Use the lead opportunity to sell synergistically rather than going for a one-product, one-shot approach? **(up to 5 points)**
5. Use leads as a way to search for information on new accounts as they build the relationship? **(up to 10 points)**
6. Offer related high-quality products/services and have a good, long-term sales history? **(up to 5 points)**
7. Follow up all leads the same week they're received and report back to you within three weeks as to the status of those leads? **(up to 10 points)**
8. Receive leads with enthusiasm and constantly ask for more? **(up to 5 points)**

TABLE 11-9 (CONTINUED)

9. Have automated account management systems for accurate and up-to-date recordkeeping? **(up to 15 points)**
10. Integrate its telemarketing efforts with field sales reps through a well-managed team effort and by sharing software and hardware? **(up to 10 points)**

TOTAL SCORE
MAXIMUM SCORE   100 points

Scoring:

80–100 points: These are the cream of the crop; send a contact to them before a competitor does.

60–80 points: Good firms that could move to the top-ranked group if you have a good lead management program to help them achieve their full potential.

50–60 points: Check their growth plans; they may be ready to add some tools that will take them to the top level.

Below 50 points: Keep looking. And don't forget: There are thousands of organizations out there to choose from. You deserve the best—especially if you've invested the time, effort, and money to design a lead generation program that will support your rep firm.

Source: Michael Marshall and Frank Siegler, "Selecting the Right Rep Firm," *Sales & Marketing Management* (January 1993), p. 83. Reprinted by permission. All rights reserved.

COMPUTING A RESELLER'S COSTS UNDER DIFFERENT SALES LEVELS

A manufacturer needs to assess the cost of different channel arrangements under different sales volume assumptions. This analysis compares the differences in costs between a direct channel and a broker. An important characteristic to consider in this cost analysis is that, while full-time sales representative salaries are a fixed expense, sales commissions to brokers are a variable expense. In conducting this analysis, it is important to make sure that all expenses are covered. Personnel expenses that could be overlooked include vacation time, personnel turnover costs, paperwork, taxes, and so on.[29]

In this example, we assume that a territory with $500,000 can be properly served by a full-time sales representative with a $40,000 salary, $8,000 in fringe benefits (at 20 percent of yearly salary), $5000 in technical support expenses (at 1 percent of sales), and $10,000 for travel and entertainment expenses (at 2 percent of sales). Total expenses under the direct distribution alternative would be $73,000. For the broker, expenses would be 10 percent commission ($50,000) plus $10,000 in technical support (at 2 percent of sales), and $10,000 for independent representative training. This would equal $70,000 (see Table 11-10). Although expenses for the full-time sales representative are about 4 percent higher than for the broker, at $500,000 in sales, the broker is less costly at the $2 million volume.

The direct distribution versus broker alternative is comparatively simple; a more difficult alternative is the use of direct distribution versus merchant

TABLE 11-10 COSTS OF DIFFERENT CHANNEL ARRANGEMENTS

(At $500,000 in sales)

Cost Element	Full-Time Manufacturer Sales Representative	Broker
Salary[a]	$ 40,000	—
Fringe benefits[b]	8,000	—
Travel and entertainment[c]	10,000	—
Commissions[d]	—	$ 50,000
Technical support[e]	5,000	10,000
Sales force training[f]	10,000	—
Ind. rep. training[g]		10,000
TOTAL EXPENSES	$ 73,000	$ 70,000

(At $2 million in sales)

Cost Element	Full-Time Manufacturer Sales Representative	Broker
Salary[a]	$160,000	—
Fringe benefits[b]	32,000	—
Travel and entertainment[c]	40,000	—
Commissions[d]	—	$200,000
Technical support[e]	20,000	40,000
Sales force training[f]	10,000	—
Ind. rep. training[g]	—	10,000
Sales manager[h]	—	—
Channel manager[i]	—	85,000
TOTAL EXPENSES	$262,000	$335,000

Assumptions
[a] One full-time sales representative needed for each $500,000 in sales.
[b] Fringe benefits equal 20 percent of salary.
[c] Travel and entertainment expenses equal 2 percent of sales.
[d] Commissions equal 10 percent of sales.
[e] Technical support equals 1 percent of sales for full-time sales representative and 2 percent of sales for broker.
[f] Fixed costs of training full-time sales representatives equal $10,000.
[g] Fixed costs of training independent sales representatives equal $10,000.
[h] One sales manager needed for every five representatives. Sales manager salary, fringes, and expenses equal $75,000.
[i] One channel manager needed when sales equal or exceed $2,000,000. Channel manager salary, fringes, and expenses equal $85,000.

wholesalers. In evaluating costs under each channel arrangement, a channel manager needs to consider the merchant wholesaler's gross margin, as well as the functions performed by the wholesaler relating to inventory storage, customer contact, granting of credit, handling product recalls, and so on.

DETERMINING THE ABILITY OF A RESELLER TO INFLUENCE SALES

The impact each reseller has on a manufacturer's overall sales was not examined in the preceding analysis, but it is possible that choice of channel reseller can have a substantial effect on sales. Resellers should be assessed by their coverage of a particular geographic territory, sales in complementary products, and total sales within specific target markets.

A wholesaler's territorial coverage of a given territory can be assessed by comparing its current number of salespeople with the number needed to effectively service a manufacturer's accounts within a specified territory. This is called an **ABC analysis** since accounts are generally categorized as A, B, and C accounts based on the required sales call frequency by type of account.

Table 11-11 shows how the number of wholesale salespeople required to adequately cover the assigned territory can be computed. In this analysis, accounts are categorized by sales potential. The highest potential account is classified as an A account; the lowest potential account is classified as an E account. Column (1) lists the average annual sales potential per account. Column (2) lists the number of A, B, C, D, and E accounts. Column (3) lists the suggested annual call frequency by type of account. The call frequency is greatest for an A account and least for an E account. Some of the E accounts can be sold through mail order or telemarketing. Column (4) calculates the required number of annual calls (column 2 times column 3). In total, a wholesaler has to make 8840 calls to adequately cover the assigned territory. If each wholesale salesperson

TABLE 11-11   NUMBER OF WHOLESALE SALESPEOPLE NECESSARY TO EFFECTIVELY COVER MARKET FOR A MANUFACTURER ABC ACCOUNT ANALYSIS

Type of Account	(1) Average Annual Sales Per Account	(2) Number of A, B, C, D, and E Accounts	(3) Annual Call Frequency	(4) = (2) × (3) Required Number of Calls
A Key account or account with very large sales potential	$70,000	40	50	200
B Above average sized account	30,000	100	25	2,500
C Average sized account	15,000	250	18	4,500
D Below average sized account	8,000	70	12	840
E Marginal account	2,000	400	2	800
TOTAL ACCOUNTS		860		8,840

Assume: Wholesaler salesperson can make 10 calls per day.
Salesperson works 200 days per year making calls.
Each salesperson can make 2,000 calls per year.

$$\text{Number of salespeople needed} = \frac{\text{Required Number of Calls}}{\text{Number of calls that each Salesperson can make}}$$

$$= \frac{8,840}{2,000}$$

$$= 4.4$$

can handle 2000 calls per year, the wholesaler needs about four or five salespersons per year to adequately cover the assigned territory. Fewer salespeople would be required if a product were complementary to products currently sold by the wholesaler's salespersons, since the wholesaler can sell multiple manufacturers' products on the same sales call.

This analysis only evaluates the total salespersons required, not additional personnel required for customer service, inventory, or credit functions. A manufacturer needs to be sure that wholesalers can handle growth when additional customers are added or when E accounts grow to become C accounts.

Another important factor is a wholesaler's performance with complementary lines sold to the same customers. Sales performance can be rated on the basis of dollar sales, unit sales, market share, or performance against a quota within the territory. The current sale of complementary products by the wholesaler can increase territory coverage for all manufacturer/suppliers as it lowers the average cost of a sales call for the wholesaler. Complementary products enable wholesalers to call on accounts that could not otherwise be profitably reached or to call on some accounts more often. Complementary accounts also enable end-users and retailer customers to benefit from one-stop shopping.

Yet another factor measures a wholesaler's ability to generate sales in specific markets through end-use analysis and other techniques. In **end-use analysis**, a manufacturer matches its desired customer profile by industry with a reseller's current sales history to each industry group. End-use analysis is generally based on a **Standard Industrial Classification (SIC)** designation, a classification system compiled by the U.S. Office of Management and Budget. The SIC assigns each firm to 11 two-digit basic industrial classifications based on its sales. Three-digit SIC codes and four-digit SIC codes contain narrower industry descriptions. For example, a two-digit code—36—represents electronic and other electrical equipment and components manufacturers (except computer equipment), a three-digit code—363—designates household appliance manufacturers, and a four-digit code—3631—classifies household cooking equipment manufacturers (see Table 11-12). Commercial research firms often sell listings of customers on the basis of their SIC code. *Dun & Bradstreet's Middle Market Directory,* for example, classifies firms on the basis of their SIC.

Table 11-12 applies end-use analysis to an electrical supply manufacturer. This table shows the percentage of a wholesaler's sales to various end-user markets. This manufacturer can evaluate prospective wholesalers based on their sales to selected SIC groupings. An ideal wholesaler would have a sales distribution to selected SIC groups that matched a manufacturer's market plans.

THE FINAL EVALUATION PROCESS

Regardless of the costs at different sales levels or the ability of a reseller to stimulate sales, there are certain knockout factors that should preclude a reseller from further consideration. Though differing from situation to situation, knockout factors could include a reseller's poor financial history, selling a directly competing product, refusing to adhere to the manufacturer's pricing policy, selling gray market goods, having a poor reputation, being unable to properly service a product, or demanding a large slotting allowance.

TABLE 11-12   END-USE ANALYSIS OF AN ELECTRICAL COMPONENTS WHOLESALER

Two-digit SIC code: 36—Electronic and Other Electrical Equipment and Components, Except Computer Equipment

Three-digit SIC code: 363—Household Appliances

Four-Digit SIC Codes	Industry Description	Percent of Company's Total Sales to Each SIC
3631	Household cooking equipment	15
3632	Household refrigerators and home and farm freezers	25
3633	Household laundry equipment	40
3634	Electrical housewares and fans	5
3635	Household vacuum cleaners	15
3639	Household appliances, not elsewhere classified	0
	Total	100

Source: SIC classifications are from *Standard Industrial Classification Manual* (Springfield, Va.: National Technical Information Service, 1987), pp. 223–225.

Pall Corporation, the world's largest manufacturer of industrial specialty filters, uses the following criteria to choose its wholesalers: entrepreneurial ability, a technically trainable sales staff, adequacy of territory coverage, and current coverage of desired markets. In addition, Pall seeks wholesalers for whom Pall will be their most important manufacturer/supplier in terms of income. Pall grants its wholesalers exclusive territories and markets.[30]

Table 11-13 develops a wholesaler profile for a manufacturer of industrial supplies that are sold to machine shops. The table differentiates between essential performance and desirable performance for each criterion. Unlike checklists, this profile is based on a specific industry. It also does not have point ratings for specific criteria.

REVISING CHANNEL ARRANGEMENTS

Even though channel decisions are of a long-term nature, they should not be viewed as unchangeable. To be effective, a channel system needs to reflect changes in consumer buying behavior, the relative importance of specific channels, and a firm's current product mix.

One approach to revising a current distribution system is to evaluate three different distribution systems: an ideal system, the existing system, and a management bounded system. The **ideal system** is customer driven, based on target markets served, and meets customer service standards. For example, an ideal system may use different marketing channels, based on different market segments and different customer service requirements for each channel. The **existing system** is a firm's current channel system. The **management bounded**

TABLE 11-13 MANUFACTURER/SUPPLIER SELECTION PROFILE FOR WHOLESALER OF INDUSTRIAL SUPPLIES

Criteria	Essential Performance	Desirable Performance
Creditworthiness	Good credit rating as stated in current Dun & Bradstreet credit report. Ability to secure credit from bank or other financial institution.	Excellent credit rating as stated in current Dun & Bradstreet credit report.
Territorial coverage	Cannot sell directly competing products. Must currently sell to major industrial firms within territory. Must visit larger accounts in territory at least 20 times per year.	Must currently sell complementary products. Has mail-order and telemarketing operation to effectively cover small accounts.
Image and reputation	Excellent reputation with both its current suppliers and customers.	
Ability to perform required services	Wholesaler needs to have large warehouse within a three-hour drive of territory. Wholesale salesperson turnover is low. Wholesaler must agree to send its salespeople to attend seminars from manufacturer.	Wholesaler has a large warehouse within a one-hour drive of territory.
Pricing strategy	Agrees to purchase goods with a functional discount of 40 percent.	
Wholesaler requirements	Wholesaler has acceptable requirements for inventory financing, cooperative advertising, and hold-harmless protection.	
Effect on other wholesalers	Wholesaler choice should not alienate existing wholesalers.	

system reflects management concerns relating to being loyal to certain types of middlemen, earning a given minimum return on investment, or limiting legal liability.[31] A **gap analysis of distribution channels** focuses on the differences among the ideal system, the existing system, and a management bounded system. The objective is to close the gap between the three systems by better enabling the existing and management bounded systems to approach the ideal system.

One means of evaluating alternative channels uses the criteria of efficiency, effectiveness, and adaptability. **Efficiency** relates to costs relative to other channels and the capacity of the channel to handle evolving end-customer demand. **Effectiveness** is measured by the channel's ability to cover a firm's target customers. **Channel adaptability** describes the channel's ability to innovate various skills and tasks while still maintaining its organizational vitality.[32] Table 11-14 ranks four different types of channels on the basis of these criteria.

By rating a firm's current channel design on these criteria, a firm can determine areas of weaknesses and suggest revisions in existing channel arrangements. For example, Goodyear determined that it needed to increase sales to mass merchants based on their high sales of non-Goodyear brands. According to Goodyear's president, "The option of selling to Sears had been discussed for years, but when we determined that nearly 2 million worn-out Goodyear tires were being replaced annually at Sears Auto Centers where there was no opportunity to replace them with Goodyears, there was no question about the action to be taken."[33]

TABLE 11-14 A RATING OF THE ALTERNATIVE CHANNEL DESIGNS FOR TIRES

Effectiveness Factor	Company-Owned Stores	Independent Tire Dealers	Oil Company Service Stations	Mass Merchandiser Auto Departments
Coverage				
1. Diversity of locations	Selective	Great	Very great	Fairly diverse
2. Sheer number of locations	Few	Many	Very many	Few
Control				
1. Of channels task performance (in selling display, pricing, installation, etc.)	Total	Medium	Low	Low
2. Of images channel conveys about the tire manufacturers' lines (reputation, claims made, suitability to customers' needs, attitudes of staff)	Total	Medium	Low	Medium
Effectiveness				
1. Coverage	Low	High	High	Medium
2. Control/competency	High	Medium	Low	Medium
Overall	Fair	Good	Poor-fair	Fair-good
Efficiency				
1. Cost	High	Low	Low	Medium
2. Capacity	Limited	Fair	Limited	Fair
Overall	Poor-fair	Fair-good	Fair	Fair

Source: Allan J. Magrath and Kenneth G. Hardy, "Selecting Sales and Distribution Channels," *Industrial Marketing Management,* Vol. 16 (1987), pp. 276–277. Reprinted by permission. Copyright 1987 by Elsevier Science Inc.

SUMMARY

1. *To determine channel objectives.* Typical objectives for a channel member can be to successively integrate the channel coverage of two firms, to secure widespread distribution in a particular channel, to reduce sales by unauthorized dealers, or to increase distribution for a product to new markets. Channel objectives can be examined by assessing the service output requirements of a firm's target customers. Intermediaries are needed to the extent that producers and end-users are unable to perform these service outputs or to perform them efficiently.

2. *To assess channel length, width, and types of intermediary requirements.* Channel length requirements specify the number of channel levels that are required to fulfill a supplier's objectives. Short channels enable a manufacturer to have a maximum of channel control; some consumers also prefer dealing directly with a manufacturer. In contrast, long channels enable a firm to reach a large number of customers, reduce a firm's financial requirements, divide channel member responsibilities among multiple channel members, and enable a consumer to purchase a large proportion of his or her needs from one source.

Channel width requirements specify the number of intermediaries that are needed at each level in the channel. Factors that determine channel width are the required level of channel investments, buyer behavior of target customers, and the volume of business in a market area. There are three degrees of channel width: exclusive distribution, intensive distribution, and selective distribution.

Decision making concerning the types of intermediaries to be used is related to channel width. The three different types of competitive environments are horizontal competition, intertype competition, and vertical competition.

3. *To evaluate market, product, manufacturer, and intermediary factors that affect channel length.* The classic theory used to prescribe channel length is Aspinwall's characteristics of goods and parallel systems theory. This theory has been expanded by Professors Miracle and Bucklin. Market factors that affect channel length are the size of the customer base, geographic dispersion, customer density, sales gestation period, level of customer, and average order size. Product factors that affect channel length are bulk, perishability, unit value, product standardization, technical nature, and gross margin. Manufacturer factors that affect a channel length are size, financial capability, desire for control, managerial expertise, and customer knowledge. Three intermediary factors affect channel length: availability, cost, and quality.

4 *To discuss the allocation of channel tasks among channel members.* The allocation of responsibilities should be based on reducing distribution costs, maximizing sales or profits, optimizing return on distribution-specific investment risks, meeting customer needs, and maintaining sources of market information. Factors that must be considered in allocating responsibilities among channel participants include the willingness of channel members to undertake certain responsibilities, the quality of the services performed by different channel members, the level of customer contact desired by the manufacturer, the importance of specific customers, and the applicability of hybrid channel arrangements.

5 *To study the selection process for specific channel resellers.* The selection process for resellers consists of preliminary screening, an interview to resolve questions and obtain additional information, a checklist, and higher cost techniques being used to further evaluate the most promising wholesalers and retailers (such as evaluating sales costs under different sales levels, and determining the ability of a reseller to influence sales). The final evaluation process must also consider possible knockout factors (such as a reseller's poor financial history) that would exclude the use of a specific reseller.

6 *To describe the process of revising channel arrangements.* Channel arrangements need to be continually evaluated and revised as necessary. One means of revising a distribution system is to examine ideal systems, the existing system, and the management bounded system. A gap analysis of distribution channels focuses on the differences among these systems. Alternative channels should be evaluated on the basis of efficiency, effectiveness, and channel adaptability.

KEY TERMS

channel design
service output
lot size
market decentralization
waiting time
product variety
service backup
channel length requirements
channel width requirements
short channel (direct distribution)
long channel (indirect distribution)
channel width
all commodity volume (ACV)
percent category volume (PCV)
exclusive distribution
intensive distribution
selective distribution
horizontal competition
intertype competition
multiple channels of distribution
dual channels of distribution
vertical competition
forward vertical integration
backward vertical integration
Aspinwall's characteristics of goods and parallel systems theory
replacement rate
gross margin
adjustment
time of consumption

searching time
red goods
orange goods
yellow goods
sales gestation period
hybrid channel arrangement

channel checklist
ABC analysis
end-use analysis
Standard Industrial Classification (SIC)
ideal system
existing system

management bounded system
gap analysis of distribution channels
efficiency
effectiveness
channel adaptability

QUESTIONS FOR DISCUSSION

1. Develop five channel objectives by examining the service output requirements of a firm's target customers.
2. Describe the tradeoffs between channel control and resource utilization that is associated with channel length.
3. Under what situation would you recommend that a firm consider a short channel?
4. Under what situation would you recommend that a firm consider a wide channel?
5. Contrast the characteristics of exclusive, intensive, and selective distribution.
6. Describe Aspinwall's characteristics of goods and parallel systems theory.
7. a. Discuss Figure 11-3.
   b. Differentiate between financial resources as a limiting factor versus as a determining factor in channel design.
8. Describe the factors that need to be considered in the allocation of responsibilities among channel participants.
9. Analyze the merits of using low-cost screening techniques early in the process of evaluating resellers.
10. What are the benefits of using a reseller checklist to evaluate resellers?
11. Evaluate the wholesaler checklist in Table 11-9.
12. How can you determine a reseller's ability to influence sales?
13. List five possible knockout factors that would disqualify a reseller from further consideration.
14. Describe the use of gap analysis for revising distribution channels.

END NOTES

1. Teri Agins, "Women Show What They Think of Pantyhose: Less and Less," *Wall Street Journal* (March 10, 1994), pp. B1, B6; Martin Everett, "When There's More Than One Route to the Customer," *Sales & Marketing Management* (August 1990), pp. 48–49 ff.; and Anthony Ramirez, "L'eggs Makes Big Switch From Plastic to Cardboard," *New York Times* (July 10, 1991), pp. D1, D7.

2. Glenn Collins, "Blending Kraft and General Foods," *New York Times* (January 5, 1995), pp. D1, D12.

3. Michael Selz, "More Small Firms Are Turning to Trade Intermediaries," *Wall Street Journal* (February 2, 1993), p. B2.

4. Jonathan Friedland, "Shoppers Talk, Black & Decker Listens, Profits," *Wall Street Journal* (January 9, 1995), pp. B1, B6.

5. See Mini Hahn and Dae R. Chang, "An Extended Framework for Adjusting Channel Strategies in Industrial Markets," *Journal of Business and Industrial Marketing,* Vol. 7 (Spring 1992), p. 32.

6. Louis P. Bucklin, *Competition and Evolution in the Distributive Trades* (Englewood Cliffs, N.J.: 1972), pp. 18–31; and Louis W. Stern and Frederick D. Sturdivant, "Customer-Driven Distribution Systems," *Harvard Business Review,* Vol. 65 (July–August 1987), p. 35.

7. See Arun Sharma and Luis V. Dominguez, "Channel Evolution: A Framework for Analysis," *Journal of the Academy of Marketing Science,* Vol. 20 (1992), pp. 1–15.

8. Thomas L. Powers, "Industrial Distribution Options: Trade-Offs to Consider," *Industrial Marketing Management,* Vol. 18 (1989), p. 157.

9. E. Raymond Corey, *Industrial Distribution Systems* (Boston: Harvard Business School, 1989), p. 7.

10. Scott McCartney, "TI's Notebook Computers Have Competitors Worried," *Wall Street Journal* (January 11, 1995), p. B4.

11. Robert J. Dolan, *Distribution Policy* (Boston: Harvard Business School, 1992), p. 4.

12. See Allan J. Magrath and Kenneth G. Hardy, "Six Steps to Distribution Network Design," *Business Horizons,* Vol. 34 (January–February 1991), p. 49.

13. Frank V. Cespedes and E. Raymond Corey, "Managing Multiple Channels," *Business Horizons,* Vol. 33 (July–August 1990), pp. 72–73.

14. *Sherwin Williams Company 1994 Annual Report,* p. 4.

15. For a discussion of the relationship of vertical integration and channel costs and profitability, see Robert D. Buzzell, "Is Vertical Integration Profitable?" *Harvard Business Review,* Vol. 61 (January/February 1983), pp. 92–103; and Saul Klein, Gary Frazier, and Victor J. Roth, "A Transactional Cost Model of Channel Integration in International Markets," *Journal of Marketing Research,* Vol. 17 (May 1990), pp. 196–208.

16. Leo V. Aspinwall, "The Characteristics of Goods Theory," in *Managerial Marketing: Perspectives and Viewpoints,* Eugene J. Kelly and William Lazer, eds. (Homewood, Ill.: Irwin, 1964), pp. 433–443.

17. Gordon E. Miracle, "Product Characteristics and Marketing Strategy," *Journal of Marketing,* Vol. 29 (January 1965), pp. 18–24.

18. Louis P. Bucklin, *A Theory of Distribution Channel Structure* (Berkeley, Calif.: IBER Special Publications, 1966).

19. V. Kasturi Rangan, Melvyn A. J. Memezes, and E. P. Maier, "Channel Selection for New Industrial Products: A Framework, Method, and Application," *Journal of Marketing,* Vol. 56 (July 1992), pp. 72–73.

20. Everett, "When There's More Than One Route to the Customer," pp. 54–55.

21. Corey, *Industrial Distribution Systems,* p. 11.

22. David Shipley, Colin Egan, and Scott Edgett, "Meeting Source Selection Criteria," *Industrial Marketing Management,* Vol. 20 (November 1991), pp. 300–301.

23. Powers, "Industrial Distribution Options: Trade-Offs to Consider," p. 157.

24. Rowland T. Moriarty and Ursula Moran, "Managing Hybrid Marketing Systems," *Harvard Business Review,* Vol. 68 (November–December 1990), pp. 146–155.

25. Cespedes and Corey, "Managing Multiple Channels," p. 73.

26. J. Davis Illingworth, "Relationship Marketing: Pursuing the Perfect Person-to-Person Relationship," *Journal of Services Marketing,* Vol. 5 (Fall 1991), p. 50.

27. Vera B. Gibbons, "The Faxable International Sales-Rep Application," *Inc.* (November 1993), pp. 95–97.

28. See V. Kasturi Rangan, Andis A. Zoltners, and Robert J. Becker, "The Channel Intermediary Selection Decision: A Model and an Application," *Management Science,* Vol. 32 (September 1986), pp. 1114–1122.

29. See Karen E. Carney, "Reputable Reps," *Inc.* (June 1994), pp. 124–125.

30. Nicholas Nickolaus, "Marketing New Products with Industrial Distributors," *Industrial Marketing Management,* Vol. 19 (November 1990), p. 289.

31. Louis W. Stern, Frederick D. Sturdivant, and Gary A. Getz, "Accomplishing Marketing Channel Change: Paths and Pitfalls," *European Management Journal,* Vol. 11 (March 1993), p. 2.

32. Allan J. Magrath and Kenneth G. Hardy, "Selecting Sales and Distribution Channels," *Industrial Marketing Management,* Vol. 16 (1987), pp. 273–278.

33. Julie Liesse, "How Goodyear Rebounded," *Advertising Age* (October 19, 1992), p. 53.

CASE 1

SNAP-ON INCORPORATED: EVALUATING CHANNEL DESIGN

Snap-On Incorporated is the largest single-source manufacturer of hand tools and service equipment for the U.S. auto service industry. The firm sells over 14,000 items which are divided into four product groups: hand tools, power tools, tool storage products, and diagnostics and shop equipment. In 1993, Snap-On reported a net income of $86 million on sales totaling $1.1 billion.

Most of Snap-On's products have been aimed at the automotive market, but many are applicable to manufacturing, assembly applications, and industrial maintenance and repair. In 1993, 83 percent of Snap-On's sales were to the professional automotive sector, 15 percent to the industrial sector, and the remaining 2 percent to non-U.S. distributors.

Snap-On's professional sector is comprised of two different markets: professional technicians and shop owners. Whereas professional technicians purchase Snap-On's tools and equipment for their own use, shop owners purchase the firm's equipment for use by multiple technicians within a service facility or garage.

Snap-On believes that it originated the mobile dealer van of marketing hand tools and equipment to professional technicians. Under this technique, a dealer visits automobile dealerships, specialty service chains (such as transmission, muffler, and tuneup specialists), and independent service stations on a weekly basis. The dealer explains the firm's new products, offers technical service, and fulfills Snap-On's warranty replacement functions. Each of Snap-On's dealers operate a van-type vehicle that houses their inventory. Dealers purchase products at a discount from list price and resell them to customers at prices of the dealer's choosing. Most dealers have a clearly defined sales route. The size of each route is based on the ability of dealers to service its accounts on a weekly basis.

Since 1991, all new dealers and a majority of existing U.S. dealers have been enrolled as franchisees of the corporation. At the beginning of 1993, approximately 2600 or 77 percent of all U.S. dealers were enrolled as franchisees. A National Dealer Advisory Council, elected by dealers, assists Snap-On in identifying and implementing enhancements to the franchise program. In some cases, a prospective dealer can work as an employee sales representative for up to one year. This program is designed primarily for franchise candidates who do not have the capital to purchase a franchise or who are uncertain of their aptitude for mobile van sales work.

A major advantage of the van form of marketing is that the service station mechanic does not have to leave the shop to purchase tools. Since most technicians are paid on a flat rate (based on each job and not per hour), the van form of distribution saves the technicians time since they do not have to leave their job to purchase tools. Another major advantage of the van form of distribution is the long-term social relationship between service technicians and the van drivers.

Other major competitors in this sector that use van type programs are Stanley (with its MAC Tools and MATCO units), Vulcan, and Cornwell. Each of these competitors offers similar financing programs, long-term warranties, and repair programs that are similar to Snap-On's. Other firms such as Sears, Roebuck and Company, Home Depot, and small hardware shops also offer auto repair products; in general, however, none offers the range of products or convenience of van operations. Snap-On realizes that the van market has been getting more competitive. In addition, better auto quality, greater emphasis on warranty sales by new car dealerships, and slower auto technician personnel turnover makes its overall market conditions less favorable.

Snap-On sells sophisticated diagnostic equipment (such as engine analyzers, air emissions testing, wheel balancing and servicing equipment, and air conditioner refrigerant recycling equipment) to service stations, auto dealers, and auto repair shops. This equipment is sold through Snap-On dealers and technical representatives that are employees of Snap-On. These technical reps also train a dealer's employees in how to use equipment. Technical reps are paid on a commission basis according to sales volume generated. Dealers receive a smaller discount than the normal level when accompanied on a sale by a technical representative. However, dealers share in the proceeds of many of the sales made wholly by technical reps to their accounts.

QUESTIONS

1. Describe Snap-On's channel system using the terms in this chapter.
2. Compare the distribution channel for Snap-On versus that for imported tools that are sold through importers and mass merchandisers. Evaluate the advantages and disadvantages of each channel system.
3. Apply Aspinwall's characteristics of goods and parallel systems theory to Snap-On's tools.
4. How should Snap-On revise its distribution system in light of poorer market conditions?

Sources: Gary Hoover, Alta Campbell, and Patrick J. Spain, eds., *Hoover's Handbook of American Business 1995* (Austin, Tex.: The Reference Press, 1994), pp. 962–963; *Snap-On Tools Corporation 1994 Annual Report;* and *Snap-On Tools Corporation Form 10-K for the Fiscal Year Ended January 1, 1994.*

CASE 2

ALBERTO-CULVER: CHANNEL STRATEGY FOR SALLY BEAUTY SUPPLY

The profitability of Alberto-Culver's traditional products, shampoos, conditioners, and hair sprays has dried up. The firm sold close to $300 million worth of Alberto VO5 products worldwide in 1994, but its profit margin has dropped substantially from its 1987 levels. Alberto-Culver has been unable to sell its more costly and higher profit margin products in the United States owing to its low-cost image, extensive competition for shelf space in U.S. drug stores and supermarkets, and the high advertising costs needed to gain consumer recognition and acceptance for its new products in domestic markets.

The bright spot for Alberto-Culver is its Sally Beauty Supply and foreign operations. Sally Beauty Supply is Alberto-Culver's fast-growing chain of 1386 wholly owned beauty products stores. This chain accounted for 52 percent of Alberto-Culver's 1994 revenues and 76 percent of its operating profits. Overall, the firm had 1994 profits of $85 million on revenues of $1.2 billion (7.1 percent of sales); Sally Beauty Supply had profits of $65 million on sales of $624 million (10.4 percent of sales).

Alberto-Culver purchased Sally in 1969 when it was a chain of 12 stores (11 of them franchised) in the New Orleans area selling beauty salon products to registered beauticians. Alberto-Culver's founder, Len Lanvin, saw Sally as a distribution vehicle through which Alberto-Culver could sell its higher margin products to the beauty salon market. Lanvin spent $1 million to acquire the chain and to purchase its 11 franchisees. He then began to expand the chain with company-owned stores.

Prior to Sally Beauty Supply, most salons purchased their hair care products from traveling salesmen. Now, only a few hair care manufacturers, such as Redken and Matrix, distribute their products in this manner. Most manufacturers of hair care products now sell their products to large distributors that concentrate their sales on large salons. Instead of copying the distribution strategy of its competitors, Sally Beauty Supply concentrates on the smaller salons that are typically ignored by these large distributors. Many large distributors require minimum purchase quantities that are too large for many smaller salons, handle smaller salons by telemarketing and catalog sales, or will not sell to smaller firms with poor or only recent credit histories.

Although Sally Beauty Salon sells hair care products to both walk-in customers and to registered beauticians, the great majority of sales comes from beauticians. Both types of customers, of course, have access to the same products, but beauticians are able to purchase the same products at a 20 to 25 percent discount. Sally Beauty Supply offers these small salon owners a wide choice of merchandise, discounted prices, and immediate access to goods ordered. It regularly stocks a full line of hair-coloring products from Clairol's professional division; this line of products is not sold in traditional distribution channels (such as retail drug stores and mass merchandisers). The small salon owners report that they feel comfortable in a neighborhood environment, value the low travel time, and like the valuable information on fashion trends and new products they receive from Sally's employees. Lastly, salons with poor credit or newly opened salons without a credit history can buy products on a cash basis from Sally.

This form of distribution has significant advantages for Sally. Specifically, Sally has low distribution costs since retailers come to Sally, pick out products, and take them directly to their own stores. This saves Sally the expenses associated with an outside sales force, picking, and delivery. Sally dominates this segment. Sally's high market share to this segment enables it to obtain better terms from its vendors. Manufacturers pay Sally fees of 3 to 7 percent for warehouse storage, in-store displays, and advertising allowances. Sally's largest competitor has less than 100 stores; Sally adds more than this quantity of stores per year.

The second major success story for Alberto-Culver is the firm's worldwide distribution network. Alberto-Culver has positioned its VO5 brand as a more costly brand abroad than in the United States. It has also benefited by using its vast foreign distribution network to market additional health and beauty aids (such as bandages and deodorant). Alberto-Culver is also seeking to add more products through its foreign distribution network; many products will be added as the result of acquisition. Internally generated cash from profitable operations, such as Sally Beauty Supply, has enabled Alberto-Culver to fund such purchases.

QUESTIONS

1. What are the pros and cons of Alberto-Culver's sales to small salons?
2. Evaluate the potential problems associated with Alberto-Culver's use of forward vertical integration.
3. Are financing resources a limiting or a determining factor on Sally's channel design? In explaining your answer, refer to Figure 11-3.
4. What factors should cause Alberto-Culver to reevaluate its channel design for Sally?

Source: Amy Feldman, "When Lenny Met Sally," *Forbes* (February 13, 1995), pp. 62–63.

CHAPTER 12

ADMINISTRATIVE STRUCTURES IN MARKETING CHANNELS

CHAPTER OBJECTIVES

1. To contrast conventional channel arrangements with vertical marketing systems.

2. To describe the characteristics of corporate marketing systems.

3. To examine the characteristics of administered marketing systems.

4. To discuss the forms of contractual marketing systems: retailer-owned cooperative systems, wholesaler-sponsored voluntary chains, and franchise systems.

5. To analyze the legal aspects of vertical marketing systems.

McDonald's has systemwide sales of over $24 billion form its over 14,000 stores. Since 1983, its profits have tripled to more than $1.1 billion. McDonald's current success is largely related to its increased market penetration in foreign markets. For example, in 1988, McDonald's had 2600 foreign stores and $1.8 billion in foreign revenues. In 1994, it had 4700 foreign stores in 73 countries with $3.4 billion in sales. In 1994, foreign operations accounted for 45 percent of McDonald's total operating income.

McDonald's success in global markets is due to a number of factors: quality of business partners, ability to adapt to local conditions, uniform product quality, and long-standing relations with important vendors.

McDonald's uses multiple channels for its foreign operations. As in the United States, both company-owned stores and franchises are used in foreign markets. About 70 percent of the company's stores worldwide are franchised. As in the United States, franchisees undergo a two-year process during which they must work in a store and complete a formal training program before gaining approval. Franchisees require $45,000 in cash and sign a 20-year contract. The contract provides McDonald's with a 4 percent royalty rate, 8.5 percent of sales for rental payments, and 4 percent for advertising. The average profitability of each foreign store is about $200,000.

McDonald's tries hard to walk the fine line in terms of being perceived as global, local, or American. While McDonald's is the most advertised single brand in the world, the company tries to use local sources for as many products as possible; it also seeks out and hires local management. For example, McDonald's initial task force in Poland had members from the United States, Russia, Germany, and Britain, but all except one representative are now Poles. The company also uses local partners to negotiate with bureaucratic government agencies. Lastly, it adapts its foreign menus to local tastes, offering vegetable burgers in Holland, black currant shakes in Poland, and salads with shrimp in Germany.

McDonald's works hard to make sure that its product quality is uniform on both a store-to-store and country-by-country basis. For example, its factory in Guenzburg, Bavaria, produces 2.5 million patties a day. Fat content in this factory is the same as anywhere in the world (20 percent or less). These patties are quick-frozen as in the United States. And as in the United States, this plant is evaluated on a monthly basis. In addition to ingredients, McDonald's pays attention to its service quality. Fourteen times a year, 200 McDonald's managers with two to five years of experience arrive from 72 countries for the intensive two-week program at its Hamburger University. This program is simultaneously translated into 20 languages. In total, some 50,000 McDonald's employees, franchisees, and suppliers have received diplomas.

McDonald's has had a long-standing relationship with many of its suppliers. In fact, some suppliers have an open-book relationship with McDonald's in which McDonald's sets their profits based on costs. Others have McDonald's as their only customer, yet they have no formal written contract with the company. Many of its vendors, such as meat supplier OSI Industries and french-fry marketer J. R. Simplot Company, have grown from small operations to firms that have annual sales of $500 million and more, based largely on sales to McDonald's. Ray Kroc, McDonald's founder, liked purchasing from smaller firms—believing they would be more responsive to its concerns. These firms grew at the same time as McDonald's. A German mustard and mayonnaise company, for example, that started with a $100 order some 20 years ago, now sells McDonald's some $40 million of condiments per year.

In this chapter, we review corporate marketing systems (in which a firm such as McDonald's operates company-owned stores), as well as franchising, where independent businesspeople can have chain-like qualities. We also explore administered marketing systems, in which a channel leader such as McDonald's sets terms for its vendors.[1]

CONVENTIONAL CHANNEL ARRANGEMENTS VERSUS VERTICAL MARKETING SYSTEMS

The previous chapter focused on channel design and selection in a **conventional channel**, where the manufacturer, wholesaler, and retailer are each independently owned. Conventional channels of distribution are the most common form of channel design. In this channel, decision making in terms of the types and variety of products offered for sale, the level of promotion, and the location of retail outlets are determined by negotiation between independent manufacturers and resellers.[2]

A conventional channel is the least formalized of channel structures. The relationship between a manufacturer and its resellers is less permanent than in other channel structures. For example, in a conventional channel, a retailer may view itself as more of a purchasing agent for its customers rather than as a selling agent for its manufacturer/suppliers. Conventional channels are also characterized by autonomous behavior among resellers and the lack of systemwide goals. Each intermediary seeks to maximize its own performance and has little or no concern for the overall performance of the total channel. For example, a wholesaler may be solely concerned about its sales to its retailer customers, not the retailer's sales to its final consumers. In a conventional channel, a reseller member would also willingly accept an offer that would maximize its profits at the expense of another reseller. Lastly, conventional channels are characterized by the highest levels of product variety.[3]

In contrast, **vertical marketing systems** are characterized by alliances or networks in which a producer, distributor, and a retailer act as a unified team rather than as independent entities. This unified approach eliminates duplicated services, establishes greater bargaining power, and unravels many of the conflicts with distributors and producers that each pursue with different objectives.[4] The shift in competition from conventional to vertical marketing systems is from independent business units, each operating in their individual selfish interest, to centralized and coordinated units operating as a whole. See

FIGURE 12-1 Contrasting conventional channel arrangements with vertical marketing systems.

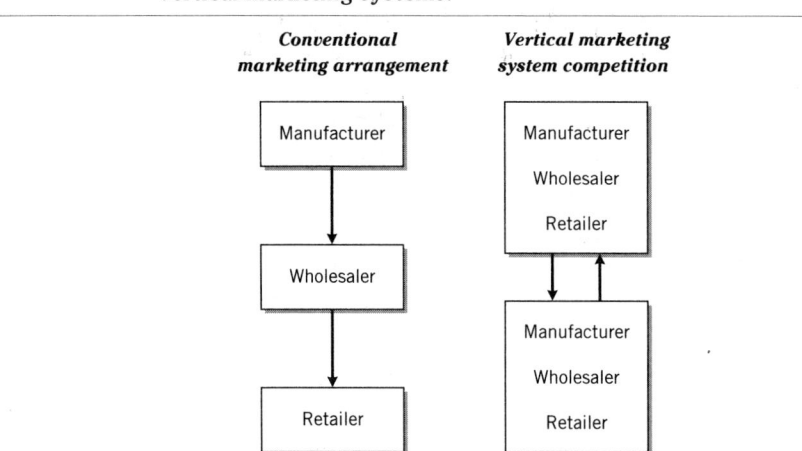

Figure 12-1 for a comparison of conventional channel arrangements with vertical marketing systems. Of major importance in vertical marketing systems is the assumption that the combined performance of all channel members as a coordinated unit is greater than the sum of independent channel members in a conventional channel.

In a vertical marketing system, power in the overall channel is centralized. Channel leadership is both formalized and determined through either negotiation, contracts, or the relative channel power of each party. Relationships in vertical marketing systems are also often based on long-term commitments, cooperation, and trust among channel members. In this manner, vertical marketing systems resemble relationship marketing. Although vertical marketing systems provide high channel coordination, they also require high investments of time and money among channel participants. Table 12-1 describes some of the major differences between conventional channel arrangements and vertical marketing systems. Although this section contrasts these alternatives, there is a high degree of overlap between a conventional marketing arrangement and a less formalized vertical marketing system.

According to Professor Kotler, vertical marketing systems have become the most prominent method of retail distribution, accounting for 70 to 80 percent of retail sales.[5] Among the benefits of vertical marketing systems for manufacturers are better inventory planning due to sharing of sales data from wholesalers and retailers; increased reseller trust developed from a long-term relationship, better control over product merchandising at the retail level, and improved coordination of marketing efforts throughout the entire channel. Among the benefits of vertical marketing systems for wholesalers and retailers are improved marketing, financial, and troubleshooting assistance from manufacturers and suppliers; association with a product that has a strong brand image; dealing with manufacturers and suppliers that take a long-term perspective with a wholesaler and retailer; and limited horizontal and intertype competition through use of exclusive or selective distribution. All resellers benefit from the division of channel activities based on the competencies of each reseller.

TABLE 12-1 DIFFERENCES BETWEEN CONVENTIONAL CHANNEL ARRANGEMENTS AND VERTICAL MARKETING SYSTEMS

Characteristic	Conventional Channel Arrangement	Vertical Marketing System
Nature of contacts	Negotiation on an individual basis	Advanced joint planning for an extended time period
Information considered	Supplier sales presentation data	Retailer's merchandising data
Supplier participants	Supplier's territorial salesperson	Salesperson and major regional or headquarters executive
Retailer participants	Buyer	Various executives, perhaps top management
Retailer's goals	Sales gain and percent markup	Programmed total profitability
Supplier's goals	Big order on each call	Continuing profitable relationship
Nature of performance evaluation	Event-centered; primarily related to sales volume and other short-term performance criteria	Specific performance criteria written into the program

Source: Ronald L. Ernst, "Distribution Channel Detenté Benefits Suppliers, Retailers, and Consumers," *Marketing News* (March 7, 1980), p. 19.

A major disadvantage of a vertical marketing system is **constrained decision making**. Through constrained decision making, decision making related to store hours, involvement in a cooperative advertising program, merchandise depth and width, and vendor selection may be severely limited by contract, or manufacturer and supplier channel power. Constrained decision making may prohibit an individual channel member from maximizing its profits or even effectively serving its clientele.

This chapter reviews three types of vertical marketing systems: corporate, administered, and contractual.

CORPORATE MARKETING SYSTEMS

In **corporate marketing systems**, all production and distribution activities are controlled by one firm through common ownership. In all other forms of vertical marketing systems and in conventional channel arrangements, channel activities are performed by individually owned firms. Since all distribution activities are performed by one firm, corporate marketing systems are distinguished by the highest possible levels of coordination and control. A manufacturer can diversify into wholesale or retail businesses, and a retailer can diversify into wholesale and manufacturing ventures through corporate marketing systems.

As discussed in Chapter 11, in **forward vertical integration**, manufacturers acquire or build up retail channels, or wholesalers acquire or develop retail channels. There are three major advantages of forward vertical integration. First, common ownership enables a manufacturer or wholesaler to control the way in which its merchandise is displayed, promoted, sold, delivered, installed, and repaired. Avon, Sherwin-Williams, and Allstate Insurance are examples of firms with forward vertical integration. For example, Allstate Insurance is sold directly by Allstate employees who only sell one brand of insurance, rather than by independent agents that sell competing brands.

Second, forward vertical integration enables a channel member to quickly determine consumer trends. According to two experts, manufacturers such as Coach and Burberry entered retailing not so much to build profits as to control or enhance their brand images and to create laboratories for new products. The ownership of retail stores by these manufacturers provided them with valuable communication with consumers.[6]

Third, forward vertical integration enables a wholesaler to refine its marketing strategy to its resellers. For example, SuperValu's chairman and president argued that its corporate store program enabled SuperValu to become a better wholesaler through determining promotional allowances offered by manufacturers.[7]

In contrast to forward vertical integration, in **backward vertical integration**, retailers purchase or develop wholesale operations, wholesalers acquire or build manufacturing operations, or retailers purchase or develop manufacturing operations. Channel members often use backward vertical integration to assure themselves a continuous source of supply. For example, it is common for large supermarket operations to own bakeries, dairies, and ice cream production facilities. Sears has an ownership interest in many of its suppliers.

A potential problem with corporate marketing systems is the extent to which a single firm can effectively operate as a manufacturer, wholesaler, and a retailer. In some cases, it may be less costly if resellers perform wholesale and retail activities and if a manufacturer monitors their performance.[8]

Many channel members utilize dual channels of distribution, with a corporate marketing system being one of the channels. For example, SuperValu, the nation's largest food distributor, is also the fourteenth largest food retailer (with 246 corporate stores as of September 1993).[9] Ralph Lauren distributes its products through its own stores, as well as department and specialty stores. However, its own stores only sell Lauren-branded products. Phillips-Van Heusen operates more than 300 outlet stores, and Harvé Benard Ltd. has 40 outlet stores. Both manufacturers widely distribute their goods to independently owned retailers.[10] Many of the major oil refiners also own and operate their own retail outlets, as well as sell through independently owned gas stations.

Some suppliers argue that their own stores have helped customers by expanding name recognition, displaying merchandise attractively, and acting as test sites for new merchandise. Some competing retailers, however, have become suspicious of competing with their suppliers.[11]

Some firms that in the past have utilized corporate marketing systems have sold off parts of their manufacturing or retail operations. For example, Hartmarx retreated from its retail operations by either closing or selling all of its retail store units. (See the accompanying "Channels in Action" box.) In 1993, Tandy Corporation sold its personal computer manufacturing operations to AST Research Inc. and also sold Lika, a printed circuit board manufacturer, in 1994. In contrast to Hartmarx which will now focus on its manufacturing operations, Tandy will now concentrate on the development of Radio Shack, Incredible Universe, and Computer City retail store units.[12] In 1994, Liz Claiborne closed its unprofitable First Issue clothing chain of 77 women's clothing stores. This resulted in a pretax charge of between $20 and $30 million.[13]

Other firms have shifted from corporate marketing systems to modular corporations wherein a manufacturer outsources production activities to independent, but closely coordinated, organizations. Modular corporations are used to reduce investment and to free up capital for uses where the firm has a competitive advantage. For example, Brooks Brothers now has all suits, slacks, and sports coats made by outside suppliers. According to the firm's chief executive officer, "Our manufacturing base is no longer absorbing precious capital."[14]

An important managerial concern is ascertaining the relative profitability of the firm's manufacturing, wholesaling, and retailing activities in a corporate marketing system. The profitability of each channel activity is based on the **transfer price**, the price set for a product sold through a company-owned channel. Although the total profits to the company will be the same no matter how they are distributed among its manufacturing, wholesale, or retail units, the transfer price determines the relative profitability of each of the firm's units. The transfer price may also affect asset allocation within the firm, as well as staff bonuses and raises in each unit. The transfer price problem is simplified when a firm sells the same products or services through dual channels (such as vertically integrated and conventional channels) and uses the conventional system market price as the transfer price.[15]

The next section will review the characteristics of administered marketing systems.

ADMINISTERED MARKETING SYSTEMS

In the second form of vertical marketing system, **administered marketing systems**, the dominant firm in the channel allocates and coordinates the responsibilities of each reseller. An administered marketing system is closest to a conventional marketing arrangement. There is no ownership linkage or formal long-term contract among different channel members. However, a much closer degree of coordination exists among channel members in an administered marketing system. This system closely follows relationship marketing. It is based on long-term relationships, trust, and the sharing of information between suppliers and resellers.

For an administered marketing system to function effectively, each channel member needs to recognize one member of the channel as the leader and to

CHANNELS IN ACTION

Hartmarx's Return to Its Roots

Hartmarx is the largest U.S. manufacturer of men's suits, sportscoats, and slacks. It manufactures such famous brands as Hart Schaffner & Marx, Pierre Cardin, Austin Reed, and Hickey-Freeman. Market analysts have estimated that Hartmarx has a 25 percent market share in the high-end men's suit market.

The firm traces its history to 1872, when three clothiers contracted with independent tailors to supply suits for their Chicago retail store. They soon began selling suits and other men's garments to other merchants. Between 1935 and 1970, the partners began purchasing such men's clothing retail chains as Wallach Brothers (New York), Hanny's (Arizona), Hickey-Freeman (Chicago, New York, and Detroit), and Field Brothers (New York). The retail chain became so powerful that in 1970, a federal antitrust decree ordered it to sell 30 of its 238 men's clothing stores and to refrain from further purchases over the next 10 years (without the court's approval). In the 1980s, it purchased Kuppenheimer's and Raleigh clothing stores (Washington, D.C.) to further diversify from the company's long-standing base in manufacturing. At one point, its retail store division had 225 stores under 35 different names. Each store group was headed by its own president.

Its diversification formula into retailing worked well until the 1990s. Retail outlets were captive outlets for the firm's clothing, and Hartmarx was able to control its retail pricing, the quality of alterations, sales force selection and training, and its store locations. Soon, however, Hartmarx began to suffer from poor sales due to the popularity of European fashions, the acceptance of more casual attire among many businesses, and the feeling among many younger customers that Hartmarx's clothing was too conservative.

Hartmarx began to close its unprofitable stores in 1990; eventually, it sold or closed almost all of its retail stores. It added Italian makers Nino Ceruti and Krizia to its manufacturing operations. Hartmarx also began to move into new distribution channels, such as producing suits under J. C. Penney's private label brand. Without its retail stores, Hartmarx is a much smaller company. Its 1994 sales were down 32 percent from their 1992 level.

Sources: Harlan S. Byrne, "Hartmarx Corp.," *Barron's* (April 5, 1993), pp. 49–50; Bruce Fox, "For Hartmarx, Hard Times Fuel Ingenuity," *Chain Store Age Executive* (September 1993), pp. 59 ff.; Gary Hoover, Alta Campbell, and Patrick J. Spain, eds., *Hoover's Handbook of American Business 1995* (Austin, Tex.: Reference Press, 1994), pp. 610–611; and Gregory A. Patterson, "Hartmarx, Having Restyled Itself, Sees Robust Profits," *Wall Street Journal* (May 31, 1995), p. B4.

yield to the leader's influence. The channel leader's role in an administered marketing system is to motivate the independently owned resellers to work together as a coordinated unit. A channel member may be recognized as a channel leader on the basis of coercive power, reward power, referent power, expertise power, persuasion power, legitimate power, and information power.

The following example explains how a manufacturer can use each of these forms of power:

- Coercive power—a manufacturer can threaten to refuse to sell products to a retailer with a poor customer service record.
- Reward power—a manufacturer can offer a complying retailer a sought-after product that is in short supply.
- Referent power—a manufacturer derives power due to the status of its brands or its retailers.
- Expertise power—a manufacturer can receive power through its superior promotional skills.
- Persuasion power—a manufacturer is accepted as channel leader on rational grounds.
- Legitimate power—wholesalers and retailers acknowledge a manufacturer's right to evaluate their performance.
- Information power—a manufacturer has valuable market research data that is sought after by resellers.

These forms of power are explained further in Chapter 13.

Two characteristics of administered marketing systems are the shifting of functions among channel resellers and the use of programmed merchandising agreements. These characteristics will now be illustrated using examples from General Electric and O. M. Scott.

An example of the shifting of functions in an administered marketing system is General Electric's (GE's) Direct Connect program. Prior to the Direct Connect program, GE used a loaded-dealer program that sought to fully stock each retail dealer. The loaded-dealer concept offered quantity discounts to get retailers to order large quantities. GE, under this strategy, assumed that large inventories of GE appliances would provide motivation for retailers to sell its GE products.

Under its Direct Connect program, GE's dealers no longer need to maintain inventories of GE's major appliances. Retailers have access to a computer program that gives them access to GE's on-line order processing system 24 hours a day. Dealers can use this system to check on a model's availability and to place an order for next-day delivery. GE's Direct Order dealers get GE's best price (regardless of order size), priority in delivery scheduling, and consumer financing through GE Credit (with the first 90 days free of interest). In exchange, Direct Connect dealers make commitments to sell nine major GE product categories, to stock carryout products (such as microwaves and air conditioners), to ensure that GE products account for one-half of their sales, to open their books for review, and to pay GE through electronic funds transfer on the 25th of the month after purchase.[16]

The Direct Connect program offers advantages for both GE and its dealers. In this program, GE gets paid quickly, is assured of dealer loyalty, and has access to excellent sales data. (In the past, GE did not know whether an order was for customer purchase or for purposes of building up inventory for the dealer.) Dealers can free up backroom inventory for more showroom space, reduce inventory investment, receive GE's best price, and achieve priority over other dealers in delivery scheduling.

Another form of the administered marketing system is the use of the **programmed merchandising agreement**. Through this agreement, a manufacturer develops a major promotional program with high acceptance by its retail dealers. Each dealer accepts the superior ability of the manufacturer to develop a total promotional program. For example, O. M. Scott, a lawn products manufacturer, provides its dealers with a comprehensive training program that covers both marketing skills and technical lawn care maintenance. Important dealers also receive tailor-made promotional programs. In a recent program, Scott sought to attract dealers to stock products in the fall which were usually pur-

CHANNELS IN ACTION

Channel Partnerships Between Manufacturers and Retailers

Increased use of brand extensions by manufacturers and the large number of new products introduced have increased the demand for retail shelf space. Retailers are increasingly evaluating shelf space profitability and asking manufacturers with poorly selling items to remove these from their shelves.

As a consequence, many manufacturers are now establishing "partnerships" with their most important retailer customers. These manufacturers are now taking on more functions that were previously reserved for retailers.

For example, Wrangler has begun a five-part Wrangler Partners Program for its key customers. In this program, Wrangler helps its retailers set up displays, assists in developing promotions, and monitors inventory levels. Wrangler monitors sales through an electronic data interchange system that determines slow- and fast-selling merchandise. According to Wrangler's vice president of retail services, "For the first time, we're doing our planning and forecasting based on consumer demands instead of retailers' orders, which takes us directly to the source." Wrangler has also developed special racks for retailers that enhance the presentation of the merchandise.

Brown & Haley, a West Coast manufacturer of fine chocolates, has also used the partnership approach to help ensure distribution. Brown & Haley was faced with the loss of Pay'n Save, one of its largest chain drug store accounts. Pay'n Save complained that Brown & Haley's line of candy was unprofitable. The manufacturer developed a plan to make the chocolate profitable for Pay'n Save based on consumer research. Brown & Haley promoted its chocolates with a campaign using phrases such as "the one the Swiss aren't neutral about," and "enough to melt an English stiff upper lip." The ads were backed up by in-store taste tests and special promotions. Brown & Haley even supplied clerks to set up and maintain displays. According to Brown & Haley's president, "The more important we are to our retailers, the less they can afford to get rid of us."

Source: Stephanie Strom, "More Suppliers Helping Stores Push the Goods," *New York Times* (January 20, 1992), pp. D1, D8.

chased by dealers in the spring. Participating dealers were eligible for a drawing to attend a World Series game. In addition, Scott had a separate contest for the best display of its products. The winning retailer received a trip to any spring training site. Both incentives were tied into Scott's corporate baseball sponsorship.[17] Such promotional offers help develop and maintain long-term relationships between Scott and its dealers. Other manufacturers that rely heavily on programmed merchandising agreements are Magnavox for consumer electronics and Corning in cookware.

The advantages of administered marketing programs include high coordination among independent channel members, focus of all channel members on a common goal, increased sharing of information, and task specialization based on a channel member's effectiveness and efficiency. A disadvantage is potential channel conflict owing to a lack of acceptance of a channel member's power.

We will now cover the last form of vertical marketing system, the contractual marketing system.

CONTRACTUAL MARKETING SYSTEMS

In contrast with administered marketing systems, **contractual marketing systems** achieve coordination among independent resellers through legal agreements that specify the responsibilities of each party. A contract formalizes work procedures, policies, and rules for each channel member. In addition, strict controls constrain a firm's level of independent decision making.[18] Con-tractual marketing systems are similar to administered marketing systems in that the functions of channel members may shift to include such activities as promotion and direct management of retail operations.[19]

The three forms of contractual vertical marketing systems are retailer-owned cooperative systems, wholesaler-sponsored voluntary chains, and franchise systems.

RETAILER-OWNED COOPERATIVE SYSTEMS

Retailer-owned cooperative systems are created when independent retailers form associations that purchase, lease, or build wholesale facilities. When retailers join a retailer-owned cooperative, they agree not only to purchase a minimum volume of merchandise, but also to purchase shares in the cooperative. (Some shares may be voting, others may be nonvoting.)

There are many variations to retailer-owned cooperative systems. For example, many food-based co-ops now have stock-based ownership. Some co-ops have divisions that are on a profit basis, and others have directors that are not members.[20] Retailer-owned cooperatives may also handle dividend payouts in different ways. Associated Food Stores, based in Salt Lake City, retains 50 percent of patronage dividends for five years. After that period, retailers can elect to leave this amount with the cooperative. Retailers then receive the prime rate less 1 percent as interest payment. If a retailer needs capital, it can then borrow it at an interest rate of 1 percent above the prime rate. Wakefern pays dividends as a share of earnings of each product department in proportion to the dollar volume done by the member with that product department.

In a major study of independents, retailer-owned cooperative systems, and wholesaler-sponsored voluntary chains in the hardware industry, dealer cooperatives were found to be more formalized than wholesaler voluntaries. The high degree of formalization reflects the cooperative's use of rules and procedures to administer the system. Instead of hierarchical authority, cooperatives are administered by effective procedures that appeal to its membership.[21] Retailer-owned cooperative systems are also characterized by power being diffused through the retailer membership.[22]

The same study also found that retailer-owned cooperatives lead the other two formats (independents and wholesaler-sponsored voluntary chains) in differentiation by emphasizing their wholesale affiliation through signage, distributor brands, and advertising.[23]

Retailer-owned wholesale cooperatives are common in the hardware field (such as with Ace Hardware, Cotter, HWI, and True Value) and in the supermarket field (such as with Topco, Associated Food Stores, Wakefern [ShopRite], Twin County, and Certified Grocers of California). In the grocery-related business, there were 53 retailer-owned cooperatives in 1991 versus 70 in 1985.[24]

An example of a retailer-owned cooperative is Florists' Transworld Delivery Association (FTD). FTD processes consumer floral delivery requests, designs promotions and new products for members, and produces supplies for members. Traditionally, a caller places an order with a local affiliated florist, the florist then sends the order through the FTD Mercury phone network to the florist that would make up the floral arrangement, and the florist then delivers the floral arrangement. In its 1993 fiscal year, FTD-member florists delivered about 18.5 million flowers-by-wire; FTD generated sales of $650 million.[25]

Another example of a retailer-owned cooperative is Topco, the nation's largest retailer-owned cooperative, with annual purchases of more than $3.5 billion. Member-owners account for more than 14 percent of all retail supermarket volume in the United States. Topco affiliation provides its members with low-cost benefits due to its high bargaining power with suppliers of groceries, perishables, operating supplies (such as shopping bags), and store fixtures. Members can also purchase shared marketing and financial services.[26]

There are several variations of retailer-owned cooperatives. In one variation, a retailer-owned cooperative sells franchises and grants members exclusive territories. This kind of group is sometimes started by franchisees that have broken away from a franchisor. For example, an estimated 100 former Mister Donut franchises have started a breakaway company, Donut Connection Cooperative. The retailer-owned cooperative handles purchasing for its members, sells franchises, and offers marketing and other services that franchisors would generally handle. The cooperative charges lower fees to members than they would have to pay as Dunkin' Donuts franchises, according to a board member. Members are given territorial protection; new members must be more than two miles from an existing unit. Dunkin' Donuts does not provide similar territorial protection.[27]

The advantages of retailer-owned cooperatives generally relate to providing independents with characteristics that are normally associated with larger chain units. Through group membership, retailer members can reduce the number of suppliers' salespeople they meet, receive quantity discounts based on pooled purchases, and have access to private brands. For example, Wakefern, a retailer-owned cooperative, has about 3000 private-label supermarket items, in addition to Elizabeth York and Farm Flavor brands.[28] Topco's private-label branded goods includes such brands as Food Club, MEGA, Pet Club, Top Crest, and Top Care. And Cotter & Company sells True Value brand products to its members to provide exclusivity, as well as to create and maintain brand and store loyalty.

The potential disadvantages of retailer-owned cooperatives relate to restrictive covenants for members, the reaction of former suppliers, and potential conflicts among members.

First, some groups have restrictive covenants penalizing members who buy elsewhere. In some cases, retailers may be able to get better buys or faster delivery from their conventional channel suppliers. Some members may also switch from one cooperative to another. The loss of a large group of members, particularly larger members, can force a cooperative into bankruptcy.[29] To reduce the threat of losing members, most retailer-owned cooperative systems have exit barriers. These **exit barriers** seek to restrict a cooperative member from leaving the group through either up-front investment requirements or the loss of rebates paid at the end of the year.

Second, a retailer's former suppliers may seek to retaliate for losing the retailer's patronage. Retaliation can take several forms. The retailer's former suppliers may withhold cooperative advertising assistance, point-of-sale materials, and inventory financing assistance directly after a retailer joins a cooperative. These suppliers can also attempt to bypass the cooperative buying group by selling directly to its members. Former suppliers can also refuse to sell to the buying group, but attempt to increase final demand for its products through promotions aimed at end-users. These suppliers may then try to show their former customers how much business they are losing through cooperative membership.[30]

Third, larger member firms may have ongoing conflicts with smaller member firms. Some large firms may believe that they are carrying the cooperative. Conflicts may also arise over the distribution of patronage dividends and over the appropriate level of retailer customer service.[31] For example, a retailer board member may be under pressure to return a cooperative's earnings as dividends rather than to reinvest it in the cooperative's facilities. Some members may also feel that cooperatives have placed more emphasis on the profitability of its warehouse unit than on service to its retailer members.

Retailer-owned cooperatives present both benefits and disadvantages to their manufacturer suppliers. Manufacturers benefit from lower distribution costs deriving from the use of a cooperative's central distribution facility versus direct store delivery. However, large-quantity discounts paid to buying group members can alienate a manufacturer's other customers as well as its wholesalers. For example, when buying groups emerged among appliance dealers, Tappan and other companies gave volume discounts to both buying groups and distributors but paid distributors a commission on territorial sales that were routed through a buying group.

We will now discuss the second type of contractual marketing system, the wholesale-sponsored voluntary chain.

WHOLESALER-SPONSORED VOLUNTARY CHAINS

In **wholesaler-sponsored voluntary chains**, independent retailers affiliate with an existing wholesaler to use a standardized storefront design, business format, name, and purchase system. As in the retailer-sponsored cooperative, voluntary chain members hope that this contractual marketing system format can deliver goods and channel support with greater efficiency and effectiveness than a conventional marketing system. In contrast to a retailer-owned cooperative, the wholesaler initiates the voluntary chain and continues to own the wholesale operation. Many marketing experts view wholesaler-sponsored voluntary chains as more hierarchically administered than retailer-owned cooperative chains. In the wholesaler-sponsored voluntary chain, the wholesaler is clearly viewed as the locus of authority and expertise, as well as the source of leadership.[32]

Except for the ownership and power difference, retailer-owned cooperatives and wholesaler-sponsored systems function in a similar manner. Members of both systems are required to purchase a given portion of their goods from a group, have standardized operating formats, and use common identification, signage, and advertising. Members of both systems also benefit from concentrated buying power, joint advertising programs, and a common identity. Lastly, both formats enable member firms to better compete against chain formats.

The strategies of these two systems are also similar. In comparing wholesaler voluntary chains with retail cooperatives, Professors Dwyer and Oh found that both systems were equally inclined to emphasize assortment, price specials, and nationally branded merchandise in their strategies.[33]

Wholesaler-sponsored voluntary chains are commonly used for hardware, auto parts, and groceries. Major wholesaler-sponsored voluntary chains include Independent Grocers Alliance (IGA), Ben Franklin Stores, SuperValu, Valu-Rite (McKesson), Drug Guild, Walgreen, Western Auto, Sentry, Trustworthy, and Pro. In the grocery-related business, there were 99 voluntary chains in 1991 versus 161 in 1985.[34]

We will now examine the specific strategies of SuperValu and McKesson, two major wholesaler-sponsored voluntary chains. SuperValu supplies its 4350 customers with more than 100 support services on an individual fee basis. The wholesaler specializes in four customer support areas: market development, financing, training, and technology. For example, SuperValu's professional development staff supports retailers with architectural and engineering services, equipment procurement, and store design. SuperValu's retail technology services relate to scanning, labor scheduling, space management, direct store delivery, and item database.[35] After SuperValu consolidated its private-label procurement and merchandising programs with Wetterau, SuperValu became the largest seller of private-label products in the United States.

McKesson's greatest strength is the 4500 independent drug stores that operate as part of its Valu-Rite voluntary chain. As a group, Valu-Rite has more drug stores than any other chain. Valu-Rite provides its retailer members with store identification, purchasing clout, sales promotions, and ancillary services (from car leasing to insurance). It links pharmacists to managed care networks. McKesson also provides its drug store members with specialized delivery services; all products are shipped in small bins that are organized by shelf location. This saves drug store owners time in restocking shelves. McKesson also acts as the buying agent for druggists in dealing with scores of generic drug producers. Finally, McKesson offers financial support to its customers.[36]

The advantages and disadvantages of wholesaler sponsored systems are similar to those of retailer-owned cooperatives. However, conflict in a wholesaler sponsored system is more likely to occur between the wholesale sponsor and its retailer members. A potential source of conflict arises when a wholesaler operates retail stores, as well as provides wholesale activities. Some retailers may see the wholesaler as taking better locations for itself, or may view a wholesaler's retail facility as a direct competitor. In contrast, the wholesaler may view its retail store as an opportunity to learn more about running a retail business or to stop a competing wholesaler from taking a preferred location.

FRANCHISE SYSTEMS

Franchise systems, the third type of contractual system, involve a contractual agreement between a franchisor and a franchisee, which allows the franchisee to conduct a given form of business under an established name and according to a given pattern of business. Most franchise contracts involve payment to the franchisor of a one-time franchise fee, a royalty fee (based on a percentage of sales). Some franchises also require that franchisees purchase selective goods and services from the franchisor, and that the franchisee pay a national advertising fee.

The widespread use of franchising today can be traced to the Singer Sewing Machine Company in the 1850s. Singer sold its products to its sales force, who in turn, had to find markets for the machines. Most early franchises involved a linkage between manufacturers and wholesalers or retailers in an effort to foster national expansion.

According to the International Franchising Association, there were 271,000 franchise establishments in 1994. Franchise sales (both franchisee- and franchisor-owned) equaled $233 billion in 1994, and 4.9 million individuals were employed by franchises in 1993.[37] These numbers do not reflect auto dealers and gas stations.

TYPES OF FRANCHISES

Franchises can be differentiated based on organizational format, type of agreement, and form of franchise expansion (see Table 12-2). It is important to recognize that this classification is not mutually exclusive. Thus, a McDonald's can be classified by service sponsor to retailer, business format franchise, and unit franchise.

TABLE 12-2 THE THREE TYPES OF FRANCHISE FORMATS

Organizational Format
- Manufacturer to retailer
- Wholesaler to retailer
- Service sponsor to retailer

Type of Agreement
- Manufacturing franchising
- Product/trademark franchising
- Business format franchising

Form of Expansion
- Unit franchising
- Conversion franchising
- Area development franchising
- Subfranchising

In terms of organizational format, franchising can occur on either a manufacturer to retailer basis (such as with General Motors and Exxon), on a manufacturer to wholesaler basis (such as with Coca-Cola), and on a service sponsor to retailer basis (such as with Hertz, McDonald's, and Midas Muffler).

Three broad types of franchising agreements are manufacturing franchising, product/trademark franchising, and business format franchising. In **manufacturing franchises**, a firm has the right to produce and market products under a franchisor's trademark. Examples of manufacturing franchising include Sealy's and Coca-Cola bottlers.

In **product/trademark franchising**, a franchised dealer distributes a franchisor's products. In this agreement format, the franchisee operates somewhat autonomously from suppliers. The dealer is able to set hours, choose locations, and set overall strategies subject to loose guidelines. Although suppliers may also sell to several retailers in a geographic area in product/trademark franchising, each dealer is generally free to sell other brands. In product/trademark franchising, retailers generally pledge to abide by sales and service policies established by their suppliers. Product/trademark franchising may also be associated with franchisees having divided loyalties among their various suppliers.[38] In product/trademark franchising, the franchisor earns the majority of its profits by selling goods and services to their outlets. Examples of product/trademark franchising include new car dealerships and retail gasoline sales (see Table 12-3).

In **business format franchising**, the relationship between franchisor and franchisee is much more structured than with product/trademark franchising. This form of franchising includes not only the product, but also operating plans, quality control, the use of prototype stores, detailed training programs, standardized operating manuals, cooperative advertising programs, and ongoing assistance and troubleshooting by the franchisor. In business format franchising, the franchisee is most dependent on the franchisor owing to the number and intensity of the franchisor-franchisee linkages. This format is more closely monitored than product/trademark franchises to ensure that a highly

TABLE 12-3 EXAMPLES OF PRODUCT/TRADEMARK FRANCHISES AND BUSINESS FORMAT FRANCHISES

Product/Trademark Franchises
  Auto and truck dealers
  Gasoline service stations
  Soft-drink bottlers

Business Format Franchises
  Restaurants
  Hotels, motels, and campgrounds
  Recreation, entertainment, and travel
  Automotive products and services
  Business aids and services
  Printing, copying, sign products, and services
  Employment services
  Maintenance and cleaning supplies
  Construction and home improvement
  Convenience stores
  Laundry and dry cleaning
  Rental services: auto and truck
  Rental services: equipment and retail
  Retailing: nonfood
  Retailing: food (nonconvenience)
  Health and beauty aids
  Real estate services
  Children's services

Source: Franchising in the Economy 1991–1993 (Washington, D.C.: International Franchise Association, 1994).

standardized format is presented at all outlets.[39] Examples of business format franchising include McDonald's, Century 21, and 7-Eleven (see Table 12-3).

A franchise can elect to expand through unit franchising, conversion franchising, area development franchising, and subfranchising.[40]

In **unit franchising**, a franchisor establishes outlets on a one-franchise-at-a-time basis. This format is often used with franchises targeted to owner/operators. In this format, a franchisee needs to reapply to the franchisor for an additional franchise in this system. This format is also generally associated with relatively slow growth.

Through **conversion franchising**, a franchisor seeks to convert an independent firm into a unit of an existing franchise system. (Some experts also include a franchisee switching from one franchise in the definition of conversion franchising.)[41] The attractiveness of the franchise's name, potential cost savings associated with joint purchasing, and improved operations are among the attractions of conversion franchising to an independent entrepreneur. Conversion franchising is generally associated with fewer methods of coordination than other forms of franchising owing to the need to accommodate existing businesses. A potential problem with conversion franchising is the difficulty in imposing constrained decision making on a firm that was independent and that has a preexisting facility that may not conform to the franchisor's prototype.

Conversion franchising is common in the hotel field, such as with Best Western Hotels or Days Inn. Another example of a conversion franchise is Snap-On Tools Corporation, which in 1991 required all new dealers to become franchisees.

In **area development franchising**, a franchisee obtains the right to develop a specific geographic area. The franchisee then builds and/or converts franchises in this geographic area. In comparison to unit franchising, area development more quickly penetrates a given market. Franchises are also generally operated by professional managers. The development of chain ownership in area development franchising has implications in terms of high franchisee power in this method. Area development franchising has been used by Wendy's, Popeye's, and Burger King. Area development is also employed in foreign franchising where the franchisor seeks a local partner.

In the last form of expansion, **subfranchising**, a franchisor appoints a master franchise which has the right to appoint single or multiple subfranchises in a given territory. The master franchise then solicits subfranchisees for its territory. Subfranchising involves two contracts: one between franchisor and master franchisee, and another between the master franchisee and each subfranchisee. The first contract establishes each party's rights, defines the territory, and specifies performance specification standards. The second contract, signed between the master franchisee and each subfranchisee, resembles a traditional franchise contract. In effect, area development franchising assigns many of the responsibilities of promotion, franchise screening, and financing to the master franchisor. In subfranchising, independent owner/operators typically manage each franchise.

METHODS OF COORDINATION IN FRANCHISING

A common characteristic of all franchising forms is the need to maintain some commonality among all units regardless of location and ownership. Commonality can be developed through legal control, economic control, administrative coordination, and secondary linkages.[42]

Legal control relates to the franchisor's right to protect its trade name and to guard against the sale of inferior products or services throughout the franchise network. In general, legal control is looser with conversion franchises than with business format franchises. A common area of legal control relates to standards designed to ensure equality of merchandise across all franchise units. Franchises that substitute inferior products and services (as in tourist areas and near major highways, where there may be little repeat business) can lower the overall value of the franchise to both franchisors and existing franchisees.[43]

Economic control relates to purchase requirements and royalty fees. For example, Southland charges its 7-Eleven franchises almost 50 percent of their profits and requires franchises to purchase their entire inventory from Southland. McDonald's requires franchises to pay 8.5 percent or more for rent.[44] In contrast, RE/MAX, a real estate conversion franchise, allows franchisees to keep 100 percent of their revenues. Franchisees in this system share certain operating expenses with the franchisor. Combined legal control and economic controls restrict the discretion of franchisees in terms of goods and services purchased, the ability to sell related products not supported by the franchisor (such as sandwiches in a Dunkin' Donuts franchise), and the ability to depart from standardized operating procedures. These restrictions constitute constrained decision making on the part of franchisees.

Administrative coordination relates to specified administrative office procedures in both conversion and business format franchises. Administrative coordination is often developed through franchise training, ongoing procedures, and periodic inspection of franchises by franchisors. In a business format franchise, these administrative coordination linkages are numerous since the entire business concept must meet the franchisor's specifications (see Table 12-4). Administrative coordination is typically linked with legal controls. A franchisor may elect to discontinue a franchise that has not met administrative coordination. (This issue is examined in detail later in this chapter in the legal aspects of vertical marketing systems.)

Secondary linkages also exist among franchisees. These may be informal and may consist of cooperative advertising arrangements and franchise associations. These secondary links have become an important means of sharing power within the system.[45]

FRANCHISOR-FRANCHISEE CONFLICT

There are a large number of potential sources of conflict in franchisor-franchisee relations. Some common sources relate to a franchisor's adding a new franchise near an existing one, developing an excellent site as a franchisor-owned unit, requiring franchisees to purchase commodity items at inflated prices, and forcing franchisees to participate in national advertising programs (which many franchisees view as facilitating the sale of franchised units for the franchisor). These and other conflict areas are identified in Table 12-5.

TABLE 12-4 FRAMEWORK FOR FRANCHISE STRATEGY FORMULATION AND IMPLEMENTATION

Type of Franchise Strategy	Type of Franchisee	Major Type of Organizational Linkages	Methods of Coordination (Extent of usage)
		Implementation	
Product/trademark	Entrepreneur	Trade name, product or service	Legal—moderate Economic—moderate Administrative—moderate
Business format	Entrepreneur	Trade name, product or service, operations, administrative procedures	Legal—tight Economic—extensive Administrative—many
Business conversion	Existing independent business	Trade name, administrative procedures	Legal—loose Economic—few Administrative—few

Source: Adapted from Richard C. Hoffman and John F. Preble, "Franchising: Selecting a Strategy for Rapid Growth," *Long Range Planning,* Vol. 24 (August 1991), p. 83. Reprinted with kind permission from Elsevier Science Ltd., The Boulevard, Langford Lane, Kidlington 0X5 1GB, United Kingdom.

TABLE 12-5 SOURCES OF CONFLICT BETWEEN FRANCHISORS AND FRANCHISEES

1. Franchisor paid royalty on the basis of sales, and may not adjust royalty rate when low price specials are promoted.
2. Franchisor may add an outlet in a territory developed by an effective franchisee.
3. Franchisor may designate the best sites for use by company-owned units. These are unavailable to franchisees.
4. Franchisor may require that commodity items be purchased from its subsidiaries, even though comparable goods and services are offered at lower cost through independents.
5. Franchisor rewards franchises that are compliant with first choice on new locations or with scarce products. Uses rewards to reduce power of franchisees.
6. Franchisor must approve buyer when franchise is sold by franchisee. Franchisor can refuse to approve multiple buyers, and then repurchase franchise at low price.
7. Franchisors typically require franchisees to buy into the national advertising program. The national advertising program increases the brand recognition of the franchise, making it easier to sell additional franchises for the franchisor. To the franchisee, the national promotional program has a high waste circulation.
8. Franchisors may not renew successful outlets after the franchise term expires.

Franchisor-franchisee relations can vary widely, ranging from cooperative to openly hostile. An example of a cooperative relationship is Blimpie's, a 149-store sandwich franchise chain. After hiring a consultant, the franchise's cofounder, Anthony Conza, learned that the franchise had expanded too rapidly and lost the trust of its franchisees. Conza flew to more than 75 cities to meet owners, formed a franchisee advisory council to get franchisees' input on key issues, launched a newsletter, and started a toll-free number to give tips to franchisees. Franchisees were also given more control over their advertising programs through the development of regional advertising cooperatives. When profitability dropped for a group of Chicago franchisees, Blimpie's even allowed franchise owners to divert their 6 percent royalty fees to advertising.[46]

ADVANTAGES AND DISADVANTAGES OF FRANCHISING TO THE FRANCHISOR

Firms typically choose franchising over ownership of wholesale or retail for two reasons: resource scarcity and administrative efficiency. The **resource scarcity** argument suggests that franchising eases access to capital and managerial resources for a rapidly expanding business. Through franchising, franchisees furnish startup capital, pay for goods based on when they are delivered to the franchisees (not when they are ultimately sold), and actively participate in the management of franchises. The **administrative efficiency** notion suggests that franchisees are more motivated than workers and require less supervision.[47]

The resource scarcity argument can be seen by examining the differences in strategy between PepsiCo's 26,800 units (Pizza Hut, KFC, and Taco Bell) and

McDonald's. Worldwide, PepsiCo owns and operates 60 percent of its restaurants, versus 80 percent for McDonald's. According to PepsiCo's chairman and chief executive, "If I were to do that [more franchising] with our international restaurants, we would reduce our capital spending [on restaurants] by more than $300 million." Eventually, PepsiCo may reduce its ownership of restaurants on a worldwide basis to 40 percent. According to a market analyst, reduced capital spending as well as money from the sale of franchises would add $1 billion to PepsiCo's cash flow after capital expenditures and dividends.[48]

Franchising also enables smaller firms with rapid growth to secure rapid market penetration and economies of scale. Unlike the owner of a unit, a franchisor's profits are based on sales, not the profitability of individual units. The franchisor also receives payments for national advertising, rent, and goods and services supplied.

The disadvantages of franchising largely relate to loss of control. In comparison to franchisee-owned units, company-owned units provide more control to the franchisor, as well as a more consistent reporting system. Those responsible for carrying out strategies are company-owned employees, not independent business owners. In addition, restrictions on the number of outlets in any territory (in some franchise contracts) may reduce the sales potential of a franchisor.

In summary, franchising enables a manufacturer or service supplier to achieve medium control at a medium cost. While it avoids the high financial investment of full ownership, the franchisor must yield some control to the franchisee.[49]

Advantages and Disadvantages of Franchising to the Franchisee

Many analysts in the past have argued that a major strength of franchising to the franchisee is the lower failure rate of franchises versus independent businesses. This finding was based on data from the International Franchising Association which stated that fewer than 5 percent of franchises fail or close per year versus a 63 percent failure rate for new businesses over a six-year period (based on Small Business Administration data).[50] This conclusion was based on studies by the Department of Commerce that surveyed franchisors, not franchisees. The 5 percent failure rate also compares favorably with estimates of independent business failures from Dun and Bradstreet. A major study by Professors Castrogiovanni, Justis, and Julian also found that the failure rate among franchises was 4 percent.[51]

Contrary evidence is found in two other studies. A researcher Bates found that of 1300 retail franchises that were started between 1984 and 1991, only 55 percent were still operating as of 1991. Of the nonretail franchises (in such fields as finance, insurance, and real estate), 73 percent were still in business. In total, 65 percent of the total franchises were operating as of late 1991 versus 72 percent of nonfranchises. The study concluded that while franchisees typically had higher sales, were better capitalized, and had easier access to borrowed funds than independents, franchisees had much lower earnings than independents. Bates concluded that the costs of fees, royalties, and required purchases may offset the benefits of franchising.[52] A second study suggests that franchise and nonfranchise groups have roughly equal failure rates.[53]

Most reports on the benefits of franchising to a franchisee discuss benefits available to independents that are generally associated with chain ownership. These include a uniform image, economies of scale, management assistance (such as technical and managerial training and troubleshooting), specialized services, ability to profit from national advertising programs, and the use of a proven operating format.

Disadvantages to the franchisee relate to inherent conflict between franchisors and franchisees, the overstating of income by franchisors, the one-sided nature of many franchise contracts, the high costs of a franchise system to the franchisee, and constrained decision making.

Conflict between franchisors and franchisees can arise, for example, when a franchisor retains the best locations for itself, or expands after a franchisee builds up its market area. In addition, although a franchisor may maximize its profitability with intensive distribution strategy, franchisee profitability may be maximized by selective distribution. One national franchise reported that 40 percent of its development group's time was devoted to resolving conflicts arising from new store introductions.[54] While most franchisees desire some form of territorial protection, the franchisee wants most intensively to develop a territory to maximize its sales and profits. Part of this conflict is due to a franchisor's income being based largely on its franchisees' sales, not profitability.

Recession and oversaturation of franchises in many markets (both geographic and by type of business) have made it more difficult for many franchises to achieve planned goals. Franchises have also been known to overstate income possibilities and to understate working hours. For example, some franchises have purchased poorly performing units at low prices in order to avoid recording a failed business on a franchise disclosure form.

Franchise contracts are also written for the protection of the franchisor, not the franchisee. According to an attorney, a contract for an international temporary agency that runs 50 pages or more has only 2 1/2 pages devoted to obligations of the franchisor.[55] In addition, franchise contracts typically stipulate that disputes must be resolved in the state of the franchisor. This requirement involves considerable expense for franchisees in terms of travel and communicating with a distant attorney. Some franchises even have clauses that give a franchisor the ownership rights to a franchisee's business phone number, client list, and equipment in the event that a franchisee wishes to terminate its franchise contract.

High costs to a franchisee can include the costs to join a franchise system, unpaid training time, royalties (that can add between 2 percent and 8 percent of gross sales), and 1 to 2 percent of sales for national advertising. In total, a single McDonald's outlet can involve a $500,000 investment.

Finally, a franchisee may face constrained decision making. Thus, a franchisee may not be able to add profitable goods and services owing to restrictions, may be forced to purchase goods and services at higher than market prices, and may be pressured to take part in national promotions that do not apply to its local market. This problem is most commonly associated with business format franchises that require standardized formats.

TRENDS IN FRANCHISING

Two important franchising trends are changes in the characteristics of franchisees and international expansion possibilities.

The International Franchising Association estimates that 30 to 50 percent of franchise applicants are currently people who lost jobs because of corporate downsizing.[56] This is substantiated by data from Francorp, a consulting firm that found that over 30 percent of all new franchisees are now ex-employees of large firms, up from 24 percent in 1992.[57]

The changed nature of franchisees has several implications for franchises. First, in contrast to franchisees in early time periods, these franchisees often have more capital to invest owing to buyout packages paid by former employers. Second, many new franchise candidates have valuable contacts that enable them to sell products and services to their old employer. Third, many new franchisees are former executives that are not used to getting what one franchise executive calls "grease under the fingernails."[58] Fourth, many new franchisees have more education (including advanced business degrees) and are less willing to accept a franchisor's total marketing program.

A second important trend is the increased globalization of franchising.[59] This is the result of NAFTA, the European Union, opportunities in many former communist bloc nations, as well as mature markets in the United States. According to the International Franchise Association, more than 83 percent of foreign outlets are currently located in Canada (9544), Japan (8975), Europe (4975), Australia (2858), and the United Kingdom (2843).[60] Research by Professor Walker found that 61 percent of franchisors he investigated had at least five years of franchising experience with at least 100 units operating domestically before expanding outside the United States.[61]

We will now explore the legal aspects of vertical marketing systems.

LEGAL ASPECTS OF VERTICAL MARKETING SYSTEMS

Much litigation has surrounded the franchisee-franchisor relationship. According to one source, since 1990, franchisee complaints filed against franchisors with the Federal Trade Commission have been growing at a rate of more than 50 percent per year.[62]

This section addresses what constitutes a franchise, tying agreements in franchising, franchise disclosure laws, and franchisee acceptance and termination. While the primary thrust of this section is on franchising, the courts have ruled that some channel relationships that are not generally considered to be a franchise are subject to franchise laws relating to disclosure, territory allocation, and termination.

WHAT CONSTITUTES A FRANCHISE

Even though they are not considered franchises, some broadly written contracts have been construed by the courts as franchise agreements subject to laws regulating franchises. Distributors may also receive the same protection from termination as franchises in many states.

Three criteria are generally used to determine whether a channel relationship is subject to federal and state franchise regulations: shared intellectual property, payment for the right to be a system member, and participation in a working system.[63] In **shared intellectual property**, the business format franchisor owns a trade or service mark that is licensed in return for royalty payments. Payment of a fee for the right to be a system member is a second criterion. While federal law generally requires an initial payment of $500, some states only require a $100 minimum fee to meet this criterion. The third criterion is the provision of marketing and operations systems for conducting a business.

For example, in a recent case, a federal judge ruled that S. B. Thomas, a baked goods unit of CPC International, had violated Connecticut franchise law. Although Thomas sought to change the territories of its independent distributors, ten distributors, in two separate lawsuits, sought to overturn these changes. Thomas maintained that it was not a franchisor, but the judge ruled that its distributors were covered by franchise law since Thomas prescribed their marketing plan.[64] Certain limousine operators, appliance distributors, and office furniture dealers have also been held by the courts to be franchises, even though none of these businesses was sold as a franchise.

TYING ARRANGEMENTS IN FRANCHISING

In a **tying arrangement**, a buyer can purchase one product (the tying product) only on the condition that it also purchases another product (the tied product). Tying arrangements are generally used to create a demand for a less popular product by tying it to a popular product. In franchise contracts, the tying product is viewed as the franchise itself, and the tied products are the supplies a franchisee must purchase to operate his or her business. Tying contracts fall under the influence of Sections 1 and 2 of the Sherman Act and Section 3 of the Clayton Act. Under the rule of reason, five elements must be present to prove an illegal tying arrangement: (1) the existence of a tying and a tied product, (2) actual coercion by the seller forcing the buyer to purchase the tied product, (3) evidence that the seller had sufficient market power to force the purchase of the tied product, (4) anticompetitive effects in the tied market, and (5) a "not insubstantial" amount of interstate commerce in the tied market.

Franchisors have generally defended tying contracts on the basis of a quality control argument that seeks to assure consistency across franchised units or on the basis of their need to provide ingredients that constituted a secret recipe. These franchisors have maintained that they have no obligation to provide a listing of product ingredients for duplication and distribution. In contrast, franchisees have argued that tying contracts require that goods and services be purchased at higher than market prices. Many franchisees would willingly allow a franchisor to test the outside suppliers' products. Some courts have ruled that a franchisor must show that there are no alternative means available to obtain the required products and services.[65]

In a case involving three Primo's pizza and sandwich restaurant franchises, the franchise agreement did not require purchase of all products from Primo's; however, it did require purchase from suppliers approved by the franchisor. The court ruled in favor of the franchisor on the basis of (1) the franchisee never submitted the names of suggested suppliers to Primo's, (2) the lasagna found in the store had not been submitted for approval to Primo's as required by the arrangement, and (3) reports of threats by Primo's managers were hearsay. To be effective, a franchisee must prove injury to competition due to a tying agreement beyond injury to the franchisee. The franchisor also must show evidence of economic pressure that influenced the purchase of particular products.[66]

FRANCHISE DISCLOSURE LAWS

The **FTC Franchise Rule**, in effect since 1979, requires franchisors to provide prospective investors with accurate and complete information regarding 23 categories of information, including the initial investment required, required fees, management experience of the franchisor, experience of the board of directors, names and addresses of operating franchises in the geographic area of prospective franchisees, a list of required purchases, circumstances under which a franchise can be terminated, and lawsuits filed by disgruntled franchisees. If profit claims are made, the FTC rule requires a franchisor to provide documentation to substantiate these claims. Federal disclosure laws are contained in a document called the Uniform Franchise Offering Circular (UFOC). Although the Federal Trade Commission sets the UFOC format, it is not responsible for franchisors that provide misleading information to prospective franchisees.

The Federal Trade Commission can grant a permanent injunction against a franchisor that files false and misleading statements under the FTC's Franchise Rule. In one action, the FTC ruled that a franchisor omitted information about the number and type of potential clients, the relationship between the franchisor and its business and personal references, the rate of return of the performance deposit, the number of states in which the franchisor transacted business, and pending litigation against the franchise.[67]

A second lawsuit, filed in May 1994, argued that Salsa's Gourmet Mexican Restaurant used fraudulent sales techniques (such as understating franchisees' costs) and made unkept promises to refund fees if promised earnings were not realized. The Federal Trade Commission won a temporary court order barring Salsa from selling any franchises without court approval. Some of the franchisees' angriest complaints related to the franchisor's alleged failure in providing training or site-selection assistance that was promised.[68]

The Federal Trade Commission oversees federal disclosure rules for franchisers, but the states may set their own tougher standards. Eighteen states have disclosure laws that require specific information to be provided to prospective franchisees prior to their investing in a franchise.[69] In many cases, state laws were motivated by the slow pace of change in federal legislation.

FRANCHISEE ACCEPTANCE AND TERMINATION

Another common area of franchise litigation is franchisee acceptance and termination. Recently, McDonald's was sued by an applicant who claimed that he conducted franchise work for a 15-month time period without pay while he underwent training. McDonald's ultimately denied the trainee a franchise.[70]

Court cases have also determined that a franchisee cannot discuss with other franchisees a prospective franchisee's business practices. The franchisor must evaluate each applicant on set criteria without discussing the potential franchisee with current franchises or the effect of a new franchisee on their business. In a recent case, the owner of a Big Apple BMW was turned down by BMW of North America for three different BMW franchises. BMW justified refusal on the ground that "their [Big Apple BMW] high volume price-discounter image is incompatible with the image of BMW." On the basis of appeal, the court found evidence of antitrust acts by more than dealer complaints. Evidence established that other BMW dealers in BMW's Eastern region "didn't want to be involved in price competition."[71]

New laws and court rulings have also made it more difficult for franchisors to terminate a franchisee without sufficient cause. As stated earlier, distributors may fall under the same protection from termination as franchises in many states.

Iowa recently passed the harshest franchise law to date, forcing franchisors to follow strict rules for franchise terminations, renewals, and transfers. The Iowa law (1) bars franchisors from opening new stores within a reasonable proximity to an existing unit of the same franchise system, (2) prohibits a franchisee from competing with a franchise in the same system after the contract term expires, unless the franchisor offers to purchase the assets of the business for fair market value, and (3) does not allow a franchisor to terminate, refuse to renew, or deny a transfer of the franchise to a new owner except for good cause.[72]

Specific acts protect franchises in certain lines of business from unfair termination. For example, the Federal Automobile Dealers' Franchise Act permits an auto dealer to bring an action in federal court to prevent a franchisor who is not acting "in good faith and without coercion" from terminating its franchise. Similarly, the Federal Petroleum Marketing Practices Act limits the permissible reasons for terminating the franchise of a motor fuel distributor or dealer. This act also provides specific procedures for terminating a franchise.

Professor Cohen, a legal expert, states that a franchisor should protect its interests in being charged with unlawful termination by communicating clearly with franchisees; documenting relationships, using appeal procedures, using the franchisor's field personnel to check on facilities, operations, and personnel of franchisee; having its field representative serve as a channel of communication with a franchisee; stating in clear terms all provisions in the franchise agreement; and retaining records (of correspondence, evaluation forms, and internal memoranda).[73]

SUMMARY

1. *To contrast conventional channel arrangements with vertical marketing systems.* In a conventional channel, the manufacturer, wholesaler, and retailer are each independently owned. A conventional channel is the least formalized of channel structures. Conventional channels are also characterized by autonomous behavior among resellers and the lack of systemwide goals. Each intermediary seeks to maximize its own performance and has little or no concern for the overall performance of the total channel.

   In contrast, vertical marketing systems are characterized by alliances or networks in which a producer, distributor, and a retailer act as a unified team rather than as independent entities. This unified approach eliminates duplicated services, establishes greater bargaining power, and unravels many of the conflicts with distributors and producers that each pursues with different objectives. Channel leadership is both formalized and determined through negotiation, contracts, or the relative channel power of each party. Relationships in vertical marketing systems are also often based on long-term commitments, cooperation, and trust among channel members.

2. *To describe the characteristics of corporate marketing systems.* In corporate marketing systems, all production and distribution are controlled by one firm through common ownership. Corporate marketing systems are distinguished by the highest possible levels of coordination and control. A manufacturer can diversify into wholesale or retail businesses (forward vertical integration), and a retailer can diversify into wholesale and manufacturing ventures through corporate marketing systems (backward vertical integration). A potential problem with corporate marketing systems is the extent to which a single firm can effectively operate as a manufacturer, wholesaler, and retailer.

3. *To examine the characteristics of administered marketing systems.* In administered marketing systems, the dominant firm in the channel allocates and coordinates the responsibilities of each reseller. There is no ownership linkage, or formal long-term contract among different channel members. However, there is a much closer degree of coordination among channel members in an administered marketing system. For an administered marketing system to effectively function, each channel member needs to recognize a channel member as a leader and to yield to the leader's influence. The channel leader's role in an administered marketing system is to motivate the independently owned resellers to work together as a coordinated unit. Two characteristics of administered marketing systems are the shifting of

functions among channel resellers and the use of programmed merchandising agreements.

4 *To discuss the forms of contractual marketing systems: retailer-owned cooperative systems, wholesaler-sponsored voluntary chains, and franchise systems.* Contractual marketing systems achieve coordination among independent resellers through legal arrangements that specify the responsibilities of each reseller. A contract formalizes work procedures, policies, and rules for each channel member. In addition, strict controls constrain a firm's level of independent decision making.

Retailer-owned cooperative systems are created when independent retailers form associations that purchase, lease, or build wholesale facilities. The advantages of retailer-owned cooperatives generally relate to providing independents with characteristics normally associated with larger chain units. The disadvantages of retailer-owned cooperatives relate to restrictive covenants for members, the reaction of former suppliers, and potential conflicts among members.

In wholesaler-sponsored voluntary chains, independent retailers affiliate with an existing wholesaler to use a standardized storefront design, business format, name, and purchase system. In the wholesaler-sponsored voluntary chain, the wholesaler is clearly viewed as the locus of authority and expertise, as well as the source of leadership.

Franchise systems involve a contractual agreement between a franchisor and a franchisee, which allows the franchisee to conduct a given form of business under an established name and according to a given pattern of business. Franchises can be differentiated on the organizational format (manufacturer to retailer, wholesaler to retailer, and service sponsor to retailer), the type of agreement (manufacturing franchising, product/trademark franchising, and business format franchising), and the form of franchise expansion (unit franchising, conversion franchising, area development franchising, and subfranchising). A common characteristic of all franchising forms is the need to maintain some commonality among all units regardless of location, and ownership. Commonality can be developed through legal control, economic control, and administrative coordination. Common sources of franchisor-franchisee conflict are a franchisor's adding a new franchise near an existing one, the developing of an excellent site as a franchisor-owned unit, requiring franchisees to purchase commodity items at inflated prices, and forcing franchisees to participate in national advertising programs (which are viewed by many franchisees as facilitating the sale of franchised units for the franchisor).

Firms typically choose franchising over ownership of wholesale or retail units based on resource scarcity and administrative efficiency.

Franchising also enables smaller firms with rapid growth to secure rapid market penetration and economies of scale. The disadvantages of franchising largely relate to loss of control. Through franchising, franchisees receive benefits that are generally associated with chain ownership. Disadvantages to the franchisee relate to inherent conflict between franchisors and franchisees, the overstating of income by franchisors, the one-sided nature of many franchise contracts, the high costs of a franchise system to the franchisee, and constrained decision making.

5. *To analyze the legal aspects of vertical marketing systems.* Even though they are not considered franchises, some broadly written contracts have been construed by the courts as franchise agreements subject to laws regulating franchises. In franchise contracts, the tying product is viewed as the franchise itself, and the tied products are supplies a franchise must purchase to operate his or her business. Tying contracts fall under the influence of Sections 1 and 2 of the Sherman Act and Section 3 of the Clayton Act. The FTC Franchise Rule requires franchisors to provide prospective investors with accurate and complete information regarding 23 categories of information. The Federal Trade Commission can grant a permanent injunction against a franchisor that files false and misleading statements under the FTC's Franchise Rule. A common area of franchise litigation is franchisee acceptance and termination. New laws and court rulings have also made it more difficult for franchisors to terminate a franchisee without sufficient cause.

KEY TERMS

- conventional channel
- vertical marketing systems
- constrained decision making
- corporate marketing systems
- forward vertical integration
- backward vertical integration
- transfer price
- administered marketing systems
- programmed merchandising agreement
- contractual marketing systems
- retailer-owned cooperative systems
- exit barriers
- wholesaler-sponsored voluntary chains
- franchise systems
- manufacturing franchising
- product/trademark franchising
- business format franchising
- unit franchising
- conversion franchising
- area development franchising
- subfranchising
- legal control
- economic control
- administrative coordination
- secondary linkages
- resource scarcity
- administrative efficiency
- shared intellectual property
- tying arrangement
- FTC Franchise Rule

QUESTIONS FOR DISCUSSION

1. Under what situation would a conventional channel arrangement be preferred over a vertical marketing system?
2. Describe three advantages of using a corporate marketing system.
3. Contrast a modular corporation with a corporate marketing system.
4. "While the total profits to the company will be the same no matter how they are distributed among its manufacturing, wholesale, or retail units, the transfer price determines the relative profitability of each of the firm's units." Explain this statement.
5. Describe the notion of channel power in an administered marketing system.
6. Contrast the operation of a retailer-owned cooperative system with a wholesaler-sponsored voluntary chain.
7. Differentiate between product/trademark franchising and business format franchising.
8. a. What are the pros and cons of the use of conversion franchising from the perspective of the franchisor?
   b. What are the pros and cons of the use of conversion franchising from the perspective of the franchisee?
9. Contrast the use of area development with subfranchising.
10. List and describe three potential sources of conflict between franchisors and franchisees.
11. a. Describe three advantages of franchising over ownership of wholesale or retail facilities to the franchisor.
    b. Describe two disadvantages of franchising over ownership of wholesale or retail facilities to the franchisor.
12. a. Describe three advantages of franchising over independent ownership of retail facilities to the franchisee.
    b. Describe two disadvantages of franchising over independent ownership of retail facilities to the franchisee.
13. Describe the applicability of tying contracts to franchising.
14. Discuss the FTC Franchise Rule and applicable state disclosure laws.

END NOTES

1. Andrew E. Serwer, "McDonald's Conquers the World," *Fortune* (October 17, 1994), pp. 103–104 ff.
2. Michael Etgar, "Effects of Administrative Control on Efficiency of Vertical Marketing Systems," *Journal of Marketing Research*, Vol. 13 (February 1976), p. 12.

3. Jeffrey C. Dilts, "A Cross-Channel Comparison of Channel Conflict," *1985 American Marketing Association Proceedings,* Robert F. Lusch, Gary T. Ford, and Gary L. Frazier, eds. (Chicago: American Marketing Association), p. 167.

4. Norton Paley, "Changing Channels," *Sales & Marketing Management* (November 1994), pp. 30, 32.

5. Philip Kotler, *Marketing Management: Analysis, Planning, Inmplementation, and Control* (Englewood Cliffs, N.J.: Prentice Hall, 1994), p. 543.

6. Walter J. Salmon and Karen A. Cmar, "Private Labels Are Back in Fashion," *Harvard Business Review,* Vol. 65 (May–June 1987), p. 104.

7. Steve Weinstein, "SuperValu: Tomorrow the World," *Progressive Grocer* (October 1992), p. 60.

8. See Erin Anderson, "Make or Buy Decisions: Vertical Integration and Marketing Productivity," *Sloan Management Review,* Vol. 27 (Spring 1986), pp. 3–19; Etgar, "Effects of Administrative Control on Efficiency of Vertical Marketing Systems," p. 12; and Lynn W. Phillips, "Explaining Control Losses in Corporate Marketing Channels: An Organizational Analysis," *Journal of Marketing Research,* Vol. 19 (November 1982), pp. 525–549.

9. *SuperValu: 1993 Distribution and Retailing Factbook,* p. 1.

10. Teri Agins, "Apparel Makers Are Refashioning Their Operations," *Wall Street Journal* (January 13, 1994), p. B4.

11. Salmon and Cmar, "Private Labels Are Back in Fashion," p. 101.

12. Stephanie Anderson Forest, "Radio Shack Goes Back to the Gizmos," *Business Week* (February 28, 1994), pp. 102, 104; and *Tandy Corporation 1994 Annual Report,* p. 5.

13. Teri Agins, "Liz Claiborne Plans to Phase Out Its First Issue Stores," *Wall Street Journal* (December 20, 1994), p. B4.

14. Shawn Tully, "The Modular Corporation," *Fortune* (February 8, 1993), p. 107.

15. See Robert E. Weigand, "Fit Products and Channels to Your Markets," *Harvard Business Review,* Vol. 55 (January–February 1977), p. 97.

16. Michael Treacy and Fred Wiersema, "Customer Intimacy and Other Value Disciplines," *Harvard Business Review,* Vol. 71 (January–February 1993), p. 87.

17. Terry Lefton, "Scott's Seeds Fall Classic Tie to Cultivate Lawncare Business," *Brandweek* (August 9, 1993), p. 9.

18. See Retha A. Price, "An Investigation of Path-Goal Leadership Theory in Marketing Channels," *Journal of Retailing,* Vol. 67 (Fall 1991), pp. 339–361.

19. Michael Etgar, "Differences in the Use of Manufacturer in Conventional and Contractual Channels," *Journal of Retailing,* Vol. 54 (Winter 1978), pp. 52–53.

20. Steve Weinstein, "Climate for Co-Ops: Partly Cloudly," *Progressive Grocer* (November 1991), p. 43.

21. F. Robert Dwyer and Sejo Oh, "A Transaction Cost Perspective on Vertical Contractual Structure and Interchannel Competitive Strategies," *Journal of Marketing,* Vol. 52 (April 1988), pp. 21–34.

22. Ibid., p. 24.

23. Ibid., p. 30.

24. Weinstein, "Climate for Co-Ops: Partly Cloudly," p. 43.

25. Patrick M. Reilly, "Competitive Floral-Delivery Networks Claim a Rose Isn't a Rose," *Wall Street Journal* (February 14, 1994), p. B1; and Richard D. Smith, "From One Little Shop, an 800-Flowers Garden Grows," *New York Times* (January 8, 1995), p. F5.

26. *Schulz Sav-O Stores, Inc. 1994 Annual Report,* pp. 8–9.

27. Jeffrey A. Tannenbaum, "Franchisees Hope to Make Big Impact at Conference," *Wall Street Journal* (January 12, 1995), p. B2.

28. Steve Weinstein, "Wakefern: A Co-Op That Works," *Progressive Grocer* (October 1991), p. 30.

29. Kenneth G. Hardy and Allan J. Magrath, "Buying Groups: Clout for Small Business," *Harvard Business Review,* Vol. 65 (September–October 1987), p. 22.

30. Ibid.

31. Weinstein, "Climate for Co-Ops: Partly Cloudy," p. 44.

32. Dwyer and Oh, "A Transaction Cost Perspective on Vertical Contractual Structure and Interchannel Competitive Strategies," p. 24.

33. Ibid.

34. Weinstein, "Climate for Co-Ops: Partly Cloudly," p. 43.

35. *SuperValu: 1993 Distribution and Retailing Factbook,* pp. 1, 6.

36. Barnaby J. Feder, "McKesson: No. 1 But a Doze on Wall Street," *New York Times* (March 17, 1991), p. F10; and *McKesson Today* (December 1993), p. 1.

37. *Franchising in the Economy 1991–1993* (Washington, D.C.: International Franchise Association, 1994), pp. 10, 11.

38. Norman D. Axelrad and Robert E. Weigand, "Franchising—A Marriage of System Members," in *The Dartnell Marketing Manager's Handbook,* 3rd ed., Sidney J. Levy, George R. Frerichs, and Howard L. Gordon, eds. (Chicago: Dartnell Corporation, 1994), p. 919.

39. See Patrick J. Kaufmann and V. Kasturi Rangan, "A Model for Managing System Conflict During Franchise Expansion," *Journal of Retailing,* Vol. 66 (Summer 1990), p. 156.

40. This section is based on Axelrad and Weigand, "Franchising—A Marriage of System Members," pp. 927–929.

41. See Meg Whittemore, "Is There a Franchise in Your Future?" *Nation's Business* (June 1992), pp. 61–70.

42. This section is based on Richard C. Hoffman and John F. Preble, "Franchising: Selecting a Strategy for Rapid Growth," *Long Range Planning,* Vol. 24 (August 1991), pp. 81–82.

43. See Mick Carney and Eric Gedajlovic, "Vertical Integration in Franchise Systems: Agency Theory and Resource Explanations," *Strategic Management Journal,* Vol. 12 (November 1991), p. 610.

44. Serwer, "McDonald's Conquers the World," p. 112.

45. Richard C. Hoffman and John F. Preble, "Franchising into the Twenty-First Century," *Business Horizons,* Vol. 36 (November–December 1993), p. 39.

46. Laurel Touby, "Blimpie Is Trying to Be a Hero to Franchisees Again," *Business Week* (March 22, 1993), p. 70.

47. See Gary J. Castrogiovanni, Nathan Bennett, and James G. Combs, "Franchisor Types: Reexamination and Clarification," *Journal of Small Business Management,* Vol. 33 (January 1995), pp. 45–46.

48. Howard Rudnitsky, "Leaner Cuisine," *Forbes* (March 27, 1995), p. 44.

49. Allan J. Magrath and Kenneth G. Hardy, *A Strategic Framework for Diagnosing Manufacturer-Reseller Conflict* (Cambridge, Mass.: 1988), p. 18.

50. Michele Galen, Laurel Touby, Lori Bongiorno, and Wendy Zellner, "Franchise Fracas," *Business Week* (March 22, 1993), p. 69.

51. Gary J. Castrogiovanni, Robert T. Justis, and Scott D. Julian, "Franchise Failure Rates: An Assessment of Magnitude and Influencing Factors," *Journal of Small Business Management,* Vol. 31 (April 1993), pp. 105–114.

52. Jeffrey A. Tannenbaum, "Retail Franchises Appear Riskier Than Other Start-Ups," *Wall Street Journal* (February 28, 1995), p. B2; and "Study: Franchising Failure Rate is 35 Per Cent," *Newsday* (March 16, 1994), p. 47.

53. Andrew E. Serwer, "Trouble in Franchise Nation," *Fortune* (March 6, 1995), p. 122.

54. See Kaufmann and Rangan, "A Model for Managing System Conflict During Franchise Expansion," pp. 155–173.

55. Serwer, "Trouble in Franchise Nation," p. 118.

56. Kirk Johnson, "Franchise Stores Lure Corporate Refugees," *New York Times* (May 13, 1994), p. A1.

57. Serwer, "Trouble in Franchise Nation," p. 118.

58. Ibid.

59. For a discussion of international franchising, see Serwer, "McDonald's Conquers the World," pp. 103–104 ff.

60. Hoffman and Preble, "Franchising into the Twenty-First Century," p. 39.

61. Bruce J. Walker, *A Comparison of International Versus Domestic Expansion by U.S. Franchise Systems* (Washington, D.C.: International Franchise Association, 1989), pp. 1–24.

62. Serwer, "Trouble in Franchise Nation," p. 118.

63. Axelrad and Weigand, "Franchising—A Marriage of System Members," p. 920.

64. Jeffrey A. Tannenbaum, "Franchise Laws Hit Firms Without Formal Programs," *Wall Street Journal* (November 24, 1993), p. B2.

65. Dorothy Cohen, *Legal Issues in Marketing Decision Making* (Cincinnati, Ohio: South-Western College Publishing, 1995), p. 276.

66. Nick L. Nicholas, "Dean O. Webb, Regency Consultants, Inc. and Primo's Partners, Ltd. v. Primo's Inc., Ferris Anthony and Carmelo Tringali," *Journal of Marketing*, Vol. 54 (July 1990), p. 95.

67. Ray O. Werner, "Federal Trade Commission v. National Business Consultants, Inc. et al.," *Journal of Marketing*, Vol. 55 (January 1991), pp. 83–84.

68. Jeffrey A. Tannenbaum, "FTC Says Franchisers Fed Clients a Line and Failed to Deliver," *Wall Street Journal* (March 14, 1994), pp. A1 ff.

69. Jeffrey A. Tannenbaum, "Senator Joins Campaign for a Franchisee's Right to Sue," *Wall Street Journal* (July 26, 1993), p. B2.

70. Tannenbaum, "FTC Says Franchisers Fed Clients a Line and Failed to Deliver," p. B2.

71. Brad Reid, "Big Apple BMW, Inc. et al. v. BMW of North America, Inc. et al.," *Journal of Marketing*, Vol. 57 (April 1993), pp. 111–112.

72. Michele Galen, Laurel Touby, Lori Bongiorno, and Wendy Zellner, "Franchise Fracas," *Business Week* (March 22, 1993), pp. 69, 71; and Meg Whittemore "Measures Target Franchise Practices," *Nation's Business* (July 1992), p. 46.

73. Cohen, *Legal Issues in Marketing Decision Making*, p. 295.

CASE 1

SHERWIN-WILLIAMS: USE OF CONVENTIONAL AND CORPORATE CHANNELS

Sherwin-Williams is divided into two segments: paint stores and coatings. The paint stores segment distributes Sherwin-Williams paint, wallcoverings, floorcoverings, window treatments, and related products through the company's 2046 company-operated specialty stores in the United States, Canada, and Puerto Rico. This segment targets do-it-yourself customers, professional painters, contractors, architects, and industrial customers whose products require a factory finish. In contrast, the coatings segment manufactures, distributes, and sells Sherwin-Williams products in five markets (coatings, consumer brands, automotive, transportation services, and specialty).

Sherwin-Williams uses multiple channels of distribution for its paints. For example, while its Sherwin-Williams brand is manufactured exclusively for sale through its paint stores segment, the company's Dutch-Boy paint line is sold through mass merchandisers. Independent paint and hardware stores get the Martin-Senour brand, and discounters (such as Wal-Mart) sell Kem-Tone. Sherwin-Williams is also the largest private-label paintmaker. For example, Sherwin-Williams produces its Easy Living and Weatherbeater brands for Sears, as well as other private-label brands for major retailers.

Sherwin-Williams's multiple brands compete with four major national brands (Benjamin Moore, Glidden, Valspar, and PPG), a few dozen regional paint manufacturers, and almost 1000 local manufacturers. Together with Sherwin-Williams, the national manufacturers comprise about half of the $13 billion per year market for paint. While the paint market grew at an annual rate of 2.5 percent per year from 1983 to 1993, Sherwin-Williams's growth rate has been more than three times the industry average.

Table 1 shows sales, operating profits, identifiable assets (those that can be directly traced to each segment's operations), and capital expenditure data (those that can be directly traced to each segment's operations). By analyzing this chart, you can determine profit margins as a percentage of sales, and return on assets by segment. The coatings segment data need to be adjusted to reflect intersegment transfers. To determine sales in the coating segments, you need to add the following sales figures to coatings that were intersegment sales: $720 million (1994), $655 million (1993), $598 million (1992), $523 million (1991), and $492 million (1990). For example, for 1994, profit margins as a percentage of sales for paint stores was 7.1 percent ($141 million divided by $1986 million). The corresponding figure for the coatings segment was 11 percent [$201 million divided by ($1100 million + $720 million)].

While Sherwin-Williams is the only brand sold by Sherwin-Williams paint stores, Sherwin-Williams's chairman and chief executive officer knows that it "cannot be dominant in the paint business with just our stores." Sherwin-Williams is currently signing supply agreements with chains like Builders Square, Grossman's, and HomeBase.

QUESTIONS

1. Evaluate Table 1.
2. a. What are the benefits to Sherwin-Williams's sales of paint through its own stores?
   b. What are the disadvantages to Sherwin-Williams's sales of paint through its own stores?
3. Could Sherwin-Williams use the modular corporation concept? Explain your answer.
4. Explain how Sherwin-Williams could determine the transfer price for its paint sold through company-owned stores.

Sources: Amy Feldman, "The House That Jack Built," *Forbes* (April 25, 1994), pp. 91–92 ff.; *Sherwin-Williams Annual Report 1994; The Sherwin-Williams Company Form 10-K for the Fiscal Year Ended December 31, 1994;* Gary Hoover, Alta Campbell, and Patrick J. Spain, eds., *Hoover's Handbook of American Business 1995* (Austin, Tex.: Reference Press, 1994), pp. 956–957.

TABLE 1 SELECTED FINANCIAL INFORMATION ON SHERWIN-WILLIAMS, 1990–1994 ($ MILLIONS)

	1994	1993	1992	1991	1990
Net Sales					
Paint stores	$1,986	$1,830	$1,682	$1,495	$1,434
Coatings	1,100	1,105	1,052	1,032	819
Other	14	14	14	14	14
Total sales	$3,100	$2,949	$2,748	$2,541	$2,267
Operating profits					
Paint stores	$ 141	$ 117	$ 91[a]	$ 82	$ 86
Coatings	201	194	174[a]	140	129
Other	8	5	6	8	4
Corporate expenses—net	(51)	(52)	(45)	(31)	(32)
Income from operations	$ 299	$ 264	$ 226	$ 199	$ 187
Identifiable assets					
Paint stores	$ 517	$ 494	$ 464	$ 449	$ 418
Coatings	$ 757	$ 730	$ 719	$ 713	$ 662
Capital expenditures					
Paint stores	$ 26	$ 29	$ 23	$ 22	$ 20
Coatings	$ 46	$ 28	$ 40	$ 22	$ 27
Operating margins					
Paint stores	7.1%	6.4%	5.4%	5.5%	6.0%
Coatings	11.0%	11.0%	10.5%	8.9%	9.8%

[a]Beginning with January 1, 1992, additional expenses associated with postretirement benefits reduced operating profits. For comparative purposes with prior years, paint stores' operating profit for 1992 was $96 million and coatings' was $178 million, excluding the effects of additional expenses.

Source: Sherwin-Williams Annual Report 1994, pp. 10–11.

CASE 2

ALPHAGRAPHICS: FROM CONFLICT TO COOPERATION

AlphaGraphics is a business format franchiser of print shops. Among the principal services conducted by its franchisees are high-speed duplication, self-service photocopying, offset printing, and desktop design and publishing. A franchisee's initial investment is between $228,700 and $413,900.

In 1994, worldwide system sales of AlphaGraphics' 316 franchisees totaled $195 million. Of its total franchises, 74 were located outside the United States. Overall, AlphaGraphics' franchisees were healthy. Systemwide sales of franchises were up 16 percent between 1993 and 1994. And average sales for U.S. stores open at least one year rose 18 percent to $745,000 in 1994 (from $635,000 in 1993).

Recently, AlphaGraphics realized that its relationship with its franchisees had deteriorated. For example, prior to the franchisor's new contract with its franchisees, about two dozen franchises withheld royalty payments. Fewer than half of the system's franchisees also submitted monthly income statements. Another group of franchisees in northern California called for a breakaway from the chain. This group eventually agreed to pay AlphaGraphics $1 million to release its members from any contractual obligations. The group paid the money to the franchisor after failing to win a fraud case in federal court.

AlphaGraphics hired Michael B. Witte as chairman in 1991. Witte, who was an executive at R. R. Donnelley & Sons prior to heading AlphaGraphics, noted that "Coming from the outside, I was used to commercial-customer relationships, and I found it curious that franchising had a rampant attitude of paternalism." After six months of negotiations with selected franchisees, AlphaGraphics offered a new contract option to all of its U.S. franchisees. When it rewrote the franchise agreement, AlphaGraphics relied heavily on input from franchisees. Witte questioned what he calls the "two myths of franchising" in rewriting the franchise contracts. These myths were, "the only way to run a franchise is through rigid controls," and "that given the opportunity, franchisees will always do the wrong thing."

AlphaGraphics thoroughly revised its contracts to be "two-sided." Nine franchisee representatives were chosen to take part in rewriting the franchise agreement. The new franchise agreement is innovative in four major areas: universal service credits, royalties, multiple-unit operations, and a franchisee buyout option.

Each franchise can use universal service credits to purchase special services. Now, 25 percent of royalty fees are set aside to pay for services of each franchisee's choosing. For example, a franchisee could use these credits to hire a computer consultant or to help with mailings. To be eligible for the service credit, a franchisee must be current on monthly payments, submit monthly financial statements, and prepare annual budgets. About 92 percent of AlphaGraphics' franchisees comply with these rules.

AlphaGraphics also revised its royalty fee structure so that instead of being a fixed rate, royalties are now on a sliding scale linked to sales volume. This enables new franchisees or franchises in developing areas to pay lower rates. Franchisees that prepare an annual business plan are also eligible to earn such incentives as lower royalty payments and additional training.

The new contract waives the $49,000 initial franchise fee for franchisees who want to open additional stores in their territories. A franchise buyout option also allows a franchisee to cancel his or her franchise agreement without cause and to buy out the contract. The settlement amount is now never more than the equivalent of three years' royalties.

More than 95 percent of the franchisees requested conversion to the new contract. According to one franchisee, "The whole relationship has become more of a partnership."

QUESTIONS

1. Discuss the use of legal, economic, and administrative controls by AlphaGraphics.
2. List and discuss the nature of franchisor-franchisee conflict for AlphaGraphics.
3. Describe the advantages and disadvantages of franchising to AlphaGraphics as franchisor.
4. Describe the advantages and disadvantages of franchising to AlphaGraphics franchisees.

Sources: Jeffrey A. Tannenbaum, "To Pacify Irate Franchisees, Franchisers Extend Services," *Wall Street Journal* (February 24, 1995), pp. B1–B2; and Meg Whittemore, "The Second Generation," *Nation's Business* (June 1994), pp. 57–64.

CHAPTER 13

CHANNEL POWER: CONFLICT AND COOPERATION

CHAPTER OBJECTIVES

1. To discuss channel power, including channel power forms.
2. To describe the methods of channel dominance and the impact of channel dominance on channel performance.
3. To explain the nature of channel conflict and its causes, and the impact of channel conflict on channel efficiency.
4. To analyze channel cooperation.
5. To evaluate conflict management and resolution.
6. To study channel satisfaction and its impact on channel performance.

According to the director of marketing services of 3M Canada, the power of major retail chains and wholesale distributors is growing. These retail chains can be viewed as channel gatekeepers, since they control the availability of a product or brands in retail stores.

The power of large chains can be seen by analyzing their impact on RCA Consumer Electronics. In the 1980s, RCA began selling its videocassette recorders, televisions, and other products to large mass merchandisers such as Wal-Mart, Sears, Kmart, and Circuit City. RCA agreed to sell direct to these chains as opposed to using its 70 exclusive distributors. Instead of obtaining the higher sales and profits that RCA had expected under this channel arrangement, RCA's new distribution strategy was unsuccessful. Its new chain customers were very aggressive in bargaining, and RCA was unable to offset its lower profit margins through additional sales. While many of these chains heavily promoted the RCA brands to achieve store traffic, they often switched customers into private-label brands in the store. These chains also did not push RCA's high-end products and more profitable models as effectively as its smaller dealers. Lastly, the high discounts demanded by large chains forced RCA to reduce its advertising levels. Ultimately, the lower promotional expenditures reduced RCA's positive brand image. Today, RCA has returned to its strategy of smaller dealers, brand advertising, and emphasis on higher-margin products.

Manufacturers have ten ways to counter the power of large retailers. These are innovation, assortment, brand-identity, profit-making, bundling, service-responsiveness, training, geographic, quality, and market-development clout. We will now examine each of these forms of manufacturer power:

- Innovation clout—Manufacturers that come out with a continuous stream of unique products can receive preferential treatment from retailers, including access to excellent shelf space.

- Assortment clout—Manufacturers should strive to dominate a product category based on sizes, flavors, types of construction, and features. High assortment clout assures high shelf space and increases a reseller's costs in switching manufacturers.

- Brand-identity clout—Brands with excellent customer franchises have high channel power through high customer traffic and brand loyalty levels.

- Profit-making clout—The use of just-in-time inventory management systems and financial support for resellers strengthens a manufacturer's power.

- Bundling clout—Package discounts and co-promotions of products from multiple divisions reduce a retailer's product and ordering costs.

- Service-responsiveness clout—A manufacturer's logistics competency (as measured by such variables as on-time delivery, backorder size, and availability of emergency delivery) increases its bargaining strength.

- Training clout—A manufacturer's superior marketing and product-based training programs offered to resellers increase its channel power.

- Geographic clout—A national or global presence provides a manufacturer with lower advertising, selling, and product development costs than a regional manufacturer.

- Quality clout—A manufacturer's recognized product quality provides brand loyalty (that becomes store loyalty), as well as a halo that resellers desire.

- Market-development clout—A manufacturer with strong market-development skills can increase consumer demand for its reseller channels.[1]

In this chapter, we explore channel power with particular reference to how manufacturers, wholesalers, and retailers can dominate the channel. Channel conflict, cooperation, and satisfaction are also studied.

OVERVIEW OF CHANNEL POWER: CONFLICT AND COOPERATION

The other chapters in this text approached distribution channels from the perspective of an economic system and were concerned largely with gaining and maintaining a long-term competitive advantage through proper channel operations and design. This chapter, in contrast, assumes a behavioral system approach to channels. Here, we approach channel management from the perspective of channel power, conflict, cooperation, and satisfaction. Much of this material relies on contributions from the social psychology and organization theory literature.[2]

CHANNEL POWER

Channel power is the ability of a channel member to control or influence the marketing strategy of an independent channel member at another level in the channel. A channel member with high power in the channel can change another channel member's behavior or make another channel member perform an activity that a channel member would not normally conduct. A manufacturer could use channel power, for example, to get a retailer to stock the manufacturer's full product line when the retailer was interested only in stocking the manufacturer's best-selling merchandise. In contrast, a retailer could use its channel power to force a manufacturer to provide it with desirable models that are in short supply.

According to marketing theorists, the existence of channel power is based on the channel members' dependency on one another. In **channel dependency**, the action of one channel member has an impact on another channel member. For example, channel members rely on each other for the performance of such channel activities as selling, channel support, physical distribution, product modification and after-sale service, and risk assumption. Channel researchers recognize channel dependency as the inverse of power. Thus, if B is dependent on A, then A has a high level of power over B.

In studying channel power, it is important to recognize that a channel member may hold power in one area but not another. The **range of power** refers to the areas within which a channel member may prescribe another channel member's behavior and expect that channel member to adhere to its desires.[3] For instance, although a franchisor may be able to force a franchisee to purchase specific goods and services, the franchisor may have little power in prescribing a franchisee's pricing levels. In contrast, a large wholesaler with a strong private-label brand may have a wide range of power in terms of developing and implementing its total marketing effort relative to its small suppliers.

There are two accepted forms of measuring channel power: potential power and exercised power. **Potential power** measures a channel member's ability to alter another channel member's behavior. In contrast, **exercised power** measures the actual alteration of a channel member's behavior.[4]

A common means of classifying channel power is the reward power, referent power, expertise power, persuasion power, and legitimate power framework that has been developed by Professors French and Raven.[5] To these five measures, Professors Raven and Kruglanski added information power.[6] Some researchers have combined these channel power forms into a coercive-noncoercive dichotomy. We will use the coercive power-noncoercive classification as the basis for organizing this section. Included in noncoercive power are reward power, referent power, expertise power, persuasion power, legitimate power, and information power.

CHANNEL POWER FORMS: COERCIVE POWER

Coercive power is based on the ability of one channel member to punish another channel member. Coercive power is the opposite of reward power and is also called the threat approach. For example, a manufacturer can threaten to discontinue selling to a retailer that provides poor customer service or that discounts its brand. A franchisor can also threaten to discontinue a franchisee based on its use of independent sources of supply. And a retailer with high market share in a given market can threaten to discontinue a manufacturer's line unless the manufacturer increases its discount structure. According to Professors Frazier and Summers, the success of coercive power is based on the magnitude of the threatened punishment, whether or not the target perceives the cost of noncompliance to be greater than the cost of compliance, and the credibility of the threat message.[7]

Some channel experts question the use of coercive power. Continued threats can force the threatened party to pursue legal action or to develop an association (such as a franchisee association or a distributors' council) to counterbalance the other channel member's power. The frequent use of threats may also magnify the level of channel conflict. Fear, anxiety, and resistance are typical responses to threats.[8] Moreover, coercive power can curtail information exchange and other positive actions among channel members that are based on mutual trust.[9] And finally, threats are a high-cost approach. For example, the costs of channel surveillance may be high. The affected party may also sever its ties with the party that has applied the threats and switch its allegiance (and that of its customers) to a competitor.

CHANNEL POWER FORMS: NONCOERCIVE POWER

As discussed in an earlier section, noncoercive power includes reward power, referent power, expertise power, persuasion power, legitimate power, and information power.

In **reward power (promises)**, a channel member can reward another who conforms to the channel member's desires. Reward power is also called a promise strategy in that there are benefits for compliance. In measuring power types, it may be difficult to distinguish between coercive power and reward power. For example, should the answer "providing service" be used to represent a reward source or should "withholding service" be used to represent a punishment?[10]

Dealers sometimes relinquish control so that they can be assured of essential resources. Thus, a dealer may yield some control to receive a manufacturer's support program. Manufacturers often feel that they must control a sizable part of the marketing mix before they are able to justify special pricing programs, training for the distributor's sales force, and so on.[11]

There are five limitations to the use of reward power. (1) Although channel member A has the ability to mediate rewards for channel member B, its range of power is limited to the specific area where A can reward B. For example, in reward power, a car manufacturer's ability to get a dealer to purchase five slow-selling models based on providing the dealer with one model in high demand is limited by its inventory of high-demand models. (2) Even though the target in reward behavior can be induced to modify its behavior, it may not change the target channel member's perceptions.[12] (3) The target may perceive the offering of rewards as suggesting that the current level of the source's performance is inadequate. (4) A target can also perceive a reward as a form of bribery. (5) Some experts argue that the offering of rewards is subject to diminishing returns; successive rewards have less impact than earlier rewards.[13]

Referent power exists when one channel member confers power on another channel member based on other brands carried or based on the channel member's overall image. Referent power is based on the desire of other channel members to identify with the first channel member. An example of referent power is a wholesaler's prestige as the exclusive distributor of an important brand or product sold by Bloomingdale's and featured in Bloomingdale's advertisements.

Expertise power is based on knowledge that one channel member attributes to another member. For example, a distributor may achieve expertise power, based on its long-term relationships with customers, and knowledge of local market conditions. Small retailers often are receptive to point-of-purchase and cooperative advertising materials that are prepared by manufacturers owing to their expertise power in promotion. As with the case of reward power, a channel member's range of expertise power is limited. For example, a manufacturer may have high expertise power in terms of advertising but low expertise power in terms of sales strategy.

Persuasion power is based on the ability of one channel member to persuade another channel member of the validity of its position. Persuasion power is based on rational appeals. Unlike reward and coercive power, a person accepts a channel member based on its role as a leader, not because of promises or threats.

In **legitimate power**, a channel member realizes that another channel member has a clear right to exercise power over it. Legitimate power is present where there is a clear power as a result of a dealership agreement or a contractual vertical marketing system. A common problem associated with legitimate power is to assume that the same degree of legitimate power exists after a former employee (where there is a direct channel of command) becomes a franchisee (where power is defined on the basis of a contract). According to Professors Frazier and Summers, legitimate power is likely to produce prompt and long-lasting compliance if the contract clearly specifies power arrangements and is viewed as fair by both parties. Where these conditions are not correct, legitimate power may increase conflict and the chance of legal battle between parties. The target can also dissolve the relationship, if the cost of complying with the contract terms is too excessive.[14]

The last form of noncoercive power is information power. **Information power** is derived by a channel member having access to factual data. Information power is not to be confused with expert power.[15] In information power, facts are accepted independently of the relationship one channel member has with another member. In information power, one channel member is persuaded to do something he or she would not do, based on objective, self-evident factual data. An example of information power would be a small retailer's access to scanner data in his or her store. These data can refute a manufacturer's claim that sales of its product increased during a major manufacturer-sponsored promotion.

SUMMARY OF POWER FORMS

Although the channel power forms were covered separately in this section, in reality, each of these forms of channel power operates simultaneously. Each channel member also uses multiple forms of power. A channel member can be weak in terms of information power but have strong overall power owing to the use of rewards and punishment. A business format franchise can be characterized by high power to the franchisor relative to the franchisee due to

Coercive power—franchisor can threaten not to renew franchise or not to approve a potential buyer of franchise.

Reward power—franchisor can offer franchisee a desirable new location based on franchisee's performance.

Referent power—franchisor's overall image contributes to its power.

Expertise power—franchisor receives power due to its knowledge of operating systems, cost structure of business, training skills, and site location knowledge.

Persuasion power—franchisor receives power due to rational appeals based on its size, financial position, and knowledge.

Legitimate power—franchisor must monitor franchisee performance as part of its responsibilities in its contract with franchisee.

Information power—franchisor has data on costs and comparative sales at other units.

Table 13-1 is a measure of a supplier's power using the coercive-noncoercive dichotomy discussed earlier. Table 13-2 is a measure of a distributor's power based on its level of responsibility regarding 17 marketing decisions and activities.

TABLE 13-1 A MEASURE OF SUPPLIER POWER

Coercive Power

Indicate your answer on a 6-point scale with the extremes being definitely agree (6) and definitely disagree (1).

My primary supplier could have made things difficult for me if I had not agreed to his/her suggestion.

My primary supplier hinted that he/she would take certain actions that would reduce my profits.

My primary supplier threatened to cancel or refuse to renew my contract.

I felt that my primary supplier would withdraw certain needed services from me.

Noncoercive Power

Indicate your answer on a 6-point scale with the extremes being definitely agree (6) and definitely disagree (1).

I felt that by going along with my primary supplier, I would be favored on some other occasions. (Reward power)

I really admire the way they run the business, so I followed their lead. (Referent power)

I trusted my primary supplier's judgment regarding the matter. (Expertise power)

It was my duty to do as requested. (Legitimate power)

Source: Adapted from Steven J. Skinner, Jule B. Gassenheimer, and Scott W. Kelley, "Cooperation in Supplier-Dealer Relations," *Journal of Retailing,* Vol. 68 (Summer 1992), pp. 188–189. Reprinted by permission.

TABLE 13-2 ITEMS USED TO MEASURE DISTRIBUTOR POWER

The distributors were asked the following question:

To market and distribute a product, several marketing decisions have to be made. In making these decisions, a distributor may have almost complete responsibility, or freedom to make a decision may be shared with the manufacturer, or the manufacturer may have almost complete responsibility. For each of the marketing decisions and activities listed below, please indicate the level of freedom or responsibility you have as compared to the selected manufacturer (in marketing the manufacturer's brand). Please check the appropriate response category.

I have almost complete responsibility.	I have more responsibility than the manufacturer.	The manufacturer and I share equal responsibility.	The manufacturer has more responsibility than myself.	The manufacturer has almost complete responsibility.

Marketing Decisions and Activities
1. Choosing geographic territories to sell in
2. Setting sales targets or goals
3. Setting selling prices to customers
4. Determining distribution policies to customers (e.g., delivery time)
5. Determining the training program for your sales force to sell the product
6. Keeping the manufacturer from selling direct in your territory
7. Product return-related issues
8. Choosing customers to sell to
9. Determining pricing policies (e.g., quantity discounts to customers)
10. Deciding to join in cooperative advertising with the manufacturer
11. Keeping the manufacturer's other distributors from selling in your territory
12. Accommodating customers' requests for product modification
13. Margins allowed by the manufacturer
14. Providing presale customer services (e.g., product information)
15. Attending sales meetings organized by the manufacturer
16. Resolving customers' product-related technical problems
17. Determining sales strategies/policies (e.g., frequency of sales calls to customers)

Source: Gul Butaney and Lawrence H. Wortzel, "Distributor Power Versus Manufacturer Power: The Customer Role," *Journal of Marketing,* Vol. 52 (January 1988), p. 55. Reprinted by permission of the American Marketing Association.

METHODS OF CHANNEL DOMINANCE

Professor Porter isolated industry, product, and customer factors associated with high supplier or buyer power. For example, Porter argues that a supplier group is powerful when the industry is dominated by a few large firms, a product has few substitutes, the buyer is not an important customer, the supplier's product is an important input to the buyer's business, suppliers have built up switching costs for the customers or the product is differentiated, and the supplier group can pose a threat of forward integration.[16] In contrast, buyers have more power when they purchase a large percentage of a seller's volume, the products purchased represent a large percentage of the buyer's total costs, they purchase standardized products, buyers have few switching costs, buyers earn low profits, buyers pose a threat of backward integration, a supplier's product quality is unimportant, buyers have full information, and buyers can influence their customers' buying decisions.[17]

This section explores the use of marketing strategies by manufacturers, wholesalers, and retailers to attain and maintain their respective channel power. The dominant member of the channel or channel leader is called the **channel captain**.

METHODS OF MANUFACTURER DOMINANCE

Table 13-3 lists some of the sources of power used by manufacturers in their quest to be channel captain. Because of space constraints, only the first eight power sources are discussed here. A manufacturer's power may be based on economic scale, high market share, brand loyalty, franchising, refusal to deal, distributor termination, vertical integration, and push money. Some of these methods, such as refusal to deal and distributor termination, are based on coercive power; others, such as franchising, are based on legitimate power; and still others, such as economic scale and high market share, are based on economic power.

Economic scale refers to a channel's power owing to its overall size. A manufacturer with large relative sales, market share, or assets generally has high bargaining power. One way for a manufacturer to increase its economic power is to find common products that are used by the entire corporation and then centralize its buying. According to the head of procurement at Chrysler, "The advantages of decentralization don't show up in purchasing."[18]

TABLE 13-3   SOURCES OF MANUFACTURER POWER

- Having high economic scale
- Having high market share in served markets
- High brand loyalty
- Using franchising
- Refusing to deal with selected wholesalers and retailers
- Threatening distributor termination
- Using vertical integration
- Using push money
- Adding another distributor to a reseller's territory
- Full-line forcing to sell slow-moving merchandise
- Tying agreements to sell slow-moving merchandise
- Offering goods in short supply to preferred wholesalers and retailers
- Offering large-quantity discounts to get retailers to concentrate purchases on major brands
- Expanding product lines so that a manufacturer's brand dominates a retailer's shelf space
- Allowing a large manufacturer's accounts to bypass traditional wholesalers

High brand loyalty, another source of power to a manufacturer, can encourage retailers to stock a new product, participate in a cooperative advertising program, and give a new product appropriate display space.

A manufacturer can maintain high power through franchising. As discussed in Chapter 12, a franchisor can dictate purchase requirements, offer a compliant franchise a preferred location, seek to terminate a franchise, threaten to add additional franchises in a franchisee's current territory, and so on. This example incorporates reward power, coercive power, and legitimate power.

A manufacturer can also legally refuse to sell to certain wholesalers and retailers under certain conditions. Mitsubishi Electronics America, one of Circuit City's top ten suppliers and the leading manufacturer of large-screen televisions, stopped supplying Circuit City. Before the split, Circuit City had been Mitsubishi's largest customer. As the president of Mitsubishi Consumer Electronics America put it: "No one wants to become hostage to a single customer."[19]

A manufacturer can terminate a distributor because of poor customer service, failure to meet sales expectations, transhipping activity, and so on. As with a franchise, a manufacturer can also elect not to renew a distributorship.

Some manufacturers and wholesalers seek to dominate a channel through vertical integration. A manufacturer can also threaten to use forward vertical integration to bypass wholesalers. After the Federal Trade Commission amended its 16-year-old ban against Levi Strauss from selling through its own stores, Levi Strauss announced its plan to open 200 retail stores between 1994 and 1999. According to Levi Strauss, its company-owned stores strategy is necessary to get Levi's traditional retailers to devote sufficient space for Levi products.[20] A manufacturer can also use factory outlets to bypass off-price retail chains.

Manufacturers can also derive channel power through push money. Manufacturers commonly use push money on brands that are doing poorly, that require more customer service, or where a manufacturer's image among customers is weak or poor. When offered directly to retail salespersons, push money may result in a manufacturer having control over a retailer's sales force.

METHODS OF WHOLESALER DOMINANCE

A wholesaler's power may be based on economic scale, private labels, gray markets, and customer loyalty. Table 13-4 identifies these and other forms of wholesaler power. Although many of these forms have been covered in previous chapters, they are analyzed here from the perspective of channel power.

As discussed in the previous chapter, a wholesaler can increase its economic power through the development of wholesaler-sponsored voluntary chains. Wholesalers can use both forward integration to bypass manufacturers and backward integration to bypass retailers. Distributors who do a large amount of business with one supplier or who have a very large market share in a geographic area secure a power advantage.

Wholesalers can also derive channel power through private labels. Unlike national brands, where loyalty is to the brand, in private-label programs, loyalty is to the brand as well as the wholesaler. Private-label programs are particularly

METHODS OF CHANNEL DOMINANCE

TABLE 13-4 SOURCES OF WHOLESALER POWER

- Having high economic scale
- Using a private-label strategy
- Using a gray market strategy
- Developing and maintaining high customer loyalty
- Tying agreements to sell slow-moving merchandise
- Using forward and backward vertical integration
- Offering large-quantity discounts to get retailers to concentrate purchases on major brands

effective as a power vehicle where the wholesaler's private label is well known, viewed by customers as providing excellent value, and where a wholesaler accounts for a large proportion of a supplier's total business.

Gray markets are yet another form of channel power for a wholesaler. By purchasing from unauthorized channels, wholesalers can ignore a manufacturer's cooperative advertising program and its minimum purchase quantities, and can even refuse to participate in a manufacturer's training program.

A distributor can also derive power through high loyalty among customers. Such a distributor can shift sales from one supplier to another. Manufacturers may be reluctant to discontinue a distributor with high customer loyalty based on fear of lost sales. Kroy Incorporated, a manufacturer of lettering equipment, attempted to drop its network of dealers and to sell direct with its own sales force. Unfortunately, Kroy underestimated the strength of its former network of dealers and the speed with which these dealers signed on with competitive suppliers. Kroy eventually reenlisted many of its dealers and began to rebuild its relationship with its former dealers.[21]

METHODS OF BUYER DOMINANCE

Table 13-5 contains a listing of selected sources of retailer power. Among the sources of retailer power that are further discussed here are store loyalty, high

TABLE 13-5 SOURCES OF RETAILER POWER

- Using store loyalty
- Increasing bargaining power through high market share
- Using centralized purchasing
- Using a private-label strategy
- Selling against the brand
- Requiring exclusive merchandise from vendors
- Using gray market distribution channels
- Requiring slotting and other fees
- Developing strong retailer trade associations

market share in served markets, private label, selling against the brand, exclusive merchandise, gray marketing, slotting and other fees, centralized purchasing, and retailer trade associations.

Large stores, particularly category killers and power retailers, have large loyalty owing to wide selection and exclusive lines of merchandise. Small stores may secure store loyalty through high levels of customer service and social relationships with consumers. A retailer can use high store loyalty to shift customer preferences from one brand to another once a customer is in the store. Retailers also serve as gatekeepers and can refuse to purchase particular brands and models.

As chains have increased their size, they have demanded slotting allowances, cooperative advertising monies, and other concessions. Smaller retailers can also expand their power through retailer-owned cooperative systems. The competition for shelf space is so great that many retailers can get away with their demands.[22] According to the vice president of a major consulting company, fast-growing retailers such as Wal-Mart and Toys "R" Us have unilaterally redefined their relationships with their suppliers. "They have extracted concessions, restricted their inventory investment, insist on high service levels, lowest possible prices, all allowable discounts, and most lenient financing terms—usually without any reciprocal benefit to their suppliers."[23]

Buyers can increase power by centralizing purchasing. Centralizing purchasing increases a retailer's bargaining power through increased order size and through eligibility for quantity discounts.

Use of a private label is an ideal way for a retailer to dominate a channel. Unlike national brands, private-label programs generate retailer loyalty. Like a wholesaler's private-label programs, a retailer's private label is particularly effective as a power vehicle where the private label is well known and perceived to be of high value by consumers, and where a retailer accounts for a large proportion of a supplier's total business.

In **selling against the brand**, retailers charge artificially high prices for the national brand to encourage consumers to purchase their private label. Often, retailers make specific price comparisons in their advertising to imply that private labels offer significantly better value. In some cases, these ads feature national brands at higher-than-market prices.

Many retailers want to push manufacturers into providing them with exclusive merchandise. Exclusive merchandise reduces price competition, generates excitement, and increases store traffic.

Like wholesalers, retailers that sell gray market goods also secure channel power. They do not have to abide by rules for authorized dealers. In many cases, gray market retailers secure cost advantages since they do not have to participate in cooperative advertising programs or meet inventory or other customer service requirements.

Slotting fees, pay to stay, and failure fees all indicate high value of shelf space in vendors due to new products seeking distribution. Retailers can use these fees as a means of rationing scarce retail shelf space. For example, in the music business, major label executives have suggested that each of the top six companies spends at least $10 million a year to secure desirable locations in major cities. Musicland Stores, a retail chain of 870 stores, reportedly charges as much as $40,000 a month to promote a new album in its stores. Much of these fees go to listening posts where potential customers can listen to a track or even an entire album prior to purchasing it.[24]

Buyers can increase power through retailer trade associations. These associations can enhance a retailer's power through joint efforts, class-action suits, and lobbying efforts on behalf of retailer members. Some research suggests that the power of trade associations is related to retail members' homogeneity of membership. Associations with homogeneous members are both stronger and better able to rally behind members' interests.[25]

WHO CONTROLS THE CHANNEL OF DISTRIBUTION?

It is not easy to generalize about who controls the channel of distribution. The balance of power must be assessed in each channel on an individual basis. A way of examining control is to examine a channel's administrative structure. Power in franchising is largely in the hands of the franchisor. This power has been somewhat eroded by the development of strong associations of franchisees, legal cases, and revised federal and state legislation. The power in wholesaler-sponsored voluntary chains is largely with the wholesaler, and the power in a retailer-owned voluntary cooperative is largely with retailer members.

Marketers should also pay particular attention to shifts in power. According to the *62nd Annual Report of the Grocery Industry,* 66 percent of chain executives, 77 percent of wholesalers, and 73 percent of manufacturers stated that a shift in power was occurring. Of those that agreed that a power shift was occurring, 62 percent of chain executives commented that it was toward retailers (versus 38 percent toward manufacturers), 66 percent of wholesalers said that it was toward manufacturers (versus 34 percent toward retailers), and 75 percent of manufacturer executives stated that the power shift was toward retailers (versus 25 percent toward manufacturers).[26] Both chain and manufacturer executives agreed that the power shift was toward retailers; in contrast, wholesalers felt that the shift in power was toward manufacturers.

In general, a manufacturer's power has increased largely through franchising and vertical integration. A wholesaler's power has grown through the development of integrated distributors, franchising, wholesaler-sponsored voluntary chains, and the increased market share of private labels in many markets. In contrast, retailer strength has increased through the use of retailer-owned voluntary cooperatives, private labeling, the increased power of franchisee associations, and the growth in importance of major chains (owing to consolidation and rapid expansion activity during the 1980s).

One channels expert argues that, although retail chains and wholesale distributors have enormous power in their gatekeeper function, manufacturers are beginning to realize their power and have begun to fight back.[27]

THE EFFECT OF CHANNEL POWER ON CHANNEL PERFORMANCE

A literature review by Professors Lewis and Lambert concluded that there is considerable evidence that a firm's dependence on another firm in the channel encourages it to perform at a higher level than if such dependence were lacking.[28] Reasons for high performance include the need for self-preservation and self-enrichment. Self-preservation recognizes that channel participants perform complementary roles. A firm's success depends on its own performance and its partner's performance. A high level of performance is necessary to preserve each firm's financial well-being. Self-enrichment describes the mutual economic gain arising from the efficient movement and exchange of products.

NATURE OF CHANNEL CONFLICTS

Perhaps no topic in channels management has been given as much attention by academics in the channel literature as channel conflict.[29] **Channel conflict** is the channel member's perception that its goal attainment is being impeded by another, with stress or tension the result.[30]

The pioneering work in conflict was conducted by Professor Palamountain, who distinguished among three different types of distribution conflict: horizontal, intertype, and vertical.[31] **Horizontal conflict** occurs among similar firms in the same level in a distribution channel. **Intertype conflict** results among different types of intermediaries at the same level in the channel. And **vertical conflict** stems from competition among different levels within a channel of distribution. Palamountain suggested that conflict was inevitable in marketing channels.

Most academic researchers agree that channel conflict, like power, is due to the functional interdependence among channel members. Yet, channel members need to cooperate with one another since they are dependent on each other to achieve their individual goals. Professor Mallen, in a classic article on channel conflict, argued that conflict is part of the exchange process, with the seller attempting to obtain the highest possible return and the buyer attempting to purchase the good for as little as possible.[32]

Conflict has been classified into five stages based on research by Professor Pondy. These stages are

Latent conflict—underlying sources of conflict.

Perceived conflict—conflict that is only perceived. No conditions of latent conflict exist.

Felt conflict—tension, anxiety, and disaffection, in addition to the perception.

Manifest conflict—behavior that blocks the goal achievement of another channel member.

Conflict aftermath—postconflict behavior.[33]

Of the perceived, felt, and manifest forms of conflict, only manifest conflict directly affects one channel's behavior toward another.

FIGURE 13-1 Modeling the levels of conflict between a manufacturer and its resellers.

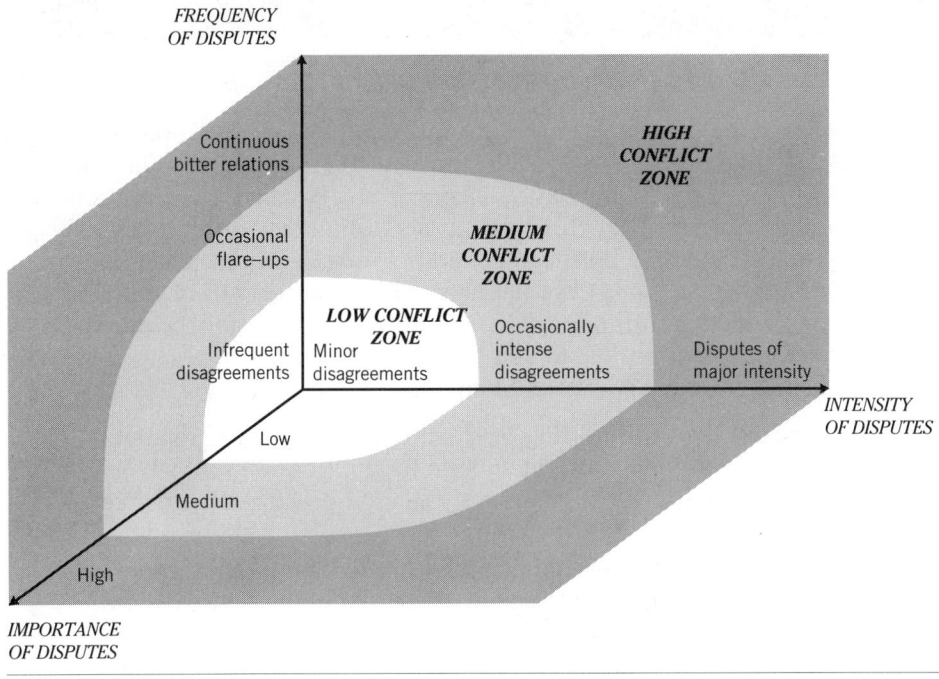

Source: Allan J. Magrath and Kenneth G. Hardy, *A Strategic Framework for Diagnosing Manufacturer-Reseller Conflict* (Cambridge, Mass.: Marketing Science Institute, 1988), p. 3. Reprinted by permission.

Channel conflict also can be classified into three dimensions, as shown in Figure 13-1. The **intensity of conflicts** dimension can range from minor flareups that are easily forgotten to major disagreements that are characterized by terminations, lawsuits, and so on. **Conflict frequency** can range from sporadic disputes and occasional disagreements to protracted, bitter relations. The third dimension is **conflict importance**, which reflects a channel member's perception of the importance of a particular dispute. When combined, the intensity, frequency, and importance dimensions determine the total degree of conflict (low, medium, or high).

CAUSES OF CONFLICT

Channel conflict is created when a company adds a new channel, reduces a wholesaler's territory, changes its discount structure, requires existing channels to perform additional services, or seeks to change the terms of a distribution agreement.

The causes of channel conflict have been typically classified by researchers as role incongruity, perceptual differences, questions concerning domain, differences in expectations, goal incompatibilities, communication difficulties, and resource scarcities among channel members.

CHANNELS IN ACTION

Channel Conflict at Mars

Mars is a privately held major manufacturer of candies, pet food, and food vending businesses. Its 1994 annual sales were estimated at $13 billion. Its brands include M&M's, Uncle Ben's rice, Milky Way, Snickers, Twix, Whiskas cat food, Kal Kan, and many others. For the past three years, according to market analysts, Mars has given up market share in both candy and pet food businesses. One analyst has computed that it gave up 1.4 market share points in the $10 billion U.S. candy market in a recent 12-month period. In Germany, its confectionery market share dropped from 30 percent in 1991 to 26 percent in 1993.

A large part of Mars's problem is related to channel conflict:

- Mars has not recognized the shifting of channel power to large retailers (such as big supermarket chains and membership clubs) and mega-wholesalers. Mars has been slow to reengineer its logistics practices to reduce costs to major resellers.

- Mars consistently is unable to supply enough products for all the orders it accepts. This makes it difficult for retailers to plan promotions. It also causes ill-will when out-of-stock situations arise. Internal task forces have been unable to resolve this problem. Market analysts attribute this problem to salespeople being encouraged to oversell units (even in peak selling periods). Mars rewards managers based on asset utilization, not customer satisfaction.

- Mars eliminated its special discount program to reduce forward buying by its wholesalers and retailers. It did not consider the importance of forward buying to reseller profitability. In retaliation, many resellers shifted shelf space competitors (such as Hershey) that have continued providing them with special discounts.

Source: Bill Saporito, "The Eclipse of Mars," *Fortune* (November 28, 1994), pp. 82–84 ff.

ROLE INCONGRUITIES

A channel member's role relates to a range of behavior that is acceptable for each channel member. In **role incongruity**, a channel member's behavior is outside of the acceptable range based on the role expectations of others. For example, a wholesaler may encounter shipment delays from a supplier that are unacceptable. In some cases, **role ambiguity** exists wherein a channel member is uncertain as to what behaviors constitute acceptable performance. A channel member needs to know the expectations of other channels, what its specific responsibilities are, and how its performance will be evaluated.

PERCEPTUAL DIFFERENCES

Perceptual differences relate to how a channel member interprets a situation or reacts to different stimuli. A retailer may think a gross margin of 40 percent is unfair, if it perceives 50 percent to be the proper discount. Channel members can also react differently to the same stimuli. For example, whereas a small independent retailer may view a manufacturer's cooperative advertising program as an important promotional tool, a large retail chain may view the program as ineffective.

A channel member can resolve conflict attributable to perceptual differences by understanding the perceptions of other channel members and by changing the reward system. In the cooperative advertising example, a manufacturer should offer different programs for small and large retailers based on an understanding of their perceptual differences. In the gross margin example, a manufacturer should consider agreeing to a 50 percent discount under the condition that retailers agree to stock large inventory levels.

Decision Domain Disagreements

Decision domain disagreements relate to a channel member's strong feeling about the specific areas of business conduct it should control. Disagreements occur when channel members do not agree on the sphere of their influence. Common decision domain disagreements relate to whether a retailer or a manufacturer has the right to determine a good's final selling price, whether a retailer has the right to transship goods, or whether a manufacturer has the right to specify inventory requirements for a distributor.

Expectational Differences

Expectational differences concern one channel member's expectations regarding the behavior of other channel members. A manufacturer, for example, may assume that a family-run wholesale lumber yard is not aggressive and will be quickly overtaken by several new Home Depot units in its trading area. Expectational differences may lead to a self-fulfulling prophecy. A prediction of poor sales by a manufacturer may result in poor sales for the manufacturer at the lumber yard based on reduced visits by its salespeople and more stringent credit controls.

Goal Incompatibilities

In **goal incompatibilities**, the goals of different channel members may not be compatible; these goals cannot be reconciled. For example, a manufacturer may seek additional shelf space for its new flavor of yogurt in order to increase its market share. In contrast, a supermarket retailer is concerned about how the new flavor contributes to additional sales. Although a shift in sales from one brand to another is the goal of a manufacturer, a retailer is much more concerned about total sales in the brand category.

Goal incompatibilities can also be seen by examining a reseller's and manufacturer's perspective on how a reseller can maximize profits. Resellers seek to maximize profits through higher gross margins, higher inventory turnover, lower expenses, and higher manufacturer allowances. Except for stimulating greater sales, a manufacturer would like to see lower margins, greater inventory, more promotional expenditures, and fewer allowances.[34]

COMMUNICATION DIFFICULTIES

Communication difficulties relate to slow or inaccurate information among channel members. Examples of communication difficulties consist of final consumers being informed of a product recall before wholesalers and retailers, or a manufacturer's being poorly informed of the sales performance of an important product in a specific channel.

To reduce some communication difficulties, some major retailers (such as Dillard's, Federated, and Younkers) have mandated that their suppliers communicate purchase orders, invoices, and, in some cases, advanced shipping notices through electronic data interchange. Beginning October 1, Younkers began mandating that its suppliers use EDI. Younkers charges $5 per carton if it does not receive EDI shipping notification, five cents per unit if there is no price on UPC tickets, and $2 per carton if that carton does not display an appropriate shipping label. Additional fees are also collected if the UPC is not marked, is incorrect, or is of poor quality.[35]

RESOURCE SCARCITIES

Resource scarcities relates to conflict over the allocation of scarce resources. An example of resource scarcities as a conflict source is a manufacturer's decision to retain its larger customer accounts as house accounts after deciding to use an indirect form of distribution.

IS CONFLICT DYSFUNCTIONAL?

Researchers are divided in opinion as to whether channel conflict promotes or distracts from channel efficiency. Those who argue that channel conflict is functional note that some conflict may stimulate innovation and discourage channel members from becoming complacent. For example, although multiple channels selling the same good may increase conflict, this strategy may maximize sales, increase customer convenience, and force channel members to be innovative. Others argue that excessive conflict may be dysfunctional and lower channel efficiency.

Several researchers have suggested that low levels of channel conflict may have little impact on channel efficiency, that moderate levels may actually increase efficiency, and that high levels of conflict may detract from channel efficiency.[36] This model is based on the notion that channel members have a tolerance zone for conflict and react to conflict when it exceeds their tolerance threshold. High levels of conflict can lead to bitter feelings, legal disputes, and the severing of relations where both parties have high switching costs.

Professors Winsted and Hunt have argued that the effect of conflict on channel efficiency is related to the source of the conflict, the level of conflict, and how conflict is managed.[37]

CHANNEL COOPERATION

Channel cooperation is the joint striving of channel members toward individual and mutual goals. Manufacturers and retailers, being dependent on each other to meet these desired goals, cooperate with each other. Channel cooperation is predicated on each channel member having compatible goals and values. Channel cooperation is the opposite of channel conflict.

Table 13-6 lists examples of manufacturer-reseller cooperation. Among the major forms of cooperation are joint promotional programs, joint inventory management assistance, exclusive products, and information sharing. In comparison to the previous section where each channel sought to dominate the channel, often at another channel member's expense, in cooperation, a win-win attitude is pervasive. In channel cooperation, each channel benefits from the use of these strategies.

TABLE 13-6   EXAMPLES OF MANUFACTURER-RESELLER COOPERATION

JOINT PROMOTIONAL PROGRAMS
- Wholesaler-retailer joint participation in cooperative advertising programs
- Manufacturer providing demonstrators for wholesalers and retailers
- Manufacturer participation in joint sales calls for wholesaler
- Manufacturer including names of distributors in its advertisements
- Manufacturer offering rebate when competition is high as opposed to price reduction
- Manufacturer forwarding inquiries to wholesaler and retailer based on location of potential customer

JOINT INVENTORY MANAGEMENT ASSISTANCE
- Manufacturer-wholesaler-retailer joint participation in electronic data interchange programs
- Manufacturer-wholesaler-retailer joint participation in just-in-time inventory management programs
- Manufacturer or wholesaler involvement in emergency shipments to resellers
- Manufacturer assistance in financing inventory for wholesalers and retailers

EXCLUSIVE PRODUCTS
- Manufacturer providing different model designations to different channel members to reduce price competition among channels

INFORMATION SHARING
- Manufacturer-wholesaler-retailer joint participation in electronic data interchange programs
- Manufacturer encouraging distributors to join distributor council

TRAINING
- Wholesaler-retailer joint participation in manufacturer's sales training programs
- Wholesaler-retailer joint participation in manufacturer's product training programs

TERRITORY PROTECTION
- Manufacturer offering protected territories to wholesalers and retailers

Joint promotional programs include cooperative advertising programs, a manufacturer providing demonstrators for wholesalers and retailers, manufacturer participation in joint sales calls for a wholesaler, a manufacturer including names of distributors in its advertisements, manufacturer rebate offers, and a manufacturer forwarding inquiries to a wholesaler and retailer based on the location of a potential customer. The use of rebates also illustrates channel cooperation. In comparison to a temporary price reduction, a rebate program has no negative impact on a wholesaler's or retailer's inventory value. As an alternative to coupons, rebates also reduce a retailer's administrative costs and minimize a manufacturer's concern about misredeemed coupons.

Joint inventory management assistance programs include joint participation in electronic data interchange programs, joint participation in just-in-time in-

CHANNELS IN ACTION

Automakers Are Finally Listening to Dealers

Auto dealers assembled in Dallas, Texas, for the National Automobile Dealers Association are now more confident of their relationship with automakers. According to a Cadillac-Saab dealer, "When I first became a car dealer, it was 'like it or leave it.' " Now, car and truck dealers are treated as knowledgeable experts on the buying behavior of consumers. Look at these examples:

- GM recently flew Cadillac dealers to Phoenix to drive the Catera, an entry-level luxury car due out in 1996. The Catera, a version of Europe's Opel Omega model, is being adapted for the U.S. market. Research and suggestions from Cadillac dealers had an important role in the product's design.

- When a customer switched from an Oldsmobile to a Buick because cloth seats were unavailable in the Olds model the customer desired, the Oldsmobile dealer complained to Oldsmobile about losing the sale. Within a two-week period, cloth seats became available for the Oldsmobile model.

- After Ford dealers complained that the 1995 Ford Contour and Mercury Mystique compact were too expensive, Ford reduced the level of options for each car. Ford also began to promote the cars as being less expensive than imports.

- In the past, many car manufacturers have pushed slow-selling cars on dealers, despite their poor appeal. Dealers who purchased large quantities of a slow-selling car were rewarded with cars in short supply. In contrast to this strategy, in January 1995, the Ford division general manager admitted to dealers that Ford should have acted sooner in slowing down production of costly Windstar minivans and slow-selling Escort compact cars.

Source: Micheline Maynard and Earle Eldridge, "Automakers Are Listening to Car Dealers," *USA Today* (February 13, 1995), p. B1.

ventory management programs, manufacturer or wholesaler involvement in emergency shipments to resellers, and manufacturer assistance in financing inventory for wholesalers and retailers. These programs minimize inventory levels throughout the entire channel, reduce lost sales to stockouts, and give consumers ready access to goods.

The offering of exclusive products can reduce both the free-rider phenomenon and price-based comparison shopping by consumers. In some cases, identical products may be given different model numbers or name designations to reduce price comparisons. In other instances, a product sold to a given retailer may have slightly different configurations. A model that has different names or model designations based on the channel in which it is sold is called a **derivative model**. For example, Packard Bell changes nameplates across retailers. It uses the Legend designation at electronics outlets such as Circuit City and Best Buy, Axcel at office superstores such as OfficeMax and Office Depot, and Force at computer superstores such as CompUSA.[38] Buying clubs often get exclusive models.[39]

Information sharing includes manufacturer-wholesaler-retailer joint participation in electronic data interchange programs, and the manufacturer encouraging a distributor to join a distributor council. Channel members can also share research findings where appropriate to multiple channel levels.

Training includes wholesaler-retailer joint participation in a manufacturer's sales and product training programs.

Lastly, channel cooperation can be increased by a manufacturer's granting wholesalers and retailers exclusive territories. A major concern among many resellers is that a territory they develop may be divided.

Table 13-7 presents an example of a channel cooperation measurement scale. This scale was designed to be used in conjunction with Table 13-1, which measures a supplier's power.

TABLE 13-7 EXAMPLE OF A CHANNEL COOPERATION MEASUREMENT SCALE

Indicate your answer on a 6-point scale with the extremes being definitely agree (6) and definitely disagree (1).

I think that if I contribute to improving company performance in the future, my primary supplier will take care of me.

My future goals are best reached by working with my primary supplier rather than against my primary supplier.

My future profits are dependent on maintaining a good working relationship with the company.

I don't feel I can count on my primary supplier to give me the kind of support (such as local advertising) that dealers working with other companies receive.[a]

[a]This question is reverse scored. Disagreeing with this statement indicates high cooperation.

Source: Adapted from Steven J. Skinner, Jule B. Gassenheimer, and Scott W. Kelley, "Cooperation in Supplier-Dealer Relations," *Journal of Retailing*, Vol. 68 (Summer 1992), p. 189. Reprinted by permission.

CONFLICT MANAGEMENT AND RESOLUTION

Channel members need to manage their relationship so that the balance between conflict and cooperation is satisfactory to each channel participant. According to one study, management of channel strategies with high conflict requires strong negotiating skills, human relations skills, and communication skills.[40]

A channel member may be able to resolve conflict by changing its strategies. For example, a manufacturer may produce different model configurations to different dealers to reduce price competition. Other methods of managing conflict include dividing markets among resellers, delineating direct sales policies to clarify conflict over large accounts, and negotiating territorial issues between regional distributors.[41] A channel member can also attempt to reduce conflict by clearly specifying which channel member is responsible for making a sale. Common boundaries are based on customer characteristics (size, end-use), geography (state, zip code), or products (do-it-yourself products sold through different channels than professional products).[42]

GENERAL METHODS OF CONFLICT MANAGEMENT AND RESOLUTION

Four methods of conflict management and resolution are persuasion, problem solving, negotiation, and politics.[43] These can apply to any form of conflict.

In **persuasion**, a channel member seeks to manage conflict by altering the other party's perspective or decision criteria relating to the focal issue(s). The intent is to move a party toward a common set of goals. For example, a franchisor can persuade a franchisee of the importance of consistency in product standards across franchises on a franchise's value.

In **problem solving**, channel participants seek to identify a solution that satisfies each party's decision criteria. Problem solving is characterized by trust and cooperation. Through problem solving, participants assemble information and share information about their goals and priorities. In problem solving, a wholesaler may acknowledge a manufacturer's right to a house account, if the manufacturer agrees to increase its use of joint sales calls with an important customer.

With **negotiation**, participants bargain. Each party gives up something. Common goals are not expected. Negotiation is characterized by a zero-sum orientation, in which what one channel member wins, the other channel member loses.

In the final form of conflict management, **politics**, channel members extend the role of bargaining to include relevant third parties who might be viewed as allies. Politics indicates the failure of the parties' ability to reach an acceptable solution on their own. The arbitration or mediation of disputes is an example of politics.

SPECIFIC METHODS OF CONFLICT MANAGEMENT AND RESOLUTION

Specific methods of channel conflict management and resolution are sensitivity training, shared tasks, and joint goal setting. These methods require the trust and commitment of channel members and are often associated with relationship marketing. In contrast, channel-wide committees, conciliation, and distributor advisory councils are administrative techniques used to manage and reduce conflict.

Through **sensitivity training**, channel personnel are trained to be aware of potential conflict areas. Individuals are also empowered to reduce conflict situations before they escalate. Sensitivity training seeks to break down barriers between companies. In addition, this form of training reveals that if the distribution system fails, so does each of its components.[44]

In **shared tasks**, channels manage conflict by developing intermediary-manufacturer partnerships through relationship marketing. A major benefit of shared tasks is enhanced channel communication and coordination of facilities.[45] For example, Deere and Caterpillar have organized joint workshops with their suppliers, and increasingly work with contracts of 24 to 36 months' duration.[46]

Joint goal setting takes into account the goals of multiple channel members. An example of joint goal setting is the development of objectives for a wholesaler's sales force based on retail sales, not wholesale sales. This approach forces a wholesale salesperson to be more concerned with point-of-purchase displays, a retailer's inventory levels, emergency shipments, and so on. A study by the Distribution Research and Educational Foundation found that 10 percent of manufacturers had joint marketing plans as of 1994. In the year 2000, 30 percent plan to use joint marketing plans with their distributors.[47]

Channel-wide committees can be part of a matrix organization. These committees are called together at periodic intervals. They differ from shared tasks in that channel members work together as part of a team on a noncontinuous basis. An adaptation of this technique is a staff exchange program, in which a manufacturer's salesperson, for example, is assigned to a wholesaler for a limited time, or vice versa.

In **conciliation**, an ombudsman position is created. The ombudsman can be a retired distributor and is now employed by a manufacturer, who has credibility with both parties.[48] Many large firms have established trade relations officials who attend trade association meetings, call on customers, and continue a dialogue.[49]

Through a **distributor's advisory council**, a channel member attempts to change power relationships by means of committees that represent the interests of specific groups. A 1993 survey of more than 700 manufacturing and distribution executives conducted by the National Association of Wholesalers found that 10 percent of manufacturers had distributor councils. In the year 2000, 20 percent plan to use distributor councils.[50] A distributor's council can serve as a forum for airing complaints, discussing emerging problems, and developing mutually acceptable solutions. It can be in the form of advisory councils or joint participation in an industry trade association.[51]

CHANNEL SATISFACTION

Channel satisfaction is the overall evaluation of the relationship between two channel members. Research by Professors Ruekert and Churchill suggests that channel satisfaction has five dimensions: social interaction, product, financial, cooperative advertising, and assistance.[52] The social interaction dimension examines interactions between intermediary and manufacturer, primarily through the sales representative that services the account. The product dimension reflects the demand for and awareness and quality of the manufacturer's products. A financial dimension looks at intermediary margins and return on investment. A cooperative advertising dimension evaluates cooperative advertising programs and allowances. The assistance dimension looks at consumer promotions, promotional support, and point-of-purchase displays. See Table 13-8 for a channel satisfaction measurement scale.

Conflict is expected to have a negative relationship with satisfaction.[53] Professors Hunt and Nevin found that noncoercive sources of power increase satisfaction and reduce conflict, while coercive sources of power reduce satisfaction and increase conflict within the marketing channel.[54]

Researchers suggest that the cooperative efforts of channel members should result in greater channel efficiency and achievement of goals, which leads to higher levels of satisfaction. In contrast, conflict is expected to have a negative relationship with satisfaction.[55] Professors Hunt and Nevin, in a classic study, argue that channel satisfaction may be related to higher morale, greater cooperation within a channel, fewer terminations of relationships, fewer lawsuits, and reduced efforts to seek protective legislation.[56] Professor Lusch also argues that satisfaction in the channel can reduce friction between parties, lower dysfunctional forms of conflict, and increase a channel's efficiency.[57]

TABLE 13-8 EXAMPLE OF A CHANNEL SATISFACTION MEASUREMENT SCALE

Indicate your answer on a 6-point scale with the extremes being definitely agree (6) and definitely disagree (1).

My primary equipment supplier is a good company to do business with.

I would not recommend that other dealers do business with my primary equipment supplier.[a]

I feel my primary equipment supplier provides the services needed to perform my business operations.

I would discontinue selling equipment manufactured by my primary equipment supplier if I could.[a]

[a] These questions are reverse scored. Disagreeing with these statements indicates high satisfaction.

Source: Adapted from Steven J. Skinner, Jule B. Gassenheimer, and Scott W. Kelley, "Cooperation in Supplier-Dealer Relations," *Journal of Retailing,* Vol. 68 (Summer 1992), p. 189. Reprinted by permission.

SUMMARY

1 *To discuss channel power, including channel power forms.* Channel power is the ability of a channel member to control or influence the marketing strategy of an independent channel member at another level in the channel. The range of power refers to the areas within which a channel member may prescribe another channel member's behavior and expect that channel member to adhere to its desires. There are two accepted forms of measuring channel power: potential power and exercised power. Channel power is commonly classified as reward power, referent power, expertise power, persuasion power, legitimate power, and information power. Some researchers have combined these channel power forms into a coercive-noncoercive dichotomy.

2 *To describe the methods of channel dominance and the impact of channel dominance on channel performance.* The dominant member of the channel or channel leader is called the channel captain. A manufacturer's power may be based on economic scale, high market share, brand loyalty, franchising, refusal to deal, distributor termination, vertical integration, and push money. A wholesaler's power may be based on economic scale, private labels, gray markets, and customer loyalty. A retailer's power may be based on store loyalty, high market share in served markets, private label, selling against the brand, exclusive merchandise, gray marketing, slotting and other fees, centralizing purchasing, and retailer trade associations.

There is considerable evidence that a firm's dependence on another firm in the channel encourages it to perform at a higher level than if such dependence were lacking. Reasons for high performance include the need for self-preservation and self-enrichment.

3 *To explain the nature of channel conflict and its causes, and the impact of channel conflict on channel efficiency.* Channel conflict is the perception on the part of a channel member that its goal attainment is being impeded by another, with stress or tension the result. Conflict has been classified into five stages based on research by Professor Pondy. These stages are latent conflict, perceived conflict, felt conflict, manifest conflict, and conflict aftermath. Channel conflict also can be classified into three dimensions: the intensity of conflict, conflict frequency, and conflict importance.

The causes of channel conflict have been typically classified by researchers as role incongruity, perceptual differences, questions concerning domain, differences in expectations, goal incompatibilities, communication difficulties, and resource scarcities among channel members.

Researchers are divided in opinion as to whether channel conflict promotes or distracts from channel efficiency. Those that argue that channel conflict is functional note that some conflict may stimulate innovation and discourage channel members from becoming complacent. Others argue that excessive conflict may be dysfunctional and lower channel efficiency. Several researchers have suggested that low levels of channel conflict may have little impact on channel efficiency, that moderate levels may actually increase efficiency, and that high levels of conflict may detract from channel efficiency.

4. *To analyze channel cooperation.* Channel cooperation is the joint striving of channel members toward individual and mutual goals. Channel cooperation is predicated on each channel member having compatible goals and values. Channel cooperation is the opposite of channel conflict. Among the major forms of cooperation are joint promotional programs, joint inventory management assistance, exclusive products, and information sharing. In comparison to the previous section where each channel sought to dominate the channel, often at another channel member's expense, in cooperation, a win-win attitude is pervasive. In channel cooperation, each channel benefits from the use of these strategies.

5. *To evaluate conflict management and resolution.* Channel members need to manage their relationship so that the balance between conflict and cooperation is satisfactory to each channel participant. Four methods of conflict management and resolution are persuasion, problem solving, negotiation, and politics. These can apply to any form of conflict. Specific methods of channel conflict management and resolution are sensitivity training, shared tasks, and joint goal setting. These methods require the trust and commitment of channel members. These are often associated with relationship marketing. In contrast, channel-wide committees, conciliation, and distributor advisory councils are administrative techniques used to manage and reduce conflict.

6. *To study channel satisfaction and its impact on channel performance.* Channel satisfaction is the overall evaluation of the relationship between two channel members. Research suggests that there are five dimensions to channel satisfaction: social interaction, product, financial, cooperative advertising, and assistance. Researchers suggest that the cooperative efforts of channel members should result in greater channel efficiency and achievement of goals, which leads to higher levels of satisfaction. In contrast, conflict is expected to have a negative relationship with satisfaction.

KEY TERMS

channel power
channel dependency
range of power
potential power
exercised power
coercive power
reward power (promises)
referent power
expertise power
persuasion power
legitimate power
information power
channel captain
economic scale
selling against the brand

channel conflict
horizontal conflict
intertype conflict
vertical conflict
intensity of conflicts
conflict frequency
conflict importance
role incongruity
role ambiguity
perceptual differences
decision domain disagreements
expectational differences
goal incompatibilities
communication difficulties

resource scarcities
channel cooperation
derivative model
persuasion
problem solving
negotiation
politics
sensitivity training
shared tasks
joint goal setting
channel-wide committees
conciliation
distributor's advisory council
channel satisfaction

QUESTIONS FOR DISCUSSION

1. Define the concept of channel power. Be sure to differentiate among range of power, potential power, and exercised power.
2. Provide three illustrations of coercive power, one each for a manufacturer, wholesaler, and retailer.
3. Describe the limitations to the use of both coercive power and reward power.
4. Differentiate among expertise, legitimate, and information power.
5. Describe three strategies a manufacturer can use to dominate a channel.
6. Describe three strategies a wholesaler can use to dominate a channel.
7. Describe three strategies a retailer can use to dominate a channel.
8. Evaluate Figure 13-1.
9. Provide an example of each of these causes of channel conflict: role incongruity, decision domain disagreements, and goal incompatibilities.
10. Is channel conflict dysfunctional? Explain your answer.
11. List and describe three strategies that channel members can use for channel cooperation.
12. Analyze the statement, "Persuasion, problem solving, negotiation, and politics are conflict management and resolution methods that can apply to any form of conflict."
13. Differentiate between the use of shared tasks and channel-wide committees in conflict management and resolution.
14. Define channel satisfaction.

END NOTES

1. Allan J. Magrath, "The Gatekeepers," *Across the Board* (April 1992), pp. 43–46.

2. See Louis W. Stern and Torger Reve, "Distribution Channels as Political Economies: A Framework for Comparative Analysis," *Journal of Marketing,* Vol. 44 (Summer 1980), pp. 52–64.

3. Robert F. Lusch and Robert H. Ross, "The Nature of Power in a Marketing Channel," *Journal of the Academy of Marketing Science,* Vol. 13 (Summer 1985), pp. 40–41.

4. Gul Butaney and Lawrence H. Wortzel, "Distributor Power Versus Manufacturer Power: The Customer Role," *Journal of Marketing,* Vol. 52 (January 1988), p. 54.

5. John R. P. French and Bertram Raven, "The Bases of Social Power," in *Studies in Social Power,* Dorwin Cartwright, ed. (Ann Arbor, Mich.: Institute for Social Research, University of Michigan, 1959), pp. 150–167.

6. Bertram H. Raven and Arie W. Kruglanski, "Conflict and Power," in *The Structure of Conflict,* Paul Swingle, ed. (New York: Academic Press, 1970), pp. 69–109.

7. Gary L. Frazier and John O. Summers, "Interfirm Influence Strategies and Their Application Within Distribution Channels," *Journal of Marketing,* Vol. 48 (Summer 1984), p. 46.

8. Robert F. Lusch, "Sources of Power: Their Impact on Intrachannel Conflict," *Journal of Marketing Research,* Vol. 13 (November 1976), p. 383.

9. Frazier and Summers, "Interfirm Influence Strategies and Their Application Within Distribution Channels," p. 46.

10. John F. Gaski, "The Theory of Power and Conflict in Channels of Distribution," *Journal of Marketing,* Vol. 48 (Summer 1984), p. 22.

11. Roger J. Calantone and Jule B. Gassenheimer, "Overcoming Basic Problems Between Manufacturers and Distributors," *Industrial Marketing Management,* Vol. 20 (August 1991), p. 217.

12. Sudhir H. Kale, "Dealer Dependence and Influence Strategies in a Manufacturer-Dealer Dyad," *Journal of Applied Psychology,* Vol. 74 (1989), p. 380.

13. Frazier and Summers, "Interfirm Influence Strategies and Their Application Within Distribution Channels," p. 46.

14. Ibid., p. 47.

15. Much of this section is from Nermin Eyuboglu and Osman A. Atac, "Information Power: A Means for Increased Control in Channels of Distribution," *Psychology & Marketing,* Vol. 8 (Fall 1991), pp. 197–213.

16. Michael Porter, *Competitive Strategy: Techniques for Analyzing Industries and Customers* (New York: Free Press, 1980), pp. 27–28.

17. Ibid., pp. 24–26.

18. Shawn Tully, "Purchasing's New Muscle," *Fortune* (February 20, 1995), p. 78.

19. Marcia Berss, "We Will Not Be in a National Chain," *Forbes* (March 27, 1995), p. 50.

20. Bill Richards, "Levi Strauss Plans to Open 200 Stores in 5 Years, With Ending of FTC Ban," *Wall Street Journal* (December 23, 1994), p. A4.

21. Kenneth G. Hardy and Allan J. Magrath, "Ten Ways for Manufacturers to Improve Distribution Management," *Business Horizons,* Vol. 31 (November–December 1988), pp. 67–68.

22. See Magrath, "The Gatekeepers," pp. 42–46.

23. Randy Myer, "Suppliers—Manage Your Customers," *Harvard Business Review,* Vol. 67 (November–December 1989), p. 161.

24. Jeffrey A. Trachtenberg, "Record Stores Lease Out Windows, Walls, Whatever," *Wall Street Journal* (April 19, 1995), p. B1.

25. Nader H. Shooshtari, Bruce J. Walker, and Donald W. Jackson, "Retail Trade Associations: Enhancing Members' Power in Relationships with Suppliers," *Journal of Retailing*, Vol. 64 (Summer 1988), pp. 199–214.

26. "62nd Annual Report of the Grocery Industry," *Progressive Grocer* (April 1995), p. 19.

27. Magrath, "The Gatekeepers," pp. 43–46.

28. M. Christine Lewis and Douglas M. Lambert, "A Model of Channel Member Performance, Dependence, and Satisfaction," *Journal of Retailing*, Vol. 67 (Summer 1991), pp. 206–207.

29. Patrick L. Schul and Emin Babakus, "An Examination of the Interfirm Power-Conflict Relationship: The Intervening Role of the Channel Decision Structure," *Journal of Retailing*, Vol. 64 (Winter 1988), p. 381.

30. John F. Gaski, "The Theory of Conflict in Channels of Distribution," p. 11.

31. Joseph C. Palamountain, *The Politics of Distribution* (Cambridge, Mass.: Harvard University Press, 1955).

32. Bruce Mallen, "A Theory of Retailer-Supplier Conflict, Control, and Cooperation," *Journal of Retailing*, Vol. 39 (Summer 1963), p. 25.

33. Louis R. Pondy, "Organizational Conflict: Concepts and Models," *Administrative Science Quarterly*, Vol. 12 (September 1967), pp. 296–320.

34. Allan J. Magrath and Kenneth G. Hardy, *A Strategic Framework for Diagnosing Manufacturer-Reseller Conflict* (Cambridge, Mass.: Marketing Science Institute, 1988), p. 6.

35. Matt Nannery, "Muscling in on Quick Response," *Today's Retail Technology* (December 1994/January 1995), p. 6.

36. See Bert Rosenbloom, "Conflict and Channel Efficiency: Some Conceptual Models for the Decision Maker," *Journal of Marketing*, Vol. 37 (July 1973), p. 29.

37. Kathryn Frazer Winsted and Kenneth A. Hunt, "Functional Conflict in Channel Systems," in *1988 American Marketing Association Educators' Proceedings*, Gary Frazier, Charles Ingene, and David Aaker, eds. (Chicago: American Marketing Association, 1988), p. 244.

38. Scott McCartney, "Computer Buyers Are Smart to Be Suspicious," *Wall Street Journal* (September 12, 1994), p. B2.

39. See "Should You Join a Warehouse Club?" *Consumer Reports* (May 1995), p. 333.

40. Magrath and Hardy, *A Strategic Framework for Diagnosing Manufacturer-Reseller Conflict*, p. 18.

41. Hardy and Magrath, "Ten Ways for Manufacturers to Improve Distribution Management," p. 68.

42. Rowland T. Moriarty and Ursula Moran, "Managing Hybrid Systems," *Harvard Business Review*, Vol. 68 (November–December 1990), p. 151.

43. Much of the material in this section is from Rajiv P. Dant and Patrick L. Schul, "Conflict Resolution Processes in Contractual Channels of Distribution," *Journal of Marketing*, Vol. 56 (January 1992), pp. 39–40.

44. George H. Lucas, Jr. and Larry G. Gresham, "Power Conflict, Control, and the Application of Contingency Theory in Marketing Channels," *Journal of the Academy of Marketing Science*, Vol. 13 (Summer 1985), p. 30.

45. See David Shipley, "What British Distributors Dislike about Manufacturers," *Industrial Marketing Management*, Vol. 16 (August 1987), pp. 153–162.

46. Paul Matthyssens and Christophe Van den Bulte, "Getting Closer and Nicer: Partnerships in the Supply Chain," *Long Range Planning*, Vol. 27 (February 1994), p. 74.

47. "The Future of the Distributor-Manufacturer Relationship," *Industrial Distribution* (February 1994), p. 22.

48. James C. Anderson and James A. Narus, "A Model of Distributor Firm and Manufacturer Firm Working Partnerships," *Journal of Marketing*, Vol. 54 (January 1990), p. 56.

49. Steve Weinstein, "Trade Relations: On the Front Lines," *Progressive Grocer* (October 1993), pp. 62–64 ff.

50. "The Future of the Distributor-Manufacturer Relationship," p. 22.

51. Allan J. Magrath and Kenneth G. Hardy, "A Strategic Paradigm for Predicting Manufacturer-Reseller Conflict," *European Journal of Marketing,* Vol. 23, No. 2 (1989), p. 104.

52. Robert W. Ruekert and Gilbert A. Churchill, Jr., "Reliability and Validity of Alternative Measures of Channel Member Satisfaction," *Journal of Marketing Research,* Vol. 21 (May 1984), pp. 226–233.

53. See Steven J. Skinner, Jule B. Gassenheimer, and Scott W. Kelley, "Cooperation in Supplier-Dealer Relations," *Journal of Retailing,* Vol. 68 (Summer 1992), p. 180.

54. Shelby D. Hunt and John R. Nevin, "Power in a Channel of Distribution: Sources and Consequences," *Journal of Marketing Research,* Vol. 11 (May 1974), pp. 186–193; and Lusch, "Sources of Power: Their Impact on Intrachannel Conflict," pp. 382–390.

55. See Skinner, Gassenheimer, and Kelley, "Cooperation in Supplier-Dealer Relations," p. 180.

56. Hunt and Nevin, "Power in a Channel of Distribution: Sources and Consequences," pp. 186–193.

57. Robert F. Lusch, "Franchise Satisfaction: Causes and Consequences," *International Journal of Physical Distribution,* Vol. 7 (1976), pp. 128–140.

CASE 1

COMPAQ AND INTEL: CHANNEL CONFLICT

There has been open evidence of channel conflict between Compaq and Intel. When Compaq's chief executive officer, Eckhard Pfeiffer, was asked about his thoughts on Intel Corporation (one of Compaq's major suppliers) at a major computer conference, Pfeiffer commented that Intel's pricing and product strategies serve only the chipmaker's interests and not those of its customers.

This is a public indication of the conflict between the goals of the manufacturer in its pull-related advertising and its customers. For example, Intel has spent $80 million on television advertising to persuade customers that they need personal computers based on its Pentium microprocessor chip. Intel hopes its advertising will get more customers to specify the Pentium chip. At this time, Intel has significant competition on its 486 microprocessor from such firms as Cyrix, Advanced Micro Devices, and other clone manufacturers. It has no direct competition on its Pentium chip. Intel's campaign is specifically designed to cast doubt in a buyer's mind about the effectiveness of 486 chips. The ad campaign occurred at a time when Compaq reported that 87 percent of its sales were from 486-based microprocessors.

In contrast, Compaq has spent $100 million on advertising to communicate to its customers the idea that it's not the chip, but the brand of personal computer, that is important. Compaq has chosen not to sell Pentium chip-based computers because of cost constraints. According to the chief executive officer of Compaq, "The sweet spot is in the $1,500 to $2,000 range, and you cannot put a Pentium product out there with a set of features we are offering for anything less than $3,000. And that is certainly not the sweet spot of the market."

There is also some conflict with Compaq concerning Intel's use of the "Intel Inside" advertising campaign. This campaign was designed to focus consumer attention on the microprocessor brand as a competitive advantage. Intel's campaign has several objectives. The campaign was designed to increase brand awareness of the Intel brand to final consumers. Intel hopes that final consumers will specify products based on its microprocessors. Intel also wants the campaign to reduce the amount of multisourcing done by personal computer manufacturers. In multisourcing, a computer manufacturer switches among microprocessor brands based on availability and cost.

In general, many small computer manufacturers like the campaign since the Intel association increases the credibility of their brands. However, Compaq doesn't like the "Intel Inside" campaign because it overvalues the Intel association over its brand name. According to Compaq's chief executive officer, "We believe that the customer is the ultimate judge on what matters to him or her. And the feedback we have is that the brand stands behind the total product, the PC, and if that is a reputable brand, then the customer, in the end, does not mind what's inside the box—everything else in the machine comes from different vendors and, at times, is exchangeable. That's what the whole industry does."

There are two parts of the "Intel Inside" campaign: cooperative advertising and point-of-purchase materials. Compaq is using the "Intel Inside" advertising campaign, in part, because of cooperative advertising dollars from Intel. However, Compaq has stopped using the point-of-purchase portion of the promotions.

Compaq's chief executive sees conflict as largely inevitable. Intel is seeking to increase sales in the field where competition is low and to increase brand awareness where competition exists. Compaq needs to sell computers at an appropriate price for its market, desires to use its own brand as a competitive advantage, and wants the option of using multisourcing of microprocessor chips. On September 14, 1994, Compaq unveiled its new line of Presario personal computers based on AMD microprocessors. Compaq plans to purchase at least 40 percent of its microprocessors from clonemakers such as AMD.

One market analyst, in learning of the Intel-Compaq discord, commented, "Like it or not [Intel and Compaq] are still joined at the hip."

QUESTIONS

1. Describe the Compaq-Intel conflict based on Figure 13-1.
2. Analyze the conflict from the perspective of the causes of channel conflict that have been discussed in this chapter.
3. Is the conflict dysfunctional to Compaq and Intel? Explain your answer.
4. How can Compaq and Intel manage and resolve this conflict?

Sources: Peter Burrows and Robert D. Hof, "Watch Out for Flying Chips," *Business Week* (September 26, 1994), p. 64; and "Eckhard Pfeiffer: An Interview with Eric Nee," *Upside* (January 1995), pp. 1–7.

CASE 2

CHANNEL COOPERATION BETWEEN SUPPLIERS AND CUSTOMERS

The sharing of tasks between suppliers and customers also applies to relationships between suppliers and industrial customers as a means of managing and resolving conflict. In some industrial firms, suppliers and customers share sensitive data relating to sales, sales forecasts, pricing, profit margins, costs, and market strategies. To protect its customers, in-house suppliers are generally required to sign a confidentiality agreement and agree to specific guidelines.

Honeywell Inc., for example, now has five suppliers working with its 20 buyers of office supplies on an in-house basis. At Honeywell, for example, some in-plant suppliers are even permitted to place orders on Honeywell's behalf with their own competitors. In other firms, in-house suppliers frequently attend meetings on a new product's production status and allow in-house suppliers access to its computer system.

There are several benefits to task sharing. By allowing suppliers into a firm's plant, a customer is often able to reduce its inventory levels and the number of its purchasing agents, and to receive cost-saving tips from suppliers that are more familiar with its needs. Honeywell, for instance, has been able to significantly reduce its inventory (it is now measured in days rather than weeks). It also received valuable suggestions to standardize some parts so that they are less costly to the manufacturer. Another firm benefited from a suggestion that it switch to a different grade of aluminum. While the original grade used had to be ordered every six months and then warehoused, the new grade could be purchased on a weekly basis, saving warehousing and interest costs.

Like all strategies, task sharing has some potential disadvantages. For one thing, suppliers may feel at risk since they may be asked to reveal their costs in a task-sharing agreement. Task-sharing agreements can also foster heavy reliance on a single customer to a supplier. Some suppliers have mistakenly assumed that by allowing task sharing, the customer was expressing a desire not to shop around for a lower price quote. When Gerber Corporation terminated its relationship with Ball Corporation, a jar manufacturer, Ball was forced to close its plant and lay off most of its 350 employees. Gerber shifted suppliers after getting a lower price quote from another firm. Finally, the risk exists to a customer of revealing a technological breakthrough to a supplier whose parent company is a direct competitor in another line of business.

Recently, Ford Motor Company responded to leaks from suppliers to newspapers about Ford's future products. Ford notified newspaper editors that any information given to them about Ford was confidential.

Wal-Mart has used task sharing with major suppliers, such as Procter & Gamble and other vendors, through electronic data interchange (EDI). Its EDI system was designed to reduce bookkeeping costs and to reduce inventory levels at both the retailer and its EDI-linked suppliers. Wal-Mart had difficulties with inventory replenishment from some of these suppliers. Some grocery suppliers were also concerned that Wal-Mart would use its data as a bargaining tool.

Fleming Companies, a major food wholesaler, has only adopted parts of Efficient Consumer Response. For example, it shares sales with some suppliers and has eliminated some warehouses as goods are shipped from vendors directly to the 10,000 stores it serves. However, Fleming still purchases goods in bulk, arguing that its increased bargaining power with suppliers due to batching purchases is a greater benefit than smaller inventories.

QUESTIONS

1. Contrast task sharing with joint goal setting as a conflict management and resolution strategy.
2. Contrast task sharing with channel-wide committees as a conflict management and resolution strategy.
3. How can a traditional department store use task sharing with an important supplier?
4. Examine task sharing from the perspective of the five dimensions of channel satisfaction discussed in this chapter.

Sources: Fred R. Bleakley, "Some Companies Let Suppliers Work on Site and Even Place Orders," *Wall Street Journal* (January 13, 1995), pp. A1, A6; and Neal Templin and Jeff Cole, "Manufacturers Use Suppliers to Help Them Develop New Products," *Wall Street Journal* (December 19, 1994), pp. A1, A8.

CHAPTER 14

CHANNELS FOR SERVICES AND INTERNATIONAL MARKETING

CHAPTER OBJECTIVES

1. To describe the development of a channel strategy for services.

2. To examine the development of a channel strategy for international marketing.

3. To analyze channel length and width decision making in international markets.

4. To discuss international physical distribution.

5. To illustrate the application of international channels and physical distribution in different regions and countries.

6. To study the legal aspects of international channels as they relate to bribery, controlled goods, distributor termination, and packaging.

In 1993, more than $1 trillion of goods and services was purchased on credit cards; some market analysts predict that credit card sales will reach or exceed $2 trillion by the year 2000. In recent years, the battle for market share in the credit card business has shifted from the United States to foreign markets, especially newly industrialized countries. In Taiwan, for example, the number of credit cards issued increased from 50,000 to 1.3 million in the 18-month period after credit and foreign exchange laws were lifted.

Visa has 323.3 million cards worldwide (and more than a 50 percent share of card volume). MasterCard has 204 million cardholders, and American Express has 35.4 million total cardholders on an international basis. Both Visa and MasterCard are owned by a consortium of financial institutions. The consortium establishes the credit infrastructure and persuades merchants to accept its cards. Member banks then issue credit cards to consumers. Citibank is the largest issuer of credit cards for both Visa and MasterCard. Citibank has locations in 39 countries outside North America. Citibank has 7 million accounts overseas versus 19 million in the United States. In 1993, these overseas cards earned about $100 million after taxes. While American Express predominantly issues cards whose balances must be paid off monthly, it is trying to build up its Optima card.

Specific problems that must be addressed in marketing credit cards on an international basis are gaining merchant acceptance, dealing with wide variations in regulations, understanding differences in consumer attitudes toward credit, and implementing a sophisticated credit system in countries with dated telecommunication systems. We will now discuss each of these issues.

A credit card issuer needs to line up merchants willing to accept cards before seeking to attract a large consumer base. Some credit card issuers have used ploys to line up retailers. In one case, the head of international banking at Poland's BIG Bank posed as a customer placing orders for a large amount of merchandise. The "customer" then refused to pay for the merchandise with cash and insisted on using a Visa card. After other BIG colleagues repeated the ploy over the next few days, the retailer eventually signed up to accept Visa International.

Regulations pertaining to credit cards also differ by country. These laws specify maximum interest rate charges, who is responsible for credit card fraud, and the rights of consumers. In some countries, considerable pressure must be exerted on regulators to allow credit card sales to be made.

There are also large differences in acceptance of credit among consumers in different countries. While most Americans seem to have little difficulty in using credit cards and paying interest charges, many Europeans prefer to use debit cards, where the purchase amount is immediately deducted from the customer's bank account, rather than a traditional credit card. According to some industry experts, Germans are especially reluctant to buy on credit. While Japanese consumers use credit cards extensively while traveling abroad to avoid carrying cash, Japanese consumers are hesitant to use cards at home. Card purchases in Japan amount to less than 1 percent of all consumer transactions. In contrast, in China, credit cards are very popular among foreigners since China does not have an efficient means of transferring money or paying bills.

Lastly, a country needs a sophisticated telecommunications infrastructure to support credit cards. The telecommunications system needs to record purchases, check for lost or stolen bad cards, and determine credit card balances. For example, Estonia does not have a suitable infrastructure to support a large-scale credit card system.

In this chapter, we study channels for services and international marketing. We examine the special characteristics of services, types of channels in services, and physical distribution issues in services marketing. We also examine selected topics pertaining to international channels such as theories of international marketing channel choice, and home and foreign market channel members, and international physical distribution.[1]

INTRODUCTION TO CHANNELS FOR SERVICES AND INTERNATIONAL MARKETING

This chapter covers two specialized areas of channel management: services and international marketing. The chapter focuses on areas where traditional channel management principles and practices need to be modified owing to the special characteristics of services and international markets. As with other chapters, we look at the development of appropriate theoretical issues that affect channel management. We also describe examples of channel management that pertain to services and international markets.

Although these two topics are covered in a single chapter, they are very important areas in terms of sales and profit potential to many firms. Many firms are now exploring the sales of services as a means of controlling the quality of installation and repair on its goods; as a means of ensuring the use of company-produced replacement parts; as a means of diversifying; and as a means of generating profits. International markets are also favored by many firms as many traditional markets in the United States have become saturated, as the standard of living improves throughout the world, and as free markets become a reality in former Communist bloc countries.

CHANNELS FOR SERVICES

The first part of the chapter analyzes channels for services. This part is divided into five sections: types of services and the special characteristics of services, channel activities of service-based intermediaries, types of service channels, physical distribution concerns in the delivery of services, and examples of services channels (banking services and car rentals).

TYPES AND SPECIAL CHARACTERISTICS OF SERVICES AS APPLIED TO CHANNEL MANAGEMENT

Prior to studying the channels for services, it is important to analyze the types of services and their special characteristics. These factors have a major influence on channel management for services.

A common three-way classification system for services is rented-goods services, owned-goods services, and nongoods services. **Rented-goods services** involve the leasing of a good for a limited time period. Examples of rented-goods services include airline tickets, apartment rentals, car leases, and hotel rooms. An **owned-goods service** involves the installation, maintenance, or repair of a good that a consumer owns. Examples of owned-goods services include lawn care, computer repair, plumbing services, and home cleaning services. Lastly, a **nongoods service** involves professional services (such as business consulting, accounting, and legal services) or services with no tangible elements (such as insurance, credit cards, and banking). Each of these types of services has different channel requirements. For example, owned-goods services are often very costly since they have to be performed on-site (in the customer's home, office, or factory). In contrast, nongoods services can be performed in more distant locations and then delivered to consumers (by mail, phone, facsimile, or on-line service). Each of the different types of services has special characteristics.

Services have four special characteristics: intangibility, inseparability, perishability, and variability in quality. **Intangibility** means services cannot be stored, transported, or inventoried. The intangibility characteristic most closely applies to nongoods services. Since intangible services such as a haircut or car wash are created and distributed simultaneously, these services can have no traditional distribution channel other than direct selling. **Inseparability** means services cannot be separated from the seller. Inseparability also implies that services must be consumed at the point of consumption. While inseparability helps foster service vendor loyalty, it makes it difficult for a consumer to transfer vendor loyalty to multiple locations. **Perishability** means that services may have a short life span. There's an old expression that states: "In the supermarket the lettuce wilts, at Broadway the curtain goes up." That is to say, after a given time, a service quickly loses its value. Although rented-goods services are especially prone to perishability, all services share this problem since services, unlike goods, cannot be inventoried. The last special characteristic, **variability in quality**, relates to differences in the quality of services over time. Variability in quality can be reduced through industrializing services (such as using machines to diagnose a problem or mechanizing service production), through systematic training programs, and through standardized procedures.

Originally, many marketing practitioners and scholars assumed that the intangibility and inseparability characteristics of services drastically affected the ability of service marketers to use certain distribution channels.[2] In the past, some marketing experts even argued that direct selling was the only possible channel for services. An indirect channel using one intermediary was the only indirect channel (such as with securities and insurance).

More recently, marketing experts began to better understand that each different type of services could have different channel arrangements. Professor Donnelly, for example, distinguished among two types of services based on whether direct contact was important. For example, although direct contact is necessary for medicine and repair services, it is not essential in banking. According to Professor Donnelly, more intermediaries are possible where direct contact is not necessary.[3]

Professors Palmer and Cole extended Donnelly's direct contact–nondirect contact dichotomy by classifying services based on flexibility in production and consumption.[4] See Figure 14-1. Services can have different degrees of flexibility in terms of where they are produced. For some services, production is inflexible, such as an historic tourist attraction that cannot be moved. Other services are costly, such as body scanners, and available at a few locations. In other cases, production is flexible such as hairdressing that can be performed in a variety of locations. Where production is flexible, services can use a "hub-and-spoke system" wherein the benefits of centralization are combined with locally accessible units. For example, the processing of loans for a bank can be made more efficient by centralizing this operation, whereas local bank offices perform sales and loan application assistance functions.

Services can have different degrees of flexibility in consumption based on how willing consumers are to travel to a service. For example, consumers are willing to travel longer distances to an historic tourist attraction than to a hairdresser. Service providers should seek to increase the accessibility of services by enabling consumers to purchase the service at a large number of locations. Service providers can also reduce the inseparability of services by designing services that can have the advantages of centralized production and flexible consumption.

Service marketers need to reexamine their service access strategies based on the desires of market segments and flexibility in production. Taco Bell, a sub-

FIGURE 14-1 Locational flexibility in production and consumption of services.

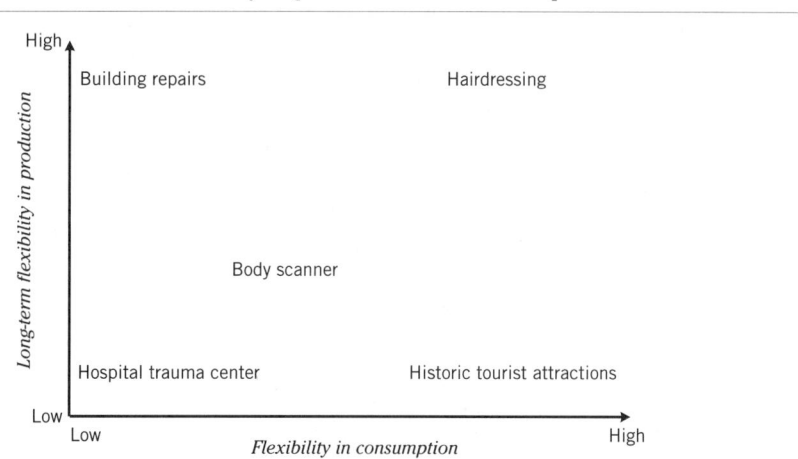

Source: Adapted from Adrian Palmer and Catherine Cole, *Services Marketing: Principles and Practices* (Englewood Cliffs, N.J.: Prentice-Hall, 1995), p. 195. © Prentice Hall, Upper Saddle River, New Jersey. Reprinted by permission.

sidiary of PepsiCo, is an example of a firm that has been able to separate the production and distribution of services. Taco Bell now has 15,000 points of access, including airport, supermarket, and school cafeteria locations. Taco Bell gained locational flexibility by performing heavy-duty food preparation in commissaries run by outside contractors.[5]

CHANNEL ACTIVITIES OF SERVICE-BASED INTERMEDIARIES

Service intermediaries engage in the same channel activities as goods marketers. Table 14-1 describes the channel activities of service-based intermediaries. A common misconception is that owned goods, rented goods, and even

TABLE 14-1 CHANNEL ACTIVITIES OF SERVICE-BASED INTERMEDIARIES

Physical possession	While there is no inventory in nongoods services, owned-goods services have tools and parts, and rented goods services have traditional goods. Rented goods intermediaries take physical possession of this inventory.
Ownership	All intermediaries (except agents and brokers) assume ownership of inventory mentioned in physical possession. In some cases, such as in airlines, wholesalers purchase excess tickets from airlines and resell them as parts of vacation packages.
Promotion	Service channel members are responsible for customer contact. Contact can be mass (such as advertising, publicity, and sales promotion) or individual (such as personal selling).
Negotiation	Service channel members, such as real estate brokers, negotiate price, terms, and commission rates with buyers and sellers.
Financing	Credit terms enable buyers to finance their purchases of services.
Risking	Risks include product obsolescence of rented goods (such as cars), seasonality, economic downturns, increased competition, and reduced demand. Risks for rented goods services are increased due to perishability.
Ordering	Rented goods services channel members order merchandise periodically from their suppliers. For example, tour wholesalers can assemble vacation packages from various sources (airlines, hotels, or car rental agencies). Channel members may have to guarantee a minimum number of sales to secure preferential prices.
Payment	Some service channel members, such as real estate brokers and insurance agents, are paid on a contingent basis based on sales performance.

nongoods service providers have no inventories. A car rental firm has a significant inventory of motor vehicles and faces more difficult variety and assortment decisions than a new or used car dealer. For example, the rental firm needs to know not only the overall mix of car types (such as economy cars, luxury cars, convertibles, station wagons, and vans), but also the particular mix desired by season and even day of week. Although the inventory of an airline wholesaler (which purchases unsold blocks of airline seats several weeks prior to a flight for resale to tourist customers) is intangible, it is costly and has very high risk owing to perishability. Muffler repair service centers also have a large inventory of replacement parts that are specifically made to fit individual auto models.

Unlike some goods-based intermediaries that resell a manufacturer's goods, some service intermediaries take an active part in the creation of a service. For example, a fast-food franchise prepares food; a muffler franchise installs parts; and a child care facility hires and supervises staff, maintains play areas, and prepares and serves meals.

TYPES OF SERVICE CHANNELS

Despite traditional thinking, many different types of marketing intermediaries are used in the distribution of services. For example, insurance can be sold through either independent agents that sell policies of competing firms or company personnel that specialize in selling the insurance policies of one firm. Although independent agents are paid based on commissions, company personnel may be compensated on the basis of a salary plus a bonus system. Many real estate brokerage firms (such as Century 21) and hotels (such as Days Inn) use franchising.

For some owned-goods services (such as plumbing repair) or nongoods services (such as tax preparation), the do-it-yourself consumer is the ultimate competitor to the service provider. Professors Fodness, Pitegoff, and Sautter suggest that two critical dimensions are the complexity of the behavior and the types of facilitating goods required. For example, a final consumer would use a travel agent where training was required, where training was inaccessible, and where facilitating goods (such as a modem for on-line access to a reservations network) were not available. On the other hand, the consumers themselves would plan a trip in which the benefits (lower costs, more convenient flight) outweighed the consumers' costs of performing the services (such as time and equipment purchases).[6]

As with goods marketing, some service providers favor direct marketing as a means of controlling the quality of the service delivery. The use of direct distribution for services also fosters the development of relationships with the service provider, enables cross selling of related products, and increases purchases of company products (as in repair services that use only company-produced parts). Direct distribution of services is appropriate when the scale of the service operation is large enough to provide profits for a single firm. However, as with the marketing of goods, direct distribution of services requires the highest degree of investment risk. For example, State Farm agents do not sell policies of competing firms. General Electric also uses company employees rather than independent repair representatives to service its appliances.

Service providers can be traditional merchant wholesalers. For example, a health maintenance organization (HMO) develops a grouping of general practitioners and specialists under one organization for use by its members. The HMO also provides a patient pool for physicians affiliated with the HMO. Thus, the HMO is an intermediary between a patient and practitioner. Tour consolidators also are merchant wholesalers that purchase and then resell packages consisting of air travel, hotel rooms, sightseeing tours, and car rentals.

The use of agents and brokers as channels for services is characterized by the independent channel member being paid on a commission schedule. Examples of service-based agents and brokers are insurance agents, travel agents, and real estate brokers. A service provider can use agents for a variety of reasons. Many consumers, for example, favor agents that represent competitive service providers. These consumers feel that agents can shop for the best value among competitive service providers (such as with life insurance and travel) and have no allegiance to any one company. Service providers can also seek to attract the customer base of a given agent. Many consumers have high confidence in their travel or insurance agent and rely on his or her judgment. In addition, there is a lower investment in establishing and maintaining an agent-based sales force than with company employees. Agents and brokers provide a ready-made sales force for a new service provider or a service provider expanding into a new geographic territory or new market.

Lastly, many service providers such as Century 21 Real Estate, Days Inn, Blockbuster Video, and Wendy's use franchising. The same benefits and disadvantages that apply to service marketing apply to the marketing of goods to both franchisors and franchisees. However, training of service franchises may be more difficult when franchisees produce the service. See Table 14-2 for examples of franchised services.

PHYSICAL DISTRIBUTION CONCERNS IN THE DELIVERY OF SERVICES

There is a high potential for savings in the delivery of services. A major study by Arthur D. Little and Pennsylvania State University found that the cost to maintain, staff, and schedule the network capacity to provide a service exceeds 75 percent of total costs for a typical service-producing organization.[7] The study found that logistics techniques can be transferred from goods to services industries. For example, there is high commonality between location analysis for retail stores and locational analysis for automatic teller machines or dental offices.

The study formulated a two-part definition of logistics: supply chain logistics and service response logistics. **Supply chain logistics** is the traditional process associated with the physical flow of materials and information. Supply chain logistics encompasses such activities as purchasing, transportation, inventory management, and materials handling, and applies equally to goods and services. In contrast, **service response logistics** is the process of coordinating nonmater-

TABLE 14-2   EXAMPLES OF FRANCHISED SERVICES

Automotive services
Business aids and services
   Accounting/tax services
   Advertising/direct mail
   Business brokers
   Check cashing/financial service centers
   Educational products and services
   Insurance
   Package preparation/shipping/mail services
   Shopping services
   Telecommunications services
Children's services
Construction and home improvement
   Construction/remodeling
   Home appliances: rental and repair
   Home inspection/radon detection
   Lawn and garden services
   Security systems
Employment services
Hotels, motels, and campgrounds
Laundry and dry cleaning
Maintenance and cleaning services
Recreation, entertainment, and travel
Printing, copying, sign products, and services
Real estate services
Rental services: auto and truck
Rental services: equipment and retail
   Formal wear rental
   Rental equipment and supplies
   Uniform rental systems
   Video/audio rental
Restaurants

Source: Franchising in the Economy 1991–1993 (Washington, D.C.: International Franchise Association, 1994), pp. 6–7.

ial activities necessary to fulfill a service in a cost- and customer service-effective manner. Service response logistics is concerned with the quality of inputs at the point of service delivery (such as ATM and the desk clerk's appearance). This form of logistics involves such functions as anticipating service needs, capacity scheduling, and provision of fulfillment channels to meet needs. Banks, for example, need to be concerned with workflows and data flows to schedule tellers, process loan applications, and optimize retail branch locations.

EXAMPLES OF SERVICES CHANNELS

Services channels can be applied to banking services and car rentals. Banking is a nongoods service, whereas car rental service is a rented-good service.

CHANNELS IN ACTION

Quaker State's Q Lube Service Stations

Quaker State is the nation's second largest retailer of motor oil, after Pennzoil. Quaker State's chain of quick-lube service stations, Q Lube, accounts for about 14 percent of the firm's total revenues. Quaker State entered the quick-lube business in 1985 through purchasing Minit Lube. The firm now has 433 stations, most of which are company-owned.

Fast-lube stations offer oil changes and lubrications to consumers without the need for an appointment, or promise to perform these services within 15 to 30 minutes of a scheduled appointment. The fast-lube business is also based on competitive pricing as semi-skilled persons can be easily trained to perform these services. Many quick-lube stations also vacuum car interiors and check brake, antifreeze, and windshield washer fluid levels as part of their service.

Originally, many new car dealers and independent garages were slow to respond to the growth of fast-lube stations. In the 1980s, these centers captured 10 percent of the oil change market. Forty percent went to gas stations and dealers, and 50 percent of consumers changed their motor oil themselves. However, dealers and independent garages soon began to take back the market share lost to fast-lube stations. Some new car dealers and garages reserved one bay for quick lubes. GM dealers even promised a free oil change and lubrication if their service was not performed during the promised time period. And more people went back to changing their own oil to save money.

To further differentiate itself from other quick lube stations, Quick Lube has recently installed a sophisticated computer system that ties all the centers together. The system reminds consumers that they are due for another oil change based on the time and mileage since their last oil change.

Sources: Agis Salpukas, "Quaker State's Quick-Change Artist," *New York Times* (August 23, 1993), p. F7; and "Speed, Service and Loyalty," *New York Times* (August 23, 1993), p. F7.

BANKING SERVICES

Some important innovations have changed the nature of channel management for banking services to the point that more self-service activities are being offered. The banks' use of self-service began with automated teller machines (ATMs) in the late 1970s. Many consumers now use ATMs to receive cash, or they use touch tone telephones to determine their checking account balance or transfer funds among their accounts. From the consumer's perspective, electronic home banking permits banking functions to be performed in a variety of locations; this practice also lowers the required number of locations to a bank. From both the bank's and consumer's point of view, electronic home banking provides 24-hour-a-day, seven-day-a-week access to selected banking services. Electronic home banking has also recently increased owing to the popularity of on-line services. Until now, many banks, for purposes of security, have been reluctant to use on-line services to enable people to apply for loans or credit cards.

Among the major banks, Chase Manhattan, Citibank, and Bank of America all offer electronic home banking. Scores of smaller banks provide similar services. In some cases, banks have joined forces with computer software firms. Many use Prodigy, an on-line network, to enable their customers to view account balances and to pay bills through their personal computer. Chase Manhattan uses Microsoft's Money software to enable the bank's customers to access its electronic services.[8]

Other banks have begun to use machines that allow customers to perform some banking services at supermarkets, office buildings, and shopping malls. Huntington National Bank, for example, has video machines in its supermarket branches. Although the machines will not dispense cash, the machines enable customers to open accounts, apply for loans, transfer funds, and speak with a banking representative 24 hours a day.[9]

As of mid-1995, fewer than 350,000 computer users banked at home according to estimates by market analysts. However, analysts expect this number to increase to 7.5 million by 1998 as more households purchase computers.[10] According to the senior vice president of marketing for Huntington National Bank, 20 to 30 percent of all retail banking will be performed over telephone lines as of 1998.

Some banking analysts are concerned that the new technologies will lessen opportunities for banks to cross-sell other services such as mutual funds, life insurance, and certificates of deposit. Other analysts caution that banks will still have to provide low-tech services for consumers uncomfortable with using home computers or for consumers without personal computers or modems. For example, Meridian Bancorp, headquartered in Reading, Pennsylvania, has hitching posts for its Amish customers' horse-drawn buggies. The bank also has two-way remote terminals for high-tech consumers who want to see and talk to bank representatives on the street.[11]

In addition to electronic home banking, many banks have begun to use a hub-and-spoke system where neighborhood branches offer services tailored to their communities (such as providing small business loans in commercial districts) and centrally located main branches provide a full complement of services. Fifth Third Bancorp, for example, uses its Bank Marts (new units mainly in new subdivisions, malls, and retail areas such as Kroger supermarkets) as spokes for deposits and withdrawals and its larger branches as hubs. The bank needs $6 million in deposits for its Bank Mart locations and $12 million for regular branches to meet profit projections. Branches that do not meet these levels will be closed.[12]

CAR RENTAL SERVICES

In contrast to banking services, car rentals are a rented-goods service. The largest car rental firm in the United States is privately held Enterprise Rent-A-Car. Enterprise has a fleet of 232,000 operating out of 2000 locations. All of Enterprise's units are company owned. In contrast, Hertz has 215,000 cars operating out of 1175 locations.[13]

Enterprise Rent-A-Car uses a totally different channel strategy than either Hertz or Avis. Both Hertz and Avis specialize in higher cost rental cars rented to both business and vacation travelers. In contrast, Enterprise Rent-A-Car is a low-cost firm specializing in the insurance replacement market (for people whose car was involved in an accident or stolen). Two-thirds of Enterprise's $1.85 billion 1994 sales were insurance related.

Enterprise's strategy is based on a low-cost philosophy that relies on the use of inexpensive locations, shorter hours, older cars, and nonpayment of commissions to travel agents. In contrast to Avis and Hertz which use decentralized airport locations that are costly in terms of rent and staffing, Enterprise uses centralized off-site locations (such as storefronts and strip shopping center locations). Although Enterprise has some locations near airports, it has no airport service desk location. Its rental facilities are also typically located 5 to 10 minutes away from major airports by shuttle bus. And while Hertz's and Avis's airport locations are open the same hours as airports, many Enterprise rental offices close at 9:00 P.M. and open at noon on Sundays. Enterprise also uses older cars. Although Hertz and Avis use cars purchased on six-month contracts (through buyback programs with the car's manufacturers), Enterprise keeps its cars for 18 months and gets better deals by favoring models that are about to be discontinued or redesigned. Lastly, unlike Hertz and Avis, Enterprise does not pay commissions to travel agents.

As a result, Enterprise can rent cars at 30 to 50 percent below its higher cost rivals. For example, Enterprise's daily rate for a midsize car in March 1995 was $27 versus Avis's and Hertz's charge of $58 in Atlanta. In Boston, a comparable car was $56 per day through Avis or Hertz and $36 through Enterprise.[14] To gain favor with insurance agents, Enterprise provides a discount of 25 percent or so to insurance agents. Enterprise also maintains close contact with new car dealers, auto body shops, and garages. The firm even has a rental booth with an attendant in large repair facilities. To improve its access to customers, an Enterprise attendant generally will drive the firm's rental car to repair stations, a customer's home, or even a hotel.

CHANNELS FOR INTERNATIONAL MARKETING

The international channel environment is a complex one. The complexity of foreign markets requires that firms intensively study each foreign environment, prepare for specific contingencies, and be able to adapt their strategy to take advantage of opportunities or to minimize problem areas. For example, although Toys "R" Us studied Mexico for several years before entering the market, it was unable to foresee the collapse of the peso in December 1994. J. C. Penney quickly postponed the opening of two of its four planned stores in Mexico during this time period.

A firm's international strategy needs to reflect the ability to obtain suitable products in each foreign market, differences in culture, the availability of channel members in different markets, and specialized channel regulations.

In some cases, a firm needs to change its product mix owing to quality considerations, local content laws (which require goods to be produced in the foreign market), quotas, high tariffs, or cultural factors that favor different goods and services. For example, because of quality considerations, Marks and Spencer's food accounts for only 10 percent of sales in Hong Kong versus 40 percent in Britain.[15]

Products sold in foreign markets also need to reflect the cultural differences present in each market. IKEA, for example, had to increase its furniture sizes from those sold in Europe in order to accommodate larger room sizes in the United States. Cultural differences also continue to exist in Europe, despite the European Union's 282 directives that seek to standardize product rules. According to a product manager at Atag Holdings NV, a diversified Dutch company that manufactures kitchen appliances, "To sell in America, you need one or two types of ceramic stove top. In Europe you need 11." Belgians, for instance, want extra-large burners, Germans like oval burners to match their oval pots, and French consumers desire small burners that are most appropriate for simmering sauces and broths.[16]

Channel member availability differs by country and even by region within a country. Sometimes, the best channel is not available because of legal restraints, the reseller's long-term relationship with other firms, or cultural differences that favor small stores. In Russia, for example, much retailing is still characterized by sidewalk kiosks and state-owned stores.[17] The term **locked-up channel** is used when a suitable channel is unavailable. In some cases, international marketers use piggybacking as a means of circumventing a locked-up channel. In **piggybacking**, the distribution channels of a manufacturer selling noncompeting goods to the same market are used. Through piggybacking, the exporter gains access to a distribution channel, while the foreign firm that provides the distribution channel is able to earn additional funds and better serve its existing customers. The foreign firm that performs the piggybacking service is generally compensated in a similar manner as a merchant wholesaler.

Regulations also differ by country. To counter the growth of superstores, France has stopped authorizing stores larger than 1000 square meters (10,800 square feet). Britain and the Netherlands have imposed **greenbelts** outside towns and cities that forbid development by superstores and other forms of retailing through strict zoning laws.[18]

In the next section, we will explore international marketing channels. First, we look at several theories of international channel choice. Second, we examine studies on the use of specific international channels. Third, we study the characteristics of specific home and foreign channel members. And fourth, we describe channel length and channel width decision making in international markets.

THEORIES OF INTERNATIONAL CHANNEL CHOICE

Four theories of international channel choice are presented here. These theories describe the effect of commitment on channel choice; channel choice as a function of risk (using factors such as political stability and legal barriers); changes in a firm's channel arrangements as it becomes more experienced in an international market; and the effect of a country's stage of economic development on channel length.

The first theory states that a firm's use of specific international channels is related to its commitment to international business. Four possible levels of commitment are ethnocentrism, polycentrism, regiocentrism, and geocentrism.[19] **Ethnocentrism** is the lowest level of commitment. In this level, the objective of international business is to dispose of surplus stock in home markets. A firm's channels in foreign markets under ethnocentrism are developed in the company's home office using identical strategies to those in the firm's domestic market. Physical distribution strategies are also as similar as possible to those used in the firm's home market. In **polycentrism**, subsidiaries are established in foreign markets, and each subsidiary designs its channel strategy independently. With polycentrism, a firm typically uses the traditional channels in each country. **Regiocentrism** designs business programs on the basis of similarities within an area; these similarities go beyond national boundaries. Lastly, in **geocentrism**, business programs are standardized throughout the world. Both regiocentric and geocentric orientations ignore national boundaries, and both use regional or global channels of distribution.

With regard to the second theory, the impact of risk on channel choice, Professors Goodnow and Hansz found that the degree of control over a firm's distribution channel declines as the risk level becomes less favorable. The authors defined risk on the basis of political stability, market opportunity, economic development, cultural unity, legal barriers, physiographic barriers, and geocultural distance.[20]

The third theory examines the impact of experience on channel choice. One model developed by Professors Johanson and Vahlne, based on the authors' observations in Sweden, suggests that a firm typically begins to export using an agent, next establishes a sales subsidiary, and may then begin production in the host country.[21] This theory suggests that firms start with the least degree of commitment strategy and gradually increase their commitment as they experience success in foreign markets. Although the Johanson and Vahlne theory implies that older firms would have more integrated international marketing channels than younger firms, other studies suggest that younger firms are more favorably disposed and active in international marketing than older firms.[22] Other studies argue that manufacturers often set up direct sales forces to get effective market share in foreign markets and then switch to the use of intermediaries. Still other authorities maintain that many firms should use export intermediaries on a permanent basis.[23]

The fourth theory examines the effect of a country's stage of economic development on channel structure. Some studies found that channels lengthen as nations develop; that channels shorten; and that channels first lengthen and then shorten.[24] While these various studies have no unifying framework, most agree that several factors influence channel length as a country's economic stage of development matures: Increased channel length and channel specialization are related to changes in the size of market demand; the intermediary choice is based on low-cost performance, market coverage, and a desired level of service; and channel length reflects a country's economic development stage, as well as social, political, and historical factors.

Professors Sharma and Dominguez found that channels first lengthen and then shorten with further economic development. These authors assume that the reversal in direction occurs when society has begun to achieve a high level of income. At this income level, competition and customer service become more important than low distribution costs.[25]

A fifth theory, transaction cost analysis, is covered later in this chapter.

USE OF SPECIFIC INTERNATIONAL CHANNELS

Three major studies recently examined the use of specific international channels. The earliest study, by Professors Bello and Williamson, found that the most widely used method of exporting by U.S. manufacturers is to sell direct to foreign distributors or end-users.[26] The authors showed that small to medium manufacturers typically lack the capital and necessary knowledge to sell directly to overseas buyers.

The second study, by Professors Seifert and Ford, examined channels used by small industrial manufacturers. Although the respondents used 19 different channel members, the two leading channels, sales representatives and export distributors, were used 51 percent of the time. The next most employed channel was the commission agent, which was used 25 percent of the time. Only eight channel members (commission agents, country-controlled buying offices, export merchants, purchasing agents, sales representatives, export distributors, export brokers, and trading companies) were mentioned more than ten times.[27]

The third study, by Professors Klein, Frazier, and Roth, examined the channels used by a group of Canadian export firms that were identified through an industry directory. Of 510 firms that responded, 121 served the market directly from Canada using company personnel, 76 sold to merchant distributors that take title to products and contact buyers themselves, 74 used commission agents, 62 firms had a wholly owned sales subsidiary, and 13 firms used a joint venture. The other firms used other channels or dual channels.[28]

Although the samples used in all three studies differ, the studies suggest that export distributors, sales representatives, and commission agents represent the most important channels.

HOME MARKET CHANNEL MEMBERS

Many authors differentiate among home market channel members and foreign market channel members based on the location of channel members that serve foreign markets. There are three home market channel member alternatives: export management companies, export merchants and agents, and direct exporting.

Export management companies are domestic firms that perform all aspects of export operations under a specific agreement. Export management companies have an established network of sales offices. These firms often work for several noncompeting firms that produce complementary products. Export management companies give a domestic firm a quick start in a foreign market since an export management company is already functioning.

Export merchants can take title or function as agents. In contrast to an export management company, export merchants retain their own identities. Export merchants often focus on one country or one region. These merchants provide limited services, focusing on the sale and distribution of goods. As a merchant wholesaler, export merchants may charge a fee for market development work. As an agent, export merchants require the manufacturer's approval on all orders. As with domestic marketing, some agents have spread themselves too thin by taking on too many lines and are not able to give adequate attention to each manufacturer.

CHANNELS IN ACTION

Small Firms Use Export Merchants to Enter Foreign Markets

Increasingly, small and medium-sized manufacturers are relying on export merchants, wholesalers that sell to foreign markets, to increase their foreign sales. Typically, these export merchants purchase U.S. goods at as much as 15 percent below a manufacturer's best price and then resell them in foreign markets. The United States Commerce Department estimates that there are now between 2000 and 2500 foreign wholesalers in the United States. Export merchants account for close to half of the members of the National Association of Export Companies.

Three examples of export merchants are International Projects Inc., Dreyfus & Associates, and Koudis International Inc. International Projects Inc. serves as an export merchant for manufacturers of pleasure boats, hospital equipment, air conditioner repair equipment, and stationery. The firm recently signed a five-year agreement with a small manufacturer of equipment that exchanges coins for paper currency. The manufacturer realized that it did not have the resources for international marketing. International Projects has annual sales of $8 million.

Dreyfus & Associates represents eight tool manufacturers in their foreign sales efforts. Dreyfus & Associates relies on foreign trade shows, a global database of 1500 distributors, and long-distance phone calls and facsimile (fax) transmissions.

Koudis International Inc. sells commercial air conditioners for its U.S. clients. The firm tracks leads generated by the United States Department of Commerce and the *Journal of Commerce.* One lead resulted in the sale of U.S. commercial air conditioners to Japan.

While export merchants can be very effective, manufacturers need to be aware of their disadvantages: (1) their use results in higher costs to buyers; (2) since they represent multiple manufacturers, they can shift their loyalty; and (3) some foreign buyers feel more comfortable dealing directly with a manufacturer.

Source: Michael Selz, "More Small Firms Are Turning to Trade Intermediaries," *Wall Street Journal* (February 2, 1993), p. B2.

In **direct exporting**, a firm carries out its foreign sales through in-house personnel. Direct exporting is carried out administratively through the use of export personnel as part of a firm's traditional sales department, a separate export department, or export sales subsidiary. A firm involved in direct exporting must have specialized personnel with knowledge of foreign markets, customs documentation, insurance requirements, and international physical distribution. Of the home market channel alternatives, direct exporting provides the highest degree of control. In some markets, such as Brazil, U.S.-based companies cannot establish their own autonomous sales forces. U.S. companies can enter the Brazilian market by forming a joint venture with a native firm.[29]

FOREIGN MARKET CHANNEL MEMBERS

The choice of foreign channel arrangements should be based on such factors as tradeoffs between cost and control, desired rate of market penetration, legal barriers in specific countries, and financial objectives.[30] The same firm could appropriately use different channels for different countries based on a country's factors. In Europe, for instance, McDonald's uses wholly owned subsidiaries. As in the United States, these subsidiaries operate company-owned stores and also license out franchises. In Asia, McDonald's uses joint ventures, usually on a 50–50 partnership, after McDonald's receives its royalty, rent, and advertising fees, which generally total 16.5 percent of sales. This joint venture allows McDonald's access into a foreign partner's connections and local expertise. In markets such as Saudi Arabia, McDonald's reduces its risk by investing none of its equity capital. McDonald's licenses its name with strict requirements as to operating standards in these markets.[31]

The methods of entry into foreign markets using foreign channel members are generally classified as exporting, joint venture, and direct ownership. A single company can use a variety of foreign market entry formulas based on the countries being targeted.

Table 14-3 describes the degree of fit of these three channel options under various circumstances. For example, exporting is a good fit when investment and political risk is high. In contrast, direct ownership is a poor fit under these circumstances. Figure 14-2 describes these three arrangements on the basis of level of control and cost of entry. Note that level of control and cost of entry are directly related. As the level of control increases, the cost of entry increases. Exporting has the lowest level of control and the lowest cost of entry. In contrast, the level of control and cost of entry are highest with direct ownership.

Exporting

The majority of world trade is handled through independent middlemen. These exporters generally have high levels of local market knowledge, contacts with foreign buyers, and the ability to provide special marketing services.[32] Many firms use exporting as a means of first entry into foreign markets due to low levels of risk and investment. There are two types of exporters: foreign distributors and foreign agents.

TABLE 14-3 THE IMPACT OF COUNTRY VARIABLES ON FOREIGN CHANNEL CHOICE

	Country Variables			
Channel Option	Local Shopkeeper Protection	Adverse Legal Environment	Foreign Ownership Restrictions	Investment and Political Risk
Exporting	Good fit	Good fit	Good fit	Good fit
Joint venture	Marginal fit	Good fit	Marginal fit	Marginal fit
Direct ownership	Poor fit	Poor fit	Poor fit	Poor fit

Source: Adapted from "Exploring Market Formulas," *Coopers & Lybrand/Chain Store Age Executive Special Issue,* Vol. 69, No. 12 (n.d.), p. 25. Reprinted by permission from *Chain Store Age Executive.* Copyright Lebhar-Friedman, Inc., 425 Park Avenue, New York, NY 10022.

Foreign distributors are independent merchants who purchase goods for their account and then resell these goods to a foreign buyer. Foreign distributors are similar to merchant wholesalers in domestic markets. These distributors sell the products of several companies. The distributor is also responsible for payment.

Foreign agents serve as an intermediary between the domestic firm and the buyer but operate under the supervision of the domestic firm.[33] Foreign agents are similar to the agents used within the United States. Foreign agents do not take title to goods, are paid on the basis of sales commissions, and are not responsible if the ultimate purchaser fails to pay.[34]

FIGURE 14-2 Evaluating foreign channel arrangements by level of control and cost of entry.

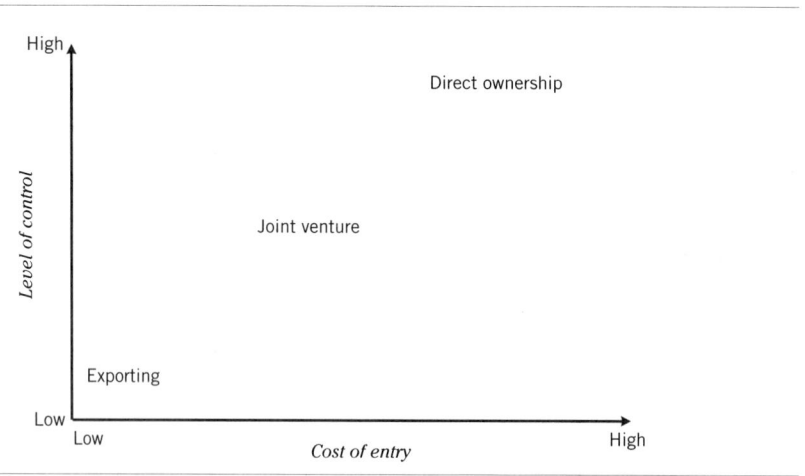

Source: Adapted from "Exploring Market Formulas," *Coopers & Lybrand/Chain Store Age Executive Special Issue,* Vol. 69, No. 12 (n.d.), p. 25. Reprinted by permission from *Chain Store Age Executive.* Copyright Lebhar-Friedman, Inc., 425 Park Avenue, New York, NY 10022.

Joint Venture

International channel joint ventures take four forms: licensing, foreign franchising, a local partner, and an original equipment manufacturer (OEM). Joint ventures enable U.S. firms to share risks in foreign channels with local firms, to utilize the business contacts and market knowledge of their foreign partners, and to gain access to foreign nationals as executives. Joint ventures are often used when direct ownership is prohibited.

Under **licensing**, a company assigns its rights to a trademark, a patent, or a store name to another firm for a royalty or fee. Licenses typically are assigned for a given number of years. Some firms use licensing when a market is too small for direct ownership but large enough to be profitable on a licensing basis. The use of licensing in retailing also facilitates expansion by small companies with prestigious names. For example, L. L. Bean licensed its name to The Seiyu Ltd., one of Japan's largest general merchandisers.

Foreign franchising enables a local entrepreneur with knowledge of a foreign country to invest in a proven retail concept in the foreign country. For the franchisor, a significant portion of the investment risk is shifted to the franchisee. Increasingly, foreign franchising is used as a vehicle for foreign expansion. In 1971, United States franchisors operated only 3365 units outside the United States; by 1988, the number was 35,000 units. In 1992, one-third of all franchises had foreign operations.[35] Many developing countries now see franchising as a means of lowering the risk for nationals to own their own business and as an important means of encouraging economic growth. For example, Mexico, Argentina, and Spain have recently begun changing distribution laws to make franchising a more viable option.

As in the United States, several strategies can be employed to expand through franchising in foreign markets. According to one strategy, a firm can sell individual franchises overseas, and according to a second, a firm can appoint a master franchisor for a foreign country or region. The master franchisor can either develop franchises for its own use or sell franchises. Through a third strategy, a domestic firm can develop a joint venture with a foreign firm. The joint venture company becomes a master franchisor. Many companies use a mix of these techniques, based on local conditions, availability of partners, and legal constraints. An example of a foreign franchise system is The Body Shop, a London-based cosmetics firm with over 1000 stores in 44 countries. Less than 10 percent of these stores are company owned.

In a **local partner** arrangement, a domestic company teams up with a foreign firm. Often the foreign partner has access to specialized distribution channels, the ability to cut though bureaucratic red tape, warehouse and distribution facilities, high brand recognition, and access to foreign capital. For example, Barney's New York, an upscale clothing-based department store, teamed up with Isetan Co., Ltd., a Japanese specialty store, to open Barney's first Tokyo outlet. In 1993, Barney's opened a second store in Yokohama.

The success of any local partner arrangement is based on choosing the right partner and maintaining a relationship of trust. For example, Wal-Mart attributes much of its success in Mexico to its joint venture partner, Cifra, Mexico's largest retailer as a local partner. On the other hand, Carrefour blames the failure of its hypermarkets in the United States on the shortcomings of its local partner.³⁶ According to a U.S. manufacturer of frozen bagel dough who picked the wrong partner in Europe, "It's like a marriage breaking up. You face all the horrible pains of divorce if it comes to that."³⁷

An **original equipment manufacturer (OEM)** is a foreign firm that sells its products to a local firm, but under the local firm's brand name. The domestic firm uses the foreign firm's brand image and distribution network. An original equipment manufacturer is similar to a private-label strategy in the United States. For example, Matsushita sells its videocassette recorders in the United States under RCA, Magnavox, and General Electric brands. The OEM strategy enables Matsushita to gain ready access to the distribution channels of these firms.

DIRECT OWNERSHIP

Direct ownership of foreign channels enables a domestic firm to maximize its control. Direct ownership is appropriate when it is legal, when a firm has access to capital, and when investment and political risk is relatively low. Direct ownership requires the largest investment in capital and resources. It also requires that a firm understand the foreign market from both a business and a cultural perspective. IKEA uses direct ownership as it expands on a global basis. In some cases, a firm that utilizes direct investment also grows internationally through acquisition. Acquisition enables the firm to obtain desirable retail sites, talented management personnel, and warehousing facilities.

CHANNEL LENGTH AND WIDTH IN INTERNATIONAL MARKETS

Certain factors affect channel length and width in international marketing. In this regard, we study transaction cost analysis, a theory that relates the development of transaction-specific assets and environmental uncertainty to channel length. For channel width, we examine the use of a formula that determines the appropriate number of channels. (You may want to refer back to Chapter 11 to reexamine general factors influencing channel length and width decision making.)

CHANNEL LENGTH DECISION MAKING

Professor Williamson contends that foreign markets are generally better off using an independent international channel in the absence of market frictions and scale economies. Independent channel member distributors are preferred for three reasons. First, independent channel members pool the demand for distribution services from several manufacturers. Second, bureaucratic structures and organizational politics are minimized. And third, an independent distributor who does not perform adequately can be replaced.³⁸ Other researchers have argued that most companies would prefer to run their own international marketing operations, but use distributors owing to low sales volume and high startup costs.[39]

One important research stream on channel length in international markets uses a transaction cost analysis (TCA) framework. In **transaction cost analysis**, firms seek to minimize the sum of transaction and production costs in making forward integration decisions. Transaction cost analysis theory argues that integrated channels are more likely to be used when transaction-specific assets accumulate. These assets include specialized knowledge and relationships based on distributing the brand over a long time period.[40] Transaction cost analysis also predicts that environmental uncertainty motivates a firm to use a more integrated mode of governance.

Transaction-specific assets are those investments that are required to complete a transaction and that have little use otherwise. These can include physical locations, specific physical assets, and specific human assets. Transaction-specific assets include specialized knowledge of market conditions and working relationships with the principal.[41] Because these assets are dedicated to a particular trading partner, their value would be lost if the particular intermediary were terminated. **Environmental uncertainty** is the extent to which an environment changes rapidly and allows a firm to be caught by surprise. In diverse environments, there are multiple sources of uncertainty in the environment.[42]

Professors Anderson and Coughlan studied distribution in foreign markets by U.S. firms in the semiconductor industry. The researchers found that products requiring the development of specialized skills and working relationships were more likely to be distributed through company channels than through independent channels.[43]

Professors Klein, Frazier, and Roth studied factors that can affect channel length in international marketing using a transaction cost analysis framework.[44] They found that hierarchical exchanges (using a foreign sales subsidiary or serving the foreign market from home) are more likely to be used when specialized knowledge and investments are necessary for international trade. Foreign sales subsidiaries were also more likely to be used when the environment is volatile. However, the authors found that channel volume and shared channel notions have a stronger relationship to channel choice than asset specificity and environmental volatility.

Professors Bello and Lohtia also studied the use of foreign distributors and foreign agents using a transaction cost analysis framework. The researchers divided assets into product assets, human assets, and specific physical assets. Diversity was also broken into two components. The researchers found that agent users make higher product and human investments. The results for environmental uncertainty suggest that low to moderate volatility in a foreign market does not affect agent or distributor choice. However, highly diverse markets favor the use of distributors.[45]

CHANNEL WIDTH DECISION MAKING

Distribution density refers to the number of outlets required to effectively sell a firm's products or services. Once the proper number of retail outlets is established, a firm can then estimate the number of wholesalers needed to service these retailers.

McDonald's uses the following formula to determine the appropriate number of McDonald's locations in a foreign country:[46]

$$\text{Potential penetration of McDonald's in country X} = \frac{\text{Population of country X}}{\text{No. of people per McDonald's in United States (25,000)}} \times \frac{\text{Per-capita income of country X}}{\text{Per-capita income of United States (\$23,120)}}$$

This formula assumes that there should be 25,000 people per McDonald's for countries with the same per-capita income as in the United States. The appropriate number of McDonald's per country should be based on the country's per-capita income as a percentage of per-capita income in the United States. Thus, a country with a population of 5 million and with 70 percent of U.S. per-capita income should have 140 McDonald's. When we apply this formula, we can determine growth prospects for McDonald's. Japan now has 1070 McDonald's but a 6100 market potential based on this formula. China has 23 McDonald's, and yet based on this formula, it has a potential for 784.

Whereas the formula may represent a good start in determining the potential for a foreign market, it has several problems. A less developed country may have proportionately less income available for McDonald's than an industrialized society. There can also be diminishing returns as more McDonald's begin to compete with each other. Moreover, the formula ignores important differences in consumer behavior within each foreign market. For example, the appropriate number of McDonald's in a foreign country should be related to the ability of shoppers to travel, the appropriateness of McDonald's menu, and the importance of the social relationship of eating (such as the importance of eating a meal as a family).[47] Finally, the formula assumes that the average size of retail outlets will be equal in all parts of the world.

The same formula can be modified to reflect ownership or usage of selected goods. For example, Latin America has 63 cars and 150 televisions per 1000 people as compared with 575 cars and 798 televisions per 1000 people in North America. And Africa has only 15 cars and 23 televisions per 1000 people.[48] In determining the market potential for each area, marketers need to determine the relative cost of these durables in each foreign country. One such measure is the number of hours a typical consumer needs to work to purchase a good.

Nondurable sales are often quoted in usage per capita by country. For example, Mexico leads the world at 333 servings of carbonated soft drinks per year per person (in comparison to the U.S. consumption of 310 servings per capita). The lowest consumption is in the Ukraine (91 servings per capita), China (3 servings), and India (2 servings).[49]

An alternative to using the McDonald's formula is to evaluate foreign markets on the basis of market saturation ratios such as average sales per retail store, average sales per retail category, and average sales per employee. Benchmarks for these ratios can be developed on a regional basis. These ratios should decline as a market becomes saturated.

INTERNATIONAL PHYSICAL DISTRIBUTION

A major concern in international channel management is physical distribution management. Physical distribution in international marketing is complicated because of the multiple locations that must be scheduled, the poor quality of the transportation infrastructure in some countries, different communications standards, and the required documentation.

International shipments must first be routed from the exporter to a port of export; then transferred to another mode of transportation for travel to the foreign destination; and again transferred to the final consumer or end-user. In some cases, special protective packaging is needed owing to moisture, road conditions, and the length of the journey. The packaging may increase the weight and bulk of packages. In some markets, such as Poland, there are shortages of trucks and warehouse space.[50]

The transportation infrastructure in foreign markets varies widely. The quality of the infrastructure affects distribution to the foreign country, as well as distribution within the country. In some countries, suppliers encounter poor-quality roads, bottlenecks at airports, and poor-quality telecommunications systems. For example, in the former Soviet Union, Procter & Gamble ships its products, mostly from Europe, by sea to St. Petersburg. The sea route is used to avoid tie-ups that trucks face at border crossings. However, getting products from warehouses to stores is still a major problem.[51]

Although electronic data interchange (EDI) is common throughout the world, each country and industry may have different protocol standards. Different standards may also be used for different types of goods. Thus, a diversified manufacturer may need multiple systems.

Common export documents are a bill of lading and a shipper's export declaration. A **bill of lading** acknowledges receipt of goods by the carrier, represents the basic contract between the shipper and carrier, and serves as evidence of title to the goods. Bills of lading may be negotiable (rights can be transferred to other parties) or nonnegotiable (called straight bills). A **shipper's export declaration** states that the shipper has authorization for export. This declaration lists the names and addresses of the principals, a description of the goods, the declared value of the goods, and the final destination of the goods. The shipper's export declarations are used to compute data relative to exports as well as to determine whether the goods shipped meet export regulations. Other documents that may be required are an **import license**, authorizing a firm to import certain goods; a **foreign exchange license**, enabling the importer to secure currency to pay for the shipment; and a **certificate of origin** which ensures collection of tariffs.

Four factors that simplify international physical distribution are the standardization of documentation, export automation software, foreign freight forwarders and customs agents, and foreign trade zones.

Fortunately, standardization of documentation in physical distribution was recently required as a result of the United States Standard Master for International Trade. Certain required information such as the export carrier and the document number are also now in the same position on all forms. The EU has also simplified shipment documentation. Export automation software has also been developed. **Export automation software** programs help create commercial invoices, country-of-origin certificates, packaging slips (written in multiple languages), and export-declaration forms.[52] Federal Express and United Parcel Service may provide automation assistance, in some cases free-of-charge, to exporters making a minimum number of shipments per day.

Many domestic firms that sell goods in foreign markets also use facilitators such as foreign freight forwarders and customs agents. A **foreign freight forwarder** is a specialist that provides transportation, shipping documentation, and customs-related services. Foreign freight forwarders also advise clients on foreign label requirements, as well as export restrictions. Forwarders are used by both large firms desiring to consolidate small shipments and by smaller firms that do not have such specialists. Another international physical distribution intermediary is a customs agent. A **customs agent** prepares necessary documentation for a good to clear customs, pays duties, and then ships the goods to their final destination. These facilitators reduce the complexity of physical distribution.

An important development in international physical distribution is the use of foreign trade zones. In a **foreign trade zone**, merchandise can be stored for unlimited time periods without the payment of duties. Duties for goods stored in a foreign trade zone are due when goods are shipped into the country where the foreign trade zone is located. Foreign trade zones are often close to airports or ports. The United States had more than 200 foreign trade zones as of 1994.[53] Foreign trade zones are considered to be outside the jurisdiction of customs. Thus, a firm using a foreign trade zone saves interest expense on duties while goods are being warehoused. There are also lower insurance costs owing to greater security in a foreign trade zone. In Wal-Mart's Savannah, Georgia, foreign trade zone, for example, Wal-Mart will pay no duties on goods imported until it ships them to stores in the United States and none if it exports them to its stores in Canada, Mexico, and South America.[54]

EXAMPLES OF INTERNATIONAL CHANNELS AND PHYSICAL DISTRIBUTION

This section provides examples of international channels and physical distribution in three areas: the European Union (EU), Eastern Europe, and Japan.

EUROPEAN UNION

The European Union (EU) is the most important economic community in the world. Its members are Austria, Belgium, Denmark, Finland, France, Germany, Great Britain, Greece, Ireland, Italy, Luxembourg, the Netherlands, Portugal,

Spain, and Sweden. On January 1, 1993, officials at most European borders stopped making passport and customs checks that once delayed the free movement of goods across member borders. Prior to this date, border crossings were so stalled that some truckers even hired specialists to fill out the required forms, while the truckers waited in local shops and bars. Now, the EU has a border-free market of 12 nations and 345 million customers.

The EU has also developed common standards for many goods. One particularly important standard is ISO9000. Developed by the International Organization for Standardization (ISO), **ISO9000** provides purchasers with a means of specifying suppliers (based on compliance with a quality assurance process), and third-party certification of suppliers. By February 1993, the EU and 56 other countries had adopted the ISO9000 series. While European Union directives require mandatory compliance with ISO9000 for a number of products (such as medical devices, construction products, industrial safety equipment, and gas appliances), many suppliers give preference to ISO9000-certified suppliers for other products.[55]

Common standards, together with the ease of goods going across borders, have facilitated cross-border shopping. In some markets, large differences in prices exist owing to varying tax and exchange rates, differences in farmer subsidies, and differences in competition.[56] For example, the excise tax on 26 gallons of beer is 0.25 European Currency Units (ECUs) compared with 1.46 ECUs in Britain. The value-added taxes (VATs) also differ by country.[57]

In terms of physical distribution, Belgium, the Netherlands, and Luxembourg dominate European transportation and distribution. It has been estimated that Rotterdam and Antwerp handle more than one-third of all U.S. container shipments to Europe. A large proportion of distribution centers have now been developed in the Netherlands. More than 170 million people, half of the EU's population, live within 300 miles of Amsterdam.[58]

EASTERN EUROPE

Eastern Europe's population of 400 million is about 10 percent smaller than the 430 million in Western Europe. The average income of Eastern Europe now approaches that of Portugal or Greece. According to some analysts, Eastern Europeans share a similar culture with Western consumers.[59]

Eastern Europe is undergoing rapid changes. For example, before economic reform, Poland's state-run food stores were operated by attendants. Customers first had to order merchandise from attendants, who then picked the ordered items. Since customers were unable to examine any items before purchase, there was little opportunity for impulse shopping. Now a new supermarket chain, Semeco-Okmess, has introduced a modern format and Western goods to Poland. Semeco-Okmess uses modern shelving, promotion racks, and conveyor-driven checkouts. More than 80 percent of the items stocked are Western foods and consumer products. Between 1990 and 1995, most of Polish retailing shifted to private stores.[60]

The transformation from communism to a free-market economy in Eastern Europe, though exciting, has produced many frustrations. There is a lack of trucks and warehouses, market research is scarce, and local managers often do not understand the basics of marketing and logistics. For example, when Unilever purchased an ice cream company in 1991 (in what was then Czechoslovakia), it did not have a reliable distribution system to get the product into retail stores. Unilever found that its ice cream often reached stores half-melted. Unilever has devoted considerable time and effort to setting up a system of wholesalers and transportation in all Eastern European countries.[61]

JAPAN

Japan's distribution system is characterized by long and complex channel arrangements as well as **keiretsu**, Japanese corporate groupings that typically contain a bank, a trading company, and over 20 groups of industrial enterprises. Both of these factors often restrict the market entry of foreign goods into Japanese channels.

Retailing in Japan is often characterized by single-product-line stores, a local neighborhood orientation, small stores, and long channels, with two or more levels of wholesalers between the manufacturer and the retailer.[62] In comparison to the United States and Western Europe, Japan has the highest number of stores per capita and per area.[63] According to Professors Goodnow and Kosenko, "the real barriers to exporting to Japan are not government regulations. Rather, they are cultural barriers inherent in the Japanese domestic distribution system."[64]

The Japanese economy is also dominated by keiretsu. The six largest keiretsu are Mitsubishi, Mitsui, Sumitomo, Fuji, Sanwa, and Dai-Ichi Kangyo. These control about half of Japan's import buying. Each keiretsu has only one member company representing each industrial sector to minimize intergroup competition. Many foreign firms have difficulty in breaking into Japanese distribution systems owing to the internal production capabilities of the keiretsu, and family ties, interlocking directorates, and management exchanges among firms.[65]

According to marketing experts, several strategies can be used to penetrate Japan's distribution system. The first strategy involves bypassing the traditional channels to penetrate a market. For example, Schick used a major cutlery wholesaler that controlled a particular channel to capture a large share of the razor blade market. A second strategy involves piggybacking. Johnson & Johnson was successful in health-care supplies by using traditional channels and building a market presence for its brands through push and pull promotional effort. A Japanese partner is a third approach. Maxwell House used a traditional channel that was controlled by Ajinomoto, a major food company, which had a strong distribution network.[66]

Japan's large-scale formats and discounting also present growth possibilities. In 1992, the law regulating large-scale development was revised based on attempts by Toys "R" Us to enter the Japanese market.[67] In May 1994, regulation of new stores (both foreign and domestic) was further relaxed. As a result, store applications increased by 50 percent. Retailers were also allowed to extend store hours.[68]

LEGAL ASPECTS OF INTERNATIONAL CHANNELS

Channel members need to be aware of local laws that pertain to exporting specific goods, allowable channel arrangements, store hours, and so on. Four legal aspects of international channels are bribery, controlled goods, distributor termination, and packaging. The laws discussed in this section relating to bribery and controlled goods are domestic laws that control international transactions. The distributor termination laws discussed relate to several European companies, and the packaging laws are German laws that affect U.S. firms selling through German retailers. The foreign examples given illustrate the complexity of the international channels legal environment. It is important that channel members hire an attorney who is well versed in each country's legal system.

BRIBERY

The Foreign Corrupt Practices Act makes it illegal for a U.S. firm to authorize payments and gifts for the purposes of influencing actions by government officials to retain business. This act applies to virtually all U.S. firms that file with the Securities and Exchange Commission. All bribes are illegal when offered in the United States or in any other country where they are expressly prohibited. This act also makes U.S. firms criminally liable for actions by distributors and agents if the U.S. firm has knowledge of a payment made to a foreign official.

A U.S. company should include within a distributorship agreement a stipulation concerning bribery by foreign distributors and agents. The U.S. firm should also develop procedures that can be used to monitor distributors and agents to promote compliance with the act.[69]

Confusion about an inadvertent violation of the act prompted passage of the **Omnibus Trade Act of 1988**. This law differentiates between transaction bribes and variance brides. **Transaction bribes (grease or facilitating payments)** made to a foreign government official to speed up a country's bureaucratic handling of an order are considered acceptable, whereas **variance bribes** made to a government official to suspend a legal norm are considered illegal.[70]

CONTROLLED GOODS

All companies are subject to the Export Administration Act regulating what goods can be exported. More burdensome regulations are imposed for some goods that the government classifies as controlled goods. U.S. firms need to secure a special license to sell these goods to specific destinations.[71] Most items that require special permission are under the jurisdiction of the Department of Commerce. Others are armaments (Department of State), atomic materials (Atomic Energy Commission), gold and silver coins (United States Department of the Treasury), narcotic drugs (Department of Justice), natural gas and electric energy (United States Federal Power Commission), and endangered wildlife (Interior Department).[72]

DISTRIBUTOR TERMINATION

In many countries (such as Germany, Austria, and France), an agreement with a distributor cannot be terminated without compensation to the distributor unless the agreement is terminated for "just cause." Precisely which actions constitute just cause vary by country. However, in most of Western Europe, failure to reach a sales quota is an acceptable reason for termination. However, in Germany, poor sales performance constitutes just cause only if both parties agree to it. In some countries, a terminated distributor can prevent its U.S. trading partner from selling products or appointing a replacement distributor until a financial settlement is completed.[73] As in domestic legislation, suppliers need to carefully document the performance of distributors.

PACKAGING

The German packaging law is widely regarded as one of the strictest laws of its type. The law is based on two underlying principles: that packaging should not be considered waste, and that those who sell new packages should be responsible for getting rid of them in an acceptable manner. The German law bans all packaging that cannot be recycled or reused. In theory, any retailer that sells anything in packages, for example, must take the package back.

In practice, Germans use a Green Dot system in which Germans pay slightly extra for a product. The additional monies go toward a collection system in which products are placed in designated household containers, get picked up, and are then reused or recycled. Stores do not have an obligation to take back packaging if it has a Green Dot. In practice, the great majority of German retail stores will not sell anything without a Green Dot.[74]

SUMMARY

1. *To describe the development of a channel strategy for services.* The types of services (rented-goods services, owned-goods services, and nongoods services) and their special characteristics (intangibility, inseparability, perishability, and variability) have a major influence on channel choice. Two ways of designing channels for services are to determine whether direct contact is important and to study the flexibility in service production and consumption. Service intermediaries engage in the same channel activities as goods marketers. Despite traditional thinking, many different types of marketing inter-

mediaries are used in the distribution of services. There is a high potential for saving in the delivery of services through the use of supply chain and service response logistics.

2. *To examine the development of a channel strategy for international marketing.* The channel environment in international marketing is a complex one. Several theories of international channel choice were studied. These are based on a firm's level of commitment to international business, risk, experience, and a country's stage of economic development. Studies suggest that export distributors, sales representatives, and commission agents are the most popular international channels. International channel members can be classified according to home market and foreign channel members. Home market channel members include export management companies, export merchants, and direct exporting. Foreign channel members include exporting (through foreign distributors and agents), joint ventures (using licensing, foreign franchising, a local partner, and an original equipment manufacturer), and direct ownership.

3. *To analyze channel length and width decision making in international markets.* Channel length can be evaluated using a transaction cost analysis framework. In transactional cost analysis, firms seek to minimize the sum of transaction and production costs in making forward integration decisions. Transaction cost analysis theory predicts that firms will use integrated channels when transaction-specific assets are high and when environmental uncertainty is high. Channel width decision making should be based on distribution density formulas and market saturation ratios.

4. *To discuss international physical distribution.* International physical distribution is complicated owing to multiple locations that must be scheduled, the poor quality of the transportation infrastructure in some countries, different communications standards, and the required documentation. Common export documents are a bill of lading and a shipper's export declaration. Four factors that simplify international physical distribution are the standardization of documentation, export automation software, foreign freight forwarders and customs agents, and foreign trade zones.

5. *To illustrate the application of international channels and physical distribution in different regions and countries.* The European Union (EU) is the most important economic community in the world. On January 1, 1993, officials at most European borders stopped making passport and customs checks that once delayed the free movement of goods across member borders. The EU has also developed common standards for many goods. A very important standard is ISO9000. In terms of physical distribution, Belgium, the Netherlands, and Luxembourg dominate European transportation and distribution.

Eastern Europe's population is 400 million, about 10 percent smaller than the 430 million in Western Europe. While the transformation from communism to a free-market economy in Eastern Europe is exciting, there are many frustrations. There is a lack of trucks and warehouses, market research is scarce, and local managers often do not understand the basics of marketing and logistics.

Japan's distribution system is characterized by long and complex channel arrangements, as well as keiretsu. Both of these factors often restrict the market entry of foreign goods into Japanese distribution channels. Retailing in Japan is often characterized by single-product-line stores, a local neighborhood orientation, small stores, and long channels, with two or more levels of wholesalers between the manufacturer and the retailer. Many foreign firms have difficulty breaking into Japanese distribution systems owing to the internal production capabilities of keiretsu, and family ties, interlocking directorates, and management exchanges among firms. Large-scale formats and discounting also present growth possibilities in Japan.

6. *To study the legal aspects of international channels as they relate to bribery, controlled goods, distributor termination, and packaging.* The Foreign Corrupt Practices Act makes it illegal for a U.S. firm to authorize payments and gifts for the purposes of influencing actions by government officials to retain business. The Omnibus Trade Act differentiates between transaction bribes and variance bribes. All companies are subject to the Export Administration Act regulating what goods can be exported. Different countries have specific laws regarding distributor termination and packaging. For example, in Germany, Austria, and France, an agreement with a distributor cannot be terminated without compensation to the distributor unless the agreement is terminated for "just cause." The German packaging law is widely regarded as one of the strictest laws of its type.

KEY TERMS

rented-goods services
owned-goods service
nongoods service
intangibility
inseparability
perishability
variability in quality
supply chain logistics
service response logistics

locked-up channel
piggybacking
greenbelts
ethnocentrism
polycentrism
regiocentrism
geocentrism
export management companies

export merchants
direct exporting
foreign distributors
foreign agents
licensing
foreign franchising
local partner
original equipment manufacturer (OEM)

transaction cost analysis
transaction-specific assets
environmental uncertainty
distribution density
bill of lading
shipper's export declaration
import license
foreign exchange license
certificate of origin
export automation software
foreign freight forwarder
customs agent
foreign trade zone
ISO9000
keiretsu
Omnibus Trade Act of 1988
transaction bribes (grease or facilitating payments)
variance bribes

QUESTIONS FOR DISCUSSION

1. Show how intangibility, inseparability, perishability, and variability affect a rented-goods service, an owned-goods service, and a nongoods service.
2. Map out a McDonald's restaurant and a gourmet restaurant based on long-term flexibility in production and flexibility in consumption. Explain your choice of locations for each restaurant.
3. Describe how the do-it-yourself consumer is a competitor for one owned-goods service and one nongoods service.
4. Differentiate between supply chain logistics and service response logistics.
5. What channel strategies can Hertz and Avis use to effectively compete against Enterprise Rent-A-Car?
6. Discuss four reasons why the international channel environment is so complex.
7. Explain the relationship between a firm's commitment to international business and channel choice.
8. Contrast a firm's use of direct exporting from its home office versus direct ownership of foreign channels.
9. a. Under what situation would you recommend that a firm use a licensing arrangement?
   b. Under what situation would you recommend that a firm use a foreign franchising arrangement?
10. Describe the use of transaction cost analysis framework in predicting channel length.
11. Evaluate McDonald's market penetration formula.
12. Describe the advantages and disadvantages of the use of foreign trade zones by a retailer such as Wal-Mart.
13. Describe the EU from the perspective of international channels and physical distribution.
14. Differentiate between a transaction bribe and a variance bribe.

END NOTES

1. Steven Lipin, Brian Coleman, and Jeremy Mark, "Visa, American Express and MasterCard Vie in Overseas Strategies," *Wall Street Journal* (February 14, 1994), pp. A1 ff.

2. James H. Donnelly, Jr., "Marketing Intermediaries in Channels of Distribution for Services," *Journal of Marketing*, Vol. 40 (January 1976), pp. 55–56.

3. Ibid.

4. This section is based on Adrian Palmer and Catherine Cole, *Services Marketing: Principles and Practices* (Englewood Cliffs, N.J.: Prentice-Hall, 1995), pp. 194–203.

5. Ronald Henkoff, "Service Is Everybody's Business," *Fortune* (June 27, 1994), pp. 52, 56.

6. Dale Fodness, Barry E. Pitegoff, and Elise Truly Sautter, "From Customer to Competitor: Consumer Cooption in the Services Sector," *Journal of Services Marketing*, Vol. 7, No. 3 (1993), pp. 18–25.

7. *Logistics in Service Industries* (Oak Brook, Ill.: Council of Logistics Management, 1991).

8. See Saul Hansell, "Banks Going Interactive to Fend Off Rivals," *New York Times* (October 19, 1994), pp. D1 ff.

9. Eleena De Lisser, "Banks Court Disenchanted Customers," *Wall Street Journal* (August 30, 1993), p. B1.

10. Daniel McGinn, "Start the Banking Revolution Without Us," *Newsweek* (May 8, 1995), p. 71.

11. Faye Rice, "The New Rules of Superlative Service," *Fortune* (Autumn/Winter 1993), p. 52.

12. Bridget O'Brian, "Bank Branches May Go the Way of Dime Stores and Dinosaurs," *Wall Street Journal* (December 6, 1993), pp. B1 ff.

13. Greg Burns, "It Only Hertz When Enterprise Laughs," *Business Week* (December 12, 1994), p. 44.

14. Annagret Burtschy, "Hitting the Road," *SmartMoney* (March 1995), pp. 80–81.

15. "Change at the Check-Out," *The Economist* (March 4, 1995), p. 16.

16. Tony Horwitz, "Europe's Borders Fade, and People and Goods Can Move Freely," *Wall Street Journal* (May 18, 1993), p. A10.

17. Celestine Bohlen, "Crash Russian Course for Procter & Gamble," *New York Times* (December 19, 1993), p. F5.

18. Cacilie Rohwedder, "Europe's Smaller Food Stores Face Finis," *Wall Street Journal* (May 12, 1993), p. B1; and Dana Milbank, "Guarded by Greenbelts, Europe's Town Centers Thrive," *Wall Street Journal* (May 3, 1995), pp. B1 ff.

19. Yoram Wind, Susan P. Douglas, and Howard V. Perlmutter, "Guidelines for Developing International Marketing Strategies," *Journal of Marketing*, Vol. 37 (April 1973), pp. 14–15.

20. J. D. Goodnow and J. E. Hansz, "Environmental Determinants of Overseas Market Entry Strategies," *Journal of International Business Studies*, Vol. 3 (Spring 1972), pp. 33–50.

21. Jan Johanson and Jan-Erik Vahlne, "The Internationalization Process of the Firm—A Model of Knowledge Development and Increasing Foreign Market Commitments," *Journal of International Business Studies*, Vol. 8 (Spring 1977), pp. 23–32.

22. See M. L. Ursic and M. R. Czinkota, "An Experience Curve Explanation of Export Expansion," *Journal of Business Research*, Vol. 12 (1984), pp. 159–168.

23. See Daniel C. Bello, David J. Urban, and Bronislaw J. Verhage, "Evaluating Export Middlemen in Alternative Channel Structures," *International Marketing Review*, Vol. 8 (1991), p. 49.

24. Arun Sharma and Luis V. Dominguez, "Channel Evolution: A Framework for Analysis," *Journal of the Academy of Marketing Science*, Vol. 20 (Winter 1992), p. 3.

25. Ibid.

26. Daniel C. Bello and N. J. Williamson, "Contractual Arrangement and Marketing Practices in the Indirect Export Channel," *Journal of International Business Studies,* Vol. 16 (Summer 1985), pp. 65–82.

27. Bruce Seifert and John Ford, "Export Distribution Channels," *Columbia Journal of World Business,* Vol. 24 (Summer 1989), p. 17.

28. Saul Klein, Gary L. Frazier, and Victor J. Roth, "A Transaction Cost Analysis Model of Channel Integration in International Markets," *Journal of Marketing Research,* Vol. 27 (May 1990), p. 201.

29. Edward R. Koepfler, "Strategic Options for Global Market Players," *Journal of Business Strategy,* Vol. 10 (July–August 1989), p. 213.

30. "Exploring Market Entry Formulas," *Coopers & Lybrand/Chain Store Age Executive Special Issue,* Vol. 69, No. 12 (n.d.), p. 25.

31. Andrew E. Serwer, "McDonald's Conquers the World," *Fortune* (October 17, 1994), p. 112.

32. Thomas F. Clasen, "An Exporter's Guide to Selecting Foreign Sales Agents and Distributors," *Journal of European Business,* Vol. 3 (November 1991), pp. 28–32.

33. John K. Keitt, Jr., "Pitfalls and Promises of Foreign Distributors," *Management Review* (May 1990), pp. 16–17.

34. For an analysis of international agents, see "The Faxable International Sales-Rep Application," *Inc.* (November 1993), pp. 95–97.

35. Alan L. Gilman, "Franchising Opens Emerging Markets," *Chain Store Age Executive* (January 1994), p. 191.

36. "Change at the Check-Out," p. 16.

37. Rob Norton, "Strategies for the Export Boom," *Fortune* (August 22, 1994), p. 129.

38. Oliver E. Williamson, "The Modern Corporation," *Journal of Economic Literature,* Vol. 19 (December 1981), pp. 1537–1538.

39. Philip J. Rosson and I. David Ford, "Stake, Conflict, and Performance in Export Marketing Channels," *Management International Review,* Vol. 20 (Number 4), pp. 31–37.

40. Oliver E. Williamson, "Transaction Cost Economics: The Governance of Contractual Relations," *Journal of Law and Economics,* Vol. 22 (October 1979), pp. 233–262.

41. Saul Klein, "Selection of International Marketing Channels," *Journal of Global Marketing,* Vol. 4 (1991), pp. 31–32.

42. Klein, Frazier, and Roth, "A Transaction Cost Analysis Model of Channel Integration in International Markets," pp. 199–200.

43. Erin Anderson and Anne T. Coughlan, "International Market Entry and Expansion Via Independent or Integrated Channels of Distribution," *Journal of Marketing,* Vol. 51 (January 1987), pp. 71–82.

44. Klein, Frazier, and Roth, "A Transaction Cost Analysis Model of Channel Integration in International Markets," pp. 196–208.

45. Daniel C. Bello and Ritu Lohtia, "Export Channel Design: The Use of Foreign Distributors and Agents," *Journal of the Academy of Marketing Science,* Vol. 23, No. 2 (1995), pp. 83–93.

46. Andrew E. Serwer, "McDonald's Conquers the World," *Fortune* (October 17, 1994), p. 104.

47. See Bob Ortega, "Wal-Mart Is Slowed by Problems of Price and Culture in Mexico," *Wall Street Journal* (July 29, 1994), p. A1.

48. Ricardo Sookdeo, "The New Global Consumer," *Fortune* (Autumn/Winter 1993), pp. 69, 73.

49. *Coca-Cola 1994 Annual Report,* p. 29.

50. Richard W. Stevenson, "Teaching the Hard Sell of Soap to Eastern Europe," *New York Times* (February 18, 1993), p. D1.

51. "Crash Russian Course for Procter & Gamble," *New York Times,* p. F5.

52. See Evan Schwartz, "Software to Carry You Through the Export Thicket," *Business Week* (May 3, 1993), pp. 158–159.

53. Philip R. Cateora and Linda J. Shea, "Export Management," in *The Dartnell Marketing Manager's Handbook,* Third Edition, Sidney J. Levy, George R. Frerichs, and Howard L. Gordon, eds. (Chicago: Dartnell Corporation, 1994), pp. 1301–1317.

54. Richard Halverson, "Logistical Supremacy Secures Merchandise—But Will It Translate Abroad?" *Discount Store News* (December 5, 1994), p. 107.

55. See H. Michael Hayes, "ISO9000: The New Strategic Consideration," *Business Horizons,* Vol. 37 (May–June 1994), pp. 52–60.

56. See Horwitz, "Europe's Borders Fade, and People and Goods Can Move Freely," pp. A1, A10.

57. Cacilie Rohwedder, "European Shoppers Save Money by Making Cross-Border Treks," *Wall Street Journal* (May 2, 1994), p. A7C.

58. Jon Jacobs, "Europe's Friendly Shipping Center," *International Business* (August 1992), p. 54.

59. Stevenson, "Teaching the Hard Sell of Soap to Eastern Europe," p. D7.

60. Simon Johnson and Gary Loveman, "Starting Over: Poland After Communism," *Harvard Business Review,* Vol. 73 (March–April 1995), p. 46.

61. Stevenson, "Teaching the Hard Sell of Soap to Eastern Europe," p. D7.

62. Rustan Kosenko and Don Rathz, "The Japanese Channels of Distribution: Difficult But Not Insurmountable," in *1988 American Marketing Association Educators' Proceedings,* Gary Frazier, Charles Ingene, and David Aaker, eds. (Chicago: American Marketing Association, 1988), pp. 233–236.

63. Arieh Goldman, "Japan's Distribution System: Institutional Structure, Internal Political Economy, and Modernization," *Journal of Retailing,* Vol. 67 (Summer 1991), pp. 156–158.

64. James D. Goodnow and Rustan Kosenko, "Strategies for Successful Penetration of the Japanese Market or How to Beat Japan at Its Own Game," *Journal of Business and Industrial Marketing,* Vol. 7 (Winter 1992), p. 42.

65. Ibid., pp. 42–43.

66. Kosenko and Rathz, "The Japanese Channels of Distribution: Difficult But Not Insurmountable," pp. 233–236; and Goodnow and Kosenko, "Strategies for Successful Penetration of the Japanese Market or How to Beat Japan at Its Own Game," pp. 42–43.

67. See "Entering New Territory: An Up-Close Look at Three Opportunities," *Coopers & Lybrand/Chain Store Age Executive Special Issue,* Vol. 69, No. 12 (n.d), p. 23.

68. "Asia: Opportunities Large and Small," *Chain Store Age Executive* (January 1995), Section 3, p. 6.

69. John K. Keitt, Jr., "Pitfalls and Promises of Foreign Distributors," *Management Review* (May 1990), p. 18.

70. Dorothy Cohen, *Legal Issues in Marketing Decision Making* (Cincinnati: South-Western College Publishing, 1995), p. 200.

71. Keitt, "Pitfalls and Promises of Foreign Distributors," pp. 17–18.

72. Cateora and Shea, "Export Management," pp. 1301–1317.

73. Keitt, "Pitfalls and Promises of Foreign Distributors," pp. 17–18.

74. Pan Demetrakakes, "European Packaging Laws: A Pandora's Box," *Packaging* (February 1993), pp. 51–52.

TRAVEL AGENTS BATTLE AIRLINES OVER COMMISSION CUTS

The year 1995 was a difficult time for the nation's 30,000 or so travel agencies. Travel agencies are facing competition from discount airlines that bypass their services, lower air fares (that result in reduced commissions), and on-line services such as Easy Sabre which allow consumers to make their own reservations.

Some discount airlines avoid paying travel agents commissions entirely, keeping their discount fares all to themselves. Since the revenues of travel agents are based directly on ticket sales (their commission is about 10 percent of a ticket's price), travel agents were hurt when air fares went down 8 percent from 1992 to 1993. Some market analysts have estimated that in 1992, airline tickets accounted for 61 percent of travel agency revenues. AMR Corporation's Sabre reservation system developed a system called Easy Sabre; this system enables air travelers to book flights from their personal computers. As of late 1994, approximately 1 million consumers used Easy Sabre. Furthermore, several companies are beginning to install travel kiosks that enable consumers to purchase airline tickets in pharmacies and supermarkets.

As if these developments were not enough bad news for travel agents, several airlines have recently announced that they will set a maximum commission (cap) on certain fares. In February 1995, first Delta, then United and USAir, and then Northwest Airlines and American Airlines in separate announcements stated that they would begin to pay travel agents a maximum commission of $50 on domestic roundtrip tickets and $25 on one-way tickets. Under this commission structure, the standard 10 percent commission would apply only to roundtrip tickets costing up to $500. In 1994, airlines paid out $6.28 billion in commission costs. Air fare commissions are the airlines' third largest expense after labor and fuel. According to the airlines, cutting commissions would benefit air travelers by resulting in lower air fares. Travel agents have several strategies to deal with the airline announcement, as well as their new market and competitive environment.

Some travel agents have begun to charge $10 to $25 fees to customers for writing low-cost airline reservations or to reissue an airline ticket. Some market analysts have estimated that it costs between $25 and $35 to process a ticket. Thus, a travel agent would lose money when selling tickets under $250. American Express, for example, has started charging some walk-in and nonrepeat customers $5 to $25 to book airline tickets that cost less than $100 and to make certain foreign hotel reservations. Others have even begun to charge fees as high as $300 for a customer who cancels an elaborate itinerary. Still others have refused to book passengers on low-cost airlines or have sought to shift them to major airlines.

Other travel agents have begun to specialize in order to further differentiate themselves and to better appeal to niche markets. In some cases, they have developed a specialty based on location (such as Hawaii); in other cases, they have appealed to special groups (such as senior citizens). More than 800 travel agents now sell cruises exclusively. Cruise travel is generally more lucrative since cruise lines pay a 12 percent commission.

Finally, some travel agents may encourage undecided vacationers to vacation abroad. Foreign air travelers pay an average commission of 13 percent on highly competitive trans-Atlantic routes. Others can seek more business accounts owing to larger average airticket sales.

A preliminary examination of the market found that many travel agents backed off of their initial demand for added fees. Customers threatened to take business to either other travel agents or directly to the airlines. For example, BTI Americas Inc., one of the nation's largest agencies with 1200 locations, decided to impose fees only in rare instances, such as very low-cost tickets. A spokesperson for the American Society of Travel Agents says that the majority of its 25,000 members are not charging fees.

The American Society of Travel Agents has announced that it will file an antitrust suit and pursue legislative options to get airlines to restore the full 10 percent commission.

QUESTIONS

1. What were the risks to the airlines of the reduced commission arrangement?
2. Contrast the pros and cons of the use of online services and airline reservations assistants versus travel agents by airlines.
3. Evaluate the strategies used by travel agents in reacting to the cut commissions.
4. Describe airline reservations based on the flexibility in production and consumption classification system.

Sources: Bridget O'Brian, "Ticketless Plane Trips, New Technology Forces Travel Agents to Change Course," *Wall Street Journal* (September 13, 1994), pp. B1 ff.; Jonathan Dahl, "Agents Ask Travelers to Start Paying Fees," *Wall Street Journal* (December 20, 1994), p. B1; James S. Hirsch, "Fare Cuts Test Travel Agents' Reliability," *Wall Street Journal* (January 19, 1994), p. B1; James S. Hirsch, "New Commission Cuts Pummel Travel Agents," *Wall Street Journal* (February 14, 1995), p. B1; Edwin McDowell, "For Travel Agents, A Tough Life," *New York Times* (August 22, 1994), pp. D1 ff.; Edwin McDowell, "Travel Agents Fight Back," *New York Times* (February 20, 1995), pp. D1 ff.; Edwin McDowell, "Travel Group Plans to Sue U.S. Airlines," *New York Times* (February 22, 1995), pp. D1 ff.; Lisa Miller, "Stung by Fee Cuts, Travel Agents Declare War on Big Airlines," *Wall Street Journal* (March 27, 1995), pp. B1 ff.; and Lisa Miller, "Travel Agents Give Clients a Break on Service Fees," *Wall Street Journal* (May 11, 1995), pp. B1 ff.

CASE 2

TOYS "R" US IN JAPAN

Toys "R" Us operates 581 toy superstores in the United States, 217 Kids "R" Us children's clothing stores in the United States, and 234 toy stores overseas. Although the firm does not divide sales and profits by Toys "R" Us and Kids "R" Us, in 1994 the U.S. market accounted for 79 percent of the firm's sales and 88 percent of its income. Analysts predict that the international profits of Toys "R" Us are growing at a 34 percent compound rate annually. In contrast, total operating profits are growing at 11 percent per year.

Even though it has an estimated market share of 20 percent of the U.S. toy market, Toys "R" Us executives view the U.S. market for toys as saturated. In 1993, the chain opened more stores outside the United States than in it, including its first stores in Australia, Portugal, Belgium, Switzerland, and the Netherlands. In addition to using direct ownership of foreign stores, Toys "R" Us has begun to make franchising arrangements in other countries.

Toys "R" Us uses a similar marketing strategy throughout the world. Its marketing strategy consists of selling diapers and baby formula at low prices to build store loyalty at an early age, using large warehouse-style stores, and employing a self-service strategy with shopping carts. Toys "R" Us is also very sensitive to cultural differences. For example, the retailer always displays the foreign version of its name alongside its U.S. logo. Toys "R" Us also caters to local toy preferences. For example, it sells porcelain dolls that are favored by Japanese girls and wooden toys preferred by German children.

The firm's operations in Japan are among the strongest of any U.S. company located

TABLE 1   SELECTED STATISTICS ON ASIAN COUNTRIES

Country	1997 Estimated GDP (in millions)	1994 Estimated Population (in millions)	1994 Urban Districts with Population over 1 Million	1990 Percent of Population in Urban Areas
Japan	4,309	125	11	77
China	649	1,192	95	26
India	317	911	20	19
Korea	424	44	5	74

Source: "Asia: Opportunities Large and Small," *Chain Store Age Executive* (January 1995), Section 3, p. 5. Reprinted by permission from *Chain Store Age Executive.* Copyright Lebhar-Friedman, Inc., 425 Park Avenue, New York, NY 10022.

there. In just a two-year period, Toys "R" Us opened 16 U.S.-style toy superstores in Japan; it plans to open an additional 19 stores in the following two-year period. Its store units in Japan are huge. While the typical Toys "R" Us store in the United States has annual retail sales of $10 million a year, its Japanese stores average between $15 and $20 million each. One supplier estimates that Toys "R" Us currently has about 4 percent of Japan's toy market and that within two years it will have close to 10 percent. (See Table 1 for data on Japan and other Asian countries.) Part of the reason for its success is that the Japanese distribution system has been dominated by small stores. The stores are costly to operate and do not stock adequate selections of merchandise.

Not everyone anticipated that the strategy Toys "R" Us used in Japan would be so successful. It took Toys "R" Us three years to negotiate to speed up the approval process for large stores. The slow process benefited Japan's small retailers. Eventually, Japan's Ministry of International Trade and Industry (MITI) agreed to limit the approval process for large-store applications to under 18 months. Initially, many large Japanese toy companies were unwilling to sell direct to Toys "R" Us stores. Eventually, most agreed because of Toys "R" Us's large market size. A third potential problem was high rental costs in Japan. Now, many property owners give preferential terms to Toys "R" Us based on traffic it generates.

QUESTIONS

1. Evaluate Table 1.
2. Under what circumstances should Toys "R" Us use foreign franchising as a means of market entry?
3. What are the benefits of the Japanese market to Toys "R" Us in contrast to the U.S. market?
4. Evaluate Toys "R" Us's channel strategy in Japan.

Sources: Gale Eisenstodt, "Bull in Japan Shop," *Forbes* (January 31, 1994), pp. 41–42; Gary Hoover, Alta Campbell, and Patrick J. Spain, eds., *Hoover's Handbook of American Business 1995* (Austin, Tex.: Reference Press, 1994), pp. 1034–1035; Annetta Miller, Lourdes Rosado, Peter McKillip, and Don Kirk, "The World "S" Ours," *Newsweek* (March 23, 1992), pp. 46–47; and Carla Rapoport and Justin Martin, "Retailers Go Global," *Fortune* (February 20, 1995), pp. 104–106 ff.

PART FOUR CASE

THERMASHIELD DISTRIBUTORS, POLAND*

INTRODUCTION

Dryvit is classified as outsulation material. Instead of insulating from inside with blown insulation, Dryvit provides insulation from the exterior surface of a building. A Dryvit contractor first attaches sheets of styrofoam to a building's exterior. Then a stucco-like acrylic material, which can be tinted in a variety of colors, is applied over the styrofoam. Although the application of Dryvit is generally associated in the United States with one-family homes, this process can be used on large office buildings that are 40 stories high. In the United States, its stucco-like appearance makes Dryvit popular in Spanish-style architecture, whereas its popularity in Eastern European countries is due largely to its insulating qualities.

The large potential market for Dryvit in Eastern Europe is based on the elimination of low-cost subsidized oil from the USSR following the collapse of the Communist bloc. Over the preceding 20 years, many buildings in Eastern Europe had been constructed without sufficient insulation. Now that former Eastern bloc nations have to purchase fuel oil on the open market, a large market for retrofitting homes and apartment buildings has developed. Poland, for instance, currently subsidizes 75 percent of the energy conservation costs for insulating existing cooperative apartment buildings. About $8 million in subsidies has been earmarked for cooperative buildings. In addition, a large market for outsulation exists for commercial and one-family homes (even though these are not subsidized).

Jan Makula, a Polish-born architect, who has lived in the United States most of his adult life, returned to Poland in 1990, following the end of the communist regime, seeking to distribute Dryvit throughout the country. Makula, aware of the poor insulation in Polish buildings, the elimination of low-cost fuel, and the large government subsidies, saw a large market for Dryvit. This case describes the overall channel strategy of Makula's firm, Thermashield Distributors, Poland, the market for Dryvit in Poland, and the characteristics of the Polish market.

---

*This case was written by Professor Victor V. Cordell, Monterey Institute of International Studies; and Barry Berman, Hofstra University.

OVERALL MARKETING STRATEGY OF THERMASHIELD DISTRIBUTORS, POLAND

As of the middle of 1994, Thermashield Distributors had an estimated 60 percent market share of the $10 million a year market for thermal retrofitting of cooperative apartments and other buildings. Thermashield's large market share was due to Makula's marketing savvy, as well as to Dryvit's superior technology. Although Makula is proud of his success, he is concerned about the firm's loss of market share in the cooperative market. Makula is also well aware that Thermashield's sales growth in 1994 was 75 percent versus the planned 150 percent level.

DISTRIBUTION ARRANGEMENTS

Jan Makula recognized that he would need to train Polish contractors and architects in the use of Dryvit materials before he would be able to sell any materials. Thus, before making a single sale, he spent $250,000 on contractors' and architects' training. Makula developed much of the training materials by translating and adapting many of Dryvit's English-language technical manuals and application guidelines.

Since Thermashield Distributors is based in Warsaw, Makula decided to handle the Warsaw market through use of a direct sales force. In Poland's other 49 voivods (Poland is divided into 50 governmental units, each called a voivodship or voivod), Dryvit is sold and installed through independently owned authorized dealers/contractors. Each of these dealers/contractors has been trained in the proper installation of Dryvit materials.

Thermashield now has a nationwide dealer network of authorized dealers/contractors. The company estimates that its dealers cover 90 percent of the Polish market for outsulation. The remaining 10 percent of the market is located in very rural areas, which Thermashield estimates would be marginally profitable in the best scenario. Each dealer/contractor has the right to use the Dryvit trademark (a contented polar bear) in its advertising. Thermashield also sells its materials to other trained contractors that do not have the status of authorized dealers. These contractors typically purchase Dryvit materials on an as-needed basis for specific jobs.

DEALER RELATIONS

There is a large difference in dealer/contractor effectiveness as judged by such criteria as sales, sales improvement, performance against quota, and installation quality. Thermashield Distributors is currently in the process of identifying its poorest dealers/contractors. The firm estimates that between 10 and 25 percent of its dealers/contractors would be in the poor performer category. Thermashield intends to discuss their inadequacies and suggest ways to improve their performance, even though as a result of this process, some of these dealers/contractors may resign as Thermashield dealers/contractors and begin to sell competing brands.

Thermashield has not decided whether it should hire a channel specialist to work with its dealers/contractors on dealer relations, joint promotions, and marketing research. However, the firm does not know whether the dealers/contractors, many of whom view themselves as craftsman, would work with a channels specialist in increasing their knowledge of marketing and business.

PRICING STRUCTURE

Thermashield's authorized dealers/contractors purchase Dryvit on the basis of a discount structure that begins at 10 percent off list price and then rises to as high as 15 percent based on volume. The discounts increase in 1 percent increments. Unauthorized dealers/contractors are not eligible for any discounts.

Reports prepared by a management consultant concluded that the 1 percent increments were too small to get dealers to increase their purchase of Dryvit. The consultant argued that Thermashield should establish a discount schedule based on a dealer's/contractor's increases in purchases from its highest level in past yearly periods. In one proposed schedule, a dealer that had a 20 percent increase in sales (such as from 2.0 to 2.4 milliards) would receive a 15 percent discount on the incremental sales (0.4 milliard) and a regular discount up to the first 2.0 milliards. If the dealer's sales declined to 1.8 milliards, the 2.0 milliard level would remain the base. One problem with this pricing structure is that it would provide the greatest discount to dealers that had poor sales performance in the past.

COMPONENT PURCHASE REQUIREMENTS FOR AUTHORIZED DEALERS/CONTRACTORS

One area of potential channel conflict between Thermashield Distributors and its authorized dealers/contractors is their use of other brands of mesh. Of the components sold by Thermashield, the firm's mesh prices are most costly relative to those of competitors. Although the mesh is subject to high tariffs and transportation costs (by virtue of being produced in the United States), it is much higher in quality than many substitute materials that are locally produced. Thermashield Distributors is aware that some dealers/contractors often order too little mesh relative to the amount of styrofoam sheeting. This practice indicates that these dealers/contractors are either using too little mesh or are combining poor quality mesh and Thermashield mesh on the same job. Thermashield Distributors is considering use of a full-line forcing strategy in which a dealer/contractor would have to order styrofoam and mesh in fixed proportions. This approach would eliminate quality concerns, but it could force some dealers/contractors to terminate their association with Thermashield Distributors.

The use of low-quality mesh could cause the styrofoam to separate from the wall. Thermashield currently guarantees all work by its authorized dealers/contractors for a 15-year period. Although Thermashield's guarantee is contingent on the contractor's use of proper materials, the use of Polish versus U.S.-produced mesh cannot be determined by nonexperts. Thermashield would also encounter a major public relations problem if it refused to honor a guarantee based on an authorized dealer/contractor using poor quality mesh.

PROMOTIONAL STRATEGY

Thermashield Distributors' promotion effort has focused largely on increasing awareness of the Thermashield name among Polish architects and contractors. Thermashield Distributors is especially careful in using the Thermashield polar bear trademark in all of its advertising. The trademark also features prominently in all advertising and print media in order to reinforce the importance of using authorized dealers/contractors. Dryvit is sold in Poland as a U.S. System based on positive country-of-origin effects. Thermashield Distributors' authorized contractors also promote the use of Dryvit through personal selling, mailers, handbills, and billboard advertising.

PRODUCT LINE

In addition to Dryvit, Thermashield Distributors is considering importing a line of paints and pigments to color the stucco-like surface. Unlike Polish-produced paints, U.S. paints contain mold and mildew protectants and so are of significantly higher quality than those generally produced in Poland.

Thermashield Distributors believes that the paint products could enhance Thermashield's brand awareness. The firm could also jointly advertise its paint and Dryvit materials, although paint would require a much more intensive distribution system than Dryvit materials. In addition to Dryvit contractors, the paint would need to be sold to professional painters, general contractors, and the do-it-yourself market.

THE MARKET FOR DRYVIT IN POLAND

Poland is in the middle of a major restructuring of its energy systems. As part of this restucturing, the country is trying to reduce its dependence on coal, improve energy efficiency, and reduce pollution. A number of reforms and programs are underway to address these problems.

One program that has been instituted is designed to increase the fuel efficiency of older buildings through outsulation. Since Dryvit is typically installed over a building's exterior, it is ideal for use in older buildings. The Dryvit process is as effective an insulator as all other available means (such as blowing insulation into voids in walls). Other opportunities for Dryvit have been found in new construction. According to some estimates, Poland has a housing shortage of 1.3 million units (over 10 percent of the current housing stock). In 1993, an estimated 95,000 apartments and single-family homes were built through a new system of housing credits.

In general, U.S.-produced building products face strong competition from European Union (EU) countries, particularly Germany. EU member products are popular in Poland because they enjoy lower duties than U.S. products. Poland is moving toward membership in the European Union and has already signed an association agreement that lowers the tariff rate with EU member nations. In addition, transportation costs are lower from EU countries due to shorter distance; all EU countries and Poland use the metric system; and German building products companies, in particular, have been very helpful in providing their Polish importers with promotional assistance and in getting certification to market German products in Poland.

U.S. firms are seeking to build market share in the Polish construction market through several vehicles. For the past eight years, a monthly magazine, *Murator,* has published articles on U.S. building technology. The American-Polish Home Builders Institute also promotes U.S. products and technologies and has recently established an exhibition facility.

MARKET SEGMENTS FOR DRYVIT

There are three primary markets for Dryvit in Poland: cooperative, commercial, and home.

Although it is difficult to estimate the size of the commercial and home market for Dryvit, the cooperative market requires competitive bids that are publicly recorded. Dryvit's dealers can easily track their sales in this segment in order to determine market share by voivod. Cooperative buildings represent the largest market segment for Dryvit in Poland, comprising 60 percent of the overall market. It is the only market for Dryvit that is subsidized. The cooperative market is very price sensitive, and not especially concerned about quality. Most experts argue that this segment would accept a poorer quality substitute with a low initial price, even if its long-term costs were high. Payoffs to cooperative officials are a common practice, but Thermashield refuses to engage in any form of bribery, although it is unsure as to whether all of its dealers/contractors follow this ethical standard.

The second largest market is the commercial market, comprising about 30 percent of Dryvit sales. Dryvit has a real market advantage in the commercial market because of this segment's higher concern for quality and lower concern for price. This is the least price-sensitive market. Unlike cooperatives that focus on the initial bid price, the commercial market is more interested in outsulation material with the lowest total cost. Dryvit's initial cost is higher than that of some competitors, but it is less likely to require maintenance and to peel or fall off a structure owing to poor adhesion. Thermashield Distributors has trained its dealers to focus on the commercial market by identifying climate-vulnerable structures in prosperous areas.

The smallest segment for Dryvit is private homes, which account for only 10 percent of the market. Thermashield Distributors recommends that its dealers specifically target neighborhoods in the better parts of towns with large concentrations of private homes. Thermashield's dealers/contractors have used mailers, handbills, and billboards as promotional media.

CHARACTERISTICS OF THE POLISH MARKET

Poland is a country of 38 million people and is one of the largest of the former communist bloc nations. It has more than three times the population of Hungary and is 45 percent larger than the combined population of Hungary,

Slovakia, and the Czech Republic combined. Of Poland's 50 voivodships, all but two (Katowice and Warsaw) have between 400,000 and 1 million inhabitants. Katowice has a population of 4 million, and Warsaw's population is 2.4 million.

On January 1, 1990, the Polish government began an economic reform to transform its former communist economy into private ownership. The economic reform plan is called the Balcerowicz Plan named after the country's finance minister. The Balcerowicz Plan sought to reduce the country's extremely high inflation rate, make the Polish currency convertible into other currencies at market prices, reduce the level of subsidies to state enterprises, and eliminate most restrictions on foreign trade. In the five-year period since its transition to a free-market economy, the Polish economy has begun to rebound. For example, the rate of inflation has decreased from almost 600 percent in 1990 to 35 percent in 1993 to 22 percent in 1995. The country's Gross Domestic Product has also increased at 5 percent in 1995 after reflecting inflation. In U.S. dollars, the GDP per capita was $2240 in 1995.

One area of the economy that is still not rosy is unemployment. Unemployment is still in the 16 percent range. The impact of unemployment, however, varies by region. Unemployment is greater than 25 percent in the northeast and in some northwestern regions. In contrast, unemployment in major cities such as Warsaw, Poznan, and Katowice is in the 8 to 10 percent range.

POLISH LEGAL ENVIRONMENT

A U.S. treaty on trade and economic relations between Poland and the United States was signed in 1990. The treaty provides investment guarantees for U.S. investors in Poland, protects U.S. intellectual property rights, and allows free transfer of profits from Poland. Under the Foreign Investment Act of 1991, and subsequent amendments to the act, any level of foreign ownership up to 100 percent is allowed. This act also guarantees the availability of foreign currency for payment of dividends to shareholders. The Overseas Private Investment Corporation (OPIC) is fully active in Poland; it provides political risk insurance and loan guarantees.

A new law has eliminated some concern over trademark protection in Poland. While the old trademark law prohibited the placing of counterfeit trademarks on goods, it provided no penalty for Polish firms that distributed counterfeit products. The revised law provides up to a one-year imprisonment or penalty to firms that sell goods with counterfeit trademarks or that place such trademarks on goods. According to one source, as much as 80 percent of clothing and 50 percent of coffee in Poland were sold under counterfeit trademarks.

An important law being proposed in Poland will require local content in all cases where public monies are used to procure commodities, services, and construction projects. Under one version of the proposed law, commodities purchased will be required to have at least 50 percent Polish content. The use of Polish labor for services will also be required. The U.S. Department of Commerce favors the proposed law since it will make it easier for U.S. firms to secure contracts.

CHANNEL INFRASTRUCTURE

Poland's road and rail networks are extensive, and its air and sea ports are generally viewed as adequate for receiving and shipping cargo, though they are in need of both modernization and expansion.

Many rural roads are in poor condition, and driving at night is made particularly dangerous by poor road conditions and lack of lighting on some roads. Poland also lacks four-lane highways that can accommodate the increased volume of motor carriers. Extensive road widening and rehabilitation are scheduled over the next 10 to 15 years. Poland has already received a $150 million loan for the modernization of its roads and bridges from the World Bank. In addition, the European Bank for Reconstruction and Development (EBRD) has approved a loan of $35 million to upgrade and improve certain portions of regular and toll-roads. Poland also has developed a program for constructing and financing new roadways at a total cost of about $6 billion. This program extends to the year 2007 and includes major north-south and east-west highways.

Railroads are also in the process of being modernized, with programs in place for maintenance of tracks, platform, and bridge repairs. Development plans have also been launched for Poland's eight major airports.

Office space in Poland is very costly. Space is quoted on the basis of square meter per month rather than square foot per year as in the United States. The range for office space is between $25 and $80 per meter per month in Warsaw. Office amenities such as modern telephones, facsimile machines, and computers are available on either a purchase or lease basis.

DISTRIBUTION CHANNELS IN POLAND

Like many countries in Eastern Europe, Poland is characterized by many small stores and an almost total lack of modern retailers such as department stores, grocery stores, and shopping centers, except for a few malls with upscale boutiques. There are an estimated 3000 small retailers in Warsaw alone.

Several means are available to establish a distribution channel in Poland. Large firms can establish a regional warehouse system, purchase trucks, and line up distributors across the country. Smaller firms often seek out a Polish distributor that will import goods and serve as the firm's representative in Poland. Many Polish distributors take on unrelated lines. For example, a Polish construction firm may act as a distributor for a disparate line of goods, as a means of increasing its income. Two important sources of Polish distributors for U.S. manufacturers are the United States and Foreign Commerce Service's (USFCS) Agent/Distributor Service (ADS) and the USFCS's Gold Key service. The ADS screens up to six potential contacts. The Gold Key service finds contacts and sets up meetings with these contacts in advance of a U.S. exporter's business trip to Poland. Background checks can be provided through the USFCS's World Trader's Data Report.

Franchising is another distribution channel that has been used in Poland. The Polish Franchise Association (PFA), established in 1992, plays an important role in Poland's franchising activity, assisting potential franchisees in selecting appropriate franchises and helping match potential Polish franchisees with foreign franchisors. Currently, only about 30 known firms have franchises in

Poland. Many of these are in services, such as low-cost hotels and fast-food restaurants. Generally, a franchisor needs to establish at least one successful project in Poland prior to seeking franchisees. A major problem associated with franchising is financing. Many Polish banks have been reluctant to lend money to finance the purchase of a franchise.

Partnerships with local businesses are a third alternative for foreign firms seeking to gain entry into Poland. Typically, the U.S. firm provides access to capital and technology, and the Polish partner provides knowledge of the Polish market and access to local governments. Many joint ventures have been established under preferential tax laws that grant partnerships freedom from taxes for three years. Although the three-year tax holiday applicable to all joint ventures has expired, tax preferences are still available, providing the venture involves foreign investment of $3 million, is in a geographic region with high unemployment, leads to the transfer of technology, and exports at least 20 percent of the firm's total sales.

Finally, firms can establish a sales office in Poland. Four types of sales offices are a site management office, a technical information office, a representative office, and an agency. A site management office can be used to oversee a project for a specific operation. A technical information office provides information about products and technical assistance, but cannot sell products or services. The services provided in a technical information office by the U.S. company must be free of charge. Representative offices can engage in any form of business activity, including foreign trade. These offices need to be fully funded by the U.S. parent company and are treated as part of a U.S. firm. Agencies are restricted to dealing in the goods and services of the parent company. They are not eligible for tax holidays. Agencies must also be registered in the name of a Polish person or firm.

English-speaking secretarial assistance is available in Poland, but Polish nationals with Western management or accounting skills are difficult to find. Former managers of state-run offices have also been slow to adapt to modern business practices. Under Polish law, for example, employers are responsible for paying an employee's social benefits (45 percent of the employee's salary), and in addition, citizens of the United States and other countries who live and work in Poland longer than 183 days per year are treated as residents for tax and social security purposes.

PROMOTIONAL MEDIA IN POLAND

The trade fair serves as a major promotional vehicle for industrial goods in Poland. Until three years ago, the trade fair business was a single event, the June Poznan International Fair. Today, there is a year-long schedule of trade fairs in major cities throughout Poland. Trade fairs specializing in building products, environmental goods and services, computers, and automotive goods have become more popular. The USFCS also has specialized trade missions and catalog shows, and displays a company's sales literature in its Commercial Library.

For consumer goods, the importance of television has increased drastically. This medium now reaches virtually every home through local channel and satellite programming. However, television is expensive. Radio is also a widely used medium. The print media are also important. Major newspapers have countrywide circulation, for the Polish people are highly literate. Business-related newspapers and magazines have also experienced wide growth.

A number of advertising agencies and public relations firms have been established in Poland.

PRICING IN POLAND

Prices for U.S.-produced goods in Poland were high based on Poland's $2240 per-capita GDP in 1995. The addition of import duties, value-added taxes, transportation costs, and high interest costs for credit have combined to increase these prices even more. In general, price levels for U.S. goods are also high compared with those from the European Union owing to differences in import duties and transportation costs.

Many market analysts suggest that U.S. firms enter the Polish market with low profit margins to build brand awareness, to conduct product trials, and to expand the size of demand. These analysts then recommend that U.S. firms slowly raise prices as the Polish economy improves.

QUESTIONS

1. Evaluate Poland as a market based on the information contained in this case.
2. Identify sources of channel conflict in this case.
3. How can the channel conflict be resolved? Make specific suggestions.
4. Develop an administered marketing system for Thermashield Distributors, Poland.
5. Evaluate the use of licensing, foreign franchising, and a local partner as channel alternatives for Thermashield.
6. Discuss whether Thermashield Distributors, Poland, should sell paint. Look at this opportunity from a channels perspective.
7. Evaluate Thermashield Distributors' current channel arrangement.

Sources: Country Data for Poland (Washington, D.C.: U.S. Department of Commerce Eastern Europe Information Center, n.d.), pp. 1–4; *Economic Trends and Outlook in Poland* (Washington, D.C.: U.S. Department of Commerce Eastern Europe Information Center, n.d.), pp. 1–6; *Energy* (Washington, D.C.: U.S. Department of Commerce Eastern Europe Information Center, 1995), pp. 1–4; *Investment Climate in Poland* (Washington, D.C.: U.S. Department of Commerce Eastern Europe Information Center, n.d.), pp. 1–5; Simon Johnson and Gary Loveman, "Starting Over: Poland After Communism," *Harvard Business Review,* Vol. 73 (March–April 1995), pp. 44–47 ff.; and *Marketing U.S. Products and Services in Poland* (Washington, D.C.: U.S. Department of Commerce Eastern Europe Information Center, n.d.), pp. 1–11.

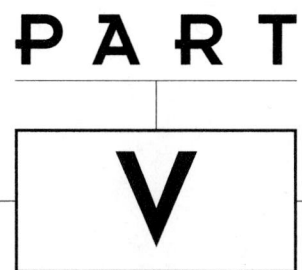

CHANNEL ASSESSMENT AND CONTROL

In Part Five, we study channel assessment and control through a variety of techniques.

CHAPTER 15

Evaluation of Channels In this chapter, we examine overall measures of channel performance, financial performance measures (Data Envelopment Analysis and financial ratios), distribution cost analysis (full-cost analysis, direct-cost analysis, and activity-based costing), and the channel audit. Channel partnerships and Efficient Consumer Response are studied as strategies to increase overall channel efficiency.

CHAPTER 15

EVALUATION OF CHANNELS

CHAPTER OBJECTIVES

1. To discuss overall measures of channel performance used by dealers and suppliers.

2. To describe the use of Data Envelopment Analysis (DEA) and financial ratio analysis.

3. To discuss distribution cost analysis.

4. To analyze the use of the channel audit.

5. To study the use of channel partnerships and Efficient Consumer Response (ECR) in increasing overall channel productivity.

According to a new study, despite their reputation as pioneers in using new methods and technologies, major retailers still need to work on supply chain management activities. The study, prepared by Andersen Consulting for the Warehousing Education and Research Council, argues that "Media reports of full-scale implementation of advanced supply-chain management capabilities are generally overstated. In fact, retailers and manufacturers are still struggling to implement technologies and operating approaches that have been available for several years." The study was based on interviews with executives at Wal-Mart, Kmart, Target, and a number of other retail firms and their suppliers.

The report also found confusion concerning logistical requirements. For example, there may be no consistency in supply chain requirements among Wal-Mart, Kmart, and Target. The lack of consistency imposes high costs on manufacturers that sell to all three chains. Furthermore, inventory and delivery requirements can differ from one department to another within the same retail firm. This lack of overall consistency plays havoc with both the retailer's and manufacturer's information systems. Other major obstacles to better supply chain management are inaccurate data and adherence to current order management and merchandise replenishment practices.

This study has made a number of specific findings with regard to the implementation of specific technologies:

- Sharing of Point-of-Sale Data—Few companies have been found that adequately use point-of-sale data. Most companies studied are at the experimentation stage in sharing point-of-sale data.

- Shipment Case Marking—Relatively few firms use shipment case marking. At one major retailer, only half of the incoming cartons have UPC case markings.

- Implementation of EDI—While electronic data interchange is close to full implementation at some mass merchants, the use of EDI is still mixed at other firms. At one mass merchant with a reputation for technological savvy, less than one-half of its invoices and purchases were sent electronically.

- Shipping Container Marking—The use of shipping container marking is at the prototype stage at many firms. The report concludes that shipping container marking will grow along with advance shipment notification.

- Advance Shipment Notification—The use of advance shipment notification is also at the prototype stage at many firms. When not properly coordinated with other systems, advance shipment notification can actually reduce the efficiency of a logistics system.

The report offers three major challenges to channel members. First, activity-based costing should be performed to ascertain which link in the supply chain can most efficiently perform each major logistical responsibility. For example, preticketing may be performed most efficiently by a vendor rather than a retailer. Second, operations need to be better integrated so that redundant activities are eliminated rather than shifted among channel members. For instance, additional inventory may not be required at the retailer, wholesaler, and manufacturer levels. Third, channel members need to focus on improvements in both operations strategies and implementation.[1]

In this chapter we focus on assessing supplier and reseller performance through use of overall measures of channel performance, financial performance measures (Data Envelopment Analysis and financial ratios), distribution cost analysis (full-cost analysis, direct-cost analysis, and activity-based costing), and the channel audit. Channel partnerships and Efficient Consumer Response are studied as strategies to increase overall channel efficiency. We will see how channel member efficiency and effectiveness can be analyzed and improved.

INTRODUCTION TO CHANNEL ASSESSMENT AND CONTROL

In this chapter, we analyze various means of channel assessment and control. It is important to differentiate among three different levels of analysis and control. The smallest level of analysis for assessment and control purposes is a product category for a given channel reseller. For example, a distributor may seek to determine the relative profitability of a private-label brand designation versus a national brand. A distributor could also seek to determine the contribution to overall profits of specific products. The next level of analysis is the profitability of a channel unit (such as a branch retail store or a manufacturer's sales office). The highest level of analysis involves determining the profitability of specific channels. Through this analysis, a manufacturer should be able to determine the relative profitability of its direct versus indirect channels. The three levels of analysis are interdependent. For example, poor overall channel performance can be due to below-average sales of a private-label good.

This chapter covers the use of channel performance measures, overall financial ratio measures, distribution cost analysis, and the management audit as channel assessment and control techniques. Other channel assessment measures dealing with customer service and physical distribution were discussed in Chapter 5, and markups and direct product profitability were covered in Chapter 9.

OVERALL MEASURES OF CHANNEL PERFORMANCE USED BY DEALERS AND SUPPLIERS

Since dealers and suppliers use different measures of channel performance, this section is divided into two separate parts: measures used by dealers and measures used by suppliers.

CHANNEL PERFORMANCE MEASURES USED BY DEALERS

Professor Spriggs studied the use of channel performance measures by medium/heavy truck dealerships. He surveyed a national sample of 888 dealer owners and managers and had a 22 percent response rate. Table 15-1 shows the number of respondents using each performance measure, as well as each measure's average performance rating. The average number of measures used was 15.8; this indicates the use of multiple measures to evaluate each dealership.[2] Among outcome-based measures, the highest degree of usage was for total dealership volume, total dealership profit, sales margins, inventory turnover, and market share. Among behavior-based measures, the service department, warranty/claims processing, buildings/facilities, office systems, and employee incentive plans were the most commonly used. The researchers found that the 34 performance measures could be summarized by five performance items: an outcome sales measure, an outcome profit measure, a behavior sales effort measure, a customer service measure, and a marketing support measure.[3]

CHANNEL PERFORMANCE MEASURES USED BY SUPPLIERS

Another study by Professors Kumar, Stern, and Achrol described reseller performance assessment from the supplier's perspective.[4] These researchers studied two firms: a motor leasing company with a network of more than 5000 dealers in the United States and Canada, and a division of a *Fortune 500* multinational manufacturer that distributes portable telecommunications equipment through about 1000 resellers.

The researchers found seven components of reseller performance: contribution to sales, contribution to profits, reseller competence, reseller compliance, reseller adaptation, contribution to growth, and customer satisfaction. Whereas reseller loyalty was originally thought to be an independent component, its scores were highly correlated to other components. See Table 15-2 for measures of reseller performance included in their final scale.

ASSESSING CHANNEL MEMBER PERFORMANCE

These two studies reveal that there are two types of measures of channel performance. One type of measure is financial such as sales, dollar profits, profit margins, and inventory turnover, and the other is behavioral such as the quality of the service department, warranty claims processing, reseller competence, and reseller adaptation. A firm needs to use multiple measures to determine overall channel member performance. In the first study, for instance, the original 34 measures could be effectively summarized by five overall measures. The second study reduced their appraisal system to seven components. Channel members should be cautioned against using any single summary measure of channel performance.[5]

TABLE 15-1 PERFORMANCE MEASURES: USAGE AND MEAN IMPORTANCE WEIGHTS FROM THE PERSPECTIVE OF THE DEALER

	Number Using	Importance
Outcome-Based Measures		
Volume ($), total dealership	188	2.04
Profit, total dealership	186	2.75
Sales margins	175	2.07
Inventory turnover	174	2.13
Market share	172	2.04
Customer satisfaction	168	2.41
Sales expenses	166	2.17
Return on investment	160	1.15
Inventory expense	160	2.33
Overall customer service level	156	2.25
Volume (units) by product type	142	1.41
Volume ($) per salesperson	141	1.57
Volume ($) to quota	129	1.24
Profit, by supplier	114	2.75
Volume ($) by product type	112	1.78
Profit by product type	99	1.43
Behavior-Based Measures		
Service department	184	2.60
Warranty/claims processing	177	2.31
Buildings/facilities	173	1.96
Office systems	156	1.79
Employee incentive plans	156	1.88
Coverage of trade area	156	2.04
Selling skills/salespeople	152	2.04
Product knowledge/salesmen	149	1.94
Dealership financial plan	147	1.91
Dealership business plan	146	1.72
Advertising/promotional programs	143	1.43
Number of customer complaints	139	1.92
Buyer credit management	123	1.45
Sales forecasts—accuracy	115	1.21
Sales calls—total	112	1.26
Calls—current customers	111	1.33
Calls—noncustomers	111	1.35
Number of product demonstrations	108	1.13

Survey Questions and Response Scales:

1. When you evaluate your dealership, there are many possible measures of performance to choose from. Please indicate which of these measures *you actually use* (at least annually) to evaluate your dealership's performance. Response: By checking all that apply.
2. Indicate which of these items *you actually review* (at least annually) in your dealership evaluation process. Response: By checking all that apply.
3. Using only the items checked in questions 1 and 2, indicate how important each of these measures are to the overall evaluation of your dealership. Response: "Extremely important" (1), "Important" (2), and Slightly important (3).

Source: Mark T. Spriggs, "A Framework for More Valid Measures of Channel Member Performance," *Journal of Retailing,* Vol. 70 (Winter 1994), p. 335. Reprinted by permission.

TABLE 15-2 MEASUREMENT OF RESELLER PERFORMANCE

Contribution to sales:
1. Over the past year, the dealer has been successful in generating high sales volume for the supplier, given the level of competition and economic growth in his market area.
2. Compared to competing dealers in the territory, this dealer has achieved a high level of market penetration for the supplier.
3. Last year, the revenue that this dealer generated from the supplier was higher than what other competing dealers within the same territory generated.

Contribution to profits:
1. The supplier's cost of servicing the dealer is reasonable, given the amount of business which the dealer generates for the supplier.
2. The dealer's demands for support have resulted in inadequate profits for the supplier.
3. The supplier made inadequate profits from this dealer over the past year because of the amount of time, effort, and energy which the supplier had to devote to assisting him/her.

Reseller competence:
1. The dealer has the required business skills necessary to run a successful business.
2. The dealer demonstrates a great deal of knowledge about the features and attributes of the supplier's products and services.
3. The dealer and his personnel have poor knowledge of competitors' products and services.

Reseller compliance:
1. In the past, the supplier has often had trouble getting the dealer to participate in its (some program important to the supplier) program.
2. The dealer almost always conforms to the supplier's accepted procedures.
3. The dealer has frequently violated [stipulations/terms and conditions] contained in his or her [contract/agreement] with the supplier.

Reseller adaptation:
1. The dealer senses long-term trends in his market area and frequently adjusts his or her selling practices.
2. The dealer is very innovative in his or her marketing of the supplier's products and services in his or her territory.
3. The dealer makes an effort to meet competitive changes in his or her territory.

Contribution to growth:
1. The dealer will either continue to be or will soon become a major source of revenue for the supplier.
2. Over the next year, the supplier expects its revenue generated from this dealer to grow faster than that from other competing [of the supplier] dealers within the same territory.
3. In the past, the supplier's business with the dealer has grown steadily.

Customer satisfaction:
1. The supplier has frequently received complaints from customers regarding this dealer.
2. The dealer goes out of his or her way to make his or her customers happy.
3. The dealer provides [customers/end-users] with good assistance in the solution of any problems involving the supplier's products and services.
    Unless otherwise noted, all items are measured on a seven-point Likert scale.

Source: Adapted from Nirmalya Kumar, Louis W. Stern, and Ravi S. Achrol, "Assessing Reseller Performance from the Perspective of the Supplier," *Journal of Marketing Research,* Vol. 29 (May 1992), pp. 251–252. Reprinted by permission of the American Marketing Association.

FINANCIAL PERFORMANCE MEASURES

This section describes the use of financial performance measures as channel assessment measures. Two types of measures are described. The first type, Data Envelopment Analysis (DEA), assesses the performance of individual stores or branches. The second type, financial ratios, evaluates overall channel performance on the basis of solvency, efficiency, and profitability.

DATA ENVELOPMENT ANALYSIS

Data Envelopment Analysis (DEA) is a technique used to evaluate the performance of specific branch locations or stores. It recognizes that not all branches or locations are equally profitable. **Data Envelopment Analysis (DEA)** evaluates factors in branch or store performance (such as sales, sales growth, profits per employee, and sales per square foot), as well as differences in technology, capacity, competition, and demographics among branch or store locations. It then compares each branch or location against units with similar attributes. Finally, all branches or locations are categorized into one of four groups: star performers (those that are most efficient and have the highest profit), branches with low-profit and low-growth potential (that have high efficiency but low profits), underperforming star branches (that have high profit but low-efficiency potential), or underperforming branches (that have low profit and low efficiency).

Figure 15-1 shows the use of the DEA matrix as a means of determining which branches or locations do best. DEA can be used to develop specific strategies for each branch. For example, funds can be more appropriately invested in an underperforming star branch than in an effectively managed branch with limited profit potential. A channel member can also determine its overall health by determining its mix of branch locations in each portion of the matrix.

FIGURE 15-1 The Data Envelopment Analysis (DEA) matrix.

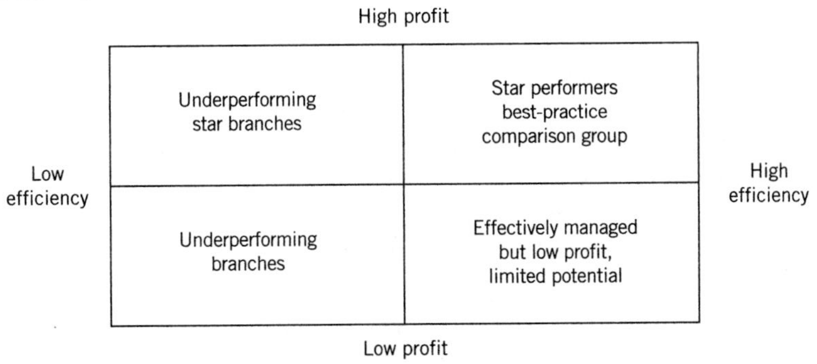

	High profit	
Low efficiency	Underperforming star branches	Star performers best-practice comparison group
	Underperforming branches	Effectively managed but low profit, limited potential
	Low profit	High efficiency

Source: Rob Norton, "Which Offices or Stores Really Perform Best? A New Tool Tells," *Fortune* (October 31, 1994), p. 38. Reprinted by permission; © 1994 Time Inc. All rights reserved.

It is also important to evaluate a firm's performance against major competitors, as well as the best performing firms in a specific industry.

OVERALL CHANNEL MEMBER FINANCIAL RATIOS

A common means of evaluating channel members is through financial ratios that focus on solvency, efficiency, and profitability.[6] These ratios can be used to evaluate suppliers, customers, and the channel member's own performance.

In comparing a firm's performance on any of these ratios, one should be cautioned to take into account variations in performance owing to geographic region and channel member size. A change in channel strategy, such as stocking up on inventory in advance of a price increase from a vendor, would also affect several of these ratios, (see Table 15-3).

Solvency Ratios

Solvency ratios measure a channel member's ability to meet its short- and long-term debt obligations. A poor solvency ratio may indicate that a firm has too much debt, may become insolvent, or may be unable to take sufficient advantage of growth opportunities owing to its low creditworthiness. A supplier may continue selling goods and services to a channel reseller with poor solvency, but may restrict the amount of the credit or carefully monitor repayment. The supplier could also seek to reduce reliance on such a reseller by using more intensive distribution. Among the major solvency ratios are the quick ratio, current ratio, and total liabilities to net worth.

The **quick ratio** divides cash and accounts receivable by a firm's current liabilities. Current liabilities include all debt that is due within one year. This quick ratio shows a firm's ability to pay off its short-run debt. The higher the quick ratio, the greater a firm's liquidity. Generally, a quick ratio of 1 to 1 or better is viewed as satisfactory.

$$\text{Quick ratio} = \frac{\text{Cash} + \text{Accounts receivable}}{\text{Current liabilities}}$$

The **current ratio** equals a firm's total current assets (cash accounts receivable less reserves for bad debt, merchandise inventory, and marketable securities) divided by its current liabilities. The quick ratio is a stricter test of a firm's liquidity than the current ratio since it does not include merchandise inventory and marketable securities. As with the quick ratio, the higher a firm's current ratio, the more solvent the firm. A current ratio of 2 to 1 or better is generally viewed as satisfactory.

$$\text{Current ratio} = \frac{\text{Current assets}}{\text{Current liabilities}}$$

The **total liabilities to net worth ratio** is computed by dividing a firm's total liabilities by its net worth. Unlike the other measures of liquidity, this ratio

TABLE 15-3 MEDIAN KEY BUSINESS RATIOS FOR SELECTED WHOLESALER AND RETAILER CATEGORIES, 1994

	Quick Ratio (times)	Current Ratio (times)	Total Liab. to Net Worth (times)	Collection Period (days)	Inventory Turnover (times)	Assets to Sales (times)	Net Profit Margin (%)	Return on Assets (%)	Return on Net Worth (%)
Wholesalers									
Farm supplies	0.9	1.8	80.0	28.8	10.9	37.8	2.0	5.0	9.9
Footwear	1.0	1.9	95.6	46.4	7.1	37.6	2.5	5.5	14.8
Hardware	1.1	2.5	72.9	40.9	6.4	38.9	2.2	5.3	10.8
Industrial machinery equipment	1.2	1.9	98.9	43.1	10.3	32.6	2.2	5.2	13.3
Industrial supplies	1.2	2.2	91.3	41.3	8.5	32.5	2.4	5.4	11.9
Jewelry, precious stones	0.9	2.1	101.1	42.0	5.9	40.0	1.8	3.9	9.4
Medical and hospital equipment	1.2	2.0	96.6	43.8	11.3	31.4	3.3	7.6	20.3
Mens, boys clothing	1.0	2.0	96.2	33.2	7.6	33.4	2.5	5.4	17.7
Photographic equipment	1.1	1.9	108.1	35.8	9.5	27.9	2.1	5.9	16.6
Stationery, office supplies	1.3	1.9	106.7	36.1	16.9	24.8	2.2	6.8	16.2
Retailers									
Apparel accessory stores	0.7	3.6	41.9	11.0	4.2	43.4	3.9	7.1	12.7
Auto dealer service station	0.3	1.4	199.9	6.9	6.9	26.4	1.6	4.9	16.7
Boat dealers	0.2	1.5	153.6	6.2	3.4	44.7	2.1	3.5	11.8
Department stores	1.3	3.9	55.0	16.8	4.3	49.5	1.5	3.0	4.9
Floor covering stores	1.1	2.2	74.1	21.9	12.9	24.8	3.7	9.5	21.6
Grocery stores	0.5	1.9	94.7	2.6	18.1	18.3	1.4	5.9	13.6
Hardware stores	0.8	3.2	58.9	17.5	4.2	45.8	2.7	4.9	9.1
Used car dealers	0.6	2.1	108.0	8.8	8.5	27.1	2.7	7.1	17.7
Shoe stores	0.5	3.3	44.5	5.8	3.6	44.0	3.7	6.9	12.4
Variety stores	0.6	3.4	45.5	6.2	4.4	37.4	2.6	6.0	11.0

Source: Industry Norms & Key Business Ratios: Desk-Top Edition 1994–1995 (New York: Dun & Bradstreet Information Services, 1995), pp. 149–172. Reprinted by permission.

looks at long-term, as well as short-term, debt. In general, a firm's total liabilities should not exceed its net worth.

$$\text{Total liabilities to net worth} = \frac{\text{Total liabilities}}{\text{Net worth}}$$

EFFICIENCY RATIOS

Efficiency ratios compute how effectively a firm uses its assets. Among the major efficiency ratios are the collection period, inventory turnover, and assets to sales ratio. In using all three ratios, a channel member can highlight areas for strategy improvement (such as increasing payments from creditors, increasing inventory turnover, or reducing inefficient assets such as poor locations).

In the **collection period**, a firm's accounts receivable are divided by its sales and then multiplied by 365 days. The collection period is an overall measure of the quality of a firm's account receivables. A firm's collection period should correspond to the credit terms offered to its customers. For example, if industry terms are generally net 30, then a collection period of 40 would be satisfactory. In this example, a collection period of 60 would indicate that the overall quality of a firm's receivables is poor. The firm should consider turning over some late-paying receivables to a collection agency, being more vigorous in collection procedures, or writing-off some questionable receivables as bad debt.

$$\text{Collection period} = \frac{\text{Accounts receivable}}{\text{Annual net sales}} \times 365$$

The **inventory turnover ratio** is computed by dividing a firm's annual net sales by its average inventory. Inventory turnover rates can differ by merchandise classification within a firm. A low inventory turnover ratio may indicate that a significant portion of a firm's inventory is either slow moving or obsolete. Inventory turnover can be increased through just-in-time inventory management, the use of floor-ready merchandise, and the application of ABC analysis to the firm's total inventory. (These techniques were discussed in Chapter 6.) On the other hand, too high a sales to inventory ratio may mean lost opportunities for sales.

$$\text{Inventory turnover} = \frac{\text{Annual net sales}}{\text{Average inventory}}$$

The **assets to sales ratio** is determined by dividing a firm's total assets by its annual net sales. This number indicates the level of assets needed to support one dollar of sales. A channel member can increase the assets to sales ratio by increasing its inventory turnover, purchasing used (instead of new) fixtures, using short-term promotions to stimulate sales, opening longer hours, and shifting channel functions that require high assets to other channel members.

$$\text{Assets to sales} = \frac{\text{Total assets}}{\text{Annual net sales}}$$

PROFITABILITY RATIOS

Profitability ratios analyze a firm's return on its assets. These include net profit margin, return on assets, and return on net worth.

The net profit margin is a widely used summary measure of a firm's profitability. The **net profit margin** is obtained by dividing a firm's net profit after tax by its annual net sales. It measures the profit per dollar of sales. All firms need sustained profitability to pay interest expenses, reduce debt, reward stockholders, and provide resources for growth opportunities.

$$\text{Net profit margin} = \frac{\text{Net profit after taxes}}{\text{Annual net sales}}$$

The **return on assets ratio** is computed by dividing a firm's net profit after tax by its total assets. This ratio calculates a firm's net profit after tax per dollar of assets. The return on assets ratio is especially important for channel members with a large asset base. A high proportion of the asset base for many wholesalers and retailers consists of inventory.

$$\text{Return on assets} = \frac{\text{Net profit after taxes}}{\text{Total assets}}$$

The **return on net worth ratio** is obtained by dividing a firm's net profit after tax by its net worth. A return on net worth of 10 percent or better is generally considered satisfactory.

$$\text{Return on net worth} = \frac{\text{Net profit after taxes}}{\text{Net worth}}$$

DISTRIBUTION COST ANALYSIS

Distribution cost analysis seeks to determine the cost levels and profitability of specific channel configurations (such as direct versus indirect channels), product lines (such as private-label brands), and customer types (such as discount stores). The three overall approaches to distribution profitability analysis are full-cost analysis, direct-cost analysis, and activity-based costing.

A survey by Professors Lambert and Sterling found that, while overall profitability reports were popular, distribution profitability analysis had low usage. For example, although 78 percent of the respondents prepared profitability reports by product line, profitability reports by channel were only conducted in 20 percent of the larger U.S. and Canadian manufacturing firms surveyed.[7]

FULL- AND DIRECT-COST ANALYSIS

Both full- and direct-cost analysis operate in a similar manner using a three-step process. These forms of cost analysis are distinguished in this section following a full explanation of this process.

TABLE 15-4 A PROFIT-AND-LOSS STATEMENT

Sales		$600,000
Cost of goods sold		250,000
Gross profit		$350,000
Salaries	$100,000	
Insurance	10,000	
Interest	30,000	
Rent	75,000	
Supplies	7,000	
Travel	9,000	
Total expenses		$231,000
Net profit before tax		$119,000

The first step in both full-and direct-cost analysis is to determine the level of all natural expenses. **Natural expenses** report costs by the names of the expenses, not their activity or function. Examples of natural expenses are salaries, rent, insurance, interest, and fuel. The profit-and-loss statement in Table 15-4 contains a listing of natural expenses. The second step is to reclassify these natural expenses into functional accounts. **Functional expenses** indicate the activity involved in the expenditure. Examples of functional accounts in distribution include selling, advertising, transportation, warehousing, and billing. Table 15-5 assigns natural expenses in Table 15-4 to functional expenses. By evaluating functional expense levels, a channel member can determine how an expense was used. For example, one can determine that increased rent went to warehouse space. The third step allocates income and functional expenses to specific channel configurations, product lines, and customer types. Table 15-6 shows channel profitability based on the classification of functional expenses to each marketing channel. In computing this table, functional expenses were allocated to each channel on the basis of the number of orders, number of sales calls, actual cooperative advertising expenditures, and costs associated with billing. Billing expenditures for specialty stores were high in this example owing to the absence of computerization.

An analysis of Table 15-6 reveals several important findings. First, gross margins differ significantly by channel. Although the firm's overall gross margin was 58.3 percent, gross profit margins for department stores were 66.7 percent as

TABLE 15-5 ASSIGNING NATURAL EXPENSES TO FUNCTIONAL EXPENSES

Natural Accounts	Total	Selling	Advertising	Transportation	Warehousing	Billing
Salaries	$100,000	$30,000	$30,000	$23,000	$10,000	$ 7,000
Insurance	10,000			5,000	5,000	
Interest	30,000			10,000	20,000	
Rent	75,000	20,000	10,000	20,000	22,000	3,000
Supplies	7,000	3,000	3,000			1,000
Travel	9,000	9,000				
Total expenses	$231,000	$62,000	$43,000	$58,000	$57,000	$11,000

TABLE 15-6 CLASSIFYING FUNCTIONAL EXPENSES INTO MARKETING CHANNELS TO DETERMINE CHANNEL PROFITABILITY

	Total	Department Stores	Specialty Stores	Discount Stores
Net sales	$600,000	$300,000	$200,000	$100,000
Cost of goods sold	250,000	100,000	100,000	50,000
Gross margin	$350,000	$200,000	$100,000	$ 50,000
Less: Operating expenses				
Selling	$ 62,000	$ 22,000	$ 30,000	$ 10,000
Advertising	43,000	25,000	11,000	7,000
Transportation	58,000	20,000	30,000	8,000
Warehousing	57,000	28,500	19,000	9,500
Billing	11,000	4,000	5,000	2,000
Total Operating Expenses	$231,000	$ 99,500	$ 95,000	$ 36,500
Net profit before tax	$119,000	$100,500	$ 5,000	$ 13,500
Net profit as a percent of sales	19.8	33.5	2.5	13.5

compared to 50 percent for both specialty and discount stores. Second, operating expenses differed by channel. Whereas total operating expenses were 38.5 percent of sales, operating expenses for department stores, specialty stores, and discount stores were 33.1, 47.5, and 36.5 percent of sales, respectively. The low overall profitability of specialty stores as compared to discount stores is due largely to higher expenses for specialty stores.

The difference between the full-versus direct-cost analysis is based on the types of expenses that are classified into particular channels. **Full-cost analysis** allocates all costs to each channel regardless of how arbitrary the expense allocation may be. Advocates of the use of full-cost analysis argue that all expenses are important. Full-cost users also like to see total profits for a firm equal to the sum of profits to each channel. Table 15-6 illustrates full-cost analysis. Note that net profit before tax in this table is the same as in the profit-and-loss statement. Also note that the overall profits for the firm equal the sum of the profits of each channel. A disadvantage of full-cost analysis is that some expenses must be allocated to channels in a somewhat arbitrary manner. For example, warehouse expenses can be allocated to specific channels on the basis of the number of orders or a channel's percentage of overall sales. Each method of cost allocation results in a different level of channel profitability.

In contrast, **direct-cost analysis** only allocates expenses that can be assigned directly to a channel or that can be traced to a given channel (such as sales force salaries when each channel is served by a separate sales force, or warehousing space when different channels have different warehouse arrangements). In direct-cost analysis, the bottom line is the contribution of each channel to unassigned expenses, not net profit before taxes. Direct-cost analysis has fewer allocation problems since only fewer expenses are allocated under this method.

The major differences between these approaches is how nontraceable common costs are handled. **Nontraceable common costs** are costs that cannot be clearly assigned to a given channel. Examples of nontraceable common costs may include marketing overhead, interest, and taxes.[8]

Both full- and direct-cost analysis are most accurate when a firm's activities are organized by channel or customer group. This would occur in a decentralized organization with a separate sales force and advertising personnel devoted to each channel.

ACTIVITY-BASED COSTING

Activity-based costing (ABC) attempts to assign costs (such as labor) directly to the good or the services that the business produces. Activity-based costing seeks to more accurately assign overhead costs by creating a cost database around activity, nonactivity, product, channel, and customer dimensions. ABC analysis should be used when overhead accounts for a large proportion of total costs. Whereas traditional accounting systems use bases like direct labor to allocate the expenses of indirect and support activities, activity-based costing

TABLE 15-7 THE STEPS IN APPLYING ACTIVITY-BASED COSTING TO DETERMINE CHANNEL PROFITABILITY

Step 1: Identify the key activities in the value chain. For a warehouse, this may be receiving, inspection, storage, staging, and shipping. Larger activities, other things being equal, should be treated separately. The costs associated with each of these components need to be estimated. The sum of these costs should equal the firm's total costs.

Step 2: Trace activity costs to the cost centers in direct proportion to the way each activity absorbs costs. Assign costs such as labor, materials and supplies, utilities, depreciation, and building-related costs from the general ledger to each activity and nonactivity component: product related, customer related, and channel related. If an appropriate driver cannot be ascertained, a special study may have to be planned and implemented.

Step 3: Assign costs from each of these activities to the individual channels. It is necessary to identify the tracking factor that relates these costs back to the appropriate channel or customer. Ideally, there should be little widespread spreading of costs. For example, inspection costs should be assigned by the complexity of the product, shipping by the number of shipments, and storage costs by the number of pallet positions reserved for the product. Cost drivers must possess three critical characteristics: They must be associated with a cost object; they must be highly correlated with the activity cost; and they must be reasonably inexpensive to collect.

Step 4: Determine customer purchases by product and by distribution channel to determine the total cost perspective for a channel. Also capture revenue information for the same channels for which costs were calculated.

Source: This section is based on Jack Haedicke, "The ABCs of Profitability," *Progressive Grocer Executive Report: Part II* (January 1994), pp. 38–40; Kenneth H. Manning, "Distribution Channel Profitability," *Management Accounting* (January 1995), pp. 44–48; and Ryan Mathews, "ABC Made Easy," *Progressive Grocer* (September 1994), pp. 37–38 ff.

segregates the expenses of indirect and support resources by activities. It then assigns those expenses based on the drivers of those activities.

Table 15-7 outlines the steps in activity-based costing to channels. Central to these steps is tracing activity and nonactivity costs to cost centers (step 2) and assigning these costs to individual channels (step 3). This process is illustrated in Table 15-8. Note that all costs are assigned either to products, channels, or customers. Also note that all costs are divided into activity and nonactivity costs.

A survey by the Institute of Management Accountants found that 29 percent of the companies surveyed used activity-based costing instead of the full- and direct-cost analysis. In addition, 56 percent used activity-based costing as an analytical technique.[9]

In the next section, we discuss the use of the channel audit as a means of assessing channel performance.

THE CHANNEL AUDIT

In a **channel audit**, firms evaluate their downstream and upstream channel relationships on a periodic basis through the use of checklists.[10] Audits are characterized by use of programmed appraisals, critical evaluations of the assumptions that underlie a firm's objectives and policies, identification of opportunities as well as weaknesses, and focus on prevention as well as cure.[11]

TABLE 15-8 COST BEHAVIOR OF ACTIVITY AND NONACTIVITY COSTS

Product Related	Channel Related	Customer Related
Activity Costs		
Schedule production	Attend trade shows	EDI and computer interfaces to customer
Setup and changeover for machine A	Order/invoice processing	Special shipping and handling requests
Test quality parameters	Sales force	Collect bad debt
	Telemarketing	Technical support for customer A
	Advertising Brand A	Prepare/deliver annual sales bid
	Arrange for shipping	
Nonactivity Costs		
Material costs	Trade discounts	Bad debt expense
Royalties	Freight	Customer rebates

Source: Kenneth H. Manning, "Distribution Channel Profitability," *Management Accounting* (January 1995), p. 46. Reprinted by permission. Copyright by the Institute of Management Accountants, Montvale, NJ 07645.

CHANNELS IN ACTION

Is That Customer Profitable?

After spending many years developing business with a computer and software manufacturer, a freight company was uncertain of the account's profitability. The freight company did not know whether the account was still profitable due to the number and size of price and service concessions made to it over the years. A thorough analysis of the profitability of this account using activity-based costing revealed that not only was this account unprofitable, but also that the freight company lost 50 percent on sales to this firm. Thus, each $100 in sales to this firm was associated with a loss of $150.

On first glance, one would assume that the freight company should either drop the account or raise its prices to sufficiently cover the high costs of servicing the account. However, by dropping this account, much of the freight company's overhead would have to be targeted at another firm. Thus, dropping the computer company account would result in an $80 million additional loss (since total costs would be reduced by $10 million, while the freight firm's overall sales would be reduced by $90 million).

The freight company decided to keep the computer company account but to reengineer the activities needed to service the freight company. The freight company carefully reevaluated its services and costs to determine whether additional costs are justified based on the customer's service quality expectations. For example, the freight company eliminated some activities that added little value to the computer customer such as measuring irregularly shaped goods. The freight firm also determined that the key to profitability of this account was to increase its market share of the computer manufacturer's business, while using the same amount of resources for that account. By obtaining better data on the computer firm's weekly production schedules, the carrier was able to eliminate dedicated flights from some terminals.

Source: Dar Wiatr, "Is That Customer Profitable?" *Across the Board* (May 1993), pp. 56–57.

THE CHANNEL AUDITING PROCESS

Several areas need to be resolved in planning and implementing the channel auditing prices. These include determining the audit frequency, choosing the type of auditor, and developing channel audit forms.

A firm should conduct a channel audit when its performance is below par, and the adequacy of its strategies has to be reassessed (such as the emergence of a new competitor, loss of a major client, difficulty with a major distributor, or a major shift in the balance of power between channel members). A firm should also audit its downstream and upstream channel members frequently to evaluate their performance and to suggest corrective actions when problems or special opportunities arise.

A channel audit can be undertaken by an internal auditor that specializes in auditing on a full-time basis, or by an individual or team that undertakes audits on a periodic basis along with their regular responsibilities. While an internal auditor knows a firm's and its channel members' policies, he or she may be subject to political pressures or time constraints. In contrast, the external auditor has few political pressures and can devote his or her time to auditing. However, the external auditor may have to spend considerable time learning about the company's channel policies and those of its suppliers and customers.

There are two types of channel audits: vertical and horizontal audits. The **vertical channel audit** focuses on one area of channels such as customer service or physical distribution. In contrast, a **horizontal channel audit** concentrates on all of a firm's channels elements. A horizontal channel audit is often called a marketing mix audit since it looks at a firm's overall channel strategy and the overall appropriateness of its channel mix.

ILLUSTRATION OF A CHANNEL MANAGEMENT AUDIT FORM

Most management audits use open-ended checklist-type questions. In some checklists, questions are grouped by subject area. Some checklists also point to each question to represent degrees of marketing effectiveness, as well as the importance of each question.[12]

Table 15-9 is an example of a channel audit form from a manufacturer's/supplier's perspective. This form is classified by subject area. The form summarizes many of the channel management concepts in this text.

IMPROVING OVERALL CHANNEL PRODUCTIVITY THROUGH CHANNEL PARTNERSHIPS AND EFFICIENT CONSUMER RESPONSE

Both the use of channel partnerships and Efficient Consumer Response (ECR) as a means of increasing overall channel productivity are designed to reduce total distribution costs while keeping customer service quality constant. In contrast, other techniques in this chapter focused on channel costs to one channel member. For example, just-in-time inventory management may not necessarily decrease total channel inventories. In some cases, it can result in redistributing inventory responsibilities from a strong customer to a weaker supplier.

Channel partnerships enable resellers and suppliers to speed up inventory replenishment, improve customer service, and reduce markdowns and the cost of distributing goods to customers. Channel partnerships often involve the use of information and communications technologies that lower costs at the same time that they improve services.[13]

TABLE 15-9 EXAMPLE OF A CHANNEL AUDIT FROM A MANUFACTURER'S/SUPPLIER'S PERSPECTIVE

Channel Structure
- Is channel coverage adequate?
- Does the firm use a low-cost channel structure?
- Does the channel plan incorporate scenarios?
- Have opportunities for multiple channels of distribution been evaluated?
- Do downstream resellers have appropriate territorial rights?
- Are conditions of termination clearly set forth to all resellers?
- Is reseller compensation adequate to attract and retain high-quality resellers?
- Does the firm periodically evaluate its resellers?

Relationship Marketing
- Are channel switching costs high for current customers?
- Does the firm demonstrate high commitment and trust to its customers?
- Is the marketing effort appropriately distributed among both new and existing customers?
- Does the firm view its customers from a long-term perspective?
- Is the focus of the company on developing and maintaining buyer loyalty (versus on a one-time sale)?
- Is the firm's use of coercive and noncoercive power appropriate?
- Is the degree of channel conflict appropriate?
- Does the firm have channel partnerships?

Customer Service
- Does the firm measure customer satisfaction on an ongoing basis?
- Has the firm communicated the lifetime value of a customer to its employees and downstream channel resellers?
- Has the firm implemented total quality management?
- Does the firm have a written customer service policy?
- Are employees appropriately empowered?

Physical Distribution
- Does the firm periodically evaluate its physical distribution quality and costs?
- Has the use of alternative transportation modes been periodically studied?
- Has the use of third-party transportation providers been evaluated?
- Has the use of freight forwarders been analyzed?
- Has the use of private versus public warehouses been studied?
- Does the firm use direct store delivery and cross docking where applicable?
- Has the firm evaluated backhauling opportunities?
- Has the firm evaluated the use of hub-and-spoke distribution systems?
- Does the firm use just-in-time inventory management?

Marketing Research and Information Systems
- Does the firm provide adequate information to its downstream and upstream channel members?
- Does the firm have computer linkages with its important channel members?
- Does the firm compile and analyze internal secondary data on a periodic basis?
- Does the firm subscribe to important sources of external secondary data?
- Does the firm measure its distribution intensity using all commodity volume and percent category volume?
- Does the firm use database marketing?

TABLE 15-9 *(CONTINUED)*

Product
- Have opportunities for scrambled merchandising been evaluated?
- Does the firm use channel members to generate and evaluate new product ideas?
- Does the firm study the fit of existing channels for new products?
- Does the firm evaluate the channel management implications of the product life cycle?
- Does the firm have an adequate product recall strategy?
- Does the firm adequately utilize product recycling?
- Is the firm's packaging strategy effective from a channel reseller perspective?
- Is the firm's packaging strategy effective from an ecological perspective?

Pricing
- Is the gross profit to each channel member fair?
- Is the firm's approach to pricing integrated?
- Has the firm evaluated the use of everyday low pricing?
- Has the firm developed ample strategies to limit the sale of gray market goods?
- Does the firm utilize price guarantees when appropriate?
- Is the firm's overall discount structure effective?
- Is the firm's pricing strategy capable of adapting to special cost, demand, or competitive conditions?
- Can the firm's pricing strategy be legally defended?

Advertising
- Is the use of pull versus push promotions appropriate?
- Does the firm's promotional strategy stimulate primary demand?
- Does the firm consider the indirect communication effects of advertising?
- Does the firm adequately utilize cooperative advertising?
- Is the firm's promotional plan to downstream resellers based on reseller size and sophistication?
- Is the firm's advertising strategy legally defensible?
- Do downstream intermediaries receive ample notice of push-oriented promotions?

Personal Selling
- Is pull versus push promotional support adequate?
- Does my sales force understand its role as teacher, reviewer, working partner, ambassador, ombudsman, and motivator?
- Does the firm have an appropriate sales training program?
- Is the sales training program ongoing?
- Does the firm utilize sales incentives?
- Does the firm use joint sales calls?
- Does the firm use telemarketing when appropriate?

Sales Promotion
- Does the firm use street money, pay-for-performance, and push money when appropriate?
- Does the firm use distributor recognition programs when appropriate?
- Do downstream intermediaries receive ample notice of push-oriented promotions?
- Is the firm's sales promotion strategy legally defensible?
- Are conditions for cooperative advertising appropriate?
- Is the use of coupons versus rebates appropriate?
- Does the firm exhibit at major trade shows?
- Are point-of-purchase displays effective?

TABLE 15-9   (CONTINUED)

Technology
- Does the firm use electronic data interchange when appropriate?
- Does the firm use scanning data?
- Does the firm use a third-party network when appropriate?
- Are appropriate channel activities computerized?
- Is case and carton scanning utilized?
- Does the firm have an ongoing technology-based training program?
- Has the firm evaluated the information superhighway as a channel?

Services Channels
- Does the channel properly reflect services intangibility, inseparability, persishability, and variability in quality?
- Does channel arrangement reflect flexibility in production?
- Does channel arrangement reflect flexibility in consumption?
- Are all channel-based activities properly delegated to intermediaries?
- Is the physical distribution arrangement for service delivery satisfactory?

International Channels
- Is channel arrangement appropriate for the firm's level of commitment to international business?
- Are home channel members appropriate?
- Are foreign market channel members appropriate?
- Have joint venture opportunities been explored?
- Have channel length and width in international markets been reassessed?
- Has the use of freight forwarders and customs agents been explored?
- Has the use of a foreign trade zone been assessed?

Channel partnerships can reduce the total system costs by:[14]

- Reducing the amount of inventory carried by all channel members.
- Using information technology to automate information capture, analysis, and dissemination (such as electronic data interchange among partners).
- Reassigning tasks such as preticketing merchandise by vendors.
- Eliminating redundancies, such as order entry by both supplier and reseller.
- Introducing supplier-managed replenishment systems.
- Using cross docking and direct store delivery.

Another way of reducing total channel costs is through Efficient Consumer Response. **Efficient Consumer Response (ECR)** is a term used in the food distribution industry to describe efforts to maximize the effectiveness of the entire supply chain. ECR gives special emphasis to the linkages among all of a firm's trading partners. For example, manufacturers need to push quick response-related technologies back into their plants and material procurement systems. The ECR Performance Measures Operating Committee (PMOC) also found that multiple trading partners often perform the same activity. ECR can also increase channel efficiency by eliminating activities that add no consumer value, by adding activities that improve communication, and by eliminating poorly performing products.[15] Among activities that increase channel efficiency are

CHANNELS IN ACTION

Channel Partnerships That Increase Efficiency

A commonly cited channel partnership is Wal-Mart's partnership with Procter & Gamble which began in 1985. This partnership is "built on trust and committed to a shared vision—meeting the customer's needs while driving out excess costs in the system by changing it." Wal-Mart's channel partnership with Procter & Gamble resulted in Procter & Gamble's inventory turnover increasing at the same time as the percentage of on-time deliveries to Wal-Mart increased. The partnership has been based on the use of electronic data interchange (EDI), a supplier-management replenishment system, and blanket purchase agreements. By eliminating order preparation tasks, Wal-Mart has reduced its buying costs. Procter & Gamble has signaled its commitment to its channel partnership with Wal-Mart by relocating some of its staff nearby Wal-Mart's corporate headquarters in Bentonville, Arkansas.

VF Corporation, Levi Strauss, and other apparel manufacturers have also developed a number of channel partnerships with discount and department stores. For example, by early 1993, VF had some 300 partners for its low-replenishment system. An important feature of these channel partnerships is the commitment by the suppliers, such as VF Corporation, to quick response inventory planning. VF Corporation completely reorganized its production processes to accommodate quick response. Early tests of reengineered merchandising and distribution processes by Kurt Associates at Dillard Department Stores, J. C. Penney, and Wal-Mart revealed significant increases in productivity. In one test, sales increased by 20 to 30 percent, inventory turnover improved by 30 percent, and in-stock performance improved from 70–75 percent to 95 percent or more.

Source: Robert D. Buzzell and Gwen Ortmeyer, "Channel Partnerships Streamline Distribution," *Sloan Management Review,* Vol. 43 (Spring 1995), pp. 85–96.

electronic data interchange, point-of-sale registers, bar codes, cross docking, scanning equipment, store replenishment software, and invoice and packaging standards. The annual cost savings of such measures has been estimated at between $24 billion and $30 billion.[16]

SUMMARY

1 *To discuss overall measures of channel performance used by dealers and suppliers.* For dealers, 34 performance measures could be summarized by five performance items: an outcome sales measure, an outcome profit measure, a behavior sales effort measure, a customer service measure, and a marketing support measure. For suppliers, there are seven components of reseller performance: contribution to sales, contribution to profits, reseller competence, reseller compliance, reseller adaptation, contribution to growth, and customer satisfaction.

2 *To describe the use of Data Envelopment Analysis (DEA) and financial ratio analysis.* Data Envelopment Analysis (DEA) is a technique for evaluating the performance of specific branch locations or stores. DEA evaluates factors in branch or store performance (such as sales, sales growth, profits per employee, and sales per square foot), as well as differences in technology, capacity, competition, and demographics among branch or store locations. All branches or locations are categorized into one of four groups: star performers, branches with low-profit and low-growth potential, underperforming star branches, and underperforming branches.

Financial ratios can be classified as solvency ratios, efficiency ratios, and profitability ratios. Solvency ratios measure a channel member's ability to meet its short- and long-term debt obligations. The major solvency ratios are the quick ratio, current ratio, and total liabilities to net worth. Efficiency ratios compute how effectively a firm uses its assets. Among the major efficiency ratios are the collection period, inventory turnover, and the assets to sales ratio. Profitability ratios analyze a firm's return on its assets. These include net profit margin, return on assets, and return on net worth.

3 *To discuss distribution cost analysis.* Distribution cost analysis seeks to determine the cost levels and profitability of specific channel configurations (such as direct versus indirect channels), product lines (such as private-label brands), and customer types (such as discount stores). There are three overall approaches to distribution profitability analysis: full-cost analysis, direct-cost analysis, and activity-based costing.

4 *To analyze the use of the channel audit.* In a channel audit, firms evaluate their downstream and upstream channel relationships on a periodic basis through the use of checklists. The channel auditing process consists of determining the audit frequency, choosing the type of auditor, and developing channel audit forms.

5 *To study the use of channel partnerships and Efficient Consumer Response (ECR) in increasing overall channel productivity.* Channel partnerships enable resellers and suppliers to speed up inventory replenishment, improve customer service, reduce markdowns, and reduce the cost of distributing goods to customers. Often channel partnerships involve the use of information and communications technologies that lower costs at the same time as improving services.

> Another way of reducing total channel costs is through Efficient Consumer Response. Among ECR activities that increase channel efficiency are electronic data interchange, point-of-sale registers, bar codes, cross docking, scanning equipment, store replenishment software, and invoice and packaging standards. The annual cost savings of such measures has been estimated at between $24 billion and $30 billion.

KEY TERMS

Data Envelopment Analysis (DEA)
solvency ratios
quick ratio
current ratio
total liabilities to net worth ratio
efficiency ratios
collection period
inventory turnover ratio
assets to sales ratio
profitability ratios
net profit margin
return on assets ratio
return on net worth ratio
distribution cost analysis
natural expenses
functional expenses
full-cost analysis
direct-cost analysis
nontraceable common costs
activity-based costing (ABC)
channel audit
vertical channel audit
horizontal channel audit
Efficient Consumer Response (ECR)

QUESTIONS FOR DISCUSSION

1. Describe the difficulties associated with the use of a single measure of channel performance.
2. Contrast Data Envelopment Analysis (DEA) with the Boston Consulting Group matrix.
3. Contrast the quick and the current ratio.
4. Show how the collection period is related to credit terms offered to customers.
5. Develop four strategies for a wholesaler to increase its return on assets ratio.
6. Differentiate between full-cost and direct-cost analysis.
7. Provide three examples of nontraceable channel-related common costs.
8. Under what circumstances should a channel member use activity-based costing instead of full-cost analysis?
9. How often should a firm conduct a channel audit? Explain your answer.
10. Prepare a vertical channel audit form to assess a firm's relationship marketing efforts.

11. Develop a vertical channel audit form to assess a firm's physical distribution activities.

12. Differentiate between assessing channel costs for one channel member versus channel costs for the entire channel.

13. Explain three sources of increased channel efficiency through use of channel partnerships.

14. Explain three sources of increased channel efficiency through use of Efficient Consumer Response.

END NOTES

1. Harrison Donnelly, "Still Struggling on Supply Chain Improvements," *Stores* (March 1995), pp. 56–57.

2. Mark T. Spriggs, "A Framework for More Valid Measures of Channel Member Performance," *Journal of Retailing,* Vol. 70 (Winter 1994), p. 334.

3. Ibid., p. 337.

4. Nirmalya Kumar, Louis W. Stern, and Ravi S. Achrol, "Assessing Reseller Performance from the Perspective of the Supplier," *Journal of Marketing Research,* Vol. 29 (May 1992), pp. 238–253.

5. Ibid., p. 250.

6. This section is based on *Industry Norms & Key Business Ratios: Desk-Top Edition 1994–1995* (New York: Dun & Bradstreet Information Services, 1995), pp. iii–vi.

7. Douglas Lambert and Jay U. Sterling, "What Types of Profitability Reports Do Marketing Managers Receive?" *Industrial Marketing Management,* Vol. 16 (November 1987), p. 298.

8. Philip Kotler, "Evaluating and Controlling Marketing Performance," in *The Dartnell Marketing Manager's Handbook,* Third Edition, Sidney J. Levy, George R. Frerichs, and Howard L. Gordon, eds. (Chicago: Dartnell Corporation, 1994), p. 752.

9. "More Companies Turn to ABC," *Journal of Accountancy* (July 1994), p. 14.

10. For a classic illustration of the use of management audits applied to channels, see William G. Browne and E. D. Reiten, "Auditing Distribution Channels," *Journal of Marketing,* Vol. 42 (July 1978), pp. 38–41.

11. Abe Schuchman, "The Marketing Audit: Its Nature, Purposes, and Problems," in *Analyzing and Improving Marketing Performance: Marketing Audits in Theory and Practice,* Albert Newgarden and Eugene R. Bailey, eds. (New York: American Management Association, 1959), pp. 11–19.

12. Leonard L. Berry, Jeffrey S. Conant, and A. Parasuraman, "A Framework for Conducting a Services Marketing Audit," *Journal of the Academy of Marketing Science,* Vol. 19, No. 3 (1991), p. 258.

13. See Don R. Vehlhaber, "Pipeline Partnerships: Strategies for Effective Supply Chain Management," *MarketShare* (Winter 1993–1994), pp. 8–11.

14. Robert D. Buzzell and Gwen Ortmeyer, "Channel Partnerships Streamline Distribution," *Sloan Management Review,* Vol. 43 (Spring 1995), pp. 90, 92.

15. Ryan Mathews, "A New Look at ECR," *Progressive Grocer* (June 1994), pp. 29–30 ff.

16. Ibid., p. 29.

CASE 1

THE USE OF ABC ANALYSIS

This case discusses the use of ABC analysis by two firms: a specialty chemical manufacturer and an industrial equipment supplier. It describes the nature of each of their problems, the data captured by ABC analysis, and the solution proposed by each firm.

The specialty chemical manufacturer supplies products to a broad range of customers in the food, consumer products, and manufacturing industries. Although the chemical firm mostly manufactured these products, some products were purchased and repackaged. All products were sold through a network of representatives, a direct sales force, and telemarketers. Customers could choose among various delivery and pricing options (including customer pickup, bulk delivery, and less-than-truckload delivery). The chemical manufacturer sought to understand the true profitability of various delivery options and customer groups.

An ABC study of revenues and costs revealed the following:

- While larger customers had lower gross profits, these customers accounted for a large percentage of the division's profitability. Large customers required less customer service, had lower bad debt, and required lower handling charges owing to the large average order size.
- The customer pickup option resulted in lower than anticipated costs owing to the lower damage claim losses and reduced costs in freight scheduling.
- The costs for selling and servicing small customers were much higher than anticipated. Many small customers had a limited ability to solve technical problems and relied heavily on the manufacturer. The gross sales generated by these customers did not cover the cost of selling and servicing these small accounts.
- Many outsourced products initially appeared to be profitable under the firm's older cost system, but the high inbound logistics costs uncovered through ABC costing showed these were unprofitable.

On the basis of ABC analysis, the manufacturer reexamined its overall strategy. Technical resources were shifted away from smaller customers. Research and development personnel also began to better track costs of service to specific accounts. The customer pickup price was lowered to attract more volume, and the company began to find other sources for its outsourced products. It developed a goal of lowering its overall handling costs by 50 percent.

The second case involves an industrial equipment manufacturer that was known for the high quality of its in-house sales force. As a result, many of the firm's competitors began to use other distribution channels to avoid direct competition. The industrial equipment manufacturer decided to undertake a study using ABC analysis to determine the value of its sales force. The manufacturer instructed its sales force to keep a detailed log that tracked sales and costs to customers and channels. The use of accurate cost data enabled the firm to estimate the impact of several changes on its overall costs and profits. The data analysis came to the following conclusions:

- Some product lines that the firm thought were profitable were unprofitable owing to higher than anticipated channel costs. On the other hand, one product line that had low margins and was thought to be a loss leader was actually relatively profitable.
- Sales costs varied widely based on customer application.

On the basis of the ABC analysis, several independent sales representatives were assigned to small and medium customers that did not require technical assistance. These reps were given a margin adequate for them to be exclusive agents for the firm. The firm dropped a product line that was the sole product purchased by a class of customers. Revenue from these single-product customers was insufficient to justify sales force costs. Finally, the price on the product thought to be a loss leader was lowered to attract additional volume.

QUESTIONS

1. Explain how full-cost analysis could have been used by the specialty chemical manufacturer.
2. Differentiate between natural and functional expenses for the specialty chemical manufacturer.
3. Develop a list of channel activity costs and nonactivity costs for the industrial equipment manufacturer.
4. a. Show how full- and direct-cost analysis could result in different conclusions for the industrial equipment manufacturer.
   b. In general, which technique would be more accurate? Explain your answer.

Source: Kenneth H. Manning, "Distribution Channel Profitability," *Management Accounting* (January 1995), pp. 44–48.

CASE 2

SIMPSON TIMBER COMPANY: THE USE OF A CHANNEL AUDIT

Simpson Timber Company's Columbia Door Division manufactures wooden flush doors that are used in home and building construction. The firm's major markets were in California, Oregon, and Washington, but it had also done well in the Midwest market (mostly the Mountain state region) which had no manufacturers of flush doors.

Simpson's Midwest territory was covered by an agent who sold Simpson doors and building products of other manufacturers to wholesalers. These wholesalers then resold the doors to retail stores and to major contractors in an 11-state region. Simpson treated the door market as a commodity, viewing price and delivery speed and reliability as most important attributes. Because of the long distance between the Midwest market and Simpson's manufacturing facility, the firm made few visits to the Midwest market. The agent provided information to Simpson on competitors' pricing and delivery schedules. The company's sales in the Midwest market were substantial, and the firm viewed the market as stable.

Several important market shifts in the Midwest market as well as in the flush door business had a major impact on Simpson. These included a shifting in emphasis of West Coast door manufacturers to the Midwest market and the increased popularity of a new Masonite door. Competitive manufacturers shifted sales to the Midwest when the West Coast building market was in a recession. Many West Coast manufacturers viewed the Midwest as a temporary outlet for sales that would have ordinarily been made in the West Coast. These manufacturers reduced their prices to gain entry into the Midwest.

A new door, made of a Masonite material that had improved scratch and nick resistance, was also developed and patented so that it could not be directly copied by Simpson. The Masonite door was beginning to be rapidly accepted by wholesalers, retailers, contractors, and end-users when

Simpson sought to produce a door equivalent to its competitor's Masonite doors, but at a lower price. Simpson's Masonite door, however, would be priced at a higher level than its traditional wood product.

Prior to introducing its Masonite door, Simpson decided to conduct a channel audit of its Midwest market. The firm developed data for the audit on the basis of phone conversations with some large Midwestern wholesalers and a market survey of high-volume users using telephone interviews. Some of the major findings of the channel audit were as follows.

- The data that Simpson had been using to determine its market share were faulty.
- Large wholesalers, in particular, were concerned about the poor support provided by Simpson's agent. For example, the agent was slow to respond to claims for faulty materials. The firm's claim procedure especially affected new customers.
- Simpson's flush doors were not represented at local and regional building trade shows. These shows were attended by major wholesalers and their customers.
- Simpson underestimated the growth in direct sales. Major home builders, large builders of building components, and large home improvement retailers were increasing their pressure to buy direct. Whereas in the past nearly 95 percent of wooden flush door sales were to wholesalers, at the time of the channel audit, industrial component and home builders accounted for 27 percent of overall sales. Further expansion of direct sales was also expected.
- Simpson's agent provided little information on competitive trends.
- While Simpson's agent represented other manufacturers' products, the "one-stop shopping appeal" of the agent was not an important decision criterion for wholesalers.

On the basis of the audit, Simpson decided to replace the agent with a direct sales office located in the Midwest. The sales office would be responsible for both the commodity door and the new Masonite-type product. The sales office's missionary work with larger retailers and contractors improved sales to these markets. The sales office also sold direct to selected accounts that did not purchase large amounts from the firm's current wholesaler.

QUESTIONS

1. How often should Simpson Timber Company use the channel audit?
2. Should Simpson use an internal or an external auditor? Explain your answer.
3. Develop an audit form to assess Simpson's agent.
4. Develop an audit form to assess Simpson's direct sales force.

Source: William G. Browne and E. D. Reiten, "Auditing Distribution Channels," *Journal of Marketing,* Vol. 42 (July 1978), pp. 38–41.

APPENDIX A

THE INFORMATION SUPERHIGHWAY AND CHANNEL MANAGEMENT

INTRODUCTION

This appendix reviews the information superhighway and channel management. The **information superhighway** is defined as a two-way interchange of information with connectability between users and services and users and other users.[1] Four types of information superhighway technologies (interactive television, the Internet, the World Wide Web, and CD-ROM-based shopping) are discussed.

In 1994, about 40 percent of U.S. households owned a personal computer, and 7 million users subscribed to interactive services such as Prodigy, CompuServe, or America Online. In addition, more than 15 million multimedia personal computers were sold, according to Dataquest, a market research firm that tracks industry developments. Dataquest predicted that number would double in 1995.[2]

On-line purchases are not new. For example, automated teller machines were introduced in the 1970s for use by consumers. Credit card purchase authorization and reservations systems, used by retailers for many years, also use a similar technology. For example, credit authorization systems require a computer terminal, a modem, and a telephone line to access a central database. Ticket and airline reservations (such as SABRE) have also used on-line access to a database through a computer network.

What distinguishes the information superhighway technologies is the ability of a traditional consumer to purchase goods and services on a twenty-four hour basis from a variety of locations. The availability of on-line shopping malls has increased the number of merchants that sell products through the information superhighway. New software has also facilitated consumer access to on-line buying services. Finally, increased graphics and video capabilities have made formats based on the information superhighway more appealing to consumers.

Shopping based on the information superhighway has several major advantages over traditional paper-based catalogs. First, the information superhighway enables a consumer to browse through the catalogs of multiple vendors. In some cases, a consumer can even respond to queries that help the consumer select a gift. Second, as opposed to traditional catalogs, information superhighway-based shopping incorporates music, animation, and video. This format is particularly effective for products that can be demonstrated in use. Third, shopping via the information superhighway also reduces the uncertainty of postage and paper cost increases that are generally associated with paper-based catalogs. Fourth, the typical computer owner has excellent demographics; among the demographic characteristics are a high degree of education, married with school-age children, and an income of $50,000 or more.[3] Fifth, interactive television, Internet, and the World Wide Web are flexible media. A vendor can immediately change its prices, offer special sales for limited time periods, and change its selection based on unseasonal weather and other events. The traditional print catalog does not have this flexibility.

The information superhighway can also be used to provide an additional customer base to a store-based retailer. It enables a small local retailer to attract and service customers on a national or even global basis. Information superhighway-based shopping also enables a retailer to sell its goods and services on a 24-hour-a-day, seven-day-a-week basis. Finally, the information superhighway enables a manufacturer or wholesaler to bypass its traditional downstream resellers and sell direct to consumers.

A firm can use multiple information superhighway-based shopping modes to access different shoppers. For example, 1-800 Flowers sells both on America Online (Internet) and the World Wide Web through its increased graphics capability, which is especially important in visualizing flower arrangements.[4]

As in any channel, information superhighway-based shopping has several disadvantages. (1) Only a small fraction of computer owners are currently on-line shoppers.[5] On-line shopping is also still comparatively small. One market research firm estimated total sales in on-line formats (both

Internet and World Wide Web) in 1994 as about $200 million. This is a very small amount compared with the $53 billion generated in annual catalog sales.[6] (2) It is difficult to use the information superhighway shopping services (in terms of downloading time and ease of searching for particular items). (3) There are large differences among consultants' predictions as to the future of information superhighway-based shopping. According to the executive director of Andersen Consulting, "Conservatively, interactive shopping will amount to 10 percent of total retail volume in 10 years." But another senior consultant projects a 5 percent market share by the year 2004.[7] (4) Some security considerations must be made in terms of providing credit card data. These problems are discussed at length in the Internet, World Wide Web, and CD-ROM sections of this appendix.

INTERACTIVE TELEVISION SHOPPING

Interactive television enables viewers to shop in their homes by pointing and clicking through on-screen catalogs. Unlike the other forms of shopping reviewed in this section, with interactive television, the consumer does not need to purchase or learn how to operate a computer. Interactive television is based on a specially equipped television set. The average cost of equipping a home for interactive television shopping is about $300.[8] As opposed to conventional television-based shopping (such as the Home Shopping Network), in interactive television shopping, the viewer selects the products displayed and their sequence.[9]

Up to one dozen interactive shopping experiments currently are under way in the United States. In one major experiment involving 4000 homes in Orlando, Florida, Time Warner and U.S. West have formed a joint venture to develop a broadband multimedia system in Orlando. Among other products, these consumers can order groceries from home based on a joint venture of Shopper Vision, a home delivery service, and Winn-Dixie, a supermarket chain. In an experiment by EON in northern Virginia, shoppers can use interactive television for banking, shopping, information services, and entertainment. The system enables shoppers even to order free samples and coupons for advertised items.[10]

A second form of interactive shopping is the interactive kiosk placed in stores or mall locations. These kiosks can be used by customers either to order merchandise or to obtain information prior to purchasing.[11] For example, consumers in Service Merchandise can use Silent Sam, its interactive monitor, to verify the in-stock status of goods and to place an order for specific merchandise. Price/Costco uses a touch-sensitive monitor that provides a color visualization of products in its Quest interactive catalog. After seeing various options, consumers can use the interactive monitor to print out an order form. These interactive kiosks lower a store's labor expense and increase the convenience for shoppers.

The next three forms—Internet, World Wide Web, and CD-ROM-based shopping—require that a consumer have access to a computer.

INTERNET

The **Internet** is a global web of computer networks that serves as a communication medium. The Internet was established about ten years ago for the purpose of linking communication among academics.

According to a market research company, 38 million computers were connected to the Internet as of the end of 1994.[12] The Internet is dominated by CompuServe, Prodigy, and America Online. Other firms are General Electric's GEnie, News Corporation's Delphi Internet Services, and Apple Computer's eWorld. The most recent major entrant is Microsoft with its Network product.[13] The oldest on-line shopping service is CompuServe's The Mall, which started in 1984. The Mall has nearly 200 merchants with total annual sales "in the tens of million dollars in 1994," according to The Mall's manager. In contrast, GEnie has 40 or so stores.[14]

All of the Internet services provide access to a variety of merchants. (Many of these are direct marketers such as Sears, J. C. Penney, Lands' End, Sharper Image, Hammacher Schlemmer, and Warner Brothers.) Most offer travel reservations systems that enable consumers to book airline reservations from their home (Prodigy, GEnie, and Delphi offer Eaasy Sabre, the on-line version of the professional service used by travel agents), and other services. The Internet has companies that sell such goods as t-shirts, books, compact disks, and legal services. An estimated 500 companies ranging from travel agencies to real estate brokers and a Volvo dealership have also set up storefronts. Unfortunately, most firms offer only product information and customer support functions. To make a purchase, a purchaser must phone a vendor.

The Internet has several advantages for resellers. Through the Internet, a manufacturer can bypass wholesalers and retailers, and a reseller can update prices and product specifications instantaneously. A reseller can also offer time-based sales or promotional offers that are valid for a limited time period. Small, local resellers can expand their trading areas to include new regions and even foreign countries. Moreover, the Internet enables shoppers to purchase goods 24 hours a day and is an especially appropriate channel for technically sophisticated products.

Internet users commonly encounter some problems. First, it takes considerable time to download data or photos from the Internet. One bank, for example, found that its first graphics took about three minutes to download. Downloading time can be even slower for computers that are not equipped with a fast modern modem. As a result, many customers who join on-line services quickly leave. This is referred to as the **churn rate**, the number of subscribers who quit per year. One research firm estimates the churn rate as more than 40 percent per year.[15] Second, the credit card numbers used on the Internet and other information may have poor security. Several shopping services now use data encryption to safeguard credit card numbers and other sensitive information. MCI and Microsoft reportedly have some form of data security. According to one industry expert, however, "There is no security on the Internet. Your conversations can be tapped, your passwords can be obtained, and your credit card number can be filched. Clearly, it's there for the reading for a clever hacker."[16]

One exciting Internet-based service is Peapod, a grocery shopping and delivery service currently available in limited supermarkets in Illinois (with Jewel Food Stores) and California (with Safeway Inc.).[17] Grocery orders are generated by consumers using software at home that enables them to "browse" electronic aisles (such as "cereals and breakfast"), to select a grocery category, or to choose a brand name. Peapod's current software displays more than 18,000 products and pieces as lists of text. This listing will soon be revamped to include pictures. Consumers can then send an order by computer, telephone, or fax. Peapod shoppers then pick and deliver the ordered goods. Shoppers at both locations pay regular store prices; in addition, these shoppers pay a delivery and service fee. Chicagoans pay $5 per delivery and 5 percent of the final bill. San Franciscans pay a flat $29.95 per month. As of the end of 1994, Peapod had 11,000 customers at both locations.[18] Peapod intends to expand its services to Boston and eventually offer these services on a nationwide basis.

WORLD WIDE WEB

The **World Wide Web** is comprised of a network of servers that use hypertext to find and access files. The World Wide Web is that part of the Internet that has multimedia capability. Many analysts argue that the World Wide Web is the most user friendly part of the Internet (with most commands being simple point-and-click mouse commands). The World Wide Web has two programs: a client program and a server program. The client program accepts keystrokes and mouse clicks, and retrieves information requested, whereas the server program provides information upon request from the client program.

Each web proprietor operates its own on-line service called a **website**. A website consists of a computer hooked up to the Internet and loaded with software that enables it to receive and answer queries from consumers. A website owner needs to follow specific rules for presenting data, text, images, and video clips. Companies can set up their own websites as a virtual storefront, or they can lease space in a cybermall from a web services provider.[19] A stand-alone site can cost as little as $5000.

Smaller companies can lease space in a mall for less than $1000, with monthly charges from $25 to $10,000 plus a royalty based on sales.[20] This fee would include a unique address for a year (or more), a one-page storefront that includes graphics, an order form, and technical assistance in preparing and maintaining that page. The mall owner also provides additional exposure by promoting its mall to other sites in the Internet.[21] According to the co-founder of eMall, a firm that manages a web-based mall, "We're like landlords of a shopping center."[22]

The World Wide Web has superior graphics and sound capabilities. Moreover, web users have excellent demographics. A study by the Georgia Institute of Technology, for example, shows that 42 percent of web users earn between $35,000 and $75,000. Single people account for 53 percent of all web users.[23] Small firms can use mall locations to generate traffic, reduce costs, and reduce technical concerns.

World Wide Web has similar disadvantages to those of the Internet. Credit card security is a particular problem with both the Internet and World Wide Web. And, too, like Internet, with World Wide Web there can be a long downloading wait.

Certain problems are unique to the World Wide Web, however. First, consumers need to fill out a complex code to locate a particular site. If the code is entered with a letter, comma, or slash in the wrong location, the user will then get an error message. This can be frustrating for many consumers. Second, the search tools are often arbitrary. For example, a consumer can contact a mattress retailer with the word "bedding" or "sleep," but not with the word "mattress." The World Wide Web does not provide any cross referencing. Third, few purchases currently are taking place from vendors' websites. Generally, consumers use the World Wide Web to obtain information. They then must call a toll-free number to order. At Sony's site, for example, a consumer can browse to learn more about camcorders. Although the site contains a picture of each camcorder model, its price, features, and even order number, no purchases can take place at Sony's website.

CD-ROM Disks

Dozens of catalogs can be stored on a single CD-ROM disk. Some firms have also distributed multiple computer programs on a single CD-ROM disk, as part of a sampling strategy. This enables consumers to test several software packages for a limited time period. After the test period, consumers can order a specific software package by paying a fee. The consumer then receives a code enabling him or her to immediately continue using the program, as well as full documentation for the software program by mail.

CD-ROM disks have some major advantages over on-line services. They are comparatively easy to use, the color images are of high-resolution, music is in stereo, a consumer can quickly search through large amounts of information, and multiple firms can share distribution costs. Two major CD-ROM suppliers are 2Market and Contentware.

The 2Market system stores more than 27 catalogs on a single CD-ROM disk. Merchants include Lands' End, 800-Flowers, Chef's catalog, Spiegel, Sony Music, and Time Warner's Warner Brothers Studio Store.[24] The 2Market can also recommend a list of gifts based on answers to questions relating to age, sex, and specific interests of recipients. 2Market is also available on America Online.

Another company, Contentware, has persuaded J. C. Penney, Spiegel, Marshall Field, and 40 other retailers to place their catalogs on its CD-ROM disk called Shopping 2000. CD-ROM enables consumers to hear previews of new music-based CDs in the Tower Records catalog and even see video clips from the Discovery Channel. Shopping 2000 disks are distributed free to some buyers of CD-ROM hardware. These disks are generally updated every three months with new vendors and products. The current version of Shopping 2000 enables consumers to order by calling a merchant on a toll-free number or by printing out an order form from the disk and then faxing the form to the merchant. In the future, personal computer owners with modems will be able to directly connect to a merchant's computerized ordering system.[25]

KEY TERMS

information superhighway
interactive television

Internet
churn rate

World Wide Web
website

ENDNOTES

1. "The Information Superhighway—Separating Hype from Reality," Direct Marketing (February 1994), p. 18.

2. Stephen C. Miller, "Point, Click, Shop Till You Drop," *New York Times* (April 20, 1995), p. C2.

3. Ibid.

4. Edward R. Silverman, "The Medium Is the Marketplace," *Newsday* (April 10, 1995), p. C1.

5. Susan Reda, "Interactive Shopping," *Stores* (March 1995), p. 21.

6. Jean Sherman Chatzky, "Will We Ever Leave the House Again?" *SmartMoney* (April 1995), p. 109.

7. Ibid.

8. Ibid.

9. "Change at the Check-Out," *The Economist* (March 4, 1995), p. 17.

10. Cyndee Miller, "Interactive TV Finally Plugged In," *Marketing News* (January 3, 1994), p. 12.

11. "Multimedia: Making It All Possible on the Desktop," *Chain Store Age Executive* (November 1993), p. 6A.

12. David A. Anderman, "Betting on the 'Net,' " *Sales & Marketing Management* (June 1995), p. 48.

13. David Kirkpatrick, "As the Internet Sizzles, Online Services Battle for Stakes," *Fortune* (May 1, 1995), p. 86.

14. Miller, "Point, Click, Shop Till You Drop," p. C2.

15. Kirkpatrick, "As the Internet Sizzles, Online Services Battle for Stakes," p. 89.

16. Jared Sandberg, "System Planned for Shopping on the Internet," *Wall Street Journal* (September 13, 1994), p. B2.

17. Peter H. Lewis, "For Ameritech, On-Line Food Shopping," *New York Times* (September 18, 1994), p. D4; and Barbara Marsh, "Peapod's On-Line Grocery Service Checks Out Success," *Wall Street Journal* (June 30, 1994), p. B2.

18. "Change at the Check-Out," p. 17.

19. See Jill H. Ellsworth, "Businesses on a Virtual Rush to the Virtual Mall," *PC Magazine* (February 7, 1995), p. 190.

20. Jill H. Ellsworth, "Three Routes to a Web Presence," *PC Magazine* (May 16, 1995), p. 224.

21. Silverman, "The Medium Is the Marketplace," p. C4.

22. Ibid., p. C5.

23. Ibid., pp. C5–C6.

24. Kevin Goldman, "On-Line Catalog Service Takes Shopping to Cyberspace," *Wall Street Journal* (November 18, 1994), p. B5.

25. Peter H. Lewis, "Greetings by PC Shopping Services Seem Belated," *New York Times* (April 24, 1994), p. D15; and Miller, "Point, Click, Shop Till You Drop," p. C2.

APPENDIX B

ETHICS IN CHANNEL MANAGEMENT

INTRODUCTION

Ethical behavior focuses on questions of fairness, the rights of participants in decisions, and conformance to moral standards.[1] This definition should not be confused with legal behavior. For example, some behavior that is legal, such as taking advantage of the high demand for plywood during a hurricane, may be legal but not ethical. Ethical standards are often higher than legal standards.

A number of ethical dilemmas arise in channel management. These dilemmas can relate to all levels of channel member relationships. A manufacturer-to-wholesaler ethical issue can relate to a manufacturer's redefining territories after the geographic area has been developed by a wholesaler, or to a manufacturer's offering a distributor a short-term contract with the expectation of switching to direct distribution after the contract has expired. A wholesaler-to-retailer ethical issue can relate to how scarce products are allocated to selected retailers, whether a wholesaler will fulfill his or her verbal promise of technical support for a new product, or whether a wholesaler will offer to bypass a retailer for a large order. A retailer-to-final consumer or end-user ethical issue can relate misrepresenting the status of gray market goods or unfairly evaluating a manufacturer's product owing to its low profit margin.

EXAMPLES OF HIGH ETHICAL STANDARDS BY CHANNEL RESELLERS

Recent examples of ethical behavior include Home Depot's sales of plywood at its traditional low prices during Hurricane Andrew (despite peak demand or poor supply conditions), some firms' engagement of voluntary consumer education programs, voluntary recycling efforts by channel resellers, and the speedy recall of Tylenol as a result of a product poisoning incident.

High ethical standards in channel management can be shown by the following actions of channel resellers:

- Providing downstream resellers with ample notice when discontinuing a product.
- Refusing to pass on unfounded rumors about a competitor's financial status.
- Giving proper territorial protection to downstream intermediaries to enable them to properly develop their territories.
- Treating oral agreements with the same degree of commitment as written agreements.
- Refusing to transship products to other wholesalers and retailers.
- Negotiating fair prices and terms with all channel members.
- Instituting an early product recall on the basis of preliminary but convincing evidence that the product is unsafe.
- Using recyclable packaging materials.
- Providing fair compensation for additional duties that a channel member needs to undertake.
- Being fair in negotiations with other channel members despite high channel power.
- Allocating scarce products to wholesalers and retailers on the basis of fair criteria.
- Listening carefully to channel member complaints and concerns and undertaking fair corrective actions.
- Keeping commitments to existing distributors and dealers even after important new channels emerge.

EXAMPLES OF UNETHICAL STANDARDS BY CHANNEL RESELLERS

The following represents unethical standards by channel resellers:

- Requiring new employees to divulge practices or trade information from their past employers.

- Lying to a dealer about a competitor's best price offer in order to achieve a lower price.
- Misrepresenting the status of gray market goods to other channel members.
- Disparaging a competitor, when you know that rumors about the competitor are unfounded.
- Accepting presents from vendors, where the level of the present may influence your behavior as a buyer.
- Granting unprotected territories to downstream intermediaries with the expectation of adding new distributors/dealers after the territory is developed.
- Looking the other way at the unethical sales practices of employees and downstream channel members that result in increased sales.
- Offering to bypass a wholesaler to receive a large order.
- Charging higher prices to poorer consumers based on their lack of shopping mobility or expertise.
- Not reporting breakage, hoping that a firm will not realize a product's damage upon delivery.

The following three examples of Honda (involving sales executives), Prudential (involving sales agents), and J. C. Penney (involving a buyer) illustrate the unethical behavior of selected employees (not of the parent company) and the firm's response. Each of these actions also had legal consequences for the affected parties. These examples were chosen based on the availability of published information. Many instances of unethical behavior are resolved by getting an employee to resign quietly and not receive public attention.

HONDA SALES EXECUTIVES

A former senior vice president in charge of Honda Motor Company's sales throughout the United States pleaded guilty in federal court to accepting bribes of up to $1 million in 1995.[2] In addition, 16 former Honda executives pleaded guilty to bribery and kickback schemes totaling up to $15 million. Two dealers, a lawyer, and an advertising executive have also pleaded guilty. The Honda executive faces up to 35 years in prison and $1 million in fines. In addition, Honda has begun legal action to recover damages from executives involved in illegal activities.

The legal case involved a bribery scheme by Honda and Acura executives to award dealerships and hot-selling cars in short supply to favored individuals. Honda and Acura dealerships were especially lucrative in the 1980s and the early 1990s owing to restraints on imports. As a result of car shortages, many Honda and Acura car dealers were able to sell these cars at above list price. Some executives were also charged with diverting Honda and dealer funds for advertising and sales training expenses.

Honda has recently taken several steps to avoid recurrence of these actions. It has established a financial disclosure policy for top executives. A committee has also been set up to review the appointments of new dealers. Finally, Honda has established a toll-free telephone number to encourage employees and dealers to express concerns of possible misconduct.

PRUDENTIAL SALES AGENTS

Prudential is investigating agents that "churned" life insurance customers into purchasing a new policy by using the cash value built up in an existing policy.[3] Insurance agents use churning as a means of receiving commissions from the sale of a new policy. These commissions are generally half of the first year's premium. In the worst case scenario, churning results in the depletion of the cash value on the insured's old policy because of the high premiums that become due as the insured gets older.

It is especially difficult to enforce churning by insurance agents. Many of the industry's 200,000 insurance agents are independent, and the job performance of corporate managers is dependent on the sales performance of their agents. As a result, many supervisors "look the other way" at churning. Many firms also disregard churning activity since it is often conducted by their best agents. These firms fear the loss of high-performing agents to competitors.

The insurance industry tries to combat churning and other unacceptable practices by developing memos on acceptable sales practices, inspecting promotional literature for accuracy, and surveying customers to determine abuses. Prudential also has developed a policy that winners of sales contests must limit the amount of insurance they sell based on the cash value of existing policies to less than 10 percent of their total sales.

A J. C. PENNEY BUYER

In a rare legal case involving prosecution against a buyer, a J. C. Penney employee admitted selling to manufacturer's representatives information on competitor's bids and selling the promise of large orders.[4] The buyer, who earned about $56,000 per year, was able to supplement his salary by as much as $1.5 million through bribes and kickbacks. What also makes the case unusual was the buyer's excellent performance. Under the buyer's direction, J. C. Penney's annual sales of tabletop merchandise increased from $25 million to $45 million per year. The person was also named "Buyer of the Year" for three consecutive years.

In July 1992, an anonymous letter informed J. C. Penney of a "special relationship" between the buyer and a manufacturers' representative from whom the buyer later admitted accepting $200,000 in bribes and kickbacks based on a percentage of sales to J. C. Penney. J. C. Penney then began a second investigation that ended in firing the buyer. Of the ten accounts known to have produced kickbacks, as many as eight involved manufacturers' representatives.

J. C. Penney has sent letters to its suppliers saying it would no longer do business with any company associated with the buyer. Penney has held suppliers accountable to the same ethical standards as its own employees. Penney also obtained a $789,000 judgment against the buyer. The buyer faces up to five years in prison and a maximum fine of twice his financial gain or twice the loss to Penney, whichever is greater.

HOW TO REDUCE UNETHICAL BEHAVIOR

A firm needs to realize the need to enforce ethical standards for its suppliers, as well as its employees. J. C. Penney's refusal to purchase additional goods from firms that bribed its former buyer and Prudential's developing sales contest standards to discourage churning are excellent examples of ethical standards applied to suppliers.[5] This section explores three principles for reducing unethical behavior. These deal with establishing of a code of ethics, enforcing standards, and seeking evidence of unethical behavior.

First, a company should establish and publicize a company code of ethics. Employees should sign a statement agreeing to these principles upon being hired and after promotion to certain positions. Wal-Mart's policy, for example, prohibits buyers from even accepting a cup of coffee from a vendor. In contrast, J. C. Penney's policy allows buyers to "accept dinners, theatre tickets, or golf dates" if these buyers anticipated a chance to reciprocate.[6] Suppliers and downstream resellers should also be made aware of these standards.

Second, a firm needs to enforce all ethical standards. It has to realize that a code of ethics has little value as a deterrent unless it is enforced. Star employees or independent resellers should not be treated differently than average performers. A firm should also pursue all of its legal alternatives such as seeking return of monies.

Third, it is also important to look for evidence of unethical behavior by hiring an internal auditor and by seriously treating any reports of unethical behavior. Some experts suggest that the auditor should report his or her findings to an audit committee of the board, rather than to a specific executive, in order to reduce the odds for different standards applied to different individuals. Among the warning signs are an employee's high life-style that is not in line with his or her salary, personal friendships between an employee and a vendor, and shifts in purchases or sales that cannot be explained.

ENDNOTES

1. Robert Allen Cooke, "Business Ethics: A Perspective," in *Arthur Andersen Cases on Business Ethics* (St. Charles, Ill.: Arthur Andersen & Co., 1988), p. 2.

2. James Bennett, "Corruption Called Broad in Honda Case," *New York Times* (April 4, 1995), pp. D1 ff.; James Bennett, "Guilty Plea in Honda Bribery Case," *New York Times* (February 8, 1995), pp. D1 ff.; and Krystal Miller, "Former Honda Executives Plead Guilty to Charges Tied to Bribes from Dealers," *Wall Street Journal* (March 15, 1994), p. A4.

3. "Some Agents 'Churn' Life-Insurance Policies, Hurt Their Customers," *Wall Street Journal* (January 3, 1995), pp. 1 ff.

4. Andrea Gerlin, "How a Penney Buyer Made Up to $1.5 Million on Vendor's Kickbacks," *Wall Street Journal* (February 7, 1995), pp. A1 ff.

5. Much of this section is from Stephen D. Willinger, "Phar-Mor—A Lesson in Fraud," *Wall Street Journal* (March 28, 1994), p. A12.

6. Gerlin, "How a Penney Buyer Made Up to $1.5 Million on Vendor's Kickbacks," pp. A1, A16.

APPENDIX C

CAREERS IN CHANNEL MANAGEMENT

INTRODUCTION

Recent college graduates (with either a minor in business, a bachelor's degree, or an M.B.A.) have excellent career opportunities in channel management with manufacturers, wholesalers, retailers, consulting firms, transportation providers, warehousing firms, and third-party logistics providers. Table 1 lists selected job titles in channel management. These range from an advertising research executive to a wholesale purchasing agent. There are also many opportunities in channel management for those who seek to start and run their own business. Among these opportunities are franchisee, retail store owner, merchant wholesaler, export wholesaler, agent, broker, management consultant, customs agent, and foreign freight forwarder. Many of these opportunities require comparatively little capital since they do not stock inventory.

TABLE 1 SELECTED JOB TITLES IN CHANNEL MANAGEMENT

Advertising research executive
Advertising support manager
Channel relations coordinator
Cooperative advertising coordinator
Customer service manager
Department manager
Franchise coordinator
Insurance agent
Insurance broker
Inventory control manager
Inventory coordinator
Logistics computer consultant
Logistics consultant
Logistics manager
Management consultant
Market research analyst
Media planner
Merchandise manager
Packaging manager
Public relations specialist
Purchasing agent
Purchasing manager
Real estate broker
Retail buyer
Retail location consultant
Sales analyst
Sales forecaster
Sales manager
Store manager
Traffic manager
Transportation manager
Travel agent
Warehousing/operations manager
Wholesale purchasing agent

People working in channels management have a wide variety of educational backgrounds and experience. A study by the Ohio State faculty found that 93 percent of logistics managers have earned at least a bachelor's degree and that 41 percent have a graduate degree.[1] In general, course work in marketing, statistics, computer science, accounting, and business law is helpful. Skills in communicating, negotiation, information management, and customer contact are also important for many positions. For careers with industrial firms or in specialized industries, specialized product knowledge and engineering skills may also be required. Students can also increase their chance of getting a particularly desirable job with a specific employer through internships at that firm during the academic year or summer sessions. As with most careers, opportunities expand for those with advanced degrees. For example, many channels managers and marketing consultants have M.B.A. degrees. Most college faculty that teach channels management courses have Ph.D. degrees in Business.

Table 2 presents the outlook for selected job titles in channels management between 1994 and the year 2005. Of 16 job titles listed, the outlook for growth is either faster or much faster than average (at least a 27 percent growth rate) for seven positions during this time period. For example, the Bureau of Labor Statistics predicts much faster than average growth for management consultants, a more than 41 percent growth rate. This forecast coincides with the experience of Andersen Consulting. This major consulting firm now does 75 percent of its business advising clients on their distribution needs, almost double the level of a few years ago.[2]

Many career opportunities in channels management are available with manufacturers, wholesalers, retailers, and providers of logistics services.

CHANNEL CAREERS WITH MANUFACTURERS

Often channel management careers with manufacturers are somewhat hidden since few manufacturers use the term *channels managers*. However, sales managers, marketing managers, advertising specialists, and pricing specialists all devote a significant amount of their time and energies toward channels management activities. Channel managers can be found in a number of departments within a large manufacturer. These include logistics, distribution, purchasing, transportation, material management, marketing research, and customer service.

TABLE 2 JOB OUTLOOK FOR SELECTED JOB TITLES BETWEEN 1994 AND 2005

Job Title	Growth Rate
Advertising manager	Faster than average
Insurance agent and broker	Average
Management consultant	Much faster than average
Manufacturers' and wholesale sales representatives	Slower than average
Marketing and sales worker supervisor	Average
Marketing manager	Faster than average
Public relations manager	Faster than average
Public relations specialist	Average
Purchasing agent	Slower than average
Real estate agents and brokers	Average
Retail buyer	Slower than average
Retail manager	Average
Securities and financial services sales representatives	Faster than average
Services sales representatives	Faster than average
Transportation manager	Slower than average
Travel agents	Much faster than average

Growth rates:
Slower than average	0–13 percent
Average	14–26 percent
Faster than average	27–40 percent
Much faster than average	41 percent or more

Source: Occupational Outlook Handbook 1994–1995 Edition (Washington, D.C.: U.S. Department of Labor, Bureau of Labor Statistics, May 1994), various pages.

The types of career opportunities in channel management with a manufacturer are based on the structure of the firm's channel arrangement, markets served, and size. For example, franchisors typically employ site location personnel, vice presidents of real estate, franchisee relations personnel, and troubleshooters. Vertically integrated manufacturers hire store managers, area managers, and operations management personnel. Firms with a large foreign sales component also employ specialists in foreign logistics, international physical distribution, and direct exporting. There are also opportunities for specialized careers such as trade advertising manager or channels coordinator in larger firms.

CHANNEL CAREERS IN WHOLESALING

There are two types of wholesaling careers: working for a wholesaler versus starting a wholesale business.[3] Table 3 lists the average compensation for specific job titles among a sample of industrial distributors. Note that these numbers are averages and that there are large variations in salaries for each position. Many individuals who currently own wholesale businesses started out working for wholesalers learning valuable product and market information. Wholesaling is often an excellent area for starting a business owing to relatively low capital requirements for manufacturers' agents, selling agents, commission agents, food brokers, and export brokers.

As with all channels careers, those wishing to pursue specialized careers should seek out larger firms (such as integrated distributors), while those desiring broader exposure should look at opportunities with small to medium wholesalers.

CHANNEL CAREERS IN RETAILING

There are generally two different types of career tracks in retailing: operations and buying. Operations careers deal with such areas as store maintenance, energy management, inventory management, credit management, and computerization. Stores with a large number of branches have career paths in operations leading from management trainees to store manager to district manager. Higher level operations positions are responsible for a larger number of stores.

Buyers purchase goods and services for resale. Many college graduates start as buyer trainees, quickly become assistant buyers, and then work their way up to general merchandise manager. In larger retailers, buying for some goods may be centralized (to increase a retailer's bargaining power), while buying for other goods is decentralized (to enable retailers to tailor merchandise assortments to specific regions). Smaller retailers may engage in cooperative buying, where noncompeting retailers pool their orders to receive better prices, or use an outside buying organization.[4]

Table 4 lists specific retailing career titles, and describes responsibilities and salary ranges for each title.

CHANNEL CAREERS IN LOGISTICS

Channel careers in logistics can be with manufacturers, wholesalers, retailers, transportation firms, warehouse operators, or other employers. An annual poll conducted by the Transportation and Logistics Research Fund of Ohio State University explores career patterns in logistics. The 1994 study listed the logistics responsibilities of the senior logistics executive in each firm. Eighty percent or more of the senior logistics executives were responsible for traffic management (95 per-

TABLE 3 AVERAGE COMPENSATION FOR VARIOUS INDUSTRIAL DISTRIBUTION TITLES BY DISTRIBUTOR VOLUME IN MILLIONS (1993)

	Distributor Volume in Millions		
Position	$1–3 Mil.	$6–10 Mil.	$20 mil.+
Chief executive officer/president	$78,733	$126,750	$149,200
Vice president—sales	62,250	65,820	109,516
Branch manager	38,167	51,980	55,265
Outside salesperson	47,500	42,825	67,036
Inside salesperson	25,500	33,000	28,615

Source: Louise King, "Distribution Outpaces the Pack," *Industrial Distribution* (November 1994), p. 36. Reprinted by permission of Cahners Publishing Company.

TABLE 4 SELECTED RETAIL CAREERS

Management trainee	Attends training program (part formal, part on-the-job). Learns store operations, assists with merchandising. Salary range: $20,000–$26,000.
Assistant manager	Has responsibility for a specific department or functions such as personnel, inventory replenishment. Salary range: $25,000–$33,000 plus bonus.
Store manager	Has responsibility for all operations and departments in a specific store. Salary range: $35,000–$50,000 plus bonus.
District manager	Liaison between store and regional groups. Responsible for a group of stores. Salary range: $40,000–$60,000 plus bonus.
Regional manager	Manages a group of stores in a large geographic region. Region may encompass several adjacent states. Salary range: $70,000–$80,000 plus bonus.
Divisional vice president	Has responsibility for several related departments or a major department in a department store. Salary range: $100,000 plus bonus.

Source: "The Climb to the Top," *Careers in Retailing* (January 1995), p. 18.

cent), warehousing (94 percent), facility location (90 percent), inventory control (80 percent), and global logistics (80 percent).[5] The median compensation (annual salary plus bonus) was $75,000 for logistics managers, $95,000 for logistics directors, and $146,000 for logistics vice presidents.[6]

SOURCES OF ADDITIONAL CAREER INFORMATION

Table 5 lists professional associations that have additional sources of channel management career information. Some of these associations also publish directories of members and listings of internship programs at selected firms.

TABLE 5 PROFESSIONAL ASSOCIATIONS THAT PROVIDE CAREER INFORMATION

American Association of Advertising Agencies
666 Third Avenue
New York, NY 10017-4056
(212) 682-2500

American Production and Inventory Control Society
500 West Annandale Road
Falls Church, VA 22046
(703) 237-8344

American Trucking Association
2200 Mill Road
Alexandria, VA 22314
(703) 838-1700

American Warehousemen's Association
1300 West Higgins, Suite 111
Park Ridge, IL 60068
(708) 292-1891

Council of Logistics Management
2803 Butterfield Road
Oak Brook, IL 60521
(708) 574-0985

TABLE 5 (*CONTINUED*)

Direct Marketing Educational Foundation
1120 Avenue of the Americas, 14th Floor
New York, NY 10036
(212) 768-7277

Food Marketing Institute
800 Connecticut Avenue NW
Washington, DC 20006-2710
(202) 452-8444

Grocery Manufacturers of America
1010 Wisconsin Avenue NW, Suite 800
Washington, DC 20007
(202) 337-9400

Independent Insurance Agents of America
127 South Peyton Street
Alexandria, VA 22324
(703) 683-4422

Manufacturers' Agents National Association
23016 Mill Creek Road
Laguna Hills, CA 92654-3467
(714) 859-4040

The Material Handling Institute
8720 Red Oak Boulevard, Suite 210
Charlotte, NC 28217
(704) 522-8644

National Association of Manufacturers
1331 Pennsylvania Avenue, Suite 1500N
Washington, DC 20004-1703
(202) 637-3000

National Association of Purchasing Management
2055 East Centennial Circle
Tempe, AZ 85285-2160
(602) 752-6276

National Automotive Dealers Association
8400 Westpark Drive
McLean, VA 22101
(703) 827-7407

National Food Brokers Association
1010 Massachusetts Avenue NW
Washington, DC 20001
(202) 789-2844

National Private Truck Council
1320 Braddock Place
Alexandria, VA 22314
(703) 838-1763

National Retail Federation
701 Pennsylvania Avenue NW, Suite 710
Washington, DC 20004
(202) 783-7971

TABLE 5 *(CONTINUED)*

Public Relations Society of America
33 Irving Place
New York, NY 10003-2376
(212) 995-2230

Sales & Marketing Executives International
458 Statler Office Tower
Cleveland, OH 44115
(216) 771-8072

Society of Logistics Engineers
8100 Professional Place, Suite 211
Hyattsville, MD 20785
(301) 459-8446

Warehousing Education and Research Council
1100 Jorie Boulevard, Suite 170
Oak Brook, IL 60521
(708) 990-0001

ENDNOTES

1. James M. Masters and Bernard J. LaLonde, *The 1994 Ohio State University Survey of Career Patterns in Logistics* (Columbus, Ohio: Transportation and Logistics Research Fund, 1994), p. 12.

2. Rita Koselka, "Distribution Revolution," *Forbes* (May 25, 1992), p. 58.

3. For a discussion of the educational requirements for a career in industrial distribution, see Louise King, "Preparing Tomorrow's Distributors Today," *Industrial Distribution* (September 1994), pp. 26–28 ff.

4. For additional information on retailing careers, see Barry Berman and Joel R. Evans, *Retail Management: A Strategic Approach,* 6th ed. (Englewood Cliffs, N.J.: Prentice Hall, 1995), pp. A1–A13.

5. Masters and LaLonde, *The 1994 Ohio State University Survey of Career Patterns in Logistics,* p. 9.

6. Ibid., p. 13.

APPENDIX D

GLOSSARY

ABC *See* Activity-Based Costing.

ABC Analysis An assessment of a wholesaler's territorial coverage of a given territory by comparing its current number of salespeople with the number needed to effectively service a manufacturer's accounts within a specified territory.

ABC Inventory Analysis A method that seeks to reduce total inventory needs by assigning different customer service-level requirements to goods based on such factors as sales and profits.

Account-Specific Advertising Specialized advertising programs that are planned for a specific retailer.

Accurate Response A new approach to forecasting for products with unpredictable demand patterns. This approach makes the supply chain fast and flexible so that managers can postpone decisions about their most unpredictable items until they have some market signals to help correctly match supply with demand.

Activity-Based Costing (ABC) An approach that seeks to assign costs (such as labor) directly to the good or the services that a business produces.

ACV *See* All Commodity Volume.

Adaptive Pricing A method that recognizes that initial prices may have to be changed to reflect differences between the planned pricing environment and actual conditions.

Additional Discounts Markdowns from a firm's initial price due to end-of-season sales, the need to move incomplete assortments of merchandise, discounts in anticipation of new models, and so on.

Additional Markups Upward adjustments to price levels due to unexpected high demand, increased list prices for new shipments, a weak dollar relative to foreign currency for imported merchandise, and so on.

Adjustment Services applied to a product to meet customers' needs or product customization requirements.

Administered Marketing Systems A form of vertical marketing system in which the dominant firm in the channel allocates and coordinates the responsibilities of each reseller.

Administrative Coordination An approach relating to specified administrative office procedures in both conversion and business format franchises. It is often developed through franchise training, ongoing procedures, and periodic inspection of franchises by franchisors.

Administrative Efficiency A notion suggesting that franchisees are more motivated than workers and require less supervision.

Affinities A term that refers to the composition of neighboring stores.

Agents Individuals who bring together a buyer and seller to complete a transaction; they are likely to be employed on a permanent basis.

Agents and Brokers Personnel who do not take title to goods or services; they are compensated on the basis of sales commissions that are typically paid for by sellers.

All Commodity Volume (ACV) A measure that weights sales and distribution intensity for products. For example, a product with 60 percent ACV in grocery stores is distributed in grocery stores that account for 60 percent of total grocery store sales in that market.

Allowable Conflict A situation that can be effectively managed without loss of sales or communication for either the company or the broker.

Always-a-Share Customers Those who share their patronage over multiple vendors.

Ambassador Role When a manufacturer's sales representative explains the manufacturer's policies and their benefit to the distributor.

Analysis The part of a marketing information system that consists of manipulating data in order to better understand a marketing-related issue.

Area Development Franchising A method for expanding a franchise whereby a franchisee obtains the right to develop a specific geographic area. The franchisee then builds and/or converts franchises in this geographic area.

Aspinwall's Characteristics of Goods and Parallel Systems Theory A theory stating that a firm's channel structure should reflect a product positioning on the basis of its replacement rate, gross margin, adjustment, time of consumption, and searching time.

Assets to Sales Ratio A ratio determined by dividing a firm's total assets by its annual net sales. This number indicates the level of assets needed to support one dollar of sales.

Asset Turnover The sales made from the equivalent of one dollar of assets.

Assurance A dimension of customer service stating that company employees should be knowledgeable and courteous.

Availability A customer service dimension that relates to in-stock rate, and percentage of orders, units, and lines filled.

Availability Rule A principle stating that functional discounts must be available to all customers, even if some customers choose not to receive them.

Backhauling Use of vendors' transportation facilities that are often not used to capacity after goods are shipped from manufacturers to wholesalers or from wholesalers to retailers.

Backward Vertical Integration A situation that exists when retailers purchase or develop wholesale operations, wholesalers acquire or build manufacturing operations, or retailers purchase or develop manufacturing operations.

Bar Code Scanners Tools that can be used to keep track of sales and inventory on hand at manufacturers, wholesalers, and retailers by reading and recording Universal Product Codes.

Benchmarking A practice that allows a firm to continually compare and measure its performance against business leaders anywhere in the world.

Bill of Lading A form that acknowledges receipt of goods by the carrier, represents the basic contract between the shipper and carrier, and serves as evidence of title to the goods.

Blurring of Gender Roles The broadening of typical household duties between male and female heads of households.

Bonded Warehouse A means of allowing tax payments (on products such as cigarettes and liquor) to be postponed until products are sold.

Breaking Bulk The wholesaler or retailer function of purchasing goods in case lots and their resale to their customers in smaller quantities. It is an important aspect of the sorting process.

Brokers Those who bring together a buyer and seller to complete a transaction; they are typically employed on a temporary basis (for a particular project or deal).

Bucklin's System of Service Outputs A concept stating that consumers prefer to deal with marketing channels that provide them with higher levels of service outputs. It identifies four service outputs that a channel member can provide: spatial convenience or market decentralization, lot size, product variety or assortment breadth, and waiting or delivery time.

Business Format Franchising A type of retail franchise that is characterized by tight control and coordination between franchisors and retail franchisees.

Buyback Allowance A reduction in price for new purchases that is based on the quantity purchased on a prior deal. It is one type of cumulative quantity discount.

Buying Allowance An off-invoice allowance which is a short-term offer of a special discount keyed to a minimum purchase requirement.

Buying Clubs (Membership Clubs) Clubs that service both wholesale and final consumers, charge retail shoppers an annual membership fee, locate in low-rental locations, and typically resemble a warehouse.

Buying Philosophy A philosophy that exists when the authority and responsibility for buying are held by buying specialists.

CAO *See* Computer-Aided Ordering.

Captive Distributors Manufacturers' sales offices and branch offices in that they are owned and operated by their manufacturers.

Cash-and-Carry Wholesalers Limited-service merchant wholesalers that do not offer credit or delivery and are self-service operations.

Cash Discounts Discounts given to wholesalers for early payment.

Category Killer An especially large specialty store that dominates other retailers in a merchandise category.

Census A method of conducting channels research whereby an entire population is questioned or observed.

Certificate of Origin An export document that ensures the collection of tariffs.

Chain-Markup Pricing Pricing that works backward from the final selling price to the final customer to determine the acceptable price levels for each reseller. In a channel consisting of a manufacturer, a wholesaler, and a retailer, the chain markup computation formula is:

1. Maximum selling price to retailer = Final selling price × [(100 − Retailer's markup)/100]
2. Maximum selling price to wholesaler = Selling price to retailer × [(100 − Wholesaler's markup)/100]
3. Maximum product cost to manufacturer = Selling price to wholesaler × [(100 − Manufacturer's markup)/100]

Chain Retailers Two or more similar retail establishments that are owned and operated by one firm.

Change Agents Wholesalers and retailers that attempt to influence the purchase decisions of intermediate and final consumers.

Channel Adaptability The channel's ability to innovate various skills and tasks while still maintaining its organizational vitality.

Channel Audit A method employed by firms to evaluate their downstream and upstream channel relationships on a periodic basis through the use of checklists.

Channel Captain The dominant member of a channel or channel leader.

Channel Checklist A list that contains specific criteria and weights for reseller evaluation.

Channel Conflict The channel member's perception that its goal attainment is being impeded by another, with stress or tension the result.

Channel Cooperation The joint striving of channel members toward individual and mutual goals.

Channel Dependency A situation that exists when the action of one channel member has an impact on another channel member.

Channel Design Decision making that involves the choice of an optimal channel arrangement.

Channel Length Requirements The number of channel levels that are required to fulfill a supplier's objectives.

Channel Management The process of planning, managing, and controlling channel activities.

Channel Overlap The extent to which two or more products share distribution channels.

Channel Power The ability of one channel member to control the marketing strategy of another member at a different level of distribution in the same channel.

Channel Satisfaction The overall evaluation of the relationship between two channel members.

Channel Specialization A concept in which channel members perform those tasks in which they have a comparative advantage.

Channel-Wide Committees An administrative technique used to manage and reduce conflict in which channel members work together as part of a team on a noncontinuous basis.

Channel Width The degree of competition at any channel level, as well as the intensity of distribution in a market area.

Channel Width Requirements The number of intermediaries that are needed at each level in the channel.

Chargebacks Coupons a retailer submitted for payment but were denied.

Closed-Loop Cycle A situation that prevails when production, distribution, collection, and recycling are controlled by one company.

Coding The numbering of each completed data form and the labeling of response categories.

Coercive Power Power based on the ability of one channel member to punish another channel member; it is also called the threat approach.

Coincident Indicators Indicators designed to track the current economy climate.

Collection Period An overall measure of the quality of a firm's account receivables. In the collection period, a firm's accounts receivable are divided by its sales and then multiplied by 365 days.

Combination Stores Stores that combine, in a single-store format, a supermarket and a pharmacy or a supermarket and a general merchandise retailer; these stores average 30,000 square feet in size.

Commission (Factor) Merchants Those who receive goods on consignment from producers, accumulate them from local markets, and arrange for their sale in a central market location.

Communication Difficulties Problems relating to slow or inaccurate information among channel members.

Communications Protocols Principles that describe in technical terms how computers interface; they are dictated by specific hardware or software.

Comparable Waste Press overruns or unsold magazines that have never reached the final buying public.

Competitive Bidding A competition-oriented pricing technique in business-to-business marketing in which a seller submits a written offer to produce a given product or service based on specifications determined by the buyer.

Completion Rate The percentage of products that were either returned or destroyed; it measures the effectiveness of recalls.

Component Life-Styles A concept stating that consumer attitudes and behavior vary by purchase situation; thus, typecasting or stereotyping people may not be particularly valid.

Computer-Aided Ordering (CAO) Computer report on the minimum in-stock inventory level for each product based on current sales patterns and vendor delivery times.

Computer-Based Sales Support Systems Systems that link salespeople (field or telemarketing) via terminals or modems to a firm's central computer. This linkage provides important customer information to the salesperson.

Conciliation An administrative technique used to manage and reduce conflict in which an ombudsman position is created.

Conclusive Research Study leading to the development of a methodology to understand the problem at hand.

Conditions for Cooperative Advertising Outline of the duration of the cooperative advertising fund, the manufacturer's maximum contribution, policies regarding approvals, the types of media that qualify, how dealers are reimbursed (credit toward future purchases or outright payment), and reasons for rejection of claims.

Conflict Frequency Conflicts ranging from sporadic disputes and occasional disagreements to protracted, bitter relations.

Conflict Importance A channel member's perception of the importance of a particular dispute.

Conglomerate Merchant (Conglomerchant) One who operates disparate retailers.

Conglomerchant *See* Conglomerate Merchant.

Constrained Decision Making A major disadvantage of vertical marketing systems for most wholesalers and retailers in which decision making related to store hours, involvement in a cooperative advertising program, merchandise depth and width, and vendor selection may be severely limited by contract, or manufacturer and supplier channel power.

Consumer Confidence Surveys Surveys that measure consumer attitudes about current business conditions. They are conducted by the Conference Board and the University of Michigan.

Consumer Contact The task of meeting and communicating with consumers. It generally occurs before the sale (as in searching for prospects), during the sale (the sales presentation), and after the sale (following up with consumers).

Consumer Demographics Such population characteristics as population, age distribution, income, number of households, marital status, and number of working women.

Consumer Life-Styles The manner in which people conduct their lives, including their activities, interests, and opinions.

Contactual Efficiency An important aspect of the sorting process that enables manufacturers, wholesalers, and retailers and their customers to reduce time and financial expenditures.

Contests A form of sales promotion requiring skill.

Contingency Plan A series of events designed to take full advantage of a business opportunity or to reduce the impact of an event that would generally be disastrous to a firm.

Contingent Event A key opportunity or threat facing a channel member.

Contractual Marketing Systems Means of achieving coordination among independent resellers through legal arrangements that specify the responsibilities of each reseller.

Controlled Observation The setting of the data collection area as part of an experiment.

Convenience Stores Stores that offer a limited line of convenience goods and services such as cigarettes, milk, candy, beer, and video rentals.

Conventional Channel A channel that exists when a manufacturer, wholesaler, and retailer are each independently owned. It is the most common form of channel design.

Conventional Department Store Store that has decentralized customer service and customer assistance, sells soft and hard goods, has greater customer service, higher merchandise depth, greater emphasis on fashion merchandise, more attractive overall store atmosphere and fixturing, and a higher proportion of sales at higher price points.

Conventional Supermarkets Stores that average 15,000 to 30,000 square feet in size and specialize in food-related merchandise. (Less than 5 percent of sales comes from general merchandise sales.)

Conversion Franchising A method for expanding a franchise whereby a franchisor seeks to convert an independent firm into a unit of an existing franchise system.

Cooperative Advertising Local advertising placed by a retailer or wholesaler that is partially or fully reimbursed by a manufacturer.

Cooperative Buying Organization An organization in which retailers share buying responsibility and costs.

Corporate Marketing Systems A type of vertical marketing system in which all production and distribution activities are controlled by one firm through common ownership.

Cost Justification Defense A way to allow sellers to pass onto their customers cost savings due to the manufacture, sale, or delivery to a buyer.

Cost-Oriented Pricing Pricing based on a reseller's examination of its total costs and addition of a suitable profit to determine its price.

Coupons Certificates prepared for manufacturers that entitle consumers to price reductions for a limited time period.

Cross Docking A situation in which a supplier ships its goods directly to the receiving dock, where these goods are divided up for each retailer's or wholesaler's branch location.

Cumulative Discount Discount given on the basis of combined purchases over a given time period.

Current Ratio Ratio that equals a firm's total current assets (cash accounts receivable less reserves for bad debt, merchandise inventory, and marketable securities) divided by its current liabilities.

Curtainside Trailers Flexible "walls" on the sides of a truck that are made of a tough fabric material. The fabric used is so durable that it will not be pierced even if a truck trailer turns on its side.

Cushion *See* Safety Stock.

Customer Resale Restriction A restriction that prohibits a wholesaler from selling to specific customers or classes of customers.

Customer Service A customer-oriented corporate philosophy that integrates and manages all of the elements of the customer interface to meet or exceed customer service quality expectations.

Customer Service Gap The difference between expectations and experiences as judged by consumers.

Customer Service Level A level that corresponds to the percentage of orders for a particular good that is in-stock.

Customized Services Services that involve the use of specially configured transportation forms, such as special trains that have been developed by some railroads.

Customs Agent One who prepares necessary documentation for a good to clear customs, pays duties, and then ships the goods to their final destination.

Customs Bonded Warehouse A special type of bonded warehouse that defers duties on imported merchandise until these goods are sold.

Cycle Stocks *See* Lot Size Stocks.

Data Analysis Evaluation of responses to data collection in the form of cross-classification tables (where the impact of changing the level of one variable on another variable can be studied), correlations, and other statistical measures and techniques.

Database The part of a marketing information system that consists of internal and external secondary data (such as shipments, coupon redemptions, and distribution intensity).

Database Marketing The creation and maintenance of a bank of information about individual customers (e.g., taken from orders, inquiries, and external lists), with the objective of analyzing consumer buying patterns and targeting promotions aimed at specific types of customers.

Data Envelopment Analysis (DEA) Evaluation of factors in branch or store performance (such as sales, sales growth, profits per employee, and sales per square foot), as well as differences in technology, capacity, competition, and demographics among branch or store locations. It then compares each branch or location against units with similar attributes and categorizes them into one of four groups: star performers, branches with low-profit and low-growth potential, underperforming star branches, or underperforming branches.

DEA *See* Data Envelopment Analysis.

Dealer Brand *See* Private Label.

Dealer Listing Promotion A specific form of push advertising in which a manufacturer's advertisement includes the names of distributors and resellers that stock its products.

Decision Domain Disagreements Disagreements that relate to a channel member's strong feeling about the specific areas of business conduct it should control.

Decline Stage The stage in the product life cycle that corresponds to a drop in industry sales and profits.

Demand-Minus Pricing A demand-oriented pricing technique useful in direct distribution where a manufacturer determines the appropriate final selling price and then works backward to compute its allowable costs. Its formula is:

Maximum product cost = Final selling price × [(100 − Markup percent)/100]

Department Stores Stores that must meet three criteria: (1) they must employ at least 50 people; (2) apparel and soft goods must account for 20 percent or more of total sales; and (3) the merchandise assortment must include each of these three groups of items: furniture, home furnishings, appliances, radios, and television sets; a general line of family apparel; and household linens and dry goods.

Derivative Model A model that has different names or model designations based on the channel in which it is sold.

Derived Demand Demand that exists when the market for organizational goods sold through manufacturers and wholesalers is affected by the ultimate demand at the final consumer level.

Desk Jobbers *See* Drop Shippers.

Diffusion Process Process that explains the manner in which different members of a population purchase a new product. It covers the entire product life cycle from product introduction to product decline.

Direct Accounts Generally large accounts or accounts that have had long relationships with manufacturers and seek to continue this relationship;

these accounts are serviced through manufacturer wholesaling.

Direct Benefits Advantages of the use of EDI that stem from the fact that the data are sent electronically from one application to another and do not rely on either business's making other changes in business practices.

Direct Communication Communication that exists in an EDI system when all trading partners communicate directly with each other.

Direct-Cost Analysis A technique that only allocates expenses that can be assigned directly to a channel or that can be traced to a given channel (such as sales force salaries when each channel is served by a separate sales force, or warehousing space when different channels have different warehouse arrangements).

Direct Distribution *See* Short Channel.

Direct Exporting A firm's conduct of foreign sales through in-house personnel. It is carried out administratively through the use of export personnel as part of a firm's traditional sales department, a separate export department, or export sales subsidiary.

Direct Marketing A form of retailing in which a customer is first exposed to a good or service through a nonpersonal medium (such as direct mail, conventional or cable television, radio, magazines, or newspapers) and then orders by mail or telephone (usually through a toll-free telephone number)—and sometimes by computer.

Direct Product Profitability Assignment of warehouse, store transportation, labor, occupancy, inventory, and other store costs to categories of products to more accurately assess their profitability.

Direct Selling Sales made on the basis of house-to-house canvassing or telemarketing.

Direct Store Delivery A situation in which goods are delivered by a vendor directly to a retailer's store location instead of to the store's private warehouse.

Display The part of a marketing information system that consists of traditional reports, exception reports, and graphics, in paper or on screen formats.

Distribution Center A privately owned major warehouse facility used to serve a regional market by consolidating large shipments from multiple vendors.

Distribution Cost Analysis Determination of the cost levels and profitability of specific channel configurations (such as direct versus indirect channels), product lines (such as private-label brands), and customer types (such as discount stores).

Distribution Density The number of outlets required to effectively sell a firm's products or services.

Distributor Recognition Awards Awards designed to motivate resellers by communicating a distributor's accomplishments at an annual meeting, awards banquet, or convention banquet.

Distributor's Advisory Council An administrative technique used to manage and reduce conflict wherein a channel member attempts to change power relationships through committees that represent interests of specific groups.

Diversified Trade Show Exhibition designed to appeal to visitors and exhibitors from a wide grouping of industries.

Diverting The practice of selling gray market goods.

Dog A product characterized by low profit and low inventory turnover.

Domestic Gray Market Goods Trademarked goods that manufacturer-authorized channel members sell to unauthorized channel members, who then resell these goods domestically.

Downscale Households Households with income of less than $25,000 in 1989.

Downstream Information An information flow between a firm and its customers (intermediaries and final consumers).

Drop Shippers (Desk Jobbers) Limited-service merchant wholesalers that perform all the traditional wholesale tasks of full-service wholesalers except that they do not handle or store goods.

Dual Channels of Distribution A situation in which the same good or service is sold through different channel arrangements.

Ecological Life Cycle of a Product Natural resource depletion in a product's manufacture, the effect of product use on the environment (air and noise pollution, and desecration of the landscape), natural resource depletion associated with a product's use (such as gasoline mileage), and the ease of product recycling.

Economic Control An approach involving purchase requirements and royalty fees.

Economic Order Quantity (EOQ) The lowest sum of inventory holding and order-processing costs per unit. The formula for computing EOQ is:

$$EOQ = \sqrt{\frac{2DS}{IC}}$$

where

EOQ = economic order quantity in units

D = annual demand in units

S = order placement costs in dollars

I = holding costs on an annual basis (as a percentage of unit costs)

C = unit cost per item in dollars

Economic Scale A channel's power due to its overall size.

ECR *See* Efficient Consumer Response.

EDI *See* Electronic Data Interchange.

Effectiveness The ability of a channel to cover a firm's target customers.

Efficiency A term referring to costs relative to other channels and the capacity of the channel to handle evolving end-customer demand.

Efficiency Ratios Ratios that compute how effectively a firm uses its assets. The major efficiency ratios are the collection period, inventory turnover, and assets to sales ratio.

Efficient Consumer Response (ECR) A term used in the food distribution industry to describe efforts to maximize the effectiveness of the entire supply chain.

Electronic Data Interchange (EDI) The systematic sharing of sales and inventory data between channel members. It is generally used in conjunction with scanning and point-of-sales systems. It enables electronic transmission and exchange of standard format documents among companies.

Electronic Scanning Either hand-held or stationary laser-based devices that read and transmit UPC data as an item is passed over or by the scanner.

Empathy A dimension of customer service stating that customers want individualized attention, and they want to be heard.

End-Use Analysis A technique whereby a manufacturer matches its desired customer profile by industry with a reseller's current sales history to each industry group.

Environmental Uncertainty The extent to which an environment changes rapidly and allows a firm to be caught by surprise.

EOQ *See* Economic Order Quantity.

Ethnocentrism The lowest level of a firm's commitment to international business. Its objective is to dispose of surplus stock in home markets.

Exception Reports Reports that flag outstanding or significantly below-planned performance and list these performance levels.

Exclusive Dealing The requirement by a seller that its customers sell only its products, or at least no products in direct competition with its products.

Exclusive Distribution A method that allows only one channel member at any level to sell a manufacturer's goods and services in a given geographic area.

Exercised Power Measure of the actual alteration of a channel member's behavior.

Existing System A firm's current channel system.

Exit Barriers Restriction of a cooperative member from leaving the group through either up-front investment requirements or the loss of rebates that are paid at the end of the year.

Expectational Differences One channel member's expectations concerning the behavior of other channel members.

Expected Value Concept The notion that long-term profitability at each bid level in competitive bidding equals the profit at that bid level times the probability of that bid being accepted.

Experimental Treatment Exposure of real shoppers in a field experiment to the controllable variable being studied.

Experimentation A controlled setting where one or more variables are manipulated.

Expertise Power Power based on knowledge that one channel member attributes to another member.

Exploratory Research The first stage in the problem definition stage of the marketing research process whereby the investigator uses unstructured or semistructured research techniques (such as discussions with consultants, analysis of published data of a similar problem in a different industry, or study of a focus group) to develop a more precise statement of the research problem.

Export Automation Software Programs that help create commercial invoices, country-of-origin certificates, packaging slips (written in multiple languages), and export-declaration forms.

Export Brokers Brokers who specialize in international trade.

Export Management Companies Domestic firms that perform all aspects of export operations under a specific agreement.

Export Merchants Those who can take title to goods or function as agents. They retain their own identities.

External Secondary Data Data generated by sources other than the channel member directly involved in conducting a market research study.

Facilitating Payments *See* Transaction Bribes.

Facilitators Consultants in a marketing channel. They typically perform more specialized functions than intermediaries.

Factor Merchants *See* Commission Merchants.

Factory Outlets Businesses owned and operated by a manufacturer to dispose of excess inventory in an out-of-the-way location so as not to alienate the manufacturer's traditional customers.

Failure Fee Fee paid to the trade after a product's launch, if the new product fails to sell at a predetermined rate.

Fair Trade *See* Resale Price Maintenance.

Family A unit of two or more related persons who live together.

Field Experiment An experiment in which the environment is more realistic but control is reduced.

Field Warehouse Building that keeps products in a special area where their movement is monitored by the public warehouse manager. These products can be used as collateral for loans.

Financial Leverage The percentage of net worth that is represented by assets.

First-Generation Information Systems Systems that consist of computerized information from a single source, such as A. C. Nielsen.

Flea Markets Retail centers that are typically open several days per week; they are often located in an unconventional retail location such as a race track parking lot or a former discount store location.

Floor-Ready Merchandise Goods that come from a vendor preticketed with a store label and bar codes, prepriced, and prehung.

Focused Trade Show Appeals to visitors and exhibitors from one industry.

Follower Brands Products that a reseller perceives to be very similar to previously introduced items.

Food Brokers Brokers who specialize in the sale of foods and related items to food service retailers.

Foreign Agents Those who serve as an intermediary between the domestic firm and the buyer but operate under the supervision of the domestic firm.

Foreign Distributors Independent merchants who purchase goods for their account and then resell these goods to a foreign buyer.

Foreign Exchange License A document that enables an importer to secure currency to pay for a shipment.

Foreign Exchange Rate Rate at which a country's currency can trade for in another country.

Foreign Franchising A means whereby a local entrepreneur with knowledge of a foreign country can invest in a proven retail concept in the foreign country.

Foreign Freight Forwarder A specialist that provides transportation, shipping documentation, and customs-related services, and also advises clients on foreign label requirements as well as export restrictions.

Foreign Gray Market Goods Foreign goods that bear a valid U.S. trademark and are imported into the United States without the approval of the U.S. trademark owner.

Foreign Trade Zone An area where merchandise can be stored for unlimited time periods without the payment of duties, which are due when goods are shipped into the country where the foreign trade zone is located.

Formality A term that refers to whether buying is a separate function within an organization with a specialized staff.

Forward Buying Retailers' and wholesalers' purchase of large quantities at special discount prices that are offered to them by manufacturers.

Forward Vertical Integration A situation whereby manufacturers acquire or build up retail channels, or wholesalers acquire or develop retail channels.

Fraction of Demand Filled from Stock The percentage of orders that can be filled from existing inventory:

Fraction of demand filled from stock = Number of orders that can be completely filled/Total number of orders

Franchise Systems Contractual agreements between a franchisor and a franchisee, which allows the franchisee to conduct a given form of business under an established name and according to a given pattern of business.

Franchise Wholesaling Affiliation of independently owned retailers with an existing wholesaler, who use a common retail strategy.

Free-Rider Phenomenon A situation in which consumers seek information from specialty stores, get the brand name and model number of the preferred product, and then seek to purchase the product at a retailer that offers a discount. This also occurs with gray markets.

Freight Forwarders Service providers that consolidate small shipments from several companies.

Frequent User Clubs Clubs used by many channel members to increase loyalty by providing free products or upgrades to loyal customers.

FTC Franchise Rule A principle that requires franchisors to provide prospective investors with accurate and complete information regarding 23 categories of information, including the initial investment required, required fees, management experience of the franchisor, experience of the board of directors, names and addresses of operating franchises in the geographic area of prospective franchisees, a list of required purchases, circumstances under which a franchise can be terminated, and lawsuits filed by disgruntled franchisees.

Fulfillment Houses Independent firms that ship premiums directly to consumers.

Full-Cost Analysis Allocation of all costs to each channel regardless of how arbitrary the expense allocation may be.

Full-Line Discount Store Concern that uses central checkouts (often shopping carts are provided), emphasizes hard goods, has lower fixturing costs, stocks soft goods that are sold on the basis of function rather than fashion, and does not typically accept mail orders or deliver merchandise.

Full-Line Forcing A situation whereby a wholesaler or retailer is forced to order, stock, and display each type of product produced by a manufacturer that is applicable to its trade area. It is a type of tying contract.

Full-Line Merchant Wholesalers *See* General-Merchandise Merchant Wholesalers.

Full-Service Merchant Wholesalers Merchants who generally conduct a wide variety of wholesale functions that include the provision of credit to customers, storage and delivery of goods, merchandising and promotional assistance, and market research.

Functional Discount Discount received by a reseller for assuming a function that would otherwise be performed by a seller (such as storage, customer service, customer contact, and selling).

Functional Expenses The activity involved (such as selling, advertising, transportation, warehousing, and billing) in an expenditure.

Functional Fit A term that deals with assessing the ability of existing channels to store, sell, repair, and service a new product.

Gap Analysis of Distribution Channels Technique that focuses on the differences among the ideal system, the existing system, and a management bounded system.

Gatekeepers Wholesalers and retailers that influence consumer diffusion of new products by controlling the availability of new products and the physical flow of goods to the consumer.

Generally Planned Purchases Purchases identified by the product category, but not by brand, prior to the shopping experience.

General-Merchandise (Full-Line) Merchant Wholesalers Merchants who generally carry almost all the items required by their customers.

Geocentrism An orientation that standardizes business programs throughout the world. It ignores national boundaries and uses regional or global channels of distribution.

Geographic-Based Buying Organization An organization that exists when buying responsibilities are divided on the basis of state or region.

GMROI *See* Gross Margin Return on Investment.

Goal Incompatibilities Goals of different channel members that are not compatible and cannot be reconciled.

Gray Market Goods Generally foreign goods purchased abroad that are not intended for the U.S. domestic market.

Grease Payments *See* Transaction Bribes.

Greenbelts Regulation forbidding development by superstores and other forms of retailing through strict zoning laws.

Greening of America The increased concern of Americans for the ecological soundness of products.

Gross Margin The total channel costs measured by the difference between production costs and the final selling price for a good.

Gross Margin Return on Investment (GMROI) A special form of return on investment pricing objectives used by many distributors and retailers. It is also known as average gross profit per dollar of inventory investment. Mathematically, gross margin return on investment equals:

$$\text{GMROI} = \frac{\text{Gross profit}}{\text{Net sales}} \times \frac{\text{Net sales}}{\text{Average inventory at cost}}$$

Growth Stage The stage in the product life cycle that corresponds to rapid sales growth due to increased product acceptance among consumers and the emergence of competition.

Hidden Assets Assets that are not reflected in a firm's balance sheet at near their market values.

High-End Strategy Retailers Merchants who seek to appeal to a consumer segment that is more concerned with high service levels than a low price.

High-Low Pricing A pricing policy whereby a reseller charges higher prices on an everyday basis, but runs frequent promotions where these goods are offered at lower prices on a temporary basis.

Hold-Harmless Agreement Agreement that a manufacturer will reimburse a distributor for product liability cases.

Horizontal Channel Audit An audit that concentrates on all of a firm's channels elements. It is often called a marketing mix audit since it looks at a firm's overall channel strategy and the overall appropriateness of its channel mix.

Horizontal Competition Competition among channel members of the same type, such as two department store chains. It is greatest with intensive distribution and least with exclusive distribution.

Horizontal Conflict Conflict that occurs among similar firms in the same level in a distribution channel.

Household Unit that consists of a person or group of persons occupying a dwelling; these persons may be related or unrelated.

Hub-and-Spoke Distribution System A popular configuration for warehouses in which small shipments are consolidated in a regional warehouse and then shipped to customers.

Human Observation A trained interviewer's/observer's recording of a subject's behavior (as in the case of a manufacturer evaluating a wholesaler's display-making capability).

Hybrid Channel Arrangement A situation in which a manufacturer can reach different segments through the same channel network (comprised of both direct and indirect channels), but perform different functions (for the entire product line) depending on the customer segment.

Ideal System A distribution system that is customer driven, based on target markets served, and meets customer service standards.

Import License Document authorizing a firm to import certain goods.

Impulse Sales Generally, nonplanned purchases.

Independent Retailer Merchant who owns and operates only one retail outlet.

Indirect Benefits Benefits that derive from leveraging EDI to enable the technology to change the way one does business.

Indirect Distribution *See* Long Channel.

Indirect Promotional Effect Indirect impact of any promotion such as advertising or trade literature aimed primarily at distributors, which may be read by consumers.

Information Power Power derived by a channel member having access to factual data.

Initial Markup A broad type of markup that uses planned levels for expenses, profit, reductions, and sales.

Initial Markup Percentage Rate used in profit planning to determine the overall markup percentage required for a reseller based on planned operating expenses, profits, and reductions (stock shortages, employee discounts, and planned markdowns):

Required initial markup percentage = Planned operating expenses + Planned profit + Planned reductions/Planned net sales + Planned reductions

Inseparability Characteristic of services whereby services cannot be separated from the seller. It also implies that services must be consumed at the point of consumption.

Inside Buying Organization An organization in which buying specialists are employees of the retailer.

In-Store Decision Rate The sum of generally planned purchases, substitute purchases, and unplanned purchases.

In-Store Materials Sales and product information materials that are provided to manufacturers and distributors for final customer use.

Intangibility Characteristic of services whereby services cannot be stored, transported, or inventoried; it most closely applies to nongoods services.

Integrated Distributors Large wholesalers that are able to undertake functions such as inventory management and market research more efficiently than some manufacturers owing to economies of scale, mechanization, and computerization.

Integrated Marketing Use of computer databases to plan and implement all aspects of promotional strategies.

Integrated Supply Contract A long-term contract that names a wholesaler as sole supplier for a firm's needs in a given product area (such as maintenance, repair, and operating supplies) and geographic area.

Intensity of Conflicts Conflicts that can range from minor flareups that are easily forgotten to major disagreements characterized by terminations, lawsuits, and so on.

Intensive Distribution Technique that allows all channel members that meet minimum credit requirements to purchase a manufacturer's goods and services.

Intermediaries Manufacturers, wholesalers, and retailers in a marketing channel. They generally take title and possession of goods, directly contact prospective customers, and offer credit to their customers.

Intermodal Transportation The use of different transportation modes for the same shipment; in some cases, the transportation also involves multiple vendors.

Internal Information An information flow that is within the firm itself.

Internal Secondary Data Market research data that have already been gathered by a firm.

Intertype Competition Competition among different types of channel members at the same level within a channel.

Intertype Conflict Conflict among different types of intermediaries at the same level in a channel.

Introduction Stage The stage in the product life cycle that corresponds to a product's commercialization and its intended sale to its full target market.

Inventory Holding Costs Costs associated with keeping inventory in stock. These costs are interest costs on inventory, insurance costs, markdowns due to obsolescence, pilferage, taxes on inventory, and warehousing costs.

Inventory Turnover The relationship between a firm's sales and the inventory required by the firm to support that sales level. It can be computed in units or in dollars (both retail and cost):

Inventory turnover (in units) = Number of units sold during a year/ Average inventory on hand during year (in units)

Inventory turnover (in $ retail) = Net annual sales in dollars/Average inventory on hand during year (at retail)

Inventory turnover (in $ cost) = Cost of goods sold during the year/Average inventory at hand at cost

Inventory Turnover Ratio Ratio computed by dividing a firm's annual net sales by its average inventory.

ISO9000 A standard developed by the International Organization for Standardization which provides purchasers with a means of specifying suppliers (based on compliance with a quality assurance process) and third-party certification of suppliers.

JIT Inventory Management Systems See Just-in-Time Inventory Management Systems.

Joint Goal Setting A method of channel conflict management and resolution which takes into account the goals of multiple channel members.

Just-in-Time (JIT) Inventory Management Systems Systems that seek to minimize inventory investment through frequent deliveries and low average order sizes from a small group of suppliers.

Kanban System System that uses cards or other objects to initiate the production or delivery of inventory.

Keiretsu Japanese corporate groupings that typically contain a bank, a trading company, and over 20 groups of industrial enterprises.

Laboratory Experiment An experiment in which a highly controlled but unnatural environment is used.

LBO See Leveraged Buyout.

Lease Terms Terms relating to the duration of a lease, renewal options, and rental amounts.

Legal Control The right of a franchisor to protect its trade name and to guard against the sale of inferior products or services throughout the franchise network.

Legitimate Power Power that exists when one channel member realizes that another channel member has a clear right to exercise power over it.

Less-Than-Truckload (LTL) Shipments Freight shipments that are under 10,000 pounds.

Level One Relationships Relationships based on financial benefits to the customer, such as a lower price due to high cumulative purchases or membership in a frequent flier or hotel club (that provides free or upgraded flights or rooms).

Level Three Relationships Relationships characterized by high levels of service customization (such as use of proprietary software, sharing of sales data, joint technical support assistance, supplier assistance in parts design, and shared inventory management responsibilities), as well as a structural change in the customer relationship.

Level Two Relationships Addition of social relationships and a medium level of service customization to a price-based relationship.

Leveraged Buyout (LBO) A situation in which a retailer is acquired by an outside firm or by the firm's existing management.

Licensing A form of international channel joint venture in which a company assigns its rights to a trademark, a patent, or a store name to another firm for a royalty or fee.

Life-Cycle Costing Procedure manufacturers can employ to study the environmental impact of the production and use of a product. With this technique, likely future costs are projected to every feature of a product's life span, from product development to eventual disposal.

Limited-Line Merchant Wholesalers See Specialty-Merchandise Merchant Wholesalers.

Limited-Service Merchant Wholesalers Merchants who do not perform all of the services that full-service wholesalers perform;

they may not provide one or more of the following functions: credit, storage and delivery of goods, merchandising and promotional assistance, and marketing research.

Local Partner An arrangement in which a domestic company teams up with a foreign firm that often has access to specialized distribution channels, the ability to cut though bureaucratic red tape, warehouse and distribution facilities, high brand recognition, and access to foreign capital.

Local Rate The rate quoted to a distributor or retailer for advertising space or time.

Locked-Up Channel Used when a suitable channel is unavailable.

Logistics A single logic that guides the usage of financial and human resources committed to physical distribution, manufacturing support, and purchasing operations.

Logistics Alliances An arrangement that allows channel members to maintain long-term alliances, coordinate tasks, and share investment requirements to lower costs and improve customer service.

Long Channel (Indirect Distribution) A channel structure in which independent channel members (manufacturers, wholesalers, and retailers) take on specified responsibilities. Long channels are generally associated with high channel specialization.

Loss Leaders Goods sold below cost (defined as either purchase costs, replacement costs, or merchandise costs plus a fixed percentage to cover overhead), depending on state jurisdiction.

Lost-for-Good Customers Customers who favor long-term commitments to one vendor, do not change vendors often, and switch vendors only with considerable reluctance.

Lot Size A service output requirement that ascribes to consumers' desire to purchase a product in small quantities.

Lot Size Stocks (Cycle Stocks) Merchandise carried whenever a firm manufactures, ships, or purchases an item in larger lots than needed for its immediate needs.

Low-End Strategy Retailers Merchants who generally seek to appeal to a price-conscious market segment through a low-cost retail format.

LTL Shipments *See* Less-Than-Truckload Shipments.

Mail-Order Wholesalers Limited-service merchant wholesalers that utilize catalogs to promote and to communicate with potential buyers.

Maintained Markup A broad type of markup that measures actual profit as a percentage of sales.

Maintained Markup Percentage Rate that uses actual operating expenses, profits, and sales data. It is computed as follows:

Maintained markup = Actual operating expenses + Actual profit/Actual net sales

Management Bounded System A system that reflects management concerns relating to being loyal to certain types of middlemen, earning a given minimum return on investment, or limiting legal liability.

Management Succession The ability of a retail operation to successfully continue to operate in the event of the sudden disability or death of a retail owner or partner.

Manufacturers' Agents Agents employed by several manufacturers with noncompeting and complementary product lines.

Manufacturers' Branch Office An office in which the manufacturers have facilities for storing inventory.

Manufacturer's Brand *See* National Brand.

Manufacturers' Sales Office An office in which a manufacturer conducts wholesale activities; it does not contain inventory.

Manufacturer Wholesaling Situation whereby the manufacturer performs all wholesale functions and owns and controls goods until they are sold.

Manufacturing Franchising A broad type of franchising agreement in which a firm has the right to produce and market products under a franchisor's trademark.

Marketability A price discrimination defense that enables a seller to lower its price to reflect a product's seasonality, perishability, or obsolescence.

Market Decentralization A service output requirement that concerns the importance of convenient locations.

Market Development Expansion into new market areas both within and outside the United States.

Marketing Channels An organized network (system) of agencies and institutions which, in combination, perform all the activities required to link producers with users to accomplish the marketing task.

Marketing Decision Support System *See* Third-Generation Information System.

Marketing Research The systematic gathering, recording, and analyzing of relevant data to reduce uncertainty in marketing decision making.

Market Penetration Increasing market share within existing markets.

Markup Percentage Rate that can be calculated mathematically as follows:

Markup percentage (at retail) = Selling price − Merchandise cost/Retail selling price

Markup percentage (at cost) = Selling price − Merchandise cost/Merchandise cost

Markup Pricing A cost-oriented pricing technique whereby channel members add operating expenses and profit requirements as a percentage of sales to determine their price. It is widely used by wholesalers and retailers.

Maturity Stage The stage in the product life cycle that corresponds to a product's reaching its sales peak (both for the company and the industry) and the highest level of product competition.

Mechanical Observation Machine measurement of behavior (such as a scanner or Nielsen television rating measurement).

Meeting Competition Defense A seller's offer of a lower price to a buyer to meet (but not beat) a competitor's lower bid.

Membership Clubs *See* Buying Clubs.

Merchandise Consistency A term relating to the differences among product lines covered.

Merchandise Depth The selection within any product line; this is described as a retailer's assortment.

Merchandise Width Different product lines stocked and sold; this is referred to as variety.

Merchandising Orientation Orientation whereby retailers combine responsibility and authority for buying and selling in a single person or group.

Merchant Wholesaling Procedure whereby independent wholesalers purchase and take title of products and undertake all wholesale functions.

Message Formats The structured data that represent forms, such as purchase orders and invoices.

Micromarketing A technique that involves satisfying the needs and wants of a special consumer segment by specifically adapting the marketing strategy to appeal to that segment's special needs.

Minimum Sum of the Cost of Inventory and Backorders A standard that seeks to minimize the total of the costs of stockouts and of carrying inventory to prevent stockouts.

Model The portion of a marketing information system that consists of interrelationships among data that can be used for prediction.

Modular Corporation A situation in which a manufacturer outsources production activities to independent, but closely coordinated, organizations.

Money Income Actual dollar income.

Motivator Role A manufacturer's sales representative's attempts to get a distributor to achieve the manufacturer's objectives.

Motor Carrier Act of 1980 Legislation that deregulated interstate trucking. It lowered barriers to entry in the motor carrier industry and encouraged competitive pricing.

Multi-Industry Exhibitor Trade Show Exhibition that appeals to the complete needs of potential customers in a given industry with exhibitors that have a wide range of products.

Multi-Industry Visitor Trade Show Show designed to attract visitors' exhibitors from many industries with a focused selection of products and services.

Multiple Channels of Distribution A type of intertype competition in which a manufacturer sells different product lines to different channel members.

National Brand (Manufacturer's Brand) A brand designation developed by a manufacturer.

National Rate The higher rate a manufacturer pays for advertising in either broadcast or print media.

Natural Expenses Costs reported by the names of

the expenses, not their activity or function. Examples are salaries, rent, insurance, interest, and fuel.

Natural Observation Observation of a person in a regular setting such as the shopping environment of a grocery store.

Negotiation A method of conflict management and resolution in which participants bargain and each party gives up something.

Net Profit Margin A widely used summary measure of a firm's profitability. It is obtained by dividing a firm's net profit after tax by its annual net sales and measures the profit per dollar of sales.

New Product Planning Process The series of steps undertaken by a manufacturer in the introduction of a new product. These steps typically include idea generation, product screening, concept testing, business analysis, product development, test marketing, and commercialization.

Noncumulative Discount Discount limited to one order.

Nongoods Service Professional service (such as business consulting, accounting, and legal services) or service with no tangible elements (such as insurance, credit cards, and banking).

Nonprice Competition Competition that exists when sellers seek to change demand on the basis of distinctive benefits, and special pre-sale, during the sale, and post-sale services. It enables a manufacturer, wholesaler, or retailer to minimize the impact of price on demand.

Nonprobability Sample A sampling approach whereby sampling units are chosen by the researcher.

Nontraceable Common Costs Costs that cannot be clearly assigned to a given channel. Examples may include marketing overhead, interest, and taxes.

Observation A form of data collection in which the behavior of respondents is observed and recorded.

OEM *See* Original Equipment Manufacturer.

Off-Price Chains Stores owned and operated by retailers that specialize in opportunistic buying of canceled orders, slightly irregular, and end-of-season merchandise that is sold in a no-frills retail setting.

Ombudsman A manufacturer's sales representative who at times must take the reseller's side.

Omnibus Trade Act of 1988 Legislation that differentiates between transaction bribes and variance bribes.

Opportunistic Buying Buyers' attempt to purchase goods at prices 20 to 50 percent below wholesale.

Opportunity Costs Costs that arise when existing relationships preclude a firm from undertaking additional relationship marketing programs with new partners.

Optional Support Modules Promotional elements offered only to specific groups of resellers based on their individual needs.

Orange Goods Goods that have medium characteristics for replacement rate, gross margin, adjustment, consumption time, and searching time.

Order Cycle Time The time span between when an order is placed and when the goods are ready for sale or use in a production process.

Order Processing Costs The costs of implementing and verifying a transaction (such as effort to prepare and validate a purchase order, merchandise inspection, and verifying products received versus ordered).

Original Equipment Manufacturer (OEM) A foreign firm that sells its products to a local firm, but under the local firm's brand name.

Outcome-Related Activities Activities pertaining to the reliability of the service (how accurately a repair was made and whether a repair was done correctly the first time).

Outlet Malls A grouping of factory outlets and off-price chains that are planned as a unit with common property management.

Outside Buying Organization An organization in which a retailer employs a private firm to perform the buying function; this firm conducts market research, evaluates trends, contacts appropriate vendors, and orders and reorders merchandise.

Overstored Trading Area Area that has too many retailers selling a specific good or service to satisfy the needs of its population.

Owned-Goods Service Service involving the installation, maintenance, or repair of a good that a consumer owns.

Parallel Channels of Distribution The distribution channels for both domestic and foreign gray market goods since at least one vendor in the channel of distribution is not an authorized distributor of the manufacturer.

Partnering *See* Relationship Marketing.

Pay-for-Performance Allowance A variation of street money in which a manufacturer provides its intermediaries with a financial incentive to reimburse them for selling its goods at a reduced retail sales price, for increasing display activity, and for generating increased sales.

Pay to Stay Fee Fee that keeps a product on a shelf for a specified period.

PCV *See* Percent Category Volume.

Pedestrian Traffic Counts The number of people passing by a given location.

Percent Category Volume (PCV) A measure that weights stores by the percentage of a relevant product category that they sell.

Perceptual Differences A term relating to how a channel member interprets a situation or reacts to different stimuli.

Perishability A term meaning that services may have a short life span. This characteristic of services signifies that after a given time, a service quickly loses its value.

Per Se Rule An action that, by its nature, is illegal. Under this rule, the complaining party only needs to show that the illegal practice occurred.

Persuasion A method of conflict management and resolution in which a channel member seeks to manage conflict by altering the other party's perspective or decision criteria relating to the focal issue(s).

Persuasion Power The ability of one channel member to persuade another channel member of the validity of its position.

Physical Distribution A concept or an approach to managing the finished goods inventory of a firm. It includes the transportation, warehousing, inventory, and order processing functions of the firm.

Physical Distribution (Total Cost) Concept The total costs of providing a given level of customer service.

Piggybacking A situation in which the distribution channels of a manufacturer selling noncompeting goods to the same market are used by international marketers.

Pioneer Brands The first entrants into a new market.

PMs *See* Push Money.

Pocket Prices The prices actually paid by a reseller.

Point-of-Purchase Displays Fixtures for stocking merchandise to increase a product's visibility and sales.

Point-of-Sale Terminals Means permitting functions such as price lookup (allowing chains to vary prices by region and by store); determining sales by item, product line, merchandise category, and salesperson; evaluating returns and exchanges; taking markdowns associated with special one-day sales; and tracking customers by zip code to evaluate a store's location.

Politics A method of conflict management and resolution in which channel members extend the role of bargaining to include relevant third parties who might be viewed as allies.

Polycentrism Situation that exists when subsidiaries are established in foreign markets and each subsidiary designs its channel strategy independently.

Post-Consumer Waste Paper that has been serviced for its intended use, collected from consumers, and diverted from landfills for reprocessing into recycled pulp.

Potential Conflict Conflict that arises when a manufacturer expects to be entering a new product category or to expand the selling area of a product.

Potential Power A channel member's ability to alter another channel member's behavior.

Poverty of Time The perceived shortage of leisure time among consumers despite the shorter time spent at work.

Power Retailers Retailers with a high market share in their merchandise category, high store loyalty, and high bargaining power relative to their suppliers.

Precision (Sampling Error) The level of uncertainty about value being measured.

Pre-Consumer Waste Paper generated in the papermaking process such as scraps and paper shavings.

Predictive Dialers Ringing of many phones simultaneously to immediately transfer an answered call to a live operator.

Premium An item of value, other than the product itself, given as an additional incentive to influence the purchase of a product.

Price Competition Competition among manufacturers, wholesalers, and retailers to increase or decrease demand on the basis of changes in price.

Price Discrimination The practice of charging different buyers different prices for goods of "like grade and quality."

Price Guarantees Guarantees protecting merchant wholesalers and retailers from a decline in a product's list price by compensating them for the difference between past and current wholesale costs multiplied by a wholesaler's or retailer's stock on hand.

Price Protection A situation in which wholesalers are reimbursed by manufacturers when a manufacturer reduces the list price of its goods.

Primary Data Information collected specifically for the purpose of the investigation at hand.

Primary Demand Demand for an entire product category.

Private Label (Dealer Brand) A brand-name designation developed by a wholesaler or retailer.

Private Warehouses Facilities owned or leased by a supplier or reseller.

Probability-Based Sample A sampling approach whereby every unit (final customer, retailer, wholesaler, or manufacturer/supplier) has an equal chance of being chosen as a member of the sample.

Problem Definition The stage in the marketing research process whereby the researcher seeks to develop a clear statement of the topic to be studied.

Problem Solving A method of conflict management and resolution in which channel participants seek to identify a solution that satisfies each party's decision criteria.

Process-Related Activities Activities that accompany a service (such as a store's cleanliness, the friendliness of its personnel, and waiting lines at cash resisters).

Process Stocks Inventory in transit that is needed because of time to get inventory from one channel member to another.

Producer-Owned Cooperatives Entities that purchase supplies; perform such wholesale tasks as storage, transportation, grading products, and arranging to sell output; and promote products through a common brand name. They are common in farming.

Product-Based Buying Organizations Organizations that utilize product-based buying specialists.

Product Life Cycle The stages in the history of a product: introduction, growth, maturity, and decline.

Product Recall Repair or replacement of products that have been produced by a manufacturer.

Product Recycling Recovery of natural resources from the return of used products and its packaging.

Product/Trademark Franchising A type of retail franchise in which franchised dealers acquire the identity of their suppliers by agreeing to sell the suppliers' products and/or operate under the suppliers' names.

Product Variety A service output requirement that measures the need to see competing brands and products.

Profitability Ratios Ratios that analyze a firm's return on its assets. These include net profit margin, return on assets, and return on net worth.

Profit-Based Pricing Objectives Objectives used by firms that set pricing objectives in terms of profits, early recovery of cash, or return-on-investment measures.

Profit Pass-Over Arrangements Arrangements whereby payment is given to a wholesaler that sells goods and services to accounts that are located outside of that wholesaler's territory by the wholesaler having those territorial rights.

Programmed Merchandising Agreement A form of administered marketing system in which a manufacturer develops a major promotional program with high acceptance by its retail dealers.

Promises *See* Reward Power.

Promotional Money *See* Push Money.

Psychographic Research Research that classifies consumers into life-styles by investigating how they live, what interests them, and what they like.

Publicity Nonpaid communication about a company or its products in the mass media.

Public Warehouses For-hire facilities that are available to any business requiring storage or handling of goods.

Pull *See* Selling Through the Wholesaler/Retailer.

Pull System System that initiates production as a reaction to present demand.

Pure Centralized Buying Organization Organization that exists when one buyer purchases all goods for all retail store units.

Push *See* Selling to the Wholesaler/Retailer.

Push Money (PMs, Promotional Money, Spiffs) An incentive paid by a manufacturer directly to a retailer's salesperson to stimulate the sale of a particular brand or specific product.

Push System System that initiates production in anticipation of present demand.

Quality A customer service dimension that includes such measures as minimum damage in transit, order-filling accuracy, billing accuracy, and shipping accuracy.

Quantity Discounts Discounts earned by wholesalers for buying specified quantities of merchandise.

Quick Ratio Ratio that divides cash and accounts receivable by a firm's current liabilities.

Quick Response Inventory Management System that allows retailers and wholesalers to receive multiple small orders from their suppliers to match sales patterns. With it, channel members can minimize inventory investment and focus on producing those items with high sales performance.

Quick Response Inventory Systems The term retailers use for just-in-time inventory management systems.

Rack Jobbers Those who provide and maintain general merchandise that is sold on a consignment basis to self-service-based mass merchants.

Range of Power A term that refers to the areas within which a channel member may prescribe another channel member's behavior and expect that channel member to adhere to its desires.

Real Conflict Conflict that affects the sales objectives and communication for one or more of a manufacturer's brands.

Real Income Income that reflects the cost of living.

Real Sales Growth Dollar sales growth in percentage minus the inflation rate for the corresponding time period.

Rebates Special money-back incentives made directly to final consumers and end-users.

Reciprocity The practice of buying goods and services from major customers; in turn, these customers then purchase goods and services from the firm.

Red Goods Goods that have a high replacement rate, low gross margin, low need for adjustment, low consumption time, and low searching time.

Referent Power Power that exists when one channel member confers power on another channel member based on other brands carried or based on the channel member's overall image.

Refusal to Deal Refusal of a manufacturer or wholesaler to sell goods to selected intermediaries.

Regiocentrism An orientation whereby business programs are designed on the basis of similarities within an area. It ignores national boundaries and uses regional or global channels of distribution.

Relationship Marketing (Partnering) Marketing based on building and maintaining long-term relationships between buyers and sellers that are based on trust and commitment.

Reliability A dimension of customer service stating that customers want companies to perform a desired service dependably, accurately, and consistently.

Reliability Measure The fraction of order or replenishment cycles with no stockouts. It is expressed mathematically as

$$\text{Reliability} = 1 - \frac{\text{Number of stockouts}}{\text{Number of replenishments}}$$

Rented-Goods Services Services that involve the

leasing of a good for a limited time period.

Reorder Point A formula that sets the inventory level at which a firm must place an order or risk a stockout. The traditional formula has three variables: order cycle time, usage rate, and safety stock.

Replacement Rate The rate at which a product is purchased by users.

Resale Price Maintenance (Fair Trade) An agreement between a supplier and a retailer stating that the retailer will not sell a particular good below a minimum price level.

Resale Restrictions A manufacturer's restriction of authorized distributors from selling its products to unauthorized distributors or authorized distributors outside its territory.

Research Design A framework or plan that guides the collection and analysis of data.

Resident Buying Offices Retailer's offices in an important buying center for a major product.

Resource Scarcities A term relating to conflict over the allocation of scarce resources.

Resource Scarcity An argument suggesting that franchising eases access to capital and managerial resources for a rapidly expanding business.

Responsiveness A dimension of customer service stating that prompt service is desired.

Retail Catalog Showrooms Showrooms that sell items via a catalog (the catalog is generally delivered to the shopper's home) in a warehouse-type setting.

Retailer-Owned Cooperatives Facilities owned and operated by their retailer members.

Retailer-Owned Cooperative Systems Systems created when independent retailers form associations that purchase, lease, or build wholesale facilities.

Retailing Those business activities involved in the sale of goods and services to consumers for personal, family, or household use.

Return on Assets Ratio Ratio computed by dividing a firm's net profit after tax by its total assets. This ratio calculates a firm's net profit after tax per dollar of assets.

Return on Net Worth Ratio Ratio obtained by dividing a firm's net profit after tax by its net worth.

Reverse Channels Movement of products from a buyer back to a manufacturer.

Reviewer Role Role of a manufacturer's sales representative in assessing a reseller's overall performance.

Review Period The frequency with which inventory counts are made.

Reward Power (Promises) A channel member's reward of another channel member who conforms to desires; there are benefits for compliance.

Role Ambiguity A channel member's uncertainty as to what behaviors constitute acceptable performance.

Role Incongruity A state that occurs when a channel member's behavior is outside of the acceptable range based on the role expectations of others.

Rule of Reason A principle stating that a court must first ascertain the reasonableness of the restraint and its effect on the overall competitive environment and then determine whether an act is illegal.

Safety Stocks Stocks used by firms to meet unanticipated variations in consumer demand or unplanned delays in order cycle time from vendors.

Sales-Based Pricing Objectives Objectives used by resellers that seek to increase sales.

Sales Below-Cost Laws Statutes that forbid the sale of goods below cost when the intent is to destroy competition or injure a competitor.

Sales Gestation Period The average length of time from the first contact to a product's purchase.

Sales Incentives Bonuses, contests, plaques, membership in an annual club of high-performing resellers, paid vacations, and other monetary and nonmonetary awards.

Sales Promotion All promotional effort that is not classified as personal selling, advertising, and publicity—often with the objective of stimulating demand.

Same-Store Sales Sales in stores open at least one year.

Sampling A data collection method by which selected respondents or observations are used to generate conclusions about a larger group.

Sampling Error *See* Precision.

Saturated Trading Area An area that has the proper

amount of retail facilities to satisfy the needs of its population.

Saturation Ratios Ratios that allow a retailer to determine the degree of market saturation. They include the number of persons per establishment, average sales per retail store, sales per capita or household, and sales per square foot of selling space.

Scenario A description of a possible or probable future event or level of an activity that is likely to occur in the future.

Scouts The first retailers to adopt a new product.

Scrambled Merchandising An extreme case of intertype competition in which a channel member adds goods and services that are not usually associated with its merchandise lines.

Seamless A term meaning that the use of multiple transportation modes and multiple vendors should be invisible to the customer.

Searching Time The amount of effort expended by customers to shop for a particular good. It is measured by the travel time and distance consumers will travel to shop for a given product.

Seasonal Discounts An incentive for wholesalers and retailers to purchase goods early in the selling season by granting an additional reduction in price.

Secondary Data Statistics not gathered for the immediate study at hand but for some other purpose. It may be internal or external.

Secondary Linkages A means of sharing power within a franchise system. These linkages may be informal and may consist of cooperative advertising arrangements and franchise associations.

Second-Generation Information Systems Systems characterized by the development of integrated marketing databases that combine data from commercial research firms with internal secondary data (such as sales, advertising, coupon redemption, and distribution effectiveness).

Selective Demand Demand for a manufacturer's brand.

Selective Distribution An attempt to balance the amount of channel member competition and degree of market coverage.

Self-Fulfilling Prophecy A situation in which a firm falsely predicts that its product is in the maturity or decline stage of the product life cycle, and consequently reduces the level of marketing support. This false prediction shortens the life of a product.

Self-Liquidating Premium A premium cost equal to or less than the price charged.

Selling Against the Brand A practice whereby retailers charge artificially high prices for a national brand to encourage consumers to purchase their private label.

Selling Agents Those who assume responsibility for the entire marketing operation of a single manufacturer.

Selling Through the Wholesaler/Retailer (Pull) A technique that emphasizes the importance of the final customer and the need for the producer to stimulate final customers.

Selling to the Wholesaler/Retailer (Push) Promotional support directed toward wholesalers and retailers to get them to stock, display, and promote a manufacturer's products.

Sensitivity Training A method of channel conflict management and resolution whereby channel personnel are trained to be aware of potential conflict areas. Individuals are also empowered to reduce conflict situations before they escalate.

Service Backup A service output requirement that assesses the importance of having a product repaired in-home or in-office.

Service Failures The expected stockouts per unit of time. This measure examines stockouts per week, month, or year:

$$\text{Service Failures} = \frac{\text{Number of stockouts}}{\text{Unit of time}}$$

Service Output Requirements used to examine a customer's distribution needs. They have been grouped into five categories: lot size, market decentralization, waiting time, product variety, and service backup.

Service Response Logistics The process of coordinating nonmaterial activities necessary to the fulfillment of a service in a cost- and customer service-effective manner.

Shared Intellectual Property A trade or service owned by a business format franchisor and licensed in return for royalty payments. It is a criterion used to determine if a channel relationship is subject to federal and state franchise regulations.

Shared Tasks A method of channel conflict management and resolution whereby channels manage conflict by developing intermediary-manufacturer partnerships through relationship marketing.

Shelf Facings Columns of the same product displayed on a shelf.

Shipper's Export Declaration Statement that the shipper has authorization for export. It lists the names and addresses of the principals, a description of the goods, the declared value of the goods, and the final destination of the goods.

Short Channel (Direct Distribution) A channel structure in which manufacturers sell their goods and services directly to final or organizational consumers without the use of independent resellers.

SIC *See* Standard Industrial Classification.

Simulation A form of data collection in which mathematical descriptions are developed to explain a given situation.

Single-Source Data Data based on household panels which seek to explain purchases (that are recorded either in stores or at the respondent's home using scanners) by correlating purchases to television viewing (which is monitored), past purchases, in-store promotions, couponing effort by manufacturers, and lifestyle and demographic data.

Size-of-Order Boundaries Boundaries specifying that the role of independent wholesalers is to serve smaller accounts; larger accounts are then served by direct distribution.

Sleeper A product characterized by high profit and low inventory turnover.

Slotting Allowance A payment given by a manufacturer to a retailer for the use of its shelf space, as well as discounts and other special deals.

Smoothing and Seasonal Stocks Stocks needed to reflect differences between production and demand.

Solvency Ratios Measure of a channel member's ability to meet its short- and long-term debt obligations.

Sorting Process A channel member function in which wholesalers and retailers resolve the conflicting orientations of manufacturers (their suppliers) and their organizational and final consumers.

Specialty-Merchandise (Limited-Line) Merchant Wholesalers Merchants who generally specialize in a narrow range of products and have an extensive assortment within that range.

Specialty Stores Stores that stock and sell one line or limited lines of related merchandise.

Specifically Planned Purchases Purchases identified by a shopper at the preshopping phase; specific items that are listed are actually purchased.

Spiffs *See* Push Money.

Stage One Program Basic product training (such as a product demonstration) for resellers.

Stage Three Program Dealers that swap roles with a manufacturer's sales staff.

Stage Two Program A joint sales call where the dealer assists the manufacturer's representative in demonstrating a new product.

Standard Industrial Classification (SIC) A system compiled by the U.S. Office of Management and Budget that classifies firms by industry based on their sales.

Status Quo-Based Pricing Objectives Objectives used by resellers that seek to minimize the impact of a new competitor, anticipated government action, or change in market condition.

Storefront System A situation in which a reseller maintains, in addition to a centralized distribution network, storefront locations where orders are taken, customer contacts initiated, spare parts maintained, and some inventory is kept.

Strategic Approach An approach that focuses on the development, implementation, and control of a long-term competitive advantage through efficient and effective channel management.

Strategic Benefits Benefits derived from the sharing of information among channel members, from open communication, and from greater trust.

Strategic Profit Model Model that assesses retailer performance on the basis of asset turnover (net sales/total assets), net profit margin (net profit/net sales), and financial leverage (total assets/net worth).

Street Money A temporary deal or discount used on a short-term basis to increase shelf space, promote sales, introduce a new product, or increase market share in a region where sales are low. It is a popular sales promotion.

Subfranchising A method for expanding a franchise whereby a franchisor appoints a master franchise that has the right to appoint single or multiple subfranchises in a given territory. The master franchise then solicits subfranchisees for its territory.

Substitute Purchases Brands or products that are switched from those that were originally planned.

Supermarkets Large departmentalized retail establishments offering a relatively broad and complete stock of dry groceries, fresh meat, perishable produce, and dairy products, supplemented by a variety of convenience, nonfood merchandise and operated primarily on a self-service basis.

Superstore (General Merchandise) Store that uses massive amounts of floor space and offers a deeper selection of products (such as personal computers and home appliances), product demonstration areas, and low prices.

Superstores (Food-Based) Stores that average 30,000 to 65,000 square feet in size and offer a large selection of general merchandise; between 20 and 25 percent of sales comes from general merchandise.

Supply Chain Logistics The traditional process associated with the physical flow of materials and information. It encompasses such activities as purchasing, transportation, inventory management, and materials handling.

Survey A form of data collection in which data are gathered from a respondent through communication. A survey can be used to measure attitudes, opinions, awareness/knowledge, behavior, demographic/socioeconomic characteristics, intentions, and motivations.

Sweepstakes A form of sales promotion based solely on chance.

Switching Costs The costs facing a manufacturer, wholesaler, or retailer that seeks to change channel arrangements.

Tabulation Calculation of summary data (averages, totals, and percents) for each response category.

Tailored Logistics Package Package that satisfies the specialized needs of different types of products and customers at a reasonable cost.

Tangibles A dimension of customer service stating that physical facilities should be attractive and clean; employees should be well-groomed.

Teacher Role A manufacturer's sales representative training of reseller's sales and support staff in sales techniques and a product's technical attributes.

Technical Problem-Solving Systems Systems that give customers access to technical data such as which products meet customer needs.

Terms Credit provided by a manufacturer/supplier for wholesalers and retailers.

Territorial Resale Restriction Restriction preventing or discouraging a wholesaler from selling outside a particular area.

Test Marketing A manufacturer's placement of a new or modified product for sale in one or more cities to observe sales performance under a given marketing plan.

Third-Generation Information System (Marketing Decision Support System) An interactive, computer-based information system designed to assist with semistructured and unstructured management decisions.

Third-Party Documentation Agencies Outside firms that are paid to document print cooperative claims.

Third-Party Network An electronic mailbox established by a service bureau through which companies can send and retrieve electronic documents.

Third-Party Transportation Service Providers An array of facilitators that operate between carriers and shippers and deliver such services as brokerage, freight forwarding, freight consolidation, warehousing, auditing of goods received against purchase orders, information processing, and fleet operations.

Timeliness A customer service dimension that relates to such factors as consistent delivery, order cycle time reliability, and minimum order cycle time.

Time of Consumption The time period during which a product is used.

Tipping Fees The price of dumping municipal waste in landfills.

TL Shipments *See* Truckload Shipments.

Total Cost Concept *See* Physical Distribution Concept.

Total Liabilities to Net Worth Ratio Ratio computed by dividing a firm's total liabilities by its net worth; it looks at long-term as well as short-term debt.

Total Quality Management (TQM) The ongoing process of improving product and service quality by examining the strategies of quality leaders, constant feedback, the use of teams, and total employee involvement.

TQM *See* Total Quality Management.

Trade Discount A discount from a product's list price given to all resellers on the basis of the level of trade.

Trade Loading The use of forward buying by manufacturers as a means of loading up resellers to increase short-term sales.

Trade Shows Periodic exhibitions in a single location of a group of manufacturers and distributors where products and services are displayed to potential buyers.

Trading Area Characteristics Demographic and life-style characteristics of the geographic area from which a retailer draws its shoppers.

Traffic Builders Products characterized by low profits but high inventory turnover.

Transactional Marketing When a customer uses multiple sources of supply, tends to frequently switch among suppliers, and buys largely on the basis of price.

Transaction Bribes (Grease or Facilitating Payments) Payments made to a foreign government official to speed up a country's bureaucratic handling of an order. They are considered acceptable.

Transaction Cost Analysis A technique involving a firm's efforts to minimize the sum of transaction and production costs in making forward integration decisions.

Transaction-Specific Assets Investments that are required to complete a transaction and have little use otherwise. These can include physical locations, specific physical assets, and specific human assets.

Transfer Price The price charged for goods and services sold through a company-owned channel.

Transportation Public transportation facilities that serve a retail location.

Trigger Point The contingent event facing a channel member which has reached a critical level and requires some action.

Troops Those who purchase a product only when scouts experience satisfactory sales levels.

Truckload (TL) Shipments A full truckload of shipments.

Truck/Wagon Wholesalers Limited-service merchant wholesalers that typically have a regular route and deliver goods at the same time they are sold.

Tying Arrangement An agreement whereby a seller conditions the sale of one product or service (the tying product) on the buyer's purchase of a second product or service (the tied product).

Understored Trading Area An area that has too few retail facilities selling a specific good or service to satisfy the needs of the area's population.

Unemployment Rate The percentage of the civilian workforce that is looking for work that is unemployed. It is perhaps one of the most visible measures of economic health.

Unit Franchising A method that allows a franchise to expand by establishing outlets on a one-franchise-at-a-time basis. It is often used with franchises targeted to owner/operators.

Universal Core Support Module Promotional programs that are applicable to all resellers.

Universal Product Code (UPC) A 12-digit number used for merchandise identification down to the lowest level (color and size for apparel).

UPC *See* Universal Product Code.

Upstream Information Information flow between a firm and its manufacturers/suppliers.

Usage Rate The rate at which a good is sold or the rate at which a good is used in a production process for a manufacturer.

VALS (Values and Life-Styles) Program An important means of classifying consumers in terms of a broad range of demographic and life-style factors. It divides Americans into eight life-style categories.

Value Chain The collection of activities performed to design, produce, market, deliver, and support its products.

Value Orientation The increased concern among consumers for the right combination of product quality, fair price, and good service.

Values and Life-Styles Program See VALS Program.

Variability in Quality Differences in the quality of services over time. It can be reduced through industrializing services, systematic training programs, and standardized procedures.

Variable Markup Policy Different markup requirements established for specific goods to reflect differences in costs, demand, and competition.

Variance Bribes Bribes made to a government official to suspend a legal norm. They are considered illegal.

Variety Store Store that sells a wide variety of low-priced general merchandise in a self-service, cash-and-carry format.

Vehicular Traffic Counts Measure of the number of vehicles passing by a given location.

Vending Machines Coin- and card-operated machinery that sells goods and services.

Vertical Channel Audit Audit that focuses on one area of channels such as customer service or physical distribution.

Vertical Competition Competition among different channel members at different levels within the channel, such as a manufacturer competing with a retailer.

Vertical Conflict Conflict resulting from competition among different levels within a channel of distribution.

Vertical Marketing System Competition A situation in which horizontally coordinated and vertically aligned establishments that are professionally managed and centrally coordinated compete against each other.

Vertical Marketing Systems Systems characterized by alliances or networks in which a producer, a distributor, and a retailer act as a unified team rather than as independent entities.

Video-Ordering Systems Systems that allow consumers to order goods and services by computer, telephone, or an in-store computer terminal.

Visibility The ability of a retail location to be seen from the road.

Waiting Time A service output requirement that reports on delivery speed.

Warehouse A physical facility used primarily for the storage of goods held in anticipation of sale or transfer within the marketing channel.

Warehouse Stores Stores that can be classified as limited assortment, warehouse, super warehouse, and hypermarket/supercenter depending on their size; they offer low prices in a no-frills setting.

Wholesaler-Sponsored Voluntary Chains A type of contractual marketing system in which independent retailers affiliate with an existing wholesaler to use a standardized storefront design, business format, name, and purchase system.

Wholesaling The buying or handling of merchandise and its subsequent resale to organizational users, retailers, and/or other wholesalers but not the sale of significant volume to final consumers.

Winner A product characterized by high profit and high inventory turnover.

Working Partner A manufacturer's salesperson who offers assistance at trade shows and works jointly with a reseller's own sales force on important sales.

Yellow Goods Goods that have a low replacement rate, high gross margin, high need for adjustment, high consumption time, and high searching time.

Zone of Tolerance Separation of desirable from adequate service levels. It varies from customer to customer and from situation to situation for the same customer.

Name Index

Abercrombie & Fitch, 117
ABF Freight System, 252
Ace Hardware, 166, 530
Achrol, Ravi S., 640, 642, 660
Adelson, Andrea, 141
Advanced Micro Devices, 585
Advertising Checking Bureau, 443
Afterthoughts Accessories, 116
Agins, Teri, 39, 512, 549
AIG Insurance, 192
Airborne Express, 255
Ajinomoto, 614
Alberto-Culver, 516–517
Albertson's, 61, 111, 120
Alderson, Wroe, 38, 39
Aleo, Joseph P., Jr., 236, 238
Allen, Frank Edward, 375
Allen, Michael, 197, 198
Allen-Edmonds, 202–203
Allstate Insurance, 524
Alpeer, Frank H., 374
AlphaGraphics, 553–554
Altman, B., 10, 108, 130
America Online, A1, A2, A4, 83, 92
American Airlines, 623
American Express, 590, 623
American Greetings Corporation, 479
American Society of Travel Agents, 624
American Standards Institute, 313
American Stores, 111
American Tourister, 223, 265
American Trucking Association, 252
Ames Department Stores, 10, 121, 131
Anderman, David A., A5
Andersen Consulting, A1, 269, 395, 638
Anderson, Erin, 39, 210, 234, 549, 609, 621
Anderson, James C., 39, 233, 234, 583
Anderson, Rolph, 40
Andreoli, Teresa, 88
Anheuser-Busch Inc., 183–184
Annin, Peter, 140
Apple Computer, A2, 191
Arlen, Jeffrey, 331
Arm & Hammer, 440
Armani, Giorgio, 108
Armstrong, Larry, 39, 235
Arnst, Catherine, 198
Artzt, Edwin L., 418
Ashley, Laura, 247
Aspinwall, Leo V., 487, 488, 492, 513
Assael, Henry, 326
Associated Food Stores, 529, 530
AST Research Inc., 43, 525

Atac, Osman A., 582
Atag Holdings NV, 601
AT&T, 207, 229
Austin Computer Systems, 190
Auto Service Industry Association, 334
Autry, Ret, 181
Avery, Susan, 327
Avis, 599–600
Avon, 58, 91–92, 524
A&W, 175
Axelrad, Norman D., 550, 551
Azzarello, Joseph A., 366

Babakus, Emin, 583
Ball Corporation, 586
Bank of America, 599
Banting, Peter M., 281
Barclay's Commercial Corporation, 10
Barmash, Isadore, 136, 144
Barnes, James H., Jr., 375
Barney's New York, 607
Barrett, Paul M., 373, 416
Barrier, Tamala L., 327
Bauer, Eddie, 83
Baum, Herbert, 69
Baxter International Inc., 25, 164, 338, 462–472
Baylor, Leslie, 281
Bean, L. L., 16, 188, 607
Bearings Inc., 150
Becker, Robert J., 514
Becton Dickinson, 496
Bello, Daniel C., 603, 609, 620, 621
Bellou, Ronald H., 251
Ben Franklin Stores, 532
Benetton, 400
Bennett, James, B3, B4
Bennett, Nathan, 550
Bennett, Peter D., 38, 88, 90, 141, 234, 236, 279, 280, 326, 458
Berg, Eric N., 256
Bergen Brunswig Company, 153, 329, 464
Berman, Barry, C6, 38, 140, 141, 181, 215, 218, 224, 626
Berry, Leonard L., 206, 217, 220–221, 233, 234, 235, 660
Berss, Marcia, 375, 472, 582
Bessen, Jim, 458
Best Buy, 575
Best Western Hotels, 536
Bethlehem Steel, 227
Bhoovaraghavan, Sriraman, 457
Biddle, David, 376
Biello, Suzanne, 90
BIG Bank, 590
Birkenstock, 16
Black & Decker, 336
Bleakley, Fred R., 587

Blimpie's, 538
Block, H&R, 83, 92
Blockbuster Entertainment Corporation, 317, 596
Bloom, Paul N., 376
Bloomberg, David J., 244
Bloomingdale's, 66, 354, 559
Blue Diamond, 166
Blumenthal, Karen, 42
BMW, 363, 544
Body Shop, The, 607
Boeing, 265
Bohlen, Celestine, 620
Boise Cascade Corporation, 217–218, 250, 464
Bombay Company, 83
Bongiorno, Lori, 550, 551
Borden, 369
Borders Books and Music, 116
Borin, Norm, 390
Bourdon, Elizabeth, 396
Bowers, Brent, 373
Bowersox, Donald J., 251, 278
Bridgestone, 377
Bristol-Myers, 329
Brokaw, Leslie, 16
Brooks Brothers, 525
Brother International, 440
Brown, Paul B., 93
Brown, Tom J., 235
Brown & Haley, 528
Browne, William G., 660, 663
Bruno's, 120
Bryant, Adam, 90, 279
BTI Americas Inc., 623–624
Bucklin, Louis P., 39, 400, 488, 492, 513
Builders Square, 116, 552
Bulkeley, William M., 326
Bullock's, 108
Burberry, 524
Burdine's, 108
Bureau of Labor Statistics, 59
Burger King, 95, 536
Burlington Northern Inc., 250–251
Burns, Greg, 620
Burrows, Peter, 39, 190, 197, 198, 457, 586
Burton, Thomas M., 472
Burtschy, Annagret, 620
Buskirk, Bruce D., 347
Buskirk, Richard H., 347
Bussell, Robert D., 513
Butaney, Gul, 562, 582
Buzzell, Robert D., 415, 657, 660
Bylinsky, Gene, 376
Byrne, Harlan S., 39, 426

Cable 1, 83
Cacique, 117
Cadbury Schweppes, 175

Calantone, Roger J., 582
Caminiti, Susan, 39, 141, 328, 472
Campanelli, Melissa, 182, 457
Campbell, Alta, 103, 144, 426, 516, 552, 625
Campbell Soup Company, 69, 347
Canada Dry, 175
Canion, Joseph R., 196
Cannon, Joseph P., 205, 376
Carey, Christopher J., 140
Carlson, Dave, 331
Carlton, Jim, 198, 375
Carman, James A., 235
Carnevale, Mary Lu, 458
Carney, Karen E., 514
Carney, Mick, 550
Carrefour, 607–608
Carroll, Paul B., 93
Carter, Bill, 326
Carter Hawley Hale, 10, 108, 130
Case Corporation, 256
Castrogiovanni, Gary J., 539, 550
Cateora, Philip R., 622
Caterpillar, 267, 400, 402, 459–460, 577
Cavusgil, S. Tamer, 416, 460
Century 21 Real Estate, 535, 595, 596
Certified Grocers of California, 530
Cespedes, Frank V., 18, 39, 416, 481, 493, 513
Champs Sports, 116
Chanel, 400
Chang, Dae R., 513
Charlier, Marj, 347, 374
Chase Manhattan, 599
Chatzky, Jean Sherman, A5
Chef's catalog, A4
Chemical Bank, 599
Chock Full o' Nuts Corporation, 345
Christie, Rick, 88
Chrysler, 337, 460–461, 563
Churchill, Gilbert A., Jr., 235, 578, 584
Circle K, 121
Circuit City, 108, 244, 245, 556, 564, 575
CIT Group, 10
Citibank, 590, 599
Claiborne, Liz, Inc., 62, 70, 142, 525
Clairol Inc., 329, 517
Claritas, 317
Clasen, Thomas F., 621
Clorox Company, 173, 363
Closs, David J., 251
Cmar, Karen A., 549
Coach, 69, 524
Coca-Cola Company, 5, 94–103, 534
Coca-Cola Research Council, 66
Cohen, Dorothy, 376, 416, 457, 544, 551, 622
Cole, Catherine, 593, 620

Cole, Jeff, 373, 587
Coleman, Brian, 620
Coleman, Sheldon, 284
Coleman, W.C., 284
Coleman Company, 284–285
Colgate-Palmolive, 419
Collins, Glenn, 512
Combs, James G., 550
Comdisco, Inc., 469
Compaq Computer, 26, 190, 191, 194, 195, 196, 249, 267, 268, 349, 404, 406, 440, 450, 585–586
CompuAdd, 190
CompUSA, 150, 575
CompuServe, A1, A2, 83
Compuserve, 92
Computer City, 525
ComputerLand Corporation, 13, 42–43, 368
Conant, Jeffrey S., 660
Concord, 403
Conference Board, 73, 74
Conlin, Joseph, 458
Connelly, Mary, 457
Conrail, 251
Consolidated Freightways, 252
Consolidated Rail Corporation, 228
Contentware, A4
Continental T.V., 176
Conza, Anthony, 538
Cooke, Robert Allen, B3
Cooperative Food Distributors of America, 313
Copacino, William C., 236, 280
Cordell, Victor V., 626
Corey, E. Raymond, 31, 39, 40, 182, 416, 494, 495, 513
Cornwell, 515
Cotter & Company, 530, 531
Coughlan, Anne T., 609, 621
Council of Logistics Management, 227–228, 244, 271
Cox, Jonathan M., 458
Cox, Reavis, 7, 38
CPC International, 542
Crate and Barrel, 83
Crew, J., 108
Crispell, Diane, 88, 89
Cronin, J. Joseph, Jr., 235
Cuneo, Alice Z., 89, 373
Curtis, Helene, 244, 245
Cutler, Blayne, 88, 89
Cuyvers, Ludo, 326, 327
CVS, 116, 117
Cyrix, 585
Czinkota, M. R., 620

Dahl, Jonathan, 624
Dai-Ichi Kangyo, 614
Daniells, Lorna M., 326
Dant, Rajiv P., 583
Dant, Shirish P., 234

Darlin, Damon, 327
Dataquest, A1
David, Miles, 457, 458
Davis, Duane L., 215, 228, 375
Davis, Tim R., 88
Day, George S., 375, 416
Days Inn, 536, 595, 596
Dayton Hudson Corporation, 54, 111, 116, 117, 142, 314
Dayton's, 116
De Lisser, Eleena, 620
Dearing, Brian, 90, 327
Deere & Company, 256, 267, 577
Dell, Michael, 186, 192, 193, 194, 195, 196
Dell Computer Corporation, 42, 152, 186–198, 358
Deloitte & Touche, 80, 82, 311, 315, 321
DeLonghi S.p.A., 357
Delta, 623
Delta Dental, 225
Demetrakakes, Pan, 622
Deming, W. Edwards, 221
Designs Inc., 242
Desposito, Joseph, 198
Deutsch, Claudia H., 89, 92, 144
Deutschman, Alan, 198
Di Benedetto, C. Anthony, 457
Dial, 435
Digital Equipment Corporation (DEC), 82, 190
Dillard Department Stores, 66, 111, 119, 120, 572, 657
Dilts, Jeffrey C., 549
Dion, Paul A., 279, 281
Direct Selling Association, 91, 133
Discount Tire Company, 377
Discovery Channel, A4
Distribution Research and Educational Foundation, 577
Dolan, Robert J., 513
Dominguez, Luis V., 513, 603, 620
Dominick's, 399
Donath, Bob, 457
Donaton, Scott, 93
Donnelley Marketing Inc., 317, 445–446
Donnelly, Harrison, 660
Donnelly, James H., Jr., 593, 620
Donut Connection Cooperative, 530
Dorin, Patrick C., 279
Douglas, Susan P., 620
Dreyfus & Associates, 478, 604
Drèze, Xavier, 399, 415
Driscoll, Lisa, 375
Drug Emporium Inc., 329, 410
Drug Guild, 532
Duff, Christina, 141, 143, 281
Duhan, Dale F., 416
Duke University Medical Center, 469, 470
Dumaine, Brian, 285

Dun & Bradstreet, 121
Dunkin, Amy, 416
Dunkin' Donuts, 530, 537
Dunn, Homer, 281
DuPont Corporation, 152, 153, 265
Duracell, 435
Durr-Fillauer Medical, 153
Dvorak, John, 39
Dwyer, F. Robert, 39, 532, 549, 550
Dwyer, Paula, 416

Eastman Kodak, 230, 237–238, 334–335, 338, 403, 464
Eaton Corporation, 336
Eckerd, 329
Eckrich, Donald W., 40
Edgett, Scott, 165, 495, 513
Egan, Colin, 165, 495, 513
Ehrlich, Elizabeth, 39
Eisenhart, Tom, 326
Eisenstodt, Gale, 625
Eklund, Christopher S., 373
Eldridge, Earle, 574
Electric Liquid Fillers Inc. (ELF), 499
Electronic Industries Association (EIA), 349
Electronics Representatives Association, 169, 172
Elliott, Stuart, 88, 93, 103
Ellsworth, Jill H., A5
eMall, A3
Emshwiller, John R., 103
English, Wilke D., 90
Enterprise Rent-A-Car, 599–600
EON, A2
Eovaldi, Thomas L., 182, 376
Eppright, David R., 90
Erickson, Greg, 376
Ernst, Ronald L., 71, 523
Etgar, Michael, 548, 549
Evans, Joel R., C6, 38, 140, 141, 181, 234
Everett, Martin, 234, 415, 458, 512, 513
Express, 117
Exter, Thomas G., 88
Exxon, 534
Eyuboglu, Nermin, 582
Ezop, Phyllis, 328

Falvey, Jack, 461
Families and Work Institute, 63
Farris, Paul W., 326, 390
Feder, Barnaby J., 127, 268, 472, 550
Federal Express Corporation, 207–208, 223, 225, 226, 242, 247, 249, 253, 255, 256, 260, 612
Federated Department Stores, 10, 108, 111, 118, 121, 130–131, 266, 320, 572
Feldman, Amy, 140, 517, 552

Field Brothers, 426
Fierman, Jaclyn, 38, 235, 328, 456, 461
Fifth Third Bancorp, 599
Filiatrault, Pierre, 234
Fingerhut Companies, 41
Fiorentini, Walter J., 458
Firnstahl, Timothy W., 235
Fisher, Marshall L., 281
Fisher-Price, 345
Fitzgerald, Mark, 93
Fleming Companies Inc., 70, 152, 153, 154, 587
Fliehman, Deborah G., 472
Florists' Transworld Delivery Association (FTD), 530
F&M, 329
Fodness, Dale, 595, 620
Food Marketing Institute, 127, 313
Footlick, Jerrold K., 88
Forbes, Christine, 181
Ford, I. David, 621
Ford, John, 603, 621
Ford Motor Company, 265, 400, 574, 587
Forest, Stephanie Anderson, 88, 198, 375, 549
47th Street Photo, 350
Fost, Dan, 326
Foust, Dean, 279
Fox, Bruce, 181, 331, 426
Francorp, 541
Frank, Robert, 280
Fraser, Margot, 16
Frazier, Gary L., 280, 513, 558, 560, 582, 603, 609, 621
French, John R. P., 558, 582
Freudenheim, Milt, 40, 373
Friedland, Jonathan, 513
Frito-Lay Inc., 54, 246, 288
Fryer, Bronwyn, 39
Fuji, 614
Fuller, Joseph B., 248, 279, 419
Furger, Roberta, 375

Galen, Michele, 141, 550, 551
Gap, The, Inc., 61–62, 108, 118, 119, 142–143, 264, 354
Garfinckel's, 108
Garry, Michael, 280, 321
Gaski, John F., 582, 583
Gassenheimer, Jule B., 561, 575, 578, 582, 584
Gateway 2000, 26, 27, 42, 190, 194, 195
Gault, Stanley C., 377
Gedajlovic, Eric, 550
Geibel, Jeffrey P., 233, 456
Gemaire Distributors, 442
General Electric (GE), A2, 83, 255, 264, 265, 314, 405, 527, 596, 608
General Medical Corporation, 153
General Mills, 419, 447

General Motors (GM), 4–5, 258, 265, 317, 357, 440, 534, 574, 598
GEnie, 83
Gerber Corporation, 586
Gerlin, Andrea, B4
Getz, Gary A., 514
Giant Food, 120
Gianturco, Michael, 416
Gibbons, Vera B., 513
Gibson, Richard, 235, 330
Gibson Greetings, Inc., 479
Gilbert, James P., 266, 280
Gill, Penny, 88, 278, 326
Gilman, Alan L., 621
Giunipero, Larry C., 280, 281
Gladwell, Malcolm, 81
Glaser, Rashi, 326
Glass, David D., 41, 121, 244–245
Glover, Donald R., 456, 457
Goldman, Arieh, 622
Goldman, Kevin, A5
Gomes, Roger, 236, 281
Goodnow, James D., 602, 614, 620, 622
Goodyear Tire & Rubber Co., 17, 23, 27, 377–378
Gopalakrishna, Srinath, 458
Graham, John L., 374
Grainger, W.W., 154
Graybar Electric, 154
Great Atlantic & Pacific Tea (A&P), 111, 351, 419, 449
Greco, Alan J., 326
Green, Gordon, 88
Greenhouse, Linda, 373
Greising, David, 219, 234, 235
Gresham, Larry G., 583
Grether, E. T., 7, 38
Grocery Manufacturers Association of America, 157, 270, 313, 397
Grossman, Laurie M., 88, 96, 375
Grossman's, 552
Grover, Rajiv, 234
GTE, 176, 320
Guadagni, Peter, 326
Guimaraes, Tom, 90
Gupta, Udayan, 10
Gutfeld, Rose, 89

Haedicke, Jack, 650
Hahn, Mini, 513
Hallmark, 432, 479
Halverson, Richard, 42, 280, 327, 622
Hammacher Schlemmer, A2
Hammond, Janice H., 281
Hammond, Walter R., 422–423
Hampton Inns, 225
Han, Sang-Lin, 234
Hanes, 62, 69
Hanny's, 426
Hansell, Saul, 620

Hansz, J. E., 602, 620
Hapoienu, Spencer L., 88
Hardy, Kenneth G., 182, 234, 427, 431, 434, 439, 456, 457, 458, 509, 513, 514, 549, 550, 569, 582, 583, 584
Harley-Davidson, 223, 265
Harris, Andrew R., 196
Hartmarx, 426, 525
Harvey, Steve, 279, 281
Hasey, Loretta M., 279, 281
Hayes, H. Michael, 622
Hayes, Thomas C., 315
Heck's, 131
Heinz, H. J., 62, 128, 417
Helferich, Omar K., 251
Heller Financial Inc., 10
Henkoff, Ronald, 279, 281, 620
Henri Bendel, 117
Herbig, Paul, 181, 458
Herman Miller Inc., 366
Hertz, 534, 599–600
Heskett, James L., 234, 235
Hewlett-Packard, 225, 265, 350, 452
Hickey-Freeman, 426
Hicks, Jonathan P., 376
Hill, Ned C., 181
Hillenbrand Industries, 223, 265
Hill's, 10
Hilton Hotels, 59
Hirsch, James S., 280, 624
Hirschman, Elizabeth C., 373
Hlavacek, James D., 488
Hoch, Stephen J., 399, 415
Hof, Robert D., 457, 586
Hoffer, George E., 375
Hoffman, Richard C., 537, 550, 551
Hofmeister, Sallie, 415, 416
Hogue, Jack T., 326
Holak, Susan L., 375
Holusha, John, 89, 376
Home Depot, 111, 117, 119, 120, 143–144, 226, 515, 571
Home Shopping Network, A2, 83, 84
HomeBase, 552
Honda, B2, 4, 24, 357
Honeywell Inc., 586
Honomichl, Jack, 326
Hooks-Super X, 329
Hooper, Laurence, 374
Hoover, Carl, 103
Hoover, Gary, 144, 426, 516, 552, 625
Horwitz, Tony, 620, 622
Howard, Bill, 235
Hudson's, 116
Huey, John, 280
Hume, Scott, 103, 326
Hunt, J.B., Transportation Services Inc., 252–257
Hunt, Kenneth A., 572, 583
Hunt, Shelby D., 233, 578, 584

Huntington National Bank, 599
Hurt, Blant, 415
Huth, William L., 90
Hwang, Suein L., 92, 374
HWI, 530
Hyatt hotels, 57

IBM, 43, 83, 92, 186, 190, 191, 195, 217, 265, 353, 354, 403
IGA, 135, 166
IKEA, 143, 601, 608
Illingworth, J. Davis, 375, 513
Illinois Central, 251
Incredible Universe, 525
Independent Grocers Alliance (IGA), 532
Individual Computer Products International Ltd (ICPI), 353, 354
Infobase Marketing, 317
Information Resources Inc. (IRI), 288, 303, 329, 348, 351, 396, 446, 483
InfoScan, 329–330
Ingersoll, Bruce, 81
Ingersoll-Rand, 486
Institute of Management Accountants, 651
Institute of Scrap Recycling Industries, 361
Intel, 357, 440, 585–586
Intelligent Electronics, 453
International Franchising Association, 533, 539, 541
International Paper Company, 365
International Projects Inc., 604
Internet, A1, A2–A3
Invacare Corporation, 25
Isetan Co., Ltd., 607
Isuzu, 24
Ivey, Mark, 198

Jackson, Barbara Bund, 214, 216, 234
Jackson, Donald W., 28, 40, 488, 583
Jackson, Ron, 379
Jacob, Rahul, 89, 234, 235, 472
Jacobs, Jon, 622
Jacques, Philip F., 425, 456
James River Corporation, 319, 432
Janssens, Gerrit K., 326, 327
Jewel Food Stores, A3
Johanson, Jan, 602, 620
Johnson, John R., 182, 373, 436, 456
Johnson, Kirk, 551
Johnson, Philip, 490
Johnson, Simon, 622, 634
Johnson & Johnson, 223, 329, 338, 440, 469, 471, 614
Jones, J. M., Company, 347
Jones, J. Morgan, 343
Jones, Kathryn, 181, 415

Jones, Marty, 434, 457
Jones, Morgan, 373, 374
Jones, Thomas O., 234, 235
Jones New York, 62
Julian, Scott D., 539, 550
Juran, Joseph M., 221, 235
Justis, Robert T., 539, 550

Kale, Sudhir H., 582
Kamins, Michael A., 374
Kansas City Southern, 251
Karan, Donna, 62, 69
Karmarkar, Uday, 281
Katel, Peter, 235
Katz, Karen L., 89
Kaufmann, Patrick J., 327, 550
Kawasaki, 265
Kay-Bee, 116
Kayser-Roth, 476
Kearney, A. T., Inc., 271
Keets, Heather, 88
Keith, Janet E., 40
Keitt, John K., Jr., 621, 622
Keizer, Gregg, 93
Kelley, Bill, 88, 89
Kelley, Scott W., 561, 575, 578, 584
Kelly, Kenneth, 347, 374
Keough, Jack, 39, 234, 428
Kerin, Roger A., 428, 456
KG Retail Stores, 242
Khermouch, Gerry, 457
Kichen, Steve, 189, 198
Kindel, Sharen, 103
King, Louise, C3, C6, 458
Kinney, 116
Kirk, Don, 625
Kirkpatrick, David, A5
Kistner, Leonard J., 457
Klein, Calvin, 62
Klein, Saul, 513, 603, 609, 621
Kleinfeld, N. R., 141
Klenier, Art, 89
KLH, 190
Kmart, 54, 61, 80, 111, 112, 116, 117, 118, 268, 284, 313, 329, 330–331, 406, 410, 556, 638
Knorr, Robert O., 280, 281
Kodak, see Eastman Kodak
Koepfler, Edward R., 621
Komatsu, 459
Konopa, Leonard J., 488
Konrad, Walecia, 89, 103
Konsynski, Benn R., 327
Kopp, Steven W., 374
Kordupleski, Raymond E., 230, 236
Koselka, Rita, C6, 278, 279, 280, 315
Kosenko, Rustan, 614, 622
Kotler, Philip, 522, 549, 660
Koudis International Inc., 604
Kraft General Foods, 69, 469, 478
Krampf, Robert F., 488
Krapfel, Robert E., Jr., 236
Krasnick, Larry, 458

Kratz, Steve, 434, 457
Kreepy Krauly, 409
Krizia, 426
Kroc, Ray, 520–521
Kroger Company, 60, 71, 95, 111, 400, 599
Kroy Incorporated, 565
Kruglanski, Arie W., 558, 582
Kumar, Nirmalya, 640, 642, 660
Kuppenheimer's, 426
Kurt Associates, 657
Kyj, Myroslaw J., 235

LaLonde, Bernard J., C6, 40
Lamb, Charles W., Jr., 90, 328
Lambert, Douglas M., 568, 583, 647, 660
Lambkin, Mary, 375
Lancaster, Hal, 198
Land O'Lakes, 166
Lands' End, A2, A4, 188
Lane Bryant, 117
Lanvin, Len, 516
Larson, Blaire M., 89
Larson, Jan, 88
Larson, Richard C., 89
Laskey, Henry A., 458
Laskin, Richard L., 234
Lauren, Ralph, 62, 70, 130, 524
Lechmere, 131
Lee, Louise, 415
Lefton, Terry, 549
L'eggs, 23–24, 27, 69, 365, 476
Leo Burnett USA, 440
Lerner's, 117
Lever Brothers, 265
Levi Strauss, 242–243, 310–311, 313, 564, 657
Levin, Doron P., 38, 39
Levin, Gary, 328
Levine, Joshua, 88
Levitt, Theodore, 339, 373
Levy, Clifford J., 327
Levy, Michael, 428, 456
Lewis, M. Christine, 568, 583
Lewis, Peter H., A5, 198, 326, 374
Lexus, 360
Liesse, Julie, 514
Lifetime Automotive Products, 493
Lika, 525
Lilien, Gary L., 488
Limited Stores, 117
Limited, The, 68, 111, 116, 117, 118, 119, 120, 142
Limited Too, 117
Linden, Fabian, 89
Lipin, Steven, 620
Little, Arthur D., 216–217, 596
Little, John, 458
Little, John D.C., 326
Loctite, 436
Lodge, George C., 376
Lohr, Steve, 198
Lohtia, Ritu, 621

Losee, Stephanie, 279, 458
Lotus, 195
Loveman, Gary W., 234, 235, 622, 634
Lowe, Larry, 416
Lowe's, 111, 120
Lubove, Seth, 141, 378
Lucas, George H., Jr., 583
Lucky Stores, 319
Lundin, Jean, 279
Lusch, Robert F., 151, 181, 578, 582, 584

MacAndrews & Forbes, 284
McCarthy, Michael J., 103
McCartney, Scott, 281, 416, 513, 583
McCrohan, Kevin F., 416
McCuistion, Tommy J., 488
McDermott, Mike, 182
McDonald's, 61, 95, 111, 127, 336, 520–521, 533, 534, 535, 536, 539, 540, 544, 605, 610
McDowell, Edwin, 624
McGinn, Daniel, 620
McGrath, Allan, 234
Machalaba, Daniel, 279, 280
Mack, Toni, 198
Mackay, Jane M., 90, 328
McKesson, 152, 532–533
McKillip, Peter, 625
McLaughlin, Edward W., 374
McNeil, 223
McQuiston, John T., 375
McWilliams, Gary, 198, 373, 376
Macy's, R. H., 10, 68, 108, 118, 121, 369, 400
Madhavan, Ravindranath, 234
Magee, John F., 236, 280
Magnavox, 176, 529, 608
Magnet, Myron, 378
Magnin, I., 108
Magrath, Allan J., 39, 182, 427, 431, 439, 456, 509, 513, 514, 549, 550, 569, 582, 583, 584
Maier, E. P., 513
Mallen, Bruce, 583
Mallory, 400
Mallory, Maria, 88, 103
Management Horizons, 68, 115
Manning, Kenneth H., 650, 651, 662
Manufacturers' Agents National Association (MANA), 157, 158, 168, 172
Marcial, Gene G., 88
Mark, Jeremy, 620
Marken, G. A., 457
Markoff, John, 39, 43
Markowitz, Arthur, 279
Marks and Spencer, 601
Marn, Michael V., 407
Mars, 570
Marsh, Barbara, A5

Marshall, Jonathan, 279
Marshall, Michael, 503
Marshall Field's, A4, 116, 354
Marshalls, 116, 117
Martin, Douglas, 89
Martin, Justin, 625
Martin Supply, 207, 208
Mary Kay Corporation, 91
Mason, Charlotte H., 343, 373, 374
MasterCard, 590
Masters, James L., C6
Mathews, Jay, 235
Mathews, Ryan, 281, 650, 660
Matrix, 516
Matsushita, 608
Matthyssens, Paul, 281, 583
Maxwell House, 614
May Department Stores, 111, 316
Maybelline, 54
Maynard, Micheline, 574
Mazda, 24
MBNA America, 224–225, 227
MCI Communications Company, A3, 207
Mead, 163
Mead Merchandising, 97
Medco Containment Services, 26
Meeks, Fleming, 328
Meier, Barry, 375
Melcher, Richard A., 181
Melville, 111, 116, 117
Memezes, Melvyn A. J., 513
Mentzer, John T., 236, 281
Mercantile Stores Company, 271
Mercedes Benz, 400, 440
Merck, 26, 329
Meridian Bancorp, 599
Merisel, 152
Merry-Go-Round, 319
Mervyn's, 68, 116, 143
Meyers Research Center, 270
MGM Grand Hotel, 127
Michelin, 377
Michman, Ronald D., 39, 181
Microsoft, A2, A3, 195
Midas Muffler, 534
Milbank, Dana, 364, 375, 376, 378, 620
Miller, Annetta, 140, 625
Miller, Cyndee, A5, 235, 328
Miller, Jacqueline, 90
Miller, Karen Lowry, 39
Miller, Krystal, B4, 39, 376
Miller, Lisa, 624
Miller, Michael W., 326
Miller, Stephen C., A4
Millstone Coffee, 490
Milsap, Cynthia R., 457
Minnesota Mining and Manufacturing (3M), 217–218, 362–363, 556
Miracle, Gordon E., 487, 488, 492, 513
Mister Donut, 530

Mitchell, Russell, 143
Mitsubishi, 24, 27, 564, 614
Mitsui, 614
MNC Financial, 227
Mobil, 127
Moncrief, William C., III, 90, 328
Montgomery, Lee, 144
Moore, James R., 40
Moran, Ursula, 513, 583
Morehead, Jere W., 182
Morgan, James I., 263
Morgan, James P., 181
Morgan, Jim, 181
Moriarty, Rowland T., 513, 583
Morris, Michael H., 215, 228, 327, 375
Morris, Robert, Associates, 149, 390, 391
Moska, Brian S., 458
Motorola, 223
Moukheiber, Zina, 141, 143
Murray, Matt, 598
Musicland Stores, 567
Myer, Randy, 582
Myerson, Allen R., 184

Nal, Amal Kumar, 280
Nannery, Matt, 583
Narisetti, Raju, 378, 458
Narus, James A., 39, 90, 233, 234, 583
Nash Finch, 70
National American Wholesale Growers Association, 313
National Assocation of Wholesalers, 577
National Association of Export Companies, 604
National Association of Hosiery Manufacturers, 476
National Association of Purchasing Management, 249
National Association of Realtors (NAR), 57
National Association of Retail Grocers of the United States, 313
National Association of Wholesaler-Distributors (NAW), 148, 152, 153, 433, 441
National Automobile Dealers Association, 574
National Council of Physical Distribution Management, 32
National Dealer Advisory Council, 515
National Food Brokers Association, 157, 169, 170–171, 313, 417
National Frozen Pizza Institute, 81
National Retail Federation, 80, 82, 390
National Semiconductor, 249

National Solid Wastes Management Association, 362
Nature Company, 83
Naumann, Earl, 235
Nautica, 23
Navistar, 316
Neal, Mollie, 233
NEC, 43, 197
Nestlé, 345, 419
Neuman, John L., 280, 281
Nevin, John R., 416, 578, 584
Newhall, Julie S., 442, 457
Newmark & Lewis, 350
News Corporation, A2
Newspaper Advertising Bureau, 441, 444
Newspaper Co-op Network (NACON), 444
Newspaper Co-op Network (NCN), 442
Nicholas, Nick L., 376, 551
Nicholls, J. A. F., 458
Nickolaus, Nicholas, 182, 328, 374, 514
Nielsen, A. C., 303, 348, 483
Nike, 70
Nino Ceruti, 426
Nissan, 4, 24
Nordstrom, 83, 119, 120, 202
Norfolk Southern, 251
Northgate Computer Systems, 195
Northwest Airlines, 623
Norton, Rob, 621, 643
Novak, Viveca, 416
Novich, Neil S., 236
Novick, Harold J., 182
Nulty, Peter, 375, 378

Obermeyer, Walter R., 281
O'Boyle, Thomas F., 280, 281
O'Brian, Bridget, 620, 624
O'Brien, Timothy L., 374
O'Callaghan, Ramon, 327
Ocean Spray, 166, 439
O'Connor, James, 419
Office Depot, 150, 575
OfficeMax, 116, 150, 575
Oh, Sejo, 549
O'Hara, Bradley S., 181, 458
Olver, James M., 326
Olympus, 400
1–800 Flowers, A1, A4
O'Neal, Charles, 280, 281
Opinion Research Corporation, 216
OPW Fueling Components, 378–379
O'Reilly, Brian, 40
Ortega, Bob, 621
Ortmeyer, Gwen, 657, 660
Osco, 329, 479
OshKosh B'Gosh Inc., 353–354
OSI Industries, 520
Oster, Patrick, 198

OTR Express, Inc., 282–283
Overnite Transportation, 252
Owens & Minor Inc., 153, 472

Packard Bell, 190, 191, 219, 575
Palamountain, Joseph C., 568, 583
Paley, Norton, 549
Pall Corporation, 319, 507
Palmer, Adrian, 593, 620
Palmeri, Christopher, 39, 88, 373
Palumbo, Fred, 458
Panczak, William, 457, 458
Parasuraman, A., 206, 217, 220–221, 234, 235, 660
Parfums Givenchy U.S.A., 400, 402, 410
Parisian, 108
Park, C. Whan, 425, 456
Parvatiyar, Atul, 233
Patch, Ken, 415
Patterson, Gregory A., 415, 426
Pay'n Save, 528
PC Flowers, 92–93
Peapod, A3
Pearl, Daniel, 280
Penhaligon's, 117
Penney, J. C., A2, A4, B3, 68, 83, 111, 120, 143, 353, 426, 600, 657
Pennzoil, 598
PepsiCo, 95, 96, 97, 98, 100, 101, 245–247, 288, 538–539, 594
Pereira, Joseph, 281, 416
Perlmutter, Howard V., 620
Perrien, Jean, 234
Perrier, 357
Peter, J. Paul, 235
Pfeiffer, Eckhard, 585
Phelps Tool & Die Company, 268
Philip Morris, 317, 345, 435
Phillips, Lynn W., 549
Phillips-Van Heusen, 524
Piirto, Rebecca, 68
Ping, Robert, 39
Pitegoff, Barry E., 595, 620
Pizza Hut, 81
Pohanka, Jack, 461
Point-of-Purchase Advertising Institute (POPAI), 114, 116
Poirer, Mark, 92
Polk, R. L., 317
Poltrack, David F., 326
Pondy, Louis R., 568, 583
Poole, Claire, 198
Popeye's, 536
Popper, Edward T., 347
Porter, Michael E., 39, 217–220, 235, 562–563, 582
Powell, Jerry, 375
Power, Christopher, 89
Powers, Thomas L., 496, 513
Preble, John F., 537, 550
Premark International, 48
Premier Health Alliance, 468

Premier Industrial Corporation, 146
Price, Retha A., 549
Price/Costco Inc., A2, 62, 83, 111, 136, 150, 190, 410, 418
Primo, 543
Prior, Teri Lammers, 490
Private Label Manufacturers Association, 351
Pro, 532
Procter & Gamble (P&G), 54, 175, 225, 247, 265, 268, 345, 363, 397, 398, 400, 418–419, 440, 587, 657
Prodigy, A1, A2, 83, 92–93
Promus, 225
Protzman, Ferdinand, 376
Prudential, B2–B3
Pruitt, Stephen W., 375
Public Service Electric and Gas Company (PSE&G), 238–239
Publix Super Markets, 111, 120
Purk, Mary E., 399, 415

Quaker Oats, 54
Quaker State, 598
Quelch, John A., 347, 360, 415, 457
Quintanilla, Carl, 235
QVC, 83, 84

Racz, Gregory N., 375
Radio Shack, 525
Raman, Ananth, 281
Ramirez, Anthony, 39, 376, 512
Ramos, Steven, 93
Ramsdale, Phil, 279, 281
Rangan, V. Kasturi, 236, 416, 513, 514, 550
Rankin, Ken, 376
Rao, Vithala R., 374
Rapoport, Carla, 625
Rathz, Don, 622
Rauch, Richard A., 141
Raven, Bertram H., 558, 582
Rawlinson, Richard, 419
Rayport, Jeffrey F., 376
Raytheon, 208, 211
RCA, 176, 556, 608
RE/MAX, 536
Rebello, Kathy, 198
Reckitt & Coleman, 440
Recycling Internation, 363
Reda, Susan, A4, 281
Redken, 516
Reebok, 152, 409
Regan, James M., 136
Rehder, Robert R., 38
Reicheld, Frederick F., 235
Reichlin, Igor, 198
Reid, Brad, 182, 376, 551
Reier, Sharon, 374
Reilly, Patrick M., 374, 549
Reilly, Robert J., 375
Reiten, E. D., 660, 663

Reitman, Valarie, 376, 419
Reve, Torger, 582
Reynolds, R. J., 352, 435
Rheem Air Conditioning and Heating Products, 442
Ricard, Line, 234
Rice, Faye, 366, 620
Richards, Bill, 582
Riche, Martha Farnsworth, 88, 89
Rifkin, Glenn, 90, 278
Rigdon, Joan E., 373
Ringer, Richard, 472
Rite Aid, 329, 419
Ritz-Carlton Hotel Company, 225
RJR Nabisco, 54, 417
Roadway Express, 252
Robinson, John P., 89
Rohwedder, Cacilie, 620, 622
Rosado, Lourdes, 625
Rose, Frank, 235
Rosenbloom, Bert, 40, 583
Rosenfeld, Donald R., 280
Rosenfield, Donald B., 236, 280
Roslow, Sydney, 458
Ross, Robert H., 582
Rossiello, Robert L., 407
Rosson, Philip J., 621
Roth, Martin S., 425, 456
Roth, Victor J., 513, 603, 609, 621
Rudnitsky, Howard, 550
Ruekert, Robert W., 578, 584
Rust, Roland T., 230, 236
Rust-Oleum, 426, 436
Ryans, Adrian B., 416
Ryder Dedicated Logistics, 252, 253

Safeway Stores, A3, 111, 118, 419
Saks Fifth Avenue, 10, 354
Salmon, Walter J., 209, 415, 549
Salpukas, Agis, 279, 280, 598
Salsa's Gourmet Mexican Restaurant, 543
Sam's Wholesale Club, 62, 136, 150, 192
Sandberg, Jared, A5
Sansolo, Michael, 42, 415
Santa Fe Pacific Corporation, 251, 257
Sanwa, 614
Saporito, Bill, 90, 140, 141, 374, 419, 570
Sara Lee Corporation, 69, 476
Sasser, W. Earl, Jr., 234, 235
Satisfaction Guaranteed Eateries, 226
Saturn, 4–5, 267–268, 461
Sautter, Elise Truly, 595, 620
Scammon, Debra L., 416
Scherreik, Susan, 280, 472
Schick, 614
Schifrin, Matthew, 415, 416, 418, 419
Schiller, Zachary, 279, 377, 378, 419

Schlender, Brenton R., 327
Schlesinger, Leonard A., 234, 235
Schlossberg, Howard, 326, 327
Schneider National Carriers Inc., 252
Schonberger, Richard J., 266, 280
Schreiber, Paul, 103
Schuchman, Abe, 660
Schul, Patrick L., 583
Schulz, David P., 40, 140, 141, 236, 279, 280, 281
Schulz, Don E., 456
Schwadel, Francine, 327
Schwader, Francine, 90
Schwartz, Evan, 622
Schwinn, 176, 350, 410
Scott, Lisa, 472
Scott, O. M., 5, 528–529
Scriver, 70
Sealy's, 534
Sears, Roebuck & Co., A2, 17, 41, 42, 54, 61, 68, 81, 83, 92, 109, 111, 119, 143, 190, 254–255, 351, 353, 357, 377, 410, 515, 524, 552, 556
Segmented Marketing Services Inc. (SMSI), 54

Seifert, Bruce, 603, 621
Seiko, 400
Seiyu Ltd., The, 607
Sellers, Patricia, 89, 90, 141, 234, 236, 279, 415, 457, 472
Selz, Michael, 42, 513, 604
Semeco-Okmess, 613
Sentry, 532
Serivner, 153
Service Merchandise, A2, 120, 121
Serwer, Andrew E., 548, 550, 551, 621
7-Eleven, 535, 536
Sfilogoj, Eric, 103
Shababb, George, 326
Shah, Reshma H., 234
Shaham, Aviv, 449, 458
Shannon, Patrick, 235
Shao, Maria, 280
Shapiro, Benson P., 236, 424, 427, 439, 457
Shapiro, Eben, 42, 103, 140, 415, 419
Sharma, Arun, 513, 603, 620
Sharper Image, A2, 16, 83
Shaw, Robert, 327, 328
Shaw's Supermarkets, 268, 321
Shea, Linda J., 622
Sheffet, Mary Jane, 374, 416
Sheffi, Yosef, 279
Sherwin-Williams, 5, 14, 67, 486, 524, 552
Sheth, Jagdish N., 205, 233
Shipley, David, 165, 396, 495, 513, 583
Shooshtari, Nader H., 583

Shopper Vision, A2
ShopRite, 166, 184, 185, 530
Shycon, Harvey N., 234
Siegler, Frank, 503
Sikora, Ed, 416
Siler, Julia Flynn, 375
Silverman, Edward R., A4, A5, 141
Simmons Market Research Bureau, 63, 448
Simplot, J.R., Company, 420
Simpson Timber Company, 662–663
Singer Sewing Machine Company, 533
Siwolop, Sana, 141
Skinner, Steven J., 561, 575, 578, 584
Smart, Tim, 373
Smart & Final, 167
Smith, N. Craig, 360
Smith Corona, 450
Smith's Food and Drug Centers, 55
Snap-On Incorporated, 515–516, 536
Snapple Natural Beverage, 94
Snyder, Glenn, 185, 280, 458
Sony, A4
Sookdeo, Ricardo, 621
Southern Pacific, 251
Southland Corporation, 118, 536
Spain, Patrick J., 103, 144, 426, 516, 552, 625
Spartan Stores, 362
Spekman, Robert E., 209, 233, 280
Spencer, Theodore, 415
Spethmann, Betsy, 457
Spiegel, A4, 83
Spitzer, Daniel M., Jr., 244
Sports Authority, The, 116, 143
Spriggs, Mark T., 416, 640, 641, 660
SRI International, 64
Sroge, Maxwell, 60, 187
Stack, Bill, 327
Stampfl, Ronald W., 373
Stanley, 515
Staples, 150
State Farm Insurance, 212, 595–596
Stationers Distributing Company, 150, 153
Steinmetz, Greg, 279
Steptoe, Mary Lou, 416
Sterling, Jay U., 647, 660
Stern, Aimee L., 207, 234, 347
Stern, Gabriella, 280
Stern, Louis W., 182, 376, 513, 514, 582, 640, 642, 660
Stern, William M., 479
Stevens, J. P., 315
Stevenson, Richard W., 621, 622
Stone, Merlin, 327, 328
Stone Container Corporation, 363
Stop & Shop, 119, 120, 121
Strauss, Levi, 142

Strom, Stephanie, 89, 90, 141, 143, 278, 279, 328, 415, 416, 528
Structure, 117
Stuart Medical Inc., 153, 471–472
Sturdivant, Frederick D., 513, 514
Subaru, 24
Sukdial, Ajay, 376
Sumitomo, 614
Summers, John O., 558, 560, 582
Sun-Maid, 166
Sun Microsystems, 260
Supermarkets General, 111
SuperValu Corporation, 70, 71, 153, 154, 315, 347, 419, 524, 532
Supply, G.E., 154
Suris, Oscar, 375
Sviokla, John J., 236
Swan Technologies, 190
Swarovski America Ltd., 410
Swenson, Michael J., 181
Sylvania, 176, 410

Taco Bell, 593–594
Tandy Corporation, 525
Tang, Y. Edwin, 375
Tannenbaum, Jeffrey A., 103, 141, 373, 549, 550, 551, 554
Tanzer, Andrew, 374
Tapellini, Donna, 198
Tappan, 531
Target, 116, 118, 143, 329, 638
Taube, Paul M., 90
Tauscher, William, 42
Taylor, Alex, III, 378
Taylor, Steven A., 235
Taylor, Thayer C., 90, 326
Teal, Thomas, 235
Teitelbaum, Richard S., 278
Templin, Neal, 373, 375, 587
Texas Instruments, 483
Thayer, Warren, 328, 331
This End Up, 116
Thom McAn, 116, 117
Thomas, S. B., 542
Thomas Group, 284
Thompson, J. Walter, 57
3M, see Minnesota Mining and Manufacturing
Thrifty, 329
Timberland Company, 272
Time Warner, A2, A4, 83
Timex, 23–24, 69
Titus, F.D., Inc., 153
Topco, 530, 531
Touby, Laurel, 550, 551
Tower, C. Burk, 416
Tower Records, A4
Toy, Stewart, 375
Toyota, 4, 24, 253, 267, 498–499
Toys "R" Us, 54, 108, 111, 117, 119, 120, 130, 369, 566, 600, 614, 624–625
Trachtenberg, Jeffrey A., 92, 582

Treacy, Michael, 549
Treece, James B., 39, 88, 89
TRI-CON, 265
Triplett, Tim, 281, 375, 458
Tropicana, 417
True Value, 530
Trustworthy, 532
TRW, 317
Tsiantar, Dody, 140
Tully, Shawn, 181, 198, 549, 582
Tupperware, 48–49, 58
Twin County, 530
2Market, A4
Tynan, Daniel, 375

Uchitelle, Louis, 90
Uniform Code Council, 310
Unilever, 419, 614
Union Carbide, 153
Union Pacific/Chicago, 251
Unisys, 190
United Airlines, 261, 623
United Parcel Service (UPS), 206–207, 252, 255, 256, 612
United Services Automobile Association (USAA), 224
U.S. Postal Service, 255
U.S. West, 83
United Stationers Inc., 153
Universal Code Council, 313
University Brands, 226
University of Michigan, 73, 74
Urban, David J., 620
Ursic, M. L., 620
U.S. West, A2
USAA, 226
USAir, 623

Vahlne, Jan-Erik, 602, 620
Vaile, Roland S., 7, 38
Valu-Rite, 532–533
Value Rent-A-Car, 24
Van den Bulte, Christophe, 281, 583
Van Heusen, 62
Vanstar, 13
Varian Associates Inc., 219
Vavra, Terry G., 327, 328
Vehlhaber, Don R., 660
Verhage, Bronislaw J., 620
VF Corporation, 657
Victoria's Secret, 117
Visa, 590
Vogel, Mark, 458
Volkswagen, 73–74
Voluntary Hospitals of America, 468
Voluntary Interindustry Communications Standards (VICS) Committee, 269
Volvo, A2
Vons, 120
Vulcan, 515
VWR, 152

Wadman, Meredith K., 373
Wakefern, 70, 166, 184–185, 530, 531
Waldenbooks, 116
Waldrop, Judith, 89
Walgreens, 111, 135, 329, 479, 532
Walker, Bruce J., 28, 40, 541, 551, 583
Walker, E. Lee, 186–187
Wallach Brothers, 426
Wal-Mart Stores Inc., B3, 41–42, 54–55, 61, 82, 108, 109, 111, 117, 118, 119, 120, 121, 127, 130, 143, 148, 150, 190, 195, 244–245, 260–261, 265, 268, 271, 284, 312, 315, 316, 329, 377, 382–383, 386, 409, 410, 418, 556, 566, 587, 607, 612, 638, 657
Ward, Bill, 282
Warehousing Education and Research Council, 638
Warner Brothers, A2
Warner, Fara, 457
Warner-Lambert, 440
Waste Management of America, Inc., 469
Wax, Alan J., 184
Weber, Joseph A., 181, 279
Webster, Frederick E., 152, 181, 182
Webster, John, 428, 456
Weigand, Robert E., 416, 549, 550, 551
Weinstein, Steve, 141, 181, 182, 185, 281, 347, 374, 376, 415, 418, 419, 457, 458, 549, 550, 584

Weisman, Katherine, 39
Weiss, Allen M., 39
Weitz, Barton, 210, 234
Welch's, 166
Weldon Tool Company, 336
Welles, Edward O., 283
Welniak, Edward, 88
Wendy's, 536, 596
Werner Enterprises, 252
Werner, Ray O., 182, 551
WESCO, 154
Western Auto, 532
Wetterau, 152, 153
Weyerhaeuser, 225
Wheatley, Malcolm, 281
Whirlpool, 336, 351
Whittemore, Meg, 550, 554
Wiatr, Dar, 652
Wiegner, Kathleen K., 43
Wiener, Joshua L., 376
Wiersema, Fred, 549
Wiesendanger, Betsy, 222, 235, 374, 457
Wilcox, Robert D., 458
Wilensky, Dawn, 351, 374
Williams, Jerome D., 458
Williams, Teresa D., 141
Williamson, Kenneth C., 244
Williamson, N. J., 603, 621
Williamson, Oliver E., 608, 621
Williams-Sonoma, 83, 320
Willinger, Stephen D., B4
Wilson, David T., 234
Wilson, Elizabeth J., 374
Wilson, Marianne, 88
Wind, Yoram, 620
Winn-Dixie Stores, A2, 111, 119, 120

Winslow, Ron, 472
Winsted, Kathryn Frazer, 572, 583
Witte, Michael B., 554
Wold, Marjorie, 182
Woodruff, David, 38, 366, 461
Woods, Wilton, 280
Woodside, Arch G., 374
Woolworth, 111, 116
WorkGroup Technologies, 187
World Wide Web, A1, A2, A3–A4
Wortzel, Lawrence H., 562, 582
Wrangler, 528

Xerox, 223, 226, 265, 478

Yoder, Stephen Kreider, 374, 375
Younkers, 572

Zahorik, Anthony J., 230, 236
Zayre, 131
Zbar, Jeffrey D., 328
Zeithaml, Valarie A., 217, 220–221, 234, 235
Zellner, Wendy, 141, 374, 550, 551
Zenith, 176, 368
Zimmerman, Denise, 327
Zinn, Laura, 10, 88, 89, 140, 141, 280
Zinszer, P. H., 40
Zipkin, Paul H., 280, 281
Zizzo, Deborah, 151, 181
Zoltners, Andis A., 514
Zweig, Jason, 374

Subject Index

ABC analysis, 505–506
ABC inventory analysis, 273–274
ABC, see Activity-based costing
Accounting data, secondary data from, 295–296, 297
Account-specific advertising, 440
Acculturation Influence Groups (AIG), 53
Accumulation, 11
Accurate response, 272
Activity-based costing (ABC), 650–651, 661–662
ACV, see All commodity volume
Adaptive pricing, 407–408
Additional discounts, 408
Additional markups, 408
Adjustment, 487
Administered marketing systems, 525–529
Administrative coordination, 537
Administrative efficiency, 538
Advertising
   account-specific, 440
   cooperative, 202, 426, 441–444, 574
   dealer listing promotions and, 430
   legal issues on, 79–80
   pull-oriented promotion and, 426, 439, 440–444
   push-oriented promotion and, 426, 427, 428, 430
Affinities, 113
African Americans, 53–54
Age distribution, 55
Agents, 147, 148, 160, 161, 162, 167–169, 174
Agents and brokers, 147, 148, 160, 161, 162, 167–169, 596
Air freight, 250, 251, 254
Airline Deregulation Act, 76
All commodity volume (ACV), 303–304, 483
Allocation, 11
Allowable conflict, 157
Always-a-share customers, 213, 214
Ambassador role, 430, 431
Analysis, 310
Antitrust legislation, 75, 76
Area development franchising, 536
Asian Americans, 53
Aspinwall's characteristics of goods and parallel systems theory, 487
Assets to sales ratio, 645, 646
Asset turnover, 119
Associations, see Trade associations
Assorting, 11

Assurance, 221
Availability, 228
Availability rule, 412

Baby boomers, 55
Backhauling, 356
Backorder reports, 298
Backward vertical integration, 70, 71, 486, 524
Bail advertising, 79, 80
Balance sheets, 296, 297
Banking services, 598–599
Bar code scanners, 80, 310–312
Behavioral approach, to channel management, 33–34
Benchmarking, 221–222
Bill of lading, 611
Blurring of gender roles, 63
Bonded warehouse, 260
Brand(s)
   follower, 344
   national, 350, 369
   pioneer, 344
   private label, 350–353, 369, 531, 564–565, 566
   selling against the, 353, 403–404, 566
Breaking bulk, 11
Bribery, international channels and, 615
Brokers, 147, 148, 160, 161, 162, 167–169, 174
Bucklin's system of service outputs, 13–14
Budgets, 295, 296
Business Electronics Corp. v. Sharp Electronics Corp., 408, 409
Business format franchising, 123, 534–535
Buyback allowance, 405
Buying allowance, 405
Buying clubs (membership clubs), 62, 128
Buying philosophy, 135

CAO, see Computer-aided ordering
Captive distributors, 163
Careers, in channel management, C1–C6, 33
Car rental services, 599–600
Case study, solving, 44–45
Cash-and-carry wholesalers, 162, 167
Cash discounts, 174
Catalog selling, 444–445
Category killer, 130, 566
CD-ROM disks, A4
Cellar-Kefauver Act, 76
Census, 305
Census of Population, 52, 59, 298, 300

Census of Retail Trade, 298, 300
Census of Service Industries, 298, 300
Census of Wholesale Trade, 294, 298, 300
Centralization, of retail buying organizations, 133–134, 566
Certificate of origin, 611
Chain-markup pricing, 391–393
Chain retailers, 122, 123
Change agents, 342
Channel adaptability, 509
Channel assessment and control, 636–663. *See also* Distribution cost analysis; Financial performance measures
   channel audit for, 651–653, 654–656, 662–663
   channel performance and, 639–642
   channel productivity improvement and, 653, 656–657
Channel audit, 651–653, 654–656, 662–663
Channel captain, 563. *See also* Channel dominance
Channel checklist, 498, 501, 502–503
Channel competition, 66–72
   horizontal, 66, 67, 485
   intertype, 64, 66, 67, 68–70, 485–486
   vertical, 66, 67, 70–71, 486
   vertical marketing system, 66, 67, 71–72
Channel conflict, 568–572, 585–586
   causes of, 569–572
   channel efficiency and, 572
   management and resolution of, 576–577
Channel cooperation, 573–575, 586–587
Channel costs, 31–32
Channel dependency, 558
Channel design and selection, 475–496, 507–517. *See also* Channel length requirements
   availability of resellers and, 497–498
   channel objectives and, 478–480
   channel structures, 8, 14–15, 17
   channel tasks allocated to channel members and, 493–496
   channel width and, 480, 483–485

SUBJECT INDEX

Channel design and selection, *Continued*
  cost of different channel arrangements and, 503–504
  evaluating resellers and, 498–507
  intermediary requirements and, 480, 485–486
  revising, 507–509
  sales affected by, 504–506
  selection, 496–507, 508
Channel dominance, 562–567
  control over channel of distribution and, 567
  manufacturers and, 563–564, 567
  retailers and, 565–567
  wholesalers and, 564–565
Channel environment, 47–93. *See also* Channel competition; Consumer demographics; Consumer life-styles; Economy; Legal issues; Technological environment
  contingency plans for, 50, 51
  marketing research monitoring, 50
  scenarios of, 49–50
Channel flows, 6, 7
Channel functions, 10–14
Channel information system reports, 310, 317–322
  computer-aided ordering reports, 321–322
  current and prospective customer lists, 319–320
  exception reports, 310, 318
  graphics in, 310, 318
  inventory management system reports, 320
  markdown reports, 319
  sales reports, 318–319
Channel information systems, 309–317, 329–331. *See also* Channel information system reports; Marketing information systems
  database marketing in, 316–317
  electronic data interchange in, 291, 312–316
  scanning-based data in, 310–312
  structure, 309
  types of, 309
Channel leaders, 526–527. *See also* Channel power
Channel length, 14
  international marketing and, 608–609
Channel length requirements, 480, 481–483, 487–493
  intermediary factors and, 488, 491
  long channel, 482–483
  manufacturer factors and, 488, 491

market factors and, 488, 489
product factors and, 488, 489–491
short channel, 481–482
theories relating to, 487–488
Channel management
  approaches to study of, 33–34
  as competitive advantage, 21–27
  definition, 21
  importance of in economy, 29, 31–33
  relationship of to other elements in marketing strategy, 27–29, 30
Channel members
  broad network of, 22, 24
  customer service provided by, 22, 25
  technology used by, 21, 24–25
Channel objectives, 478–480
Channel organization, 27–29. *See also* Channel design and selection
Channel overlap, 337, 338
Channel partnerships, 528, 653, 656, 657
Channel performance
  assessing, 639–642
  channel power and, 568
Channel power, 19, 556–562. *See also* Channel dominance
  channel performance and, 568
  coercive power, 558–559, 561
  distributor power, 562
  information power, 526, 527, 560, 561
  legitmate power, 526, 527, 560, 561
  manufacturer power, 556–557, 563–564
  noncoercive power, 559–560, 561
  persuasion power, 526, 527, 560, 561
  referrent power, 526, 527, 559, 561
  reward power, 526, 527, 559, 561
  supplier power, 561
  wholesaler power, 564–565
Channel productivity, improving, 653, 656–657
Channel profits, 31
Channel relationships, 17–21
  divided loyalty, 17–19
  high switching costs, 20–21
  long-term, 19–20, 26
  selling to and selling through intermediaries, 19
Channel satisfaction, 578
Channel selection, 496–507, 508. *See also* Channel design and selection
Channels manager, 28–29
Channel specialization, 14

Channel structures, 8, 14–15, 17. *See also* Channel design and selection
Channel tasks, 493–496
Channel-wide committees, 577
Channel width, 14
  international marketing and, 609–610
Channel width requirements, 480, 483–485
Chargebacks, 447
Churn rate, A3
Clayton Act, 76, 542
Closed-loop cycle, 363
Coding, 307
Coercive power, 526, 527, 558–559, 561
Coincident indicators, 72
Collection period, 645, 646
Combination stores, 128
Commercial research firms, 302–305
Commission agents, 603
Commission (factor) merchants, 147, 148, 162, 163, 168
Communication difficulties, 572
Communications protocols, 314
Company-based research reports, 296, 297
Comparable waste, 361
Competition-oriented pricing, 386, 393–394
Competition, *see* Channel competition
Competitive advantage
  channel management as, 21–27
  value chain analysis and, 217–220
Competitive bidding, 393–394
Completion rate, 357–360
Component life-styles, 63–64
Comprehensive analysis, channel selection and, 498, 501, 503–506, 507
Computer-aided ordering (CAO), 321–322
Computer-based sales support systems, 82
Computers, *see* Technological environment
Conciliation, 577
Conclusive research, 292–293
Conditions for cooperative advertising, 441
Conflict frequency, 569
Conflict importance, 569
Conflict management and resolution, 576–577. *See also* Channel conflict
Conglomerate merchant (conglomerchant), 116–117
Constrained decision making, 72
  franchisee and, 540–541
  in vertical marketing systems, 523

Consumer confidence surveys, 73, 74
Consumer contact, 13
Consumer demographics, 52–58
  age distribution, 55
  households, 56–57
  income distribution, 55–56
  marital status, 57–58
  population growth, 53–55
  working women, 58, 59, 63
Consumer Goods Pricing Act, 76, 408
Consumer life-styles, 58–66
  blurring of gender roles, 63
  component life styles, 63–64
  greening of America, 60–61
  poverty of time, 59–60
  VALS, 59, 64–66
  value orientation, 61–62
Consumer Product Safety Commission, 76, 357
Consumer Products Safety Act, 76
Consumer protection legislation, 75–76
Consumer spending, 73
Contactual efficiency, 11
Contests, 445, 450
Continental T.V. v. GTE, 176
Contingency plans, 50, 51
Contingent event, 50, 51
Contractual marketing systems, 529–533. *See also* Franchise systems
  retailer-owned cooperative systems, 162, 166, 367, 529–532
  wholesaler-sponsored voluntary chains, 532–533
Controlled goods, 615–616
Controlled observation, 306
Convenience stores, 126
Conventional channel, 521–523. *See also* Vertical marketing systems
Conventional department stores, 130–131
Conventional supermarkets, 128
Conversion franchising, 535–536
Cooperative advertising, 202, 426, 441–444, 574
Cooperative advertising utilization reports, 298
Cooperative buying organization, 135
Cooperative systems, retailer-owned, 162, 166, 367, 529–532
Cooperative wholesalers, 162, 166
COPIAT (Coalition to Preserve the Integrity of American Trademarks), 400
Corporate marketing systems, 523–525, 526
Cost analysis, of arrangements, 503–504

Cost justification defense, 411
Cost-oriented pricing, 386–391
  direct product profitability, 389–390, 391
  gross margin data and, 390–391
  initial markup percentage, 387
  maintained markup percentage, 387–388
  markup pricing, 387–388
Coupons, 397, 403, 408, 445, 446–447
Credit advertising, 79, 80
Cross docking, 259
Cumulative discount, 405
Current ratio, 644, 645
Curtainside trailers, 253
Cushion, *see* Safety stock
Customer correspondence, 296, 297
Customer lists, 319–320
Customer resale restriction, 176
Customer satisfaction reports, 298
Customer service, 214–232, 238–239. *See also* Relationship marketing
  channel members providing, 22, 25
  definition, 214–216
  direct versus distributor channels and, 165
  economics of, 216–217
  evaluation model, 214, 215
  physical distribution and, 227–229, 244
  principles of, 224–227
  SERVQUAL and, 220–221
  suppliers evaluated based on, 229–230
  total quality management and, 221–224
  value chain analysis and, 217–220
Customer service gap, 214
Customer service level, 228
Customized services, 250
Customs agent, 612
Customs bonded warehouse, 260
Cycle stocks, *see* Lot size stocks

Data analysis, 307
Database, 309
Database marketing, 316–317
Data Envelopment Analysis (DEA), 643–644
Data sources, *see* Primary data; Secondary data
Dealer brand, *see* Private label (dealer brand)
Dealer listing promotion, 430
Dealers, channel performance measures used by, 640, 641
Decision domain disagreements, 571
Decline stage, of product life cycle, 340, 341, 354–355

Demand
  primary, 425
  selective, 425
Demand-minus pricing, 391–392
Demand-oriented pricing, 386, 391–393
  chain-markup pricing and, 391–393
  demand-minus pricing and, 391–392
Demographic characteristics, *see* Consumer demographics
Department stores, 130
Derivative model, 575
Derived demand, 73
Desk jobbers, *see* Drop shippers
Diffusion process, in product life cycle concept, 342–343
Direct accounts, 175
Direct benefits, of electronic data processing, 314–315
Direct communication, 314
Direct-cost analysis, 647–650
Direct distribution, *see* Short channel
Direct exporting, 605
Direct marketing, 113, 133
  for service delivery, 595–596
Direct ownership, foreign markets and, 606, 608
Direct product profitability, 389–390, 391
Direct selling, 113, 133
Direct store delivery, 258–259
Discounts, 404–407, 411–412
  additional, 408
  functional, 174, 404–405, 411–412
  integrating structure of, 406–407
  pay-for-performance incentives, 404, 435
  promotional allowances, 404, 452
  quantity, 405
  rebates, 404, 408, 445, 447–448, 574
  seasonal, 405–406
  street money, 404, 435
  trade, 404
  wholesalers and, 174
Discriminatory pricing, *see* Price discrimination
Display, channel information system and, 310. *See also* Channel information system reports; Point-of-purchase displays
Distribution center, 258
Distribution cost analysis, 647–651
  activity-based costing, 650–651, 661–662
  direct-cost analysis, 647–650
  full-cost analysis, 647–650

Distribution cost data, 295, 296
Distribution density, 609–610
Distribution, relationship marketing and, 210. *See also* Physical distribution
Distributor recognition awards, 437
Distributors, power of, 562
Distributor's advisory council, 577
Diversified trade show, 448, 449
Diverting, 399–400, 417–418
    gray market goods and, 398–403
Documentation standardization, international physical distribution and, 611–612
Dog, 389, 391
Dollar, value of, 74–75
Domestic gray market goods, 398, 399
Doubleday rule, 412
Down-scale households, 56
Downstream information, 291
Drop shippers (desk jobbers), 162, 167
Dual channels of distribution, 15, 17, 22, 23, 486

Eastern Europe, 613–614
Ecological life cycle of a product, 60
Economic control, 536–537
Economic order quantity (EOQ), 272–273, 274
Economic scale, 563
Economic trends, 72–74
Economy, 72–75
    channel management and, 29, 31–33
    trends, 72–74
    value of dollar and, 74–75
ECR, *see* Efficient Consumer Response
EDI, *see* Electronic data interchange
Editor & Publisher Market Guide, 52
EDLP, *see* Everyday low pricing
Effectiveness, 509
Efficiency, 509
Efficiency ratios, 645, 646
Efficient Consumer Response (ECR), 270, 656–657
80/20 rule, 273
Elderly, marketing to, 55
Electronic data interchange (EDI), 81–82, 291, 312–316
    international channel management and, 611
    relationship marketing and, 209, 210
    wholesalers using, 153
Electronic scanning, 311
Empathy, 221
Employment
    in channels, C1–C6, 33
    unemployment rate and, 72–73
End-use analysis, 506, 507
Environment
    greening of America and, 60–61
    product recycling and, 356, 360–365
Environmental uncertainty, 609
EOQ, *see* Economic order quantity
Ethics, B1–B4
Ethnic groups, 53–55
Ethnocentrism, 602
European Union (EU), 541, 612–613
Everyday low pricing (EDLP), 243, 397–398, 399, 418–419
Exception reports, 310, 318
Exclusive dealing, 77, 79, 367
Exclusive distribution, 14, 15, 17, 21, 22, 23, 484
Exclusive products, 573, 575
Exercised power, 558
Existing system, 507
Exit barriers, 531
Expectational differences, 571
Expected value concept, 394
Experimental treatment, 307
Experimentation, 306–307
Expertise power, 526, 527, 560, 561
Exploratory research, 292, 293
Export Administration Act, 615
Export automation software, 612
Export brokers, 162, 169
Export distributors, 603
Exporting, 605–606
Export management companies, 603–604
Export merchants, 604
External sales force, 444
External secondary data, 293, 297–305

Facilitating payments, *see* Transaction bribes
Facilitators, 6
Facility inspection reports, 298
Facility structure, 244, 246. *See also* Warehouse decision making
Factor merchants, *see* Commission (factor) merchants
Factors, 10
Factory outlets, 62, 132
Failure fee, 345
Fair trade, *see* Resale price maintenance
Family, 56
Federal Automobile Dealers' Franchise Act, 544
Federal Petroleum Marketing Practices Act, 544
Federal Trade Commission, 369, 411, 541, 543–544, 564

Federal Trade Commission Act, 76
Field experiment, 306–307
Field warehouse, 260
Financial leverage, 119, 120–121
Financial performance measures, 643–647
    Data Envelopment Analysis, 643–644
    efficiency ratios, 645, 646
    profitability ratios, 645, 647
    solvency ratios, 644–646
Financial ratios, *see* Financial performance measures
First-generation information systems, 309
Flea markets, 132
Floor-ready merchandise, 271
Focused trade show, 448, 449
Follower brands, 344
Food and Drug Administration, 356–357
Food brokers, 162, 168–169, 173
Food-oriented retailers, 126–128
Forecasting, 49–50
Foreign agents, 606
Foreign Corrupt Practices Act, 615
Foreign distributors, 606
Foreign exchange license, 611
Foreign exchange rate, 74–75
Foreign franchising, 607
Foreign freight forwarder, 612
Foreign gray market goods, 398–399, 400
Foreign market channel members, 605–608
Foreign trade, 75
Foreign trade zone, 612
Formality, 133, 134
Forward buying, 395–396, 397
Forward vertical integration, 70, 486, 524, 564
Fraction of demand filled from stock, 229
Franchise systems, 123–124, 367, 533, 564
    advantages/disadvantages of, 538–541
    conflict in, 537–538
    coordination in, 536–537
    definition, 542
    disclosure rules for, 543–544
    foreign, 607
    franchisee acceptance and termination and, 544
    legal issues of, 541–544
    for service delivery, 595, 596, 597
    trends in, 541
    tying arrangements and, 542
    types of franchises, 533–536
Franchise wholesaling, 162, 166
Free-rider phenomenon, 129, 401, 575
Free samples, 445, 449–450

Freight forwarders, 255
  foreign, 612
Frequent user clubs, 449
FTC Franchise Rule, 543
Fulfillment houses, 449
Full-cost analysis, 647–650
Full-line discount store, 131
Full-line forcing, 77, 79, 368
Full-line merchant wholesalers,
  see General-merchandise (full-line) merchant wholesalers
Full-service merchant wholesalers, 161, 162, 164–166
Functional approach, to channel management, 33
Functional discounts, 174, 404–405, 411–412
Functional expenses, 648
Functional fit, 337

Gap analysis of distribution channels, 508
Gatekeepers, 340, 342
Gender roles, see Blurring of gender roles
Generally planned purchases, 115
General-merchandise (full-line) merchant wholesalers, 162, 164
General-merchandise retailers, 129–132
Geocentrism, 602
Geographic-based buying organization, 134
Globalization, see International channels
GMROI, see Gross margin return on investment
Goal incompatibilities, 571–572
Governmental units, secondary data from, 298, 299–300
Graphics, in channel report, 310, 318
Gray market goods, 398–403, 410, 565, 566
  distribution of, 78, 79
  foreign exchange rate and, 75
Grease payments, see Transaction bribes
Great Income Reshuffle, The, 56
Greenbelts, 601
Greening of America, 60–61
Gross margin, 390–391, 487
Gross margin return on investment (GMROI), 385–386
Growth stage, of product life cycle, 340, 341, 346–349

Hidden assets, 118
High-end strategy retailers, 124–126
High-low pricing, 395–397
Hispanics, 53

Hold-harmless agreement, 172
Home market channel members, 603–605
Horizontal channel audit, 653
Horizontal competition, 66, 67, 485
Horizontal conflict, 568
Horizontal integration, 77, 79
Households, 56–57, 63
Hub-and-spoke distribution systems, 260–261
Human observation, 306
Hybrid channel arrangement, 496

Ideal system, 507
Implementation of findings, in marketing research, 308
Import license, 611
Impulse sales, 114–116
Income distribution, 55–56
Independent retailer, 121–122
Indirect benefits, 315–316
Indirect distribution, see Long channel
Indirect promotional effect, 425
Industry deregulation legislation, 76
Information power, 526, 527, 560, 561
Information sharing, channel cooperation and, 573, 575
Information superhighway, A1–A5
Initial markup, 388
Initial markup percentage, 388
Inseparability, 592
Inside buying organization, 135
Institutional approach, to channel management, 33
In-store decision rate, 115
In-store materials, 450
Intangibility, of services, 592
Integrated distributors, 154
Integrated marketing, 452
Integrated supply contract, 150
Intensity of conflicts, 569
Intensive distribution, 14, 15, 484
Interactive kiosk, A2
Interactive television, A1, A2
Intermediaries, 6
  channel length and, 488, 491
  functions of, 10–14
Intermodal transportation, 255–257
Internal information, 291
Internal sales force, 444
Internal secondary data, 293–297
International channels, 591, 600–616, 624–625
  channel choice and, 601–603
  channel length and, 608–609
  channel width and, 609–610
  direct ownership and, 606, 608
  Eastern Europe and, 613–614
  European Union and, 612–613
  exporting, 605–606

foreign market channel members and, 605–608
franchising and, 641
home market channel members and, 603–605
Japan and, 614
joint ventures and, 605, 606, 607–608
packaging and, 611, 616
physical distribution and, 602, 611–612
Russia and, 601
specific international channels and, 603
wholesalers and, 152
International channels, legal issues of, 615–616
  bribery, 615
  controlled goods, 615–616
  distributor termination, 616
  packaging, 616
Interstate Commerce Commission, 251, 252
Intertype competition, 64, 66, 67, 68–70, 485–486
Intertype conflict, 568
Interviews
  for channel selection, 498, 500–501
  for surveys, 306
Introduction stage, of product life cycle, 340, 341–346
Inventory holding costs, 272
Inventory management, 244, 261–274
  ABC inventory analysis, 273–274
  channel cooperation and, 573, 574–575
  economic order quantity, 272–273, 274
  Efficient Consumer Response, 270
  inventory turnover, 262–264
  inventory types and, 261–262, 263
  just-in-time, 209, 265–269
  reorder point, 270–272
  reports, 320
  technological developments and, 80–82
Inventory records, secondary data from, 296, 297
Inventory turnover, 262–264
Inventory turnover ratio, 645, 646
Invoices, 295, 297
ISO 9000, 613

Japan, 614
JIT, see Just-in-time (JIT) inventory management system
Joint goal setting, for conflict management and resolution, 577

Joint venture, 605, 606, 607–608
Junk bonds, 118
Just-in-time (JIT) inventory management systems, 209, 265–269

Kanban system, 267
Keiretsu, 614
Kiosk, interactive, A2
Kmart Corporation v. Cartier, Inc., 410

Laboratory experiment, 306–307
LBO, *see* Leveraged buyouts
Lease terms, 114
Legal issues, 75–80, 81. *See also* International channels, legal issues of; Pricing, legal issues of; Product management, legal issues of
   of advertising, 79–80
   antitrust, 75, 76
   consumer protection, 75–76
   of franchising, 541–544
   industry deregulation, 76
   of promotion, 80, 443, 452–453
   unfair trade practices, 75, 76

Legitimate power, 526, 527, 560, 561
Less-than-truckload (LTL) shipments, 252
Level one relationships, 206
Level two relationships, 206–207
Level three relationships, 206, 207–208
Leveraged buyouts (LBOs), 118, 121, 131
Licensing, 607
Life-cycle costing, 61
Life-styles, *see* Consumer lifestyles
Limited-line merchant wholesalers, *see* Specialty-merchandise limited-line merchant wholesalers
Limited-service merchant wholesalers, 161, 162, 166–167
Local partner, for international joint ventures, 607–608
Local rate, 441–442
Locked-up channel, 601
Logistics, 247–248
   channel careers in, C3–C4
Logistics alliances, 243
Long channel (indirect distribution), 14, 15, 482–483
Loss leaders, 409
Lost-for-good customers, 213, 214
Lot size, 480
Lot size stocks (cycle stocks), 262, 263
Low-cost channel of distribution, 22, 25–26

Low-end strategy retailers, 124, 125–126
LTL shipments, *see* Less-than-truckload (LTL) shipments

Mail-order sales, 78, 79
Mail-order wholesalers, 162, 167
Mail questionnaire, 306
Maintained markup, 388
Maintained markup percentage, 388–389
Management bounded system, 507–508
Management succession, 123
Manufacturer-reseller cooperation, 573
Manufacturers
   channel careers in, C2–C3
   channel length and, 488, 491
   power of, 556–557, 563–564, 567
Manufacturers' agents, 162, 168, 169
Manufacturers' branch office, 162, 163
Manufacturer's brand, *see* National brand
Manufacturers' sales office, 162, 163
Manufacturer/supplier-wholesaler contracts, 153, 169–177
Manufacturer wholesaling, 159, 160, 161, 162, 163
Manufacturing franchises, 534
Marital status, 57–58
Markdown reports, 319
Marketability, 411
Market coverage, channel width and, 483
Market decentralization, 480
Market development, 54–55
Marketing channels
   activities of, 6–8
   components of, 5–8
   definition, 5–8
Marketing decision support system, *see* Third-generation channel information system
Marketing information systems, 50, 288–289, 308–309. *See also* Channel information systems; Marketing research
   marketing research vs., 308–309
Marketing personnel, channels-related decisions analyzed by, 29, 30
Marketing research, 289–308
   channel environment monitored by, 50
   in channels management, 290–291
   data analysis in, 307
   definition, 289–290

   implementation of findings in, 308
   marketing information systems vs., 308–309
   primary data in, 291, 305–307
   problem definition in, 291, 292–293
   recommendations for action in, 307–308
   secondary data in, 291–292, 293–305
Market penetration, 54
Market saturation, 117–118
Markup percentage, 387
Markup pricing, 387–388
Markups
   additional, 408
   gross margin data and, 390–391
   initial markup percentage, 387
   maintained markup percentage, 387–388
   markup percentage, 387
   markup pricing, 387–388
   variable, 388
Mass distribution, 11–12
Materials handling, 244, 246
Maturity stage, of product life cycle, 340, 341, 349–354
Maxicode, 311
Mechanical observation, 306
Meeting competition defense, 411
Membership clubs, *see* Buying clubs
Merchandise consistency, 124
Merchandise depth, 124, 125
Merchandise width, 124, 125
Merchandising orientation, 135
Merchant wholesaling, 147, 148, 160, 161, 162, 163–167, 174, 596
Mergers and acquisitions
   railroads and, 251
   wholesalers and, 153–154
Message formats, 314
Michael Haleblan, N.J. Inc. v. Roppe Rubber Corp. et al., 176
Micromarketing, 54
Minimum sum of the cost of inventory and backorders, 229
Model, 310
Modular corporation, 151–152
Money income, 55
Monsanto v. Spray-Rite Service Corp, 408–409
Motivator role, 430, 431
Motor Carrier Act of 1980, 76, 252
Motor carriers, 245–246, 250, 251, 252–253
Mueller standard, 412
Multi-industry exhibitor trade show, 448, 449

SUBJECT INDEX S-7

Multi-industry visitor trade show, 448, 449
Multiple channels of distribution, 69, 485–486

NAFTA, see North American Free Trade Agreement
National brand (manufacturer's brand), 350, 369
National Highway Traffic Safety Administration, 356
National rate, 441–442
Natural expenses, 648
Natural observation, 306
Negotiation, 576
Net profit margin, 119, 120, 645, 647
New product planning process, 335–339, 340, 341–346
Noncoercive power, 559–560, 561
Noncumulative discount, 405
Nongoods service, 592
Nonprice competition, 384
Nonprobability sample, 306
Nonstore-based retailers, 132–133
Nontraceable common costs, 649–650
Nontraditional channels, 22, 23–24
North American Free Trade Agreement (NAFTA), 152, 541

Observation, 306
OEM, see Original equipment manufacturer
Off-price chains, 62, 113, 131–132
Ombudsman, 430, 431
Omnibus Trade Act of 1988, 615
On-line shopping, A1–A2
Opportunistic buying, 131, 135–136, 137
Opportunity costs, 208
Optional support module, 429
Orange goods, 487
Order cycle time, 271
Order processing costs, 272–273
Original equipment manufacturer (OEM), 608
Outcome-related activities, 216
Outlet malls, 62
Outside buying organization, 135
Overstored trading area, 117–118
Owned-goods service, 592
Ownership, in retailing, 121–124

Packaging, 365–366
 environmental concerns and, 61
 international channels and, 611, 616
 recycling and, 362, 363
Parallel channels of distribution, 399
Partnering, see Relationship marketing

Pay-for-performance allowance, 404, 435
Pay to stay fee, 345
PCV, see Percent category volume
Pedestrian traffic counts, 113
Percent category volume (PCV), 304, 483
Perceptual differences, 570–571
Periodicals, with channels management, 301–302
Perishability, of services, 592
Per se rule, 176
Personal interview, 306
Personal selling
 pull-oriented promotion and, 439, 444–445
 push-oriented promotion and, 427, 430–434
 in relationship marketing, 211
Persuasion, for conflict management and resolution, 576
Persuasion power, 526, 527, 560, 561
Physical distribution, 9, 242–250. See also under Distribution; Inventory management; Transportation decision making; Warehouse decision making
 customer service in, 227–229
 definition, 243
 international, 602, 611–612
 logistics, 247–248
 physical distribution concept, 248–249
 poor, 245–246
 service delivery and, 596–597
Physical distribution (total cost) concept, 248–249
Piggybacking, 601
Pioneer brands, 344
Pipelines, 250, 251, 254
PMs, see Push money
Pocket prices, 407
Point-of-purchase displays, 450
Point-of-sale terminals, 80–81
Politics, for conflict management and resolution, 576
Polycentrism, 602
Population growth, 53–55
Post-consumer waste, 361
Potential conflict, 157
Potential power, 558
Poverty of time, 59–60
Power, of channel leader, 526–527. See also Channel power
Power retailers, 150, 151, 566
Precision (sampling error), 306
Pre-consumer waste, 361
Predatory pricing, 382–383
Predictive dialers, 445
Preliminary screening, channel selection and, 498, 499
Premiums, 445, 449

Price comparisons, 79–80
Price competition, 383–385
Price discrimination, 75, 76, 78, 79, 410–411
Price guarantees, 403
Price protection, 174
Pricing, 381–419. See also Cost-oriented pricing; Demand-oriented pricing; Discounts; Pricing, legal issues of
 adaptive, 407–408
 channel-related decisions and, 30
 competition-oriented, 386, 393–394
 everyday low, 243, 397–398, 399, 418–419
 gray market goods and, 398–403
 high-low, 395–397
 integrated approach to, 394–395
 legal issues on, 79, 80
 objectives of, 385–386
 price guarantees and, 403
 price vs. nonprice competition and, 383–385
 relationship marketing and, 211
 selling against the brand and, 353, 403–404, 566
 terms and, 406, 411
Pricing, legal issues of, 78, 79, 408–411
 discounts, 411–412
 gray market goods, 410
 predatory pricing, 382–383
 price discrimination, 75, 76, 78, 79, 410–411
 resale price maintenance, 408–409
 sales below-cost laws, 409
 terms, 411
Primary data, 291, 305–307
Primary demand, 425
Private label (dealer brand), 350–353, 369, 531, 564–565, 566
Private warehouses, 257–259
PRIZM, 59
Probability-based sample, 306
Problem definition, in marketing research, 291, 292–293
Problem solving, for conflict management and resolution, 576
Process-related activities, 216
Process stock, 261, 262, 263
Producer-owned cooperatives, 162, 166
Product-based buying organization, 134
Product life cycle, 339–355
 decline stage, 340, 341, 354–355
 defusion process in, 342–343
 evaluation of, 355

Product life cycle *Continued*
  growth stage, 340, 341, 346–349
  introduction stage, 340, 341–346
  maturity stage, 340, 341, 349–354
Product management. *See also* New product planning process; Packaging; Product life cycle; Product management, legal issues of; Reverse channels
  channel length and, 488, 489–491
  channel-related decisions and, 30
  relationship marketing and, 210–211
Product management, legal issues of, 76–78, 334, 367–369
  exclusive dealing, 367
  full-line forcing, 368
  private label strategy, 369
  reciprocity, 368
  refusal to deal, 368–369
  slotting allowances, 369, 452
  tying agreements, 334, 367–368
Product recall, 356–360
Product recall notices, 298
Product recycling, 356, 360–365
Product/trademark franchising, 123, 534, 535
Product variety, 480
Professional associations, *see* Trade associations
Profitability ratios, 645, 647
Profit-and-loss statements, 296, 297
Profit-based pricing objectives, 385
Profit passover arrangements, 174–175
Programmed merchandising agreement, 528–529
Promises, *see* Reward power
Promotion, 421–461. *See also* Pull-oriented promotional strategy; Push-oriented promotional strategy
  channel cooperation and, 573, 574
  channel-related decisions and, 30
  legal issues of, 80, 443, 452–453
  promotional allowances and, 404, 442, 452
  reimbursement for expenses and, 452–453
  relationship marketing and, 211–212
Promotional allowances, 404, 442, 452
Promotional money, *see* Push money
Psychographic research, 64

Publicity
  pull-oriented promotion and, 439, 450–451
  push-oriented promotion and, 427, 437–438
Public warehouses, 257, 260
Pull, *see* Selling through the wholesaler/retailer
Pull-oriented promotional strategy, 426, 438–452. *See also* Promotion
  advertising, 426, 439, 440–444
  improving, 451–452
  personal selling, 439, 444–445
  publicity, 439, 450–451
  sales promotion, 439, 445–450
Pull system, 267
Purchasing, centralizing, 134–136, 566
Pure centralized buying organization, 133–134
Push, *see* Selling to the wholesaler/retailer
Push money, 435–437
Push money (PMs), 564
Push-oriented promotional strategy, 425–438. *See also* Promotion
  advertising, 426, 427, 428, 430
  budgeting for, 428
  effectiveness of, 429–430
  improving, 438
  personal selling, 427, 430–434
  publicity, 427, 437–438
  sales promotion, 427, 434–437
Push system, 267

Quality
  customer service and, 228
  of services, 592
  total quality management and, 221–224
Quantity discounts, 174, 405
Quick ratio, 644, 645
Quick response inventory systems, 82, 265. *See also* Just-in-time (JIT) inventory management systems

Rack jobbers, 162, 165–166
Railroads, 250–251
Rand McNally Commercial Atlas & Market Guide, 52
Range of power, 558
Real conflict, 157
Real income, 55–56
Real sales growth, 109
Rebates, 403, 404, 408, 445, 447–448, 574
Recall programs, *see* Product recall
Reciprocity, 77, 79, 368
Recommendations for action, in marketing research, 307–308

Recycling, *see* Product recycling
Red goods, 487
Referent power, 559, 561
Referrent power, 526, 527
Refusal to deal, 77, 79, 368–369
Regiocentrism, 602
Relationship marketing (partnering), 20, 202–214, 237–238, 268. *See also* Customer service
  advantages and disadvantages of, 212–213
  definition, 202, 204
  distribution and, 210
  implications of, 208–212
  levels of, 206–208
  popularity of, 209
  pricing and, 211
  product planning and, 210–211
  promotion and, 211–212
  transactional marketing vs., 204–206, 208–209, 210, 211, 212–214
Reliability, 221
Reliability measure, 229
Rented-goods services, 592
Reorder point, 270–272
Replacement rate, 487
Reports, *see* Channel information system reports
Resale price maintenance, 78, 79, 408–409
Resale restrictions, 77, 79, 175–177
Research design, 305
Resellers, 496–507
Resident buying offices, 135
Resource scarcity
  channel conflict and, 572
  franchising and, 538–539
Responsiveness, 221
Retail catalog showrooms, 131
Retailer-owned cooperative systems, 162, 166, 367, 529–532
Retailers
  high- and low-performance, 119–121
  non-store based, 132–133
  power of, 367, 565–567
  relationships with suppliers and customers, 17–19
  roles of, 17
Retailing, 8, 9, 107–144
  buying organizations, 133–137
  channel careers in, C3
  characteristics of, 112–116
  conglomerate merchants, 116–117
  definition, 107, 109
  food-oriented retailers, 126–128
  general-merchandise retailers, 129–132
  immediacy and, 112
  impulse sales, 114–116

leveraged buyouts and, 118
location and, 112–114
low coverage sales, 114
market saturation and, 117–118
ownership and, 121–124
sales, 33, 109–112
seasonality and, 116
strategy and, 124–133
trends, 116–121
Return on assets ratio, 645, 647
Return on investment, 119
Return on net worth ratio, 645, 647
Reverse channels, 356–365
    product recall and, 298, 356–360
    product recycling and, 356, 360–365
Reviewer role, 430, 431
Review period, 272
Reward power (promises), 526, 527, 559, 561
Risk, international channels and, 602
Robinson-Patman Act, 76, 369, 410–411, 443, 452
Role ambiguity, channel conflict and, 570
Role incongruity, channel conflict and, 570
Rule of reason, 176
Russia, 601

Safety stocks, 262, 263
Sales
    of retailers, 33, 109–112
    technological developments relating to, 80–82
    of wholesalers, 33, 147–148, 154–155, 159
Sales-based pricing objectives, 385
Sales below-cost laws, 409
Sales force, in pull-oriented promotion, 444–445
Sales gestation period, 489
Sales incentives, in push-oriented promotion, 433–434
Sales & Marketing Management's Survey of Buying Power, 52
Sales promotion
    pull-oriented promotion and, 439, 445–450
    push-oriented promotion and, 427, 434–437
Sales reports, 318–319
Sales representatives, 603
Sales training programs, 432–433
Same-store sales, 111–112
Sampling, 305–306
Sampling error, *see* Precision
Saturated trading area, 117
Saturation ratios, 117
Scanning-based data, 310–312
Scenarios, of channel environment, 49–50

Scouts, 342–343
Scrambled merchandising, 64, 69–70, 118, 150
Seamless, intermodal transportation as, 257
Searching time, 487
Seasonal discounts, 405–406
Secondary data
    on consumer demographics, 52
    on consumer life-styles, 59
    in marketing research, 291–292, 293–305
Secondary linkages, 537
Second-generation channel information systems, 309
Securities and Exchange Commission, 615
Selective demand, 425
Selective distribution, 15, 17, 484–485
Self-fulfilling prophecy, 355
Self-liquidating premiums, 449
Selling against the brand, 353, 403–404, 566
Selling agents, 162, 168
Selling through the wholesaler/retailer (pull), 19, 20, 426. *See also* Pull-oriented promotional strategy
Selling to the wholesaler/retailer (push), 19, 20, 425–426. *See also* Push-oriented promotional strategy
Sensitivity training, 577
Service backup, 480
Service failures, 229
Service output requirements, 479–480
Service response logistics, 596–597
Services, channel strategy for, 590–600, 623–624
    activities of intermediaries and, 594–595
    banking, 598–599
    car rentals, 599–600
    physical distribution and, 596–597
    types of service channels, 595–596, 597
SERVQUAL, 220–221
Shared intellectual property, 542
Shared tasks, for conflict management and resolution, 577
Shelf facings, 339
Sherman Antitrust Act, 76, 334
Shipper's export declaration, 611
Shipping records, 296, 297
Short channel (direct distribution), 14, 15, 481–482
SIC, *see* Standard Industrial Classification
Simulation, 307
Single-person households, 56, 57

Single-source data, 302–305
Size-of-order boundaries, 175
Sleeper, 389, 391
Slotting allowances, 345–346, 347, 369, 452, 566
Smoothing and seasonal stocks, 262, 263
Solvency ratios, 644–646
Sorting process, 11
Specialty-merchandise limited-line merchant wholesalers, 162, 165
Specialty stores, 129–130
Specifically planned purchases, 114–115
Spiffs, *see* Push money
Stage one program, of reseller training, 432
Stage two program, of reseller training, 432–433
Stage three program, of reseller training, 433
Staggers Rail Act, 76
Standard Industrial Classification (SIC), 506, 507
Standardization of documentation, international physical distribution and, 611–612
Standard Rate & Data Service, 52
Status quo-based pricing objectives, 386
Storefront system, 259
Strategic approach, to channel management, 34
Strategic benefits, of electronic data processing, 316
Strategic profit model, 119–121
Street money, 404, 435
Subfranchising, 536
Substitute purchases, 115
Supermarkets, 126–128
Superstore
    food-based, 350
    general merchandise
    general-merchandise, 128
Suppliers
    channel performance measures used by, 640, 642
    customer service assessing, 229–230
    power of, 561
Supply chain logistics, 596
Surveys, 306
Sweepstakes, 445, 450
Switching costs, 20–21

Tabulation, 307
Tailored logistics package, 248
Tangibles, 221
TCA, *see* Transaction cost analysis
Teacher role, 430, 431
Technical problem-solving systems, 82

Technological environment, 80–84
  channel members and, 22, 24–25
  computer-aided ordering, 321–322
  information superhighway and, 80
  problem solving and, 82
  sales and inventory and, 80–82
  video-ordering systems and, 83–84
  wholesalers and, 152–153
Telemarketing, 444–445
Telephone Consumer Protection Act of 1991, 444–445
Telephone interview, 306
Television, *see* Interactive television
Terms, 174, 406
Territorial resale restriction, 175–176
Territory protection, channel cooperation and, 573, 575
Test marketing, 339
Third-generation channel information system (marketing decision support system), 308, 309
Third-party documentation agencies, 444
Third-party network, 314
Third-party transportation service providers, 254–255
Timeliness, customer service and, 228
Time of consumption, 487
Tipping fees, 362
TL shipments, *see* Truckload (TL) shipments
Total cost concept, *see* Physical distribution (total cost) concept
Total liabilities to net worth ratio, 644, 645, 646
Total quality management (TQM), 221–224
TQM, *see* Total quality management
Trade associations, 367
  career information from, C4–C6
  secondary data from, 299
  of wholesalers, 497–498
Trade discount, 174, 404
Trade loading, 396
Trade shows, 448–449
Trade zones, 612
Trading area, 117
Trading area characteristics, 113
Traffic builders, 389–390, 391
Traffic counts, 113
Training
  channel cooperation and, 573, 575

sales training programs, 432–433
Transactional marketing, 203–204
  relationship marketing vs., 204–206, 208–209, 210, 211, 212–214
Transaction bribes (grease or facilitating payments), 615
Transaction cost analysis (TCA), 603, 609
Transaction-specific assets, 609
Transfer price, 525
Transportation decision making, 114, 244, 250–257
  air freight, 250, 251, 254
  intermodal transportation, 255–257
  international channel management and, 611
  motor carriers, 245–246, 250, 251, 252–253
  pipelines, 250, 251, 254
  problems in, 245–246
  railroads, 250–251
  third-party providers, 254–255
  waterways, 250, 251, 253
Transshipping, 176–177
Trigger point, 50, 51
Troops, 342–343
Truckload (TL) shipments, 252
Trucks, *see* Motor carriers
Truck/wagon wholesalers, 162, 167
Tying arrangements, 77, 79, 334, 367–368
  in franchising, 542–543
Tying managements, 334

Understored trading area, 117
Unemployment rate, 72–73
Unfair trade practices legislation, 75, 76
Uniform Franchise Offering Circular (UFOC), 543
United States Standard Master for International Trade, 611
U.S. v. Colgate, 368–369
Unit franchising, 535
Unit pricing, 78, 79
Universal core support module, 429
Universal Product Code (UPC), 80, 310–312
Upstream information, 291
U.S. v. Arnold Schwinn, 176
Usage rate, 271

VALS (Values and Life-Styles) program, 59, 64–66
Value chain analysis, 217–220
Value orientation, 61–62
Variability in quality, of services, 592
Variable markup policy, 388

Variance bribes, 615
Variety store, 130
Vehicular traffic counts, 113
Vending machines, 113, 132
Vertical channel audit, 653
Vertical competition, 66, 67, 70–71, 486
Vertical conflict, 568
Vertical integration, 77, 79, 486
  backward, 70, 71, 486, 524
  forward, 70, 486, 524, 564
Vertical marketing systems, 521–554. *See also* Contractual marketing systems
  administered marketing systems, 525–529
  competition and, 66, 67, 71–72
  conventional channel vs., 521–523
  corporate marketing systems, 523–525, 526
Vertical trade show, 449
Video-ordering systems, 83–84
Visibility, 114

Waiting time, 480
Warehouse, 257
Warehouse clubs, 113
Warehouse decision making, 244, 257–261
  hub-and-spoke distribution systems, 260–261
  private warehouses, 257–259
  problems in, 246
  public warehouses, 257, 260
Warehouse stores, 128
Waste reduction, recycling and, 356, 360–365
Waterways, 250, 251, 253
Website, A3
Wheeler-Lea Amendment, 76
Wholesalers
  power of, 564–565
  relationships with suppliers and customers, 17–19
  roles of, 17
  trade associations of, 497–498
Wholesaler-sponsored voluntary chains, 367, 532–533, 564
Wholesaling, 8–9, 145–185
  agents and brokers, 147, 148, 160, 161–162, 167–169, 174
  broadening merchandise lines and, 150
  channel careers in, C3
  characteristics of, 156–158
  computerization and, 152–153
  definition, 147
  full-service merchant wholesalers, 161, 162, 164–166
  international expansion and, 152
  large distributors and, 153–154

layers of, 156
limited-service merchant wholesalers, 161, 162, 166–167
location of establishments and sales, 159
manufacturer downsizing and, 150–151
manufacturer/supplier-wholesaler contracts, 153, 169–177
manufacturer wholesaling, 159, 160, 161, 162, 163
merchant wholesaling, 147, 148, 160, 161, 162, 163–167, 174
modular corporation and, 151–152
power retailers and, 150, 151
sales, 33, 147–148, 154–155, 159
statistics on, 154–155
trends, 148–154
wholesaler representation of multiple manufacturers and, 156–158

Winner, 389, 391
Women, in work force, 58, 59, 63
Working partner, sales representative as, 430, 431

Yankelovich Monitor, 59
Yellow goods, 487

Zone of tolerance, 216